SWEDEN

*Torneälven*

*Umeälven*

Gulf of Bothnia

Lake
Onega

Lake
Ladoga

● Åbo
● Helsingfors
Vyborg ●
Petrograd ●

*Volkhov*

● Stockholm

Lake
Mälaren

*Saaremaa*

*Gotland*

Öland

*Dvina*

*Volga*

Moscow ●

R U S S I A

U R A L   M T S.

*Baltic
Sea*

*Neman*

nholm
enmark)

Minsk ●

*Vistula*

Warsaw ●

*Bug*

Kiev ●

*Dnieper*

*Don*

*Oder*

*Vistula*

Carpathian Mts.

*Southern Bug*

*Dniester*

*Donets*

*Volga*

AUSTRIA-
HUNGARY

Budapest ●

*Tisza*

*Prut*

*Siret*

Kuban'

CAUCASUS MTS.

*Caspian
Sea*

*Maros (Mures)*

*Drava*

*Sava*

Belgrade ●

ROMANIA

Bucharest ● *Danube*

inaric
Alps

SERBIA

*Morava*

Balkan Mts.

Black Sea

NTENEGRO

BULGARIA

*Maritsa*

Constantinople ●

Sea of
Marmara

ALBANIA

*Vardar*

GREECE  *Aegean
Sea*

OTTOMAN
EMPIRE

PERSIA

N

*Ionian
Sea*

Athens ●

HIALEAH GARDENS
MEDIA   DISCARD   91

*Crete*

*Cyprus*

| 0 | | 200 | | 400 mi. |
| 0 | 200 | 400 km | | |

# EUROPE
## SINCE 1914
### ENCYCLOPEDIA OF THE AGE OF WAR
### AND RECONSTRUCTION

# EDITORIAL BOARD

# EUROPE
## SINCE 1914
### ENCYCLOPEDIA OF THE AGE OF WAR AND RECONSTRUCTION

## Volume 2

## Child Care to Futurism

*John Merriman and Jay Winter*

EDITORS IN CHIEF

**CHARLES SCRIBNER'S SONS**

*An imprint of Thomson Gale, a part of The Thomson Corporation*

Detroit • New York • San Francisco • New Haven, Conn. • Waterville, Maine • London • Munich

**Europe since 1914: Encyclopedia of the Age of War and Reconstruction**

John Merriman
Jay Winter
Editors in Chief

**LIBRARY OF CONGRESS CATALOGING-IN-PUBLICATION DATA**

Europe since 1914: encyclopedia of the age of war and reconstruction / edited by John Merriman and Jay Winter.
p. cm. — (Scribner library of modern Europe)
Includes bibliographical references and index.
ISBN 0-684-31365-0 (set : alk. paper) — ISBN 0-684-31366-9 (v. 1 : alk. paper) — ISBN 0-684-31367-7 (v. 2 : alk. paper) — ISBN 0-684-31368-5 (v. 3 : alk. paper) — ISBN 0-684-31369-3 (v. 4 : alk. paper) — ISBN 0-684-31370-7 (v. 5 : alk. paper) — ISBN 0-684-31497-5 (e-book)
1. Europe–History–20th century–Encyclopedias. 2. Europe–Civilization–20th century–Encyclopedias. I. Merriman, John M. II. Winter, J. M.
D424.E94 2006
940.503–dc22
2006014427

This title is also available as an e-book and as a ten-volume set with
Europe 1789 to 1914: Encyclopedia of the Age of Industry and Empire.
E-book ISBN 0-684-31497-5
Ten-volume set ISBN 0-684-31530-0
Contact your Gale sales representative for ordering information.

Printed in the United States of America
10 9 8 7 6 5 4 3 2 1

# CONTENTS OF THIS VOLUME

# CONTENTS OF OTHER VOLUMES

**VOLUME 4**

## N

## O

## P

**VOLUME 5**

## T

## U

# MAPS OF EUROPE SINCE 1914

The maps in this section illuminate some of the major events of European history in the twentieth and early twenty-first centuries, including World War I and World War II, the Holocaust, the breakup of Yugoslavia, and the formation of the European Union.

WWI in Europe

- Allies, 1918
- Central Powers
- Neutral nations
- Farthest advance by Central Powers
- 1914 border

**Versailles Settlement**

■ Newly-formed nations
— Boundaries, 1923

ICELAND

ATLANTIC OCEAN

0    200    400 mi.
0    200    400 km

NORWAY

SWEDEN

FINLAND

Christiania (Oslo)

Stockholm

Helsinki
Tallinn
Petrograd

ESTONIA

North Sea

Riga
LATVIA

Moscow

DENMARK
Copenhagen

Baltic Sea

LITH.
Kaunas

IRISH FREE STATE

UNITED KINGDOM

Danzig

East Prussia (Ger.)

UNION OF SOVIET SOCIALIST REPUBLICS

London
Amsterdam

Berlin

Warsaw

NETH.
Brussels

GERMANY

POLAND

BELG.

LUX.

Prague

Krakow

Paris
Saar

CZECHOSLOVAKIA

Vienna

Budapest

FRANCE

Bern
SWITZ.

AUSTRIA

HUNGARY

ROMANIA

Venice

Bucharest

Black Sea

Belgrade

PORTUGAL

ANDORRA

YUGOSLAVIA

BULGARIA

Madrid

ITALY

Rome

Sofia

Lisbon

SPAIN

Tirane

Constantinople

ALBANIA

GREECE

TURKEY

Tangier (International Territory)
Gibraltar

Athens

Spanish Morocco

Mediterranean Sea

Morocco (Fr.)

Algeria (Fr.)

Tunisia (Fr.)

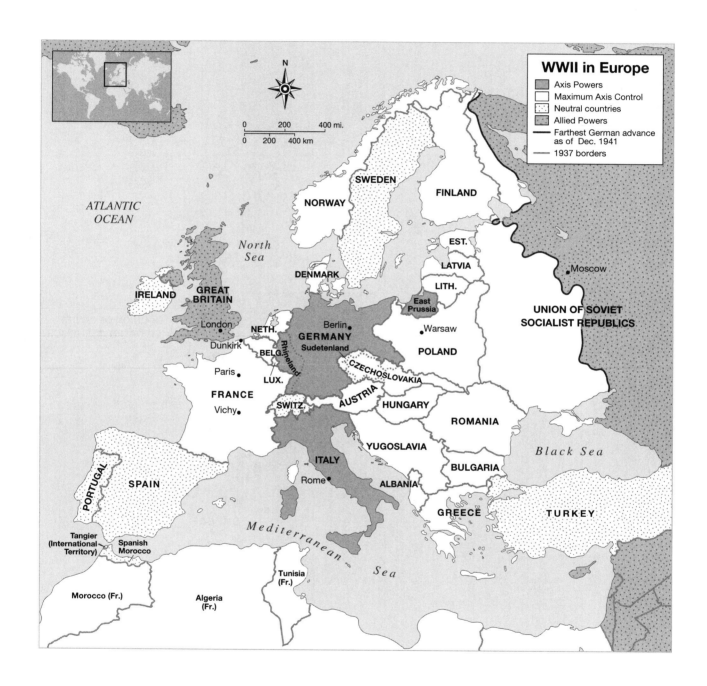

**WWII in Europe**

- Axis Powers
- Maximum Axis Control
- Neutral countries
- Allied Powers
- Farthest German advance as of Dec. 1941
- 1937 borders

ATLANTIC OCEAN

North Sea

SWEDEN

NORWAY

FINLAND

EST.

LATVIA

Moscow

DENMARK

LITH.

IRELAND

GREAT BRITAIN

London

East Prussia

UNION OF SOVIET SOCIALIST REPUBLICS

NETH.

Berlin

Warsaw

Dunkirk

GERMANY

POLAND

BELG.

Rhineland

Sudetenland

Paris

LUX.

CZECHOSLOVAKIA

FRANCE

AUSTRIA

HUNGARY

Vichy

SWITZ.

ROMANIA

Black Sea

YUGOSLAVIA

ITALY

BULGARIA

PORTUGAL

SPAIN

Rome

ALBANIA

Mediterranean Sea

GREECE

TURKEY

Tangier (International Territory)

Spanish Morocco

Morocco (Fr.)

Algeria (Fr.)

Tunisia (Fr.)

0   200   400 mi.

0   200   400 km

N

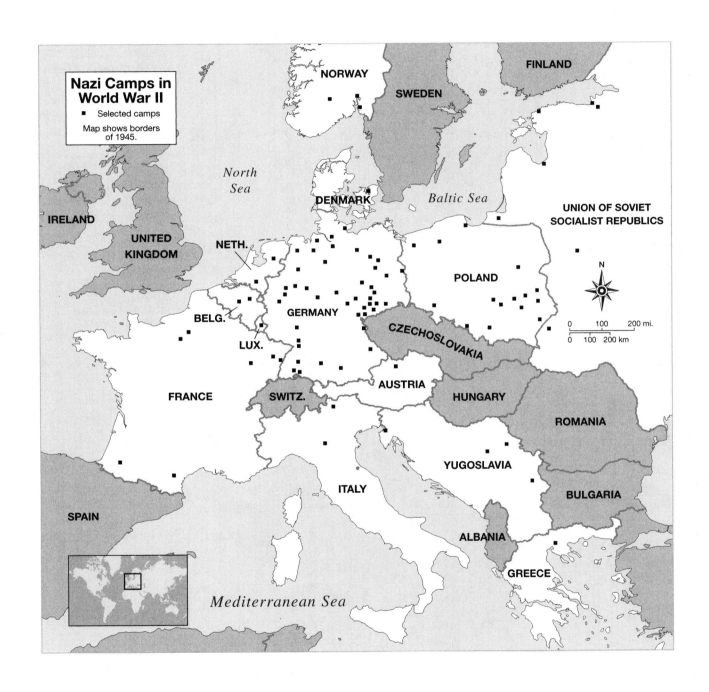

## Nazi Camps in World War II

■ Selected camps

Map shows borders of 1945.

NORWAY

SWEDEN

FINLAND

*North Sea*

*Baltic Sea*

DENMARK

IRELAND

UNITED KINGDOM

NETH.

UNION OF SOVIET SOCIALIST REPUBLICS

N

BELG.

GERMANY

POLAND

LUX.

0    100    200 mi.

0   100   200 km

CZECHOSLOVAKIA

FRANCE

SWITZ.

AUSTRIA

HUNGARY

ROMANIA

YUGOSLAVIA

ITALY

BULGARIA

SPAIN

ALBANIA

GREECE

*Mediterranean Sea*

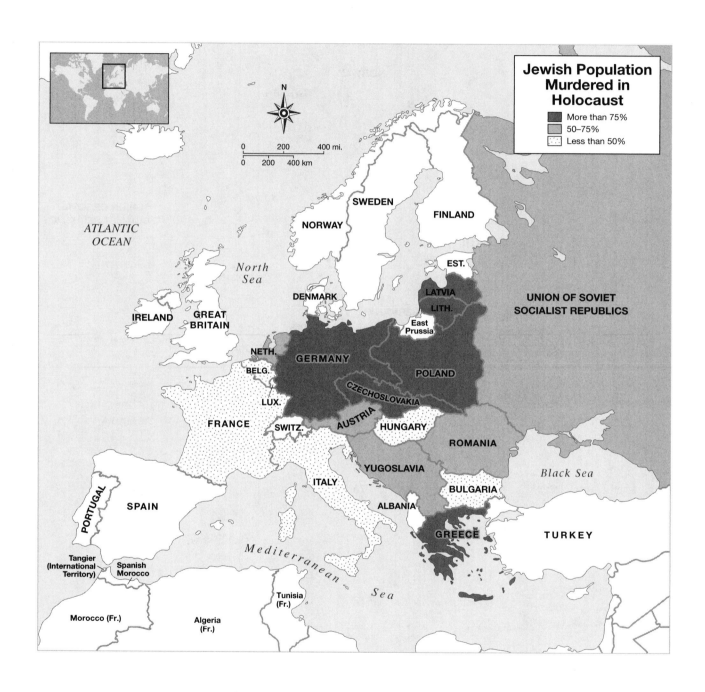

Jewish Population Murdered in Holocaust

More than 75%
50–75%
Less than 50%

## Post 1945 Europe

Communist nations — Iron Curtain
Non-Communist nations ⊛ Capital

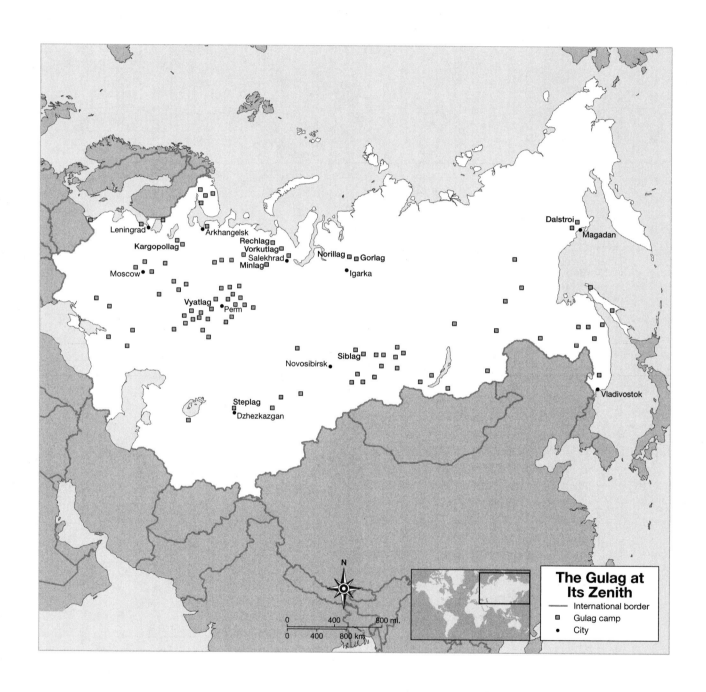

Leningrad

Arkhangelsk

Kargopollag

Rechlag
Vorkutlag
Salekhrad
Minlag

Moscow

Norillag  Gorlag

Igarka

Dalstroi
Magadan

Vyatlag
Perm

Novosibirsk  Siblag

Vladivostok

Steplag
Dzhezkazgan

**The Gulag at
Its Zenith**

——— International border

☐ Gulag camp

● City

N

0     400     800 mi.

0   400   800 km

**Yugoslavia Before the Breakup**

— International border
—·—·— Republic border
—— —— Autonomous area border
⊛ National capital
• Republic or autonomous area capital

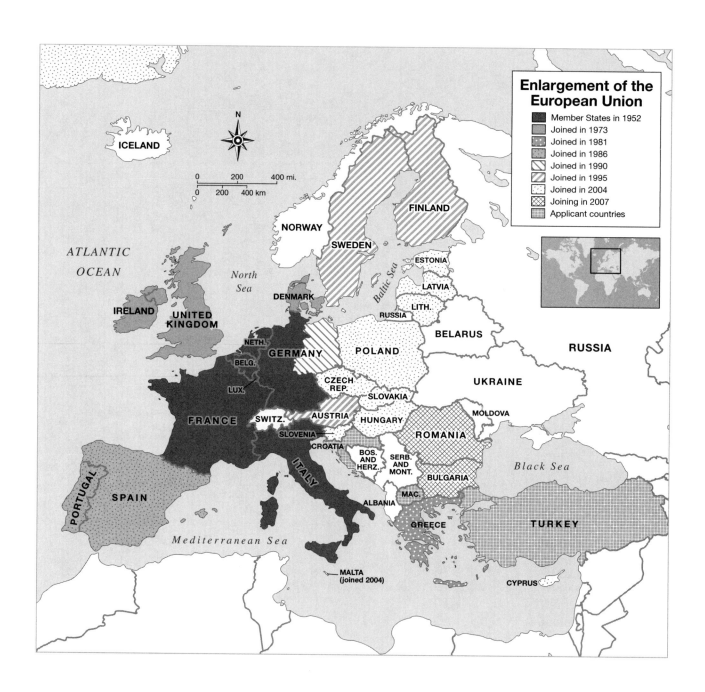

**CHILD CARE.** Child care has always been problematic. In nineteenth-century industrial society, child care was a social necessity resulting from mothers working. At the time, solutions were most often found on an individual basis, by having the children looked after by relatives, neighbors, or a nanny. As early as 1844, Firmin Marbeau in France conceived the idea of a model day care center, which constituted the first stage in the development of a comprehensive education system for working-class children, including "mothers' schools" for women who were obliged to work. The nursery, which was supposed to substitute for mothers during working hours, was to become a powerful instrument of control over social and family life, aiming to turn working women into worthy mothers and housewives. The idea was soon to be taken over in other countries.

In the twentieth century, the period between the two world wars was a time of paradoxes. Interest in the family had never been so vivid, and the role of the mother became a central issue. The obsession with demography sparked by massive loss of life during World War I gave rise to the widespread conviction that work outside the home was incompatible with a woman's natural destiny as mother and wife, and care for the child became a key political issue. The nineteenth-century conception of the child as an asset gave way to the idea of the child as a responsibility and subsequently to the child as an "idol," demanding total physical and psychological commitment on the part of the mother. As a result, motherhood came to be viewed as a vocational activity, a fundamental social function requiring careful monitoring and management, and national associations were created for the training of mothers and the protection of children. The nursery consultations and home visits set up by these bodies clearly reflected an intention to exert control over social and family life.

Numerous moralists viewed these nurseries as a necessary evil that ought to be resorted to only in case of absolute necessity and not advocated as a standard solution. An interview with applicant families prior to admission was often required, allowing the service providers to monitor the environment within which the child grew up. Evening meals, most often limited to soup, were distributed, a practice that lasted into the 1970s. Children could now be entrusted to private child minders, host families, or neighbors in return for payment. In certain villages and the suburbs of large cities, child care even evolved into a specialized activity.

The availability of child care facilities played a key role in the maintenance of women on the labor market after the birth of a child. In most European countries, given the growing ratio of women, and especially young mothers, in the workforce, the post–World War II years witnessed increasing state intervention in the domain of family politics and the development of different forms of child care.

**Child care workers from the St. Margaret Day Nursery take children for a walk, London, May 1937.** ©HULTON-DEUTSCH COLLECTION/CORBIS

Thus, for example, several Western European countries devoted a substantial effort to facilitating child care, whether in the form of extended funding for parental leave or a considerable increase in the provision of public child care. In Sweden, parental leave was instituted in 1974, and the provision of public care centers has kept growing ever since (from 2 percent in the 1960s to 10 percent in the early 1970s and 50 percent in 1994). In 1995 a law obliged boroughs to provide access to a care center for all children aged one to six. In the Netherlands, where public accommodation for children under three was practically nonexistent in the early 1980s, an active public policy allowed the creation of seventy thousand additional places in a very short time span.

But in the years since the 1980s, a period marked by increasing unemployment and the crisis of the welfare state, these policies have been called

into question, and one cannot but observe a breakdown in both the quality and quantity of child care centers. Moreover, since the downfall of the communist regimes, whose impressive network of child care facilities was the object of a specific government policy, a reduction in the number of centers has been felt throughout Eastern Europe as well.

It would be an error, however, to believe that the opposition between the traditional view advocating the return of mothers to the home to look after their children and a more progressive view, emphasizing the equal distribution of domestic and family responsibilities between fathers and mothers, coincides with the traditional split between right- and left-wing political tendencies. Thus in Sweden it was a right-wing government dominated by conservatives that passed a bill obliging boroughs to provide accommodation in a collective facility for every child aged one or more, while in France it was under François Mitterrand's socialist presidency that the AGED (Allocation de Garde d'Enfant à Domicile) was introduced, encouraging parents to provide care for their children at home.

Yet throughout Europe the growing proportion of women in the workforce and the evolution of social perspectives and pedagogy have led to an ever increasing demand for child care outside the home. In 2000, if one excepts the Scandinavian countries, which have always been in the vanguard of child care policies, the highest rate of children from three to six entrusted to outside care was in France, Belgium, and Italy. In France in the late twentieth century, 95 percent of all children in this age bracket attended a nursery school, and a range of other facilities was offered for children of school age. But the accommodation of children under three in state-financed facilities in Europe is more limited, whatever the country. In countries like England or Germany, family matters are generally regarded as belonging to the private domain, and as a result, such facilities as are available are private or depend on arrangements within the family. In the Mediterranean countries, where the social structure is still heavily marked by intergenerational solidarity, the public authorities have little say in the care provided for young children. The ratio of children under three accommodated in public-service facilities is 3 percent in Italy and practically nil in Spain, Ireland, and Germany. By contrast, Sweden, Denmark, and to a lesser degree France, Holland, and Belgium have favored the development of small-scale child care structures. In Denmark over 50 percent of the children under three are looked after in publicly financed structures, compared to 30 percent in Belgium and Sweden. In France the number of places available to children under three in collective structures has grown from 36,000 in 1969 to 267,000 in 1999, and demand keeps growing. Throughout Europe, one may also observe the appearance of individual or neighborhood initiatives like parent-managed care centers, in which parents take turns caring for each others' children to compensate for the deficit in public-service facilities.

In Germany the traditional mother-child relationship has prevailed in the western half of the country. Child care centers are still rare and recourse to kindergartens has been a late development. In the 1960s only one-third of the children between four and six would attend a nursery school, as the medical discourse on the risk of contamination and illness and family beliefs about the psychological hazards of early separation between mother and child long prevailed over arguments favorable to entrusting young children to collective care.

Thus concerns about child care have varied from one country to another, conditioned notably by differing political and institutional environments, and have been associated with health, hygiene, economic, demographic, or pedagogical issues or shaped by ideas such as the role of the mother in the household or equality between men and women. Together or separately, all these issues have come to determine family policies. Early-childhood policies have always been fraught with heavy gender connotations, as the domain of child care has long remained a female prerogative and has, as a result, been credited with only minor economic and cultural value.

*See also* **Childhood and Adolescence; Domestic Service; Welfare State.**

BIBLIOGRAPHY

Bock, Gisela, and Pat Thane, eds. *Maternity and Gender Politics: Women and the Rise of the Welfare State, 1880s–1950s.* London, 1991.

European Commission Network on Childcare. *A Review of Services for Young Children in the European Union, 1990–1995.* Brussels, 1996.

Fenet, Francine, Frédérique Leprince, and Liliane Périer. *Les modes d'accueil des jeunes enfants.* Paris, 2002

Heinen, Jacqueline, ed. *La petite enfance: pratiques et politiques.* Paris, 1998.

VALÉRIE PIETTE

---

# CHILDHOOD AND ADOLESCENCE.

The twentieth century might well be called the century of the child and the adolescent. The Swedish reformer Ellen Key chose New Year's Day of 1900 to publish her *Century of the Child*, and it was followed four years later by G. Stanley Hall's *Adolescence*. The idea of the child has a long history, but the concept of the adolescent was a late-nineteenth-century creation. Both were nourished by the European and American urban middle classes, which saw themselves as creating new civilization in which childhood and adolescence would have a unique status, superior not only to that assigned them by the peasant and working classes but by all previous societies, western as well as nonwestern. These concepts would be only partially realized until the post–World War II era, when in developed countries the treatment of children and adolescents became relatively standardized according to urban middle-class notions of both age and gender. For the relatively brief period from 1950 to 1980, it was possible to talk in gendered ways about *the* child and *the* adolescent in Western European societies, but by the beginning of the twenty-first century the universality of both categories was again in question.

## CHILDHOOD, ADOLESCENCE, AND IDEOLOGY

It is important to note that childhood and adolescence are normative notions based less on what children and adolescents actually are than on an ideology of what they ought to be. Both are based on a notion of life as a linear, irreversible passage through a series of strongly gendered stages, a nineteenth-century evolutionary concept that assumed that both individuals and peoples develop through time. According to this view of the world, nonwestern peoples were childish, new nations were youthful, and older European nations were mature. These modern concepts of human development were reinforced by equally novel notions of gender. In earlier periods, less had been made of differences between boy and girl infants. As late as 1900, boys were dressed in skirts and their hair allowed to grow long until they were properly "breeched" (put into trousers) and ceremoniously shorn. Even in the twentieth century, childhood was gendered feminine, something boys needed to be distanced from if they were to grow up to be "real" men. The greater number of rites of passage associated with male adolescence than with female reflected the expectation that boys would put away childish, girlish things. Indeed, for most of the twentieth century, when people spoke of youth they were usually referring to males. In the work of G. Stanley Hall and his successors, female adolescence was given little attention, as if women

moved from childhood to adulthood in a seamless sequence culminating in marriage, contrasting sharply with the discontinuous, often troubled lives of young men. Male adolescence became associated with hypermasculinity, and with delinquency, political radicalism, and violence. Fears of female deviancy focused mainly on sexuality. These powerful stereotypes held sway in Europe for most of the twentieth century and only at the turn of the twenty-first century are they being challenged.

The appeal of these stereotypes must be understood in the context of significant demographic, economic, social, and political trends in Western European societies in the twentieth century. Following a pattern initiated by the middle classes, Europeans reduced their fertility while at the same time extending their longevity. The result was that each successive cohort of children and adolescents was smaller. The proportion of younger to older age groups fell significantly, while both childhood and adolescence became increasingly refined into smaller subgroups—babies and infants, preteens and teens—each of which was accorded its own special status and treatment. Although fewer in number, children and adolescents loomed ever larger in European consciousness. By the 1960s and 1970s, the prophecies of Key and Hall seemed to have been realized.

This trend was reinforced by changes in the economy, which removed first children and then adolescents from the labor market and from the world of adults. Trends that had begun before 1914 accelerated during the Depression and culminated after 1945 in a situation where young people's primary function became consumption rather than production. Children became the target of advertising aimed at getting adults to spend on their behalf, and a new teenage market in clothes, music, and sport developed. Among poor and immigrant populations, children remained a source of economic support for families, but compulsory schooling removed virtually all children and a growing proportion of adolescents from full-time employment. By the 1960s, both children and adolescents were largely dependent on their families, an unprecedented condition and one that depressed the European fertility rate still further. Families, now smaller than ever before, were keeping their offspring at home longer than previous

**Children with their teacher in class, Mont, France, 1950.** The enactment of compulsory education laws proved a major factor in shaping the nature of childhood in the twentieth century. ©HULTON-DEUTSCH COLLECTION/CORBIS

generations had, reinforcing the identification of children (especially girls) with the private realm of home and family, breaking their long-standing connection with workplaces, streets, and the public sphere.

### AGE SEGREGATION

Outside of families and kin groups, the world of children and adolescents was sharply segregated from that of adults. Already segregated by schooling, they were now served by an array of social services keyed to their perceived special needs. The medical specialty of pediatrics spawned new fields of child and adolescent psychology. The growth of the welfare state brought with it new agencies concerned exclusively with the care of young people. Beginning in the 1920s, special courts were established to deal with juvenile delinquency. Likewise, the publishing, music, and film industries became

segmented along age lines. Radio and later television offered special programming for children and teenagers. Censorship of media came to be justified in the name of protecting innocent children and vulnerable juveniles. In a similar way, age minimums applied to drinking, smoking, and driving reflected increasingly strict age segregation in all social activities.

Never before had European society been so age segregated, with the result that adults began to worry about losing touch with the younger generation. An awareness of peer group influence, reflected in a concern with juvenile delinquency, had been growing since the late nineteenth century but reached a peak after 1945, when, despite all evidence of growing conformity, a series of moral panics about juvenile crime and deviancy swept through Europe. By this time, both children and youth had assumed enormous symbolic power.

They had become a kind of litmus test of social well-being and national vitality. The bodies of young athletes were assigned enormous national and racial significance in the Olympics before and after World War II. In an effort to rejuvenate itself in the wake of its defeat in 1940, France invested enormously in its youth. During the Cold War, youth was everywhere on the frontline, symbolizing either the supposed strength or weakness of the contending powers.

Children and adolescents took on unprecedented iconic power in the course of the twentieth century. Children came to stand for an innocence that was assumed to be lost in the course of maturation. Paradise had once been seen as a place; now it was a stage of life. Adult nostalgia for lost childhood was reflected in the proliferation of child-centered holidays such as Christmas and in popular photography, which focused almost exclusively on children. Only the home, and a home under the supervision of a competent mother, was thought sufficient to preserve this paradise. Thus although child-protection laws proliferated, they stopped short of regulating family life, despite the evidence that child abuse was more common in private than in public life.

The symbolic status assigned to adolescents was different. The teen years were increasingly described as tumultuous and rebellious. Despite evidence that modern adolescents were no more violent or radical than earlier generations, they were recruited symbolically as well as physically by various self-described leftist and rightist "youth" movements during the 1920s and 1930s. Youth continued to serve a similar function in the 1960s, but even in quieter times adolescence was still used to represent what was unacceptable, if not illegal. The threatening image of the juvenile delinquent came to symbolize everything that Europeans had come to see as unacceptable in the adult male. In a similar way, sexual fear came to be focused on the teenage unwed mother, despite evidence of declining illegitimacy rates throughout the Western world. The functions that demons and witches had once performed in earlier societies were transferred to the teenager. Even as children came to symbolize innocence lost, teenagers represented newfound evils.

## CHRONOLOGIZATION

Normativized notions of *the* child and *the* adolescent reached their apogee from 1950 to 1980 and found their clearest expression in the work of psychologists such as John Bowlby and Erik Erikson and in a postwar sociology bent on revealing universal laws of human development. Until Phlippe Ariès published his *Centuries of Childhood* in the early 1960s, both childhood and adolescence had been treated as timeless. In retrospect, however, these static, essentialized notions can be seen as a way of denying or containing the very changes that were sweeping through Western capitalist societies and would soon affect communist Europe. Postwar Europe was experiencing an education revolution that had already transformed its age and gender systems. By the 1960s, virtually all female as well as male adolescents were in secondary education; by the 1990s a sizable proportion of young people would continue on to a university or technical education. By then it was common to distinguish older youth from adolescents and even to talk about a stage of young adulthood prior to marriage.

The new service-oriented, information-based economy was closely tied to the welfare state that had emerged during the era of the Cold War. In addition to expanding the duration of schooling, the welfare state institutionalized child and youth welfare services, standardized age minimums, and policed the boundaries between the young and old. European societies had gained an unprecedented measure of social security, but at the cost of increased regulation of its citizens' lives. In addition, the maintenance of military service after 1945 ensured that the lives of young men were especially controlled, but young women were no less affected by the strict moral and sexual codes of the period.

An unprecedented degree of age conformity had been achieved, reflected in the increasing uniformity with which people of all classes and ethnic groups moved through schooling, into work, and then into marriage. What Martin Kohli has called the "chronologization" of European life reached its apex by the 1980s. Even as other standards of behavior became less rigid, age norms took on ever greater influence. In terms of dress, musical taste, and other markers of status, lines were now drawn between generations rather than within generations on a class or ethnic basis. It would not be an exaggeration to say that in Europe class discrimination was displaced by age discrimination.

## BOUNDARY EROSION

But all this was about to change. By the 1980s, the fertility rate in some parts of Europe dropped close to or below the replacement level. Many people were already delaying having children, but some were now deciding against having children altogether. In many places, the fertility rate among immigrants was much higher than that among the native born; and because people were living so much longer, the proportion of children and youth became ever smaller. Children were still regarded as precious, but with the collapse of communism throughout Eastern Europe, state support was drastically reduced and child poverty increased dramatically. But Western European economies were also feeling the effects of the restructuring of capitalism that had become associated from the 1970s onward with the term *globalization*. As manufacturing shifted to third world countries, male workers' wages in Europe stagnated and unemployment increased. Married women entered the workforce in larger numbers to compensate. Western European welfare states softened the effects of loss of jobs and income, but everywhere young people again began to take up paid work in order to earn spending money to sustain their status as consumers. It was now not uncommon to combine work and school at the secondary and post-secondary levels.

The boundaries between age groups were visibly eroding. Media and advertising targeted ever younger age groups, exposing them to language and images once reserved for their elders. Sexual maturity was occurring at earlier ages and access to tobacco, alcohol, and drugs became easier. New categories—preteens and tweens—emerged to describe this precocity. Even as the lines between children and teenagers blurred, adolescence seemed to merge with adulthood. Teenagers moved into the spaces once occupied by their elders, and young adults, now postponing marriage to their thirties, seemed less mature than earlier generations. Age norms that had once seemed fixed by nature suddenly seemed uncertain, open to negotiation.

Even as age norms were flexing, they were also becoming more diverse as Europe itself became more heterogeneous in the late decades of the twentieth century. Patterns of age groupings had been different in Eastern and Western Europe, and differences remained in the expanded European Union. New immigrant groups, especially from Muslim countries, further diversified the age cultures of host countries. In France and Germany, difference was increasingly the occasion for tension and outright conflict. Everywhere there was a sense that childhood and adolescence were changing. Some observers even thought they were disappearing. Both became less strongly gendered as the perceived differences between males and females were reassessed. The movement of women into previously male spheres of activity, including the military, was partly responsible. Evidence of female aptitude for violence and gang behavior, as well as the growing awareness of the feminine side of many males, eroded both age and gender boundaries. At the end of the century, discussions of adolescent homosexuality and bisexuality further loosened the grip of old essentialized stereotypes of age and sex.

All these changes have highlighted the mutable nature of both childhood and adolescence. They have not only prompted an abundance of psychological and sociological studies but triggered much valuable historical research, which throws light on the changing nature of age relations. Whatever the future of childhood and adolescence may be, these categories will no longer be able to be viewed as universal or static, exempt from the contingencies of time and space. Henceforth one will have to speak of Europe's multiple childhoods and adolescences.

*See also* **Child Care; Consumption; Demography; Education; Gender; Old Age; Sexuality.**

BIBLIOGRAPHY

Ariès, Philippe. *Centuries of Childhood: A Social History of Family Life.* Translated by Robert Baldick. New York, 1962.

Fass, Paula S., ed. *Encyclopedia of Children and Childhood: In History and Society.* 3 vols. New York, 2004.

Gillis, John R. *Youth and History: Continuity and Change in European Age Relations, 1770–Present.* Revised ed. New York, 1981.

Hall, G. Stanley. *Adolescence: Its Psychology and Its Relations to Physiology, Anthropology, Sociology, Sex, Crime, Religion, and Education.* 2 vols. New York, 1904.

Jobs, Richard. *Riding the New Wave: Youth and the Rejuvenation of France after the Second World War.* Ph.D. diss., Rutgers University, 2002.

Key, Ellen Karolina Sofia. *The Century of the Child.* New York, 1909.

Kohli, Martin. "Die Internationalisierung des Lebenslauf." *Vierteljahresheft fuer Soziologie und Sozialpsychologie* 1 (1985): 1–29.

Levi, Giovanni, and Jean-Claude Schmitt, eds. *A History of Young People in the West.* Vol. 2. Translated by Camille Naish. Cambridge, Mass., 1997.

Mitterauer, Michael. *A History of Youth.* Oxford, U.K., 1993.

JOHN R. GILLIS

# CHIRAC, JACQUES (b. 1932), French politician.

Jacques Chirac is the great survivor of modern French politics. Over a career spanning forty years he has held every major office, culminating in his election as president in 1995. Born in 1932 to a middle-class family, Chirac studied at the prestigious École Nationale d'Administration (ENA), the training ground of high civil servants. He became an aide to the Gaullist Prime Minister, Georges Pompidou (1911–1974), who nicknamed Chirac the "bulldozer" because of his great energy. Pompidou encouraged Chirac to enter politics and he was elected for the rural department of the Corrèze in 1967. In 1967 he was given his first ministerial post, and when Pompidou became president in 1969 Chirac was promoted to various senior ministerial positions.

After Pompidou's premature death in 1974 Chirac backed the centrist candidate Valery Giscard d'Estaing (b. 1926) over the Gaullist Jacques Chaban-Delmas (1915–2000), claming that he considered Giscard the conservative candidate best placed to prevent the victory of the Left. Many Gaullists saw this as treason, but Giscard rewarded Chirac by appointing him prime minister. Relations between the two men quickly deteriorated and in 1976 Chirac became the only prime minister of the Fifth Republic to resign rather than being dismissed by the president. Now he set about taking over the Gaullist party (renamed the Rally for the Republic, RPR), and turned it into the instrument of his ascent to power. He challenged Giscard increasingly openly, defeating his candidate for the mayoralty of Paris in 1977. Paris became Chirac's second power base along with the Corrèze. In a notorious speech in December 1978 Chirac came close to denouncing Giscard's pro-Europeanism as treason. In 1981 Chirac stood in the presidential election and came third in the first round. He studiously avoided recommending that his voters transfer their votes to Giscard in the second round. This is widely credited with having aided the Socialist François Mitterrand (1916–1996) to beat Giscard narrowly in the second round. Having betrayed Chaban in 1974 Chirac betrayed Giscard in 1981. By 1986 Mitterrand's popularity was waning, and in the parliamentary elections of that year the RPR won the largest number of votes. Mitterrand appointed Chirac prime minister, leading to the first "cohabitation" in the Fifth Republic between a president from one party and a prime minister from another. Chirac came to power committed to reversing the nationalizations carried out by the socialists. Much of this program was carried out, but he was politically outwitted by Mitterrand, who skillfully took credit for the popular measures of Chirac's government while distancing himself from the unpopular ones. When Chirac stood against Mitterrand in the presidential election of 1988 he was comfortably beaten by him in the second round. When the pattern repeated itself in 1993 and the Right again won the legislative elections Chirac held himself in reserve and let one of his colleagues become prime minister in his place. Finally in 1995 he was elected president against the Socialist Lionel Jospin (b. 1937) by a comfortable margin.

As president Chirac quickly ran into trouble. Although having promised in the elections to remedy the "social fracture" caused by unemployment, his government carried out public expenditure cuts. This led to a massive wave of strikes in the autumn of 1995 and the government had to backtrack. In April 1997 Chirac took the gamble of dissolving parliament and to everyone's surprise the Left won the elections. Chirac was now forced into "cohabitation" with Jospin as his prime minister.

Having been president only two years, he found himself powerless. In the 2002 presidential election, Chirac stood again, coming top in the first round. To universal amazement, the extreme Right candidate Jean-Marie Le Pen (b. 1925) pushed the Socialists into third place. In the second round, therefore, Chirac won an unprecedented majority of 82 percent as left-wing voters rallied to him in order to bar the way to Le Pen. Chirac failed to exploit this extraordinary situation. Although he won domestic popularity for opposing the Iraq War in 2003 he was increasingly dogged by allegations of corruption dating back to his period as mayor of Paris. In 2005 he called a referendum on the European constitution, recommending that people vote for it. The "no" vote won comfortably. This was widely seen as a vote more against Chirac than against the constitution. Chirac did not resign and merely replaced his prime minister. But he seemed an increasingly discredited and ageing figure, although possibly still nursing dreams of standing for president again.

The paradox of Chirac's career is that although he is excellent at achieving and holding power, he has never known what to do with it. He has been a master of the politics of patronage, and it is from this that the accusations of corruption have stemmed. There is no discernible ideological consistency in his career. If he can in any sense be called a Gaullist, it is the pragmatic Gaullism of Pompidou over the historic Gaullism of Charles de Gaulle (1890–1970). He has been variously anti-European (1978) and pro-European (2005); he talked the language of Thatcherite economics in 1986 and the language of social welfarism in 1995. It has often been remarked of Chirac that he was ideally suited to the Fourth Republic, where the executive had limited power and the name of the game was survival. In the Fifth Republic, where the executive has potentially great power, that is not enough.

*See also* **France; Giscard d'Estaing, Valéry; Le Pen, Jean-Marie; Mitterrand, François; Paris.**

BIBLIOGRAPHY

Jarreau, Patrick. *La France de Chirac.* Paris, 1995.

Michaud, Yves. *Chirac dans le texte: la parole et l'impuissance.* Paris, 2004.

Tessier, Arnaud. *Le Dernier septennat: 1995–2002: Jacques Chirac.* Paris, 2002.

Tuppen, John. *Chirac's France 1986–88: Contemporary Issues in French Society.* New York, 1991.

JULIAN JACKSON

---

**CHRISTIAN DEMOCRACY.** Christian Democracy has a good claim to be considered the most successful and one of the most durable and influential political forces in twentieth-century Europe. From the 1890s to the 1990s, parties claiming a primarily Christian inspiration for their political actions garnered mass support in elections and occupied positions of power in municipal, regional, and national governments. This success was all the more remarkable given the strong downward trend in religious practice in many (although not all) areas of Europe during much of the twentieth century. Despite social and cultural secularization, Christian Democratic parties were highly adept at winning support for their distinctive political message of moderate democracy, social justice, and Christian morality. This was particularly so in the predominantly Catholic areas of central Europe. Although Christian Democratic parties emerged almost everywhere in Europe, from Poland and the Baltic States in the east to Spain and Portugal in the southwest, their heartland always lay in a band of territories stretching from the Low Countries (Belgium and the Netherlands) in the north through western Germany and eastern France to Austria, Switzerland, and northeastern Italy. In these areas, Christian parties in their various permutations were, for much of the twentieth century, the dominant political force and exerted a formative influence over the structures of state and society.

**DEFINITION**

It is not easy to define who exactly was or was not a Christian Democrat during the twentieth century. Historians and political scientists, and especially those who are sympathetic to Christian Democracy, have a tendency to incorporate all broadly progressive Christian political movements into a Christian Democratic tradition—a tradition that reached its apogee in the powerful Christian Democratic parties that dominated the politics of many Western European states for roughly twenty-five years after the end of the World War II (1945). Such an interpretation, however, risks neglecting the diversity that existed within Christian politics in twentieth-century Europe.

Not all Christian political parties can accurately be described as democratic. Indeed, many, especially in the first half of the century, were explicitly anti-democratic in their inspiration and political ideology. Moreover, the durable confessional fault line between Catholicism and the various Protestant churches of Europe was reflected in differing patterns of political engagement. Especially after 1945, Christian Democratic parties in mixed Catholic and Protestant states, such as Germany, made much of their openness to Christians of all denominations, but Christian Democracy was always a primarily Catholic movement. The connection between Christian belief and political commitment was more individual and less automatic in the Protestant churches than in the more hierarchical and unitary structures of Catholicism. Religious practice remained high in some largely Protestant societies, notably in Scandinavia, and Protestant churches, such as the Anglican Church in the United Kingdom, often occupied a privileged position in state and society, but in none of these largely Protestant states did Christian Democratic parties become a major political force.

**ORIGINS**

It is more accurate to regard Christian Democracy as a particular form of Catholic political engagement that, although initially only a minority presence in Catholic ranks, came strongly to the fore after 1945. Its origins lay in the Catholic milieu of late-nineteenth-century Europe. The term *Christian Democrat* first came to be used by Catholic social and spiritual organizations in Belgium, France, and Germany in the 1880s and 1890s, for whom the word *democrat* represented not a commitment to democracy but a wish to reach out to the ordinary people often neglected by middle- and upper-class Catholic organizations. Their ambitions were more social than political. Inspired by the encyclicals, or public statements, issued by the popes, such as "Rerum Novarum" (New kingdom), published by Leo XIII in 1891, these activists, many of whom came from privileged backgrounds, sought to alleviate the material sufferings of the poor, especially in the new urban and industrial centers.

These paternalist forms of charity went together, however, with an emerging vision of a new social and economic order in which the competitive individualism and secularism of liberal capitalist society would be replaced by Catholic values of harmony and cooperation. Thus, before 1914, Christian Democrats began to develop organizations such as cooperatives, agricultural syndicates, and trade unions, within which a new generation of Christian Democratic workers, small-scale farmers, and white-collar employees was formed. Tentatively at first, their ambitions became more political. Christian Democratic trade unions competed with their larger socialist rivals for the support of workers, and Christian Democratic activists made their entry into Catholic political parties such as the Zentrumspartei (Center Party) in Germany and the Catholic Party in Belgium, which had emerged in the late nineteenth century to defend Catholic interests in local and national politics. Christian Democracy was, however, only a minority current in pre-1914 European Catholic politics. The German and Belgian parties, as well as the Christlich-Soziale Partei (Christian Social Party) in Austria, continued to be dominated by a middle-class elite and committed to the protection of the Catholic Church's institutional interests.

This largely remained the case during the interwar years. The democratic reforms enacted in many European states after World War I, such as the establishment of the Weimar Republic in Germany, created a more favorable environment for Christian Democracy. Membership in Christian trade unions increased rapidly, notably in Germany, Italy, and France, and the established Catholic parties were obliged to open their ranks more fully to Christian Democrats in order to reach out to a mass electorate. The dominant trend in Catholic politics during the interwar years was, however, away from the practical and incremental economic and social reforms favored by Christian Democrats. Instead, many Catholics were drawn toward the more militant rhetoric of spiritual reconquest favored by the papacy or toward ideologies of the extreme Right. In Italy, the short-lived progressive Catholic party, the Partito Popolare Italiano (Italian Popular Party), was swept away by the Fascist seizure of power in

1922, and in Spain the Confederación Española de Derechas Autónomas (Spanish Confederation of Autonomous Right-Wing Groups), the principal Catholic political party during the Second Republic (1931–1936), collapsed in the turmoil of the Civil War (1936–1939), during which many Catholics supported the Nationalist forces led by General Franco. In Germany, the Nazi Party won a lower proportion of the votes in Catholic areas of Germany, and along with most Catholic political organizations Christian Democrats opposed the militantly nationalist and populist tone of Nazi electoral rhetoric. But with Hitler's accession to power in January 1933 and the subsequent concordat between the Nazi regime and the papacy in July 1933, Christian Democratic groups were obliged to either disband or continue their activities discreetly within the institutions of the Catholic Church.

## HEYDAY

Given this history, it is at first sight surprising that Christian Democratic parties should have emerged so powerfully onto the European political stage after 1945. In Italy, the new Catholic party, Democrazia Cristiana (Christian Democracy), won an impressive 35 percent of the vote in the first postwar elections (1946), and the party's initial leader, Alcide De Gasperi, was prime minister of the new Italian state until 1953. In Belgium and the Netherlands, the Christelijke Volkspartij–Parti Social Chrétien and Katholieke Volkspartij, respectively, rapidly became major parties in the postwar political system, as did the Österreichische Volkspartei in Austria. Perhaps most dramatic was the success of the Christian Democratic parties in France and Germany. In France, where political polarization between supporters and opponents of the republic had hitherto hindered the development of an autonomous Christian Democratic politics, the Mouvement Républicain Populaire (MRP), established in 1944 by Christian Democratic activists, won 28 percent of the vote in the 1946 elections, making it the principal electoral rival to the Communist Party. In Germany, the Catholic Church was one of the few remaining social organizations after the final collapse of Nazism. Christian Democratic politicians established a new party, the Christlich-Demokratische Union (Christian Democrat Union, CDU), in

1945, which with its sister party, the Christlich-Soziale Union (Christian Social Union, CSU) in Bavaria, became the leading political force in the new Federal Republic of Germany (West Germany, created in 1949). The CDU and CSU dominated West German politics in the 1950s and 1960s, and the Catholic leader of the CDU, Konrad Adenauer, became the first chancellor of the new German state.

The emergence of Christian Democracy after 1945 was largely due to changes within Catholic political ranks. The engagement of many Catholic political groups with the extreme Right during the 1920s and 1930s left the way open for a new generation of Christian Democratic activists to come to the fore. These were predominantly younger people, often from intellectual backgrounds, who had been formed in the Catholic spiritual and social organizations that had proliferated in the interwar years. Some had been active in the Resistance against German occupation during the war, and most shared a strong belief in the need to create a modern, Christian-inspired politics that accepted the defining framework of parliamentary democracy. This new mood of openness was accompanied, however, by more traditional Catholic mentalities. Fear of communism—both of the Soviet Union and of the national Communist parties—had been intensified by the events of the war years, prompting a mentality of Catholic solidarity against the threat of communist rule or of a popular front of socialist and liberal anticlerical forces. Another element of Christian Democracy's appeal was that many of the traditional right-wing parties had been discredited by fascism and the center-right ideology of the Christian Democratic parties appealed to many electors who no longer had a political home. The Christian Democratic parties therefore skillfully combined appeals to Christian unity with a strong rhetoric of anticommunism and policies designed to appeal to social groups such as farmers and the middle classes that had formerly tended to vote for the political right.

This formula was a successful one. By the end of the 1950s, it was possible to speak of Christian Democratic dominance in the politics of Western Europe. With the notable exception of France, where the MRP declined rapidly during the 1950s, Christian Democratic parties were a major governmental force in Germany, Austria, Switzerland, Italy, Belgium, the Netherlands, and Luxembourg. It is perhaps no accident that, apart from Austria and Switzerland, these states were also signatories of the Treaty of Rome (1957), which established the European Economic Community (EEC). The EEC's moderate parliamentary democracy and economic free market combined with substantial welfare provisions and economic protection for the professions and agricultural producers bore the imprint of its Christian Democratic founders. Thus, although the leaders of the Christian Democratic parties remained careful to emphasize their commitment to a Christian social and political ideal, they were by the 1960s increasingly secular parties of the center-right, drawing their support from rural and small-town Europe as well as from the middle classes and from technical and white-collar employees who had benefited from the high levels of postwar economic growth.

## DECLINE AND TRANSFORMATION

By the end of the 1960s, Christian Democratic parties were on the wane. Social Democratic parties were competing effectively for elements of their electorate, and the profound changes in the character of Catholicism initiated by the Second Vatican Council (1962–1965) eroded the close connection between religious practice and political commitment. Many Christian trade unions broke away from the parties, and Catholic militants engaged in the new forms of social protest that swept across Europe during the late 1960s and early 1970s. In Italy, Democrazia Cristiana remained a powerful bulwark against the threat of a Communist electoral victory, but elsewhere the 1970s was an era of marked decline for Christian Democratic parties. The unity of purpose and the mentality derived from a Christian identity that they had once built on were no longer as powerful and Christian Democratic parties were obliged to find new identities and ways of winning electoral support.

They did so with varying degrees of success. In Italy, Democrazia Cristiana effectively disappeared in the realignment of political forces that took place in the 1990s. But in Germany, and to a lesser degree in Belgium and the Netherlands, the Christian Democrats proved to be much more

resilient. Under the long chancellorship of Helmut Kohl (1982 to 1998), the CDU and CSU once again dominated the government and they presided over the reunification of the country after the collapse of the German Democratic Republic (East Germany). As Kohl's success demonstrated, however, the power of Christian Democracy depended on maintaining the support of those middle-class and rural voters who had long formed the core of its supporters, as well as on emphasizing such themes as prudent economic management and the construction of a united Europe, which could win over less committed voters. In this way, Christian Democratic parties were able to live on, even when the distinctive political and social ideology that had given rise to Christian Democracy had largely come to an end.

*See also* **Adenauer, Konrad; Catholicism; Common Agricultural Policy; Resistance; Vatican II.**

BIBLIOGRAPHY

Buchanan, Tom, and Martin Conway, eds. *Political Catholicism in Europe, 1918–1965.* Oxford, U.K., 1996. A collection of essays on the development of Catholic politics from the World War I onward, organized by nation.

Conway, Martin. *Catholic Politics in Europe, 1918–1945.* New York and London, 1997. A study of the interwar evolution of Catholic politics.

Gehler, Michael, and Wolfram Kaiser, eds. *Christian Democracy in Europe since 1945.* London, 2004. The foremost single-volume study of Christian Democracy in its post-1945 heyday.

Kalyvas, Stathis. *The Rise of Christian Democracy in Europe.* Ithaca, N.Y., and London, 1996. An important account of the emergence of Christian Democracy.

Kselman, Thomas, and Joseph A. Buttigieg, eds. *European Christian Democracy: Historical Legacies and Comparative Perspectives.* Notre Dame, Ind., 2003. A series of analytical and reflective essays on the Christian Democrat phenomenon.

Lamberts, Emiel, eds. *Christian Democracy in the European Union, 1945/1995: Proceedings of the Leuven Colloquium, 15–18 November, 1995.* Leuven, Belgium, 1997. A comprehensive collection of informative essays on Christian Democrat parties, paying particular attention to their role in the European Union.

Van Hecke, Steven, and Emmanuel Gerard, eds. *Christian Democratic Parties in Europe since the End of the Cold War.* Leuven, Belgium, 2004. A collection of essays on the evolution of Christian Democracy at the end of the twentieth century.

Warner, Carolyn M. *Confessions of an Interest Group. The Catholic Church and Political Parties in Europe.* Princeton, N.J., 2000. An analysis of the political strategies of the Catholic Church and its connection with Christian Democracy.

MARTIN CONWAY

---

**CHRISTO** (b. 1935), Bulgarian-born artist known for environmental art installations created in collaboration with his wife, Jeanne-Claude.

Since their first collaborative project in 1961, *Dockside Packages* (Cologne, West Germany), Christo and Jeanne-Claude (who use only their first names) have repackaged the ecological contexts of urban and rural environments through experimental transformations. Creating a fusion of artistic and societal engagement, they have engineered dozens of heroically scaled, transitory site-oriented works emerging out of the pop idiom of the 1960s and earth art movement of the early 1970s. Critical acclaim and enthusiastic endorsements are shared by aesthetic theorists, avid collectors, and supportive curators as well as civic and public leaders for expanding art's definition into new dimensions of social and community activism. The ensuing public discourse—Is it art? What does it mean?—becomes an essential element of the artistic process. Arguing before zoning boards and town councils, they encourage a dialogue between highbrow critics and Everyman. Less sympathetic observers have questioned their relentless self-promotion, claiming these stunts have relied on media promotion fueled by a Dada-inspired, antiart populism stripping away artistic boundaries. Accepting no commercial sponsors or corporate donations, they express a determination to "work in total freedom."

With constantly innovative uses of industrial materials called "hardware," they achieve disquieting acts of subterfuge and transformation. Landmark buildings, geological sites, public parks, and other iconic locations are characteristically wrapped in tarpaulins, draped in canvas, or concealed in thousands of square meters of fabrics and ropes, each given new but only temporary physical identities. Because these projects are expected to live by creation, not merely as sketchbook dreams,

Christo and Jean-Claude dismiss being called conceptual artists. Documentary films and elaborate "not for profit" funding schemes have gained them an enviable reputation as Robin-Hood-like artists-provocateurs.

Fatefully entwined, their destinies began at the same hour on 13 June 1935 when they were both born, but in dramatically diverse political circumstances. Christo (Christo Vladimirov Javacheff, born and raised in Gabrovo, Bulgaria) grew up in an educated, comfortable family of textile industrialists. Jeanne-Claude (Jeanne-Claude Denat de Guillebon) was born in Casablanca, Morocco, to a prominent French military family. She enjoyed an affluent childhood pampered in the milieu of colonial North Africa as her father rose to the rank of general. Christo's early years in the People's Republic of Bulgaria, a repressive satellite state of the communist Soviet empire, left an indelible impression. An ongoing quest for artistic freedom can be traced back to his memories of censored, restricted art in this era of Stalinist-driven socialist realism. An underlying motif would become permeating invisible borders, walls, and fences analogous to his origins behind the Iron Curtain. Between 1953 and 1956 Christo was quickly recognized for his superior drawing skills at the conservative Fine Arts Academy of Sofia. Ironically, his formative years were in complete isolation from postwar avant-garde movements and styles between Paris and New York. Escaping to the West from Prague to Vienna in a freezing, unheated freight train on 10 January 1957, Christo literally arrived without any possessions. He attended the Vienna Fine Arts Academy, stayed temporarily in Geneva, and arrived in Paris in 1958. The penniless Bulgarian artist met the privileged socialite in the Latin Quarter as their journeys merged into a single artistic persona.

Early influences can be traced to a transition from abstract expressionism to pop in commonplace, man-made materials used by Jasper Johns and Robert Rauschenberg. *Wrapped Bottles and Cans* (1958–1959) were Christo's first "packaged objects" establishing the theme of material alteration. *Wrapped Bottles and Cans* began an extended series of related "wrappings." While insisting their purpose is "more about altering an environment," the idea for wrapping was an underlying motif culminating in 1975 with the "wrapping" of the

***The Pont Neuf Wrapped, Paris, 1975-1985.*** Installation by Christo and Jeanne-Claude. REPRODUCED BY PERMISSION

Pont Neuf in Paris. Furthermore, they are quick to rectify misconceptions noting that it is "totally idiotic" to label them erroneously as "wrapping artists." Appreciating their use of "fabric, cloth, and textiles" in a manner that is "fragile, sensual, and temporary" enforces the notion that "wrapping is not at all the common denominator of the works."

Following the art world's shift from the lethargy of Paris, they established their permanent residence and studio in New York in 1964, and he became a U.S. citizen in 1973. A prescient *New York Times* review (2 May 1964) mentions the newly landed Christo's "pet trick . . . wrapped packages prompting curiosity." The astonishing future direction for Christo and Jeanne-Claude's career trajectory, utilizing hundreds of thousands of square feet of tarpaulin, miles of woven nylon fabrics, steel cables and ropes, and tons of steel and concrete, each project with a multimillion-dollar budget, has shaped one of the unique artistic résumés of the twentieth century.

Major projects often require an evolutionary process requiring a span of years or even decades from initial germination to realized completions. During the intial "software" period, the project evolves through preparatory drawings, collages, and scale models. As momentum gathers, Christo and Jeanne-Claude move toward "crystallization" of the project and oversee construction of the project's "hardware," inventing engineering and construction blueprints. The projects ultimately reach completion for days or a few weeks at a time under the glare of news media coverage and fine art photography and documentary cinematography capturing the moment. This is an "aesthetic decision" allowing the artists to "endow the works of art with the feeling of urgency to be seen, and the tenderness brought by the fact that it will not last."

Among their most noteworthy experimental projects are: *Wrapped Kunsthalle* (Bern, Switzerland, 1968); *Wrapped Museum of Contemporary Art* (Chicago, 1969); *Valley Curtain* (Rifle,

Colorado, 1970–1972); *Wrapped Roman Wall* (Rome, 1974); *Running Fence* (Sonoma and Marin Counties, California, 1972–1976); *Surrounded Islands* (Biscayne Bay, Miami, 1980–1983); *The Pont Neuf Wrapped* (Paris, 1975–1985); *The Umbrellas* (Ibaraki, Japan, and California, 1984–1991); *Wrapped Reichstag* (Berlin, 1971–1995); *Wrapped Trees* (Riehen-Basel, Switzerland, 1997–1998); *The Gates* (Central Park, New York City, 1979–2005); and *Over the River* (Arkansas River, Colorado, in progress at this writing.) Recognized as global artists, Christo and Jeanne-Claude are remarkably unpretentious, humorous, and humbled by their celebrity. They continue to enlighten and amuse, creating beguiling and intellectually unpredictable intersections between art and life. A ceaseless itinerary sparks this sprawling legacy of artistic prophesy alighting on four continents.

*See also* **Avant-Garde.**

BIBLIOGRAPHY

Chernow, Burt. *Christo and Jeanne-Claude: A Biography.* Epilogue by Wolfgang Volz. New York, 2002.

Fineberg, Jonathan. *Christo and Jeanne-Claude: On the Way to the Gates.* New Haven, Conn., 2004.

Laporte, Dominique. *Christo.* Translated by Abby Pollak. New York, 1986.

Schellmann, Jorg, and Josephine Benecke. *Christo Prints and Objects 1963–1995: A Catalogue Raisonné.* Munich and New York, 1995.

Vaizey, Marina. *Christo.* Barcelona, 1990.

PHILIP ELIASOPH

---

# CHURCHILL, WINSTON (1874–1965),
British politician, prime minister from 1940 to 1945 and 1951 to 1955.

After a long and controversial career, Winston Churchill became prime minister in May 1940, just as the German offensive in the west began. His inspiring leadership during the following year in which Britain stood alone against Adolf Hitler (1889–1945) was crucial in preventing a Nazi victory in World War II. After Russia and the United States entered the war in 1941, Churchill was one of the three leaders of the "grand alliance" that eventually defeated Germany in 1945. For these reasons, since 1945 Churchill has been popularly regarded as the most important figure in modern British history.

Churchill was a complex and fascinating figure, and his talents and drive were admired as much as his ambition and judgment were mistrusted. His industriousness, inquisitiveness, and ingenuity made him the master of any topic that he addressed or any government department that he was appointed to. As a cabinet minister he was an exasperating colleague, full of ideas and constantly intruding into areas outside his own responsibilities. His character and style revealed many childlike qualities: belligerent without malice, generous to opponents once defeated, fascinated by new inventions, and rushing in a whirlwind of energy from one topic to the next. He had an extraordinary command of the English language, both as an orator and as the author of many volumes of biography and history. However, his egotism, impetuousness, and lack of proportion frequently led to difficulties and sometimes to disaster. Churchill's recovery from these setbacks was due to the brilliance, audacity, stubbornness, and unfailing courage that rested upon his belief in his own abilities and destiny. He changed his party allegiance twice—on both occasions gaining swift advancement—and his individualist and buccaneering approach made other politicians wary and suspicious. He was thought to be an unprincipled adventurer, and until 1940 he was a leader with few followers.

## THE MAKING OF A POLITICIAN, 1874–1900
Churchill's family background was crucial in shaping his personality and outlook. He was a direct descendant of John Churchill (1650–1722), 1st Duke of Marlborough, the brilliant general of the early eighteenth century. Winston was born on 30 November 1874 at Blenheim Palace; his father, Lord Randolph Henry Spencer Churchill (1849–1885), was the younger son of the seventh duke, and his mother was Jennie Jerome, an American heiress and beauty. Winston's American connection fostered his democratic instincts and his belief in the importance of an Anglo-American "special" relationship. Lord Randolph had a meteoric political career in the 1880s, becoming chancellor of the exchequer in 1886. However, he fell from power a few months later and then succumbed to the

degenerative disease that led to his death at the age of forty-five in 1895. Winston's relationship with his parents was distant and difficult—they had little time for him, and Lord Randolph was constantly critical and dismissive of his son. Even so, Winston idolized him, and his death was a devastating blow.

Churchill did not excel at school, and rather than going to university he entered the Royal Military Academy at Sandhurst in 1893. From 1895 to 1899 he served as a cavalry officer, pulling strings to get postings to wherever there was a chance of the limelight. He saw action on India's northwest frontier in 1897 and took part in the last great cavalry charge of the British army at the Battle of Omdurman in 1898. He wrote press reports during both campaigns, and his dispatches formed the basis of his first books. He had begun to earn his living by writing, and in 1899 he resigned from the army. When the Boer War broke out Churchill went to South Africa as a well-paid war correspondent, but got too close to the action and was captured in November 1899. His dramatic escape from prison in Pretoria was a bright spot during a period when the war was going badly for Britain, and it made him a popular hero. In the 1900 general election, Churchill became one of the youngest and best-known members of the House of Commons.

## LIBERAL FORTUNES AND MISFORTUNES, 1900–1924

Churchill's first period as a Conservative member of Parliament (MP) lasted less than four years. He began by attacking his government's plans to reform the army and was one of the strongest opponents of the campaign for tariff reform launched by Joseph Chamberlain (1836–1914) in 1903. However, the Conservative defenders of free trade soon became a beleaguered minority, and on 31 May 1904 Churchill formally "crossed the floor" of the House of Commons and joined the Liberal Party. He was almost unique in doing so, and it earned him lasting antagonism from many in his former party. Whatever his motive, it was an opportune move, as the next decade was one of defeat for the Conservatives and success for the Liberal Party.

In December 1905, the Liberals formed a government in which Churchill became the undersecretary for the colonies, with sole responsibility for representing the department in the Commons. He became a Privy Councillor (PC) on 1 May 1907, a clear sign of his rising prominence. When Herbert Henry Asquith (1852–1928) succeeded to the premiership in April 1908, Churchill was promoted to the cabinet as president of the board of trade. He rapidly emerged as a radical and energetic social reformer, introducing Labor Exchanges to help the unemployed find work, and he forged a close partnership with the chancellor of the exchequer, David Lloyd George (1863–1945). In February 1910, Churchill was promoted to the prestigious office of home secretary, where again he introduced reforms.

Churchill was deeply absorbed in his own career, and his social life revolved around politics. He had little time to spare for romance, but in 1908 he met Clementine Hozier, and they were married on 12 September. She came from an aristocratic background, but there was little money and she was brought up in modest circumstances. Churchill was devoted to Clementine, and does not seem to have had any interest in other women after their marriage, which produced one son and four daughters, one of whom died in infancy. Clementine often gave her husband sound advice, which he usually ignored. Family life could be stormy: there was much affection but also frequent emotional rows, and Churchill's relationship with his three older children—especially with his son, Randolph—became difficult as they entered adulthood in the 1930s.

On 24 October 1911, Churchill was unexpectedly moved from the Home Office to become first lord of the admiralty, the minister responsible for the Royal Navy. This was not a demotion: the admiralty was a key post at this time, due to the naval challenge from Germany and the antagonisms that were to lead to war. Churchill threw himself into his new task with typical enthusiasm, and his advocacy of a larger construction program led to a struggle with Lloyd George over the 1914 budget in which both men threatened resignation. Churchill built on the earlier reforms of Admiral John Arbuthnot Fisher (1841–1920) and did much to energize and strengthen the fleet, including encouraging the early naval air service.

When war came in July 1914 he used his initiative to mobilize the fleet and prevent the chance of a surprise attack, but then recklessly attempted a futile defense of Antwerp. He recalled Fisher from retirement to act as the navy's senior officer, but their relationship deteriorated as Churchill interfered in operational decisions. The breaking point was Churchill's diversion of resources from home waters to support his pet project of knocking out Germany's ally, the Ottoman Empire, through an attempted invasion at Gallipoli. In May 1915, Fisher's resignation forced Asquith to create a coalition government with the Conservatives, who insisted upon Churchill's removal from the admiralty. He spent six unhappy months in the unimportant post of chancellor of the Duchy of Lancaster, while the Gallipoli campaign turned into a humiliating disaster. Although this was not his fault, Churchill shouldered much of the public blame for the fiasco. His political career appeared to be over, and he sank into a depression that was only slightly lifted by his discovery of painting, which became a lifelong source of relaxation. Marginalized and unpopular, he resigned from the government on 11 November 1915, and for several months in 1916 served as a battalion commander on the western front.

Churchill was one of the few leading Liberals to support Lloyd George when he ousted Asquith from the premiership in December 1916. In July 1917, Lloyd George felt secure enough to offer Churchill a government post, despite a chorus of Conservative disapproval. He served as minister of munitions from July 1917 until January 1919, as secretary for war and air for the following two years, and then as colonial secretary from February 1921 until the fall of Lloyd George's government in October 1922. During this period he forcefully advocated intervention in Russia against the Bolshevik government, but this was another policy failure that tarnished his reputation. By the time the coalition government was overthrown by a revolt within the Conservative Party, Churchill was detached from the Liberals and without any clear party connection. In the general election that followed in November 1922 he was also defeated at Dundee, the Scottish seat that he had represented since 1908. Once again, Churchill seemed to be in the wilderness and without a political future.

## CONSERVATIVE STATESMAN AND TROUBLEMAKER, 1924–1939

Churchill remained out of Parliament for two years, during which time he moved back toward the Conservative Party. This was a logical consequence of the rise of the Labour Party and the continuing decline of the Liberals, for since 1918 antisocialism had become Churchill's main theme. In the general election of October 1924, Churchill returned to the House of Commons as Conservative MP for Epping, a safe seat in the north London suburbs, and he held this seat for the rest of his political career. Many Conservatives continued to have reservations about this former coalitionist, but even those who had welcomed his return were staggered by the next development. The Conservatives had won a landslide victory, and the prime minister, Stanley Baldwin (1867–1947), offered Churchill the prize position of chancellor of the exchequer. He held this post throughout the government until its defeat in 1929. The chancellorship was one of the happiest phases of Churchill's career, but he never made the mark here that he had in his previous posts. His budgets were ingenious but had little impact on the level of unemployment. Despite some doubts, Churchill followed orthodox opinion and restored Britain to the gold standard in 1925, but the adoption of the prewar exchange rate was a mistake that added to Britain's economic stagnation. He was sidelined during the General Strike of May 1926, due to fears that his pugnacity would inflame the situation. Despite being chancellor, he was never likely to succeed Baldwin as Conservative leader—he continued to oppose the protectionist tariffs that most Conservatives wanted, and was constantly suspected of plotting with Lloyd George to revive the former coalition.

After the Conservatives went into opposition in 1929, Churchill drifted apart from the rest of the leadership. This was partly because he needed to restore his finances, which had suffered heavily in the stock market crash. Churchill was well paid for lecture tours, especially in the United States, and for his newspaper articles and books—which included his history of World War I, *The World Crisis,* and a life of his ancestor, *Marlborough,* each in several volumes. He spent much of his time writing at the manor house of Chartwell in the Kent countryside, which he had bought in 1922 without consulting Clementine. During the "wilderness years" of the 1930s, Churchill became an infrequent attendee at the House of Commons, apparently mainly interested in attacking the Conservative leadership. Not surprisingly, his motives were questioned and he was met with hostility. In fact, the issues he took up during the 1930s were the result of strong convictions, but his views over India seemed outdated (he was opposed to the native population having a significant role in the central government) and his warnings about Germany and the need for rearmament appeared alarmist and likely to increase tensions rather than reduce them. Baldwin's support for political reform in India caused Churchill's resignation from the Conservative leadership in January 1931, while still in opposition. He was therefore not included in the National Government formed in the economic crisis of August 1931, and remained out of office until 1939. From 1931 to 1935, Churchill led the resistance of the Conservative right wing against the proposed legislation on India, losing much of his political credibility in the process. The lowest point came in December 1936, when his lone support for King Edward VIII (1894–1972) in the abdication crisis led to him being howled down in the House of Commons; once again, his career seemed to be over.

Churchill's wild statements and ill-judged tactics over India reduced the impact of his more sober warnings of the dangers of German rearmament and Hitler's ambitions. He was consistent in urging swifter British rearmament, especially of the air force, and his speeches were strengthened by the information that sympathizers in the armed forces and civil service secretly passed to him. His opposition to the government's policy of "appeasement" was less consistent than his memoirs later suggested, but by the time of the Czech crisis in 1938 Churchill had become a rallying point for dissenters. In the immediate wake of the popular Munich agreement, he was under considerable pressure, and there were moves against him in the Epping constituency. However, after Hitler exposed the pact as a sham by occupying Prague in March 1939, Churchill's prestige and popularity rose as the credibility of the prime minister, Neville Chamberlain (1869–1940), ebbed away. When war came in September 1939, Chamberlain had no choice but to offer a key post in the Cabinet.

**Winston Churchill (left) with British information minister Brendan Bracken, surveying damage to the House of Commons following bombing by German planes, May 1941.** ©BETTMANN/CORBIS

Churchill returned to the admiralty; it was a sign of his rehabilitation that the signal "Winston's back" sent to the fleet increased morale and confidence.

### HIS "FINEST HOUR": WORLD LEADER IN WAR AND PEACE, 1939–1955

During the months of "phony war" in the winter of 1939–1940, the navy was the most active and effective service. Churchill's popularity rose, and when the failures of the Norway campaign forced Chamberlain to resign on 10 May 1940, he was the only credible replacement. Churchill combined the posts of prime minister and minister of defense, and formed a new coalition government that included the Labour Party. For the next five years he concentrated all of his efforts upon winning the war and largely ignored domestic politics, although he became leader of the Conservative Party in October 1940 after the unexpected collapse of Chamberlain's health. Churchill felt that his whole life had been a preparation for this moment of national peril, and that he was "walking with destiny." As France collapsed in the summer of 1940 and Britain faced bombing and possible invasion in the autumn, Churchill's resolute leadership was of vital importance. He was frank and realistic, while making it clear that the contest was not simply between nations, but a struggle with evil for the future of the whole world. Through a series of powerful broadcasts and speeches, he came to personify the will to fight on regardless—"we shall never surrender." His individualist career and detachment from party was now his greatest asset, and his determination and strength of character made him the one indispensable figure. His popularity remained high throughout the war, an instantly recognizable figure with his constant cigar, spotted bow ties, walking stick, and famous two-fingered "V for Victory" sign. As well as rallying public morale, Churchill energized the administrative and military machine: "action this day" was his response to critical issues. He could be demanding and abrasive to work for, but was also decisive and inspirational, producing a stream of ideas.

His second vital role was in constructing the wartime alliance. Through a correspondence that had begun in 1939 and several face-to-face meetings, he forged a close relationship with the American president Franklin Delano Roosevelt (1882–1945). This led to vital American financial and material support in the lend-lease program begun in 1941, and American assistance with protecting the transatlantic convoys that brought the food and munitions needed to continue the war. Defeating Hitler had absolute priority, and when Germany invaded the Soviet Union in June 1941, Churchill swiftly welcomed the Soviets as an ally. After the American entry into the war in December 1941, much of Churchill's attention was given to inter-allied diplomacy and summit meetings. From 1941 to 1944, British efforts were concentrated upon North Africa and then the Mediterranean theater, as Churchill once again vainly sought the "soft underbelly" of the enemy. In the closing stages of the war, Britain's role began to be eclipsed by the growing strength of the superpowers, and Churchill became increasingly concerned about the Soviet Union's postwar intentions.

When Germany surrendered in May 1945, Churchill was feted as the national savior. His defeat in the general election in July was a shock and bitter disappointment, but he was seen as a war leader rather than a peacetime reformer, and the Conservative Party was deeply unpopular. The outcome was a landslide victory for the Labour Party, and a depressed Churchill became leader of the opposition. During the next few years he spent much time writing his war memoirs and traveling, and his international prestige remained huge. He was concerned by the hardening Soviet grip upon Eastern Europe and feared an American return to isolationism; his "iron curtain" speech at Fulton, Missouri, on 5 March 1946 gave early warning of the communist threat and marked the coming of the Cold War. Churchill left much of the detailed work of the revival of the Conservative Party to the able lieutenants that he had appointed, and endorsed the new party policy despite his doubts about it.

Postwar economic problems and the resulting austerity program were the main cause of Churchill's return to power in October 1951 with the small parliamentary majority of seventeen. He set out to show that the Conservatives could govern moderately, accepting almost all of Labour's measures and spending extensively on the welfare state and the housing program. This was the beginning of the period of "affluence," with prosperity bringing an end to wartime controls and a rise in consumerism, although generous settlements of industrial disputes contributed to difficulties later in the decade. Churchill believed that his wartime prestige would enable him to negotiate with the Soviet leadership, and he relentlessly pursued the mirage of a three-power conference to achieve détente. He suffered a stroke in June 1953 that was concealed from the public, but despite a good recovery his powers were clearly fading. He repeatedly postponed making way for his heir apparent, Sir Anthony Eden (1897–1977), but was eventually pressured into standing down. Churchill resigned as prime minister on 5 April 1955. He had been awarded the Nobel Prize for literature in 1953 and a year later accepted the Order of the Garter, becoming Sir Winston Churchill, but he declined other honors. His final years were a slow decline marked by depression; he retired from the House of Commons in October 1964, and after a severe stroke died on 24 January 1965, receiving a state funeral.

See also **Chamberlain, Neville; Edward VIII; Hitler, Adolf; Stalin, Joseph; World War I; World War II.**

BIBLIOGRAPHY

*Primary Sources*

Churchill, Winston S. *My Early Life: A Roving Commission.* London, 1930. Autobiography covering his life up to 1900.

———. *The World Crisis 1911–1918.* 5 Vols. London, 1931. History of World War I.

———. *Marlborough: His Life and Times.* 4 Vols. London, 1933. Biography of Churchill's famous ancestor.

———. *The Second World War.* 6 Vols. London, 1948– 1954. War memoirs combined with a history.

———. *A History of the English-Speaking Peoples.* 4 Vols. London, 1956–1958. Combined history of Britain, the British Empire, and the United States.

*Secondary Sources*

Addison, Paul. *Churchill on the Home Front, 1900–1955.* London, 1993. A study of Churchill's domestic political career.

Ball, Stuart. *Winston Churchill.* London, 2003. Recent succinct biography.

Best, Geoffrey. *Churchill: A Study in Greatness.* London, 2001. Good medium-length biography.

Blake, Robert, and Wm. Roger Louis, eds. *Churchill.* Oxford, U.K. 1993. Essays on many aspects of Churchill's career.

Charmley, John. *Churchill: The End of Glory.* London, 1993. Controversial revisionist account, critical of Churchill's wartime priorities.

Churchill, Randolph S. (Vols. 1 and 2); Gilbert, Martin (Vols. 3–8). *Winston S. Churchill.* 8 vols. London, 1966–1988. The hugely detailed official life, begun by Churchill's son; the first five volumes also have companion volumes of documents.

Gilbert, Martin. *Churchill: A Life.* London, 1991. Single volume summary of the official life.

James, Robert Rhodes. *Churchill: A Study in Failure 1900–1939.* London, 1970. Stimulating analysis of Churchill's career up to World War II.

Jenkins, Roy. *Churchill.* London, 2001. Substantial life written by an experienced senior politician.

Ramsden, John. *Man of the Century: Winston Churchill and His Legend since 1945.* London, 2002. Discussion of Churchill's reputation in his lifetime and since.

STUART BALL

---

# CIANO, GALEAZZO (1903–1944), Italian politician.

The only son of the naval hero and Fascist political leader Costanzo Ciano, Galeazzo Ciano was born in Livorno, on 18 March 1903. He is best known for his service as foreign minister (1936–1943) under Benito Mussolini (1883– 1945), in which role he helped link Fascist Italy to Nazi Germany. His father's political connections were essential to his own political success. Costanzo Ciano left active service in May 1919 and joined the Fascists in 1920. Mussolini appointed him as navy undersecretary in November 1922; communications minister from 1924 to 1934; and Chamber of Deputies president from 1934 to 1939. Corrupt and greedy, Ciano accumulated great wealth, acquiring a count's title in 1928.

## EARLY CAREER

Snobbish and pampered as a child, Galeazzo Ciano disdained Blackshirt violence. Displaying modest journalistic and writing talent, he gained a law degree in 1925, then entered the foreign service with his close friend Filippo Anfuso. Ciano served in Brazil, Argentina, and China, returning to Rome in September 1929. His father, Mussolini's secretly designated successor, successfully proposed that Galeazzo wed Mussolini's daughter, Edda. They married in April 1930 then departed for China. After their 1933 homecoming, Mussolini appointed Galeazzo as his press and propaganda chief. In this position, he shaped public opinion for Mussolini's impending Ethiopian invasion.

Despite respiratory ailments, Ciano assumed command of a bomber squadron in Eritrea in August 1935. In October, during the Italo-Ethiopian War, he attacked Ethiopian towns. In December, using medical leave, he fled looming disaster from Ethiopian counteroffensives and Italian diplomatic isolation. Ciano encouraged Mussolini's January 1936 agreement with Adolf Hitler (1889–1945), in which Mussolini exchanged gradual abandonment of Austria for German diplomatic and economic support. Italian victories in Africa drew Ciano back to Ethiopia in February. After carrying out daring missions he returned to Italy and was rewarded with medals and Fascist Grand Council membership. Mussolini appointed him foreign minister and heir apparent on 11 June 1936.

Ciano assigned Anfuso to his cabinet, directed diplomacy dictatorially, and implemented pro-German policies. From July 1936, alongside Germany, he championed supporting the nationalists in Spain's civil war. Ciano's successful October meeting with Hitler, Mussolini's Rome-Berlin Axis proclamation in November, and the December dispatch to Spain of an expeditionary corps reflected Mussolini's goals: Mediterranean-Balkan predominance.

Ciano and Anfuso oversaw operations in Spain. But defeat at Guadalajara in March 1937—"my ugliest day," Ciano noted (author translation)— revealed miscalculations. In Spain, Italy further exhausted resources that had already been diminished in Africa, while Germany expanded, annexing Austria (March 1938), Sudetenland (September 1938), and Bohemia and Moravia (March 1939). The nationalist victory in Spain and the Italian invasion of Albania, both in April 1939, hardly compensated for Italy's losses, both in resources and in power relative to Germany.

Western documents stolen from embassies gave Ciano advantages unwarranted by Italian power. Taken together, the stolen information and the policy of appeasement adopted by western governments help to explain Ciano's diplomatic successes: the Belgrade Pact (March 1937), Nyon conference (September 1937), Easter Accords (April 1938), First Vienna Award (November 1938), and Neville Chamberlain's Rome visit (January 1939). Ciano sought to divide the democracies, circumscribe Germany, and delay war pending Italian readiness. Meanwhile, Anfuso, long a German spy, informed Berlin.

## SHIFTING POLITICAL FORTUNES

Apparent Axis solidarity masked deep antagonisms. Mussolini and Ciano feared Hitler; yet Nazi might overawed them when they toured Germany in September 1937. Hitler flattered Mussolini, and the German foreign minister Joachim von Ribbentrop (1893–1946) pressed alliance on Ciano when Nazi leaders inspected Italy in May 1938. During the Sudetenland crisis, in September 1938, Mussolini backed Hitler almost to war despite Ciano's trepidation. That crisis and the end of appeasement in March 1939 persuaded Mussolini to ally with Germany. In exchange, Hitler promised peace until 1943. Mussolini then discovered Hitler's Polish invasion plans. Enraged, Mussolini nonetheless plotted parallel conquests of Greece and Yugoslavia. Mussolini and Ciano expected that the Pact of Steel, signed 22 May 1939, would protect their aggression.

Costanzo Ciano's death that June, along with the Duce's missteps, weakened Galeazzo's certainty that Mussolini was always right. By August he convinced Mussolini that their army could not invade the Balkans while resisting western offensives. Mussolini sent Ciano to Hitler to urge negotiations over Poland. Hitler refused. Ciano persuaded Mussolini to declare "nonbelligerence" when war exploded in Europe. Both expected a lengthy conflict that would enrich Italy, exhaust the belligerents, and facilitate eventual intervention alongside Germany. Ciano's December 1939 Chamber speech suggests that his opportunism had replaced the Duce's ideological attraction to Nazism. But in March 1940 Mussolini decided Germany would prevail soon and promised Hitler imminent support. Ciano, fearing defeat, plotted a coup with the king. German victories in the spring dissuaded them. Like Mussolini, they expected a British surrender after the French collapse. Mussolini declared war on 10 June 1940.

Ciano shifted with Axis fortunes. He backed the poorly planned invasion of Greece (October 1940). Then, after enforced air service in the disaster, he again plotted Mussolini's overthrow in May 1941. Operation Barbarossa renewed Ciano's bellicosity. Defeats at El Alamein and Stalingrad reawakened Ciano's conspiring. He believed that Winston Churchill (1874–1965) and Franklin Delano Roosevelt (1882–1945) would support his removal of Mussolini and then negotiate peace. Instead, in February 1943 Mussolini dismissed Ciano, who accepted the ambassadorship to the Vatican. There, Ciano rewrote his diaries—minimizing his guilt, maximizing Hitler's and Mussolini's—and conspired with Fascist leaders and the king against Mussolini. At the Grand Council, on 25 July 1943, the majority denounced the Duce's policies. The king had Mussolini arrested, and the regime collapsed.

Fearing imprisonment, Ciano sought refuge in Spain via Germany. But after Hitler had placed Mussolini atop a puppet Fascist republic, he turned on Ciano. Condemned for treason, Ciano attempted to trade his doctored diaries for escape. Hitler refused. Ciano died bravely before a firing squad in Verona on 11 January 1944. Ciano's fascinating, dishonest diaries and more accurate diplomatic papers appeared posthumously.

*See also* **Axis; Ethiopia; Fascism; Germany; Italy; Mussolini, Benito; Nazism; World War II.**

BIBLIOGRAPHY

*Primary Sources*

Ciano, Galeazzo. *Diplomatic Papers: Being a Record of Nearly 200 Conversations Held during the Years 1936–42 with Hitler, Mussolini, Franco, Goering, Ribbentrop, Chamberlain, Eden, Sumner Welles, Schuschnigg, Lord Perth, François-Poncet, and Many Other World Diplomatic and Political Figures, Together with Important Memoranda, Letters, Telegrams, etc.* Edited by Malcolm Muggeridge. Translated by Stuart Hood. London, 1948.

———. *Documents on German Foreign Policy, 1918–1945, from the Archives of the German Foreign Ministry.* Washington and London, 1949–1983.

———. *Diary, 1937–1943.* Edited by Renzo De Felice (1980). Translated by Robert L. Miller. New York, 2002. Sometimes inaccurate translation of *Diario, 1937–1943.*

*Secondary Sources*

Guerri, Giordano Bruno. *Galeazzo Ciano: Una vita, 1903–1944.* Milan, 1979.

Moseley, Ray. *Mussolini's Shadow: The Double Life of Count Galeazzo Ciano.* New Haven, Conn., 1999.

BRIAN R. SULLIVAN

---

**CINEMA.** The power of cinema as a mass cultural medium in the twentieth century cannot be overstated. When the German writer Walter Benjamin wrote about the revolutionary power of cinema in "The Work of Art in the Age of Mechanical Reproduction" (1936), his words were suffused with a sense of loss for the value of "original" art objects as they are replaced by their infinitely reproducible representations. Benjamin's nostalgia seems all the more prescient in light of digital technology, which obscures even the necessity for reality as the basis of cinematic representation—we no longer need to film anything *real* at all—when whole worlds can be created by manipulating digital images on a computer.

Moreover, when we think of the movies, we immediately think of Hollywood, its name in shining lights on a hill. Yet European filmmakers have played a crucial role in shaping the form and scope of cinematic expression from its very inception, and over the course of the twentieth century, cinema has become a centerpiece of modern artistic and popular culture around the world.

**BACKGROUND TO 1914**

In 1839 the first still photographs were taken by Louis Daguerre and his associate, Joseph Niépce. Within forty years, Eadweard Muybridge had found a way to do series photography with his famous studies of galloping horses. He was followed by Étienne-Jules Marey, who invented the "chronotopic gun" to record animal movements, and the development of celluloid film was not far behind. In 1891 Thomas Edison's assistant, W. K. L. Dickson, developed the kinetoscope (considered to be the world's first motion-picture camera), and by 1894 the first kinetoscope parlors had opened to the public. It was two French photographic equipment manufacturers from Lyon named Auguste and Louis Lumière, however, who invented the first widely used camera, the *cinématographe*, which could also be used to print and project film. The Lumière brothers thus established the standard speed for silent film (sixteen frames per second), and other versions of the kinetoscope and the *cinématographe* emerged almost simultaneously in Germany and Great Britain. Lumière camera operators spread out around the world, filming and exhibiting short vignettes of foreign landscapes and everyday life.

The earliest films were often referred to as *actualités,* since filmmakers such as the Lumières made little attempt to embellish or edit filmed scenes in any significant way. But another

Frenchman, Georges Méliès, had been present at the first Lumière screenings in France and recognized the (literally) fantastic potential of the new cinematic medium. He began making narrative films, and developed many of the basic cinematographic elements that are in use today, including the fade-in/out, superimposition through double exposure, stop-motion photography, and the dissolve. As the twentieth century began, Méliès's films became more and more fantastic, including his famous *Trip to the Moon* (1902), as well as versions of the *Arabian Nights* (1905) and *Twenty Thousand Leagues under the Sea* (1907).

European filmmakers also helped to determine the standard ("feature") length of films: four very popular foreign films, all released in the United States between 1911 and 1914 (and all between four and nine reels long), helped to stretch the attention span of the average audience member to the ninety-minute to two-hour length with which we are familiar today. This new breed of films was expansive and epic, often with prestigious literary or theatrical precedent (e.g. *The Loves of Queen Elizabeth* [1912], starring Sarah Bernhardt, and *Quo Vadis?* [1913]). Italy followed the international success of *Quo Vadis?* with another huge epic, Giovanni Pastrone's *Cabiria* (1914). Unfortunately, Italy's success in the international cinema market had peaked by 1919, and its film industry had nearly collapsed by the mid-1920s.

In France, meanwhile, several filmmaking concerns made important contributions to the growing medium: a company named Pathé Frères, formed in 1896, achieved massive dominance in the international film market during the first decades of the century, while a smaller company founded by the inventor Léon Gaumont produced films made by the first female filmmaker, Alice Guy, and serial films by the director Louis Feuillade. Pathé broke new ground in several areas of the new industry, becoming one of the first companies worldwide to vertically integrate (that is, to hold a controlling interest at all levels of the business, from production to exhibition); Pathé also innovated such editing practices as hand-stenciling color onto certain release prints, a practice it continued through the early 1930s.

In Great Britain, cinema proliferated quickly, aided by the inventor R. W. Paul's widespread sale of projectors; the more films people saw, the more demand increased. The British filmmakers at the turn of the century were remarkable for their willingness to experiment with the *actualité* form, adding "trick" elements and other innovations in editing. The rich history of films from Scandinavian countries began before its famous proponent Ingmar Bergman was even born: films produced by Nordisk, in Denmark, were among the most popular and highly regarded of the first two decades of the twentieth century.

## WORLD WAR I AND THE RISE OF NATIONAL CINEMA SYSTEMS

For all the ingenuity and growth in European cinema to 1914, the United States would come to dominate markets at home and abroad by the early 1920s, aided by the war in Europe. The onset of war in 1914 forced two of the biggest players in international cinema, France and Italy, to severely diminish their production; American firms saw their opportunity and seized it, pouring money into production values that would be recuperated in domestic and international revenues. The European film industries were crippled not only by the distraction of war but also by a closing down of borders between national cinemas, so that technical and stylistic advances no longer passed freely from one country to another. Thus did each nation begin to develop its own distinctive features and style, some strains of which would continue throughout the twentieth century.

German cinema before 1912 was fairly nonexistent due to cultural resistance to the form, which was considered derivative compared to theater and morally questionable in terms of content. The first successful movement in German cinema, then, called the *Autorenfilm* (the "authors' film") justified its worth by borrowing its prestige from literary and theatrical predecessors—and in that sense really was derivative, and it predictably lost steam. Germany relied heavily on imports from other countries, including Denmark, but fear of anti-German sentiment conveyed in such films provoked Germany to ban all foreign films in 1916, almost completely isolating German cinema.

Russia's film industry was also somewhat slow to develop, and during World War I became as cloistered as Germany's film system. The result of such segregation from the rest of the world for Germany and Russia would be unique qualities with which we still associate these national cinemas, though in the case of Russia, many of these innovations would have to wait until after the Bolshevik Revolution in 1917, which brought Russia's burgeoning film industry to a screeching halt.

From Great Britain to Russia, Europe from 1914 to 1919 had one main preoccupation: war. The effect of this period in European cinematic history should not be underestimated, not only because it forced countries into their own corners of filmmaking but also because the themes and content of films made during this period inevitably shifted toward promotion of the war effort in each particular nation. Newsreels proliferated as a form, and American films filled the screens of European playhouses. European countries such as Denmark took advantage of their politically neutral status to gain a greater share of other European markets, and innovative Swedish directors such as Victor Sjöström enjoyed widespread acclaim for complex narrative innovations and use of landscape.

## DAWN OF A NEW AGE: THE 1920S AND 1930S

Following World War I, several of the twentieth century's most important filmmaking movements took shape in Europe. In Weimar Germany, most of the industry was gathered up by the government conglomerate Universum Film Aktiengesellschaft (UFA) in 1917. Such consolidation allowed for a distinctive and consistent development of film style, and the eventual result was expressionism. Yet preceding expressionism in the immediate postwar context of Germany was a spate of huge costume dramas meant to compete with Italy's epic historical films of the teens. The director Ernst Lubitsch, later known in the United States for his "Lubitsch touch," made his first films during this period in Germany.

Concurrently, a new strain of German cinema was taking shape: in 1918 the Austrian artist Carl Mayer and Czech poet Hans Janowitz presented a harrowing tale of madness, murder, and abuse of power to the then independent production company Decla-Bioskop (it did not merge with UFA until 1921). At first Fritz Lang was slated to direct *The Cabinet of Doctor Caligari* (1919), but it was

ultimately assigned to the filmmaker Robert Wiene. Wiene sought to render his narrator's madness in visual terms, which he accomplished by having eminent contemporary expressionist artists execute the sets. The sets were extremely stylized, with distorted shapes and lighting painted directly onto the backdrops; combined with chiaroscuro setups in the actual lighting, the total effect was haunting, filled with shadows and dark corners. Wiene thus "expresses," or makes visible, the inner darkness and hallucinatory distortion of his characters' minds.

Expressionist films would dominate German cinema over the next decade, when several of its masterpieces were made. Fritz Lang's *Destiny* (1921; *Die Müde Tod*), for example, tells the story of a young woman who bargains with Death for the life of her lover, while Lang's next film, *Dr. Mabuse, the Gambler* (1922; *Doktor Mabuse, Der Spieler*), is one step more lurid, reverting from a journey through the ages (*Destiny*'s setting) to the dank underworld of the gangster. Lang made one of his last and most famous silent films, *Metropolis,* in 1927. This dystopic tale of a mechanized future pushed Lang's—and UFA's—resources to the limit: Lang and his team made a number of technical innovations and trick shots in order to represent the enormous scale of this future world; UFA, on the other hand, was helped to bankruptcy by the effort, and it would take many years for audiences and critics to recognize the brilliance of Lang's frightening vision.

The other key director of German expressionism is F. W. Murnau, whose film *Nosferatu, a Symphony of Horrors* (1922) is remarkable for the way its expressionistic elements are integrated into the acting, lighting, and cinematography rather than relying on highly stylized sets as in Lang's *Metropolis* or Wiene's *Caligari*. Murnau perfected the use of low-angle lighting to create expressive distortion of shadows cast by Nosferatu, rendering the vampire all the more menacing. Shot on location in eastern Europe, *Nosferatu* would cast its own shadow of influence on a wide range of filmmakers to follow, including Orson Welles and Werner Herzog (who made his own version of *Nosferatu* in 1979, starring Klaus Kinski and Isabelle Adjani). With *The Last Laugh* (1924), Murnau left expressionism largely behind, turning to a much more realistic mode, a trend in the mid-1920s known as "the new objectivity" (*Die Neue Sachlichkeit*). By the end of the 1920s, Murnau had immigrated to Hollywood, like so many other European directors of his vintage.

In France, parallel systems of film production materialized, divided into mainstream and more avant-garde experiments in film. A system of "cine-clubs" also began in France during the 1920s, founded by the novelist, director, and film critic Louis Delluc. Delluc believed that cinema could be studied and appreciated on a level with other art forms, and called for the formation of exhibition and viewing practices that would include lecture, discussion, and debate about contemporary films. The importance of the advent of cine-clubs in France and their proliferation around the world during the twentieth century cannot be overestimated; their support of films and film movements outside of mainstream cinematic entertainment often constituted the difference between a film's success or failure, and it helped to reinforce the concept of cinema as "the seventh art" in France.

In 1920s Europe, cine-clubs provided a venue for avant-garde artists of various modernist movements to experiment with cinematic form. There were impressionist filmmakers—not to be mistaken with the nineteenth-century group of French painters—who sought to express inner states without resorting to the stylization of the German expressionists (Germaine Dulac, Jean Epstein, Marcel L'Herbier), abstract graphic experiments (Hans Richter and Viking Eggeling), dadaist films (Marcel Duchamp, Francis Picabia, Man Ray, René Clair), early surrealist shorts (Fernand Léger, Dulac, and Antonin Artaud). Two crucial European films of the decade were made in France by Spaniards, Luis Buñuel and Salvador Dalí: *Un chien andalou* (1928; An Andalusian dog) and *L'age d'or* (1930; The golden age—it should be noted that Dalí's role was much less in this film). Both *Andalou* and *L'age d'or* are remarkable for their disjointed narrative "structures" and juxtaposition of bizarre images to represent dream imagery; they are likewise suffused with an eroticism and antiauthoritarian spirit that continue to captivate filmmakers and viewers today.

The director Abel Gance, while certainly avant-garde (in the sense of being ahead of his time) in many respects, and though he was working at the same time in France, only skirted the edges of the various groups just mentioned. Yet his contribution to European cinema is considerable. Gance considered the American director D. W. Griffith a spiritual father and endeavored to make films of the sweep and grandeur of Griffith's *Intolerance* (1916). In several films of the late 1910s and early 1920s, Gance cultivated his skill at associative (metaphorical) editing (*J'accuse!* 1919; *La roue* [1922–1923; The wheel]). With *Napoleon* (1927), Gance uses a dizzying array of effects and techniques to render Napoleon a monumental historical figure; at several moments in the twenty-eight-reel original cut (the first of six intended parts), Gance employs a three-camera triptych process in order to enlarge the screen to three times its normal width.

Other influential directors of the 1920s and early 1930s include Danish-born Carl Dreyer, whose 1928 *Passion of Joan of Arc* is still considered one of the finest films in the history of cinema for its use of dramatic close-up to draw the spectator into Joan's suffering; Jean Vigo (*À propos de Nice*, 1930; *Zero for Conduct*, 1933; *L'Atalante*, 1934), whose early death cut short a brilliant career and partnership with the cinematographer Boris Kaufman (brother of Dziga Vertov); and René Clair, who made among the most successful transitions to sound with the musical comedies *Under the Roofs of Paris* (1930), *The Million* (1931), and the astonishingly hopeful *A nous la liberté* (1931), a film that depicts the plight of the industrial worker in the era of the Great Depression (it is often compared to Charlie Chaplin's *Modern Times*).

Finally, no discussion of the silent era in Europe would be complete without examination of one of its most (literally) revolutionary cinematic movements: along with the Bolshevik Revolution in 1917 came a radical new kind of filmmaking, known as Soviet "montage," so named for its emphasis on editing as the focal point for the production of meaning in cinema. In August 1919 the Russian film industry was nationalized and the State Film School was founded. Some of the Soviet era's key figures soon gathered there, including Lev Kuleshov and Vsevolod Pudovkin. During the civil war years (1918–1920), most

**A poster by Anton Lavinsky for Russian director Sergei Eisenstein's film *Battleship Potemkin*, 1926.** RUSSIAN STATE LIBRARY, MOSCOW/BRIDGEMAN ART LIBRARY

state-sponsored filmmaking was devoted to propagandistic (often newsreel) material to be sent out and exhibited on agit-trains and other modes of transporting Lenin's message to the countryside. An agreement with Germany (the Rapallo Treaty) in 1922 effectively ended the embargo of film production materials to the USSR, and production sites were set up in numerous areas of the Soviet Union. Though a vast majority of the films exhibited in the USSR during the early 1920s were imports, the indigenous film industry slowly began making inroads.

The first centralized distribution entity of the Soviet era, Gosinko, was largely replaced by another organization, Sovinko, when the former proved unsuccessful at reviving the flagging film industry during the early 1920s. Yet in 1925 it was Gosinko that produced one of the most influential films in cinema history: Sergei Eisenstein's *Potemkin*, which is an epic rendering of a popular uprising that took place on the battleship *Potemkin*

in 1905. Its denouement on the steps of Odessa is cut in an extraordinary rhythm that captures both the suspense and the relentless onslaught of the massacre it depicts. Eisenstein went on to have a long and varied career in Soviet film, ranging in style and content from *Strike* (1925), depicting a factory strike in tsarist Russia (filmed on location with actual workers in place of actors), to *Ivan the Terrible, Parts 1 and 2* (1944, 1958), a massively scaled biography of Ivan IV.

One of the USSR's other key filmmakers also originated during the revolutionary and civil war period: Dziga Vertov (né Denis Kaufman) began by working on agitprop documentaries during the late 1910s and early 1920s, developing a theory and approach to documentary filmmaking that would result in *Kino-Eye* (1924), *Man with a Movie Camera* (1929), and an astounding, sprawling work about the first Soviet Five-Year Plan called *A Sixth of the World* (1926).

## 1930 TO WORLD WAR II

In "Evolution of the Language of Cinema," the French film critic and cofounder of the journal *Cahiers du cinema*, André Bazin, argues that sound inherently nudged cinematic style toward realism, since it is less "flexible" than the visual image—that is, its syntax cannot as easily be changed. As national cinemas around the world made the transition to sound, transformations occurred on every level of production, from business infrastructure to style. Sound required new shooting setups for cameras suddenly immobilized by cumbersome devices for muffling the sound of their operation; exhibition spaces had to be outfitted with technology to project sound in theaters. In the early sound era, several versions were made of each film, but this proved too costly to be a sustainable solution. Then dubbing became quite common (and is still commercially accepted today by Italian audiences, for example), whereas in the Netherlands and Scandinavia films were (and are) almost always shown in their original version.

As the United States moved to sound technology between 1928 and 1932, several American companies set their sights on the European market as well. While RCA and General Electric were largely successful in Great Britain, industry forces based in Germany banded together to develop competing sound technology and to sue American companies in European courts for copyright infringement. The resulting corporate battle would not be resolved until 1930, when all of the international industry players met in Paris to negotiate which areas of Europe (and the world) would be controlled by whom. The agreement proved to be fragile, finally collapsing in 1939 as World War II loomed, but the net result for Europe was significant: the resistance to American dominion over sound technology prevented Hollywood from completely overwhelming the European film industry during the 1930s.

In Great Britain, several strains of filmmaking took advantage of the new dimension of cinematic representation: Alfred Hitchcock's films, for instance, only became better once sound was added. One of his early classics, *Blackmail* (1929), was even promoted as Britain's first full-length sound film, though that claim is still disputed.

In *Blackmail*, the lingering influence of expressionism is clearly present (in a trade agreement, Hitchcock had made his first two films in the 1920s as a contract director in Germany). During his British period, Hitchcock made several innovations, including the use of sound to reflect a character's stream of consciousness.

Another important development in 1930s Britain was a move toward social realism, an approach to and an ethics of filmmaking exemplified by the Scottish filmmaker John Grierson. Grierson founded the British documentary movement and has been credited with coining the term *documentary*. Profoundly influenced by predecessors Robert Flaherty and Sergei Eisenstein, Grierson sought to reveal the inherent drama in the struggles of everyday working people. He started the Empire Marketing Board Film Unit (and in 1933 the GPO Film Unit), gathering a group of bright young filmmakers around him, and together they produced such films as *Drifters* (1929), *Industrial Britain* (1933), *Granton Trawler* (1934), *Song of Ceylon* (1934), and *Night Mail* (1936). He was eventually appointed Canadian film commissioner and founded the National Film Board of Canada.

Instead of turning to nonfiction to represent the difficult social realities of the 1930s, French filmmakers infused narrative fiction film with harsher themes and stylistic techniques, an inclination known as poetic realism. The directors Jean Renoir, Marcel Carné, Jacques Feyder, Julien Duvivier, and Pierre Chenal all made films in this mode. Several of the most influential films of the period starred Jean Gabin (*Pépé le Moko*, 1937; *The Lower Depths*, 1936; and *Daybreak*, 1939) and Michel Simon (*Boudu Saved from Drowning*, 1932; *The Last Turn*, 1939), and both men starred in Carné's *Port of Shadows* (1938; *Quai des brumes*). While rendered differently by each director, films associated with poetic realism tend to deal with societal outsiders, petty criminals, and poor working-class people. Both Gabin and Simon use their bodies and facial expressions to convey deep humanity despite the heaviness and pessimism of the era. The atmosphere of these films is dank and foreboding, though Renoir's films sometimes bucked the inclination toward fatalism expressed by other filmmakers of the 1930s (for instance, *Boudu* maintains a somewhat comic tone, while *The Lower Depths* retains a much darker tone and message).

Indeed, Jean Renoir was the most significant and influential talent to emerge from France during the pre–World War II period. His films from the 1930s constitute their own pantheon of touchstones for generations of filmmakers to follow: such future luminaries as Luchino Visconti and Satyajit Ray (considered the "father" of modern Indian cinema) worked as his assistants over the years, and an entire generation of new-wave filmmakers consciously integrated aspects of his style. Several months before the premiere of Renoir's film *The Rules of the Game* in July 1939, the director was asked what "the rule" of the game in the title was. He answered that he sought "to show that for every game, there is a rule. If one plays otherwise, one loses the game." *Rules of the Game* recounts the story of a group of Parisians who gather at a marquis's country home for the weekend. With astonishing sympathy and skill, Renoir wanted to show what it was like to be "dancing on a volcano"—that is, how a fading class of people try to live on the eve of another world war. The film was somewhat misunderstood at first (due in part to the shortened version that was released in 1939), but it has since become one of the world's most beloved films. In the British film periodical *Sight & Sound*'s 2002 decennial survey of the "Ten Greatest Films of All Time," *The Rules of the Game* was once again prominently featured, extolled for its ability to "cast a spell over you." In 2000 the French educational system used *The Rules of the Game* as one of its main subjects for the *baccalaureat*, the exam that all French students take to graduate from high school.

It was also during the 1930s that Henri Langlois, George Franju, and Jean Mitry founded the Cinémathèque Française, an organization dedicated to the preservation and exhibition of film. The Cinémathèque would prove to be instrumental in French film culture, as it not only saved fragile celluloid films from being discarded or lost but also served as a purveyor of taste (primarily Langlois's), as well as providing a physical and intellectual space in which young cinephiles could come together to watch and discuss films.

Socially and politically conscious filmmaking was also prevalent in certain Scandinavian countries and Belgium during the 1930s. As in France, cine-clubs served as vital informal conservatories for directors such as Joris Ivens (the Netherlands), Charles Dekeukeleire, and Henri Storck (Belgium). All made films that were prescient in their warnings about fascism in Europe. In Sweden, on the other hand, the film industry foundered both commercially and creatively during this period, losing considerable talent to Hollywood (Victor Sjöström, Mauritz Stiller, and Greta Garbo, among others).

Like Murnau, Lubitsch, and Erich von Stroheim before him, Fritz Lang would also eventually make the move to Hollywood, but not before directing two of the most important films of the early sound era: *M* (1930), a film written by his wife, Thea von Harbou, and based on a series of actual child murders in Germany; and *The Last Will of Dr. Mabuse* (1933). The latter film was banned by the newly elected National Socialists for its supposed subversive content. The Nazis recognized the power of cinema to shape the masses, though their focus was on state-sponsored documentary film rather than on narrative fiction film. Two state-sponsored documentaries of monumental scale were made with virtually unlimited resources by Leni Riefenstahl during the 1930s: the first, *Triumph of the Will* (1935), depicts the 1934 Nazi Party rally at Nuremburg, while the two-part *Olympia* (1938) amplifies the 1936 Olympics held in Berlin. The German film industry was controlled from 1933 to 1945 by the propaganda minister Joseph Goebbels, but it was not formally nationalized until 1942.

Though Benito Mussolini came to power in 1922, Italy was also somewhat slow to exploit the mass propagandistic potential of cinema. The 1920s and 1930s were relatively fallow decades creatively in Italy, as the industry continued to adjust to the loss of the prestigious position it held internationally during the pre–World War I era of historical epics. Apart from LUCE (L'Unione Cinematogràfica Educativa), a governmental body formed in 1924 to oversee the production of newsreels, Mussolini did not attempt to nationalize Italy's film industry during the 1920s. This is not to say that Mussolini underestimated the power of film; he just held a long-term view for the redevelopment of Italian cinema. In 1935 a centralized governmental agency was formed to supervise the distribution and exhibition levels of the industry, the ENIC (Ente Nazionale Industrie Cinematorafiche), and in the mid-1930s Mussolini authorized the establishment of two entities that continue to affect Italian cinema today: a national film school (Centro Sperimentale di Cinematogràfia) and the Cinecittà studios in Rome.

It would take several years, however, before such infrastructural changes would transform the quality and diversity of cinematic output in Italy. The 1920s and 1930s were dominated by melodramas and *telefono bianco* (white telephone) comedies—so named for the inevitable appearance of a white telephone in nearly every film, symbolic of middle-class affluence. At the newly formed Centro Sperimentale, the film school director Luigi Chiarini gathered together students such as Roberto Rossellini, Giuseppe De Santis, and Michelangelo Antonioni, all of whom would become key figures in Italian cinema after World War II. Several important film journals also cropped up during the 1930s, including *Black and White* (which remains a forceful voice in Italian cinema today) and *Cinema,* which was run by Benito Mussolini's son, Vittorio Mussolini. As in so many other European countries during the period, Mussolini also enforced strict quotas on foreign films, banning American films completely in 1940, as the world once again went to war.

The effort to stem the dominance of Hollywood has been a persistent dilemma throughout the history of European cinema. As in Italy, protectionist measures were periodically put in place by European countries, primarily by way of quotas on the number of American films that could be shown in relation to indigenous cinematic production; national subsidization of film industries has also proven to be effective in countering the economic power conferred by Hollywood studios. Europe has also suffered from a drain of talent to the United States at various moments of the twentieth century, most often due to the double contingencies of economic and political exile. As a result, though, the influence of European directors, cinematographers, editors, and actors on the medium of cinema as a whole is undeniably vast.

Without attempting to be exhaustive, European directors who transformed the face of Hollywood include Lubitsch, von Stroheim, Murnau, Lang, Sjöström, Hitchcock, Mihaly Kertesz (Michael Curtiz), Billy Wilder, Jean Renoir, Detlef Sierck (Douglas Sirk), Max Reinhardt, Max Ophüls, Robert Siodmak, Otto Preminger, and Fred Zinnemann.

During World War II in Europe, some cinematic production was curtailed, as might be expected where resources were scarce and populations were living under siege. European films made during wartime were mostly funded by governments for their escapist or propagandistic value. The Italian director Roberto Rossellini, for instance, directed three films between 1940 and 1943 (*The White Ship,* 1941; *A Pilot Returns,* 1942; *Man of the Cross,* 1943) with the support of Mussolini's Fascist regime. Rossellini, who would go on to make some of cinema history's most acclaimed humanistic films immediately following the war, "contorted" himself (his word) to fit the demands of wartime Italy. Interestingly, 1942 and 1943 were among the most commercially successful years ever for Italian film. According to the film scholar Tag Gallagher, the total number of films produced had increased sixfold since the mid-1930s, and audience numbers nearly doubled.

In occupied France, on the other hand, film production was completely halted at first. German films were given the most screen time, but French audiences did not respond enthusiastically, driving attendance downward during the first years of the occupation. In May 1941, Germany reauthorized French film production, and since American films were prohibited and Germans poured money into productions, the French film industry became more commercially successful than ever. At the same time, filmmakers involved in the Resistance continued to pool their energy and resources to make films, forming the Comité de Libération du Cinéma Français (Committee for the Liberation of French Cinema) in 1943. The committee members, including Jean Grémillion and Jacques Becker, were among the many Resistance fighters who filmed the liberation of Paris in August 1944. By then, Allied bombing had destroyed much of the crucial infrastructure of the French film industry:

five studios, including warehouses storing films, and over three hundred theaters were destroyed.

## POSTWAR EUROPE

The Vichy government centralized systems of production and controlled distribution and exhibition by barring films with objectionable content during the war. As in Italy, however, fascist control resulted in the foundation of a French national film school (the Institut des Hautes Études Cinématographiques) in 1943. Many other outlets for cinematic culture went underground during the war, including several film journals and the Cinémathèque Française.

Just as before the occupation, the postwar French film production system was dominated by smaller firms; though the two vertically integrated companies, Pathé and Gaumont, survived the war, capital was scarce in France after the war for all players. To make matters worse, the French government relaxed quotas on American films in 1946, further reducing the potential box office take (and thus investment capital into French film projects). During the same year, however, the French government also established the CNC (the Centre National de la Cinématographie), an entity dedicated to industry regulation, including government subsidization of French films. The result was an increased recognition and support of artistic and even documentary filmmaking, instead of allowing the market to be flooded with strictly conventional commercial fare. By 1948–1949, the French had restored protectionist measures, including quotas on American films, and founded the governmental publicity agency Unifrance to bolster their efforts at promoting cinema as the "seventh art": Unifrance's charter was to promote French film abroad, including the coordination of films to be exhibited at film festivals around the world. Testament to France's cultural commitment to cinema is the fact that the CNC, Unifrance, and the Cinémathèque Française (discussed earlier) all continue to exist today.

French film of the late 1940s and 1950s has been called "cinema of quality" (*cinéma de qualité*), a term that refers to the reliance in the postwar period on literary adaptations with high production values filmed on studio sets. It would be this impulse of "quality," of finely honed scripts and careful symbolization, against which the new-wave filmmakers would later set themselves. Important French filmmakers of the period include Marcel Carné and Jacques Prévert (*Children of Paradise*, 1945); Claude Autant-Lara, with the assistance of the screenwriting duo Jean Aurenche and Pierre Bost (*Devil in the Flesh*, 1947); and René Clement (*Forbidden Games*, 1952; also written by Aurenche and Bost). Three directors who do not quite fit into the "quality" mold but are nonetheless of note are Robert Bresson, Jean Cocteau, and Henri-Georges Clouzot, whose films (*Ladies of the Bois de Boulogne* [1945] and *Diary of a Country Priest* [1950]; *Beauty and the Beast* [1945] and *Orpheus* [1950]; *Le corbeau* [1943; The raven], and *Les diaboliques* [1955], respectively) influenced both the new wave to come and innumerable directors working beyond the boundaries of France. Jacques Becker, who was an assistant to Renoir during the 1930s, also made his masterpiece, *Casque d'or* (1952; The golden coach), during this period. Finally, toward the end of the 1950s, two more key players in French cinematic culture made films with lasting impact: Georges Franju's *The Keepers* (1958), his first feature, which was a quasi-documentary story of a man confined in an insane asylum, and Jean-Pierre Melville's *Bob le flambeur* (1955), a kind of muted, French version of noir filmmaking. France of the 1950s even spawned a comic genius: though he only made a few films, Jacques Tati's *Holiday* (1949), *Monsieur Hulot's Holiday* (1953), and *My Uncle* (1958) are still considered among the most inspired comedies of all time, expertly combining the physical comedy of Chaplin with a tender satire that is unique to Tati.

For other European countries, the postwar period was not nearly as varied. Sweden and Denmark made a quick recovery from the war and began to specialize in art films, for which both national cinemas remain known today. The British film industry, for its part, was whittled down to a few vertically integrated companies (the most powerful was the Rank Organisation). As in France, many postwar British films consisted of "prestige" literary adaptations, including works by Laurence Olivier (*Hamlet*, 1948; *Richard III*, 1955), Gabriel Pascal (*Caesar and Cleopatra*, 1946), and newcomer David Lean, whose Dickens adaptations serve as an instructive prelude to his epic period pictures of the 1960s, *Lawrence of Arabia* (1962) and *Doctor Zhivago* (1965).

In the newly divided Germany, an interesting situation developed in the capital, Berlin. While East and West had completely separate spheres of film production, distribution, and exhibition, strange pockets of cross-influence developed. As the film scholar Katie Trumpener explains, "border" movie theaters in West Berlin during the postwar period were often populated by East Berliners who would sneak across the city divide in order to see Western (during the Allied occupation, primarily American) films. American films totally dominated the West German market from 1945 to 1949—a prerogative of American occupation that also took place in Japan during the same period—and American financial interests also "occupied" the emerging West German production system by replacing the old centralized UFA system with numerous smaller firms. These new film companies focused their attention on the domestic market, generating primarily light entertainment fare, including *Heimat* (homeland) films that consisted primarily of domestic dramas of German village life.

The dominance of American films in postwar Germany is an extreme example of the proliferation of American cinema throughout the European market after 1945; American companies saw an opportunity as Europe rebuilt and reorganized, and took it. By 1948 several countries had reinstated (or increased) protectionist measures initiated during the 1930s: France, for example, put strict limits on American imports in 1948 and required that French films be shown a minimum of twenty weeks a year in all theaters. Britain and Italy passed similar laws in 1948–1949, also opting for a combination of quotas and minimum required screen time for domestic output. In the early 1950s European film companies also began combining resources to form larger European coproductions, a practice that continues today in an attempt to counter American blockbuster films.

In the USSR and Soviet bloc countries, Soviet political control ran deep into its various national film industries, and production funds were relatively scarce. The cultural policy permitting only socialist realist art was reinstated and enforced even more vigorously than before World War II. The first epic production of the postwar period in the Soviet Union, Sergei Eisenstein's *Ivan the Terrible, Part 2* was banned for its depiction of a ruthless authoritarian regime. Most of the important filmmakers from the interwar period—Eisenstein, Dovzhenko, and Pudovkin included—only made one or two films after 1945. Little of interest was made during Stalin's final years of life, until the "thaw" that began in 1953 when Stalin died. From 1953 to 1958, until Nikita Khrushchev came to power, Soviet film production increased and censorship was somewhat relaxed.

Nonetheless, the most interesting films made in Eastern Europe during the Cold War came from outside the Soviet Union: during the 1950s and 1960s, the Łódź Film Academy in Poland (which was founded in 1948 to churn out Stalinist propaganda) turned out some of the most important filmmakers of the twentieth century. Andrzej Munk (*Man on the Tracks*, 1956; *Eroica*, 1957) and Andrzej Wajda (*A Generation*, 1954; *Kanal*, 1957; *Ashes and Diamonds*, 1958) have influenced generations of filmmakers in Poland and beyond. Both took a hard, deromanticized look at the lost illusions of the postwar period. Wajda's *Ashes and Diamonds*, for instance, tells the story of a non-communist resistance fighter who must assassinate a Communist Party official. Though the resistance fighter, Maciek, seems to die with a futility equal to his own murderous act, he transfixed audiences, subverting the overt pro-Communist message. A young film student named Roman Polanski also attended the Łódź Film Academy and acted in Wajda's *A Generation*. His first feature, *A Knife in the Water* (1962), made him both famous and infamous (a dialectic that would plague his entire career): it was nominated for an Academy Award for best foreign film in 1963 and earned a place on the cover of *Time* magazine, but in Poland it was cited by the governing Gomułka regime as one of the reasons to shut down the Łódź Film Academy altogether, which it did in the early 1960s. Other Soviet bloc countries, including Czechoslovakia and Hungary, also denounced the "subversive" content of Polish cinema during the late 1950s, effectively silencing their own freedom of expression.

Perhaps the most influential innovation of European cinema in the postwar period emerged not from the production phase of filmmaking at all but from its distribution and exhibition practices: international film festivals such as Cannes,

Venice, and Berlin would serve as crucial proving grounds for a select stratum of the international cinema market. Festivals also insisted on the recuperation of cinema as an art, and not simply or principally a commercial product. Festivals also reinforced national identity and prestige in a fragile, healing postwar European culture. The Venice, Cannes, Locarno (Switzerland), and Karlovy Vary (Czechoslovakia) film festivals were all restored in 1946, and Berlin (1951), San Sebastian (Spain, 1954), London (1957), Barcelona (1959), and Moscow (1959) followed over the next decade.

Like a handful of other European directors, the Swedish filmmaker Ingmar Bergman gained worldwide renown after World War II through the international art film festival circuit. Bergman's deeply personal and often existential films appealed intensely to this highly educated, cosmopolitan audience. Though many critics consider his first masterpiece to be *Summer Interlude* (1951), Bergman gained international recognition with his highly allegorical tale *The Seventh Seal* (1957), in which a medieval knight plays a game of chess with Death during the plague. *The Seventh Seal* won the Special Jury Prize at Cannes in 1957, tied with Andrzej Wajda's *Kanal*. In Bergman's next film, *Wild Strawberries* (also 1957), another character confronts death, but this time the journey is much more contemporary and personal, expressed in dreams and flashbacks. From his 1966 film *Persona* to his 2003 feature, *Sarabande*, Bergman has continued to probe the larger human questions of identity, familial and romantic relationships, and, of course, mortality.

International film festivals also helped to "discover" an emerging movement in Italian postwar cinema that would come to be known as Italian neorealism. Directors and screenwriters associated with Italian neorealism include Luchino Visconti, Roberto Rossellini, Vittorio De Sica, Giuseppe De Santis, and Cesare Zavattini (who coined the term). Neorealist filmmakers wanted to move away from the artifice of the classical Hollywood style; instead they shot on location, used primarily nonprofessional actors, and sought to expose the drama they saw in everyday life. Zavattini wrote that "the ideal film would be ninety minutes of the life of a man to whom nothing happens" (Cook, p. 367). Yet we should not assume that

neorealist filmmakers did not construct their films very carefully, or that neorealist films are devoid of melodrama or pathos. In many ways, Rossellini's *Rome, Open City* (1945) consists of a conventional melodramatic plot; likewise, De Sica's *Bicycle Thieves* (1948), which is often held up as the epitome of neorealist cinema, is composed of painstakingly controlled shots, many of which use a method of shooting called depth of focus, which refers to shots filmed with fast lenses that allow both the foreground and the background to remain in focus, creating the illusion of depth in the visual field.

The critic André Bazin hailed depth of focus as a revolutionary technique in the 1930s and 1940s, since, he argued, it draws spectators into a relation with the image closer to that which we enjoy with reality. Bazin claimed that such closeness invites a more active mental attitude on the part of the spectator, as "it is from his attention and his will that the meaning of the image in part derives" (Bazin, vol. 1, p. 36). Bazin also asserted that depth of focus reintroduces the fundamental ambiguity of meaning in reality: "[t]he uncertainty in which we find ourselves as to the spiritual key or the interpretation we should put on the film is built into the very design of the image" (vol. 1, p. 36). Bazin believed that the problem with Hollywood's tendency toward invisible editing is that classical continuity, which makes action appear to be smooth and continuous, relies on abstract mental logic or time rather than real time. Moreover, he asserted, photographic media actually add to or transform reality instead of acting as reality's substitute: so we should understand the force of neorealism to be in assisting the *creation* of reality (a "new" reality) rather than the perfect representation of it. Neorealism's divergence from the prevalent idea that filmmaking (and its attendant technologies) will and should move progressively toward "a total and complete representation of reality" is the movement's most radical—and most crucial—quality, according to Bazin (vol. 1, p. 20). In a revision to Zavattini's original summation of neorealism as "ninety minutes of the life of a man to whom nothing happens," Bazin describes De Sica's *Bicycle Thieves* in the following sentence: "a man is walking along the street and the onlooker is amazed at the beauty of the man walking" (Bazin, vol. 2, p. 67). In the film, we see that De Sica is not so much optimistic about the world as he is tender and sympathetic toward its inhabitants.

We should not forget that Europe was devastated both physically and psychically following World War II. In England, air raids had destroyed close to 25 percent of the country's film theaters, while Germany lost almost 60 percent of its film production infrastructure. The 1950s would also bring a competing technology in the form of television, as well as a sharp increase in leisure activities that drew audiences out of dark theaters and into national sport (athletic) centers—as well as outdoors—throughout Europe. Just as in the United States, European film concerns worked to develop new technologies that would regain movie spectators' attention. Innovations in wide-screen and improved color and sound were all intended to compete with American films and to attract larger audiences. Many European countries focused on "prestige" pictures, and several older directors who had fled Europe during the war returned to make films in their home countries during the 1950s (Renoir, Ophüls, Dreyer, Lang, etc.). British cinema during the 1950s consisted of such strains as literary adaptations ("prestige" films) by David Lean, international art house films by Carol Reed, and beautifully rendered extravaganzas by Michael Powell and Emeric Pressburger.

## 1960S EUROPE

In 1960 Karel Reisz's *Saturday Night and Sunday Morning* announced the beginning of yet another strain in British film, which would come to be known as "new cinema" or social realism. Directors associated with "new cinema" took their inspiration from Italian neorealists, the British Free Cinema movement of the 1950s, and from a brand-new movement brewing on the other side of the English Channel. Tony Richardson (*A Taste of Honey*, 1961; *The Loneliness of the Long Distance Runner*, 1962), John Schlesinger (*A Kind of Loving*, 1962; *Billy Liar*, 1963), and Lindsay Anderson (*This Sporting Life*, 1963) all made films in this mode during the early 1960s. The films usually took place in the Midlands of England, depicting the struggles—and speaking in the language—of working people. Unlike the saturated colors of Powell and Pressburger's films just a few years earlier, blacks and gray tones dominate the color palette of British social realist cinema.

Also on the eve of the 1960s, a more exuberant revolution was launched in French cinema: a group of young film-critics-turned-filmmakers, who would come to be known as the "new wave" (*la nouvelle vague*), made their first feature-length films (Claude Chabrol, François Truffaut, Jean-Luc Godard, Jacques Rivette, and Eric Rohmer all made first features between 1958 and 1962). This loose affiliation of directors emerged from their association writing for the film journal *Cahiers du cinema* in the 1950s. Many of their films, particularly those of Godard, have a more intellectualized or "thought-out" quality as a result. Some film scholars point to Chabrol's *Le beau serge* (1958) as the first new-wave film, since it contains many of the qualities later associated with the movement, but two films that premiered between 1959 and 1960 truly inaugurated the political authorship (*politique des auteurs*) of the new wave.

First, in 1959, François Truffaut's *400 Blows* premiered. *400 Blows* is the story of a young boy, Antoine Doinel, making his way through a difficult childhood. His working-class parents are too preoccupied with their own unhappiness to pay much attention to Antoine; the cramped shots of the small apartment the three share are sharply contrasted by the high crane shots and light music that give a sense of openness and possibility to Antoine the moment he steps outside into the street. The film ends with a freeze frame of the young teen as he runs away from reform school and toward the liminal space at the ocean's edge on a barren stretch of beach; we share his profound uncertainty as to where he will go next. Luckily for us and for him, Truffaut went on to make three more films centering on the life of Antoine, all played by the same actor (Jean-Pierre Léaud). We see Antoine through romance, marriage, a child, divorce—and throughout, Truffaut films his subject with a remarkable combination of honesty and compassion.

Jean-Luc Godard's first film, *Breathless,* appeared just one year after *400 Blows* and was inspired by a script idea Truffaut gave to Godard about a petty thief who inadvertently kills a police officer and returns to Paris to collect money and to convince his American girlfriend to join him on the run. The resulting film is a dazzling feat of visual jazz: it follows its own unexpected rhythm, slowing down to endless takes when you least expect it, and then speeding up and cutting out action when it seems most essential (when the protagonist kills the policeman, for example). One of the techniques Godard used to shorten or create ellipses in the narrative action is called a "jump cut," a cut from one shot to another in which an action does not quite match up with the previous image, calling our attention to the constructed nature of film. It is much more widely used in films today due to Godard's considerable influence.

Other filmmakers of the new wave, including Jacques Rivette and Eric Rohmer, would also develop distinct signature, or authorial, styles over the years. With the exception of Truffaut, who died in 1984 at the age of fifty-two, all of the original French new-wave directors have continued to make films into the twenty-first century. Other filmmakers who were more tangentially associated with the new wave, such as Alain Resnais (*Night and Fog*, 1955; *Hiroshima mon amour*, 1959; *Last Year at Marienbad*, 1961), Chris Marker (*La Jetée* [1962; The pier], *Le joli mai* [1963; The lovely month of May], *Sans soleil* [1982; Sunless]), and Agnès Varda (*Cleo from 5 to 7*, 1961; *Far from Vietnam*, 1967; *Vagabond*, 1985), have also continued to make films into the twenty-first century.

Italian film after neorealism also struck out in new political and aesthetic directions. An important figure of neorealism, Luchino Visconti, embodies the transformation: after inaugurating neorealism with his 1943 film *Ossessione* and creating one of its crowning achievements in 1948 with *La terra trema* (The earth trembles), Visconti turned to increasingly sumptuous and dissolute subjects, including a story set during the Austrian occupation of Italy in the mid-nineteenth century (*Senso*, 1954) and another nineteenth-century study of decadence and the loss of power, set in Sicily during the Risorgimento (unification) of Italy (*The Leopard*, 1963). In both films, Visconti explores the beauty of the decaying aristocratic class structure in which he was born while simultaneously damning it (Visconti was a committed, if complicated, Marxist).

Federico Fellini likewise began his career firmly rooted in the idealism and aesthetics of neorealism, where he began as a screenwriter on Rossellini's *Rome, Open City* (1945), and *Paisà* (1946). His first directorial efforts, *The Young and the Passionate* (1953) and *La strada* (1954), strongly reflect his neorealist background. But by 1959, when he found huge commercial and critical success with *La dolce vita*, Fellini had already moved toward the world of the magical and the absurd. In *8½* (1963), his eighth-and-a-half film, Fellini weaves together an epic tapestry of one man's life, Guido, as he struggles to make a big-budget film. Through a series of flashbacks, fantasies, and dreams, we are transported into Guido's interior world, culminating in a long celluloid parade of every character in his life (and the film) at the end.

Michelangelo Antonioni, on the other hand, moved from neorealist tendencies in *Il grido* (1957; The cry) to a much more minimalist, abstract, architectural form of filmmaking. More than any other European director in the postwar period, Antonioni learned to exploit the newer widescreen techniques for the purposes of art rather than mere spectacle, and the resulting films are breathtaking in their vastness and evocation of existential emptiness (*L'avventura* [1961; The adventure], *La notte* [1961; The night], *L'eclisse* [1962; Eclipse], *Il deserto rosso* [1964; The red desert].

Pier Paolo Pasolini was no less philosophical than Antonioni, but his filmmaking was much more visceral and radically politicized: Pasolini was a well-known writer before he ever became a director, and his first two films, *Accattone!* (1960) and *Mamma Roma* (1962), are based in the Roman slums he had previously depicted in novels. A committed Marxist, Pasolini used the film medium to attack the authority of the Catholic Church and the state with increasing vehemence during the 1960s and early 1970s (*La ricotta*, 1963; *The Gospel According to Matthew*, 1964; *Hawks and Sparrows*, 1966; *Salò or the Hundred and Twenty Days of Sodom*, 1975). In 1975, shortly before the release of his brutal and highly controversial film *Salò*, Pasolini was murdered, cutting short one of the most luminous and provocative cinematic oeuvres of the twentieth century.

Bernardo Bertolucci worked as an assistant director on Pasolini's first film, *Accattone!* and has often referred to Pasolini, along with Jean-Luc Godard, as a cinematic father figure. Bertolucci's second feature, *Before the Revolution* (1964), is the story of Fabrizio, who is trying to decide whether to commit to his radical political beliefs or to retreat to the familiar comfort of his bourgeois milieu. Over and over again, Bertolucci presents us with characters who must choose between a tough moral-political stance and the ease of conformity, as exemplified in his most famous and most recent films, respectively—*The Conformist* (1970) and *The Dreamers* (2003).

With the exception of Luis Buñuel (who spent relatively little time making films in Spain over his fifty-year career), Spanish cinema was not well known outside of Spain until the 1960s. Until then, films were generated by monopolistic entities, directors from the national film school IIEC (Instituto de Investigaciones y Experiencias Cinematográficas), and the Spanish government's newsreel service. In 1962 a new director general of cinema was named, who reorganized the national film school (and gave it a new acronym, EOC) and created greater opportunities for governmental subsidization of new film productions. The result was a string of formidable feature pictures in the 1960s made by directors such as Luis Garcia Berlanga, Carlos Saura, Miguel Picazo, and Basilio Martín Patino. However, true "opening" of Spanish cinema would not occur until the "soft dictatorship" period in the two years preceding Franco's death in 1975.

## 1970S TO THE 2000S

Unlike in France and Italy (but perhaps more like in Spain), cinema in the new West German state sputtered in fits and starts during the 1960s, and even with support from a group organized at the Oberhausen Film Festival in 1962—that called for a "new" German cinema and successfully petitioned the West German government to fund young filmmakers—German cinema would not capture the world's attention until the early 1970s.

In the 1970s, though, German film collectives made up for lost time: members of the Author's Film Publishing Group included Rainer Werner Fassbinder (*The Bitter Tears of Petra von Kant,* 1972; *Ali: Fear Eats the Soul,* 1974; *The Marriage of Maria Braun,* 1979), Alexander Kluge, and Wim Wenders, while Werner Herzog (*Aguirre: The Wrath of God,* 1972; *Stroszek,* 1977; *Nosferatu,* 1979) received funds to make his first film from the Young German Film Board that came out of the Oberhausen initiative in the mid-1960s. The husband-wife team of Volker Schlöndorff (*The Sudden Wealth of the Poor People of Kombach,* 1974; *Coup de grâce,* 1976; *The Tin Drum,* 1979) and Margarethe von Trotta (*Summer Lightning/A Free Woman,* 1972; *The Lost Honor of Katharina Blum,* 1975) also contributed some of the most important films of the period. The tone of the New German Cinema is somewhat pessimistic, expressing disenchantment with Germany's past and uncertainty about its future. It also represents a generation very much "infiltrated" by American culture since the occupation, maintaining an uneasy relationship with America's cultural imperialism. The New German "character" is embodied by the protagonist in Wim Wenders's *Kings of the Road* (1976): a young film projector mechanic named Bruno wanders along the East German border maintaining old, broken-down projectors in old, broken-down movie theaters. Bruno is laconic, his face impenetrable; long minutes tick by with no words at all. He meets another young man, nicknamed "Kamikaze" for a failed suicide attempt that brings about the first encounter between them, and they decide to travel together, American road-movie style. Yet the film contains an ambivalent relationship to America throughout: the commercialization of film is wrecking small-town German movie theaters, while American rock and roll and constant homage to American films and filmmakers by way of visual quotations provide energy and momentum to the film.

Just two years later, Helke Sander's *Redupers, The All-Around Reduced Personality* (1978) would blend fiction and documentary to tell the story of Edda (played by Sander herself), a single mother and photographer who joins a women's photography collective in West Berlin. The collective has just received a grant to document West Berlin from a feminist perspective, but instead of seeing differences between West and East through her camera, Edda/Helke only sees parallels. She does not fit in anywhere and wanders the city not unlike Wenders's

Bruno, and the film refuses to grant its protagonist—or the audience—answers about the future.

The 1970s proved to be a catalyzing decade across Europe for artistic innovation in film. In post-Franco Spain, Carlos Saura, Juan Bardem, and Luis Berlanga continued to make politically oriented films of various kinds (symbolic, satire, thriller), and Victor Bice directed the internationally lauded masterpiece *Spirit of the Beehive* (1973), in which a traveling projectionist shows *Frankenstein* in a small town, activating the imagination of two young girls. By the end of the 1970s, the director Pilar Miró would test the boundaries of censorship in post-Franco Spain with his film *The Cuenca Crime* (1979), for which Miró was charged with defamation. When Miró was exonerated and the film was finally released, it broke all domestic box office records.

It was also during the 1970s that Pedro Almodóvar began making films with a Super-8 camera and screening them in Madrid's underground clubs. With an exuberant feel for the perversions and manias that drive us, Almodóvar has become Spain's most consistently successful and provocative filmmaker. Though his films are populated with surprisingly lovable drug-addicted nuns, prostitutes, and transvestites, Almodóvar has been showered with nominations and awards from all over the world since his breakout film *Women on the Verge of a Nervous Breakdown* in 1987. He has been nominated for a number of Academy Awards, Césars (France's Oscar), BAFTAs (the U.K.'s Oscar), and European Film Awards. He has also won Oscars for *All About My Mother* (1999) and *Talk to Her* (2002), and multiple European awards and prizes.

Before Almodóvar, relatively few directors in the sound era found that they could cross national borders as easily as those in the silent era; many of those who did have been mentioned over the course of this essay. This was in part a problem of language, as previously discussed. The filmmakers who had international success gained it primarily through festivals and the international art house circuit. Yet Almodóvar and other filmmakers at the turn of the twenty-first century face a major paradigm shift at the level of both markets and audiences to a global economy and culture.

The importance of this shift to the present and future of cinema should not be underestimated.

For very strong national film cultures such as France, globalization provides more possible venues for coproduction and distribution. Yet the infrastructure that remains in place maintains distinct national features that exist nowhere else in the world. France still produces over two hundred films a year, a remarkable number for a country of its size; France also has more major female film directors than any other country in the world (Chantal Akerman, Catherine Breillat, Claire Denis, Diane Kurys, Colline Serreau, Agnès Varda, to name just a few). The French government also continues to subsidize and regulate the contemporary film industry through a tax on every movie ticket sold. Other countries in Europe have struggled more to find a place in global film culture: with the exception of Tom Twyker (*Run Lola Run*, 1998; *Winter Sleepers*, 1997; *Heaven*, 2002), Germany has not regained the prominence—domestically or globally—that it enjoyed during the 1970s.

Since the 1990s, there has also been a marked increase in "crossover" directors: filmmakers who seem to work easily in more than one country or language. The brilliant Polish filmmaker Krzysztof Kieslowski, for instance, began his career at the Łódź Film Academy and initially made documentaries and shorter works meant for Polish television (*Camera Buff*, 1979; *The Decalogue*, 1988). In the 1990s Kieslowski made four films in France, the last three of which formed a trilogy called *Three Colors* (1993–1994). The trilogy is a meditation on the "postmodern condition," on parallel lives and chance intersections. In Kieslowski's films, characters take tiny, awkward steps toward connection in an otherwise alienating world. His actors are often shot as small figures against a vast background.

At the beginning of a new century, European cinema has become more complex—and more vital—than ever. In the British director Stephen Frears's *Dirty Pretty Things* (2003), the main characters are Nigerian and Turkish immigrants, played by a British-Nigerian and a French actor, respectively (Chiwetel Ejiofor and Audrey Tautou). The cast also includes actors from Croatia, Spain, and China; the two primary languages spoken in the film are English and Somali.

*Dirty Pretty Things* is a thriller about, among other things, the global trafficking of human organs, and the daily struggle of immigrants to survive in West London. How do we classify such a film? Is it British? Is it international, as its distribution credits would suggest? Is it "global," based on its cast and content?

The story of European cinema in the twentieth century would tell us that it is all three, and more: European cinema is both transformed by culture and transformative in its proliferation and mass appeal. Released in 2001, the British film *Harry Potter and the Philosopher's Stone* was seen by 59,032,893 spectators in Europe alone. It calls to mind the description of Jean Renoir's 1939 film *The Rules of the Game*: astonishing for its ability to cast a spell over us all.

*See also* **Almodóvar, Pedro; Bardot, Brigitte; Buñuel, Luis; Chaplin, Charlie; Cocteau, Jean; De Sica, Vittorio; Dietrich, Marlene; Fellini, Federico; Film (Documentary); French New Wave; Godard, Jean-Luc; Kracauer, Siegfried; Lang, Fritz; Ophüls, Marcel; Pabst, Georg Wilhelm; Pasolini, Pier Paolo; Propaganda; Riefensthal, Leni; Rossellini, Roberto; Tarkovsky, Andrei; Wajda, Andrzej; Wenders, Wim.**

BIBLIOGRAPHY

Andrew, Dudley. *Mists of Regret: Culture and Sensibility in Classic French Film.* Princeton, N.J., 1995.

Bazin, André. *What Is Cinema?* Translated by Hugh Gray. 2 vols. Berkeley, Calif., 2005.

Benjamin, Walter. "The Work of Art in the Age of Mechanical Reproduction." In *Illuminations,* edited by Hannah Arendt and translated by Harry Zohn, 217–251. New York, 1968.

Bondanella, Peter. *Italian Cinema:From Neorealism to the Present.* 3rd ed. New York, 2001.

Bordwell, David, and Thompson Kristin. *Film History: An Introduction.* 2nd ed. Boston, 2003.

Cook, David A. *A History of Narrative Film.* 4th ed. New York, 2004.

Elsaesser, Thomas. *European Cinema: Face to Face with Hollywood.* Amsterdam, 2005.

Fowler, Catherine, ed. *The European Cinema Reader.* London, 2002.

Gallagher, Tag. *The Adventures of Roberto Rossellini.* New York, 1998.

ANNE M. KERN

---

**CITIZENSHIP.** The construction of Europe as a political entity started immediately after World War II, motivated by the belief that only creation of a genuinely European citizenship would put a definitive end to the violence and atrocities that had ravaged the old continent throughout its history. As of 2005 the European Union (EU) included twenty-five nations that maintain peaceful relations among themselves. Europe has thus attained the first and principal objective of its foundational figures. However, a consensus exists that the EU has not yet become a real political community. Most of its inhabitants do not consider themselves "citizens of Europe." A major reason for this is the fact that the leaders of the principal member-states do not always agree on the type of citizenship to be promulgated. Since the nineteenth century, each nation has developed differently and created its own definition of citizenship. The past still weighs on the present, obstructing reflection and action on the part of those who militate on behalf of a politically unified Europe.

### THE ROLE OF LANGUAGE

World War I may be considered a turning point in the history of European citizenship. In destroying the old empires and consolidating the ascendancy of nation-states, it represented the beginning of the new era. But the war also marked the outcome of a long historical process that occupied peoples and nations during the nineteenth century. During the nineteenth century, indeed, each nation created its own vocabulary to express the concept. To translate the English word *citizenship,* French offers a choice of two words: *citoyenneté* and *nationalité.* The same is true for the German language, with *Bürgerschaft* and *Staatsangehörigkeit.* Like other Latin languages, French uses *nationalité* to designate both the common origin of inhabitants and the concept of state affiliation, while English and German employ two different terms to more clearly differentiate these two notions.

The history of nations explains these linguistic differences. In England, the wealthy landowners, in contesting the arbitrary character of the monarchy, had obtained the right to appoint their parliamentary representatives. In that country, the concept of citizenship was associated from the start with defense of individual liberties and with obtaining new rights, but it did not call into question the oath of allegiance of the "subjects of His Majesty." With reference to this specific case in *Citizenship and Social Class* (1950), the political scientist Thomas Humphrey Marshall (1893–1981) proposed a definition that remains famous and is still discussed in textbooks in the early twenty-first century. Emphasizing the gradual enlargement of rights granted to citizens, he suggested that in the wake of the civil and political rights obtained during the eighteenth and nineteenth centuries, the second part of the twentieth century marked the start of a new phase, based on the emergence of social rights granted by the welfare state.

Marshall's view, however, did not take into account individual histories of the other major European states. The French definition of citizenship was profoundly influenced by the Revolution of 1789. In that country Jean-Jacques Rousseau's (1712–1778) conception prevailed. In his *Contrat social* (Social contract) in 1762, Rousseau criticized the English for not sufficiently or carefully enough separating political and civil rights. Taking Athens as his model, Rousseau believed that citizenship should be defined by active participation in the life of the state. He advocated replacing monarchies with republics that were defined as sovereign communities, the members of which submit to the laws of the state, as subjects, but also as citizens who collectively contribute to the development of laws and legislation. Rousseau's influence explains why the French often approached the concept of citizenship from the perspective of participation in the nation's political life, and for a long time they were preoccupied with determining who should belong to this civic community and who must be excluded. The struggles of workers' movements and feminists to extend the right to vote to the lower classes and to women should be viewed in this context.

History also explains the distinctive vocabulary for German citizenship. While in France and England the monarchic state had imposed sovereign power over all its subjects since the seventeenth century, the German Holy Roman Empire, first adumbrated by Charlemagne (r. 768–814), had collapsed in the Middle Ages, leading to a multitude of separate states and principalities. In this context, the monarchic state's first priority was to impose its law

upon all its subjects. This was why the Prussian king, Frederick William II (r. 1786–1797), enforced the *Allgemeines Landrecht* (General State Law) in 1794. The nobility consented to obey this code but, in exchange, the king acknowledged they enjoyed privileges and continued to place heavy burdens on the peasants. Principles of citizenship such as individual liberty and equality, as a consequence, took hold only slowly in the German states. The bourgeoisie, as the class that included individuals who benefited from the *droit de cité,* or citizenship rights accorded city-dwellers, played a major role in this emancipation process. It is no accident that German is the only European language in which the terms for *citizen* and *bourgeois* are virtually synonyms.

In the early years of the nineteenth century the German vocabulary for citizenship acquired a new word, *Volkstum.* Philosophers, who were intellectuals drawn mostly from the upper class, had greeted the French Revolution in 1789 with enthusiasm. However, occupation of German territories by Napoleon's army forced the Germans to revolt against French domination. From that point on the battle for freedom was no longer a struggle against an arbitrary power and privileged class (the nobility), but also a fight to emancipate an oppressed nation. Henceforth it was not enough to know who was a citizen and who was not. Nations must now define themselves and set out criteria by which they could be identified and distinguished each from the another. One fruit of this effort was *Volkstum,* a word invented by the philosopher Friedrich Ludwig Jahn (1778–1852) to designate the "national character" of a people by applying three criteria—language, custom, and, most important of all, "the vital impulse," defined as the "spiritual principle" that stamps a nation as unique. French writers and historians of the Romantic period (1820–1840) agreed with and endorsed this definition. They translated *Volkstum* with a new French word, *nationalité,* in hopes of clarifying France's own particular characteristics.

During this period the "principle of nationality" became popular throughout Europe. It legitimized the struggles for national sovereignty for which small groups of militants were fighting. The defeat of the Revolutions of 1848 brought about brutal repression of these subversive movements. But they continued to gather strength in the

**An open-air parliament, in Glarus, Switzerland, April 1939.** During the annual gathering, citizens vote on municipal issues. ©Bettmann/Corbis

decades that followed, attacking the power of old empires from within. This would be one of the chief causes of World War I.

At this time, in the German language, another word, *Staatsangehörigkeit,* appeared; it designated citizenship not by allegiance to a nation but rather to a state. Prussian civil servants first employed the term in the context of arguments with neighboring countries concerning measures to control vagrancy and begging. The Prussian state, wishing to care only for its own poor, passed a law in 1842 that more clearly defined which individuals would benefit from its protection. The law specified that the legal status of the Prussian subject was transmitted by paternity from father to child. Thus, Prussia relied on the *jus sanguinis* (right of blood), which had been used in 1804 by the Napoleonic Civil Code to specify French status and which was later adopted by most European countries. The

noteworthy exception was England; that country remained faithful to the feudal principle of the *jus soli* (right of territory), by which birth within a state confers nationality.

### THE POLITICAL STAKES

Until the end of the nineteenth century citizenship and nationality were viewed from two different angles. Philosophers and political activists were principally concerned with what it meant to belong to a nation or a people, while magistrates and bureaucrats were interested in the problem of who belongs to a state. The years between 1880 and 1914 were a vital period in the history of citizenship because these two concerns were ever more closely linked. Workers gradually won the right to vote and various social rights. But, at the same time, governments obliged citizens to enlist in the military and do battle for their nation.

Given these circumstances, one can understand why the right to citizenship became a major political issue. Increasing migration and a terrible economic depression beginning in the mid-1870s provoked the government to intervene in social matters. Most European countries passed laws on immigration and citizenship that revealed a protectionist impulse in public policy-making. Such laws established strict lines of demarcation that separated nationals, who benefited from them, and foreigners, who did not. Citizenship laws also enabled nations to increase their populations by turning foreigners into citizens by a wave of a judicial magic wand. At a time when a nation's power was still measured by the number of soldiers it could enlist in its military, no state was prepared to deprive itself of this resource. By contrast, because leaders were ever more concerned by citizens' *loyalty* to their nation, the right of citizenship also functioned to exclude those suspected of not sharing the feeling that they belonged to the national community.

These new laws regarding citizenship, which would remain in force through the rest of the twentieth century, must be above all understood as instruments in the service of state power. Arguments used to justify them were often found in the writings of philosophers and historians. But governments used such arguments only if they served their interests. The case of Switzerland clearly revealed that linguistic or religious criteria were not employed to define citizenship when the powers that be judged them inopportune. The notion of "Swiss citizenship" entered the legal vocabulary during a constitutional revision in 1874. From that point on, only the Helvetian confederation could decide on the rules pertaining to political and civic matters insofar as they applied to the Swiss themselves. However, the *droit de cité communal,* a retention from the ancien régime, remained a determining factor in acquiring citizenship. Anyone who did not enjoy its privileges was considered a "stateless person" (*heimatlose*).

The major issue that brought about citizenship reform in France in 1889 was concern over the declining birthrate. Since the 1860s France has been a destination for immigrants. The republican regime wanted to avoid the formation of ethnic minorities; the army needed new soldiers. In

Algeria French colons wished to reinforce discrimination against the local population but they also wanted to prevent Italian and Spanish immigrants from becoming a majority. This led the government to grant greater importance to the *droit du sol* (citizenship for all those born on French soil with at least one parent born in France) as a way to convert those born on national soil into French citizens.

Germany was unique in that it was a destination for immigrants, including a large Polish community in eastern Prussia, and at the same time a country of emigration, with some 3.5 million Germans in other countries. The main goal of the German citizenship law voted in 1913, known as the Delbrück Law, was to reinforce the bond of nationality beyond the country's borders. Individuals born of German parents were to be considered German citizens. Contrary to what was often claimed, such a reinforcement of the *jus sanguinis* did not represent the wish to apply a "German conception" of the nation. Rather, the law aimed to better protect the interests of a country losing inhabitants to emigration at a moment when receiving countries were striving to "nationalize" the foreign population within their borders. In 1891, for example, Brazil decided that all immigrants living on its soil were henceforth Brazilian citizens, unless they expressed the wish to retain their former nationality. As early as 1912 Italy also reinforced the *jus sanguinis,* allowing all native Italians living abroad to retain their original citizenship.

The legal status of individuals thus became, during the years preceding World War I, a central issue that constituted a form of rivalry among nations. These laws not only demarcated a rigid boundary between the national and foreign populations but also fomented discrimination within the national population as a whole by establishing a variety of intermediate categories of individuals who were denied full citizenship, such as women, stateless persons, naturalized citizens, natives of the colonies, and others.

Another reason that right of citizenship became a major problem was that the fact of belonging to a nation was not only a judicial issue. During this period bureaucracy had made major strides. The state intruded ever more deeply into all the spheres of daily life of its citizens. Everywhere in Europe bureaucrats accomplished the huge task of creating systems of identification and thorough and precise registers of citizenship. This was the era that saw the first modern identity papers and population census reports, from which statistics could be extracted and maps created to reveal the ethnic composition and distribution of the populations.

## WORLD WAR I AND THE "PEOPLES' RIGHT TO SELF-DETERMINATION"

During World War I citizenship and nationality were connected in a highly repressive way. Passage of the Delbrück Law a few months before hostilities began was perceived in France and England as a warlike act that aimed to destabilize other European countries by seeking support from German and Austro-Hungarian immigrants. This was the reason why, with the beginning of the war, foreign nationals from those countries were confined in internment camps. Similarly, the Allies adopted laws refusing citizenship to immigrants from enemy countries. These decisions, justified by the war, remained in force during the next several decades. In France the law of denaturalization would later be used against previously naturalized communist activists. Internment would also be applied during World War II, including the detention of Germans fleeing Nazi persecution.

In 1854, at the time of the Crimean War, Napoleon III (r. 1852–1870) had refused to imprison the numerous Russians then living in France, contending that he was at war with princes, not people. This kind of reasoning could no longer apply after the principles of citizenship were established because each citizen is considered a representative of his or her nation. After World War I this logic spread to the whole of Europe. It is estimated that the peace treaties signed in 1919–1920 affected the citizenship of about one hundred million individuals. A change of such magnitude had not occurred since the Napoleonic era. "Peoples' right to self-determination," officially proclaimed in January 1918 by U.S. president Woodrow Wilson (1856–1924), became a bedrock of international law. In the name of the "principle of nationalities," the great powers became the supreme arbitrators for determining which groups "really" constituted a nation and which did not,

based on ethnic, linguistic, or religious criteria—which, in fact, those nations had never themselves respected in the course of their own histories. Considering the extraordinary diversity of populations living in eastern Europe and the Balkans, these criteria could only be applied in an arbitrary way. Groups that could not obtain the status of sovereign nation became "minorities" with rights guaranteed by the League of Nations, but the new nation-states considered them to be threats to their integrity. The principle of national homogeneity, legitimized by the great powers, fueled tensions that led to armed conflicts, notably between Greece and Turkey in 1919–1922. Massive population transfers occurred in the Balkans and in Asia and were most often enforced without taking into account the will of those involved.

The totalitarian parties that came to power between the two world wars followed to extremes the logic of belonging to a state and the concept of national homogeneity that had been created in the nineteenth century. The Bolsheviks, Italian Fascists, and Nazis each adopted laws of denationalization to be used against enemies of the regime. In Germany laws depriving Jews of the protection of the German state created a "legal" framework for the persecutions and thereby inaugurated a process that led to the Holocaust. Unlike British or French legislation that applied only to individuals guilty of treason, the Nazi laws were applied collectively and based on racist criteria that principally targeted Jews. The Reich Citizenship Law of 15 September 1939 stipulated that henceforth only nationals of "German blood" were to be considered citizens of the Reich. Anti-Semitic laws adopted in France by the Vichy government during World War II employed the same logic. Similarly, totalitarian regimes justified massive population transfers with arguments about homogeneity of the peoples as an extension of the principle of nationalities. This was why, as the historian Eric Hobsbawm has emphasized, Adolf Hitler (1889–1945) was a "Wilsonian nationalist" when he organized the transfer of Germans living abroad to Germany as well as when he decided to eliminate the Jews. Nevertheless, one must not forget that the Allies stood up for "peoples' right to self-determination" as a means to favor peace and put an end to ethnic clashes, while the Nazi regime applied its policies of homogeneity to physically eliminate millions of people.

What made the Stalinist Soviet Union unique with regard to the physical extermination of civilians was its supposed universal destiny and project for constructing a worker's state. Social and economic arguments, rather than ethnic categories, were used to justify mass repression, such as the elimination of the kulaks (wealthy peasants). The fifteen republics that constituted the Soviet Union represented as many "nations," each with its own territory, language and, at least in theory, a significant measure of autonomy. After 1932 nationality defined in ethnocultural terms became an element in the personal identity of everyone in the Soviet Union, and was duly so registered by official census reports. This institutionalization of nationality would seriously fuel the violence that erupted after the collapse of the Soviet regime in the early 1990s. The same process could be observed in other communist countries, notably in Yugoslavia.

## EMERGENCE OF EUROPEAN CITIZENSHIP

The establishment of principles of national citizenship thus may be viewed as a series of missteps that in a sense facilitated the tragic paroxysms of Nazi barbarism and the horror of World War II. As soon as peace returned, consequently, there were numerous international initiatives to establish durable and definitively pacific relations between peoples. The Universal Declaration of Human Rights, adopted by the United Nations in 1948, is among the most appealing demonstrations of this collective effort to support the emergence of a universal citizenship. Establishment of the European Union was undertaken with the same basic rationale, even though the various nations did not renounce their sovereignty. On the contrary, it is most striking that postwar citizenship laws adopted by the European states extended their own traditions. The West Germans continued to abide by the Delbrück Law and by the *jus sanguinis*, because, according to them, inhabitants were still Germans even if living in another sovereign land. In the same way, the United Kingdom retained the right of soil and all people within the empire were granted Britain citizenship and were subjects of the Crown. France, which became one of the principal destinations for immigrants between the two world

wars, reinforced the principles built into its 1889 citizenship law.

However, in the postwar decades, citizenship legislation in the various European nations gradually converged. Two reasons explain this phenomenon. The first involved the integration of nations in the European Union. This was accomplished, to be sure, more by creating a large common market than by the construction of a genuine political union. However, elimination of the customs duties was one step in a process that finally enabled people to circulate freely within the European Union—a decision taken by the several states that signed the Schengen treaty in Luxembourg in 1985. Borders separating nations now designated their interior limits while the real boundaries that protect European space moved to the perimeter of the Union. European citizenship was reinforced in 1992 by the Maastricht Treaty, signed in the Netherlands, which granted citizens of one EU nation the right to live and work in another member nation, and in certain cases even vote in local elections. Another essential element in the process of integration was the adoption of a single currency in 2002. Money had long been a fundamental component of state sovereignty and an essential factor in identifying citizens as belonging to a specific national community. The relative ease with which Europeans accepted the euro was a genuine victory over the past. The final element in the progress of European citizenship concerns the judicial and administrative spheres. Even if unaware of it, Europeans in the early twenty-first century abide by laws that were established, in most cases, by high-ranking civil servants of the European Commission in Brussels, by elected members of the European Parliament in Strasbourg, and by members of the Court of Justice in Luxembourg.

However, until the beginning of the twenty-first century, it has not been possible to create a common accord that would regulate European citizenship. Not all authors agree as to the reasons for this stumbling block. Many think that citizenship expresses one's national identity, so that the past still weighs too heavily on the present to allow the major European states to agree, now or in a near future. But other researchers, on the contrary, believe that nothing, in principle, should prevent a unified law of citizenship. Most European nations have become destination countries for immigrants. However, in the modern world, governments cannot allow the constant multiplication, generation after generation, of great numbers of individuals who do not "belong" to their nations. Since the 1970s most European governments have thus modified their right to citizenship in a way that most resembled the system that France, the oldest of the immigrant-destination nations, adopted at the end of the nineteenth century. This system, while based on the *jus sanguinis,* still leaves an important place to the *jus soli,* which allows the immigrants' children to join the national community. Since World War II the Netherlands, Belgium, and Spain have legislated measures along these lines.

But the growing convergence of European law around citizenship is exemplified by the legislation Germany adopted in 1999. The Germans now made a place for the *droit du sol.* The British response represents rapprochement of a different kind. As noted, traditionally, the right of citizenship in England was based on the subjects' oath of allegiance to their monarchy. Everyone under the jurisdiction of former colonies had, as a consequence, the right to freely inhabit British soil. To gain greater control over African and Asian immigration, however, the government has in recent years modified the law by giving full benefits of citizenship only to British citizens born in the United Kingdom.

In the early twenty-first century, in all nations that comprise the European Union, three categories are distinguished vis-à-vis the right to citizenship: citizens of the various nations, citizens of Europe, and non-Europeans.

*See also* **European Union; France; Germany; Holocaust; Immigration and Internal Migration; Maastricht, Treaty of; Minority Rights; Soviet Union; Switzerland; United Kingdom; World War I; World War II.**

BIBLIOGRAPHY

Anderson, Benedict. *Imagined Communities: Reflections on the Origin and Spread of Nationalism.* London, 1983.

Arlettaz, Gerald, and Silvia Arlettaz. *La Suisse et ses étrangers: Immigration et formation nationale, 1848–1933.* Lausanne, 2004.

Bade, Klaus J. *Migration in European History.* Translated by Allison Brown. Malden, Mass., 2003.

Brubaker, Rogers. *Nationalism Reframed: Nationhood and the National Question in the New Europe.* Cambridge, U.K., and New York, 1996.

Cafruny, Alan, and Glenda Rosenthal, eds. *The Maastricht Debates and Beyond.* Boulder, Colo., and Burnt Mill, Harlow, U.K., 1993.

Gellner, Ernest. *Nations and Nationalism.* Ithaca, N.Y., 1983.

Grawert, Rolf. *Staat und Staatsangehörigkeit; Verfassungsgeschichtliche Untersuchung zur Entstehung der Staatsangehörigkeit.* Berlin, 1973.

Hansen, Randell, and Patrick Weil, eds. *Towards a European Nationality: Citizenship, Immigration, and Nationality Law in the EU.* Basingstoke, U.K., and New York, 2001.

Heckmann, Friedrich, and Dominique Schnapper, eds. *The Integration of Immigrants in European Societies: National Differences and Trends of Convergence.* Stuttgart, Germany, 2003.

Hobsbawm, E. J. *Nations and Nationalism since 1780: Programme, Myth, Reality.* Cambridge, U.K., 1990.

Jahn, Friedrich Ludwig. *Deutsches Volksthum.* 1810. Hildesheim, Germany, and New York, 1980.

Klausen, Jytte, and Louise A. Tilly, eds. *European Integration in Social and Historical Perspective: 1850 to the Present.* Lanham, Md., 1997.

Kocka, Jürgen, and Allan Mitchell, eds. *Bourgeois Society in Nineteenth-century Europe.* Oxford, U.K., and Providence, R.I., 1993.

Koselleck Reinhart. *Futures Past: On the Semantics of Historical Time.* New York, 2004.

Lucassen, Jan. *Migrant Labour in Europe, 1600–1900: The Drift to the North Sea.* London and Wolfeboro, N.H., 1987.

Marshall, Thomas Humphrey. *Citizenship and Social Class and Other Essays.* Cambridge, U.K., 1950.

Noiriel, Gérard. *Etat, nation et immigration: Vers une histoire du pouvoir.* Paris, 2001.

Rosanvallon, Pierre. *Le Sacre du citoyen: Histoire du suffrage universel en France.* Paris, 1992.

Rousseau, Jean-Jacques. *On the Social Contract.* New York, 2003.

GÉRARD NOIRIEL

---

**CIVIL SERVICE.** Centuries pass, and the customary view of the civil service does not change. After the works of Honoré de Balzac, Charles Dickens, and Nikolai Gogol in the nineteenth century and the satires of Georges Courteline at the turn of the twentieth century, subsequent literary efforts portrayed the civil servant as unskilled, irresponsible, corrupt—indeed, often enough all three at once. Sometimes there is an element of tragedy, and the civil servant finds himself inside depersonalized or totalitarian environments. Works by Robert Musil, Franz Kafka, Václav Havel, and Alexander Solzhenitsyn have described the distress of the isolated individual facing terrifying bureaucratic or police systems. Unfortunately, certain of these descriptions are not wrong.

## CHANGING ROLES OF CIVIL SERVICE

As with all myths, that of the civil service has some truth. With Alexis de Tocqueville, Karl Marx, Max Weber, and later Hannah Arendt and Michel Foucault, political philosophy has continued to investigate the rise of technocratic civilization concomitant with the entry of the masses into political life. In addition, it is clear that the number of public-sector employees in Europe increased considerably over the course of the twentieth century. Precise figures are not easy to come by, considering the dissimilar criteria among countries for determining who is a civil servant. The number of civil servants in Italy grew tenfold, from 2.2 percent of the active population in 1880 to 22 percent in 1980, but "only" by four and a half times in France during this same period. In the whole of Western Europe, the salaries of civil servants represented an increasing percentage of government expenses. At the beginning of the 1990s, in the ten most industrialized countries in the European Union (EU), civil servants of state and regional agencies (public utilities excluded) accounted for between 5 percent and 8.5 percent of the population, though as high as 13 percent in Denmark.

Remuneration of those traditionally considered civil servants—such as police, magistrates, and administrative officials—does not represent the greatest cost to taxpayers. The most numerous public employees are teachers, postal employees, nurses, social administrators, technicians, and all the various social-service professionals; these occupations became the states' responsibility over the course of the twentieth century. The two world wars led all the countries involved to develop government services in charge of industrial mobilization, weapons manufacture, and administration of the workforce. The postwar state had to take care of widows and orphans, organize the reconstruction of ravaged regions, manage enormous financial deficits, and seek to maintain peace. All these tasks and more fell to the state. This was why, after 1945, many European countries—whether by choice or, on the eastern part of the Continent, under Soviet influence—opted for nationalization and the establishment of vast public state-run enterprises, notably energy, transportation, communication, and banking. Add to these the great expansion of social services.

A tendency to reverse public-sector growth has been at work since the 1980s, particularly in central and Western European countries. However, even here, for all the haste to stop the proliferation of administrative systems, it was not possible to create the tabula rasa that had been the hope of the more radical proponents of anti–big government associated with Margaret Thatcher and Ronald Reagan. The centuries-long history of the geopolitical construction of Europe, with its empires and nation-states, generated influential models. If we follow Tocqueville, Napoleon I (r. 1804–1814, 1815), by inventing the Civil Code and the *préfet* (high-ranking civil servant of local administration), essentially continued the centralization process already begun under the ancien régime, and he was always prepared to invent new taxes to finance war.

The colonial influence was equally important. By the seventeenth century Spanish and Portuguese administrations managed and controlled vast New World possessions. In 1813 the East India Company opened a training school for future civil servants serving the colonial regime. This model, created with the help of Sir Charles Edward Trevelyan and Thomas Babington Macaulay, was copied in 1853–1855 by the British government, leading to creation of a civil service that put an end to the old patronage system in the public sphere. Such comparisons can only be pushed so far. If bureaucracies in four of the continental empires on the eve of World War I—the German, Austro-Hungarian, Russian, and Ottoman—shared an authoritarian character, only Germany, inheriting the long tradition of Prussian cameralist policies, could be considered efficient. In fact, only Germany would recover from the troubled period between the two wars, albeit at the price of Nazi ideology.

Insofar as the civil service during the interwar period is concerned, two major confrontations should be noted. First, on a political basis, there grew an opposition between parliamentary democracy and authoritarianism or totalitarianism. But there also developed increasing tension between efficiency and loyalty. The nature of their mission—to put the law to work—made civil servants lay claim to professionalism, which could in turn lead them to question, in ways subtle and unannounced, the policy of the powers that be. The history of the civil service in Europe during the twentieth century can be understood as a gradual quest for independence from the political system and, at the same time, the outcome of efforts on the part of politicians to find a means to control the public bureaucracy.

## CIVIL SERVICE STATUTES

Careers in civil service at once organized and symbolized the establishment of a cadre of professionals that serve the res publica (commonwealth). As to recruitment and training, advancement, remuneration, and discipline, the tendency to regimentation and codification was present at the beginning of the century and continued during the interwar years. Although the first civil service statutes were legislated in the middle of the nineteenth century—they may be dated to 1852 in Spain, 1853 in Piedmont—many were introduced in the years just before and after World War I. Thus, for example, the Italian civil service statutes were passed in 1923, at the beginning of the fascist period, and remained in effect until 1957, well after that period ended. Irish statutes were passed in 1924, Swiss statutes in 1927; in the Netherlands, legislation dates to 1929. France and England were two exceptions. France did not pass civil service legislation until 1941, during the Vichy regime of Marshal Philippe Pétain; it was revised after the war in 1946. In spite of its extensive civil service, England still has no comparable general statute.

A comparison of the situation in Britain and France, the two oldest and largest democracies in Western Europe, remains instructive. In Britain, without a written constitution and with administrative issues long left to the prerogative of the Crown, the government had a vast field of action, and various innovations evolved into permanent features. By the mid-nineteenth century, the ideal training for high-ranking civil servants was based on the study of humanities and excluded all specialized professional knowledge; a Civil Service College was established only somewhat later. Similarly, the ways in which the civil service functioned and their employees were represented by unions were conceived as early as 1916 and put into operation three years later with the advent of the National Whitley Council. In France, on the contrary, these issues brought about a debate on principles among lawyers, politicians, and functionaries. Banned by the law, civil service unions were unofficially tolerated as early as 1924. In 1945 the École Nationale d'Administration (ENA) was established to train high-ranking civil servants; it took over a task previously entrusted to a private institute, the École Libre des Sciences Politiques, better known as Sciences-Po.

In both Britain and France, as in other liberal democracies, in the early twenty-first century legislation guarantees that public servants be treated equally. For appointments and careers in administration, discrimination on the basis of race, religion, gender, or political orientation is banned. Freedom of speech is granted to civil servants who, however, must respect a code of conduct, indeed, of loyalty to the government. The possibility of running for elective office varies from one country to another, and the most permissive in this regard is France, while in England civil servants are forbidden to run for public office.

Although liberalism as a policy model is today found throughout Europe, this was not always the case. During the 1930s, competing ideologies—Nazism, fascism, Stalinism, and the dictatorships in the countries of central Europe—all rejected political pluralism. So it was that Adolf Hitler (1889–1945), for example, put into effect the "Law for the Restoration of the Professional Civil Service" shortly after coming to power in 1933. This legislation permitted a purge based on racial and political criteria and completely deprived civil servants of political freedoms. Although the bureaucracy, which had basically never warmed to the republican regime, at first welcomed the Nazis, it rapidly began to suffer from the polycratic exercise of power in the Hitlerian administration and the rise of the SS (Schutzstaffel). An organization of coercion and terror that eventually coordinated and directed a new level of administration—that of mass murder—the SS never had reason to complain of lack of collaboration from other sectors of the state bureaucracy.

## ADAPTABILITY: DEMOCRACY AND DICTATORSHIP

In a general way, the civil service adapted readily to the numerous transitions from democracy to authoritarian regimes and dictatorships in the twentieth century. Authoritarian regimes were often prompt to denounce bureaucracy and punish civil servants, sometimes with extreme violence—in the Soviet Union, for example, under Joseph Stalin. But in spite of accusations of cowardice, sabotage, and lack of enthusiasm, civil servants remained loyal. Beginning in the 1930s a new class of civil servants appeared. Corruption, nepotism, and outrageous political activism became the rule in Italy and the Soviet Union—two good examples even though ideologically opposed to one another. This was the "managerial" era, according to an influential model conceived by the American political theorist James Burnham; adapted to circumstances in Europe by the Yugoslavian vice president and writer Milovan Djilas and the French social philosopher Cornelius Castoriadis, this model became a severe critique of the bureaucracy's usurpation of power, such as occurred in the Soviet-dominated states of Eastern Europe.

In this context, the liberal principles associated with political and religious neutrality in public service on one hand, and of equal access to civil service on the other hand, were questioned at both ends of the political spectrum. For those in favor of an authoritarian state, political pluralism, which implies refusal to expel civil servants whose loyalty might be questioned under a liberal democratic regime—only underscored the perennial weakness of administrations unable to develop a powerful executive system. For Marxists, on the contrary, equality in the civil service seemed chimeric, merely a formal freedom given lip service. In fact, only slowly did women gain access to jobs in civil service, particularly management positions; democratization, when it came to recruiting civil servants, improved only very slowly. Of course, by comparison with past eras, when to be a servant of the state was such an honor that it did not warrant a salary, the advent of entry exams and remuneration opened doors to the less fortunate. Still, the weight of entrenched administrations remained significant, restricting the ability of politicians in power to control the state apparatus presumably at its disposal. Thus was reborn the specter, which the French revolution had tried to put to rest, of a takeover of national sovereignty by privileged, intermediate corporations.

## AFTER WORLD WAR II

Government expanded after 1945 to an even greater degree than in the wake of World War I. As Tocqueville had observed in 1850, "War . . . must invariably and immeasurably increase the powers of civil government; it must almost automatically concentrate the direction of all men and the control of all things in the hands of the government" (p. 650). The war's end did not lead to a decline in numbers in the public-sector workforce. The terror apparatus and systems to control public opinion were indeed destroyed—at least in Western Europe, even while central and Eastern Europe remained under Soviet influence. But new problems arose for postwar governments. The resources of countries destroyed by years of conflict had to be mobilized to rebuild infrastructure and housing; restart manufacturing; manage debts; and provide care for prisoners, deportees, and returning refugees. In addition, for France and Britain, the situation in their colonial holdings would soon prove to be an issue.

Such circumstances made it impossible to return to the liberal economic policies that had proved inefficient during the crisis years of the 1930s, all the more since state intervention also owed to political considerations. Nationalization of monopolies and state planning thus became the order of the day both in Western Europe, with Charles de Gaulle in France and the Labour Party in Britain ascendant, and in Eastern Europe. Thus, the three decades following the war saw a revival of Keynesian economic policies, largely under state direction; this activity slowed only when it started to generate too much tension as a result of inflation. This kind of stop-and-go growth pattern ended with the very strong showing, in the early 1980s, of the resolutely antigovernment monetary models such as that propounded by Margaret Thatcher.

Even when governed by left-wing parties, most countries in Western Europe proceeded with privatizations, justified on both ideological and budgetary grounds, with a free-market model imposed by the European Union as the foundation of economic policy. France was only a temporary exception to this process. After having greatly increased the number of its civil servants and the boundaries of government in public services in 1982, France began, within a few short years, in the mid-1980s, to gradually disengage from state intervention, a move that proved scarcely popular in a state where government ownership had powerful connotations. At the same time, even in the *sphère régalienne* (the police, army, justice, diplomacy), private-sector management methods emerged, with the diffusion of ambitious but confusing concepts such as "governance" and "new public management." The old ministerial type of administration was viewed as fossilized, centralized, and routine. In its place, although too Manichaean in rhetoric and somewhat artificial in practice, were new attitudes of flexibility and efficiency of agencies in which civil servants were evaluated and remunerated commensurate with their ability to fulfill objectives set by the government or legislature.

Although the education system has not entirely developed along the same lines, the systems of transportation, telecommunications, postal service, and energy are today almost completely open to competition while the civil service settles for a role as regulator, in some areas more comfortably than in others. Since the 1990s, the collapse of the static economies in Eastern Europe encouraged advocates of deregulation. On 1 May 2004 the Europe Union's admission of eight of those nations underscored their ability to adapt to the competitive capitalist system. However, to the disappointment of some, the new management principles have only been partially established in administrative systems (particularly Austro-Hungarian and Russia) that were shaped by the dual tradition in which bureaucracies of the old empires were reinforced by almost a half-century of authoritarian socialism. At the end of the 1990s, two Baltic republics, Latvia and Estonia, had extensively to refurbish their administrative practice, using as inspiration the

North American model as well that of Hungary and, to a lesser degree, of the Czech Republic. It is not simple to erase the past, particularly when such overburdened and backward-looking structures as the administrative systems are its incarnation.

Whether we consider the short military-political twentieth century that lasted from 1914 to 1989, or the long technological twentieth century, which began with the industrial revolution in the 1880s and ended with the twenty-first-century communications revolution, Europe saw the implementation of many state systems. There were authoritarian models, dating to the empires of the nineteenth century, and liberal administrations of the pre-1914 era that some countries hoped to revive in the interwar years. There were also the totalitarian states of Hitler, Stalin, and others. The state as economic partner was put to use during the period from 1950 to 1970, rebuilding the old continent. Even if some convergences seem to appear—notably in terms of decentralization—deep differences remain between the various European administrative systems that originated within heterogeneous historical experiences. However, the three processes traditionally associated with the evolution of the civil service in the twentieth century—professionalization, bureaucratization, and specialization—are still relevant criteria at the beginning of the twenty-first century. To this must be added the never-easy alliance between politics and administration—an ambiguous and ambivalent relationship.

*See also* **Bourgeoisie; Parliamentary Democracy; Totalitarianism.**

BIBLIOGRAPHY

Broszat, Martin. *The Hitler State: The Foundation and Development of the Internal Structure of the Third Reich.* Translated by John W. Hiden. London, 1981.

de Monzie, Anatole, Henri Puget, and Pierre Tissier, eds. *Encyclopédie française.* Vol 10: *L'état moderne: Aménagement, crise, transformations.* Paris, 1935.

Finer, Herman. "Civil Service." In *Encyclopedia of the Social Sciences,* vol. 3, edited by Edwin R. A. Seligman. New York, 1935.

Heyen, Erk Volkmar, ed. *Jahrbuch für europäische Verwaltungsgeschichte,* no. 1/1989 to no. 16/2004. Baden-Baden, Germany, 1989–2003.

Peters, Guy, and Jon Pierre, eds. *Handbook of Public Administration.* Thousand Oaks, Calif., 2003.

Tocqueville, Alexis de. *Democracy in America*. Edited by J. P. Mayer, translated by George Lawrence. Garden City, N.Y., 1969.

Weber, Max. *Economy and Society: An Outline of Interpretive Sociology*. Edited by Guenther Roth and Claus Wittich. Translated by Ephraim Fischoff and others. Berkeley, Calif., 1978.

Marc Olivier Baruch

---

**CIXOUS, HÉLÈNE** (b. 1937), one of the francophone world's most influential contemporary thinkers and writers.

Daughter of Jewish parents, Hélène Cixous (pronounced "seek-sue") was born on 5 June 1937 in Oran, Algeria. She has described her "luck" at being born during "the blazing hotbed between two holocausts" (1991, p. 17) since much of her future thinking, writing, and creative activity were to have their deepest roots in this historical accident. Raised as a Jewish child in Algeria during the German occupation of France and thus denied access to formal schooling, Cixous learned to read and write in a neighbor's informally organized "school" for children like herself. She has always claimed to know from a very early age that she would spend her life somehow with words and books. Cixous's earliest influential reading (texts she often describes as her "Grandmother texts") included the Bible, the epics (*Gilgamesh*, the *Iliad*, the *Odyssey*), William Shakespeare, Franz Kafka, as well as the German poets Rainer Maria Rilke, Friedrich Hölderlin, and Heinrich von Kleist. When Cixous went on to do doctoral work in France, however, it was the English-language writer James Joyce who received her major critical attention. *The Exile of James Joyce* (1969) is the English translation of her 1968 thesis. Later on in her career as a professor of English (and women's studies) within the French university system, Cixous would discover the works of the Brazilian writer Clarice Lispector and bring them (through their publication by Antoinette Fouque in her *Editions des femmes*) to the attention of an international reading public. Thomas Bernhard, Anna Akhmatova, Marina Tsvetaeva, Paul Celan, Ingeborg Bachmann, Osip Mandelstam, Primo Levi—and many of the most read philosophers and critical theorists of the twentieth century (Georges Bataille, Martin Heidegger,

Jacques Derrida) can also be considered decisive readings for Cixous. Indeed, Derrida and Cixous were not only longtime friends (both having been born in Algeria and having come to France at almost the same time) but literary collaborators (*Veils*, a "twinned" text, was published jointly in 2002). It was the outbreak of the Algerian War (1956) that saw Cixous's departure from Algeria and her definitive move to France. She completed her *licence* at Bordeaux (where she read English and American literature) and in 1959 became the youngest ever *agrégée de lettres* in France.

The tumultuous events of May 1968 in France led to major reforms in the French university system, and Cixous (by this time a professor of English literature in Paris) was asked by the government of the day to become *chargée de mission* for the setting up of an experimental Université de Paris VIII at Vincennes (today Saint-Denis). In 1974, she founded the Centre de recherches en études féminines at Paris VIII and became the center's first director. Her creative writing career had already had its beginnings nearly a decade before (in 1967) with the publication of a collection of short stories, *Le Prénom de Dieu* (The first name of God). In 1969 her first novel, *Dedans* (Inside), won the Prix Médicis.

During the 1960s and early 1970s, a time of tremendous growth of feminism worldwide, Cixous was initially associated with various French feminist groups (Psych et Po, for example) yet early on attempted to distance herself from belonging to any organized group, preferring instead to concentrate on her teaching and writing, where she developed the seminal concept of the "libidinal economy" and articulated what that concept meant in terms of women's lives, women's writing, and *"écriture féminine."* Criticized by some feminists as being too "essentialist" with her emphasis on "writing the body," Cixous nonetheless is best known for her formulation of several of feminism's most fundamental tenets: the crucial need for woman to discover her voice and the critical importance of multiplicity in woman's *jouissance*. In two widely read and anthologized pieces, *The Newly Born Woman* and "The Laugh of the Medusa," Cixous locates a linkage between writing, femininity, and transformation, "between the economy of femininity. . . . and a link between this 'libido of the other' and writing" (Cixous and Clément, p. 91–92).

Resistant always to any label such as "theorist" or "feminist," Cixous is self-described primarily as a writer. Since her earliest publications of the mid-1960s she has produced almost one new book per year, an oeuvre that includes scholarly and philosophical works, creative fiction (short stories, novellas, novels, "texts"), political essays and journalistic pieces, lifewriting (a contemporary creative autobiographical form of writing very much in evidence in her work of the early 2000s), and many plays. Indeed, her collaboration with Ariane Mnouchkine of the Théâtre du Soleil dates from the early 1980s and in the early twenty-first century is perhaps her work with the widest audience.

*See also* **Derrida, Jacques; Feminism; France.**

BIBLIOGRAPHY

Cixous, Hélène, and Catherine Clément. *The Newly Born Woman.* Translated by Betsy Wing. Minneapolis, Minn., 1986.

Cixous, Hélène. *"Coming to Writing" and Other Essays.* Translated by Sarah Cornell et al. Cambridge, Mass., 1991.

Conley, Verena Andermatt. *Hélène Cixous: Writing the Feminine.* Rev. ed. Lincoln, Neb., 1991.

———. *Hélène Cixous.* Toronto, 1992.

Penrod, Lynn Kettler. *Hélène Cixous.* New York, 1996.

Sellers, Susan. *The Hélène Cixous Reader.* New York, 1994.

Shiach, Morag. *Hélène Cixous: A Politics of Writing.* London, 1991.

LYNN KETTLER PENROD

---

# CLEMENCEAU, GEORGES (1841– 1929), French politician.

It is conceivable that only two names from the history of France in the twentieth century will be remembered—General Charles de Gaulle, because he was the symbol of the Resistance after France's 1940 defeat during World War II, and Georges Clemenceau, because he was the symbol of France's victory in World War I. Clemenceau was not destined to be a military leader, however.

Born in 1841 in Vendée, which was a "White" region, that is, deeply royalist and Catholic,

Clemenceau belonged to a bourgeois "Blue" (republican and atheist) family. He began studying medicine under the Second Empire, during which he forcefully displayed his republican sentiments, thereby earning himself several weeks in prison. Fresh out of medical school, he left for the United States because he could no longer tolerate living in imperial France—and also because he had recently suffered a serious disappointment in his love life. He lived in the United States from 1865 to 1869 and learned to speak English, a skill that was uncommon in France at that time. Also while in the United States, he married a young American woman with whom he had three children and whom he divorced in 1892.

Clemenceau's political career began in 1870 after the fall of the empire, when he was named mayor of the Parisian district of Montmartre—a title he continued to hold when the revolutionary Commune movement broke out there. Although he was not lacking in sympathy for some of its ideas, such as its commitment to social progress and its refusal to accept France's defeat at the hands of Germany in 1870, he could not sanction its use of violence. In March 1871 he was elected deputy but resigned in protest when Alsace-Lorraine was handed over to Germany.

This was not the end of his political career, however, which was to last for nearly another fifty years—one of the longest France has ever known. It began on the far left: though a republican himself, Clemenceau was a fierce enemy of republican moderates and orchestrated the end of numerous ministers' careers. Throughout his life he was feared for his tongue—he was one of the great orators of his time and never hesitated to cut down even his friends with epigrams—his sword, because he loved to fight duels, and his pen. Indeed he was one of the most incisive journalists of his time and dearly loved to write.

Because Clemenceau was not always careful about the company he kept, attempts were made to compromise him in the Panama affair, in which French politicians were bribed to support the canal project. The scandal lost him his seat as deputy for the Var in the 1893 elections, and he did not return to parliament until 1902, as senator for the same department. His years away from the legislature, however, proved to be among the most important of his life because he was one of the most vocal supporters of Captain Alfred Dreyfus, who had been unjustly convicted of treason. He wrote thousands of articles arguing for the captain's rehabilitation. Although he considered himself to be on the far left, and though he had a more heightened social consciousness than most politicians of his time, Clemenceau was never a follower of socialism. In a famous speech of 1884, as this current was gaining strength, he clearly stated that he was opposed to it. Furthermore, when this "radical" (who did not want to join the Radical Party when it was founded in 1901) became a minister for the first time in 1906 at the age of sixty-five, then premier from 1906 to 1909, he devoted a considerable portion of his energy to suppressing social movements. Dubbed the "strikebreaker," this man of the left was hated by leftist workers at the time and would remain so for the rest of his life. As a self-styled patriot, however, he was much more cautious when the international politics of the day were at issue. In truth, he was not among France's greatest government ministers and was headed for retirement in 1914, when war broke out.

Refusing to take part in the coalition government known as the Sacred Union because he held both its members and the president of the Republic, Raymond Poincaré, in low esteem, and convinced of Germany's total responsibility for the war (he remained unequivocal on this point until his death), Clemenceau called for will and determination to win the war and condemned those he suspected of weakness, pacifism, and defeatism. When the situation became critical in 1917, especially in terms of morale, Poincaré reluctantly called upon Clemenceau to take charge of the government. From 16 November 1917 onward, the "fearsome old man" (he was seventy-six) infused the country with his energy and led it to victory. He became immensely popular as a result but securing the peace proved vastly more difficult. Although more moderate than he was reputed to be (unlike Marshal Ferdinand Foch, he quickly renounced the idea of dismembering Germany) and having little belief in the Wilsonian ideas of perpetual peace and the League of Nations, he advocated measures intended to shield France from future aggression. Also contrary to what was frequently reported, he managed to find areas of compromise with President Woodrow Wilson as the months of negotiations ran on. The resulting treaty, however, was dealt a severe blow when the United States Senate refused to ratify it.

He ran for president of the Republic in 1920, wishing to oversee the enactment of the Treaty of Versailles, but many Catholic politicians refused to vote for an elderly man with a history of anticlericalism, and numerous other enemies he had made during his political career also withheld their support. Thus removed from political life, Clemenceau devoted his time to travel (though never in French colonial territories, because he had always been a staunch enemy of France's colonial enterprises) and to writing. In 1922 he returned to the United States to defend the Treaty of Versailles and the need for its adoption. He enjoyed an enthusiastic reception but failed to convince. His last book, *Grandeurs et misères d'une victoire* (*Grandeur and Misery of Victory*), was published posthumously in 1930. In it, he engages in polemical defenses of his own work, against the recently deceased Marshal Foch. Clemenceau died in Paris on 24 November 1929 at the age of eighty-eight and was buried in his native region of Vendée. His statue on the Champs-Elysées in Paris is one of the city's most prominent memorials.

*See also* **France; Reparations; Versailles, Treaty of.**

BIBLIOGRAPHY

Becker, Jean-Jacques. *Clemenceau, l'intraitable.* Paris, 1998.

———. *Clemenceau en 30 questions.* La Crèche, France, 2001.

Duroselle, Jean-Baptiste. *Clemenceau.* Paris, 1988.

Monnerville, Gaston. *Clemenceau.* Paris, 1968.

Watson, David Robert. *Georges Clemenceau, A Political Biography.* London, 1974.

Wormser, Georges Marcel. *La République de Clemenceau.* Paris, 1961.

JEAN-JACQUES BECKER

# COAL MINING.

In 1912–1913 the European coal industry reached its peak. At that time coal was the unchallenged energy supply not only for heavy industry and transportation but also for public and domestic heating. In Great

Britain coal represented 95 percent of total energy consumption and was also used to produce electricity and gas. Coal mining remained a labor-intensive activity based on a male labor force. The United Kingdom alone counted more than one million coal miners before World War I, the most important group of workers (10 percent of the country's male labor) both in numbers and in trade union power. Coal mining was also a major industry in France, Belgium, Germany (Ruhr, Saarland), Poland (Upper Silesia), the Austro-Hungarian Empire, and Ukraine (Donetsk).

## FROM UNCHALLENGED POSITION TO STRUCTURAL DECLINE

The history of coal mining in twentieth-century Western Europe contrasts with that of Eastern Europe and the United States. After World War I coal output in Western Europe entered a long phase of stagnation and, after a period of recovery from 1945 to 1958, a structural decline. For instance, Great Britain produced 292 million tons in 1913 (a level it would never reach again), 245 million in 1930, 220 in 1950, 128 in 1975, and 50 million in 1996. The picture is the same for all other Western European countries. In Eastern Europe, by contrast, output continued to increase after World War I. Poland, the largest producer except for the Soviet Union, produced 32 million tons in 1920, 38 in 1930, 78 in 1950, 172 in 1975, and still 137 million in 1997.

In Western Europe coal mining suffered from a slowdown of demand because of technological improvements to reduce energy consumption in heavy industry and transportation as well as the growing competition of American coal on the international market. While Great Britain was the major coal exporter in the world in the late nineteenth century, the United States took the lead in the 1920s. Moreover, on the European continent itself British coal had to struggle with the growing export of cheap, high-quality coal from Poland. The British coal position also was challenged by France and Germany. The collieries of Nord-Pas-de-Calais that suffered heavy damage in the war were modernized in a major program of reconstruction. French coal output increased from 41 million tons in 1913 to 55 in 1930 and reached its peak in 1958 with 60 million tons. The recovery of German coal mining after World War I was even

more impressive thanks to the efforts of cartels such as the Rhenish-Westphalian. German coal mining was mechanized: in the Ruhr 66 percent of coal output was cut by machines in 1926 as against 22 percent in Britain. The German output increased from 118 million tons in 1924 (after the occupation of the Ruhr) to 188 million tons in 1939. Finally, during the interwar period new coalfields were opened, such as the Campine in Belgium, and Dutch coal mining expanded rapidly (Dutch production was only 2 million tons in 1913 but reached 14 million in 1937). Meanwhile American and Polish coal mining were concentrated in large concessions big enough to invest in mechanization, while most of the collieries in Western Europe were still too small, fragmented in innumerable concessions (areas of land granted by governments to mining companies) dating from the mid-nineteenth century.

The stagnation of demand in the 1920s made clear the fact that West European coal mining suffered from an excess of capacity, insufficient productivity, and too much expensive coal. With the economic crisis of the 1930s its precarious position grew still worse except in the German Reich. British output fell from 262 million tons in 1929 to 210 in 1933.

Miners, however, remained a strong group able to paralyze a country by strike actions. The labor-intensive character of coal-mining operations encouraged miners' trade unions to fight for social provisions, higher wages (such as the British minimum wage legislation of 1912), better working conditions, and reduction of working hours per day (the British Coal Mines Regulation Act of 1908, known as the "Eight Hours Act"). With a very high level of trade union participation, unions were well placed to apply pressure to industrial affairs. Owners also were organized, in associations such as the Mining Association of Great Britain. The coal industry was thus characterized by repeated miners' strikes. In Great Britain the movement culminated with the strike and lockout of 1926. Though the strike ended in defeat for the miners, the sector did not recover. Many other actions were taken by coal miners' trade unions in the Weimar Republic, Belgium, and France. At the same time, coal increasingly became the source of political and even military intervention: the Ruhr coalfields were occupied by French and Belgian troops in 1923 to force Germany to pay war reparations.

**A miner works with a pony and cart to haul coal, Durham, England, 1934.** ©HULTON-DEUTSCH COLLECTION/CORBIS

World War II and its aftermath, reconstruction, created such a huge demand for coal that it provoked, as Régine Perron has written, the "myth of scarcity," in which Jean Monnet (one of the founding fathers of the European Coal and Steel Community, or ECSC) and others warned that Western Europe would suffer deeply from a shortage of coal in the following decades. Therefore the goal was to increase output and improve productivity as quickly as possible. A "battle for coal" ensued in 1945–1946, especially in Belgium and France. In the first years of the ECSC the High Authority continued to encourage production, but the energy market was dramatically changing due to the competition of cheap, abundant coal from the United States and Poland and, after 1958, the challenge of oil and natural gas, which remained low-cost until 1974. (Civil nuclear energy remained a marginal supplier until the

1970s). Drastic changes in the energy market were not peculiar to Europe; between 1950 and 1970 the world's energy consumption is estimated to have tripled. Even with increased energy consumption, however, the production of coal declined in Europe because coal was too expensive and oil increasingly competitive.

In 1958–1959 the demand for coal fell, paving the way for the structural decline of coal mining in Western Europe. In the short term (1958–1960), many companies had to struggle with increasing stocks and excessive capacities. In the long run, restructuring the entire sector became a priority: closing unprofitable collieries, concentrating production on larger concessions (as in Campine in Belgium), accelerating mechanization, improving the quality of the product, and finally, reducing the number of coal miners. This meant the

**Striking coal miners picket near Buckingham Palace, London, 1959.** ©Hulton-Deutsch Collection/Corbis

disappearance of an enormous occupational class, with its know-how, its strike tradition, its own culture. For instance, the 1.1 million coal miners Great Britain counted in 1913 fell to 700,000 in 1945, 300,000 in 1975, and fewer than 11,000 in 2000.

From the early 1960s onward all the countries of Western Europe adopted national planning, supported by the High Authority of the ECSC, to reduce and even to stop coal mining. Indeed, since World War II coal mining had been under state control as a strategic sector. In Great Britain the nationalization of the sector (already envisaged by the Coal Mines Act of 1930) became effective in 1947 with the creation of the National Coal Board. France nationalized the coal industry by the law of 17 May 1946 and the creation of Charbonnages de

France. In the Netherlands coal mining was under state control from the beginning, while in Belgium private companies were placed under strict state control after 1959.

In the 1980s, after some attempt to maintain production during the oil crisis, the exhaustion of most of the coalfields, more severe safety regulations, and new environmental protections made European coal too expensive in comparison with coal imported from China or South Africa. In the early 1970s the Netherlands was the first to decide to close down its coal-mining operations; the last colliery was closed in 1992 in Belgium, after social conflicts of great violence, then in 1994 in Portugal and 2005 in France. While Germany has not yet made the decision to close its last pits as of 2006, Great Britain is engaged in a drastic reorganization of its coal-mining industry. Spain, Poland, Bulgaria, and Romania also have started to reduce the number of collieries.

## MODERNIZATION AND MECHANIZATION
The fact that coal mining was a sector in decline in Western Europe does not imply obsolete technology. On the contrary, since the end of World War II the idea was to increase productivity by closing mines that were not suitable for mechanization and to modernize the most profitable ones.

The traditional system of work organization to cut coal at the coal face was the room-and-pillar system that was used in coalfields presenting disturbed geological configuration. However, the longwall method, imported from the United States, was used in England (Yorkshire, Lancashire) and later in countries such as Poland, where the coal seam permitted it. The advantage was that the longwall method permitted the mechanization of coal cutting. American mechanical coal cutters with loaders were introduced into the Midlands in 1936.

However, this method was inappropriate for most of the coal mines on the Continent (except in Poland) due to geological constraints. Consequently coal cutting had to be done by hand with pneumatic picks. In the Ruhr however, mechanical coal cutters were developed during World War II. The German face conveyor or armored flexible conveyor became one of the key inventions of modern mining and by the 1960s it had been installed on all major longwall faces in Britain.

Safety conditions were greatly improved by the introduction of the powered roof support in the mid-1960s and by new techniques in tunneling and shaft sinking. However, one of the most important improvements of the twentieth century was electrification. After the 1902 international exhibition in Düsseldorf, electricity not only revolutionized coal mining itself (with electric headlamps for miners and fixed lighting in the galleries) but ushered in the age of the coal-fired power station.

Modernization and the closure of obsolete coal mines dramatically increased productivity (see table 1). Increased productivity also resulted from improvement in safety conditions, especially after the tragedy of Courrières (Nord-Pas-de-Calais) in 1906, which cost the lives of eleven hundred miners.

**TABLE 1**

**Output in the coal industry of the principal European producer countries, 1960–1975 (in kilos of coal per miner and day)**

|      | Germany | United Kingdom | France | Belgium |
|------|---------|----------------|--------|---------|
| 1960 | 2,126   | 1,994          | 1,798  | 1,577   |
| 1965 | 2,815   | 2,621          | 2,039  | 1,874   |
| 1970 | 3,941   | 3,469          | 2,643  | 2,630   |
| 1975 | 4,062   | 3,493          | 2,761  | 2,426   |

SOURCE: Rolande Trempé, "La politique de la main-d'œuvre de la Libération à nos jours en France." *Revue Belge d'Histoire Contemporaine* 19, nos. 1–2 (1988): 76.

## COAL MINING AND MIGRANT WORKERS
Coal mining companies had always been confronted with the difficulties of recruiting and keeping workers. This problem became severe after World War I, when miners and other young workers deserted the collieries for healthier and better-paid occupations. Consequently the companies had to recruit foreign workers, usually on a temporary basis (guest workers). In France the first Italians were accommodated in the basin of Briey in 1905. After the war they were followed by Poles and Czechs. In the small coalfield of Albi, Czechs and Poles account for 40 percent of the manpower of the miners in 1925. They flowed especially into Nord-Pas-de-Calais. Recruitment of foreign workers increased dramatically after World War II. The coalfields of Europe became a multiethnic society formed by people who shared the same occupational know-how and who forged a local culture that had no equivalent in other industries or other places. However, in Europe, coal miners are now part of history, not of the future.

*See also* **General Strike (Britain); Industrial Capitalism; Strikes; Trade Unions.**

BIBLIOGRAPHY

Ashworth, William. *The History of the British Coal Industry.* Vol. 5: *1946–1982: The Nationalized Industry.* Oxford, U.K., 1986.

Leboutte, René. *Vie et mort des bassins industriels en Europe, 1750–2000.* Paris, 1997.

Michel, Joël. *La mine: Une histoire européenne.* In *La Documentation française,* bimestriel no. 8010. Paris, 1999.

Perron, Régine. *Le marché du charbon, un enjeu entre l'Europe et les Etats-Unis de 1945 à 1958.* Paris, 1996.

Supple, Barry. *The History of the British Coal Industry.* Vol. 4: *1913–1946: The Political Economy of Decline.* Oxford, U.K., 1987.

RENÉ LEBOUTTE

---

**COBRA.** CoBrA was born in Paris during the 1948 International Conference of the Center for the Documentation of Avant-Garde Art, organized by the group Surréalisme Révolutionaire (SR). At the conference the artists Joseph Noiret and Christian Dotremont (Belgium); Asger Jorn (Denmark); and Karel Appel, Constant Anton Nieuwenhuys ("Constant"), and Corneille Guillaume van Beverloo ("Corneille") from Holland joined forces to reproach Surréalisme Révolutionaire's dogmatic and theoretical tendencies. The dissidents got together later at the Café Notre-Dame, where they composed the manifesto *La cause était entendue* (The cause was understood). Several days later, Dotrement proposed a name for the group, CoBrA, composed of the initial letters of Copenhagen, Brussels, and Amsterdam. In their eyes, the only way to pursue an international collaboration was in the nature of an experiment. CoBrA championed the power of violence and spontaneity by mixing primitivism and oceanian arts with certain forms of automatic production inherited from surrealism.

The group brought together some twenty or more artists and writers, including Henry Heerup, Egill Jacobsen, and Carl-Henning Pedersen from Denmark, and later the Belgian painter Pierre Alechinsky. The activities of its founding artists prior to the group's formation furnished springboards for the young movement, including the theoretical and technical explorations of the Surréalisme Révolutionaire in Belgium, the abstract-surrealist group Høst in Denmark, and the Dutch Experimental Group. They shared a common Marxist consciousness that drew them all in one way or another toward communism. Wishing to create collective works that allied writers and painters from every country, they began a series of "Meetings in Bregnerød" on 18 August 1949, in a student lodging in north Copenhagen. The meetings produced a wall mural in the living room, while Dotrement and Edouard Jaguer from France began writing *Les artistes libres* (Free artists), a series of journals whose covers were created by the artists who wrote them.

Tensions escalated when the group's first exhibition was held in Amsterdam in November 1949, leading to the withdrawal of the poets in the Dutch Experimental Group, and leaving only Appel, Constant, and Corneille as the remaining Dutch members. Dotrement represented another subject of discord because he exercised too much influence over the content of the magazine *CoBrA*, for which he was the editor in chief. Furthermore, at the Amsterdam Conference adjoining the exposition he successfully proposed transforming the group into an Experimental Artists Internationale (EAI), which was meant to welcome artists from all countries under the condition that they avoid the three great standards of formalism: naturalism, the old surrealism, and abstract art. Jorn retorted that it was necessary to maintain different national identities and reproached Dotrement for failing to clearly break with the Belgian Communist Party, which was following the party line set in Moscow. Dotrement completed his break with the party in May 1950 by publishing the pamphlet " 'Le réalisme-socialiste' contre la révolution" ("Socialist-Realism" against revolution).

For their part Appel, Corneille, Constant, and Jorn set up shop in Paris in September 1950 and mounted expositions at the Collette Allendy Gallery, the Maeght Gallery, and the Salon des Surindépendants. They deviated from the CoBrA principles in order to almost imperceptibly revive abstract formalism, a current that Dotrement and Alechinsky remained aloof to, moving instead to Copenhagen at the close of 1950 and then to Malmö. The following year Jorn left the group, but illness brought him together with Dotrement again for a brief period at the Silkeborg Sanitarium, where out of the ashes of CoBrA they produced a series of "word-paintings" dedicated to the life of the invalid. Just as Alechinsky was organizing a CoBrA exposition in Liège on 8 November 1951, three years after the signing of the manifesto "The Cause Was Understood," Dotrement sent him a letter announcing the dissolution of the group.

The group's failure was due to a number of reasons. In reality, the Danes, Dutch, and Belgians created it at a moment when their paths were crossing but not destined to converge. The Dutch were defining themselves by demarcating their national culture, and Jorn sought recognition for Scandinavian thought at the same level as Latin thought, whereas the Belgians considered the group's literary surrealism a subject of exoticism, though all the while adhering to it. The bridge between poets and plastic artists was never fully complete—on the whole the painters remained painters, and the writers remained writers. Furthermore, although in its origins CoBrA sought to be an anti-Parisian movement, it could not thumb its nose at the French capital for long. Far from leading to the group's downfall however, this illustrates the welcome and hospitality extended to the group's principles by artists living in Paris.

Still a certain spirit of the group persisted, and almost ten years after its dissolution Jorn and Constant rejoined Guy Debord as the core of Situationist Internationale, a synthesis of art and literature, with political goals. Jorn and Alechinsky joined forces again at the dawn of the 1960s, leading Alechinsky to follow new directions in the pictorial domain. As for Dotrement, he continued to defend the spirit of CoBrA through experimental collective works and his calligraphic poems, or *Logogrammes*. CoBrA remains a wonderful encounter between European artists, assembled at the core of a diverse group and nurtured to maturity by a strong pictorial program that attempted to forge its own path outside the dictates of the Paris School.

*See also* **Avant-Garde; Painting, Avant-Garde; Surrealism.**

BIBLIOGRAPHY

Andersen, Troels, et al. *COBRA: Copenhagen, Bruxelles, Amsterdam: Art expérimental, 1948–1951.* Munich and Lausanne, France, 1997. Exposition catalog.

Jaguer, Édouard. *Cobra au coeur du XXe siècle.* Paris, 1997.

Lambert, Jean-Clarence. *Le règne imaginal: Les artistes Cobra.* Paris, 1991.

Miller, Richard. *Cobra.* Paris, 1994.

VIRGINIE DEVILLEZ

# COCTEAU, JEAN (1889–1963), French poet, playwright, novelist, choreographer, draftsman, painter, and film director.

Jean Cocteau, the son of a well-to-do bourgeois family that patronized the arts, began at a very young age to associate with the poets and writers in vogue at the time, including Catulle Mendès, Anna de Noailles, Charles-Pierre Péguy, Edmond Rostand, Laurent Tailhade, and Marcel Proust. He also developed a taste for writing when he was very young. At twenty he published his first collection of poems, *La Lampe d'Aladin* (Aladdin's lamp), followed by *Le Prince frivole* (1910; The frivolous prince) and *La danse de Sophocle* (1912; Sophocles' dance).

A great lover of ballet, music, and the theater, he attended the performances of the Russian Ballet in Paris, where he met Sergei Diaghilev, director of the Ballets Russes, for whom he composed *Le dieu bleu* (1912; The blue god) with Reynaldo Hahn. In his reflections on aesthetics, *Le Potomak* (1919), he explained how the anticonformist performance of Igor Stravinsky's *Sacre du printemps* (1913; *Rite of Spring*) by the Ballets Russes shattered his comfortable life as a dandy and convinced him that the poet must find utterly unconventional ways to express himself. He therefore decided to become an avant-garde artist, fearless about scandalizing the public and about pushing the boundaries of art. He was convinced that all the performing arts, including theater, the circus, film, ballet, and opera were excellent vehicles for poetry. He befriended penniless artists in Montmartre and Montparnasse, artists whose audaciousness exasperated the bourgeoisie, and became a zealous propagandist for the new art invented by Pablo Picasso, Max Jacob, Guillaume Apollinaire, Diaghilev, Stravinsky, Erik Satie, Blaise Cendrars, Moïse Kisling, and Amedeo Modigliani. He created a profusion of poems, plays, screenplays, and critical manifestos.

Cocteau collaborated with Picasso and Satie on the ballet *Parade* (1917), also for the Ballets Russes, which Apollinaire characterized as "surrealist." In 1920 he created *Le boeuf sur le toit* (The ox on the roof) and in 1921 composed *Les mariés de la Tour Eiffel* (The newlyweds of the Eiffel Tower). He also wrote the ballets *Les biches* (1924; The hinds) with Darius Milhaud and Francis Poulenc, and *Les fâcheux* (1924; The nuisances), in collaboration with Georges

**COCTEAU'S FILMOGRAPHY**

*Cocteau fait du cinéma* (1925)
*Le sang d'un poète* (1930)
*La belle et la bête* (1945)
*L'aigle à deux têtes* (1947)
*Les parents terribles* (1948)
*Orphée* (1949)
*Coriolan* (1950)
*La Villa Santo-Sospir* (1952)
*Le testament d'Orphée* (1959)

Auric and Louis Laloy. Both ballets were produced by Diaghilev. In *Le coq et l'arlequin* (1918; The cock and the harlequin), he defended Satie's "uncluttered art" (*art dépouillé*), in opposition to the work of Claude Debussy and Richard Wagner. Cocteau was fascinated by the avant-garde in all its forms: he celebrated airplanes and machines in his poetry and even did aerial acrobatics with Roland Garros—an experience he would later translate into poetic telegrams (with irregular spaces between words) in his *Le Cap de Bonne Espérance* (1918; The Cape of Good Hope). He contributed to the magazine *Dada* as well. Cocteau served as an ambulance driver for the Red Cross on the Belgian front in 1916 and later turned his war experiences into a collection of poems entitled *Discours du grand sommeil* (1922; Discourse on the great sleep), as well as a novel, *Thomas l'Imposteur* (1923; Thomas the imposter). The surrealists' hostility toward him led him to give up avant-garde theater and from then on, heavily influenced by Raymond Radiguet, he produced more traditional works, defending that new traditionalism in a manifesto, *Le secret professionnel* (1922; Professional secrets). His output during the interwar years and beyond is stunning in its diversity: he produced novels, works of criticism, memoirs, plays, drawings, paintings, and films. Depressed and plagued by emotional problems, he turned to opium, the ravaging effects of which he depicted in *Opium* (1930) after undergoing detoxification in 1925. During this time he corresponded with Jacques Maritain, who tried to convert him to Catholicism, and broke definitively with the surrealists.

Even more than personal interpretations of classical myths, the guiding thread of Cocteau's creative work was his memories of childhood and adolescence. Thus the starting point for his novel *Les enfants terribles* (1929; *The Holy Terrors*) was the memory of a snowball fight at the Lycée Condorcet, during which the hero, Paul, is wounded by the demonic student Dargelos. The scene brings to mind the relationship between a teenage brother and sister that ends with both of them committing suicide. His poem *L'ange Heurtebise* (1926; The angel Heurtebise) as well as the play (1927) and film version of *Orphée* (1949; Orpheus) depict an angel ensnaring the poet. The sphinx in *La machine infernale* (1934; The infernal machine) plays a similar role. Cocteau portrayed the tragic fate of the human being who comes from nothing and, after the short and absurd interlude of life, sinks back into nothingness. All his works play with open and closed space, this world and the one beyond, illusion and reality, order and chaos. Only poetry offers immortality, and the poet creates works of art that explain the world after death.

In 1930 Cocteau made his first film, *Le sang d'un poète* (The blood of a poet), which was autobiographical and piqued the curiosity of psychiatrists. This was followed by *L'éternel retour* (1943; Eternal return) and *La belle et la bête* (1945; *Beauty and the Beast*), a visual enchantment for spectators, who thronged to the theaters to applaud this lyrical and technical triumph, then by *L'aigle à deux têtes* (1947; Two-headed eagle), *Orphée* (1949), and finally *Le testament d'Orphée* (1959; The testament of Orpheus), which was his last film and a true will and testament, a virtual catalog of all his poetry, dreams, anxieties, fantasies, and hallucinations. He conceived all his films as a vehicle for his friend the actor Jean Marais.

Cocteau pursued his poetic work in *Le chiffre sept* (1952; The Number Seven) *Clair-obscur* (1954; Chiaroscuro), and *Le Requiem* (1962; Requiem), as well as in two volumes of his theatrical writings, published in 1948 (*Théâtre I* and *Théâtre II*). He designed works for Murano glassblowers and for stained-glass windows (including the Church of Saint-Maximin in Mctz) and painted thc frescocs of Saint Peter's Chapel in Villefranche-sur-Mer, of Saint Blaise des Simples in Milly-la-Forêt, of Notre Dame de France in London, of The Mare Tower of the Notre Dame Chapel in Jerusalem, as well as wall murals in the Villa Santo Sospir in Saint-

**Jean Cocteau prepares a mask for his theater productions, 1930.** ©Hulton-Deutsch Collection/Corbis

Jean-Cap-Ferrat, the city hall in Menton, and the restaurant-bar of the Hôtel Mont-Blanc in Megève.

This scandalous provocateur did not fail to receive numerous official honors. In 1949 he was made Chevalier of the Legion of Honor. In 1955 he succeeded Colette at the Belgian Royal Academy for French Language and Literature and was accepted into the Académie Française. In 1956 he was made *doctor honoris causa* at Oxford University and in 1957 he became an honorary member of the National Institute of Arts and Letters. In 1960 he was elected *prince des poètes*, France's poet laureate. In 1961 he was named Commandeur of the Legion of Honor.

Long reputed to be frivolous and superficial, Cocteau is, in his words, being "reconsidered" (*envisagé*) by academics, after having first been "deconsidered" (*dévisagé*) by them.

*See also* **Apollinaire, Guillaume; Cinema; Picasso, Pablo; Surrealism.**

BIBLIOGRAPHY

Bernard, André, and Claude Gauteur, eds. *The Art of Cinema / Jean Cocteau*. Translated by Robin Buss. London, 1992. Translation of *Du cinématographe*.

Caizergues, Pierre, ed. *Jean Cocteau aujourd'hui*. Paris, 1992.

Fraigneau, André. *Cocteau on the Film: A Conversation Recorded by André Fraigneau*. Translated by Vera Traill. New York, 1954. Translation of *Jean Cocteau. Entretien autour du cinématographe* (1951).

Rolot, Christian, ed. *Le cinéma de Jean Cocteau-Hommage à Jean Marais*. Montpellier, 1994.

Touzot, Jean. *Jean Cocteau*. Lyon, 1989.

———. *Jean Cocteau: Le poète et ses doubles*. Paris, 2000.

MARYSE FAUVEL

## COHN-BENDIT, DANIEL (b. 1945), French student leader of the revolution of May 1968.

Daniel Cohn-Bendit was born just four days before the end of World War II in Montauban, France on 4 April 1945, to German Jewish parents who had fled Nazi Germany during the war. His father had been a successful lawyer prior to the Nazi seizure of power and had made a name for himself defending leftist individuals. Because of his father's association with the German Left and Jewish heritage, the family was forced to flee to France during the war. Cohn-Bendit's parents returned to Germany after 1945, but the family never felt completely settled in either country and young Daniel finished his primary and secondary schooling in West Germany. His own sense of both German and French citizenship would later explain his commitment to internationalism and the European Community. After passing his high school exams in 1965, he chose to attend university in France with the assistance of a German repatriation scholarship.

Having grown up in a bilingual environment, Cohn-Bendit had no trouble studying at the new branch of the University of Paris located in Nanterre. While attending Nanterre, Cohn-Bendit was influenced by one of his teachers, Alain Touraine (b. 1925), a young sociologist interested in the "sociology of action" who specialized in labor movements in Latin America. Cohn-Bendit agreed with his teacher and felt that sociologists had a duty to put their thoughts into action. To the chagrin of his professors, he became associated with a small group of students known as the *enragés,* or "the angry ones," who frequently disrupted classes and demanded university reforms. In January 1968, in a famous confrontation with François Missoffe, France's Minister for Youth and Sports, Cohn-Bendit compared the minister to the leader of the Hitler Youth. This relatively minor incident turned Cohn-Bendit into "Dany the Red" due to his red hair, cheeky comments, and assumed leftist leanings at Nanterre.

In February of 1968, Cohn-Bendit went to West Berlin to attend a Vietnam Congress with other student leaders of the growing European antiwar movement. The congress celebrated the recent Tet Offensive and one of the key spokesmen was the Marxist Rudi Dutschke, who headed West Germany's Socialist German Student Union (SDS). Cohn-Bendit greatly admired Dutschke and may have also earned the nickname "Dany the Red" from his association with "Red Rudi" Dutschke.

On 22 March 1968, Cohn-Bendit and a dozen others occupied the faculty lounge in the administration building at Nanterre and demanded university reforms and the right to use classrooms to hold discussions about the Vietnam War. The resulting disciplinary hearings and repressive measures taken by the school president only increased the supporters of Cohn-Bendit's group that came to be known as the 22 March Movement. The fact that Cohn-Bendit and his peers chose to name their group after the date of their initial occupation is indicative of their disregard for established student associations or more doctrinaire Marxist student organizations. Historian David Caute has suggested that Cohn-Bendit and the 22 March Movement's politics were closest to the French Situationists, who believed that revolutions cannot be controlled and that the role of the revolutionary is therefore simply to create situations that will lead to another chain of events ultimately altering political and social life. Cohn-Bendit and the 22 March Movement's actions eventually forced the closing of the university at Nanterre.

By the beginning of May 1968, Cohn-Bendit had become a public figure, using his own disciplinary hearings to rally students all over Paris to the movement. On 2 May, the police invasion of the Sorbonne roused a universal outcry among young people, workers, and the residents of the Latin Quarter; Dany the Red was seen with a megaphone all over the city at rallies and sit-ins. Using his broad smile and good sense of humor, Cohn-Bendit had a perfect sense of the moment and drew legions of support precisely because he did not come across as an angry dogmatic revolutionary.

The May events of 1968 proved to be the most spectacular in Western Europe, and Cohn-Bendit's playful mocking of authority made him the perfect spokesman to antagonize President Charles de Gaulle (1890–1970) French workers would later stage a general strike and by 22 May had shut down France. De Gaulle later used Cohn-Bendit's West German citizenship as a reason to deport him and he was expelled from the country at the end of May. Cohn-Bendit remained active in the New Left in Frankfurt, and in the 1980s joined the Green Party. He would later be elected to the Frankfurt City Council and was a member of the European Parliament in the early twenty-first century.

*See also* **May 1968; 1968; Student Movements.**

BIBLIOGRAPHY

Caute, David. *The Year of the Barricades: A Journey Through 1968.* New York, 1988.

Cohn-Bendit, Daniel. Personal Web page. Available from http://www.cohn-bendit.de.

Fraser, Ronald. *1968: A Student Generation in Revolt.* London, 1988.

Kurlansky, Mark. *1968: The Year that Rocked the World.* New York, 2004.

STUART J. HILWIG

---

**COLD WAR.** The Cold War is the name for the overarching rivalry between the United States and the Soviet Union that came to define the epoch from the end of World War II in 1945 until the collapse of the Soviet Union in 1991. At its center—part cause, part effect—was the postwar division of Europe and especially of Germany, whose unification in 1989–1990 was a decisive moment in the endgame of the Cold War. But the Cold War extended far beyond Europe to become a global competition between the superpowers, as well as communist China, involving a nuclear arms race that teetered, at times, on the brink of devastating war.

**TERMINOLOGY**

The term *Cold War* was popularized by the American columnist Walter Lippmann in his book of that title published in 1947. But in October 1945 the British author George Orwell, pondering the implications of the new atomic bomb, had already predicted an epoch in which a great power could be at once "*unconquerable* and in a permanent state of 'cold war' with its neighbours" (pp. 9–10). The term, in fact, has a long lineage, having been used to characterize Hitler's war of nerves against France in the 1930s and the international arms race before World War I. It was even used by the medieval Castilian writer Don Juan Manuel, who wrote: "War that is very strong and very hot ends either with death or peace, whereas cold war neither brings peace nor gives honour to one who makes it" (quoted in Halliday, p. 5).

The other term that entered common usage in the 1940s was *superpowers,* coined in 1944 by the American political scientist William T. R. Fox to denote countries with "great power plus great mobility of power" (p. 21). At this time Fox identified three such superpowers—the United States, the Soviet Union, and Britain. Although Britain was an important factor in the early Cold War, its rapid imperial and economic decline soon exposed the fact that there were only two real superpowers in the postwar world. Their competition gave the Cold War its essential bipolar dynamic.

**HISTORIOGRAPHY**

For a generation the field of Cold War historiography was dominated by American authors. Early writings were predominantly sympathetic to the policy of the U.S. government, blaming the Cold War largely on Soviet territorial expansionism and portraying American policy as reactive. Although differing on the relative importance of ideology as against power politics in Soviet thinking, this so-called orthodox school held sway in the 1950s and early 1960s. Its exemplars included the scholar and policymaker Arthur M. Schlesinger Jr. During the 1960s, however, a "revisionist" critique gained momentum, fed by contemporary political debate about the Vietnam War and by the firstfruits of American archives. Historians such as William Appleman Williams argued that an American policy of economic expansion bore a large measure of responsibility for the Cold War. Anxious to promote an "open door" for its trade, finance, and ideas, the United States, they argued, had been trying to redesign the world in its own image, to create an informal American empire.

In the 1980s historians such as John L. Gaddis sketched out a "postrevisionist" view. Although taking elements from both previous approaches, including recognition of the assertive nature of American policy, this interpretation tended to be a more nuanced, archivally based restatement of traditionalism. Another leading postrevisionist, the Norwegian scholar Geir Lundestad, developed the argument that if Cold War Western Europe was part of an American empire, this was "empire by invitation"—sought, even welcomed, by the Europeans.

Lundestad also exemplified another trend in Cold War historiography during the 1980s—the entry of non-American, Western scholars into the debate as European archives were opened. Following Lundestad's lead, they showed that the British, French, and even West Germans were not mere objects of U.S. and Soviet foreign policies but had their own agenda and sometimes set the pace and tone of Cold War policy. This was an "international" approach to the Cold War.

The 1990s saw a "postcommunist" turn in the historiography, with the collapse of the Soviet bloc and the selective opening of its archives. The former East German party files became accessible for the whole period from 1945 to 1991; Poland, Hungary, and the Czech Republic made available important new material on key Cold War crises. Although this new documentation is patchy, particularly for Russia, it has shed important light on the "other side" of the Cold War, and scholars are still absorbing the implications.

## ORIGINS

Not merely the interpretation of the Cold War but its periodization depends a good deal on one's overall approach. Revisionists, for instance, were often inclined to date it back to 1917, the year of the Russian Revolution and the United States' entry into the European war. As such, the Cold War was a struggle of revolution versus counterrevolution. On the other hand, the two powers had little to do with each other after the end of the Russian civil war and the United States' retreat from European commitments.

What really brought them into contact was their alliance of wartime necessity against Hitler and especially the presence from 1945 of U.S. and Soviet troops in the heart of defeated Germany. With the two powers now face to face and forced to work together on postwar peacemaking, their fundamental ideological differences really began to matter. Each still wanted cooperation, but on its own terms, and events in 1945 showed just how far the other side would go.

The biggest problem was what to do about Germany itself, occupied by America, Britain,

France, and the Soviet Union as prelude, it was assumed, to creating an independent, denazified German state. However, the Allies could not agree on the terms for a peace treaty. Having lost perhaps twenty-eight million in the war, the Soviets were naturally determined to keep Germany down. The Americans, remote from Europe and suffering only three hundred thousand dead, were more interested in rebuilding the German economy as a motor for European recovery.

The defeat of Hitler's Reich also left the Red Army in control of large areas of Eastern Europe. Joseph Stalin (1879–1953) understood the Yalta Conference of February 1945 to signify that he was being given a free hand in "his" part of Europe, just as he left the British and Americans predominant in the West. But they expected that he would conform to the "open door," democratic values for which they proclaimed the war had been fought. The imposition of Communist-dominated governments in Poland, Bulgaria, and Romania in 1945 was therefore a deep shock. Stalin, in turn, regarded Western protests as a breach of promise and as sinister evidence that his erstwhile allies posed a threat to basic Soviet interests.

The year 1945 was not just the end of the Second World War; it also marked the beginning of the nuclear age. In August 1945 the United States dropped two atomic bombs on Japan to end the Asian war. Stalin's response was to galvanize the Soviets' own atomic project, giving it top priority for manpower and resources. Revisionist historians sometimes argued that if Washington had been more willing to share atomic secrets with Moscow, this might have reduced Cold War friction. But even a leader less paranoid than Stalin would not have rested easy as long as atomic weapons remained an American monopoly. Nuclear rivalry exacerbated the underlying mistrust.

During 1945, the new American president, Harry S. Truman, agreed to the governments of Poland, Bulgaria, and Romania on essentially Stalin's terms, with the addition of a few token noncommunists. But his suspicion of Soviet conduct deepened during 1946, not only in Europe but also in places such as Iran, Turkey, and Korea. Winston Churchill, the wartime British prime minister, helped conceptualize the new worldview with his speech at Fulton, Missouri, on 5 March 1946 warning of an

"Iron Curtain" coming down across Europe. On both sides, memories of the previous war were pervasive. The Americans and British saw events as a possible replay of the 1930s, with aggression escalating into another world war if the response was appeasement; the Soviets feared another surprise attack from the West, akin to 1941, and Stalin played on this to justify renewed repression at home.

### THE PARTITION OF EUROPE, 1947–1949

The crucial year was 1947. The British, in economic crisis, informed Washington that they could no longer provide financial aid to Turkey and Greece, where the communists were gaining ground in a brutal civil war. Calling on Congress to pick up the tab, Truman spoke of a world divided between "democracy" and "totalitarianism," and committed the United States to supporting "free peoples" everywhere. The Truman Doctrine of 12 March 1947 ideologized the Cold War.

The second big American initiative that year was the Marshall Plan. With Western European recovery faltering because of a grave shortage of dollars, the U.S. secretary of state George C. Marshall spoke out at Harvard University on 5 June. Marshall promised that if the Europeans drew up a joint recovery program, the United States would provide financial assistance. Marshall's offer did not in principle exclude the Soviets, who turned up at the ensuing conference at Paris in July with a hundred-strong delegation. But when Stalin discovered that the aid would not be unconditional, as in the war, and that the Americans saw it as a lever for opening up nationalist economies, he recalled his delegation and warned satellite countries such as Poland and Czechoslovakia that participation would be regarded as a hostile act against the Soviet Union. The Marshall Plan went ahead for Western Europe alone, while much of Eastern Europe became an exploited Soviet colony. In many ways July 1947 was the moment when the Iron Curtain really came down.

The divide became political as well. May 1947 saw new coalition governments formed in France, Italy, and Belgium, without the communists. Over the next year, union movements across Western Europe split into communist and noncommunist groupings. Meanwhile, Eastern European states were Stalinized, with only Moscow loyalists left in power, and command economies were rapidly imposed.

With the great powers deadlocked over its future, Germany remained essentially a barter economy in which the main medium of exchange was cigarettes. The country was potentially the engine of European economic recovery, and the British and Americans decided they must start to revive their zones of Germany without Soviet agreement. After the communist takeover of Czechoslovakia in February 1948, the French—hitherto more fearful of the Germans than of the Russians—also fell into line. Faced with a new currency in western Germany, Stalin tried to intimidate the West by imposing a blockade of Berlin in June 1948. To his surprise, the Americans and British responded with an airlift that kept the city supplied through the winter until he conceded defeat in May 1949.

By this time the Western allies had agreed on the basis of a new western German state. The Federal Republic of Germany came into existence in May 1949, even though the Allied occupation continued. The Berlin crisis also accelerated talks about transatlantic cooperation. The North Atlantic Treaty, signed in April 1949, was an unprecedented American peacetime commitment to the security of Europe and a sign of how far the world had moved since 1945.

### MILITARIZING THE COLD WAR, 1949–1955

Later in 1949, however, the initiative again shifted away from the West. In August the Soviet Union tested its first atomic bomb, based on information transmitted by Soviet agents about the device tested by the Americans in 1945. And in October the Chinese communists, victors of the long and savage civil war, proclaimed the new People's Republic of China.

In Stalin's eyes these two events signaled a shift in the "correlation of forces." They emboldened him to approve the bid by his North Korean allies to bring the whole of their country under communist control. The Korean War, which broke out in June 1950, had a dramatic effect on Europe. The Atlantic allies, fearful that it presaged a similar offensive in Western Europe, galvanized their own rearmament and turned the treaty into a proper military alliance (the North Atlantic Treaty Organization—NATO), with its own command structure under American leadership. Despite strong opposition in Congress, the United States

**Civil defense workers test protective radiation suits and radiation detectors, Bonn, West Germany, 1954.** ©Bettmann/Corbis

committed four new combat divisions to European defense, in return demanding that the Europeans accept the rearmament of West Germany.

The French were deeply alarmed at the revival of German military power. For nearly four years the allies explored the idea of a European Defense Community in which German forces would simply be part of a multinational army. After this proposal was rejected in the French Assembly in August 1954, the allies eventually agreed to admit a rearmed West Germany into NATO. Its forces would not have an independent existence, and the government also renounced atomic, biological, and chemical weapons.

The Soviets also viewed the revival of West German power with grave suspicion. In the spring of 1952 Stalin proposed new talks leading to a

Germany that would be united, rearmed but neutral. When the West rejected this as a spoiling tactic, the Soviets sealed off their part of Germany from the west. Having argued in 1952–1953 about whether East Germany was an asset or a liability now that they had looted most of its assets, the Soviet leaders were panicked by the riots across the country in June 1953. In a marked change of policy, they started to build up the East German regime. When West Germany joined NATO in May 1955, the Soviets countered by drawing their satellites, including East Germany, into their own military system, known in the West as the Warsaw Pact.

Only a few European countries stayed aloof from the two rival alliances. Switzerland and Sweden maintained their traditional neutrality. In

Austria, the four occupying powers withdrew in May 1955, under a treaty that left the country united, independent, and nonaligned. And Yugoslavia's leader Josip Broz Tito had successfully broken away from Moscow's orbit to develop a looser communist economy with aid from the West. But these were rare exceptions. Ten years after the end of Hitler's Reich, most of Europe had been divided into two armed camps.

**FIRST THAW AND NEW DIVISIONS, 1955–1961**
Stalin's death in March 1953 heralded a thaw. The new collective leadership was anxious to reduce tension with the West, and it negotiated an armistice in the deadlocked Korean War. The two sides also looked for advantageous ground on which to stage a "summit" conference—a term popularized by Churchill—and eventually met at Geneva in July 1955.

But the occasion was largely symbolic. Despite growing concern about the nuclear threat now that both sides were developing hydrogen bombs, the arms race was spiraling out of control. Britain had joined the nuclear "club" in 1952; France followed in 1960. In November 1953 the first battlefield nuclear weapons were introduced into West Germany, presaging the "nuclearization" of war at the tactical as well as the strategic level. In November 1956 the brutal Soviet repression of the Hungarian revolt marked a return to confrontational politics.

This was not, however, the acute tension of the early 1950s. Under the Soviet leader Nikita Khrushchev (1894–1971), the slogan was "peaceful coexistence," which meant an intensified competition by all means short of war. Khrushchev was anxious to reduce the arms burden on his own economy. Like the Americans, his aim was to cut down conventional forces and rely more heavily on the deterrent effect of nuclear weapons. The successful launching of Sputnik, the first artificial Earth satellite, in October 1957 suggested that the Soviets were ahead in the development of long-range missiles. Hitherto the Soviets had no long-range aircraft to deliver their nuclear bombs against the United States; now, it seemed to panicky Americans, they could hit Washington within thirty minutes. On the back of this technological triumph, Khrushchev boasted that the Soviet Union would outstrip U.S. per capita output within fifteen years.

Khrushchev exploited his advantage by trying to force an agreement about Berlin, still occupied by the four wartime allies and as such the only point where East Germans could escape to the West. After a series of crises from November 1958, Khrushchev decided to stop the hemorrhage of young talent by blocking off the Soviet zone of the city. Barricades and barbed wire on 13 August 1961 quickly became a twelve-foot-high concrete wall, flanked by minefields, watchtowers, and searchlights. Despite West German anger, the West accepted the fait accompli: a divided Germany seemed an acceptable price for a more stable Europe. But the Berlin Wall cost the Soviets dear in propaganda terms. To those who did not grasp what was at stake between "the free world and the Communist world," President John F. Kennedy (1917–1963) declared, "Let them come to Berlin."

**CUBA, VIETNAM, AND THE PRAGUE SPRING, 1962–1969**
East Germany was a Soviet showpiece in the Cold War. Another, more recent, was Cuba. After Fidel Castro (b. 1926) and his guerrillas seized power from a corrupt Americanized regime in 1959, they became increasingly dependent on Soviet aid as they turned the country into a socialist state. Cuba was only ninety miles from America, and Kennedy did his best to overthrow the Castro government. In the autumn of 1962 Khrushchev responded by introducing medium-range nuclear missiles into Cuba. He tried to do so secretly, but American spy planes detected the buildup and Kennedy went public on 22 October, announcing a blockade of the island. After an increasingly frenzied week of negotiation, Khrushchev, aware that the U.S. nuclear arsenal was far superior to his own, backed down and pulled out the missiles. This massive humiliation, played out on the world stage, was a major factor in his enforced resignation in 1964.

But Kennedy's advantage was short-lived. He was assassinated in November 1963, having already laid the groundwork for America's own nemesis—Vietnam. After the French pulled out of this divided country in 1954, the United States propped up the anticommunist regime in the south with massive amounts of aid, and in 1960 the North embarked on a massive guerrilla war. Kennedy, seeing Vietnam as a Cold War test case of American virility, began to introduce "military advisors." Although the Soviets were not anxious to escalate the conflict, the increasingly radical government of China, now bitterly at odds with Russia, provided aid to the North, and Moscow had to follow suit or lose face in the communist world. With South Vietnam in danger of collapse in 1965, Kennedy's successor, Lyndon B. Johnson (1908–1973), committed combat troops and started massive bombing of North Vietnam. But his escalation failed to end the conflict and also caused immense popular protest in America and across the world.

The growing anti-American feeling in Western Europe was reflected at the top of the Western alliance. Critical of what he saw as excessive American domination, the French president Charles de Gaulle (1890–1970) withdrew his country from NATO's integrated command system in 1966.

But the 1960s also brought another reminder of the nature of Soviet rule. Reformers in Czechoslovakia under Alexander Dubček (1921–1992) promoted democratic change in what became known as the "Prague Spring." Eventually Warsaw Pact troops reimposed Soviet control in August 1968—another military success that was also a propaganda disaster. The 1960s ended with both sides in the Cold War having lost the moral and ideological high ground.

## THE RISE AND FALL OF DÉTENTE, 1969–1979

Johnson's successor, Richard M. Nixon (1913–1994), sought to break the Cold War deadlock, which was now pulling down America's once all-powerful economy. The first goal of Nixon and his national security advisor Henry Kissinger (b. 1923) was to extricate America from Vietnam without loss of face. Part of that strategy was to bomb the North Vietnamese even more heavily than Johnson had. But Nixon also managed to detach North Vietnam from its communist patrons, through pathbreaking visits to Beijing (February 1972) and Moscow (May 1972)—the first time an American president had visited either communist capital. At Moscow he also concluded the Strategic Arms Limitation Treaty (SALT I) in an effort to slow the arms race. This started a flurry of superpower summits with the Soviet leader Leonid Brezhnev (1906–1982) that marked the heyday of

**A soldier guides the positioning of a NATO missile, Verona, Italy, 1957.** ©DAVID LEES/CORBIS

détente (French for "relaxation of tension"). It reflected the fact that both sides were now roughly equal in nuclear arsenals and that each could see real benefits from a reduction of the arms race.

Détente had a European dimension as well. In 1970–1972 the new Social Democrat–led government in West Germany under Willy Brandt negotiated a series of treaties with its eastern neighbors. These included de facto recognition of the East German government (to permit divided families to pay visits across the border). And in July 1975 thirty-five nations concluded the Conference on Security and Cooperation in Europe with some pathbreaking agreements. Thirty years after the war, the Western countries effectively accepted Soviet hegemony in Eastern Europe. But in return the Soviet bloc committed itself to honoring basic freedoms of speech, information, and travel. This would prove a time bomb ticking away beneath the edifice of communist rule.

In January 1973, as part of détente, a Vietnam peace agreement was initialed in Paris. Although American troops pulled out, Nixon hoped to maintain the South Vietnamese regime through massive economic aid and the threat of U.S. airpower. But as scandal engulfed his administration in 1973–1974, Congress cut back military appropriations, and in April 1975 South Vietnam was overrun.

It was not until 1977, with the presidency of Jimmy Carter, that détente resumed momentum with renewed negotiations on arms limitation. The SALT II treaty was initialed at a Carter-Brezhnev summit in Vienna in June 1979. By this time, however, Carter was becoming seriously alarmed at the expansion of Soviet influence, particularly in Africa, and the opening of full diplomatic relations with China in January 1979 was intended in part as a warning to Moscow.

But what really ended détente was the crisis in Afghanistan. Factional and tribal feuds in this Soviet client state escalated into civil war during 1979. At Christmas, the Red Army was sent in to restore order, only to be sucked into a brutal eight-year guerrilla war that became Moscow's equivalent of America's Vietnam. In response Carter withdrew the SALT II treaty from Senate ratification, banned many economic and cultural contacts with the Soviets, and called on American athletes to boycott the 1980 Olympic Games in Moscow.

### THE "NEW COLD WAR," 1980–1985

The freeze deepened in 1981 with the crisis in Poland, whose fierce anti-Russian nationalism had been fueled by the country's fervent Roman Catholicism. In October 1978 Karol Wojtyła (1920–2005), the archbishop of Kraków, was elected Pope John Paul II, becoming a rallying point for opposition to communist rule. Equally important was the burgeoning free union movement, led by Lech Wałęsa (b. 1943), which adopted the collective name "Solidarity." In December 1981 the Polish government, under intense pressure from Moscow, imposed martial law and rounded up Solidarity's leaders.

For Carter's successor, Ronald Reagan (1911–2004), Poland was yet more evidence of the need to confront what he famously called "an evil empire." Reagan presided over a zealously anticommunist administration, determined to restore American power. His presidency saw a new arms buildup and a vigorous campaign against communist-backed movements in Central America.

But the president was not a straightforward cold warrior. He genuinely believed that nuclear deterrence—mutually assured destruction, or MAD—was an abomination and hoped to replace offensive missiles with comprehensive antimissile defense systems. In March 1983 he gave his backing to the so-called Strategic Defense Initiative (SDI), nicknamed "Star Wars," but the prospect of a new, high-tech twist to the arms race seriously alarmed the Soviets. SDI also upset Reagan's European allies, who feared being left outside America's strategic umbrella.

Western Europe was even more upset by the introduction of new theater nuclear missiles. This deployment had been agreed to back in 1979, as a counter to updated Soviet SS-20 missiles. But when NATO's cruise and Pershing missiles were deployed, they provoked mass protests and sit-ins across Western Europe. The early 1980s saw the worst NATO crisis of the whole Cold War. It was only because of firm conservative governments in Britain and West Germany that the deployments went ahead. In the mid-1980s NATO seemed the more brittle of the two alliance blocs.

### THE GORBACHEV REVOLUTION AND THE SOVIET COLLAPSE, 1985–1991

Appearances were deceptive, however. The Soviet Union was in a state of zero growth, and the arms race with the United States was consuming perhaps one-sixth of GDP. The root problem was the command economy, ruled by a central but ineffectual plan, administered by a vast bureaucracy, and riddled with corruption. During the 1970s and 1980s the Western economies had painfully transcended the era of "heavy metal"—the so-called rustbelt industries such as coal, steel, and automobiles—to develop new service economies and begin the computer-driven information technology revolution. But the Soviet economy was starved of consumer goods, and its few computers were mostly pirated from America. As the West entered the information age, the Soviets were still locked in the industrial age.

In April 1985 leadership passed to a new generation. Mikhail Gorbachev (b. 1931) was energetic, bright, and university trained. His predecessors had been shaped by the era of Stalinism and World War II, which engendered paranoid concepts of stability and security. By contrast, Gorbachev had seen the West and was influenced by concepts of social democracy developed in West Germany and Scandinavia. The key, in his view, to a radical restructuring (perestroika) of the Soviet system was to reduce the arms burden on the economy. Gorbachev seized the initiative in what was nothing less than a diplomatic revolution.

Geneva in November 1985 started a new flurry of superpower summits, at which Gorbachev made most of the concessions. The meeting in Washington in December 1987 agreed to remove all intermediate-range nuclear forces, including the SS-20, cruise, and Pershing missiles that had caused such trouble a few years earlier. It was also the first time the superpowers had agreed to reduce their missile stocks, instead of merely slowing their expansion. Gorbachev also agreed to a regime of on-site inspections—a novel development for the secretive Soviets and evidence of his new philosophy of openness and transparency (glasnost).

Meanwhile, Gorbachev was encouraging reform across the Soviet bloc, anxious to replace the gerontocratic leaderships with younger reformers who would mobilize domestic support for change. But this message had been heard before, in 1956 for instance, and then the Kremlin sent in the tanks when reform got out of hand. Only slowly did Gorbachev's rhetoric that "unity does not mean uniformity" inspire confidence, validated by actions such as the Soviet withdrawal from Afghanistan in 1988–1989. Of critical importance in promoting reform across Eastern Europe was the nucleus of opposition groups whose existence had been guaranteed by the Helsinki agreement of 1975.

The two countries in the vanguard of reform were Poland and Hungary. The Polish Communist government conceded free elections in June 1989, and these resulted in a Solidarity-led coalition government. In Hungary, reformers within the Communist Party took control, rehabilitating the leaders of the 1956 revolt, and symbolically opened the country's border with Austria. This offered an unprecedented loophole for East Germans, thousands of whom fled west and then claimed their right to West German citizenship.

Faced with another hemorrhage of young talent, a new reformist Politburo in East Germany bowed to mounting popular unrest and announced travel concessions on 9 November 1989. This was intended as a limited, regularized program, but thousands flocked to the border crossing in Berlin and the massively outnumbered guards let them through. Over the next few days two or three million East Germans went to and fro across the Berlin Wall. The Iron Curtain had fallen, and the East German regime lasted only a few more weeks.

By the end of November, mass rallies and strikes had toppled Communist rule in Czechoslovakia in what became known as the "Velvet Revolution." Only in Romania did the end of the brutal regime of Nicolae Ceaușescu (1918–1989) involve significant bloodshed, with the dictator and his wife summarily executed on Christmas Day.

Few had anticipated that the end of the Soviet bloc would be so quick and relatively peaceful. Gorbachev's refusal to use force, in marked contrast to his predecessors, was of decisive importance. But so was the communications revolution. News of the upheavals in Poland and Hungary were relayed around the bloc by West German TV and radio, emboldening protestors even in Ceaușescu's police state. The revolutions of 1989 marked the triumph of communication as much as the failure of communism.

Gorbachev's reformism had unleashed a whirlwind that was now beyond his control. As West Germany moved rapidly to absorb East Germany, leading to formal unification in October 1990, the Soviet Union itself fell apart. Gorbachev's attempt to introduce elements of a market economy led to roaring inflation. New powers for the Soviet republics and the legitimation of noncommunist parties made politics less easy to control. And the erosion of the union led to a backlash in Russia, the largest republic and bankroller of the rest, where Gorbachev's rival Boris Yeltsin was firmly in control. After hard-liners tried an unsuccessful coup in August 1991, Gorbachev's remaining power ebbed fast. On Christmas Day 1991, the red flag was lowered on the Kremlin flagpole as the Soviet Union ceased to exist.

## CONCLUSION

Stated simply, the Cold War ended in 1989–1991 when most of the world's communist regimes collapsed, Germany was reunited, and the Soviet Union ceased to exist. In that sense, the West and especially the United States won the Cold War. This was certainly the verdict of many American conservatives.

But other factors mattered as well. Leaders, for instance, were crucial, particularly in the Soviet Union: the Cold War grew out of Stalin's paranoid sense of insecurity; conversely, Gorbachev's belief that security was not a zero-sum game helped bring it to an end.

The Cold War was also a phase in social history. It was made possible by the development of mass media, particularly television and film, and their use by governments to shape public ideology in the Soviet Union and the United States. The explosion of new electronic media under looser official control ushered in a new historical era. Equally important in the Soviet bloc was the growth of an educated middle class, which made Stalinism increasingly difficult to maintain.

At the time, the Cold War seemed an all-encompassing phenomenon, particularly to Americans. Yet much associated with the Cold War has outlived it. The People's Republic of China—the world's most populous country and a coming power of the twenty-first century—is still a communist state, albeit in modified form. Final verdicts on Marxism-Leninism will depend heavily on how China evolves. And although the Cold War and the atomic bomb came of age together in 1945, the problem of nuclear weapons has survived the Soviet collapse. Evaluating the Cold War and its legacies will preoccupy historians for decades to come.

*See also* **Arms Control; Berlin Wall; Eastern Bloc; Gorbachev, Mikhail; Korean War; Marshall Plan; NATO; 1989; Solidarity; Soviet Union; Sputnik; Warsaw Pact.**

BIBLIOGRAPHY

*Primary Sources*

Cold War International History Project. Its Web site features translated primary source material from former communist states and numerous research papers based upon it. Available at http://wilsoncenter.org.

Hanhimäki, Jussi M., and Odd Arne Westad, eds. *The Cold War: A History in Documents and Eyewitness Accounts.* Oxford, U.K., 2003. An excellent reader, richly documented and thoughtfully analyzed.

Orwell, George. *The Collected Essays, Journalism, and Letters of George Orwell*, edited by Sonia Orwell and Ian Angus. Vol. 4. London, 1968.

*Secondary Sources*

Crockatt, Richard. *The Fifty Years War: The United States and the Soviet Union in World Politics, 1941–1991.* London, 1995. A good overview.

Fox, William T. R. *The Super-Powers: The United States, Britain, and the Soviet Union.* New York, 1944.

Gaddis, John. *We Now Know: Rethinking Cold War History.* Oxford, U.K., 1997. An early synthesis of the period 1945–1962, drawing on communist sources.

Halliday, Fred. *The Making of the Second World War.* 2nd ed. London, 1986.

Reynolds, David. *One World Divisible: A Global History since 1945.* New York, 2000. Sets the Cold War within larger global patterns.

Westad, Odd Arne, ed. *Reviewing the Cold War: Approaches, Interpretations, and Theory.* London, 2000. A stimulating set of essays.

DAVID REYNOLDS

---

## COLIJN, HENDRIKUS (1869–1944), Dutch politician.

Hendrikus Colijn was a farmer's son born on 22 June 1869 in Burgerveen, a small agricultural village just south of Amsterdam. In 1886 he volunteered for military service and six years later became a second lieutenant in the Royal Dutch Indian Army. He distinguished himself in the Aceh Wars and also as a civil servant. He retired as a major in 1907, when he was appointed secretary of the government of the Dutch East Indies. After a successful career in the colonial civil service, he returned to the Netherlands in 1909 to become member of parliament for the Protestant Anti-Revolutionaire Partij and in 1911 he was appointed as minister of war. In his characteristic energetic way he began the reorganization of the army. After the fall of the government in 1913 he became president of the Bataafsche Petroleum Maatschappij in 1914. His international position allowed him to represent

Dutch interests during World War I, when the Netherlands stayed neutral.

Despite pressure to resume a political career, he remained in business as president of the Koninklijke Petroleum Maatschappij and a director of Royal Dutch Shell. He returned to parliament in 1922 and became minister of finance in 1923; in 1925 he led his first cabinet, which fell after only a couple of months. He remained in the Dutch parliament while at the same time being active in all kinds of international economic organizations and involved in the modernization of the administration of the Dutch East Indies. During the economic crisis he pleaded for a severe retrenchment policy, which he was finally able to implement in 1933 as head of his (second) broad coalition cabinet. Colijn was convinced that the only solution to the crisis was austerity, and he strove to balance the budget and maintain the strength of the guilder. This served to increase unemployment, however, thus making even greater demands on the Dutch exchequer. His stringent welfare cuts provoked riots in July 1934 in a working-class district of Amsterdam, where the police use of armored vehicles to suppress the revolt led to seven fatalities. Under strong international pressure and criticism from his Catholic coalition partners he was forced to devaluate the Dutch guilder in September 1936. At the same time his defense cuts became more and more controversial as international tension grew. His political career came to an end in August 1939 when his fifth cabinet fell. He nevertheless remained active in international diplomacy until the Germans invaded Holland in May 1940.

At the beginning of the German occupation he criticized the Dutch government for going into exile in London and pleaded for an acknowledgment of the German hegemony in Europe. However he remained too wedded to a Protestant morality to reach an accommodation with Nazi ideology and soon dissociated himself from the Germans. In June 1941 he was taken hostage and deported in March 1942 to Ilmenau (Thüringen) where he enjoyed a relative liberty until he died of a heart attack on 18 September 1944.

Characterized by a colleague as "excessively admired [and] whole-heartedly vilified" (Jan Blocker in De Volkstrant, 11 April 2004, p. 16), Colijn distinguished himself from his more parochial conservative Protestant fellow politicians through his wide experience in business and diplomacy. Profoundly influenced by his years in the Dutch Indian Army, he was committed to principles of law and order and highly critical of democracy. He misjudged the rising nationalism in the Dutch Indies and the dangers of National Socialism in Europe. Although an admirer of Benito Mussolini, the Fascist dictator of Italy, he played an important role limiting the impact of National Socialism on the Dutch public, thus paradoxically criticizing democracy while at the same time maintaining its credibility. In his lifetime, his rhetorical qualities and his firmness made him very popular even among the liberal opponents who agreed with his economic policies. His self confidence, however, also led to failure, as can be seen in his unsuccessful struggle against the economic crisis that severely damaged the Dutch economy and sustained high levels of unemployment much longer than necessary during his six-year regime. After the war, Colijn was largely remembered for his stubborn defense of the gold standard. He was vilified for his colonial policies and his lack of sympathy for the plight of the Dutch unemployed. The image of the steady steersman who had protected his people from the evils of modernization was further undermined when his biographer revealed that during his military career Colijn had been responsible for atrocities in the Dutch East Indies during the so-called Lombok expedition of 1894. At the time, his ruthlessness had been applauded, but in the changed climate of the 1990s, it was seen as a further stain on his character.

See also **Dutch Colonial Empire; Netherlands.**

BIBLIOGRAPHY

Primary Sources

Colijn Archives in The Historical Documents Centre for Dutch Protestantism of the Vrije Universiteit Amsterdam.

Secondary Sources

Langeveld, Herman J. Hendrikus Colijn, 1869–1944. Vol. 1, 1869–1933: Dit leven van krachtig handelen. Amsterdam, 1998.

———. Hendrikus Colijn, 1869–1944. Vol. 2, 1933–1944: Schipper naast God. Amsterdam, 2004.

DICK VAN GALEN LAST

## COLLABORATION.

With the development of nation-states after 1789, civilians and even more so authorities were expected to be loyal with regard to their country. Cooperation with a foreign occupier was considered high treason and made punishable by law. In the long nineteenth century, the balance of power ensured that this phenomenon did not occur. During World War I, the warring parties tried to detach national minorities of the enemy from their patriotic loyalty, and thus some collaboration movements developed, but they remained marginal phenomena. During World War II, the far-reaching cooperation of parts of the population not only with the German, Italian, and Japanese occupiers, but also with Allied occupiers, was an important phenomenon, whereby the collaborators of one side were the allies of the other. After World War II, the phenomenon also existed in contexts of occupation and colonization.

The focus herein is on collaboration with Nazi Germany during World War II. The notion of Collaboration (with a capital C) is often found having this meaning, so that the term immediately takes on a subjective and morally loaded interpretation, especially in languages other than English. In English, collaboration (with a small c) is a neutral term with which the many and divergent forms of cooperation of an occupied nation with an occupier can be denoted. In the standard literature and in this article too, the terms *cooperation* and *accommodation* are used for this concept.

A distinction should also be made between the occupied nation's cooperation with the occupier to make everyday life possible, and collaboration, that is, the purposeful cooperation of groups and individuals to help realize the occupier's policies. Only a small part of the population was prepared to do the latter, a part that was approximately as large as the part of the population that appeared to be prepared to actively offer resistance. The major part of the population adjusted to occupation circumstances, which to a certain extent implied cooperation with the occupier. The Hague Convention of 1907 actually prescribed that the occupied authorities had to cooperate with the occupier insofar as that cooperation did not infringe the laws of the occupied country. In practice, this principle did not result in a clear dividing line between legally permitted cooperation and unlawful cooperation. The fortunes of war affected the boundary between what was considered morally acceptable and morally unacceptable or, in other words, the difference between collaboration and cooperation. When in 1943 the fortunes of war turned definitively to Germany's detriment, cooperation was less approved of than at the beginning of the war, when Germany seemed set for long-term domination of continental Europe.

The circumstances of occupation also affected collaboration and cooperation. There were essential differences between western Europe on the one hand and parts of eastern Europe and the Balkans on the other. At the same time, the occupier's divide-and-rule policy aimed to exploit the occupied countries and the definitive dominance of Germany and Nazification of the "Germanic" core territory. There were differences in the degree to which force and violence were employed to achieve these objectives. In western Europe, the occupying powers were prepared to negotiate with part of the administrative elite, because parts of the social and economic fabric should not be too highly disrupted to exploit them efficiently. The occupiers made room for enforced cooperation, whereby the local elites sometimes succeeded in mitigating the consequences of the occupation, if only because violence stayed within limits. This "policy of the lesser of two evils" was not unideological, because the degree to which the local elites were prepared to negotiate depended on their attitude to a new (social) order or, in other words, on their adherence to liberal-democratic principles. Moreover, the "policy of the lesser of two evils" appeared to be a slippery slope down which organizations and people in positions of authority slid across the boundary into collaboration. But in general their intentions differed from those of the collaborators who supported the Nazification project for ideological, political, or personal reasons. The notion of "collaborationism"—mainly used in the French literature—is appropriate for this ideology-driven collaboration. Not every collaborator, however, was driven by ideological motives. Personal motives frequently played a part. Because of the relatively stable social context in which collaboration developed, collaborator violence remained within

A cage at the zoo is used to contain men suspected of being Nazi collaborators as they await trial in Belgium, September 1944. ©Bettmann/Corbis

limits. Only at the end of the occupation did more excesses occur, which are called "criminal" collaboration.

In large parts of eastern Europe and the Balkans, the occupier pursued the rapid destruction of civil society and total subjugation of the indigenous population to enable a German-Germanic colonization. Stirring up internal civil wars by exploiting national, ethnic, and religious differences was part of this strategy. Therefore, for the subjugated population, cooperation with the occupier was often a survival strategy, one that was detached from ideological considerations and often the consequence of local circumstances and coincidence. Almost inevitably, collaboration with the occupier implied excessive violence so that collaboration and criminal behavior became synonymous.

The fate of the Jewish population and Gypsies went beyond the difference between east and west.

The Nazis pursued their total destruction from 1941 on. But whereas Jews and Gypsies from western Europe were deported to Poland to be murdered there, in the Balkans and eastern Europe this often happened in situ with the cooperation of collaborators. These were peaks in the already high curve of violence.

The use of excessive violence and the genocidal policy of Nazi Germany deepened the moral rejection of those who collaborated with that regime. At times the term *traitors* is used as a synonym for collaborators. *Traitors* in the narrow sense refers to collaborators who literally gave away compatriots to the occupier and/or exposed them to persecution. In the broad sense it concerns those who cooperated with the occupier for political-ideological reasons. The collaborators' political organizations were the core of the multiple forms of cooperation.

## POLITICAL ORGANIZATIONS IN WESTERN EUROPE

In western Europe, collaboration was embodied in the first place by fascist (in a generic sense) organizations that supported the National Socialist new order. These were minority movements that could attract only a few percent of the population. Some had been in contact with the Third Reich from before the war and were therefore often considered as a German "fifth column" in their own country. Nevertheless, these organizations were always also ultranationalistic. Confronted with German imperialism in the new ordering of Europe dictated by Berlin, the leaders of these movements put the expected, promised, or acquired positions of power before their nationalistic convictions. They were also all prepared to cooperate with the SS, a political organization founded by Heinrich Himmler aimed at the annexation of the territory considered as German and the formation of a Germanic-German elite. Local fascist leaders could acquire positions of power only to the degree that they were prepared to cooperate in the German exploitation of their country. Their followers were brought into the German war machine and the occupation of their country. Thus political collaboration always led to other forms of collaboration in the field of administration, economy, the military, and the police.

In Norway, the leader of the Nasjonal Samling (NS; National Unity), Vidkun Quisling, led a putsch immediately after the German invasion on 9 April 1940. This fact highly impressed the largely still unoccupied Europe. Quisling's name became a synonym for treason and collaboration, so that *quislings* still lives on as a term for collaborators during World War II, especially in the English language. Quisling was rejected en masse by the Norwegian population, which is the reason why a German *Reichskommissar* was appointed. With the latter's help, the NS infiltrated the Norwegian government and Quisling was appointed prime minister on 1 February 1942. The members of his party were then brought in at all levels of the Norwegian administration. The seizure of power by the NS was very substantial, especially at a local level.

Because Denmark offered hardly any military resistance to the German invasion, the country supposedly retained its neutral status, and the prewar parties and politicians remained in charge. The Danish state was forced to far-reaching *samarbejdspolitikken* (cooperation) with Germany, but formally retained its sovereignty. In March and May 1943, national and local elections were even held, in which the Danmarks Nationalsocialistiske Arbejderparti (Danish Nazi Party) gained only 2 percent of the votes, drawing some support only among the German minority in Jutland. Even when the Danish government resigned and the country became officially occupied in mid-1943, the Danish Nazi Party played only a minor role.

In France, after the French armistice on 22 June 1940, the Vichy regime (so-called because its headquarters were situated in the town of Vichy) came into being under the leadership of Marshal Philippe Pétain, who had been appointed leader of the government and who from then on was to govern an unoccupied zone as head of state. The Vichy regime enjoyed formal sovereignty, which was possible only because Pétain was prepared to carry out far-reaching cooperation with Germany. The French head of state literally used the term *collaboration* after his meeting with Adolf Hitler on 24 October 1940, by which he meant the French state's cooperation with Germany. Under prime ministers Pierre Laval and François Darlan, the Vichy regime developed de facto into a police state; it handed over Jews to the Nazis, and was unable to offer protection to its own population, culminating in the German military administration taking over all of France in November 1942. The rank and file of the Vichy regime consisted of conservative right-wing forces, some of whom were convinced fascists and/or favored Germany's final victory. Cooperation very quickly became collaboration (or "collaborationism" in the French context of the notion). In France, there were also some collaborating political parties: the Parti Populaire Français under the leadership of Jacques Doriot and the Rassemblement National Populaire under the leadership of Marcel Déat, which mainly supplied manpower for the eastern fronts and against armed resistance by their own compatriots. Finally, collaborating factions were active in the Breton and French-Flemish regionalist and nationalistic movement.

After the capitulation on 15 May 1940, a civilian government was established in the

**Danish soldiers escort a suspected Nazi collaborator to trial, Copenhagen, 1945.** ©HULTON-DEUTSCH COLLECTION/CORBIS

Netherlands that cooperated with the Dutch administrative machinery. Anton Mussert, the leader of the Nationaal-Socialistische Beweging (NSB; National Socialist Movement), claimed political power in vain. Only after the new order–minded Nederlandse Unie (Netherlands Union)—a popular movement that soon had hundreds of thousands of members—did not cooperate adequately did the occupier force the NSB into the Dutch administration.

In Belgium, because of the presence of the head of state in the occupied country, a military government of occupation was installed after the capitulation on 28 May 1940, which meant that Hitler officially still kept the political future of Belgium open. When no modus vivendi resulted from a meeting between the Belgian king and Hitler in November 1940, the occupation administration gave support to the Vlaams Nationaal Verbond (Flemish National Union), a Flemish-

nationalistic, pan-Dutch, and fascist party. The party was allocated administrative positions and mainly gained power in local governments. It was not given any official governmental power and had to tolerate that the SS leaders founded a Greater-German countermovement. This was initially the Flemish SS and then, from 1941, the German-Flemish Labor Community. Because the Nazis did not consider French-speaking Belgians and Walloons as Germans, the leader of the Rex fascist party, Léon Degrelle, received little support. His military and political star rose only when he volunteered as a soldier for the battle on the eastern front. Degrelle was able to convince Hitler that the Walloons should be considered as Romanized Germanics. He joined the Waffen-SS and founded a military recruitment reserve and a police force against the Belgian resistance. On 12 July 1944 Belgium was annexed to the German Reich in the shape of a Reichsgau Flandern ([German] Province of Flanders) and Reichsgau Wallonien ([German] Province of Wallonia).

The Grand Duchy of Luxembourg was actually annexed as early as 1940, and military conscription was introduced in 1942. The Volksdeutsche Bewegung (Movement of German Peoples) under the leadership of Damian Kratzenberg grouped together annexionist collaborators. It remained a small movement in spite of the fact that civil servants were obliged to join.

## POLITICAL ORGANIZATIONS IN EASTERN EUROPE AND THE BALKANS

World War II started with the German invasion of Poland in September 1939 and the destruction of Polish civil society. The German occupation of western Poland and from 22 June 1941 the whole of Poland did not offer any starting point for a Polish collaboration movement. Only individual collaboration was tolerated, among other things in the extermination of Polish Jews.

Even before Poland, Czechoslovakia was the first victim of German imperialism. The Nazis envisaged the destruction of civil society in the Czech Republic so that Czech fascist factions were not given any room for establishing a political collaboration movement worth mentioning. Under the leadership of Josef Tiso, the Slovak nationalists of Andrej Hlinka's Slovak People's Party reformed Slovakia into a German protectorate on 14 March 1939. Slovakia was a military ally of Germany, but it retained its autonomy, and Tiso enjoyed wide support among the population until 1943.

There was a similar situation in Croatia, which was made into a German protectorate under the leadership of the fascist Ante Pavelić a few days after the German invasion of Yugoslavia on 10 April 1941. With his Ustaše militias, he purged Croatia of Jews, Gypsies, and Serbs. In the entire territory of the multiethnic Yugoslavian state a bloody civil war developed, whereby sometimes tactical alliances were concluded with the German, Italian, and Bulgarian occupiers. This strategy did not develop into a stable collaboration policy. The same picture was to emerge in Albania and Greece, where the Italian, Bulgarian, and German occupations provoked and provided the framework for civil war.

Hungary, Romania, and Bulgaria were allies of the Axis Powers, so that there was no such thing as collaboration movements in the strict sense of the term. The changing extreme-right regimes had their own agenda. They retained their sovereignty, although they had to take into account fascist movements and organizations supported by Germany inasmuch it was expedient to German interests. When Hungary was occupied by German troops on 19 March 1944, the German-minded fascist Arrow Cross Party was given free rein only when the Hungarian regime wanted to break the alliance with Germany. In addition to military security, the extermination of the Jews, with which Hungarian collaborators cooperated, was high on the German agenda.

Collaboration in the Baltic states, Byelorussia, Ukraine, and the other occupied territories of the Soviet Union showed a similar pattern. The German troops were greeted as liberators from Joseph Stalin's regime by some parts of the population, including members of the ethnic-German minorities, the *byvshie liudi* ("former people" of tsarist elites), and victims of Soviet repression. The Nazis' racism prevented any stable political cooperation. Attempts to establish or revive political structures such as the Byelorussian National Committee and the Organization of Ukrainian Nationalists were nipped in the bud. Berlin considered the Slavic population as *Untermenschen* (inferior people), not as potential allies. They wanted to colonize the territory, plunder it economically, and drive out, exterminate, or enslave the local population. The German occupational powers exploited the ethnic discrepancies in a divide-and-rule strategy that resulted in complex and violent internal conflicts. Widespread anti-Semitism among the Baltic and Slavic population was exploited in the extermination of the Jewish population. The battle against "Judeobolshevism" was an ideological basis for collaboration. In addition, the war against communist partisans was critical for considerable police collaboration. When in 1943, as a result of the turning fortunes of war, there was yet more room for political cooperation, it was largely limited to the use of local populations and Russian prisoners of war (POWs) in military and paramilitary formations that were employed behind the front in the war against partisans. Attempts to bring about a

**A barber shaves the head of a woman as members of the Free French Resistance supervise, Bourg-Blanc, France, 1944.** After the liberation, women suspected of engaging in sexual relationships with German soldiers were frequently subjected to this form of public humiliation. ©HULTON-DEUTSCH COLLECTION/CORBIS

political movement around the Russian army general and POW Andrei Vlasov misfired. As early as 1942 Vlasov had made an offer to form a "liberation army" consisting of Russian POWs. Only in November 1944 did he receive a green light to form the Russian Liberation Army, which was deployed on the eastern front.

## FORMS OF COLLABORATION

Political collaboration was often the basis for other forms of collaboration. Supplying manpower for the war and occupation activities was a way of proving loyalty to the occupier while simultaneously acquiring a local basis for power. The recruitment of personnel for military units,

paramilitary guard units, and all kinds of administrative and economic control services often happened through the organizations of political collaborators, which did not prevent the event of an inflow of apolitical collaborators who committed themselves for reasons of livelihood, personal opportunism, or adventurism. In the transfer of information to the occupier, personal motives often played a part, while certain forms of administrative and police collaboration involved the systematic leaking of sensitive information to the occupier and therefore gave rise to "structural betrayal."

Political collaboration was framed by cultural and ideological collaboration by intellectuals, artists, and writers who used their talents to legitimize the cooperation with the occupier. Their collaboration consisted of the distribution of ideas that often had concrete implications. They inspired and legitimized others to collaborate. In particular, the battle on the eastern front against "irreligious bolshevism" gave rise to varied and extensive propaganda that stimulated many to volunteer for the German army.

By signing conscription contracts, military collaborators became subjected to German martial laws, whereby they were bound for a certain period or even for the duration of the war. Turning one's back on collaboration implied desertion for them. In the beginning of the war and before the Nazi attack on the Soviet Union, military collaboration was not yet a reality. Serving in the then still victorious German army was considered an honor that was reserved only for "Germanics." The SS recruited volunteers in occupied "Germanic" countries for the Waffen-SS. After Operation Barbarossa, all over occupied Europe anti-Bolshevik legions were founded that were also deployed in the Wehrmacht. In the racist Waffen-SS too there was an influx of non-Germans. SS units were founded in the Balkans, the Baltic states, Central Asia, and Caucasia. At the end of the war the Waffen-SS had approximately two hundred thousand non-Germans. Even more military collaborators fought in the Wehrmacht. Particularly in the Balkans and eastern Europe the volume of military collaboration was very great. But because of the specific conditions in which they aligned themselves with the occupier and under which they operated, military collaborators could easily change sides by defecting to the partisans or the Red Army, which happened frequently starting in 1943.

Economic collaboration is the most complex form of collaboration because it was (and is) very difficult to draw the line between what was perceived as permitted and nonpermitted cooperation. Direct supplies of arms and war infrastructure were generally labeled as collaboration, while indirect industrial cooperation was considered to be unavoidable, as was voluntary work by employees in German industry. A special form of economic collaboration was the exploitation of stolen Jewish property.

## RETRIBUTION

After the retreat of the occupier, collaborators were the target of the population's revenge and the reckoning of the Resistance with its enemies. In the days immediately after the liberation there were more or less spontaneous waves everywhere whereby collaborators were traced, taken prisoner, and sometimes killed. The degree to which society was stabilized during the war and had been the scene of violence also determined the volume and violence of this cleanup. Visual forms of collaboration—for example, uniformed military or paramilitary collaborators—were easy targets. Certain forms of collaboration evoked popular fury, such as certain visual forms of economic collaboration (the so-called war profiteers) or the "horizontal collaboration" of women who had entered into sexual relationships with the occupier. Punishment sometimes consisted of a well-defined repertoire, such as destruction of property or shaving off women's hair. Betrayal was also judged a great sin, but was often far more difficult to prove.

The so-called popular repression came to an end when the postwar regime took hold again because, among other things, the monopoly on violence returned to the hands of the authorities. This was the starting signal for judicial repression whereby collaborators had to justify themselves in court. All over Europe collaborators were punished. Thousands of death sentences were pronounced and executed. Hundreds of thousands of collaborators ended up imprisoned for shorter or longer periods of time. There were great differences in judicial procedures between countries, depending on events during the occupation, the legal tradition, and whether or not a constitutional state was founded after the Nazi dictatorship. On this subject there were again major differences between the West European democracies and the new dictatorships in Eastern Europe and the Balkans.

Collaborators often remained pariahs in society after the completion of their legal punishment, although that was largely dependent on the degree to which they were able to construct a socially accepted legitimization for their actions during the occupation. Thus collaborators were sometimes rehabilitated by nationalistic movements if they were able to present their collaboration as a national war of liberation. By contrast, certain forms of collaboration that were pardoned in the postwar period were not accepted later on because of a changed social climate. Thus involvement in the extermination of Jews became more heavily reckoned starting in the 1960s, which resulted in trials and sentences through the end of the twentieth century.

*See also* **Occupation, Military; Pétain, Philippe; Quisling, Vidkun; Resistance; Vlasov Armies.**

BIBLIOGRAPHY

Andreyev, Catherine. *Vlasov and the Russian Liberation Movement: Soviet Reality and Émigré Theories.* Cambridge, U.K., 1987.

Burrin, Philippe. *France under the Germans: Collaboration and Compromise.* Translated by Janet Lloyd. New York, 1996.

Hoidal, Oddvar K. *Quisling: A Study in Treason.* Oxford, U.K., 1989.

Lagrou, Pieter. *The Legacy of Nazi Occupation: Patriotic Memory and National Recovery in Western Europe, 1945–1965.* Cambridge, U.K., 2000.

Paxton, Robert O. *Vichy France: Old Guard and New Order, 1940–1944.* New York, 1972. Reprint, with new introduction, New York, 2001.

B. DE WEVER

---

# COLLECTIVIZATION.

The collectivization of Soviet agriculture accompanied rapid industrialization during Joseph Stalin's First Five-Year Plan (1928–1932). Collectivization was meant to create a large-scale socialized agricultural economy based on state and collective farms. While state farms were to replicate nationalized industry with state ownership and the employment of a salaried workforce, collective farms were to be profit-sharing organizations, in which farmers tilled and managed the land collectively. Collectivization was intended to radically transform the rural sector, displacing communal forms of peasant land tenure as well as ridding the countryside of a rural bourgeoisie (the "kulaks"), capitalism, and the market.

The Communist Party viewed collectivization as a solution to agrarian backwardness and the industrial development of the nation. By the late 1920s, when the state turned toward forced industrialization, the peasantry (some 85 percent of the population) had emerged as a key economic resource to be tapped for the capital funding of industrialization by way of taxation, grain levies for export, and labor (voluntary and forced) for industry and the extraction of raw materials. The collective farm was to be a control mechanism for the economic exploitation of the peasantry.

Through collectivization, the state also sought hegemony over the countryside and the eradication of the peasantry as a semiautonomous cultural entity. Collectivization therefore entailed not only the creation of collective farms and the taking of grain, but also the implementation of a series of ancillary policies that aimed to destroy peasant self-government, to curtail and control the peasant market, to suppress religion, and to remove all sources of traditional village leadership and authority by way of the so-called liquidation of the kulaks as a class. Dekulakization, as it was known, was an endeavor to decapitate village authority structures and to remove undesirable elements in order to break down village cohesion and minimize peasant resistance.

Implemented in the midst of the crisis atmosphere of the late 1920s, collectivization was imposed with brute force, largely by workers and urban communists mobilized for work in the countryside. Based on a Marxist-Leninist reading of the rural community, the Communist Party attempted to divide the village by exploiting social tensions and cleavages; it failed, however, to understand the strength and cohesion of what was largely a precapitalist, communal peasantry. This ideological misreading, along with counterproductive policies against religion and the kulaks and the use of outside forces to implement collectivization, served to unite the peasantry against the state. In 1930 peasants fought collectivization in a wave of resistance that included close to fourteen thousand mass disturbances (mostly riots) encompassing as many as two million participants and over one thousand murders of and just under six thousand assaults against rural officials and peasant activists. In the end, peasant resistance was no match for the superior forces of the state. Collectivization would be largely completed by the end of the First Five-Year Plan.

## DEKULAKIZATION

The policy of dekulakization was auxiliary to collectivization. Local activists employed dekulakization to intimidate peasants into joining collective farms (lest they be subject to the fate of the kulak) and to halt the flight of peasants seeking to escape repression and leave for the cities. In all, in 1930 as many as 337,563 peasant families were subject to some form of dekulakization. Kulaks were divided into three categories. The first category, consisting of supposed "counterrevolutionary kulak activists," was to be quickly liquidated by way of the incarceration of heads of households in concentration camps or, when deemed necessary, execution. Their families were subject to property confiscation and internal exile. The second category was made up of the remaining elements among the "kulak activists," especially the wealthiest kulaks; following property expropriations, they and their families were to be exiled to distant parts of the Soviet Union beyond or within their native regions. Those in the third category were subject to property expropriation and left largely in place, but were not allowed to join collective farms.

Repression in fact was not limited to the largely mythical rural bourgeoisie, but instead struck all manner of peasant and nonpeasant in the village, including poor and middle-class peasants, the families of Red Army soldiers and industrial workers, members of the rural intelligentsia (i.e., teachers, agronomists, doctors), people with ties to the old regime or anticommunist political parties, and, in general, anyone who dared to criticize or object. The total number of kulaks deported in 1930 and 1931 ranges from 356,544 families (1,679,528 people) to 381,026 families (1,803,392 people). These figures do not include those peasants designated as third-category kulaks, nor those who fled the countryside. If one includes the smaller exiles of 1932 and 1933, the total number of people exiled would surpass two million. The major regions of exile were the remote hinterlands of the Urals (128,233 families), Western Siberia (69,950 families), the Northern Region (58,271 families), Kazakhstan (50,879 families), and Eastern Siberia (26,555 families). Once there, deported peasant families built and lived in "special settlements" (*spetsposelenie*, later *trudposelenie*) administered by the secret police and gulag. Death rates through the first half of the 1930s were massive, in the hundreds of thousands, as a result of famine and disease. Employed in forestry, mining, fishing, and other industries, the special settlers became forced laborers for the extraction of the Soviet Union's natural resources so crucial for industrialization and hard-currency-earning exports. They were forbidden to return home until 1954 and officially "rehabilitated" only in the early 1990s.

## THE AFTERMATH

The short-term consequences of collectivization included a huge influx of peasants into the labor force, massive social fluidity, and the disruption of agriculture on a scale that led to a major famine in 1932 and 1933. The Stalinist state and the collective farm system triumphed in the end, but their triumph did not spell the end of the peasantry. Passive resistance and other weapons of the weak became endemic mechanisms of coping and survival for the peasantry within the collective farm. Agriculture stagnated, becoming the Achilles' heel of the Soviet economy, weakened by low productivity, poor management, massive peasant indifference, and official neglect. Like the peasant commune before it, the collective farm became a bulwark against change, as much a subsistence shelter for peasants as a control mechanism for the state. Over time, the collective farm became the quintessential risk-aversion guarantor that peasants had always sought. Socioeconomic leveling, a basis subsistence, and some degree of cultural independence, demographic isolation, and feminization of the village maintained and even strengthened certain aspects of village culture and tradition. The constant and historic insecurity of peasant life ironically bonded the peasant to the collective farm. State attempts at decollectivization, after the fall of the Soviet Union, were resisted and blocked by a peasantry grown accustomed to the collective farm.

## INTERPRETATIONS

The classic Soviet historiographical view proclaimed collectivization to be a "revolution from above with support from below." This view derived largely from Stalin's own pronouncements concerning collectivization in official party histories. This view was first challenged within the Soviet Union during the Khrushchev years (1953–

A propaganda photo shows workers eating lunch in the fields at the Lenin's Way collective farm in the Soviet village of Vilshanka, August 1939. ©BETTMANN/CORBIS

1964), when a series of historians suggested that Stalin committed "mistakes" both in the implementation of collectivization and in the assumption that the peasantry welcomed the new policy; the mistakes resulted in widespread violence and peasant suffering. These views were largely muted during the Brezhnev years (1964–1982), only to resurface during Mikhail Gorbachev's perestroika (1985–1991) and after. At that time, the historians of the Khrushchev years returned to a critical analysis of collectivization, for the first time discussing the famine of 1932 and 1933 and its victims as well as the deportation of the kulaks.

Western historians were far more skeptical of Stalinist claims regarding collectivization. The earliest Western studies tended to view collectivization as "necessary" to industrialization: the collective farms facilitated the state's access to peasant grain, thereby providing a source of capital for industrialization through grain exports. This viewpoint was challenged in the late 1960s and 1970s by scholars who argued that collectivization in fact made a negative contribution to industrialization as capital flowed not from countryside to town, but in the reverse direction. The construction and modernization of a new agricultural system proved costly to the state, and the damage wrought by collectivization reduced agricultural output.

In the 1970s Western historians explored the social history of collectivization, challenging in no uncertain terms Stalinist arguments about class war in the village and advanced social stratification. Historians were divided, however, on ways of seeing the village. Some have implicitly viewed the countryside through a Marxist-Leninist lens, while arguing that social stratification was minimal and class war a reality only in the Stalinist imagination. Others have explicitly rejected Marxist-Leninist conceptions of the village, turning instead to an understanding of the Russian village as an overwhelmingly precapitalist, communal peasantry made up of small family productive units. In both cases, scholars agree that social support for collectivization within the village was minimal and class war all but nonexistent. In the 1980s Western historians continued their explorations of the social basis of collectivization, suggesting that the regime relied on urban sources of support to implement collectivization; others investigated the massive social fluidity caused by collectivization as millions of peasants headed for the cities.

From the late 1980s, the study of collectivization has benefited from the partial opening of Soviet archives and the declassification of key documentation. This has allowed both Western and Russian historians to explore in depth Stalin's role in decision-making and the evolution of state policy, the scope and dynamics of peasant resistance, the famine of 1932 and 1933, and the expropriation and deportation of the kulaks. The opening of the archives has revealed the extent to which collectivization was formative to the rise of the Stalinist police state. The liquidation of the kulaks as a class represented the first mass deportation and use of forced labor of the Stalin era, setting the precedent for and marking the beginning of the rise of the Soviet secret police as a vast economic empire and a state within a state.

Collectivization was the Soviet state's first major project in social engineering on a massive scale. In its goals of transforming peasants into collective farmers and eradicating peasant culture, collectivization represented what James C. Scott has called the "imperialism of high-modernist, planned social order," so characteristic of the twentieth century. At the same time, dekulakization was an early model of the murderous, excisionary population politics aimed against supposed enemy or alien segments of the population so characteristic of the worst of the excesses of twentieth-century European dictatorships. Yet, while collectivization and dekulakization can be seen as sharing features in common with the most repressive aspects of twentieth-century European modernity, it is also important to recognize that the overwhelmingly agrarian nature of the early Soviet Union, its vast geography, and its underdeveloped provincial governmental structures set it apart from Western European polities. The result was a unique Soviet modernity characterized by modernist intentions carried out in the context of rather unmodern conditions and by a state that relied on repression as a substitute for rule by routine administrative and legal institutions.

*See also* **Five-Year Plan; New Economic Policy (NEP); Purges; Soviet Union; Stalin, Joseph.**

BIBLIOGRAPHY

Davies, R. W. *The Socialist Offensive: The Collectivisation of Soviet Agriculture, 1929–1930.* Vol. 1 of *The Industrialization of Soviet Russia.* Cambridge, Mass., 1980. Authoritative and thorough study of the collectivization campaign.

Davies, R. W., and Stephen G. Wheatcroft, eds. *The Years of Hunger: Soviet Agriculture, 1931–1933.* Vol. 5 of *The Industrialization of Soviet Russia.* New York, 2003. Treatment of the famine, making use of newly declassified archival documents.

Fitzpatrick, Sheila. *Stalin's Peasants: Resistance and Survival in the Russian Village after Collectivization.* New York, 1994. A survey of the collectivized village.

Lewin, M. *Russian Peasants and Soviet Power: A Study of Collectivization.* Translated by Irene Nove. Evanston, Ill., 1968. Reprint, New York, 1975. Classic study of the peasantry and the state in the years leading to collectivization.

Millar, James R., and Alec Nove. "A Debate on Collectivization: Was Stalin Really Necessary?" *Problems of Communism* 25, no. 4 (1976): 49–62. An introduction to the debate on collectivization's contribution to industrialization.

Scott, James C. *Seeing Like a State: How Certain Schemes to Improve the Human Condition Have Failed.* New Haven, Conn., 1998. A pioneering study of the modern state's attempts to transform society in conditions of what Scott calls "high modernism."

Shanin, Teodor. *The Awkward Class: Political Sociology of Peasantry in a Developing Society; Russia, 1910–1925.* Oxford, U.K., 1972. Classic study and critique of sociology of the Russian village.

Viola, Lynne. *Peasant Rebels under Stalin: Collectivization and the Culture of Peasant Resistance.* New York, 1996. Outline and analysis of peasant resistance during collectivization, making use of newly declassified archival documentation.

Ward, Chris. *Stalin's Russia.* 2nd ed. London, 1999. Includes an excellent discussion of the historiography on collectivization.

LYNNE VIOLA

# COLLINGWOOD, R. G. (1889–1943), English philosopher, archaeologist, and historian.

Born in the English Lake District, Robin George Collingwood was until the age of thirteen educated by his parents. His father was a scholar, archaeologist, and artist and his mother was an artist as well. Collingwood's early education laid the foundation for his later career. After attending Rugby School, he studied classics at University College in Oxford. From 1912 until 1935 he was tutor of philosophy at Pembroke College, and from 1927 until 1935 university lecturer in philosophy and Roman history. In 1935 he was appointed Waynflete Professor of Metaphysical Philosophy at Magdalen College. He had to resign this position in 1941 because of ill health and died in 1943 at Coniston.

Collingwood's scholarly reputation is as curious as it is unique, in that in his own lifetime he was primarily esteemed as an archaeologist and main expert on Roman Britain, whereas after his death he is especially known as a philosopher. His most important contribution to archaeology was a complete edition of the Roman inscriptions of Britain, on which he worked for many years, posthumously edited by R. P. Wright and published as *Inscriptions on Stone* (1965), volume 1 of *The Roman Inscriptions of Britain*. But he also wrote *The Archaeology of Roman Britain* (1930), the first handbook in the field. On the history of Roman Britain he wrote *Roman Britain* (1923; rev. eds. 1932 and 1934) and, with J. N. L. Myres, *Roman Britain and the English Settlements* (1936).

Collingwood's reputation as a philosopher started after World War II with the posthumous publication of *The Idea of History* (1946; rev. ed. 1993), edited by his pupil T. M. Knox. This book, a collection of lectures, essays, and part of an unfinished book, has attracted the attention of both historians and philosophers and has had a lasting influence on discussions of the philosophy of history. The relevance of Collingwood's philosophy is much wider, however. The scope of the subjects he dealt with is unparalleled and includes, besides the philosophy of history, studies on the philosophy of religion, art, nature, politics, metaphysics, and philosophical method. Since 1978 more than four thousand pages of manuscripts have been deposited at the Bodleian Library in Oxford. They show new dimensions of the wide-ranging philosophical interests of Collingwood, including extensive lectures on ethics and studies on cosmology and anthropology. Parts of the manuscripts have meanwhile been published, both separately and as additions to revised editions of Collingwood's philosophical books.

A predominant theme in Collingwood's philosophy is the idea of the unity of mind in opposition to its progressive fragmentation. This subject is worked out in *Speculum Mentis* (1924), in which a distinction is made between four "forms of experience" (art, religion, science, history), with philosophy playing a specific role in their assessment and interrelation. Collingwood believed that mind should be studied on its own terms, which led him to disparage the pretensions of psychology. The study of mind should be aimed at self-knowledge, which can only be accomplished by the study of history and philosophy. In opposition to positivism, Collingwood championed dialectical thinking in dealing with these subjects, influenced by Hegel and more in particular by his Italian contemporaries Benedetto Croce, Giovanni Gentile, and Guido de Ruggiero.

Collingwood worked out some interesting philosophical theories. An antirealist in epistemology, he developed a "logic of question and answer," implying that knowledge is conceived as an interaction between a subject and his or her "reality." In *An Essay on Philosophical Method* (1933; rev. ed. 2005), he expounded a theory on the nature of philosophical concepts, explaining that, in contrast with scientific concepts, they exhibit a "scale of forms" in which their generic essence is realized in varying degrees. Of special interest is his theory of "absolute presuppositions," as worked out in *An Essay on Metaphysics* (1940; rev. ed. 1998). The nature of these presuppositions is conceived as the bedrock of all "relative" presuppositions. They are unverifiable and operate as the mostly unconscious frameworks of one's thoughts and actions. Collingwood's lasting involvement with art culminated in *The Principles of Art* (1938), in which an expressionist theory of "art proper" is developed against instrumental modes of art as "craft." In his final book, *The New Leviathan* (1942; rev. ed. 1992), he deals with the concept of civilization. Collingwood considered it his "war effort" and as a defense against the barbarism of fascism and Nazism.

Though initially underestimated as a philosopher, Collingwood's contributions to philosophy are increasingly acknowledged as of great significance. The growing interest in his philosophy is enhanced by the remarkable correspondence of some of his views with certain well-known philosophical theories. Collingwood's theory of absolute presuppositions, for instance, can be seen as an anticipation of Thomas Kuhn's theory of paradigms (though Collingwood's theory is of a wider scope), and there is a noticeable similarity between Collingwood's views and those of Ludwig Wittgenstein on mind and language.

*See also* **Croce, Benedetto; Wittgenstein, Ludwig.**

BIBLIOGRAPHY

Boucher, David. *The Social and Political Thought of R. G. Collingwood.* Cambridge, U.K., 1989.

Donagan, Alan. *The Later Philosophy of R. G. Collingwood.* Oxford, U.K., 1962.

Dray, William H. *History as Re-enactment: R. G. Collingwood's Idea of History.* Oxford, U.K., 1995.

Dussen, W. J. van der. *History as a Science: The Philosophy of R. G. Collingwood.* The Hague, Netherlands, 1981.

Johnston, William M. *The Formative Years of R. G. Collingwood.* The Hague, Netherlands, 1967.

Mink, Louis O. *Mind, History, and Dialectic: The Philosophy of R. G. Collingwood.* Bloomington, Ind., 1969.

Rubinoff, Lionel. *Collingwood and the Reform of Metaphysics: A Study in the Philosophy of Mind.* Toronto, 1970.

W. J. VAN DER DUSSEN

---

**COLONIALISM.** The term *colonialism* encompasses all of the diverse efforts by which colonizers seek to maintain their rule over colonized territory and to benefit from this exercise of power. Colonialism entails the reduction or elimination of autonomy for colonized people and the concomitant extension of control by the colonizers. These developments, almost by definition, take place in terms of political independence. In the narrowest possible sense, this means that one state (called the metropole) legally defines a territory it has taken over as a colony, claims sovereignty over it, and administers it. However, events since 1914—the beginning of World War I—demand that the term include diverse policies and practices by which the government of one state exercises its sovereignty to impose limitations on the actions of the elites and inhabitants of another territory. Alongside explicitly political questions of self-rule, the ways in which modern Europeans, in particular, pursued colonialism require that the concept include not just political domination but also the domination of economics, education, culture, and language. What distinguished modern colonialism from the empires or forms of domination exercised in other times and by other cultures, to quote the historian David Abernethy, was "the persistent effort of Europeans to undermine and reshape the modes of production, social institutions, cultural patterns, and value systems of indigenous peoples" (p. 10). Closely related to that was the role that sharp and institutionalized distinctions between colonized and colonizers played in European overseas colonialism.

**THE COLONY AND THE METROPOLE**
Whether it is judged by the narrowest or the broadest definition, twentieth-century colonialism was inextricably linked to the existence, expansion, and then almost total disappearance of the overseas empires that a number of European states acquired as part of the "new imperialism." The late nineteenth century saw the reinvigoration of assertions by political leaders and pundits throughout Europe that their state should seek to control and govern other areas of the globe. This process of building or expanding an empire is called imperialism. By 1914 the United Kingdom, France, the Netherlands, Germany, Belgium, Italy, and Portugal—along with the non-European latecomers the United States of America and Japan—together had divided up and were ruling almost all of Africa and South, Southeast, and East Asia, along with most of Oceania. In addition to territories that they had conquered under the ideological promptings of the new imperialism, Britain, France, the Netherlands, Spain, and Portugal also continued to control and govern previously conquered overseas territories. The most notable were areas where large-scale European settlement had taken place, such as Canada, Australia, New Zealand, and

**Edward, Prince of Wales, with the Begum of Bhopal during his visit to India, 1922.** In what they called an "indirect" form of administration, the British relied on the cooperation of local leaders to control their colonies in India. ©HULTON-DEUTSCH COLLECTION/CORBIS

South Africa (the so-called white dominions of the British Empire), French Algeria, the Dutch East Indies (in present-day Indonesia), and Portuguese holdings on the African coast.

The growth, maintenance, and eventual decline of these modern empires not only shaped the world outside of Europe, the practices and certainties of colonial rule also helped form the institutions that connected modern European states to their own people, including nationality, citizenship, parliamentary rule, and popular sovereignty. As the twentieth century opened, all Europeans struggled to navigate the conflicts that the institutionalization of liberal ideas such as individual rights, rational debate, the will of the people, representative government, and universalism provoked. In the overseas colonies, governments that at home embraced liberal principles (to varying degrees) ruled over people who had little access to citizenship or its attendant rights. The existence of large empires offered various ways to defuse such tensions (above all through nationalist mobilization at home), terrains from which resources to support metropolitan ambitions could be drawn (whether Indochinese rubber, Congolese precious metals, or colonial conscripts and recruits), and laboratories where solutions to metropolitan problems could be tried out (in areas ranging from urban design in French-ruled Morocco to legal reform and crowd control in British India).

Beginning at the end of World War I and accelerating after World War II, the resistance of colonized peoples to their limited options and lack of autonomy received international attention. Their struggles both suggested that Europeans had betrayed their ideals in the pursuit of empire and, more radically, that the practice of empire revealed many of the contradictions inherent in European modernity.

## JUSTIFICATIONS FOR COLONIALISM

As the twentieth century opened, colonialism continued to enjoy a largely positive reputation among European statesmen and among most of the writers who paid attention to it. Discussions centered less on exploiting the economic and military potential that empire offered than they had in previous decades. The concept of careful and respectful colonialism now overshadowed that of openly ambitious and rapacious imperialism. Most arguments for maintaining European control in overseas territories asserted that it was good for all involved and that it both offered proof of and contributed to the dynamism, vision, and strength of the colonizing society. They pointed to economic and strategic concerns and claimed that colonialism increased patriotic unity and moral regeneration at home.

For the British, whose control of some one-fourth of the world's habitable territory dwarfed that of its competitors, the empire often appeared as a structure that, if the right men ran it according to proper rules, could reinforce traditional hierarchies at home. Most of the men whom the Colonial and India Offices recruited to run imperial affairs were members of the aristocratic and Oxford- and Cambridge-trained elites; their practice of colonial governance helped ensconce powers and privileges that the extension of capitalism, popular democracy, and mass culture were undermining within the British Isles. Despite the intense struggles within Britain for female suffrage, for example, women were barred from virtually all posts in the India Office.

The colonizers' "civilizing mission" provided the most popular moral explanation for colonial rule. Some advocates couched their arguments in terms of obligations—what the British writer Rudyard Kipling identified as the "white man's burden" to assist the darker, and supposedly lesser, peoples of the world. Others, such as French defenders of the *mission civilisatrice,* insisted that their nation, thanks to its universalist values, was willing and able to reshape and improve other peoples and societies by making the colonized more like their colonizers. Colonialists were certain that Europeans alone could bring the building blocks of progress to the backward people whom they, through conquest, had made their wards. At the most basic level, colonialists pointed to the benefits of modern technology and European-imposed order—what a British medical official in Kenya called "the railroad and the hall of justice."

The pursuit of truth, and particularly of scientific knowledge, offered another justification of colonial rule. Its proponents spoke in terms of the interest of all humanity. European governments and businesses, eager to exploit the economic potential and consolidate political control of their overseas possessions, supported scholars and scientists whose work facilitated these endeavors. In this way, colonialism directly shaped the questions that ground modern Western universities, while, fortuitously, the universities in return lent it scientific authority. Studying the colonized world catalyzed the formation of new disciplines such as anthropology and revitalized others, including orientalism and geography. The flourishing field of imperial history, as the British historian Dane Kennedy notes, although often rigorous in its research methods, had as its main purpose "to contribute historical insights into past exercises in overseas power that could be used to inform and inspire contemporaries to shoulder their obligations as rulers of a world-imperial system" (p. 345).

Through analogies drawn from the natural sciences, European scholars created a systematized depiction of the world that explained why those countries that ruled were, in virtually every domain, superior to those whom they ruled. For example, beginning in the mid-nineteenth century, both social Darwinism and a pseudoscientific form of racism proposed and espoused the recognition of hierarchies among racially distinguished populations, hierarchies that they claimed were anchored in nature and demonstrable by science. Most other social models inspired by scientific methods also offered strong support for European colonialism.

## PRACTICES OF RULE: DEFINING TERRITORY

The ways in which twentieth-century metropoles ruled their colonial holdings varied within empires as well as between them. A key concern was how to define the land in question. The diversity of colonial legal frameworks can be explained less by the exigencies of rationality or efficiency than by the metropolitan powers' efforts to convince their own citizens that colonial suzerainty was natural and necessary. Other noteworthy factors included the need to convince colonial subjects of the same and tensions between different government bureaucracies over who had the authority to exercise colonial control. Existing legal frameworks ranged from annexation to diverse forms of protectorate status. France proclaimed the area around the North African port city of Algiers, which it had seized from the Ottoman Empire in 1830, to be an extension of France, and after 1848 French governments managed Algeria through domestic ministries. However, the French designated other holdings as colonies, including Cochin China, the Indochinese provinces that the Second Empire conquered in 1862 as part of Emperor Napoleon III's efforts to re-create Napoleonic glory. The British Empire defined many of its possessions as crown colonies, which gave the British government, through the Colonial Office, control over all areas of government. The French eventually governed most other parts of Indochina as protectorates, in which the colonizers had legally guaranteed privileges concerning, for example, religion and economics and controlled foreign affairs.

Protectorate status entailed leaving established local rulers in place, as France did with the sultan of Morocco after 1912; it also meant that the authority of the colonial power, although usually great, did not include actual sovereignty. The British used the protectorate model both in areas long under their control, such as Biafra (in present day Nigeria), and in more recent colonial possessions, such as Zanzibar (off the coast of southeast Africa). With the transfer by the British Foreign Office of authority over Zanzibar to the Colonial Office in 1913, its previous role in governing protectorates came to an end. Sudan, the only territory where the Foreign Office still governed after 1913, was called a condominium, meaning that the British shared sovereignty with Egypt, which itself was under British domination after 1882, and became a protectorate in 1914.

Well into the twentieth century, British privileges in some protectorates continued to be managed by royal chartered companies, such as the British South Africa Company, which officially governed Southern Rhodesia until 1922, when it became a colony. Chartered companies were given the right to exploit any sources of profit they could find and in return were expected to exercise effective administrative control over the territory. Through this mechanism, metropolitan officials sought to avoid having to spend money while still holding onto ultimate control. By the early twentieth century, the failure of these efforts had become apparent: in order to squeeze out profits, the companies had proved willing to engage in the violent brutalization of local populations, which metropolitan public opinions were no longer ready to support.

A final type of colonial domination arose after World War I, when the new League of Nations established a system of mandates, which assigned sovereignty over territories formerly ruled by Germany and the Ottoman Empire to states in the victorious alliance. For example, Belgium took over governance of the former German colony Rwanda-Burundi, and Britain became the mandatory power for the former Ottoman province of Palestine. Unlike protectorates, where the colonizing power simply assumed control of another polity's sovereignty, the mandate system assigned the mandatory power formal responsibility for the subjects or citizens of its mandate but assigned ultimate responsibility over the territory to the League of Nations. In practice, however, the mandatory powers treated their mandates as they did their other colonies.

## DIRECT VERSUS INDIRECT RULE

However the colonizers defined the lands in question, the two most important models under which European states claimed to govern their colonial possessions were direct and indirect rule. Under the direct model, officials in the metropole

The 18th Senegalese Regiment of the French Colonial Infantry shown in formation at the Oasis of Gabes, Tunisia, preparing to confront invading Italian forces, 1938. ©BETTMANN/CORBIS

determined the approaches and rules used to govern the colonies and colonial officers worked to displace traditional local authorities. Direct rule was most often associated with the French Empire, but in the early twentieth century it was also proclaimed by the Netherlands in the Dutch East Indies; Belgium after it transformed the Congo Free State into the Belgian Congo in 1908; Germany until it lost its colonies after 1918; and Portugal, which defined its African colonies as overseas provinces. Germany and Portugal both used direct rule in hopes of transforming their southern African colonies through settlement. In Portuguese Angola and Mozambique, white settlers had almost feudal powers over the administration of justice, administrative and police powers, and taxation. France, however, claimed to embrace direct rule in order to transform inhabitants in its new colonies either into French people or into people who would be like the French. In protectorates, such as Laos or Tonkin (in Indochina), France left in place some traditional authorities as

figureheads but filled all administrative jobs with French functionaries. In the Belgian Congo, under the guise of a deeply paternalistic policy of direct rule, a combination of Belgian government officials, the Catholic Church, and Belgian private companies established the most extensive colonial administration in sub-Saharan Africa.

British leaders proclaimed that the principle of indirect rule underwrote their relationship with the inhabitants of their empire. Distinct but overlapping administrations—the Colonial Office, the India Office, and the Foreign Office—oversaw such policies in specific territories around the world, and each had its attendant corps of civil servants. To manage the empire's "crown jewel," India, the British had established a viceroy, called the raj, with an associated India Office and India Service, which governed India, Ceylon, and Burma, and later much of the Persian Gulf and Indian Ocean territories. Britain directly administered substantial parts of the Indian subcontinent while leaving roughly one-third of the territory under the control of some five hundred princely states. Relying on what imperialist scholars identified as "traditional" social structures, indirect rule both made local leaders into crucial elements of imperial government and placed groups of the local population into rigidly defined and distinct groups. As in the United Kingdom, the British imposed a strict hierarchy among people in India. In South Asia, this meant taking an existing but spottily and unevenly applied form of social organization, the caste system, and strengthening and generalizing its workings. An official warrant of precedence assigned dozens of strictly hierarchized ranks to everyone in the Raj, British or "native." At the top of this hierarchy, the British monarch held the title of emperor (or empress) of India. In this way, the British proclaimed that their rule was the legitimate continuation of the Mughal Empire, which they had conquered and ousted. The belief that they were strengthening traditional forms affirmed legitimacy among the colonized and reassured the British elites that respect for status played a crucial role in the superiority of Britain over other countries.

The varied models under which colonizing powers claimed to govern did not reflect significant differences in how the colonized experienced their colonization, or in the extent to which colonial officials interfered in the affairs of local peoples. Both had far more to do with the colonial power's interest in a given area, with how many Europeans were there, and with who those Europeans were. Administrative and academic efforts to define both the policies used and the people ruled in colonial possessions had as much, if not more, to do with the debates and developments within Europe than with actual practice or existing reality in the colonies. The idea that there was a stark opposition between direct and indirect forms of colonial rule resulted, above all, from competition between European states as each sought to identify the strengths and weaknesses of its colonial system, and thus its version of European modernity, by comparing them to others.

## PRACTICES OF RULE: CONTROLLING PEOPLE

The European conquest of power had been relatively easy, especially during the massive late-nineteenth-century expansion into Africa, since machine guns, telegraph lines, other forms of technology, and a disregard for African lives allowed European armies and their local allies to kill or devastate everyone who stood in their way. In most new colonies, however, very few Europeans actually remained in place to maintain control, and so the colonizers relied on local collaborators to exercise sovereignty. Divide-and-rule policies proved a particularly efficient way to maintain colonial dominance. At a basic level, the boundaries that European countries agreed upon between their colonies often both lumped mutually hostile groups together into one territory and split up communities who previously had enjoyed close connections. A dramatic example of the latter phenomenon took place in the Horn of Africa, where the Somali people found themselves divided among British, Italian, French, and Ethiopian control.

The Belgian claim that two elements of the social structure of Rwanda-Burundi were distinct "ethnic groups," Tutsis and Hutus, highlights a slightly more subtle form of divide and rule. The Belgians celebrated the Tutsis as natural rulers, just as French republicans in Morocco and Algeria considered the Berbers more democratic, more egalitarian, and less imbued with Islamic religiosity than the Arabs. In each case, the colonizers took popularly recognized traits and created a stereotype that would legitimize stark differences in treatment, privileges, and possibilities between groups. Members of privileged groups who decided to participate had special access to the benefits that colonial administrations offered, including education, entry into the administration or armed forces, and economic opportunities.

Peoples who, on the contrary, sought to resist colonial rule, or even just unfair decisions, suffered directly and brutally. In German Southwest Africa (Namibia), the 1904 revolt by the Herero people against the favoritism shown to colonial settlers was met by massive violence, in which some two-thirds of the population died, the state seized all Herero lands, and the surviving Herero were banned from owning livestock. The British, as they sought to impose their League of Nations mandate in Iraq, responded to violent resistance by first Arabs and then Kurds with history's first large-scale use of aerial bombing in 1920–1921.

The number of victims, and in particular the number of civilians killed and mutilated, led even British officials who wholeheartedly supported the takeover of Iraq (for example, Gertrude Bell) to protest the tactics' inhumanity. Even nonviolent protest could inspire harsh retribution, as it did, for example, when British troops killed 379 of Gandhi's followers who had dared to demonstrate for home rule in Amritsar, India, in 1919. Such tactics gave support to complaints that colonialism, by turning nonwhites into lesser forms of humanity, did not bring civilization but undermined it.

## WORLD WAR I AND MODERN COLONIALISM

World War I brought to bear on Europeans the troops, the tools (such as machine guns), and the tactics (in particular the targeting of civilian populations) that had contributed so much to European colonial expansion. Even more dramatically, the competition between different European economic and political systems, which had often been invoked to explain the necessity for imperialism abroad to European publics, was now used to explain the need for total victory at any cost. Types of devastation and violence that had occurred in the colonial world on a smaller scale, and that remained largely out of the metropolitan public eye, were applied to and decimated Europeans. Oddly, one of the war's effects was to reinvigorate colonialism. Most obviously, the Versailles Treaty brought the Arab lands of the now defunct Ottoman Empire under the control of France and Great Britain, expanding European colonial practices into the Near and Middle East and turning Germany's overseas empire in Africa and Oceania over to the control of the victorious alliance's members. Also important was the use the victors made of their overseas empires during the fighting, in particular the participation in combat of colonial troops from Britain's "white dominions" and from French West and North Africa.

Their colonial subjects' role in the war reaffirmed for European politicians the importance of their empires, but the conflict also catalyzed resistance to colonialism. Both colonized elites and hundreds of thousands of soldiers from the colonies witnessed the disconnect between colonialist propaganda about European civilization and the war's savagery. Germany's defeat and Britain and France's near-defeat gave encouragement to their critics in the colonies. More directly, the minimal recompense that French and British politicians offered for the blood debt of colonial troops vitiated any hope in the colonies for an extension of British liberty in India, or assimilation as equal members into the French Republic. These three understandings played key roles in catalyzing subsequent criticism of colonial rule.

At the same time, by leading to the disappearance of the Russian, Ottoman, and Austro-Hungarian empires, World War I seemed to sound the death knell for land-based empires and affirmed the triumph of the nation-state model of governance. U. S. president Woodrow Wilson's 1917 and 1918 proclamations of peoples' right to self-determination helped guarantee that one of the most durable effects of modern colonialism would be the extension of the nation-state model of government throughout the lands that Europeans had colonized. National independence became the rallying cry of anticolonial militants across the globe.

Other goals and ideals also mobilized critics of colonial rule, although nationalism eventually overshadowed them. Christianity, Islam, pan-Africanism, and trade unionism, among others, catalyzed various groups to protest imperial abuses or to reject colonial rule altogether. In 1919, for example, African American activists and intellectuals brought together a Pan-African Congress in Paris. In Africa, and notably in South Africa and Kenya, labor movements played increasingly crucial roles in nurturing anticolonial thinking. The organizational model and the message of the Bolshevik revolution (1917) also offered inspiration. More concretely, the Third International, or Comintern (founded in 1919), provided guidance, training, and connections, which allowed communists to invigorate, take over, or lead many anticolonial movements, particularly in Asia. Until the mid-1930s, communist activists within Europe also worked aggressively to advance critiques of overseas colonialism.

## THE INTERWAR PERIOD (1918–1939)

In the 1920s and 1930s, as Britain and France continued to expand their empires, they also sought to consolidate them. In the 1920s they did this by privileging arguments about the beneficial effects of colonial rule on the colonized. These arguments took on new importance when the Great Depression, which hit colonized territories exceptionally hard, made it clear that, despite claims that European rule uplifted backward native societies, colonialism had done little to modernize the colonial economies.

The British embrace of the concept of developmentalism sought to counter evidence that colonial rule was impeding both economic and political progress. The French proclaimed that their efforts aimed to "realize the potential" (*mise en valeur*) of their overseas possessions, not just economically, but through the establishment of new infrastructures, such as schools, transportation networks, and hospitals, and by bringing enlightenment through education. The British had extended substantial autonomy to the settler-controlled governments of their "white dominions" and, under pressure from anticolonial nationalists, now moved to extend limited versions of autonomy to India and elsewhere. By the 1930s, the end of colonialism was the acknowledged goal of both the British and the French empires, the former imagining a distant future when Britain would husband the independence of all of its colonies, the latter evoking an equally distant future when all its subjects would become citizens of Greater France. To these ends, in all the French and British colonies of sub-Saharan Africa, forced labor continued to be used in order to pursue the "development" (or *mise en valeur*) of the colonial societies.

In the early 1930s, in the midst of international economic catastrophe, metropolitan discussions of colonialism celebrated the benefits it provided for everyone involved. This was spread through many films and novels and by political decisions such as the publicity campaigns trumpeting the new British Commonwealth or "one hundred million Frenchmen," and the costly promotion of Colonial Expositions in London (1924) and Paris (1931). The latter both gloried in the rainbow of peoples within Greater France, from the reproduction of Angkor Wat to the "African" village complete with villagers, and depicted the empire as a harmonious society that saved its subjects from violence and brought them into progress.

The rise of fascist powers in Europe partly explains the urgency with which the French and British embraced their empires in the 1930s. In the same context, European Communist Parties dropped their commitment to ending colonialism immediately in favor of antifascist mobilization to defend democracy and the Soviet Union. Across the world, Japan's conquest of Manchuria in 1931 began a stunning series of colonialist expansions by what would become members of the fascist Axis: Japan conquered most of China after 1937; Italy conquered Ethiopia in 1935 and 1936; Germany conquered central, western, and then eastern Europe after 1939; and Japan expanded into Oceania and Southeast Asia after December 1941. These years marked the farthest extension of colonial rule in modern times. Fascist ideological explanations for their expansion, which combined depictions of each state's colonial designs as preordained—the Nazi Lebensraum; the Italian Fascist Mare Nostrum; the Japanese Greater East Asia Co-Prosperity Sphere—and highly elaborate definitions of racial hierarchies, affirming the racial superiority of the colonizer, pushed to their extremes preexisting justifications for European colonialism.

## RACE AND TWENTIETH-CENTURY COLONIALISM

In the twentieth century, arguments for continued European domination constantly referred to supposedly scientific racial categories. Race also became the most important marker of difference between people within the colonial world. Even critics of colonialism participated in affirming racial difference. One of the best known depictions of the horror associated with European overseas rule is Joseph Conrad's *Heart of Darkness* (1902), based in part on the author's experiences on the Congo River in 1890. Conrad's novella undeniably sought to reveal the evil inherent in colonial rule. As the Nobel Prize–winning Nigerian novelist Chinua Achebe pointed out in 1977, however, it was also typical of the wildly popular genre of colonial travel narratives and follows the genre's convention of presenting the colonial world as a space where the white protagonist could come to terms with greater truths. Conrad's narrative depends on his readers' identification with Marlow, the narrator, whose struggles and moral enlightenment occur against a

**Women are taught to use irons at a school in Leopoldville, Belgian Congo, c. 1957.**
Bringing the benefits of Western civilization to non-Western peoples was one rationale offered
for colonialism in the twentieth century. ©Hulton-Deutsch Collection/Corbis

background provided by dehumanized black bodies—often just black limbs glimpsed at the edge of the river. Although explicitly critical of colonial practices, *The Heart of Darkness* inevitably celebrated the new possibilities for growth and reflection that colonialism offered to the colonizers and wholly dismissed any possibility that the colonized Africans could be historical actors.

Other forms of difference, such as status, continued to matter intensely in the colonies, and in the metropoles race was often less important in shaping popular thought and legal categorization than class or gender. After 1900, however, all empires witnessed the growing importance of racial thinking. One immediate and self-reinforcing result was that the number of interactions across the legal categories dividing colonizers from colonized declined. Sexuality was one of the most important areas where the need for separation could be staked out, a situation the English writer E. M. Forster captured well in his 1930s novel

*A Passage to India,* with its miscommunications, its sexual tensions, its obscure caves, and its hint of rape. In societies such as the Dutch East Indies, official and elite acceptance of marriages and sexual relationships across racial lines receded. Forms of white solidarity also increased as connections and shared concerns among Europeans in diverse colonies increasingly overcame divisions of class, status, gender, or ethnicity. In British settler colonies, such as Kenya and Rhodesia, as well as in India, fears, often overwrought, about the potential for anti-colonial violence—with sexual attacks against white women the primary fantasy—led British authorities to distribute guns to white men and women and to organize basic training in armed self-defense.

The interwar period saw the role of race and European-ness consolidated by both the increasing certainties of racist political movements within Europe and the growth of nationalist movements that rejected the domination of Europeans in the colonies. By working to overcome ethnic and language differences among citizens of the same European state and emphasizing a struggle for survival between nations, imperialism had in part created the possibility for European nationalist ideologies to become attached to racial communities. The flourishing of British identity is the best known example: In the metropole, nationalist propaganda fomented popular support by presenting imperial rule as a natural trait of all British—rather than English—people, at the same time that Scottish, Welsh, and Irish people played a disproportionate role in the overseas military, economic, and settlement activities that formed the second British Empire. As they emerged to dominate political life within Europe, fascist and right-wing nationalist organizations gained in popularity among Europeans overseas. In Java, the Dutch colonial community, long mocked by racists because racially mixed children and marriages were widespread at all economic levels, saw the growth of Fatherlands Clubs and of membership in the National Socialist Union. In French Algeria, anti-Semitic bile targeting indigenous Jews, who had gained full French citizenship in 1870, offered fertile grounds for racist nationalist groups born in the metropole and provided arguments that blocked reform projects, such as the Blum-Violette Bill of 1936, aimed at giving French citizenship to more Muslims.

## THE POST-1945 FAILURE OF DERACIALIZED COLONIALISM

In the years after World War II, official European colonialism sought to distance itself from any reliance on racism. To leaders in Britain and France, their empires were crucial to claiming an important role on a world stage, which increasingly appeared to have room for only two principals: the United States of America and the Soviet Union. Although most British and Dutch colonies across Asia almost immediately gained independence (1947–1949), the French in Indochina and all colonial powers in Africa sought to hold on to their possessions. The British and especially the French aggressively sought to introduce limited forms of democracy and provide social welfare possibilities as the anchors for a new, deracialized colonialism. The French in sub-Saharan Africa extended full social rights to people who all were now citizens of the new French Union. This meant that African labor

unions were able to obtain minimum wage rates and family allowances for their members at the same levels as metropolitans.

Such reforms did not quell demands for the end of colonialism, however, but neither the French nor the British gave up easily and the chilling number of colonized people who died as a result highlights the continued importance of racist presumptions. In the best known exercise of brute force, the French killed at least 250,000 Muslim Algerians in failed efforts to crush the Algerian Revolution (1954–1962). Early-twenty-first-century work suggests that British repression against the Kikuyus in Kenya, pursued under the guise of defending British civilians against Mau Mau depredations (thirty-two white settlers died), led to tens of thousands of Kikuyu deaths. But by 1963, with Kenya's independence, some forty-two former colonies had entered the United Nations.

In contrast, the Portuguese continued to embrace racist explanations, and to hold Angola, Mozambique, and Guinea-Bissau until 1974, and white minority regimes maintained and strengthened colonial-era racial policies in Rhodesia until it became Zimbabwe in 1979 and in South Africa, which the African National Congress finally freed from apartheid in 1991. With the British departure from Hong Kong in 1997, all of the most significant European colonies had been decolonized.

## THE COLD WAR AND COLONIALISM

The Cold War put an end to twentieth-century colonialism, in part by creating a new context and in part by redefining what colonialism meant. In order to affirm its anticolonial bona fides and pursue its international aims, the United States intervened to force its British and French allies (along with the Israelis) to end their 1956 takeover of the Suez Canal and to convince the French to sign a treaty with Ho Chi Minh's North Vietnam in 1954. The Soviets, particularly under Nikita Khrushchev, moved to embrace Third World struggles and numerous postcolonial regimes in order to consolidate their own revolutionary claim to be on the side of the oppressed. It was also the Cold War that narrowed the general understanding of colonialism, focusing on formal independence, as the Americans and Soviets both sought to claim victory with each transfer of power in the former colonies.

Left-wing analysts subsequently argued that the continued influence of the former colonial powers amounted to neocolonialism. Examples of this included the presence of large numbers of troops in former colonies, French control of the currency of most in its former African colonies, as well as the economic and military activities of the United States in Latin America and Indochina. Liberal and right-wing politicians and writers targeted Soviet domination of Eastern Europe, which the 1956 invasion of Hungary consolidated as an empire in the same months as the Suez Crisis erupted. It was not until the Cold War ended that the latter claim, at least in institutional terms, was widely accepted. Indeed, as the post–Cold War world continues to develop, we may see a redefinition of colonialism. Already, scholarly work on Russian expansion in the nineteenth century emphasizes the need to think more rigorously about whether there was something distinct about overseas imperialism. As some scholars take up the tasks of the earlier imperialist historians—providing material to support, for example, the extension of American control over Afghanistan in 2001 or Iraq in 2003—while others interrogate the continued influence of colonialist thinking, new questions will certainly arise.

*See also* **Algeria; Algerian War; British Empire; British Empire, End of; Cold War; Communism; Fascism; French Empire; German Colonial Empire; League of Nations; Portuguese Empire; Russian Revolutions of 1917; Suez Crisis; Versailles, Treaty of; World War I; World War II.**

BIBLIOGRAPHY

Abernethy, David B. *The Dynamics of Global Dominance: European Overseas Empires, 1415–1980.* New Haven, Conn., 2000.

Adas, Michael. *Machines as the Measure of Men: Science, Technology and Ideologies of Western Dominance.* Ithaca, N.Y., 1989.

Arendt, Hannah. *The Origins of Totalitarianism.* Vol. 2: *Imperialism.* New ed. New York, 1973.

August, Thomas. *The Selling of Empire: British and French Imperialist Propaganda, 1890–1940.* Westport, Conn., 1985.

Betts, Raymond. *France and Decolonization, 1900–1960.* New York, 1991.

Blue, Gregory, Martin Bunton, and Ralph Crozier, eds. *Colonialism and the Modern World: Selected Studies.* Armonk, N.Y., 2002.

Burton, Antoinette, ed. *After the Imperial Turn: Thinking with and through the Nation.* Durham, N.C., 2003.

Chafer, Tony, and Amanda Sackur, eds. *Promoting the Colonial Idea: Propaganda and Visions of Empire in France.* New York, 2002.

Chatterjee, Partha. *The Nation and Its Fragments: Colonial and Postcolonial Histories.* Princeton, N.J., 1993.

Clancy-Smith, Julia, and Frances Gouda, eds. *Domesticating the Empire: Languages of Gender, Race, and Family Life in French and Dutch Colonialism.* Charlottesville, Va., 1998.

Conklin, Alice. *A Mission to Civilize: The Republican Idea of Empire in France and West Africa, 1895–1930.* Stanford, Calif., 1997.

Cooper, Frederick. *Colonialism in Question: Theory, Knowledge, History.* Berkeley, Calif., 2005.

Cooper, Frederick, and Ann Laura Stoler, eds. *Tensions of Empire: Colonial Cultures in a Bourgeois World.* Berkeley, Calif., 1997.

Kennedy, Dane. "Imperial History and Post-Colonial Theory." *Journal of Imperial and Commonwealth History* 24, no. 3 (1996): 345–363.

Lebovics, Herman. *True France: The Wars over Cultural Identity, 1900–1945.* Ithaca, N.Y., 1992.

MacKenzie, John M. *Propaganda and Empire: The Manipulation of British Popular Opinion, 1880–1960.* Manchester, U.K., 1984.

Osbourne, Michael A. *Nature, the Exotic, and the Science of French Colonialism.* Bloomington, Ind., 1994.

Sherman, Daniel J. "The Arts and Sciences of Colonialism." *French Historical Studies* 23, no. 4 (2000): 707–729.

Stoler, Ann Laura. *Carnal Knowledge and Imperial Power: Race and the Intimate in Colonial Rule.* Berkeley, Calif., 2002.

Wesseling, H. L. *Imperialism and Colonialism: Essays on the History of European Expansion.* Westport, Conn., 1997.

TODD SHEPARD

---

**COMITÉ NATIONAL DES ÉCRIVAINS.** The Comité National des Écrivains, or National Writers' Committee, was founded in June 1941 with the goal of bringing into the French Resistance writers from different political and religious tendencies. The 1943 poem "La rose et le réséda" by one of its founding members, Louis Aragon (1897–1982), represents the CNE, and the Resistance, as an ideal community uniting Stalinist and Gaullist writers, Catholics, Jews, Protestants, and atheists. The early members reflect this diversity: Louis Aragon, a former surrealist, was a member of the French Communist Party; Jean Paulhan (1884–1968) was director of publication at Gallimard; Jacques Decour (1910–1942) taught German and was a member of the French Communist Party; the Catholic writer François Mauriac (1885–1970) belonged to the Académie Française; Édith Thomas (1909–1970), a novelist, hosted the CNE meetings in her apartment during the Occupation; and Jean-Paul Sartre (1905–1980) joined in 1943, even though the Communists had always been suspicious of his enthusiasm for Martin Heidegger. By the end of 1943 the CNE had some two hundred members, united in their efforts to save the honor of French letters.

Along with creating a united front opposed to the Nazi occupation of France, the CNE also sought to regulate the professional conduct of writers during the war. The CNE favored clandestine publications, strongly discouraged writers from publishing in journals approved by the Nazi occupiers, and frowned on the literary abstention favored, for instance, by the poet René Char. The founding members of the CNE—Aragon, Paulhan, and Decour—created the clandestine journal *Les lettres françaises*. The first issue was slated for publication in February 1942, but the arrest and execution of Jacques Decour delayed publication until September of that year. From then on, *Les lettres françaises* appeared every month and published anonymous manifestos, poems, and literary articles by the intellectual Resistance in France, along with occasional texts from representatives of the French literary canon: Victor Hugo, from *Les châtiments* in particular; Guy de Maupassant, who had lived through and denounced another occupation; Alphonse de Lamartine; and Guillaume Apollinaire. The CNE also cooperated closely with the clandestine publishing house Les Éditions de Minuit. Founded in 1942, Minuit published dozens of literary texts during the war, including Mauriac's *Le cahier noir* (1943), the volume *L'honneur des poètes* (1943–1944), edited by Paul

Éluard, and Vercors's immensely popular *Le silence de la mer* (1943).

The main business of the CNE, however, was denouncing collaborationist writers. The very first issue of *Les lettres françaises* singles out for retribution the *Nouvelle revue française*, France's most prestigious prewar literary journal, directed during the occupation by Pierre Drieu la Rochelle. In November 1943 the CNE requested permission from the postwar Liberation authorities to create a council dedicated to examining and judging the conduct of writers during the Occupation. This request for judicial authority was never granted, but the CNE asserted its influence by creating blacklists of tainted writers. The first list was published in September 1944 and contained the names of writers whose punishment included execution for treason (Robert Brasillach), imprisonment (Charles Maurras), and a ban on publishing for several years (Jean Giono, Jacques Chardonne, and Paul Morand).

In September 1944, the CNE published a "Manifesto" in *Les lettres françaises* calling on French writers to "remain united in victory...and in the righteous punishment of the impostors and traitors." Although the manifesto was signed by some sixty writers, the ideal of a national unity that transcended political, religious, and generational divides was already beginning to disintegrate. Soon after the Liberation of Paris, François Mauriac denounced what he saw as the arbitrariness of the purge tribunals and of the CNE's blacklists. As Mauriac stated in his famous debate with Albert Camus, the CNE and the French nation were too quick to find scapegoats who could expiate the crimes of the community. Mauriac was expelled from the CNE in 1948. Jean Paulhan, who resigned from the CNE in 1946, went even further. For Paulhan, in 1945 the members of the CNE were engaged in nothing more than a seizure of power that perfectly mirrored that of the collaborationist intellectuals in 1940.

By the end of the war, *Les lettres françaises* was one of the most widely read intellectual journals in Europe, with a circulation of approximately 190,000. Benefiting from the prestige of its members, the CNE embarked on an ambitious campaign to promote French literature in France and abroad. But in the 1950s, the CNE's drift toward

Stalinism, the inflammation of old rivalries between writers, and the rise of competing publications such as *Les temps modernes* and *Critique* transformed the CNE from a clandestine republic of letters into one more instance of Cold War polarization in France.

*See also* **Aragon, Louis; France; Resistance; Sartre, Jean-Paul.**

BIBLIOGRAPHY

Conley, Verena. *Littérature, Politique et communisme: Lire "Les Lettres françaises" 1942–1972.* New York, 2004.

Judt, Tony. *Past Imperfect: French Intellectuals 1944–1956.* Berkeley, Calif., 1992.

Kaplan, Alice Yaeger. *The Collaborator: The Trial and Execution of Robert Brasillach.* Chicago, 2000.

Mauriac, François. *Le baillon dénoué, après quatre ans de silence.* Paris, 1945.

Novick, Peter. *The Resistance versus Vichy: The Purge of Collaborators in Liberated France.* New York, 1968.

Paulhan, Jean. *De la paille et du grain.* Paris, 1948.

———. *Lettre aux directeurs de la Résistance.* Paris, 1952.

Rousso, Henry. "L'épuration en France. Une histoire inachevée." *Vingtième Siècle* 33 (January–March 1992): 78–105.

Sapiro, Gisèle. *La guerre des écrivains: 1940–1953.* Paris, 1999.

Simonin, Anne. *Les Éditions de Minuit, 1942–1955: Le devoir d'insoumission.* Paris, 1994.

Verdès-Leroux, Jeannine. *Au service du Parti: Le parti communiste, les intellectuels et la culture (1944–1956).* Paris, 1983.

Watts, Philip. *Allegories of the Purge: How Literature Responded to the Postwar Trials of Writers and Intellectuals in France.* Stanford, Calif., 1998.

PHILIP WATTS

# COMMON AGRICULTURAL POLICY.

The Treaty of Rome (1957), the founding document of the European Economic Community (EEC), committed its signatories to establishing a Common Agricultural Policy (CAP) and set out a list of contradictory objectives for that policy. The motivations for this policy were politically strong. In 1959 agricultural workers formed 24 percent of the employed labor force in France, a similar proportion in the German Federal Republic, and 33 percent in Italy. Their electoral judgments counted, particularly in Germany and Italy, where they were closely tied to the Christian Democratic political parties. And agricultural exports were an import contribution to Dutch and Italian trade. Even so, the idea of enforcing a common trading and pricing policy on so great a number of small-scale farmers would probably not have become so important were it not that in every member state of the Community agriculture had already been receiving a wide range of state subsidies—for output, for new investment, for veterinary services, for fuel, for exports—as well as being favored by the tax system. During the throes of the Great Depression there had been little support for the idea of a free domestic market in agricultural products; in the food shortages of the aftermath of World War II, there was even less. Sales were regulated in some member-states of the EEC, notably Germany and the Netherlands, by producers' associations such as the Deutscher Bauernverband, or, in the Netherlands, the Stichting voor de Landbouw. Everywhere in the EEC, ministries of agriculture functioned rather like national agricultural corporations managing the sector with state largesse.

One notable aspect of the CAP, however, was that although the common market of the EEC was shaped with the intention of sweeping away barriers to trade within the Community, the effect of the CAP was to increase the extent of regulation and controls on traded agricultural produce within the market and to sustain high levels of protection on the same products against nonmember states. Since the CAP came into effect the standard of living of those still employed in the sector has greatly improved, fulfilling one of the CAP's intentions. For most of the agricultural produce that can be produced in Europe's climate, the EC/EU is more or less self-sufficient.

Financial support for agriculture has dominated the Community's budget. Expenditure on agriculture and fisheries amounted to 80.6 percent of the 1973 general budget. Agreement on budgetary reform in 1988 led to a steady decline in this share. In 1999 it was only 45.5 percent. There are, however, other items in the budget that provide some measure of support for agriculture. Until 1970 the budgetary contributions of the member-states were related through a system of "keys" to their Gross Domestic Output. Persistent demands by France that the Community be financed through its own resources (*ressources propres*) led to a fundamental change in 1970. The customs dues raised by the Common External Tariff were allocated to these "own resources." Levies on agricultural produce crossing internal frontiers, their purpose being to standardize prices within the Community, were also allocated to the Community's own budget. One percent of the Value Added Tax (VAT) collected in all the member-states was allocated in the same direction. Lastly, direct financial contributions from the member-states had to be made to bring the Community's own resources up to a maximum of 1.27 percent of the Community's GNP in 1999. That last step carried with it, of course, the implication that the European Community had some attributes of a nation.

## DEVELOPMENT

In many parts of the Community, agriculture is a small-scale activity. The number of separate enterprises under supranational management through common community rules made the task of managing almost impossible. One result was that the CAP took up such a large share of the funding that other policies were underfunded. Furthermore, national contributions to the common budget dominated political arguments between the member states, and often within them. One result of the CAP has been to preserve small farms throughout a half century of change in the organization of European industry and services—change that has been driven by trade liberalization and increasingly open markets. It would be difficult to argue that in the early stages of the EEC this was not politically and socially a wise choice. As subsidized enterprises tend to do, however, the system has partially outlived its usefulness.

The European Agricultural Guidance and Guarantee Fund (usually referred to by its French acronym FEOGA), although in 2006 only a minor cog in the subsidization machinery, was the major distributor of subsidies until the 1990s. Its expenditures supported farmers' incomes by subsidizing the prices of more than two-thirds of the EC's agricultural products through guaranteed prices and sales. This involved purchasing and storing produce that could not otherwise attract the fixed price and frequently selling it later to Eastern European countries or providing it as food aid to the third world. Some products continue to be directly subsidized, and many products remain protected by import regulations. Final EC prices are fixed annually by the national ministers of agriculture acting as an EC committee. Since ministries of agriculture have acted in all countries as supporters of farmers' pressure groups, the prices have been high. Excess production has been one result.

Like developed non–European Union (EU) countries that export agricultural produce, the European Union subsidizes agricultural exports. This practice has led to high-level trade disputes with the United States, Australia, and Argentina. It has led also to clamorous protest from those who believe exports from the poorest third-world countries should be encouraged by subsidies rather than made more difficult by subsidies to producers from rich European and American states. In 2006 export subsidies constitute a much smaller share in the CAP's subsidy expenditure than at any time in the CAP's history.

## CHANGE

Community subsidies for exports take the form of "restitutions," which are, in plainer English, refunds allowing exporters to close the gap between Community prices and the price at which they will have to sell in the unsubsidized world. In 1986 such restitutions absorbed about 40 percent of the FEOGA guarantee fund. In 2005 they amounted to less than 20 percent of the same fund and are due for further reduction. Protest over the extent and size of agricultural subsidies has been increasing within the European Union since 1984, when the first serious attempts were made to hold agricultural expenditure to a lower rate of increase than that of the union's overall budget. Efforts to reduce EU food surpluses have been slow and controversial because the financial consequences do not fall equally on the member states. In the 1990s some countries, particularly the United Kingdom, used EU subsidies to stop production on less fertile land. Restrictions on domestic milk production have been in operation since 1986. Similar procedures have been cautiously adopted for cereal farming, a sector which for the first twenty years of the CAP was notorious for its large share of export subsidies, which it obtained because of the influence of large-scale grain farmers in national farmer's organizations in France and the United Kingdom. Further financial restrictions came in 1988, when the rate of growth of annual agricultural expenditure was fixed at no more than three-quarters of the growth of total EC expenditure.

In the 1990 world trade talks, usually known as the Uruguay Round, the United States led a challenge to the European Union, calling for a 75 percent cut to its agricultural subsidies. The talks collapsed over this issue. The European Union's response fell far short of the United States' demand. It was not clear that the United States' own extensive agricultural subsidies were as low as the level it demanded from the European Union.

It is difficult to predict the extent to which the 1990s policy changes within the CAP will survive in the greatly enlarged European Union of the twenty-first century. Attempts to freeze farm spending between 2000 and 2006 were rejected by Germany, although the level of spending was increased only slightly and part of the increase was to help the new member states to adapt to the new, and for them unexpected, harsher regime. They had been expecting to benefit from the extensive and proliferating programs of agricultural subsidy. The special program of subsidization, the Special Assistance Programme for Agricultural and Rural Development (SAPARD), that they were offered, was directed toward increasing investment in farming methods, marketing techniques, conservation, village preservation, rural heritage projects, and other matters that seem of more immediate concern to farmers in western Europe. (The list does not include many of the easier pickings that had earlier been provided for western European farmers.)

The CAP should be understood as a lingering consequence of the Great Depression of the 1930s, which cemented agricultural protection firmly into place and stimulated increases in food output across Europe as a way of reducing imports. The complex interplay between national government policies and farmers' own bureaucracies has only since 1990 slowly adapted to fit the agricultural sector into a less regulated trade regime. The European Union's reactions have not been slower than those in other parts of the world, especially when the political complexity of its constitutional arrangements are taken into account. Indeed, it may well be that the most potent force for change has not been international pressure but internal dissent among the early EU members, where agricultural labor is now only a very small part of the total labor force and has far less political leverage with national governments.

The CAP's contribution to the construction of the European Community also has to be recognized. It presided over an unprecedented movement of labor out of the agricultural labor force and into other branches of the labor force. Between 1951 and 1959, at least 350,000 agricultural workers per year left the land and were absorbed into other jobs. Such a large change would not have been possible without a rapid growth in manufacturing. One consequence was a sharp improvement in labor productivity in the agricultural sector. The determination of governments in the 1930s to keep people on the land was swept away. In the more backward sectors of the European Union, labor productivity in agriculture improved the most spectacularly. In the German Federal Republic, it improved by 5.5 percent annually between 1949 and 1959, in France by 4.9 percent, and in Italy by 4.7 percent. United Nations estimates suggest that the improvement of total productivity in Europe was greatest in the northwest, where labor markets were tightest. In that region, about two-thirds of the investment in agriculture went to labor-saving machinery. The CAP made changes in total productivity throughout the German economy relatively easy, resolving one of the worst problems of the 1930s and in doing so making domestic politics far more peaceful. The same can be said about its political impact in France and Italy.

*See also* **Agriculture; European Coal and Steel Community (ECSC); European Union; Rome, Treaty of.**

BIBLIOGRAPHY

Hill, Brian E. *The Common Agricultural Policy: Past, Present, and Future.* London, 1984.

Milward, Alan S. *The European Rescue of the Nation-State.* 2nd ed. London, 2000.

Tracy, Michael. *Government and Agriculture in Western Europe, 1880–1988.* 3rd ed. New York, 1989.

ALAN S. MILWARD

# COMMONWEALTH.

The British Commonwealth is the world's oldest political association of states. Composed of independent and self-governing nations formerly belonging to the British Empire, membership in the Commonwealth is voluntary, requiring only adherence to basic standards of good internal governance. From its origins as an association of dominions within the empire, to its rapid expansion during decolonization in the 1960s, the Commonwealth has never lived up to the aspirations of its more ambitious supporters, but it survives because of the modest benefits associated with membership, and as a symbol of connections and ideals associated with the empire and with British parliamentary democracy.

## ORIGINS

In its modern usage, the term *Commonwealth* is best understood as referring to the family of nations originating in the British Empire. It was first used before the American Revolution to refer to Britain's colonies, and British statesmen in the nineteenth century occasionally employed the phrase to refer to colonies within the empire. By the early twentieth century, the word *colony* was found to be demeaning to the status of Australia, Canada, New Zealand, and the group of states that would shortly form the Union of South Africa. All four had achieved internal self-government and were approaching practical if not formal independence. In 1907 the Canadian prime minister, Wilfred Laurier (1841–1919), led these nations and Britain in discussions, which concluded that henceforward they would be known as the *Dominions*.

The Dominions, in turn, became the core of the Commonwealth. The originators of this concept—notably, the British author Lionel Curtis (1872–1955) and the South African statesman Jan Smuts (1870–1950)—hoped their reconfiguration of the empire would offer a solution to the dangerous predicament that Britain faced in the early twentieth century. By this time, Britain had passed the peak of its relative power, and was facing potent European rivals, especially Germany. If Britain was to keep pace with these powers, it was essential that the Dominions share the cost of equipping the Royal Navy. But as the Dominions were self-governing, and in many cases far away from most of Britain's rivals, they could not be forced or easily frightened into contributing. Furthermore, if they chose to do so, they would naturally expect to have a voice in the making of British policy.

The solution, in the view of Curtis, was imperial federation. He argued, ultimately correctly, that the empire faced a choice between union and disintegration. Few were so ambitious. But Curtis's logic was widely shared, and had been the basis of earlier proposals, such as the efforts of Joseph Chamberlain (1836–1914) after 1903 to promote the unity of the empire through tariff reform. Where Curtis and those of similar mind differed from Chamberlain was in their emphasis, exalted and even utopian, on the concept of self-government and how it could be squared with a sharing of imperial burdens through the Commonwealth. Put cynically, the Commonwealth would bring federation on the sly; put idealistically, it would remake the identities of the nations within the empire so they would cooperate willingly with each other.

World War I both proved the loyalty of the Dominions and empire to Britain and put new strains on their ties. Britain declared war on behalf of the Dominions and the Indian Empire, all of which fought and sustained thousands of casualties for the Allied cause. This experience, added to the economic and political stresses of the war, produced restiveness in India and gave the Dominions powerful additional reasons to think of themselves as being the home not merely of Britons living abroad, but of different, albeit friendly, nationalities. At the Versailles Peace Conference, the Dominions were represented both by the British and in their own, separate delegations, a further sign that they were close to practical independence.

## FORMAL EMERGENCE OF THE COMMONWEALTH

In recognition of this fact, the 1920s witnessed the formal emergence of the Commonwealth. When Ireland was partitioned in 1922, the Irish Free State was defined as having the same status as the other Dominions, in "the group of nations forming the British Commonwealth of Nations." This was the first formal use of this style. The year 1922 also brought the Chanak Crisis, which threatened

**Dominion delegates to the Imperial Conference, 1926.** Front row, from left: Irish president William Cosgrave, South African prime minister Barry Hertzog, Canadian prime minister Mackenzie King, British prime minister Stanley Baldwin, Australian prime minister Stanley Bruce, New Zealand prime minister J. G. Coates, and Newfoundland prime minister W. S. Monroe. Second row: the Mararajah of Burdwan, British lord chancellor Frederick Edwin Smith, British chancellor of the exchequer Winston Churchill, and British lord president of the council Arthur James Balfour. ©HULTON-DEUTSCH COLLECTION

war between Britain and Turkey. When the British seemed to presume publicly that the Dominions would naturally offer military support, they were met by private protests from Australia and a public nonresponse from Canada. The implication was that, unlike 1914, Britain could no longer make foreign policy for the Dominions.

By the time the Dominions gathered for an imperial conference in 1926, domestic politics in Canada, South Africa, and the Irish Free State had given these Dominions an even more vigorous desire to assert their status as separate and equal nations. The result was the famous definition of the Commonwealth produced by a committee chaired by Arthur, Lord Balfour (1848–1930) of Britain: "They are autonomous Communities within the British Empire, equal in status, in no way subordinate one to another in any aspect of their domestic or external affairs, though united by a common allegiance to the Crown, and freely associated as members of the British Commonwealth of Nations." When this definition was legalized by Britain in the Statute of Westminster of 1931, it made the Dominions as independent as they wished to be: the right of free association implied the right not to be associated at all.

In the 1930s, the British sought to manage this implication. In the Indian Empire, the

Government of India Act of 1935 brought provincial self-government; the measure was scorned by leaders of the Indian nationalist movement, but it brought the Congress Party to power in many areas. The British hoped the act would moderate, and so frustrate, the nationalists; it had the potential to do so, but only by giving them power and a platform to press for more changes. In Ireland, the 1936 External Relations Act, followed by a referendum in 1937, all but made it a republic by eliminating any substantial role for the Crown. The British found it better to accept these developments than risk the disintegration of the Commonwealth by opposing them. Most seriously of all, throughout the decade, Dominion reluctance to become involved in a second great European war gave the British government another reason to appease Fascist Italy and Nazi Germany.

It would be too simple to describe this as merely an era of imperial disintegration: the 1932 Ottawa Conference, for example, brought a partial fulfillment of Chamberlain's dream of imperial unity by instituting imperial tariff preferences. More broadly, many in Britain, and in the Commonwealth, viewed the institution with pride, finding in it a broadly applicable model for the development of peaceful cooperation between democratic states. But no matter how artfully described, the reality was that the Commonwealth had become a way to slow and accommodate the drift of the Dominions away from Britain, not a means by which self-government in the Dominions could be reconciled with wholehearted support for Britain's role as a great power.

Britain's cautious handling of the Commonwealth restricted its European diplomacy, but it did help to ensure that when Britain declared war in September 1939 all the Dominions except Ireland did likewise. But this was not 1914: only Australia merely assumed that Britain's declaration applied to it, and South Africa entered the war by the narrowest of margins. And, when Japan entered the war against Britain in 1941, Australia and New Zealand realized what Canada had long known: only the United States could protect them. This meant that the Commonwealth could not be a self-sufficient economic unit, nor unite politically, nor even defend itself. It was the end of any possibility that the Commonwealth would ever

attain the unity to which a generation of Britons had aspired.

But though the entry of Australia, New Zealand, and Canada into the war initially widened the war almost beyond Britain's strength, their willingness to fight proved that these members of the Commonwealth, at least, retained their loyalty to Britain, both as the ancestral homeland of many of their citizens and as a great parliamentary democracy. These nations, with Britain itself, were the core on which the Commonwealth built in the twenty years following World War II, when the age of decolonization began with the independence of India and Pakistan in 1947, followed by Ceylon and Burma in 1948.

Burma never entered the Commonwealth, and in 1949 the Commonwealth for the first time lost a member when Ireland departed as a republic at midnight on 17–18 April. But this was more than balanced by the decision of the prime minister Motilal Nehru (1861–1931) of India, five days after Ireland's exit, that India, though a republic, would remain in the Commonwealth. In recognition of the end of the Indian Empire, the term *Dominion* had been abandoned in favor of *Commonwealth Members* in 1948. Nehru's declaration implied that the Commonwealth would continue to add new members, but on the basis of their right to conduct their internal affairs as they wished.

Over the following decades, the Commonwealth indeed grew rapidly. At the Commonwealth heads of government meetings, known by the inelegant neologism *CHOGM*, there were eight leaders in 1948, eleven in 1960, twenty-one in 1965, thirty-one in Singapore—at the first official CHOGM—in 1971, forty-two in 1981, and fifty-two in 1999. In the middle decades of the century, the British repeatedly rejected the possibility that many of the smaller territories within the empire could ever be viable, independent states, or that they could ever be full Commonwealth Members. But just as repeatedly, the British found no easy way to draw the line. Thus, as the empire contracted, the Commonwealth expanded apace.

### DECOLONIZATION

The watershed year was 1960. Since 1945 the British Empire had clearly been moving toward its end, but even in the late 1950s the British believed their African Empire might last into the 1970s. In 1960 the context of imperialism was irrevocably changed by France's grant of independence to thirteen territories and by the passage of United Nations Resolution 1514 on ending colonialism. Like the French, Britain picked up the pace of decolonization. Ghana had become the first African member in 1957. In 1960 Nigeria, Africa's most populous state, became an independent Commonwealth Member, and in the same year, Prime Minister Harold Macmillan spoke in the South African parliament of the "winds of change" that were blowing through the continent.

For the next thirty years the Commonwealth struggled with the dilemmas of decolonization. One problem, as the number of potential republics within the Commonwealth grew, was to describe the relationship between the British Crown and the Commonwealth. This was handled with surprising ease in 1949 at a meeting of Commonwealth prime ministers, who agreed that the Crown would be "the symbol of the free association" of Commonwealth Members and, "as such, Head of the Commonwealth." Thus, if and when a Commonwealth Member decided to become a republic, it would not necessarily have to reconsider its status within the Commonwealth.

Other difficulties posed by decolonization were resolved less neatly. The most intractable of these centered around questions of citizenship and race. In 1961, foreshadowing later disputes, the apartheid state of South Africa left the Commonwealth because it refused to treat the newly independent African members, and their diplomatic representatives, as equal members of the Commonwealth. For many believers in the Commonwealth, the departure of South Africa was a shattering blow, confirming that the old Commonwealth was no more.

That Commonwealth had held it as a principle that the internal policies of a particular member were not a legitimate subject of concern for the rest of the Commonwealth. The new Commonwealth seemed to promise only angry, public disputes over domestic policies. Yet the departure of South Africa, and, more broadly, the rapid expansion of the Commonwealth into a multiracial grouping, also prompted the last outburst of enthusiasm for it. In previous decades, the Commonwealth supposedly exemplified peaceful cooperation between sovereign Anglophone democracies; now, in the era of decolonization, it promised to be a model of cooperation between races around the world.

In its fullest bloom, this idealism did not survive the 1960s. Among British conservatives, the Commonwealth was already losing its appeal. Some criticized the effective abolition of the Crown connection, believing that it had produced a Commonwealth that stood for nothing more than its own existence. Others realized that maintenance of the Commonwealth, or indeed the empire, as a genuine political unit implied that Africans and Asians would have the unrestricted right to emigrate to Britain. In a series of acts, starting with the 1962 Commonwealth Immigrants Act, consecutive British governments sought to assert control of their borders while giving offense to neither Commonwealth Members nor liberal opinion and Commonwealth supporters at home.

**INTERNAL POLICIES**

The multiracial appeal of the Commonwealth meant that the Left was the home of much of the remaining Commonwealth idealism. But the British and the Commonwealth faced an unavoidable dilemma. If the Commonwealth were to stand for democratic values, for racial cooperation, and for friendly association and mutual aid between rich and poor nations, it had to concern itself with the internal policies of its members. Furthermore, at least for a time, most of the policies in question would inevitably be those of Britain, because it was the most visible and important nation in the Commonwealth, and of South Africa and Rhodesia (since 1980 Zimbabwe), which were led by minority white governments.

For a time, the struggle was bitter. In 1966 Kenneth Kaunda (b. 1924), of Zambia, spoke of "throwing Britain out of the Commonwealth" because of its handling of Rhodesia. Harold Wilson (1916–1995), the British Labour prime minister, complained that "We are being treated as if we were a bloody colony." In 1971 at the Singapore CHOGM, rhetorical unanimity was achieved with the adoption of a new definition of the Commonwealth, which stated that the Commonwealth supported peace, liberty, and international cooperation, and opposed racial discrimination, colonial domination, and wide disparities of wealth.

**Nigerian tribal chiefs attend the opening ceremonies of the Commonwealth Heads of Government Meeting in Abuja, December 2003.** ©YVES HERMAN/POOL/REUTERS/CORBIS

These platitudes about the role of the Commonwealth in international affairs disguised the fact the Commonwealth was now primarily concerned with its own internal affairs. In 1965 the Commonwealth Secretariat was established to administer economic and international affairs. Such a secretariat had long been a goal of British imperialists, but not until it became clear that the Commonwealth had little real power did its members allow it to develop central institutions of this sort. More such institutions were soon created: the Commonwealth Foundation, also in 1965; in 1971, the Commonwealth Fund for Technical Co-operation. These organizations were well intentioned but they were a sign of the Commonwealth's impotence, not its importance.

Until 1980 the most important issue facing the Commonwealth was how to deal with Rhodesia, which had unilaterally declared its independence in 1965 under the leadership of Prime Minister Ian Smith (b. 1919). The initial British response was to impose sanctions, which were not successful. At a Commonwealth conference in 1966 Wilson managed to win a "last chance" for Smith, but most of the other heads of government did not support the British approach, which Smith then rejected. In the end, it took a civil war to bring down the white minority regime. At the 1979 Lancaster House Conference, the Commonwealth secretary-general Sonny Ramphal (b. 1928) and African leaders persuaded rival African politicians in Rhodesia to accept a British plan for elections. After an overwhelming victory, Robert Mugabe (b. 1924) took office, and the new nation of Zimbabwe gained its independence in 1980.

The road to majority rule in South Africa was even more painful. After South Africa withdrew from the Commonwealth in 1961, the Commonwealth had to decide what connections its members would keep up with the apartheid regime, and what measures it would take to bring about majority rule. Sporting boycotts were the most visible means of expressing disapproval of South Africa. In 1977 the Gleneagles Agreement isolated the regime from Commonwealth sports, the Commonwealth Games having by this time become the organization's most important symbol and event.

In the 1980s, CHOGMs regularly endorsed sanctions against South Africa, and just as regularly recorded the dissent of British Prime Minister Margaret Thatcher (b. 1925), who believed that sanctions would be counterproductive. For this, she was vilified: more nations boycotted the 1986 Commonwealth Games, held in Edinburgh, than competed in them. But Commonwealth sanctions, combined with the more important pressure exerted by the African National Congress and other foreign powers and international organizations, finally led to a 1994 all-races election, the election of Nelson Mandela (b. 1918) as president, and the return of South Africa to the Commonwealth.

By the mid-1990s, it was obvious that the most persistent violators of the 1971 principles, now reinforced by the 1991 Harare Commonwealth Declaration, were in Africa and Asia. In 1995 military-ruled Nigeria was suspended from the Commonwealth. This suspension was lifted in 1999 but was followed by the suspension of Pakistan, where the democratically elected government had been overthrown by the military. In 2000 Fiji was suspended; its membership was restored the following year. In 2002 Zimbabwe was suspended, and in 2003 this suspension was extended, whereupon the dictatorial regime of Robert Mugabe left the Commonwealth. In 2004 Pakistan's suspension was lifted, though the commitment of its leaders to democracy was uncertain. As of mid-2005, the Commonwealth had fifty-three members.

The political record of the Commonwealth Members is uneven, and except in the cases of Rhodesia and South Africa, there is little reason to think that the Commonwealth itself has played a central role in advancing human rights. Its most successful institutions are not those charged with promoting economic development, or popular knowledge of the Commonwealth, but the Commonwealth Games and the Commonwealth War Graves Commission. And there is no likelihood that the Commonwealth will assume the leading role in international affairs that was projected for it in the 1920s and 1960s. Yet it retains its attractiveness as a modestly effective international organization, and a symbol—and occasionally more than a symbol—of the connections made by the British Empire, and of the values associated with parliamentary democracy.

*See also* **British Empire; British Empire, End of; Decolonization; India; Pakistan; United Kingdom.**

BIBLIOGRAPHY

Brown, Judith, and William Roger Louis, eds. *The Twentieth Century.* Vol. 4 of *The Oxford History of the British Empire,* editor-in-chief William Roger Louis. Oxford, U.K., 1999.

Darwin, John. *The End of the British Empire: The Historical Debate.* Oxford, U.K., 1991.

Hall, Hessel Duncan. *Commonwealth: A History of the British Commonwealth of Nations.* London, 1971.

Hancock, William Keith. *Survey of British Commonwealth Affairs.* Vol. 1: *Problems of Nationality, 1918–1936.* London, 1937. Vol. 2: *Problems of Economic Policy, 1918–1939.* Part 1, London, 1940; and part 2, London, 1942.

Mansergh, Nicholas. *Survey of British Commonwealth Affairs: Problems of External Policy, 1931–1932.* vols. 1–2. London, 1952, 1958.

———. *The Commonwealth Experience.* 2nd ed. 2 vols. London, 1982.

McIntyre, William David. *The Commonwealth of Nations: Origins and Impact, 1869–1971.* Minneapolis, Minn., 1977.

———. *A Guide to the Contemporary Commonwealth.* Houndmills, U.K., 2001.

Miller, J. D. B. *Survey of Commonwealth Affairs: Problems of Expansion and Attrition, 1953–1969.* London, 1974.

Moore, Robin James. *Making the New Commonwealth.* Oxford, U.K., 1987.

TED R. BROMUND

# COMMONWEALTH OF INDEPENDENT STATES.

It was the collapse of the Soviet Union in late 1991 that brought to life an active but essentially dysfunctional international organization called, rather misleadingly, the Commonwealth of Independent States (CIS). Initially, it was only the three initiators of dismantling the USSR—Belarus, Russia, and Ukraine—that formed this loose alliance on 8 December 1991, but within the month seven other former Soviet republics (Armenia, Azerbaijan, Kazakhstan, Kyrgyzstan, Moldova, Turkmenistan, and Uzbekistan) joined by signing the Alma-Ata Declaration. The three Baltic states (Estonia, Latvia, and Lithuania) refused to be associated with this organization, and Georgia, while initially declining the invitation, had to join in December 1993, needing Russia's help in a violent internal crisis.

From the very start, the member states have had quite different views on the aims of their union, from the minimalist approach of handling a "civilized divorce" (as formulated by Ukraine) to the ambitious agenda of advancing multidimensional integration. This agenda is outlined in the CIS Charter, adopted in January 1993, and hundreds of other documents signed by heads of states and governments. Implementation, however, has been at best haphazard and more often nonexistent.

Russia was expected to be a "natural" leader of this ambivalent grouping, whose members had plenty of shared tragedy in the past but did not fancy much of a common future. Moscow managed to sort out the immediate problems related to the heritage of the USSR, from dividing the external debt and property to distributing quotas on tanks according to the Conventional Forces in Europe (CFE) Treaty (1990) and securing for itself the monopoly on nuclear weapons. Further leadership became uncertain and centered mostly on maintaining contacts among the political elites through regular summit meetings and supporting networks. It was only in the second half of the 1990s that Moscow showed interest in more ambitious integrative projects seeking to assert its dominance across the post-Soviet space. The top priority was given to building an alliance with Belarus, formatted as a union with a charter (1997) and a treaty (1999) that set the goal of building a confederal state. The Belarus leadership pursued its own interests in these "brotherly" ties but showed

little interest in wider cooperation, despite hosting the CIS headquarters in Minsk.

A particular focus of political networking has been on the regional security developments, first of all in the Caucasus and Central Asia. In May 1992, six states (Armenia, Kazakhstan, Kyrgyzstan, Russia, Tajikistan, and Uzbekistan) signed the Collective Security Treaty (CST); Azerbaijan, Belarus, and Georgia joined in 1993, but in 1999, when the treaty was to be renewed, Azerbaijan, Georgia, and Uzbekistan effectively seceded. A key aim of the Russia-led security cooperation was to manage violent conflicts in the CIS area, but the plans for joint peacekeeping forces were never realized, and the organization merely issued mandates for Russian peacekeeping operations in Tajikistan (1992–1997) and Abkhazia (ongoing since 1994). Besides establishing regular meetings between defense and interior ministers, this framework was moderately successful in facilitating the export of Russian weapons and the education of officers in Russian academies, as well as in building a joint air defense system. Since autumn 2001, Moscow has sought to intensify security cooperation in the CIS, seeing it as a response to the limited deployment of American and NATO forces in Kyrgyzstan and Uzbekistan. While the Antiterrorist Center has not become an efficient structure, several joint military exercises were held between 2002 and 2004, and the status of the CST was upgraded in May 2002 to the Collective Security Treaty Organization.

Priority attention in the CIS has been given to the economy, and it is in this area that the results are particularly unimpressive. The initially proclaimed ambition to establish an economic union was undermined already in 1994 by the failure to retain the ruble as the common currency. In the first half of the 1990s, all post-Soviet states were hit by severe economic crises, and none of them showed serious interest in trying to find a common way out. Russia sought to advance its economic influence by signing a customs union with Belarus and Kazakhstan in 1995 and expanding it the next year to a free trade zone, which included also Kyrgyzstan and eventually Tajikistan. At the Chisinau summit (October 1997), Russia was criticized for hindering the implementation of the CIS agreements by its selective approach. Its ability to provide economic leadership, however, was undermined by the Russian financial meltdown in August 1998, which affected all its partners. For that matter, all CIS member states engaged in accession negotiations with the World Trade Organization (WTO) without any coordination or attempts at synchronizing their efforts. It was only in 2003 that Moscow launched a new initiative in this area, convincing Belarus, Kazakhstan, and Ukraine to remove most of the barriers for cooperation in the framework of a United Economic Space.

This project was a part of Russia's wider efforts to consolidate its leadership in the CIS area by combining closer bilateral ties with a variety of multilateral frameworks. The foundation for these efforts was created by Russia's strong economic growth, driven primarily by the energy sector, but the core content was shaped by the closer cooperation between post-Soviet regimes that were all backing away from the path of democratic reforms and developing various forms of semi-authoritarianism. The successful uprising against the regime of Eduard Shevardnadze in Georgia in November 2003 appeared to be an anomaly in this general trend, but the "orange revolution" in Ukraine in November–December 2004 had a devastating effect on Russia's policy. Moldova's prompt reorientation toward the European Union in February 2005 showed that a regime change was not a necessary precondition for abandoning the CIS frameworks. The collapse of the regime of Askar Akaev in Kyrgyzstan in March 2005 demonstrated that Russia had no reliable instruments for supporting its allies against internal challenges.

Facing this chain of failures and setbacks, Moscow had to reconsider the usefulness and viability of the CIS, even if it continued to insist on its "civilizing mission on the Eurasian continent" (as President Vladimir Putin asserted in his April 2005 address to the Parliament). It appears entirely possible that Moscow could opt for dismantling this umbrella structure and concentrate its efforts on key bilateral relations, first of all with Belarus, and also with Armenia and Kazakhstan. In Central Asia, Russia would then seek to assert its key role in the Central Asian Cooperation Organization (which it joined in May 2004) and coordinate its policy with China in the Shanghai Cooperation Organization (established in June 2002). The key issue for the future for these overlapping and inherently unstable structures is Russia's own political trajectory and its commitment to rapprochement with Europe.

*See also* **Russia; Soviet Union; World Trade Organization.**

BIBLIOGRAPHY

Allison, Roy. "Russia and the New States of Eurasia." In *Contemporary Russian Politics: A Reader,* edited by Archie Brown, 443–452. Oxford, U.K., 2001.

Dwan, Renata, and Oleksandr Pavliuk, eds. *Building Security in the New States of Eurasia: Subregional Cooperation in the Former Soviet Space.* Armonk, N.Y., 2000.

Kreikemeyer, Anna, and Andrei V. Zagorski. "The Commonwealth of Independent States." In *Peacekeeping and the Role of Russia in Eurasia,* edited by Lena Jonson and Clive Archer, 157–171. Boulder, Colo., 1996.

Light, Margot. "International Relations of Russia and the Commonwealth of Independent States." In *Eastern Europe and the CIS,* 23–35. 3rd ed. London, 1996.

"Vozroditsya li Soyuz? Budushchee postsovetskogo prostranstva." *Nezavisimaya gazeta* (23 May 1996): 4–5.

PAVEL K. BAEV

**COMMUNISM.** As a term, *communism* became adopted among networks of revolutionary artisans in western Europe during the 1830s and 1840s, denoting both the distinctiveness of their own political movement and the main quality of the society they hoped to create. Bespeaking a collectivist or cooperative ideal of the good society, it was always linked to a passionate critique of emerging capitalism as a type of society based on private property, necessary inequality, and unregulated market relations. With the rise of the European labor movements between the 1860s and 1890s, *communist* became largely supplanted by *socialist* and *social democratic,* but that earlier language of the 1840s still left some permanent traces. Most famously expressed in the *Communist Manifesto* of Karl Marx and Friedrich Engels in 1847–1848, these traces included the idea of an inner core of revolutionaries seeking the general overthrow of society, the ideal of a future cooperative and egalitarian world, the fundamental critique of capitalism, and a politics focused sociologically on the massed agency of the working class.

## FORMATION OF COMMUNIST PARTIES

These resonances were not properly reclaimed until the European socialist movement was thrown into crisis by the First World War. After the initial disorientation of July–August 1914, bitterly contested divisions were opened in each national party around issues of support for the war. Vladimir Lenin in particular embraced the rhetoric of "communism" as a means of separating himself from the given leaderships of the Second International, the federation of socialist parties and trade unions founded in 1889. As the antiwar Left regrouped through conferences in the Swiss villages of Zimmerwald and Kienthal between September 1915 and April 1916, and popular discontent proliferated through the winter of 1916–1917, the appeals of such language grew. For Lenin and the "Zimmerwald Left," the need for a split and refoundation became paramount: opposing the war required unequivocal revolutionary opposition to capitalism; supporting the war ("social patriotism") spelled reformism and betrayal of the movement's best traditions. Massive working-class unrest unfolded across most of Europe between April and September 1917, reaching a spectacular climax in the Russian Revolutions of February and October. Riding this wave of success, the victorious Bolsheviks changed their name from the Russian Social Democratic Labor Party to the Communist Party in March 1918. As revolutionary turbulence engulfed the Continent at the end of the war in November 1918, with principal storm centers in Italy and Germany, divisions now widened between the older socialist parties, whose leaderships pursued broadly reformist and pragmatic strategies of reform, and the new militancies increasingly inspired by the success of the Bolsheviks in Russia.

In April 1917 a major break had been wrought in Germany when the Social Democratic Party (SPD) expelled its large left-wing opposition, who then regrouped as the Independent Social Democratic Party (USPD). Smaller breakaways occurred elsewhere, while in Germany, Austria, Greece, Hungary, the Netherlands, and Poland during 1918 small Communist parties were formed

as such. The launching of the Third International in March 1919 then drew representatives from these early initiatives to the founding congress in Moscow, augmented by delegations from most of the Russian Empire's former territories and from Turkey, Persia, China, and Korea. They were also joined by individual revolutionaries from various parts of Europe, representing mainly themselves. Further Communist parties were now launched in Bulgaria, Yugoslavia, and Spain.

Yet so far each of these new parties remained isolated fragments and sects. Effective rivalry with the old socialist parties required attracting large sections, even majorities, of their supporters into the new camp. This was especially true of the strong central and northern European "social democratic core" of the German-speaking countries, the Czech lands, and Scandinavia, where socialist parties won more than 25 percent of the popular vote in national elections before 1914, but it also applied to the major countries of France, Italy, Britain, and Spain. Yet even the German USPD, the largest of the new left-wing formations issuing from the wartime divisiveness, still balked at a final break with the past. Neither of the two largest parties moving strongly to the "maximalist" left during 1918–1919, the Italian Socialist Party and the Norwegian Labor Party, were ready to affiliate with the new Communist International. Nor were the strong left oppositions in parties like the Swiss, Czech, or French. On the other hand, the revival of the pre-1914 Second International at Bern in February 1919 was not a success. After only a year all but the German SPD, the British Labour Party, and the moderate socialist parties of Sweden, Denmark, Belgium, and the Netherlands had abandoned it, including the large left-wing parties of Italy, France, Austria, and Norway. If the new communism was to take off, these were the parties it needed to win.

Thus a further process of radicalization was required across Europe before most left-wing socialists were willing to take the plunge and identify themselves with communism. This could involve either disillusionment with a moderate socialist party whose intransigence drove radicals to the left, as happened in Germany via the conflicts between the SPD and USPD, or else the exhaustion of other left-wing alternatives, such as

**Delegates pose for a group photograph at the opening of the first congress of the Third International, Moscow, March 1919.** Vladimir Lenin can be seen in the second row, just right of center. ©Hulton-Deutsch Collection/Corbis

the syndicalist chimera of the general strike in France or Italy. But the main impetus came from a drastic radicalizing of popular militancy during 1919–1920, which brought new cohorts of working-class revolutionaries into politics and overwhelmed the reservations of more seasoned voices on the left. This last effect was most apparent in Germany and Italy. In response to the new revolutionary upswing in western Europe, accordingly, the Third International's Second Congress in July 1920 issued a renewed call for affiliation on the basis of "Twenty-One Conditions," which now defined who qualified to become a Communist Party (CP). In a series of dramatic congresses, beginning with the USPD in October 1920 and continuing with the French socialists (December), the Italians (January 1921), and the Czechs (May), some of Europe's largest socialist parties voted to join the Communist International. In the course of 1920–1921 this process was repeated elsewhere, until each European country had acquired its national CP, however tiny and marginal within the national polity. For a while some left-wing

socialists sought to hold a middle ground between the Second and Third Internationals, most notably the large and prestigious Austrian Socialist Party. But by 1923 the differences had hardened. Socialists and Communists faced each other from two angrily distinct and mutually hostile camps.

**DEFINING THE MOVEMENT**

What did this new communism signify? Most simply put, it stood for "revolution" as against "reform." In the period from 1917 to 1923, it stood above all for the successful making of a revolution. The Bolsheviks had seized state power, won their civil war, and consolidated a socialist regime. Abstracting further from this experience, the communist model of revolutionary change seemed to entail a strategy of armed insurrection coordinated by the leadership of a disciplined revolutionary party, profiting from extreme social polarization and collapse of the liberal center. Given such polarization of the class struggle, a pitched confrontation against the recalcitrant forces of reaction was then thought to be inevitable, culminating in a "dictatorship of the proletariat." In contrast with the inevitabilist understandings of most pre-1914 socialists, for whom revolution was the natural consequence of the maturing of capitalist contradictions, the ripening of the economy for socialist control, and the amassing of unstoppable working-class majorities in elections, this Bolshevik model of revolutionary change was also *voluntarist*. Rather than waiting for the objective logic of history to do its work, revolutionaries could now make their own opportunities; socialist revolution was no longer the necessary exit from the inevitable capitalist crisis but could be conceived as a creative political act.

Further linked to this loosening of economic determinism was an argument about "Russian backwardness." That is, revolutions could be made not only in the most completely industrialized societies but also where extremes of uneven development (an exceptionally mobilized working class, an exceptionally exploited peasantry) had concentrated social tensions to the point of rupture. In Lenin's formulation, Russia was "the weakest link in the imperialist chain"; once it snapped the effects would certainly be transferred elsewhere. Other features of Bolshevik success, such as their willingness to take up the demands of the peasantry or their advocacy of national self-determination, were less immediately inspiring for revolutionaries farther to the west. But two final perspectives advanced by Lenin and his main ally in these years, Leon Trotsky, were crucial. One was internationalism, the idea that Russian backwardness would cease to be an impediment to the building of socialism providing revolution also occurred in the more industrialized societies to the west. The other was the role of the soviets—factory-, neighborhood-, and city-based participatory organs of direct democracy—whose historical superiority the Twenty-One Conditions now aggressively asserted against parliamentary institutions.

During the period from 1919 to 1923 the idea of the soviets was perhaps most important of all. In the manifestos issued by the founding congress of the Third International, communism was contrasted with the moribund system of "bourgeois democracy," which not only right-wing socialists ("social patriots") but also many on the left sympathetic to the revolutionary camp ("the amorphous, unstable Socialist center") were still

defending. Against parliaments and the classic liberal freedoms were counterposed the soviets or workers' councils as "the conditions and forms of the new and higher workers' democracy." For Lenin and the Bolsheviks, as for all genuine revolutionaries willing to take the communist road, the dictatorship of the proletariat had become the instrument of working-class emancipation, just as "insurrections, civil wars, and the forcible suppression of kings, feudal lords, slave owners and their attempts at restoration" had previously been the unavoidable means of the bourgeoisie's ascent. Under the circumstances of Europe's current revolutionary crisis, therefore, forming an international revolutionary vanguard in the form of the new CPs, to be coordinated via the Third International, had become the utmost priority.

Through this process of popular radicalization, conflict among socialists, and contentious differentiation, the category of *communism* reentered European political discourse with a clear set of meanings. By the early 1920s it denoted the main home of revolutionary politics, whose goal was the violent overthrow of capitalism rather than its peaceful and piecemeal transformation via ameliorative regulation, constitutional action, and cumulative reform. Yet by the end of 1923, that sharpness of contrast between Communists and their socialist rivals—between polarized confrontation and the pragmatics of negotiation, between the immediacy of revolution and a politics of the long haul, between attacking the system and working within it—was already becoming blurred. The "actuality of the revolution," as the Hungarian Communist Georg Lukács called it, had started to recede. If in 1920–1921 Communist politics meant soviet as against parliamentary state forms, by 1923–1924 the new parties were being drawn once more into participating in the given political order—in parliaments, elections, and the entire institutional world of the reviled "bourgeois democracy." Lenin and the Bolsheviks found themselves conceding the necessity of parliamentary, trade union, and other "legal" forms of action, in however tactical or cynical a form. Furthermore, once the new parties started expanding, their new heterogeneity of support posed unavoidable problems. The disciplined adherence to a unified outlook imagined by the Twenty-One Conditions quickly dissolved amid the actual diversity of beliefs the new cohorts of supporters brought with them—embracing everything from council communism and syndicalism to parliamentary socialism of the pre-1914 variety and an extreme ultraleftism that refused truck with parliaments of any kind. Indeed, the strongest of the new parties in Germany, Italy, and Czechoslovakia faced mobilized constituencies of young working-class militants who were angrily resistant to *any* suggestion of a coordinated political line. Making disciplined Communists out of such volatile and localistic insurgencies would be no easy thing.

## CENTRALIZATION AFTER 1923

Accordingly a new phase in the early history of communism opened with the exhaustion of immediate revolutionary hopes after late 1923, as the new parties began retooling themselves for a different kind of politics. This transition had three main dimensions. One was organizational consolidation. Most of the new parties, especially the large and prestigious German KPD, suffered from massive and rapid turnovers of membership, frequent changes of leaders, and volatile oscillations of political line; the ability to hold local militants to the policies of the party central was also slight. Thus pressures grew for a tightening of internal discipline behind the approved party line: there was less tolerance for dissenters; earlier diversity of outlooks became flattened; relations with other left-wing organizations were severed; successive leaderships were disgraced and expelled. Wagons were circled against a hostile capitalist world. This drive for "democratic centralism" took bolshevism as its model. Between the Fifth Comintern Congress of 1924, which issued detailed instructions for reshaping each party in the Bolshevik image ("bolshevization)," and the next congress of 1928 the European Communist parties were dragooned into much stricter uniformity of organization, as leaderships demanded higher degrees of internal discipline and overall conformity to a single political line. As a result, by 1928 many of the founding Communists had gone. Conversely, in most parties extraordinarily long-lasting leaderships were now locked into place. Examples included Ernst Thälmann in the KPD (from 1925 until his arrest by the Nazis in 1933 and murder in 1944); Maurice Thorez in the French PCF (1930–1964); Harry Pollitt in the

British CPGB (1929–1956); Klement Gottwald in the Czechoslovak KSC (1929–1953), and Palmiro Togliatti in the Italian PCI (1926–1964).

Second, the same years saw a ruthless imposing of Moscow's dominance through the Comintern, the association of Communist parties (Communist International) established in 1919. This was preceded by the power struggle inside the Soviet Communist Party (CPSU) in 1923–1924 following Lenin's illness and death, which by 1925–1926 brought Joseph Stalin to undisputed leadership. The failure of revolution to occur in the advanced capitalist West combined with the Soviet Union's embattled isolation to produce a severe contraction of internationalist perspectives. Under the policy of "socialism in one country" announced by Stalin in January 1926, European Communists regrouped around the overriding priority of defense of the Soviet Union. But compelling arguments for ensuring the survival of the one successful revolution slid easily into the rationalizing of Soviet self-interest and thence into uncritical conformity with Soviet demands. The independent importance of the other CPs became demoted and their roles redefined. The autonomy of the Comintern was taken away, differences across national contexts were ignored, and its executive committee was brought under Soviet control. Despite misgivings, even the shrewdest and most independently minded of European Communists, such as Togliatti or Lukács, fell into line, not least because by this time extreme political repression had driven their own parties into exile and underground. The Soviet leadership's immense authority precluded effective opposition.

Third, this process of "Stalinization" in the European CPs sealed the finality of the split within socialism. The divisiveness of the war years, driven to a high pitch of rhetorical and actual violence via the revolutionary conflicts of 1917–1923, was given lasting institutional form by the welding of the new CPs into rigidly demarcated formations. Those parties emerged from the mid-1920s as austerely revolutionary organizations, digging themselves down into redoubts of proletarian militancy, bitterly denouncing social democrats for betraying the revolution, and uncritically upholding Soviet superiority. Henceforth Communists dourly patrolled the ideological walls separating themselves from socialists and other parts of the Left, an attitude entirely reciprocated by their socialist opponents, for whom anticommunism remained the defining glue of their own creed. At another level, the CPs discharged a hard task remarkably well by shaping the chaotic radicalism of the postwar years into more stable organized form. But in the event a peculiarly rigidified set of political cultures became the unfortunate result. The Sixth Comintern Congress in 1928 was again the decisive event, enforcing new standards of uncritical obedience to its decisions, instating Moscow-loyalist leaderships inside the individual parties, and demanding strict separation from other parts of the Left. Under the terms of this so-called left turn the Sixth Congress opened the period of communism's most extreme ultraleft isolation, insisting on a new period of revolutionary opportunity and denouncing social democrats ("social fascists") as the main enemy.

It was mainly from this period, 1928–1935, that the familiar stereotypes of the Communist politician were to come: secretive, manipulative, and disciplined; rigidly loyal to Moscow; never deviating from the line; using democracy for his own purposes; seeking allies mainly in order to outmaneuver and undermine. The bolshevization process, brought to its ugly climax in 1928, sharpened the boundaries separating Communists from other parts of the Left. The various CPs emerged with new leaders, often trained in Moscow, especially if the party was illegal and underground. They were now much smaller in membership. They recruited new cohorts of workers with little previous labor movement background. Moreover, the new rules of discipline imparted a distinctive quality to life inside the party. Becoming a Communist demanded a special loyalty, which spread into all parts of a militant's life, especially where the party remained a small cadre organization. It required full-time daily commitment, marking Communists off from other workers. Passionate identification with the Soviet Union and the discipline of international solidarity were also a vital part of the positive appeal, but opened the way to a knee-jerk dependence on Moscow's authoritative leadership. Here the rules of "democratic centralism" also spelled a collectively embraced authoritarianism. All of these characteristics came to define "Stalinism" as a distinctive political culture, which reigned more completely in some national parties than others.

This never reached straightforwardly down into the local working-class cultures where Communist popular strengths were embedded. But equally, no party leadership or full-time apparatus kept free of its constraints.

In the Soviet Union itself, the most extreme version of a centralist and bureaucratic party-centered regime took shape. Tolerance for dissent, whether inside the CPSU or in society at large, had always been uncertain during the 1920s, despite a certain loosening under the New Economic Policy (NEP) adopted in March 1921. But at the end of that decade the drives for industrialization and collectivization of agriculture now imposed a brutally coercive climate of policing, public values, and interventionist state power. After the assassination of Sergei Kirov, a potential rival to Stalin, in December 1934, a grand-scale state terror unfolded, marked by a series of grotesque show trials in 1936–1938, by a thoroughgoing purge of the party, Red Army, and other institutions, and by the sheer scale of the victims—for example, 680,000 executed during 1937–1938 alone, 3,000,000 imprisoned. By these means a massive turnover of leadership was effected: of 1,966 delegates to the Seventeenth Party Congress in February 1934, only 59 were present at the Eighteenth Congress in 1939; of 139 Central Committee members, only 24 remained, with no less than 98 convicted of treason and shot. The Soviet Communist Party of the mid-1920s was already profoundly different from the Bolshevik revolutionaries who seized power in 1917, but the thoroughly Stalinized apparatus emerging from the Great Purges was now entirely removed from that earlier Bolshevik heritage. Stalin himself had secured an extraordinary concentration of personal power.

The democratic impoverishment of the Comintern's internal regime, the appalling violence of the Great Purges, foreign Communists' uncritical adulation for Stalin, the instrumentalizing of the European CPs for the purposes of Soviet foreign policy—all these features of Communist history painted a bleak picture by the late 1930s. Yet, paradoxically, this was a period of enormous Soviet prestige. By its remarkable feat of forced industrialization, massive projects of social engineering, and apparent harnessing of natural and human resources for the pursuit of the collective good, with all the utopian fervor of building a "new civilization," socialist construction in the Soviet Union attracted widespread Western admiration during the 1930s, often from the unlikeliest of quarters. This prestige acquired particular momentum from two sources. On the one hand, Soviet planning seemed to record exceptional successes at a time when the 1929 stock market crash had thrown Western capitalism into a crisis that many radicals believed might be terminal. On the other hand, the Soviet Union seemed the only international source of resistance to the threat of fascism.

## THE POPULAR FRONT

That dual context of the 1930s—catastrophic unemployment and a massive failure of the capitalist system, combined with the rise of Nazism and the broader right-wing assaults on democracy—formed the setting of a remarkable European Communist advance. After a period of willfully magnified isolation between 1928 and 1933–1934, the CPs responded belatedly but creatively to the destruction of democracy in Germany and Austria by seeking to emerge from their isolation. With the PCF in France setting the pace, a new strategy of coalition building was adopted, taken up first by Communists in Italy, Czechoslovakia, Poland, and Spain, before being adopted officially by the Seventh Comintern Congress in July 1935. This was the new Popular Front strategy, which called for the broadest possible democratic alliances against fascism. Such People's Fronts were to be based on all those forces that the Comintern had repudiated so decisively in 1919 at its birth—not only the immediate socialist rivals but also the previously reviled forces of bourgeois democracy, including liberals, radicals, and republicans; peace movements; humanitarian organizations; where possible the churches; and even conservative groups open to the defense of democracy. Communists should now support any government willing to uphold democratic rights. This was vital for the forming of international coalitions against the further advance of Nazi Germany, not least for the protection of the Soviet Union itself.

Although in each case it later went down to defeat, this strategy won its greatest initial victories in France and Spain, forming the French Popular Front government of 1936–1937 and rallying the Second Republic against the Nationalist uprising in the Spanish civil war (1936–1939). Associated especially with the Bulgarian Communist Georgi Dimitrov and the Italian Palmiro Togliatti, key figures in the Comintern of these years, the rhetoric of the Popular Front recast socialism as the highest form of older progressive traditions rather than their implacable opponent. Communists now affirmed the importance of universal humanist values ("civilization versus barbarism"), invoked their own country's authentic popular democratic traditions, and took their stand on the common ground of democracy. Through the fight against fascism, moreover, such a broad democratic Left could use this strategy to begin accomplishing the transition to socialism. Rather than stressing the revolutionary climacteric of the insurrectionary seizure of power on the model of 1917, the Popular Front strategists proposed a different perspective: building popular support patiently over a longer term; drawing progressive aspirations from all parts of society; commanding ever greater public influence via existing institutions; building the working-class movement's moral authority into the democratic foundations of the transition. Such a theory of revolution refocused attention away from armed struggle and pitched confrontations and toward changing the system from within by incremental gains.

For Communists this approach marked a decisive departure from the form of revolutionary politics to which they had committed themselves from 1917 to 1923. It allowed for the repairing of bridges to social democracy. With the exception of France and Spain, however, socialists refused to be drawn into coalition. More fundamentally, the Popular Front had failed as an international strategy: the governments of Britain and France rejected an alliance with the Soviet Union; in September–October 1938 Hitler's demands on Czechoslovakia had been disgracefully appeased; and the Spanish civil war was lost. When the Eighteenth Congress of the CPSU convened in March 1939, Europe's Communists seemed more isolated and embattled than ever before. Illegality had become the norm of Communist existence: the CPs in Germany, Austria, Italy, Spain, Portugal, Czechoslovakia, Yugoslavia, Greece, Bulgaria, Romania, and Hungary were all underground. With the outbreak of World War II, the PCF too was banned, soon to be joined by the

**A man is arrested by London policemen during a communist march, 1936.** Despite the clear excesses of Stalinization, communist parties in Europe were strengthened in the 1930s by the rise of fascism and by the apparent failure of capitalism manifested in the Great Depression. ©HULTON-DEUTSCH COLLECTION/CORBIS

CPs in those countries invaded by Nazi Germany and in Switzerland. The small CPs in Britain and Sweden were then the only ones remaining aboveground. The split between Communists and socialists seemed as bitter as ever. The signing of the Nazi-Soviet Nonaggression Pact on the very eve of war made the collapse of the Popular Front strategy complete.

### POSTWAR STRENGTH

This situation was transformed by the Nazi invasion of the Soviet Union on 22 June 1941, which at last brutally imposed the conditions for an international anti-Hitler alliance. With the confusing interlude of the Nazi-Soviet Pact now behind them, Communists could rally for cooperation with socialists and other progressives, country by country, in the interests of the primary antifascist cause, a stance that socialists finally reciprocated. First under the auspices of the national resistance movements and then during the liberation in 1944–1945, when the postwar coalition governments began to be formed, Communists emerged with unprecedented positions of recognized legitimacy and political strength. Partly riding the transnational popularity of the Red Army and Soviet Union, the CPs briefly entered the accepted political arena in most of Europe. As stalwarts of the European resistance, they prospered in postwar elections, becoming the Left's majority force in Italy, France, Czechoslovakia, Yugoslavia, Albania, Bulgaria, and Greece, and recording their highest ever successes in democratic elections everywhere else. They also participated in postwar coalition governments, not only in the "People's Democracies" of Eastern Europe where the regional presence of the Red Army provided obvious sanction, but also in the West. The first postwar elections brought palpable evidence of popular desires for change, borne by rhetorics of national reconciliation and new beginnings. Between the autumn of 1945 and summer 1946, accordingly, in Scandinavia, the Low Countries, Italy, and France, varying configurations of Socialists, Communists, and Christian Democrats commanded around three-quarters of the popular vote. In Belgium, Italy, and France, Communists joined in forming the postwar reforming governments.

Four points may be made about this dramatic growth of Communist strength. Most obviously, it marked a decisive break from the Bolshevik origins. The violent and insurrectionary model of revolutionary change associated with 1917 was set aside, to be replaced by a broad democratic conception of restructuring. Communists wished to build the new society inside the frame of the old, both prefiguratively by exemplary institutions and behaviors in the working-class movement and legislatively by reforms. This new gradualist approach was predicated on several key recognitions: the lower than expected ceilings of left-wing electoral support (which seldom reached more than 40 percent of the popular vote, usually far less); the resulting necessity of coalitions with nonsocialist forces; and the inevitability of strategic moderation and slowness of forward advance. Confrontational violence, disrespect for pluralism, and resort to coercion could only isolate Communists from the rest of society; breadth of consensus was essential to the Left's success. Consequently, Communists needed to take their stand unequivocally on the ground of democracy, building on their own society's "national-popular" traditions. This new version of communism became broadly ascendant across Europe, varying inevitably party by party, during the brief moment of antifascist unity from 1943 to 1947. It was developed most consistently by Togliatti and his supporters in the PCI. One of its main theoretical inspirations was the earlier leader of the PCI, Antonio Gramsci, who had died in Mussolini's prisons in 1937.

Second, the main lasting features of the postwar settlements in Europe owed a great deal to Communist support and participation. From their new positions of influence Communists threw their weight behind the process of reconstruction in 1945. The resulting achievements included new constitutions, especially in France (1946) and Italy (1947), which restored parliamentary democracy, civil rights, and the rule of law, enfranchised women in France, Italy, and Belgium for the first time, and introduced progressive taxation, antitrust laws, and public ownership. The unifying themes of the broader settlements included comprehensive social security, full employment, planned modernizing of the economy, and moral renewal via attacks on Nazi collaborators and the "old gang" of discredited pre-1939 elites. Country by country, the postwar social reforms were mainly laid down during 1945–1946, while Communists were still accepted members of the consensus. Those reforms also ranged across public health and public housing, food programs and family allowances, education, the length of the working week, and the full restoration of trade union rights. Altogether this was a structural transformation that framed Western European political action well into the 1970s and in some ways beyond. It was fundamentally a part of the new Communist program.

Third, the popular communism of the mid-1940s was a dramatically new phenomenon. On the eve of the Nazi invasion of the Soviet Union, the CPs had been almost without exception small and persecuted cadre parties, marginal to their national polities, at daggers drawn with socialist rivals, still in thrall to the insurrectionary memories of 1917–1923, and beholden to Moscow loyalism. In contrast, the Communists recruited through the resistance movements knew nothing of the founding years or the bolshevization drive; they escaped the machinery of Stalinist socialization, which wartime circumstances effectively interrupted; their outlook was shaped by the cooperative logic of antifascism rather than the earlier culture of sectarian isolation; and they were inspired by ideals of national reconstruction. At most they looked back to the Popular Front campaigns, which in many respects prefigured this antifascist élan. The growth in Communist popularity could be startling—the PCI grew from barely 5,000 members to over 1,750,000 between mid-1943 and late 1945—making the new CPs entirely different from the small and battered circles of militants ten years before. The potential for tensions with those earlier generations, or with the old Moscow-loyalist leaders who resurfaced from prisons and exile, was a serious problem, and after spring 1947 the impact of the Cold War restored such Stalinists to influence, forcing the new "National Communisms" into recession. In Eastern Europe that process acquired deadly force, as after 1947–1948 Stalin unleashed vicious and systematic assaults on the legitimacy of these "national roads to socialism."

Fourth, the onset of the Cold War—via the Truman Doctrine and Marshall Plan aid in the West, through the attack on "Titoism" and the purging of the Eastern European CPs in the East—abruptly severed the politics of antifascist unity and banished communism once again to the margins. In Italy, France, and Belgium, Communists were expelled from the coalition governments in May 1947. More generally, the split between Communists and Socialists was crudely reopened, making anticommunism into the litmus test of loyalty to the main political consensus in the West. Some CPs, such as the French and a number of smaller parties, embraced this renewed isolation with Stalinist alacrity; others, like the Italian or the smaller British and Scandinavian parties, sought ways of keeping alive the newly fashioned politics of democratic participation. When Soviet communism entered its own crisis with the dramatic onset of destalinization after the death of Stalin in 1953, leading to the Polish and Hungarian uprisings of 1956, the ideas of 1943–1947 slowly reemerged. But it required the subsequent sociocultural changes associated with the next pan-European upheaval of

**Communist leaders (left to right) Palmiro Togliatti, Harry Pollitt, and Maurice Thorez photographed at a party conference in Milan, January 1948.** Communist leaders, most notably the three pictured here, were an influential force in shaping the new governments of Western Europe during the postwar period. ©HULTON-DEUTSCH COLLECTION/CORBIS

1968, encompassing Czechoslovakia, Poland, and Yugoslavia in the East, and especially France, Italy, and West Germany in the West, before these continuities were properly resumed.

### THE COLD WAR

If the antifascist momentum of 1943–1947 gave the new national communisms in East and West a broadly convergent character, the consequences of the Cold War brought a new bifurcation. The Eastern European CPs were the real casualties of Stalin's purges after 1948. They were crushed as creative movements and in the process completely remade: a quarter of the region's aggregate party membership was expelled between 1948 and 1952, or some 2.5 million Communists, with perhaps a

quarter of a million imprisoned. In 1945 liberation from Nazism had promised not only social transformation but also new measures of democracy and well-being. But instead the Stalinizing of Eastern Europe now imposed a brutal and hard-faced normalizing. Power became centralized in the party-state's inner leadership, with no constitutional checks or legal opposition, with a captive press and an administered public sphere, and with a local political life frozen into paranoid conformity, whether inside the governing CPs or out. This assertion of political monopoly and single-party rule was the first of three fixed features of Soviet rule in the East. The second was Soviet-style economics, first elaborated after 1928–1929 through the Soviet Union's own experience of heavy industrialization, collectivizing of agriculture, and the use of the five-year plan. The principles of collective property, bureaucratic management, and central planning were instituted across Eastern Europe between 1947 and 1949 and proved subsequently nonnegotiable. Pressures for economic reform—most dramatically in Hungary in 1956 or Czechoslovakia in 1968—always halted at the inviolability of state ownership and the command economy, whether directed toward regional and sectoral decentralization, profit mechanisms, new accounting methods, enterprise autonomy, or self-management. The third feature was the military dimension. The Stalinizing of Eastern Europe rested on the iron fist of Soviet military rule, based on Europe's geopolitical division in 1945–1949, solidified into NATO and the Warsaw Pact.

These were the three fixed points in the Soviet system from the late 1940s to the mid-1980s. The pivotal initiative in Soviet destalinizing, Nikita Khrushchev's denunciations of the crimes of Stalin in his "secret speech" to the CPSU's Twentieth Congress in February 1956, which might have opened the way for a process of internal change, stopped strictly short of attacking Stalin's main policies. Each of these was left carefully intact, whether "socialism in one country" and bolshevization of the Comintern, central planning, industrialization and collectivization of agriculture, or democratic centralism and the one-party state. As the main Communist reform movements learned to their cost—in Hungary in 1956, Czechoslovakia in 1968—these were the boundaries that could never be overstepped. Thus once the new government of Imry Nagy restored the multiparty system and took Hungary out of the Warsaw Pact, the Red Army immediately invaded; likewise, though the Prague Spring meticulously reaffirmed Czechoslovakia's membership in the Warsaw Pact, the ending of single-party rule had the same inevitable result. While decisively impeding regenerative reform inside Eastern Europe itself, moreover, these same fixed features of Soviet rule proved huge liabilities for the Left in the West, whose advocacy for socialism was disastrously handicapped by the unattractiveness of these "actually existing socialisms."

For Communists in Western Europe, the combined trauma of 1956—first Khrushchev's revelations, which opened the possibility of change, then the invasion of Hungary, which left everything still the same—began an uneven process of separating themselves from the Soviet Union and the liabilities of Stalinism. The crisis itself saw a massive hemorrhaging of CP support: between 1956 and 1958 the PCI lost four hundred thousand members, the CPGB eight thousand, or a quarter of the whole. In some smaller CPs (Austria, Germany, Portugal), Moscow loyalists simply hunkered down. But a far larger number of parties moved toward greater independence, usually after losing members and often via splits (Scandinavia, Spain, Greece, Switzerland, Britain, Ireland, the Low Countries). In the largest parties of Iceland, Italy, and France, 1956 worked with the grain of existing history. The smallness of the country allowed the Icelandic People's Alliance to avoid the vagaries of international communism altogether. But if the PCI used the crisis to enhance its own autonomy, the PCF simply flaunted its Moscow orthodoxy. French Communist dissent broke on the rock of Stalinist party discipline. But after the initial securing of party unity by defeating the dissenters at the PCI's Eighth Congress in December 1956, Togliatti moved firmly toward reestablishing a distinct set of Western European Communist perspectives. He tactfully rejected Moscow's single and unqualified leadership, proposing a new concept of "polycentrism" instead, affirming the importance of "national roads to socialism" and reclaiming the experience of 1943–1947.

During the 1960s an uneasy standoff ensued, as Western Communists edged toward greater autonomy without repudiating either the Soviet Union or their own Stalinist pasts. Once the Czechoslovak reform movement (the "Prague Spring") had galvanized such renewed and heady hopes for the East, the Warsaw Pact's invasion in August 1968 shattered any remaining belief in the Soviet Union's benevolent leadership. On the one hand, the Soviet invasion ended socialism's Eastern European prospects. In the Soviet imperium's first quarter century, from 1944 to 1970, reform movements had always involved complex synergies between social pressures and inner-party renewal; Communist traditions had themselves fueled the Hungarian Revolution and the Prague Spring.

But this was the possibility brutally terminated on 20 August 1968. Henceforth dulled conformity, social apathy, bureaucratic privilege, Moscow loyalism, and at best a kind of technocratic ambition became generalized across Eastern Europe's governing Communist cultures. After 1968, no democratic impulse could begin from the region's Communist parties; reform politics would come in opposition to the CPs rather than through them. This change was dramatically apparent in the key remaining oppositional episode of Eastern European Communist history, the remarkable rise of *Solidarność* (Solidarity) in Poland in 1980–1981, with its preceding explosions of 1970 and 1976.

On the other hand, Western European Communists broke decisively with the Soviet Union. In contrast with 1956, Soviet actions in 1968 were almost universally condemned. At the CPSU's Twenty-Fifth Congress in February 1976 and a Conference of European CPs in East Berlin in June, the criticisms were reaffirmed: Western Communists demanded "equality and respect for the autonomy of all parties," together with support for individual and collective freedoms under socialism. A shared position coalesced around the Italian, British, and Swedish speakers, and in East Berlin an unprecedented debate ensued. The official document validated internal debate, international nonalignment, and "dialogue and collaboration with democratic forces." The old Bolshevik or "Leninist" talk, where the CPs were "vanguard forces" with "identical objectives" and "a common ideology," was gone. Instead, the Soviet Union was asked to respect the "equality and sovereign independence of each party" without interfering in its "internal affairs." Each CP should be free to work out its own "national road."

## EUROCOMMUNISM

Concurrent with the loosening of Communist conformities and the accumulating critique of Stalinism was a remarkable revival of critical Marxist thought, sometimes beginning inside the organized Communist frameworks of East and West, sometimes occurring outside them altogether. That revival was intimately connected in the later 1960s with both the growth of student radicalism in the greatly expanded higher education systems of Western Europe and the broader intellectual-cultural ferment of the time. The practical import was dramatized by the Paris "May events" of 1968. But these were only the most spectacular moment of a European-wide political crisis linked to student insurgencies, the rise of a new feminism and associated social movements, and the pan-European strike wave of 1967–1975. Such new radicalisms issued a challenge not only to the established liberal norms of political life in Western Europe but also to the Communist parties as the main guardians of an anticapitalist critique. By the mid-1970s certain of those CPs, essentially the most consistent of the Soviet Union's critics since 1968 (and those drawing the clearest lessons from 1956) were enunciating a creative response. Through intensive consultations between 1975 and 1977, inspiring similar ideas among Communists in Britain, Scandinavia, and other smaller countries, the important Italian, Spanish, and French CPs arrived at a common outlook. Tagged as "Eurocommunism," the resulting program sought to sustain a commitment to socialist transformation by further distancing Western European Communists from the Soviet model, committing them unambiguously to democratic pluralism and opening them to the new post-1968 radicalisms.

As a programmatic strategy, Eurocommunism was a failure. When the French Left's common program fell apart in September 1977, the PCF reverted to sectarianism, and in the 1978 elections its vote was surpassed by the Socialists for the first time since 1945; after the Socialist electoral victories of 1981, the PCF never recovered, sinking to a terminally marginal place in the polity. Having been the mainstay of resistance to Franco's dictatorship, the Spanish Communists made a vital contribution to Spain's democratic transition, brokering the key negotiations of 1975–1977 and defending the parliamentary parameters of the ensuing consolidation; yet this never translated into electoral success, and by 1979 the party had become permanently outflanked by the newly created Socialist Party. The strongest Eurocommunist showing was in Italy, where in 1976 the PCI recorded its highest ever electoral success (34.4 percent) while pressing hard for a fundamental realignment of Italian society. Appealing to the heritage of Togliatti, Gramsci, and 1943–1947, its new leader Enrico Berlinguer sought to draw the ruling Christian Democrats into his "historic compromise," both to defend Italy's constitution against a threatening social polarization and to initiate a fresh stage of democratic restructuring. By decisively repudiating the old language of the "dictatorship of the proletariat," taking its stand forthrightly on the ground of democracy, patiently building new coalitions, and casting off the handicaps of Moscow, the PCI hoped to shed its permanent opposition and demonstrate its right to govern. But Berlinguer was outmaneuvered by the Christian Democrats. By the 1979 elections the PCI had lost 1.5 million votes. Abandoning the historic compromise, the party returned to opposition.

In other respects Eurocommunists produced lasting results. In Italy and Spain they defended democratic constitutions against serious right-wing destabilization. They also brought southern Europe finally into the fold of social democracy. While Scandinavia, the Low Countries, and German-speaking Europe formed a north-central European "social democratic core" in the first two-thirds of the twentieth century, Mediterranean Europe had a different labor movement, one shaped by anarcho-syndicalism and then in the Cold War by strong CPs marginalized by regimes of the Right. Only by the 1970s were southern European Lefts winning leverage on government via organized labor followed by electoral growth. Socialists in France, Spain, and Portugal now challenged the primacy of the CPs in this regard, but Communists themselves adopted perspectives indistinguishable from the more ambitious forms of social democracy in Scandinavia and elsewhere. Eurocommunists also rejected the traditional Leninist model of the cadre party, seeking broader-based forms of social-movement-type organizing more akin to the politics encouraged by 1968. Democratic centralism was dismantled and the parties opened toward diverse currents and issues; concurrently, the historic identification with the industrial working class was exchanged for broader social appeals, particularly to women and the university educated. Thus Eurocommunists not only embraced pluralism, multiparty competition, free elections, and parliamentary government for both West and East, but they also prioritized issues that could

not be subsumed within class-struggle perspectives based on industrial workers, including everything from the big identity axes of gender, ethnicity, religion, and race to problems of youth, sexuality, ecology, international relations, and a cultural politics embracing both uplift and entertainment.

Most importantly of all, Eurocommunists finalized the break with the Soviet Union. The crises of 1956 and 1968 in Hungary and Czechoslovakia had given the earlier impetus for this independence, and the next Eastern European upheaval in Poland in 1980–1981 proved terminal. Support for Solidarity's challenge to Soviet rule was the final test of Western Communist independence. Thus if the PCF at best equivocated in the face of this Polish struggle for democracy, the PCI gave a ringing endorsement. In a series of debates and resolutions, the Italian Communists drew a thick line beneath the epoch of the Bolshevik Revolution: "We must accept that this phase of development (which began with the October Revolution) has exhausted its driving force, just as the phase which saw the birth and development of socialist parties and trade union movements mustered around the Second International [before 1914] also ran out of steam." As Berlinguer continued: "The world has moved on. . . . The point is to overcome the present by looking ahead."

After these two final episodes—Eurocommunism's disappointments in the West, the suppression of Solidarity in the East—communism really had run out of steam. The advent of Mikhail Gorbachev to the leadership of the Soviet Union in 1985 still initiated an extraordinary process of change. But what thereby began as socialist restructuring and democratic renewal ended in the implosion of state and society. Gorbachev hoped to move Soviet communism into a modernized future, recuperating non-Stalinist reform traditions going back to the 1920s and much of the Khrushchev era. For inspiration he drew both on the Prague Spring and on Swedish social democracy. Beneath the twin watchwords of perestroika (restructuring or radical reform) and glasnost (openness), he sought a democratized Soviet Union and a revived CP, reinvented as a social democratic party committed to market socialism. In the process he courageously dismantled all three of the pillars of Soviet rule in Eastern Europe: the military security system of the

Warsaw Pact, the command economy, and the Communist Party's sole political rule. The end of the Cold War, marketization, and multiparty democracies were the result. But in the process all distinctiveness of the communist tradition was gone. The remaining denouement—dissolution of the Soviet Union in December 1991, following the Eastern European revolutions of autumn 1989—brought formal closure to a process already long decided. Communism was at an end.

*See also* **Anticommunism; Antifascism; Bolshevism; Destalinization; Eastern Bloc; Eurocommunism; Lenin, Vladimir; Popular Front; Russian Revolutions of 1917; Social Democracy; Socialism; Soviet Union; Warsaw Pact.**

BIBLIOGRAPHY

Alexander, Martin S., and Helen Graham, eds. *The French and Spanish Popular Fronts: Comparative Perspectives.* Cambridge, U.K., 1989.

Ali, Tariq, ed. *The Stalinist Legacy: Its Impact on Twentieth-Century World Politics.* Harmondsworth, U.K., 1984.

Anderson, Perry. "Communist Party History." In *People's History and Socialist Theory,* edited by Raphael Samuel, 145–156. London, 1981,

Andrews, Geoff, Nina Fishman, and Kevin Morgan, eds. *Opening the Books: Essays on the Social and Cultural History of the British Communist Party.* London, 1995.

Banac, Ivo, ed. *The Effects of World War I: The Class War after the Great War: The Rise of Communist Parties in East Central Europe, 1918–1921.* Brooklyn, N.Y., 1983.

Berlinguer, Enrico. *After Poland: Towards a New Internationalism.* Nottingham, U.K., 1982.

Bull, Martin J., and Paul Heywood, eds. *West European Communist Parties after the Revolutions of 1989.* Basingstoke, U.K., 1994.

Fowkes, Ben. *The Rise and Fall of Communism in Eastern Europe.* London, 1993.

Gruber, Helmut. *International Communism in the Era of Lenin: A Documentary History.* Ithaca, N.Y., 1967.

———. *Soviet Russia Masters the Comintern.* Garden City, N.Y., 1974.

Gruber, Helmut, and Pamela Graves, eds. *Women and Socialism, Socialism and Women: Europe Between the Two World Wars.* New York, 1998.

Gundle, Stephen. *Between Hollywood and Moscow: The Italian Communists and the Challenge of Mass Culture, 1943–1991.* Durham, N.C., 2000.

Hobsbawm, Eric. "Fifty Years of People's Fronts." In *Politics for a Rational Left: Political Writing 1977–1988,* 103–109. London, 1989.

Hobsbawm, Eric, and Giorgio Napolitano. *The Italian Road to Socialism.* Translated by John Cammett and Victoria De Grazia. London, 1977.

Jensen, Jane, and George Ross. *The View from Inside: A French Communist Cell in Crisis.* Berkeley, Calif., 1984.

Leonhard, Wolfgang. *Child of the Revolution.* Translated by C. M. Woodhouse. Chicago, 1958.

Loebl, Eugen. *Stalinism in Prague: The Loebl Story.* Translated by Maurice Michael. New York, 1969.

Lukács, Georg. *Record of a Life: An Autobiographical Sketch.* Edited by István Eorsi. Translated by Rodney Livingstone. London, 1983.

Macintyre, Stuart. *Little Moscows: Communism and Working-Class Militancy in Inter-War Britain.* London, 1980.

Naimark, Norman M., and Leonid Gibianskii, eds. *The Establishment of Communist Regimes in Eastern Europe, 1944–1949.* Boulder, Colo., 1997.

Rees, Tim, and Andrew Thorpe, eds. *International Communism and the Communist International, 1919–1943.* Manchester, U.K., 1998.

Rosenhaft, Eve. *Beating the Fascists? The German Communists and Political Violence, 1920–1933.* Cambridge, U.K., 1983.

Rupnik, Jacques. "The Roots of Czech Stalinism." In *Culture, Ideology, and Politics: Essays for Eric Hobsbawm,* edited by Raphael Samuel and Gareth Stedman Jones, 302–320. London, 1983.

Samuel, Raphael. "The Lost World of British Communism." *New Left Review,* no. 154 (November–December 1985): 3–53.

———. "Staying Power: The Lost World of British Communism, Part Two." *New Left Review,* no. 156 (March–April 1986): 63–113.

———. "Class Politics: The Lost World of British Communism, Part Three." *New Left Review,* no. 165 (September–October 1987): 52–91.

Sassoon, Donald. "The Rise and Fall of West European Communism 1939–1948." *Contemporary European History* 1 (1992): 139–169.

Spriano, Paolo. *Stalin and the European Communists.* London, 1985.

Suny, Ronald Grigor. *The Soviet Experiment: Russia, the USSR, and the Successor States.* New York, 1998.

Vidali, Vittorio. *Diary of the Twentieth Congress of the Communist Party of the Soviet Union.* Translated by Neil Amter Cattonar and A. M. Elliot. Westport, Conn., 1974.

Wheaton, Bernard. *Radical Socialism in Czechoslovakia: Bohumír Šmeral, the Czech Road to Socialism, and the Origins of the Czechoslovak Communist Party, 1917–1921.* New York, 1986.

Williams, Kieran. *The Prague Spring and Its Aftermath: Czechoslovak Politics, 1968–1970.* Cambridge, U.K., 1997.

GEOFF ELEY

---

**COMPUTER REVOLUTION.** In the early twenty-first century, the computer revolution is exemplified by a personal computer linked to the Internet and the World Wide Web. Modern computing, however, is the result of the convergence of three much older technologies—office machinery, mathematical instruments, and telecommunications—all of which were well established in Europe in the twentieth century.

### EARLY INFORMATION TECHNOLOGIES

Office machinery was first developed in the United States in the last quarter of the nineteenth century. Office machines mitigated clerical drudgery and facilitated the systematic organization of large-scale offices. The most important machines were typewriters, calculators, punched-card accounting machines, and filing systems. American companies such as Remington Typewriter, Burroughs Adding Machine, and International Business Machines (IBM) were the most prominent firms, and all established European subsidiaries. Several major European manufacturers such as Imperial Typewriter (Britain), Olivetti (Italy), Mercedes (Germany), and Bull (France) became established in the opening decades of the twentieth century.

The modern electronic computer was invented in the United States in 1946. As originally conceived, the computer was a mathematical instrument designed for the solution of numerical problems. As such, the electronic computer was the culmination of a line of development that began with Charles Babbage (1792–1871), who was followed by such pioneers as Leonardo Torres y Quevedo (1852–1936) in Spain, Louis Couffignal (1902–1966) in France, Konrad Zuse (1910–1995) in Germany, and Alan Turing (1912–1954) in England. In the 1950s the scope of the computer broadened to include data processing, as well as mathematical problem solving. The office-machine giant IBM quickly dominated the computer industry worldwide. As well as hosting several IBM subsidiaries, Europe sustained an indigenous computer industry with firms such as Britain's ICL, Machines Bull, Siemens, and Olivetti.

Electric telegraph systems were simultaneously developed in many countries around the middle of the nineteenth century. Telegraphs were initially used for signaling on the newly built railways, but soon found a lucrative market for the transmission of news, market, and financial information. The International Telegraph Union, established in Bern, Switzerland, in 1865, created standards for the international transmission of messages. The early years of the twentieth century saw the development of national telephone systems. There were several European telecommunications manufacturers that became successful multinational operators, including Siemens and Telefunken in Germany, Ericsson in Sweden, and General Electric in Britain. The telephone was widely used in business throughout Europe by about 1910, but domestic diffusion varied greatly; in some countries of Europe it was not until the 1970s that telephones were routinely available in homes. In the 1960s and 1970s telephone systems were fully automated, dispensing with connections made by human operators, and the international range was extended so that it became possible to dial direct to most advanced countries.

### THE COMPUTERIZATION OF SOCIETY

From the mid-1960s on, computers and telecommunications became increasingly integrated, enabling many businesses to conduct transactions in "real time." The most visible manifestations of this new way of conducting business included airline reservation systems, automated teller machines, and barcode scanning in supermarket checkouts. Less visibly, the electronic data interchange (EDI) movement enabled firms to interact electronically, eliminating the economic friction of paper-based systems. For example, when a supermarket checkout registered the sale of an item, this information would be transmitted to the supplier of the item so that stocks could be replenished automatically. In the 1980s "just-in-time" operations revolutionized manufacturing: manufacturers and their suppliers became electronically entwined so that inventories could be eliminated and orders for components and subassemblies delivered on demand.

In the 1970s the development of microelectronics and the invention of the microprocessor transformed not only business computing but also consumer electronics. The most popular consumer items of the early 1970s were video games, hand-held calculators, and digital watches. Video-game hardware manufacture was initially an American phenomenon, and was later dominated by Japanese producers. Europe, however, was well placed to develop video-game software both to appeal to indigenous tastes and for international markets. The development of the pocket calculator saw the rise of new producers such as Sinclair in the United Kingdom, and the demise of the old-line calculating machine manufacturers. Digital watches were initially expensive gadgets that appealed largely to technologically fixated males. As the technology matured, however, digital watches became cheaper, more reliable, and more accurate than their mechanical predecessors. In the second half of the 1970s the mechanical watch industry, especially in Switzerland, was devastated, and manufacturers had to reposition their products as fashion accessories and luxury items for discerning buyers.

The personal computer emerged as a consumer item in the late 1970s. The first machines, such as those made by Apple, Commodore, and Tandy, were imported from the United States, but European manufacturers soon entered the market producing their own designs. Few if any of these personal computer firms came from the traditional computer industry. In 1981 IBM, the leading business computer manufacturer, entered the personal computer market with two important consequences. First, the imprimatur of IBM legitimated personal computing for businesses, which had not until then generally viewed desktop computers as being capable of serious information processing. Second, the entry of IBM established a standardized "PC," which caused a massive shakeout and consolidation of the industry. By the end of the decade most PCs were being supplied by a small number of multinational firms, predominantly American and Japanese, although Europe supported a number of second-tier players such as Siemens and Olivetti.

## VIDEOTEX AND THE INTERNET

Although Europe was relatively unsuccessful as a computer manufacturer, it was very successful in adopting and adapting information technology to improve its industrial competitiveness and information infrastructure. By far the most important European development—though ultimately only partly successful—was videotex, which promised an Internet-like experience a full decade before the Internet came to prominence.

During the period from 1979 to 1984, national videotex systems were developed in some fifteen countries including Britain, France, and Germany in Europe and also Canada, Australia, and Japan (but not the United States). Videotex was intended to provide an information service for businesses and consumers. The videotex technology was developed in the United Kingdom and was based on the teletext system devised there for broadcast television in the early 1970s. National videotex systems were developed in complex public–private partnerships, with the network infrastructure funded and controlled by the national PTTs (postal, telegraph, and telephone authorities), augmented by private-sector information and equipment suppliers. With the single exception of France, in every country where videotex systems were developed, after an initial burst of enthusiasm, they failed to take off as consumer services and gradually faded away or became purely business systems. France, however, launched its national videotex system Télétel as a *grand project* in 1982. Télétel was seen as a means of modernizing and complementing France's aging telephone infrastructure—and the "killer application" would be an online telephone directory. The French government provided inexpensive terminals for telephone users, and by 1988 there were 4.2 million terminals and 9,500 information providers. The French initiative showed, long before the Internet euphoria of the 1990s, that a government could kick-start an information revolution. The failure of videotex elsewhere had multiple causes: the technology was expensive and somewhat immature, and the nonparticipation of the United States undermined its credibility. By the early twenty-first century, France was in the uncomfortable position of migrating to the global Internet.

Although the Internet is generally perceived as an American invention, in fact it is built on a constellation of technologies and standards that were negotiated and developed worldwide over a thirty-year period, starting in the second half of the 1960s. One of the underlying technologies of the Internet, for example, is packet-switched communications, which was initially developed in the National Physical Laboratory in the United Kingdom in the 1960s. Many of the computer networking concepts on which the Internet is based were first elaborated in the Geneva-based International Organization for Standardization. Europe's most important contribution to the Internet was the invention of the World Wide Web by the British-born computer scientist Tim Berners-Lee, while working at the CERN European Particle Physics Laboratory in 1991. Up to that time the Internet had been primarily used by the technical and scientific communities, but the World Wide Web opened it up to ordinary citizens by means of point-and-click software that was very easy to use.

Europe has been an enthusiastic adopter of the Internet. By 2005 nearly 50 percent of European Union citizens had access to the Internet, and the rest of Europe was catching up fast (with about 17 percent having access). In the future the Internet will have massive but unpredictable consequences for Europe, as for the rest of the world. For example, the Internet is already enabling firms to reach global markets for which their small size and remoteness were formally insuperable barriers. The Internet has enabled the "outsourcing" of labor—from which some countries benefit, while others lose out. And the adoption of American English as the lingua franca of the Internet poses a significant challenge to Europe's diverse cultural heritage.

*See also* **Science; Technology.**

BIBLIOGRAPHY

Campbell-Kelly, Martin, and William Aspray. *Computer: A History of the Information Machine.* 2nd ed. Boulder, Colo., 2004.

Coopey, Richard, ed. *Information Technology Policy: An International History.* Oxford, U.K., 2004.

Naughton, John. *A Brief History of the Future: Origins of the Internet.* London, 1999.

Randell, Brian, ed. *Origins of Digital Computers: Selected Papers.* 3rd ed. Berlin, 1982.

Rojas, Raúl, ed. *Encyclopedia of Computers and Computer History.* 2 vols. Chicago, 2001.

MARTIN CAMPBELL-KELLY

---

**CONCENTRATION CAMPS.** Concentration camps are sites for the forcible detention and isolation of large numbers of people outside judicial control or international conventions. They tend to be set up in periods of war or internal turmoil and, in contrast to prisoner-of-war camps, are used to confine civilians, usually people regarded by those in power as (potential) opponents or as a threat, and often with a view to their eventual removal. The establishment of concentration camps is linked to the modern bureaucratic-militaristic state and its attempts to maintain the dominance of the ruling elites and to create some homogeneity. The term is often used synonymously for the camps set up by the Nazis first in Germany and later in the occupied territories of Europe. In fact, the origins of concentrations camps go back much further, and conversely, not all the camps established by the Nazis were of the concentration camp type.

**EARLY CONCENTRATION CAMPS**

The military internment camps used in 1838 by the U.S. Army mostly in Tennessee to detain several thousand Cherokee Indians before their forced resettlement under the Indian Removal Act can be seen as early examples of the kind of detention centers that later became known as concentration camps. The term itself was first coined in the Third Cuban War of Independence (1895–1898), when the Spanish governor, General Valeriano Weyler y Nicolau, ordered the Cuban rural populations to relocate to "campos de concentración" to avoid being treated as insurgents. The British army used the same term for the camps they set up during the Second Boer War (1899–1902) for Boer women and children as well as their black workers to cut off civilian support for the Boer forces.

SS colonel Karl Koch, commandant of the Buchenwald concentration camp, with his wife and son. ©CORBIS

Common features of all these camps were that people were detained there as members of a specific group rather than as individuals, that this was done on the basis of an administrative act rather than as the result of a judicial process, and that there was usually no procedure to challenge the internment. The human rights of those internees were ignored and violated. Treatment was harsh and often arbitrary, and most camps were characterized by overcrowding, poor sanitary conditions, malnourishment, and, as a consequence, diseases and a high mortality rate.

War and upheaval in the early twentieth century brought internment camps of this type also to Europe. During World War I, the Austro-Hungarian Empire used them in its Balkan border regions to confine Serbs and other (pro-Serbian) Slavs who were regarded as potentially disloyal and

destabilizing. The largest of these camps was at Doboj in northern Bosnia, which held some forty-five thousand people between 1915 und 1917. In Finland, after the Civil War of 1918, the victorious "Whites" (nonsocialists) set up camps to confine tens of thousands of people who were suspected of belonging to the "Reds" and seeking a Soviet-style revolution. Two camps run by the Prussian state government in Germany between 1921 and 1923 to detain "unwanted" foreigners until their deportation were officially called "concentration camps." Many of those detained there were Jews from eastern Europe.

### CONCENTRATION CAMPS IN NAZI GERMANY
It was the Nazis who gave the concept *concentration camp* its definitive and most notorious shape.

Under their regime, concentration camps became a central element of the repressive system and the racial state. The Nazi concentration camps imparted to the twentieth century some of its defining images that achieved almost iconic character, such as the gate and ramp of Auschwitz-Birkenau, or the skeletal survivors behind the barbed-wire fences of Bergen-Belsen.

The system of Nazi concentration camps started out in an ad hoc and widely improvised way. An emergency presidential decree of 28 February 1933 following the burning of the Reichstag laid the foundations for imprisonment without trial outside the regular penal system. Subsequently, thousands of political opponents of the Nazis, most of them communists, social democrats, and trade unionists, were taken into so-called protective custody (*Schutzhaft*). Camps to hold them were set up and run, often in administrative rivalry, by the SS (Schutzstaffel), the SA (Sturmabteilung), the political police, and other local and regional state agencies. The first SS camp was established on the order of the Reichsführer-SS, Heinrich Himmler (1900–1945), on 21 March 1933 at Dachau near Munich, but it was only in 1934 that all "protective custody" camps came under the control of the SS. Himmler appointed Theodor Eicke (1892–1943), the commandant of Dachau, as head of the inspectorate of concentration camps and SS guard units (Inspektion der Konzentrationslager und SS-Wachverbände) and ordered him to reorganize and standardize the concentration camp system. Apart from Dachau, all the other camps were disbanded in the mid-1930s and new purpose-built concentration camps, modeled on Dachau, were set up to take their place.

With the consolidation of their rule, the Nazi regime placed not only political opponents in concentration camps but also social outsiders whose nonstandard behavior was seen as unacceptable in the racially pure and socially regulated "national community" (*Volksgemeinschaft*). They included beggars, vagrants, the so-called work-shy, alcoholics, people with a string of criminal convictions, pimps, prostitutes, homosexuals, Jehovah's witnesses, and Sinti and Roma. From 1938, especially following the *Kristallnacht* (Night of Broken Glass) pogroms of 9–10 November 1938, Jews, too, were incarcerated in concentration camps.

After the outbreak of war, the number of concentration camp prisoners soared. The largest intake were now Jews and political prisoners, most of the latter suspected members of the national resistance movements against the Nazi occupation. Following the invasion of the Soviet Union, tens of thousands of Soviet prisoners of war also ended up in concentration camps. In January 1945, the SS registered almost 715,000 concentration camp prisoners, the highest total number at any one time; less than 10 percent of them were Germans.

Concentration camps were only those camps that came under the Inspektion der Konzentrationslager. The Nazis still established a multitude of special detention camps where conditions were similar but which were outside this administrative and organizational system, such as labor education camps, forced labor camps, forced ghettos, police imprisonment camps, transit camps, and civil internment camps. Some of these were open to inspection by representatives of international organizations such as the Red Cross. Special cases were the extermination camps Chelmno, Treblinka, Sobibor, and Belzec, which were set up to implement the "Final Solution." They were not part of the regular concentration camp system either, but there was considerable overlap, as two concentration camps, Auschwitz-Birkenau and Majdanek-Lublin, also had gas chambers installed.

*Labor deployment* Hard work was an important element of concentration camp imprisonment from the very beginning and was intended to discipline and drill the inmates. In the early years most of the work that they were forced to do served no meaningful purpose, but from the mid-1930s economic considerations gained greater prominence among the higher echelons of the SS. The concentration camp prisoners were increasingly recognized as an asset that the SS could exploit to their own advantage by deploying them for menial tasks in the the ambitious civil and military construction projects that the regime embarked on.

During the war, deployment shifted from construction to the armaments industries, and concentration camp prisoners became part of the reservoir workforce used to replace the German workers drafted into the Wehrmacht. Most were hired out to state and private firms in need of manpower, which in the last years of the war comprised nearly all prominent German firms. The concentration camp system was now an important element of the huge economic empire of the SS. In order to coordinate their economic interests more effectively, the SS Business Administration Main Office (*Wirtschaftsverwaltungshauptamt*, WVHA) was established in early 1942, and the inspectorate for concentration camps became part of it as its Section (*Amtsgruppe*) D. Subcamps of the existing concentration camps were established near those plants that employed large numbers of prisoners, and as a result the concentration camp system became a vast network spanning much of Europe. In 1945 there were some 1,200 satellite camps (*Außenlager*) and work commandos (*Außenkommandos*), which together held more prisoners than the 25 main concentration camps (*Hauptlager*), whose main task had become one of distributing prisoners to where they were needed.

However, despite their economic importance especially in the final years of the war, the deployment of concentration camp prisoners was not ruled by rational considerations of productivity or cost-efficiency, but work always remained primarily a means to humiliate, terrorize, and ultimately annihilate the prisoners. Apart from few exceptions, they were put to work under horrific conditions and driven until their strength was totally depleted in a system perhaps best described as "terror work" (Sofsky). In the last stage, most of those deployed in underground factories such as the one producing the V2 weapons, did not last longer than a few weeks.

***Treatment of concentration camp prisoners*** In the early years of Nazi rule, conditions were not unlike those in the pre-Nazi concentration camps. Many prisoners were released after a period of detention, and there were no systematic killings. Deaths that did occur were usually the result of abuse and maltreatment of individual prisoners by their SS guards.

However, from the beginning, imprisonment in concentration camps was meant to break the inmates as individuals. Various measures were used to achieve this, and they became more brutal as time went on. Prisoners had to give up all personal possessions, had their hair shaved off, were made to wear a special outfit that identified them as concentration camp prisoners (the "zebra uniform"), and had their names replaced by identification numbers (which were later tattooed onto their arms). Daily roll calls, often lasting for hours, and severe punishment for even the slightest violation of the camp rules set by the SS added to the rule of terror and unpredictability that characterized these camps.

Rising prisoner numbers meant that conditions in the camps deteriorated markedly and death rates rose sharply. With the outbreak of war, concentration camps were not just sites of mass-scale confinement but became also sites of murder—not as individual acts of arbitrary violence but as deliberate policy. This included the execution of prisoners without trial and the killing of thousands of Soviet prisoners of war (POWs) in Buchenwald, Sachsenhausen, and Auschwitz concentration camps. A number of prisoners were subjected to medical experimentation before they were killed. In addition, there was what has been called "indirect mass annihilation," the deliberate policy of induced starvation, brutal treatment, and total physical exhaustion through "terror work" eventually leading to death. This policy reached its climax when the camps in the east were hurriedly vacated before the advancing Red Army and the prisoners herded to camps in the *Reich* where those who had not died during these transports or marches were left to perish. The best known of these receiving camps is Bergen-Belsen near Hannover, which became an enduring symbol of the final phase of the Nazi concentration camps because of the photographs and film footage taken by the British when they liberated the camp in April 1945.

Prisoners were classified according to why they had been sent to the camps, and from 1936 they were given different colored badges, mostly triangles, which they had to wear on their clothes; for Jews it was the yellow Star of David. The treatment of the prisoners varied considerably according to their category. German criminal and political prisoners generally held the highest social position and had the best chances of getting preferential work assignments or positions of supervising or even commanding other inmates. The Jews were at the lowest rung of the concentration camp hierarchy, and the treatment that they received was worse than that of any other group. After the outbreak of war, their chances of survival were by far the

A Russian prisoner points an accusing finger at a guard during the liberation of his concentration camp by Allied forces, April 1945. ©CORBIS

lowest. Located only marginally higher on the social scale were homosexuals, Sinti and Roma, and Russians. Some of the prisoner-functionaries in the camps executed their task with brutality similar to the SS, whereas others tried to use their positions to help their fellow prisoners. The dividing line between perpetrators and victims often became blurred: "a grey zone, with ill-defined outlines which both separate and join the two camps" (Levi, p. 27).

Despite all the attempts of the SS to dehumanize the concentration camp prisoners and isolate them, something like a "camp society" did emerge in most camps. This was easiest in the early period of Nazi rule, when the process of developing solidarity was helped by the fact that most of those imprisoned were political opponents of the Nazis,

but even during the final stages of the war, when conditions became increasingly unbearable, testimonies of survivors cite many examples of mutual support. There were also attempts of small groups to engage in resistance activities.

It is impossible to give a precise number of the people who perished in the concentration camps; estimates range from 700,000 to as many as 1,100,000 out of a total of some 1.7 million. Most of these deaths were not the result of outright executions but of the conditions of the imprisonment. In addition, up to three million Jews plus tens of thousands of non-Jews were systematically killed in the extermination camps, largely by gas.

*The legacy of the Nazi concentration camps*
Those who survived the concentration camps kept

**Bodies of prisoners lie in the open at the camp at Nordhausen, Germany.** Upon reaching the camp in April of 1945, U.S. soldiers found over 3,000 dead and only a handful of survivors. AP/WIDE WORLD PHOTOS

the scars of their physical and psychological wounds for years, most of them until their death, and even the second generation was affected by this experience. There were also widespread feelings of guilt over having survived while so many others had perished. Many perpetrators never faced prosecution for the crimes they committed. The Allies tried the upper echelons of Nazi and military officials at Nuremberg, but most of the "ordinary" SS men and women returned to normal life after the end of the war. Postwar Germany, west and east, had problems facing up to the Nazi past. There was a general will not to remember too closely, and while cemeteries at the sites of the former concentration camps were cared for, it was a considerable time before proper memorials were set up that provided information on the crimes committed

there. It was only after German unification in 1990 that a wider discourse opened up about the place of the Nazi concentration camps in public memory, and how what is basically unrepresentable can be remembered.

## CONCENTRATION CAMPS OUTSIDE NAZI GERMANY

Just as the Nazis did not invent concentration camps, they were not the only ones to use them during this period. In the Soviet Union, camps to detain mainly political opponents date back to the 1920s, and this practice still continued after 1945: the so-called gulag system, as it became known after the branch of the Soviet security service NKVD. During World War II, members of ethnic and other minorities whose loyalties were doubted were also subjected to camp imprisonment or relocation to closed settlements.

In the Spanish civil war (1936–1939), the antirepublican forces led by General Francisco Franco set up concentration camps, such as San Pablo de Cardeña near Burgos, to incarcerate members of the prorepublican International Brigades who were not immediately executed after their capture. When prorepublican refugees from Spain entered France in early 1939, they were placed in special internment camps, the largest of which was Gurs at the foothills of the Pyrenees. The Vichy government of unoccupied France retained Gurs after 1940 and used it for the detention of political opponents and, increasingly, Jews, many of whom were handed over to the Germans. While conditions in all these camps were appalling, they were broadly in line with pre-Nazi concentration camps.

This was different from the camps established during World War II in Mussolini's Italy, by the pro-Nazi Ustaša régime in Croatia, and by Romania under Marshal Ion Antonescu, mainly in Transnistria. These were run on lines similar to the Nazi concentration camps, although they never achieved the same kind of murderous "efficiency." One of the most notorious camps was in Jasenovac, Croatia, where tens of thousands of Serbs, Jews, and Sinti and Roma were murdered.

## CONCENTRATION CAMPS AFTER 1945

The end of the Nazi regime did not mean the end of large-scale and arbitrary internment in camps established only for this purpose. Soviet military government placed political opponents of the new regime in their zone of occupation in Germany in "special camps" (*Sonderlager*), often set up, as in Buchenwald, at the recently liberated Nazi concentration camps. In Poland and Czechoslovakia, the ethnic German populations were rounded up after the end of the war, and many of them were confined in camps before their forced resettlement into what remained of Germany. Following their successful coup in 1967, the Greek military junta interned thousands of political opponents whom they suspected of "leftist" sympathies.

All these camps were detention camps where people were confined as members of specific political or ethnic groups and without proper judicial process. However, there has been disagreement over whether they could by right be called concentration camps, not least in the light of the specific connotation that this term obtained during the Nazi period. As a result, more descriptive terms, such as labor or detention camps, have usually been used to avoid an immediate Nazi association. Camps outside Europe were more readily branded as concentration camps, such as the so-called reeducation camps set up in Cambodia after the Khmer Rouge led by Pol Pot seized power in 1976.

In the post–Cold War period, there seems to be a gradual return to the use of the term in the somewhat wider sense of pre-1933. There was broad agreement that the camps set up by all the warring ethnic groups during the collapse of Yugoslavia, and in particular during the Bosnian War of 1992–1995, constituted concentration camps, with the abuses against the internees, the purposeful killings, and the conscious intent of ethnic cleansing. However, it needed film footage from the Bosnian Serb–run Logor Trnopolje camp in northern Bosnia to galvanize the international community into active intervention in this conflict. The pictures were so effective because they showed Muslim and Croat prisoners emaciated and behind barbed wire, which immediately evoked the scenes of Bergen-Belsen after its liberation in April 1945. The fact that they shook the world in a way that other pictures of human suffering in such camps during this war did not showed yet again the long shadow that the Nazi concentration camps cast over the twentieth century and beyond.

*See also* **Auschwitz-Birkenau; Buchenwald; Dachau; Forced Labor; Genocide; Gulag; Holocaust; Yugoslavia.**

BIBLIOGRAPHY

Armanski, Gerhard. *Maschinen des Terrors: Das Lager (KZ und GULAG) in der Moderne.* Münster, Germany, 1993.

Bauman, Zygmunt. "Das Jahrhundert der Lager." *Die Neue Gesellschaft / Frankfurter Hefte* 41, no. 1 (1994): 28–37.

Benz, Wolfgang, and Barbara Distel, eds. *Geschichte der Konzentrationslager, 1933–1945.* 2 vols. already published, several more in preparation. Berlin, 2001–.

Drobisch, Klaus, and Günther Wieland. *System der NS-Konzentrationslager, 1933–1939*. Berlin, 1993.

Gilbert, Martin. *The Macmillan Atlas of the Holocaust*. London, 1982.

Gutman, Yisrael, and Avital Saf, eds. *The Nazi Concentration Camps: Structure and Aims—the Image of the Prisoner—the Jews in the Camp: Proceedings of the Fourth Yad Vashem International Historical Conference*. Jerusalem, 1984.

Herbert, Ulrich, Karin Orth, and Christoph Dieckmann, eds. *Die nationalsozialistischen Konzentrationslager: Entwicklung und Struktur*. 2 vols. Göttingen, Germany, 1998.

Kaminski, Andrzej J. *Konzentrationslager 1896 bis heute: Eine Analyse*. Stuttgart, Germany, 1982.

Kogon, Eugen. *Der SS-Staat: Das System der deutschen Konzentrationslager*. Munich, Germany, 1946.

Levi, Primo. *The Drowned and the Saved*. Translated by Raymond Rosenthal. London, 1988. Translation of *I sommersi e i salvati* (1986).

Orth, Karin. *Das System der nationalsozialistischen Konzentrationslager: Eine politische Organisationsgeschichte*. Hamburg, Germany, 1999.

Pohl, Dieter. *Verfolgung und Massenmord in der NS-Zeit, 1933–1945*. Darmstadt, Germany, 2003.

Schwarz, Gudrun. *Die nationalsozialistischen Lager*. Frankfurt am Main, 1990.

Sofsky, Wolfgang. *The Order of Terror: The Concentration Camp*. Translated by William Templer. Princeton, N.J., 1997. Translation of *Die Ordnung des Terrors: Das Konzentrationslager* (1993).

Tuchel, Johannes. *Konzentrationslager: Organisationsgeschichte und Funktion der "Inspektion der Konzentrationslager," 1934–1938*. Boppard am Rhein, Germany, 1991.

Wippermann, Wolfgang. *Konzentrationslager: Geschichte, Nachgeschichte, Gedenken*. Berlin, 1999.

RAINER SCHULZE

---

# CONSCRIPTION.

Conscription, also known as the draft, is the compulsory enrollment of personnel, especially for the armed forces, based on national laws. Although ancient societies used conscription systems, and some forerunners existed in seventeenth-century Scandinavia, the beginnings of modern universal conscription are generally assigned to Revolutionary France with its *levée en masse* in 1793 and the Loi Jourdan-Delbrel of 1798. The *levée en masse* was not only an extraordinary measure to cope with both the necessities of the war since 1792 and the internal resistance to the Revolution; it was also a revolutionary means to mobilize the population. It created a myth of mass mobilization. While the German states, especially Prussia, introduced this system in their military reforms of 1806 to 1813 and kept it during peacetime, France after 1814 heavily restricted involuntary recruitment.

Starting in the 1860s, conscription was again high on the agenda in Europe, not only because of the instability of international relations, but also because of the consequences of nation building and industrial progress. Prussia and the German states cancelled all exemptions from 1867 on, the same year that Austria-Hungary introduced universal conscription after its defeat in the Austro-Prussian War of 1866; and France reintroduced it in 1872 after its own defeat in the Franco-Prussian War (1870–1871). In Russia military service was part of the peasants' serfdom. Following Russia's defeat in the Crimean War and enactment of the 1861 land reform, military recruitment had to be put on a new basis, introduced in an 1874 law. Service in the Imperial Army still remained extremely long and harsh. Switzerland introduced conscription nationwide in 1874, but kept a specific militia system that embraced all men up till the age of sixty. In Italy conscription was introduced in 1907.

Universal conscription became a central factor of the security policy of these states. It also turned out to be a major institution of political socialization in the age of the national states, and thus a homogenizing experience for men from different regions, and even those speaking different languages. While for the longest time there were exemptions for certain ethnic groups and certain strata of society, this tendency declined toward the turn of the century. Even Great Britain, where a broad anticonscription mood prevailed, debates on mass recruitment evolved during the Boer War (1899–1902) and prior to World War I. International tensions, especially those arising since 1904, led to an intensified policy of conscription in most European states.

## WORLD WAR I
In the summer of 1914 universal conscription and volunteer recruitment led to the buildup of mass

armies on an unprecedented scale. Over sixty million men were mobilized during World War I in Europe; almost nine million soldiers lost their lives.

Even in France, where the draft evasion rate had been almost 50 percent before the war, mobilization of men succeeded almost completely: only 1 percent failed to answer their call-up papers. With the murderous battles on the western front in 1916, mobilization had to be extended. Great Britain introduced universal conscription that year (although Ireland stayed exempt until April 1918), while Germany launched an overall mobilization of all men between the ages of seventeen and sixty for Patriotic Auxiliary Service (Vaterländischer Hilfsdienst). German military and industrial mobilization at this time contradicted each other. The Imperial Army even had to release more than three million soldiers in 1916 and 1917 in order to maintain a high level of industrial employment. Russia, on the other hand, extended conscription, so that at the end of 1916 even families' breadwinners had to join the army. This was one of the reasons for the disintegration of its Imperial Army, a process that had already started by 1915, and that stemmed from social inequality inside the army, unresolved problems of land reform, and logistical headaches in the army. This disintegration became a major factor leading to the two Russian Revolutions in 1917. While Pope Benedict XV (r. 1914–1922) criticized conscription in general, western and central European states were forced to legitimize mobilization through promises of welfare and political participation. Welfare for families, widows, and veterans had to expand on a broad basis. In Germany and Britain, the suffrage was reformed at the end of the war.

### THE INTERWAR PERIOD

After 1918, most European states, except Great Britain, either kept or developed conscript armies. Only the defeated states—Germany, Austria, Hungary, and Bulgaria—were restricted to volunteer armies. The interwar period saw two different developments: a decline of conscription in the democracies and the buildup of enormous mass armies by the dictatorships. In Russia, after the communist takeover in 1917, the Bolsheviks for a short period resorted to volunteer recruitment for

**TABLE 1**

**Mobilized men during World War I in Europe**

| Country | Number of mobilized men | Percentage of all war-able men |
|---|---|---|
| Austria-Hungary | 9,000,000 | 78 |
| Belgium | 292,000 | 15 |
| Bulgaria | 600,000? | 55 |
| France | 8,100,000 | 81 |
| Germany | 13,200,000 | 81 |
| Great Britain and Ireland | 6,100,000 | 53 |
| Greece | 335,000 | 33 |
| Italy | 5,600,000 | 55 |
| Montenegro | 50,000 | 100 |
| Portugal | 100,000 | 8 |
| Romania | 750,000 | 39 |
| Russia | 15,800,000? | 39 |
| Serbia | 750,000? | 63 |
| Total | 60,677,000 | 39 |

SOURCE: Gerhard Hirschfeld, Gerd Krumeich, and Irina Renz, eds. *Enzyklopädie Erster Weltkrieg*. Paderborn, Germany, 2003, p. 664.

their new Red Army (Rabochye-Krestyanskaya Krasnaya Armiya), but already during the early stages of the Russian civil war (1918–1920), they returned to conscription. Thereby, they incorporated officers of the Imperial Army into the new Red Army. By 1920, the Red Army constituted the largest military force in the world, with 5.5 million enlisted men and women. Even after the civil war the Soviet leadership kept a giant army, the size of which rose from 600,000 soldiers in 1924 to 1.8 million in 1939. The age of liability to conscription was set at between twenty-one and thirty, and the men, predominantly from working-class or poor peasant families, had to serve for two years.

Per the terms of the Treaty of Versailles of 1919, Germany was forced to abolish conscription and keep a professional army of one hundred thousand men. Adolf Hitler's rise to power in 1933, however, brought fundamental changes. In 1935, to support the new Wehrmacht, he reintroduced universal conscription entailing two years of military service preceded by a half year of duty in the Labor Service (Reichsarbeitsdienst). All spheres of society were militarized, and male youth received paramilitary training in the Hitler-Jugend. Austria after 1919 was obliged to keep only a small professional army of less then thirty thousand men. It reintroduced conscription in 1936, but the new army was soon integrated into the Wehrmacht.

The Italian army after the war was once again enlarged to face the conflict over Trieste in 1920. The army was demobilized only in 1922. The new fascist regime did not intensify conscription, which in first place affected the southern Italian peasantry. Even during the Italo-Ethiopian War of 1935 to 1936, the army did not expand.

During World War I, Polish men had been recruited into three different armies, the German, Austro-Hungarian, and Russian. Independent Poland in 1919 introduced universal conscription for its own army, which was heavily enlarged by volunteers in the Polish-Russian War of 1919 to 1920. The army held a comparatively high portion of 256,000 men in peacetime, which was raised to almost one million during the crisis of August 1939.

In the western democracies, conscription came to an end after World War I. Britain abolished universal conscription, generally considered an extraordinary measure interfering in the citizens' lives. In France during the 1920s pacifist thinking prevailed, and in 1926 obligatory military service was reduced from three years to one. That year the international pacifist movement signed its first anticonscription manifesto, thus hoping to reduce the risk of war.

All this changed after the Nazis came to power in 1933. In the face of Hitler's aggressive foreign policy, starting in 1935, but also because of the rise of right-wing militant movements all over Europe, conscription again became an important part of national security policy. Reluctantly, even the British government reintroduced it in early 1939.

## WORLD WAR II

Conscription during World War II differed heavily from the developments during World War I. On the one hand, conscription antedated the outbreak of war; on the other hand, conscription was ended in those areas that came rapidly under German control from 1940 until the spring and summer of 1941. Thereafter the Nazis themselves faced a manpower shortage. The newly created Waffen-SS conscripted men from Germany and from ethnic German minorities in Europe. Thus almost eighteen million men were recruited into the armed forces. In 1945 male youths and the elderly were mobilized for service in the Volkssturm militia without any prior military training.

**TABLE 2**

**Percentage of the male population aged twenty to forty-four in the military**

| Country | 1950 | 1960 | 1970 |
|---|---|---|---|
| Belgium | 4.7 | 7.3 | 5.9 |
| France | 8.4 | 13.5 | 5.8 |
| Italy | 3.8 | 3.8 | 4.6 |
| Netherlands | 12.7 | 8.1 | 5.3 |
| Sweden | 3.0 | 3.2 | 3.1 |
| United Kingdom | 7.6 | 6.1 | 4.2 |
| West Germany | – | 3.4 | 4.5 |

SOURCE: Peter Flora, Jean Alber, et al., eds. *State, Economy, and Society in Western Europe, 1815–1975: A Data Handbook.* Vol. 1. Frankfurt, 1983, p. 251.

The Soviet Union, which entered World War II on 17 September 1939, steadily increased the size of the Red Army from an initial force of 4.3 million men. Despite the loss of parts of the population after the German occupation of the western territories, the Soviet authorities were able to mobilize between thirty-five and forty million soldiers, among them approximately eight hundred thousand women, between 1941 and 1945. Irregular forms of conscription emerged in occupied eastern European countries, enforced by partisans, who forcibly recruited new personnel among the rural population.

The British conscription law recognized conscientious objection. It was also lenient in handling those who tried to avoid military service. In 1941 the government extended mobilization to civilians through the National Service Act, which established obligatory labor service for all men between eighteen and fifty years of age and for all women between the ages of twenty and thirty. The Nazi leadership, in order to avoid internal discontent, waited until 1944 to include women in compulsory labor systems.

In sum, an estimated seventy-five to eighty-five million men were mobilized in European armies during World War II (including those from non-European Russia). More than twenty million of these people died, at least half of them members of the Red Army.

## COLD WAR ERA

The end of World War II led to general demobilization and an enormous task of reintegration and rehabilitation of those who had served as conscripts during the war. The Red Army (known as the Soviet Army starting in 1946) was kept at considerable strength in order to sustain Soviet influence in most of Eastern Europe and to counterbalance the strategic advantage of U.S. nuclear weapons. Germany and Austria were completely demilitarized, unlike the former Axis allies Hungary, Romania, and Bulgaria. Conscription right after the war was unpopular, but even the British did not immediately return to a professional army.

From 1947 on, the Cold War dominated security policy and thus the debate on conscription. The British National Service remained in force until 1960; its last conscripts ended their duties in 1963. Every man at the age of eighteen was to serve eighteen months in the army. These men were required both for service in Europe, and therefore for deterrence against the Soviet Union, and for deployment in colonial conflicts. By the mid-1950s the strategy of the North Atlantic Treaty Organization (NATO) was shifted to focus on nuclear deterrence, thus also aiming to reduce the enormous costs of conventional forces. The shift in strategy during the late 1960s gave more weight to conventional warfare, but the plans for expanding the armies were not realized. Instead negotiations on troop reductions prevailed.

In France, conscription was widely accepted only after 1948. Nevertheless, conscripts were generally not deployed in the First Indochina War of 1946 to 1954. But conscription was used in the Algerian War of 1954 to 1962, and the French army had one million men in uniform by 1960. Public debate on the necessity of conscription intensified during the 1960s and 1970s.

In both the Federal Republic of Germany and the German Democratic Republic, planning for rearmament had already started by 1950. On Soviet orders the East German authorities in 1952 installed a paramilitary force, the so-called Kasernierte Volkspolizei, which was turned into the National People's Army (Nationale Volksarmee) in 1956. Public opinion in West Germany was sharply divided on rearmament, which finally started in 1956 with the buildup of the Federal Forces (Bundeswehr), a new conscript army, which did not recruit citizens of West Berlin. Universal conscription came only later, in 1962. A similar development occurred in Austria, where a new conscript army was introduced in 1955, after the nation had regained its sovereignty.

Only after Joseph Stalin's death in March 1953 did the size of the Soviet Army fall, from 5.3 million men to 3.6 million at the end of 1958. In 1960 Nikita Khrushchev started another troop reduction, but stopped it during the crisis over Berlin. Conscripts of the Soviet Army were deployed abroad, often in other member countries of the Warsaw Pact (1955). During the 1970s and 1980s a crisis of morale developed, caused by bad pay, poor housing, and brutal treatment, and visible in high rates of criminality and suicide. Especially starting in the mid-1980s, draft evasion increased considerably. This problem did not change after Mikhail Gorbachev's 1989 troop reductions and the transformation of the Soviet Army into the Russian Army in 1992.

In the immediate aftermath of World War II, the Eastern European armies predominantly relied on the personnel of wartime communist underground movements. In Hungary, which had fought on the Axis side during the war, an army was established only in 1949. At the end of the 1950s, when the Soviet Army was reduced in size, the Warsaw Pact countries had to enlarge their national armed forces. When conscription restarted at the end of the 1940s, the communist regimes tried to shift the traditional patterns of recruiting by enacting preferences for young men from working-class or peasant backgrounds. The recruits could join either the regular army, the internal troops of the ministries of the interior, or the border troops. Soldiers in Warsaw Pact armies were to a considerable degree deployed in the economy, such as in construction work or in harvesting. Political education and indoctrination were constant features of Warsaw Pact armies. All states, in addition to their armies, kept paramilitary militias or territorial defense forces made up of older men and at times of women. Yugoslavia did not join the Warsaw Pact, but kept its giant army, which numbered 500,000 in 1951, under national control. It was finally reduced to 180,000 men during the 1980s. Nevertheless, Yugoslav conscripts were kept under constant communist indoctrination.

## POST–COLD WAR DEVELOPMENTS

After the end of the Cold War and the dissolution of the Warsaw Pact in 1991, army sizes in Western and Eastern Europe were seriously reduced. The Soviet Army, in Europe divided into Russian, Ukrainian, Belarusian, Moldovan, and Baltic armies, withdrew its troops from the former Warsaw Pact countries. Several former Warsaw Pact members joined NATO (Hungary, the Czech Republic, and Poland in 1999; Bulgaria, the Baltic states, Romania, Slovakia, and Slovenia in 2004), and they thus now must use NATO standards of military service and training. All of these nations have considerably downsized their armies, reduced the length of service, and thus diminished the role of conscription in defense strategy.

After 1989 criticism of conscription was on the rise again. Both the reduction of dangerous political tensions inside Europe and troop reductions strengthened the arguments for a professional army. France began to revise its conscription policy in 1992 and finally started the process of turning its army into a volunteer force in 1997. Conscription ended in several European states, first in Belgium and the Netherlands, and since 2000 in France, Spain, Portugal, Slovenia, the Czech Republic, Hungary, and Italy. Other countries were in the process of planning to introduce professional armies.

## GENERAL FEATURES OF CONSCRIPTION

Conscription is the most serious obligation a citizen has to fulfill, because it includes the loss of individual freedom and the risk of being killed. Thus conscription was always under debate within societies and among politicians. In societies with a functioning public sphere these discussions were led in public; in authoritarian or totalitarian systems draft evasion was the only way to express dissent.

In contrast to the nineteenth century, the significance of conscription for nation building and for the development of notions of citizenship declined during the twentieth century. Only new or reborn states such as Poland in 1918 or Ukraine or Slovakia in the post–Cold War era consider conscription to be part of modern state-building. Nevertheless, the idea of the citizen-soldier, born in the revolutionary era, was still alive in the French tradition, as well as during the revolutions of 1917 to 1919, and in the West German debates on army reform during the 1960s and 1970s. For conscripts, army service constitutes an important agent of conservative socialization. In the army, some critics believe, governments obtain full control of the young male population.

Conscription is always dependent on the demographic structure of societies, especially on the availability of men between the ages of approximately seventeen and thirty. For example, in France until 1940 there was much concern about the country's demographic disadvantage in relation to Germany, with the latter's more dynamic population growth. Only in exceptional cases, as occurred in the Soviet Union and Great Britain during World War II, were women recruited for special branches of the army. In the 2000s, there were discussions in Sweden as to whether military conscription should be applied equally to men and women. A second important factor in the way conscription operates is the maintenance of standards of physical and mental fitness for military service. Countries with poorly structured economies in particular had problems in recruiting physically able young men; since the late twentieth century the general decline of physical fitness among youth has affected the conscription rate. Several countries had or have specific conscription rules according to the level of education, thus exempting men with higher education or reducing the length of their service.

Especially during the first half of the twentieth century social inequality often determined recruitment. While the professional officer corps had a disproportionate number of men from the aristocracy and upper strata of society, general conscription predominantly aimed at men of peasant origin. Especially in wartime, workers were recruited to a lesser extent, because they were considered important for the war economy. Only communist armies tended to deliberately recruit workers or sons of workers' families. After World War II these socially differentiated patterns of recruitment faded away, because of the rapid urbanization in Europe and the diminution of political tensions, but with certain notable exceptions as in the Yugoslav civil war in the 1990s.

Ethnicity played an important role in conscription, especially up to World War II. During World War I all the empires, but especially Austria-Hungary and Russia, mobilized large numbers of minorities. Then the successor states had to cope with large minorities in their armies. Only the Red Army and later on the Yugoslav armies were able to integrate these centrifugal forces under communist coercion from the 1940s until the late 1980s.

The question of conscription has always been connected to conscientious objection. Most conscript armies introduced exemptions for specific, especially religious, groups such as Jehovah's Witnesses or Quakers; even the Red Army exempted certain groups of conscientious objectors until 1939. Prussia lifted all these regulations in 1867, and draft evasion was severely punished in Germany until 1945. During the Nazi period draft evaders were sent to concentration camps. The West German Basic Law of 1949 introduced an "alternative service" for conscientious objectors according to the British model. Since the 1990s this practice has been adopted by several European states.

*See also* **Armies.**

BIBLIOGRAPHY

Flynn, George Q. "Conscription and Equity in Western Democracies, 1940–1975." *Journal of Contemporary History* 33, no. 1 (1998): 5–20.

———. *Conscription and Democracy: The Draft in France, Great Britain, and the United States.* Westport, Conn., 2002.

Foerster, Roland G., ed. *Die Wehrpflicht: Entstehung, Erscheinungsformen und politisch-militärische Wirkung.* Munich, 1994.

Frevert, Ute. *A Nation in Barracks: Modern Germany, Military Conscription, and Civil Society.* Translated by Andrew Boreham with Daniel Brückenhaus. Oxford, U.K., 2004.

Joenniemi, Pertti, ed. *The Changing Face of European Conscription.* Burlington, Vt., 2005.

Mjøset, Lars, and Stephen Van Holde, eds. *The Comparative Study of Conscription in the Armed Forces.* Amsterdam, 2002.

Moran, Daniel, and Arthur Waldron, eds. *The People in Arms: Military Myth and National Mobilization since the French Revolution.* Cambridge, U.K., 2003.

Sanborn, Joshua A. *Drafting the Russian Nation: Military Conscription, Total War, and Mass Politics, 1905–1925.* DeKalb, Ill., 2003.

DIETER POHL

# CONSTITUTIONS.

Constitutions are documents that set forth and describe the fundamental organizing principles of a state, the rights possessed by citizens of the state, the institutions that exercise public authority and the allocation of powers among those institutions, the allocation of responsibilities between the national government and subnational levels of government, and the means by which the constitution may be amended.

Constitutions are typically prepared after the demise of an existing state and its succession by one or more new states or in order to transform an existing state into a new state. Representing as they do the reconstitution of public authority in an existing or a newly created state, constitutions invariably present, even if only implicitly, a diagnosis of the institutional flaws that existed in the previous regime and were assumed by those drafting the new constitutions to have contributed to the failures—perhaps even demise—of that regime as well as a prescription, again often only implicit, for how to ensure that those failures do not occur again. But they may of course also contain provisions that, under certain circumstances, have consequences that were unanticipated by their authors.

Since 1914, Europe has experienced three periods of especially intensive preparation of new constitutions—after World War I, after World War II, and after the demise of the Soviet Union and the communist-dominated regimes of Central and Eastern Europe. In all three periods, new constitutions were prepared after the demise of the regimes that were defeated in the wars and the creation of new states in their place—for example, after the defeat of the German Empire and Austria-Hungary in World War I, after the defeat of Nazi Germany and Fascist Italy in World War II, and after the demise of the Soviet Union, Yugoslavia, and Czechoslovakia and the demise of communist regimes in other countries in the 1990s. There were, however, other notable moments at which new constitutions were prepared, such as after the demise of a military-dominated dictatorship and subsequent abdication of a monarch in Spain in 1931, after the death of Francisco Franco (1892–1975), the Spanish head of state, in 1975, and after the return of Charles de Gaulle (1890–1970) as prime minister of France in 1958.

## CONSTITUTIONS AS DIAGNOSIS AND PRESCRIPTION: THE CASE OF GERMANY

Most of the European constitutions drafted since World War I have been drafted by constituent assemblies composed of the representatives of parties elected for that purpose or already sitting in representative institutions. That they typically provide both a diagnosis of the past and a prescription for the future is suggested by the content of many of the constitutions drafted over the past century. None illustrates that better than the constitution of the German Republic (1919–1933) and the Basic Law (*Grundgesetz*) of the Federal Republic. And the fate of the short-lived republic illustrates, also, that constitutions can, despite the best of intentions, have unintended and even tragic consequences.

One week after the Armistice that ended World War I, the German emperor (kaiser), William II (1859–1941), abdicated and the leaders of the parliament (Reichstag) declared Germany a republic. An election for a constituent assembly was called for 19 January 1919. In the election the Social Democratic Party, the Catholic-based Center Party, and the Democratic Party won a substantial majority of the seats in the assembly.

The empire created in 1871 was a federation of German states in which the king of Prussia was the emperor, the minister president of Prussia, the largest state, was the chancellor (*Kanzler*), the states were represented in the upper chamber of the parliament (the Reichsrat), and males voted for representatives of parties who sat in the lower chamber (the Reichstag). Despite the facade of democratic politics, the empire was an executive-dominated, authoritarian regime. The chancellor was accountable to the emperor, not to the parliament. The emperor could dissolve the parliament. The parliament did not have the right to question the government and could not initiate legislation. In addition, although parties existed, the opposition—most notably the Social Democratic Party, which drew substantial support from industrial workers, and the Catholic-based Center Party—were subjected to legal restrictions during much of the late nineteenth century (e.g., via the anti-socialist laws in the case of the Social Democrats) and harassment, intimidation, and attacks on their institutions (e.g., via the Kulturkampf in the case of the Center and other Catholic parties).

The Weimar assembly replaced the executive-centered empire with a republic in which sovereignty was vested in the people, civil liberties were guaranteed in the constitution, the government was formed in and accountable to the parliament, and the parliament had the right to initiate legislation, question the chancellor, and vote or withhold confidence in the government. Article 22 of the new constitution stipulated that the lower house of the parliament was to be elected by universal, equal, direct secret suffrage of all men and women over twenty in accordance with the principle of proportional representation. According to Article 109, all Germans were equal before the law. In marked contrast to the empire, Article 135 of the Weimar constitution guaranteed full liberty of faith.

Perhaps more than any other until then, the Weimar constitution appeared to maximize liberal values and democratic institutions and accountability. And yet, within fourteen years, on 30 January 1933, Adolf Hitler (1889–1945) came to power—peacefully, appointed chancellor at the head of a government formed by his National Socialist German Workers Party (NSDAP) and the German National People's Party (DNVP)—bringing with him the seeds of the Holocaust and the imperial pretensions that would eventually lead to World War II.

While many political, economic, social, cultural, and international factors contributed to the coming to power of Hitler and the Nazis, the Weimar constitution itself contributed to that outcome. For one thing, its requirement that the seats in the Reichstag be allocated by proportional representation and the use of a national list system resulted in an exceptionally low threshold of representation—well under 0.5 percent of the national vote—that removed any incentive for parties to coalesce and dispersed the seats in the Reichstag among many parties. As a result, no party came close to having a majority and parties that sought to govern could do so only by forming coalitions with other parties. For the first decade of the republic, coalitions were able to obtain the support of a majority in the parliament. But once the Social Democratic Party, the largest in the republic, withdrew from the government in March 1930 in a dispute over the funding of unemployment compensation, it became impossible to form a coalition that enjoyed the support of a majority in the parliament.

At that point, a second flaw in the constitution became apparent—its retention, despite the democratic form of government, of an unusual degree of power in the office that replaced the emperor as the head of state. The Weimar constitution replaced the emperor with a president who was to be directly elected (Article 41) for a term of seven years (Article 43). The president could dissolve the Reichstag, which would result in an election within sixty days (Article 25); issue emergency decrees, impose martial law, and suspend the rights of citizens in order to ensure the state's performance of its duties and restore public order and security (Article 48); and appoint and dismiss the chancellor (Article 53).

Lacking a parliamentary majority, the government that took office after the March 1930 resignation of the Social Democratic-led government attempted to use the president's decree powers in Article 48 to pass a financial bill. But it was defeated and so President Paul von Hindenburg (1847–1934) dissolved the Reichstag and called new elections. In the election of 14 September 1930, the NSDAP won 18.3 percent, a substantial increase over the 2.6 percent it had won in 1928, and became the second-largest party in the chamber. Without the Communists, who won 13 percent, the Nazis, and the Social Democrats, who obtained almost 25 percent of the vote, a parliamentary majority did not exist. As a result, government lapsed into rule by presidential decree and a series of unsuccessful efforts by presidential appointees to form a government that could command a majority.

The turn to presidentialism provided additional legitimation to that office beyond what already existed as a result of direct election. And as that office became increasingly powerful relative to the parliament, it was not surprising that Hitler decided to challenge Hindenburg when the president, despite his age—eighty-four—ran for reelection in 1932. In the first ballot on 13 March 1932, Hitler obtained

30 percent of the vote and deprived Hindenburg of a first-ballot victory. Hindenburg won reelection in the run-off ballot on 10 April 1932, but Hitler, with 36.8 percent of the vote, had doubled the Nazi vote, compared with the election of September 1930.

The president's advisers sought Hitler's support for a new government formed by the parties of the center-right of the political spectrum but not including the Nazis. Hitler agreed, providing new elections were called. In the election on 31 July 1932, many of those who had voted for Hitler in the presidential election voted for the NSDAP. In fact, it received 37.3 percent, almost the same vote Hitler had received in the second round of the presidential election. With the NSDAP now constituting the largest party by far in the parliament, Hitler demanded the position of vice-chancellor as the price of support for a government. Hindenburg refused, but without the NSDAP and the Communists it was impossible for any grouping of parties to form a parliamentary majority, so the president dissolved the parliament and called another election on 6 November 1932. The NSDAP vote dropped slightly, to 33.1 percent, but it was still the largest party by far, and the president's advisers asked Hitler under what circumstances he would support a government. He demanded that he be appointed chancellor. Hindenburg refused and appointed instead the defense minister, General Kurt von Schleicher (1882–1934). But both the NSDAP and the DNVP refused to support Schleicher and so, seeing no other alternative, in late January 1933 Hindenburg appointed Hitler chancellor of an NSDAP-DNVP government.

The Hitler-led government took office on 30 January 1933. Less than two months later, using a fire in the Reichstag as a pretext, a new election was called on 5 March 1933, in which the NSDAP won 44 percent of the vote and the DNVP 8 percent. Commanding a majority in the Reichstag, the government put through an Enabling Act that gave the government all of the parliament's powers for four years, thus terminating the Weimar Republic.

After the defeat of Nazi Germany in World War II, the victors—the United States, the United Kingdom, France, and the Soviet Union—divided the country into four occupation zones. In December 1946 the United States and the United Kingdom combined their zones into a new entity called Bizonia, and a year later France was persuaded to join its zone to Bizonia. In February 1948, at a meeting in London to prepare the distribution of assistance through the American Economic Recovery Program (better known as the Marshall Plan after the U.S. secretary of state George Marshall, who had proposed the plan), the three Western occupying powers agreed to transform Bizonia into a federal, democratic state.

At Frankfurt on 1 July 1948 the military governors of the three occupation zones met with the minister presidents (i.e., prime ministers) of the twelve states within the zones—the other five states were located in the zone occupied by the Soviet Union—and recommended that the ministers convene a constituent assembly before September to draft a constitution for the state and put it to a referendum for approval. The ministers were less than enthusiastic, fearing that to do so would permanently divide the country, and agreed, instead, to convene a Parliamentary Council to draft a Basic Law, rather than a constitution, that would be ratified by the states. The council, consisting of delegates of the twelve states, met in Bonn from September 1948 and completed preparation and adoption of the Basic Law (*Grundgesetz*) in May 1949. Several months later, the five states in the Soviet zone were transformed by the Soviet Union into the German Democratic Republic (GDR) in October 1949, thereby creating the institutional and legal basis for a division of Germany into two states that would remain until the five states of the GDR entered the Federal Republic on 3 October 1990.

Just as the constituent assembly that met in Weimar in 1919 had sought to correct the deficiencies of the empire, so too the Parliamentary Council that met in Bonn in 1948–1949 sought to correct the deficiencies of the Weimar constitution. It stipulated that those who abused the freedoms granted by the law to fight the democratic order would forfeit those rights (Article 18). It created a "democratic and social federal state" (Article 20). It stipulated that acts tending to or undertaken with the intention of disturbing peaceful relations among states and preparing for aggressive war were unconstitutional (Article 26). In order to prevent the centralization of power that occurred in Hitler's Germany, it recreated a federal system of states and empowered the states through both the allocation of competences and the representation of their governments in the Bundesrat, the upper chamber of the bicameral legislature (Articles 30 and 70). It created a parliamentary form of government with a strong bicameral legislature and a weak, indirectly elected president (Article 54). It stipulated that the Bundestag, the new lower house, could express its lack of confidence in the chancellor only by a majority vote for a successor (Article 67).

The Basic Law did not explicitly mandate a change in the electoral system used in the Weimar Republic. But the electoral statute that was adopted was designed to prevent the dispersion of votes and proliferation of parties that occurred with the republic's form of proportional representation. It established a dual-ballot electoral system in which one-half of the seats in the Bundestag were filled by representatives elected on a first-past-the-post basis in single-member districts and one-half were filled from party lists in each state for which voters expressed a preference. But it stipulated that only parties winning a district seat or 5 percent of the party vote could receive seats from the party lists, thereby favoring the large parties and underrepresenting or excluding altogether small parties and inducing them to coalesce with larger ones. (In 1953 the threshold was raised from 5 percent of a state list to 5 percent of the second-ballot vote for the party in the entire electorate. And in 1956 the minimum number of district seats required in order to qualify for seats from the party list according to the national vote was raised to three.) Taken together, these institutional changes played a large role in facilitating the development of two large parties—the Christian Democratic Union and the Social Democratic Party—that were able, with one or more smaller parties, to form stable majorities for long periods, thereby avoiding the parliamentary instability that characterized the last years of the Weimar Republic.

## RECONSTITUTING THE STATE IN SPAIN, FRANCE, AND ITALY

In Spain, after the resignation in 1930 of General Miguel Primo de Rivera (1870–1930), who had seized power and established a dictatorship in 1923, the king, Alfonso XIII (1886–1941), decided to hold municipal elections. The elections, in April 1931, produced a massive vote for parties favoring a republic, and the king abdicated. Two months later, on 28 June 1931, a constituent assembly was elected and drafted the constitution that created the Second Republic. In an assembly dominated by the Republican and Socialist parties, it was perhaps not surprising that the constitution would establish a "democratic republic of workers of all classes." And in a country in which the Catholic Church had been a political, economic, and social power for so long, it was not surprising that the constitution would be sharply anticlerical. Article 26 stipulated that much of the property owned by the church was to be taken by the state, that public salaries for priests and the church's role in education were terminated, that orders such as the Jesuits that required a vow of loyalty were prohibited, and that divorce was legal. The explicitly class-based and anticlerical provisions of course contributed to the mobilization of Catholic and conservative opposition to the republic and to a deepening ideological polarization that eventually led, in 1936, to a military insurrection led by General Franco against the republic and the civil war of 1936–1939.

In France, the Third Republic, which had been formed in 1875, had been brought to a close with the vote by the Chamber of Deputies and Senate in July 1940, one month after the German invasion, to grant full governing power to Marshal Philippe Pétain (1856–1951). On 21 October 1945, a provisional government headed by Charles de Gaulle (1890–1970) called an election to elect representatives who would either constitute a restored Chamber of Deputies of the Third Republic or a new constituent assembly. De Gaulle urged the latter but demanded that the assembly have a limited duration of seven months and that the constitution it prepared be submitted to a referendum. The voters chose to create a constituent assembly that would, as de Gaulle wished, be limited to seven months' duration and would submit its draft to a subsequent referendum.

On 5 May 1946, a draft constitution supported by the Communists, the largest party in the assembly, and the Socialists was rejected in a referendum. Following new elections and negotiations among the major parties, a slightly modified constitution was put to a referendum on 13 October 1946 and approved by 54 percent of the voters, thereby constituting the Fourth Republic. The constitution created a "secular, democratic and social republic" (Article 1), an indirectly elected president (Article 29), and a parliamentary form of government in which the prime minister and government must receive the confidence of the National Assembly (Article 45). While it left the mode of election to be determined by law, it clearly expressed a preference for proportional representation (Article 6).

Italy had been a monarchy since the country's unification in 1861. The country had been ruled, at least nominally, by King Victor Emmanuel III (1869–1947) from 1900 until his abdication in May 1946, even throughout the two decades from October 1922 until July 1943 when Benito Mussolini (1883–1945) and the Fascists controlled the state. On 2 June 1946, Italian voters were asked to decide in a referendum whether they wished to retain the monarchy or preferred creating a republic. Fifty-four percent voted for a republic and elected a constituent assembly that drafted and, on 11 December 1947, approved the constitution creating a new republic. As in France, it created an indirectly elected president (Article 83) and required that the government enjoy the confidence of both houses of parliament (Article 94). And it stipulated that the lower house, the Chamber of Deputies, would be elected by proportional representation (Article 56).

In the wake of Franco's death in Spain in November 1975, the nature of the regime was uncertain. He had made Prince Juan Carlos de Borbón (b. 1938) his designated successor as head of state, but it was far from clear in what direction, if any, the regime would evolve. But led by Adolfo Suárez (b. 1932), and with the guidance of King Juan Carlos I, the post-Franco government engineered a gradual and peaceful transition to a democratic regime. In 1976 political parties were legalized, and in December of that year the government called a referendum that overwhelmingly approved the transitional process toward democracy outlined by the government. On 15 June 1977, an election was held for a constituent assembly. On 6 December 1978, after having been approved by an overwhelming margin in the assembly, 88 percent of the voters approved the new constitution in a referendum. Three weeks later, King Juan Carlos I signed and promulgated the new constitution that created a democratic and parliamentary form of government in a state that was a constitutional monarchy.

## PRESIDENTIAL CONSTITUTIONS

In at least two notable instances, constitutions were prepared not by constituent assemblies elected by voters or indirectly elected assemblies such as the German Parliamentary Council but, rather, by political executives. Not surprisingly perhaps, the constitutions prepared by sitting executives greatly enhanced the power of the executive at the expense of the legislative branch.

In France, de Gaulle had abruptly quit as head of the provisional government in January 1946, in part because of his frustration with the political parties in the constituent assembly. On 16 June 1946 he spoke at Bayeux and criticized the parties and the constitution they had wrought, and called for one that concentrated power in the presidency. While his supporters organized politically and participated in the Fourth Republic, de Gaulle remained aloof from politics, living at his country home in the small village of Colombey-les-deux-Églises in the east and writing his memoirs.

Making use of various forms of proportional representation to elect the National Assembly, the Fourth Republic had experienced a fragmentation of partisan support that made it exceptionally difficult to form stable governments. After the Communist Party, which was the largest party and remained so throughout the Fourth Republic, withdrew from the government in May 1947, it became difficult if not impossible to form stable majorities, and over the next eleven years twenty different governments held office. In addition to their short life expectancy, governments in the Fourth Republic were severely weakened by their involvement in two colonial wars, the first in French Indochina from 1946 until 1954 and the second, from 1954, in Algeria.

In the spring of 1958, with the war against the Algerian National Liberation Front (FLN) in its fourth year and the French government's resolve to continue the war weakening, the French military, with the vocal support of the large settler community, created a Committee of Public Safety in Algiers and called for de Gaulle's return to power, assuming—incorrectly as it turned out—that de Gaulle would keep Algeria as an integral part of France. De Gaulle indicated he was available, and President René Coty (1882–1962) invited him to return as prime minister, which he did on 1 June 1958.

But de Gaulle returned on one condition—that he be empowered to revise the constitution. His aides, led by Michel Debré (1912–1996), rapidly prepared a new constitution that substantially increased the power of the president. According to the new constitution, which was approved by 79 percent of the voters in a referendum on 28 September 1958, the president was given the responsibility to ensure that the constitution was observed, the public authorities functioned properly, and the country's independence was maintained (Article 5). The president would appoint the prime minister and, on the latter's proposal, the ministers of the government (Article 8). He presided over the government (Article 9), had the power to veto legislation (Article 10), could submit a proposed law to a referendum and, if it passed, promulgate it (Article 11), could dissolve the parliament and call new elections (Article 12), was the commander in chief and in charge of the military (Article 15), could take whatever measures were required to defend the republic when it was threatened (Article 16), could negotiate and ratify treaties (Article 52), and could initiate an amendment of the constitution (Article 89). In December 1958, de Gaulle was elected president by an electoral college consisting of members of parliament, departmental councils, mayors, and councilors of the communes.

In the early years of the Fifth Republic, de Gaulle mobilized support for the major initiatives of the government, and for himself personally, by calling referendums on Algerian self-determination (8 January 1961), Algerian independence (8 April 1962), and direct election of the president (28 October 1962). Legislative elections were held immediately following the 1958 referendum that approved the constitution and the 1962 referendum instituting direct election of the president, thereby transferring to the party led by de Gaulle's supporters and colleagues a good deal of the support for him expressed in the referendums. Ironically, de Gaulle, who was elected to a second seven-year term in December 1965, was defeated in a referendum on Senate and regional reform on 27 April 1969, after which he resigned.

Another instance in which a sitting executive prepared a constitution that greatly enhanced the power of the president occurred in the Russian

Federation in 1993. The Russian Federation was the successor to the Russian Soviet Federated Socialist Republic, one of the fifteen that, together, constituted the Union of Soviet Socialist Republics (USSR). At the Nineteenth Party Conference of the Communist Party of the Soviet Union (CPSU) in 1988, Mikhail Gorbachev (b. 1931), who had been elected general secretary of the Central Committee of the CPSU in March 1985, initiated a series of political institutional reforms that transformed the Soviet Union and, many would say, contributed to its demise. Over the next two years, the Supreme Soviet of the USSR was transformed into a standing legislature; a Congress of People's Deputies was created, from which the Supreme Soviet was elected; multiple candidacies in the elections for the Congress were tolerated; the Central Committee of the CPSU voted, following a vote by the Congress, to remove Article 6 of the USSR constitution, which gave the CPSU a leading role in the state; elections were held for the Supreme Soviets in which multiple candidacies were allowed; and several republics declared sovereignty or outright independence.

Boris Yeltsin (b. 1931) had been brought to Moscow to be Central Committee secretary for construction in 1985 and was soon elevated to first secretary of the Moscow City Party and a position in the Politburo of the CPSU. He was dropped from both positions in 1987 after criticizing the slow pace of Gorbachev's perestroika (restructuring) but made a political comeback in 1989–1990. Elected to the Congress and Supreme Soviet in 1989 and then to the Supreme Soviet of the Russian Republic in 1990, he was elected chair of the latter in May 1990. One month later, the Russian Supreme Soviet followed the lead of the Baltic republics and others and declared its sovereignty in the Union.

Faced with declarations of sovereignty or independence by most of the republics, Gorbachev sought in 1990–1991 to renegotiate the Union Treaty. In March 1991, a referendum was held in nine republics to preserve the USSR as a "renewed federation of equal sovereign republics." At the same time, the electorate of the Russian Republic was asked whether it wanted direct election of the chairman of the Supreme Soviet. More than 70 percent said yes, and on 12 June 1991 an election was held and Yeltsin won, obtaining 57 percent of the vote.

The Union Treaty was to be signed by nine of the fifteen republics on 20 August 1991. Fearing the de facto breakup of the Soviet Union, the heads of some of the most important ministries and agencies, including defense, interior, and state security (the KGB), attempted unsuccessfully to carry out a coup. In the wake of the coup attempt, the three Baltic republics declared their independence. The Ukrainian Supreme Soviet declared the republic independent on 24 August 1991, and in October it unanimously rejected the Union Treaty. On 1 December 1991, in a referendum in which 84 percent of Ukrainian voters participated, more than 90 percent voted in support of Ukrainian independence. One week later, Yeltsin, Leonid Kravchuk (b. 1934) of Ukraine, and Stanislav Shushkevich (b. 1934) of Belarus met in Minsk, declared the USSR treaty null and void, and invited the other republics to join them in a Commonwealth of Independent States. On 25 December 1991 Gorbachev resigned as state president—he had resigned as general secretary of the CPSU on 24 August 1991—and the USSR ceased to exist.

After the demise of the USSR and transformation of the RSFSR into the Russian Federation, Yeltsin, who had played a major role in thwarting the August 1991 coup, sought to pursue a program of rapid economic reform. But he and his government soon encountered considerable resistance from within the Congress and Supreme Soviet. By early 1993 there was so much opposition to Yeltsin that a motion to impeach him nearly won. In September 1993, Yeltsin dismissed the Supreme Soviet and Congress, and the Supreme Soviet responded by terminating his presidency. The Constitutional Court upheld the Supreme Soviet's action but Yeltsin refused to leave office. When the leaders of the parliament refused to vacate the White House, he used military force to drive them out.

Meanwhile, Yeltsin had set his aides to work drafting a new constitution. The latest version of the USSR constitution, which dated from 1977, was obviously no longer applicable, and the federation had obtained independence without any constitutional structure other than what it inherited from the Russian Republic. Not surprisingly, in view of the deep hostility that had arisen between the presidency and the legislature in 1992 and 1993, the constitution prepared by Yeltsin's advisers provided for an exceptionally strong president and shifted public authority from the legislative to the executive branch. According to the constitution, which was put to the voters in a referendum on 12 December 1993 and approved by 58 percent, the president is the guarantor of the constitution and the sovereignty and independence of the federation and defines the basic domestic and foreign policy guidelines of the federation (Article 80). He appoints the prime minister, presides over meetings of the government, decides on the resignation of the government, appoints and dismisses the deputy prime ministers and ministers, nominates the judges of the Constitutional and Supreme Courts, and forms and heads the Security Council (Article 83). He can dissolve the House of Representatives (the Duma) and call elections and referendums (Article 84). He is responsible for the federation's foreign policy and negotiates and signs treaties (Article 86), is the head of the military and can introduce martial law (Article 87), can impose a state of emergency (Article 88), and can issue binding decrees and orders (Article 90). Regarding his relations with the House of Representatives, if it rejects his nominee for head of government three times he can appoint the head, dissolve the House, and call new elections (Article 111). And if the House passes two nonconfidence resolutions within three months, he can dismiss the government or dissolve the House (Article 117).

In the period since the demise of the communist-dominated regimes of Central and Eastern Europe and the Soviet Union, many of the states have succeeded in establishing democratic institutions. Most of the states in Central and Eastern Europe, seeking to join the European Union (EU) and aware that the EU's criteria for membership include the establishment of a democratic policy, have succeeded in establishing democracy and the rule of law. But most of the former republics of the Soviet Union except for the Baltic states have turned, instead, toward a form of executive-centered politics marked by an exceptionally strong president, a weak legislature, a weak judiciary, and an absence of secure guarantees for individual rights and liberties. Since 1993, the Russian Federation has exemplified this mode of politics, and to a very large degree its turn toward executive-centered authoritarianism is the result of,

and dates from, its adoption of the constitution drafted by the presidency in December 1993.

## CONSTITUTIONS AND THE VERTICAL ALLOCATION OF AUTHORITY

If the relationship between the executive and legislative branches figures prominently in all constitutions, an equally important relationship involves that between the national government and subnational levels of government. Broadly speaking, constitutions create either unitary systems of government—that is, systems in which all responsibility and authority lies with the national government, although it may delegate or devolve some of its authority to subnational levels—or federal systems of government in which subnational units have constitutionally defined competences and powers. There are, however, intermediate arrangements, as in the case of unitary systems that devolve some degree of authority to subnational units or regions. France, Italy, and the United Kingdom have all enacted limited devolutions of authority to subnational units such as regions.

Occasionally, constitutions have been drafted primarily for the purpose of altering the existing arrangements between national and subnational governments. Among the notable examples are the 1971 and 1974 constitutions of the Socialist Federal Republic of Yugoslavia and the 1993 constitution of Belgium. The 1974 constitution, one of the longest and most complicated ever written, dealt with relations between the six republics of the federal republic—Serbia, Croatia, Slovenia, Bosnia-Herzegovina, Macedonia, and Montenegro—and the two autonomous regions within Serbia, Vojvodina and Kosovo, as well as the sharing of power by the republics and regions in a collective presidency. Designed by Tito (Josip Broz; 1892–1980), the leader of the League of Communists since 1939, prime minister from 1945 until 1953, and president since 1953, to prepare for his passing from the scene and partly to contain the resurgent nationalism that had appeared in Croatia in the early 1970s, the constitution created a collective presidency in which the six republics and two provinces had equal weight, diminished the power of Serbia in the collective presidency, increased the power of Vojvodina and Kosovo in the Serbian parliament, and increased the autonomy of those regions—all of which would, a decade later, provoke the first upsurge of Serbian nationalism, which in turn fueled a drive for secession in Slovenia and Croatia and started the descent into the wars of the 1990s.

The 1993 Belgian constitution represented the culmination of a quarter century of discussion over the relations among the linguistic and cultural regions of the country and between the regions and the national government. It replaced the unitary state with a federal state made up of communities and regions (Article 1) and created three communities—the French, Flemish, and German (Article 2); three regions—the Walloon, the Flemish, and Brussels (Article 3); and four linguistic regions—the French, Dutch, bilingual Brussels, and German (Article 4). It restricted the power of federal authorities only to matters that were formally attributed to it by the laws and the courts and reserved power in all other matters to the communities and regions. In creating a multiplicity of subnational jurisdictions possessing considerable authority while substantially limiting the powers of the national government, the constitution has moved perhaps further than any other in reversing the traditional dominance of the national government over the subnational units.

While most constitutions are quite unambiguous in creating either a federal or a unitary system, the Spanish constitution of 1978 was unusual in creating the possibility of substantial regional autonomy without precisely defining its extent. Article 117 provided for the organization of the state into municipalities, provinces, and autonomous communities, the latter to be formed voluntarily by contiguous provinces (Article 143). Articles 146 and 147 stipulated that the assembly of the provinces can then draft the statutes of the autonomous community, including its competences. Article 148 elaborates a large number of domains of policy in which the autonomous community may assume competences, and Article 150 allows the state to transfer or delegate to the autonomous community matters that are within its competence. In so doing, the constitution allows both variation across the country in the presence or absence of autonomous communities and a variation among the communities in the scope of their autonomy.

## THE ANOMALOUS CASE OF THE UNITED KINGDOM

Almost every state has a written constitution. There are, however, some notable exceptions. The United Kingdom, for example, does not have a written constitution in the sense of a single constituting document. A reflection of the exceptionally long, uninterrupted existence of the English, and subsequently British, state, the most important reconstitution of public authority occurred in the seventeenth century, beginning with the civil war of 1640–1649 and culminating with the Convention Parliament of 1689, its Declaration (later Bill) of Rights, toleration act, declaration that King James II had abdicated, and transfer of the monarchy, limited in its powers, to the Dutch stadtholder, William of Orange (1650–1702) and Mary (1662–1694). Those events having taken place long before the practice, epitomized by the American and French postrevolutionary constitutions of the late eighteenth century, of describing all aspects of the forms and exercise of public authority in a single written document, the British constitution consists of all the acts, norms, and practices since 1688 that, taken together, define the rights of citizens, the powers of the monarch, the means by which a government is formed, the institutional structure of Parliament and its relations to the monarchy and the government, and the place of Scotland, Wales, and Northern Ireland in the United Kingdom.

## A CONSTITUTION FOR THE EUROPEAN UNION?

In December 2001, the heads of state and government of the European Union (EU), meeting at Laeken, Belgium, issued the Laeken Declaration on the Future of the European Union. Noting that the EU stood at a crossroads, a defining moment in its existence as the enlargement of its membership to include the formerly communist states of Eastern Europe and the consequent unification of Europe approached, the leaders stated that the EU had to become more democratic, more transparent, and more efficient. It had to bring its citizens, especially the young, closer to its institutions; it had to redesign institutions that, for the most part, were created for the European Coal and Steel Community in 1952 and European Economic Community in 1958— both of which consisted of only six states, France, Germany, Italy, Belgium, the Netherlands, and Luxembourg—so they could function effectively for a union of thirty or more member states; and it had to develop the capacity to play a role in the world commensurate with its size.

In order to pave the way for an Intergovernmental Conference that would address these and other challenges, the leaders announced they had decided to convene a European Convention consisting of representatives of the national parliaments, the European Parliament, the European Commission, and the member states to consider the key issues for the EU's future development and identify the various possible responses. They suggested the convention should consider simplifying the four complex treaties that governed the EU, review the distinction made in the Treaty on European Union between the Union and the Community and the three pillars (the European Community and intergovernmental cooperation in justice and home affairs and in foreign and security policy), consider whether a Charter of Fundamental Rights agreed upon in 2000 should be incorporated into the treaties, and examine whether this simplification and reorganization "might not lead in the long run to the adoption of a constitutional text in the Union" and, if so, "what might the basic features of such a constitution be?" (Laeken Declaration).

The convention, composed of fifteen representatives of the heads of state or government, thirty members of the national parliaments of the fifteen member states, sixteen members of the European Parliament, two representatives of the European Commission, and two representatives of the national parliaments and one representative of the government of each of the thirteen accession candidates, as well as a president—former French president Valéry Giscard d'Estaing (b. 1926)—and two vice presidents, convened on 28 February 2002. Over the next sixteen months, the convention drafted a Treaty Establishing a Constitution for Europe that introduced a large number of changes in the institutions of the EU that were designed to enhance its democratic legitimacy and increase its efficiency both within the union and vis-à-vis the rest of the world.

The constitutional treaty was presented to the European Council in July 2003 and an Intergovernmental Conference began on 4 October 2003. After a protracted dispute over a proposed change in the weight of the member states in voting within the council and several other issues, the now twenty-five member states agreed to the treaty on 18 June 2004. The treaty was officially signed in Rome on 29 October 2004 and then referred to the member states for

ratification. As with any treaty of the EU, all of the member states would have to ratify it in order for it to take effect.

By late May 2005, nine member states had ratified the treaty, starting with Lithuania in November 2004, then Hungary in December 2004, Slovenia in February 2005, Italy and Greece in April 2005, and Germany, Austria, Slovakia, and Spain in May 2005. But on 29 May 2005, in a referendum in France in which more than 69 percent of the registered voters participated, 54.7 percent of the voters rejected the treaty. Three days later, on 1 June, in a referendum in the Netherlands in which more than 63 percent of the registered voters participated, 61.7 percent of the voters rejected the treaty.

Recognizing the legal reality that the treaty could not take effect until all of the member states approved it, the leaders of several member states that had planned referendums and in which approval of the treaty was far from assured immediately announced postponement of the referendums. Meeting two weeks after the French and Dutch referendums, the leaders of the EU called for a "period of reflection" and agreed to reconsider the situation in June 2006. Several member states nevertheless continued with the ratification process: Latvia and Cyprus in June 2005, Malta in July 2005, Luxembourg—after a referendum that endorsed the treaty—in October 2005, and Belgium in a series of votes extending from April 2005 to February 2006. As a result, by the latter date, a total of fourteen of the twenty-five member states had approved the treaty. But it was clear to all that the treaty would not take effect until France and the Netherlands reversed their votes—and it was far from clear whether, and if so under what circumstances and when, that would happen, just as it was not at all clear that, in the event the referendums were rescheduled and held in all of the member states that postponed them, the treaty would be approved.

*See also* **Citizenship; European Constitution 2004–2005; Parliamentary Democracy.**

BIBLIOGRAPHY

Brenan, Gerald. *The Spanish Labyrinth: An Account of the Social and Political Background of the Spanish Civil War.* 2nd ed. Cambridge, U.K., 1950.

Brown, Archie. *The Gorbachev Factor.* Oxford, U.K., 1996.

Conradt, David P. *The German Polity*. 7th ed. New York, 2001.

Elster, Jon, and Rune Slagstad, eds. *Constitutionalism and Democracy*. Cambridge, U.K., 1988.

Elster, Jon, et al. *Institutional Design in Post-Communist Societies: Rebuilding the Ship at Sea*. Cambridge, U.K., 1998.

Eyck, Erich. *A History of the Weimar Republic*. Translated by Harlan P. Hanson and Robert G. L. Waite. 2 vols. Cambridge, 1963.

Friedrich, Carl J. *Constitutional Government and Democracy*. 4th ed. Waltham, Mass., 1968.

Gunther, Richard, Giacomo Sani, and Goldie Shabad. *Spain after Franco: The Making of a Competitive Party System*. Berkeley, Calif., 1988.

LaPalombara, Joseph. *Democracy, Italian Style*. New Haven, Conn., 1987.

Lijphart, Arend. *Patterns of Democracy: Government Forms and Performance in Thirty-six Countries*. New Haven, Conn., 1999.

Lijphart, Arend, and Carlos H. Waisman, eds. *Institutional Design in New Democracies: Eastern Europe and Latin America*. Boulder, Colo., 1996.

Linz, Juan J., and Alfred Stepan, eds. *The Breakdown of Democratic Regimes: Europe*. Baltimore, 1978.

Linz, Juan J., and Arturo Valenzuela, eds. *The Failure of Presidential Democracy*. Vol. 1: *Comparative Perspectives*. Baltimore, 1994.

Newton, Michael T., with Peter J. Donaghy. *Institutions of Modern Spain: A Political and Economic Guide*. Rev. ed. Cambridge, U.K., 1997.

Safran, William. *The French Polity*. 6th ed. New York, 2003.

Sartori, Giovanni. *Comparative Constitutional Engineering: An Inquiry into Structures, Incentives, and Outcomes*. 2nd ed. New York, 1997.

Shugart, Matthew S., and John M. Carey. *Presidents and Assemblies: Constitutional Design and Electoral Dynamics*. Cambridge, U.K., 1992.

*Treaty Establishing a Constitution for Europe*. Luxembourg, 2005.

Walter Hallstein Institute for European Constitutional Law, Humboldt University, Berlin. "European Constitutional Law Network." Berlin, 2006. Available at http://www.ecln.net.

Williams, Philip M. *Crisis and Compromise: Politics in the Fourth Republic*. Garden City, N.Y., 1966.

DAVID R. CAMERON

# CONSTRUCTIVISM.

Constructivism was an avant-garde movement in twentieth-century art that embraced the fine arts from painting to architecture, with parallel movements in literature, theater, and film. The term was first coined in 1921 by artists in Russia, where it was closely associated with the utopian idealism generated by the Russian Revolution of October 1917 and the civil war (1918–1920). The term was used to describe an entirely new kind of creative activity in which artistic skills were harnessed not to create works of art but to design practical objects of everyday use and total environments for the new society. This movement is identified as Russian or Soviet constructivism. The term *constructivism* was subsequently used in Europe during the 1920s and later to describe a geometric abstract art in which the precision of the forms and their mathematical qualities evoke associations with science, engineering, and technology and with progressive social and scientific values. This broader movement is called international constructivism.

Soviet constructivism originated with the Working Group of Constructivists (Rabochaya gruppa konstruktivistov) set up in Moscow in March 1921, consisting of the critic Alexei Gan (1895–1940) and the artists Varvara Stepanova (1894–1958), Alexander Rodchenko (1891–1956), Karl Ioganson [Karlis Johansons] (1890–1926), Konstantin Medunetsky (1900–1934), and the brothers Vladimir (1899–1982) and Georgy Stenberg (1900–1933). Proclaiming a new synthesis of art, industry, and politics, the group relegated their purely artistic explorations to the role of "laboratory work," aspiring to extend their creative experiments with abstract forms into the real environment by participating in the industrial manufacture of useful objects. They organized their work according to three principles: *tektonika* ("tectonics," or the functionally, socially, and politically appropriate use of industrial material within communist society), *construction* (the organization of this material for a given purpose), and *faktura* (the conscious handling and manipulation of material).

The concept of construction derives from the technique of building up a sculpture from distinct material elements, instead of modeling or carving the form. Invented by Pablo Picasso (1881–1973),

**Model of the Monument to the Third International**
by Vladimir Tatlin, 1920. The artist is in the foreground holding a pipe. BRIDGEMAN ART LIBRARY

it was developed further in Russia by Vladimir Tatlin (1885–1953) in his *Counter Reliefs* of 1914 and then in his revolutionary *Model for a Monument to the Third International* (1920), intended to be the functioning headquarters for the organization dedicated to fomenting world revolution. The exhibition of the *Model* in Moscow in December 1920 inspired the formation of the constructivist group.

The constructivists developed and promoted their ideas within the Moscow Higher Artistic and Technical Workshops (VKhUTEMAS—Vysshie [gosudarstvennye] khudozhestvenno-tekhniche-skie masterskie), which were set up in 1920 to train artists for industry. Many figures, like Lyubov Popova (1889–1924) and Gustav Klucis (1895–1944), became associated with constructivism, while Moisei Ginzburg (1892–1946) and Alexander Vesnin (1883–1959) extended its principles into architecture. The practical results of the

constructivists' aspirations can be seen in designs for workers' clothing, furniture, textiles, posters, and graphics as well as in stage productions. Notable examples are Popova's set design for Fernand Crommelynck's (1886–1970) farce *The Magnanimous Cuckold* of 1922 (in which a machine replaced the traditional set, and theatrical costumes were replaced by so-called production clothing or *prozodezhda*), Rodchenko's Workers' Club of 1925, and the Vesnin brothers' design for the Leningrad Pravda building (1924). By the late 1920s the lack of official and market support led to a general decline of constructivism, despite a late flowering of photography and photomontage, used for communist propaganda.

International constructivism as a self-conscious movement was initiated at Düsseldorf in May 1922 when the International Faction of Constructivists was organized by Theo van Doesburg (1883–1931) representing Dutch De Stijl, Hans Richter (1888–1976), and El Lissitzky (1890–1941). The faction's declaration emphasized their rejection of subjectivity and individualism in favor of a more scientific and objective approach, which involved "the systematization of the means of expression" and "art as a method of organization that applies to the whole of life." Whereas the Moscow constructivists rejected art, the international constructivists saw art as an activity that embraced the making of works of art as well as the design of useful objects. Whereas the Russian constructivists were committed to communism, the international constructivists adopted a non-aligned political radicalism. The movement gained ground in Germany during the 1920s, where it was stimulated by the *Erste russische Kunstausstellung* of October 1922; the presence of Russian émigrés such as Lissitzky and Naum Gabo (1890–1977); and the activity of Hungarian artists such as László Moholy-Nagy (1895–1946), who had been inspired by the Moscow constructivists and the communist ideals of the short-lived Hungarian Revolution of 1919. Constructivist movements of various complexions were also active in Poland and Czechoslovakia. After the 1920s it becomes more difficult to disentangle constructivism from the broader history of non-objective art. In the early 1930s, as the repressive regimes of Germany and the Soviet Union effectively destroyed modernism, Paris became a haven for abstract painters and sculptors. By the end of the decade, the center of constructivism had shifted to Britain. After World War II a new generation of artists in America and Western Europe explored the aesthetic possibilities of constructivism's visual language and its scientific and mathematical resonances.

*See also* **Architecture; De Stijl; Lissitzky, El; Modernism; Moholy-Nagy, László; Painting, Avant-Garde; Theater.**

BIBLIOGRAPHY

Bann, Stephen, ed. *The Tradition of Constructivism.* London, 1974.

Gough, Maria. *The Artist as Producer: Russian Constructivism in Revolution.* Berkeley, Calif., 2005.

Kiaer, Christina. *Imagine No Possessions: The Socialist Objects of Russian Constructivism.* Cambridge, Mass., and London, 2005.

Lodder, Christina. *Russian Constructivism.* New Haven, Conn., and London, 1983.

CHRISTINA LODDER

---

**CONSUMPTION.** All human societies consume. What distinguished Europe in the twentieth century was the rapidly expanding meaning, scope, and significance of consumption in politics, economy, culture, and everyday life. At the beginning of the twentieth century, consumer advocates in France and England hoped a "century of the producer" would give way to a "century of the consumer," where civic-minded consumption would advance welfare and ethics. By the 1950s and 1960s Europeans, like Americans, began to wonder whether they were becoming a new social system: a consumer society. By the 1990s *consumer culture* and *consumerism* became widely used both to describe a hedonistic postmodern lifestyle and to support a politics of choice.

The growing political and academic as well as commercial recognition of consumption as a distinct, even hegemonic phenomenon resulted from four overlapping dynamics: the politics of needs; the transformation of material comfort; the unprecedented proliferation of new goods and technologies; and the expansion of dream worlds and lifestyle consumption. Instead of a model of successive paradigm shifts (from scarcity to affluence; or from collective consumption to individualistic hedonism), these four dynamics overlapped, unfolding alongside each other. What changed was the balance between them as the meanings, objects, and practices of consumption evolved.

**MEANINGS**

In the course of the twentieth century Europeans attached to "consumption" a growing range of goods, symbols, values, and practices. These included provisioning, using, wasting, and imagining consumption as well as shopping or the act of purchase. Consumption can take place in a number of sites and through different social systems (collective provisioning or market). The nineteenth-century association of the consumer with the literal using-up of essential foodstuffs (bread) and resources (gas and water) widened into more diverse forms and practices. In France in the 1920s, *la cooperation nouvelle* addressed "consumers of health" and marketed family holidays. In Britain already in the 1930s, it came to include "consumers of art" and "consumers of education." Keynesian demand management put consumption at the center of political economy. The consumer's new status was captured by the satirical magazine *Punch* in 1934 that made a boy proclaim: "I want to be a Consumer. . . . I've never had aims of a selfish sort. . . . I want to be a Consumer, and help to further Trade."

In socialist countries, critique of bourgeois consumption ushered in attempts to build a collective art of socialist consumption. In capitalist countries, concerns with private commercial forms of consumption increasingly marginalized earlier collective and business meanings (such as firms consuming coal), a trend reaching its peak in the "affluent" 1960s. Following American models, consumer advice bureaus now covered tourism and book clubs, car repair and fashion, and even marriage brokers. Since the 1990s, neoliberalism has exported the language of "choice" and the "sovereign consumer" from the market to the public sector. Most notably in Britain, public policy seeks to make patients, welfare recipients, and users of police demanding "citizen-consumers." The twentieth century closed with a similar project with which it began, although now proceeding from the domain of the market rather than civil society: the fusion of consumption and citizenship.

## NEEDS AND CONSUMER POLITICS

Europeans entered World War I with an uneven and underdeveloped sense of being consumers. Notwithstanding the expansion of commercial culture in the modern period and economists' attention to consumer preferences, consumption was mainly considered a problematic, even unproductive, inferior activity. It was first in Victorian and Edwardian Britain that democratic ideas were mobilized by taxpayers to position themselves as public-minded consumers. Significantly, consumers first articulated a voice over articles that were considered necessaries and were being exhausted in the literal sense of consumption (bread, water, gas). Consumer cooperatives, including women's groups, developed in the second half of the nineteenth century into a European network. But mobilization and identity-formation was uneven. Powerful societies in Manchester and Glasgow stood in contrast to more particularist and labor-oriented groups on the Continent; the large *Konsumverein* in Hamburg was called "Produktion"; outside Denmark, consumer cooperatives barely touched rural people. Socialist politics and corporate traditions of land, labor, and nation retarded a similar equation of consumers with the public interest in France, Germany, and Italy; in battles over high food prices, consumer interests were easily portrayed as a mere sectional interest.

Battles over trade policy at the beginning of the twentieth century and World War I catapulted consumption to the center of European societies, producing an unprecedented mobilization of consumers that would shape consumer politics and sensibilities for the next half century. Some of this mobilization was initiated by the state. War committees of consumers were set up in German cities, Vienna and Budapest, with the aim of educating consumers and limiting inflation and scarcities. Planners, like Walther Rathenau, identified consumption as an instrument of collective welfare, ethics, and national development. Most mobilization, however, came from below. From Barcelona to Berlin and The Hague, cities became sites of food riots. Even in Britain, which escaped severe crises of provision, the war led to the political education of citizen-consumers. If most experiments with consumer representation did not survive the end of war, consumers across Europe were now increasingly looking toward the state (not the market) to regulate trade and provide secure access to healthy food at stable prices.

The politics of food security played itself out differently conditioned by ideological as well as material differences. Conditions in Berlin were worse than in Paris or London but they also revealed a fragmented, antagonistic view of consumer interests that fueled social conflict and the collapse of the state. In contrast to an organic, inclusive representation of the consumer as public interest in Britain, poor housewives in Berlin attacked pregnant mothers and soldiers' wives for their greater entitlements. In Soviet Russia, on the other hand, scarcities helped the legitimacy of the new Soviet state. In Petrograd (formerly St. Petersburg) people only ate half as much in 1920 as in 1913, hated the tasteless canteen food, and sought to evade the Bolshevik shutdown of shops. Yet, problems of provision here strengthened a belief that state intervention was necessary and that social justice required the rooting out of bourgeois elements.

Consumer cooperatives emerged from the war stronger than ever, expanding their membership and share of the food sector, and, in Britain, forming a political party allied to Labour. Social democratic parties in the 1920s favored marketing boards, quotas, and other forms of regulation to stabilize agricultural production. Greater nutritional awareness prompted by the discovery of vitamins and biochemical knowledge emphasized the centrality of "essential foods" (especially milk) and led to popular demands on states to provide basic nutritional standards.

Western Europeans largely escaped the famines and chronic malnutrition haunting many other areas. Still, periodic scarcities and fear of hunger left a lasting imprint on people's identity as consumers. Daily rations in Essen, Germany, in 1918 for a "normal consumer" were almost half that later estimated by the League of Nations for inactive people. Barter, black markets, and home provisioning were as important as market systems of provision. Refugees, unemployed, children, elderly, and urban inhabitants without access to allotments

**A milkman in Yorkshire, England, delivers milk to a customer, 1930.** Wartime scarcities and greater awareness of nutritional concerns led to demands for stabilization of the production and supply of essential commodities such as milk in the interwar period. GETTY IMAGES

were suffering most. This sense of vulnerability, revived after World War II by the extreme scarcities of 1944–1948, formed the mental background to the general support of agricultural protection and subsidies culminating in the Common Agricultural Policy of the European Union.

Alongside economic nationalism and imperialism, food security also generated new transnational networks and global awareness. Much of the consumption in Central Europe after World War I was organized through intermediate organizations. In 1922 the American Relief Administration fed more than eight million people a day in the Soviet Union. Humanitarian aid after World War II meant survival for thousands in Western and Central Europe. Trade cycles, nutritional science, and the world depression (1929–1932) made internationalists turn

to consumption as the vehicle for simultaneously advancing public health, absorbing excess production, and stabilizing international relations. "Freedom from Want" became a rallying cry for European social movements as well as a pillar of U.S.-Allied diplomacy. World War II left a new global awareness on the minds of many organized consumers. Scarcities were not just an Indian or Soviet problem: Europe was part of a global food problem.

Food security came late to Europe and overshadowed more spectacular, hedonistic aspects of consumption. Partly, this resulted from an expanding sense of needs and nutritional standards. Sugar, meat, and milk became necessities. The unemployed in the world depression were not starving, but nutritional knowledge highlighted a "hidden famine" caused by lack of vitamins and calcium. Consumption cemented a new democratic culture of social citizenship. In the West it only slowly became marginalized by a culture of choice, markets, and commodification during the Cold War. In the late 1940s, as many Britons supported rationing and fair shares as those wanting to abolish them.

The long preoccupation with food security also reflected the persisting vulnerability of many groups. Most Europeans in the 1950s were not part of a mass consumer society with leveled tastes. Social and regional contrasts remained significant. Until the late 1950s, West German workers lived frugally: real coffee was a luxury and chicory the main substitute. Only one-quarter of West Germans could afford to eat meat daily. By 1963 the typical working-class family still spent 35 percent of its budget on food. In Italy expenditure on food fell below 50 percent of the average household budget in the 1950s; for poor southerners it remained 75 percent. In 1959 the communal boards that operated the *cucine popolari* and provided food parcels and clothing still assisted over four million people in Italy. Regional gaps in Italy, Spain, and Portugal only narrowed in the 1960s to 1970s, facilitated by migration, industrial and service jobs, and a shrinking peasantry.

Attention to improvements in the standard of living conventionally focuses on the 1860s to 1890s, when the price of food fell rapidly thanks to declining costs of shipping. Europeans had to wait for the period from the 1960s to the 1990s for another significant improvement, following increased wages, the concentration of retailing, and the integration of food chains. In Greece the food share of household expenditure was still 30 percent in 1970 compared to 20 percent in Great Britain, Denmark, and Austria: by 1990 this figure had almost halved. An industrial worker in West Germany had to work over four hours for a pound of coffee in 1958, but only eighteen minutes in 1993. If for the majority of Europeans food security has became a distant concern, it remains alive for disadvantaged groups. The United Nations estimated that 1.5 million families in Britain could not afford an adequate diet in 1994.

## MATERIAL CULTURE AT HOME

Underneath the ups and downs of the politics of food, the home was transformed into a primary site of consumption practices and technologies. Accident figures in the European Union in 2000 are telling: domestic products and faulty usage caused about twenty million accidents, more than were caused at work or leisure.

By the late twentieth century, the largest share of consumption was dedicated to the home; from 20 percent in Portugal to 28 percent in Nordic countries. Housing, the use of water and energy, household durables, home maintenance, and gardening dominated consumption routines and expenditure. The home was the main space accommodating an ever-increasing number of objects and technologies. Consumption practices moved into the home (bathing, listening to the radio, using the computer) while production vacated it. In interwar Slovenia, industrial workers raised their own vegetables and kept chickens and rabbits. By the 1980s self-provisioning had become the distinction of a privileged alternative lifestyle. Even farmers rarely consumed what they produced and instead relied on the market; an exception was Poland, where every second individual farm still worked primarily to feed its own family in 1998. Technologies like the sewing machine briefly prompted a countertrend—by 1983, 52 percent of West German households had an electric sewing maching, 18 percent still had a mechanical one. But in the long-term, the productionist evacuation of the home is clear. The obesity boom in the early twenty-first century partly reflects declining food preparation skills. New domestic skills are increasingly consumption skills (computer games, warming up prepared foods)—not production skills; cooking, gardening, and home improvement have moved from being everyday life skills to advertised forms of lifestyle entertainment.

Material and cultural dynamics converged in this consumerist revalorization of the home. Modern German kitchens in the 1920s were initially advertised through the language of productivity, but by the 1950s, through representations of comfort and beauty: hard-working housewives were replaced by images of leisurely women. Clearly, work did not disappear from the home with the washing machine. Rather, technologies have rearranged the time and significance attached to different practices in the process of laundry:

ironing, drying, and sorting have expanded even as washing itself has become less labor-intensive. A study of British couples in 1999 found that women spent four hours per day on household tasks, men three hours; women did more washing and cooking, men more pet care. The expansion of domestic consumption alongside increased female labor participation has arguably advanced gender inequalities: working women in two-income families continue to shoulder most chores.

The modernization of the home facilitated the erosion of class and regional consumption communities. This came in two stages. First, the expansion of a common culture of ordinary consumption. Gas and water had been early sites of Victorian consumer protests, and it was the expansion of domestic utilities that initiated the second stage: the democratization of consumption routines following the expansion of consumer durables. Cultures of consumption did not so much progress from needs to wants. Rather, they produced an ever-expanding conception of needs. Previous luxuries, like a hot bath or refrigeration, became standardized conveniences. The expansion of the domestic consumption of water, gas, and electricity was stunning. In Berlin only 4 percent of all households had electricity in 1910, but 76 percent did in 1933.

In Western Europe, many urban dwellers had access to a common toilet by 1900 but the convenience of a private toilet inside one's flat only became normal in the interwar years and after. Semidetached housing made bath, toilet, and running hot water first accessible to some working class-families in Britain in the 1930s. Most Europeans had to wait for another generation; in West Germany only every other home had a bath as late as 1960. Smaller towns and rural areas lagged behind large cities. Even in France and Germany the outhouse and lack of running water was not unknown in rural areas in the 1960s. Central heating spread rapidly in the postwar years. In Western Europe, by 1996, 81 percent of households had central heating, 97 percent had hot running water; Central-Eastern Europeans are only slightly behind, with the exception of Bulgaria and Romania.

The connection of homes to utilities helped privatize consumption practices—the personal bath replaced the public bath. It also intensified practices.

In early twentieth-century France even schoolteachers, those evangelizers of personal hygiene, still only washed their hair once a month. In the 1980s to 1990s daily showers rapidly became the norm for ever more Europeans. More frequent and intensive cleaning of the body revolutionized water consumption. Households today consume the largest share of public water supply: 35–40 percent of all domestic water consumption is used for bathing and showering. Changing lifestyles have had major consequences for the environment and urban infrastructures.

New communication technologies and household durables reinforced the importance of the domestic sphere. The car functioned as an extension of family life—the weekend outing, the holiday in Spain or Italy. Radio and television created new familial consumption experiences. These undermined commercial forms of public entertainment (the cinema) as well as collective leisure activities sponsored by church, towns, or social movements. By 1936 there were twenty-eight million radios in Europe—compared to twenty-three million in the United States. In the 1960s Western Europe picked up with the American expansion of television; 66 percent of British households had a television at the beginning of that decade, 90 percent at the end.

Washing machines have likewise privatized services. Since the 1960s, most clothes have been washed at home, not sent away or washed in a communal washhouse. The electrical industry in the interwar years promoted a cult of cleanliness to sell timesaving appliances. Class structures and the low income of working-class women meant that the diffusion of washing machines in Europe lagged behind the United States by one or two generations; before the 1950s they were limited to some middle-class households. In the long run, the rise of appliances and the decline of domestic services narrowed the gulf of consumer culture between classes. By the early 1960s, every other household in the United Kingdom and every third in Germany had a washing machine; by 1995, 88 percent of EU households did; dryers and dishwashers, by comparison, were still found in only every fifth household.

New technologies had contradictory effects on how people spent their time and money. In 1955, European cinemas attracted four billion visits. Attendance fell steadily to six hundred million by 1990 (a mere two visits per person per year), while TV viewing steadily increased; by 1974 Britons spent half their free time in front of the "telly."

New technologies and the new needs they foster have had important cultural spillovers for older consumption routines. The TV dinner promoted prepared food and altered the rhythm of the family meal. In 1960s Italy, the program *Carosello*, which mixed commercials with cartoons, meant children began to go to bed after this nine o'clock show. New consumption practices can coexist, interpenetrate, or compete with each other. The rise of TV, for example, has not meant the decline of the radio. In the 1990s, Europeans continued to listen to as many minutes of radio as they watched TV. What has changed was the social context—most listening was in the morning. Nor has TV been impregnable to new technologies, such as personal computing. People who spend less time on other leisure activities because of Internet use primarily reduced their time watching television and reading books, much less the time spent with family, friends, or sport.

Especially since the 1960s, advances in chemistry, engineering, design, and information technologies have resulted in an unprecedented expansion and thickening of the material world consumption, from Tupperware to electric kitchen tools, pocket-sized music-players to computing toys. A "craze for novelties" already attracted attention in the eighteenth century. What was new in the second half of the twentieth century was the accelerating speed and scope of product innovation. Cycles of acquisition, use, and disposal quickened—the "throwaway society" was coined in 1955. Within a few years computers replaced typewriters, and CD and DVD marginalized the vinyl record. The shifting balance between objects and humans had contradictory effects for the domestic world of consumption. Some consumer durables like the dishwasher free up time for sociability. The multiplication of the same object, however, can also dissolve the familial into more lonely forms of consumption. With the purchase of a new television, the second set frequently moved into the children's room. In the former East Germany in 2003, 55 percent of six-to-thirteen year olds had their own set: they watched an hour more TV than friends without a set and suffered from a decline in social skills.

The expansion of domestic consumption was not an inevitable, market-driven process but shaped by politics and ideologies. In Nazi Germany, the radio had the full backing of the propagandist Josef Goebbels for providing relaxing entertainment and strengthening a depoliticized private sphere. In the 1950s traditional elites, especially the Catholic Church, initially opposed consumerism, fearing it would destroy the family. Christian Democratic ministers like Ezio Vanoni in Italy and Ludwig Erhard in Germany won with an alternative prescription: consumerism cemented the family by liberating people from basic material drives and freeing mothers from housework, thus enabling families to spend more time with each other. Conservative women's groups spread the gospel of domestic happiness through consumerism. Governments provided tax credits to assist families' purchase of new consumer durables. The family was an indirect beneficiary of export-led growth policies during the economic miracle. Low investment in collective consumption, transport, and services made the family and private forms of consumption like the car, kitchen, and entertainment at home more vital than ever.

The most self-conscious and aggressive experiment seeking to reverse the long-term expansion of domestic consumer culture was socialism. After the Russian revolution, Soviets targeted the private home and commercial markets as twin expressions of bourgeois capitalism. Communes and housing cooperatives tried to reform the *byt* or daily life. Soft furnishings were condemned as hazardous to health, dangerous remnants of prerevolutionary culture, household objects attacked as oppressive. New cities like Magnitogorsk promoted communal living, public baths, and collective leisure activities. In the end, socialist attempts to transform consumption routines were as impressive for the resistance they caused as for their ambition. The replacement of Christian with socialist objects in the home was greeted with grumbling or opposition. Individuals in collective living quarters often resorted to consuming food in the last corner of privacy remaining: their bed. In Magnitogorsk, many preferred to live in mud huts, which may

Cover of a special edition of the French magazine *La Maison Française*, titled I'm Equipping My Kitchen, 1950. The connection of homes to utilities throughout the middle of the twentieth century led to a marked increase in the purchase of timesaving appliances in the post-World War II period. BRIDGEMAN ART LIBRARY

have been primitive but afforded domestic privacy, than in the new collective barracks. In the early 1930s, the Communist Party took a U-turn in the program of domestic transformation: people's private objects and consumption practices were accepted. The primary role of women was to support the male worker and industrial productivity by managing a clean and comfortable private home.

In the 1950s and 1960s, consumption became a symbolic site of mutual observation and competition between rival social systems. Tellingly, Richard Nixon and Nikita Khrushchev conducted a "kitchen debate." In 1958 Walter Ulbricht pinned the superiority of socialism on the promise that East Germany would overtake its Western neighbor in per capita consumption of food and consumer goods. Socialist consumers were to benefit from a new "selling culture," new industrial

inventions, and domestic comfort. Initially, in the mid-1950s the campaign to mechanize housework considered public spaces (such as launderettes at work) as well as private households, and the East German state sought the advice of female consumers. By the early 1960s, however, the growing competitive orientation toward the West led to a producer-oriented fixation on appliances in the home; in 1958 only 1.6 percent of East German households had a washing machine, by 1967 this had risen to 38 percent. Department store combines (*Konsument*) and mail-order catalogs were also introduced. Yet, investment in consumer industries was too limited and price reform too cautious to allow for an expansion of consumption akin to that in West Germany. From the early 1960s the share of consumption in GNP declined. The two-tier system between rationed goods and more expensive goods eroded popular trust in the socialist ideal of more equitable consumption. Engagement with consumer culture was stopgap. In the late 1960s the regime initiated a youth fashion plan that sought to engage with teenage culture, only to divert resources once bottlenecks in other textile branches emerged. Planning directives and political personalities, not consumers and their changing tastes, directed policy. Increased imports of consumer goods in the 1980s were financed through ever-advancing debt. Ultimately, the East German state was overwhelmed by the desires it had helped to unleash.

"MASS CULTURES"

The interwar years initiated an unprecedented commercialization of film, music, and other spheres of culture that transformed the mental and sociological nature of consumption. New forms of media consumption like cinema and radio and their expanding audiences were tied to anxieties of "mass consumption" and to the erosion of European culture by American commercial civilization. Already in late nineteenth century France, Gustave Le Bon argued that mass markets created dangerous new means of manipulating the gullible masses. From right to left, interwar commentators warned of the ephemeral nature of mass consumption and the power and commercial rationale of the culture industries that uprooted the uneducated, suggestible masses from their traditional values only to leave them in the grip of cheap pleasures, easy preys for authoritarian regimes; critics ranged from F. R. Leavis in England to José Ortega y Gasset in Spain, to Frankfurt School scholars in American exile. Just as industrial society shifted toward mass production, so consumption too appeared to shift from individual to standardized mass practices and desires.

Certainly, film and phonograph expanded the virtual stimuli and behavior introduced in the late nineteenth century by the department store, the flaneur, and window shopping, allowing ordinary Europeans to escape into readily available dreamworlds. The political uses of consumption were not lost on the Nazi state. Mass entertainment was partly distraction, partly promoted as a collective experience of joy designed to strengthen a national community: the most successful years for German film and dance were the early years of World War II. Yet, "mass consumption" was not intrinsically connected to manipulation, nor to the creation of soulless individuals in a lonely crowd. Cinemas, like department stores, opened public spaces for isolated groups, especially women. Commercial music was successful because it was linked to dance halls and clubs that offered new forms of sociability and feelings of liberation.

Centralization, standardization, and mass production created pressures for greater uniformity. At the same time these released opportunities for creativity and more pluralistic tastes. Music is an example. Regional leisure cultures gave way to more uniform national practices in the interwar years. Radio raised expectations across class and region about the acceptable standards of musical performance, assisting in the creation of shared national cultures. The velocity of cultural production and consumption accelerated with the rapidly changing number of hits and musical fashions. The phonograph made a greater variety of music available to working and middle classes. Popular music dominated commercial radio, a trend that public radio was unable to ignore; 56 percent of minutes broadcast during an average Sunday on Radio Luxembourg in 1935 was popular song and dance music, another 35 percent comedy songs and light orchestra; only 0.5 percent was classical music, and only 9 percent nonmusic related.

In the interwar years, amateur music gave way to professional, organized musical production; one British agency in 1938 controlled three hundred bands playing in two thousand halls. In the 1960s to 1980s, with the growing availability of cheap, electrical instruments (the guitar, then the synthesizer), the divide between producers and consumers of culture became once again more porous, as listeners learned they could make music too. Punk in the late 1970s emerged from a simple if sometimes violently staged belief that musical production had ceased to be the monopoly of commercial producers and trained musicians. Music became part of a lifestyle, a shift that minimized established traditions of musical training and reinforced a performative and rebellious aspect of consumer culture. As continuous cycles in the evolution and commercialization of popular and subcultures have shown, "mass culture" always creates opportunities for transgression and resistance that undercut a logic of standardized uniformity. What was new in the 1980s and 1990s in music, fashion, and other parts of youth culture was the accelerating speed in the cycle of style creation, commercial marketing, transgression and, again, creation.

From a long-term perspective, critics may have overestimated the passive gullibility of consumers and underestimated the creative, diversifying dynamic of "mass consumption"; the potential for resistance, self-discovery, or the pursuit of new identities, such as in subcultures, gay communities, or the designing of one's own personality through a creative or ironic appropriation of brands and fashions. The expansion of cultural consumption has not only created new genres (video art, rock, culture jamming) but also widened access to older genres like opera and museums. But critics were correct in fearing the erosion of cultural authority, not least their own: there is perhaps no other area in twentieth-century Europe where the democratization of consumption has done more to erode class hierarchies of taste and expertise than music.

Tourism and the pursuit of luxury emerged as key phenomena in more democratic forms of consumption since the mid-1950s. Their development reflects the dialectic between commercialized standardization and playful, hedonistic, and ephemeral aspects of contemporary consumption. Tourism has grown by over 7 percent per year since the 1950s to become the world's largest industry. The 1950s to the 1970s saw the rise and fall of standardized mass tourism; the first charter flight from Berlin to Mallorca took off in 1956. Spain received 1.5 million tourists in 1952, 43 million by 1984. Standardization has since been overshadowed by more personalized forms of cultural consumption and orchestrated encounters with difference: the personalized, exotic trip; short-term luxury breaks; cultural city breaks; and sustainable tourism. Tourism in particular is about consumption as pleasure, self-expression, and the transcendence of new wants. If consumption has become about identity, tourism has played an integral part in socializing people into sensual consumers yearning for fantasy and authenticity, self-discovery, and enchantment. The growing significance of this commodified form of hedonism and fantasy has also, however, reinforced social inequalities and exploitation. Forty-six percent of Europeans were not able to go on holiday at all in the late 1990s—especially unemployed, retired persons, and manual workers. Abroad, the hedonistic pursuit of self and pleasure has boosted sex tourism; in Thailand, popular with Europeans, an estimated 800,000 children are in prostitution.

One powerful engine behind mass consumption was the influence of the American model of a classless consumer society. American products, ideas, and tastes became a prominent part of Europeans' lives—the most popular TV series in the 1970s and 1980s were American (*Bonanza, Dallas, Dynasty*); in 2002, U.S. movies were responsible for 70–80 percent of all box office receipts; American-style malls have risen up outside many European cities; EU consumer protection in the 1970s initially borrowed from John F. Kennedy's speech of 1962. Still, Americanization amounted less to a wholesale imposition of American taste and objects than to a creative dialogue, admittedly on an uneven politico-economic playing field. This dialogue could result in imitation, fusion, or rejection. Images of a classless, consumerist American way of life were a central branch of anticommunist cultural diplomacy after World War II in the Marshall Plan, America Houses, traveling exhibits, and the Voice of America. One-half million Italians passed in awe through an "American Way" supermarket exhibit in Rome in 1956. In practice, however, European consuming cultures retained significant differences. A supermarket opening in Florence in 1961 was greeted by demonstrations and boycotts from shopkeepers and some residents. As late as the early 1980s, Italians and the French bought only 2 percent and 14 percent of their food in supermarkets; compared to 32 percent in Germany and 70 percent in the United States. One-quarter of French people in the early twenty-first century shop at least once a week in a local market.

The American convergence of consumption and citizenship met with different responses. If in the 1920s German experts had been skeptical of American mass consumption, they embraced American marketing and its fusion of opinion polling and commerce after World War II. In France, by contrast, there was resistance to the conflation of political and consumer culture. Postwar Britain was divided between supporters of fair shares and those embracing choice and consumerism; some championed advertising as the friend of democracy and freedom, others criticized it for undermining civic culture with selfish materialism. Europe, moreover, was not only the recipient of American models, but an active contributor through multilateral global relations, including a Japanese/British strand promoting savings.

New national idioms emerged where American and indigenous styles became fused. This was true for music, but also for fashion and advertising. British menswear stores combined more egalitarian American marketing with an indigenous appeal to the gentleman. Many European advertisers remained skeptical of American methods as out of tune with the taste regimes of their own imperial cultures. Into the 1950s, empires provided alternative cultural systems, with their own genres (Empire film) and purchasing promotion (Empire advertising). Immigration and postcolonial developments have helped diversify many areas of consumption from food to fashion that are as important as trends of Americanization. "Mass consumption" and "*Konsumterror*" have been continuous targets for new social movements and terrorists since the 1960s. At a popular level, Europeans have responded with different sensibilities to the relative decline of their cultural industries and regional traditions. Seventy-five to seventy-eight percent of young people in Italy, Ireland, and Portugal were interested in the screening of European films in 2000, but only just over 40 percent in Sweden, Germany, and the United Kingdom. Popular resistance to "McDonaldization" and the preservation of local food culture has been greatest in France and in Italy, the hub of the "slow food" movement.

## CONVERGENCE AND DIVERGENCE

A comparison of European consumers in the early twenty-first century with their grandparents or great-grandparents points to significant trends of convergence. Most Europeans enjoy unprecedented affluence and comfort. Like most citizens of the "developed world," they share a material culture involving television, stereo, telephone, automobile, and, increasingly, virtual modes of communication. Most live in private homes with hot water, central heating, electricity, refrigerator, and washing machine. Even in Eastern Europe by the late 1990s, 90 percent of households had refrigerators, 75 percent color televisions, over 50 percent automatic washing machines, and almost every other person used a computer and had a car; only Romania significantly lagged behind. In 2003 Estonia had as many mobile-phone users as France. Working time has declined, consumption time has increased; working hours in Western Europe fell by over one-third in the twentieth century. Differences within as well as between societies have become less pronounced compared to the situation on the eve of World War I, where, for example, the average Milanese ate fifty-three kilograms of meat per year, but those in Trapani (Sicily) only three kilograms. Meat, fresh fruit, and vegetable consumption has increased across Europe since the mid-1970s; outside France, 40 percent or more of Europeans are overweight or obese.

Whereas consumption tended to reinforce class and status communities in the first half of the twentieth century, more recently it has helped to dissolve these into more fluid and pluralistic relationships. Gender and generational hierarchies have become looser. The recognition of the elderly and children as "active consumers" and the sexualization of childhood are twin features of this trend. Young Europeans have a shared image of the body: 50 percent of fifteen-year-old girls either diet or think they ought to. Consumer desires transcend income differences: Romanians are even more concerned with consumption than affluent Western Europeans.

With the collapse of socialism, markets and retail concentration have become the defining modes of provision for Eastern as well as Western Europeans. Outside Italy and Spain, the small retailer has become a marginal presence; in Sweden 80 percent of local dairies and distribution centers closed between 1960 and 1994. While the variety of manufactured and synthetic products has increased, biodiversity for apples and potatoes has diminished. Street festivals like the love parades record a shared transnational hedonism. The consumer has also shot to the fore within the European Union (EU). The Treaty of Rome (1958) only mentioned the consumer in passing in relation to the common agricultural policy, but since 1975 the European Commission has sought to establish a market-based citizen-consumer. Consumption is a vital source of income for European states; most Europeans do not realize that they pay as much tax on consumption as on their income. In the 1980s and 1990s several governments began to export choice and consumerism from market into public services, especially the United Kingdom.

Nonetheless, visitors touring Europe in the early twenty-first century would find it difficult to square their experiences with ideas of globalization or postmodernity. Instead of a common material culture or a symbolic totality of objects and meanings, different groups and countries continue to have distinct cultures of consumption. In addition to "glocalization" or creolization, remarkable contrasts remain between and within societies. In proportion of their household budget, Greeks and Spaniards spent twice as much on restaurants and hotels than Scandinavians. Britons, Danes, Dutch, and Germans spent twice the share on recreation and culture as their Mediterranean neighbors. Austrians and Britons spent twice as much money on their pets as do Germans and Italians. In many societies, eating remains a crucial source of sociability, but in Austria 50 percent of consumers eat alone. Italians and Finns consume twice as much water as people in France or Flanders. Advertising spending (as percentage of GDP) is twice as high in Holland, the United Kingdom, and Greece as in Italy, Ireland, and France.

How (and how much) people consume remains in part determined by income and national welfare systems. In France, health-related consumption has

**A man serves customers at a restaurant in Mykonos, Greece, 1989.** Despite the globalization of consumer markets, regional differences in European consumption persist. For example, Greeks and Spaniards spend twice as much in restaurants and hotels as do Scandinavians. ©DAVE G. HOUSER/CORBIS

shot up dramatically since the 1960s. Athenians spend twice as much on leisure as their rural neighbors. Pensioners significantly improved their standard of living in France in the 1970s to the 1990s and now consume as much as younger cohorts, whereas in Britain they experienced impoverishment and consume 25 percent less. More than half of Germans rent their home, while 80 percent own theirs in Spain, Ireland, and Italy; this has implications for related aspects of domestic consumption (home improvement, gardening). Scandinavians are well ahead in consuming new communication technologies (mobile phone, Internet).

The uneven advance of consumerism is captured in contrasting approaches to credit and saving. National legislation and financial institutions have shaped the availability and use of consumer credit. In the United Kingdom, consumer credit rose from 50 percent to 70 percent of the national income (1988–2001); Britons were twice as likely to have a credit card as Germans, while 22 percent of Italians did not even have a bank account. Between 1970 and 2000 the household saving rate (percentage of disposable income) fell dramatically in Italy (from 32 percent to 11 percent), Portugal (15 percent; 9 percent), and the United Kingdom (5 percent; 3 percent), but was stable in France (15 percent; 14 percent) and Germany (12 percent; 10 percent)—in the United States it declined from 8 percent to 0 percent.

And Europeans continue to spend their time differently. The average Finn and Swede spend seventeen minutes on the phone per day, whereas Danes and Belgians are concise with only four to five minutes. Reading remains a popular pastime in the United Kingdom, Ireland, and Scandinavia, much less so in Portugal. Mediterranean people spend one hour more per day in front of the TV than Nordic people. Germans, Dutch, and Austrians predominantly listen to international music, while national music continues to amount to half the music sales in Italy, France, Finland, and Greece. Regional trends remain pronounced in cultural consumption. In 1996 average residents in Lyon and Manchester went nine times to the cinema, three times more than those in Seville, Marseille, Vienna, and Berlin. There are three times as many visits to the theater per resident in Copenhagen than in Berlin or Rome. Danes visit amusement parks twice as often as Italians. The Irish and Danes are compulsive renters of video; not so Italians, Germans, Swedes, and Portuguese.

Cultural patterns shape tourist desire as much as income or climate. Mediterranean people spent over 80 percent and Scandinavians half their holidays in their home country, while over two-thirds of Irish, Germans, and Austrians prefer to go abroad. Greeks like hotels, Dutch prefer campsites or rented apartments, Swedes and Finns tour-operated holidays. The Irish in 1999 spent more on their holidays than any other Europeans (except Luxembourgers)—three times as much as Swedes and Portuguese.

In general, the democratization of taste appears to have proceeded in two different directions. Britain is close to American dynamics of cultural specialization: activities like listening to the radio, reading, and sport became the preference of smaller groups of people who pursued them, however, more intensely. Countries like Norway and Holland, by contrast, displayed a trend toward greater cultural homogeneity: the rise or fall of consumption practices is more inclusive, a shared social trend. Thus in the United Kingdom and United States people listened less to the radio in 2000 than in 1975, but those who especially liked the radio intensified their habits, whereas in Norway and Holland both groups reduced their listening time.

Consumers' expectations of retailers, governments, and consumer movements also continue to differ. Sixty percent of Finns and Swedes think price one of the three most important factors when buying food, but only 18 percent of Greeks, who privilege quality, taste, and family preference. Trust in supermarkets is very high in the United Kingdom and Holland, whereas Scandinavians, French, and Germans place it in small producers and farmers. Risk sensibilities and perceptions of "the consumer interest" continue to differ, partly reflecting different national regimes of regulation and consumer politics. In Norway, there is a low sense of a distinct consumer interest, and the state is expected to act on people's behalf. In France, consumer groups have been more populist and confrontational, whereas in Germany they tended to be more technocratic and corporatist. In Britain, a more pluralist vein emerged, with consumer movements stressing the diversity of consumer interests to be protected and consulted. In contrast to British and German consumers, it is Danish and Dutch consumers who see the representation of consumer interests as a principal task of consumer movements, rather than just issuing practical advice. With the decline of the cooperative movement since the 1950s, membership in consumer organizations differs more than ever—25 percent in Holland and Sweden, but only 2 to 3 percent elsewhere. Nor has the democratization of the European market meant an equally "free" play of consumption. In Sweden, advertising aimed at children is banned, in Ireland smoking in public. Privatization and regulatory policies affecting the consumption of utilities continue to differ in spite of general directives by the European Union on liberalization and the consumer interest.

In an oligopolistic setting like Germany, where four conglomerates dominate the market for electricity, consumers pay twice as much as in the British market.

## APPROACHES TO CONSUMPTION

Outside the dominant branch of neoclassical economics, consumption mainly attracted negative scholarly readings until the late twentieth century. It was viewed either as a source of class division and inequality or as a source of manipulation by which capitalists and dictators sought to pacify citizens into passive "masses." Thorstein Veblen in 1899 focused on the "conspicuous" consumption of a parasitic "leisure class": the display of consumer goods served to buttress superior status. In the 1960s Pierre Bourdieu presented consumption as a "structuring structure," a classifying as well as classified system, which re-created social distinction and class cultures. The Frankfurt School and American scholars such as Vance Packard and Stuart Ewen emphasized the power of advertising, mass media, and producers in manipulating people through dreamworlds and material objects. With the declining importance of class, the democratization of taste, and the expansion of consumerist discourse and practices came more diverse and positive appreciations of consumption in the 1980s and 1990s. Instead of a "passive dupe," fields as diverse as cultural studies, anthropology, and management highlighted the consumer as an "active" coproducer of meaning, taste, and self-identity. The pleasures, creativity, and benefits of consumption were re-appreciated, their aesthetic and emancipatory potential for individuals, outsiders, and subcultures celebrated. The triumph of markets and the political language of choice have been mirrored in the more positive scholarly readings of consumers as agents and of the opportunities available in commercial culture for the creation of personal and collective identities. Early twenty-first-century sociologists of ordinary consumption have dug beneath the spectacular or conspicuous landscape of consumption to retrieve more mundane, routine practices (washing, eating) and their relation to changing technological systems. After the initial reaction against a productivist bias, scholars are also reintegrating production into their analysis. Social scientists are discussing consumption in areas well beyond the sphere of shopping, ranging from media consumption and tourism to social services.

Historians have broadly followed these trends, but only part of the way. Consumption was initially approached through an interest in retailing or mass-production, critical of the shift from collective leisure to commercial consumer culture. Social historians looked at consumption through the lens of "social distinction," emphasising the reproduction of habitus and structures of inequalities. The influence of cultural studies in the United Kingdom and United States was to highlight transgressive, creative, or emancipatory features. Attention to gender highlighted the liberating aspects of cinemas, department stores, and boutiques in providing women with access to the public sphere. Generational shifts have received far less attention. More recently, scholars have highlighted the contribution of consumers to democratic politics and civil society. How political and commercial domains interact remains underexplored, although new work on consumer identity and knowledge is a starting point. Unlike medieval and early modern colleagues, most modern historians writing on consumption still say little about routine practices, technologies, and the environment.

### IMPLICATIONS
The implications of consumption for public life and environment remain dominant tropes and moral dilemmas of political debate and social mobilization. For much of the twentieth century, cultural and political elites as well as intellectuals attacked "consumerism" as a shallow and alienating form of individualist materialism that dissolved communal solidarities, political commitment, and critical thought. Twentieth-century European history shows the problems with such a zero-sum equation of consumption and citizenship. As well as allowing for apolitical escapism, consumption has given excluded groups access to public spaces. In the early twentieth century, consumer mobilization shaped civic sensibilities. Since the interwar years commercial and political domains have become more interactive and mutually constitutive, but alongside trends of depoliticizing individualization, consumption, and market research have also been mobilized for progressive purposes, such as the use of opinion polls to highlight the political centrality of family, identity, and personal well-being. Formal political engagement may have declined, but the expansion of consumption-oriented lifestyles also helped to broaden the terrain of political culture, including environmental, generational, and gender politics. The increase of consumption has not merely amounted to more goods but to new facilities of symbolic expression. As a source of identity, consumption has been the main beneficiary from the collapse of more totalizing ideological projects (fascism, nationalism, socialism) and the loosening of class and gender hierarchies. Feeding into more pluralistic forms of public life, consumption may not bundle the collective energies of previous larger collective projects, but from a democratic point of view this may not be a bad thing. Cultural consumption has fostered civil society, and new information technologies have introduced new spaces of mutuality. In former socialist societies, like East Germany, the goods and symbols of consumption are being fashioned into in a new politics of identity.

Much of the critique of "consumerism" originates in a critique of neoliberal "choice." The rise of "choice" in political discourse, however, must not be conflated with the experience and practices of consumption in everyday life. A British study in 2004 found that the majority of people did not experience "choice" in their weekly shopping, but frustration. Shopping involves forms of sociality, not just self-centered hedonism. Consumption, moreover, is broader than shopping. The ongoing intensity of recurrent moralistic debates about the death of the public may in itself be good evidence against the thesis that consumption has eroded politics.

The environment shows a less ambiguous picture of the public costs and benefits of convenience and affluence. Europe has played an important part in the causal connection between consumption in the developed North and global environmental problems. Eighty percent of resources are now consumed by the 10 percent of people living in the North. Since 1950 the richest one-fifth on the planet has doubled its consumption of energy and meat and quadrupled car ownership while the poorest fifth has barely changed at all. However, it is the lack of recycling and sustainable consumption in the affluent North rather than consumption as such that has carried global costs. Some European societies have been at the forefront of addressing this problem, as well as causing it. Europe's carbon dioxide emissions declined with the shift from coal; in 1995 it was 8.5 tons per person (21 in the United States). In many continental European cities car-sharing and public transport policy has reduced car use. Dutch people have a high car ownership but take 30 percent of their urban trips by bicycle. A major environmental culprit has been energy consumption in the home, which increased by 9 percent in the 1990s while industrial and agricultural use declined. The gains from increased efficiency of many products (washing machines use four times less water in 2000 than in the early 1970s) has been outweighed, however, by increasing ownership numbers, the rise of single-person households, and new wasteful technologies; in Holland 13 percent of all energy consumption in the home feeds the stand-by function of appliances. Most Europeans continue to be oblivious to how much water and energy they consume and pay for. Household waste in Holland increased by 55 percent between 1985 and 1998. Germany, Holland, and the Scandinavian countries have led sustainability initiatives, increasingly relying on civil society as well as on state initiatives, such as tax policies, eco-labeling, recycling, and pay-as-you-throw-away schemes; in 2002 Holland, 9,210 households participated in a nongovernmental organization initiative and achieved a 26 percent reduction in their household waste. More neoliberal countries, like Britain, with less homogenous cultures of consumption and policies of privatizing public services have lagged behind in sustainable consumption. In spite of the revival of alternative politics of consumption among the young, it is disproportionally those over over sixty-five who separate waste. How to decouple consumption and growth from environmental damage is becoming a central concern of formal politics as well as social movements and "alternative" consumers.

*See also* **Americanization; European Commission; European Union; Globalization; Leisure; Public Health; Tourism.**

BIBLIOGRAPHY

Baudrillard, Jean. *The Consumer Society: Myths and Structures.* London, 1998. Originally published in French in 1970.

Brewer, John, and Frank Trentmann, eds. *Consuming Cultures, Global Perspectives.* Oxford, U.K., and New York, 2006.

Buchli, Victor. *An Archaeology of Socialism.* Oxford, U.K., and New York, 1999.

Daunton, Martin, and Matthew Hilton, eds. *The Politics of Consumption: Material Culture and Citizenship in Europe and America.* Oxford, U.K. 2001.

de Grazia, Victoria. *Irresistible Empire: America's Advance through 20th-Century Europe.* Cambridge, Mass., 2005.

de Grazia, Victoria, with Ellen Furlough, eds. *The Sex of Things: Gender and Consumption in Historical Perspective.* Berkeley, Calif., and London, 1996.

*Eurostat* and Official Publications of the European Union. *Trends in Europe and North America: The Statistical Yearbook of the Economic Commission for Europe.* New York, 2003.

Goubert, Jean-Pierre. *The Conquest of Water: The Advent of Health in the Industrial Age.* Translated by Andrew Wilson. Princeton, N.J., 1989.

Gronow, Jukka, and Alan Warde, eds. *Ordinary Consumption.* London and New York, 2001.

Haupt, Heinz-Gerhard. *Konsum und Handel: Europa im 19. und 20. Jahrhundert.* Göttingen, 2002.

Kotkin, Stephen. *Magnetic Mountain: Stalinism as a Civilization.* Berkeley, Los Angeles, and London, 1995.

Miller, Daniel, ed. *Acknowledging Consumption: A Review of New Studies.* London and New York, 1995.

Mort, Frank. *Cultures of Consumption: Masculinities and Social Space in Late Twentieth-Century Britain.* London and New York, 1996.

Sassatelli, Roberta. *Consumo, Cultura e Società.* Bologna, 2004.

Schor, Juliet B., and Douglas B. Holt, eds. *The Consumer Society Reader.* New York, 2000.

Trentmann, Frank, ed. *The Making of the Consumer: Knowledge, Power and Identity in the Modern World.* Oxford, U.K., and New York, 2005.

Veblen, Thorstein. *The Theory of the Leisure Class: An Economic Study of Institutions.* 2nd ed. New York, 1953.

FRANK TRENTMANN

# CONVENTION ON GENOCIDE.

The Convention on the Prevention and Punishment of the Crime of Genocide was adopted by Resolution 260 A (III) of the United Nations General

Assembly on 9 December 1948 in Paris. One-third of the member states quickly ratified the convention, allowing it to enter into force. By contrast, in 1998 only two-thirds of the member states of the United Nations (then numbering more than two hundred) had ratified it—relatively few by comparison with other texts on human rights. Even many of the signatories expressed reservations, particularly on the definition of genocide and on penal aspects, such as the difficulties of extradition.

The two first articles go to the heart of the matter:

Article I: The Contracting Parties confirm that genocide, whether committed in time of peace or in time of war, is a crime under international law which they undertake to prevent and to punish.

Article II: In the present Convention, genocide means any of the following acts committed with intent to destroy, in whole or in part, a national, ethnic, racial or religious group, as such:

(a) Killing members of the group;

(b) Causing serious bodily or mental harm to members of the group;

(c) Deliberately inflicting on the group conditions of life calculated to bring about its physical destruction in whole or in part;

(d) Imposing measures intended to prevent births within the group;

(e) Forcibly transferring children of the group to another group.

This formulation was a major innovation in international law. The concept of genocide was absent from the Nuremberg trials (1945–1946), because at the time only the concept of "crimes against humanity" was recognized under international law. Article 6c of the statutes of the International Military Tribunal that convened at Nuremberg incorporated the text of the London Agreement of 8 August 1945, which added "crimes against humanity" to crimes against peace (Article 6a) and war crimes (Article 6b): "namely, murder, extermination, enslavement, deportation, and other inhumane acts committed against any civilian population before or during the war; or persecutions on political, racial or religious grounds in execution of or in connection with any crime within the jurisdiction of the Tribunal, whether or not in violation of the domestic law of the country where perpetrated." The convention of 1948, in nineteen articles, built on the declaration unanimously passed by the United Nations General Assembly in 1946 that genocide was "a crime under international law, contrary to the spirit and aims of the United Nations and condemned by the civilized world."

These moral and legal steps were the direct outcome of World War II. In 1941 Winston Churchill had spoken of a "crime without a name" to describe the horrors of the slaughter of Jews and others by Nazi Germany. The Polish Jewish refugee jurist Raphael Lemkin had given that crime a name in 1943. He called it *genocide*—compounded from the Greek *genos* (race) and the Latin *occidere* (killing)—and published it in his seminal work *Axis Rule in Occupied Europe* (1944). Lemkin summarized his thoughts in different texts when he was appointed an advisor to the American justice at the Nuremberg trials, Robert Jackson.

The international legal definition of the crime of genocide is found in Articles II and III of the Convention on Genocide, which describe the mind of the genocidal agent, who manifested the "intent to destroy, in whole or in part, a national, ethnical, racial or religious group, as such," and the acts of the genocidal agents. Describing genocide and the perpetrators of genocides was necessary to establish the character of the crime and the criminals responsible for it. The convention allowed for consideration of past crimes, "Recognizing that at all periods of history genocide has inflicted great losses on humanity." This meant that retroactive legal action was possible. The notion of genocide has since been applied both to later atrocities, such as the massacre of Tutsis in Rwanda in 1994, and to earlier ones, such as the massacres of Armenians in 1915.

The Convention on Genocide marked the beginning of a new era in international thinking about mass crimes, largely through the creation of a new category of legal and moral analysis, the category of genocide. Each genocidal catastrophe since then has been seen in terms of its specificity—the historical context of the crimes—and its universality: the desire to eradicate a part of humanity. As Lemkin put it, "the practice is ancient, the word is new." What distinguished genocides from mass killings and ethnic cleansing throughout history is that death is no longer a means to a political end, but an end in itself. Once the possibility of wiping out entire peoples was established as a criminal reality, then the notion that genocide touches everyone at the core was chillingly persuasive.

One problem in the emergence of the term that persists is how to define genocidal intent. Most such massacres are carried out in secrecy; hence the establishment of intent is a difficult, though not impossible, matter. Similarly, there is the problem of partial genocides, the destruction of parts of groups, such as the Anatolian Armenians in 1915 but not those living near Istanbul. Does the fact that some people of a particular group were left alone diminish the force of the claim that the murder of others of the group constituted genocide?

Clearly, while the 1948 convention remains an important foundation, it may seem outmoded in a world that is ever more fragmented; and yet, its utility and significance have been confirmed since the crimes in the former Yugoslavia and in Rwanda in the 1990s. While not a fully developed legal concept, genocide is a term that describes the limits of humanity and inhumanity reached in the twentieth century and beyond.

*See also* **Genocide; International Law; Nuremberg War Crimes Trials; War Crimes.**

BIBLIOGRAPHY

Prevent Genocide International. Available at http://www.preventgenocide.org. Includes texts on genocides.

Schabas, William A. *Genocide in International Law.* Cambridge, U.K., 2000.

Schaller, Dominik J., and Jürgen Zimmerer, eds. "Raphael Lemkin: The 'Founder of the United National's Genocide Convention' as a Historian of Mass Violence." Special issue, *Journal of Genocide Research* 7, no. 4 (2005).

Yale University. Avalon Project. "The Nuremberg War Crimes Trials." Available at http://www.yale.edu/lawweb/avalon/imt/imt.htm.

ANNETTE BECKER

---

# CORPORATISM.

Corporatism was an ideology and model of social, economic, and political organization especially with extreme-right and fascist regimes in the 1930s and during World War II. The system of industrial relations in Western Europe between 1950 and 1975 was labeled as *neo-corporatism*.

## ORIGINS

Corporatism started as an ideological project, propagated by Catholics in the last quarter of the nineteenth century, referring to an idealized medieval society, without class conflict. Corporatism can be defined as a dual antagonism: antiliberal and antisocialist. In political liberalism the individual faces the state, without intermediary structures, which had been abolished with the French Revolution. Political participation is a right of the individual and only the state can impose rules, which, in principle, apply to all citizens. In corporatist ideology an individual belongs to a community based on his or her occupation and these communities are the foundations of society ("organic" society). Corporatism implies a degree of transfer of regulatory power from the state to organizations enabling them to impose rules on the members of the occupational community. The transfer of state power can vary, the highest stage being a corporatist parliament. Legally binding collective wage agreements are a weaker type of corporatism. Corporatism also was an answer to socialism, stressing class collaboration initially by integrating employers and workers in one organization as the medieval guilds ("mixed trade unions"), later by systems of social consultation. Corporatism hampered the solidarity of the working class since the principle of organization was not class but occupation (or economic sector). Corporatism was a means to enclose the working class as well. From an economic point of view, corporatism was more antiliberal than anticapitalist. In contrast to socialism, the private property of the means of production was not put into question and corporatism was a way to regulate the economy on another basis than laissez-faire liberalism and socialist state intervention.

These basic ideas were developed in the papal encyclical *Rerum Novarum* (1891), which favored the growth of Catholic trade unions, positioning themselves as an alternative to socialist unions. The corporatist ideal could be put into practice by means of councils for collective bargaining with representatives of the trade unions and the employers' organizations. This system was quite common after World War I, when the labor movement became a political force. This process of democratization had two basic components: universal (male) suffrage and the recognition of the trade unions. Systems of collective bargaining at sector level and advisory social and economic councils were introduced. The former decided on wages and working conditions while the latter advised government and parliament on social and economic policy. By means of these institutions trade unions and employers' organizations were integrated into the structures of the state. In Belgium *commissions paritaires* (joint commissions) were established in the key sectors of the economy. In the Netherlands the Hoge Raad van Arbeid (supreme labor council) with representatives of the labor unions, employers' organizations, and independent scholars was founded in 1919. In Weimar Germany a national economic council and collective bargaining at sector level were part of the postwar political pacification and was even constitutionalized.

## THE GROWTH OF CORPORATISM

The extent to which these systems match the ideal definition of corporatism is debatable, but groups advocating corporatist ideology saw these institutions as the starting point for a more ambitious reform. This was the case in the Netherlands where Catholic organizations elaborated a system of joint industrial councils in 1919–1920. The joint industrial councils would have far-reaching regulatory power in the social and economic field giving the labor unions employee participation on economic matters. This issue split the Catholic movement, employers arguing that the economy was the monopoly of business and that participation should not go beyond wages and working conditions. At the same time, the radicalization of the Dutch workers, of which the project was a manifestation as well as a reaction against, came to an end. The Belgian Catholic trade union campaigned for a corporatist program inspired by the Dutch example. It was an alternative to socialism as well, which grew rapidly in the wake of the war.

Corporatist programs were also part of the crisis of liberalism, which emerged after World War I and came to a climax in the 1930s, when corporatism, elaborated again in the encyclical *Quadragesimo Anno* (1931), was seen as an answer

to the crisis. Attempts were made to introduce corporatist reform within parliamentary systems. The initiative came from Catholic organizations, for example, in Belgium and Switzerland. The idea was to make a separate structure for decision making on social and economic policy, based on the system of industrial relations already referred to. Basically, this corporatism had two political purposes: social pacification and a reform of the state. The economic crisis of the 1930s made economic regulation seem inevitable. Corporatism could avoid direct state intervention, which did not match the Catholic state theory built on the principle of subsidiarity. A corporatist organization, based on parity, protected business against a parliament and a government dominated by the labor movement. Through the corporatist structure, trade unions and employers' organizations obtained political power, direct or indirect, depending on the type of corporatism. This explains the support of the socialist trade unions for moderate corporatist projects, and projects with a corporatist component as Hendrik De Man's labor plan in Belgium.

## AUTHORITARIAN CORPORATISM

Besides this corporatism compatible with parliamentarism, authoritarian corporatism was put forward by Far Right and fascist movements as an alternative to democracy. In the ideology of the Far Right corporatism had been present since the 1920s. The concept was rather vague because there was no model that could be followed until 1926 when Benito Mussolini introduced corporatism as part of Italy's fascist state. This corporatism was based on a single trade union and a single employers' organization. Membership was compulsory. In the corporations at sector level, representatives of both organizations were equally represented but the leader was appointed by the state. A national corporatist council was established as an advisory board to the ministry of corporations. Strikes were illegal and a labor magistrate dealt with social conflicts. Corporatism was a means to exclude the nonfascist trade unions. In 1926 the fascist union obtained the monopoly of workers' representation. In 1927 the new social organization was laid down in the Labor Charter, a feature of most authoritarian corporatist regimes. In Portugal and Spain a type of corporatism strongly resembling the

Italian model survived until 1974 and 1975, respectively.

Portuguese corporatism was the most elaborate and illustrates how authoritarian corporatism actually worked. The labor statute and a corporatist constitution were promulgated in 1933, but the corporatist structure was only completed in the 1950s. The foundations of corporatism were *gremios* and *syndicatos*. All the employers of the sector were members of a *gremio*. *Gremios* were preexisting employers' organizations or were created by the state. *Gremios* represented the employers and negotiated with the *syndicatos* (trade unions). *Syndictos* were, like the *gremios,* single organizations. To frustrate working-class solidarity, they were organized at the district level and not at the national level (in 1931 the General Confederation of Labor, or CGT, had been disbanded). In the countryside *casos du povo* (people's community centers) were established at the level of the parish, matching the corporatist ideal of mixed organizations: the farmers were members, while the landowners were patrons and held power. In 1937 the Portuguese system changed: landowners had their *gremios* and the *casos do povo* played the same role as the *syndicatos* in industry. The fishery included *casos dos pescadores* (fishermen's centers), mixed organizations of workers, employers, and harbormasters, but workers were dominated by the other groups. These basic structures were established in the 1930s, but paradoxically the corporations were only created in 1956. Since 1936 the Organization of Economic Coordination (OEC) regulated the economy and was the link between the basic corporatist organizations and the state. The OEC enabled the state to control the economy. This was one of the reasons why the formation of the corporations lasted twenty years. In the meantime, a set of collaborative agencies promoted the corporative idea. The *Unia Nacional,* headed by A. O. Salazar, composed of bureaucrats and officials, had to mobilize support for the regime. A paramilitary organization was assigned to defend the social order and the corporatist idea. This social order had been defined in the labor statute, which strongly resembled the Italian charter. The socialist and communist unions had been outlawed before 1933 and the formation of the new *syndicatos* was a priority for the regime, which saw the working class as a threat. In contrast to the labor unions, private employers' organizations continued to exist and corporatism was advantageous to business: business dominated the OEC and the corporatist system favored monopolies and cartels. The standard of living of the Portuguese workers lagged behind and social security remained underdeveloped. The corporations had a political representation, the Chamber of Corporations, and were members of the Council of State, a top-level advisory body.

In the three southern European countries (France, Italy, and Spain), corporatism was a pillar of an authoritarian regime and state and party had a firm grip on the system. The same situation applied to corporatism in central and Eastern Europe: Bulgaria, Albania, Yugoslavia, the Baltic states, Romania, Greece, Poland, and Austria under Engelbert Dollfuss.

The social organization of Nazism differed from the "southern" model to the extent that the factory and not the sector prevailed. The factory was defined as a "community of labor," where labor and capital had to work together for the sake of the company. The *Führerprinzip* (leader principle) gave the employer, the *Führer* of his "community of labor," a dominant position. The role of the trade union, the German Labor Front, was rather limited at the factory level. The interests of the workers had to be defended by the State Trustee of Labor, a civil servant for whom maintaining social peace was the primary task. It can be debated to what extent the social and economic organization of Nazi Germany can be labeled "corporatism," because the state played a dominant role. This was especially true in the social field. The economy was organized in Reichsgruppen, compulsory statutory trade organizations that had the monopoly for the representation of business interests. In the Reichsgruppen workers had no representation at all. The stronghold of the state on the corporatist structure was in the end a feature of all the authoritarian corporatist regimes. There was a difference between worker's and business organizations, however. While the latter could maintain a certain degree of autonomy, and there often was a symbiosis between the private employers' organizations and the official corporatist structures, the trade unions lost their autonomy and were subordinated to party and state.

World War II expanded corporatism because corporatist structures following the Nazi model were introduced in occupied countries. In Vichy France a social system based on corporatism was established following the principles of a labor charter.

## NEO-CORPORATISM AND "FORDISM"

Although corporatism lost legitimacy with the defeat of fascism and Nazism, it did not disappear but was transformed: a system of collective bargaining and statutory trade organization became part of the model of democracy that took shape in the aftermath of the World War II. Organized labor and employers' organizations were integrated in the state through a specific set of institutions next to government and parliament, for social and to a lesser extent economic policy-making. These institutions consisted of councils for social consultation and collective bargaining and advisory economic and social councils. This "neo-corporatism" was a result of a tradeoff between employers and trade unions on one side and the state and organized interests on the other. The first tradeoff, following liberation from Nazi occupation, was in some countries laid down in solemn declarations of labor and employers' leaders as the Social Pact in Belgium or as the Foundation of Labor in the Netherlands. Workers' organizations did not question capitalism, as employers enhanced social progress and trade union participation. The second tradeoff was not subject to codification but developed with the actual functioning of the system. Trade unions participated in policy making and were responsible for the implementation of the decisions that had been taken, implying control over the rank and file. This was labeled "interest intermediation" by political sociologists of neo-corporatism. From the liberation to the economic crisis of the 1970s a new type of economic regulation, called "Fordism," emerged in Western Europe. Economic growth was based on mass consumption and the increasing purchase power of the workers, which was financed by gains in labor productivity. Neo-corporatism served as a mechanism to adjust wages and labor productivity in order to maintain profitability. The economic doctrine underpinning this economic

policy was Keynesianism, stressing state intervention in the economy. The parliamentary system had originally been designed to contain state intervention, thus neo-corporatism served to adapt the structure of the liberal state to this new role. Social policy was no longer decided in parliament but in special (parity) councils and advisory bodies that guaranteed trade unions and employers' organizations direct involvement in social and economic policy making. The economic crisis of the 1970s caused a shift in economic thought from Keynesianism to neoliberalism, questioning neo-corporatism as incompatible with free market capitalism. By the end of the twentieth century, however, systems of industrial relations based on wage moderation agreed on by employers' organizations and labor unions, such as the Dutch "polder model," emerged. These systems, which were often codified in a social pact, had corporatist characteristics as well.

*See also* **Fascism; Labor Movements; Trade Unions.**

BIBLIOGRAPHY

Bähr, Johannes. *Staatliche Schlichtung in der Weimarer Republik: Tarifpolitik, Korporatismus und industrieller Konflikt zwischen Inflation und Deflation, 1919–1932.* Berlin, 1989.

Barkai, Avraham. *Das Wirtschaftssystem des Nationalsozialismus. Ideologie, Theorie, Politik, 1933–1945.* Frankfurt, 1988.

Costa Pinto, António. *The Blue Shirts: Portuguese Fascists and the New State.* New York, 2000.

Grant, Wyn, Jan Nekkers, and Frans Van Waarden, eds. *Organising Business for War: Corporatist Economic Organisation during the Second World War.* New York and Oxford, U.K., 1991.

Kuypers, Ivo. *In de schaduw van de grote oorlog. De Nederlandse arbeidersbeweging en de overheid, 1914–1920.* Amsterdam, 2002.

Le Crom, Jean-Pierre. *Syndicats, nous voilà! Vichy et le corporatisme.* Paris, 1995.

Luyten, Dirk. *Ideologisch debat en politieke strijd over het corporatisme tijdens het interbellum in België.* Brussel, 1996.

Maier, Charles S. *Recasting Bourgeois Europe: Stabilization in France, Germany, and Italy in the Decade After World War I.* Princeton, N.J., 1988.

Mason, Timothy W. *Social Policy in the Third Reich: The Working Class and the National Community.* Providence, R.I., and Oxford, U.K., 1993.

Schmitter, Philippe C., and Gerhard Lehmbruch, eds. *Trends towards Corporatist Intermediation.* London and Beverly Hills, Calif., 1979.

Schütz, Roland, and Regina Konle-Seidl. *Arbeitsbeziehungen und Interessenrepräsentation in Spanien: vom alten zum neuen Korporatismus?* Baden-Baden, Germany, 1990.

Visser, Jelle, and Anton Hemerijck. *A "Dutch Miracle": Job Growth, Welfare Reform and Corporatism in the Netherlands.* Amsterdam, 1997.

Weber, Quirin. *Korporatismus statt Sozialismus: die Idee der berufsständischen Ordnung in der schweizerischen Katholizismus während der Zwischenkriegszeit.* Freiburg, Germany, 1989.

Wiarda, Howard J. *Corporatism and Comparative Politics: The Other Great "Ism."* Armonk, N.Y., and, London, 1997.

———. *Corporatism and Development: The Portuguese Experience.* Amherst, Mass., 1977.

Williamson, Peter J. *Corporatism in Perspective: An Introductory Guide to Corporatist Theory.* London, 1989.

KIRK LUYTEN

**CORSICA.** This island of 8,722 square kilometers, situated in the Mediterranean Sea some two hundred kilometers off the southern coast of France, is a veritable mountain in the middle of the sea. Sparsely populated (with 260,000 inhabitants in 1999), it belongs to the Italian sphere of influence, but became French when the Republic of Genoa provisionally ceded it to France in 1768. In reality, it constitutes a kind of autonomous territory within the kingdom of France. During the Revolution, Corsica was designated a department when all of France was divided up for administrative purposes; and under the empire that followed, the most famous Frenchman of the day, Napoleon Bonaparte, was Corsican. As a result, the island gradually became better integrated with France. All the same, throughout the nineteenth century and for the first part of the twentieth, Corsica had a completely different political organization from continental France, which, whatever its formal institutions, was actually based on clientelism, or "clanism." Broadly speaking, government authorities let well enough alone as far as political life in Corsica was concerned and were not particularly concerned with fraud that had taken place when establishing voter registration rolls. Economically, the island was poor, but population growth was easily absorbed by continental France and the colonies. Corsicans played an important role in colonial ventures, as well as in the French army and administrative apparatus.

In the 1960s this traditional equilibrium, both human and economic, was upset by the end of the colonial enterprise and the return of many Corsicans who had been living in North Africa. In addition, a new generation emerged that sought to bring the island out of its economic isolation so that young people might remain there and find work. An independence-minded nationalist movement developed in Corsica during this time, spawned by what came to be called the "Aléria incident" of 22 August 1975, when two policemen were killed during an assault on a wine and spirits store occupied by "regionalist" militants, who would soon take the name "nationalists" under the leadership of two brothers, Edmond and Max Siméoni.

At the dawn of the twenty-first century, the question of Corsica's status had been a recurrent theme in French political life for more than twenty-five years. A wave of successive governments, and in particular their interior ministers, sought to settle the question, shifting back and forth between negotiation and repression. As just one example, the interior minister under the government of Lionel Jospin, Jean-Pierre Chevènement, appointed an iron-fisted prefect who wanted to bring the island firmly under the control of French law in all aspects of everyday life. His mission ended in farce when he sought to have the police set fire to an illegal beachfront restaurant. Chevènement resigned when he felt the government was making too many concessions.

The trouble is that no government can envision ceding a portion of its national territory and yet independence is precisely what the nationalists seek. The vast majority of Corsicans are caught between the French government and the nationalists: they do not want independence but they rarely demonstrate, for fear of being the victims of a terrorist attack themselves or because custom prevents them from denouncing those nationalists who are guilty of violence, even though they disapprove of them. There are a number of reasons why a majority do not favor independence: a portion of the Corsican population lives on the Continent; there have been numerous marriages between Corsicans and continental French; no other French department receives as many subsidies, both legally and through back channels; and no other French department has a higher ratio of civil servants and welfare recipients. This last argument is less persuasive for the young, among whom the nationalist movement finds the majority of its recruits.

Corsica has experienced violence, only occasionally punctuated by periods of calm, since the nationalist movement began. In its first fifteen years, more than five thousand acts of armed violence were recorded, including almost daily bombings that attacked the "symbols of the French state" such as public buildings, police stations, and "colonizers," both those from continental France and *pieds noirs,* Corsicans who had returned from the colonies. The modern farms built by Algerian repatriates on Corsica's east coast, for example, were destroyed by nationalist attacks. In 1976 a number of diverse groups united into the Front de Libération Nationale de la Corse (FLNC; National front for the liberation of Corsica); but in the ensuing years it was plagued by incessant schisms caused by disputes about strategy or divergent material interests. Many nationalist groups turned into regular mafias, which led to scores of settling of accounts, at times constituting a veritable civil war. Violence reached an extreme on 6 February 1998, when the island's most senior French civil servant, its regional prefect, Claude Erignac, was assassinated.

This constant unrest is obviously highly unfavorable to economic activity. Potential investors flee the island, and agriculture and industry are extremely limited. The paradox is that, aside from the public sector, the only significant economic activity is tourism, favored by the climate and scenic beauty. This is true to such an extent, in fact, that, contrary to the wishes of its nationalists, the island has come to depend primarily on tourism. For two months every year, Corsica is overrun by some two million visitors.

Over time the violence has wearied the majority of the population, and the demand for "Independence Now!" is fading in nationalist circles. Furthermore, the progressive installation of new institutions such as the Territorial Assembly, granted significant powers, is slowly transforming conditions in Corsica, and it is conceivable that the island is headed toward a broad-based autonomy.

*See also* **France; Italy.**

BIBLIOGRAPHY

Andréani, Jean-Louis. *Comprendre la Corse.* Paris, 1999.

Becker, Jean-Jacques. *Crises et alternances, 1974–2000.* New ed. Paris, 2002.

Tafani, Pierre. *L'État de la France, un panorama unique et complet de la France.* 2 vols. Paris, 1993–2001.

JEAN-JACQUES BECKER

**COUNCIL OF EUROPE.** The Council of Europe, established by the London Treaty of 1949, was the first of the supranational European institutions. Starting as a group of ten Western European states, it has constantly expanded in accordance with the democratization process in European countries and in 2005 comprised forty-five member states, covering all of Europe: the twenty-five members of the European Union; some other Western European states, such as Switzerland, Iceland, and Norway; and Turkey and the states that have emerged from the breakdown of the former Yugoslavia and the former Soviet Union.

Despite its ambitious objectives, with cooperation extending potentially to every sphere other than defense, the Council of Europe is weak in its institutional procedures. With the exception of the European Court of Human Rights, which is its most innovative body, the council contains only standard intergovernmental institutions. These comprise a Committee of Ministers, which assembles foreign affairs ministers twice a year and can adopt recommendations without binding force; a parliamentary assembly; and a committee of local and regional authorities, comprising elected representatives of the member states with consultative powers only. Unlike the European Union, the Council of Europe does not have a supranational executive and does not adopt legally binding standards. Accordingly, its field of operations is limited to exchange of experiences, discussion concerning democracy, and technical assistance in countries undergoing a transition to democracy. The council is an international body that operates only at a level of influence in domains such as the development of the state of law and democracy, combating racism, and the protection of minorities. Nevertheless, some of the conventions that it has adopted—particularly those relating to the protection of regional minorities and languages—have given rise to bitter disputes in countries that are experiencing ethnic tensions or that cherish a tradition of republican integration.

The only sphere in which the Council of Europe's activities have demonstrably expanded is the protection of human rights. The European Convention for the Protection of Human Rights and Fundamental Freedoms, adopted in 1950, did not add any rights to those already safeguarded within the internal systems of the member nations, but it did specifically establish a supranational mechanism for safeguarding those rights. The European Court of Human Rights, established in 1959 and based in Strasbourg, is the cornerstone of this mechanism, which has gradually led to the formation of a true European rule of law. The process was hybrid at the outset: the council's member states were not obliged to ratify the convention and even if they did ratify it they could still withhold from individuals living on their soil the right to address their petitions directly to the European Court. Moreover, court pleadings were subject to political screening before being conveyed to the court. A Commission of Human Rights, made up of independent members but elected by the Committee of Ministers, decided on the admissibility of the petitions and sought to reach an amicable settlement with the state concerned before referring it to the court, which meant that only 2 percent to 3 percent of petitions were actually examined by the judges.

Since 1998 the procedure has been simplified, and it resembles a federal judicial review. Member states are now obliged to grant individuals living on their soil—whether they are nationals or not—the right to address their petitions directly to the European Court once they have exhausted the avenues of internal appeal. The court examines these petitions and gives definitive and binding judgments that are nevertheless devoid of sanction apart from possibility that the condemned state could be expelled from the Council of Europe, which is an entirely hypothetical scenario. The European Court in Strasbourg has as many judges as member states—in 2005, forty-five—who are elected for six-year terms by the parliamentary assembly, at the recommendation of the Committee of Ministers. Although these judges enjoy relatively weak guarantees of independence compared with the members of other supreme courts (a short, renewable term and the correlation between the number of states and judges may have given rise to fears that the judges would not dare to oppose the principal states), the European Court has been innovative in its case law. Basing itself on the theory that its task is not only to protect but also to develop and promote the European heritage of fundamental rights, the court seeks to advance, through its judgments, the traditional rights of the convention in accordance with the development of custom and practice. With the support of human rights organizations that encourage private parties to address petitions to it, the court seeks to extend the fundamental rights to states in which the rule of law is least well established by regularly condemning torture, discrimination, and judicial guarantees that it considers inadequate. More generally, it aims to carry out pioneering work by extending the scope of Europe's traditional rights in domains such as sexual freedom, political pluralism, and labor organizing.

Relations between the Council of Europe and the European Union are almost nonexistent, although the twenty-five members of the union also belong to the council. Although the European Parliament—a European Union institution elected by direct vote—shares its benches in Strasbourg with the parliamentary assembly of the Council of Europe, which is made up of national authorities, that is roughly where the contact ceases. The two courts—the Luxembourg court, which is a European Union institution, and the Strasbourg court—follow each other's case law closely and seek to avoid inconsistencies, but they are not associated by any formal agreement. However, the constitutional treaty of the European Union, signed in 2004, includes a provision that the European Union should itself be a member of the

Council of Europe, making it possible for the acts of European Union institutions to be examined by the court in Strasbourg, which would make it the supreme European court in the domain of fundamental rights.

*See also* **European Court of Justice; European Parliament; European Union; Human Rights.**

BIBLIOGRAPHY

Gearty, C. "The European Court of Human Rights and the Protection of Civil Liberties: An Overview." *Cambridge Law Journal* 52 (1993): 89–127.

Lawson, Rick, and Matthijs de Bloijs. *The Dynamics of the Protection of Human Rights in Europe.* Boston, 1994.

PAUL MAGNETTE

---

**COUNTERINSURGENCY.** Insurgency has been the subject of extensive study, ongoing debate, and endless controversy. Like most forms of irregular war, it confounds efforts at precise definition. Long associated with communist "wars of national liberation," insurgency has been widely considered illegitimate by Western governments, who often faced such conflicts as their empires collapsed after the World War II. The tendency of the United States since the attacks of 11 September 2001 to label all forms of political violence below the level of conventional war as "terrorism" adds to the confusion surrounding this form of conflict.

The emotional connotations surrounding the term, its imprecise use, and its confusion with terrorism point to the need for clear definitions of *insurgency* and its corollary, *counterinsurgency.* Such clarification must precede any historical overview of this most persistent form of conflict.

**DEFINING TERMS**

*Insurgency* is a campaign to gain control of a state from within through a combination of propaganda, guerrilla warfare, and terrorism. *Guerrilla warfare* refers specifically to the military activities of insurgents, usually against military units and police of a threatened state. Analysts distinguish between *insurgent guerrillas* and *partisan guerrillas* (usually referred to simply as *partisans*) who operate behind enemy lines and in support of regular forces resisting an invasion. Guerrillas operate out of uniform in small bands using hit-and-run tactics. They attack isolated government outposts, ambush small military and police units, and disrupt communications within a state. Faced with superior force, they disappear into the general population, which either actively supports them or at least acquiesces to their presence.

Terrorism, like guerrilla warfare, is a weapon in the insurgent arsenal. Calculated to spread fear, such acts aim to disrupt the normal functions of a state. Insurgents will assassinate officials, bomb government buildings, and murder members of the general population who support the existing order as a warning to others. In contrast to contemporary religious terrorism, insurgent terrorism seeks to make a dramatic statement without producing mass casualties. Both prefer symbolic targets and foster the impression that they can strike anywhere at any time. Insurgents, however, find killing people they seek to win over to their cause counterproductive. Two historical examples make this contrast abundantly clear. When the Irgun Zvai Leumi bombed the King David Hotel in Jerusalem in 1946 as part of their campaign to expel the British from Palestine, they phoned in a warning before detonating their bomb. More than ninety people died when the British ignored the warning, but killing them was not as important to the insurgents as destroying a symbol of British power. When Al Qaeda attacked the World Trade Center in 2001, it sought both to destroy a symbol of American economic strength and to kill as many people as possible.

The political objective of gaining control of a country links guerrilla warfare and terrorism into a coherent insurgent campaign. Insurgencies usually occur within states characterized by significant degrees of misrule and popular discontent with the status quo. Insurgents seek to exploit such discontent by persuading disaffected people that conditions would improve once the insurgents gain power. They communicate their agenda, which usually includes an attractive list of reforms and social programs, through propaganda. To succeed, insurgents need not persuade that many people to support them. They require only the active support of the few and the tacit acceptance of the many. Most people with a poor standard of living (absolute or relative), limited opportunities, and few political rights will be fence-sitters during insurgency, struggling to survive while waiting to see who will make their lot better.

*Counterinsurgency,* as the name suggests, consists of those efforts by a threatened state to defeat insurgency. Any counterinsurgency campaign, however, that merely reacts to insurgent attacks will fail. For this reason, one of the gurus of Western counterinsurgency, Sir Robert Thompson, objected to the term entirely. A threatened state must, first and foremost, identify and address the causes of unrest that foster the insurgency in the first place. These sources of discontent may be economic, social, political, or any combination of the three. Like the insurgents who threaten it, a reforming government will try to sell its program to disaffected people through propaganda. Unlike the insurgents, though, the state will actually have to show some progress in improving conditions. Meeting the needs of its people is, after all, the raison d'être for any government. Because such measures aim to regain the trust of a disaffected population, this aspect of counterinsurgency is often referred to as "winning hearts and minds."

Because a reforming government is even more vulnerable to attack than a repressive one, it must take measures to protect people, institutions, and critical infrastructure from terrorism and guerrilla warfare. Given the extent of such vulnerability, the state must also undertake offensive action against the insurgents. In doing so, it must make every effort to use force in a limited and selective manner. An overreliance on force will alienate people further and drive them into the arms of the insurgents.

## TYPES OF INSURGENCY

The foremost practitioner of insurgency and the man who wrote the first practical guide for conducting it was the Chinese communist leader Mao Zedong (1893–1976). In his decades-long struggle to overthrow the government of Chiang Kai-shek, Mao adopted a phased approach to Karl Marx's general theory of proletarian revolution, which he later articulated in his book *On Guerrilla Warfare* (1937). Mao envisioned and implemented a strategy specifically designed for China's demographic situation. He planned to secure an isolated area as a base, win support of

the country's vast rural population through propaganda, engage in guerrilla operations, and then, when his movement was strong enough, engage Chiang Kai-shek's regular forces, which were often tied down protecting urban areas. Mao would thus "drown the cities in a sea of peasants."

Mao's victory in 1949 led many insurgents to emulate his methods. Few actually succeeded, and those who did enjoyed the advantage of attacking "soft colonial targets." Only Fidel Castro pulled off a truly Marxist insurgency against the decidedly corrupt government of Fulgencio Batista y Zaldívar in Cuba. Mao's success had the unfortunate effect of convincing the West that all insurgencies were communist-inspired. By far the largest number and the most successful were primarily anticolonial, even if the insurgents espoused communist doctrine. Failure to distinguish between these two motivations had tragic consequences for the United States in Vietnam.

## COLONIAL COUNTERINSURGENCY CAMPAIGNS

The World War II left European colonial powers severely weakened. Virtually all of them had suffered defeat at the hands of the Germans and/or Japanese, shattering the myth of Western military invulnerability. Asia in particular saw the emergence of revolutionaries who had fought the Japanese and who were not about to accept the restoration of colonial powers. The postwar anticolonial insurgencies produced distinctively national counterinsurgency responses. The French and British experiences in particular provide a vast body of information and a stark contrast in opposing strategies.

*French counterinsurgency* France experienced by far the most extensive and humiliating experience in World War II. Defeated by the Nazi blitzkrieg in 1940, the country suffered four years of occupation, during which the Japanese overran its colony in Indochina. A communist resistance movement led by Ho Chi Minh fought the Japanese and determined to secure independence after the war. The Vietminh organization launched a highly effective campaign, assassinating pro-French village leaders while winning the support of local people.

**Vietnamese soldiers attack the French position at Dien Bien Phu, 1954.** The failure of the French counterinsurgency campaign in Vietnam was sealed by the unsuccessful attempt to establish a garrison at Dien Bien Phu. ©DIEN BIEN PHU MUSEUM/REUTERS/CORBIS

In combating this threat, the French made every mistake a counterinsurgency campaign can make. They deployed a heavily armed, mechanized, road-bound army to fight lightly armed, mobile guerrillas. They relied on brutality and excessive firepower and tied their forces down in cities and fortified garrisons, thus losing touch with the Vietnamese people. The climax came in 1954, when the frustrated French tried to establish a fortified outpost at Dien Bien Phu. They sought to draw the insurgents into battle and destroy them with heavy artillery. General Vo Nguyen Giap, however, turned the tables on the French, cutting off the garrison and overrunning the position.

This stunning defeat led to French withdrawal from the northern part of Indochina, but it did not lead to reform of French methods. Within a few years the nation found itself tied down in yet another desultory conflict in Algeria. Despite some successes, French forces again relied on repressive methods that alienated Algerians, French citizens at home, and the international community. The inevitable ignominious withdrawal occurred in 1962.

***British counterinsurgency*** Britain enjoyed a greater degree of success in its counterinsurgency campaigns than the French or any other colonial power. This success derived from trial and error during more than a century of "imperial policing" and from some unique features of British common law. British counterinsurgency strategy rested on four broad, flexible principles: minimum force, winning hearts and minds, civil-military cooperation, and tactical flexibility. English common law dictated that use of force to subdue unrest had to be the least amount necessary to achieve an immediate result. Limitations on the use of force led the British to address the causes of unrest that led to insurgency in the first place, in an effort to "win the hearts and minds" of the disaffected population. Once people saw their lives improving, they might support the government rather than the insurgents, even to the point of providing intelligence to the security forces. To implement the counterinsurgency strategy, the British relied on local committees of police, military, and civil officials. They applied the same decentralization to military operations, in which junior and noncommissioned officers enjoyed considerable latitude in discharging their duties.

The British achieved their greatest success against communist insurgents in the Federation of Malaya (1948–1960). Like the French, the British had experienced a humiliating defeat by the Japanese. The Marxist Malayan People's Liberation Army, which the British had trained and equipped to fight the Japanese, launched an insurgency against colonial rule after the war. They gained support of Chinese peasants who lived a subsistence existence in squatter villages along the jungle fringes. To separate the insurgents from this support, the British relocated the population into new, protected villages with better homes, running water, medical clinics, and schools. They offered the Chinese land and citizenship. This approach produced the intelligence that allowed small units to pursue the insurgents deep into the jungle.

Critics of the British approach maintain that it was achieved under favorable circumstances and, in any event, represented little more than a holding action. To be sure, British counterinsurgency did not produce an unbroken string of victories, as the withdrawal from Palestine in 1947 and South Arabia in 1967 indicate. However, a Malayan-style victory in Oman (1970–1975) and what appears to be success in Northern Ireland suggest that the success of British counterinsurgency derives from more than fortuitous circumstances and good luck.

**OTHER INSURGENCIES**
While most insurgencies target colonies, two occurred within Europe itself. Basque separatists in Spain sought an independent homeland consisting of Basque provinces in Spain and France. Catholic insurgents in Northern Ireland pursued unification of the province with the Irish Republic

Basque Fatherland and Liberty, better known as ETA from the Basque acronym, drew support from a Basque population deprived of its language, culture, and institutions by the dictatorship of

Francisco Franco (1892–1975). ETA launched its campaign in the 1960s with attacks on police and government institutions within the Basque region and Madrid. The insurgents' greatest success came with the assassination of Franco's handpicked successor, Admiral Louis Carrero Blanco, in 1973. This success also marked the beginning of ETA's decline. The reestablishment of democracy following Franco's death in 1975 resulted in a new Spanish constitution that granted the Basque provinces limited autonomy, use of the Basque language, and cultural independence. Continued violence in spite of these concessions, particularly a bombing that killed twenty-one in Barcelona in 1987, turned public opinion against ETA. Improved counterinsurgency methods, including an extradition treaty with France, contributed further to ETA's decline. The organization declared a cease-fire in 1998, and although it announced an end to the cease-fire in late 1999, ETA was much less visible in the first years of the early twenty-first century. The Northern Ireland insurgency began in 1969 as a civil rights movement against what had become an apartheid regime oppressive of Catholics. The Provisional Irish Republican Army (PIRA) gained control of the movement and launched an insurgency against British rule. After initial blunders, including the Bloody Sunday massacre of 1972, the British rediscovered their traditional approach to counterinsurgency, combining economic development and political reform with selective use of military forces. The PIRA's failure to achieve military success led them to seek a political settlement. Both sides agreed to a cease-fire in 1994 and the Good Friday Accords in 1998. Despite some setbacks, this settlement has held.

**IRAQ AND BEYOND**
The war in Iraq has made it painfully clear that insurgency remains one of the most persistent forms of conflict. Unfortunately, the conduct of this war shows that conventional armed forces have learned little from past wars. The American-led coalition was ill prepared for a protracted war and only slowly adapted to what was finally acknowledged as an insurgency rather than mere terrorism. A few participants, however, most notably the British and the Dutch, took their own painful historical experience to heart and applied a more

patient, comprehensive approach to the struggle. If the counterinsurgency experience of the last century is any guide, this is the only approach that will work.

*See also* **Algeria; Basques; ETA; Palestine; Vietnam War.**

BIBLIOGRAPHY

Beckett, Ian F. W., and John Pimlott, eds. *Armed Forces and Modern Counter-insurgency.* New York, 1985.

Mockaitis, Thomas R. *British Counterinsurgency, 1919–1960.* London, 1990.

Nagl, John A. *Counterinsurgency Lessons from Malaya and Vietnam: Learning to Eat Soup with a Knife.* Westport, Conn., 2002.

O'Neil, Bard. *Insurgency and Terrorism: From Revolution to Apocalypse.* 2nd ed. Washington, D.C., 2005.

Thompson, Robert. *Defeating Communist Insurgency: The Lessons of Malaya and Vietnam.* London, 1965.

THOMAS R. MOCKAITIS

---

# CRAXI, BETTINO (1932–2000), Italian politician.

Leader of the Italian socialist youth movement, member of the central committee of the PSI (Italian Socialist Party) from 1957 and supporter of the movement toward autonomy, Bettino Craxi, who was born in Milan in 1934, entered the leadership of the party in 1965 and was among the promoters of the unification between the PSI and the Social Democrats. A deputy from 1968 and vice-secretary of the PSI from 1970, he was elected its national secretary in 1976. He followed a political line aimed at reinforcing the autonomy of the PSI, especially from the PCI (Italian Communist Party), against which he entered into an open polemic with the express intent of "re-equilibrating" the forces of the Left; at the same time, he formed a sometimes conflicted alliance with the Christian Democrats.

His criticism of Marxism, rehabilitation of liberal socialism, and accentuation of libertarian principles and socialist humanism, present in the tradition of the PSI, were the result of a reflection undertaken in harmony with the accelerated changes occurring in Italian society. The turnaround was emphasized even in the new symbol of the party (a red carnation), which was added at the Congress of the PSI of 29 May 1978, when Craxi was reelected secretary.

After the end of the historic compromise the socialists of Craxi chose to return to government with the DC (Christian Democrats), thus terminating all dialogue with the Left and indeed initiating a violent offensive against the Communists. Craxi, who was at the time the undisputed leader of the party, made maximum use of the coalition-forming power of the PSI to place himself before the Catholic party as a preferred partner for ensuring the "governability" of the country.

From August 1983 to March 1987 (4 August 1983–27 June 1986 and 1 August–3 March 1987), Craxi remained at the helm of a five-party coalition, composed of the DC, PSI, PSDI (Italian Socialist-Democratic Party), PLI (Italian Liberal Party), and PRI (Italian Republican Party). On 8 February 1984 at the Villa Madama, with Cardinal Agostino Casaroli (1914–1998), he signed the new Concord between Italy and the Holy See.

During the first Craxi government, the *Achille Lauro*, an Italian cruise ship, was hijacked on 7 October 1985 by four men from the Palestinian Liberation Organization while the ship was sailing from Alexandria to Port Said, Egypt. The hijackers directed the ship to sail to Tartus, Syria, and demanded the release of fifty Palestinians then in Israeli prisons. Refused permission to dock at Tartus, the hijackers shot one wheelchair-bound passenger—an American Jew named Leon Klinghoffer—and threw his body overboard. The ship headed back to Port Said, and after two days of negotiations, the hijackers agreed to abandon the ship for safe conduct and were flown toward Tunisia aboard an Egyptian commercial airliner. The plane was intercepted by U.S. Navy fighters and was directed to land at the naval air station of Sigonella, a NATO base in Sicily, where the hijackers were arrested by the Italians after a disagreement between U.S. and Italian authorities. Craxi and the minister of foreign affairs, Giulio Andreotti (b. 1919), refused U.S. president Ronald Reagan's requests for extradition of the hijackers, declaring that the Italian government had jurisdiction over its own territory, even though the territory in question was a NATO naval base. The decision was probably due both to security concerns about terrorists taking revenge against Italian targets and to an Italian tradition of diplomacy with the Arab world. The hijackers' leader, Abu Abbas, fled to Yugoslavia and was convicted in Italy in absentia.

Long a representative of the PCI at the Socialist International and a member of the European Parliament, Craxi served as a representative of the Secretary General of the United Nations, Javier Pérez de Cuéllar (b. 1920), responsible for problems of debt in developing countries (1989), and then as a special counselor for issues regarding the development and consolidation of peace and security. From the beginning of the 1980s, however, the first scandals began to break over the PSI: in 1981, in the course of investigations of the P2 (the Masonic lodge headed by Licio Gelli [b. 1919]), leading members of the Socialist Party were implicated. Among the documents confiscated from P2, record was found of a Swiss account, the "Protection" account, which was destined in the 1990s to set judges on the trail of the illicit financial dealings of Craxi and his collaborators. In 1983 the arrests of several provincial and regional assessors from Turin and Savona set the stage for a mudslide that would sweep over the entire governing elite, and above all the PSI of Craxi, which became a virtual symbol of the corruption.

The year 1992 marked the beginning of *Mani Pulite* (clean hands), the inquest on kickbacks paid by businessmen to officeholders in order to obtain contracts. The investigation, undertaken by public prosecutors of the Republic of Milan, in particular judge Antonio di Pietro (b. 1950), gave a mortal blow to already tormented parties. On 2 May 1992 the Socialist ex-mayors Paolo Pillitteri (b. 1940), Craxi's brother-in-law, and Carlo Tognoli (b. 1938) were subpoenaed, but the operation did not spare even members of the DC and the PDS (the new name of the Communist Party). On 14 July 1992 the Socialist ex-foreign minister Gianni de Michelis (b. 1940) was also subpoenaed. The Enimont case (January 1993), called the "mother of all kickbacks," revealed how the leading parties in government distributed kickbacks. The scandal led to the suicides of several Italian businessmen, while in Parliament subpoenas began to arrive for all the ministers of the parties of the governing majority, including the party leaders. In the Senate Craxi denounced in vain the collective responsibility of politicians and captains of industry, all of whom were aware of the illegal system of party financing. In February 1993 Craxi resigned from the secretariat of the PSI.

In May 1994 he moved to Hammamet, Tunisia, where he would not miss an occasion to send advice and admonishments and to express his concerns for the fate of Italy and socialism, which was on the route to dissolution (on 13 November, the PSI was disbanded). On 29 July 1994 Craxi and Claudio Martelli (b. 1940), his understudy, were condemned in the affair of the "Protection" account. From then on Craxi was considered a fugitive, though he continued to call himself an exile. The Tunisian government always supported him, refusing to grant his extradition. On 27 October 1995, together with Martelli and other government leaders, he was condemned in the Enimont trial.

On 27 October 1999 his health worsened and there was discussion about the possibility of suspending his sentence to allow him to return to Italy for medical care. After a kidney procedure, he died on 19 January 2000 in Hammamet, of cardiac arrest.

*See also* **Crime and Justice; Di Pietro, Antonio; Italy.**

BIBLIOGRAPHY

Bohn, Michael K. *The Achille Lauro Hijacking: Lessons in the Politics and Prejudice of Terrorism.* Washington, D.C., 2004.

Cafagna, Luciano. *La grande slavina. L'Italia verso la crisi della democrazia.* Venice, 1993.

Cassesse, Antonio. *Terrorism, Politics, and the Law: The Achille Lauro Affair.* Princeton, N.J., 1989.

Colarizi, Simona, and Marco Gervasoni. *La cruna dell'ago: Craxi, il Partito socialista e la crisi della Repubblica.* Rome, 2005.

Intini, Ugo. *Craxi, una storia socialista.* Milan, 2000.

Statera, Gianni. *Il caso Craxi. Immagine di un presidente.* Milan, 1987.

MARIA TERESA GIUSTI

---

# CRIME AND JUSTICE.

**CRIME AND JUSTICE.** Although most countries within Europe had at least rudimentary statistics on crime and disorder by the beginning of the twentieth century, drawing cross-national comparisons is a hazardous enterprise. Laws varied between countries, as did the ways in which those laws were implemented and criminal statistics classified. Changes over time and between countries in access to telephones or cars, inevitably had an impact on the willingness and the ability of the public to report crimes, as indeed did their relationships with the police. Political concerns also meant that crime data for Soviet bloc countries was rarely reliable. That said, there appears to have been a steady increase in reported crime throughout the twentieth century, albeit the pace of change varied. In Ireland, for example, the postwar rise in recorded crime was far greater in (British) Northern Ireland than in the Irish Republic; in England and Wales the postwar increase began much earlier than it did in the Netherlands.

However, it was not until the widespread deployment of victim surveys in the 1980s that researchers were able to draw direct comparisons. The first International Crime Victimisation Survey (ICVS) was completed in 1989, and repeated in 1992, 1996–1997, and 2000, providing a partial, but nonetheless welcome basis for addressing crime concerns within Europe. This reveals that car-related crime and other property crime predominate, and interpersonal crime, including robbery, is less common. Over the twenty-year period, risk of crime appears to have been relatively high in England and Wales and the Netherlands, lower elsewhere, with Northern Ireland notably having low rates for conventional crimes despite political unrest. In general, public attitudes are positively correlated with levels of risk. For example, "fear" of crime has been relatively high in England and Wales, and early-twenty-first-century falls in concern over burglary parallel a decline in levels of burglary, with risk halving in England and Wales in the 1990s. Among former Eastern bloc countries, government corruption appears to be a particular problem. Official statistics and data from the ICVS also indicate a rise in crime during the 1990s, but partly as a result of the greater publicity given to crime and disorder issues, public concern increased markedly. This in turn affects considerations about appropriate policing styles and sentencing strategies.

## POLICY AND PRACTICE

The political map of Europe has changed dramatically since 1914. Two world wars and their aftermath, and the emergence of the Soviet empire and its dissolution, have shifted both national boundaries and alliances. This clearly has an impact upon criminal justice policy. Invading powers, principally Nazi Germany and the Soviet Union, imposed their own models of policing and control on their satellites, and one of the first priorities of the governments of liberation was to reestablish their own systems. Other influences, both within and outside Europe, have also applied. The Council of Europe and the European Union (EU) have each been instrumental in encouraging members (and in the latter case prospective members) to attain minimum standards. From outside, international bodies such as the United Nations, Amnesty International, and Interpol, and countries such as the United States, have equally attempted to influence core criminal justice policies within European nation-states. Such approaches have been supplemented with the expansion of the global village, whereby policy makers consciously examine examples of good practice from abroad and assess how they might be adapted for home consumption.

Nevertheless, the concept of a European approach to crime and disorder is a misnomer. National traditions have been modified, in many cases overturned, but national distinctions are still evident. There are still more differences in the approaches of European countries to crime and disorder than there are similarities.

## POLICE SYSTEMS

By the early twentieth century, all European nations had at least one professional police system. However, differences in the ways these were structured and controlled and the range of responsibilities accorded the police were marked. As Brian Chapman noted, on much of continental Europe there was a long tradition of powerful, centralized police organizations. Within Nazi Germany and the Soviet Union, consequently, the police systems that achieved notoriety were variants of a traditional model, rather than a new invention. The specter of this all-powerful weapon of state control was a major reason why a modern police system was so strongly resisted in England, and why the model of policing adopted there in the nineteenth century was so different.

For example, Raymond Fosdick, a New York police administrator who toured Europe at the beginning of the twentieth century, contrasted systems of continental Europe with those of England and Wales and the United States. Although scarcely a scientific analysis, his account highlighted a number of differences between the typical Continental force and the situation in England and Wales. In the former, the police was centralized, in the latter locally based; in the former, a paramilitary body, in the latter routinely armed only with a truncheon; in the former, responsible for a range of administrative roles in addition to crime control, in the latter adopting a service-orientation to crime control.

Nevertheless, as Fosdick acknowledged, there were considerable variations within continental Europe, with perhaps the most extreme examples in western Europe to be found in France, Italy, and Spain. However, in none of these countries was there only one centralized and all-powerful force. This was partly because, following the French Revolution, rulers were reluctant to ascribe too much power to one body, so one centralized paramilitary force was often counterbalanced with either a second national body or a plethora of local urban forces. Interestingly, because the major threats to control were seen to come from abroad, across national boundaries, or from within, with mass marches on the capital, the more centralized and militaristic police forces invariably covered the countryside. In France, for example, the *gendarmerie* was responsible for maintaining order in rural areas, being housed in police barracks locally and supported in emergencies by the *gendarmerie mobile*. In contrast, local forces policed the larger cities, before being incorporated into a second centralized force, the *police nationale,* in 1966.

In other parts of Continental Europe, a local input was more evident. In Germany, for example, there was a commitment to county (or lander) autonomy. The West German police system was also radically changed in the postwar period by the Allies, with administrative responsibilities scaled down and the structure demilitarized In the Netherlands, before reform in the 1990s, the power and wealth of the cities meant that the

balance between urban forces and a national *gendarmerie* covering the countryside was rather different than in France. Scandinavian police systems have also tended to be localized, although the Swedish system was centralized between 1965 and 1984.

On mainland Britain, the paid police evolved somewhat differently. The vast array of county and metropolitan forces spawned in the nineteenth century was rationalized in the twentieth century, with amalgamations eventually leading to forty-three forces in England and Wales and eight in Scotland. From the beginning, officers were uniformed. While in the United States early developments comprised a resistance to uniforms, these being seen as militaristic reminders of a colonial past, in Britain uniforms were seen as necessary to guard against the secret police system favored in much of Continental Europe. Unlike on the Continent, officers were also "citizens in uniform," with minimal special powers, and welfare/service roles were incorporated. However, despite the community policing imagery, barriers were established between police officers and the communities they policed: for example, community influence was more restricted than in the United States and police personnel were often recruited from other areas of the country.

Caution is also required before conceptualizing a British model of policing. From the beginning, the police in Ireland was molded differently. The problems of maintaining control in a hostile environment resulted in a paramilitary police force run from London, and formed the blueprint for subsequent colonial forces formed throughout the British Empire. Following partition, the Irish Republic maintained a centralized system, but "civilianized" the police. In the North, the newly formed Royal Ulster Constabulary continued the paramilitary tradition. In the early twenty-first century it is in the process of reform, following the 1999 *Patten Report,* but the difficulties of radically changing police traditions are evident. Elsewhere in the British Isles, separate autonomous police forces exist on the Isle of Mann, Guernsey, and Jersey, the latter in particular epitomizing a community-based system.

At the other extreme, the police system created in Vladimir Lenin's Soviet Union was more akin to the traditional Continental model, with a paramilitary centralized militia subordinate to the powerful secret police. This model was imposed across the Eastern bloc in the late 1940s, where it became known as the repressive police. When these countries and parts of the Soviet Union gained their independence in the 1980s and 1990s, the new governments were committed to police reform. In this endeavor they variously solicited advice from the United States and Western European neighbors, and attempted, among other things, to sever the link between government and operational policing, reduce the administrative responsibilities of the police, advance community policing, decentralize, and civilianize the police. Undoubtedly changes have occurred, but they have lost momentum, partly due to increased popular concern about crime and safety. Additionally, U.S. influence, epitomized in the funding of an Eastern European police college in Budapest, has emphasized the war against organized crime, and especially the international drug problem, rather than the need to democratize and decentralize the police. The entry of many former Eastern bloc countries into the European Union at the turn of the twenty-first century, and scrutiny of police systems in those under consideration, may however lead to future modifications.

Certainly the European Union has had a significant impact on national arrangements. Trevi, for example, was established in 1975–1976 as an intergovernmental cooperative mechanism between member states that established working parties composed of senior officers from different European police forces to plan joint operations. The Schengen Treaty of 1962, expanded most notably through the 1984 Fontainebleau Declaration, espoused as its basic principle the desirability of freedom of movement within the European Union, but in recognizing that this facilitated the movement of illegal goods and services, also sought to enhance international police cooperation. The United Kingdom has not been a party to Fontainebleau, but in much of Europe the principle of greater cooperation has been accepted, initially through Trevi and later through the Schengen Convention of 1990 and the 1991 Maastricht Treaty. More recently, the European Drugs Unit, created in 1994, developed into a full-scale European Police Office (Eoropol), providing cross-border

coordination mainly in relation to drugs, immigration, terrorism, people trafficking, forgery, and vehicle trafficking, and the European Police College (CEPOL) was established in 2001. Ironically, moves to facilitate cooperation have also served to emphasize differences and, on occasions, have led to conflict, a case in point being German and Swedish concern over the more liberal Dutch approach to drug control.

Other changes appear to be more a response to local circumstances than international concerns. For example, local police units have been introduced in France, Italy, and Spain, to supplement centralized systems. Other changes include the removal of a range of noncrime responsibilities from the police in France under the presidency of François Mitterrand. However, while it is tempting to see these as indicative of a convergence across Europe there is little evidence of any consistency here. Rather, it appears that governments have used their autonomy to respond to national issues where they arise. For example, in Germany the significance of the national police has faded as border patrols have become less necessary, and the Dutch system, never excessively centralized, was changed due to controversy over area variations in police costs, and is now structured in a way that is more akin to England and Wales. This suggests that in discussing police systems in Europe there is a need to be mindful of the differences between counties, as well as the caveat that increased cooperation is quite different from harmonization or convergence.

**THE PENAL SYSTEM**

Differences between different European countries are equally evident in terms of alternative ways of dealing with known offenders. While the nineteenth and twentieth centuries saw prison replacing capital and corporal punishment as the ultimate sanction, and imprisonment becoming a sentence in its own right rather than prisons being a place of detention prior to trial, fine payment, or deportation, it was viewed very differently in different European countries at various points in time. In England and Wales, efforts were made to reduce the prison population in the interwar period and then briefly during the 1970s and late 1980s, but generally the English system is characterized by expansionism. During the "Troubles" in Northern Ireland the prison population also reached record proportions, although since the Northern Ireland agreement it has fallen dramatically. However, in neither case has the use of imprisonment come close to the situation in the United States.

Elsewhere in Europe, the use of imprisonment as a sanction against political dissent reached its extreme in the Soviet Union and other Eastern bloc countries. If the police were the first arm in maintaining totalitarian regimes, the prison systems provided a second arm. Social and political dissent was met by an extensive and brutal penal system. Traditionally a high proportion of the population was imprisoned, sentences were relatively long, and inmates confined in large, overcrowded institutions characterized by dire living standards and harsh regimes.

As with the police, one of the main priorities of the emerging new democratic governments was to reduce the use of imprisonment. To achieve this, amnesties, conditional release, and squashed convictions had an immediate impact, while long-term changes were attempted by modifying sentencing patterns, decriminalization of some former crimes, and the expansion of community sentences like probation. Nevertheless, the political will to change has been more evident in some countries, such as Poland, the Czech Republic, and Hungary, than in others, including the Baltic States, Moldova, Ukraine, Belarus, and Russia. Moreover, even in the former more radical countries, policy changes have been challenged by a public increasingly concerned about crime and disorder.

In the postwar period, the most distinctive reductionist example in Europe was the Netherlands, where the rate of imprisonment fell from the 1950s to the early 1990s, a policy commonly attributed to the pragmatic and liberal approach adopted by policy makers who, unlike in the United States and Britain, were not under pressure from a public demanding more punitive sentencing. This low rate was not due to a lower rate of sentencing, but to a high rate of cases being discontinued, combined with use of short sentences. However, Dutch policy changed dramatically in the 1990s, with imprisonment rising and an apparent end to Dutch tolerance. As a result, by 2002, the rate had risen to 100 per 100,000 population, lower than the European average but above that in all Scandinavian countries as well as Belgium, France, and Switzerland, among others. At the other extreme, England and Wales have traditionally had a relatively high rate of imprisonment by Western European standards, although this does not appear to have had any effect on their crimes rates. Nevertheless, imprisonment has become a more popular sanction in Europe in the late twentieth and early twenty-first centuries. It thus seems that while rates of imprisonment, in Western Europe at least, are well behind those in the United States, the move is toward an increased use of custody.

Traditionally, probation has been considered the natural alternative to imprisonment. However, although it emerged in the nineteenth century in the United States and Britain as a means for providing community support for offenders, in much of Europe its origins are more recent. In countries with a civil law tradition, suspended sentences, usually without any conditions of supervision, were more common, and probation has been introduced along with a growing array of noncustodial alternatives. Electronic monitoring has also been imported from the United States, and while it is not a common sentencing choice it is now deployed in a range of European countries, including England and Wales, Scotland, the Netherlands and Sweden. However, as in the United States, an expansion in more demanding and punitive community sentences appears to have been at the expense of other noncustodial sentences, rather than as a replacement to prison. There is therefore persuasive evidence that sentencing policies in Europe are becoming increasingly punitive, reflected in both an increased willingness to imprison and an expansion in community punishment. That is not to ignore the expansion of more constructive alternatives such as mediation and restorative justice. Moreover, variations between the nations of Europe in their approach to prison and its alternatives are still considerable.

## SUMMARY

The structure and role of the police and the operation of the penal system within countries of Europe depend on both crime and disorder and public perceptions of "the crime problem" and on social and political traditions, adjusted as they have been by wars, fought-for independence, and the forging of alliances. However, while criminal justice systems have been subject to extensive change, and convergence can be identified in police operations, the changing nature of probation, and expanding prison populations, there are nonetheless considerable differences. New policies and practices are adopted partly as a result of international pressures and the search for examples of good practice abroad, but they are also the result of internal pressures. In consequence, considerable differences remain in the ways that different countries within Europe perceive and confront their crime problems.

*See also* **Death Penalty; Drugs (Illegal); European Court of Justice; International Law; Police and Policing.**

BIBLIOGRAPHY

Downes, David. *Contrasts in Tolerance: Post-War Penal Policy in the Netherlands and England and Wales.* Oxford, U.K., and New York, 1988.

Dunkel, Frieder. "Imprisonment in Transition: The Situation in the New States of the Federal Republic of Germany." *British Journal of Criminology* 35 (1995): 95–113.

Fairchild, Erika S. *German Police: Ideals and Reality in the Post-War Years.* Springfield, Mass., 1988.

Hamai, Koich, et al. *Probation around the World: A Comparative Study.* London, 1995.

Jasinski, Jerzy, and Andrzej Siemaszko, eds. *Crime Control in Poland.* Warsaw, 1995.

King, R. D. "Russian Prisons after Perestroika." *British Journal of Criminology* 34 (1994): 62–82.

Mawby, R. I. *Comparative Policing Issues: The British and American Experience in International Perspective.* London, 1990.

———. "The Changing Face of Policing in Central and Eastern Europe." *International Journal of Police Science and Management* 2, no. 3 (1999): 199–216.

Mawby, R. I., ed. *Policing across the World: Issues for the Twenty-first Century.* London, 1999.

Pakes, F. J. "League Champions in Mid Table: On the Major Changes in Dutch Prison Policy." *Howard Journal of Criminal Justice* 39, no. 1 (2000): 30–39.

Ruggiero, Vincenzo, Mick Ryan, and Joe Sim. *Western European Penal Systems: A Critical Anatomy.* London, 1995.

Rutherford, Andres. *Prisons and the Process of Justice.* London, 1984.

Tonry, Michael. *Penal Reform in Overcrowded Times.* London, 2001.

van der Laan, P. H. "Electronic Monitoring in Europe: Outcomes from Experiments in England and Wales, the Netherlands and Sweden." *CEP Bulletin* 13 (1999): 8–10.

Walmsley, Roy. *World Prisons Population List.* 5th ed. London, 2003.

Whitfield, Dick. *Tackling the Tag: The Electronic Monitoring of Offenders.* Winchester, U.K., 1997.

Zvekic, Ugljesa. *Criminal Victimisation in Countries in Transition.* Rome, 1998.

R. I. MAWBY

## CROATIA.

In 1914 all the Croatian regions were part of the Austro-Hungarian Empire. Croats were the majority in two such regions (with strong Serb minorities). The "kingdom of Croatia-Slavonia" in the north, with its capital in Zagreb, was attached to Hungary and enjoyed some degree of autonomy, with its own institutions: the *ban* (viceroy) and the *sabor* (parliament). Along the Adriatic, in the south, Dalmatia, belonging to Austria proper, also had its own provincial parliament but without autonomy. The two regions were essentially rural. Dalmatia was particularly poor, isolated, and depopulated because of emigration. Croats asked for, and never obtained, the union of the two provinces. There were also Croats in Bosnia and Istria.

Croat opinion was divided between the "Croat-Serb coalition," the more bourgeois party, heir to the "Yugoslav Movement" of the nineteenth century, and the purely Croat parties that were more popular, particularly the "Croatian Peasants Party" of Stjepan Radić (1871–1928). Thanks to poll-tax suffrage, the former held the majority in both Chambers. In 1910 Radić's party only had nine deputies in the parliament of Zagreb (out of seventy-seven).

During World War I most Croat soldiers fought loyally in the Austrian army. In the case of an Allied victory, many feared the division of the region between Serbia and Italy (which had in fact been the intention of a secret inter-Allied agreement signed in London in 1915). To avoid this, a possible solution was for all of the regions where Croats lived to unite with Serbia, in the name of the Yugoslav idea. This was the choice made in 1914 by a few Croatian politicians, mostly from Dalmatia. Exiled in Paris, they founded a "Yugoslavian committee" in 1915 that sought to negotiate with Serbia and to be recognized by the Allies as legitimate representatives of Slovene, Croat, and Serb subjects of the Habsburgs.

In October 1918 Austria collapsed. The Serbian army liberated Serbia and marched west. The Italians progressed along the Adriatic. The threat of division became greater. The parliaments of all the southern Slavic provinces of the empire sent delegates to Zagreb. They founded a "National Committee of Slovenes, Croats, and Serbs" (SHS) presided over by Anton Korošec (1872–1940), a Slovene, but dominated by Svetozar Pribićević (a Croatian Serb). They proclaimed the independence of the "SHS State" and their desire to unite with Serbia. Only one delegate, Radić, who favored an independent republic of Croatia, protested. The delegation went to Belgrade where it agreed to the fusion of the two States: SHS and Serbia, into one "Kingdom of Slovenes, Croats, and Serbs" (later called "Yugoslavia"), proclaimed on 1 December 1918 by the regent and future king, Alexander Karadjordjević (1888–1934). The state's structure as either a federation or a union, was to be decided by a future constituent assembly.

**THE MONARCHY OF YUGOSLAVIA (1918–1941)**
At first, the union of Croatia and Serbia was welcomed. It seemed the only alternative to division and anarchy. Moreover, a part of the Croat elite embraced the idea of a "Yugoslavian people" uniting Croats and Serbs as equals. But very quickly the methods employed by the Serb army and bureaucracy, the disadvantageous currency exchange rate, the suppression of autonomous Croatian institutions, and the Serb seizure of all key positions fed discontent. As of 1919, in the constituent assembly elected by universal suffrage, Radić's Peasants Party won more than half of the Croat vote, and the Communists also did well. But Radić's followers boycotted the vote on the constitution and the Communist Party was banned. It was therefore a truncated assembly that voted for the constitution of 1921. The latter established a rigorously centralized system, based on the Serbian model, and gave the king great power.

The following twenty years were characterized by the ongoing conflict between Belgrade's centralizing will and Croats' resistance. The Croat elite quickly renounced the Yugoslav ideal of the preceding generation and joined the masses of farmers in protest against the regime. Several times, the army fired on peaceful Croat demonstrators, and Croatian intellectuals were assassinated. In 1928, on the floor of the parliament in Belgrade, Radić and two other representatives were shot down by one of their Montenegrin colleagues.

The king suspended the constitution and promulgated another even more centralizing document. Ante Pavelić (1889–1959), a Croatian extremist representative, sought asylum in Italy, where, under the protection of Benito Mussolini (1883–1945), he founded the Ustaše (insurgent) movement, a terrorist organization. In 1934 he had King Alexander assassinated when the monarch was visiting Marseille, France. The dictatorship continued under the prime ministers appointed by the king's successor, Prince Regent Paul (1926–1976).

An attempt at conciliation was made in 1939. The royal government concluded an agreement with Vladko Maček, successor of Radić, creating a "banovina [province] of Croatia" that would be largely autonomous and would include a part of Bosnia. In April 1941 Yugoslavia was invaded by Nazi Germany and collapsed in a matter of days.

**THE USTAŠE REGIME (1941–1945)**
The Germans wanted an independent Croatia. Maček, the main Croat leader, refused to collaborate with them. The Ustaše took power. They proclaimed the "Independent State of Croatia" (NDH). Their leader, Pavelić, became chief of state, "poglavnik" (führer). The new state encompassed all of Bosnia but had to relinquish a part of Dalmatia to Italy.

The Croat population welcomed the country's independence as if it had been liberated. But the enthusiasm for the Croat state did not translate into adhesion to Ustaše policy. Strong resistance quickly took shape.

The NDH was a typical fascist state: a one-man dictatorship marked by a single-party system, arbitrary decisions, violence, concentration camps, and

**Dubrovnik, Croatia, photographed in 2005.** The ancient port city of Dubrovnik, a center of Slavic culture during the medieval period, was heavily damaged in the fighting that followed the breakup of Yugoslavia. A subsequent rebuilding effort restored the city to its position as a resort and tourist destination. ©PHILIPPE GIRAUD/GOODLOOK/CORBIS

massacres. But its nationalism learnt to live with complete submission to Germany and Italy. The single party, the Ustaše, was not a party of the masses. It remained a small violent group that did not have much influence upon society.

Because the NDH encompassed all of Bosnia, only 53 percent of the population was Catholic Croat, but 17 percent was Muslim and 30 percent Orthodox Serb. The regime decided to lean on the first two groups and to eliminate Serbs, who were expelled, converted to Catholicism by force, or killed. This program was put into effect with village massacres and deportations to death camps. Jews and Roma (Gypsies) were exterminated. The casualty count has often been exaggerated, but it was established that approximately three hundred thousand Serbs died during the war in Croatia and Bosnia: some died in combat or in other war-related ways, but probably at least half died in these systematic killings.

This policy naturally triggered armed resistance, first among the Serbs who were its primary target, but also among many Croats and Muslims. The rebels divided into two enemy movements: the "chetniks," Serb royalists under General Dragoljub Mihailović (1893–1946), and the communist "partisans," led by the Croat Josip Broz (1892–1980), known as Tito. The "chetniks," all Serbs, massacred Croat and Muslim populations and collaborated with the Italians and sometimes with the Germans. The "partisans" were open to all ethnic groups, their organization the sole conduit that Croatian resisters, who were more and more numerous, could turn to. Soon, Pavelić's government controlled less than half of its territory. The partisans—who recruited from every group, were more effective, and were supported not only by the Soviet Union but also eventually by the Western Allies—were victorious. In May 1945 they finished conquering Croatia and took Zagreb.

## COMMUNIST YUGOSLAVIA (1945–1990)

In its beginning, the regime was very harsh. Thousands of prisoners were executed without trial (the Bleiburg massacre), and Catholic priests were murdered. Archbishop Alojzije Stepinac (1898–1960) was sentenced to solitary confinement. A single-party regime was established, Stalinist methods were put into effect, and the economy was entirely nationalized.

But on the institutional level, the new power got off on a different footing than did the monarchy before the war: it was federalist and not unitarian. Croatia (minus Bosnia but including Istria, which was taken away from Italy) became one of six federated republics. The Croat and Serb nations were recognized.

As of 1948, after the breakup between Tito and the USSR, the regime distanced itself from Stalinist methods. The state economy was replaced with a self-management policies. During the 1960s and 1970s economic growth was rapid. Industry and tourism increased, as did the emigration of workers, especially to Germany. With the end of the 1960s and some liberalization of the regime, a movement appeared demanding full acknowledgment of Croatian specificity. In 1971, with the wide support of the population, the communist leaders began reforms to that end. It was the "Croatian Spring," a movement repressed by Tito, who fired those communist leaders and ordered more than one thousand arrests.

In 1974 a new constitution established an almost confederate regime that gave much power to the six republics and to the two autonomous provinces. A large number of the demands of the Croatian Spring were met. After Tito's death in 1980, in spite of the economic deterioration, Croatia was at peace until 1989.

Decentralization displeased the Serbs, who were scattered across several republics and provinces. They wanted to strengthen the central power, or the attachment to Serbia of all regions where Serbs lived (including in Croatia). This demand, first expressed by the opposition, was adopted and supported in 1986 by Slobodan Milošević (1941–2006), a new Serb Communist leader, who, in 1989, abolished the autonomy of the two provinces of Kosovo and Voivodine. The other republics felt threatened.

## THE EXPLOSION OF YUGOSLAVIA AND THE WAR OF INDEPENDENCE (1990–1995)

The conflict deepened in 1990 when, after the fall of communism in neighboring countries, the Yugoslav republics also organized free elections. The communists won the elections in Serbia and Montenegro. In Croatia, the winner was a new nationalist party, the HDZ (Croatian Democratic Community). Franjo Tudjman (1922–1999), its leader and a former partisan who had been jailed several times under Tito, was elected president. His policy displeased Croatian Serbs, who openly rebelled in the summer of 1990.

In 1991 Milošević blocked the functioning of the federal presidency in order to prevent the pending election of a Croat, Stipe Mesić. Federal troops supported the armed rebellion of the Croatian Serbs. Croatia, following Slovenia's example, organized a referendum and proclaimed its independence on 25 June 1991. Belgrade answered with war: first in Slovenia, which the Yugoslavian army evacuated two weeks later, and then in Croatia, where the fighting lasted six months (July 1991–January 1992).

Rural regions where Serbs were the majority, called Krajina (borderlands), proclaimed a "Republic of Serbian Krajina" (RSK), which separated itself from Croatia. The federal army, using artillery and aviation, and aided by local militias and volunteers from Serbia, gained increasing control of the ground, occupying eventually a third of Croatia, from which all Croats were thrown out (three hundred thousand refugees, massacres, much destruction). Dubrovnik and Osijek were besieged and bombarded, as well as Vukovar, which was taken in November and where many Croat prisoners were murdered.

Croats had little to resist with but still managed to raid federal barracks for weapons. In some regions, they also chased away or massacred Serbs. They succeeded in preserving their main cities and the integrity of their territory.

European attempts at mediation remained ineffective for six months. In December of 1991, the European Union, at the behest of Germany, decided to recognize Croatia's independence. Fighting stopped in January 1992. According to the "Vance plan" (named after the American mediator Cyrus Vance [1917–2002]), the regions of Croatia conquered by the Serbs were placed under the military occupation of United Nations troops but remained under the control of the RSK. In violation of this plan, the Croats who had been chased out were not allowed to return.

From 1992 to 1995 war raged in Bosnia. The Croats of Bosnia armed themselves against the Serbs, but very quickly began fighting Bosnians as well: Tudjman also wanted to annex a portion of Bosnia. In 1994 the United States succeeded in stopping the fighting and convinced each side to join with the other against the Serbs. The Croatian army made rapid progress in Bosnia, and in two very quick military operations (May and July 1995), reconquered almost all of the Krajina, from which the Serb population was evacuated by order of their own leaders. This victory facilitated the conclusion of the Dayton Agreements, which put an end to the war in Bosnia and enabled Croatia to peacefully recover that portion of its territory (Vukovar) that was still occupied.

**POSTWAR PERIOD (FROM 1995)**
Croatia has definitely secured its independence and reunited its territory. It was ruined by the war, but reconstruction went quickly, and the economy began to grow again, thanks especially to tourism. Tudjman's rule became more and more personal, authoritarian, and nationalistic, but the president died in December 1999 and the HDZ, his party, lost the 2000 elections. The new president, Mesić, who was very hostile toward nationalism, established, in two successive administrations (the first was dominated by the Socialists until the elections of 2003 and the next involved a renewed HDZ), a policy of democratization and reconciliation with Croatia's neighbors aimed at, eventually, Croatia's membership in the European Union.

*See also* **Bosnia-Herzegovina; Milošević, Slobodan; Sarajevo; Serbia; Tudjman, Franco; World War I; World War II; Yugoslavia.**

BIBLIOGRAPHY
*Primary Sources*

Maček, Vladko. *In the Struggle for Freedom.* Translated by Elizabeth and Stjepan Gazi. University Park, Pa., 1957. Translation of *Memoari.* Memoirs of one of the principal Croat leaders between the two world wars.

Mesić, Stipe. *The Demise of Yugoslavia: A Political Memoir.* Budapest and New York, 2004. Translation of *Kako je srušena Jugoslavija: Politički memoari.* Testimony of the last president of Yugoslavia, before he became the second president of Croatia.

Tomac, Zdravko. *The Struggle for the Croatian State: Through Hell to Democracy.* Translated by Zrinka Kos et al. Zagreb, Croatia, 1993. Testimony of a Croat politician, minister in 1991–1992.

Tudjman, Franjo. *Horrors of War: Historical Reality and Philosophy.* Translated by Katarina Mijatovic. New York, 1996. Translation of *Bespuča povijesne zbiljnosti: Raaprava o povijesti i filozofii zlosilja.* Very controversial historical-philosophical book by the first president of Croatia.

*Secondary Sources*

Adler, Jasna. *L'Union forcée: La Croatie et la création de l'Etat Yougoslave (1918).* Chêne-Bourg, Switzerland, 1997. Every detail about this single decisive year.

Banac, Ivo. *The National Question in Yugoslavia: Origins, History, Politics.* Ithaca, N.Y., 1984. In-depth study of the aspirations and national policies of various peoples, including Croats.

Goldstein, Ivo. *Croatia: A History.* Translated by Nikolina Jovanović. London, 1999.

Hory, Ladislaus, and Martin Broszat. *Der kroatische Ustascha-Staat, 1941–1945.* Stuttgart, 1964. Focuses on foreign politics and minority persecution.

Krulic, Joseph. *Histoire de la Yougoslavie de 1945 à nos jours.* Brussels, 1993. Meticulous study of the evolution of the Communist Party.

Macan, Trpimir, and Josip Šentija. *A Short History of Croatia.* Zagreb, Croatia, 1992.

Magaš, Branka. *The Destruction of Yugoslavia. Tracking the Break-up, 1980–92.* London, 1993. This book brings well-constructed answers to the most controversial questions. Croatia holds it dear.

Magaš, Branka, and Ivo Žanić, eds. *The War in Croatia and Bosnia-Herzegovina, 1991–1995.* London and Portland, Ore., 2001. Collaborative book to which various historians from various countries as well as Croat and Bosnian politicians and soldiers have contributed.

Melčić, Dunja, ed. *Der Jugoslawien-Krieg: Handbuch zu Vorgeschichte, Verlauf und Konsequenzen.* Opladen, 1999. International collaborative book, the most complete and critical studies: cultural facts, political history, statistical figures.

Peroche, Gregory. *Histoire de la Croatie et des nations slaves du Sud 395–1992.* Paris, 1992. Croatian point of view on Croatia's history.

Ramet, Sabrina P. *Nationalism and Federalism in Yugoslavia, 1962–1991.* 2nd ed. Bloomington, Ind., 1992.

———. *Balkan Babel: The Disintegration of Yugoslavia from the Death of Tito to the Fall of Milošević.* 4th ed. Boulder, Colo., 2002. The two books by Ramet survey the last forty years of history and answer certain cultural and institutional questions.

Tanner, Marcus. *Croatia: A Nation Forged in War.* New Haven, Conn., and London, 1997. The best documented and most complete general study. Two hundred pages devoted to the twentieth century.

Tomasevich, Jozo. *The Chetniks.* Stanford, Calif., and Cambridge, U.K., 1975.

———. *War and Revolution in Yugoslavia, 1941–1945: Occupation and Collaboration.* Stanford, Calif., 2001. Tomasevich's two books paint an exhaustive picture of World War II in Croatia and Bosnia and all of its complexity.

PAUL GARDE

---

# CROCE, BENEDETTO (1866–1952), Italian intellectual and political theorist.

Benedetto Croce was a proudly independent scholar with an astonishing reach that included philosophy, history, political thought, and literary criticism. Born to a wealthy family in the Abruzzi, he lived in Naples after 1886, except when participating in Roman political life—as a senator beginning in 1910 and as minister for education in Giovanni Giolitti's brief postwar government. After Benito Mussolini assumed dictatorial power in January 1925, Croce became the regime's leading critic.

Through his books and his essays for his journal *La critica* (1903–1944), Croce sought to develop a publicly accessible philosophy adequate to the positivistic culture of modern industrial society, which no longer met human needs for religious meaning. Yet he did not believe, with Hegel, that philosophy could rationally comprehend all of reality. Philosophy's role was to offer an orientation or "faith" that would preserve a sense of the absolute without any claim to knowledge outside human experience. The various modes of human action—aesthetic, logical or scientific, practical, and ethical—were distinct moments whose interaction might be appreciated contemplatively but which could not be rationally grasped together.

His first major work, the *Estetica* (1902; Aesthetics), presented humanity as a spectacularly creative species with vast powers of intuition that allowed it to shape history just as poets and artists shaped their works. The book led to a Croce cult among young intellectuals over the next decade, which, however, broke apart in 1914 when he refused to back Italian intervention into World War I.

After the war, Croce was slow to recognize fascism's intrinsic illiberalism and dictatorial trajectory. Traumatized by the cataclysmic impact of the war, the Bolshevik Revolution, Italy's *biennio rosso* (two red years, 1919–1920), and the birth of Italian Communist Party in 1921, he was among those members of the liberal establishment seized by a "return to order" mentality that blinded them to the danger Mussolini represented.

The war itself had a profound effect on Croce's political ideas. He was never a nationalist, but the war led him to a heightened emphasis on the inevitability of struggle and war, which was a universal, human passion. He came to believe that individuals have a duty to act on behalf of their country quite independently of any universalist ideals they might also hold. What especially worried him during the war was that the Italian state might be enfeebled because it had succumbed to the antiwar propaganda of the socialists and the Catholics. A similar logic fed his initial support for Mussolini, whose politics had been made necessary by the chaos of the war but that, he hoped, would cleanse Italy of various utopianisms and thereby prepare the way for a more mature liberal state.

Croce never offered a sociological or political analysis of fascism but simply responded to it at the level of pragmatic politics. Before 1925, he wrote several journal articles offering guarded support for the regime. Then, after Mussolini assumed dictatorial power and Giovanni Gentile, his former collaborator on *La critica,* launched a "Manifesto of the Fascist Intellectuals," Croce responded with a "Manifesto of the Anti-Fascist Intellectuals" (May 1925), for which he gained hundreds of intellectual supporters. This attitude prevailed until the regime fell in July 1943, at which point he developed a more historical and philosophical assessment of the regime as a "parenthesis" in Italian history.

Croce rejected Italy's "ethical state" tradition, which had culminated in Gentile. For him, the ethical state was a *statolotria* (state worship) that rested upon a confusion between public and private spheres. Yet he supported the early Fascist regime because he believed its suspension of normal constitutional liberties in order to combat threats from the Left would ultimately strengthen the liberal state. Even the violence of Fascist *squadrismo* and the crisis precipitated by the murder of the Socialist Giacomo Matteotti in 1924 did not overly concern him because, like Machiavelli, he was convinced that politics was necessarily bound up with evil. Only when he saw that fascism was succeeding in establishing itself as a regime that would supplant the liberal state rather than serving as an ugly prelude to a new version of it did he move into the opposition.

During the years of the regime, he wrote some of his most important works: *Storia d'Italia dal 1871 al 1915* (1928; History of Italy from 1871 to 1915), *Storia d'Europa nel secolo decimono* (1932; History of Europe in the nineteenth century), and *La storia come pensiero e come azione* (1938; History as thought and action). Although his continued presence in Italy, which included his role as a senator in a lifeless parliament, may have helped legitimate the regime, these works operated as subtle critiques of fascism. Moreover, he did not shy away from oppositional public stands. In 1929 he was the only senator to oppose the Lateran Accords with the Vatican, and he was an outspoken opponent of the "racial laws" of 1938.

After the war, Croce took part in two cabinets and was elected to the Constituent Assembly in 1946, but he mostly devoted himself to scholarship and to the Institute for Italian Historical Studies until his death in 1952.

*See also* **Fascism; Italy; Mussolini, Benito.**

BIBLIOGRAPHY

Casale, Giuseppe. *Benedetto Croce between Naples and Europe.* New York, 1994.

D'Amico, Jack, Dain A. Trafton, and Massimo Verdicchio, eds. *The Legacy of Benedetto Croce: Contemporary Critical Views.* Toronto, 1999.

Jacobitti, Edmund E. *Revolutionary Humanism and Historicism in Modern Italy.* New Haven, Conn., 1981. The wider context of Croce's early thinking.

Rizi, Fabio Fernando. *Benedetto Croce and Italian Fascism.* Toronto, 2003. A more recent study of a vexed question.

Roberts, David D. *Benedetto Croce and the Uses of Historicism.* Berkeley, Calif., 1987. Penetrating analysis of Croce's philosophy of history.

WALTER L. ADAMSON

# CUBAN MISSILE CRISIS.

The Cuban Missile Crisis of October 1962 is the closest the world has ever come to full-scale nuclear war, and fear of the narrow means by which true disaster was averted frightened European and North American leaders into changes that dramatically altered the international system. Thereafter the Cold War entered a more stable phase, as the superpowers shifted from direct confrontation to a series of proxy wars fought over the ensuing generation throughout the developing world. Washington and Moscow each recognized a need for diffusing their mutual tensions in the wake of the crisis, while their European and Asian counterparts generally developed a greater desire for an alternative to seemingly moribund Soviet and U.S. leadership.

## THE CRISIS

Cuba was the focus of the crisis, but the roots of this conflict lay in long-standing Soviet and U.S. antagonism and insecurities. The country had become a thorn in the side of U.S. leaders following Fidel Castro's seizure of power in 1959. Analysts in Washington debated Castro's faith in communism, but whatever his leanings, U.S. policy makers believed their reputation in Latin America could not tolerate a truly radical state only ninety miles from Florida. Castro's threats to nationalize foreign property on the island might seem a dangerous example to revolutionary groups throughout a region long considered a U.S. sphere of influence, they reasoned, while Cuba was simply too close for comfort for U.S. leaders ever vigilant against communist outposts. President Dwight D. Eisenhower endorsed Castro's overthrow as early as January 1960, a year before breaking diplomatic relations with his regime. By the time John F. Kennedy took office the following year vowing to "oppose aggression or subversion anywhere in the Americas," plans for a U.S.-supported invasion by Cuban exiles were already advanced, and the new president approved the operation with minimal oversight.

The failed Bay of Pigs invasion of April 1961 proved one of Kennedy's greatest fiascos. He publicly took full responsibility but swore thereafter to hold more tightly to the reins of power lest others drive his administration to ruin. He appointed his most trusted advisors, including his brother, Attorney General Robert F. Kennedy, to oversee Cuba policy, making Castro's removal one of his highest priorities. Cuba's affect on U.S. security and prestige, the president believed, threatened to tilt the Cold War's delicate balance in communism's favor.

Correctly believing that U.S. leaders sought his fall from power, Castro sought Moscow's protection, a move the Soviets embraced. Premier Nikita Khrushchev in particular sought greater parity in U.S.-Soviet relations by the early 1960s and believed Washington's greater nuclear strength, including its nuclear missiles stationed along the Soviet border in Turkey, ensured that the Americans held the better hand in any superpower clash. The two communist leaders therefore decided in May 1962, for reasons both believed were defensive, to deploy to Cuba some eighty nuclear missiles, with range enough to place virtually the entire continental United States—including the newly constructed American missile fields in the Dakotas—within Moscow's sights. "Installation of our missiles in Cuba would, I thought, restrain the United States from precipitous military action against Castro's government," Khrushchev later recounted, and "equalized what the West likes to call the 'balance of power'," (Khrushchev, pp. 493–494). Washington saw things differently. Soviet missiles in Cuba offered the Kremlin a true first-strike capability, including the ability to destroy Washington without warning while decimating America's missile deterrent as well. Surely the Kremlin would not risk this

dangerous move, Kennedy's intelligence team incorrectly determined a full five months *after* Khrushchev ordered the missile deployment. If Cuba should "become an offensive military base of significant capacity for the Soviet Union," Kennedy publicly warned, "then this country will do whatever must be done to protect its own security and that of its allies" (*Public Papers*, 1962, p. 674).

Kennedy was therefore infuriated to learn, on 16 October, that a U.S. spy plane had captured photos of Soviet missile-site construction in Cuba. His national security team hastily developed three options for removing the threat: invasion, negotiations, or blockade of the island. While his more hawkish advisors called for an immediate strike, on 22 October Kennedy announced a "quarantine" around Cuba. Soviet leaders vowed their ships would not respect the American blockade, and Khrushchev warned that Kennedy was pushing "mankind towards the abyss" (Hunt, p. 239). Soviet ships eventually halted just short of the quarantine line two days later, but as missile-site construction continued in Cuba, each side continued to prepare for war.

Cooler heads eventually prevailed. Public blustering continued, but private discussions—including secret meetings between Robert Kennedy and the Soviet ambassador, Anatoly Dobrynin—eventually developed a usable compromise. The Soviets would remove the missiles following a U.S. pledge not to invade Cuba, while Kennedy promised to remove his missiles from Turkey (after a politically prudent six-month interval). "I am not going to war over worthless missiles in Turkey," Kennedy privately explained (LaFeber, 1994, p. 601). By 28 October full-scale war had been averted, though revelations during the late 1990s demonstrated that nuclear war was in fact closer than ever realized. Unbeknownst to Washington, Soviet commanders in Cuba had full authorization to employ nuclear arms in defense against a U.S. invasion, and one can only imagine the consequences of U.S. landing forces in Cuba being met with nuclear fireballs. "Where would it have ended?" asked former Secretary of Defense Robert McNamara in 1992 upon learning of this near-catastrophe: "in utter disaster" (LaFeber, 1994, p. 601). Only Castro seemed displeased by the peaceful

The U.S. Navy destroyer *Vesole* sails alongside the Soviet freighter Polzunov as the U.S. crew inspects missiles being returned to the Soviet Union, November 1962. ©BETTMANN/CORBIS

conclusion of the crisis. Having been ready to sacrifice his country's existence for the sake of its independence, indeed having urged Khrushchev to strike the United States, Castro felt betrayed by what he termed the Kremlin's "surprising, sudden, and unconditional surrender" (Suri, p. 40). It would take several years and millions in aid before he would trust the Soviets again.

**THE AFTERMATH**

The ramifications of this near brush with disaster dramatically changed the course of the Cold War, and Europe's role in the conflict especially. Kennedy proved shaken by the nearness of the conflict and resolved thereafter to limit the risk of nuclear warfare. He authorized a direct "hot line" between the White House and the Kremlin so that leaders could communicate directly during any future crisis, and a U.S.-led ban on atmospheric nuclear tests

followed. In retrospect, a decreased U.S. emphasis on potential flash points of superpower conflict followed as well, replaced by low-scale responses to communist insurgencies throughout the formerly colonized world. In areas such as Southeast Asia and Central America, subsequent U.S. policy makers would put this "flexible response" strategy to the test without fear of a nuclear exchange.

Soviet leaders drew similar and different conclusions from the conflict, shaped by their perception that they had lost the confrontation because of the very disparity of power that the missile deployment in Cuba had been designed to eliminate in the first place. On the one hand, Khrushchev left the conflict as shaken as Kennedy. What was needed was a "relaxation of tension," he told his U.S. counterpart. Others within his government preached strength, however. "You Americans will never be able to do this to us again," one Soviet diplomat warned, and while U.S. leaders focused on countering communist insurgents throughout the developing world, Soviet policy makers thereafter focused primarily on narrowing the nuclear gap (Garthoff, pp. 133–134). By the mid-1970s neither side could be said to have had a real advantage in this arena, especially as each possessed the ability destroy the other (and the world) numerous times over. Khrushchev did not survive in power long enough to oversee this transformation, however, but was instead deposed in October 1964. "You insisted that we deploy our missiles on Cuba," one accuser charged, "and carried the world to the brink of nuclear war." Yet "not having any way out, we had to accept every demand and condition dictated by the U.S." (Fursenko and Naftali, p. 354). The great irony of Khrushchev's departure is that he ultimately left the Soviet Union with the very international stability, built on a foundation of nuclear parity, that he had long sought, though the burden of matching the wealthier Americans would eventually cripple the Soviet economy.

The Cuban Missile Crisis altered European and Asian diplomacy as well. Chinese leaders forged ahead with their own nascent nuclear program in its wake, determined never again to let Moscow take the lead in the East–West conflict. Relaxation of U.S.–Soviet tensions, illustrated by their mutual support for the Limited Test Ban Treaty, proved that both countries only sought "domination of the world by the two great despots," China's foreign minister charged, while Mao Zedong later vowed that Beijing's nuclear threat guaranteed that "the Chinese people will never accept the privileged position of one or two superpowers" (Suri, pp. 75–76).

France's Charles de Gaulle would not have put the idea any differently. The Cuban crisis reinforced his long-standing view that French power was needed as a counterweight to Soviet and U.S. balancing, and he was particularly incensed when Kennedy chose to only "inform" him of events during the crisis rather than "consult" (LaFeber, 1991, p. 228). He rejected the Limited Test Ban Treaty as a U.S.–Soviet ploy to limit France's "right to possess its own arms," and within a year he removed his military from full participation in the North Atlantic Treaty Organization (NATO)

and vetoed Britain's application for entry into the European Common Market. British membership would be as Washington's "Trojan Horse," he charged, and "the end would be a colossal Atlantic community dependent on America and directed by America" (LaFeber, 1991, pp. 228–229). Cuba proved to de Gaulle that an independently strong France was needed for a true balance of powers, even if limits on French international cooperation followed.

British leaders had already reached a similar conclusion on the need for an alternative to bipolarity and on the central importance of nuclear weapons to true great power status because, as Prime Minister Harold Macmillan quipped, "We must rely on the power of the nuclear deterrent, or we must throw up the sponge!" (Nunnerly, 1972, p. 117). Macmillan's government was particularly infuriated with Washington's public expectation of unwavering support during the Cuban crisis, but unlike de Gaulle, British analysts determined to work to reform superpower relations from within rather than to break outright with the Americans. This faith in the special relationship was put to the test in December 1962, when Washington threatened cancellation of its promised Skybolt missile. Britain's nuclear deterrent, its sole remaining claim to great power status, required this U.S. aid, and an irate Macmillan ultimately persuaded Kennedy to supply Polaris missiles in their place. The damage to their relationship of these twin blows, Cuba and Skybolt, was immense, leading British leaders too to fear Washington's rising hegemony. "The United States didn't want a partner," one British official exclaimed in frustration. "They wanted a satellite" (LaFeber, 1994, p. 603).

Not every state chose nuclear parity as the answer to the East–West divide. German leaders in particular, whose history made development of this fearful weapon simply impossible, feared in particular their geographic peril. Set between the warring superpowers, indeed divided by them, German leaders pushed hardest for détente following 1962, because as Chancellor Konrad Adenauer explained even before the Cuban stalemate, any future war in Europe "would be a nuclear war ... without any profit for the survivors" (Suri, p. 26). His was a common sentiment throughout the Continent, and with a wall bisecting the ancient capital of Berlin since 1961, German leaders led the charge following the Cuban Missile Crisis toward East–West reconciliation, even though it would take until the end of the decade for terms such as *détente* or *Ostpolitik* to enter the diplomatic lexicon. "There is no hope for us," West Berlin Mayor Willy Brandt concluded after the Cuban Missile Crisis, "if there is no change," and Germans on both sides of the Iron Curtain must "break through the frozen front between East and West" (Suri, p. 217).

Castro left the crisis the only real winner, while superpower bipolarity endured its death-blow. The tense October days allowed the Cuban leader to solidify his tenuous hold on power, and for the remaining decades of the Cold War he remained a favorite ally in Moscow and notorious in Washington. Neither Kennedy nor Khrushchev survived in power long after the affair, and their departure symbolized the way the Cuban Missile Crisis, in many ways the low point of the Cold War brought on by the logic of a world divided in two, revealed to observers throughout the world, and to Europeans especially, the need to find a third way.

*See also* **Arms Control; Cold War; Nuclear Weapons; Soviet Union.**

BIBLIOGRAPHY

*Primary Sources*

Chang, Laurence, and Peter Kornbluh, eds. *Cuban Missile Crisis, 1962: A National Security Archive Documents Reader.* Washington, D.C., 1997.

Kennedy, John F. *Public Papers of the Presidents: John F. Kennedy. 1961, 1962.* Washington, D.C., 1962, 1963.

Kennedy, Robert F. *Thirteen Days: A Memoir of the Cuban Missile Crisis.* New York, 1999.

Khrushchev, Nikita. *Khrushchev Remembers.* Translated and edited by Strobe Talbott. Boston, 1974.

May, Ernest, and Philip Zelikow, eds. *The Kennedy Tapes: Inside the White House during the Cuban Missile Crisis.* New York, 2002.

*Secondary Sources*

Beschloss, Michael. *The Crisis Years: Kennedy and Khrushchev, 1960–1963.* New York, 1991.

Fursenko, Aleksandr, and Timothy Naftali. *One Hell of a Gamble: Khrushchev, Castro, and Kennedy 1958–1964.* New York, 1997.

Garthoff, Raymond L. *Reflections on the Cuban Missile Crisis.* Washington, D.C, 1989.

George, Alice L. *Awaiting Armageddon: How Americans Faced the Cuban Missile Crisis.* Chapel Hill, N.C., 2003.

Hunt, Michael. *Crises in U.S. Foreign Policy.* New Haven, Conn., 1996.

LaFeber, Walter. *America, Russia, and the Cold War, 1945–1990.* New York, 1991.

——. *The American Age: United States Foreign Policy at Home and Abroad since 1750.* New York, 1994.

Nash, Philip. *The Other Missiles of October: Eisenhower, Kennedy, and the Jupiters, 1957–1963.* Chapel Hill, N.C., 1997.

Nunnerly, David. *President Kennedy and Britain.* New York, 1972.

Scott, L. V. *Macmillan, Kennedy, and the Cuban Missile Crisis.* London, 1999.

Suri, Jeremi. *Power and Protest: Global Revolution and the Rise of Détente.* Cambridge, Mass., 2003.

Taubman, William. *Khrushchev: The Man and His Era.* New York, 2003.

JEFFREY A. ENGEL

---

**CUBISM.** Cubism is neither a movement nor an identifiable group. It is an artistic tendency that appeared between 1907 and 1909, created by Pablo Picasso (1881–1973) and Georges Braque (1882–1963). The term comes from an article by the critic Louis Vauxcelles, published in the *Gil Blas* issue of 14 November 1908, about an art exposition at the Kahnweiller gallery that featured the Braque paintings that were refused by the Salon d'Automne. It became more than a simple term, as it started an aesthetic revolution that put into question the way we see and conceive of a painting.

Critics and historians agree on this point: the *Demoiselles d'Avignon* (1906–1907) was the first cubist painting. Picasso gave birth to a painting technique that changed the face of the twentieth century. In this painting, Picasso demonstrated common artistic concerns with Paul Cézanne (1839–1906), whose retrospective he was able to see in 1907 at the Salon d'Automne: he focused on a new way of depicting three-dimensional objects within the flat space of the canvas, without having to rely on light and shadow. Moreover, cubism was inspired by African and Iberian (particularly noticeable in the right-hand portion of the *Demoiselles d'Avignon*) arts, and by Cézanne's theory that

***Three Musicians.*** Painting by Pablo Picasso, 1921. Created after more than a decade of cubist experimentation, *Three Musicians* is considered among the most eloquent expressions of the style. DIGITAL IMAGE ©THE MUSEUM OF MODERN ART/LICENSED BY SCALA/ART RESOURCE, NY

advocated treating "nature in terms of spheres, cylinders, and cones." There were three distinct stages: precubism (1907–1909), analytical cubism (1909–1912), and synthetic cubism (1912–1925). These categories were established based on the evolution of the works of Braque, Juan Gris (pseudonym of Jose Victoriano Gonzalez, 1887–1927), and Picasso.

Braque's *Grand Nu* and the landscapes he painted at L'Estaque (*Le viaduc de L'Estaque,* 1908) also testify to this willingness to give solidity and density to shapes and motifs without the help of lighting effects. In 1908 Braque and Picasso changed the terms of depiction by reducing reality to fundamental shapes and volumes (such as in Braque's *Guitare et compotier,* 1909). These aesthetic experiments led them to analytical cubism, in which perspective is abandoned in favor of a multiplication of sight line angles in order to represent the multiple facets of an object. Picasso and Braque therefore achieved simultaneous views of an entire object through geometric forms (as in Picasso's *Portrait de D. H. Kahnweiler,* 1910, and Braque's *Nature morte au violon,* 1911). They took a decisive step in the history of representation by going beyond appearance to come up with a total vision and an art that deeply changed the face of iconography. Volumes, space, and colors find themselves balanced on a fine line between reality and abstraction.

Picasso and Braque also changed the way a painting is observed by simultaneously introducing letters or numbers (Picasso in *Ma jolie,* 1911–1912, and Braque in *Le Portugais,* 1911–1912) in trompe l'oeil while re-implementing reality in the canvas by using materials other than paint (paper reproducing wood, caning, pieces of newspaper, matchboxes). In 1910 Braque used nails. In 1912

Picasso produced the first cubist collage with *La Nature morte à la chaise cannée* while in the same year Braque was experimenting with the "glued paper" technique in his *Compotier et verre*.

Thus, the two painters created an ambiguity within the way a painting is read. This study of different planes was also noticeable in their use of oval-shaped canvases for their paintings, such as *La table et la pipe* by Braque (1912–1913). Their research abolished the idea of imitation of reality and made cubism a conceptual art form according to the formula invented by Guillaume Apollinaire (1880–1918). Picasso and Braque established a new relationship between reality and representation, between the essence and the concept.

Synthetic cubism was born out of the new relationship that Picasso and Braque had with the subjects of their paintings, in the sense that the object would be completely stripped of anything superfluous (Braque, *Clarinette* [1913] and *Violon* [also 1913]). The entire representation is no longer needed, the object is depicted by a fragment—that is, its essential characteristics. Thus, Picasso migrated toward the essence of the object in order to determine its defining characteristic. The depiction of a glass in a few essential strokes in *La bouteille de Marasquin* in 1914, remains an emblematic example because the object is no longer three-dimensional, but flat.

During the first years of cubism, Picasso and Braque did not show their work much, except at the Kahnweiler and Uhde galleries. However, other artists such as Gris, Albert L. Gleizes (1881–1953), and Jean Metzinger (1883–1956) developed a cubism style of their own. Gleizes and Metzinger wrote a book titled *Du cubisme* that was published in 1912. The painters (Louis Marcoussis, Andre Lhote, Henri Le Fauconnier, Férat) became members of the "Puteaux group" formed around the Duchamp brothers (Marcel Duchamp, Jacques Villon, and Raymond Duchamp-Villon), and participated in the Salon de la Section d'Or in 1912. Apollinaire invented the expression *orphic cubism* for Robert Delaunay's series *Les fenêtres*, in 1913. Fernand Léger and Francis Picabia would also contribute important innovations. There is also cubist sculpture, the first of which was by Picasso, and its influence was echoed in the installations of Alexander Archipenko, Duchamp-Villon, Henri Laurens, and Jacques Lipchitz.

*See also* **Modernism; Painting, Avant-Garde; Picasso, Pablo.**

BIBLIOGRAPHY

Antliff, Mark, and Patricia Leighten. *Cubism and Culture.* New York, 2001.

Apollinaire, Guillaume. *Cubist Painters: Aesthetic Meditations, 1913.* New York, 1944.

Barr, Alfred Hamilton, Jr. *Cubism and Abstract Art.* Cambridge, Mass., 1936, 1986.

Cooper, Douglas, and Gary Tinterow. *The Essential Cubism, 1907–1920: Braque, Picasso and Their Friends.* London, 1983.

Johnson, Robert Stanley. *Cubism and La Section d'Or: Reflections on the Development of the Cubist Epoch, 1907–1922.* Chicago, 1990.

Rosenblum, Robert. *Cubism and Twentieth-Century Art.* London, 1960.

CYRIL THOMAS

---

# CURIE, MARIE (1867–1934), Polish scientist.

Marie Skłodowska Curie was not only an internationally renowned physicist and chemist, she was also one of the first women to have held such an important place in the scientific community.

Marie Skłodowska was born into a cultured family in Warsaw during the Russian domination of Poland. Her father was a professor of physics and her mother was the director of a high school for girls. She was a brilliant student. However, the political persecution of her father and the illness and death of her mother interrupted her studies, obligating her to make a living as a tutor in the countryside and in Warsaw. The rest of her scientific education was self-taught, especially in the framework of the "Flying University," whose goal was, unbeknownst to the Russians, to help young Poles expand their culture. So the young woman became a member of a clandestine and anticlerical movement whose journal, *Pravda,* promoted the cult of science.

In October of 1891 she joined her sister, who had become a doctor in Paris, and enrolled at the Sorbonne to pursue scientific studies—which, at the time, was not commonplace for a woman. She took first place in the bachelor's degree of science in 1893, with a major in physics, and second place in the bachelor's degree of mathematics in 1894. It was then that she met the young scientist Pierre Curie (1859–1906), a teacher's assistant and then a professor at the School of Industrial Physics and Chemistry. She married him in 1895. The following year, she received first place in the physics and chemistry *agrégation* exams, which enabled her to teach in secondary education. In 1897 her daughter Irène was born, and Marie began her thesis on X rays, recently discovered by Wilhelm Conrad Roentgen (1845–1923). She defended "Research on Radioactive Substances" in 1903 and worked on electricity and magnetism with her husband.

Following discovery of the properties of uranium salts by Antoine Henri Becquerel (1852–1908), Marie and Pierre attempted to measure the ionization power of the radiation emitted by these salts with the help of the electrometer invented by Pierre. During the experiments of 1898, Marie noticed that the thorium composites held the same properties and that two uranium minerals (pitchblende and chalcolite) are radioactively stronger than the uranium metal. The Curies broke down the pitchblende into two elements called polonium (July 1898) and radium (November 1898) and worked to discover their properties. They obtained a small quantity of radium chloride from uranium residue in 1902 and determined the atomic weight of radium. This earned them the Berthelot medal from the Academy of Sciences and the Gegner Prize, followed by other international awards.

In 1903 the Curies and Becquerel received the Nobel Prize for their discovery of radioactivity and came out of anonymity to become not only famous but also respected members of the scientific community. Marie was then appointed to teach a class at the College of Science, where she was able to develop the theories that would make up her *Traité de radioactivité* (Treatise on radioactivity), which establishes the link between matter and electricity. In 1904 their second daughter, Eve, was born. That same year, the French industrialist Armet de

**Marie Curie in her laboratory, c. 1920.** ©Hulton-Deutsch Collection/Corbis

Lisle founded a factory and offered a laboratory to the Curies, which considerably improved their research conditions.

After the accidental death of her husband in 1906, Marie Curie, who had resumed teaching, continued working in the same environment, and then at the Radium Institute, created in 1910 through an agreement between the Academy of Sciences and the Pasteur Institute. Her affair with the physicist Paul Langevin (1872–1946) caused a scandal in 1911; she received the Nobel Prize for Chemistry, but failed to be elected to the Academy of Sciences by one vote. The radioactivity pavilion was inaugurated in Warsaw two years later. During World War I, Marie Curie participated in the creation of radiological units and in the training of nurses in charge of applying radiological techniques. After the war, she was able to continue her research thanks to American donations, particularly at the Radium Institute, and after 1920, with help from her daughter Irène. In 1922 Marie became a member of the International Commission on Intellectual Cooperation of the League of Nations. She was received at the

Academy of Medicine in the same year. Two years later, she published *L'isotopie et les éléments isotopes* (Isotopy and isotopic elements), a biography of Pierre Curie, and a new treatise on radioactivity. Irène Curie and her husband, Frédéric Joliot, discovered artificial radioactivity in 1933. Marie Curie died in 1934.

*See also* **Nobel Prize; Poland; Science.**

BIBLIOGRAPHY

*Primary Sources*

Curie, Marie. *Radioactivité.* 2 vols. Paris, 1935. Published posthumously.

———. *Oeuvres de Marie Curie.* Warsaw, 1954. Curie's original works, published by her daughter Irène.

*Secondary Sources*

Bensaude-Vincent, Bernadette, and Isabelle Stengers. *Histoire de la chimie.* Paris, 1993.

Boudia, Soraja. *Marie Curie et son laboratoire-sciences et industrie de la radioactivité en France.* Paris, 2001.

Dussart, Remi. *Marie Curie.* Paris, 2001.

Pflaum, Rosalynd. *Grand Obsession: Madame Curie and Her World.* New York, 1989.

Quinn, Susan. *Marie Curie: A Life.* New York, 1995.

Reid, Robert. *Marie Curie, derrière la legende.* Paris, 1979.

SOPHIE LETERRIER

---

**CYCLING.** From the time of the invention of the first pedal-driven cycle in 1839 to the present day cycling has functioned across Europe as an important form of transport, a leisure pursuit, and a competitive sport.

The first major cycling boom took place in the 1890s and was enabled, as all subsequent developments in cycling have been, by technological advances. While the bicycle, in various forms, had been a common sight, it was the invention of the chain drive in 1874 and the pneumatic tire in 1888 that made cycling safe, relatively comfortable, and efficient. By the time of World War I, bicycles were being mass-produced in Britain, France, and Italy and were a common form of transport for urban and rural dwellers. In the pre-1914 period cycling

had also moved into the sporting arena. The first track-racing world championships had been started in 1895, and a year later cycling was included in the list of events for the inaugural Olympic Games in Athens. The most famous race in cycling, the Tour de France, began in 1903. Originating as a means to promote the sporting newspaper *L'Auto,* the Tour grew so that it was symbolic of the French nation as opposed to a mere cycle race. The model of a major national or regional race gave rise to similar events elsewhere in Europe. The Tour, the Giro d'Italia (1909), and the Vuelta a España (1935) are now considered the Three Grand Tours in cycle racing. To date, only four cyclists (two French, a Belgian, and an Italian) have ever won all the three Grand Tours across the duration of their career, and no cyclist has ever managed to win all three in a single calendar year. In addition to the national tours, a series of one-day races also began in the decades leading to World War I: The Paris–Roubaix (1896), the Tour of Flanders (1913), and the Liège–Bastogne–Liège (1892).

European cyclists have, until recent years, dominated the major cycling-tour events. In one-day events such as the Tour of Flanders, the winners' roll contains only European nationals, and even the Tour de France, a far more globally recognized sporting event, did not feature a non-European winner until 1989 (the American Greg Le Monde). American Lance Armstrong has dominated the race like no one else in history, and in 2005 won the Tour for a record-breaking seventh time.

The Tour de France lies at the heart of European cycling. The race around France, as conceived by the editor of *L'Auto,* Henri Desgrange (1865–1940), meant that the Tour, from its first running in 1903, captivated the public attention. Symbolically the Tour covers the various regions and landscapes of France and coincides with the start of the school holidays and the celebration of Bastille Day on 14 July. It is a race that manages to combine a national psyche with a sporting event. It has worked, especially in the era of television coverage, as a showcase for the French countryside and its tourist opportunities. Originally the Tour was based around teams that were sponsored by bicycle manufacturers, and the event helped sell the bicycle to an ever-wider audience. Food and drink

**Participants in the Tour de France pass the fourteenth-century papal palace in Avignon, France, during the 1951 tour.** ©Bettmann/Corbis

manufacturers slowly replaced these sponsors, and in 1930 the decision was made to organize national teams. This experiment changed the nature of the Tour, and was abandoned temporarily due to the outbreak of hostilities in 1939. After the war the teams were once more organized around national identity, but these gave way to commercial concerns from the late 1950s.

The Tour has always been a legendary event and is globally known. It is now covered across the globe, and since the 1960s and the advent of television coverage its stars have become heroes beyond the confines of France. It was commonly argued in the 1990s that the Tour was third, as a mass sporting spectacle, behind only the Olympics

and the football (soccer) World Cup, in terms of spectator numbers, global media reach, and sponsorship income. In 1998 this image was badly dented when a series of drug scandals dogged the Tour and leading riders and teams came under scrutiny. Many individual riders were banned and teams fined. It was presumed that the Tour would enter a crisis because of the drug issue, and that major sponsors and media outlets would desert the race. In many ways the opposite has proved to be true. While it is clear that the Tour has been badly tainted because of its links with various forms of doping, many supporters and commentators have accepted that the sheer physical efforts required to cycle around France and through two mountain ranges require superhuman, even unnatural, efforts. As a result the Tour remains the preeminent and most identifiable cycle race in the world.

At the organizational level, in the same manner as the origins of the main riders, cycling has also been dominated by Europeans. The strength of the European nations was evident as early as 1900 when the International Cycling Union (UCI) was founded in Paris. The founder members were Belgium, France, Italy, Switzerland, and the United States. Under the auspices of the UCI, the first Road World Championships were staged in 1927, Cyclo-Cross World Championships in 1950, and the inaugural Indoor Cycling World Championships in 1956. The growing commercial opportunities afforded to elite cyclists became evident in 1965, when the UCI reorganized so that it became the umbrella organization for the International Amateur Cycling Federation (FIAC: headquarters in Rome) and the International Professional Cycling Federation (FICP: headquarters in Luxembourg). In 1992 the FIAC/FICP distinction was removed, and the UCI as a single body moved its headquarters to Lausanne. All the eight presidents of the UCI since 1900 have been drawn from the cycling strongholds of Belgium, France, Italy, the Netherlands, Spain, and Switzerland. Despite the traditionally European focus of the UCI, it has embraced change in the world of cycling and has promoted a series of new initiatives, including, in 1993, the first BMX World Championships, and successfully lobbied for the inclusion of mountain biking (1996) and BMX racing (2008) in the Summer Olympic Games.

Bicycles have not only been used in a sporting setting. Since World War I they have been one of the most important and affordable means of transport. Under the advent of mass car ownership, which was dependent on the relative levels of industrialization, modernization, and wealth, the bicycle dominated until the time of World War II. Until that period, European companies including Phillips in Germany, Raleigh in Britain, and Bianchi in Italy dominated cycle manufacture. After 1945 the main focus for bicycle production shifted to the Far East, and countries such as China now dominate the market in total numbers of bicycles built. In the late 1990s, for example, China alone produced 30 million bicycles, compared to the European Union's total of 11.3 million. Within the European Union there is, however, only a limited appetite for imported bicycles from outside Europe. In 1998 Germany was the biggest recorded European manufacturer, producing 5.3 million bicycles, followed by British, French, and Italian companies. In the same year the whole European Union imported 4.4 million bicycles. Bicycle ownership in Europe remains highest in Italy, Germany, and the Netherlands with 26.5, 63, and 16.5 million bicycles in circulation.

*See also* **Leisure; Tourism.**

BIBLIOGRAPHY

Alderson, Frederick. *Bicycling: A History.* Newton Abbot, U.K., 1972.

Dauncey, Hugh, and Geoff Hare, eds. *The Tour De France, 1903–2003: A Century of Sporting Structures, Meanings, and Values.* London and Portland, Ore., 2003.

Henderson, Noel. *European Cycling: The 20 Classic Races.* Brattleboro, Vt., 1989.

Holt, Richard. *Sport and Society in Modern France.* London and Oxford, U.K., 1981.

MIKE CRONIN

---

# CYPRUS.

In the history of Cyprus the period 1914 to 2004 is marked by two distinct but interrelated eras: from 1914 to the independence of the island from British rule in 1960 and the postcolonial period from 1960 onward. Both periods share a common characteristic, war and its related traumas. Among other similarities, this is the one that binds and at the same time segregates the island's Greek- and Turkish-speaking communities. It is by understanding this trauma that the sociocultural history of the island can be understood.

## THE EARLY YEARS OF BRITISH COLONIAL RULE

The annexation of Cyprus to Britain took place in November 1914, a few months after World War I broke out and following a period of occupation by Britain from 1878, the year that saw Cyprus change rulers after three hundred years of Ottoman rule (1571–1878). The transition was under a special agreement with the Ottoman Government following its defeat by Russia. The English politician Benjamin Disraeli (1804–1881), who was instrumental in the British takeover of Cyprus from the Ottoman Empire, explained the move as paramount because Cyprus was seen as the key to Western Asia. The strategic positioning of the island would prove significant in its later history.

World War I saw a considerable number of Cypriots taking part in the war effort as auxiliaries for the British army. It was during the period of the war and during the 1920s and 1930s that various efforts for unification with Greece, *enosis,* became a more prominent figure of the sociopolitical landscape. At the same time the Turkish-speaking minority (other minorities that constitute the population of Cyprus are the Maronite, Armenian, and Latin communities) demanded unification with Turkey. The British government twice (in 1912 and 1915) offered Cyprus to Greece in exchange for Greece allowing military bases on its mainland and joining the Allied forces. The Greek government rejected both offers because they were seen as sacrificing Greece's neutrality. It is important to note that the British offers were part of the political situation in the area at a time when the war effort in the Balkans was not progressing in favor of the Allies. World War I was to change the previous political alliances in the region and British support for Turkey.

However, with the emergence of Germany militarism during the period before World War I, Britain's ties with Russia strengthened, resulting in Turkey seeking an alliance with Germany and hence, the offer of Cyprus to Greece during the period of the war. Because of the possibility of unification with Greece, Greek Cypriots' volunteering for the war effort took an added meaning in terms of their contribution being recognized as a step toward unification. These expectations were squashed with the outcome of the war in favor of the Allied forces. Once more the ever-changing political situation in the region would prescribe the future of Cyprus. The Communist revolution in Russia created new strategic considerations and the important positioning of Cyprus would hinder the dream of enosis.

It was during this period—the inter-war years—that the British saw an opportunity within the Turkish-speaking population of Cyprus to apply their colonial divide-and-rule policy. The colonial government employed increasing numbers of Turkish Cypriots for the day-to-day administration of Cyprus and in order to oppose the increasing demands of Greek Cypriots for enosis. During the 1920s the economic situation in Cyprus worsened and, together with the tense situation in the area because of the Greek war effort in Turkey, the proclamation of Cyprus as Crown Colony in 1925, and the celebrations of fifty years of British rule on the island in 1928, the demands for enosis strengthened. However, it is the establishment of communism in the 1920s and its international influence that is also paramount for the cultural history of the island at the time. The mid-1920s saw the establishment of the first trade unions and the first Communist Party in Cyprus. These provided a challenge to the dominance of the church and the moneyed right-wing party. Most important, despite the many efforts of the British colonial administration to keep the two communities apart, the trade unions and the Communist Party brought them together, fighting their unfair economic treatment in the hands of the British administration, by joining together in demonstrations and strikes in an attempt to gain better working conditions and higher wages.

**DISCONTENT AND UPRISING**

The worsening economic conditions of the early 1930s in Cyprus, due to a great extent to the worldwide depression, together with the imposition of a new tax bill on the island and the rejection by the British government of constitutional changes, led to the first major uprising in October 1931. Demonstrations led to riots and attacks on official buildings, culminating in the burning of the Colonial Government House in Nicosia. The British army suppressed the uprising, a number of people were imprisoned or exiled, and new laws were introduced that curbed any demonstrations of Greekness. Also banned were the trade unions and various publications that were seen as inciting nationalistic ideas. What such actions failed to address were the economic circumstances that contributed to the uprising. An important outcome of the events was the new attitude of the colonial government toward the two communities. From this point onward they were referred to as Orthodox and Muslim. Such division would have detrimental effects for bi-

**Turkish soldiers parachute into Cyprus on the first day of the invasion, 22 July 1974.** ©BETTMANN/CORBIS

women donated their wedding rings and other jewelry for a special collection fund.

A visit to the island by the British Prime Minister Winston Churchill (1874–1965) in 1943, echoing a similar visit in 1907, brought renewed hopes that Britain would acknowledge the contribution of the island to the war effort and provide some concessions. New economic-relief measures were introduced that brought economic prosperity in the 1950s as well as relaxation of the laws imposed in the 1930s. Attempts to reintroduce the legislative assembly and some form of self-government failed and was followed by demonstrations and strikes by the trade unions. Once again external events were to influence the destiny of the island. The Cold War and the events in Palestine were to increase even more the strategic importance of the island. For the British military establishment any discussion of withdrawal from Cyprus was unimaginable because of the volatile situation in the Middle East and the Suez Canal in particular.

Instead the divide-and-rule policy was further enforced within the two communities. The Turkish community started demanding the return of Cyprus to Turkey. In 1950 the Greek Cypriot community staged a referendum and later took the case of Cyprus to the newly formed United Nations. At the same time Archbishop Makarios III (1913–1977) emerged on the political and religious scene of the island. In collaboration with the extreme right-wing general Georgios Grivas (1898–1974), the EOKA (Greek Initials for National Organization of Cypriot Fighters) underground organization started the independence struggle in April 1955, which also aimed at unification of the island with Greece. The EOKA struggle was very much modeled on European resistance movements against the Nazi occupation. The measures adopted by the colonial administration against EOKA, which was branded as a terrorist group, were concentration camps and detention without trial, use of torture, curfews, and executions. The struggle provided the Greek-speaking community for the first time with its own heroes. Their commemoration provided the first large-scale erection of memorials on the island and their memory provided the foundations for the building of postcolonial national identity.

communal relations because the division was from now on based on religious affiliations. By doing so the colonial government tried to intervene in the strong bi-communal relationship that was building up during this period through the trade-union movement.

The outbreak of World War II saw a relaxation in the draconian measures imposed during the 1930s. The war also brought renewed aspirations for the Greek-speaking community. Initial victories of the Greek army over Mussolini's advancing army at the Albanian border sparkled the renewal of Greekness within the Greek-speaking community, which, in this instance, was not suppressed by the colonial administration. On the contrary, it was used in the recruitment campaign for the Cyprus Regiment. Large numbers of men volunteered and

The British government, relying on the inter-communal crisis brought about by the EOKA uprising, increased pressure for the acceptance of a settlement in Cyprus that offered limited self-government with the involvement of Greece and Turkey in the local affairs of the island. The plan was rejected in favor of a second plan proposed by Greece and Turkey during a six-day conference in Zurich in February 1959. The agreement excluded the union of Cyprus with any other country or its partition and, most alarmingly, provided for the permanent presence on the island of Greek and Turkish troops. Britain also retained two sovereign areas of the island for military use.

**INDEPENDENCE AND ETHNIC CONFLICT**

The struggle also codified the bi-communal conflict that was supported by the constitution agreed upon by Britain, Greece, and Turkey, all of which became guarantors for the independence of the island. Makarios, who during the EOKA struggle was exiled by the British administration in 1959, became the first president of the republic. Soon after independence the bi-communal conflict resurfaced starting in 1963 and culminating with the division of the island in 1974 following a military coup on the island, supported by the Greek military government, to overthrow Makarios. The coup provided the opportunity for Turkey to claim its guarantor powers under the 1960 constitution in order to protect the Turkish minority on the island. The Turkish military advancement established the Turkish Republic of North Cyprus, thus dividing the island into two: The Greek-speaking south and the Turkish-speaking north with enforced movements of population within the two communities. These events were once again related to the strategic positioning of Cyprus, especially the U.S. fear that Cyprus would fall into Communist hands and the consequences of this for the oil crisis in the Middle East. The Turkish republic failed to be recognized by the international community.

The two communities remained completely separated until the opening of the border in April 2003, a year before Cyprus joined the European Union. A United Nations–led settlement of the problem was turned down at a referendum by the Greek community. As a result, only the south part of the island joined the European Union. Bi-communal rapprochement initiatives that started in the 1990s are still continuing and have had a considerable impact on bi-communal relations. It is, however, in the understanding, acceptance, and incorporation of the traumatic past of the two communities that hopes for reconciliation can be found.

*See also* **Balkans; Greece; Labor Movements; Turkey; World War I; World War II.**

BIBLIOGRAPHY

Efthyvoulou, Alex, and Marina Vryonidou-Yiangou. *Cyprus 100 Years.* Nicosia, Cyprus, 2000.

Georghallides, George Stavros. *Cyprus and the Governorship of Sir Roland Storrs: The Causes of the 1931 Crisis.* Nicosia, Cyprus, 1985.

Holland, Robert. *Britain and the Revolt in Cyprus, 1954–1959.* Oxford, U.K., 1998.

Panteli, Stavros. *A History of Cyprus: From Foreign Domination to Troubled Independence.* 2nd ed. London, 2000.

Purcell, Hugh Dominic. *Cyprus.* New York, 1969.

Volkan, Vamik D. *Cyprus: War and Adaptation. A Psychoanalytic History of Two Ethnic Groups in Conflict.* Charlottesville, Va., 1988.

GABRIEL KOUREAS

**CZECHOSLOVAKIA.** Czechoslovakia was a small country in central Europe that declared its independence on 28 October 1918 and dissolved into the Czech Republic and Slovakia on 1 January 1993. Czechoslovakia was formally created at the Paris Peace Conference of 1919 through the joining of the Lands of the Bohemian Crown (Bohemia, Moravia, and Silesia), several counties of Upper Hungary inhabited largely by Slovak speakers, and Sub-Carpathian Ruthenia. All these territories had belonged to the Habsburg Empire, with the Bohemian Crownlands having been part of the post-1867 Austrian half of the empire, and the others having been part of the Hungarian half. Partly as a result of these territorial origins, partly for historical reasons stretching back into the medieval period, and partly because of the Czechoslovak leadership's successful lobbying at the Peace Conference, the state emerged with substantial German and Hungarian minorities, which represented 22 and 5 percent of the state's population in 1930, respectively.

## THE INTERWAR PERIOD

Despite the potential for ethnic conflict, the interwar Czechoslovak Republic was, by all accounts, a successful state. Initial secessionist urges among ethnic Germans living in the border regions waned when Czechoslovakia's economic success and political stability encouraged them to adopt a more positive attitude toward the republic. During the interwar period Czechoslovakia maintained a more steadfast commitment to democracy than any of its neighbors or any of the states of eastern Europe. Under the guidance of its most visible personage, Tomáš Garrigue Masaryk (president from 1918 to 1935), Czechoslovakia enacted several pieces of progressive legislation, including social and unemployment insurance schemes, institution of the eight-hour workday, and housing and agrarian reform. Legislation was shepherded through the parliament by an institution known as the *pětka*, composed of members of the leaderships of the major political parties, and, if they reached an impasse, by caretaker governments. After initial deflationary hardships, the economy embarked on almost a decade of strong growth, bringing a generalized prosperity, although there were significant regional differences in the standard of living, with western regions faring better than those to the east. Internationally, Czechoslovakia was a supporter of the Versailles system, having alliance treaties with France, the Soviet Union, and Romania and Yugoslavia (in the Little Entente), and was a pillar of support for the League of Nations.

The years of economic growth and political calm came to an end with the onset of the Great Depression in Europe in 1931 and the rise of Nazi Germany. Czechoslovakia's German population increasingly came to support Konrad Henlein's (1898–1945) Sudeten German Party, which received financial and other support from the Nazi regime and won almost two-thirds of the German vote in the local elections of 1935. Similarly, tensions rose among the state's Hungarian population. These led to a series of international discussions aimed at resolving the Czech-German conflict that culminated in the Munich Accords, signed by the leaders of Nazi Germany, Italy, Great Britain, and France on 30 September 1938. Its terms forced Masaryk's successor, Edvard Beneš (president from 1935 to 1948) to cede eleven thousand square miles of Czechoslovak territory inhabited largely by ethnic Germans to the Nazi state. Similarly, the first Vienna Award (2 November 1938) gave some four thousand six hundred square miles in Slovakia and Sub-Carpathian Ruthenia to Germany's ally, Hungary.

## WORLD WAR II

The "Munich betrayal," as Czechs still see it, by the western powers, effectively meant the end of the democratic interwar Czechoslovak state. A nominally independent Slovak state under Nazi tutelage came into existence on 14 March 1939 and the following day, as German troops entered that territory, the remaining Czech lands became the Protectorate of Bohemia and Moravia. President Beneš, who had fled to London, successfully organized a government-in-exile, gaining recognition from the Allies during the course of 1941 and 1942. Although the war years were not as difficult for inhabitants of the Protectorate or Slovakia as for those other areas of eastern Europe, the hardships eventually provoked domestic resistance movements. In the Protectorate, Czechoslovak parachutists assassinated Reichsprotektor Reinhard Heydrich (1904–1942) in 1942, while in Slovakia a large-scale uprising began on 29 August 1944, mobilizing sixty thousand troops and lasting two months. Finally, the citizens of Prague rose up on 5 May 1945, as Soviet and, in southwestern Bohemia, American troops were completing the liberation of the country.

## THE RISE OF COMMUNISM

The immediate postwar years were filled with political, social, and economic turmoil as the state sought to reintegrate its Czech and Slovak halves and to reestablish itself. Following approval by the Allies at the Potsdam Conference (17 July–2 August 1945), President Beneš issued a decree revoking the citizenship of close to three million ethnic German citizens of prewar Czechoslovakia, resulting in their sometimes-violent expulsion. This decree also affected ethnic Hungarian citizens, whose expulsion was halted by the Communist

A Czech woman in the Sudetenland weeps while giving a Nazi salute at the arrival of German troops, 1938. ©CORBIS

Party's assumption of power. The expulsions were the source of continuing tension between Czechoslovakia (and, later, the Czech Republic and Slovakia) and their neighbors. The property of the expelled populations became the basis for a wide-ranging land reform. Czechoslovakia also experienced a reorientation in foreign policy after Beneš signed a twenty-year alliance treaty with the Soviet Union in December 1943. The ceding of Sub-Carpathian Ruthenia to the Soviet Union followed in June 1945.

Domestically, a leftward political shift was evident in a number of measures, including the nationalization of key sectors of the economy and larger individual enterprises, resulting in 62 percent of the workforce being employed in the public sector. It was also evident in the political makeup of the National Front government, in which the right wing, whose parties had been banned, was absent. In this constellation, the Communist Party was by far the dominant force, winning 38 percent of the vote in the elections of May 1946 and installing its chairman, Klement Gottwald (1896–1953), as prime minister. Tensions between the Communists and their opponents worsened markedly in late 1947 and a political crisis erupted in February 1948 when several noncommunist ministers resigned. The crisis was resolved when Beneš approved Gottwald's government reorganization plan on 25 February 1948, a plan that included only Communist ministers and fellow travelers from the other parties, effectively making Czechoslovakia a communist state. Following the highly suspicious suicide of the noncommunist foreign minister, Jan Masaryk (son of the former president), on 10 March 1948, an ill President Beneš refused to sign the new Communist constitution and abdicated on 7 June 1948. He died on 3 September of that year, leaving the presidency to Gottwald.

### 1948–1960

The first years of Communist rule brought enormous change and considerable suffering. Beginning in 1948 the Communists deepened the nationalization program and embarked on the collectivization of agriculture, while internationally the state was a founding member of the Council for Mutual Economic Assistance and the Warsaw Treaty Organization. The regime also quickly began a purge of (often only suspected) political enemies in the state apparatus, the military, and leading roles in the economy. These purges were followed by the trials, imprisonments, and occasionally executions of those deemed opposed to the new regime. The victims included many religious leaders, members of noncommunist political parties, Slovak nationalists, and army personnel who had served in the west during World War II. Finally, these pseudo-judicial proceedings came to be directed against party members themselves, culminating in a show trial with strong anti-Semitic overtones involving the General Secretary of the CPCz, Rudolf Slánský (1901–1952), and thirteen other important communists in November of 1952, in which Slánský and ten of his codefendants were executed. President Gottwald died on 14 March 1953 and was succeeded by Antonín Zápotocký (president from 1953 to 1957), who was succeeded in turn by Antonín Novotný (president from 1957 to 1968).

Czechoslovak premier Klement Gottwald at a meeting of the Trade Union Council in Prague, February 1948, on the eve of his successful coup. ©BETTMANN/CORBIS

Developments in the Czechoslovak economy also had political consequences. Growth was impressive in the 1950s, although the economy was increasingly centralized and growth was concentrated in heavy industry. A currency reform was carried out in 1953, despite the fact that it triggered protests across the country, most notably in the industrial city of Plzeň (Pilsen). The reform, coupled with Gottwald's death before the onset of Soviet leader Nikita Khrushchev's initial destalinization push, allowed the regime to weather 1956. By improving the standard of living Czechoslovakia avoided the political turmoil experienced in neighboring Poland and Hungary. It was against this backdrop of general quiescence and the absence of destalinization that President Novotný promulgated a new constitution in 1960. It further centralized decision-making and declared that socialism had been achieved, formally changing the state's name to the Czechoslovak Socialist Republic to reflect this.

## THE PRAGUE SPRING

Shortly after the introduction of the 1960 constitution Prague's Stalinist leaders encountered difficulties. Initially, these were economic, with growth slowing in the early 1960s and actually declining in 1963. Here, in the wake of Khrushchev's intensification of the destalinization campaign in 1961, the regime began to encourage limited reforms. Dissatisfactions spread, however, in the mid-1960s, as ferment began among intellectuals, students, and the released victims of the show trials of the 1950s. During the course of the decade, Novotný, who occupied both the presidency and the Communist Party chairmanship, managed to alienate most of the important constituencies in the polity and was forced to relinquish his party position on 5 January 1968.

His replacement as party secretary, Alexander Dubček, was a Slovak who actively encouraged reform in the early months of 1968, producing the flowering known as the "Prague Spring."

Czechoslovak society became involved in wide-ranging discussions about democratization, federalization, and economic reform and formed new civic associations to support what became called "socialism with a human face." Censorship began to break down, and the public began to express reformist opinions that went far beyond those the regime was willing to consider, given that the leadership was split among reformers, centrists, and conservatives who had been weakened by the replacement of Novotný as president by Ludvík Svoboda (president from 1968 to 1975) in late March. Further, over the course of the months leading into the summer, Czechoslovakia's communist allies expressed increasing concern over developments in the state, fearing that the reform process had escaped the party's control and demanding the reinstitution of censorship and other changes designed to stifle reform. Tensions began to peak in late July when Leonid Brezhnev and much of the Soviet leadership met personally with Dubček and the Czechoslovak leadership and demanded a set of changes. When these changes were not enacted to the Soviet leadership's satisfaction, and a looming party congress was expected to result in the sweeping victory of reformers, Czechoslovakia was invaded by troops from the USSR, East Germany, Poland, Hungary, and Bulgaria on the night of 20–21 August 1968. The invasion was the source of the Brezhnev Doctrine, which, although never explicitly acknowledged as such, required socialist states to militarily intervene in any state where socialism was perceived as under threat.

Although the invasion was a success militarily, it failed politically, as conservative forces had not prepared the way for the replacement of the reformers, the feared party congress met in secret and condemned the invasion, and the public rallied in support of the leadership. In such conditions, the Soviet leadership was forced to negotiate with its Czechoslovak counterpart. Dubček and his associates, who had been taken to Moscow, were forced to sign the Moscow Protocol, which bound them to carry out a list of demands. Only when these steps were taken would the Soviet Union consider the situation in Czechoslovakia "normalized" and begin withdrawing its troops. Over the course of the months after the invasion Dubček sacrificed virtually all of the reforms he had championed. By the time of his resignation as Communist Party of Czechoslovakia (CPCz) head, on 17 April 1969, the only major reform that remained standing was the federalization of the state into Czech and Slovak halves, adopted by the parliament on 28 October 1968.

## NORMALIZATION

Dubček's successor as CPCz leader was another Slovak, Gustáv Husák (1913–1991), who also succeeded Svoboda as president, ruling from 1975 until 1989. The final two decades of Communist rule, known as the period of "normalization," after the term from the Moscow Protocol, are closely associated with his name. The period is notable for five features. First, the regime undertook a wide-ranging purge of the party and institutions of economic and public life. Second, the era was exemplified by political changelessness and a general sense of dreariness. Third, the regime's strategy for gaining the acquiescence of an initially hostile citizenry was to encourage consumerism and a withdrawal into private life. This proved quite successful while the economy grew through the mid-1970s, but by 1977 the economy began a slide into the stagnation that characterized the 1980s, sapping the approach's viability, although living standards remained higher than almost anywhere else in the Eastern bloc. Fourth, a large and active secret police force and networks of informers made Czechoslovakia one of the most restrictive societies in Eastern Europe. Finally, the strictness of the regime inhibited the founding and growth of dissident movements. The most important of these was Charter 77, whose most notable figure was the playwright Václav Havel (b. 1936). It was founded in 1977 and had more than one thousand two hundred signatories by the mid-1980s.

## THE VELVET REVOLUTION AND THE VELVET DIVORCE

On 17 November 1989, after many Czechs and Slovaks had become aware of the changes taking place elsewhere and other organizations had begun to spring up alongside Charter 77, a government-sponsored student parade turned into a demonstration calling for freedom and democracy. The movement rapidly gained support and, after days of massive demonstrations across the country and a highly successful nationwide general strike on 27 November, the CPCz entered into negotiations with opposition leaders. These culminated on 10 December, when Husák announced the formation of a largely noncommunist government and resigned his post. Havel succeeded him as president, while Dubček returned to serve as speaker of the parliament. That this took place without violence has led to it being called the "Velvet Revolution."

After elections in June 1990 the country began the difficult process of postcommunist transition. In addition to the difficulties of reforming all spheres of public and economic life, the nature of the relationship between the two republics needed to be addressed. With an eye to this, the state changed its official name to "The Czech and Slovak Federative Republic." More importantly, however, differences between the two republics in approaches toward fiscal and privatization issues, among others, and the desire for more autonomy or even independence among many Slovaks caused political tensions. These peaked after the June 1992 elections, which brought a party advocating closer relations between the republics to power in the Czech lands, whereas in Slovakia the victorious party favored a much looser, essentially confederal, arrangement. These two parties began meeting shortly after the elections and, after much intense negotiation, the decision was reached to divide the country. Despite the fact that a majority of Czechs and Slovaks opposed the end of Czechoslovakia, the Czech Republic and Slovakia came into existence on 1 January 1993, with this "Velvet Divorce" mirroring the "Velvet Revolution" in its lack of violence.

*See also* **Beneš, Eduard; Charter 77; Czech Republic; Dubček, Alexander; Eastern Bloc; Gottwald, Klement; Havel, Václav; Hungary; Masaryk, Tomáš Garrigue; Prague; Prague Spring; Slánský Trial; Slovakia; Sudetenland; Velvet Revolution; Warsaw Pact.**

BIBLIOGRAPHY

Abrams, Bradley F. *The Struggle for the Soul of the Nation: Czech Culture and the Rise of Communism.* Lanham, Md., 2004.

Leff, Carol Skalnik. *National Conflict in Czechoslovakia: The Making and Remaking of a State, 1918–1987.* Princeton, N.J., 1988.

Lukes, Igor. *Czechoslovakia between Stalin and Hitler: The Diplomacy of Edvard Beneš in the 1930s.* New York, 1996.

Mamatey, Victor S., and Radomír Luža, eds. *A History of the Czechoslovak Republic, 1918–1948.* Princeton, N.J., 1973.

Musil, Jiří, ed. *The End of Czechoslovakia.* Budapest and New York, 1995.

Renner, Hans. *A History of Czechoslovakia since 1945.* London and New York, 1989.

Skilling, H. Gordon. *Charter 77 and Human Rights in Czechoslovakia.* London and Boston, 1981.

Suda, Zdeněk. *Zealots and Rebels: A History of the Ruling Communist Party of Czechoslovakia.* Stanford, Calif., 1980.

Williams, Kieran. *The Prague Spring and Its Aftermath: Czechoslovak Politics 1968–1970.* Cambridge, U.K., and New York, 1997.

BRADLEY ABRAMS

**CZECH REPUBLIC.** Located in the geographical center of Europe, the Czech Republic is a landlocked country with an area of 78,866 square kilometers (30,500 square miles). The country shares borders with Germany, Poland, Austria, and Slovakia. The topography ranges from plains to highland and mountainous regions that cover almost 46 percent of the territory. The Czech Republic is composed of two historically distinct provinces, the Czech lands (Bohemia) and Moravia. The capital and largest city is Prague (Praha), which is situated in the heart of Bohemia. Brno, the second largest city, is the cultural and political center of Moravia.

The Czech Republic's population of 10,230,000 (as of 2001) people is for the most part ethnically homogeneous: Czechs and Moravians make up 94 percent of the population. Ethnic Slovaks make up the largest minority group at 2 percent of the population, followed consecutively by Roma, Poles, and Germans. Czech, a member of the west Slavic branch of the Slavic languages, is the native language of the majority of the population, although Slovak, Romany, and German are also strongly represented in minority communities.

Roman Catholics comprise the largest religious group in the Czech Republic, with almost 40 percent of the population. Protestant denominations, including Hussites, Czech Brethren, and others, comprise approximately 5 percent. Eastern Orthodox believers make up 3 percent; 40 percent of Czech citizens claim no official religious affiliation. The country's Jewish population—357,000 in 1930—was devastated during the Holocaust and further depleted by emigration after the war.

The Czech Republic is divided into fourteen administrative regions, including one for the city of Prague. The government is organized as a multiparty parliamentary democracy. The bicameral parliament consists of a two-hundred-member chamber of deputies and a senate with eighty-one members. Deputies are elected to four-year terms, and one-third of the senators may come up for reelection every two years. The leader of the government is the prime minister and the head of state is the president, who is elected to a five-year term by both chambers of parliament. The writer and playwright Václav Havel was the first president of the Czech Republic, serving two terms from 1993 to 2003. In 2003 parliament elected the economist and former prime minister Václav Klaus as president.

Both the Czech Republic and its former federal partner, Slovakia, came into existence as separate independent countries on 1 January 1993. Explanations for the amicable and bloodless breakup of Czechoslovakia, popularly called the Velvet Divorce, vary widely and include historic, economic, constitutional, and political factors. The root causes of the breakup are found in the formation of Czechoslovakia in 1918. The ancient linguistic and ethnic heritage common to both nations was not enough to overcome the economic disparity and separate historical development of the two peoples. The Czech lands inherited from the Habsburg Empire the majority of the country's industrial base, whereas Slovakia, which for centuries had been under the Hungarian Crown, was largely underdeveloped.

The period of Slovak independence (1938–1945) is also a contributing factor. Although established by the Third Reich, the limited period of independence engendered a separate Slovak political identity. Prewar Czechoslovakia, minus Ruthenia, was reconstituted in 1945. Constitutional provisions affecting the status of Slovakia within Czechoslovakia in the postwar era further contributed to a Slovak feeling of separateness. After the communist takeover in 1948, a new constitution established a separate Slovak parliament, or national council, and a Slovak Communist Party. The constitution of 1968 elevated Slovakia to full federal status beginning in 1 January 1969 and established a minority veto in the federal parliament, meaning that a small minority block voting along nationalist lines could defeat important legislation. Although the minority veto had little impact during the socialist era, during the postcommunist period it created problems for the federation. Rather than uniting the two nations, the development of separate Slovak political institutions and full federal status, together with the minority veto, reinforced the separate Slovak political identity.

After the communist regime collapsed in 1989, differences between Czech and Slovak approaches to economic reform deepened the political divide. Czech politicians held strongly to policies promoting the rapid development of a market economy, whereas Slovakia's leaders endeavored to slow down market reform. Ultimately, Czech politicians saw fewer advantages to preserving the federation than to proceeding with economic reforms without Slovakia. Although public opinion supported the preservation of the federation, both Czech and Slovak political leaders took measures toward separation. In July 1992 the Slovak national council approved a declaration of sovereignty for the Republic of Slovakia. On 25 November 1992 the federal assembly passed a bill dissolving the federation.

*See also* **Communism; Czechoslovakia; Havel, Václav; Holocaust; Romanies (Gypsies); Slovakia.**

BIBLIOGRAPHY

Elster, Jon. "Transition, Constitution-Making and Separation in Czechoslovakia." *European Journal of Sociology/Archives Europennes de Sociologie* 36, no. 1 (1995): 105–134.

Hilde, Paal Sigurd. "Slovak Nationalism and the Break-up of Czechoslovakia." *Europe-Asia Studies* 51, no. 4 (June 1999): 647–665.

Leff, Carol Skalnik. *The Czech and Slovak Republics: Nation Versus State.* Boulder, Colo., 1996.

Official website of the Czech Republic. Available at http:www.czech.cz.

Příhoda, Petr. "Mutual Perceptions in Czech-Slovak Relationships." In *The End of Czechoslovakia,* edited by Jiří Musil, 128–138. Budapest, 1995.

Wolchik, Sharon L. "The Politics of Transition and the Break-Up of Czechoslovakia." *The End of Czechoslovakia,* edited by Jiří Musil, 225–244. Budapest, 1995.

MICHAEL LONG

# D

**DACHAU.** Dachau was the longest continually existing Nazi concentration camp. Of about 200,000 prisoners who were registered at the camp, more than 41,500 died there. Dachau attained especial notoriety as the camp where pseudo-medical experiments were conducted, where prominent prisoners were held, and where postwar trials took place.

## ORIGINS
The antecedents of the Dachau concentration camp date back to World War I. Prior to 1914 Dachau was a town of about five thousand residents located ten miles northwest of Munich. In 1915 the Bavarian government built a new munitions factory there because of the abundant supply of water. The nearly eight thousand munitions workers were demobilized in 1919 under the terms of the Treaty of Versailles. Many remained in the area, and in 1927 Dachau had the highest unemployment rate in Germany. In 1933—before Hitler became chancellor on 30 January—local officials requested that the Bavarian government set up a "militia or work conscription camp" on the abandoned factory grounds.

Heinrich Himmler (1900–1945), the head of Adolf Hitler's SS (Schutzstaffel), chose the Dachau munitions factory as the site of a prison camp to intern political opponents while the Nazis consolidated their power. (Such camps were anticipated in the Nazi constitution drafted for their November 1923 coup d'état attempt.) On 21 March 1933

newspapers announced that the next day a "protective custody camp" would be opened in Dachau. It could hold five thousand inmates, to include "all communist functionaries, and as necessary Reichsbanner [an organization of veterans that tried to curb the violence of the Nazi SA] and marxists" for "as long as necessary" to achieve the "pacification of the national populace."

## SCHOOL OF VIOLENCE
Himmler's personal role in Dachau was crucial for the future of the Nazi concentration camp network. Initially Dachau was the only camp under SS control (the SA [Sturmabteilung] controlled other early camps). As the SS grew, it took over the entire camp system. Theodor Eicke (1892–1943), a World War I veteran Himmler named commandant in June 1933, became Inspector of the Concentration Camps in 1934. Eicke spread his system of organization with its draconian punishments to the entire camp system. He mentored Rudolf Höss, who became commandant of Auschwitz in 1940. A dozen camp commandants were trained in Dachau. Of Dachau's six main commandants, one was killed at the front, three committed suicide, and two were sentenced and executed after the war.

## POPULATION AND DEATH RATE
The early camps served to neutralize political opposition and utilized prisoner labor but mostly for make-work projects. Lethal violence was commonplace from the start. By the end of May 1933 a

**TABLE 1**

### Number of officially recorded deaths in Dachau

| Time period | Number of deaths recorded by the Dachau camp | Additional documented deaths | Totals |
|---|---|---|---|
| March 1933–May 1938 | 150 | | |
| June–Nov. 1938 | 68 | | |
| 11 Nov. 1938–Feb. 1939 | 243 | | 2,318 |
| Jan. –April 1939 | 342 | | |
| 1940 | 1,515 | | |
| 1941 | 2,576 | ca. 4,500 | |
| 1942 | 2,470 | (Soviet POWs) | 9,546 |
| 1943 | 1,100 | | 1,100 |
| Jan. –Aug. 1944 | 1,154 | | |
| Sept. –Dec. 1944 | 3,640 | 2,946 | 7,740 |
| Jan. –May 1945 | 15,384 | 2,966 | 18,350 |
| Red Cross registered deaths not in col. 1 | | 3,309 | 3,309 |
| **Total** | **28,642** | **13,721** | **42,363** |

SOURCES: Col. 1: Kimmel, pp. 372, 385, after Smikalla's reckoning based on *Die Toten von Dachau*. Col. 2: Zamecnik, pp. 399f. Note: Zamecnik's addition on p. 400 is off by 4.

**TABLE 2**

### Number and size of work detachments

| Year | Number of branch camps | Approximate total of inmates in new branch camps |
|---|---|---|
| 1933–1939 | 3 | 120 |
| 1940 | 6 | 260 |
| 1941 | 4 | 170 |
| 1942 | 26 | 2,300 |
| 1943 | 6 | 5,300 |
| 1944 | 86 | 32,000 |
| 1945 | 40 | 600 |

Note: Most large branch camps continued to exist until 1945

SOURCE: Martin Weinmann, ed., *Das nationalsozialistische Lagersystem* (Frankfurt, 1990), pp. 554–558.

dozen men had been tortured to death or murdered, with Jews being singled out for the most brutal treatment.

Dachau's inmate population rose from 2,000 to 2,600 by the end of 1933, then fell to 1,300 by the end of 1934. In early 1935 Himmler convinced Hitler to expand the camp system instead of dissolving it. Beginning in 1936 three camps were constructed with a design capacity of six to eight thousand inmates each. Dachau was completely rebuilt between January 1937 and August 1938. The prisoners' section was a 250-by-600-meter enclosure with thirty-four barracks and a service building, with a much larger compound for SS guards and troops in the adjacent munitions factory buildings. With the addition of two new categories of prisoner, "asocials" and "criminals," and the March 1938 annexation of Austria, the number of inmates rose to 3,500 by July 1938. The November 1938 *Kristallnacht* pogroms added 11,911 Jewish inmates to Dachau, so that 14,232 were imprisoned as of 1 December 1938. Large releases reduced the total to 3,300 to 3,900 after April 1939. From September 1939 to February 1940 all but about a hundred inmates were sent to other camps so that Dachau could be used to train SS combat troops.

During the war years the number of foreign inmates surpassed the number of Germans. Of the thirty-seven nations of origin represented in the camp, Poland had the largest total with about 35,000, followed by Russians and Hungarian Jews. In 1940 Dachau became the central camp for clergymen, with 2,720 ultimately registered. One barracks (later several more) housed the prisoner infirmary, others a camp store and library for German inmates. In the summer of 1940 a two-chamber crematory began operating in the camp. A much larger building with a gas chamber and an eight-chamber crematory was constructed between May 1942 and April 1943. Although there is no evidence that the gas chamber was used for the systematic mass murder for which it was designed, prisoner reports smuggled out at the time and testimony after the war indicate that experimental and test gassings were conducted there. Why was it never used for systematic gassings? Just as it was completed in 1943 prisoner labor for the war effort was given priority, then near the end of the war death by starvation and disease kept the eight ovens working at capacity.

## WORK DETACHMENTS

In 1943 living conditions were improved so that inmates could contribute to the war effort. External sub-camps were set up to utilize prisoner labor at more distant locations. Of 188 total work detachments, only thirty were based in the main camp. Eleven of the external camps were for women only (on 24 November 1944, 5,044 women were registered). Thirteen of the external camps had 1,000 to 4,300 inmates; ninety-one had fifty or fewer. The

**Journalists view bodies following the liberation of Dachau, May 1945.** The victims shown here had been alive at the time U.S. soldiers first arrived but succumbed to disease or starvation soon afterward.

BMW plant in Allach was one of the largest external labor camps, averaging 3,800 inmates from March 1943 until the end of the war. One inmate worked for the mayor of Dachau, and two for the mayor of Munich. On 22 April 1945 there were 27,649 prisoners registered in the main camp, 37,964 in subcamps. About 43,000 were categorized as political prisoners, 22,000 as Jews. At liberation some of the barracks, designed to accommodate 360 inmates, held nearly 2,000.

Doctors conducted lethal human experiments in Dachau. From February 1942 to April 1945 about a thousand inmates were infected with malaria, from April to August 1942 inmates were subjected to ultra-low air pressure, from August 1942 to May 1943 others were frozen in ice baths, and from July to September 1944 they were forced to drink seawater. An inmate brothel was set up in 1944.

### RESISTANCE

Brutal punishments and a system of spies made prisoner resistance essentially impossible. However, political prisoners (mostly communists) managed to occupy most of the crucial administrative positions delegated to inmates. These included the labor detachment office and the infirmary, as well as the positions of barracks- and room-elders for most barracks. They used informal networks of personal trust to improve and save the lives of many inmates, especially in comparison with camps where criminals fulfilled the prisoners' administrative functions. There was also a network of clandestine radios, and prisoners participated in secret religious and cultural activities, such as the ordination of a priest and literary discussion groups. In the spring of 1945 prisoners in the various national groups came together to form an international camp leadership that took over the running of the camp after liberation. Survivors in this Comité International de Dachau fought to preserve the camp as a memorial site, and still participate in its administration.

## LIBERATION

On 26 April 1945, the SS began the evacuation of the camp with a march of 7,000 inmates, south toward Hitler's "Alpine redoubt" (which did not exist). On 28 April some escaped inmates joined with townspeople to take over city hall, but the uprising was put down by the camp's SS garrison. On 29 April the U.S. army's Forty-fifth and Forty-second Divisions arrived within hours of each other and liberated the camp, killing forty to fifty of the 560 surrendering SS men. Of the 3,000 corpses found in the camp, about 2,200 were added to a mass grave of 4,000 that the SS had started, and 700 to 800 were cremated. Another 2,200 who died after liberation were buried in the town cemetery.

## POSTWAR

In July 1945 the U.S. army used the prisoner and SS compounds to intern up to thirty thousand German suspects. From November 1945 to December 1947 eleven concentration camp and atrocity trials were conducted in Dachau. The last internees were released in August 1948. The Bavarian state took over the camp and converted it into a residential settlement for two thousand refugees from Eastern Europe. A museum set up in the large crematory building in 1945 was removed in May 1953, but re-established in 1960 after heavy lobbying by survivors. A memorial site with a much larger museum opened in 1965 after the last refugees were moved out. The museum was renovated and expanded from 1995 to 2003.

*See also* **Auschwitz-Birkenau; Buchenwald; Concentration Camps; Holocaust.**

BIBLIOGRAPHY

Distel, Barbara, et al. *The Dachau Concentration Camp, 1939 to 1945: Text and Photo Documents from the Exhibition.* Munich, 2005. This richly illustrated catalog of the memorial site museum begins with four scholarly essays about the camp's history.

Kimmel, Günther. "Das Konzentrationslager Dachau." In *Bayern in der NS-Zeit,* edited by Martin Broszat, vol. 2, pp. 349–413. Munich, 1979. Scholarly overview.

Marcuse, Harold. *Legacies of Dachau: The Uses and Abuses of a Concentration Camp, 1933–2001.* New York, 2001. The most comprehensive account available in English.

Zámečník, Stanislav. *Das war Dachau.* Luxembourg, 2002. This meticulous historian-survivor's monograph is the most reliable scholarly work about the camp.

HAROLD MARCUSE

**DADA.** "Let us rewrite life every day. What we are celebrating is both buffoonery and a requiem mass" (Ball, p. 56). When the German poet Hugo Ball set down those lines in his diary on 12 March 1916, he invoked both Christian liturgical prayers for the salvation of the souls of the dead ("requiem mass") and the comic performances of clowns and acrobats ("buffoonery") as points of reference for what he and a group of fellow poets and artists had been doing of late in the newly established Cabaret Voltaire in Zurich, Switzerland.

## DADA IN ZURICH

Named in honor of the eighteenth-century French philosopher Voltaire, author of the satirical novel *Candide, or Optimism* (1759), and founded by Ball, along with the German poet and cabaret singer Emmy Hennings, the Alsatian artist Jean Arp, the Romanian poet Tristan Tzara, and the Romanian artist Marcel Janco, the Cabaret Voltaire opened on 5 February 1916 and lasted only until late June of that year. The naming of the Cabaret Voltaire was a gesture that acknowledged the political and philosophical despair as well as the artistic ambitions of Ball and his collaborators, including, in addition to those named above, the Swiss artist Sophie Taeuber, the German poet and medical student Richard Huelsenbeck, and the German artist, writer, and filmmaker Hans Richter. "The ideals of culture and of art as a program for a variety show—that is our kind of *Candide* against the times," wrote Ball (p. 67). As a group, Ball and the others sought to invent new ways of composing both art and life in neutral Switzerland, a location in which they were at once insulated from and haunted by the perils and terrors of World War I. Speaking of the effects of their performances and exhibitions, Ball wrote: "The horror of our time, the paralyzing background of events, is made visible" (p. 65).

As announced in a press notice in the Zurich papers of 2 February 1916 that Ball cites in his diary, the Cabaret Voltaire was founded as an experiment intended "to create a center for artistic entertainment" that would be open to "suggestions and contributions of all kinds" from the "young artists of Zurich" (p. 50). Arp, Ball, Hennings, Huelsenbeck, Janco, Richter, Taeuber, and Tzara variously contributed paintings, masks, and other objects that were exhibited on the walls of the nightclub's cramped rooms; so-called sound-poems or verses without words, including Ball's "Gadji beri bimba" (1916), that were recited on the nightclub's makeshift stage by authors in outlandish masks and costumes, often accompanied by drumming that was meant to evoke African musical traditions; simultaneous poems that were declaimed by several performers at once ("L'amiral cherche une maison à louer" [1916] by Huelsenbeck, Janco, and Tzara being the most famous of those); and experimental dance performances that drew on new theories of expressive movement promulgated by the choreographer Rudolf von Laban, with whom Taeuber and the German dancer Mary Wigman, herself a pioneer of modern dance and occasional Cabaret Voltaire performer, studied.

A journal called *Cabaret Voltaire* that was published on 4 June 1916 contained the first appearance in print of the word *Dada* in connection with the Zurich group's avant-garde art, poetry, and performances. The title *Dada* was soon attached to a periodical, collections of poetry by Huelsenbeck, and exhibitions of art by Arp, Richter, Janco, and others. Precisely how or when the word *Dada* was discovered or invented as a name for the performances, poems, and works of art produced by the Zurich group in spring 1916 has not been established, but it is clear that part of the word's appeal was its multilingual evocativeness: "*Dada*," wrote Ball on 18 April 1916, "is 'yes, yes' in Rumanian, 'rocking horse' and 'hobbyhorse' in French. For Germans it is a sign of foolish naïveté, joy in procreation, and preoccupation with the baby carriage" (p. 63). March 1917 saw the opening of an art gallery, the Galerie Dada, that succeeded the Cabaret Voltaire as the center of Zurich Dada activities. At around that same time, Huelsenbeck returned to Berlin and quickly sought to establish the German capital as a center of Dada activity.

## DADA IN GERMANY

In the midst of the acute material deprivation and increasing social and political tension brought on by World War I, Huelsenbeck began to collaborate in Berlin with the artists George Grosz and John Heartfield and the writers Wieland Herzfelde and Franz Jung, and in early 1918 they joined him in founding the "Club Dada," which also counted the architect and writer Johannes Baader, the artists Raoul Hausmann, Hannah Höch, and Otto Schmalhausen, and the writer Walter Mehring among its members. In Germany Dada took on a more aggressively political character, with the Berlin dadaists and their counterparts in Cologne, prominent among the latter the artists Max Ernst and Johannes Theodor Baargeld, advocating radical political change in the wake of the abdication of Kaiser William II and the November Revolution of 1918. Grosz, Heartfield, Herzfelde, and Jung were all founding members of the German Communist Party, and German Dada journals (including *Der Ventilator* [The fan], published in Cologne, and *Jedermann sein eigner Fussball* [Every man his own football], published in Berlin) as well as several major Dada exhibitions held in Cologne and Berlin in 1919–1920, addressed contemporary political events and attempted to establish connections between the German dadaists' experimental artistic techniques, most prominent among them collage and photomontage, and their critiques of contemporary politics and culture. A spring 1920 exhibition in Cologne was temporarily shut down by the police in connection with charges of obscenity, and the largest of the German Dada exhibitions, the so-called Erste Internationale Dada-Messe (First International Dada Fair), which was held in Berlin in summer 1920, resulted in the trial of several of its organizers on charges of having "insulted the military" with the inclusion of works such as Grosz's portfolio of lithographs, *Gott mit uns*

(God with us; 1920), which satirized the practices of military authorities during and after World War I, and a sculptural assemblage consisting of a stuffed German officer's uniform with a plaster pig's head that hung from the ceiling in the exhibition and bore the name *Prussian Archangel* (1920).

## DADA IN PARIS AND THE SHIFT TO SURREALISM

Just as Huelsenbeck bore the word *Dada* to Berlin, Tzara carried it to Paris, arriving there from Zurich in January 1920. Through personal correspondences, the collaborative production and international dissemination of Dada publications, and word of mouth, key players in what would become the Paris Dada movement were already aware of much of what had gone on at the Cabaret Voltaire and the Galerie Dada in Zurich, and they were even more familiar with the events and inventions of the New York Dada movement, in which the Parisian artists Marcel Duchamp, Jean Crotti, and Francis Picabia had participated, along with the American artist Man Ray and others, while living in the United States during World War I. Early in 1919, Picabia collaborated with Tzara in Zurich on the publication of issues of the journals *Dada* and *391*. Around the same time, the Parisian poet André Breton made contact with Tzara to praise his 1918 "Dada Manifesto." Several months later, Breton and fellow poets Louis Aragon and Philippe Soupault published the first issue of *Littérature*, which would become a key organ of Paris Dada and, eventually, one of the major journals of the surrealist movement that would succeed Dada in Paris as the French capital's primary avant-garde movement in literature and the arts. Dada in Paris was more oriented to literature and the making of art-world scandals than to politics and the visual arts, and one of its centers of activity was the bookstore Au Sans Pareil, site of several key Dada exhibitions, including an important show of Ernst's Dada works in late spring 1921.

By 1923 the various European Dada movements—which had spread from Zurich, Berlin, Cologne, and Paris to Hanover and elsewhere in Germany, and to Holland, Czechoslovakia, Hungary, and Russia—had more or less come to an end. Ball had retreated from Dada and from public life in

general in 1920, turning his attention instead to the study of early Christian saints and pursuing his own devotion to Catholicism; the Berlin dadaists variously oriented their work toward politics and the so-called new objectivity in painting; Baargeld studied for a doctorate in philosophy and economics; and Ernst moved to Paris, where he became a key participant in the surrealist movement.

*See also* **Aragon, Louis; Arp, Jean; Ball, Hugo; Breton, André; Cabaret; Duchamp, Marcel; Grosz, George; Surrealism; Tzara, Tristan.**

BIBLIOGRAPHY

Ball, Hugo. *Flight Out of Time: A Dada Diary.* Edited and with an introduction by John Elderfield. Translated by Ann Raimes. Berkeley, Calif., Los Angeles, and London, 1996.

Dickerman, Leah, ed. *Dada: Zurich, Berlin, Hannover, Cologne, New York, Paris.* New York, 2005.

Huelsenbeck, Richard. *Memoirs of a Dada Drummer.* Edited by Hans J. Kleinschmidt. Translated by Joachim Neugroschel. Berkeley, Calif., Los Angeles, and London, 1991.

Motherwell, Robert, ed. *The Dada Painters and Poets: An Anthology.* 2nd ed. Cambridge, Mass., 1989.

Richter, Hans. *Dada: Art and Anti-Art.* Translated by David Britt. London and New York, 1997.

Tzara, Tristan. *Seven Dada Manifestos and Lampisteries.* Translated by Barbara Wright. London, 1981.

BRIGID DOHERTY

---

# DALADIER, ÉDOUARD (1884–1970), French politician.

Édouard Daladier, having given up all political activity in the last decade of his life, was already mostly forgotten when he died at the age of eighty-six, though he had been one of the prominent figures in French politics during the 1930s and, except for the period from July 1926 to March 1930, had served in the government continuously from 1925 to 1940. The son of a baker from Carpentras in the south of France, he was intellectually very gifted, placing first in the history *agrégation*, the French teaching certification examination, of 1909. But he devoted very little time to teaching. In 1911, at the age of twenty-seven, he was elected mayor of his native town of

Carpentras. He served in World War I, achieving the rank of infantry lieutenant, and received the Croix de Guerre with four citations for bravery. The war marked him profoundly. After it ended, he devoted himself entirely to politics. A member of the Radical Party, he was elected deputy of the Vaucluse region in 1919 and continuously reelected until 1940. He very quickly stood out from the mass of deputies. After the victory of the Cartel des Gauches (Left-wing cartel) in 1924, Premier Édouard Herriot, also a professor (of literature)—Daladier had been his student in Lyon—appointed him minister for the colonies. Although these two men were both part of the Left and members of the Radical Party, their political views were quite different. Herriot was a moderate radical and Daladier more of a leftist. He was closely allied with the socialists, though he never believed in socialism.

Daladier played his major political role during the 1930s, concerning himself with three major issues: the incapacity of certain institutions to prevent permanent governmental instability; the economic and social troubles related to the world crisis; and the increasing external threats occasioned by the Nazis' rise to power in Germany. The France of Édouard Daladier's time was in crisis. As premier in 1934, he had to face the growing lawlessness of the far-right leagues. On 6 February, he was forced to resign. This only convinced him that in order to face the danger, the Radical Party over which he had presided had to strengthen its ties with other leftist forces. Despite Herriot's great reluctance, Daladier became an active supporter of the Popular Front, standing with the socialists and the communists. After the electoral victory of the Front, he was appointed vice president in Léon Blum's government, formed in June 1936.

Nevertheless, Daladier progressively distanced himself from the Popular Front—a growing number of radicals were disconcerted by its revolutionary aspects. Moreover, he had been interested in military issues for a long time and served as minister of war, and then of national defense, almost continuously from 1933 to 1940. He was aware of the contradiction between social measures such as reducing the workweek to forty hours and the large industrial effort necessary to rebuild the army, which had been more or less abandoned since World War I.

When he once again became premier in 1938, he severed his ties with the Popular Front and, with Paul Reynaud, his minister of finance, set about "putting France back to work." He set in motion a huge rearmament effort but was nevertheless still unable to provide the army with competent leaders. Still traumatized by the memories of the enormous number of casualties at the beginning of the war in 1914, he leaned toward a policy of defense.

Reluctantly, and with few illusions about its success, Daladier signed the Munich agreement with Adolf Hitler in September 1938 because he could not count on the support of the United Kingdom and because France was not ready for war. In November, he thwarted a general strike called to protest the government's intentions to modify existing social laws. He was enjoying great popularity when, in March 1939, Germany annexed what was left of Czechoslovakia. Daladier was determined to stand his ground. When Germany attacked Poland on 1 September 1939, France and the United Kingdom responded by declaring war. After a few days of hesitation, the French Communist Party officially came out in support of the German-Soviet pact signed that August and requested negotiations with Germany. Daladier dissolved the party and emerged as the leader of the powerful anticommunist wave that hit France at the time.

On the military level, however, the Allies chose a strategy of defense, as they were convinced that over time they would achieve considerable material superiority. This was the "phony war," which ended with the German offensive of May 1940. Daladier, accused of not waging war energetically enough, had been replaced in March by Paul Reynaud. After the 1940 defeat, Daladier would have liked to continue the fight from abroad, but a majority of deputies handed power over to Marshal Philippe Pétain, who signed the Armistice in June. Daladier was arrested under orders of the Occupation government in Vichy and was among those who stood accused at the Riom trials of being responsible for the war. But the trials were soon suspended under German pressure after a vigorous defense was mounted, especially of

Daladier. He was handed over to the Germans and remained in detention until the end of the war.

Despite the violent allegations against him by the then very powerful Communist Party, which never forgave him for his attitude toward them in 1939, Daladier returned to France and to his old post of deputy for Vaucluse in June 1946. The Radical Party, however, was only a shadow of its former self, and it fused into a coalition of left-wing parties, the Rassemblement des Gauches Républicaines, an alliance of circumstance with little power. And while Herriot managed to become president of the National Assembly, Daladier never again played an important role. He made his presence felt with his opposition to the European Defense Community (EDC), paradoxically holding the same views as the communists. He was mayor of Avignon from 1953 to 1958 but, like many others, was swept out of office that year by the Gaullist wave and lost his seat as deputy. He never again sought to reclaim it.

Daladier was nicknamed the "Bull of the Vaucluse," but his determined attitude hid the fact that he was never able to be the man of action that everyone expected.

*See also* **Blum, Léon; France; Munich Agreement; Popular Front; World War II.**

BIBLIOGRAPHY

Berstein, Serge. *Histoire du Parti radical.* 2 vols. Paris, 1980–1982.

Borne, Dominique, and Henri Dubief. *La crise des années trente (1929–1938).* Paris, 1989.

Du Réau, Elisabeth. *Édouard Daladier.* Paris, 1993.

Rémond, René, and Janine Bourdin, eds. *Édouard Daladier, chef de gouvernement, avril 1930–septembre 1939.* Paris, 1977.

JEAN-JACQUES BECKER

---

# DALÍ, SALVADOR (1904–1989), Spanish painter, sculptor, and graphic artist.

Born and raised in the Spanish province of Catalonia, situated in the country's northeast corner, Salvador Dalí was destined to win worldwide fame. Indeed, as a result of his continual self-promotion, Dalí is probably the best known of all the surrealists—the only one who achieved celebrity status during his lifetime. Although he published numerous writings, his most important contributions were concerned with surrealist painting. While his name conjures up images of melting watches and flaming giraffes, his mature style took years to develop. By 1926, Dalí had experimented with half a dozen styles, including pointillism, purism, primitivism, Marc Chagall's visionary cubism, and Giorgio de Chirico's metaphysical art. The same year, he exhibited the painting *Basket of Bread* at the Dalmau Gallery in Barcelona, inspired by the seventeenth-century artist Francisco de Zurbarán. However, his early work was chiefly influenced by the nineteenth-century realists and by cubist artists such as Pablo Picasso and Georges Braque.

The publication of André Breton's first *Manifeste du surréalisme* in 1924 made an indelible impression on Dalí. Although Catalonia and the rest of Spain were seething with avant-garde activity, Dalí was excited by what was taking place in France. Moving to Paris in 1929, he joined the French surrealists and participated in their various activities. Except for vacation trips to Catalonia, he remained there for many years. Quickly assimilated into the French movement, Dalí contributed a whole series of articles and paintings to journals such as *La révolution surréaliste, Le surréalisme au service de la révolution,* and *Minotaure.* While Breton, the leader of the surrealists, eventually came to despise the artist, whom he accused of rampant commercialism, he was extremely impressed by his talent initially. "For the first time perhaps," he announced in 1929, "Dalí has opened our mental windows wide." Calling his art "the most hallucinatory in existence," Breton advised the surrealists to cultivate voluntary hallucination like the painter (vol. 2, pp. 308–309; author's translation).

By this date, Dalí's art had evolved beyond his earlier obsession with strange objects and had acquired a visionary character. It would undergo a radical transformation during the next few years as the artist experimented with a new hallucinatory aesthetics that made his former efforts seem pale by comparison. Taking a leaf from the poet Arthur Rimbaud's book, who taught himself to see a mosque in place of a factory, Dalí boasted he was able to imagine a woman who was simultaneously a horse. By accustoming himself to voluntary

***The Metamorphosis of Narcissus.*** Painting by Salvador Dalí, 1937. ART RESOURCE, NY

hallucination, he was able to reshape reality according to the dictates of his desire. This experience, which foreshadowed the invention of his famous paranoiac-critical method, testified to the triumph of the pleasure principle over the reality principle. At the same time, Dalí's obsession with putrefaction and scatological subjects increased, and he began to explore Freudian themes overtly in paintings such as *The Great Masturbator* (1929) and in the movie *An Andalusian Dog*, created the same year with the Spanish filmmaker Luis Buñuel. By 1934 Dalí had managed to violate every conceivable artistic taboo and had perfected the outrageous persona that would contribute to his notoriety.

While voluntary hallucination produced excellent results, it was essentially a conscious process. Inspired by the psychoanalyst Jacques Lacan, who published a thesis on paranoia in 1932, Dalí developed a method of incorporating involuntary hallucinations into his art. Defined by Dalí as a "spontaneous method of irrational knowledge based on the irrational-critical association of delirious phenomena" (Ades, p. 126), the paranoiac-critical method furnished the artist with an endless number of paintings. In the early 1930s, he became obsessed with Jean-François Millet's *The Angelus* (1858), which he cited over and over in his works, and with the story of William Tell. Toward the end of the decade, Dalí began to juxtapose pairs of images to illustrate the theme of involuntary transformation. In *The Metamorphosis of Narcissus* (1937), for example, two identical constructions are placed side by side. The image of Narcissus admiring himself in the water is juxtaposed with several objects that closely resemble him. In other paintings, two images are superimposed in such a way that each is continually transformed into the other, creating a deliberate confusion between figure and ground. In *The Slave Market with the Disappearing Bust of Voltaire* (1940), a statue of the French philosopher in the foreground dissolves to reveal three servants standing in the background, who dissolve again to depict Voltaire in the foreground. Dalí would exploit these and other hallucinatory techniques brilliantly during the next fifty years, broadening his repertoire to include mystical and scientific themes while remaining faithful to his original inspiration.

*See also* **Breton, André; Chagall, Marc; Cubism; Painting, Avant-Garde; Surrealism.**

BIBLIOGRAPHY

Ades, Dawn. *Dalí.* London and New York, 1995. The best book on the subject.

Alexandrian, Sarane. *Surrealist Art.* Translated by Gordon Clough. London and New York, 1985.

Breton, André. *Oeuvres complètes.* Edited by Marguerite Bonnet et al. 3 vols. Paris, 1988–1999.

Finkelstein, Haim. *Salvador Dalí's Art and Writing, 1927–1942: The Metamorphosis of Narcissus.* Cambridge, U.K., 1996.

Neret, Gilles, and Robert Descharnes. *Dalí 1904–1989.* Translated by Michael Hulse. New York, 1998.

WILLARD BOHN

---

# D'ANNUNZIO, GABRIELE (1863–1938), Italian author, soldier, and political leader.

Gabriele D'Annunzio was born in Pescara, a provincial coastal town in the region of the Abruzzi in Italy on 12 March 1863. A poet, novelist, political activist, and dramatist, he was also known for his flamboyant and rather anarchic lifestyle and for his numerous amorous adventures with high-society women. As a novelist, he was greatly inspired by the works of Friedrich Wilhelm Nietzsche (1844–1900), the late-nineteenth-century German philosopher who challenged the foundations of traditional morality and Christianity.

## POLITICAL ACTIVISM

D'Annunzio was an ardent nationalist and favored the intervention of Italy into the First World War on the Allied side. His enthusiasm was shared by the poet Filippo Tommaso Marinetti (1876–1944), the founder of the futurist movement (1909), who believed war to be the only hope for a healthy world. D'Annunzio was a controversial figure for over fifty years; he was considered to be a promoter of fascism, even when all evidence showed his contempt for the Fascists and for their leader Benito Mussolini (1883–1945), who led Italy from 1922 to 1943. D'Annunzio in fact regarded Mussolini as his social and political inferior. D'Annunzio's political views were quite equivocal and so was his relationship with the Fascist regime. The scholar Paolo Alatri sees the poet during this period as a pacifier attempting to create a bridge between left-wing agitators fighting for their rights and Mussolini's followers ready to beat their opponents into insensibility.

D'Annunzio was above all an individualist who was impervious to public criticism and followed his own poetic instincts. In his mid fifties during the First World War, he flew bombing raids over Austria and a few months later captained a torpedo boat raid into enemy Dalmatia. D'Annunzio was always on the watch for actions that would allow him to enter into the legends of posterity. When the war concluded, on the pretext of an established Italian culture already in place, the poet and his private army, called the *Arditi,* invaded the city of Fiume (in present-day Croatia) in September 1919 and transformed it into a city-state called Carnaro, which he ruled like a Renaissance prince. While ruling the city of Fiume, D'Annunzio issued the Carnaro Charter, a document stating that schools should be free of religious propaganda and influence and guaranteeing freedom of the press and of trade union associations. The Charter was in a sense the antithesis to the course of actions taken by Mussolini's government in the years to come. However, the situation in Fiume deteriorated to a point of anarchy, leading the population of the city to speak out against the occupation and against the immoral attitude of the legionaries. After stiff resistance, D'Annunzio left Fiume on 18 January 1921, when international opinion forced his expulsion and when an Italian naval shell hit his window, barely missing his head. His nationalistic ideals and his willingness readily to use armed force were viewed by the public as important examples for Mussolini and for his March on Rome in 1922.

## POET AND PLAYWRIGHT

As a poet, D'Annunzio made his debut at the age of sixteen when he published *Primo vere* (1879), but it was not until he published *Halcyon* in 1903 that his international reputation as one of the great Italian poets was confirmed. *Halcyon* is a carefully

**Gabriele D'Annunzio, right, during his service with the Italian Air Force.** BRIDGEMAN ART LIBRARY

organized sequence of eighty-eight lyrics, which to gain their full effect must be read as a whole. *Halcyon* is a reminiscence of a summer spent by the poet in Tuscany, part of the time with his legendary lover, the actress Eleanora Duse. The poems evoke specific times and locations that stir emotions linked to memories and myths associated with each place. However, D'Annunzio's birthplace was the most significant inspiration in his writings. The Abruzzi region, with its well-defined background culture rife with chthonic myths (concerning the underworld) and dark superstitions, permeated nearly all of his creative output. This regional influence was so pervasive in his writings that epithets such as the "Abruzzese" or the "Pescarese" are recognized in Italy as synonymous with D'Annunzio.

For centuries an atmosphere of legend and mystery had surrounded his homeland. The wall formed by the rocky Apennines on one side and the bordering of the Adriatic Sea on the other isolated this region, allowing its strong folkloric traditions to be preserved. Allusions to folklore and myths are to be found in his works, particularly in the collection of short stories *Le novelle della pescara* (1902; Tales of Pescara) and in his novel *Il trionfo della morte* (1894; Triumph of death). This novel is also the one work in which the author focuses on his long-lasting devotion to his mother.

In his fictional representation of rural life, D'Annunzio was spurred by the paintings of his friend the artist Francesco Paolo Michetti (1851–1929), who began his career as a painter in 1877. It was this artistic marriage that led D'Annunzio to write his most successful play, *La figlia di Iorio* (1904; The Daughter of Iorio, 1907), based on the painting *Daughter of Iorio* (1895) by Michetti.

During his playwriting career, he confided in his mistress, Eleonora Duse (1858–1924), who by 1885 was regarded throughout the world as Italy's greatest actress. D'Annunzio's eight-year relationship with Duse was a tempestuous affair later explored in his novel *Il fuoco* (1900; The Flame of Life, 1900). As a dramatist, his aim was to create a new type of theater based largely on classical themes that could be solidly linked to the present in a modern and original way rather than merely revive the past. To Duse he confided a sense of tediousness that he felt about the bourgeois drama that proliferated on the stages of fin-de-siècle Italy. Breaking the mold of contemporary Italian drama, D'Annunzio created tragedies such as *La città morta* (1898; The Dead City, 1902), *Il sogno d'un mattino di primavera* (1897; The Dream of a Spring Morning, 1902), and *Il sogno d'un tramonto d'autunno* (1898, The Dream of an Autumn Sunset, 1904), which were meant to arouse an apathetic Italian audience with what he considered a new genre.

D'Annunzio spent the later part of his life at his home in Gardone Riviera, on Lake Garda. He died in 1938 and was given a state funeral by Mussolini.

*See also* **Fiume; Italy; Marinetti, F. T.**

BIBLIOGRAPHY

Klopp, Charles. *Gabriele D'Annunzio.* Boston, 1988.

Tumini, Angela. *Il mito nell'anima: Magia e folklore in D'Annunzio.* Lanciano, 2004.

Valesio, Paolo. *Gabriele D'Annunzio: The Dark Flame.* Translated by Marilyn Migiel. New Haven, Conn., 1992.

Winwar, Frances. *Wingless Victory: A Biography of Gabriele d'Annunzio and Eleonora Duse.* New York, 1956.

Woodhouse, John. *Gabriele D'Annunzio: Defiant Archangel.* Oxford, U.K., 1997.

ANGELA TUMINI

**DANZIG.** *See* **Gdansk/Danzig.**

**DARDANELLES.** The Dardanelles Strait is the deep-water channel connecting the Aegean Sea with the Sea of Marmara in Turkey. The strait must be considered in conjunction with the Bosphorus Strait, the waterway connecting the northern end of the Sea of Marmara with the Black Sea. Together these channels constitute one of the most strategic waterways in the world.

Prior to 1914 the Dardanelles was greatly overshadowed by its northern counterpart, the Bosphorus, which was the gateway to Istanbul, the capital of the Ottoman Empire, and to the Black Sea. The two channels came to be the focal point of the so-called Eastern Question, the question being what would happen to Istanbul and the rest of the Ottoman lands after what was then seen as the inevitable collapse of the Ottoman Empire. For Britain and France, the primary issue was containing Russia, whose traditional goal was to take Istanbul and the Straits, thereby guaranteeing access to the Mediterranean. The Eastern Question was so interwoven with the fate of the Dardanelles and the Bosphorus that the term was often interchangeable with the Straits Question.

The Dardanelles leapt to the forefront of history with the Dardanelles campaign of World War I (19 February 1915–9 January 1916), also known as the Gallipoli campaign, named after the peninsula on the northern shore of the strait that saw the heaviest fighting. Heavily fortified by the Turks and their German allies, the strait proved impossible to overcome by naval bombardment and land forces, and the Dardanelles became the site of one of the most spectacular defeats for the Allies in the Great War. Largely the brainchild of Winston Churchill, then first lord of the admiralty, the aim of the campaign was to force the strait and make a dash for Istanbul, thereby knocking the Ottoman Empire out of the war and extending a helping hand to Russia, Britain's hard-pressed ally.

The critical naval attack occurred on 18 March when an Allied force consisting of some twenty heavy warships entered the strait and heavily bombarded the shore batteries. The day proved a disaster for the Allied fleet, with the loss of three battleships and damage to many more. On the French ship *Bouvet* alone, which struck a mine and went down in two minutes, the captain and 639 seamen were drowned. Taking stock, the Allied command decided that a naval attack alone would never tax the Turkish defenses enough to penetrate the strait. Therefore on 25 April the greatest amphibious landing military history had yet seen began. The Allied force consisted of seventy-five thousand men under the command of General Sir Ian Hamilton. The bulk of the force was made up of thirty thousand Anzac (Australian and New Zealand Army Corps) soldiers, who would become a legend during the campaign.

The other legend of the Dardanelles campaign was the Turkish General Mustafa Kemal, who would go down in history as Atatürk, the founder of modern Turkey. Mustafa Kemal was to be a crucial figure in the campaign. Highly critical of the way the German officers in the high command were running the campaign, Mustafa Kemal turned out to be a talented officer. It was largely through his decisive command, matched by failures in Allied intelligence and preparation, that the Anzac landing on 25 April failed. The campaign then became a sort of extension of the trench warfare that was seen on the western front, except for the fact that at some points only ten yards separated the two trenches. The fierce battles were often broken by truces, when both sides would bury their dead. It was said that the courtesy and civility with which the two sides treated each other was the last time chivalry was seen in trench warfare. There was a constant exchange of gifts, the Turks throwing over grapes and sweets, the Anzacs responding with tinned food and cigarettes.

By mid-May it had become clear that neither side was in a position to dislodge the other. The last major Allied push came on 6 August when a fresh force was landed on the Dardanelles beaches.

**Australian troops charge Turkish positions during the Dardanelles campaign, 1915.** ©CORBIS

In fierce fighting during August some forty-five thousand Allied troops died. In the last week of September Bulgaria joined the war on the German side, drastically altering the power balance in the Balkans. On 1 January 1916 the Allies began to withdraw from the peninsula. The Dardanelles campaign was to go down in history as one of the bloodiest encounters of World War I, with the casualties on both sides estimated at over half a million. It turned Allied strategy back to the western front, where the bloodshed would continue for another two and a half years.

*See also* **Atatürk, Mustafa Kemal; World War I.**

BIBLIOGRAPHY

Anderson, M. S. *The Eastern Question, 1774–1923: A Study in International Relations.* London, 1966.

Fromkin, David. *A Peace to End All Peace: Creating the Modern Middle East, 1914–1922.* London, 1989.

Moorhead, Alan. *Gallipoli.* New York, 1956.

SELIM DERINGIL

---

# DARLAN, FRANÇOIS (1881–1942), French admiral.

Jean-François Darlan, Admiral of the Fleet, a title he had ordered put back into use for himself and which has never been used since, remains a very controversial figure. Different historians have attributed contradictory and dubious intentions to him, so one must turn to the facts instead.

As a member of a navy family that had dabbled in politics (his father had been a deputy for Lot-et-

Garonne and minister of justice from 1896 to 1897), he joined the navy as well but saw little action, at least at sea. During World War I he almost always fought on land, and in the years that followed was often a state minister. He had a reputation for leaning toward the Left, which was rare in the navy, and it was Léon Blum who appointed him Admiral Chief of Staff in 1937. He is a bit excessively glorified as the creator of the large fleet France possessed at the outbreak of World War II in 1939. The ill winds of the day worked against anything more than its limited use in combat, however. A portion of the fleet was destroyed in the raid on Mers El-Kebir in July 1940 by the British, who were afraid it would fall into the hands of the Germans. The majority of the fleet, however, was scuttled in the port of Toulon in November 1942, when the Germans invaded the "Free Zone."

Admiral Darlan was a high-profile figure under the collaborationist Vichy government. He had been tapped as minister of the navy by Marshal Philippe Pétain on 16 June 1940, during the last government of the Third Republic. But it was only after the 1940 defeat that he acceded to the highest ranks. An Anglophobe, as French sailors traditionally were, especially after the events at Mers El-Kebir, he quickly became convinced of the need to collaborate with Germany, whose victory appeared certain. His position was in fact very close to that of Pierre Laval, and when a plot was hatched in December 1940 to supplant Pétain's second-in-command, who held the real reins of power, Darlan replaced him as deputy prime minister and designated successor. Although some said Darlan privately had reservations about the National Revolution, in practice he was a fervent supporter, and it was during his government that a whole series of its measures were taken, including the creation of the General Committee on the Jewish Question, the passage of the second set of anti-Semitic laws, the special tribunals for judging members of the Resistance, and the Work Charter. Above all, it was during Darlan's tenure that a marked increase in collaboration with the Germans occurred. In the hope of forging a political accord, to which the Germans had no intention of agreeing, Darlan offered military cooperation, which included giving the Germans access to airfields in Syria and the ports of Bizerte and Dakar. As events unfolded after the Soviet Union and the United States entered the war, however, these attempts failed to gain concessions from the Germans, who feared Admiral Darlan would change sides and whom they felt was not the man they needed. They reinstated Laval to his position of power in April 1942, though Darlan remained commander of the army.

His fate was determined somewhat by chance, since he happened to find himself in Algiers during the Anglo-American landing in North Africa in November 1942. It was an opportunity for him to switch sides—he intended to maintain a Vichy-style regime while at the same time rallying the leaders of the colonial territories, as well as other exiled French forces to the Allied cause, even though he had recently ordered those forces to fire on the Allies. He was engaged in a highly complex and ambiguous game, virulently opposed by the Gaullists, when he was assassinated by Bonnier de la Chapelle, a young member of the Resistance with monarchist tendencies. Was this an isolated act or the result of a conspiracy? The truth will never be known, given the local authorities' evident haste to execute the admiral's murderer by firing squad. In continental France, the public was not fooled—Darlan, too visible to be able to switch sides at the necessary moment as others managed to do, was a Vichyist and a collaborator who had been executed for his acts.

*See also* **Blum, Léon; France; Laval, Pierre; Pétain, Philippe; World War II.**

BIBLIOGRAPHY

Couteau-Bégarie, Hervé, et C. Huan. *Darlan.* Paris, 1989.

Paxton, Robert. "Un amiral entre deux blocs." *Vingtième siècle, revue d'Histoire* (October–December 1992): 3–19.

Sirinelli, Jean-François, ed. *Dictionnaire historique de la vie politique française au XXe siècle.* Paris, 1995.

JEAN-JACQUES BECKER

# DAWES PLAN.

**DAWES PLAN.** The Dawes Plan was an international agreement regarding Germany's payment of war reparations following World War I.

## REPARATIONS, 1919–1923

The Treaty of Versailles obligated Germany to pay reparations for damages done to Allied life and property during World War I. The treaty specified no total sum, nor did it determine how the receipts were to be divided. Reparations were apportioned among the major creditor powers—France, Belgium, Britain, and Italy—at a conference at Spa in July 1920. The total sum to be paid in money and in kind was set at a conference in London in April 1921. There a schedule of payments was established (the London schedule), and an ultimatum was sent to the German government. After months of incomplete efforts to meet the schedule, Germany was declared to be in default. At the initiative of Raymond Poincaré, the premier of France, engineers and troops from France and Belgium occupied the Ruhr district of Germany in January 1923 to impose sanctions and to collect reparations-in-kind from the coal mines there. German railroad and mine workers adopted a strategy of passive resistance, went on strike, and were supported by payments from the government. The serious inflation that had begun in Germany in June 1922 became astronomical. The chancellor and foreign minister, Gustav Stresemann, unilaterally ended passive resistance in September. The British Foreign Office took the lead in setting up an international committee of experts to examine the problem of reparations.

## THE DAWES COMMITTEE

Two committees convened in Paris on 14 January 1924 and issued their reports on 9 April. The most important was chaired by Charles G. Dawes, a prominent businessman from the American Midwest, director of the office of the budget, future vice president, and subsequent winner of the Nobel Peace Prize. It was composed of leading banking figures and financial experts from each of the major creditor powers and the United States. The task before it was to devise a scheme Germany could pay. That there was consensus regarding the plan the committee produced owed much to the good judgment and the negotiating skills of the other American member, Owen D. Young, a lawyer from upstate New York and chairman of the board of directors of the General Electric Company and of the Radio Corporation of America.

## PROVISIONS OF THE PLAN

What came to be known as the Dawes Plan did not reduce Germany's total reparation obligation as determined in 1921, nor did it alter the ratio by which it was distributed. It changed the rate at which Germany would pay. Germany was scheduled to pay a series of graduated annuities beginning at 1 billion gold marks per year in 1924–1925 (approximately one-half of the London schedule) and increasing to 2.5 billion in 1928–1929 (the standard Dawes annuity). These figures amounted to 1.8–3.2 percent of German national income. This was a level that Young thought high enough to indemnify France and to prevent German industry and commerce from dominating the world economy. Funds from German transportation, excise, and customs revenues were earmarked for the reparation account. To prevent a recurrence of inflation, the German central bank was reorganized and placed under the supervision of both German and foreign officials. An agent general for reparations was appointed to see that payment of the annuities would not weaken the economy and that the transfer abroad of large sums of currency would not threaten the stability of the mark. S. Parker Gilbert, a lawyer from New York and undersecretary of the U.S. Treasury, was named to this post. To the consternation of the Germans and the British, an end to the military occupation of the Ruhr was not made part of the plan. Dawes in particular was willing to see it continue as a means of coercing German payment. However, the direct exploitation of the Ruhr mines and the customs barrier between the Ruhr and the rest of Germany imposed during the 1923 occupation were ended. The report of the experts affirmed the fiscal and economic unity of the Reich. Sanctions could be imposed in the future only in the event of what was termed a "flagrant failure" to perform the terms of the plan.

## CREDITOR AND DEBTOR ADVANTAGES

The Dawes Plan was not inherently unsatisfactory to the reparation creditors. They gained what had eluded them since the end of the war—Berlin's voluntary agreement to pay reparation. And because the Dawes Plan did not reestimate Germany's total debt, they were spared a payment schedule based on estimates of German capacity in the aftermath of a financial crisis. Meanwhile it held potential advantages for Germany. Stresemann expected access to foreign capital, sustained Anglo-American mediation in favor of Germany, an end to the military occupation of the Ruhr, the beginning of the end of the military occupation of the Rhineland, and further downward revision of reparations before the payment of the first full Dawes annuity was due. He regarded the Dawes Plan as provisional, a temporary settlement, and envisioned a full examination of Germany's capacity to pay by the year 1928. This was in fact what Young intended. The American expert did not think that Germany could transfer the standard Dawes annuity. He expected the plan to become unworkable at that time, and a new scheme devised.

## CONSEQUENCES

The Dawes Plan was adopted at a conference attended by the creditors and Germany in London in July–August 1924. There Édouard Herriot, the new French premier, agreed that France would withdraw all troops from the Ruhr within one year and, at American and British insistence, not again impose sanctions against Germany unilaterally. In 1925–1926 the governments of Belgium, Italy, and France settled their respective war debts to the United States, and France settled its debt to Britain. (Britain settled its debt to the U.S. government in 1923.) With the creditor powers certain of their war debt obligations, a second committee of experts was convened to determine a permanent reparations settlement. Headed by Young, it reported in June 1929. The Young Plan reduced German payments below the standard Dawes annuity. They were scheduled out to 1988, the year French war debt payments to the United States were to end. Payment of both reparations and war debts ended in the aftermath of a conference in Lausanne in 1932—without the formal consent of the United States.

See also Reparations; Versailles, Treaty of; World War I.

BIBLIOGRAPHY

Jacobson, Jon. "The Reparation Settlement of 1924." In *Konsequenzen der Inflation*, edited by Gerald D. Feldman, Carl-Ludwig Holtfrerich, Gerhard A. Ritter, and Peter-Christian Witt, 79–108. Berlin, 1989.

Leffler, Melvin P. *The Elusive Quest: America's Pursuit of European Stability and French Security, 1919–1933.* Chapel Hill, N.C., 1979.

Moulton, Harold G. *The Reparation Plan.* New York and London, 1924.

Schuker, Stephen A. *The End of French Predominance in Europe: The Financial Crisis of 1924 and the Adoption of the Dawes Plan.* Chapel Hill, N.C., 1976.

JON S. JACOBSON

---

**DAYTON ACCORDS.** The Dayton Accords marked the end of wars in Bosnia-Herzegovina and Croatia that lasted from 1991 to 1995 and provided a roadmap for Bosnia's postwar development. The Accords were officially called "The General Framework Agreement for Peace (GFAP)," contained eleven annexes, and were 130 pages long. The negotiations at the Wright-Patterson Air Force Base in Dayton, Ohio, began 1 November 1995 and the Agreement was initialed in Dayton on 21 November. It was formally signed in Paris on 14 December and endorsed by the UN Security Council on 15 December 1995. Implementation of the accords began when the NATO-led Implementation Force (IFOR) deployed into Bosnia and Herzegovina on 20 December and when the first High Representative arrived in Sarajevo on 21 December 1995.

The Accords were a watershed. The Balkan wars shaped a generation of diplomats and soldiers from the United States, Europe, and the United Nations. They spurred efforts to address difficult conditions underlying intrastate conflict after the end of the Cold War. Most directly, the Accords ended a war that had lasted for more than three years.

## THE ONSET OF WAR

The war's origins were in the violent unraveling of the Socialist Federal Republic of Yugoslavia, which followed elections in 1990 that made regional leaderships ethnically accountable. The leaders of Yugoslavia's six constituent republics did not agree on the constitution for a democratic Yugoslav federation. A brief armed conflict leading to Slovenian independence gave way to a more difficult war in Croatia in the second half of 1991. In this conflict rebel Serbs seized one-third of Croatian territory with support from the Yugoslav National Army (JNA). The UN negotiator, the former U.S. Secretary of State Cyrus Vance (1917–2002) negotiated a plan that allowed approximately 14,000 UN troops to deploy to oversee the reintegration of this territory back into Croatia. Progress quickly stalled as rebel Serbs called for greater-Serb unification and refused to support implementation of the Vance Plan.

The situation in Bosnia was especially fragile, as the election of November 1990 amounted to an ethnic census in a multiethnic republic that lacked a clear, titular nation. By autumn 1991 a delicately balanced coalition government among Serb, Croat, and Bosnian Muslim parties broke down. The disputes included Bosnia's relationship to the rump Yugoslavia, the departure of the Serb Democratic Party delegation (led by Radovan Karadžić [b. 1945]), and the formation of multiple Serb Autonomous Regions with support from the JNA. By March 1991, the Croatian president, Franjo Tudjman (1922–1999), had already discussed the partition of Bosnia-Herzegovina with the Serbian president, Slobodan Milošević (1941–2006).

Several Western governments recognized the Bosnian government's declaration of independence on 6 April 1992 following a referendum that was boycotted by most Serbs in Bosnia. Bosnian Serb military forces, which were armed with weapons inherited from the JNA, launched a military campaign that rapidly captured about 70 percent of Bosnia's territory. In an attempt to homogenize Bosnia's ethnically complex social geography, the Serb military engaged in ethnic cleansing and created prisoner camps. The radical Croatian Defense Council (HVO) subsequently launched offensives in Herzegovina and central Bosnia.

**FROM DIPLOMATIC FAILURE TO DAYTON**
International negotiators were initially ineffective at ending the war. The United Nations Security Council established an arms embargo that favored the well-armed Bosnian Serb Army against the poorly equipped Army of the Republic of Bosnia-Herzegovina, created six poorly defended "safe areas" for civilians, and addressed the provision of humanitarian assistance and protection of civilians. The UN deployed twenty-six thousand lightly armed troops in the UN Protection force (UNPROFOR). These troops were scattered throughout Bosnia-Herzegovina in support of humanitarian efforts. But these troops were neither in position to compel compliance with the UN mandate nor to bring the war to a close.

In the period between 1991 and 1995 diplomats from the European Community, the United Nations, and a Contact Group consisting of the United States, Russia, Great Britain, France, and Germany drafted a series of peace plans that were based on extensive postwar power-sharing. However the Serb, Croat, and Muslim leaders were unable to reach a consensus on any of them. Only in the summer of 1995 did American diplomats take the initiative to lead the negotiations to end the war. The increasing assertiveness of Serb forces by mid-1995 culminated in the conquest of Srebrenica on 11 July. In the largest single post–World War II European massacre, more than seven thousand Muslim males were separated from their families and executed by Bosnian Serb forces under the command of General Ratko Mladić (b. 1943). In response to the subsequent NATO air intervention that lasted from 30 August until 21 September, a Bosniak-Croat offensive won back significant territory from the Bosnian Serbs, which set the stage for a cease-fire on 12 October. This also led to negotiations on the basis of "Joint Agreed Principles" that were signed in Geneva, Switzerland, on 8 September by foreign ministers from Bosnia-Herzegovina, Yugoslavia, and Croatia.

The negotiations in Dayton, Ohio, were led by the U.S. ambassador Richard Holbrooke (b. 1941) and included the secretary of state, Warren Christopher (b. 1925), and diplomats from France, Germany, the United Kingdom, Russia, and the European Union. The negotiations only peripherally involved the principals from the conflict. The three heads of delegations were the Bosnian Muslim president, Alija Izetbegović (1925–2003), the Serbian president, Milošević, and the Croatian president, Tudjman. The Bosnian Serb leaders Karadžić and Mladić did not come because they had already been indicted for war crimes by the International Criminal Tribunal for the former Yugoslavia (ICTY), and the Bosnian Croat leader, Kresimir Zubak (b. 1947), was present, but Presidents Tudjman and Milošević gave assurances that their Bosnian subordinates would sign the agreement.

## THE DAYTON ACCORDS

The three weeks of negotiations forced each party to make significant political concessions. The Serbs accepted that Republika Srpska would remain part of Bosnia. Croat hard-liners did not win a specifically Croat entity. The Bosnian Muslims accepted a decentralized state that the party that controlled 49 percent of the territory (Serbs) had gained through an aggressive war. An initial success in the negotiations, on 11 November, over the return of the Serb-controlled territory in Eastern Slavonia to Croatia set the stage for the conclusion of the agreement ten days later under great American pressure.

It was hoped that the Dayton Accords would end the fighting once and for all, facilitate a quick transition to stable rule, and restore Bosnia's multi-ethnicity. They covered all military and civilian aspects of the peace, including a constitution, and provided international military and civilian oversight of the Bosnian government in its implementation of the GFAP. The implementation succeeded in ending the fighting, but more than a decade after the Dayton Accords were signed the Bosnian government continued to prepare itself for accession into the European Union. Serbia's pathway to Europe is longer still, and blocked by the fact that Bosnian Serb leaders accused of war crimes and crimes against humanity continue to evade justice.

*See also* **Bosnia-Herzegovina; Croatia; Izetbegović, Alija; Karadžić, Radovan; Milošević, Slobodan; Mladić, Ratko; Sarajevo; Serbia; Srebrenica; Tudjman, Franjo; Yugoslavia.**

BIBLIOGRAPHY

Annan, Kofi. *Report of the Secretary General Pursuant to General Assembly Resolution 53/35 (1998): The Fall of Srebrenica.* United Nations publication A/54/549, 15 November 1999.

Burg, Steven L., and Paul S. Shoup. *The War in Bosnia-Herzegovina: Ethnic Conflict and International Intervention.* Armonk, N.Y., 1999.

Chollet, Derek. The *Road to the Dayton Accords: A Study in American Statecraft.* New York, 2005.

Gow, James. *Triumph of the Lack of Will: International Diplomacy and the Yugoslav War.* New York, 1997.

Holbrooke, Richard. *To End a War.* New York, 1998.

Office of the High Representative. "The General Framework Agreement for Peace in Bosnia and Herzegovina." Available at http://www.ohr.int/dpa/default.asp?content_id=380.

Ramet, Sabrina P. *Balkan Babel: The Disintegration of Yugoslavia from the Death of Tito to the Fall of Milošević.* Boulder, Colo., 2002.

MARK BASKIN

---

**D-DAY.** The term *D-Day* in general denotes the unnamed day on which a military offensive is to be launched. In particular, D-Day refers to 6 June 1944, the day on which the Allied forces invaded France during World War II, and to the following victory over Germany; in this connection D-Day stands for the greatest logistical achievement in military history as well.

## D-DAY IN MILITARY HISTORY

The preparations for the cross-channel invasion finally began after the Quadrant Conference at Quebec in August 1943. On 18 December 1943 Dwight D. Eisenhower became supreme Allied commander and Bernard L. Montgomery was appointed invasion commander. The plan for Operation Overlord, as the invasion was to be known, was for a landing in Normandy between Cherbourg and Le Havre. The site was chosen for three main reasons: First, the coastline was favorable to a seaborne operation, with beaches and few cliffs. Second, the landing beaches were well in range of the Allied fighter airplanes. And third, the German army high command expected an invasion at the Strait of Dover, and therefore massed its most intact divisions, including all tank divisions, in that region. To further persuade the German generals that the landings would be made north of the Seine, the Allies created an entire phantom army, said to be based around Dover in southeast England opposite the Strait of Dover and commanded by George S. Patton.

In fact, during the first six months of 1944 the United States and Great Britain gathered an impressive land, naval, and air force in the south of England, the initial landing force concentrated between Falmouth and Newhaven. This invasion force consisted of five infantry divisions: two American (the First and Fourth Divisions), two British (the Third and Fiftieth Divisions), and one Canadian (the Third Division). Seven more divisions were held in reserve. These troops were assigned to go ashore on beaches code-named, from west to east, Utah, Omaha, Gold, Juno, and Sword. Two American airborne divisions (the 82nd and the 101st) were to land behind the western end of the assault area, with one British airborne division (the Sixth) at the eastern end.

On D-Day, 6 June 1944, one day after the originally scheduled date, the Allies landed around 155,000 troops in Normandy; 57,500 Americans on the Utah and Omaha beaches; 75,000 British and Canadian soldiers on the Gold, Juno, and Sword beaches; plus nearly 23,500 British and American airborne troops. The troops had been delivered to the landing zones by an armada of nearly 900 merchant vessels and over 4,000 landing ships and landing craft, which had been marshaled and escorted by more than 1,200 naval combat ships. Some 195,700 personnel were assigned to the operation. In the air, nearly 12,000 fighter, bomber, and transport aircraft supported the landings, against which the Luftwaffe (the German air force) was able to deploy fewer than 400 planes. On this day, the Allied pilots flew over 14,000 sorties, and only 127 aircraft were lost. In the airborne landings on the flanks of the Utah and Sword beaches, more than 3,000 aircraft and gliders of the U.S. Army Air Force (USAAF) and the Royal Air Force (RAF) were used on D-Day.

By the end of 11 June (D-Day plus 5), more than 320,000 troops, nearly 55,000 vehicles, and over 100,000 tons of supplies had been landed on the beachhead. Two weeks later, the Allied troops could fall back upon nearly 200,000 vehicles and 600,000 tons of stores. Most supplies had to be landed on the beaches because the two artificial harbors, known by their code name Mulberry, were each the size of Dover harbor, and the five smaller harbors, known as Gooseberries, were not in place as scheduled. The Americans abandoned their Mulberry when a heavy storm destroyed much of the half-finished floating structure on 19 June; the British harbor (Mulberry and a Gooseberry), near Arromanches-les-Bains (Gold Beach), was not in use until July. Nevertheless, the enormous logistical effort not only enabled the Allied forces to land on the Normandy beaches but also to develop an overwhelming weight of firepower, break out of the beachhead, and then fight and win a battle of attrition against the German troops.

On the ground in mid-July, as many as thirty-one Allied divisions and numerous independent brigades, with 770,000 American soldiers and 591,000 from the British Empire, faced 420,000 German troops who had no hope of getting additional men and material. The Seventh German army had lost 117,000 troops during battle in Normandy but by 24 July had received only 10,000 reinforcements. More than 3,500 Allied tanks stood opposite 475 German panzers (tanks). And in the air, up to 13,000 Allied aircraft faced a mere 1,000 Luftwaffe airplanes. The successful invasion of the Continent on D-Day meant the foreseeable end of World War II in Europe. Logistics and reinforcements had been a major key to this great victory.

## D-DAY IN EAST AND WEST

D-Day and what followed was a great victory for the Western Allies, but not so for the Soviet Union. The former Soviet—and today Russian—attitude to the Normandy invasion has always been that the United States, Great Britain, France, and the other Western Allies have never given proper recognition to the part played by the Soviet troops in the defeat of Germany and its armies. The Soviets had always been of the opinion that they played a much bigger role in defeating Germany than the Western Allies did. Indeed, the Soviet Union lost an estimated twenty-five million citizens in World War II. By comparison, total military and civilian casualties for the United States and Great Britain are estimated at around seven hundred thousand. And in addition to this, the Soviets felt that they had been let down by their Western Allies. From the moment that the Soviet Union was attacked by the German Wehrmacht (army) on 22 June 1941, Moscow called upon its allies to open a second front against Germany. But it took three years before the invasion came off. When the Western Allies finally landed on the Normandy beaches in June 1944, the Soviets maintained that it was too late, and that as a result of this imprudent delay the war had dragged on and millions of lives, especially Russian lives, were lost unnecessarily.

Russian politicians and historians blamed that mainly on the British prime minister, Winston Churchill, whom they were convinced disliked the

**American soldiers wade ashore at Normandy under heavy German fire on D-Day, 6 June 1944.**
NATIONAL ARCHIVES AND RECORDS ADMINISTRATION

Soviet Union. This belief was bolstered by the fact that when General Eisenhower had suggested that a second front be opened in the summer or fall of 1942, President Franklin D. Roosevelt agreed, but Churchill refused. Had he agreed, and had the second front opened then, Russian officials are persuaded that World War II in Europe would have ended not later than 1943. The Soviet Union celebrated 8 May 1945 as the day the war ended, and today Russia does so as well.

The French undoubtedly admired the stunning success of the Normandy campaign. They felt relief to be free but also a touch of humiliation that rescue had come from across the Channel. Being indebted to the Americans and the British for their liberation was, and is still, hard for the Grande Nation, especially since it was so bitterly defeated by the German army in 1940.

For the Germans, D-Day was not their worst defeat. As a turning point of war, the surrender of the Sixth Army at Stalingrad counted much more, and in retrospect the bombing of the German cities was the greatest catastrophe. As a result of the Second World War, a majority of German society has developed a profound antimilitarism. Today, German conscripts often serve in the army with reluctance. The army itself, deprived of a role, has lost almost all of its self-respect, a situation for which there is no precedent in German history, not even after the defeat on D-Day.

For the Americans, the British, and the Canadians, the invasion of the Continent was the beginning of the end of the war in Europe, and it seems that today the memories of D-Day (often reduced to the Omaha Beach landing in the United States, particularly since the release of the movie *Saving Private Ryan*) are of more importance than the capitulation of Germany and the actual end of the war in Europe on 8 May 1945.

**U.S. soldiers wait in foxholes for the order to move inland during the D-Day invasion, 1944.** GETTY IMAGES

## POSTWAR COMMEMORATIONS

Not surprisingly, ceremonies commemorating the anniversaries of the Allied landings in Normandy were held every year. Usually, celebrating D-Day was a private event; some veterans of the invasion met in Normandy and remembered the heavy fighting. But in the later years of the twentieth century, the D-Day commemoration had become more and more part of world politics. The fortieth anniversary in 1984 was overshadowed by political conflict between the Western democracies and the Soviet Union over Soviet missiles that were threatening Western Europe. For that reason, D-Day was celebrated as triumph of democracy. In his address at the Normandy invasion ceremony at Omaha Beach, President Ronald Reagan underlined the cause of freedom for which so many gave so much. The president pointed out that, when the Allied forces marched into Germany, they came not to prey on a brave and defeated people, but to nurture the seeds of democracy among those who yearned to be free again. He reaffirmed the unity of democratic peoples who fought a war and then joined with the vanquished in a firm resolve to keep the peace. Furthermore, the president made it clear that the Western democracies would always be prepared, so they might always be free. Ten years later, the fiftieth anniversary of D-Day was celebrated as a triumph of the Western Allies over Germany, and over the former Soviet Union as well, as the president of Russia had not been invited to Normandy. Because the British and French leaders at that time, Prime Minister Margaret Thatcher and President François Mitterrand, had been very skeptical about German reunification (which took place in 1990), the commemoration ceremonies demonstrated the power, not of the United States, but of the European Allies Britain and France, to the now-reunited Germany.

The sixtieth anniversary of D-Day had to cope with differences between the Western Allies—the United States and Britain on one side, France on the other—over the Iraq war. The ultimate message of the day was that modern leaders have to honor what the troops who took part in the Normandy landings died for by standing together in the cause of freedom and democracy. President George W. Bush took the opportunity to strengthen the ties between the United States and Europe, saying that the Allies were bound together by the sacrifices that were made on D-Day to help liberate the European continent. The President emphasized that the alliance was strong and was still needed. It was the first time that a Russian president and a German chancellor had been invited to a D-Day ceremony. The intended message to the (Islamic) world was: Franco-German reconciliation shows that hatred has no future and there is always a road to peace.

## D-DAY AND EUROPEAN-AMERICAN RELATIONS

D-Day has always had a special meaning for the Western Allies of World War II because it represented a huge common struggle, as President Franklin D. Roosevelt put it in his D-Day prayer, "to preserve our Republic, our religion, and our civilization, and to set free a suffering humanity." There have been, there are, and there will be (as in every relationship), differences between the United States and Europe, based on different views of politics, economics, culture, religion, and philosophy. But D-Day offers both sides a chance to put current differences aside. The shared commemoration of the Normandy invasion in which Germany, the previous enemy, is now included serves to remind Europeans and Americans of their common values and accomplishments. D-Day ultimately has become a symbol of the transatlantic alliance.

See also **Warfare; World War II.**

BIBLIOGRAPHY

*Primary Sources*

Bryant, Arthur, Sir. *Triumph in the West, 1943–1946: Based on the Diaries and Autobiographical Notes of Field Marshal the Viscount Alanbrooke.* London, 1959.

Eisenhower, Dwight D. *Crusade in Europe.* Garden City, N.Y., 1948. Classic memoirs of the commander of the European Theater of Operations.

*Secondary Sources*

Boog, Horst. "Invasion to Surrender: The Defence of Germany." In *World War II in Europe: The Final Year,* edited by Charles F. Brower, 115–140. New York, 1998. Study of the war in the West from the German point of view.

Chandler, David G., and James Lawton Collins, Jr. *The D-Day-Encyclopedia.* New York, 1994.

Hall, Tony, ed. *D-Day, Operation Overlord: From Its Planning to the Liberation of Paris.* London, 1993. Very useful collection of articles.

Keegan, John. *Six Armies in Normandy: From D-Day to the Liberation of Paris.* London, 1982; rev., 1994. Detailed and innovative study of the Normandy campaign.

Overy, Richard J. *Why the Allies Won.* London, 1995. The study stresses the importance of technological innovation and structural responsiveness in winning World War II.

Vogel, Detlef. "German and Allied Conduct of the War in the West." In *Germany and the Second World War,* Vol. 7: *The Strategic Air War in Europe and the War in the West and East Asia, 1943–1944/45,* edited by Horst Boog, Gerhard Krebs, and Detlef Vogel. Oxford, U.K., 2006. Official German history of the Second World War, in translation.

JÜRGEN LUH

---

# DEATH PENALTY.

Hundreds of books and articles have focused on the political and judicial aspects of the death penalty. However, few historical studies have been devoted to the theme. Debates between abolitionists, retentionists, and supporters of the death penalty, national investigations into the social profile of people condemned to death, and the pardon policies and execution practices of states remain largely unstudied.

## WAVES OF ABOLITION FOR ORDINARY CRIME

During the nineteenth century many countries maintained the death penalty for capital offences, especially murder. At the beginning of the twentieth century, the main trend in European criminal law was the progressive abolition of the death penalty for murder (see figure 1).

**FIGURE 1**

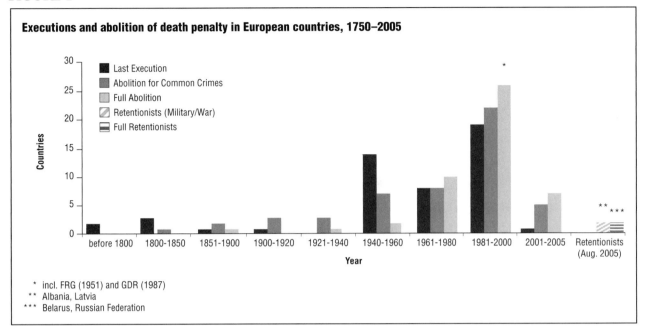

Executions and abolition of death penalty in European countries, 1750–2005

* incl. FRG (1951) and GDR (1987)
** Albania, Latvia
*** Belarus, Russian Federation

The first country to abolish capital punishment for ordinary crime was Portugal in 1867, soon followed by the Netherlands, Romania, Italy, and Norway. After World War I, they were joined by Sweden, Denmark, and Switzerland, all neutral countries during the war. The period 1918–1950 constituted a break in the abolition process. Dictatorial states reintroduced the death penalty. The Italian Rocco code in 1930, German codification under the Nazi regime, Spain under Francisco Franco (1892–1975), and Portugal under Antonio de Oliveira Salazar (1889–1970) introduced capital punishment for ordinary crimes. Having abolished the death penalty for ordinary crime in 1917, the USSR reintroduced this "supreme measure of social defense" in 1920.

After World War II, the fall of the fascist dictatorships was accompanied by the abandonment of capital punishment in Italy (1944) and in the Federal Republic of Germany (1949). People's democracies under the supervision of the USSR reintroduced the death penalty in the ordinary justice system, not only for murder but also for economic crimes and used it essentially as a way of purging political opponents. At the end of the 1980s, the collapse of Soviet domination of Eastern European countries led to the rapid abolition of the death penalty in criminal codes. A moratorium on executions was proclaimed in the German Democratic Republic in 1987, in Romania in 1989 after the execution of Nicolae Ceauşescu (1918–1989), in Hungary and the former Czechoslovakia in 1990, and afterward in many former communist countries, except Belarus and the Russian Federation.

## DEATH PENALTY IN "EXCEPTIONAL" CIRCUMSTANCES

However, many countries, while proclaiming themselves abolitionists in civil matters, maintained the death penalty for military crimes or for state security concerns. Generally speaking, Europe in the first half of the twentieth century had been the setting for an upsurge in public executions, a consequence of the two world wars and occupations, involving a harshening of military law against soldiers and an extension of military law to civilians.

***War and military court executions*** During World War I, armies at war used the death penalty against their own soldiers. Provisional figures show that 346 Commonwealth soldiers were executed for capital offenses (306 from the United Kingdom, 25 Canadians, 10 Australians, and 5 from New Zealand); nearly 600 in the French army (430 in 1914–1915 and 45 during the mutinies of 1917); 48 in the

TABLE 1

**Afterwar political retribution: Death sentences and executions in some European countries (1944-1950)**

| | Estimated Population (1950)+ | Death sentences | Executions | Execution rate (100 verdicts) | Execution rate (100000 h.) | Verdict rate (100000 h.) |
|---|---|---|---|---|---|---|
| Norway | 3,265,000 | 65 | 37 | 57% | 1.13 | 1.99 |
| Denmark | 4,271,000 | 78 | 46 | 59% | 1.08 | 1.83 |
| Netherlands | 1,011,400 | 152 | 40 | 26% | 0.40 | 1.50 |
| Belgium | 8,639,000 | 2,940 | 242 | 8% | 2.80 | 34.03 |
| France* | 41,829,000 | 7,037 | 1,536 | 22% | 3.67 | 16.82 |
| Italy** | 47,105,000 | 5,000 | 50 | 10% | 0.11 | 10.61 |
| Austria | 6,935,000 | 43 | 30 | 70% | 0.43 | 0.62 |
| Hungary | 9,338,000 | 322 | 146 | 45% | 1.56 | 3.45 |
| Czech Provinces | 8,925,000 | 723 | 686 | 95% | 7.69 | 8.10 |
| Slovakia | 3,460,000 | 65 | 27 | 42% | 0.78 | 1.88 |
| Bulgaria | 7,250,000 | 2,618 | 1,576 | 60% | 21.74 | 36.11 |

* estimated figures: add around 9,000 summary executions

** estimated figures: add around 10,000 summary executions

SOURCES: + US Census, international database; Déak, Gross, Judt, *The Politics of Retribution*, p.301; Frommer, *National Cleansing*, p.91.

German army; 750 in Italy; and in Belgium, 12 soldiers and 4 Belgian and 4 German citizens.

Based on a systematic study of British files, Gerry Oram's study *Worthless Men: Race, Eugenics, and the Death Penalty in the British Army during the First World War* (1998) confirms that the purpose of military law was not to achieve justice but rather to maintain discipline in the army. Yet the army's policy on discipline and the death penalty varied greatly between the different divisions. French executions after the mutinies of 1917 are put in a broader perspective in *Fusillés pour l'exemple, 1914–1915* (2003), André Bach's study of French military executions in 1914 and 1915. Bach underlines the fact that after the massive executions of 1914–1915 the French parliament passed an act limiting the excesses of military justice with regard to executions, which contributed to mitigating the repression after the 1917 mutinies. In occupied countries like Belgium and northern France, 332 suspected spies (including Edith Cavell) and members of intelligence networks were executed by German martial courts despite the Hague Convention. In Britain, eleven German spies were shot at the Tower of London. After the Easter Rising in Ireland, at least fifteen Irishmen were executed by a martial court. The last one, Roger David Casement (1864–1916), was found guilty of high treason by the Central Criminal Court (Old Bailey) and hanged. This last case is a reminder that a state of war paves the way for using the death penalty against civilians.

In World War II, during the military action, every belligerent nation used the death penalty against its own soldiers in cases of treason, espionage, or desertion. During the period 1941 to 1953, forty-seven soldiers were sentenced to death and executed by British courts-martial, and twenty people were executed under the 1940 Treachery Act or the High Treason Act. According to various sources, the U.S. army executed between seventy and ninety-six soldiers during the European campaign, while the German army executed between thirteen thousand and fifteen thousand individuals during the war.

*Occupations, civil wars, and dictatorships* In civil wars and military occupations, capital punishment and execution of civilians are utilized in a similar way. The traditional distinction between civilians and the military was seriously challenged in the first half of the twentieth century in Europe by the massacres of the so-called franc-tireurs in August 1914 in the west and the pogroms in the troubled years of 1917–1921 in the east, as well as the civil war in Finland. During the Finnish civil war (1918) nine thousand people were killed in action, and eighty-nine hundred were executed or murdered, while twelve thousand died in prison camps. The same situation applied to the Spanish civil war (1936–1939) and the Greek civil war (1944–1949). Dictatorships focused on controlling their minorities. In the USSR, after the assassination of Sergei Kirov (1886–1934), the decree of 1 December 1934 created an exceptional procedure with a direct death sentence for "terrorism," paving the way for the Great Terror. In 1937–1938, nearly half of the 1,575,000 civil servants, scientists, intellectuals, and clergymen arrested, that is, 681,692 people, may have been executed. The death penalty was also used by a special military court in order to purge the officers of the Red Army. Nazi Germany preferred direct action against "political opponents"—such as *Kristallnacht* (Night of Broken Glass; November 1938), when Jewish-owned businesses throughout Germany were ransacked and destroyed—and it developed a network of concentration and extermination camps as "alternatives to the death penalty."

Continental Europe under Nazi rule (1939–1945) was characterized by the upsurge in illegal and extralegal "executions" performed by special units such as the Einsatzgruppen (Special Action Groups) in eastern Europe or the collaborators' milices in western occupied countries. After 1942 both civil and military courts handed down capital sentences and ordered the execution of so-called bandits, terrorists, and resistance fighters. In 1944–1945 the German "Volksgerichte" executed 8,500 Germans as political dissenters or those suspected of defeatism following summary trials.

***Political retribution*** After World War I, France and Belgium's courts condemned people to death for "uncivil behavior," but not a single execution was performed. War crimes remained largely unprosecuted by international courts. The introduction of unprescribed crimes in 1944 paved the way for international political repression. The International Military Tribunal in Nuremberg prosecuted twenty-four accused (one committed suicide before the trial, another was not tried due to health reasons). Out of the twenty-two defendants, twenty-one were convicted and one was acquitted. On Monday, 30 September 1946, twelve were sentence to death; ten were executed. One had been tried in absentia, and his remains were found later; another committed suicide after sentencing.

In various countries, members of the military who had committed war crimes and "collaborators" who had committed murder were sentenced to death by various ad hoc courts. There were disparities in summary executions (around nine thousand in France, ten to fifteen thousand in Italy), but even state policies of sentencing and execution varied considerably. In the former Axis countries, Germany, Italy, and Austria, a special court for "denazification" issued death sentences. In Austria, the Volksgerichte sentenced forty-three people to death, of whom thirty were executed. In Italy, out of five thousand to ten thousand death sentences, forty to fifty people were executed. French Cours de Justice handed out 6,763 death sentences, with 767 or 791 executions, but at least 769 executions performed by courts-martial and military tribunals should be added to this). In the Netherlands, Belgium, and Norway the death penalty was reintroduced or reactivated, resulting in 152 sentences and forty executions in the Netherlands, and 2,940 sentences and 242 executions in Belgium by 1950, by firing squad. In Norway, thirty-seven out of sixty-five death sentences were carried out against Norwegians and Germans; in Denmark, forty-six out of seventy-eight. In Hungary, the people's courts handed down 322 death sentences up until March 1948, of which 146 were performed, in the Czech provinces, 686 out of 723, in Slovakia 27 out of 65, and in Bulgaria 1,576 out of the 2,618 sentenced to death. Even in "neutral countries," military courts handed down death penalties. In Switzerland, seventeen of the thirty-three people condemned to death in 1939 and 1945 were executed. In summary, combining sentencing and execution rates shows that some countries developed a stiff legal retribution policy (Bulgaria and Belgium), others were more lenient (Austria, Italy, and the Netherlands).

## EUROPEAN COLONIES AND THE DEATH PENALTY

A persistent black hole in the history of the death penalty is its use in European colonies. In German Southwest Africa (present-day Namibia), capital punishment was used by the Germans among the Hereros. In the Kenya Protectorate, the British executed 1,090 suspected Mau Mau fighters. In addition to traditional capital punishment cases (murder and rape), the death penalty was applied to political offenses and witchcraft. Belgians used public hanging against blacks convicted in the Belgian Congo until the 1950s. For the European colonial powers, the utilization of capital punishment as both a penal and a political tool reveals the

**Protestors demonstate against the planned execution of a condemned prisoner outside Wandsworth prison, London, 1935.** ©HULTON-DEUTSCH COLLECTION/CORBIS

dichotomy between an empire's desire to pursue a civilizing mission and create "citizens" and its need to control "native subjects" (e.g., South Africa). Decolonization processes coincided with the progressive abandonment of the death penalty by Western European countries.

After World War II, international organizations like the United Nations, the Council of Europe, and the European Union placed the question of capital punishment in the context of human rights and promoted the suppression of death penalties in the legal systems of their affiliated states, thus enshrining the victory of abolitionists in European countries. In 1994 the Council of Europe made the abolition of the death penalty a preliminary condition for any country wishing to join it. In 1998 the European Union decided that the abolition of capital punishment was a precondition for membership, stressing that "the death penalty has no place in the penal systems of modern civilized societies."

*See also* **Chemin des Dames/Mutinies; Collaboration; Colonialism; Crime and Justice; Denazification; Einsatzgruppen; Nuremberg War Crimes Trials; Occupation, Military; War Crimes.**

BIBLIOGRAPHY

Babington, Anthony. *For the Sake of Example: Capital Courts-Martial, 1914–1920.* London, 1983.

Bach, André. *Fusillés pour l'exemple, 1914–1915.* Paris, 2003.

Council of Europe. *The Death Penalty: Abolition in Europe.* Strasbourg, France, 1999.

Courtois, Stéphane, Nicolas Werth, Jean-Louis Panné, et al. *The Black Book of Communism: Crimes, Terror, Repression.* Translated by Jonathan Murphy and Mark Kramer; consulting editor, Mark Kramer. Cambridge, Mass., 1999. Translation of *Le livre noir du Communisme: Crimes, terreur, et répression* (1997).

Deák, István, Jan Gross, and Tony Judt, eds. *The Politics of Retribution in Europe: World War II and Its Aftermath.* Princeton, N.J., 2000.

Evans, Richard J. *Rituals of Retribution: Capital Punishment in Germany, 1600–1987.* Oxford, U.K., 1996.

Frommer, Benjamin. *National Cleansing: Retribution against Nazi Collaborators in Postwar Czechoslovakia.* New York, 2005.

Mikhlin, Alexander S. *The Death Penalty in Russia.* Translation with a foreword by W. E. Butler. London, 1999.

Oram, Gerard. *Worthless Men: Race, Eugenics, and the Death Penalty in the British Army during the First World War.* London, 1998.

Takala, Hannu, and Henrik Tham, eds. *Crime and Control in Scandinavia during the Second World War.* Oslo, 1989.

XAVIER ROUSSEAUX

# DEBUSSY, CLAUDE (1862–1918), French composer.

Achille-Claude Debussy was born in Saint-Germain-en-Laye, France, on 22 August 1862. He may be considered one of the foremost composers in Western music of the concert hall, and he influenced church, film, and jazz music. Debussy's family was unstable, and he received no formal education of importance. He attended the Conservatoire de Paris from 1872 to 1884, studying composition with Ernest Guiraud (1837–1892) and organ briefly with César Franck (1822–1890). Debussy won the coveted Prix de Rome for composition in 1884 and traveled to Rome for intensive study, but as a cultural rebel he despaired of what he considered an outmoded musical language among the academicians. The 1889 Exposition Universelle in Paris enabled him to hear authentic Asian music, and with that his feeling for polyphonic sonority caught fire. In the 1890s he lived the bohemian life in Paris with Gaby Dupont (1866–1945), appreciating the iconoclastic spirit of the cabaret, and

indulged a profusion of decadent impulses, ranging from Rosicrucianism to the esoteric sensuality of Pierre Louÿs (1870–1925), whose 1899 *Chansons de Bilitis* he set to music. Debussy left Gaby to marry Lilly Texier that year, but in 1904 he began life with Emma Moïse Bardac (1862–1934), a beautiful and artistic woman of wealth. In 1905 Emma and Debussy divorced their spouses. Their daughter, Emma-Claude, the composer's only child was born in 1905; they married in 1908. A sometime conductor and pungent critic, Debussy often struggled to make ends meet but was aided by his publisher, Jacques Durand (1865–1928).

Arguably the most important compositions of Debussy's youth were the opera scene in Théodore de Banville's *Diane au bois* (1886; Diana of the wood) and the lyric poem for voices and orchestra *La damoiselle élue* (1888; Blessed damozel), after Dante Gabriel Rossetti; both show Debussy's early Pre-Raphaelite sensibility. His orchestral *Prélude à l'après-midi d'un faune* (1894; Prelude to the afternoon of a faun) was written in response to a poem by Stéphane Mallarmé and has become his most-heard composition. Its coordination of tone color as an agent in structure, ambivalence toward conventional use of themes, and revolutionary tonal language led the way in twentieth-century modernism. The revolutionary if "noiseless" opera *Pelléas et Mélisande* (1893–1902) was received with enthusiasm by young moderns such as Maurice Ravel (1875–1937) but was disparaged by the old guard for its unconventional lyricism, which seemed to turn traditional opera on its head. This symbolist opera established Debussy as the foremost avant-garde musician in France in the early part of the century, and its structure includes leitmotifs derived from Richard Wagner (1813–1883) but absorbed within a compositional method altogether his own. Debussy's *Trois Nocturnes* (Three nocturnes) for orchestra of 1899; his "symphonic sketches" *La mer* (1905; The sea); the 1913 ballet *Jeux* (Games); pathbreaking piano sets including the Japanese-flavored *Estampes*, the *Images,* and twenty-four *Preludes* for piano; and song sets on texts by Banville, Paul Verlaine, and Mallarmé: all confirmed the composer's standing. Of these, some commentators argue that *La mer* signals the creative high point of his career.

Debussy left an indelible mark for all succeeding composers with his psychologically evocative harmonies, alternately tonal (modal, pentatonic, octatonic, or mixed) or chromatic (in a way, following Richard Wagner). Critics also point to the *Douze Études* (Twelve Études) for piano (1915), which, unlike the vast majority of Debussy's works, convey no extra-musical associations, but instead pose abstract technical problems.

An early biographer, Louis Laloy, said insightfully that Debussy learned more from poets and painters than from musicians. Thus the composer responded to the impressionism of the painters Claude Monet (1840–1926) and Edgar Degas (1834–1917) by combining the strength of his design with an apparent spontaneity and sensuality. Debussy used stream of consciousness and abhorred anything blatant, a stance that recalled the symbolist poets as well, and with them he was moved by Wagner's depth psychology and interconnections among the arts. Debussy anticipated the harsh, dark emotions of the central European expressionists, whose sensibilities he shares, and who haunt parts of the opera *Pelléas* Debussy sketched with its settings of Edgar Allan Poe's *Fall of the House of Usher* and *Devil in the Belfry*. French folk song, nationalist and ethnic influences from the Orient, Spain, and Russia, and African American music figure in his kaleidoscopic but exquisitely structured idiom.

Debussy the modernist was constantly evolving stylistically, surpassing and frequently confusing even his admirers; in his inclusivism and in his challenge to expected evolution in musical history, he anticipated postmodernism. A reference to the French classical traditions of Jean-Philippe Rameau (1683–1764) and François Couperin (1668–1733), emphasizing clarity and the modification of old forms, occupied certain works, from his youth to the end of his life, notably in the incomplete set of chamber sonatas of 1918. Even the world of childhood and its simplicity marked his music, as in the 1908 piano suite *Children's Corner,* dedicated to his young daughter, "Chouchou." He defended Mediterranean values vigorously as World War I proceeded and remarked that certain of his last works were an offering to France's war effort, such as songs based on the poetry of François Villon (1431–1463?) and Charles d'Orléans (1391–1465).

As obscure a forum as the (Indiana) *Daleville Journal,* in announcing his death in April 1918, recognized Debussy's role as the twentieth-century progenitor in music: "His work was not understood or even liked by all, but the world will not forget who led the way."

*See also* **Expressionism; Modernism.**

BIBLIOGRAPHY

Briscoe, James. *Claude Debussy: A Guide to Research.* New York, 1990.

Briscoe, James R., ed. *Debussy in Performance.* New Haven, Conn., 1999.

Howat, Roy. *Debussy in Proportion: A Musical Analysis.* Cambridge, U.K., 1986.

Lockspeiser, Edward. *Debussy: His Life and Mind.* 2 vols. London, 1962–1965. Cambridge, U.K., 1978.

———. *Debussy.* 5th rev. ed. London, 1980.

Parks, Richard S. *The Music of Claude Debussy.* New Haven, Conn., 1990.

Smith, Richard Langham, ed. *Debussy Studies.* Cambridge, U.K., 1997.

Trezise, Simon, ed. *The Cambridge Companion to Debussy.* Cambridge, U.K., 2003.

JAMES R. BRISCOE

**DECOLONIZATION.** The term *decolonization* took on its current meanings in the mid-twentieth century, when vast European overseas empires, largely built or consolidated in the late nineteenth century, existed and then almost completely disappeared. For this reason, *decolonization* usually refers to the end of direct European control of non-European territories and implies both a chronological period and a process. Some scholars date the beginning of this period from the British agreement in 1922 to restore the authority of the monarchy in Egypt, although it is more usually thought of as beginning at midnight 15 August 1947, with Indian and Pakistani independence. The end of British rule in Kenya in 1963 closed the five-year high point of decolonization, when over thirty European dependencies became independent states, although the independence of Portuguese colonies in 1974 was certainly part of the same larger cycle. Most commentators agree on including the end of white-minority rule of Rhodesia (now Zimbabwe) in 1979, while there is some debate about whether the disappearance of apartheid in South Africa (and of South African rule over what became Namibia) fits within the same narrative.

A number of scholars claim that the period of decolonization ended in 1997, when the United Kingdom returned Hong Kong to China. Activists, politicians, and scholars, however, also have invoked the decolonization process to describe other ongoing efforts—besides changes in sovereignty—to break with what they view as variants of colonialism, in fields like economics, language policy, human rights, literary criticism, and the writing of history. Events in central and Eastern Europe and the former Soviet Union since 1989 have encouraged further interrogations about whether the process of decolonization is necessarily linked to overseas colonies, while developments since 2001 in places like Afghanistan and Iraq have raised questions about why we presumed that the period of decolonization signaled the end of colonial empires. Such debates have emphasized that decolonization played a central role in the post-1945 history of Europe in general, and of Europe's former colonial powers in particular. They also remind us that one effect of decolonization was to obscure that role—as well as the decisive contribution of colonialism to European modernity.

### THE CAUSE OF DECOLONIZATION

What caused the post-1945 collapse of various types of formal control by European states over overseas territories and peoples remains a subject of intense scholarly debate. Certain historians focus on how anticolonial nationalists won struggles for national liberation, overcoming the resistance of the colonizers. Others propose, to the contrary, that colonial authorities in most cases pursued a "transfer of power" over state institutions to local interlocutors, relying on negotiations, collaboration, and occasionally confrontation to impose the most amenable outcome possible. Each theory explains, in general terms, certain cases: for example, Palestine/Israel (1948), Burma (1948), Vietnam (1945–1975), and Algeria (1962), the former, or India/Pakistan and most of French

sub-Saharan Africa (1960), the latter. Analyses of changing international political and economic conditions, however, have made clear the limits of heroic narratives, which describe how visionary nationalist leaders carried the day. Such partial explanations served more to establish or comfort postindependence political legitimacy in former dependencies than to describe pre-independence realities. Similarly, archival studies in the imperial home countries (or "metropoles") and on the ground of the conditions and terms under which "transfer" actually happened make the rational-actor model on which it depends untenable. European leaders, in particular Charles de Gaulle (1890–1970) of France and Harold Macmillan (1894–1986) of Great Britain, actively fabricated (most obviously in their memoirs) the extent to which they had precipitated events that, in fact, had been imposed on them.

A number of historians argue that the economics of empire became too costly for metropolitan politicians and voters to bear. After 1945 the need to invest in welfare states, refocus armed forces around nuclear weapons, and rebuild international prestige through novel policies supposedly made expenditures on old-style empires unfashionable as well as untenable. The French Empire, with its geographic focus in vast underpopulated and inaccessible regions of sub-Saharan Africa, had always required significant levels of state spending, which grew exponentially after the post–World War II establishment of the French Union. In the same period, British expenses also began to overtake gains. Retrospectively reasonable, such arguments do not reflect what decision-makers argued at the time. It is noteworthy, for example, that in 1956 a well-known French journalist, Raymond Cartier, used economic arguments to advocate French withdrawal from sub-Saharan Africa. As Cartier opined: "Black Africa for us is, like everything, a ledger. What is it worth? What does it cost? What does it offer? What hopes does it inspire? What sacrifices is it worth?" (quoted in Shepard, p. 38). Yet it is more important that almost nobody in France took up what were called *cartiériste* explanations. For Conservative British ministers in the 1950s, "prestige and economics," in the historian Frank Heinlein's words, "were rather intimately linked" (p. 88). They were convinced that pulling out of their costly West African colonies would give

**Indian workers, followers of Mohandas Gandhi, protest British rule through nonviolent means by lying on the ground in front of their workplace, April 1930.** ©BETTMANN/CORBIS

an impression of weakness that would lead to unstoppable decline, with catastrophic consequences for Britain's well-being. For similar reasons, all European colonial powers actively resisted giving up their empires until decolonization brought them to an end; decolonization occurred, in part, as previously convincing arguments for empire came to seem unimaginable.

## GENEALOGY OF THE TERM
*DECOLONIZATION*

While attempts to identify causes remain contentious, scholars have reached wide agreement around the use of the term *decolonization* to describe what happened. The word seems to have first appeared in an 1836 French-language tract, "Decolonization of Algiers," in which the journalist Henri Fonfrède calls on the kingdom of France to end the six-year-old occupation of territory in North Africa. Liberal anticolonialists in Great Britain and on the Continent continued to use the term through the 1850s; with the rise of the new imperialism, however, it disappeared from

circulation. In the late 1920s, a few social scientists and communists began to employ the term *decolonization*. They did so either to analyze how British efforts to expand self-rule in India contributed toward the coming of an international proletarian revolution (a theory that the Sixth Congress of the Communist International condemned in 1928), or to assess such developments as signs of the decline of the West. On 14 June 1927, for example, the term *decolonization* appeared for the first time in the *Times* of London in a report on a speech by the Belgian scholar Henri Rolin, titled "Development of Colonies: Native Advance to Self-Government," while in 1926 the Indian Communist leader Manabendra Nath Roy used the word to describe the British policy of granting concessions to bourgeois Indian nationalists (*The Future of Indian Politics*). In both cases, the term did not imply independence. The work of Moritz Bonn, a proponent of the decline argument, finally imposed the word *decolonization* among European scholars. Indeed, a number of historians, following Bonn himself, mistakenly identify the German economist empires," as well as designations that appear mainly in archived documents, like the British Colonial Office's use of "constitutional advances," or the India Office's evocations in the 1930s of "diarchy" and in 1945–1947 of "demission." Contemporary anticolonial critics proposed numerous names as well. In the 1950s, the Senegalese essayist and historian Abdoulaye Ly described what he saw happening as "a ring of fire burning all along the Tropics," while in 1956 the French anthropologist Georges Balandier referred to "the insurrection of poor and dominated peoples," in order to argue that "this is the event that defines the twentieth century." It was in French that the word *decolonization* first began to circulate widely. French-language writers regularly began to invoke decolonization in reference to the Algerian Revolution (1954–1962), and to a far lesser extent the independence of French sub-Saharan colonies (1957–1958) and the Belgian Congo (1961). In popularizing it, they changed the term's meaning.

The most influential commentator was the revolutionary theorist Frantz Fanon, in the articles and books he wrote while working with the Algerian National Liberation Front (FLN). Like earlier writers, Fanon used *decolonization* to describe specific situations in particular colonized territories (he usually discussed "decolonizations"). Unlike them, however, he believed that the Algerian Revolution demonstrated that such movements were immediately necessary and were the only hope for true human progress. Situating the people he described as "the colonized" in the history-making role that Marxists assigned to "the proletariat," Fanon summoned the "wretched of the earth" to take action. Radical critics like Fanon claimed that struggles for decolonizations could expose the violence and oppression inherent in the emergence of Europe's modern imperialist nation-states. Fanon also predicted that they might portend the birth of a new era when "the last shall be first." This did not occur. Many scholars today employ the term *decolonization* to indicate merely the end of European states' formal colonial empires, whatever cause they may attribute it to. Others, however, use it to explore and critique the gaps between what happened in terms of national sovereignty and what was hoped for in terms of freedom.

**Demonstrators protest the French occupation in the Fez Medina quarter of Rabat, Morocco, 1954.**
©BETTMANN/CORBIS

as the inventor of the term. By the 1950s, European and American scholars and politicians hesitantly applied it to describe specific shifts of sovereignty in particular territories. Like the French ethnologist Henri Labouret, who in 1952 published the first book with *decolonization* in its title (*Colonisation, colonialisme, décolonisation*), most Western scholars argued that such developments were wrongheaded, at least in the short term, and could be avoided through wise political choices made in Europe's imperial capitals. In English, the word itself remained rather technical and little used. The second appearance of the term in the *Times* of London, for example, was in August 1958, while it first showed up in the *New York Times* (twice) in 1959.

Since then, however, *decolonization* has subsumed other descriptions of what happened to European overseas empires after 1945, some widely used, such as the aforementioned "national liberation" and the "transfer of power," or the "end of

In analyzing decolonization in European history, not only does each of these interpretations remain available to scholars: from the end of World War II through the end of the Cold War, these distinct understandings of what was happening and, more important, the certainty that something dramatic was happening invested decolonization with crucial and multiple roles. European histories of decolonization, that is, are at once analyses of one of the twentieth century's foundational "events," and windows into how an array of extremely diverse phenomena together came to be considered as an event: a coherent process with wide-ranging implications that took place in a specific period. Understanding how this second development happened helps explain why, paradoxically, the enormous changes that anticolonial activists, ideas, and the end of formal colonialism sparked in Europe anchored the myth that modern European history happened only in Europe, and not also in the relationships Europeans have had with the rest of the world.

## POST-1945 HISTORICAL CONTEXTS OF DECOLONIZATION

At the end of World War II, two developments placed the question of colonialism—and whether it could continue—at the heart of European concerns. The first was the success of anticolonial nationalists in South and Southeast Asia ("Monsoon Asia") and the Middle East, who confronted their colonizers with demands for immediate independence. The second was the new shape of world power politics that emerged from World War II, namely the Cold War and the sharp decline in the influence of Europe's colonial powers. The first development produced a cascade of independence days across colonized Asia between 1947 and 1949, events that made imaginable the idea that the decolonization of certain colonial dependencies would lead to outright independence. Officials, however, still refused to consider the possibility that all but a few colonies would soon become independent. Within a decade, the need for the "decolonization" of virtually every colony had become a widely invoked argument; by 1965 the imminent completion of what now appeared to be a stage of historical progress appeared obvious.

***The end of colonial rule in Monsoon Asia and the Middle East*** Between 1942 and 1949, nationalists in Monsoon Asia and the formerly Ottoman Arab Middle East used, in various combinations, mass actions, international pressure, armed struggle—or the possibility of armed struggle—and the weak position of their colonial overlords to quickly obtain independence over all or part of the territory they claimed as their own. British India, by far the largest and richest European colony, provided the model. Already, the nationalist Indian National Congress had succeeded during the interwar period in extending its base of support well beyond its Western-looking urban core. This had allowed the party to take advantage of British reforms, which accepted the broadening of self-rule in certain colonial dependencies in the hopes of preventing any threat to British control over what mattered to them. Alfred Milner (1854–1925), one of the preeminent British imperialists of the era, used the phrase "Why worry about the rind if we can obtain the fruit?" to explain his support for meeting anticolonial protests with the extension of local control over purely internal questions. The "fruit" he referred to was control over foreign policy and external trade.

World War II offered leaders of the Congress an opportunity to again highlight the hypocrisy of British resistance to Indian independence. The conflict also provided a context in which their attempts to put pressure on colonial authorities proved particularly effective. In September 1939, when Viceroy Linlithgow (Victor Alexander John Hope) declared that India, too, was at war with Britain's enemies, the Congress responded by arguing that "India cannot associate itself in any war said to be for democratic freedom when that very freedom is denied her," requesting instead a clear statement of the British government's war aims and immediate and significant moves toward self rule. Throughout the war, the Congress pursued mass protests in support of these demands, and by 1942 the British had agreed to establish full self-government when the war ended; this eventually led to the establishment of two republics, India and Pakistan. With relatively little conflict, and with the active collaboration of conservative local politicians, the United States of America granted the Philippines independence in 1946,

**Congolese prime minister Patrice Lumumba and Belgian premier Gaston Eskens sign the act of independence, Leopoldville, June 1960.** ©BETTMANN/CORBIS

and the British gave up sovereignty over Ceylon (later Sri Lanka) in 1948. In 1943 the Free French government recognized Lebanese independence, while in 1946 the British recognized the full sovereignty of the government of Transjordan (present-day Jordan). In both British Burma and the Dutch East Indies, the transition was more conflictual. After the Japanese defeat, and in relatively short order, the nationalist leaders Aung San, in Burma (1948), and Ahmed Sukarno, in Indonesia (1949), used the political authority and armed relays they had developed during the war (with Japanese assistance) to force their European suzerains to recognize their country's independence. In Indonesia, these efforts proved particularly difficult, as Dutch forces launched an aggressive military campaign to destroy the Indonesian Republic that nationalists

had proclaimed in 1945. Only strong U.S. pressure led the Dutch to agree to independence. In Syria, the French responded with massive military force to large-scale demonstrations that nationalists had organized against French rule in May 1945, demonstrations meant to coincide with the end of the antifascist war in Europe. (Similar demonstrations and even more severe repression began in French Algeria on V-E Day [8 May 1945].) In this case, international pressure (the British prime minister Winston Churchill threatened to invade) forced the French to end fighting, recognize Syrian independence, and withdraw their troops in April 1946. The newly formed United Nations, which had called on the French to evacuate Syria in February 1946, soon was deeply involved in developments in neighboring Palestine. Unable to stop

Zionist violence against Arab civilians, British institutions, and personnel—and under intense pressure from the U.S. president Harry S. Truman to accept the establishment of a Jewish homeland—the British handed over control of their League of Nations mandate in Palestine to the United Nations. When the British pulled out on 14 May 1948, Zionist leaders proclaimed the State of Israel, which was attacked by its Arab neighbors the next day in the name of anticolonialism. By 1949, when all the states involved had signed armistices, Israel had emerged victorious, no Arab state had emerged in Palestine, and some seven hundred thousand Arab refugees had been forced to leave their homes.

***The Cold War and anticolonialism*** After 1945 there were only two great powers, the United States and the USSR, and both claimed to oppose colonialism. Each had strong ideological and historical reasons for its opposition. The Soviet Union's self-definition as a worker's state guided by Marxist-Leninist principles connected it to many of the most influential anticolonial activists and movements; Vladimir Lenin (1870–1924) himself had penned one of the most frequently cited critiques of imperialism; and the Soviet-run Comintern and Third International had each provided training, resources, and political solidarity with anticolonial activists through the interwar period. Still, anticolonialism was not a priority for Soviet leaders in 1945. As part of their 1930s embrace of a "popular front" strategy to fight fascism, European communists already had muted their support for immediately ending colonial rule. After 1945, the fixation of Soviet dictator Joseph Stalin (1879–1953) on protecting his country from threats in Europe led the Soviets to play little active role in fomenting anticolonial struggles. The United States, born in the first modern anticolonial revolution and proud of this history, had only begun to explicitly promote anticolonialism abroad in 1932, with the election of Franklin Delano Roosevelt (1882–1945) as president. This new approach became clear in dealings with the Philippines, the most important U.S. colony. Whereas previous administrations had rejected any discussion with local "agitators," Roosevelt sent officials to meet with Filipino nationalists in order to establish an explicit timetable for independence. During World War II, American officials repeatedly affirmed that colonialism needed to end, or as a top advisor to President Roosevelt stated in early 1942: "The age of imperialism is dead." Their British allies, in turn, repeatedly refuted such claims, with Churchill affirming in December 1944 that " 'Hands off the British Empire' is our maxim."

Between 1947 and 1951 the emergence of the Cold War led U.S. policy makers to focus on strengthening their European allies against the perils of Soviet invasion and domestic communism. This made it easy to ignore indigenous nationalist demands altogether, particularly in Africa, and actively to support the continuation of European colonial control. Whereas Indonesian nationalists' role in crushing communist activities had encouraged United States efforts to pressure the Dutch to leave, the growing importance of communists among Vietnamese antinationalists had the opposite effect on United States policy toward Indochina. This shift was particularly blatant, given that Roosevelt himself repeatedly had identified French rule there as typifying the worst excesses of colonialism: financial neglect; repression of political activity; and the consolidation of a feudal-style agricultural system. The British quickly responded to U.S. shifts, and used their 1948 declaration of the Malayan Emergency, made in the name of countering a communist insurgency (1948–1960), to sideline their earlier policy of extending autonomy. The British also began to argue that their continued control of Asian colonies was meant, in fact, to build up local nationalisms as bulwarks against spreading communism.

## EUROPEAN EFFORTS TO REINVENT OVERSEAS COLONIALISM

At the end of World War II, every European colonial power saw the continuation of their control of overseas dependencies as deserved—as well as necessary for their political and economic well-being. British and French political leaders viewed holding on to their empires as fundamental to their respective claims to play a central role in the post-war political order. Yet even countries that had no such illusions affirmed that their colonies still mattered. Most Italian leaders, for example, expressed shock when, under the terms of the Paris Peace Treaty of 1947, their country renounced all claims over the colonies it had ruled until the defeat of

Benito Mussolini's Fascist regime. The famed liberal thinker and deputy Benedetto Croce (1866–1952) went before parliament to denounce this effort to take away regions that Italy "had acquired by her blood, and administered and elevated to civilized European standards by her genius and expenditure of her all too scarce financial resources." Dutch politicians saw reestablishing and maintaining their control of Indonesia as vital to their country's postwar renaissance. "The nightmare of the loss of Empire," in the Dutch historian H. L. Wesseling's words, troubled their hopes of creating a "new society out of the ruins" of defeat and occupation by the Nazis (quoted in Seton-Hall, pp. 171 and 126).

## "DERACIALIZED" IMPERIALISM

After they took power in 1945, Britain's Labour Party leaders took pride in hewing to a middle path, which avoided both the old-style imperialism still popular among Conservative leaders and the ardent anticolonialism of the Far Left. Although one prominent minister announced in 1946 that his colleagues were "great friends of the jolly old Empire," the government preferred to emphasize that their commitment to extending egalitarian politics to all British subjects had produced something wholly different from what had gone before. As one Labour Party publication proclaimed in 1948: "Imperialism is dead, but the Empire has been given new life." While Belgian governments saw little need to reform their paternalistic rule over their African colonies, and the Portuguese dictatorship actually reinforced appeals to racism in its dependencies, leaders of France and Great Britain worked to establish a "deracialized" imperialism. Against strong opposition from local British authorities and settlers, London tentatively extended eligibility for certain welfare programs to African workers in Kenya, while other officials sought to reinvent the Commonwealth to include "nonwhite" states, whether the republics of India and Pakistan or current colonies. Most anticolonial nationalists, it was hoped, would be satisfied with extensions of autonomy and participation in the Commonwealth, rather than independence. In reforms that paralleled but went further than British reforms, French legislators after 1945 proposed a new federal system, termed the French Union, to knit together and govern the French Republic and Empire. These decisions had some significant effects, with the end of both "native codes" and forced labor across the French Union the most obvious.

Both the United Kingdom and France joined their overseas efforts to transform their empires with redefinitions of national belonging that offered new possibilities for people from the empire to enter, work, and live in the metropole. The Constitution of the Fourth Republic created French Union citizenship, which put all French nationals and colonial subjects in the same category, eliminating the latter term altogether from official language. As part of an effort to solidify the connections between Britain and what remained of its empire, the nationality law of 1948 affirmed that all inhabitants of the empire/Commonwealth had British nationality, with equal rights to entry and employment within the United Kingdom. Between 1946 and 1962, taking advantage of these and other new rights—and of Britain's desperate need for workers to staff the postwar economic boom—some four hundred thousand people of color moved to Great Britain. At the same time, Britain also acted to cement connections by encouraging Britons to emigrate elsewhere in the empire/Commonwealth. Between 1945 and 1962, hundreds of thousands British people did so; many left their islands for the "white dominions," but significant numbers settled in Kenya and other colonial possessions. The Portuguese government, under the dictatorship of Antonio de Oliveira Salazar (1889–1970), also sought to use emigration to invigorate its empire, or *Ultramar*. As a result, the white population of Angola quadrupled between 1940 (44,083) and 1960 (172,529), while that of Mozambique tripled in the same period, rising from 27,400 to 97,200.

## THE "THIRD WORLD" AND THE INTERNATIONAL POLITICS OF DECOLONIZATION

While British and French leaders were trying to invent new forms of transnational unions, commonwealths, federations, and the like, critics of colonialism mobilized successfully to demand national independence. Although anticolonial activism historically had taken many different forms and proposed diverse goals, by 1945 nationalists held center stage. While previous Pan-African Congresses, for example, had pushed for racial unity and antiracism,

**Jomo Kenyatta is sworn in as prime minister of Kenya, Nairobi, 1963.** GETTY IMAGES

the 1945 meeting in Manchester, England, came out in support of mass nationalism and independence. With the collapse of the French Union in 1956 and the independence of Ghana (formerly the British Gold Coast) in 1957, even those anticolonial politicians or union activists who had sought to take advantage of possibilities opened by postwar French and British reforms embraced the necessity of independence. Only after independence was achieved could new forms of interstate cooperation emerge.

The "Third World," a continent-spanning space that began to be invoked in the 1950s, rather than communities put in place by their former colonizers—or, for that matter, by the superpowers—appeared for many to be the most important venue to build such connections. The French demographer Alfred Sauvy invented the term *Third World* for a 1952 magazine article, which claimed that there were currently "Three Worlds" (industrialized capitalist states; industrialized socialist

states; the rest). He concluded by invoking the French Revolution, to warn the first two "worlds" that "this ignored, exploited, and distrusted Third World, just like the Third Estate, wants to be something" ("Trois mondes, une planète," *Observateur* 118 [14 August 1952]; author's translation). In August 1955, the leaders of twenty-nine newly independent or emancipated African and Asian states met for the Asian-African Conference at Bandung, Indonesia. Among the most notable attendees were Gamal Abdel Nasser (1918–1970), an Arab nationalist who had overthrown the British-supported Egyptian monarchy in 1952, and Chou En-lai (1898–1976), premier of the People's Republic of China, marking the first time since the 1949 communist takeover that China staked out an independent role on the world stage. The most important certainty to emerge from this gathering was that these states had a shared understanding that colonialism had to end, and that they were willing to do what they could to achieve this goal. Concurrently, nationalist politicians such as Kwame

Nkrumah, in soon-to-be independent Ghana, Félix Houphouët-Boigny in the Ivory Coast, or Jomo Kenyetta in Kenya, used political alliances, astute bargaining, and convincing claims of popular support to transform themselves, in the descriptions of colonial officials, from thugs to unavoidable partners—often in a very short period of time.

Against urgent claims from Bandung and local nationalists that all forms of colonial rule should end immediately, European leaders continued to insist that there were multiple colonialisms, and thus multiple paths out of the current situation. Such claims increasingly appeared simply irrational. In this late 1950s context, the Americans and the Soviets again turned their attention to the colonial question. Each sought to draw what the Indian leader Jawaharlal Nehru (1889–1964) termed the "nonaligned" countries of the world away from the other, efforts that the growing number of UN debates on colonialism made strikingly visible. Both also sought to check efforts by the Chinese to position themselves as the ultimate defender of Third World causes. United States policy makers had become increasingly certain that no further European state was likely to "fall" to communism. Concurrently, U.S. analysts began to give increasing attention to the destabilizing effects of struggles for decolonization in Africa, and grew concerned that Soviet influence there could threaten U.S. interests. With the election of John Fitzgerald Kennedy (1917–1963) to the presidency, the United States once again began to give strong verbal support to ending overseas colonial rule. The Soviets, too, increasingly embraced struggles they had previously dismissed as merely "nationalist" or "bourgeois." In the early 1960s, Nikita Khrushchev (1894–1971) waxed enthusiastically about what the historians Vladislav Zubok and Constantine Pleshakov term the "wave of national liberation in Asia, Africa, and Latin America," and reoriented Soviet foreign policy in their direction (p. 206).

In those same years, most European states finally left their last important colonies, with Belgium leaving the Congo in 1960, France acceding to Algeria's liberation, Holland finally accepting Indonesia's claims to Dutch New Guinea in 1962, and the United Kingdom freeing Kenya in 1963. Leaders of each country presented these decisions, which they energetically had fought to prevent, as obvious. The British prime minister Harold Macmillan's famous "Winds of Change" speech, which he delivered in February 1960 before the parliament of the Union of South Africa, announced and laid out rationales for the end of Britain's support for white minority rule of territories in its Commonwealth, and for the decolonization of all colonized territories. De Gaulle and other French politicians affirmed that Algeria's independence was part of the "tide of History" named decolonization, an inevitable development that wise politicians could only recognize, not alter. Just months after Algerian independence, de Gaulle pointed to the United Kingdom's failure to decolonize fully as a sign of its lack of commitment to building Europe—one key reason, the French president explained, why Britain should be kept out of the European Community.

## FORGETTING EUROPEAN EMPIRES

It suggests how important empires had been to the building of modern states that, once their colonies were gone, European countries actively sought to efface as many signs as possible of their imperial past. Across Western Europe, economic developments facilitated this forgetting, since expectations of postcolonial disaster proved unfounded. Indeed, the opposite was true, as European economies flourished in the decades following the end of their empires. Such a result was particularly dramatic in Belgium and Holland, where control over, respectively, Congo and Indonesia had been seen as vital to the national economy. In the Netherlands, per capita income increased at an average of about 3.5 percent between 1950 and 1970, which was seven times more than during the first forty years of the century. Against this background, Europeans worked to exclude empire from their past as well as their present. In the United Kingdom, arguments that Britain had chosen to decolonize and done so far more successfully than other nations, the French in particular, worked to obscure both the enormous effort British officials had expended to avoid such a development and the hundreds of thousands who had died in the process of Britain's successful decolonization (in India/ Pakistan, Palestine/Israel, Malay, and Kenya, most notably). Most French people embraced interpretations that insisted that empire had never been very important, anyway. Concurrently, many on the right celebrated Charles de Gaulle "the decolonizer," who had extricated France from the incompetence of his predecessors; some on the left heralded antitorture activists who had reminded their countrymen during the Algerian War that colonialism was antithetical to French republicanism—ignoring the fact that every French Republic had embraced colonial rule.

European states rewrote 1940s laws that had extended membership in the national community to colonial subjects. The United Kingdom quickly sought to end the immigration of nonwhites from the Commonwealth. Reversing the 1948 Nationality Act, the 1962 Commonwealth Immigrants' Act restricted immigration possibilities for people without direct blood ties to Britain. Laws in 1968 and 1971 further reinforced such restrictions. The French, unlike the British, encouraged immigration from their former colonies. Yet in response to the 1962 exodus from Algeria, de Gaulle's government stripped non-European Algerians of their French nationality. The flip-side of European efforts to exclude former colonial subjects from citizenship was the need to welcome significant numbers of settlers and officials repatriated from newly independent colonies. Some 250,000 people left Indonesia and "repatriated" to Holland between 1945 and 1958 while, after the independence of Portuguese colonies in 1974, some 500,000 *retornados* settled in the former metropole—a significant increase in population. In the months before and after Algerian independence, France confronted what observers termed "the exodus," as close to one million people left Algeria to come to metropolitan France. In each of these countries, the reintegration of repatriates of European descent was far more successful than expected—at least in economic terms. While predictions that the *retornados* would provide a ready constituency for Portuguese Far-Right groups proved unfounded, French repatriates began to emerge as a political force in the 1980s. These so-called *pieds noirs* were particularly visible in support of anti-immigrant politicians, such as Jean-Marie Le Pen of the Front National. Like the British politician Enoch Powell, whose 1968 "Rivers of Blood" speech catalyzed anti-immigrant activism in the United Kingdom, Le Pen had strongly defended empire before decolonization (in 1957 he gave up his seat in the

National Assembly to join the army in Algeria). As with the mid-1990s Dutch politician Pim Fortuyn, Le Pen and Powell both trafficked in popular resentment that immigrants from countries that had not wanted European rule were now living in the former metropoles (since the early 1960s, Far-Right writers had warned that Europe, in turn, was being "colonized" by foreigners). In the Dutch case, for example, some 115,000 people from Surinam immigrated to the Netherlands during the 1970s—and many arrived just before the South American territory gained independence from the Dutch in November 1975. With little evidence, such politicians affirmed that maintaining access to welfare benefits, rather than to work or opportunities, was what drew immigrants.

## VIOLENCE

In part as a way to respond to anti-immigrant arguments, activists and scholars have mapped more complicated postcolonial connections, which tie so many immigrants to the countries in which they and their descendants live. These analyses add nuance to fundamentally economic explanations for why people immigrated; they also can trouble xenophobic definitions of national or European identity. Discussions about the violence that decolonization entailed have been particularly tense.

Violence was central to decolonization, although the intensity, effects, and constancy of violence, actual or threatened, differed dramatically between colonies and over time. A number of anticolonial movements pursued strategies premised on violent struggle, or employed violent tactics. Among the most noteworthy were Zionist groups that began targeting Arab civilians, then British forces, before embracing blind terrorism in their successful struggle for a Jewish homeland; the ethnic-Chinese communists who used the tactics they had honed during World War II as the Malayan People's Anti-Japanese Army to begin fighting the British in 1948, and whom the British crushed by 1956; the Mau Mau rebellion, which emerged among Kikuyus in Kenya to resists white settlers' seizure of land and, between 1952 and 1960, butchered close to two thousand African civilians, two hundred members of the police and British armed forces, and thirty-two white settlers; their supporters were decimated in return; and the guerrilla armies that—variously aided by the Chinese,

From left: Rhodesian prime minister Abel Muzorewa, Dr. S. Mundawarana, and former prime minister Ian Smith attend the Zimbabwe Rhodesian Constitutional Conference in London, September 1979. ©BETTMANN/CORBIS

Cubans, and/or Soviets—took up arms against the Portuguese in Angola (1961), Guinea-Bissau (1963), and Mozambique (1964). In the name of responding to anticolonial violence, all of the European colonial powers generalized and intensified use of the types of lethal force they had always relied on overseas. The French government, to take the most well known case, embraced the use of torture and "exceptional justice" against suspected Algerian nationalists. These choices were presented as necessary responses to the use of terrorist attacks by the National Liberation Front (FLN). The military also introduced the use of napalm and pursued efforts to relocate peasant populations in Army-controlled camps. French violence sparked a wide-ranging international debate about its morality and legality. There was concurrent discussion of FLN tactics, as Paris distributed images of Algerian civilians whose throats had been slit, or emasculated soldiers—and accused their American allies of giving assistance and support to these terrorists,

whether through anticolonial rhetoric or by allowing FLN representatives to speak and travel across the United States. By the war's end, an estimated three thousand European civilians were dead from the fighting, as were nearly eighteen thousand French soldiers. The numbers of Algerian dead are more uncertain: estimates from the Algerian government reached one million plus, while more recent demographic and archival studies point to at least 350,000 Algerian dead as a result of the war.

MEMORIES OF DECOLONIZATION

Other debates took place long after the actual violence had ended. In the 1980s, when one of the Netherlands most prominent historians, Louis de Jong, published his study of Dutch efforts to prevent Indonesian independence, public outcry forced him to change the Dutch title of one chapter from "Misdaden" (war crimes) to the officially approved "Excessen" (excesses). In France, there have been repeated public scandals around the use of torture by French forces in Algeria, and political groups like the "Natives of the Republic," founded in 2004, have begun to draw links to the colonial past to criticize current conditions. In Belgium, debates about Adam Hochschild's *King Leopold's Ghost* (1998), which analyzes the horrors associated with the late-nineteenth-century Congo Free State, informed harsh assessments of Belgian complicity in the genocidal violence that wracked another former colony, Rwanda, in the 1990s. In Great Britain, on the contrary, public recognition, however limited, of the violence of the imperial past has not extended to decolonization. Caroline Elkins's demonstration in her 2004 book that the British campaign to crush Mau Mau led to some 100,000 dead in detention camps, in addition to the 12,000 to 20,000 dead in combat, has been the object of scholarly, but not political debate.

## CONCLUSION

Anticolonial struggles brought to the fore and turned to their own use many of the presumptions on which colonialism had depended. Among the most well-known, and the most effective, were the ways that nationalists embraced concepts central to Europeans' self-definition as humanity's avant-garde, such as the institution of citizenship, rule by the will of the people, and national independence, to expose how colonial rule both denied them to the colonized and depended on racist presumptions to justify their absence. Subsequent European debates about the violence that decolonization entailed and postcolonial immigration continue to engage with such challenges. Decolonization has also forced politicians on the left and the right to offer new understandings of the nation and its place in the world, in order to explain the absence of empire. Some Far-Left activists have referred to decolonization to demand the breakup of "colonial" states like the United Kingdom, Spain, and France, to support the claims of "colonized" populations within Europe, such as immigrants, or to provide models of political action, whether through affirmations that oppression confers revolutionary status on groups like women or homosexuals, or by adopting terrorist tactics. The Far Right has called on Europeans to reject their "colonization" both by immigrants from Africa and the United States. Meanwhile, at the same time as scholars insist on the importance of colonial histories to understanding the European present, cultural shifts—both popular, as in French rap music, or officially recognized, as with "multicultural" Britain—make clear that sharp distinctions between European and non-European cultures are untenable. Culturally and politically, Europeans continue to grapple with the often uncomfortable truth that the hierarchies—racial and other—on which colonialism depended, and the sharp distinctions between colonized and colonizer on which anticolonial struggles and the success of decolonization relied, have given way to more complicated relations—of power, between people, and to the past.

*See also* **British Empire, End of; Colonialism; Dutch Colonial Empire; French Empire; German Colonial Empire; Portuguese Empire.**

BIBLIOGRAPHY

Atieno Odhiambo, E. S., and John Lonsdale, eds. *Mau Mau and Nationhood: Arms, Authority, and Narration.* Oxford, U.K., 2003.

Betts, Raymond F. *Decolonization.* New York, 1998.

Birmingham, David. *The Decolonization of Africa.* London, 1995.

Césaire, Aimé. *Discourse on Colonialism.* Translated by Joan Pinkham. New York, 2000.

Chatterjee, Partha. *The Nation and Its Fragments: Colonial and Postcolonial Histories.* Princeton, N.J., 1993.

Cooper, Frederick. *Colonialism in Question: Theory, Knowledge, History.* Berkeley, Calif., 2005.

Darwin, John. *Britain and Decolonisation: The Retreat from Empire in the Post-War World.* New York, 1988.

Elkins, Caroline. *Imperial Reckoning: The Untold Story of Britain's Gulag in Kenya.* New York, 2005.

Fanon, Frantz. *Toward the African Revolution: Political Essays.* Translated by Haakon Chevalier. New York, 1967.

Heinlein, Frank. *British Government Policy and Decolonisation, 1945–63: Scrutinising the Official Mind.* London, 2002.

Howe, Stephen. *Anticolonialism in British Politics: The Left and the End of Empire 1918–1964.* Oxford, U.K., 1993.

Kahler, Miles. *Decolonization in Britain and France: The Domestic Consequences of International Relations.* Princeton, N.J., 1984.

Le Sueur, James D., ed. *The Decolonization Reader.* New York, 2003.

Low, D. A. *Eclipse of Empire.* Cambridge, U.K., 1993.

Seton-Hall, Hugh, ed. "Imperial Hangovers." Special issue of *Journal of Contemporary History* 15, no. 1 (January 1980).

Shepard, Todd. *The Invention of Decolonization: The Algerian War and the Remaking of France.* Ithaca, N.Y., 2006.

Young, Robert. *White Mythologies: Writing History and the West.* New York, 1990.

Zubok, Vladislav, and Constantine Pleshakov. *Inside the Kremlin's Cold War: From Stalin to Khrushchev.* Cambridge, Mass., 1996.

TODD SHEPARD

---

**DEGENERATE ART EXHIBIT.** When it opened on 19 July 1937 under the auspices of Joseph Goebbels's Propaganda Ministry, the Degenerate Art Exhibit (Entartete Kunstausstellung) marked a major escalation of the campaign the National Socialists had been waging against modern art since the 1920s. In his political tract *Mein Kampf*, Adolf Hitler (1889–1945) had condemned the "Art Bolshevism" of his age represented in cubism, dadaism, futurism, and the "hallucinations" of "insane and degenerate men." Founded in 1927 by Alfred Rosenberg, editor of the Nazi Party organ *Völkischer Beobachter*, the Combat League for German Culture (Kampfbund für deutsche Kultur) agitated against modernism, "non-Aryan art," and the politically engaged art of the Left and instead promoted art in a traditional representational style that extolled the *völkisch* values of "German blood and soil," pre-industrial lifestyles, and "healthy" German racial consciousness. Within months of Hitler's appointment as chancellor, the National Socialists acted on their anti-modernist rhetoric. In accordance with the law for Restoration of Professional Civil Service enacted in April 1933, Jews and other individuals who lacked "political suitability" were purged from positions at public art institutions. Officials applied the same racial and ideological criteria to determine eligibility for the Reich Chamber of Culture, the compulsory professional organization established by law in September 1933, whose seven chambers encompassed all sectors of cultural activity, including journalism. As the Culture Chamber processed new applications and reviewed its membership rolls over the next four years, it systematically denied Jews, communists, socialists, and "undesirables" the right to participate in any area of artistic expression in the "new Germany."

Acting on Goebbels's directive, Adolf Ziegler, president of the Visual Arts Chamber within the Culture Chamber, assembled the Degenerate Art Exhibit from 730 paintings, sculptures, prints, and books of graphic art removed from thirty-two public collections as part of a comprehensive operation that culminated in the seizure of more than sixteen thousand artworks from museums and galleries throughout Germany by 1938. The 112 artists featured in the exhibit were the most prominent representatives of modernist art movements ranging from impressionism, cubism, expressionism, Dada, to new objectivity and the Bauhaus: Oskar Kokoschka, Otto Dix, Max Beckmann, Wassily Kandinksy, and Ernst Barlach, the exiles George Grosz and John Heartfield, as well as the foreign artists Pablo Picasso and Marc Chagall. Ziegler targeted members of the expressionist group Die Brücke (the Bridge) especially, exhibiting over fifty pieces by Karl Schmidt-Rottluff, followed by Ernst Ludwig Kirchner (thirty-two), Emil Nolde (thirty), and Otto Mueller (thirty-two). Although the exhibit's rhetoric emphasized the link between Jews and "Art Bolshevism," only six of the featured artists were actually Jewish; and only four women artists were included, with just one work each.

By restricting admission to adults, the exhibit organizers underscored the "offensive" nature of the objects, which were crowded together in nine rooms carrying such labels as "barbarism of representation," "mockery of the German woman," and disrespect for the military and "racial consciousness." In the excess of commentary accompanying the artworks, quotes by Hitler and other proponents of *völkisch* art equated expressionism with mental illness and associated Jews, bolshevism, and modernism with the "decadent culture" of the Weimar Republic. Frequently the artists' own revolutionary manifestos were used to incite a negative response. Captions also indicated artists who had held faculty positions at state academies until 1933, such as Dix and Paul Klee, and highlighted artworks that collections had either commissioned or purchased with taxpayers' money.

The Degenerate Art Exhibit opened in Munich's Archeological Institute across from the House of German Art (Haus der Deutschen Kunst)

**Degenerate Art exhibit, 1937.** This section featured a quote by George Grosz: "Take Dada seriously! It's worth it." The painting on the left is Kurt Schwitters's *Merzbild*; beneath it is a sculpture by Rudolf Haizmann. The two smaller paintings are Paul Klee's *Sumpflegende* (below) and Kurt Schwitters's *Ringbild* (above). To the right are two pages from the periodical *Der Dada*. BILDARCHIV PREUSSISCHER KULTURBESITZ/ART RESOURCE, NY

and was conceived as the negative counterpart to the six hundred examples of German paintings and sculptures in the approved, neoclassical, *völkisch* style that comprised the first Great German Art Exhibit (Große Deutsche Kunstausstellung), which Hitler himself had inaugurated the previous day, on 18 July 1937. To the great astonishment of its organizers, the sensationalist Degenerate Art Exhibit attracted five times as many visitors as the Great German Art Exhibit and set a record for a modern art exhibit, with over two million visitors attending its four-month start in Munich. Between 1938 and 1941, the exhibit traveled with slight modifications in its makeup to Berlin and eleven other cities in Greater Germany, with more than one million additional visitors.

In 1991 the Los Angeles County Museum re-created the Degenerate Art Exhibit with 172 of the artworks from the Munich opening and featured a lecture series and photographs of the original exhibit to provide the historical context. The re-created Degenerate Art Exhibit traveled to the Chicago Art Institute and even inspired a cabaret production by the Irondale Ensemble Project in 1998.

*See also* **Beckmann, Max; Chagall, Marc; Dix, Otto; Grosz, George; Nazism; Picasso, Pablo.**

BIBLIOGRAPHY

Barron, Stephanie, ed. *"Degenerate Art:" The Fate of the Avant-Garde in Nazi Germany.* Los Angeles and New York, 1991.

Cuomo, Glenn R., ed. *National Socialist Cultural Policy.* New York, 1995.

Petropoulos, Jonathon. *Art as Politics in the Third Reich.* Chapel Hill, N.C., 1996.

GLENN R. CUOMO

# DELORS, JACQUES (b. 1925), French economist and politician.

Jacques Delors's name remains associated with a "golden age" of European integration: president of the European Commission from 1985 to 1994, he embodied the relaunch of the dynamics of integration that took place with the Single European Act (1987) and the Treaty of Maastricht (1992).

Born into a modest Parisian family, Delors began his career as a civil servant in the Banque de France at the age of nineteen. Involved with trade unions and think tanks inspired by liberal Catholicism, he became in the 1950s a supporter of Catholic philosopher Emmanuel Mounier's "personalist" philosophy. Modernizing France, deepening democracy, opening the Catholic Church, and decolonizing Algeria were the major concerns of this generation who found in Pierre Mendès-France a model of political commitment. In the 1960s, inspired by the Scandinavian model, Delors became an expert in social affairs and trade unionism—a "social engineer," in his own words—first in the Commissariat Général au Plan (a governmental agency for planning) and then as a personal advisor for social affairs to the Gaullist prime minister Jacques Chaban-Delmas.

In 1974, convinced that the regime of the Fifth Republic led to bipolar politics and that his social and democratic ideals could only be defended within the *Union de la gauche* (Union of the Left), Delors joined François Mitterrand's Socialist Party. After a few years dedicated to university teaching and the promotion of lifelong learning—one of Delors's constant political ambitions—he became a member of the European Parliament in 1979 and the minister for finance of Mitterrand's first government in 1981. In this coalition of the Communist and Socialist parties, which symbolized the end of the Gaullist era and the first alternation of power since 1945, Delors was the face of the moderate Left, concerned with the fight against inflation and with gradual social progress. In 1983 Delors convinced Mitterrand that, in order to fight inflation and the devaluation of the franc, France should stay within the European Monetary System and adopt austerity measures, opposing the socialist Left's pleading for the "national way toward socialism." His name became synonymous with the *tournant de la rigueur,* which meant the end of the old-guard socialism, the choice for Europe, and the acceptance of market economics.

Jacques Delors's European career began in 1984, when he became president of the European Commission. The European Economic Communities (EEC) were deemed in a state of sclerosis. The 1960s had been dominated by Charles de Gaulle's unwillingness to deepen European integration, the 1970s by the first enlargement to Britain, Ireland, and Denmark and the incapacity of the nine member states to coordinate their policies to face the consequences of the oil crises. This period had, nevertheless, seen much reflection on the relaunch of European integration and the creation of flexible mechanisms of cooperation in the field of monetary policies and foreign affairs. When he became president of the commission, Delors knew the willingness to relaunch the EEC was widespread among the governments, and floated three ideas that had been widely discussed in the previous decade: monetary unification, coordination of defense policies, and institutional reform. Realizing that none of these three plans gathered a consensus, and unconvinced by the federalist strategy

supported by the European Parliament, he chose to resume the "functionalist" mechanism of the founders. The governments should first agree on an ambitious yet realistic objective—completing the common market contemplated by the Rome treaty—and then make the necessary reforms of the decision-making rules, extending the scope of qualified majority voting. Delors knew this objective was supported by business organizations that would put pressure on the governments, and he hoped the realization of the "single market" would prompt new discussions on economic and monetary unification. Agreed to by the ten governments and the Spanish and Portuguese candidates, this strategy was codified in the Single European Act signed in 1987 and paved the way for an intensive legislative program of market deregulation and reregulation known as the "Objective 1992." Moved by his social ideals and his close contacts with trade unions, Delors also tried to relaunch, but with less success, a European social dialogue meant to counterbalance the deregulative effects of the formation of the single market.

After the fall of the Berlin Wall in 1989, Delors was again one of the kingpins of a second relaunch of European integration. Although the Treaty of Maastricht was primarily the outcome of a big bargain among the governments, the Delors report on monetary unification, written by a group of central bankers he chaired, helped them reach an agreement on this ambitious objective.

The last years of Delors's mandate as president of the commission, and the years that followed, were devoted to broad reflections on the future of European integration. After having refused to be the French Socialist Party's candidate for the presidential elections of 1995, for he believed there was no majority for his policies, Delors became an acute observer of and respected commentator on European integration. While supporting the accession to the European Union of the former socialist states of central and eastern Europe, he pleaded for the creation of an "avant-garde" of states that would deepen integration in the field of economic and social policies. He was less enthusiastic as far as foreign and defense policies were concerned. Convinced that the European nations are vital spheres of solidarity and democracy, he had always believed that the EU should be a "federation of nations" instead of a federal state: if the market and economic policies could be deeply integrated, foreign policies were too deeply marked by the individual histories of the European nations to be dealt with through similar methods and should remain the object of primarily intergovernmental coordination. Besides, Delors showed little interest in the constitutionalization of the European Union. His Christian and social ideals led him to see economic growth and solidarity as the major priorities of his time and to trust functionalist mechanisms of integration more than the federalist plans. In this respect, Delors bore witness to the persistence of the founders' distinctive doctrine.

*See also* **European Commission; European Union; Maastricht, Treaty of.**

BIBLIOGRAPHY

Delors, Jacques. *L'unité d'un homme.* Paris, 1996.

Delors, Jacques, with Jean-Louis Arnaud. *Mémoires.* Paris, 2004.

Drake, Helen. *Jacques Delors: Perspectives on a European Leader.* London, 2000.

Ross, George. *Jacques Delors and European Integration.* Cambridge, U.K., 1995.

PAUL MAGNETTE

---

# DEMOGRAPHY.

All the components of population growth—mortality, fertility, and migration—underwent fundamental changes in Europe during the twentieth century. The century represents a transition toward a completely new demographic regime and a break with the past. The steep decline of mortality, interrupted only by military conflicts, was the result of an epidemiologic revolution. The fertility transition led to the advent of a new reproductive regime characterized by small families; further declines by the beginning of the twenty-first century even threatened to lead to a regression of population size, while the resulting aging was expected to place an unbearable burden on social support systems. Net migration, finally, which had long been negative for Europe, became positive during the second half of the twentieth century.

## MORTALITY

The secular decline of mortality had started to pick up speed before 1914 after the discovery of the germ theory of disease and the resulting improvements in public and private sanitation. It was interrupted by World War I, which caused over ten million European deaths, and by the influenza epidemic of 1918, which may have caused two million European deaths. (As in the case of other estimates of mortality in times of war and catastrophe, the figures have large margins of error because the systems of data collection typically break down as a result of crises.) There were other high mortalities before World War II but more restricted in scope: the civil war in Russia from 1918 to 1920, the famines of 1921 and 1933 in parts of Russia and Ukraine (2.6 million people may have died from the 1933 famine in Ukraine alone), or the Spanish civil war (over 300,000 deaths). The toll of World War II for Europe may be estimated at more than forty million, but this would include civilian deaths and the victims of genocide, including approximately six million Jews and 250,000 Gypsies. The total number of war deaths (civilians and military, including prisoners of war) may have reached twenty six million for the USSR (including those of Asian origin), between 4.6 and 6 million for Germany, 5.8 million for Poland (15 percent of the population), and 1.5 million for Yugoslavia. England lost 300,000, France 600,000, and Italy 450,000 people. Several smaller countries of eastern Europe (Romania, Hungary, Czechoslovakia, and Greece) each lost more than 400,000 people, comparatively a very large toll. The second half of the century, however, was relatively free of wars with European participation, with the exception of the civil wars attending the breakup of Yugoslavia during the 1990s, which may have caused 200,000 deaths.

In 1910 the average expectation of life at birth for Europe (excluding Russia) amounted to forty-eight years for both sexes together, with highs at fifty-seven in Sweden, Denmark, and Norway and lows close to forty in eastern Europe. (Tables 1 and 2 show expectation of life at birth for both sexes in a selection of countries during the twentieth century.) Infant mortality was below one hundred deaths under age one per thousand births in the three Scandinavian countries by the beginning of the century but was still at least twice as high in Germany, Austria, and most of eastern and southern

**TABLE 1**

| Expectation of life at birth in years, selected European countries: Males | | | | | |
|---|---|---|---|---|---|
| Country | 1910 | 1930 | 1960 | 1985 | 2000 |
| Belgium | 48.9 | 54.5 | 66.3 | 71.1 | 74.6 |
| Denmark | 55.6 | 61.5 | 70.4 | 71.6 | 74.5 |
| England & Wales | 51.5 | 58.3 | 68.0 | 71.7 | 75.4 |
| France | 48.5 | 54.3 | 67.0 | 71.3 | 75.2 |
| Germany | 47.4 | 58.4 | 66.9 | 71.0 | 75.0 |
| Hungary | 39.1 | 48.7 | 65.9 | 65.3 | 67.2 |
| Italy | 44.3 | 51.0 | 66.5 | 72.4 | 76.6 |
| Netherlands | 52.9 | 63.8 | 71.3 | 72.7 | 75.5 |
| Norway | 55.0 | 62.8 | 71.2 | 72.8 | 76.0 |
| Poland | – | 48.2 | 64.8 | 66.5 | 69.7 |
| Romania | 39.9 | 41.2 | 63.6 | 66.9 | 67.7 |
| Russia | 34.7 | 42.0 | 65.6 | 64.2 | 59.0 |
| Spain | 40.9 | 48.4 | 66.9 | 73.1 | 75.5 |
| Sweden | 55.2 | 62.3 | 71.4 | 73.8 | 77.4 |
| Switzerland | 50.6 | 59.2 | 68.7 | 73.5 | 76.9 |

Note: Boundaries of the time. For Russia, European part of USSR in 1930, entire USSR in 1960. For the United Kingdom in 1910, 1930, and 1960, figures are for England and Wales only.

SOURCE: Bardet and Dupâquier, 1999, p. 134; Sardon, 2004, pp. 312–313.

Europe. Wars did not interrupt and may even have stimulated medical innovation, and the general trend of expectation of life was steadily upward, except for the countries of eastern Europe where it stagnated or even receded after 1960. The century witnessed a revolution in the mortality regime, which has received the name of *epidemiologic transition*. The expression refers to a movement from a situation dominated by infectious diseases to one where people die mostly from chronic and degenerative conditions. In the 1910s childhood diseases and gastrointestinal and respiratory infections were the most lethal, and tuberculosis was the most important single cause of death that affected young adults as well as persons of other ages; in 2000 mortality was largely cardiovascular in nature (strokes and heart conditions) or the result of cancers. The changes resulted from a variety of factors, and the exact causal relation is hard to pin down. Medical progress certainly played an important role, particularly the development of vaccines that could be administered routinely to small children. Mortality from several infectious diseases, however, was strongly reduced before effective medication had been discovered; thus measles came down before the introduction of an effective vaccine and tuberculosis before the use of streptomycin for its treatment. Public health and sanitation improved and contributed to erasing the prevailing excess

mortality of the cities over the countryside. Health education familiarized the public with simple hygienic measures, while increases in the standard of living improved living conditions and nutrition. A great medical breakthrough occurred with the development of antibacterial drugs from the late 1930s onward. The decline was remarkably similar in all countries throughout most of the century, although trends started to diverge in eastern Europe during the last quarter of the period.

By the 1960s there had been a great deal of convergence of mortality levels among European countries. It appeared that the great mortality transition was over and that the era of infectious diseases was over. Infant mortality had decreased from levels around one hundred deaths of children under age one per thousand births at the eve of the Great War to levels around twenty per thousand in the 1960s. The decline would continue in northwestern Europe, to average levels close to five deaths per thousand births by the year 2000, with extreme values of three in Iceland and six in Ireland. In eastern Europe, however, infant mortality remained at higher levels, in excess of fifteen per thousand in Romania and Russia. On the whole, however, infant and child mortality had reached such low levels by the 1960s that further improvement had only a moderate impact on the expectation of life.

TABLE 2

**Expectation of life at birth in years, selected European countries: Females**

| Country | 1910 | 1930 | 1960 | 1985 | 2000 |
|---|---|---|---|---|---|
| Belgium | 52.5 | 59.3 | 72.2 | 76.8 | 80.8 |
| Denmark | 58.5 | 63.2 | 74.1 | 77.5 | 79.3 |
| France | 52.2 | 59.3 | 73.5 | 79.4 | 82.7 |
| Germany | 50.7 | 61.3 | 72.2 | 77.4 | 81.0 |
| Hungary | 40.5 | 51.8 | 70.2 | 73.2 | 75.7 |
| Italy | 45.7 | 54.4 | 71.4 | 78.8 | 82.5 |
| Netherlands | 55.2 | 65.2 | 75.2 | 79.2 | 80.5 |
| Norway | 58.8 | 65.7 | 75.7 | 79.4 | 81.4 |
| Poland | – | 51.4 | 71.0 | 74.8 | 77.9 |
| Romania | 40.1 | 42.6 | 67.1 | 72.6 | 74.6 |
| Russia | 37.8 | 46.8 | 73.1 | 73.3 | 72.2 |
| Spain | 42.6 | 51.6 | 71.7 | 79.4 | 82.7 |
| Sweden | 57.6 | 64.4 | 75.2 | 79.7 | 81.7 |
| Switzerland | 54.0 | 63.0 | 74.2 | 80.0 | 82.6 |
| United Kingdom | 55.4 | 62.4 | 73.9 | 77.6 | 80.2 |

Note: Boundaries of the time. For Russia, European part of USSR in 1930, entire USSR in 1960. For the United Kingdom in 1910, 1930, and 1960, figures are for England and Wales only.

SOURCE: Bardet and Dupâquier, 1999, p. 134; Sardon, 2004, pp. 312–313.

If the increase in the duration of life before 1960 was principally the result of declines of mortality before age fifty, after 1960 it became increasingly the result of the improved survival at older ages. New causes of deaths became prominent that were linked to behavior and particularly deadly among young adults, such as tobacco smoking and automobile accidents, and late in the century HIV/AIDS. Contrary to predictions, however, expectation of life at older ages continued to increase steadily in most countries, without appreciable slowdown. By the end of the century the expectation of life at birth exceeded seventy-five years for men and eighty years for women in the countries of northwest and southern Europe, but it was lagging behind by around ten years for men and seven years for women in most countries of eastern Europe. Russia, with an expectation of life at birth of fifty-nine years for men and seventy-two years for women, had slid back to the lowest levels in Europe and below its own level in 1960.

The extension of life for the older population was the dominant factor of change in the mortality regime during the second half of the twentieth century. It was characterized by a reduction of chronic degenerative diseases, particularly of cardiovascular conditions. It is unclear to what extent this development was the result of changes in lifestyle, of the prevention of self-inflicted conditions such as alcoholism, smoking, and accidents, of the better tracking and management of chronic diseases, of new medications or surgical procedures, or of the long-term effect on the organism of reduction of childhood diseases that occurred many years earlier. Interestingly, Mediterranean countries (Italy, Spain, and France, which were among the relatively high-mortality countries of Europe at the beginning of the twentieth century) had among the highest expectations of life in Europe in the early twenty-first century despite relatively high tobacco consumption. This resulted mainly from a relatively low prevalence of cardiovascular diseases and is probably related to lifestyle and diet rather than to the effectiveness of the public health system. On the other hand, the former communist countries of eastern Europe, which benefited to the full from the reduction of infectious diseases before 1960, were unable to adapt to the changes in behavior that would curb man-made diseases and improve the personal management of health and did not benefit from the decline of cardiovascular diseases that took place in the rest of Europe.

**FERTILITY**

The secular decline of mortality had a considerable positive impact on the growth rate of Europe and compensated for the simultaneous decline of fertility. On the eve of the First World War, practically all European countries (with the exception of Ireland and Albania) had become engaged in what is known as the *fertility transition*. The latter term refers to the widespread adoption of methods of family limitation by couples in the population at large, which resulted in the progressive control of marital fertility. The methods were still crude (mostly withdrawal) and relatively ineffective, but the motivations were powerful. For selected countries through the century, table 3 shows total fertility, that is, the number of children a woman would have by the end of childbearing if she were exposed to the fertility of the specific period.

There were many reasons for the changes in the pattern of reproduction. They certainly included the decline of mortality, which made it possible for couples to attain the same final family size, and for populations to maintain their size and growth, with fewer births. A concern for the health of mothers and children and for the economic prosperity of couples helped shift the emphasis from the quantity of children to their quality. Confronted with the fertility decline in a context of military conflict and labor force needs, some nations of Europe attempted to reverse the trend by legislating access to contraceptive information (as in a law passed by the French assembly in 1920) or by promulgating policies in favor of the family (most notably in Sweden).

The Great Depression provided additional economic reasons to postpone births or avoid them altogether. During the early 1930s, total fertility would reach levels below two children per woman for England and Wales, Germany, Sweden, and Switzerland. The decline continued until 1935 for many countries and past that date for some, particularly in eastern Europe, but a recovery had started here and there by the late 1930s. In all countries, the generations of women born between 1920 and 1945 had in excess of two births on average. The Second World War concealed the long-term tendency for a time, but it became clear after the war that the long decline of fertility was over and that a resurgence of childbearing was taking place. This was widely characterized as the "baby boom." At first the rise was interpreted as the making up of births postponed during the depression and the war, but the reversal of the

trend toward decline persisted during the 1960s, resulting in total fertility rates in excess of 2.5 children per woman for the decade in northwestern, central, and southern Europe. The phenomenon was explained in part by a marriage boom, characterized by more people marrying and doing so at a younger age. For example in the Netherlands, the mean age at first marriage of women declined from twenty-six years in 1948 to less than twenty-three years in 1975. Even in Ireland, a country with a high marriage age and a high proportion of people never marrying, the behavior of couples reflected the new popularity of marriage as on the Continent. It appeared, then, that the European countries had reestablished a demographic equilibrium between the birthrate and the death rate that would result in moderate growth or constant population size in the long run. The impression was deceptive, though, as a large proportion of the births were unwanted, with children born to very young couples who hardly could afford them and had no access to effective contraceptive methods—even though the resort to illegally induced abortions was increasing.

Toward the mid-1960s many laws regulating the diffusion of contraception were relaxed. Later, starting in the 1970s, abortion was progressively legalized in most European countries. Increasingly the states of noncommunist Europe adopted a laissez-faire policy in matters of reproduction. Military might, a primary consideration in 1914, ceased to be a determinant of public policy. The excesses of populationism and eugenism during the interwar years (ranging from the prevention of contraceptive access to forced sterilization of less desirable members of the population including ethnic minorities in Nazi Germany) inspired great caution on the part of governments with regard to interference with reproductive freedom. The generalization of family allowances occurred on social rather than demographic grounds.

Reproduction in eastern Europe followed a distinctly different course from the rest of the Continent. Traditionally, contrasted marriage patterns had prevailed on both sides of a line running from the Adriatic to the Baltic Sea. Marriage was earlier and more universal in eastern Europe, and this resulted in a pattern of early family formation. The secular decline of fertility had started later and

TABLE 3

**Total fertility rate (children per woman), selected European countries**

| Country | 1910-14 | 1930-39 | 1960-64 | 1980-84 | 2000 |
|---|---|---|---|---|---|
| Belgium | – | 2.09 | 2.63 | 1.60 | 1.66 |
| Denmark | 3.54 | 2.17 | 2.58 | 1.44 | 1.77 |
| France | 2.45 | 2.15 | 2.82 | 1.88 | 1.89 |
| Germany | 3.80 | 2.01 | 2.47 | 1.38 | 1.38 |
| Hungary | 4.50 | 3.27 | 2.24 | 2.01 | 1.32 |
| Italy | 4.35 | 3.05 | 2.51 | 1.55 | 1.24 |
| Netherlands | 3.86 | 2.70 | 3.17 | 1.52 | 1.72 |
| Norway | 3.72 | 3.05 | 2.93 | 1.69 | 1.85 |
| Romania | – | 3.95 | 2.10 | 2.22 | 1.31 |
| Poland | – | 3.20 | 2.76 | 2.31 | 1.34 |
| Russia | 5.80[a] | 3.87 | 2.67 | 2.10 | 1.21 |
| Spain | 4.29 | 3.19 | 2.87 | 1.89 | 1.24 |
| Sweden | 3.42 | 1.80 | 2.30 | 1.64 | 1.54 |
| Switzerland | 3.00 | 1.88 | 2.58 | 1.53 | 1.50 |
| United Kingdom | 2.95 | 1.88 | 2.85 | 1.80 | 1.65 |

Note: Boundaries of the time. For Russia, USSR until 1980–84. For Germany, data for 1960–64 and 1980–84 are for the FDR only.

SOURCE: Bardet and Dupâquier, 1999, p. 196; Sardon, 2004, pp. 292–293

continued into the 1980s; there was little evidence of a baby boom. As a result of national policies, access to contraception remained more limited than in western Europe and abortion became a common technique of birth control, while generous regimes of family allowances and marriage support encouraged medium-size to large families. Several countries attempted to raise their fertility by restricting access to abortion where it had become the main technique of birth control. In Romania, a change in the law in 1967 resulted in a spectacular but momentary peak in fertility, followed by a long decline at higher levels than in most countries of the region.

Contrary to most forecasts, the decline of fertility resumed in the noncommunist European countries after 1964 and eventually led to levels that could not ensure replacement in the long term. At prevailing mortality levels it would take an average of 2.1 children per woman to ensure the replacement of a generation. By the early 1980s only Ireland, Greece, and Portugal, plus all the countries of communist eastern Europe except East Germany, had total fertility rates above two. In West Germany, the rate dropped below 1.3 in 1985; Spain (1.6) and Italy (1.4) were not far behind. Among younger cohorts of women, childlessness was rising rapidly. Eastern Europe engaged in a new demographic regime of very low fertility after

the collapse of the communist regimes. The eastern part of Germany that used to be the Democratic German Republic even attained the record low total fertility level of 0.84 children per woman in 1995 but recovered slightly thereafter.

The changes were aided by innovations in birth control technology. Hormonal contraception diffused from the mid-1960s on, at the same time as intrauterine devices. These methods were especially adapted to the prevention of births early in the reproductive lives of women. As a backup in case of contraceptive failure, safe techniques were developed to induce abortion. Northern, western, and central Europe adopted a change in reproductive behavior that has received the name of *second demographic transition*. It was characterized by new approaches to marriage and celibacy, leading to below-reproduction levels of fertility. The normative sequence in Europe had long followed a well-established pattern: courtship, wedding, sexual relations, one or two children following promptly upon marriage, and the avoidance or postponement of subsequent births. Extramarital births were frowned upon, and an ideal of monogamy and conjugal fidelity was promoted, if not always conformed to. Scandinavian countries, where cohabitation was more common that elsewhere in Europe, led the way in adopting new patterns of nuptiality. These were characterized by the postponement of a formal wedding while the couple was already cohabiting and possibly having children, or even by the complete forsaking of any marriage ceremony. On the one hand, the age at marriage went up (in the Netherlands, for example, from 22.6 years in 1975 to 27.5 in 1995 for women, and the increase was very similar in France). On the other hand, an increasing proportion of couples lived together without being married. In 2000 the proportions of extramarital birth reached 56 percent in Sweden and exceeded 40 percent in Denmark, France, and Norway. Increasingly the laws of European countries have granted recognition of equal rights to children born outside of marriage and accepted new forms of legal unions, as for example the civil solidarity pacts in France that provide rights to nonmarried, stable partners. Even in the countries of southern Europe, where the traditional forms of marriage continue to prevail, and in eastern Europe, the age at marriage has been going up, and the birth of children occurs typically at an older age of the parents. Meanwhile the number of divorces has increased, and cohabitations are less stable than formal marriages.

There has been much speculation on the reasons behind the second demographic transition and the collapse of fertility levels. Inferred psychological causes have included the growth of individualism and the decline in importance of the family as a provider of services and resources in welfare states. Concerns for sustainable growth, the preservation of the environment, quality of life, and the rights of women have become important shapers of policy. The main factor, however, appears to have been rising female schooling and labor force participation. During the second part of the twentieth century the male breadwinner system of the past increasingly yielded to the two-earner family. Those countries that have attempted to reduce the conflict for women between working outside the home and having children, for example by providing free childcare facilities or other benefits, appear to have been better able to sustain their fertility levels than those where the assistance to working mothers has lagged behind.

The effect of low fertility on population growth has more than compensated the effect of the decline of mortality. However, its impact has been concealed to some extent by the increase in the flow of migrants to Europe after the Second World War.

## MIGRATION

The large streams of European migration that contributed to the settlement of America, as well as Australia and New Zealand, essentially dried up during the First World War and were greatly reduced between the wars, particularly when the Great Depression eliminated the overseas demand for foreign labor. Intracontinental migration and refugee movements were considerable, however, as a result of the world wars, of the boundary changes imposed at the Treaty of Versailles in 1919, and of the civil wars and ethnic conflicts of the period. The Russian Revolution and the expulsion of minorities in eastern and central Europe may have resulted in the forced displacement of 10 million persons after the First World War; the conflict between Greece and Turkey resulted in the resettlement of 1.5 million ethnic Greeks, and the Spanish civil war led to the departure of a half-million refugees. The Second World War gave rise to even larger population movements. As many as 30 million people were forced to move between 1939 and 1948, including some 10 million ethnic Germans expelled from eastern Europe. The creation of a political division between the Western world and the communist countries resulted in substantial flows of refugees, particularly between East and West Germany before and even after the establishment of the Berlin Wall in 1961 (for a net movement of 4.1 million persons), and in 1956–1957, 1968, and 1980–1981 on the occasions of the uprisings in Hungary and Czechoslovakia and the imposition of martial law in Poland. In excess of 320,000 Russian Jews migrated to Israel and the United States between 1970 and 1989. In the early 1990s close to 5 million people fled from the various countries that had made up Yugoslavia; most of the moves were temporary, however.

Germany adopted a right of return for people of German origin living abroad and does not consider them as migrants. In addition to postwar refugees, before the disappearance of the Iron Curtain, West Germany negotiated the repatriation of close to three million ethnic Germans from Russia and Poland; others came from Austria, the

TABLE 4

| Total population (in thousands), with growth ratios, selected European countries | | | | | |
|---|---|---|---|---|---|
| Country | 1920 | 1960 | 2000 | 1960/1920 | 2000/1960 |
| Belgium | 7,406 | 9,129 | 10,239 | 1.23 | 1.12 |
| Denmark | 3,079 | 4,565 | 5,330 | 1.48 | 1.17 |
| France | 38,900 | 45,684 | 58,744 | 1.17 | 1.29 |
| Germany | 61,770 | 72,543 | 82,163 | 1.17 | 1.13 |
| Hungary | 7,980 | 9,984 | 10,043 | 1.25 | 1.01 |
| Italy | 37,006 | 50,200 | 57,680 | 1.36 | 1.15 |
| Netherlands | 6,820 | 11,556 | 15,864 | 1.69 | 1.37 |
| Norway | 2,635 | 3,567 | 4,478 | 1.35 | 1.26 |
| Poland | 26,746 | 29,776 | 38,654 | 1.11 | 1.30 |
| Romania | 15,541 | 18,403 | 22,455 | 1.18 | 1.22 |
| Spain | 21,289 | 30,327 | 39,733 | 1.42 | 1.31 |
| Sweden | 5,905 | 7,471 | 8,861 | 1.27 | 1.19 |
| Switzerland | 3,877 | 5,295 | 7,164 | 1.37 | 1.35 |
| United Kingdom | 46,596 | 52,164 | 59,623 | 1.12 | 1.14 |

Note: Boundaries of the time. Some of the countries gained or lost some territory in the intervening periods. For Germany in 1960, sum of GDR and FRG.

SOURCE: Bardet and Dupâquier, 1999, p. 196; Sardon, 2002, pp. 129–130.

Balkans, and other parts of the world. Between 1945 and 1992 the Federal Republic of Germany integrated about twenty-four million foreign-born persons. By providing labor, the influx contributed to the success of German industry in the postwar era and sustained population growth at a time when fertility had become very low. Italy and Spain also freely readmitted individuals of national origin, particularly from Latin America.

The dissolution of colonial empires (Dutch, British, French, and Belgian) resulted in the return migration of European settlers as well as in a flow of migrants from former territories to the former mother countries or to other parts of Europe. England had a policy of free access from countries of the Commonwealth until 1971. With the economic boom of the 1960s and 1970s, a demand for labor resulted in the hiring of "guest workers" from Yugoslavia, Turkey, and North Africa, who progressively replaced migrants from European countries such as Italy, Spain, Portugal, Greece, and Ireland. These countries had themselves become countries of immigration, or return migration, by the end of the century. Whereas the labor movements from countries outside of the European Union consisted at first of men alone, in a second stage their impact was multiplied by family reunification.

Migration streams have doubly contributed to European population growth: first by the migrants themselves, second by their higher-than-average fertility. By 2000 there were 18.5 million foreigners recorded, or about 7 percent of the population of the European Union. The assimilation of some ethnic minorities has proven difficult, and at the turn of the century, with the growth of unemployment in the European Union and a shift of public opinion against migration, increasing legal restrictions have been placed on new arrivals. Undocumented entries and refugee movements have continued, however, and at the turn of century the number of undocumented aliens in the European Union was estimated in excess of 3 million. Meanwhile immigration from eastern Europe has become more important. Poland in particular has become a major supplier of skilled, temporary labor to western Europe.

**POPULATION GROWTH AND AGING**

European population growth was sustained throughout the twentieth century, as shown in table 4. As a whole, the population of Europe grew from 422 million in 1900 to 548 million in 1950 and 727 million in 2000. Growth was moderate in contrast with that of most other parts of the world, so that the share of Europe in the world population totals was cut in half, from 24 percent at the beginning of the century to 12 percent in 2000. The geopolitical advantages of large populations are uncertain, however. The Continent is densely populated as it is, and it has accommodated its population while preserving its environment and its living patterns. No European city features among the twelve largest in the world, and the proportion of the urban population residing in moderate-size cities, or less than 500,000, has remained stable at slightly above 60 percent. In itself, the relaxation of population pressure would cause little concern to the nations of Europe were it not for the impact of the decline of fertility on the age distribution of the population.

Despite fertility below replacement for a number of years, the large number of young women in the population (resulting from the higher fertility at midcentury) resulted in a continued excess of births over deaths. This effect of a favorable age distribution has been termed *population momentum*. The situation has now been reversed in many countries, and only immigration prevents the shrinking of their populations. In the year 2002, deaths exceeded births in the all the countries of the former USSR and of eastern Europe, as well as in Germany, Greece, and Italy, while positive population growth still prevailed in the former three countries; eastern Europe was losing, rather than attracting, migrants. Both negative natural increase and absolute decline of population are likely to become more common in the twenty-first century, as the reproductive age groups are thinned down by the low fertility of the last quarter of the twentieth century. In 2000 the number of European women between ages twenty and forty largely exceeded the female population under age twenty, thus presaging a sharp reduction in the future number of births.

No country is willing to face the large absolute decline of its population that would result from present levels of the birthrate, or, alternatively, the cultural and political consequence of the level of migration from countries outside Europe that would be necessary to prevent the collapse of population numbers. For example, with a continuation of present fertility and migration levels, the population of Italy would decline from fifty-eight million in 2000 to forty-six million by 2050 and twenty-nine million in 2100. Moreover, the percentage of the population above age sixty-five would become close to 40 percent (from its 2006 level of 18 percent). The level of migration necessary to halt

the decline would be so high that it would progressively replace the population of Italian stock.

The effect of low fertility on population aging is of major concern to the governments of Europe. The proportion of the population over age sixty-five in 2000 was 14.7 percent for Europe as a whole, compared with 8.2 percent in 1950 and a projected 23 percent in 2030. As the baby boom cohorts are reaching the age of retirement, the proportion of old-age dependents relying on pension schemes is bound to increase rapidly. These schemes, however, are usually based on the "pay-as-you-go" principle, meaning that a contribution levied on the working population supports the retirement of the older population. As the ratio of the retired to those in the labor force increases, this becomes a source of financial problems for the sponsoring states. This is compounded by the fact that the proportion of the oldest old (age eighty-five and above) is increasing too, thus increasing the cost of state-supported medical insurance schemes.

Thus, in the early years of the twenty-first century it is increasingly obvious to governments and public opinion that the low fertility of European countries is not sustainable in the long run. What should be done to restore fertility levels that will ensure the reproduction of the population is not obvious. Various measures have been suggested, ranging from more generous family allowances to privileges accorded parents on the labor market and special family voting rights. Nations are turning to the example of Scandinavian and French family policies aiming to enhance the compatibility of motherhood and family life with labor force participation. For example, the German parliament passed laws entitling all children age three and older to a place in a kindergarten. The effect of such measures, however, will at best only be perceptible with time; at best, they would only alleviate the consequences of aging in the long run.

*See also* **Abortion; Decolonization; Divorce; Immigration and Internal Migration; Sexuality.**

BIBLIOGRAPHY

Bardet, Jean-Pierre, and Jacques Dupâquier, eds. *Histoire des populations de l'Europe.* Vol. 3: *Les temps incertains, 1914–1998.* Paris, 1999. Extensive discussion by

European specialists, with chapters on the components of demographic change and on individual countries.

Demeny, Paul. "Population Policy Dilemmas in Europe at the Dawn of the Twenty-first Century." *Population and Development Review* 29, no. 2 (2003): 1–28.

Fassman, Heinz, and Rainer Münz, eds. *European Migration in the Late Twentieth Century: Historical Patterns, Actual Trends, and Social Implications.* Laxenburg, Austria, 1994.

Meslé, France, and Jacques Vallin. "Mortality in Europe: The Divergence between East and West." *Population-E* 57, no. 2 (2002): 157–198.

Sardon, Jean-Paul. "Recent Demographic Trends in the Developed Countries." *Population-E* 57, no. 2 (2002): 111–156; *Population-E* 59, no. 2 (2004): 263–314.

United Nations. *Policy Responses to Population Decline and Ageing.* Special issue of *Population Bulletin of the United Nations,* nos. 44–45. New York, 2002.

ETIENNE VAN DE WALLE

---

# DEMONSTRATIONS. 
The taking over of public space by religious or social groups or by crowds of rioters and insurrectionists is a traditional form of collective expression and protest. Street demonstrations, which occur more in some countries than in others, are usually organized by religious or social groups and are to be distinguished from riots and mob assemblies, in more than one way. The street protests typical of mobs are spontaneous, seeking immediate redress for their causes and objectives (which are often confused). As a result, they often entail violence. Conversely, demonstrations that avoid violence (or at least attempt to do so) and express demands while asserting a group's identity allow time for politics to occur. Immediacy and urgency give way to a necessary examination of available options. Such demonstrations presuppose the existence of parties that possess if not a strategy then at least a capacity to control a crowd and impose rules that reflect what is particular to crowd behavior. They arise, therefore, only with the emergence and support of parliamentary democracies. However, they do not exclude the possible resurgence of violent protest, for example, the riots that took place in certain French suburbs in November 2005.

## WORKERS' RIGHTS, UNIVERSAL SUFFRAGE, AND THE NEW FORMS OF PROTEST

The decision to stage joint struggles on 1 May 1889 and on following days for the eight-hour workday constituted an opportunity to expand the forms that protests could take and set the scene for demonstrations in the twentieth century. These types of protests varied by country: large demonstrations in the heart of London in 1890; ritualized processions in Germany, Austria-Hungary, Italy, and Belgium, sometimes occurring in the rural areas; and in France the lodging of petitions with public authorities. Such protests were often better tolerated than other practices and constituted an opportunity to learn the methods of orderly public procession—for demonstrators and police alike. Parades by organizations, consecration of flags, and protests in support of strikes (by and for miners in particular) enjoyed a similar level of tolerance, with the same results.

In 1886 Belgian demonstrators helped obtain universal suffrage. Demonstrations to that same end were organized in Finland (1904–1906); Sweden, Saxony, Hamburg, and Austria (1905–1906); and then in Prussia (1908–1910). Since these protesters were demanding the rights of full citizens, they strove to evince their respectability during the orderly processions by dressing in their Sunday best (as had those who had taken part in suffrage demonstrations in France on the eve of the Revolution of 1848). After universal suffrage was achieved, the movements disappeared because they were not viewed as an alternative to voting. They were at times prohibited as a possible threat to public order but not because they were deemed illegitimate.

Things appeared in a different light in France, however, where universal suffrage was granted in 1848. The Third Republic (1871–1940) tended to view as illegitimate any organization or movement that stood between voting citizens and their elected officials. Universal suffrage was considered the sole legitimate expression of the sovereign people, the only way to be heard by government authorities. Therefore, the public authorities were suspicious of the movements that sought to make themselves heard through demonstrative means. This suspicion, which persisted for some time, was particularly acute toward "street movements," which had made and unmade regimes in France since the Revolution of 1789. The Third Republic therefore did not include the right to assembly among the democratic liberties it guaranteed in the 1880s, unlike those countries where freedom of assembly was more easily conceded, precisely because street protests did not compete with universal suffrage, which was introduced later, and did not have the same symbolic charge. The successive constitutions of the French Republics recognized the citizen's right to "speak his mind" but without once postulating freedom of assembly as the term is used today. Tolerance of public demonstrations in France depended on the judgment of local mayors. In Italy, despite the fact that universal suffrage arrived rather late, tolerance of public demonstrations similarly depended on local mayors.

## WORLD WAR I AND ITS AFTERMATH

Over time, public demonstrations, whether urban or rural, whether marches or group assemblies, multiplied, making specific demands or calling for group recognition at the local, national, or transnational level. And although fueled by the energy of many different actors, demonstrations were increasingly led by workers' organizations to address their issues.

The unifying symbols behind the workers' movement spread from one country to another. When Paris mobilized in force against war beginning in 1912, it borrowed from London and Berlin the model of tolerating assemblies on different rostrums in public parks. National approaches were also taking shape everywhere, with explicit or implicit rules and rituals that owed their specificity to each country's laws, unique methods for maintaining public order, distinct cultural and historical crosscurrents, and the relationships pertaining between its political culture and the army and organized religion. These approaches came to represent a unifying framework for all forms of demonstrations held within a specific country, above and beyond the diversity of their actors and objectives.

The political role played by demonstrations became markedly more diverse after 1918. In the parliamentary democracies of northern and western Europe, they became permanently entrenched as ritualized modes of expression for established groups, taking on a festive atmosphere that celebrated group identity. Or they served to support strikes, which did not always rule out the use of violence. They had no

political autonomy. In the crisis-ridden regimes of Italy (immediately following World War I) and Weimar Germany (for a longer period of time), demonstrations devolved into violence. But the victory of the Fascist and Nazi regimes signaled the disappearance of all but official parades. (Street action would also lead to the downfall of Eastern European communist regimes in 1989.) The disappearance of these totalitarian regimes restored to the demonstration its conventional functions.

## FRANCE, AN EXCEPTION TO THE RULE

In France, demonstrations have long had very complex characteristics. Although demonstrations were frequent there from the turn of the twentieth century on, despite the fact that they were not fully legalized until 1935, they played no role whatsoever in the rise and fall of successive regimes in 1940, 1944, and 1958. But they were a major component in the crises plaguing the dominant political systems in February 1934 and May 1968. In both instances, widespread demonstrations were the instigating factor in the resulting political crises, as well as one of the means by which the crises were overcome. Indeed, it was those forces capable of mobilizing people in the streets in the name of the Republic's values (antifascist in 1934, Gaullist in 1968) that prevailed in both situations and determined the political nature of the outcome. They did so by implicitly evoking the "right" to insurrection, already firmly recognized in the nation's history and imagination. Demonstrations therefore appear in this light as one of the modes of consent that France has developed to navigate a history marked by the insurmountable fracture of 1793. Regimes in the twentieth century were no longer toppled by street protests. Instead, major crises, constituted in large part by mass demonstrations, were resolved within the regime's existing framework. The management of a crisis via demonstrations became a sign of the limits each political force sought to impose upon itself. The act of demonstrating signified that struggle would take place in the domain of hegemonic mastery rather than that of violence, by signaling adherence to constitutive social codes and thereby avoiding crises of regime change.

This status for the demonstration was de facto modified in the 1980s by the combined effects of the Fifth Republic's constitution and the new constellation of political and social forces arrayed by the rise to power of France's Socialist Party leader François Mitterrand. Exponentially increasing numbers of demonstrations were frequently accompanied by specific demands by delegations, usually at the national level, and became a customary mode of action designed to intervene directly in public policy. Some of these protests were aimed at specific laws under consideration or at cabinet-level secretaries and ministers. Almost all of them prevailed over the incendiary legislation and even over the minister responsible for introducing it (for instance, the right-wing demonstrations in 1984 against the Savary Law intended to undermine private sector education, or the union protests in 1995 against the Juppé plan for retirement pension reform). What was new, when compared with the preceding decades, was that these demonstrations were not considered political crises caused by the governments in question. Instead, because they were allowed to take place, they surreptitiously came to represent a kind of referendum instigated by the populace rather than by a specific legislator. As such, they were furtively added to the list of constitutional liberties, on the condition that they not disturb the peace, and were better tolerated inasmuch as they came to appear as an available option for peacefully managing social or urban crises, just as they had previously managed political ones. Demonstrations became one phase in the process of restoring public order—a means to lower the level of violence.

## PROTESTS IN THE 1960S AND BEYOND

From the 1960s on, transnational movements acting through street mobilization assumed new forms, often borrowed from the battery of tools developed in North America. They converged around specific issues, such as the antinuclear movement and the fight against the Vietnam War, which were preludes to the protests of May 1968. This crisis period placed unusual demands upon the methods of street protest (e.g., the student barricades in Paris); after the crisis passed, new movements, focused on environmental and social issues, generated previously unknown forms of mobilization, such as ACT UP's "Die-Ins," gay pride activities, and "technoparades." Antiglobalization protesters later took up the same tactics, redefining the space and time of protests and the methods as well. International gatherings and the globalization of images via the Web and the news media have played a role in coordinating events worldwide (witness the global protest day against the war in Iraq in February 2003) and in diffusing shared visual and audio cues.

In those countries where the tradition of using public space for political ends has long been weak and constricted by the legalistic organizations of the majority party, these initiatives have produced spectacular effects, fueled by the energies of organizations devoted to the antiglobalization movement, such as the Direct Action Network in the United States and Reclaim the Streets in the United Kingdom, which have garnered widespread mobilizations and other "street parties" that represent a radical break with British militant traditions. Nothing of the sort has occurred in France, where the emergence of new means of direct action has been hindered by an atmosphere overly steeped in history (and older traditions of protest). Inversely, in other countries, the resurgence of the extreme Right and the rise in terrorism after 2000 has led some governments to resort to loyalist demonstrations, met by massive counterdemonstrations in the case of the war in Iraq. Of one point, however, we can be certain. National modes of expression have yet to disappear.

*See also* **1968; Labor Movements; May 1968.**

BIBLIOGRAPHY

Tarrow, Sidney. *Power in Movement: Social Movements, Collective Action, and Politics.* Cambridge, U.K., 1994.

Tartakowsky, Danielle. *Le pouvoir est dans la rue: Crises politiques et manifestations en France.* Paris, 1998.

DANIELLE TARTAKOWSKY

**DENAZIFICATION.** The idea of purging the German state apparatus in the wake of the Allied victory was agreed to at the Potsdam Conference (17 July–2 August 1945). The so-called Potsdam Agreement urged the removal of all Nazi influence not only from the state apparatus but also from German society at large, its culture, press, economy, and judicial system. The agreement expressed no more than a general principle, however, and the actual denazification process changed over time in response to the political constraints affecting the Allied occupiers; it also varied according to the occupation zone concerned.

In all zones, nonetheless, denazification meant an immense enterprise of social engineering, the prelude to which was the mass arrest of a proportion of the male population of Germany. Thus some 183,000 people were confined in internment camps between May 1945 and January 1947. Of these an estimated 86,000 were freed. These figures refer solely, however, to the three Western Occupation Zones.

This internment was legally underpinned by the so-called Law of Liberation from National Socialism and Militarism (March 1946), endorsed by the Inter-Allied Council for Berlin, which defined categories of guilt and envisaged the judicial sanctions to be taken against each. Classification, triage, incarceration, and sanction: the clear intention was that the social engineering of purge be meticulously controlled and administered in a manifestly consistent way. In reality the practice of the different occupying forces quickly diverged.

The Soviet Occupation Zone was undoubtedly the most affected by repressive measures. The Soviets imprisoned in special camps anyone suspected of involvement in the party or state organization of the Third Reich, and no fewer than forty-two thousand people lost their lives in a purge of striking swiftness and comprehensiveness. The reasons for the Soviets' particularly energetic attention to denazification had much to do with the ideology and legitimacy of the socialist state they wished to build. Conditions in the special camps were especially harsh, and the entire process of denazification was supervised by the NKVD, the Soviet secret police. The repression was thus characterized by secrecy and violence, but it might at the same time be seen as serving a ritual function necessary and preparatory to the reintegration, in the context of a society in chaos, of compromised elites whose experience remained indispensable to material and state reconstruction.

The U.S. approach to denazification was distinguished by the sheer scale of the arrests and the number of indictments. The simplest cases were dealt with by means of a questionnaire comprising 131 questions, a procedure that later elicited a blistering retort from Ernst von Salomon in his book *Der Fragebogen* (1951; The questionnaire), which revisited the experience of the German generation marked by World War I—a generation that supplied the chief protagonists in the Nazi tragedy.

Once they had answered the questionnaire, suspects were classified according to five categories— major offenders, offenders, lesser offenders, followers, and exonerated persons—as defined in the aforementioned Law of Liberation. No fewer than nine hundred thousand cases were tried by the 545 denazification courts set up in the U.S. Occupation Zone; most cases were assigned to German judges. But if the American approach to denazification was characterized by its massive scale and bureaucratic tendencies, it also underwent a distinct evolution. Under the direction of High Commissioner John McCloy, and in the context of the first tensions of the Cold War, the Americans put the brakes on denazification from 1948 on. By that time the construction of the Federal Republic of Germany created a pressing need for the talents of the wartime generation, and the Americans demonstrated a pragmatism in this regard that lends a measure of credibility to the charge, formulated by the East Germans, that denazification was never completed, through collusion between defeated and victorious capitalists.

The French and British adopted an even more pragmatic approach than the Americans. They too based their work on a five-class categorization, leaving the two less-serious classes of suspects to German courts and releasing the majority of their detainees without ever seriously investigating their activities during the Nazi period.

These practical differences in the approaches of the occupying powers are reflected in the statistics for their respective zones. Of 250,000 people imprisoned overall, some 86,000 were freed in 1947. But whereas the American, British, and French together released between 42 and 53 percent of 183,000 detainees, the Soviets for their part continued to hold 88 percent of their 67,000 prisoners captive. Their policy was thus marked at once by its breadth and its harshness.

Generally speaking, denazification wavered between two imperatives: one, ethical and witness-bearing in nature, demanded prosecution and punishment for Nazi crimes; the other, of a pragmatic order, argued for more lenient treatment in the light of Germany's absolute need to rebuild.

**U.S. soldiers escort German citizens to view the grisly scene at Buchenwald, April 1945.** Visitors are shown a pile of bones, the remains of about 400 victims; nearby stands a portable gallows. ©Bettmann/Corbis

Approaches to denazification differed, but (with the possible exception of the Soviet and East German variant) they were an intelligible response to the situation. In West Germany proceedings against presumed Nazis became rare during the 1950s but picked up once more thereafter with a wave of trials. By that time, however, denazification had given way to the simply judicial (and indeed very systematic) prosecution of selected Nazi crimes.

*See also* **Nuremberg Laws; Occupation, Military; Potsdam Conference.**

BIBLIOGRAPHY

Frei, Norbert. *Adenauer's Germany and the Nazi Past: The Politics of Amnesty and Integration.* Translated by Joel Golb. New York, 2002.

Kuretsidis-Haider, Claudia, and Winfried R. Garscha, eds. *Keine "Abrechnung": NS-Verbrechen, Justiz und Gesellschaft in Europa nach 1945.* Leipzig, Germany, 1998.

Meyer, Kathrin. *Entnazifizierung von Frauen: Die Internierungslager der US-Zone Deutschlands, 1945–1952.* Berlin, 2004.

Moeller, Robert G. *War Stories: The Search for a Usable Past in the Federal Republic of Germany.* Berkeley and Los Angeles, 2001.

Reichel, Peter. *Vergangenheitsbewältigung in Deutschland: Die Auseinandersetzung mit der NS-Diktatur von 1945 bis heute.* Munich, 2001.

Teschke, John P. *Hitler's Legacy: West Germany Confronts the Aftermath of the Third Reich.* New York, 1999.

CHRISTIAN INGRAO

**DENMARK.** The Danish Commonwealth in 1914 included in addition to Denmark overseas dependencies such as the Faeroe Islands, Greenland,

and Iceland. The Faeroe Islands and Greenland are still parts of the Danish Commonwealth, even though with extensive home rule, while Iceland in 1918 left the commonwealth, but remained linked to Denmark by a personal union. This last link was broken, too, when Iceland declared itself sovereign in 1944. The three Virgin Islands in the Caribbean— Saint Croix, Saint Thomas, and Saint John—had been colonies of Denmark. However, after long-winded negotiations, they were sold to the United States in 1917 because the United States feared that they would otherwise fall into German hands.

At the outbreak of World War I Denmark proper had about 2.8 million inhabitants. About 57 percent made a living from agriculture and fishery. In 2004 the population totaled 5.3 million, and just 5 percent made their living from agriculture and fishery. Those figures testify to the fact that the Danish society—like most other western societies—over those ninety years underwent a fundamental modernization and industrialization.

In 1914 the average Dane died at the age of fifty-five, while in 2004 he or she could expect to live until the age of seventy-five. Around 1900 the average woman gave birth to four children; in 2000 the birth rate was only 1.7 per woman. The dramatic fall in fertility can mainly be ascribed to the fact that women in great numbers joined the regular labor market in the postwar period. Although the birthrates seemed to be going up again at the beginning of the twenty-first century, it is still a fact that the indigenous population is unable to reproduce itself. However, the gap is compensated for by growing immigration from abroad: the number of immigrants grew from a total of one hundred thousand in 1984 to three hundred thousand in 2004. Most of the new immigrants are refugees from Third World countries and have very different cultural backgrounds.

## POLITICAL LIFE

Since 1849 Denmark's constitution has been defined as a democracy with restricted monarchy. Legislative power rests with the popularly elected parliament, while executive power rests with the government, formally appointed by the monarch, but politically responsible to parliament.

The so-called Change of System in 1901 ended a long political conflict on the issue of the king's right to choose his ministers freely, regardless of the majority in parliament. On this occasion King Christian IX (r. 1863–1906) silently accepted the parliamentarian principle according to which the government must be in accordance with the majority in parliament, and, after many years with a massive majority, the Liberals were, for the first time, allowed to form a government. For the following kings, however, it seemed difficult to come to terms with this reduced role, and only after yet another serious constitutional crisis in 1920, during which the country for a few weeks was on the brink of revolution, King Christian X (r. 1912–1947) openly recognized the rules of parliamentarism. Eventually, the principle was included in the revised constitution of 1953, which also replaced the two-chamber system with a one-chamber parliament and allowed conditional female succession to the throne. This constitution continues in force in the early twenty-first century.

Having written off revolutionary ideology already before World War I, the Social Democratic Party came into power for the first time in 1924 and remained so for most of the twentieth century. This party has therefore left its indelible impression on the country's transition into a modern industrial state and on the development of the welfare society. In a landslide election in 2001, however, the party lost power to a bloc of liberals and conservatives, which remained in power as of 2006. This change in the political landscape indicates that the long era of social-democratic dominance may finally be running out—not unrelated to the transformation of industrial society into the postmodern communication society.

## NEUTRALITY IN THE SHADOW OF GERMANY

Since the defeat in 1864 Denmark's foreign policy had been one of unarmed neutrality, even though it leaned toward Germany due to Denmark's exposed position at the edge of the great continental power.

The outbreak of World War I in 1914 left Denmark in a dangerous position. For Germany, control of the Danish straits was vital in order to keep the British Royal Navy out of the Baltic. There was therefore an obvious risk that Germany would occupy the weakly defended Danish coastlines in order to keep the straits under control, and this would mean Denmark's direct involvement in the war. After difficult deliberations during the first days of the war the government therefore decided to let the Danish navy close the straits with sea-mines, thus denying the Royal Navy access and, at the same time, reassuring the Germans and preventing them from taking steps that could harm Danish neutrality. However, this step also implied a dangerous double game: at the same time the government discreetly let the British government know that the mines were in fact unarmed.

By this delicate diplomacy Denmark was, indeed, allowed to preserve its neutrality and keep out of the war and Danish food producers earned large profits from food export to the warring nations, in particular to Germany. By means of a very strict policy of regulation the government, at the same time, showed itself capable of keeping the heated war economy fairly under control. At the end of the war the Danish production system was certainly worn down due to failing investments and lack of imported raw materials, but, compared with other nations, Denmark came through the war relatively unharmed.

The interwar years were marked by political instability and growing economic problems that turned into an acute crisis during the Great Depression. At the same time the liberal government was forced to step down and leave power to a coalition of social democrats and social liberals under the joint leadership of the social democratic Prime Minister Thorvald Stauning (1873–1942) and the social liberal Foreign Minister Peter Munch (1870–1948). This coalition stayed in power until the German occupation in 1940 and eventually succeeded in creating broad political consensus on a long-term strategy of survival for the Danish society in the shadows of the emergent Nazi Germany.

This strategy was intended to preserve the neutral and pacifist course that had brought Denmark safely through World War I, secure a balanced foreign trade in accordance with the neutrality principle, and enable the civic society to resist attacks from extremist totalitarian forces.

As already mentioned, Danish neutrality was not unbiased, but aimed first and foremost at convincing Germany that Denmark would never be found among Germany's enemies. This line should not be interpreted as sympathy for Hitler's Germany, but rather as a means of surviving in its shadows. In the same way, the declared pacifism was a down-to-earth recognition of the fact that a military defense of Danish territory against a strong invader was impossible. Therefore—so was the belief—the best defense was to strengthen the internal cohesion of the Danish society by strengthening democratic institutions and social solidarity. Such considerations led, in the early 1930s, to the passing of a large complex of reform laws that neutralized the worst effects of the world crisis and laid the foundations for the coming welfare state.

## UNDER GERMAN OCCUPATION, 1940–1945

Danish neutrality came to an abrupt end when, in the early morning of 9 April 1940, Germany launched a military attack on Denmark, taking the government and the population by complete surprise. After a few hours of sporadic resistance the government yielded and, under protest, decided to carry on under the new conditions.

Initially the German troops in Denmark behaved rather discreetly, and Danish authorities also went far in their policy of appeasement toward the apparently invincible Nazi Germany. But, as the fortunes of war began to change in the course of 1942–1943, a popular resistance movement grew up, mainly inspired and supported by the British sabotage organization Special Operations Executive. The mounting wave of sabotage culminated in August 1943 with an open popular rebellion against the occupants and the official policy of appeasement and collaboration. Confronted with harsh German demands for draconian countermeasures, the government finally decided to resign and leave the floor to the Germans.

At this juncture the official Danish policy had finally collapsed and for the rest of the occupation a state of open war existed between the ever-growing Resistance and the occupation forces. In October 1943 the Germans decided to eliminate the Danish Jews, but—due to a leak in the German administration—about seven thousand Danish Jews, efficiently helped by legal and illegal circles in Denmark, escaped to Sweden, while only a few hundred were sent to German concentration camps. Thanks to the active resistance movement Denmark was granted recognition as a de facto member of the Allies and, after the war, was also among the signatory powers of the United Nations Pact. The breakdown of neutrality during the German occupation eventually led to Danish membership of the NATO Pact in 1949, and the country has since then been a member of the western alliance.

## THE WELFARE STATE

The blueprint for the Danish welfare model was drawn soon after the war by the young social democratic ideologist and later prime minister through the 1960s, Jens Otto Krag (1914–1978), and began to take shape in the 1960s, when the consequences of war and depression had finally been surmounted. It was eventually developed into the comprehensive social-security system that takes care of every Danish citizen from cradle to grave.

The model is universal in the sense that it includes all citizens regardless of social and economic status. Furthermore, it is exclusively tax-financed. This is also the essential weakness of the system, insofar as it depends on the willingness of the Danes to bear one of the highest tax rates in the world. This willingness depends again on a high general income level, but nowadays wages are under pressure from a globalized labor market. Thus there is much to indicate that the system will have to undergo considerable changes in the future in order to adapt to the realities of a globalized economy. This will imply great political challenges, too, because the welfare model is in fact the essential manifestation of the inner cohesion and solidarity that for the most of the twentieth century allowed the survival of Danish society.

## THE FOOT-DRAGGING EUROPEANS

Denmark joined the European Economic Community (EEC)—later European Union (EU)—in 1973 together with Britain and, like the British, the Danes remained functionalists in their attitudes to the Union in the sense that they wanted cooperation in economic matters but remained suspicious about the political project. In relation to the visions of a great, unified Europe the Danes were—and still are—hesitant Europeans and, typically enough, all subsequent referenda on specific issues have in reality turned out to become voting for or against the Union in general. After more than thirty years of membership, however, Danish economy and legislation is so closely interwoven with the EU system that nobody can imagine in earnest that Denmark should quit the Union.

## DENMARK IN A CHANGING WORLD

At the beginning of the twentieth century Denmark was essentially an old-fashioned, inward-looking agrarian society with a rather primitive social structure. After World War I the process of modernization hit the country with full force and, over a few decades, transformed it to a modern industrial state with a sophisticated social-welfare system comparable to those in other western societies. Now, at the beginning of the twenty-first century, the postindustrial Danish society has—for good and for evil—become an integral part of a close-knit world community, the so-called global village. Only the future can tell whether the Danes will still be able to meet those challenges without losing the specific qualities that enabled them to survive as a nation and face the trials and changes of the unstable twentieth century.

See also **European Union; Germany; Holocaust; United Kingdom; World War I; World War II.**

BIBLIOGRAPHY

Christiansen, Nils Finn, Niels Edling, Per Haave, and Klaus Petersen, eds. *The Nordic Welfare Model—A Historical Reappraisal.* Copenhagen 2004. A good recent assessment of the debate over the welfare state.

*Denmark.* Edited by the (Danish) National Encyclopaedia. Copenhagen, 2001. Includes much useful information about all aspects of the Danish society.

Jespersen, Knud J. V. *No Small Achievement: Special Operations Executive and the Danish Resistance, 1940–1945.* Odense, Denmark, 2002. A discussion of the role and achievements of the armed resistance against the German occupation based upon the archives of British sabotage organization.

———. *A History of Denmark.* Houndmills, Basingstoke, Hampshire, U.K., and New York, 2004. A general survey of the history of Danish society from 1500 to the present.

Johansen, Hans Christian. *Danish Population History, 1600–1939.* Odense, Denmark, and Portland, Ore., 2002. An excellent survey with many useful figures.

KNUD J. V. JESPERSEN

**DEPORTATION.** Forcible and violent mass deportations of civilian populations to remote areas are a phenomenon that twentieth-century totalitarian regimes often resorted to. Typically, the deported groups were nationally, ethnically, religiously, or racially distinct, and their deportation was part of a campaign of annihilation that the deporting regime conducted against them. Almost always, the deported population was transferred by violent means to areas of settlement that were unsuited to its ways of life and livelihood. In the course of the deportation, the deportees suffered grave economic damage, loss and disintegration of their social and community framework, severe violence, and loss of lives. In many cases, deportation was the first stage in a process of ethnic cleansing or genocide. Its purpose was to induce the deported group to eradicate itself by assimilating into the population at large or to destroy it in the literal, physical sense, resulting in its disappearance as a group with an identity and characteristics of its own.

The first salient case of deportation as part of such a process was the removal of the Armenians in the Ottoman Empire during World War I. The Ottoman regime, led by a group of reformist officers known as the Young Turks, regarded the Armenians as an ethnic and national collective that obstructed the fulfillment of the Ottoman national and economic goals. In April 1915 hundreds of Armenians affiliated with their national intelligentsia were executed in order to deprive the Armenian population of its natural leadership. Afterward, the Ottoman government ordered the deportation of approximately one million Armenians from Anatolia to the areas of Syria and Mesopotamia. The deportation escalated into an act of genocide in which lengthy death marches resulted in mass mortality. As the victims of the deportation made their way across arid zones and deserts, their Turkish military escorts subjected them to gunfire, abuse, and brutal acts of rape. Hundreds of thousands died of starvation, illness, and murder. The number of victims of the Armenian deportation and genocide is estimated at between 800,000 to 1.2 million.

Another example of mass deportation with ethnic-cleansing characteristics is that perpetrated by the Soviet dictator Joseph Stalin (1879–1953) against the Ukrainian peasant class in the 1930s. To promote collectivization and shatter the Ukrainian peasants' resistance, the Soviet regime began in 1930 to deport hundreds of thousands

of Ukrainian civilians to faraway areas of settlement in Central Asia, Siberia, and northern Russia. Ostensibly the deportations were directed against prosperous peasants, known as kulaks, only, but in reality encompassed peasants from many different backgrounds. The deportations were accompanied by total destruction of the agricultural and rural infrastructure in Ukraine. Sometimes the peasants themselves, in their struggle against the authorities, elected to destroy their own farms and slaughter their work animals to keep them out of the hands of the Soviet apparatus. More than 1,800,000 Ukrainian peasants were driven off their land in 1930–1931 and forcibly resettled far away. More than 380,000 deportees died during the deportation or in their places of resettlement as a result of the harsh conditions that they found there. These deportations, which continued on a small scale throughout the 1930s, obliterated the independent Ukrainian peasant class and brought the economic and community system in Ukraine to total collapse. The ghastliest result of the deportation policy was the severe famine that gripped Ukraine in the early 1930s, claiming as many as seven million victims, according to current estimates.

The Polish population that had settled in areas that came under Soviet sovereignty after 1920 also became victims of brutal deportations in the 1930s. During the great Stalinist terror (1937–1938), some 110,000 ethnic Poles who dwelled in Belarusian and Ukrainian territory were executed, and additional hundreds of thousands were deported to Central Asia or northern Russia, where they were interned in Soviet forced-labor camps, the gulag, or in labor and penal colonies.

## NAZI DEPORTATIONS, 1939–1942

The Nazis' Jewish policy stressed from the beginning the need to banish Jews from the German society and nation. By the late 1930s, this policy rested on deliberate pressure from the economic authorities, the police, and/or the SS (Schutzstaffel) to induce Jews to emigrate from the German Reich. The first deportation of Jews from Germany took place on 28–29 October 1938. Some seventeen thousand Jews who held Polish citizenship and were living in Germany were rounded up in a coordinated Gestapo action and driven across the Polish border to the vicinity of

Zbaszyn. The Polish government blocked the deportees' entrance, trapping them in a no-man's-land along the German-Polish frontier with no systematized source of sustenance. Jewish relief organizations, foremost the American Jewish Joint Distribution Committee, saw to their needs.

After World War II began, the deportation policy became a basic element in the Nazis' plans for the German-occupied areas in eastern Europe. By late October 1939, the SS chief of the Gestapo, Heinrich Himmler (1900–1945), the ex officio "Reich Commissar for the Strengthening of Germandom," had issued guidelines for a grandiose scheme involving a demographic upheaval in the occupied Polish territories. According to the guidelines, within four months more than 550,000 Jews living in the areas of western Poland that had been annexed to the German Reich (the Wartheland area) were to be deported, as were hundreds of thousands of Poles in these areas who were deemed hostile to Germany. It was decided to transfer the deportees to the General Government, the area in central Poland that the Nazis intended to transform into a reserve for racially inferior population groups. These groups, according to the Nazi ideology, were to become a pool of labor and an economic resource to be exploited for the economic utility and the needs of the German Reich.

The deportations started in late 1939. In the Wartheland area, a main target for Germanization, mass expulsions of Poles and Jews began, and ethnic Germans from the Baltic countries were transferred to the area for resettlement in the localities that had been cleansed of Poles. By spring 1941, the Germans had deported about four hundred thousand Poles and Jews from the Wartheland, southeastern Prussia, and eastern Upper Silesia. Preparations for the resettlement of the deportees in the General Government were not made, and those removed were not allowed to ease their absorption in the resettlement areas by bringing possessions. The Jews, who accounted for 13 percent of the deportees, faced an especially dire situation; they had to find living quarters in the congested ghettos where the Nazis had interned the Jews who lived in the General Government area.

The deportation plan that the SS officer Karl Adolf Eichmann (1906–1962) had prepared for the Jews in occupied Poland was even more far-reaching. By October 1939, Eichmann had set forth a program for the deportation of more than seventy thousand Jews from eastern Upper Silesia to the Lublin area, east of the Vistula (Wisla) River. Shortly afterward, he also began to include on the deportation trains Jews from the protectorate of Bohemia and Moravia and from Austria. In this scheme, known as the Nisko and Lublin Plan or the Lublin Reservation, Eichmann aimed to transform the chosen area (eastern Poland, along the Soviet border) into a territorial reserve to which the Jews of the Reich would be expelled. However, after only several thousand Jews were sent to the camp that had been established in the Lublin area, Hitler struck down the plan in March 1940, ruling that this kind of a territorial solution to the Jewish problem was inapplicable. In summer 1940, the Lublin Plan was succeeded by a new deportation scheme, the Madagascar Plan. The idea now was to transform the faraway eastern African island of Madagascar into a massive, isolated ghetto, where the millions of Jews living in the Nazi-controlled areas in Europe would be concentrated. This plan, too, was shelved in early 1941 after its utter inapplicability became blatantly clear.

These deportation attempts were initial pilot steps toward a comprehensive program, known as Generalplan Ost, that took shape progressively in 1941–1942. The intent now was to create a new ethnic and demographic order in the areas that Germany had occupied in eastern Europe. It was related to the expansionist aims and the creation of Lebensraum (living space) for the German nation that the Nazi ideology prescribed. The plan called for extensive ethnic cleansing in the areas that Germany was about to occupy in the Slavic east of Europe—Poland, Russia, and Ukraine. These areas were to undergo intensive Germanization and the disappearance of their Slavic population within ten years, with the exception of a carefully selected minority suited for assimilation into the "Aryan" race. Some fifty million Slavs in these areas would be deported to the east, beyond the Ural Mountains, and a minority of several million would remain in eastern Europe as a labor force for the German economy. Within the framework of this ethnodemographic upheaval, the Jewish question would find its final solution.

**Deportees prepare a meal outdoors, Zbaszyn, Poland, 24 December 1938.** In November of 1938, the German government ordered that a large number of Jews living near the Polish border be deported to the camp in Zbaszyn, where they were confined until they could find new homes outside Germany. ©BETTMANN/CORBIS

In January 1942 Himmler set the plan in motion by promoting a German settlement project in the southwestern part of occupied Lithuania. In March 1942 he also approved a German colonization venture in the Polish territories around Zamość, in Lublin District. In November–December 1942, about one hundred thousand Poles were deported from this area brutally and without time to prepare. They were to be replaced with ethnic Germans from Ukraine.

Deportations of Jewish and non-Jewish populations also took place in western Europe in 1940. After the defeat of France and the annexation of Alsace-Lorraine to the German Reich, about seventy thousand French whom the Germans defined as undesirable, including thousands of Jews, were deported from the annexed territory to areas controlled by the Vichy government. In October 1940, police raided villages in the Baden and Saarpfalz areas and rounded up all Jews without forewarning. About 6,500 Jews were concentrated and deported to the Vichy zone in the south of France, where they were placed in camps that the French authorities had established for them.

### DEPORTATIONS AND THE "FINAL SOLUTION"

When the decision about the Final Solution was made in the autumn of 1941, the next phase of the deportation of European Jewry began. The destinations now were extermination centers in eastern Europe. The deportation of German Jews to various ghettos in Poland, Lithuania, Latvia, and Belarus began in September 1941. Some fifty thousand Jews had been deported by the end of 1941; many of them had been murdered immediately upon reaching their destinations, along with the local Jews. Those remaining were placed in the ghettos of Łódź, Warsaw, and Riga. The person responsible for organizing the transports from Germany, Austria, and (later) from western Europe, Slovakia, Hungary, Greece, Italy, Bulgaria, and Croatia, was one of Eichmann's aides, a young SS officer of Austrian origin named Frantz Novak. Novak had amassed experience in the technical organization of deportation trains during the deportation actions in Poland in 1940–1941, and when mass deportations of Jews to extermination began, it was he who coordinated and organized the evacuation trains. As a result of his organizational efforts, more than seven hundred deportation trains delivered Jews to death camps.

The first deportations of Jews to extermination took place in the middle of January 1942. The destination was Chełmno, in western Poland, the first extermination camp activated in Poland. The establishment of the Belzec, Sobibor, and Treblinka camps and the installation of extermination facilities in Auschwitz marked the completion of the mass extermination system. Once this was done, mass deportations of Jews in Poland and from the other European countries for extermination began. The deportation of Jews in Lublin District started in spring 1942. The great deportation of Jews from the Warsaw ghetto took place that summer, as approximately 350,000 were transported to Treblinka for extermination within a few weeks. Deportation transports began to leave Slovakia in late March 1942; by the end of the summer, fifty-eight thousand Jews had been taken to Auschwitz. Initial deportations from France set out in the spring of 1942. Transports from the Netherlands and Belgium began in July 1942, and 5,500 Jews from Croatia were deported to Poland for extermination in August 1942.

In summer 1941, Romania, Germany's ally, formulated its anti-Jewish policy under the influence of the policy that was taking shape in Germany. The Romanian dictator, Ion Antonescu (1882–1946), decided to solve the problem of the Jewish population in the areas that his country had annexed in Bessarabia and Bukovina. First, Romanian military forces and SS murder units murdered more than 150,000 Jews in these areas. Afterward, Romania issued a deportation order for the remaining Jews, alleging that they had collaborated with the Soviet Union during the Soviet occupation of these territories in 1939–1941. From September 1941, some 150,000 Jews were deported from Bessarabia and Bukovina to Transnistria, a salient between the Bug and Dniester Rivers in Ukraine. The deportation was typified by horrific death marches, as its Romanian military and police escorts murdered deportees ruthlessly.

A second large wave of deportations of Jews from western Europe to the death camps in Poland began in early 1943. That spring, Greece joined the roster of countries from which Jews were being deported. Some forty-six thousand Jews, a large majority of whom came from Salonika, were sent to Auschwitz for extermination during these months. In late 1943, as the Wehrmacht (the German army) entered Italy to stop the Allied armies that were advancing from the south and prevent them from occupying the entire country, the Nazis began to deport Jews from Rome and locations in northern Italy. In 1944 mass extermination deportations continued in almost all places where Germany's declining situation on the fronts allowed them to take place. A new wave of deportations of Jews from Slovakia began that year. In August 1944 the last large concentration of Jews in Poland, the seventy thousand who were still living in the Lodz ghetto, was deported. The Germans' last large murder deportation took place in Hungary. When the Wehrmacht rushed into Hungary in March 1944 to frustrate its ally's intention to secede from the war, Adolf Eichmann and members of his unit reached Budapest and, from the middle of May to July 1944, engineered the deportation of some 440,000 Jews from Hungary in conjunction with units of the Hungarian gendarmerie. Most of the deportees met their death in Auschwitz.

The mechanism that the Germans used to deport European Jewry to extermination in 1942–1944 did not require the establishment of a special and sophisticated logistical and transport system. Eichmann's department, which handled the logistical aspects of the deportations, relied on cooperation with officials at the German foreign ministry and its representatives at the German embassies in the German-allied countries and in satellite states such as Vichy France and Slovakia. Furthermore, local police forces and auxiliary units in these countries collaborated in the deportations and provided assistance. They did so in the service of their own interests; there was no deep German involvement, as there had been, for example, in Romania and Hungary. The German transport ministry, together with the Reich railroad authority, made special trains available for deportation needs. In Poland, the local railroad authority, integrated into the Reich rail network after the occupation in 1939, participated in the transport of Jews to extermination. Record-keeping, planning, and payment for the "special trains" that delivered the deported Jews to death were worked out between Eichmann's unit and the general railroad system even during the most difficult periods of the war, when needs on the eastern front placed the rail system under severe pressure. In many cases, especially during the deportations from Germany and western Europe, Jews were hauled to the east in ordinary passenger trains under group-fare arrangements. Most of the extermination deportations, however, were carried out in sealed freight cars; the internal reckoning for payment treated them as freight transport.

The Gypsies in the Reich territories were also subjected to a policy of deportation as part of a genocidal solution after the war began. The first groups of Romanies (Gypsies) who were defined as criminal or asocial elements were evicted from Berlin in May 1940, shortly before the invasion of France. By the autumn of that year, 2,850 Romanies had been deported to the General Government. In autumn 1941, after the systematic murder of Jews in eastern Europe began, the deportation of five thousand Roma from the Burgenland in Austria got under way. These Gypsies were deported to the Lodz ghetto, where they were concentrated in a separate area and were among the first to be deported to extermination from the ghetto when it began in late 1941. On 16 December 1942 Himmler issued an order for the deportation of Sinti and Romanies to concentration camps. These deportations began in the spring of 1943 and continued until summer 1944. Although Gypsies were deported from all Nazi-ruled areas that they inhabited, the actions against them were sporadic and uneven. Some

twenty-two thousand Gypsies reached Auschwitz, where 19,500 perished in the gas chambers or died of starvation and disease.

## EXPULSIONS IN EASTERN EUROPE, 1944–1948

After World War II, deportations and forced emigration were used extensively in eastern Europe to regulate the ethnic and national tensions that had been typical of these areas before 1939. Another element in this phenomenon was the wish of the peoples who had suffered from the terrors of Nazi occupation and enmity to settle scores with Germany. As the war wound down, the leaders of the three leading victors—the Soviet Union, Britain, and the United States—in conjunction with the governments-in-exile of Poland and Czechoslovakia, agreed that the problem of German populations in the two last-mentioned countries, which Germany had occupied during the war, had to be solved. The solution chosen was the expulsion of millions of Germans who were living in the areas that had just been annexed to Poland, at Germany's expense, under the agreements concluded at the Tehran and Yalta conferences, and in western Czechoslovakia. Between 1945 and 1948, some eleven million Germans left Poland, Czechoslovakia, the Baltic countries, and Romania, and moved to Germany; nearly all of them settled in the British and the American occupation zones. This powerful outflux of humanity began before the end of the war, as Germans fled in an unprecedented fashion because of fear of the approaching Red Army, and it continued immediately after the surrender of Germany. What followed was a mass expulsion of Germans from the countries that had just been liberated in eastern Europe. Some two million German civilians are believed to have died in the course of these escape and expulsion actions.

The Germans were not the only group expelled forcibly from Poland after the war. In April 1946 Polish military forces embarked on the violent expulsion to the Soviet Ukraine of the Ukrainian population that was still dwelling in various parts of eastern Poland. This action, too, was influenced by the wish to avenge Poland for the role of Ukrainians in supporting the Nazi occupation during the war and in perpetrating severe violence against ethnic Poles. Roughly 260,000 Ukrainians were evacuated against their will, but even afterward the Polish authorities believed that too many Ukrainians remained in the country, estimating their numbers at 75,000 or as many as 200,000. In spring 1947 an operation began to remove and resettle these Ukrainians in western Prussia, in order to place them at the greatest possible distance from the Polish-Ukrainian frontier. Approximately 140,000 Polish citizens of Ukrainian origin were displaced and settled in the new areas that had been allocated to them.

*See also* **Concentration Camps; Germany; Holocaust; Jews; Nazism; Refugees; Romanies (Gypsies).**

BIBLIOGRAPHY

Browning, Christopher R. *The Origins of the Final Solution: The Evolution of Nazi Jewish Policy, September 1939–March 1942*. Lincoln, Neb., 2004.

Dadrian, Vahakn N. *The History of the Armenian Genocide: Ethnic Conflict from the Balkans to Anatolia to the Caucasus*. Providence, R.I., 1995.

Hilberg, Raul. *Sonderzüge nach Auchwitz*. Mainz, Germany, 1981.

Ther, Philip, and Ana Siljak, eds. *Redrawing Nations: Ethnic Cleansing in East-Central Europe, 1944–1948*. Lanham, Md., 2001.

DANIEL BLATMAN

---

**DEPRESSION.** The cyclical downturn in the U.S. economy that began in summer 1929 has overcome all rivals to the title Great Depression. It challenged and overturned the confidence of Americans at the end of a decade in which the United States had stamped its political and economic dominance on the world. The pictures of long lines of hopeless men with no job to look for, of crowds besieging banks with no money to pay out, serve as a potent reminder of the fallibility of economic institutions and of prosperity. They still serve as a prompter to the American conscience and as a permanent stimulus to explain why the Depression occurred. However, what made it so great a depression was that neither its causes nor its consequences were limited to the United States. It was a worldwide phenomenon whose length, depth, and violence revealed the extent of the

United States' involvement in and dependence on the international economy.

## ORIGINS OF THE DEPRESSION: THE UNITED STATES

The conclusion that the Great Depression's origins lay in the United States is often drawn from the long decline in prices on the Wall Street stock exchange after September 1929. The decline accelerated violently in the panic selling of 24 and 29 October, still the two worst days in the history of the U.S. stock exchange, when twenty-eight million shares were sold. When the market temporarily stopped falling in November, however, its level was as high as it had been in mid-1928. Only about 8 percent of the population owned stocks, and they were the wealthy, so that any fall in national consumption from this event was small. Furthermore, the stock market financed only about 6 percent of gross private national investment. But longer periods of declining stock prices were still to come in 1931, and the downward trend continued into 1933.

So long a trend was evidently a deflationary force in the economy, but it was by no means the greatest such force. More influential for the whole economy were the declining prices for foodstuffs and other primary products. The falling incomes from farming in 1931 left farmers unable to pay their debts, provoking numerous bank failures. Repossessions from those failures drove the stock market down from April that year until shares in manufacturing were barely more than a quarter of their value in November 1929.

There is some evidence that the fall in the stock market was related to certain aspects of consumption in the 1920s, notably the purchase of automobiles, radio equipment, and housing, acquisitions that depended on credit. Sales of U.S. automobiles for export began to decline a year before the onset of the stock market crash, for domestic consumption as early as March 1929. Domestic purchases had fallen by one-third by September 1929. The housing market began to slow down in summer 1929. Nevertheless, the steepness of the general economic downturn in 1929 was not so exceptional, compared to other downturns, as to indicate the subsequent length and severity of the

Depression. The Wall Street crash undoubtedly did reveal some of the risks of new methods of selling consumer goods as well as the inequalities of personal income distribution in the United States, but such factors were not sufficiently influential to account for the totality of what followed, although they played their part in the bank crashes. Consumer durables did not suffer the biggest falls in sales and output.

The Depression's severity is sometimes attributed to errors of monetary policy in the United States. The growth of money supply was deliberately reduced by the Federal Reserve Bank from 1928 to check stock market speculation. Supply fell by 33 percent between August 1929 and August 1933. Shortage of liquid funds is blamed for the many bank failures in 1931. Authorities, however, believed monetary policy to be too lax because interest rates were lower than in earlier cyclical downturns in the decade. It is difficult to see how an increase in the money supply to the American economy in late 1930 could have prevented the abandonment by other countries of the existing international trade and payments machinery, especially the United Kingdom's departure from it in September 1931, when it gave up the gold standard. The outstanding characteristic of the Great Depression was its international scope. Country after country was caught in a vortex of declining output, earnings, and employment, and this makes the contribution of monetary policy in the United States, while it may have been unwise, too small a factor to account for so cosmic an event.

Of the major industrial countries, the United States and Germany were the hardest hit. Even in those more lightly hit—Sweden and the United Kingdom, for example—the decline in industrial production was severe. Beyond industrialized America and western Europe, however, foodstuff and raw material suppliers, such as Argentina, Brazil, Australia, and New Zealand, suffered declines in agricultural output, with severe drops in gross domestic product. The relentless devaluation of bond earnings was matched by a relentless and more widespread fall in agricultural profits. In other aspects too the American deflation marched in step with a worldwide deflation.

**TABLE 1**

**Falling industrial production and gross domestic product (GDP), 1929–1932, percentage change**

|  | Industrial Production | GDP |
|---|---|---|
| United States | -44.7 | - 28.0 |
| Germany | -40.8 | - 15.7 |
| France | -25.6 | - 11.0 |
| Italy | -22.7 | - 6.1 |
| Sweden | -11.8 | - 8.9 |
| UK | -11.4 | - 5.8 |

SOURCE: Aldcroft, 1978, p. 81.

**ORIGINS OF THE DEPRESSION IN GERMANY**
The First World War established financial links between the United States and Germany that go some way to explaining the similarity of their experiences from autumn 1929 onward. There are those who see the origins of the Great Depression in these links or, indeed, in Germany itself. The postwar adjustment to a world in which the First World War had promoted the protection of new industrial developments made life more difficult for Europe's two major industrial producers, Germany and Britain. Those difficulties were reflected in their balance of payments problems after 1918, but for Germany these were exacerbated by the imposition of so-called reparations to be paid to the victors. The American insistence on the repayment by its allies in the war of all loans to them from the United States added an extra burden on the international payments system. It encouraged, moreover, the biggest borrowers, France and the United Kingdom, to demand reparations payments from Germany in full in order to repay their American loans. The weight of these transfers on the German economy, the temptation not to resist inflation of the currency too strenuously, when it might make reparations a lighter burden or even persuade the Allies that it was an impractical solution, played their part in the spectacular collapse of the exchange value of the German mark. Its value against the dollar fell from 103.65 in January 1920 to 414,000 at the end of July 1923 and to 3,300,000 in August 1923. The social disorder that long adherence to the gold standard had averted triumphed in defeat, occupation, and hyperinflation, soon to be followed by the political disorder of the National Socialist Party.

The actual sum required in reparations after the hyperinflation was between 50 and 125 million pounds sterling annually. To pay such a sum in manufactured exports to the protectionist United States was not seriously contemplated in Washington. Insofar as it was paid, it was so from the stream of dollar capital imports into Germany for postwar reconstruction. New capital issues, specifically for Germany, guaranteed or controlled by the U.S. government amounted to $176.3 million in 1928. Corporate issues without government guarantee or control amounted to $10.1 million. In 1930 government guaranteed issues amounted to $143.3 million; non-guaranteed issues to $23.5 million (figures from Secretariat of the League of Nations, pp. 320–321.) These transfers were established on a flexible basis in 1924 by the Dawes Plan, which through its transfer committee tailored the sums annually to what seemed feasible. The Dawes Plan constituted an official framework for American capital exports to Germany. With this seeming extra security, capital imports into Germany amounted to about 3 billion marks per year over the period 1924–1927. In that period the peak year for reparations payments amounted to almost 1.6 billion marks in 1927.

The inflow of American capital began to shrink in 1928 after an increase in American interest rates and a deepening unease about economic conditions in Germany. Opinion remains divided about whether the downturn in the German economy in 1929 was domestic in origin, resulting from a decline in investment, or external, from the recall of American capital investment due to, or perhaps earlier than, the onset in 1929 of the Wall Street crash. The evidence points more to international origins. In either case, the German response was to cut back on commodity imports, wages, and public expenditure. The government of Heinrich Brüning could see no way forward to meet the cost of imports plus reparation payments other than through cuts deep enough to preserve a balance of payments surplus, which was in fact achieved in 1932. By that date the world's two biggest manufacturing producers and exporters, the United States and Germany, were locked together in spiraling deflation, falls in industrial output, and steeply declining national product. A devaluation of the mark to stimulate German exports would have made the dollar value reparations more expensive to meet.

The Young Plan of 1929–1930, in a last attempt to preserve international cooperation in the payment of reparations, further reduced the German government's room for maneuver. Under the Dawes Plan the transfer of payments had been allowed only if the German balance of payments was not endangered. The Young Plan imposed a binding scheme for repayment spread over a longer period but removed in doing so the safeguard against transfers when the German balance of payments was threatened. In theory, this should have deterred foreign lenders, but while net capital imports fell, total capital imports were still high in 1930 and 1931. The lack of any obvious explanation of this trend only strengthened the German government's commitment to a balanced budget, achievable only by a deflationary policy, worsening the international crisis. This policy did produce substantial export surpluses for paying reparations to a similarly deflationist United States.

## THE NECESSITY AND THE FAILURE OF INTERNATIONALISM

In retrospect the Dawes Plan appears as the one instance of an internationalized solution that offered a way forward to the United States, to Germany, and thus, if the framework could have been extended, to America's other European debtors. After the events of 1929 it was perhaps too late. Perhaps, also, genuine internationalism could not have been born from so violent an event as the Franco-Belgian invasion and occupation of the Ruhr and the Rhineland in January 1923, intended to compel Germany to pay the reparations. The devaluation of the German mark was one consequence, well illustrating the fundamental reality that effective international trade and payments machinery depends absolutely on international political cooperation. It was lacking.

For ten countries to be recompensed by operations from Germany, for the United States to be repaid by its wartime allies, the prewar machinery for international trade settlements—the gold standard—would be put under heavy strain because of the economic and political boundary changes resulting from the First World War. Evidently, if war debts and reparations were to be repaid, Germany had to remain a prosperous and stable society, if only because it was one of the world's three major trading powers. Instead, it was riven by recriminations, denunciation of reparations, bitter internecine political struggle, and, by 1931, the climb to power of the National Socialist Party, threatening to end the democratic constitution and to overturn the Treaty of Versailles. Yet about three-quarters of the borrowing by German credit institutions and by local governments was from the United States, and the flow continued even in 1931.

America's wartime allies could not congratulate themselves on having restored by their own political decisions a durable framework of politico-economic cooperation. Faced with the fragmentation of the Habsburg Empire into its ethnic component parts, with the replacement of the Russian Empire by the Soviet Federation and then the Soviet Union, governed by self-proclaimed international revolutionaries, western European states were mainly concerned to preserve their prewar socioeconomic governing practices. In particular this meant continuing to depend mainly on established import and excise taxes for revenue so that the balance of the fiscal burden did not fall proportionately more heavily on the middle class than it had before the war, a political stance that strengthened their commitment to obtaining reparations from Germany in lieu of tax reform at home. The same conservative longing for the prewar world led in the direction of reestablishing a settlements mechanism for international trade as close as possible to the prewar gold standard, by which the price of gold was kept within narrow limits and either gold or foreign currencies convertible into gold within these limits were kept as central bank reserves and used to settle international debts.

The important question was at what rate the exchange between gold and national currency would be reestablished. Most countries, taking account of the changes in trade patterns caused by the creation of new countries out of the Habsburg Empire, expected initial difficulties in returning to the prewar system and selected lower exchange rates against gold and the dollar than the prewar rate. New countries also aimed at a low rate. The United Kingdom did not. In its own conservative gesture toward its major role in the prewar trade and payments system, it returned to the prewar pound/dollar exchange rate, increasing the price of its exports against those of European competitors.

There was no effort to coordinate internationally the rates of exchange that countries chose. While the new British rate forced deflation on the United Kingdom, France experienced a persistent inflation and currency depreciation until 1926, when the franc was "stabilized" with the backing of legislation shaped to prevent further inflation. This disorderly return to a form of gold standard among the world's major traders became a barrier to their attempts to escape from the worldwide deflation of 1929. It did more to sustain the Depression or, through trade competition, enforce it on others. While the French economy grew vigorously with inflation until 1926–1927, French foreign investment in the United States and the United Kingdom was high. The 1926 stabilization of the franc pushed the United States and the United Kingdom into further difficulties as gold flowed back into France, but the Bank of France was unable, because of the 1926 legislation, to readjust its exchange rate for fear of stimulating inflation.

The variety of national experiences in the timing and depth of the Great Depression reflects the haphazard return to separate national visions of the past and future. A significant element in British post-1918 trade deficits was the decline in Britain's prewar staple exports, already declining after 1890: textiles, cotton thread, ships, coal, and pig iron. In 1928 British shipbuilding was utilizing only about half of its total capacity, cotton about three-quarters. Most of the activity in such industries being regional, the pattern of unemployment was much more regional than, for example, in the United States or Germany. The regions officially characterized as "old industrial"—the north of England, southern Wales, and central Scotland—contributed 50 percent of net national industrial output in 1924, but only 38 percent in 1935. In the Midlands and southern England newer industries, especially automobiles and chemicals, contributed 29 percent of net industrial output in 1924 and 37 percent in 1935. In those newer industrial regions consumer goods sales grew and housing construction boomed, in contrast to the United States' experience. Nevertheless, on the national scale mass unemployment accounted for more than half the British people living in "primary poverty" in 1936, a measure of the slowness with

**Scots march from Dundee to London to protest unemployment and hunger in the United Kingdom, 1932.**
©HULTON-DEUTSCH COLLECTION/CORBIS

which the United Kingdom adjusted to post-1918 trading conditions.

## THE COLLAPSE OF THE GOLD STANDARD

In addition to the adjustment problems after the First World War and the tendency of the restored gold standard to impede recovery from the deflationary pressures that announced themselves in 1929 in the industrialized nations, the low level of prices of primary products was a further persistent source of deflationary pressure on the larger world economy. While the price of agricultural goods fluctuated markedly in the mid-1920s, the overall terms of trade between developed, industrialized states and states that produced mainly raw materials and food moved in favor of the industrialized states in the interwar period. As a market for manufactured exports, the world's primary product producers were weakening before and throughout the Great Depression. Forty percent of British exports, the great body of which were manufactured goods, were exported to primary producers while at the same time declining industries such as cotton thread and textiles were facing increasing competition from slowly industrializing primary producers such as India.

Many large primary producing counties were heavily dependent on a narrow range of products. Raw wool accounted for about 41 percent of Australian exports by value, cotton for about 80 percent of the value of Egyptian exports. From other primary producers foodstuffs dominated exports: 75 percent of Cuba's exports was sugar, 71 percent of Brazil's was coffee. It is not surprising that such primary producers were among the first to abandon the gold standard. Argentina, Brazil, Australia, and New Zealand all did so before 1930. The main markets for the industrialized countries were each other. The fall in their exports to primary producers was of too small a total value to weigh against the value of the interchange between developed economies, but the poverty of the agricultural producers was one more barrier to escaping from deflation.

The manufacturing economies held out longer on the gold standard. The collapse of the Credit Anstalt bank in Austria in 1931 led in July to the imposition of exchange and trade controls by Hungary. In the same month Germany also imposed exchange and trade controls. In September the United Kingdom abandoned a century of the pursuit of free trade when it left the gold standard and simultaneously devalued the pound sterling against the gold dollar by 30 percent while preparing a general tariff. The exchange rate of the pound, technically floating, was thenceforward determined by the Bank of England's management of the floating rate. As the 1930s turned increasingly toward war, quantitative trade controls, mainly import quotas, supplemented protectionism. In Germany and much of central Europe, annual bilateral trade agreements strictly controlled the goods traded and the value of their currency. The new German Reichsmark, for example, was not convertible. France and Germany became insignificant trading partners of each other. British trade, directed by tariff preferences and the retention of sterling as a convertible currency within the Commonwealth, increased with distant Australia and New Zealand and decreased with neighboring European industrial producers. None of these outcomes was conducive to recovery. Protection of domestic agriculture from foreign imports became general in Europe and the United States. It was to be well into the 1950s before these trade barriers began to be carefully and slowly reduced and the automatic convertibility of European currencies into gold/dollars began to be reinstated.

The search for national causes of the Great Depression, whether in the United States or Germany or elsewhere, seems a somewhat limited enterprise when so much evidence shows that the system of international settlements was so

## TABLE 2

| Increase in gross domestic product (GDP), 1932/33–1937/38 | |
| --- | --- |
| United States | 46.6% |
| Germany | 67.5% |
| France | 7.9% |
| United Kingdom | 25.7% |
| Sweden | 38.3% |
| Belgium | 9.8% |
| Italy | 20.8% |
| Netherlands | 12.2% |

SOURCE: Aldcroft, 1978, p. 81

defective, without central authority or agreed objectives, while being so effective at transmitting deflation to each and every one of the main trading nations. Consider but the case of the United Kingdom, whose central bank had played so facilitating a role in the pre-1914 gold standard. With large prewar surpluses on goods, turned by 1920–1924 into a small deficit, and with a deficit on long-term capital flows, it was in no position to return to the exchange rate against the dollar of the years when it had been seen as a manager of the system. There was no manager of the system in the interwar period.

To blame the United States, as some do, for not stepping into the role of "hegemon" is greatly to exaggerate the authority that a hegemon could have exerted in so divided a world. Hegemony would in any case have been no substitute for international agreement but only a prop to it. International agreement had to wait for a much greater sense of common purpose, such as came in the Cold War of the 1950s, furthered, no doubt, by the terrible consequences of the National Socialist government in Germany.

## RECOVERY

If the first step toward recovery was to break the constraints of the gold standard, one would expect the countries that stayed on gold until the late 1930s to show a lower rate of recovery than those that left it. France, Belgium, and the Netherlands, three countries that stayed longer on gold, do show a lower level of recovery by 1937/38 than others. The spectacular recovery of Germany to full employment and high levels of output reflects the extent of concentration on rearmament, broadly defined. The two countries that had suffered the worst falls in output, Germany and the United States, showed the biggest gains, although in the United States this recovery was much less attributable to rearmament than in Germany. Yet by summer 1938 there were undeniable indications of another economic downturn. It would be no exaggeration to say that the threat of another world war led to a more convincing upturn in 1941 in the United States.

A more apt comparison is between France and Belgium on the one hand and the United Kingdom on the other. Breaking the shackles of the gold standard in the way that the United Kingdom did was a serious blow to international cooperation; Britain could be fairly accused of pursuing a beggar-my-neighbor policy. It is not, though, necessarily true that all countries that abandoned the gold standard were making things harder for those, like France, who remained on it, for they were relinquishing gold for those who sought, like France, to acquire it. Furthermore, the evidence from all countries, including those that left the gold standard, is that reflation was undertaken only cautiously. The theoretical demonstration by the British economist John Maynard Keynes that increased public expenditure was necessary for a return to economic equilibrium after so catastrophic a slump made more impact toward the end of the decade than at the start of the recovery. Concentration of expenditure on rearmament and public works, as in Germany, cut off the economy from its long-established trade relations with neighboring states that stayed on gold. German trade with France was insignificant by 1937. British trade and income recovered only slowly. Even after six months of war and military conscription and seven years of increasing rearmament expenditure, about a million working-age men in Britain were still registered as seeking work in early 1940. Only in Germany did public works expenditure, on express highways and on the stimulation of the automobile market, produce large increases in employment by 1935/36. Its objective, however, was not a return to equilibrium, at least not within Germany's existing frontiers. Germany imposed such draconian controls on the national currency as to make it unwanted beyond the national frontier. Fear of hyperinflation gnawed at the heart of all countries that had experienced it

in the 1920s. In these circumstances the increase in money supply that freedom from the gold standard permitted helps to explain less than half the adjustment to higher capacity utilization of manufacturing plants in the major industrial countries by September 1939. The shadow of the Great Depression thus hovered over all who had been caught in its coils, whatever their subsequent governments or their actions in seeking recovery.

*See also* **Bretton Woods Agreement; Capitalism; Inflation.**

BIBLIOGRAPHY

Aldcroft, Derek H. *From Versailles to Wall Street, 1919–1929.* London, 1977.

Eichengreen, Barry. *The European Economy, 1914–1970.* London, 1978.

———. *Golden Fetters: The Gold Standard and the Great Depression, 1919–1939.* New York, 1992.

Fearson, Peter. *The Origins and Nature of the Great Slump 1929–1932.* London, 1979.

Friedman, Milton, and Anna J. Schwartz. *A Monetary History of the United States, 1867–1960.* Princeton, N.J., 1963.

Mouré, Kenneth. *The Gold Standard Illusion: France, the Bank of France, and the International Gold Standard, 1914–1939.* Oxford, U.K., 2002.

Secretariat of the League of Nations. *The Course and Phases of the World Economic Depression.* Rev. ed. Geneva, 1931.

Sering, Max. *Germany under the Dawes Plan: Origin, Legal Foundations, and Economic Effects of the Reparation Payments.* Translated by S. Milton Hart. London, 1929.

Temin, Peter. *Did Monetary Forces Cause the Great Depression?* New York, 1976.

ALAN S. MILWARD

---

# DERRIDA, JACQUES (1930–2004), French philosopher.

Jacques Derrida was a French philosopher who had a career equal in international status to that of Jean-Paul Sartre (1905–1980). Both were controversial, prolific writers and indefatigable champions of human rights and democratic values. And both were concerned with questions of ethics, difference, and otherness.

Although Derrida's interest in topics like forgiveness, hospitality, and friendship was inherently existential, his thinking stems from a current in French intellectual history that developed via Martin Heidegger (1889–1976) in opposition to Sartrean existentialism. In the 1940s, Georges Bataille (1897–1962), Maurice Blanchot (1907–2003), and Emmanuel Levinas (1906–1995) had called certain philosophical assumptions into question, among them, Cartesian reflection theory (typified by the phrase "I think, therefore I am") and Hegelian dialectics (typified by oppositions that achieve synthesis), both of which were central to Sartre's *L'être et le néant* (1943; *Being and Nothingness*). Bataille thought that Hegel's dialectical oppositions did not achieve synthesis without leaving some remainders that could not be accounted for and that Sartre had overlooked this. Levinas thought that the "I think" of reflection theory could not adequately account for the difference of other people, whereas Sartre generally assumed all others are fundamentally symmetrical to the self. And Blanchot argued in refutation of Sartre's writings on literature, that "writing is my consciousness without me," hence demystifying Sartre's assumption that a text is the direct translation of an author's views and feelings.

In 1967 Derrida published three books that changed the intellectual landscape of philosophy: *La voix et le phénomène* (1967; *Speech and Phenomena*), *L'écriture et la différence* (1967; *Writing and Difference*), and *De la grammatologie* (1967; *Of Grammatology*). Essentially, these are the first books to advance "deconstruction," the dismantling of hierarchical oppositions in order to overturn established values. Derrida's work is based, in part, on the insights initiated by Bataille, Levinas, and Blanchot some thirty years earlier. Derrida touches on a major thread of intellectual history that involves prejudices in favor of "voice" (interiority) versus its transcription into "writing" (exteriority). The problem with "writing" is that it is disseminative (miscreant, polymorphous perverse, uncontainable, viral, open ended, multisourced), whereas "voice" is seated in a particular consciousness (intentionality, psychology, the existential situation of the author). Derrida's thesis in *Of Grammatology* was that since Gutenberg (that is, since the invention of a printing press using movable type) "writing" has been increasingly replacing "voice" and that this is indicative of philosophy's

overcoming of metaphysics, something that even major philosophers like Edmund Husserl (1859–1938), Martin Heidegger, and Sartre had not quite noticed.

Another break with Sartre concerns social contract theory. Sartre saw modern European social relations as alienated and in his Marxist phase of the 1950s investigated notions of the group and the collective in order to combat alienation. Derrida is suspicious of alienation as a concept because it begs the question "What is a social relation?" Unlike Sartre, Derrida did not believe that Marxism had the answer. Instead, in *Of Grammatology* he turned to Jean-Jacques Rousseau (1712–1778) in order to reopen this question. In work on Franz Kafka (1883–1924) in the early 1980s, Derrida related issues of social relation to questions of law, in particular, Kafka's famous parable of the man before the law. Derrida took the "impossibility" of the relation to law as the universal condition of any social contract, given that a contract involves some kind of law (implicit or explicit) that is not ever entirely rational. Among much else, Derrida has considered the vicissitudes of the social relation (or contract) in terms of the signature, the gift, forgiveness, hospitality, and perjury.

In *Politiques de l'amitié* (1994; *The Politics of Friendship*), Derrida queried the notion of the friend in terms of the paradoxical law: "O friends, there is no friend." In *Donner le temps. 1: Fausse monnaie* (1991; *Given Time*) he investigated the gift as a social "principle without principle" in that the performativity of giving is not codifiable in terms of law, even though patterns or norms of gift exchange can be established. In *Monolinguisme de l'autre; ou, La prothèse d'origine* (1996; *Monolingualism of the Other*), Derrida investigated the social relation in terms of a social contract with language: that one speak (or perform) only one language, hence coming under its law or rule, despite the paradoxical corollary that this language really is not ever one's own and that its law is alien. In all of these instances, performativity is key since it can never be entirely objectified, rationalized, or accounted for.

By the 1990s Derrida had become something of a cultural icon. In France his portrait appeared on postage stamps, and several films about him have been made, among them, *Derrida* (2002) by

Kirby Dick and Amy Ziering Kofman. Derrida gave numerous radio interviews during his life, was prominent in the French press, was falsely arrested (in 1981) in Prague by Communist authorities for trafficking in drugs (really, Derrida was being punished for conducting a seminar), was a founder and director of the Collège Internationale de Philosophie, became the occasion for a flap at Cambridge University over his being awarded an honorary doctorate (various analytical philosophers objected on methodological grounds), and in 1987 Derrida found himself at the center of a controversy over the honor of Paul de Man (1919–1983). A professor at Yale University and fellow practitioner of deconstruction, de Man had concealed a shadowy life under Nazism that came to light after his death when a researcher exposed articles de Man had written for a fascist Belgian newspaper. Among Derrida's last books was *Voyous: Deux essais sur la raison* (2003; *Rogues*), a book that studies political rhetoric, in particular, the phrase *rogue state*.

*See also* **Postmodernism; Sartre, Jean-Paul.**

BIBLIOGRAPHY

Bennington, Geoffrey, and Jacques Derrida. *Jacques Derrida.* Translated by Geoffrey Bennington. Chicago, 1993.

Caputo, John. *The Prayers and Tears of Jacques Derrida: Religion without Religion.* Bloomington, Ind., 1997.

Gasché, Rodolphe. *The Tain of the Mirror: Derrida and the Philosophy of Reflection.* Cambridge, Mass., 1986.

Rapaport, Herman. *Heidegger and Derrida: Reflections on Time and Language.* Lincoln, Neb., 1989. Reprint, 2004.

Royle, Nicholas. *Jacques Derrida.* London, 2003.

HERMAN RAPAPORT

# DE SICA, VITTORIO (1901–1974), Italian actor and film director.

Born in Sora, Italy, on 7 July 1901 into a lower-middle-class family, Vittorio De Sica directed at least 25 films and acted in more than 150. He spent his childhood years in Naples and then moved with his family to Rome in 1912. He began his career as an actor in the early 1920s, when he joined Tatiana Pavlova's theater company. He made his cinema debut in 1918 in a supporting role in *Il processo Clémenceau* (The Clemenceau affair) by Alfredo De Antoni, but starred only in 1932 in *Gli uomini, che mascalzoni!* (*What Scoundrels Men Are!*) by Mario Camerini. Interestingly, that last film was part of a series inspired by the Hollywood model of light comedies, but the scenes were filmed outdoors, rather than on a set. De Sica became famous for playing in elegantly romantic comedies directed by a number of filmmakers including Vittorio Cottafavi (*I nostri sogni/Our Dreams*, 1943) and Amleto Palermi (from *La vecchia signora/The Old Lady*, 1932, to *La peccatrice*, 1940).

In 1939 he decided to become a film director. His first experience behind the camera came with *Rose scarlatte* (1940; *Red Roses*), an adaptation of a successful play. Then he improved with *Maddalena, zero in condotta* (1940; *Maddalena, Zero for Conduct*), *Teresa venerdi* (1941; *Doctor Beware*), and *Un Garibaldino al convento* (1942; *A Garibaldian in the Convent*). All these films stand apart from Italy's political situation before and during the war. If De Sica had no sympathy for the fascist regime, he did not use his popularity to argue against Benito Mussolini (1883–1945). However, he claimed that for the last eight months of the war he hid two Jewish families in Rome.

The turning point of De Sica's career was the meeting with Cesare Zavattini (1902–1989), a screenwriter and filmmaker. Their first collaboration began with *I bambini ci guardano* (1944; *The Children Are Watching Us*). They shared a common interest in the destiny of the Italian cinema in the postwar period and Zavattini, in particular, thought that the taste for reality came not from one side of the belligerents, but from the two of them, the defeated as well as the victors.

Thus, De Sica and Zavattini together wrote four major films: *Sciuscià* (1946; *Shoeshine*), *Ladri di biciclette* (1948; *The Bicycle Thieves*), *Miracolo a Milano* (1951; *Miracle in Milan*) and *Umberto D* (1952). Together with the films directed by Luchino Visconti (1906–1976), Roberto Rossellini (1906–1977), and Giuseppe De Santis (1917–1997), these masterpieces mark the renewal of a taste for reality, a period of cinema usually called "neorealism." André Bazin, in the most powerful text ever written on De Sica ("De Sica as Director," 1952), claims that there

**Lamberto Maggiorani as the father and Enzo Staiola as the son, in a scene from *The Bicycle Thieves*,** 1948.
PRODUZIONE DE SICA/THE KOBAL COLLECTION

are not so many differences between all these film-makers. They used location shooting, nonprofessional actors, and other techniques to present situations as realistically as possible. It was often by choice but sometimes by necessity. Nevertheless, what makes De Sica different from the others, especially Rossellini, is his sensibility and the way he directed the cast: "It is through poetry that De Sica's realism takes its full meaning," writes Bazin, adding, "The neorealism is an ontologic stance before being aesthetic." Far from Visconti's aesthetics of decadence, De Sica always offered a humanist view of the poor, the outcast people of the Italian society.

*Shoeshine,* a story of the disintegration of a friendship between two Italian youths who fall victim to the state's juvenile detention system, won a special Academy Award in 1947. The award citation reads: "The high quality of this motion picture, brought to eloquent life in a country scarred by war, is proof to the world that the creative spirit can triumph over adversity." *The Bicycle Thieves,* which won an Academy Award for best foreign film and is certainly De Sica's highest achievement, tells a simple story: Ricci, an unemployed man, lines up every morning looking for work. One day, an advertisement says that there is a job, but only for a man with a bicycle. "I have a bicycle!" Ricci cries out, but actually he does not, for it has been pawned. Eventually, he finds one, but it happens to be stolen. At the end of the film, Ricci is tempted to steal a bicycle himself, continuing the cycle of theft and poverty. What is striking in the film is not so much the social description as the way the characters are confronted with ethical or moral choices in their personal life.

In *Miracle in Milan* and *Umberto D* De Sica continues to explore the plight of the poor and dispossessed. For Bazin, *Umberto D* is especially interesting in the way De Sica works with time and the narrative and not only on the representation or interpretation of social issues: "The stakes are to make spectacular and dramatic the very time of life, and the natural duration of a human being to whom nothing particular happens" (p. 326; translated from the French).

*See also* **Cinema.**

BIBLIOGRAPHY

*Primary Sources*

De Sica, Vittorio. *Lettere dal set*. Edited by Emi De Sica and Giancarlo Governi. Milan, 1987.

*Secondary Sources*

Bazin, André. *What Is Cinema?* Translated by Hugh Gray. Berkeley, Calif., 1967–1971.

Brunetta, Gian Piero. *Storia del cinema italiano*. Vol. 3: *Dal neorealismo al miracolo economico, 1945–1959*. 4th ed. Rome, 2001.

Cardullo, Bert. *Vittorio De Sica: Director, Actor, Screenwriter*. Jefferson, N.C., 2002.

Darretta, John. *Vittorio De Sica: A Guide to References and Resources*. Boston, Mass., 1983.

CHRISTIAN DELAGE

---

# DESTALINIZATION.

Destalinization, a term of Western origin, refers to the dismantling of various aspects of the politics, judicial system, economy, social values, and cultural life of the Soviet Union that were associated with the legacy of Joseph Stalin (1879–1953).

## CHRONOLOGY AND ORIGINS

The chronology of destalinization is not settled, but it is most often presumed to have begun right after Stalin's death in March 1953. It is possible to distinguish two periods when Stalin's legacy was debated most intensely—one from 1953 through 1964, coinciding with Nikita Khrushchev's term as first secretary of the Communist Party of the Soviet Union, and the other one from 1985 through 1991, when Mikhail Gorbachev headed the party on the eve of the USSR's collapse.

Destalinization was rooted in World War II. Victory in the war brought about a new sense of self-worth in people who had fought and seen that the country's fate depended on them. After 1945 many, especially the intelligentsia, hoped that the regime's repressive policies would be relaxed, burdens on the collectivized peasantry would be alleviated, the militarized economy would be modified toward the people's everyday needs, intellectual life would be liberalized, and in general the government would show some degree of appreciation for the citizens' contribution to victory. Frustrated in the late 1940s, these hopes and expectations nonetheless survived, and the pressing desire for change prepared ground for the actual changes of the 1950s.

Judging by how quickly reforms were implemented after March 1953, the need for them had become clear to many of the country's leaders while Stalin was still alive. Some scholars even propose an embryonic "destalinisation under Stalin" (Gorlizki, p. 2), discerning it in the changes within the party apparatus at the Nineteenth Party Congress (1952) and in the rhetoric of "collective leadership" and "inner-party democracy" that developed in the press on the eve of the congress. One of the first socially critical publications, Valentin Ovechkin's sketch *Raionnye budni* (District routine), which exposed the deplorable state of the agricultural sector, also came out in 1952.

## DESTALINIZATION UNDER KHRUSHCHEV

Drastic changes, however, began only after Stalin's death. The first and most significant area of destalinization was the ending of mass reprisals and the release of prison camp inmates. In the spring of 1953 an amnesty for about 1.2 million criminal convicts was launched. The Kremlin-associated doctors who were earlier accused of conspiring against the country's top leadership (the so-called Doctors' Plot) were freed in April 1953. From 1954 to 1956 followed a wave of several hundred thousand releases of political prisoners from the camps. Parallel to that, the powers of the repressive organs were curtailed, and a (relatively small) number of special police officers were fired and/or sometimes prosecuted for having mistreated prisoners in the past. Prison camps, even though they persisted, were considerably reduced in size, and their regime temporarily became somewhat milder.

Release of prisoners accused of political crimes was in some cases accompanied by rehabilitation, which presumed restoring a person's juridical competence and reestablishing his or her reputation as a loyal member of Soviet society. In cases of former party members, the restoration of party membership was of key importance for rehabilitation. Occasionally, but by far not always, the rehabilitated ex-prisoner would receive material compensation, such as salary due for the years of unjust imprisonment, a room or an apartment, and/or reinstatement at a previous job. Those released but not rehabilitated faced much worse prospects for social reintegration, because they were often denied jobs and residence in their hometowns, especially those from Moscow and Leningrad.

According to research published in the 1990s and early 2000s, Soviet society showed mixed reactions to the release of prisoners. While many had always believed in their innocence, there were quite a few who continued to regard the former convicts as enemies or at least displayed a degree of suspicion toward them. Mistrust and rejection created additional obstacles for the former victims' return to normal life.

Just as mixed were people's reactions to another critical aspect of destalinization—the removal of Stalin's omnipresent images and praises for him from the press, art, and school textbooks. Conducted under the slogan of struggle against "the cult of personality," this iconoclastic campaign brought about not only relief and joy but also a good deal of confusion and disorientation among Soviet citizens, whose world of symbols was now falling apart.

The crucial moment in destalinization came in February 1956, when Khrushchev delivered his famous "secret speech" before the dead-silent delegates of the Twentieth Party Congress in Moscow. This revolutionary speech attacked Stalin for creating his own worship in the country, for unleashing mass terror against innocent people (mostly party members were mentioned as victims), and for committing serious blunders in state leadership. With his speech, Khrushchev put a decisive seal of approval on the release and rehabilitation of camp prisoners, as well as on the dismantling of the Stalin cult. One other important consequence of the Twentieth Congress was the return of several nationalities, deported during World War II as "unreliable," to their original areas of residence.

At that time, the secret speech was published in the West but not in the Soviet Union. Yet the text was read aloud at meetings of local and institutional party organizations all across the country, and although the meetings were supposed to be held behind closed doors, it was not impossible for someone interested to gain entry. The content of the speech thus became an open secret. Again, reactions in the audiences were mixed—joyful relief, guilt for compliance with the past terror, denial, desire for self-vindication, and widespread confusion as to what would happen to the country next. A violent outburst of protest against the public denigration of Stalin broke out in his home country, Georgia.

Perhaps the one most common reaction to the secret speech was shock, because the indictment of the recently deified Stalin now became official and was verbalized by the country's top leader. It was this shock that suggested the most serious limit for destalinization—the issue of legitimacy. It was under Stalin that the Soviet system had taken shape in its essential features, and most of the Soviet period to date had been spent under Stalin. Therefore, the open denunciation of Stalin could not but expose to doubt the legitimacy of the Soviet system itself. This logic was not lost on numerous officials who felt the need to proceed alertly, if at all, about admitting the blunders and crimes of the past. The urge to maintain the legitimacy of the Soviet order dictated caution in further attacks on Stalin. Between 1953 and 1961, the press, both political and literary, kept the theme of the terror heavily understated, either passing it over in silence or referring to it in very reticent, elusive language.

At the same time, other important aspects of the Stalinist order came under attack in these years. The party restated its commitment to collective leadership, opposing it to the much-criticized "cult of personality," which now became a politically acceptable euphemism for the Stalin years. In the countryside, taxes on agricultural produce were lowered, debts written off, and it became easier for peasants to travel or move to cities, an improvement that greatly softened the restrictions on peasant mobility imposed during collectivization in the early 1930s. A series of reforms in industrial management was launched, with many of the Stalin-era central branch ministries dismantled (1957) and their powers transferred to the local "councils of the economy" (*sovnarkhozy*). Correspondingly, the attack on the ministerial bureaucracy became a prominent theme in the newspapers and literature, culminating in the publication by the journal *Novy mir* of Vladimir Dudintsev's novel *Not by Bread Alone* (1956), which became a sensation thanks to its unprecedentedly bold and comprehensive criticism of Stalin-era industrial management. Yet another important area of liberalization was relations with the West, where in 1954 and 1955 the first cultural exchange programs were launched and travel abroad became somewhat easier for a (very limited) number of Soviet citizens. The mid-1950s were also the moment when, after a long gap, the Soviet audiences were for the first time exposed to abstract art, via Western art exhibits and the reopening of the turn-of-the-century art collections at home.

The 1956 uprisings against the Soviet regime in Poland and especially Hungary, provoked by revelations about the Stalin terror, urged the Khrushchev leadership to tighten up ideological control within the country, which, together with the Suez Crisis of 1956, slowed down the Soviet rapprochement with the West. Further alienation came with the 1958 press campaign against the poet Boris Pasternak (1890–1960), after he had been awarded the Nobel Prize—largely for his novel *Doctor Zhivago*, which fundamentally reinterpreted Russia's experience of the revolution and the civil war. Despite all these setbacks, the processes of parting with Stalin's legacy did not stop in the late 1950s: much of the intellectual fermentation in the country continued, and so did its exposure to Western influences.

Destalinization received a powerful boost in 1961 at the Twenty-Second Party Congress, when Khrushchev resumed his attack on Stalin and the past terror. The Twenty-Second Congress dealt a final blow to the public commemoration of Stalin's name and image: in 1961 places named after him were renamed, his monuments were destroyed (except in his birthplace of Gori), and his mummified body was taken out of the Lenin Mausoleum and reburied in a simpler grave by the Kremlin wall.

This time the attack on the terror was publicized more boldly, and quite a few rehabilitations made their way to the newspapers. In the period from 1961 to 1964, publications about the mass reprisals became much more numerous and outspoken than ever before. Encouraged by this legitimization of remembrance, thousands of people began sending written memoirs about the Stalin terror to the Central Committee and to various periodicals. In particular, many manuscripts were sent to *Novy mir*, thanks to the high prestige and the semi-oppositional reputation of this journal, whose editor, Alexander Tvardovsky (1910–1971), paid great attention to the terror theme. Only a few were published, and yet these texts, especially Alexander Solzhenitsyn's *One Day in the Life of Ivan Denisovich* (1962), powerfully influenced the ways in which thousands of people thought about their country's past and present.

## DESTALINIZATION AFTER KHRUSHCHEV

Khrushchev's removal from power in October 1964 put a gradual end to this brief outburst of fairly open and critical reassessment of the Stalin past. Publications mentioning the terror did not cease immediately; and yet from 1965 on their number went down and their language became ever more evasive. It was then that many people began fearing a "re-stalinization," the restitution of Stalin's name and a return to the repressive policies of his time. In 1966 concerns about the terror coming back manifested themselves in the intelligentsia's revulsion against the trial of the writers Andrei Sinyavsky (1925–1997) and Yuli Daniel (1925–1988), who were arrested and imprisoned for publishing their works in the West. Much of Sinyavsky's and Daniel's writing also dealt with the legacy of Stalin's terror and the possibilities of its return.

The terror never came back, nor did the formal rehabilitation of Stalin, but the new leaders of the country, above all Leonid Brezhnev (head of the party from 1964 to 1982), did put the debate about Stalin's legacy on hold, sensing its explosive nature. Nevertheless, the interpretation of the Stalin past, and hence, essentially, the entire Soviet experience, remained a major concern for many people who in the 1970s retreated into private family and friendly circles to discuss these issues.

The continuing importance of the Stalin theme became clear in the late 1980s, when Mikhail Gorbachev launched his reforms, greatly liberalizing the intellectual climate. The old discussions about Stalin and Stalinism revived with new force and vigor in the late 1980s and early 1990s. Many literary works of the 1960s that had never seen light before were now published, together with new books and films about the past, providing food for thought and innumerable discussions, open and private. It may be safely concluded that the debate about the Stalin past was one of the major factors that, through revelations about the scope of terror and the massive disenchantment with the Soviet order, brought the USSR to its collapse in 1991.

Born in the mid-1950s, the term *destalinization* has by now become somewhat narrow and obsolete. It prompts the reader to view the Soviet system as a single-handed creation and epitome of Stalin's will, thus following the "cult of personality" reasoning for the country's problems that the Khrushchev leadership advanced in the 1950s and early 1960s. While having some validity, this term tends to obscure the fact that the Soviet system, together with all attempts to reform it, had deep-seated historical and structural origins in society and culture, which extended far beyond Stalin's personality, and of which Stalin himself might be but a product. Future research may replace the term *destalinization* with one or several more adequate characteristics for the complex and important developments that Soviet society went through between 1953 and 1991.

*See also* **Denazification; Gulag; Khrushchev, Nikita; Purges; Soviet Union; Stalin, Joseph; Terror.**

BIBLIOGRAPHY

*Primary Sources*

Artizov, A. N., Iu. V. Sigachev, V. G. Khlopov, and I. N. Shevchuk, comps. *Reabilitatsiia: Kak eto bylo; Dokumenty Prezidiuma TsK KPSS i drugie materialy.* 3 vols. Moscow, 2000–2004.

Eimermacher, Karl, and Vitalii Iu. Afiani, eds. *Doklad N. S. Khrushcheva o kul'te lichnosti Stalina na XX s'ezde KPSS: Dokumenty.* Moscow, 2002.

*Secondary Sources*

Adler, Nanci. *The Gulag Survivor: Beyond the Soviet System.* New Brunswick, N.J., 2002.

Gorlizki, Yoram. "Party Revivalism and the Death of Stalin." *Slavic Review* 54, no. 1 (1995): 1–22.

Jones, Polly, ed. *The Dilemmas of Destalinisation: A Social and Cultural History of Reform in the Khrushchev Era.* London and New York, 2006.

Smith, Kathleen E. *Remembering Stalin's Victims: Popular Memory and the End of the USSR.* Ithaca, N.Y., 1996.

Taubman, William. *Khrushchev: The Man and His Era.* New York, 2003.

Taubman, William, Sergei Khrushchev, and Abbott Gleason, eds. *Nikita Khrushchev.* Translated by David Gehrenbeck, Eileen Kane, and Alla Bashenko. New Haven, Conn., 2000.

Toker, Leona. *Return from the Archipelago: Narratives of Gulag Survivors.* Bloomington, Ind., 2000.

Tompson, William J. *Khrushchev: A Political Life.* New York, 1995.

van Goudoever, Albert P. *The Limits of Destalinization in the Soviet Union: Political Rehabilitations in the Soviet Union since Stalin.* Translated by Frans Hijkoop. London, 1986.

Zubkova, Elena. *Russia after the War: Hopes, Illusions, and Disappointments, 1945–1957.* Translated and edited by Hugh Ragsdale. Armonk, N.Y., 1998.

DENIS KOZLOV

---

**DE STIJL.** De Stijl (literally, The Style) was a movement founded in the neutral Netherlands in 1917 by the painter, philosopher, poet, savant, and tireless proselytizer Theo van Doesburg (1883–1931), with the significant contribution of Piet Mondrian; it was also the name of a magazine, published in Leiden from 1917 to 1931. The movement encompassed a fluctuating and tenuously connected group of adherents who shared selective goals but interpreted them according to their own personal viewpoints and invariably fell out with the volatile Van Doesburg after a time. At first exclusively Dutch, after 1921 advocates were drawn from an international cadre of artists and activists.

**Schroeder House, designed by Gerrit Rietveld, 1923.** Foto Marburg/Art Resource, NY

De Stijl shared with the avant-garde configurations that proliferated in the first three decades of the twentieth century a radical and somewhat utopian agenda that sought to reunite art with life and, indeed, saw aesthetic transformation as the chief medium for social change. Its signature aesthetic elements included a preference for abstract geometric form, the orthogonal, and the flat plane; the incorporation of modular composition; the use of primary colors along with black, white, and gray; and the subordination of the natural to the mechanistic. All these motifs symbolized De Stijl's new worldview, which acknowledged the ethical as well as the physical impact of recent scientific, technological, and political revolutions on human existence, experience, and conduct. The group speculated about the notion of space-time; the conquest of nature and the triumph of the machine were among its aims. Through the reform of music, dance, literature, and arguably most of all, design in two and three dimensions (from typography to city planning, from furniture to film), a restorative harmony was to be born. Thus Manifesto 1 (1918) averred that "the war is destroying the old world with its contents. The new art has brought forward what the new consciousness of time contains: a balance between the universal and the individual" (quoted in Overy, p. 47).

De Stijl emphasized the dominance of the spiritual, which was embodied in an abstract formal language, and sought a global equilibrium characterized by *eenheid in veelheid,* unity in diversity. This would be manifest in the *Gesamtkunstwerk,* the total work of art, an ideal that inspired many architects and designers in the later nineteenth century and on into the twentieth. By placing the beholder within, rather than before, the work of art, artists, architects, and craftspersons would collaboratively create an environment that integrated opposites such as vertical and horizontal, male and female, the individual and the communal, and that would both result in and reflect concord.

Unlike some other contemporary constellations, De Stijl was not overtly political in the sense of favoring a particular party, though most of those associated with it were left-leaning when not actually communist. At various times Van Doesburg forged connections with futurism, Russian constructivism, the Bauhaus, and even Dada, whose embrace of the irrational and the anarchic would seem to be at odds with De Stijl's deliberate and disciplined procedures. Such links illustrate both the broadly representative position of De Stijl within the avant-garde and the fruitlessness of characterizing the movement in simple black-and-white terms. Published in the periodical were works and words from spokesmen as various as the Italian Filippo Marinetti and the Russian El Lissitzky. Van Doesburg himself assumed multiple personae and could, it seems, entertain antithetical beliefs simultaneously; born C. E. M. Küpper, he also wrote Dada poetry as I. K. Bonset and as a futurist called himself Aldo Camini. From 1921 to 1923 he spent time at the first Bauhaus, in Weimar, and when its founder, Walter Gropius, did not invite him to become a professor, he taught a rival independent course that would influence subsequent Bauhaus designs. De Stijl's production of fluid and flexible space and its integration of interior and exterior were subsumed into the rhetoric of International Style architecture.

Sources of De Stijl include the British Arts and Crafts movement, which similarly included moral considerations in its innovations in design and practice, and cubism. Perhaps the most influential single figure was Frank Lloyd Wright (1867–1959), who recognized the consequences of the intervention of the machine in the building process. Wright's right-angled designs with hovering planes inspired a number of De Stijl projects, most notably those by Robert van't Hoff (1887–1979), Gerrit Rietveld (1888–1964), Jan Wils (1891–1972), J. J. P. Oud (1890–1963), and Cornelis van Eesteren (1897–1988). Wright's work had been introduced to the Netherlands by H. P. Berlage (1856–1934), the doyen of Dutch architecture, whose rejection of historicism and search for socioartistic "unity in diversity" provided a powerful theoretical background.

Emanating from a small country during and immediately after World War I, De Stijl nevertheless had a widespread international impact. It has had a seductive staying power, manifested particularly in architecture and design, that surpasses most of its progressive contemporaries.

*See also* **Architecture; Lissitzky, El; Mondrian, Piet.**

BIBLIOGRAPHY

*De Stijl.* Facsimile edition. 3 vols. Amsterdam, 1968. Volumes 1 and 2 reproduce all the numbers of the magazine, while volume 3 provides English translations of many of the texts.

Friedman, Mildred, ed. *De Stijl: 1917–1931: Visions of Utopia.* Oxford, U.K., 1982.

Jaffé, Hans Ludwig C. *De Stijl 1917–1931: The Dutch Contribution to Modern Art.* Amsterdam, 1956. Paperback edition: Cambridge, Mass., and London, 1986.

Overy, Paul. *De Stijl.* Revised and expanded edition. London, 1991.

Troy, Nancy J. *The De Stijl Environment.* Cambridge, Mass., 1983.

HELEN SEARING

---

**DIANA, PRINCESS OF WALES** (Diana Frances Mountbatten-Windsor, née Spencer; 1961–1997), British princess and international icon.

Diana Spencer was the youngest daughter of Edward Spencer, then Viscount Althorp, subsequently the eighth earl of Spencer, and his wife Frances, née Burke Roche. She had two elder sisters and a younger brother. When her parents divorced in 1969, the custody over the children remained with the father. Until 1975, Diana lived in Sandringham, Norfolk, thereafter in the Spencer family seat at Althorp in Northamptonshire. She was educated at a preparatory school in Norfolk and a boarding school in Kent. At sixteen she went to finishing school in Switzerland, and in 1979 she moved to London, where she briefly worked at a kindergarten.

On 29 July 1981, in a spectacular wedding ceremony staged and widely perceived as a modern fairy tale, the twenty-year-old Lady Diana Spencer married the heir to the British throne, Charles, Prince of Wales (b. 1948), in London's St. Paul's Cathedral. More than a billion people around the world were estimated to have followed the event on either television or radio. Young, photogenic, and endowed with an often radiant smile, the new Princess of Wales easily took up the traditional royal roles of public appearances and charity work. She soon became one of the most popular members of the royal family. By giving birth to two sons, William

**Princess Diana visits children injured by land mines in Angola, January 1997.** AP/WIDE WORLD PHOTOS

(b. 1982) and Henry (b. 1984), she also fulfilled the most important dynastic role assigned to any princess, namely securing the line of succession.

Diana separated from her husband in 1992 and obtained a divorce in 1996. During the breakdown of her marriage, she embarked on a carefully planned media campaign in order to win public support and to cast a new role for herself outside the royal family. Particularly influential for the reshaping of her persona was her collaboration with the biographer Andrew Morton, who published the first edition of *Diana: Her True Story* in 1992. Although the direct involvement of the princess only became known after her death, more than two million copies of the book were sold in less than a year. Morton's narrative centered around the antithesis between the warm, tactile, and caring femininity of Diana and the cold, withdrawn, and cynical masculinity of Charles and the rest of the

royal family. Reversing the romantic fairy tale staged at her wedding, Morton presented Diana as the innocent victim of a royal public-relations campaign disguised as a love story. In a 1995 television interview seen by more than twenty-three million viewers in Britain alone, Diana replied to the question of whether her husband's long-term mistress, Camilla Parker-Bowles (b. 1947), had been "a factor" in the breakdown of her marriage: "Well, there were three of us in this marriage, so it was a bit crowded."

On 31 August 1997 Diana died following a car accident in the Pont de l'Alma underpass in Paris. While her severely injured bodyguard survived, Diana's romantic companion Dodi Al Fayed and his driver, who was later found out to have alcohol in his system, also died in the accident. French police investigations concluded that Diana's car had been traveling at excessive speed and that another car, which could never be found, had also been involved in the accident. Diana's premature death led to an overwhelming outpouring of public grief. In Britain, more than a million bouquets of flowers were laid in her honor, and hundreds of thousands of people stood in queues to sign books of condolence. An estimated 2.5 billion television viewers around the world followed the funeral service at Westminster Abbey on 6 September. She was buried on an island within an ornamental lake at Althorp.

The main reason for the unprecedented dimensions of the reactions to Diana's death was that in the course of her much publicized separation from the royal family the meanings of her persona had dramatically multiplied. No longer in the exclusive service of the British monarchy, she had become a multifaceted global icon who appealed to a great variety of individuals and groups, ranging from AIDS and land mine victims to people who had experienced similar matrimonial breakdowns. Descriptions such as the "people's princess" or the "queen of hearts" reflect the supranational and almost universally applicable meaning Diana had acquired by the time she died.

Despite much speculation about negative or even fatal effects of Diana's death on the future of the British monarchy, the institution proved to be remarkably resilient and stable. In 2005 Prince

Charles was even allowed to marry his long-term mistress Camilla Parker-Bowles.

*See also* **United Kingdom.**

BIBLIOGRAPHY

Berghahn, Sabine, and Sigrid Koch-Baumgarten, eds. *Mythos Diana: Von der Princess of Wales zur Queen of Hearts.* Giessen, Germany, 1999.

Davies, Jude. *Diana, a Cultural History: Gender, Race, Nation, and the People's Princess.* Houndmills, U.K., 2001.

Morton, Andrew. *Diana: Her True Story, in Her Own Words.* Rev. ed. New York, 1997.

Richards, Jeffrey, Scott Wilson, and Linda Woodhead, eds. *Diana: The Making of a Media Saint.* London, 1999.

ALEXIS SCHWARZENBACH

# DIEN BIEN PHU, BATTLE OF.

Dien Bien Phu (13 March–7 May 1954) was the last battle fought by the French Army in the twentieth century. It was also the last battle waged with forces drawn from other parts of the French Empire (which had been reorganized as the "French Union" in 1946). The defeat there, furthermore, signaled the beginning of the empire's definitive dismantlement: the fall of Dien Bien Phu inflicted a profound psychological shock on metropolitan France, instigated the demise of the Laniel government (1953–1954) and the rise of Pierre Mendès-France to power (prime minister, 1954–1955), as well as the signing on 21 July 1954 of the Geneva Accords, which ended France's engagement in Vietnam and drew up its partition, originally meant to be provisional.

## THE FRENCH POSITION

From a bird's eye point of view of the Dien Bien Phu basin-turned-battlefield in 1954, the strategic choices made by the French command over the course of the previous year appear rather stupefying. In order to loosen the pressure being exerted by the Vietminh on the Tonkin Delta, and also to forestall an attack on Laos, General Henri Navarre had envisioned creating a kind of acute abscess 350 kilometers west of Hanoi near the Laotian border, supplied from the air and designed to force the Vietminh to engage in a full frontal battle where they would be wiped out. To this end the basin was occupied in an air operation spread out over three days, which dropped a total of six battalions of paratroopers and one artillery group that refurbished a preexisting airfield, and then held their positions in anticipation of the first wave of reinforcements.

In March 1954 this Northwest Operational Task Force, under the command of Colonel Christian de Castries, was composed of 10,800 men, 40 percent of whom were from the Foreign Legion. The Vietminh commander, General Vo Nguyen Giap, met this challenge by concentrating several divisions around the basin, an additional several thousand "coolies," and above all two hundred pieces of artillery (including antiaircraft cannons and rocket-launchers), whose transport and assembly in the jungle could not have taken place without unheard of physical effort on the part of the Vietnamese, combined with the Vietminh's singularly supple ingenuity, whose work completely evaded French aerial observation. Also contrary to general-staff estimations, enemy supply lines using bicycles, hand-carted across the jungle, proved equally efficacious as logistical support.

Furthermore, the Vietminh artillery completely evaded French counterattacks once the bombardment began on 13 March 1954 (leading the chief of French artillery, Colonel Charles Piroth, to commit suicide in his bunker). The Vietminh made the airfield their primary target, thereby rapidly cutting off the French garrison at its umbilical cord, since it was unable to evacuate its wounded, who then became dependent on parachute-drop operations rendered highly unreliable by inclement weather and the effectiveness of enemy antiaircraft fire.

With the fall of the uppermost line of hills dominating the camp's line of entrenchment (all dubbed, ironically, with feminine code names), the battle was lost in the first ten days. "Beatrice," on the northwest side of the basin, was the first to go, followed by "Gabrielle," in an isolated spot on the north side of the entrenchment. Finally "Dominique," "Eliane," "Huguette," and "Claudine," the rest of the northern trenches, fell too.

## CONDITIONS IN THE GARRISON

By 20 April, despite counterassaults intended to prevent the basin's total destruction, the net area under French control was reduced by half, from an initial eight square kilometers to just four The fighting force itself was reduced to 9,940 men, including 1,670 lightly wounded who remained at their posts, and 800 heavily wounded who could not be evacuated, and who therefore had to be herded into muddy shelters, rain soaked by the slightest downpour. The fate of the wounded was atrocious, and weighed heavily on the morale of the entire garrison, which by 13 April had lost nearly 5,000 men, both wounded and dead, including almost 160 officers. The airlift of an additional four battalions of reinforcements composed of nine hundred paratroopers and a significant number of irregular troops, failed to stem the losses. The emotional and physical exhaustion was such that soldiers were reported to have died without even incurring a single wound. Despite the presence of a certain number of deserters who managed to hide inside the encampment, the battle raged on until 7 May based entirely on the heroics of the garrison itself, which by that date was holding on to little more than their HQ perimeter and a few final footholds situated to the south of the airfield: Dien Bien Phu was in this respect a true soldier's battle. The basin fell with no formal capitulation: the shooting simply stopped as a way of signifying to the enemy the cessation of combat.

## TRENCH WARFARE

On both sides, the fight hinged primarily on trench warfare. The Vietminh gained ground on the French positions by digging parallel trenches and inching their way forward across the length of the basin. The French meanwhile sought to defend their positions by burying underground bunkers, whose remnants are still visible on the ground. The fact that spontaneously in their letters and notebooks French soldiers so frequently compared Dien Bien Phu to Verdun in 1916 is easily explained by this mode of entrenched confrontation, the omnipresence of mud, and the defensive nature of the battle being waged against an enemy benefiting from superiority in manpower and materiel. Had not their fathers fought like this during World War I? As it had been for them, just forty years earlier, was it not necessary therefore to just "hold on?" De Castries, promoted to the rank of general while the battle raged on, would invoke it himself by referring to Dien Bien Phu as a Verdun without

its "Sacred Way," the sole supply and escape route left open to the French in 1916.

Unlike Verdun, however, the entrenched camp's survivors, save the most seriously wounded, were forced to head east on foot, toward captivity in Vietminh outposts near the Chinese border. These 9,500 men (including 700 wounded), in a wretched physical and moral state, exhausted by 56 days of battle, many suffering from dysentery, were made to walk 600 kilometers in 40 days. This is considered one of the worst death marches ever inflicted on a group of soldiers in the twentieth century, to which was added the incredibly high death rates in the camps themselves: fully two-thirds of the prisoners taken at Dien Bien Phu would be dead before their liberation came in the fall of 1954.

*See also* **French Empire; Indochina; Vietnam War.**

BIBLIOGRAPHY

Bruge, Roger. *Les hommes de Dien Bien Phu*. Paris, 1999.

Corvisier, André (under the direction of). *Histoire Militaire de la France*. Volume 4: *De 1940 à nos jours*. Paris, 1992.

Grauwin, Paul. *J'étais médecin à Dien-Bien-Phu*. Paris, 1954.

STÉPHANE AUDOIN-ROUZEAU

---

**DIET AND NUTRITION.** The European diet in the early twentieth century can be divided into four main regional types—northern, central, eastern, and southern—each based on a distinctive pattern of agricultural production and trade. Northern and southern Europe represent the extremes, the former distinguished by a high average consumption per head of animal foods, fats, and sugar and the latter by a heavy dependence on plant foods—cereals, fruits, vegetables, and olive oil—with small usage of meat and dairy products. The four regional patterns are differentiated in Table 1.

## THE CHRONOLOGY OF CHANGE

European diets in the twentieth century have been shaped by environmental factors but also, increasingly, by socioeconomic factors. Although

**TABLE 1**

### European regional diets in calories per capita per day, c. 1914

| | Northern | Central | Eastern | Southern |
|---|---|---|---|---|
| Cereals | M | H | VH | VH |
| Roots, incl. potatoes | L/M | H | M/H | L |
| Sugar | VH | M | L | L |
| Fruit and vegetables | VL | L | L/M | VH |
| Meat, eggs | VH | H | M | L |
| Milk and milk products | VH | H | L | VL |
| Fats | VH | H | M | M |
| Total calories | VH | H | H | M |

KEY: VL, very low; L, low; M, moderate; H, high; VH, very high.

SOURCE: Paul Lamartine Yates, *Food, Land and Manpower in Western Europe* (London, 1960), Chapter 2 and Table 2.1.

traditional foods continue to be important, food patterns have become increasingly more diverse while at the same time tending to converge regionally and across income groups. The key determinants of dietary change have been, first and foremost, rising real income associated with a demand for quality, variety, convenience, and built-in services. Food availability per head has grown in line with rising agricultural production and trade, and with increased output of processed and preserved foods. Dietary change is closely correlated with social change (urbanization, smaller families, and more working women); with heightened consumer awareness of the relationship between food and health; with the demand for food services; with changes in food retailing; and with the globalization of the food industries. Kitchen routines have been revolutionized by technical change in the form of cast iron stoves (from the later nineteenth century), refrigerators and freezers (after World War II), and more recently the microwave oven.

Since 1914 European food patterns have undergone a succession of changes, beginning in the northern industrialized countries and spreading after World War II to the less developed regions. The period between the wars was one of marked contrasts. Diets in northern Europe became more varied, with fewer cereals and more animal foods, imported tropical and Mediterranean produce, and processed foods. Most households in eastern and southern Europe, meanwhile, were increasing their consumption of starchy foods. Many suffered

severe shortages in the 1930s, when upward of one-quarter of the peasant population of east and southeast Europe is estimated to have been seriously undernourished. In many Romanian homes, the typical diet consisted almost entirely of corn polenta, with very little bread, meat, or milk, and as a result vitamin-related diseases, such as pellagra, were prevalent. As late as the 1950s, many peasants in central Greece and the Greek islands struggled to fill the "hungry gap" that came after their stocks of grain had been exhausted in early spring and before the threshing out of the next harvest at midsummer.

With the end of rationing in the early 1950s, food supplies soon recovered to prewar levels and in most countries, except in the laggard Eastern Bloc, by the end of the decade had comfortably exceeded them. Driven by rising incomes, new food products, and the vigorous promotional campaigns of food manufacturers, traditional consumption patterns began to break down. Changes within food categories were often more socially and dietetically significant than changes between categories. Cereal consumption per head was declining at the same time as wheat was displacing corn (maize) and rye as the principle bread grains in central and eastern Europe and in parts of the Mediterranean, and ready-to eat cereals were replacing cooked meats and bread as breakfast foods in the northern countries. In Britain, consumers increasingly preferred wholegrain and multigrain breads, which they had given up in the eighteenth century, to white bread. Bread and potatoes were giving ground to rice and pasta. Important shifts occurred also within the animal foods category, from beef and sheep meat to pork and poultry, and in dairy products from whole milk and butter to low-fat milk, flavored milks, chilled desserts, and cheese. The American milk bar (soda fountain), after a promising debut in Britain in the 1930s, made little progress in the postwar period.

By the beginning of the twenty-first century, total calorie consumption was generally higher than in the prewar period, the most impressive advances having been made in southern and eastern Europe, where it approached or exceeded the European Union (EU) 15-member country average of 3,500 calories. In northern Europe it had leveled off. Per capita cereal consumption continued to decline but in the Mediterranean remained

TABLE 2

### Dietary trends in northern, southern, and eastern Europe, 1962–2002

| | Total Calories Cal/Cap/Day (Number) | | | Animal Products Cal/Cap/Day (Number) | | | Vegetable Products Cal/Cap/Day (Number) | | | Vegetables Cal/Cap/Day (Number) | | | Cereals, Excluding Beer Cal/Cap/Day (Number) | | | Milk Products, Excluding Butter Cal/Cap/Day (Number) | | | Fruits, Excluding Wine Cal/Cap/Day (Number) | | |
|---|---|---|---|---|---|---|---|---|---|---|---|---|---|---|---|---|---|---|---|---|---|
| | 1962 | 1982 | 2002 | 1962 | 1982 | 2002 | 1962 | 1982 | 2002 | 1962 | 1982 | 2002 | 1962 | 1982 | 2002 | 1962 | 1982 | 2002 | 1962 | 1982 | 2002 |
| **N. Europe** | | | | | | | | | | | | | | | | | | | | | |
| France | 3,261 | 3,421 | 3,654 | 1,030 | 1,272 | 1,357 | 2,231 | 2,148 | 2,297 | 102.5 | 81.8 | 100 | 945 | 806 | 886 | 316.8 | 377.8 | 387.8 | 94.4 | 81.2 | 101.4 |
| Germany | 2,945 | 3,364 | 3,496 | 950 | 1,134 | 1,070 | 1,996 | 2,229 | 2,426 | 32.3 | 48.6 | 66.3 | 718 | 731 | 836 | 237.4 | 249.4 | 317.1 | 121.5 | 138.9 | 141.2 |
| Sweden | 2,811 | 2,974 | 3,185 | 1,001 | 1,070 | 1,074 | 1,810 | 1,904 | 2,112 | 22.4 | 32.9 | 54.5 | 590 | 651 | 799 | 375.3 | 454.5 | 427.4 | 97.6 | 94.1 | 105.1 |
| United Kingdom | 3,267 | 3,158 | 3,412 | 1,316 | 1,224 | 1,043 | 1,951 | 1,934 | 2,369 | 42.2 | 61.4 | 66.1 | 778 | 647 | 849 | 360.2 | 339.8 | 349.2 | 86.7 | 73.3 | 113.2 |
| **S. Europe** | | | | | | | | | | | | | | | | | | | | | |
| Greece | 2,772 | 3,402 | 3,721 | 401 | 706 | 811 | 2,370 | 2,696 | 2,911 | 69.6 | 146.2 | 148.5 | 1,280 | 1,093 | 1,073 | 205.3 | 319.2 | 362.5 | 192.8 | 173.8 | 201.5 |
| Italy | 2,979 | 3,390 | 3,671 | 478 | 841 | 952 | 2,500 | 2,549 | 2,718 | 73.1 | 102.9 | 93.4 | 1,291 | 1,134 | 1,165 | 178.6 | 282.3 | 276.7 | 131.5 | 148.3 | 156.5 |
| Portugal | 2,563 | 2,820 | 3,741 | 341.5 | 547 | 1,089 | 2,221 | 2,273 | 2,652 | 59.8 | 77.5 | 108.9 | 1,162 | 942 | 1,024 | 92 | 144 | 301 | 110 | 71.7 | 168.6 |
| **E. Europe** | | | | | | | | | | | | | | | | | | | | | |
| Bulgaria | 3,243 | 3,644 | 2,848 | 430.6 | 784.5 | 696.8 | 2,812 | 2,859 | 2,151 | 60.1 | 75 | 84.4 | 1,893 | 1,553 | 1,085 | 133.2 | 255.6 | 250.4 | 139.8 | 116 | 56.2 |
| Poland | 3,280 | 3,302 | 3,375 | 896.8 | 996 | 882 | 2,383 | 2,306 | 2,492 | 48.4 | 66.1 | 66.7 | 1,405 | 1,170 | 1,190 | 331.5 | 283.8 | 205.3 | 26.1 | 56.5 | 61.4 |
| Romania | 2,892 | 3,008 | 3,455 | 429 | 679 | 708 | 2,463 | 2,328 | 2,747 | 49.5 | 113.7 | 94.6 | 1,788 | 1,203 | 1,651 | 196.3 | 231.5 | 347.8 | 36.9 | 93.5 | 69.1 |

SOURCE: Food and Agriculture Organization of the United Nations. *Food Balance Sheets*. Rome, 1962–2002. Earlier data extracted from country entries; 2002 data is available from http://faostat.fao.org/faostat/collections?version=ext&hasbulk=0

significantly above the EU average of 1,085 calories. Consumption of animal foods grew rapidly up to the 1970s, after which its growth began to slow or in some places decline. Eastern Europe registered a sharp downturn in animal protein intake in the early 1990s in the aftermath of the collapse of the former Communist regimes. Most Mediterranean countries saw gains of 80 percent to 100 percent or more between 1962 and 2002. The consumption of milk products has moved erratically but in most countries far exceeds prewar levels. Fruit and vegetable consumption has risen but is still substantially lower in northern and eastern than in southern Europe. In the north, exotic fruits such as bananas, citrus fruit, and peaches are increasingly preferred to indigenous fruits. The southern hemisphere supplies large quantities of fresh fruits and vegetables during the winter. Table 2 shows the main dietary trends in selected countries across the northern, southern, and eastern regions.

## IMPACT OF FACTORY FOODS

Arguably, the outstanding feature of the postwar diet has been a huge increase in the consumption and variety of proprietary branded foods. Indeed, the overwhelming majority of food items on sale in the large modern supermarkets of the early twenty-first century did not exist in 1914. An estimated ten thousand new grocery items, packaged and branded, are introduced each year in Britain, of which 90 percent are withdrawn within two years. These include growing numbers of so-called socially engineered or niche foods, designed to meet the specific needs of groups of consumers identified by market research. In the early postwar years, the pace was set first by canned foods, then by fast frozen foods, and since 1990 chilled, ready-to-eat meals. Although slow to take hold in southern and eastern Europe, sales of processed foods are accelerating there due to growing affluence and the spread of supermarket. At the turn of the twenty-first century large sections of the European food industry are controlled by North American multinational firms, which, since World War II, have been a seminal force in the reshaping of European eating habits.

Since 1970 a rising share of food budgets has been expended on catered meals and takeaway foods, including fast foods. The first McDonalds restaurant in West Germany opened in 1973, in Britain in 1973, and in the former East Germany in 1990. McDonalds had four hundred outlets in Germany in 1992 and one thousand in 2003; in the same period, Russia went from fewer than ten McDonalds to more than eighty. McDonalds, Pizza Hut, Kentucky Fried Chicken, and Burger

King, all American owned, are the largest restaurant chains. Starbucks, the first of the new-style coffee shops, opened branches in central Europe in 2002. Since the 1970s, foreign foods—of North and Central American, Mediterranean, and Far Eastern origin—modified to suit local tastes, have come to occupy an established position in European diets and now seriously challenge native cuisines. Chicken tikka masala, an Indian-style dish specially tailored for the British market, has replaced the traditional roast or steak and chips as the nation's favorite food.

Diversification and convergence are dominant themes in modern food history. Although under threat, customary foods and food habits still form the basis of most culinary regimes. Thus meals are social events in Spain, Italy, and Portugal; Portugal and Greece prefer light meals, but Sweden, Belgium, and Germany prefer heavy. Attitudes toward fast foods vary, with France and particularly Italy fighting vigorous rearguard actions in defense of traditional cooking. Research confirms, however, a growing similarity in consumption patterns across Europe, especially among younger consumers.

## FOOD AND HEALTH

Although Europeans may be eating enough to satisfy their physiological requirements, it is an open question whether the right foods in the correct quantities are being eaten. Since the 1950s, evidence has been steadily mounting of a causal link between diseases such as diabetes, cancer, and cardiovascular problems and foods such as refined carbohydrates and unsaturated fats. Highly processed foods, together with fast foods, are believed to constitute a particular risk.

In 1950 coronary heart disease was primarily a disease of men in the affluent classes; in the early twenty-first century it affects all classes, including the younger age groups and particularly low-income groups. Western degenerative diseases are shown to be closely correlated with high levels of blood cholesterol, a deficiency of essential fatty acids, and excessive sodium. Refined sugars, highly refined white flour, hydrogenated vegetable oils, and synthetic food additives are also identified as potential risks. Low-fiber diets are believed to be a causative factor in the development of colon

cancer, diabetes, and peptic ulcers and are believed to inhibit the absorption of proteins and fats.

The three basic classes of nutrient—carbohydrates, proteins, and fats—and their role in building and repairing the body and as sources of dietary energy were discovered by German physiologists in the mid-nineteenth century. After 1900 it was recognized that they were necessary but not sufficient to maintain bodily health. Between 1915 and 1925, British and American scientists identified many of the key vitamins but not as yet their precise functions or methods of action. By the 1930s, dairy products, eggs, cod liver oil, and seeds had been identified as rich sources of vitamin A, which was essential for the growth of children, and fresh vegetables had been identified as accessible sources of vitamin C. White flour was understood to be deficient in vitamin B and because vitamin C was destroyed by heating it was understood to be absent from most dried and canned foods. Research revealed important differences in the biological value of plant and animal protein, depending on the presence of certain classes of amino acids.

By 1939 the relationship of food and health to income could be explored scientifically. The two world wars were a perfect laboratory for nutritionists, allowing them to observe the effects of food shortages and rationing schemes on the general population. In World War I, for example, Denmark responded to the Allied blockade with a prescribed diet of vegetables, wholegrain bread, and milk products, with little or no meat or spirits, which is claimed to have resulted in a dramatic fall in death rates. World War II saw scientific research applied in the construction of national feeding programs. Britain, it was said, was never so well fed, nutritionally speaking, as during rationing.

The search for the perfect diet—one that would meet philosophical and religious as well as nutritional needs—predated the discovery of vitamins. Aversion to animal foods, especially meat, spawned a clutch of vegetarian and cereal-based diets, along with "nature cures," such as that designed by Dr. Max Bircher-Brenner at Zurich soon after 1900, which consisted of raw fruit and vegetables. Slimming diets and slimming foods, such as rye biscuits, were first formulated in the 1920s. In the same decade, organically grown foodstuffs were promoted as healthy and spiritually uplifting alternatives to foodstuffs grown by modern scientific methods. In the 1930s, health food shops selling herbal remedies and dietary supplements could be found in most major towns and cities across Europe. By this stage, scientific eating, in the form of patent preparations such as breakfast cereals, "natural" foods such as salad and nuts, and the "milk and greenstuffs" diet promoted by the American biochemist and discoverer of vitamin A Elmer McCollum had an enthusiastic following among a section of the educated middle classes. Spinach was for a time much acclaimed as an energy food on the spurious grounds that it was up to ten times richer in iron than any other green vegetable. By the 1950s, most countries were providing schoolchildren with free or subsidized milk, and specific regimens and supplements were prescribed for expectant and nursing mothers and the aged.

The postwar period saw the formulation of countless dietary regimes addressing a wide range of medical conditions, including eating disorders and behavioral problems. Of these, the most celebrated was the so-called Mediterranean diet, which was high in fruit, vegetables, nuts, seeds, grains, and olive oil and relatively low in meat, dairy products, and animal fats. This became famous as a result of the Seven Nations Study published in 1970 by Ancel Keys. A long-term study of eleven countries, it confirmed that elderly people who followed it and who kept active and didn't smoke lived longer than those who did not. The high-protein Atkins diet, designed for weight watchers, continued to provoke controversy in the early twenty-first century. Low carbohydrate–high protein diets date from the 1950s but were criticized as deficient in vitamin B and liable to cause acidity. The marketplace became increasingly congested with proprietary dietary programs supported by a plethora of confusing scientific advice. Health concerns have been a factor in the falling consumption of sugar, saturated fats (especially lard and butter), and some refined carbohydrates and in the growing popularity of low-fat dairy products, high-fiber foods, complex carbohydrates, wine (promoted as a potent source of anti-oxidants), and specialized "functional" foods fortified with specific nutrients and trace elements, claiming to deliver health benefits above and beyond those normally supplied.

Whereas in the early postwar years the World Health Organization was concerned mainly with undernourishment, by the turn of the new century it had identified obesity as a serious late-twentieth-century disorder, affecting particularly the developed countries, where in many cases more than half the population is classified as overweight and up to one-quarter as clinically obese. The highest levels occur in northwest and central Europe, with the largest proportion of obese children in the seven-to-eleven age group being found in Spain, Italy, and Greece, where diets have moved dramatically away from the traditional Mediterranean model since 1980. By 2030 an estimated thirty million Europeans will require treatment for diabetes and other weight-related diseases. Better diets, the World Health Organization contends, could prevent 30 percent to 40 percent of cancer cases in Europe.

## FOOD SAFETY

Deteriorating standards of food safety have also been a matter of growing concern. After almost a century of steady improvement, by 1960 most foodstuffs on sale were pure and unadulterated within the terms of the regulatory guidelines, bovine tuberculosis had been largely eliminated, and microbial food-borne diseases, although an ever-present threat, seemed to be under control. Subsequently, a sharp rise occurred in reported incidents of *salmonella* and *campylobacter* (the most common infections, found mainly in animal products, especially poultry), listeriosis (associated with uncooked meat, raw milk, and soft cheeses), and on a small scale *clostridium botulinum*. A new disease, variant Creutzfeldt-Jakob disease (CJD), linked to Bovine Spongiform Encephalopathy (BSE) in cattle, was first reported in Britain in 1996. By mid-2001, ninety-nine cases had been confirmed in Britain, three in France, and one in Ireland. Other food safety concerns include pesticide residues, food irradiation, chemical additives, and genetically modified foods.

The growth in reported food-linked infections is attributed to the extreme length and complexity of the modern food chain and to catered meals and industrially processed foods, especially meat and milk products. Poor culinary hygiene in handling frozen and reheated foods is a particular problem in low-income households that may be unable to afford hygienic aids, may lack clean hot water, and may have limited knowledge of food risks.

*See also* **Agriculture; Alcohol; Consumption; Public Health; Rationing.**

BIBLIOGRAPHY

Askegaard, Søren, and Tage Koed Madsen. "The Local and the Global: Exploring Traits of Homogeneity and Heterogenuity in European Food Cultures." *International Business Review* 7 (1998): 549–568.

Collins, Edward. "Why Wheat? Choice of Food Grains in Europe in the Nineteenth and Twentieth Centuries." *Journal of European Economic History* 22 (1993): 7–38.

Collins, Edward, and Derek J. Oddy. "The Centenary of the *British Food Journal*, 1899–1999: Changing Issues in Food Safety Legislation and Nutrition." *British Food Journal* 100 (1998): 434–550.

Food and Agriculture Organization of the United Nations. *Food Balance Sheets.* Rome, 1955–2002: 2002 data is available from http://faostat.fao.org.

Griggs, Barbara. *The Food Factor.* London, 1998.

Sutton, John. *Sunk Costs and Market Structure: Price Competition, Advertising, and the Evolution of Concentration.* Cambridge, Mass., 1991.

Trager, James. *The Food Chronology: A Food Lover's Compendium of Events and Anecdotes from Prehistory to the Present.* New York, 1995.

Warriner, Doreen. *The Economics of Peasant Farming.* London, 1939.

World Health Organization. *Food and Health in Europe: A New Basis for Nutrition.* Copenhagen, 2002.

Yates, Paul Lamartine. *Food, Land and Manpower in Western Europe.* London, 1960.

TED COLLINS

---

# DIETRICH, MARLENE (1901–1992), German-born screen actress.

Maria Magdalena Dietrich was born in Berlin on 27 December 1901, and died in Paris on 6 May 1992. On her request she was buried in Berlin next to her mother. After moving to the United States in the early 1930s, Dietrich took the position that if Nazis defined what it meant to be German, then she was not German. During the filming of *Knight without Armour* (1937), directed by Jacques Feyder, she was approached by Nazi agents who tried to persuade her to return to Germany. She refused. Subsequently her films were banned in Germany, and she began to be viewed as a traitor by many of her countrymen. In 1939 she became a U.S. citizen, and during World War II she entertained Allied troops in Africa and Europe with standards like "Falling in Love Again" and "Lili Marlene." She also gave anti-Nazi broadcasts in German. In recognition of her wartime commitment, she was awarded the American Medal of Freedom and was named a Chevalier of the French Legion of Honor. In one of her last films, *Judgment at Nuremberg* (1961), she plays the wife of a Nazi officer, a small part in what was considered by Stanley Kramer an homage to Hollywood's lost glory days as well as a work of memory of World War II and of the Nuremberg Trials.

What made the glory of Marlene Dietrich was not her political commitment: in the twentieth century, she became one the most glamorous stars of the German and American motion pictures industry. As a young violinist, she aspired first to become a concert musician but physical limitations prevented her from continuing playing, which proved to be a profound disappointment. Choosing instead to pursue acting, she auditioned for drama school in Berlin at age twenty-one. After having appeared in German cabaret productions and some minor films, she met the director Josef von Sternberg who offered her what was to become the memorable character of Lola Lola in *The Blue Angel* (1930). In this first German "talkie" film, she sings: "Ich bin von Kopf bis Fuß auf Liebe eingestellt" ("From head to toe, I'm made for love"). In *The Haunted Screen* (1952), the classic book on German cinema of the 1920s, Lotte H. Eisner paid attention to the shadowed expressionism of that film's photography. (The cinematographer Günther Rittau had worked previously with Fritz Lang on *The Nibelungen* in 1924 and on *Metropolis* in 1927.) Later, Siegfried Kracauer, in his book *From Caligari to Hitler* (1947), underlined the mixture of architectural fragments, characters, and nondescript objects and argued that *The Blue Angel* raised the question of social immaturity of the German middle class. He wrote that "Lola Lola was a new embodiment of sex," and that Dietrich's "impassivity encouraged [one] to look for the secret hidden beyond her insensitive selfishness and her cold insolence" (pp. 215–218). The film was an international box-office success and the starting point of a

**Marlene Dietrich in a scene from _Morocco_, 1930.**
PARAMOUNT/THE KOBAL COLLECTION

close collaboration between Dietrich and Sternberg, which proved short but intense.

The same year, Sternberg directed Dietrich in _Morocco_, where she plays a singer named Amy Jolly, dressed in white tie, top hat, and tails. She arrives from Paris to work at Lo Tinto's cabaret and meets a legionnaire, Tom Brown, who is played by Gary Cooper. In 1931 Sternberg and Dietrich collaborated on the film _Dishonored_, which tells the story of the Austrian Secret Service sending its most seductive agent to spy on the Russians; then _Shangai Express_ (1932) and _Blonde Venus_ (1932), which was followed by _The Scarlet Empress_ (1934) and their final film, _The Devil Is a Woman_ (1935). In all these pictures, Dietrich appeared as a woman of mystery and a symbol of erotic allure for several generations. Far different from other contemporary film stars, such as Greta Garbo and Rita Hayworth, Dietrich was ambiguous in her style, playing androgynous and suggestively bisexual characters.

During this phase of her career, Dietrich appeared like a creature of Sternberg's creation, but when their six-year collaboration ended, she felt free to explore other roles, like the one in which she plays Frenchy, opposite James Stewart, in the western _Destry Rides Again_ (1939), directed by George Marshall. Dietrich also worked with great filmmakers such as Alfred Hitchcock (_Stage Fright_, 1950) and Billy Wilder (_A Foreign Affair_, 1948), in which she plays a former Nazi café singer in occupied Berlin, and _Witness for the Prosecution_ (1950), which was also directed by Wilder.

Ultimately, Dietrich conquered the Las Vegas and Broadway circuits in the 1960s, and made a world tour in the 1970s, after which she settled into a life of relative seclusion in Paris. In her last film _Just a Gigolo_ (1978), directed by David Hemmings, she returned to the Weimar period of German history and costarred with another famous singer, the British rock star David Bowie.

_See also_ **Cinema; Germany; Kracauer, Siegfried.**

BIBLIOGRAPHY

_Primary Sources_

Dietrich, Marlene. _Nehmt nur mein Leben . . . : Reflexionen._ Munich, 1979.

_Secondary Sources_

Kracauer, Siegfried. _From Caligari to Hitler: A Psychological History of the German Film,_ edited and introduced by Leonardo Quaresima. Princeton, N.J., 2004.

Salmon, André. _Marlène Dietrich._ Paris, 1932.

Spoto, Donald. _Blue Angel: The Life of Marlene Dietrich._ New York, 1992.

Studlar, Gaylyn. _In the Realm of Pleasure: Von Sternberg, Dietrich, and the Masochistic Aesthetic._ New York, 1992.

Sudendorf, Werner, ed. _Marlene Dietrich: Dokumente-Essays-Filme._ 2 vols. Munich, 1977–1978.

CHRISTIAN DELAGE

# DIMITROV, GEORGI (1882–1949), Bulgarian statesman.

Georgi Dimitrov, born 18 June 1882 in Kovachevtsi, Bulgaria, was a major figure of the Bulgarian and international communist movements. At age twelve he started work as a printer in Sofia and enrolled actively in the trade-union movement, organizing the first mass strike in Bulgaria, the coal-miners' strike in Pernik (1906). By 1909 he became secretary of the Revolutionary Trade Union Federation. In 1902 he joined the Bulgarian Workers' Social Democratic Party and was a member of its Central Committee from 1909. After the party split in 1903 over issues of strategy and tactics, Dimitrov sided with the revolutionary wing ("narrow socialists"), which was renamed the Bulgarian Communist Party (BCP) in 1919. As member of parliament from 1913 to 1923, Dimitrov was highly critical of Bulgaria's policies during the Balkan Wars and World War I. He voted against the war credits in 1915 and denounced Bulgarian nationalism, activities for which he served brief prison sentences. Eager to internationalize the Bulgarian movement, Dimitrov took part in the First (1909) and Second (1915) Balkan Social Democratic Conferences. In 1921 he participated in the Third Congress of the Communist International (Comintern) and was elected as a member of the executive bureau of the Profintern.

In September 1923, together with Vasil Kolarov (1877–1950), Dimitrov led a communist uprising against the military junta, which had ousted Alexander Stamboliyski's (1879–1923) agrarian government (1919–1923) in June 1923. This uprising, long hailed in the mainstream communist literature as the first antifascist revolt, produced bitter discussions within communist circles at the time. The Communist Party had announced its "neutrality" in the face of the coup d'état, a formula that was just a cover for the weakness of the left-wing forces. However, the Moscow-based Comintern, still hoping to foment a "permanent revolution," criticized the Bulgarian communists for their passivity and ordered them to rise. After acrimonious debates, which divided the leadership of the BCP, the faction represented by Dimitrov and Kolarov prevailed. Accusation of quiescence to the dictates of the Comintern and conscious adventurism were raised by other communists, based on the fact that the uprising was organized hastily and in the most remote western province of Bulgaria, from where Dimitrov and Kolarov quickly escaped into emigration, whereas the subsequent "White Terror" threw the country into bloody reprisals.

With a death sentence from the military regime, Dimitrov was forced into emigration. He was a member of the foreign bureau of the BCP, a member of the executive committees of the Comintern and the Profintern, and secretary of the Balkan Communist Federation. In 1929 he settled in Berlin as head of the West European bureau of the Comintern. The Reichstag Fire of 27 February 1933 provided Adolf Hitler (1889–1945) with a pretext for outlawing his Communist opponents, and Dimitrov was accused, alongside other Communist leaders, of plotting the fire. Arrested in March 1933, Dimitrov stood trial between 21 September and 23 December 1933 in Leipzig, leading his own defense. This was a defining moment in his life and career. His brilliant rhetoric and remarkable political courage, as well as the worldwide protests, won him acquittal from the Nazi court, but he was kept in prison. Granted Soviet citizenship, Dimitrov was allowed to leave for Moscow in February 1934.

At the Seventh Congress of the Comintern in 1935, he was elected general secretary of the organization until its dissolution in 1943. Dimitrov formulated his theory of fascism and was the decisive force behind overcoming a number of dogmatic and sectarian communist attitudes, especially against social democracy. He was the chief promoter of popular-front movements against Nazism. While in Moscow, Dimitrov fostered the foundation of Bulgaria's Fatherland Front (1942), the popular antifascist coalition. He returned to Sofia on 6 November 1945, a year after the Communist-led takeover of 9 September 1944, and a year before the promulgation of the people's republic. Elected prime minister by the Grand National Assembly (November 1946), he became general secretary of the BCP (December 1948). Negotiations with Josip Broz Tito (1892–1980) to form a Balkan federation were stalled by Joseph Stalin (1879–1953) in 1948. Dimitrov formulated the general lines of development following a Stalinist model and presided over the destruction of the noncommunist and intra-party oppositions. Still, the open Stalinist grip on the country occurred after his death on 2 July 1949 and after the show trial against the popular former executive secretary of the BCP, Traicho Kostov in December 1949, although it had been already prepared with Dimitrov's participation. The very circumstance that Dimitrov was not alive at the time of the trial against and the subsequent assassination of the very popular Kostov, coupled with the rumors that he himself might have fallen victim to Stalin, explains why, in the aftermath

# SOVIET UNION AND COMMUNISM

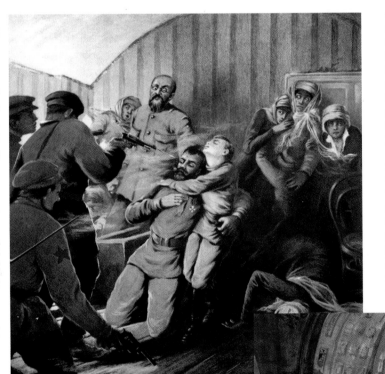

**LEFT:** *The Execution of Tsar Nicholas II and his Family at Ekaterinburg, 17 July 1918.* Illustration by S. Sarmat from a French history by H. de Weindel, 1923–1924. The execution of Nicholas and his family, considered a political necessity by a government facing civil war, was viewed as proof of Bolshevik barbarity in western Europe, particularly since Nicholas's wife, Alexandra, was a granddaughter of Queen Victoria and first cousin to both Kaiser William of Germany and King George of England. ARCHIVES CHARMET/THE BRIDGEMAN ART LIBRARY

**BELOW:** *The Assault on the Winter Palace, 7 November 1917.* Early-twentieth-century painting by Georgiy Savitsky. The capture of the tsar's Winter Palace in Petrograd by the Red Guard quickly came to be regarded as the pivotal point of the Russian Revolution, signaling the fall of Kerensky's provisional government and the assumption of power by the Bolsheviks. In fact, the events at the Winter Palace were much less dramatic than portrayed in art of the period. TRETYAKOV GALLERY, MOSCOW, RUSSIA/NOVOSTI/BRIDGEMAN ART LIBRARY

**BELOW LEFT:** *Petrograd Red 7 November.* Poster by Sergei Vasilevich Chekhonin, 1919. The revolution in its early phases was supported by Russian artists, who manifested their sentiments through propaganda posters. Here Chekhonin uses modernist techniques to create a homage to the sailors of the Baltic fleet who participated in the seizure of Petrograd. THE STAPLETON COLLECTION/BRIDGEMAN ART LIBRARY

**TOP RIGHT:** *On the Eve of the World Revolution, Down with the Bourgeoisie.* Soviet poster, date unknown. A worker representing the communist revolution prepares to destroy figures representing the bastions of capitalist power: the church, monarchy, and the bourgeoisie. BARBARA SINGER /BRIDGEMAN ART LIBRARY

**BOTTOM RIGHT:** Cover of the German satirical journal *Simplicissimus,* 21 November 1927. Leon Trotsky is shown being attacked by red wolves, a comment upon his expulsion from the Communist Party earlier that month. The caption reads: "Lucky Lenin, you are their saint but they are eating me up." BIBLIOTHÈQUE NATIONALE, PARIS/ARCHIVES CHARMET/BRIDGEMAN ART LIBRARY

**LEFT: A poster promoting the first Five-Year Plan, 1932.**
A major goal of Stalin's first Five-Year Plan was to accomplish complete collectivization of the Soviet economy. By 1940 private ownership of property had been all but eliminated through increasingly repressive state measures. DEUTSCHES PLAKAT MUSEUM, ESSEN, GERMANY/ARCHIVES CHARMET/BRIDGEMAN ART LIBRARY

**BELOW:** *The Construction of the USSR.* Photomontage by Alexander Rodchenko c. 1920. Rodchenko was a prominent figure in the Russian avant-garde of the early twentieth century and a pioneer in the technique of photomontage, used here to create a compelling vision of early Soviet history. MUSEUM OF THE REVOLUTION, MOSCOW, RUSSIA/GIRAUDON/BRIDGEMAN ART LIBRARY

**TOP RIGHT:** *Starving Crowds Leaving their Homeland.* Lithograph by Georges Carrey c. 1924. A major drought in western Russia in 1921–1923 led to widespread famine, which was exacerbated by the policies of Lenin's government. The situation drew sympathy from western powers but was also used to discredit socialism elsewhere in Europe. ARCHIVES CHARMET/BRIDGEMAN ART LIBRARY

**MIDDLE RIGHT:** **Women harvest hay on a state farm near Krujë, Albania, in the 1980s.** Under the regime of Enver Hoxha, Albania developed some of the most repressive policies in the Eastern Bloc and in fact broke with Soviet officials over the issue of destalinization in 1961. By 1989, it had become the poorest and most isolated nation in Europe. © SETBOUN/CORBIS

**BELOW:** *Workers of the First Five Year Plan Period: Construction of Drieproges Hydroelectric Station.* Painting by Karp Trokhimenko. Beginning in the 1930s, socialist realist painters such as Trokhimento sought to further the aims of the Soviet government by presenting idealized portraits of communist life. Here Trokhimenko celebrates Joseph Stalin's efforts to dramatically increase the pace of industrialization in the Soviet Union between 1928 and 1933. ODESSA FINE ARTS MUSEUM, UKRAINE/BRIDGEMAN ART LIBRARY

LEFT: *1 May, Stalin Holds a Child in His Arms.* Painting by Fedor Reshetnikov, 1952. The contradictions of Soviet ideology are abundantly clear in this painting by a noted exemplar of socialist realism: the aging Stalin, whose policies by this time had resulted in the deaths of millions, is depicted as a most benevolent figure. ARCHIVES CHARMET/BRIDGEMAN ART LIBRARY

BELOW: **A street vendor sells vegetables in Moscow, November 1987.** Soviet leader Mikhail Gorbachev announced his policy of perestroika, or restructuring, which permitted some forms of free enterprise, in May of 1987 in an attempt to address critical problems in the Soviet economy. © BERNARD BISSON/CORBIS

**BELOW: Solidarity protestors in Poland, 1987.** Public support for the independent Polish trade union Solidarity, which was officially outlawed by communist officials, grew rapidly throughout the 1980s. By the end of the decade the Polish government was forced to legalize the union and Solidarity representatives were able to defeat Soviet-backed candidates in limited free elections. © PETER TURNLEY/CORBIS

**OPPOSITE PAGE: A man uses a hammer and chisel to help dismantle the Berlin Wall, December 1989.** The most renowned symbol of the separation of the Eastern Bloc from the West was rendered pointless and was soon dismantled as the Soviet Union crumbled and Soviet citizens traveled freely to western Europe. © OWEN FRANKEN/CORBIS

of the destalinization process and the rehabilitation of Kostov, his reputation did not suffer. His embalmed body was preserved in a mausoleum in Sofia until its removal by his family in 1990. The mausoleum was demolished by the Bulgarian government in 1999, although the building's destruction was controversial.

*See also* **Bulgaria.**

BIBLIOGRAPHY

*Primary Sources*

Dimitrov, Georgi. *The Diary of Georgi Dimitrov, 1933–1949.* Introduced and edited by Ivo Banac. New Haven, Conn., 2003.

Dimitrov, Georgi, and Joseph Stalin. *Dimitrov and Stalin: 1934–1943: Letters from the Soviet Archives.* Edited by Alexander Dallin and F. I. Firsov. New Haven, Conn., 2000.

*Secondary Sources*

Bell, John D. *The Bulgarian Communist Party from Blagoev to Zhivkov.* Stanford, Calif., 1986.

Oren, Nissan. *Bulgarian Communism; The Road to Power, 1934–1944.* New York, 1971.

Rothschild, Joseph. *The Communist Party of Bulgaria: Origins and Development, 1883–1936.* New York, 1959.

MARIA TODOROVA

---

# DI PIETRO, ANTONIO (b. 1950), Italian magistrate and politician.

The Italian magistrate and politician Antonio Di Pietro was born in Montenero di Bisaccia. Having served in the police force at the Ministry of the Interior and then entered (1981) into the Magistracy, he came to the Public Prosecutor's Office of the Republic of Milan in 1985 as an assistant district attorney specializing in organized crime as well as crimes against the public administration and information technology. After achieving satisfactory results in various investigations, he launched the *Mani Pulite* (clean hands) probe in 1991. *Mani Pulite* unfolded in the broader context of the "Tangentopoli" (bribesville) scandal and was intended to reveal the extensive and continuous series of crimes committed by public officials and business leaders. *Mani Pulite* began from an apparently marginal investigation of a Socialist executive, Mario Chiesa, president of the Pio Albergo Trivulzio, a retirement home. Chiesa was caught red-handed on 17 February 1992, immediately after having pocketed an envelope containing seven million lire, a portion of the kickback that a cleaning service had paid to win its contract. (The agreement stipulated a payment of 10 percent on a contract worth one hundred forty million lire.) Following the interrogation of Chiesa (who was expelled from the PSI, or Italian Socialist Party), the investigation spread and uncovered the full extent of the phenomenon, which served to finance political parties. Over the following months subpoenas were issued to various Italian political figures for corruption and violations of the law on party-financing. The suspects included the ex-mayors of Milan, Carlo Tognoli (b. 1938) and Palolo Pillitteri (b. 1940); the minister of transport, Carlo Bernini (b. 1936); and the Socialist ex-foreign minister Gianni De Michelis (b. 1940), who was investigated for corruption relating to a series of contracts in the Veneto region.

In light of the rapidly growing scope of the inquiry, the heads of the prosecutor's office of Milan, Gerardo D'Ambrosio and Saverio Borrelli, decided in April to flank Di Pietro with assistant district attorney Gherardo Colombo, first, and then Pier Camillo Davigo. The so-called pool of *Mani Pulite* was born. On 15 October 1992 the administrative secretary of the PSI, Vicenzo Balzamo (who would die eleven days later of a heart attack), confirmed the rumors of a formal indictment for corruption and violation of the law on party-financing, while in December, even Bettino Craxi (1934–2000) was accused (the alleged crimes included complicity in corruption, receiving stolen goods, and violation of the law on party-financing). Tangentopoli provoked the crisis and collapse of several parties—causing the dissolution of the PSI, the DC, or Christian Democrats, and PSDI, or Italian Social Democratic Party—and the so-called end of the First Republic.

In 1992 dramatic events unfolded in the course of the investigations: the suicides of Renato Amorese, secretary of the PSI at Lodi, and the deputy Sergio Moroni, a regional-level party leader, were followed by those of Gabriele Cagliari, ex-president of the ENI (National Hydrocarbon

Agency), and Raoul Gardini, head of Enimont, from the Ferruzzi group. The year 1993 saw the trial of Sergio Cusani, a Socialist financier, for the Enimont "super-kickback," billions of lire distributed to the various political parties in proportion to their size and importance (of which two hundred million went to the justice-loving Lega Nord). Members of the PCI/PDS (Italian Communist Party) were also implicated. On 6 December 1994, availing himself during the judicial audience of an innovative computerized system, Di Pietro concluded the "Enimont" investigation, which would result in the condemnation (on 27 October 1995) of Craxi, Claudio Martelli and De Michelis (PSI), Arnaldo Forlani and Paolo Cirino Pomicino (DC), Renato Altissimo (PLI, or Italian Liberal Party), Umberto Bossi (Lega Nord), and Ugo La Malfa (Italian Republican Party). After resting the prosecution's case Di Pietro announced his resignation from the magistracy, which he made official on 2 May 1995.

On 7 May 1995 he was placed on the list of those under investigation, charged with embezzlement by the head of the financial police (Guardia di Finanza), Giuseppe Cerciello (himself accused of corruption and condemned on 9 November with other leaders of the Financial Police). On 22 February 1996 Di Pietro was absolved of all accusations in a preliminary hearing. In May 1996 he was named minister of public works in the administration of Romano Prodi (17 May 1996–9 October 1998), a position he resigned on 14 November.

In November 1997 Di Pietro was elected Senator of the Republic. On 21 March 1998, he founded the Italy of Values (L'Italia dei Valori) movement, whose first priority was the collection of signatures for the referendum on the abolition of the proportional quota. On 19 February 1999 the Italy of Values movement joined the movement of the Democrats (i Democratici). On 13 June 1999 Di Pietro was elected to the European Parliament, and on 2 February 2000 he became the head of the Senate faction of the Democrats. On 9 February he joined a Senate constitutional-affairs commission on Tangentopoli, charged with establishing the parameters of a law sanctioning a commission of inquest on Tangentopoli. In February 2000 he created "The Observatory on

Legality and the Issue of Morality," to promote the issue of morality in Europe as the ethical underpinning of a restored political framework. On 3 May 2000 he founded his own autonomous movement, the "Lista Di Pietro—Italia dei Valori," in both the Senate and the European Parliament, which he represented in the elections of April 2001 (winning 1,443,057 votes for the House and 1,139,566 for the Senate).

On 7 February 2002 he was elected president of the delegation of the European Parliament at the commissions for cooperation with Asiatic countries (EU-Kazakhstan, EU-Kirghizistan, EU-Uzbekistan) and as a member of the delegation for the relations with Tajikistan, Turkmenistan, and Mongolia. In June 2002 he published the book *Mani pulti. La vera storia* (Clean hands. The true story). In addition to his contributions to daily papers and national and foreign magazines, Di Pietro has published various works in the fields of law and information technology as well as civic-education texts for use in secondary schools, such as *Diventare grandi, Costruire il futuro* (1995).

*See also* **Craxi, Bettino; Crime and Justice; European Parliament; Italy; Northern League.**

BIBLIOGRAPHY

Di Pietro, Antonio. *Memoria*. Milan, 1999.

Guarnieri, Carlo. *Magistratura e politica in Italia*. Bologna, 1993.

Losa, Maurizio. *Uno uomo scomodo: intervista ad Antonio Di Pietro*. With an introduction by Giorgio Bocca. Bergamo, 1996.

Valentini, Gianni, ed. *Intervista su Tangentopoli*. Rome-Bari, 2000.

MARIA TERESA GIUSTI

---

**DISARMAMENT.** The elimination of all weapons and armed forces, typically known as disarmament, was a widespread but elusive goal in the twentieth century. It should not be confused with arms control—the limitation of the numbers and types of weapons—though the two terms are often used synonymously. Disarmament enjoyed the support of many statesmen and a number of important mass movements, but self-preservation and the

logic of great-power relations repeatedly under-mined its idealistic foundations and prevented serious progress. Technological development and the proliferation of ever-more-deadly varieties of weapons—especially biological, chemical, and nuclear—also meant that far more and far deadlier weapons were available worldwide at the end of the century than at its beginning. Yet despite this record of failure, there have been a few major successes, offering advocates lessons and hope for the future.

The most common argument used in favor of disarmament is that it reduces the likelihood of war. The fewer weapons states have, the logic goes, the fewer their means to attack their neighbors and the lower their chances of winning a war. Similarly, disarmament's supporters argue that without restraints on weapons and armed forces, states can easily fall into arms races, which further increase the chance of war. The classic example here is the Anglo-German naval buildup in the first decade of the century, which, by straining relations between the two countries, helped set the stage for the First World War. Particularly since the development of nuclear weapons, some advocates have taken a moral position in favor of disarmament, arguing that it is unethical for states even to possess weapons capable of killing millions and destroying entire countries.

Disarmament's opponents take issue with these positions. In their view the causes of wars run deeper than the numbers of weapons on both sides. In fact arms races are the result, not the cause, of the international tensions that can lead to war. Moreover, given that the state's primary goal is to protect its citizens, it would be foolish to disarm in the face of real threats. This logic was especially powerful in the Cold War, when nuclear deterrence provided the foundation for the period's "long peace."

Even after the Soviet Union's collapse, the debate about disarmament continued apace. Advocates expanded their focus to include small arms and other weapons less lethal but more widespread than nuclear weapons, winning a major victory with the 1997 Ottawa Treaty banning antipersonnel land mines. Controversially, the U.S. government used disarmament as one of its major arguments to justify the 2003 invasion of Iraq. At the beginning of the twenty-first century the debate about the wisdom of disarmament—in Iraq and beyond—rages on, and so long as states have armed forces, it will continue to do so.

## WORLD WAR I AND THE TREATY OF VERSAILLES

The disarmament of Germany was a major feature of the Paris Peace Conference (1919–1920), which the victors convened to end the First World War. In the aftermath of the bloodiest war in history, politicians, journalists, and academics argued that the prewar Anglo-German naval arms race had been one of the chief causes of the conflict. It was therefore essential to limit or reduce the size and scope of states' armed forces in order to prevent future wars. But rather than proceeding with disarmament multilaterally, the victors decided to impose it on the defeated powers, particularly Germany.

Germany had invaded France twice in the fifty years prior to the peace conference, which meant its ability to act aggressively in future had to be reined in. The Allied politicians who led the conference—David Lloyd George of Great Britain, Georges Clemenceau of France, and Woodrow Wilson of the United States, collectively known as the "Big Three"—agreed that measures to constrain German military power were necessary but disagreed about their severity. Clemenceau took the most extreme position. Like many of his compatriots, the French premier believed that the very existence of Germany posed a serious threat to French and even European security. In his view Germany had to be dismembered. Failing that, he wanted Germany's industrial heartland, the Rhine valley, to be amputated from the rest of the country and transformed into an independent republic. Lloyd George and Wilson took a far less aggressive line. The British prime minister firmly believed that a stable, unified Germany was essential to the Continental balance of power. Imposing a Carthaginian peace on the defeated country would destabilize the Continent and potentially open the door to French domination. Wilson, uninterested in the "old diplomacy" of the balance of power, likewise sided against Clemenceau, offering the League of Nations instead as the guarantor of postwar peace.

**Members of the League of Nations Disarmament Conference convened in Geneva, September 1924.** Among the issues discussed at this historic session was enforcement of the terms of the Treaty of Versailles regarding the disarmament of Germany. ©CORBIS

They eventually reached a compromise. The Treaty of Versailles imposed an elaborate system of shackles on German military power in order to destroy the country's capacity to wage aggressive war. During the war the Imperial Navy had numbered more than seventy ships, but the vast majority of these had been scuttled in 1919 during their internment in Scotland. According to the treaty, Germany's postwar navy could have no more than twenty-four ships, including, at most, six battleships. Submarines, which had proven such an effective weapon against the Allies, were forbidden outright. The army, four million strong during the war, would be capped at one hundred thousand, down even from its prewar strength of seven hundred thousand. Germany could have no tanks, heavy artillery, or general staff. The Rhineland

would be demilitarized and occupied by Allied troops for fifteen years. The Allies would control the Saar and its rich coalfields for the same period. Finally, in order to prevent a large segment of the population from acquiring military training, conscription was banned. These were tough measures indeed, and despite early acquiescence, Germany resisted them with increasing ferocity as time went on.

## WASHINGTON NAVAL CONFERENCE

Two years later the United States convened an international conference on the military and political situation in East Asia and the Pacific. The conference opened in Washington, D.C., in late 1921, the first conference in history whose primary goals were disarmament and arms control. It was also the

**Members of the Women's International League prepare stacks of disarmament petitions for shipment to the League of Nations headquarters, London, January 1932.** ©HULTON-DEUTSCH COLLECTION/CORBIS

first international conference held in the United States, testament to the country's ascent to world-power status. Secretary of State Charles Evans Hughes used the rhetoric of disarmament and peace in his invitations, but his goals were more pragmatic than idealistic. Above all, he wanted to check British and Japanese power in the Pacific, and this is exactly what he achieved.

Besides the United States, eight countries took part: Britain, Japan, France, Italy, the Netherlands, Belgium, Portugal, and China. Between November 1921 and February 1922 they produced three major agreements. The most important of these was the Five-Power Treaty, also known as the Naval Limitation Treaty. According to its terms, the United States, Britain, and Japan would maintain a 5:5:3 ratio in capital ship tonnage, and the

French and Italian navies were each allowed an absolute maximum of 175,000 tons for their capital fleets. As a consequence, twenty-six U.S., twenty-four British, and sixteen Japanese ships (either already built or under construction) were scrapped. This was a major change for British policy, given London's long-standing faith that naval superiority was the only way to ensure the security of Britain and its empire. The formal acceptance of naval parity with the United States amounted to an acknowledgment that the British simply could not afford to compete with the Americans in any kind of naval arms race.

The same group of countries, minus Italy, also negotiated the Four-Power Treaty, further confirmation of U.S. strategic ascendancy in the Pacific. They agreed not to expand their Pacific possessions and to consult each other in the event of any disagreement about them. This rhetoric was soothing, but it imposed no binding obligations. The agreement's real significance lay in the fact that it ended the Anglo-Japanese Alliance, a mutual defense pact dating from 1902. Concerned about their rivalry with the Japanese in the Pacific, the Americans had insisted on the cancellation of the pact in order to avoid a confrontation with the British should war break out with Japan. London preferred to maintain the alliance, which eased the burden of its Pacific commitments, but it feared being dragged into a U.S.-Japanese war on Tokyo's side. The British therefore bowed to U.S. demands and accepted the Four-Power Treaty, even though it offered nothing like the firm security guarantees of the old alliance.

The final agreement, which involved all of the countries present at the conference, addressed the problem of foreign possessions in China. The Nine-Power Treaty obliged its signatories to respect Chinese integrity, independence, and sovereignty and to consider the future of extraterritoriality. But like the Four-Power Treaty it required no serious action. Echoing the United States' long-standing open door policy, it also gave the countries the right to do business in China on equal terms.

With the unsurprising exception of the Chinese, everyone involved deemed the conference a success. To varying degrees, it was. More importantly, it reflected not an idealized vision of disarmament or pacifism but rather the realities of great-power politics.

**LONDON CONFERENCE**
The London Conference of 1930 continued the work begun in Washington. The Washington Conference had limited the construction of capital ships, but the great powers continued to compete in building midsize warships, known as cruisers. By 1930 the pressure on governments to disarm had increased substantially, not least because of the necessity of cutting spending. In these conditions cruiser competition was scarcely sustainable. British Prime Minister Ramsay MacDonald therefore invited the Americans, Japanese, French, and Italians to London to discuss limits on mid- and small-size warships and to review the agreements

they had signed in Washington some eight years before.

The conference opened in late January 1930 and ran for three months. Negotiations were hotly contested and quickly reached an impasse. Benito Mussolini's Fascist government insisted that it would reject any proposal that did not grant it at least parity with France. France, concerned as ever about foreign attack, refused to accept parity with Italy unless a naval version of the 1925 Locarno Pact—in which Britain guaranteed France's eastern border—were signed to protect its Mediterranean coast. The British in turn dismissed any thought of undertaking new security commitments when it could not afford to maintain its preexisting ones. Besides, Britain's major interests in the Mediterranean—the Levant and Suez Canal—lay in the east, not the west. If this was not enough to sink any hope of agreement, the British and French both insisted that any new security pact would require U.S. support, something that was hardly forthcoming.

Despite the failure to include the French and Italians, the British, Americans, and Japanese managed to conclude a three-way settlement. They extended 1922's 5:5:3 ratio to cruiser, destroyer, and submarine tonnage and declared a five-year moratorium on battleship construction. In addition, the British yielded to a U.S. demand that neither country be allowed more than fifty cruisers. In practice this meant that the British fleet would be pared down to match the size of the U.S. fleet rather than requiring the Americans to build up to the British level. Washington achieved full naval parity on the cheap, and the British made progress toward financial solvency, even if at the cost of security.

**LEAGUE OF NATIONS DISARMAMENT CONFERENCE**
Disarmament was one of the chief objectives of the League of Nations, which the Treaty of Versailles had established in 1919. Article 8 of the League's Covenant committed members to reducing armaments "to the lowest point consistent with national safety," but by the early 1930s none of the members had acted on this pledge. A general disarmament conference had first been proposed for 1925, but it did not actually meet until 1932 due to a lack of enthusiasm. Even after its opening in Geneva in

A London policeman talks to demonstrators outside a NATO meeting convened to discuss strengthening nuclear capabilities, May 1950. ©HULTON-DEUTSCH COLLECTION/CORBIS

February of that year its prospects for success were slim.

Its rationale was the same as that of the Washington and London Conferences, but its scope extended beyond strictly naval questions. Due to continued economic woes, most governments were under serious fiscal strain. In these circumstances, the prospect of curbing spending on ground, sea, and air forces was most welcome. Strategic concerns played a role too. Germany, under the increasingly unstable Weimar Republic, was determined to throw off the remaining shackles of Versailles and reestablish itself as a full and equal European state. Many in the British government sympathized with these demands, feeling that German rehabilitation was long overdue. From London's point of view a strong and stable Germany was essential as a counterweight to

France. Naturally the French could not tolerate the security threat that German equality would pose and so were reluctant to agree to any limitations at all. On top of this basic conflict, disagreements about the definitions of the various kinds of armaments made progress extremely difficult. Having reached a standstill, the conference adjourned in June 1933. When it reconvened in October, Germany—led by Adolf Hitler and the Nazi Party—withdrew, refusing to consider any limitations on German power. The conference effectively collapsed, though officially it limped on until 1937, by which point all hope of disarmament was lost thanks to the increasing likelihood of another major war.

### THE ATOMIC BOMB

The arrival of atomic weapons at the end of the Second World War raised the stakes of disarmament to levels that had previously been unthinkable. Even before the bombings of Hiroshima and Nagasaki, the prospect of weapons able to destroy cities caused serious apprehension, including among those working to build them. The first atomic weapons were developed in the strictest secrecy through a joint U.S.-British-Canadian wartime effort known as the Manhattan Project. In 1939 Albert Einstein, a pioneer in the field of nuclear physics, urged U.S. president Franklin D. Roosevelt to establish the project. Einstein feared that without a concentrated, government-directed Allied effort, the Germans might develop the bomb first. But once the bomb had been built and the war won, he worried that nuclear weapons could cause untold future damage if not properly controlled. He insisted that scientists had to make "governments aware of the unspeakable disaster they are certain to provoke unless they change their attitude towards each other and towards the task of shaping the future" (Einstein, p. 200). Atomic war was too terrible to contemplate, and governments therefore had to make every effort—especially by disarming—to avoid war. J. Robert Oppenheimer, the American scientist who had headed the Manhattan Project, shared Einstein's feelings. He said that the physicists who built the bomb "have known sin; and this is a knowledge which they cannot lose" (Bird and Sherwin, p. 388).

Official U.S. support for nuclear weapons remained strong despite this high-profile concern. President Harry S. Truman regarded the development of nuclear weapons and energy as the pinnacle of modern science, and the U.S. press was generally sanguine about the peacetime benefits of nuclear power. Geopolitically the bomb seemed to offer the United States an important advantage over the Soviet Union in a relationship that was growing increasingly tense. The U.S. government cast atomic weapons as one of the pillars of national security, though the U.S. public was divided over their use. The key ethical questions surrounding the construction and use of nuclear weapons first arose in the mid-to-late 1940s, and have persisted ever since. How could such a destructive weapon of war provide a basis for a durable peace? Was it moral to threaten the use of such weapons, or even to possess them? The logic of nuclear deterrence,

then only slowly coming into shape, was unpalatable indeed.

## CAMPAIGN FOR NUCLEAR DISARMAMENT AND EARLY ANTINUCLEAR MOVEMENTS

The development of the Soviet atomic bomb in 1949—several years ahead of U.S. predictions—and the detonation of the first hydrogen (or thermonuclear) bombs in 1953 and 1954, by the Soviet Union and the United States respectively, only intensified the debate. These new types of weapons were hundreds of times more powerful than the bombs dropped on Japan. It was obvious that a U.S.-Soviet war had the potential not only to destroy both countries but to make entire continents uninhabitable. In this context, President Dwight D. Eisenhower announced his "New Look" defense strategy, the cornerstone of which was "massive retaliation." Given the costs of the Korean War and defense spending in general, he was eager to cut the military's budget and therefore proclaimed massive retaliation the basis of U.S. defense policy. Any Soviet attack on NATO, conventional or otherwise, would be met with a full-scale nuclear response. Any European war would automatically be a nuclear war.

These developments spawned considerable public outcry in Europe and, to a lesser extent, in North America. In a 1955 press conference the British philosopher Bertrand Russell issued a document known as the Russell-Einstein Manifesto, named for two of its most prominent signatories. It warned that unless statesmen took decisive action to resolve their disputes peacefully, a war waged with thermonuclear weapons was a serious possibility. Such a war would destroy whole cities and make the entire planet uninhabitable. Every person on earth, warned the manifesto, was "in imminent danger of perishing agonizingly." Its signatories urged leaders: "Remember your humanity, and forget the rest."

Three years later, a number of prominent Britons, including Russell, founded the Campaign for Nuclear Disarmament (CND), which institutionalized the manifesto's ideas. Its platform was simple: governments should give up their entire nuclear arsenals unilaterally. Besides Russell himself, the historians A. J. P. Taylor and E. P. Thompson, the publisher Victor Gollancz, and the politician and polemicist Michael Foot were among its original members. To promote its cause it staged massive public rallies—often in London's Trafalgar Square—that attracted crowds numbering in the thousands. At one of its first protest marches, from London to Aldermaston, the site of Britain's main nuclear weapons research and manufacturing facility, it unveiled its logo, which was popularized in the 1960s and has since become internationally known as the "peace symbol."

CND's membership grew dramatically and quickly. By the early 1960s it claimed the support of as much as a third of Britain's population. Yet after the Cuban missile crisis (1962) and the signing of the Nuclear Test Ban Treaty (1963), and with the rise of public opposition to the Vietnam War in the mid-to-late 1960s, CND's prominence and membership waned. Protests continued, but on a much smaller scale than before. It is difficult to say whether the group had any significant impact on British policy in these early years. When the Labour Party leader Harold Wilson became prime minister in 1964, he simply ignored pressure to give up Britain's modest nuclear stockpile, even though many prominent party members were themselves supporters of CND and staunch advocates of unilateral disarmament.

## DISARMAMENT IN THE 1980S

The disarmament cause fell by the wayside during the late 1960s and through the 1970s, largely because protesting the Vietnam War absorbed the energy of most disarmament advocates, who typically were to the left of the political spectrum. Yet disarmament gained a new urgency in the late 1970s and early 1980s as the end of détente and worsening superpower relations raised the specter of nuclear war once again. As important as the conflict between the superpowers, however, was the clash between Western governments and large segments of their own populations over the wisdom of nuclear deterrence, the foundation of Western defense policy.

In December 1979, NATO announced the deployment of Cruise and Pershing 2 nuclear missiles to Western Europe, including Britain, West Germany, the Netherlands, and Italy. The effort was both a response to the Soviet deployment of new SS-20 nuclear missiles across Eastern Europe

in 1977 and an American attempt to demonstrate a continued commitment to the defense of Western Europe. Huge protests erupted in Western Europe, reinvigorating the dormant antinuclear movement. In Britain, CND membership increased twentyfold in the early 1980s, and the Labour Party, which had accepted nuclear weapons in the 1960s, featured unilateral disarmament as a key plank in its 1983 election campaign. In West Germany more than two million people signed an antinuclear petition organized by opposition political and clerical leaders. In 1981 and 1982 hundreds of thousands gathered for protest rallies in Bonn, the federal capital. Yet neither the British nor German disarmament campaigns, as large as they were, succeeded in reversing official policy. Margaret Thatcher's Conservatives and Helmut Kohl's Christian Democrats won their respective elections in 1983, cementing the British and West German commitments to NATO and the new deployments. The missiles began to arrive later that year.

Despite this defeat, unexpected support for the disarmament cause came shortly thereafter from President Ronald Reagan, a resolute hawk who had vigorously defended the NATO missile deployments. It is debatable whether Reagan advocated disarmament out of genuine personal conviction or as an attempt to assuage hostile European public opinion. In any event, after the war scare following NATO's 1983 Able Archer exercises, he formulated what became known as the "zero option."

At his 1986 Reykjavik, Iceland, summit meeting with the Soviet leader, Mikhail Gorbachev, Reagan, much to the consternation of many top members of his administration, offered to withdraw all Pershing missiles from Europe if the Soviets would do the same with their SS-20s. In addition, both sides would destroy almost their entire stockpiles of nuclear weapons, keeping only one hundred each. Rather than gradual reductions, both sides would move effectively to zero right away. Gorbachev, sobered by the recent Chernobyl disaster and eager to reduce Soviet military spending, responded enthusiastically. It seemed that the most significant disarmament agreement of the twentieth century was within reach. However, Reagan refused to accept one of Gorbachev's key conditions—that the United States cancel the Strategic Defense Initiative (SDI), its program of ballistic missile defense research—and the deal fell

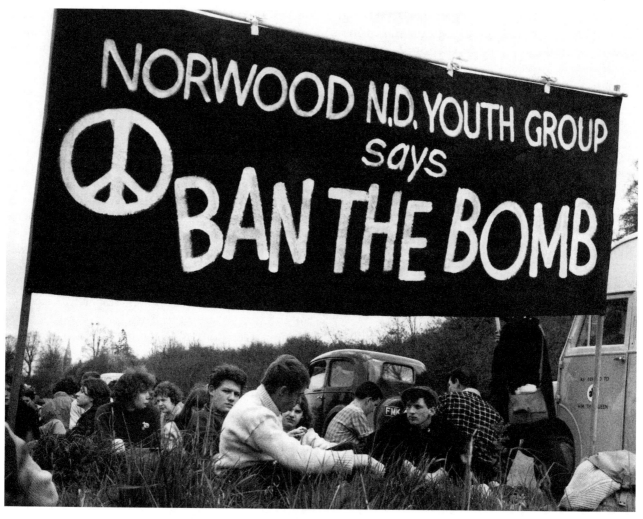

**Young people protest nuclear weapons at a rally in England, 1968.** ©Hulton-Deutsch Collection/Corbis

through. Gorbachev nevertheless persisted, and after agreeing to negotiate on the European missiles in isolation from SDI, the two sides came to agreement. In December 1987 they signed the Intermediate Nuclear Forces Treaty, which pledged the elimination of the Cruise, Pershing 2, and SS-20 missiles. Though it applied to only a fraction of their overall nuclear stockpiles, this was the first time that the superpowers had agreed to cut their arsenals instead of just limiting their expansion.

## COLLAPSE OF THE SOVIET UNION AND AFTER

With the collapse of the Soviet Union and the end of the Cold War, even greater progress was made in reducing the superpowers' nuclear stockpiles. These cuts were achieved through the Strategic

Arms Reduction Treaties—known as START 1 and START 2—of 1991 and 1993. START 1 reflected the waning tensions of the Cold War. It stringently limited the kinds of missiles and warheads that the two sides could possess and led them to destroy large portions of their arsenals. After the USSR's dissolution, the treaty's obligations devolved to the successor states of Russia, Belarus, Ukraine, and Kazakhstan. With the help of U.S. disarmament specialists, all but Russia have since destroyed the Soviet weapons they inherited.

START 2 banned Multiple Independently Targetable Reentry Vehicles (MIRVs), a technology that allowed many nuclear warheads to be placed on a single missile, each aimed at a different target. However, because the United States did not ratify it until 1996 and Russia until 2000, the treaty stagnated and failed to live up to its promise. In 2002 it was superseded by the Strategic Offensive Reductions Treaty (SORT). Rather than eliminating MIRVs entirely, the United States and Russia agreed to reduce their total warhead stockpiles to between seventeen hundred and twenty-two hundred. Despite the significant progress that has been made since the end of the Cold War, and despite the diminished importance of nuclear deterrence, complete nuclear disarmament—as envisioned variously by CND, Ronald Reagan, and Mikhail Gorbachev—remains elusive.

Disarmament has been much debated since the attacks of 11 September 2001, particularly with reference to Iraq. After the Gulf War of 1991, the United Nations imposed strict disarmament rules on Saddam Hussein's regime. The country was forbidden from manufacturing or possessing any kind of weapons of mass destruction, whether chemical, biological, or nuclear. Teams of UN inspectors were charged with verifying Iraqi compliance. But over the course of the 1990s Hussein refused to disarm and interfered with the inspections, leading to more than a dozen Security Council resolutions restating the original requirements and calling for immediate cooperation. Nevertheless, no serious action against Iraq was taken.

The situation reached a crisis point only in 2003, following renewed U.S. demands for complete disarmament and unfettered access for UN inspectors. President George W. Bush threatened to overthrow the Iraqi government if it failed to meet them. The Bush administration cited Hussein's recalcitrance in the face of these demands as one of the main reasons for the U.S.-led invasion of Iraq in March 2003. In the ensuing months, however, no Iraqi weapons of mass destruction were found, calling into question one of the war's chief justifications.

Disarmament efforts continue to focus on weapons of mass destruction rather than on conventional weapons. Though Iraq no longer has such weapons, the problem of disarmament remains acute. At the top of the agenda is the spread of nuclear weapons to both states (e.g., Iran and North Korea) and nonstate actors (e.g., Al Qaeda and other Islamist terrorist groups). Disarmament was and remains among the most elusive ideals of modern international relations, and despite past progress, there is no sign that success will come any time soon.

*See also* **Al Qaeda; Arms Control; Atomic Bomb; Islamic Terrorism; League of Nations; Nuclear Weapons; Terrorism; United Nations; Versailles, Treaty of.**

BIBLIOGRAPHY

Bird, Kai, and Martin J. Sherwin. *American Prometheus: The Triumph and Tragedy of J. Robert Oppenheimer.* New York, 2005.

Dingman, Roger. *Power in the Pacific: The Origins of Naval Arms Limitation, 1914–1922.* Chicago, 1976.

Einstein, Albert. *Out of My Later Years.* New York, 1984.

Gaddis, John Lewis, ed. *Cold War Statesmen Confront the Bomb: Nuclear Diplomacy since 1945.* Oxford, U.K., 1999.

Kitching, Carolyn. *Britain and the Problem of International Disarmament, 1919–1934.* New York, 1999.

———. *Britain and the Geneva Disarmament Conference: A Study in International History.* New York, 2003.

Larsen, Jeffrey A. *Historical Dictionary of Arms Control and Disarmament.* Lanham, Md., 2005.

Lettow, Paul. *Ronald Reagan and His Quest to Abolish Nuclear Weapons.* New York, 2005.

Minnion, John, and Philip Bolsover, eds. *The CND Story: The First 25 Years of CND in the Words of the People Involved.* London, 1983.

Russell, Bertrand. *Has Man a Future?* New York, 1962.

MICHAEL COTEY MORGAN

**DISPLACED PERSONS.** A new phenomenon developed throughout the twentieth century in Europe: that of refugees and displaced persons. During and immediately after both world wars, the victims of these forced movements—mainly civilians—could be counted by the millions.

Prior to World War I, many Jews from the tsarist empire and Central Europe, Turks, Bulgarians, and Southern Slavs were forced to leave their countries. They did not know where to go and were not easily accepted in other countries. During, and especially after, World War I, the number of displaced persons increased. The collapse of empires (Hohenzollern, Habsburg, tsarist, and Ottoman) and the strengthening of nation-states led to massive migration. Poles, Balts, Germans, and Russian victims of the Bolshevik

**Displaced persons from various countries gather at a dispersal point in Ansalt, Germany, awaiting repatriation, 1945.** ©HULTON-DEUTSCH COLLECTION/CORBIS

Revolution and civil war numbered among the peoples fleeing from violence and destruction. Nearly 350,000 Armenians fled to Europe to escape from the Turks. Overall, nearly six million people were displaced between 1914 and 1919, including the prisoners of war liberated in Central Europe and Germany.

This was a difficult challenge for Europe to face. The League of Nations set out to address the problem. From 1920 on, the high commissioner nominated by the League of Nations, Norwegian-born Fridtjof Nansen (1861–1930), planned assistance for Russian prisoners of war, for the victims of the Russian civil war, for the Armenians, and later for the Greeks and Turks who were exchanged against their will through the implementation of the 1923 Lausanne Treaty.

The fact displaced persons were seen as "stateless persons" worsened their plight. Regardless of whether or not they had left their country of origin, they did not have a passport and were not entitled to any kind of protection or rights. To ease their circumstances, Nansen convinced the League of Nations to create a special passport known as the "Nansen passport." By 1924 thirty-eight states had agreed to it, effectively putting an end to the tragic uprootedness of its beneficiaries.

This development was jeopardized by the worldwide economic crisis of the 1930s and the development of totalitarian regimes or dictatorships in Europe. The number of displaced persons and refugees increased steadily. Jews under Nazi Germany's Nuremberg Laws faced a very serious threat. By the end of 1937, 135,000 German Jews were seeking refuge elsewhere in Europe, in the United States, or in Palestine. The Spanish civil war forced 450,000 people to flee to France in the spring of 1939.

**Displaced women and children arrive in Berlin, December 1945.** ©BETTMANN/CORBIS

During World War II, between 1939 and the end of 1946, displacement grew: sixty million people, adults and children alike, were affected. Military action, in Belgium and France in 1940 for instance, was responsible for the displacement of hundreds of thousands of civilians. At the end of the war, it was the Germans' turn to take to the roads, fleeing from the Soviet Red Army. But Hitler's Germany, with its "New Order," had implemented throughout Europe a barbaric and racial plan whose main victims were the Jews. There were few survivors in the camps, and most chose to leave Europe.

The Allies entering Germany, the liberation of all types of prisoners (including prisoners of war), the arrival of German civilians coming from the east, and the flight of victims of the regime of Joseph Stalin (r. 1929–1953) combined to create a chaotic situation. Overall, between the end of World War II and 1959, twenty million adults and children were described as refugees and displaced persons.

In 1946 the first General Assembly of the United Nations gave priority status to the issue of refugees. This task became more formidable after 1947 with the deterioration of relations between the Western Allies and the communist world. In 1949 the UN General Assembly set up the UN High Commissioner for Refugees (UNHCR). Through this specialized agency, the 1951 Geneva Refugee Convention—the first of its kind—was agreed upon. It stated the fundamental standards in assisting refugees and displaced persons. At first, it relied on the definition which had been used since 1946: *displaced person* applies to a person "who has been deported from, or has been obliged to leave, his country of nationality or of former habitual residence, such as persons who were compelled to undertake forced labor or who were deported for racial, religious or political reasons."

The Convention also provided a definition for the word *refugees,* as formulated in its 1967 New York Protocol. A refugee was defined as "a person who is outside his/her country of nationality or habitual residence; has a well-founded fear of persecution because of his/her race, religion, nationality, membership in a particular social group or political opinion; and is unable or unwilling to avail himself/herself of the protection of that country, or to return there, for fear of persecution." The main difference between displaced persons and refugees was that the latter had crossed a border.

From the 1960s on the issue ceased to be exclusively European in scope and spread to the rest of the globe, in particular to former colonial territories. The UNHCR's estimate of the number of refugees and displaced persons at the end of the twentieth century was twenty to twenty-five million. Europe now accounts for a much smaller share of the global total, even in terms of displaced persons and refugees being hosted.

In Michael Marrus's words, the twentieth century was the "age of refugees." In Europe, the phenomenon was directly related to the two world wars and, as Hannah Arendt claimed, to the rise of totalitarianism. It deeply affected the European conscience, so much so that it contributed to an "urge for compensation": a strengthening of the family and the post-1945 baby boom.

*See also* **League of Nations; Refugees; United Nations; World War I; World War II.**

BIBLIOGRAPHY

Arendt, Hannah. *The Origins of Totalitarianism.* New York, 1951.

Marrus, Michael R. *The Unwanted: European Refugees in the Twentieth Century.* 2nd ed. Philadelphia, 2002.

Mazower, Mark. *Dark Continent: Europe's Twentieth Century.* London, 1998.

United Nations Refugee Agency home page. Available at http://www.unhcr.ch.

BERNARD DELPAL

**DISSIDENCE.** While the term *dissidence* refers generally to disagreement with a given viewpoint or center of power, in terms of mid- to late-twentieth-century European history it has also come to refer specifically to a political resistance movement against the socialist state of the Soviet Union and against its satellite states in Eastern and Central Europe. The Soviet origins of this movement are to be found in the period following the death in March 1953 of Soviet leader Joseph Stalin, who had ruled from the late 1920s with a degree of political control that led to the radical repression of public discourse, and a degree of terror that led to the imprisonment and death of innumerable Soviet citizens. That Stalin appeared to be heading toward renewed abuses of power just before his death gave extra impetus to early post-Stalinist political discontent, which manifested itself particularly in the realm of literature. Individuals such as Vladimir Pomerantsev argued for "sincerity in literature" in the Soviet literary journal *Novy Mir* (December 1953), while the Village Prose literary movement (including such authors as Fyodor Abramov, Valentin Rasputin, and a little later Alexander Solzhenitsyn) opened a critical discussion of state policies in rural Russia.

### DISSENT AMONG THE URBAN ELITE

Broader stirrings of political discontent soon manifested themselves in the *kompanyas,* or informal private gatherings, of the urban, educated Soviet elite. Private discussions, lectures, and musical events all provided opportunities for an increasingly complex critical discourse. The emergence among this same group of samizdat, or self-publishing, in the face of rigid state censorship of officially published materials facilitated further dissemination and consolidation among them of ideas and information that, despite the liberalization of the so-called Thaw period under Nikita Khrushchev, still remained untenable as public political discourse. As many sought to understand the meaning of their political system and its history, early samizdat materials included poetry, novels, and memoirs, many of them about the experience of Stalinism. Other samizdat included forbidden or censored materials in politics, literature, the sciences, the humanities, and the social sciences. Several samizdat journals were founded as well, including the literary journal *Syntax,* published by Alexander Ginzburg in 1959 and 1960 until he was arrested

**Czech playwright Václav Havel, photographed in 1976.**
A leader of the dissident group Charter 77, Havel was
imprisoned by the Czech Communist government from 1979
to 1983. After the fall of the Soviet Union, he was elected
president of Czechoslovakia and later of the Czech Republic.
©THE BETTMANN ARCHIVE/CORBIS

and imprisoned. Other resistance to the Soviet state
in this early period included student demonstrations
in 1956 as well as public literary and artistic gatherings in the late 1950s and the early 1960s.

Expansion and consolidation of the dissent
movement was triggered in the Soviet Union in
1965 by the trial of two prominent Moscow literary
figures who had published work in the West that
could not be published in the Soviet Union due to
censorship, Yuli Daniel and Andrei Sinyavsky. Both
men were condemned to substantial terms in prison
camps, arousing considerable anger among the *kompanyas*. Both men while imprisoned began to send
back to their Moscow family, friends, and supporters
new information about political prisoners they were

discovering in the prison camp system; relatively few
among the urban educated elite had been aware of
the large number of Soviet political prisoners more
than a decade after Stalin's death. This information,
along with the samizdat publication of former political prisoner Anatoly Marchenko's *My Testimony*,
about his own prison experience, led to a growing
awareness of more widespread resistance to the
Soviet state, especially among ethnic and religious
minorities in the Soviet system; it led as well to
increasing solidarity of the urban Russian movement
with other dissenters in the Soviet Union.

**ETHNIC AND RELIGIOUS MOVEMENTS**

Prominent among the non-Russian ethnic dissent
movements was a growing Ukrainian nationalist
movement that was rooted in the revival of Ukrainian
cultural life during the late 1950s and the 1960s. The
Baltics (Lithuania, Latvia, and Estonia) had come
under Soviet control only with the Nazi-Soviet Pact
of 1939; despite the decimation of their populations as
multitudes of ethnic Balts were exported from the
region upon the Soviet takeover, they too experienced
revivals of national folklore, literature, and art that by
the 1960s contributed to growing national self-consciousness and dissent. In the Caucusus, Georgian and
Armenian nationalist dissident movements took shape
in the 1960s as well. The role of samizdat in the
expansion of ethnic self-awareness and growing
nationalism among all of these ethnic groups was vital.

Members of other ethnic groups had very specific reasons for resistance. The Crimean Tatars had
suffered deportation from their native lands during
World War II, as had the Meshki from their territory
in southern Georgia; both groups sought the right
to return to their lands. Some Soviet Germans, who
had suffered persecution since World War II, wished
to leave the Soviet Union. Some ethnic Jews, many
of whom had experienced severe disenchantment with
the Soviet system due to Stalin's virulent anti-Semitism
in the last years of his life, also sought the right to
leave the Soviet Union. Those seeking religious
freedom included Baptist, Pentecostalist, Seventh-
Day Adventist, Jewish, and Russian Orthodox worshippers. Against the background of the official
Soviet policy of atheism, they, like other dissenters,
formed networks and produced samizdat for
spreading information and building interest and
support. Participants in all of the ethnic and

religious dissident movements experienced arrest and imprisonment by the threatened and hostile Soviet state.

Central to the growth of solidarity among these greatly varied movements was the expansion of information networks. Perhaps of greatest importance was the publication inside the Soviet Union of the Moscow-based samizdat dissent newsletter *Chronicle of Current Events,* first published in 1968; the *Chronicle's* founders and supporters collected and publicized detailed information about the locations, official crimes, and sentences of political prisoners across the Soviet Union. Also of great importance was the dissident development of ties with Western news correspondents and other Westerners based primarily in the capital city of Moscow who were willing to help the movement by publicizing its cause outside the Soviet Union. Foreign reporting on dissent increased popular and political interest in the topic in the West. Contact with Western journalists had an impact inside the Soviet Union as well, as such U.S.-supported organs as Radio Free Europe/Radio Liberty and Voice of America beamed previously published or broadcast information about the dissident movement back into the Soviet Union shortly after its dissemination in the West.

## COMMON GOALS AND CAUSES

Given the variety and complexity of the Soviet dissent movements, it would be difficult to argue for a single ideological purpose among Soviet dissenters. Yet perhaps one reason for the impact of the movement as a whole despite its manifest internal contradictions was the ability of those at the Moscow center of power and communications to articulate goals that could be supported by all or at least most other dissenters. Alexander Esenin-Volpin of Moscow argued that the Soviet Constitution of 1936 guaranteed a wide range of rights that its citizens should band together to defend; this theory helped to give dissenters of all stripes a sense of legal legitimacy as they continued their campaign against the Soviet state through meetings, demonstrations, circulation of letters and petitions, and publication of trial materials. Esenin-Volpin also demanded what he called *glasnost,* or transparency, especially in the trials of dissenters. This argument, going back to

imperial Russia in the nineteenth century, held that the state should render its deliberations, decisions, and actions open to public scrutiny. Particularly appealing to the numerous dissenters of the professional class were the arguments of the renowned Soviet physicist Andrei Sakharov that progress could best be achieved in the Soviet Union through intellectual and professional freedom and peaceful coexistence with the Western world. Sakharov received the Nobel Peace Prize in 1975.

Another approach that could be supported by a variety of dissenters and other members of the educated elite as well was a small but vibrant voluntary charity movement to help political prisoners of all sorts, as well as their families, by collecting and redistributing money, food, clothing, reading material, and other urgently needed material goods. This spontaneous movement was eventually largely replaced by a single organization, the Fund for Aid to Political Prisoners. Author Alexander Solzhenitsyn donated all of his substantial Western royalties for his famous prison camp study *The Gulag Archipelago* to create the fund in 1974. Its first chairman was Alexander Ginzburg. The fund soon became a target of the Soviet secret police (KGB), who sought to damage its reputation for selfless charity by planting forbidden Western currency in the apartment of Alexander Ginzburg. Ginzburg was put on trial and imprisoned for this manufactured crime; the Soviet state targeted later leaders of the fund with similar determination. Among many other activities supporting prisoners, the Fund for Aid to Political Prisoners helped to finance efforts to uncover and publicize Soviet abuses of psychiatry against political prisoners. The information that the Soviet state was punishing Soviet dissidents by imprisoning them in psychiatric hospitals was initially disbelieved by Western psychiatric professionals but ultimately did a great deal to discredit Soviet efforts to repress dissent.

Yet another cause that most participants in the varying Soviet dissent movements could support was that of human rights generally in the Soviet Union. The first human rights association, the Initiative Group to Defend Human Rights in the USSR, was formed in May 1969. A second group, the Committee for Human Rights in the USSR, was founded in 1970. The Helsinki Accords (Final Act of the Conference on Security and Cooperation in Europe) signed in 1975

**Avital Scharansky, wife of Soviet dissident Anatoly Scharansky, holds a protest in New York City, 1985.**
©BETTMANN/CORBIS

legitimized and greatly strengthened the human rights movement in the Soviet Union; this diplomatic agreement among the United States, Canada, the Soviet Union, the countries of Western Europe, and Turkey, essentially exchanged Western acquiescence to the sphere of Soviet control in Eastern and Central Europe for a Soviet commitment to respect human rights in the territories of the Soviet sphere. In 1976 the Moscow Helsinki Watch Group was established with strong ties to Western human rights networks; other Helsinki Watch groups were formed soon thereafter in Ukraine, Lithuania, Georgia, and Armenia. A significant U.S. actor on the Western side was Robert Bernstein, president and CEO of the U.S. publisher Random House and founding chair of Human Rights Watch in 1978. Also in the United States, the Helsinki Commission, or Commission for Security and Cooperation in Europe, was established with nine senators, nine congressional representatives, and one representative each from the Departments of State, Defense, and Commerce.

Another U.S. figure to support Soviet and Soviet bloc dissenters was President Jimmy Carter, who during his period in office (1977–1981) made human rights a centerpiece of his foreign policy, and who intervened personally on behalf of several individual political prisoners.

## EASTERN AND CENTRAL EUROPE

The situation of dissenters was different in the so-called Soviet bloc of Eastern and Central Europe to some extent because while Soviet dissidents were struggling against their own political system, those in Eastern and Central Europe were struggling in part against foreign (Soviet) control, as well as against those of their compatriots who had been co-opted by Soviet power to rule in its place. After the Soviet Union had taken control of most of the lands of Eastern and Central Europe following World War II, there had been a series of significant uprisings in that region: in East Germany in 1953, in Hungary and Poland in 1956, and in Czechoslovakia in 1968. The Czech revolution of 1968 reached the highest levels of the Czech government and was both deeply threatening to the Soviet authorities and inspiring to dissenters throughout the Soviet sphere. Under the leadership of Alexander Dubček, Czechoslovakia took substantial steps toward a reformed socialist system under the motto "socialism with a human face." Soviet leader Leonid Brezhnev responded by invading the country and returning it to what was described as "normalization" under more rigorous Soviet control.

In the period following, dissent took a variety of forms in Eastern Europe. It tended to focus around the networks of intellectual or artistic life, with the distribution of underground printed or typed materials and the establishment of underground "universities," or private seminar series. Religion could also play a significant role, as in the cases of Catholicism in Poland and the Slovak lands of Czechoslovakia, and Protestantism in East Germany. A number of complex and substantial dissenting discourses developed throughout the region, as intellectuals struggled with the questions of whether and how to resist Soviet and other state encroachment on society and on individual liberties. In Poland, the journalist Adam Michnik argued for what he called the "New Evolutionism" (1976). Poles could expect no advantage from radical, violent action, he wrote, as the Soviets would crush them, and dissenting intellectuals could not expect to carry the day themselves, but would need the support of the working class that was so important to the socialist Polish state. Personal commitment to action rather than passivity, to the possible rather than the ideal, to improving one's life and community, were the foundations of his model for resistance.

Czech playwright Václav Havel argued for "living in truth" as a means of resisting the distortions of language and communication that were part and parcel of Soviet political co-optation and control of the Czechoslovak state. Like Michnik, he believed resistance to the state lay in the simple, everyday commitment of individuals to active integrity, articulating this belief most famously in his essay "The Power of the Powerless" (1979). Hungarian intellectual dissent was early influenced by the Budapest school of the Marxist theorist György Lukács, and thus such thinkers as Janos Kis and György Bence originally sought to criticize Hungarian socialism in Marxist materialist terms (*Towards an East European*

*Marxism,* 1978). Other important materialist critiques of socialism in Hungary included Ivan Szelenyi and György Konrad's *Intellectuals on the Road to Class Power* (1979). In East Germany, the former Communist Party member Rudolph Bahro also argued for Marxist reform, in his book *The Alternative* (1977).

A major development in active political Eastern European dissent was the formation of a Polish resistance movement that did indeed, as Michnik had recommended, coordinate the energies of intellectuals with those of workers. At the heart of this intellectual-worker alliance were KOR, or the Worker's Defense Committee, established in 1976, and the Solidarity union, led by Lech Wałęsa and resulting from a vast outbreak of strikes in 1980 that ultimately drew ten million Polish workers. The visit of the Polish Catholic pope John Paul II in 1979 had served as one inspiration for the development of this vast Polish resistance movement, which by 1981 was having a considerable impact on Polish government policies. General Wojciech Jaruzelski's seizure of political power in a coup in December 1981 put a substantial crimp in KOR and Solidarity activities. Whether or not the coup had saved Poland from a Soviet invasion like that of Czechoslovakia in 1968 was a topic of intense debate.

Another significant moment in Eastern European dissent took place in Czechoslovakia, where writers and musicians played a role in building toward the formation of a dissident organization established in 1977, Charter 77. The arrest and trial in 1976 of members of the underground rock group Plastic People of the Universe on a variety of charges, including gross indecency and moral offensiveness, inspired an outburst of support from Czech intellectuals. Among their most famous defenders was Václav Havel, who wrote in a widespread underground essay entitled "The Trial" that at a time of such oppression by the state, "there are only two things one can do: gamble everything, or throw in the cards." The "Chartists," as signatories of Charter 77 were called, chose to gamble everything, forming a human rights organization that, like the Helsinki Watch Group of the Soviet Union, demanded the observation of the Helsinki Accords on human rights. The Czechoslovak state took sharp action against Charter 77, but it persisted and gained in membership over the following years.

## THE GLASNOST ERA

By the early to mid-1980s, dissent in the Soviet Union suffered considerable depredations as many dissidents were either imprisoned or exiled to the West or internally (such as Andrei Sakharov to the Soviet city of Gorky in 1980), and as internal conflicts among the various movements began to manifest themselves more strongly. The Soviet state's policy of discrediting dissidents as opportunistic, more interested in material gain through exposure to Westerners and Western life than in reforming society, also had an effect. But it was in the Soviet Union that the state leadership began to move toward acceptance of the dissident critique of state control and politicization of individuals and society, under the leadership of Mikhail Gorbachev. In 1987 Gorbachev implemented his policy of glasnost in order to open public discourse. He also brought to an end Soviet support for the East European satellite governments, allowing the forces of dissent and revolution to take over in Eastern Europe in 1989 without threat of Soviet invasion. The Soviet Union itself proved incapable of surviving open public discourse as a body politic, as some of the debates that had simmered among the great variety of dissidents surged to the surface of public discourse, along with many other tensions in Soviet society. Above all, ethnic and nationalist discontent, including a growing Russian nationalist movement that involved, among others, such early Village Prose authors as Valentin Rasputin, had an impact, leading to the disintegration of the Soviet Union as a multiethnic empire in 1991.

The impact of Soviet and Soviet bloc dissent on the post-Soviet period has not yet been settled by history. In Poland and Czechoslovakia, two former dissenters, Václav Havel and Lech Wałęsa, became major political leaders in the 1990s. More broadly, while the dissident emphasis on individual responsibility to speak out and to take action against injustice laid an evident groundwork for post-Soviet discourse on civil society in Central and Eastern Europe and in the former Soviet Union, it will take generations for the ideas and the history of dissenters to work themselves out in the region that bred them.

*See also* **Havel, Václav; Radio Free Europe; Samizdat; Solidarity; Solzhenitsyn, Alexander; Wałęsa, Lech.**

BIBLIOGRAPHY

Alexeyeva, Ludmilla. *Soviet Dissent: Contemporary Movements for National, Religious, and Human Rights.* Translated by Carol Pearce and John Glad. Middletown, Conn., 1985.

Falk, Barbara J. *The Dilemmas of Dissidence in East-Central Europe: Citizen Intellectuals and Philosopher Kings.* Budapest and New York, 2003.

Rubenstein, Joshua. *Soviet Dissidents: Their Struggle for Human Rights.* 2nd ed. Boston, Mass., 1985.

BARBARA WALKER

**DIVORCE.** Unlike the Protestant view, Catholic doctrine considers marriage as an indissoluble sacrament. At the end of the eighteenth century, the monopoly on matrimonial cases that the Catholic Church was still claiming to exercise in many European countries was severely shaken. Among other questions, the controversy was strong over the opportunity to allow divorce, within a conception of marriage based on contract, favoring the affection between spouses rather than the strategies of alliances between families. In France the revolutionary law of 1792 made divorce possible through three procedures: certain determinate causes; mutual consent; and incompatibility, even when just one spouse alleged an incompatibility of temperament. This permissive and egalitarian law was abrogated by the Civil Code of 1804—applicable for various periods in a number of European countries after the Napoleonic conquests—which signified a return to an earlier order typified by inequality between husband and wife. The principle of divorce was maintained, in the name of the religious liberty, but the grounds were reduced. The civil code established a limited number of faults (the wife's adultery; the husband keeping a concubine in the matrimonial home; cruelty; and condemnation to certain penal sanctions). Divorce by mutual consent was also provided for, but made very difficult to obtain and was full of disadvantages for both the parties. This procedure by mutual consent was in fact preserved for one main reason: to allow the dissimulation of "scandalous" causes, for the sake of family order. It was only in 1857 in England and Wales, outside the influence of the French Civil Code, that divorce was made available in a new nonecclesiastical court. The new procedure, which replaced the need for a private act of

Parliament, rested exclusively on the grounds of fault, which was categorized differently for men and women. In Germany, it was only thanks to the coming into force of the first German Civil Code (BGB 1900) that uniform divorce legislation became applicable, on the grounds of fault as well.

In some European countries divorce, which had been provided for during relatively liberal periods, was suppressed following the imposition of authoritarian regimes. For example, in Portugal divorce was introduced in 1910, abrogated in 1940, and reintroduced in 1975; in Spain it was introduced by the Republicans, suppressed under the regime of Francisco Franco, and reestablished in 1980. In Russia, civil divorce was only possible after the Bolshevik Revolution (1917) and in Austria, after the Anschluss (1938). Accused of contributing to the destruction of the family, already allegedly imperiled progressively by women's emancipation and the decline of marital power, divorce became a major political issue, and, for a long time, moralists and even sociologists considered it a "social evil," criticizing the damage provoked by rare examples of liberal legislation (for example, in the United States and the Soviet Union). This distaste explains why most European countries first organized divorce around the notion of some fault committed by one of the spouses. The view was that marriage, seen as an institution, should only be broken in extremely serious cases, and legislators hoped that these would be rare. Belgium was an exception by admitting mutual consent, which was organized according to the restrictive logic of the Code Napoleon. Some countries, such as Norway, also recognized divorce on the grounds of insanity, which strictly speaking could not be considered as a fault.

## CATHOLICISM AND DIVORCE

Catholicism continued to influence the issue of divorce in Europe during the twentieth century. Papal encyclicals repeated indefatigably the sacred character of marriage, with clear impact on secular law, as some countries only introduced divorce very late (Italy, 1970; Ireland, 1996) or even still refuse to allow it in the early twenty-first century (Malta, despite its membership in the European Union, although the situation there may change, as it did in Ireland). The secularization of marriage, as a civil contract, became predominant, even in non-Catholic countries (Greece, 1920). Strictly speaking, judicial separation—which does not authorize remarriage—remains the only possibility for observant Catholics, if apart from exceptional cases of annulment as illustrated by the famous case of Caroline of Monaco (1992).

## PREWAR AND POSTWAR EUROPE

For a long time, the divorce rate in Europe remained very low. Divorced spouses were often socially ostracized and remarriages were disapproved of. Progressively, however, the notion of fault appeared inadequate in contrast with the extreme complexity of conjugal life. Collusion and condonation between spouses to disguise mutual consent in the form of a fault was widespread. For their part, judges played an important role, interpreting legal categories so as to widen the grounds for divorce and to soften the inequalities of which married women were the victims. These changes, brought about by case law, were in some countries little by little incorporated into statutes. After World War I, certain legislation equalized the position of both spouses (England and Wales, in 1923 and again in 1937), simplified procedures (Soviet Union, 1926), or introduced new grounds for divorce: the recognition of the irretrievable breakdown of the marriage (already admitted in Norway from 1909 and in Switzerland from 1912) and the existence of separation for a certain length of time (Denmark, 1922; Finland, 1929). So it was that before World War II, some countries had mixed systems, where fault and no-fault divorce coexisted.

The divorce rate rose spectacularly after World War II, feeding the debate on the grounds and the procedures that ought to be favored. Many regretted that the notion of fault contributed to poisoning the relationship between spouses and forced them to express their requests in terms of culpability. In the 1960s, the whole of family law underwent some dramatic reform (affiliation, matrimonial property, marital power, and the incapacity of married women), mainly under the impulse of rising feminism. Divorce could not escape this process. Women's liberation movements fought for the promotion of divorce by mutual consent. Following the example of Scandinavian countries, the United Kingdom, under the rather paradoxical influence of the Anglican Church (articulated in the report *Putting Asunder,* 1966) emphasized breakdown of marriage, seen in some cases as an "empty legal shell to be destroyed with the maximum fairness and the minimum bitterness, distress and humiliation." This logic spread throughout the Continent: the recognition of the failure of a marriage, often demonstrated by a specified period of separation, progressively replaced the need to demonstrate fault (Netherlands, 1971; Sweden, 1973; Belgium, 1974; Germany, 1976; Scotland, 1976). In the early twenty-first century this "divorce-failure" (*divorce-faillite*) has been generalized, often based on a two-stage procedure (a separation for an ever shorter period followed by the divorce itself), sometimes in the general frame of extremely simplified procedures (Sweden, 1973; England and Wales, 1973). Nevertheless, in some systems, powers have been reserved to judges to dismiss the petition for divorce if their evaluation is that the dissolution of the marriage would have consequences that are too heavy, materially or morally, for the children or for the "innocent" spouse—the one who has not brought the action. This "hardship clause," by shifting the emphasis from grounds to consequences, in effect reintroduced fault by the back door.

In the early twenty-first century one tends to say that in some European countries (Belgium and France, among others), one out of three marriages ends in divorce and even, in some big cities, one out of two. This statistical frequency is often connected with factors that need to be carefully examined. Such statistics tend to foster representations of gender relationships and prejudice judgments over the supposedly negative consequences of women's emancipation. It is the case for married women's employment, even if it is clear that to be able to earn a living increases women's independence and hence their possibility to start a divorce procedure. Female emancipation and the influence of women's liberation movements are often referenced. It is true that in 70 percent of European divorce cases, women take the initiative to petition for a divorce. Everywhere spouses are encouraged to reach an agreement on how to share property and how to exercise parental responsibility (alimony, guardianship of children, and rights of visitation).

The court procedure, which most legislation tends to make less contentious, is often accompanied by a familial mediation.

## DIVORCE AND FAMILIES

In the eighteenth-century debate, where all the arguments that were going to be used in the nineteenth and the twentieth centuries were already developed, it was the idea of happiness and of the personal fulfillment of husbands and wives that promoted the need for allowing dissolution of marriage. By the same token, marriage, once viewed primarily as an institution that supported society and the state, became founded more on affection between spouses. This ideology of love has rendered conjugal unions more fragile, as such unions could be ended legally, bringing into question the notion of the universal, durable heterosexual couple. Just as the nuclear family was being made possible by the rise of individualism, it faced the ever greater risk of dissolution.

By bringing matrimonial life to an end, divorce often results in a single person, on the one hand, and a single-parent family, on the other, most often headed by a woman. Some gender studies are now seriously questioning whether no-fault divorce has an altogether beneficial effect for women, though it had been a major feminist objective. In all European countries, the great majority of divorces that are based on a specific grounds result in the mother assuming guardianship of the children, confirming the traditional female role in the field of education, often presented as a privilege. For some years, associations of fathers have expressed their sense of unfairness with regard to the alleged tendency of courts to deprive them of full parental responsibility. But the number of fathers who in fact apply for guardianship remains low (less than 20 percent in France). If the grounds for divorce are not any more at the center of important controversies, the effects of the breakdown are being treated as a worrying social issue. Failure to pay alimony is a common problem and one that is difficult to resolve. The tendency seems to be for the state to meet the initial payment of these rather large sums when one spouse does not do so (Scandinavian countries; Belgium, 2004). Beyond that, the increase in the divorce rate has multiple consequences worthy of a full inventory, as, for example, the reorganization of housing provision (in some big cities, single-person homes are in the majority).

In some parts of Europe, the majority of the pupils come from broken homes. Divorce leads to a reorganization of family relationships, giving rise by the same token to new forms of kinship and alliance and to new questions should these recomposed families break up in their turn. A new legal and sociological definition of family could well be needed. The increase in the divorce rate is contributing to a trivialization of the dissolution of marriage to such an extent that one can state that divorce is now a part of marriage.

*See also* **Catholicism; Demography; Sexuality.**

BIBLIOGRAPHY

Boele-Woelki, Katharina, Bente Braat, and Ian Sumner, eds. *European Family Law in Action.* Antwerp, Belgium, and New York, 2003.

Chester, Robert, ed., with Gerrit Kooy. *Divorce in Europe.* Leiden, Netherlands, 1977.

Glendon, Mary Ann. *Abortion and Divorce in Western Law.* Cambridge, Mass., 1987.

Meulders-Klein, Marie-Thérèse. *La personne, la famille et le droit, 1968–1998: Trois décennies de mutations en occident.* Brussels, 1999.

RÉGINE BEAUTHIER, VALÉRIE PIETTE

---

# DIX, OTTO (1891–1969), German painter.

Like many among the avant-garde, the young German painter Otto Dix greeted the onset of war in August 1914 with a sense of excitement, and he joined the army not as a conscript but as a volunteer. He was in favor of what he viewed as a just and purifying struggle that offered the prospect of Nietzschean redemption. From its early enthusiasms to cruel disenchantments, he plunged into the war and followed it until the end.

At the front, Dix was fascinated. He spun out his real-world research and attempted to overcome the contradiction between the aesthetics and destructiveness of modern warfare. But disenchantment and *Zerrissenheit* (best translated as "torn-to-pieces-hood") gradually shaped the warp and woof of his representations. His drawings show the trenches, excavations left by shrapnel shells, ruins, broken staircases that lead nowhere. Topless trees and their stump branches were reminders of headless and mutilated soldiers, vanished at the desolate front.

Although not a committed dadaist, Dix agreed to participate in the movement's 1920 International Fair in Berlin, where he exhibited his images of the ravages of the war as they appeared in the city streets. One sees the bodies of the demobilized soldiers who are yet still "at war" in canvases such as *War Cripples, Self-Portrait, Prague Street, Match Seller, The Skat Players,* and *The Barricade.* Each of these works of Dix from 1920 portrays wounded survivors of the conflict, those massacred and torn apart by World War I and then the German Civil War, all amid the detritus of civilization, fine art and kitsch alike. Huge, horrible prostitutes remind one of the monstrosity of the front, of Eros and Thanatos.

Dix wanted to force his contemporaries to confront the cruelty of war itself and the brutality of postwar political life. His paintings trumpet the traumatic shock and mutilation, the prostheses and broken faces; they refuse to sanitize the conflict. *Prague Street* (1920) shows two war cripples passing one another, each without seeing the other, as before the war, while the bourgeois and the beggar are only two double-jointed puppets in a two dimensional space, parallel to the plaster torsos in the window of a shop selling erotic objects, between sado-masochism and the monstrance of horror. A dog holds in its mouth a newspaper with the words *Juden Raus* (Jews out). The world had come a long way since 1914.

Only in the second half of the 1920s did Dix return to the front and his wartime experience, particularly in a series of etchings he called *Der Krieg* (The war), in which he exposed the devastation that battle wreaked on bodies and souls. Skeletons are torn apart by shells, bodies melded into the upthrust soil, suicides; screams of distress and whispers of the dying wounded can be heard.

Like Max Beckmann (1884–1950), Dix employed the medieval triptych, which suggested the Trinity and offered the possibility of picturing shattering visions of the horror and grief fused with Catholic mysticism in terms of spiritual abandonment, the sufferings of martyrdom, and the imitation of Christ and the Virgin Mary. Form and content

**The Skat Players.** Painting by Otto Dix, 1920. THE ART ARCHIVE/DAGLI ORTI. © 2001 ARTISTS RIGHTS SOCIETY (ARS), NEW YORK/VG BILD-KUNST, BONN.

coalesce perfectly. His *War Triptych* (1929–1932) reveals, like the Isenheim Altarpiece of Matthias Grünewald (c. 1480–1528), three episodes in a soldier's life—departure for the trenches, the battle, and the return. The predella of the triptych shows soldiers who seem to be sleeping in their shelters, but the viewer sees they are dead under their shrouds. For them, there will not be a resurrection—and this is the message Dix, now a pacifist, wanted to convey.

In 1937 Nazis organized an exhibition of what they called "degenerate art" to prove the moral corruption of Weimar Germany. Works of Dix and George Grosz (1893–1959) were among the most prominent. Dix's art was opposed in every way to the aesthetic and social values of Nazism. It was neither respectable nor orderly, offered no message of comfort or security but instead screamed out with the despair of men caught in the turmoil of personal and collective drama. With his grasp of the significance of war, his works were subversion on canvas.

After exhibiting his paintings, the Nazis put some canvases in storage and destroyed others, including *War Cripples* and *The Trench,* as "insulting to the heroes of the Great War." Dix now underwent exile in his own country. He served in the 1939–1943 war and was a prisoner in Alsace. He would return again to the subject of the Great War in the 1960s but indirectly, perhaps only metaphorically, in his religious painting.

*See also* **Beckmann, Max; Dada; Degenerate Art Exhibit; Grosz, George; World War I.**

BIBLIOGRAPHY

Barron, Stephanie, ed. *Degenerate Art: The Fate of the Avant-Garde in Nazi Germany.* Los Angeles, 1991.

Becker, Annette, and Philippe Dagen. *Otto Dix: Der Kreig/ The War.* Milan, 2003.

Eberlé, Matthias. *World War I and the Weimar Artists: Dix, Grosz, Beckmann, Schlemmer.* Translated by John Gabriel. New Haven, Conn., 1985.

Los Angeles County Museum of Art. *Entartete Kunst.* Los Angeles, 1937. Exhibition catalog.

McGreevy, Linda. *The Life and Works of Otto Dix: German Critical Realist.* Ann Arbor, Mich., 1981.

Tate Gallery. *Otto Dix, 1891–1969.* London, 1992. Exhibit catalog.

ANNETTE BECKER

# DJILAS, MILOVAN (1911–1995), leader of Montenegro.

Milovan Djilas was born the fourth of nine children to the peasants Nikola and Novka Djilas on 12 June 1911 in the mountains along the Albanian frontier in Podbišće, Montenegro. His childhood, as revealed in the first volume of his memoirs, *Land without Justice* (1958), was punctuated by the Balkan Wars (1912–1913); World War I (1914–1918); and the formation of Yugoslavia, including Montenegro, in 1918. After completing elementary and secondary school in Montenegro he entered Belgrade University to study literature in 1929, the same year that the royal dictatorship of King Alexander Karadjordjević (r. 1921–1934) was established in Yugoslavia.

Under the influence of the Great Depression and other postwar problems facing Yugoslavia, problems stemming from underdevelopment, multinationalism, and a lack of a democratic tradition, Djilas became a communist during his university years and was soon imprisoned as an agitator by the dictatorship in 1933–1936. He served in prison with top Yugoslav communist leaders, including Tito (Josip Broz, 1892–1980), Moša Pijade (1890–1957), and Alexander Ranković (1909–1982), and saw it as a school for revolutionaries. After Djilas's release he immediately went underground and also married a fellow Montenegrin communist student, Mitra Mitrović, in 1937; they had a daughter in 1947. Djilas was appointed to the Central Committee and Politburo of the Yugoslav Communist Party in 1938 and 1940, respectively. During World War II, in the Yugoslav Revolution and War of National Liberation, he was in charge of the Montenegrin theater and the editor of the Party newspapers *Borba* (The struggle) and *Nova Jugoslavija* (The new Yugoslavia). As a lieutenant general of the partisan resistance in 1944 Djilas headed up a diplomatic mission to Moscow and first met Joseph Stalin (1879–1953). His encounters and eventual disillusionment with the Soviet dictator and communism are captured in Djilas's *Conversations with Stalin* (1962). His prewar and war experiences also were recounted in the second and third volume of his memoirs, *Memoir of a Revolutionary* (1973) and *Wartime* (1977), respectively.

In 1945–1954 Djilas rose to become the vice president of Yugoslavia and president of the Federal Assembly and second in power only to Tito. Following the Yugoslav-Soviet split and break with Stalin in 1948, along with Edward Kardelj (1910–1979) and Boris Kidrić (1912–1953), Djilas was an architect of socialist "self-management," a cornerstone of "Titoism," Yugoslav national communism, and Yugoslavism. In 1950 he divorced his first wife and married his second, Stefića, a former Croat partisan, in 1952. They had a son in 1954.

Djilas's disillusionment with communism had already begun during World War II. He actively began to critique Stalinism in theory and practice in 1948 and Titoism in 1953. He worked diligently and almost foolhardily to democratize and decentralize Titoism. After numerous official warnings from Tito and other Yugoslav leaders Djilas was stripped of all official posts by the Third Plenum of the League of Yugoslav Communists, the Yugoslav Communist Party, in January 1954 and resigned his membership in the League in March. His first imprisonment under communism followed in 1956–1961. With the publication of *The New Class* (1957) in the West, Djilas quickly became communism's most famous critic at the height of the Cold War.

To Djilas, the "new class," comprising self-serving party bureaucrats that supported and were partners in the communist dictatorship, was the ultimate contradiction of communism, which after the revolution was supposed to yield a classless democratic society. This class grew out of and sustained itself on the control and not the ownership of the means of production. In *The New Class*, Djilas condemned the reality of communism but not the Marxist ideology. His final break with Marxism came with the publication of *The Unperfect Society* (1969) after his second imprisonment under communism in 1962–1966. In this book, he pointed out that human beings by their nature were not "imperfect," capable of perfection, but "unperfect," incapable of perfection. Marxism and all other universal ideologies (e.g., Christianity) were horribly flawed in that the sought to foster human perfection at the expense of human freedom. As he had done first at the end of the *New Class*, in *The Unperfect Society* he still came down favorably on the side of the more democratic varieties of Eurocommunism developing in France and Italy.

With the death of Tito in 1980 Djilas quickly published his not wholly uncomplimentary appraisal of the Yugoslav leader, *Tito: The Story from Inside* (1980). His two volumes of postwar memoirs, *Rise and Fall* (1985) and *Of Prisons and Ideas* (1986) followed. In addition to his overtly political works, beginning in 1953 Djilas also published numerous novels and collections of short stories, many of them written in prison. His *Njegoš* (1966), a major biography of the nineteenth-century founder of modern Montenegro, ranks among Djilas's major writings such as *The New Class, Conversations with Stalin,* and *The Unperfect Society,* and has helped to earn him a leading position in Yugoslav literature. Montenegro remained an important theme in his

life and work. Milovan Djilas died in Belgrade on 20 April 1995.

*See also* **Eurocommunism; Montenegro; Tito (Josip Broz); Yugoslavia.**

BIBLIOGRAPHY

*Primary Sources*

Djilas, Milovan. *The New Class: An Analysis of the Communist System.* New York, 1957.

———. *The Unperfect Society: Beyond the New Class.* Translated by Dorian Cooke. New York, 1969.

*Secondary Sources*

Reinhartz, Dennis. *Milovan Djilas, A Revolutionary as a Writer.* Boulder, Colo., and New York, 1981.

DENNIS REINHARTZ

# DÖBLIN, ALFRED (1878–1957), German physician and writer.

Alfred Döblin ranks with Thomas Mann (1875–1955) and Franz Kafka (1883–1924) among the three most significant German prose writers of the twentieth century. Although during his life—except for a brief period at the end of the Weimar Republic (1918–1933)—Döblin's reputation fell short of his two competitors, it has risen constantly since his death. The Nobel Prize–winning author Günter Grass (b. 1927) has referred to him as "my teacher."

Born on 10 August 1878 in Stettin, Pomerania (present-day Polish Szczecin), Döblin was the fourth of five children of Jewish parents. When the boy was ten, his father deserted the family, an experience that traumatized Döblin for the rest of his life and left its mark on his works. Following his university studies in Berlin and Freiburg, he practiced medicine in Regensburg and Berlin.

With his short stories and one-act plays Döblin had a great impact on the German literary scene during the first decade of the twentieth century. His works appeared in expressionist journals such as Herwarth Walden's *Der Sturm.* In 1912 he published *Die Ermordung einer Butterblume* (The murder of a buttercup), a collection of novellas; the title story is one of the most famous expressionist prose texts. On a walk through the forest the protagonist beheads a buttercup with his walking stick. Driven by guilt, he plants a buttercup in his home and opens a bank account for it. Following the flower's demise the man returns to the forest and kills flowers at his delight. With such depiction of schizophrenic bourgeois behavior Döblin found the central theme for his entire oeuvre: critique of modern man's neurotic actions and alienation from nature.

Döblin's first novel to appear in print was *Die drei Sprünge des Wang-Lun* (1915; The three leaps of Wang-Lun), which was followed by three more novels by 1920. In these works Döblin developed what in his theoretical writings he called his "lapidary style" (*steinerner Stil*), a mode of writing in which the auctorial "I" disappears behind the epic material. He carried this style, which he also called "epic," to extremes in the novel *Berge, Meere, und Giganten* (Mountains, oceans, and giants), published in 1924 and depicting a futuristic world of political dictatorship and inhuman technology.

It seems that Döblin felt the limitations of his "epic" style when he wrote a novel that was to become his most famous work and also one of the greatest novelistic achievements of German literature during the Weimar Republic. *Berlin Alexanderplatz* (1929), with its reference to the main square of the German capital, has a realistic touch, but it also opened the then outgoing style of expressionism to the incoming "New Matter-of-Factness" (*Neue Sachlichkeit*). The plot centers on a Berlin worker named Biberkopf ("Beaver Head"), who entangles himself in criminal actions and thereby reflects the negative consequences of modern capitalism. The social ills of the Weimar Republic are set in parallel to visionary scenes of guilt and suffering with biblical references. While Biberkopf stubbornly adheres to his habits, the narrator suggests the possibility of another ending, in which an improved protagonist emerges as the "new man" of expressionism. It is this latter aspect that the filmmaker Rainer Werner Fassbinder (1946–1982) stressed in his 1970 fifteen-hour adaptation of the novel. *Alexanderplatz* is also one of the first large-city novels in German literature, whose epic tapestry has been compared to John Dos Passos's *Manhattan Transfer* (1925) and James Joyce's *Ulysses* (1922).

Döblin became one of the most outspoken social and cultural critics of the Weimar Republic. In 1924 he was chosen chair of the Schutzverband Deutscher Schriftsteller (German writers organization). He strongly opposed oppressive government actions, among them the censorship law (Schmutz- und Schundgesetz) of 1926; and he used both radio and press to warn against the rise of the political right. Following his election into the most prestigious German cultural institution, the Preußische Akademie der Künste, in 1928, Döblin became one of its most outspoken members. When the novelist Heinrich Mann and the artist Käthe Kollwitz were ousted from the Akademie under political pressure, Döblin led the opponents' protest.

After the rise to power of Adolf Hitler (1889–1945), Döblin fled Germany. Following a few months in Switzerland, he and his family moved to France and became French citizens. In 1940, with the help of an Emergency Rescue Committee visa, they reached the United States, thereafter living consecutively in Los Angeles and Hollywood. In 1941 Döblin converted to Catholicism. As soon as the war was over, he joined the French occupation forces in Baden-Baden and participated in Germany's "reeducation" by selecting manuscripts for publication.

From 1946 to 1951 Döblin published *Das Goldene Tor* (The golden gate), one of the most prestigious postwar German periodicals; and in 1949 he became a cofounder of the Mainzer Akademie der Wissenschaften und der Literatur. His novels written during and after his exile have gradually, but increasingly, found positive reception. Having repeatedly changed his residence between Germany and France during his final years, he died in Emmendingen near Freiburg im Breisgau on 26 June 1957.

*See also* **Hesse, Hermann; Kafka, Franz; Mann, Thomas.**

BIBLIOGRAPHY

*Primary Sources*

Döblin, Alfred. *Berge, Meere, und Giganten.* Berlin, 1924.

———. *Alexanderplatz, Berlin: The Story of Franz Biberkopf.* Translated by Eugene Jolas. New York, 1931. Translation of *Berlin Alexanderplatz* (1929).

———. "The Murder of a Buttercup." Translated by Patrick O'Neill. In *Early Twentieth Century German Fiction,* edited and introduced by Alexander Stephan. New York, 2003.

*Secondary Sources*

Dollinger, David B. *The Berlin Novels of Alfred Döblin: Wadzek's Battle with the Steam Turbine, Berlin Alexanderplatz, Men without Mercy, and November 1918.* Berkeley, Calif., 1988. Succinct analyses of the mentioned works with focus on the tension between the individual and society.

Dollinger, Roland, Wulf Köpke, and Heidi Thomann Tewarson, eds. *A Companion to the Works of Alfred Döblin.* Rochester, N.Y., 2004. In-depth analyses of Döblin's major works by critics and literary historians.

Köpke, Wulf. *The Critical Reception of Alfred Döblin's Major Novels.* Rochester, N.Y., 2003. A comprehensive review of the reception of several of Döblin's novels.

Kort, Wolfgang. *Alfred Döblin.* New York, 1974. The only English biography in book form to date, with general discussion of Döblin's oeuvre.

HELMUT F. PFANNER

---

## DOCUMENTARY. *See* **Film (Documentary).**

---

## DOLLFUSS, ENGELBERT (1892–1934), Austrian politician and chancellor (1932–1934).

A member of Austria's Catholic and conservative Christian Social Party, Engelbert Dollfuss rose through the ranks of agrarian politics, serving in the 1920s as secretary of the Lower Austrian Peasant Federation, as director of the Lower Austrian Chamber of Agriculture in 1927, as minister of agriculture and forestry in 1931, and finally becoming chancellor of Austria in 1932. Dollfuss's conservative coalition government brought an end to interwar parliamentary politics by suspending the parliament in March 1933 and banning competing parties from the left and right. Dollfuss and his sympathizers maintained that the politically polarized parliament had "dissolved itself."

Dollfuss's political philosophy had roots in the Catholic Church's *Rerum Novarum* (1891), whose vision of a return to a corporate society was reaffirmed by Pope Pius XI in his 1931 encyclical *Quadragesimo Anno.* It shared with other nationalist Catholic movements in Europe a suspicion of the forces of modernity: industrialization, secularization, urbanization, and the individualism of liberal democracy. In Austria, support for the Catholic corporate state was strong in the countryside and in the farming milieu from which Dollfuss came. With the post-Habsburg Republic of Austria (founded in 1918) lacking a strong "national" identity, political Catholicism became a central feature for German-speaking Austrian patriots looking to differentiate themselves from pan-German nationalists and from the socialists who dominated Viennese municipal politics. Upon assuming the chancellorship, Dollfuss quickly put together an antisocialist cabinet. In 1933 the Dollfuss government banned the Communist Party and the Austrian branch of the National Socialist Party. The same year, Dollfuss formed the Fatherland Front, a political organization that sought to replace political parties with a new social order built on seven overarching, harmoniously integrated professional and occupational bodies.

After Austria's brief civil war in February 1934, in which Socialists and their Republican Guard battled Christian Socials and the conservative Heimwehr (home guard) militia, Dollfuss banned the Social Democratic Party and labor unions. In May of that year he established an authoritarian corporate state (*Ständestaat*) backed by the Catholic Church and billed as a "patriotic" alternative to the class-fragmented politics of the republic. The tenets of the corporate state were spelled out in a new Austrian constitution of May 1934. Under the new constitution, the church regained influence over marriage law and the administration of schools. To relieve Austria's struggling economy, Dollfuss accepted a large loan from the League of Nations on condition that Austria not join a customs union with Nazi Germany.

In foreign relations, Dollfuss tried to navigate a position for an independent Austria by securing support from Benito Mussolini. In August 1933 he met with Mussolini in Riccione, Italy, to form an alliance. Mussolini urged Dollfuss to create a fascist state modeled on his own; Dollfuss himself never adopted the term *fascist.* He also reached a concordat with the Vatican, and through the Protocols of Rome entered into closer economic cooperation with Italy and Hungary. Despite these measures intended to protect Austria from German aggression, members of the banned National Socialist Party disguised themselves in army and police uniforms and stormed the federal chancellery in Vienna on 25 July 1934. In the putsch attempt, supported by the Reich government in Berlin, Dollfuss was fatally shot. Putschists took over state radio in Vienna and announced the false news that Dollfuss had handed over the government. The Nazi putsch was defeated, and the Austrian corporate state outlasted Dollfuss. Kurt Schuschnigg, also of the Christian Social Party, succeeded him as chancellor and ruled until March 1938, when Austria was annexed by Nazi Germany.

Dollfuss occupies an ambiguous position in Austrian history. On one hand, he dismantled the postwar parliamentary system in favor of an authoritarian state ruled by his Fatherland Front. On the other hand, sympathizers credit him with standing up to German nationalists by banning the Austrian Nazi Party and refusing to enter into coalition with Hitler's Germany. In this version of history, Dollfuss was a patriot who tried to preserve the independence of Catholic Austria. To understand Dollfuss's position on the political right, historians have usefully noted that there were indeed two forms of fascism in Austria: the fascism of the pan-Germanists and the "Austrofascism" of Dollfuss and conservative Catholics. In the polarized politics of interwar central Europe, some have argued that Dollfuss tried to steer an Austrian "third way" that rejected both Marxism and pan-Germanism.

*See also* **Austria; Vienna.**

BIBLIOGRAPHY

Bischof, Günter, Anton Pelinka, and Alexander Lassner, eds. *The Dollfuss/Schuschnigg Era in Austria: A Reassessment.* New Brunswick, N.J., and London, 2003.

Kitchen, Martin. *The Coming of Austrian Fascism.* London, 1980.

Rath, R. John. "The Dollfuss Ministry: The Demise of the Nationalrat." *Austrian History Yearbook* 32 (2001): 125–147. Last in the author's series of five noted articles in the *Austrian History Yearbook* that seek to reassess the Dollfuss legacy.

MAUREEN HEALY

---

# DOLTO, FRANÇOISE (1908–1988), French psychoanalyst.

Françoise Dolto (née Marette) was born in Paris, where she grew up in a middle-class family. The death of her elder sister due to cancer played a key role in her career choice. From an early age, she aspired to join the medical profession and take care of children, but throughout her youth this ambition met with family resistance. Her mother saw no future for a girl other than in marriage. Françoise turned to dressmaking and decorating china. In 1929 her mother finally agreed to let her study nursing, but Françoise soon began taking medical classes. This is where she met Mark Schlumberger, who had been analyzed and trained in Austria and England and who advised her to read Sigmund Freud. In 1934 she started a series of analyses with René Laforgue, who in turn encouraged her to participate in seminars with Spitz, Nacht, and Loewenstein.

Even before World War II, Dolto had come to believe that a number of the childhood diseases she dealt with had an unconscious psychological origin. She completed her studies at the Paris Faculty of Medicine and graduated in 1939 with a thesis entitled "Psychoanalysis and Pediatrics." In September of the same year, she opened a practice as a general practitioner and pediatrician. In 1942 she married Boris Dolto (1899–1981), a rheumatologist and founder of the French School for Orthopedics and Massage, who enthusiastically adhered to the ideas developed by his wife. The couple had three children: Jean-Chrisostome, who was to become popular as a singer under the name of Carlos; Grégoire, an architect; and Catherine Dolto, a sociologist, physician, and successful author of children's books.

Françoise Dolto was a member of the Freudian School in Paris, and her theories were controversial. Children's psychoanalysis was still in its early stages and was surrounded by criticism, even from other analysts. Dolto reported that one psychoanalyst complained that if the psychoanalysts started dealing with children soon no adults would be seeking treatment and the profession would run out of patients. Yet Dolto remained unshaken in her conviction that human beings communicate with their environment from the very beginning, even in the womb, and that children should be viewed within the dynamic of their personal and family histories.

Although she had planned a career as a pediatrician, Dolto became a psychoanalyst and made a significant contribution to the development of child psychoanalysis. She consulted in several institutions, including the Trousseau Hospital (1940–1978) and the Etienne Marcel Center (1962–1985). A member of the Psychoanalytical Society of Paris since 1938, she followed Jacques Lacan in the famous 1953 rift, which led to the founding of the French Psychoanalytical Society. In 1964 she took part, with Lacan, in setting up the French School for Psychoanalysis, which later became the famous Freudian School of Paris.

She also publicized her thoughts on the world of childhood through radio broadcasts and subsequently in best-selling books. Her status was enhanced by her talent for using the media, and she came to be regarded as France's "favorite grandmother." She spoke and wrote in a language accessible to all, seeking to de-dramatize situations and avoid prescriptive attitudes. (She told anxious parents that being bored in class is a sign of intelligence.) Her success as a communicator encouraged her to retire as a psychoanalyst and devote herself to the shaping and spreading of knowledge as a pedagogue.

In the media, Lacan and Dolto became the public idols of psychoanalysis. Young parents relied on her books, which ran into many reprints. Her views replaced those of the U.S. pediatrician Benjamin Spock, first in France and then throughout Europe, but her success earned her the jealousy, and sometimes the enmity, of fellow psychoanalysts. A famous but controversial clinician, in 1979 she opened the Maison Verte (Green House), which sought to develop early social contact in children by inciting them to speak, play, and de-dramatize their problems. The initiative met with great success, and other Maisons Vertes opened in Europe and throughout the world. In the early twenty-first century, Dolto-inspired places continue to spring up, including Maisons Vertes, after-school neighborhood centers where children are cared for, children's hotels, and meeting centers for the children of divorced parents.

A committed Christian, Dolto attempted to reconcile her faith with the practice of psychoanalysis. In 1977 she published *L'evangile au risque de la psychanalyse* (The gospel at the risk of psychoanalysis). Françoise Dolto died in Paris on 25 August 1988.

*See also* **Freud, Sigmund; Lacan, Jacques; Psychoanalysis.**

BIBLIOGRAPHY

*Françoise Dolto, aujourd'hui présente: Actes du colloque de l'Unesco, 14–17 Janvier 1999.* Paris, 2000.

Ledoux, Michel H. *Introduction à l'œuvre de Françoise Dolto.* Paris, 1993.

Sauverzac, Jean-François de. *Françoise Dolto: Itinéraire d'une psychanalyste: Essai.* Paris, 1993.

VALÉRIE PIETTE

**DOMESTIC SERVICE.** Even though they were regarded with suspicion, domestic servants were an indispensable element in the households of the triumphant nineteenth-century bourgeoisie. The affluent middle classes, who had enjoyed a spectacular rise thanks to widespread industrialization and urbanization, became increasingly vocal in their demand for an abundant domestic workforce. Initially, domestic service was assimilated within the larger category of the proletariat, but it came to constitute a separate sector as legislation assigned workers to more clearly defined categories. During the twentieth century, the rate of feminization in this sector increased until women constituted 80 to 95 percent of the domestic workforce in some European countries. From the late nineteenth century onward, the declining status of domestic service became a cause for general concern, and in response constant attempts were made to maintain the volume of the sector's workforce by increasing its professionalization or by turning to an immigrant workforce from more and more distant countries. Complaints of a crisis in the availability of domestic servants became a commonplace topic of conversation among bourgeois housewives in many nations.

## ROLE AND CONDITIONS OF WORK

Although the crisis in domestic service was an international phenomenon, the number of women entering into service remained high. In 1920, servants in Switzerland accounted for 14 percent of women in the workforce; in Germany in 1925, 11 percent of working women were domestic servants. During the Depression of the 1930s, the scarcity of domestic servants was felt even more acutely on the Continent. When in response to the economic crisis governments sought to limit women's work through both persuasion and coercion, household and domestic employment were exempted from the measures.

The demand for servants rose as new social categories acquired wealth. The upper middle classes and the aristocracy were no longer the only potential employers, and the emergence of a massive class of employers only increased the demand for domestic servants. Prior to the widespread adoption of the automobile as a status symbol, the domestic servant was valued as an external sign of wealth by a class that sought to separate itself from its working-class origins.

Various solutions were proposed to remedy the relative penury of servants. In the nineteenth century these were initiated primarily by individuals and in the twentieth by governments. During the 1920s, girls became less willing to enter domestic service, for a variety of reasons. Among these, the inferior social status of the occupation ranked high, followed by working conditions, including long working hours and the lack of comfort and leisure, and psychological and social factors, such as isolation from one's family, the lack of hope for improvement of one's situation, and the limited prospects for marriage. Although numerous surveys documented the reasons girls were unwilling to enter domestic service, solutions were hard to find. One remedy was sought at the level of semantic symbolism. It was felt that the vocabulary of domestic service, heavily fraught with disparaging connotations, must change. The words *maid* and *servant* were replaced by euphemisms such as *domestic worker* or, more elegantly, *lady's help*, or in French *employée de maison* or *auxiliaire ménagère*, and in German *Hausgehilfin*.

Domestic workers were, almost as a matter of course, excluded from the legal benefits to which other workers were entitled, including working

contracts in Belgium in 1900 and industrial law in England and Poland in 1928. In countries where domestic work was included in the general laws protecting workers (for example, Spain in 1931), domestic employees were still generally excluded from laws that specified working and resting hours. Some exceptions must be noted, however. In Switzerland, a 1920 law on working hours imposing nine-hour periods of rest applied equally to domestic employees and to other workers. A 1918 Czech law specified daily and weekly rest periods. Throughout the period between the two world wars, recurring attempts were made on the Continent to regulate domestic work by means of public law, but they were rarely successful. In Belgium, five different bills were submitted, but none was approved. Only in the second half of the twentieth century did legislation specifically regulating domestic service appear (in Belgium, for example, in 1970).

## UNIONS AND IMMIGRATION

One attempt to make domestic work more attractive was the provision of vocational training for girls of rural or working-class origins. Throughout Europe, initiatives were taken to develop the teaching of domestic economy and household skills. But although in the nineteenth century the very idea of a society without servants was inconceivable except to a few visionaries, in the first few decades of the twentieth century the scarcity of domestic help came to be accepted, albeit grudgingly. The idea of scientific work management, already well implanted in the United States, played a key role in this awareness and thus the development of scientific domestic engineering, introduced in Europe by the Americans Lilian Gilbreth and Christine Frederick and taken over by the French Paulette Bernège and the German Erna Mayer, ran parallel to the scarcity of domestic workers.

Domestic service remained a solitary and unstructured form of employment, making it difficult to organize. Only a few unions emerged: in Finland, domestic employees' unions were first organized in 1900 and were grouped into a federation in 1905. Similar unions appeared in Denmark, Sweden, the Netherlands, Austria, and Lithuania.

The primary response to the shortage of domestic servants was to draw on an immigrant workforce. Legislation on immigration, although generally

**Students at a training school for domestic workers in London learn to arrange place settings, 1937.** ©HULTON-DEUTSCH COLLECTION/CORBIS

restrictive with regard to the workforce as a whole, displayed greater leniency for this category of workers. In Switzerland in 1928, 28 percent of domestic servants were immigrants, compared with 13 percent in other occupations. As a result, the statistics in some large cities show more female than male immigrants. With time, the areas from which domestic workers were recruited grew. Initially, southern European countries (Italy, Spain, Portugal) supplied domestic workers for northern countries. So, later, did Eastern European countries (Poland, Hungary, Bulgaria), and numbers rose steeply after the fall of the Berlin Wall in 1989 and the extension of the European Union's borders. But recruitment spread well beyond the European continent as Filipino and Peruvian servants came to be in high demand.

In the early twenty-first century, attempts to evade new laws governing domestic work caused domestic work to become increasingly clandestine, giving rise to the emergence of a substantial black-market economy in Europe. The phenomenon is universally acknowledged but impossible to assess statistically. Both national and European authorities are trying to combat this underground economy by various means (see *Resolution of the European Parliament on the Normalization of Domestic Work in the Informal Economy,* 30 November 2000), but despite their attempts concern over domestic slavery is growing. An uncountable number of servants are locked away in their employers' homes, where they are subjected to catastrophic conditions, including systematic confiscation of their passports upon their arrival, painful working and living conditions, sequestration, and physical violence—conditions against which these modern-day slaves are totally unprotected. In response, the Council of Europe in June 2001 encouraged the governments of member states to severely repress this new form of the slave trade.

*See also* **Immigration and Internal Migration; Trade Unions.**

BIBLIOGRAPHY

Anderson, Bridget. *Doing the Dirty Work? The Global Politics of Domestic Labour.* London, 2000.

Gubin, E., and Valerie Piette, eds. *Domesticité.* Special issue, *Sextant* 15–16 (2001).

Sarti, Raffaella. "Da serva a operaia? Transformazioni di lungo periodo del servizio domestico in Europa." *Polis* XIX (1 April 2005): 91–120.

VALERIE PIETTE

# DORGELÈS, ROLAND (1886–1973),

prominent French literary figure.

From a provincial middle-class family, Roland Dorgelès (born Roland Lécavelé) was a Parisian journalist and bohemian, friendly with artists and writers, who became well-known as the author of the popular and widely translated novel of World War I, *Les croix de bois* (1919; *Wooden Crosses,* 1921). Dorgelès drew on his military experience, first as an infantryman and later in the air force; he was injured in a plane crash in 1917. Although he began work on *Wooden Crosses* during the war, censorship delayed publication until 1919. While the immediate postwar period was less favorable to war novels than had been the case during the conflict, the book nonetheless was a singular success that won the Femina Prize for the year's best novel; the Prix Goncourt, however, went to *A l'Ombre des jeunes filles en fleurs* (*Within a Budding Grove*) by Marcel Proust (1871–1922). Nevertheless, a decade later, Dorgelès was invited to join the Académie Goncourt.

Although fiction, *Wooden Crosses* offered a realistic description of army life and the horrors of war. Dorgelès liked to say: "I hated the war but love those who made it." Although his work was less political than that of Henri Barbusse (1873–1935) and less accurate than the diaries of Maurice Genevoix (1890–1980), Dorgelès enthralled his readers with his narrative sweep. His work also reflected the resentment of soldiers who sometimes felt abandoned and even betrayed on the home front. This was a view he expressed again in *Le réveil des morts* (1923, The rising of the dead), in which, during a dream, the main character envisions dead soldiers confronting living people; the novel has similarities with *J'accuse,* the Abel Gance (1889–1991) film of 1918–1919. The 2003 publication of Dorgelès's war correspondence has revealed biographical elements relevant to the discord between soldier and civilian. The letters indicate that, while he was at the front, Dorgelès's mistress betrayed him and left him for another man. They also indicate that to some extent he reconciled this personal bitterness and realistic vision of the war with a measure of patriotism.

Moreover, Dorgelès did not readily leave the war behind. In addition to his published work, during the interwar years he presided over the *Association des Ecrivains Combattants* (Association of military veterans and writers). In 1927–1928, he also defended his views on the literature of war over those of critic Jean Norton Cru, whose famous work *Témoins* (1929, Witnesses) favored unvarnished "moral accounts."

Dorgelès's career as a journalist provided him with a steady income, and in 1932 Raymond Bernard (1891–1977) directed a screen adaptation of *Wooden Crosses* starring Charles Vanel (1892–1989), one of the famous actors of his time. The film was partly shot on the original battlefields with actors who were, like the star, themselves war veterans.

Dorgelès traveled widely with his Russian wife, Hania Routchine, visiting Asia and the Soviet Union, writing numerous books that combined expository with narrative writing. One such work was *Vive la Liberté!* from 1937, a condemnation of bolshevism published after a trip to the Soviet Union. When it came to colonialism, Dorgelès was clearly less critical, even apologetic, in such works as *Sur la route mandarine* (1925; *On the Mandarin Road,* 1926), *Sous le casque blanc* (1941, Under the white helmet), and others.

During the brief French military resistance to the Germans in World War II, Dorgelès worked as reporter for the newspaper *Gringoire* and used this material in a book entitled *La drôle de guerre, 1939–1940* (1957, The phony war)—even claiming he had originated the expression used ever since to describe the period from 9 September 1939 until the French collapse on 10 May 1940. Loyal to the "hero of Verdun," Dorgelès moved increasingly to the right and penned several texts favorable to Philippe Pétain (1856–1951). However, he left *Gringoire* in 1941 when the newspaper became outspokenly and strongly anti-Semitic.

In the great debate at war's end, Dorgelès supported amnesty for the intellectuals who had collaborated with the Germans. He continued his career but without his former success, renowned but lacking the moral authority he had enjoyed between the two wars. The "Christian anarchist" and veteran became obsolete and unfashionable. Dorgelès was increasingly remembered as the author of one book, *Wooden Crosses.*

*See also* **France; Pétain, Philippe; World War I; World War II.**

BIBLIOGRAPHY

*Primary Sources*

Dorgelès, Roland. *Souvenirs sur les Croix de Bois.* Paris, 1929.

———. *Les Croix de Bois.* Paris, 1919. Reprint, Paris, 1962.

———. *Le Cabaret de la Belle Femme.* Paris, 1919. Reprint, Paris, 1967.

———. *Je t'écris de la tranchée: Correspondance de guerre.* Paris, 2003.

*Secondary Sources*

Dupray, Micheline. *Roland Dorgelès: Un siècle de vie littéraire français.* Paris, 1986.

Nicolas Beaupré

# DRIEU LA ROCHELLE, PIERRE
(1893–1945), French writer.

Along with Robert Brasillach (1909–1945) and Louis-Ferdinand Céline (pseudonym of Louis-Ferdinand Destouches, 1894–1961), Pierre Drieu la Rochelle is undoubtedly the French writer who best exemplifies certain French intellectuals' swerve toward fascism, anti-Semitism, and collaboration with the Nazi occupiers. Of the three, moreover, it was he who was the most prominent literary figure at the time, even though he could not lay claim to the talent and the posterity of a Céline, instead describing himself as an "uneven writer."

Drieu la Rochelle was born into a middle-class Paris family originally from Normandy. His hated father, although he practiced the honorable profession of lawyer, had nonetheless drawn his family into debt. Drieu's family and early environment in Normandy were central in his works, especially at the beginning of his literary career. *État civil* (1921; Civil status), *Le Jeune Européen* (1927; European youth), and above all *Rêveuse Bourgeoisie* (1937; Daydreams of the bourgeoisie) treat in their respective ways his love-hate relationship with this environment, which as an adult and a writer he would perceive as decadent.

In 1910 he enrolled at the École Libre des Sciences Politiques (ELSP; Free School of Political Science), but he failed his final exams in 1913. He then enlisted ahead of the draft to do his military service. The war of 1914–1918, in which he was wounded twice, was a formative experience for him. Exaltation and myth prevailed over horror and reality. It was at this time that he wrote and published his first book—the collection of poems *Interrogation* (1917)—at the prestigious Nouvelle Revue Française publishing house. After 1919 his wartime experiences were continually re-created and reused in his works, especially in *Gilles,* his autobiographical novel of 1939. *La comédie de Charleroi* (1934; *The Comedy of Charleroi,* 1973), published at the time of his definitive conversion to fascism, allowed him to portray himself as a warrior and a man of action and to present the war as a seminal moment.

In 1917, for reasons of convenience and money, he married a young woman of Jewish descent, Colette Jeramec, the sister of a schoolmate. After he became a fascist and an anti-Semite, Drieu stated that because of his wife's Jewish ancestry the marriage had never been consummated. More generally, this first marriage marked the beginning of a complicated relationship to women. His second marriage, in 1927, was scarcely more successful. Drieu was a misogynist lover of women, so to speak. Marriages, love affairs, and flings almost invariably ended—or even began—as fiascoes, even though he liked to pass himself off as a debauched seducer (*L'homme couvert de femmes* [1925; A man buried in women]).

From after the war until the beginning of the 1930s, Drieu established friendships and then quarreled with members of the Paris literary elite: he counted André Malraux (1901–1976), Emmanuel Berl (1892–1976), Louis Aragon (1897–1982), Jean Paulhan (1884–1968), and others among his friends, at least for a time. His social skills and reputation, along with his relations with Otto Abetz (1903–1958) Hitler's ambassador to Paris, enabled him to assume the editorship of the prestigious *Nouvelle Revue Française* (*NRF*) during the war and transform it into a showcase for literary collaborationism while attempting to maintain in it some semblance of quality. Meanwhile, this lover of theory had converted to an anti-Semitic fascism that he presented in *Socialisme fasciste* (1934, Fascist socialism). He had previously gone through phases of Nietzscheanism, Maurrasism, nationalism, Europeanism, and nonconformism, and had been tempted by dadaism and surrealism. He sought out other fascist intellectuals, such as Ernst von Salomon (1902–1972), and pursued a career as a militant journalist for various organs of the extreme Right. In 1936 he joined the Parti populaire français (PPF; French people's party), the fascist party of Jacques Doriot (1898–1945), with whom he quarreled two years later, then reconciled in 1942. Meanwhile, in 1940 he had chosen collaboration out of conviction while others did so out of opportunism. He thus agreed without hesitation to represent intellectual France in Nazi literary congresses in Germany.

In 1943 his life was again marked by failure when he decided to fold the *NRF,* which was a mere shadow of what it once had been. At the approach of the defeat, overcome by disgust, this writer who had enjoyed depicting his fascination with death and his suicidal tendencies committed suicide on 15 March 1945.

*See also* **Aragon, Louis; Brasillach, Robert; Céline, Louis-Ferdinand; Dada; Malraux, André; Surrealism.**

BIBLIOGRAPHY

Andreu, Pierre, and Frédéric Grover. *Drieu la Rochelle.* Paris, 1979.

Balvet, Marie. *Itinéraire d'un intellectuel vers le fascisme: Drieu la Rochelle.* Paris, 1984.

Desanti, Dominique. *Drieu la Rochelle: Du dandy au nazi.* Paris, 1978. Reprint, Paris, 1992.

Lecarme, Jacques. *Drieu la Rochelle ou le bal des maudits.* Paris, 2001.

Leibovici, Solange. *Le sang et l'encre: Pierre Drieu la Rochelle: Une psychobiographie.* Amsterdam, 1994.

NICOLAS BEAUPRÉ

---

**DRUGS (ILLEGAL).** Illegal drugs represent only a selection among a range of psychoactive substances. Historically they were natural products such as coca and opium, which were used for religious, medical, or recreational purposes. Opium plays the most prominent role in the history of illegal drugs. It was a remedy sold over the counter for two centuries before it gradually became more regulated, first restricted to the pharmacists' shops in the mid-nineteenth century and then losing its role in medicine during the twentieth century. Opium and later its extract, morphine, were shown to have an extraordinary potential for pain relief as well as having a positive influence on mood. It was the excessive smoking of opium that first created concern. The intoxicating effect, consequences for mental and physical health, and addictive potential became the model criteria for the determination of whether a psychoactive substance is considered a dangerous, and therefore potentially illegal, drug.

Heroin, amphetamines, and LSD all went from being considered useful medicines to becoming illegal drugs. Amphetamines were widely used by soldiers during World War II, and in the years to follow they were popular stimulants used for self-medication. LSD was introduced as a promising new drug in psychiatric treatment before it became a recreational drug favored by the counterculture of the 1960s. By the end of the twentieth century a number of new synthetic drugs had been developed, of which ecstasy is the most well-known.

### A CHANGING PROBLEM

What became the youth drug problem in the 1960s had been at the start of the twentieth century something quite different. There was fear that use of opium among immigrant groups in Europe and the United States could spread to the national population. Established opium dens for habitual users were more or less abolished after World War I. During the years to come the drug problem was related to three groups of users: those addicted because of long-term use or misuse of prescription drugs; medical professionals who had easy access to controlled substances; and groups such as artists, the aristocracy, and soldiers, who were inclined to use drugs recreationally.

Illegal drug use and addiction in the youth population became a dominant public concern beginning in the 1960s. Drugs in general, and especially cannabis and LSD, became important elements of the popular youth movement. During the 1970s and 1980s the use of heroin increased dramatically in a number of European countries. Cocaine, ecstasy, and LSD were key ingredients of the club (or "rave") culture of the 1990s.

## THE INTERNATIONAL DIMENSION

The principles for regulating these illegal drugs were to a large extent determined by international cooperation beginning in the early twentieth century. Regulation and control of the opium trade became one of the first themes for collective action by independent national states in nonpolitical international affairs. The anti-opium protest movements, especially in countries as Britain and the United States, at the beginning of the 1900s contributed to the political pressure that convinced the international community to create a number of enduring international control instruments.

The first conference on the opium trade was held in Shanghai in 1909, followed by conferences in The Hague in 1911–1912, which resulted in the Hague International Opium Convention of 1912. Smoking of opium had caused the popular concern, but the handling of the problem in the international arena was to a large extent determined by the interests of trade. The colonial powers, Britain and the Netherlands, wanted to protect their monopolies. France, Switzerland, and Germany wanted to protect their pharmaceutical industry. The initiatives of the League of Nations for further regulation of the drugs market resulted in the Geneva International Opium Convention of 1925. That convention settled a system for state monopolies for import, distribution, and sale of raw materials of opium and coca products and a system for control of production and sale of the derivates as morphine and cocaine. Cannabis was included on the list of substances that should be used only for medical and scientific purposes. The Convention obliged the participants to develop legal sanctions against actions offending the rules of the convention.

The success of decreasing the legal production and market created the opportunity for profitable clandestine cultivation and manufacture of illegal drugs. In 1936 the League of Nations agreed on the first treaty designed to suppress the illicit drug traffic. The initiatives to set up this convention stemmed from the organization that later became known as INTERPOL.

The United Nations (UN) followed in the track of the League of Nations when they negotiated the Single Convention on Narcotic Drugs in 1961. The convention is, together with the Convention on Psychotropic Drugs from 1971 and the Convention against Illicit Traffic in Narcotic Drugs and Psychotropic Substances from 1988, the basis for international cooperation today. The Single Convention settled the area of drug policy. It signified the prohibition of cannabis and made recommendations to the parties that they should provide facilities for the treatment, rehabilitation, and care of drug addicts. It states which substances should be regulated and it restricts legal use of these substances to medical and scientific use only.

## CONTROLLING DRUGS ON THE NATIONAL LEVEL

At the core of the handling of illegal drugs is the boundary drawn between substances deemed to be therapeutic and the ones whose use is legally proscribed and punished. This boundary is in no way fixed. Some sketches from different European countries can give an indication of the number of factors that influence how these distinctions are made as well as their practical effects.

The principles of the three UN conventions have been muddled through the different national institutional systems of the European countries. Thus, the policies on illegal drugs vary considerably among the European countries. Legal traditions, the professional knowledge base, role of the professions in the legal process, and the status of elites in relation to the public are among the factors that contribute to these differences. The drug policy of a particular nation indicates how its social and governmental infrastructure responds to crime, deviance, subcultures, and social and health problems. It is a commonality among nations, however, that drug use as a form of rebellion among students and cultural elites in the 1960s became a symptom of social marginalization, poverty, and bad health through the 1970s.

The Hague Convention was the basis for the first Opium Laws of the European countries. These laws mainly regulated import, export, and the medical profession's handling of opium, cocaine, and morphine. The potential for conflicts around these laws was highly determined by the traditions for use of these drugs in treatment and for recreation. In Britain the Dangerous Drugs Act of 1920 at an early stage became a battleground for the Home Office and the Ministry of Health. The Home Office wanted to use the law also to control the practices of the medical profession. Brit Bergersen Lind's historical study of drug control in Norway shows that the very limited experience of recreational use made the sharing of responsibilities much easier. The health authorities were in the Norwegian context given full responsibility over the legal distribution of these substances.

Early-twenty-first-century regulations of illegal drugs for the most part have their roots in the 1950s and 1960s. Many countries experienced an escalation of repression of the counterculture and associated drug use during the 1970s and 1980s. Norway represents a very strong illustration of this. The use of illegal drugs was criminalized in 1968. In 1972 and 1981 the maximum penalty for serious drug crimes by professional criminals was raised first from six to ten years, and then subsequently to fifteen years. In 1984 the structure of the laws was changed so that more criminal offenses were placed into the Penal Code. Finally the maximum penalty was raised to the absolute limit, twenty-one years, for particularly aggravated drug crimes. The raising of the penalty levels were most of all aimed at combatting drug trafficking, but some changes were also made in order to hold the users more accountable. By 1984 most of the legal basis for regulating illegal drugs was included

in the Penal Code and the crimes were defined as felonies. Only use and possession for personal use were accepted as misdemeanors.

The differences between the laws of the different nations revealed differences in the drug-policy climates in those countries. Countries including Italy, the Netherlands, Austria, and Spain had an explicit differentiation between "soft" and "hard" drugs and between users and traffickers in their laws, whereas France, Norway, and Sweden did not make these distinctions. The balance between penal provisions and administrative measures also varied considerably. Finally, the expediency principle that allows the police authorities to make priorities between cases and not prosecute minor offenses has de facto legalized possession and consumption of illegal drugs in some countries, for instance the Netherlands.

European integration has contributed to a growing space for regulation and administrative measures in drug policy within the European Union, especially from the early 1990s. Nicholas Dorn and Simone White conclude in 1999 in a study of twelve European countries that the balance between administrative and criminal measures in national policy still varies but that most countries restricted the clear criminal measures to drugs trade, selling and possession of larger amounts, or activities involving more dangerous drugs. In cases of nuisance, administrative and criminal measures were mixed, whereas administrative measures dominated in the handling of local planning, licensing, and possession of illegal drugs in general.

From the end of the 1990s most changes in the European laws on drugs have moved the systems in a more liberal direction. Possession and use of drugs have either changed status from a crime to an offense or have been fully decriminalized in countries as Italy, Spain, Greece, and Portugal. Others, such as Britain and Belgium, restrict this lenience to cannabis only.

### THE HARD AND SOFT DRUGS CONTROVERSY

In practical policy and legal practices hard and soft drugs are treated differently in the European countries. That cannabis should be included in the international conventions on illegal drugs at all was contested from the beginning. Experts commonly recognize that cannabis does not have the same medical and psychological risks as do most of the other drugs on the list of illegal drugs, but in the political debates cannabis still has an important symbolic status. It is considered to be a gateway drug that easily leads to further drug problems for individuals.

The most well-known examples of de facto legalized trade in soft drugs are the "Free City of Christiania" in Denmark and the coffee-shop policy of the Netherlands. In 1971 some large barracks situated almost in the center of Copenhagen were abandoned by the military. Shortly thereafter they were occupied by squatters, who nicknamed them "The Free City of Christiania." In the beginning this was a clearly politicized social experiment opposing the established way of life. There has been a continual debate about Christiania among the Danish public, but all the same the "Pusher Street" in Christiania has survived for more than thirty years as a permanent venue for open trade in hashish. This history has not only to do with the Danish permissiveness in moral questions. It has most of all to do with the principle of making a separation between hard and soft drugs that was set down in the legal practice by the attorney general in 1969 and supported by the chief medical officer of the capital. It is thus possible for the police not to intervene in Christiania as long as hard drugs are not being sold.

The role of the elite of the public services is quite similar in the Netherlands. The Dutch chiefs of police and justice officials recommended legalization of cannabis in the late 1960s. They argued for the necessity of concentrating police resources on drug trafficking rather than on petty crime. The Baan Committee's report of 1972 settled the principle that the regulation and level of punishment in drug cases should be determined by the health risk posed by the particular drug. Experts in the Netherlands agreed on the conclusion that cannabis was less dangerous than other drugs. During the 1970s and 1980s the system of retail sale of cannabis in coffee shops developed, and by the early 1990s the government planned to legalize production of Dutch cannabis (*nederwiet*). These plans were stopped, however, and Paulette Kurzer (2001) argues that there have been considerable differences between popular belief and the attitudes of the elite toward the drug question. The reaction in the society together with pressure from the European Union have led to an increasingly restrictive regulation of the coffee shops and a much stronger focus on nuisance during the 1990s. But still the Netherlands stands out as the one European country that actually has a strategy for a regulated legal trade in cannabis.

## MAINTENANCE TREATMENT AND HARM REDUCTION

The medicalization of the drug problem is best illustrated by strategies for maintenance treatment and prescription practices. Among the best-known strategies for this is the "British system" and the recent heroin trials in Switzerland. The British system has a long history while the Swiss trials are clearly a part of the movement toward harm reduction from the early 1990s.

The Rolleston Committee report from 1926 settled, according to Berridge (1999), a partnership between the professional ideology of doctors and the aims of legal control. This was the start of the so-called British system that most of all was based on an establishment of a therapeutic relationship between a doctor and a patient who agreed on the patient's being ill and in need of treatment. The system worked pretty well until the late 1950s when prescribed drugs started to flow into a growing illegal market for recreational use. The Brain Committee of 1966 prepared the introduction of specialized drug dependence units (called clinics) in 1968. They were designed to provide maintenance treatment for heroin and cocaine. By the start of the 1980s it was clear that the clinics neither met the goal of making the addicts accessible for treatment nor stopped the supply of legal drugs to the illegal market. There was also a growing doubt about the practices from a professional point of view, and most practitioners preferred to discontinue the administration of injectable heroin in favor of oral methadone. Even if the practices of the clinics were quite contested by the mid-1980s, the system represented a very useful infrastructure for the rapid change needed when the HIV epidemic occurred. The choice of strategy when confronted with this new threat associated with intravenous drug use was well-founded in the previous tradition of public health. Medically assisted treatment, advice, and information as well as needle exchange programs could be administered through the clinics. By the end of the century the administration of oral methadone and increasingly buprenorphine came to dominate the treatment of opiate dependent patients. Numbers from 2002 show that only 1 percent of these patients receive injectable heroin.

The background for the Swiss heroin trials was somewhat different. During the 1980s Switzerland was confronted with some of the largest open drug scenes in Europe. Heroin trials were started in the early 1990s and were shown to have a very efficient positive impact on the problem of drug crimes and health problems among the addicts. Compared to the British system, the Swiss treatment is much more controlled and puts the patient under a strict set of rules. It has made heroin addiction into "a painstakingly monitored illness" (Aarburg and Stauffacher, p. 41). Switzerland experienced a rapid increase in the prevalence of heroin addiction up to 1993/94, followed by a gradual decline in the following ten years. Thus the Swiss authorities consider their treatment strategy as quite successful. Medically assisted treatment, especially with methadone, has become an important part of harm-reduction strategies in Europe. Together with securing the supply of clean syringes, establishing injection rooms, and providing addicts with information, medical involvement in drug policy has contributed to the limitation of the spreading of HIV as well as other infectious diseases.

## DRUG POLICY BEYOND THE NATIONAL STATES

Drug policy was among the first topics for international cooperation, as shown by the international conventions. It has also proven to be a very fertile soil for cooperation in Europe. It is easy to agree on the necessity of cooperation, and, in spite of differences in practical policy, to fight drugs is deemed a good cause. Among the Nordic countries the cooperation was set up in the early 1970s, through meetings between the Nordic ministers, cooperation in epidemiological research, police cooperation, and special services for youth from other Nordic countries in Copenhagen.

The Pompidou Group was set up in 1972 as a cooperative effort between the six members of the European Economic Community (EEC) and the United Kingdom. It started as a multidisciplinary cooperation program on drugs covering health,

education, information, enforcement, and legislation. To state the necessity of international cooperation not only in control but also in handling the drug problem as a social problem and a problem of public health was an important contribution of this cooperation. In 1980 the Pompidou Group become a "partial agreement" under the Council of Europe. Since 1982 experts have cooperated to develop administrative monitoring systems for the assessment of public health and social problems related to drug abuse. This cooperation evolved over the years through cooperation in school surveys and a multicity study of drug indicators.

When the European Union decided to set up its own drug-monitoring institution, the European Monitoring Centre for Drugs and Drug Addiction, in 1993, it could build on the traditions from the Pompidou Group. The EMCDDA consolidated the monitoring effort in Europe and drew national civil services into a more comprehensive cooperation on epidemiological studies as well as other aspects of prevention and treatment in the drug field.

The European Union's involvement in drug policy and enforcement expanded after the Maastricht Treaty of 1992, first through cooperation between police forces and customs. Drug trafficking and international crime became a focus of police cooperation among the EU member states beginning in the mid-1980s. The Europol Drug Unit was set up in 1993 before the negotiations about the Europol convention finished. Measures to control the trade in the precursors of illegal drugs and to prevent money-laundering were put in place by the early 1990s. Together with the cooperation in research and knowledge production, these elements express a European approach to illegal drugs. The problem of illegal drugs should be handled with a wide range of strategies from fighting international crime to implementing knowledge-based strategies for treatment, prevention, and harm reduction.

*See also* **AIDS; Amsterdam; Police and Policing.**

BIBLIOGRAPHY

Aarburg, Hans-Peter von, and Michael Stauffacher. "From Law Enforcement to Care: Changed Benefits and Harm of Heroin Use in Switzerland through a Shift in Drug Policy." In *European Studies in Drugs and Drug Policy,* edited by Tom Decorte and Dirk Korf, 21–46. Brussels, 2004.

Albrecht, Hans-Jörg, and Anton van Kalmthout. *Drug Policies in Western Europe.* Freiburg, Germany, 1989.

Berridge, Virginia. *Opium and the People: Opiate Use and Drug Control Policy in Nineteenth and Early Twentieth Century England.* Rev. ed. London, 1999.

Bruggeman, Willy. "Europol and the Europol Drugs Unit: Their Problems and Potential for Development." In *Justice and Home Affairs in the European Union: The Development of the Third Pillar,* edited by Roland Bieber and Joerg Monar, 217–230. Brussels, 1995.

Bruun, Kettil, Lynn Pan, and Ingemar Rexed. *The Gentlemen's Club: International Control of Drugs and Alcohol.* Chicago, 1975.

Dorn, Nicholas, and Simone White. "Drug Trafficking, Nuisance and Use: Opportunities for a Regulatory Space." In *Regulating European Drug Problems,* edited by Nicholas Dorn, 293–290. The Hague, 1999.

Fjær, Svanaug. "Rules or Values? Production of Knowledge and the Question of Institutionalization in European Drugs Cooperation." *Contemporary Drug Problems* 28, no. 2 (2001): 307–331.

———. "From Social Radicalism to Repression: The Construction of the Norwegian Drug Policy in the 1970s." In *Public Health and Preventive Medicine, 1800–2000: Knowledge, Co-operation and Conflict,* edited by Astri Andresen, Kari Tove Elvbakken, and William H. Hubbard. Bergen, Norway, 2004.

Garde, Peter. "Denmark: Regulating Drug Trafficking, Nuisance and Use." In *Regulating European Drug Problems,* edited by Nicholas Dorn, 67–86. The Hague, 1999.

Hakkarainen, Pekka, Lau Laursen, and Christoffer Tigerstedt, eds. *Discussing Drugs and Control Policy: Comparative Studies on Four Nordic Countries.* Helsinki, Finland, 1996.

Hartnoll, Richard. *Drugs and Drug Dependence: Linking Research, Policy and Practice.* Strasbourg, France, 2004.

Kurzer, Paulette. *Markets and Moral Regulation: Cultural Change in the European Union.* Cambridge, U.K., 2001.

Lind, Brit Bergersen. *Narkotikakonflikten: Stoffbruk og Myndighetskontroll.* Oslo, Norway, 1974.

Strang, John, and Michael Gossop, eds. *Heroin Addiction and the British System.* London, 2005.

SVANAUG FJÆR

# DUBČEK, ALEXANDER (1921–1992), Czech politician and reformer.

Alexander Dubček was born in Uhrovec, Czechoslovakia (now in the Slovak Republic). His parents had lived in the United States prior to World War I, in Chicago, Illinois, and in Cleveland, Ohio. Both had been active in the socialist movement of Eugene Debs but had returned to Czechoslovakia after the war. Dubček's father, Stefan, was one of the founders of the Czechoslovak Communist Party. In 1925 Dubček's family moved to Kirghizia (now Kyrgyzstan) to help build socialism in the Soviet Union. They returned to Slovakia in 1938, when Dubček was seventeen, and he promptly joined the illegal Communist Party of Czechoslovakia. During World War II, he was an anti-Nazi guerrilla and participated in the Slovak National Uprising in 1944. After the war he rose rapidly through the ranks of the Slovak Communist Party, becoming a member of the Slovak Party Central Committee in 1951. In 1955 he was sent to study at the Moscow Political College, where he graduated with honors in 1958. In 1962 he was named a full member of the Central Committee of the Czechoslovak Communist Party and later first secretary of the Slovak Communist Party.

In the early 1960s, the country suffered an economic downturn and in 1965 the hard-line first secretary of the Czechoslovak Communist Party, Antonín Novotný, was compelled to introduce a set of measures to decentralize state control over the economy. The Soviet Union refused to support Novotný, largely viewing his policies as ill advised, and aware of the growing disenchantment within the Czechoslovak Communist Party with his leadership. Dubček led a group of reformers who in October 1967 presented a long list of grievances against the government. This was followed later in the fall by popular protests against the Novotný government. In January 1968 the Czechoslovak Party Central Committee ousted Novotný and replaced him with Dubček. A key supporter of Dubček was Gustav Husak, also a Slovak, who was named Dubček's deputy. During the resulting Prague Spring (March to August 1968), Dubček attempted to reform the Communist Party and allow "socialism with a human face."

Dubček announced a series of liberalizations that included the abolition of censorship and the right of citizens to openly criticize the government. As a result, newspapers began publishing stories on official corruption, implicating many Novotný supporters. Further reforms allowed for collective

**Alexander Dubček, 1989.** ©PETER TURNLEY/CORBIS

bargaining by trade unions and for farmers to form independent cooperatives. Industrial enterprises were also provided greater freedom to negotiate wages and prices. In April 1968 the Communist Party Central Committee openly criticized the disgraced Novotný for economic mismanagement and launched measures to liberalize the Communist Party itself, proclaiming that members have "not only the right, but the duty to act according to [their] conscience."

Dubček was careful not to antagonize the Soviet Union. Remembering the 1956 Soviet invasion of Hungary, where the reformers under Imre Nagy had sought to take Hungary out of the Warsaw Pact, Dubček made it clear that, despite the internal reforms, he would make no changes in Czechoslovak foreign policy. The country would remain firmly in the Soviet orbit. Nonetheless, the Soviet leadership became increasingly suspicious of the Dubček-led regime and on 21 August 1968 Warsaw Pact forces invaded Czechoslovakia. In order to avoid bloodshed, Dubček ordered the troops not to resist. After the invasion, Dubček and others were subsequently "invited" to meet with Leonid Brezhnev and Alexei Kosygin in Moscow, after which

Dubček announced the end of the reforms. In April 1969 Dubček was replaced as party first secretary by his deputy, Gustav Husak. The following year he was expelled from the party and for the next eighteen years he worked as a forestry official in a lumberyard. He was forbidden to converse with anyone outside his immediate family without permission.

Following the collapse of the communist government after the Velvet Revolution of November 1989, Dubček was rehabilitated. In November 1989 he spoke at a rally in Bratislava and later stood with the newly elected Czechoslovak president Václav Havel in Prague while huge crowds cheered. On 28 December 1989 Dubček was unanimously elected chairman of the Federal Assembly, and he was reelected in 1990. He was awarded the Sakharov Peace Prize in 1989 and he published two books, *The Soviet Invasion* (which documented the events in 1968) and his autobiography, *Hope Dies Last.*

Dubček suffered serious injuries in an automobile accident in 1992 and died as a result of those injuries at age seventy, on 7 November 1992.

*See also* **Brezhnev, Leonid; Czechoslovakia; Havel, Václav; Nagy, Imre; Prague Spring; Slovakia; Velvet Revolution; Warsaw Pact.**

BIBLIOGRAPHY

Dubček, Alexander. *Hope Dies Last: The Autobiography of Alexander Dubček.* New York, 1993.

Golan, Galia. *Reform Rule in Czechoslovakia: The Dubček Era, 1968–1969.* Cambridge, U.K., 1973.

Henderson, Karen. *Slovakia: The Escape from Invisibility.* London, 2002.

Kalvoda, Josef. "The Rise and Fall of Alexander Dubček." *Nationalities Papers* 8 (1980): 211–217.

Kirschbaum, Stanislav J. *A History of Slovakia: A Struggle for Survival.* New York, 1995.

Shawcross, William. *Dubček.* New York, 1971.

JOHN ISHIYAMA

# DUCHAMP, MARCEL (1887–1968), French artist.

Marcel Duchamp became one of the most influential artists of the twentieth century for a succession of provocative works that helped reorient the production and reception of art. Duchamp's turn from painting to a range of procedures, his designation of everyday objects as art, and an insistent lack of stylistic unity challenged assumptions about the status of the original and the relevance of aesthetic judgment.

Born in the Normandy region of France, Duchamp grew up in a family rich in artists, including two older brothers, Jacques Villon and Raymond Duchamp-Villon, who participated in the cubist movement, and a younger sister, Suzanne Duchamp, who also painted. Duchamp's early paintings, produced after joining his brothers in Paris in 1904, demonstrate his interest in Paul Cézanne (1839–1906), fauvism, and then cubism. Several of these were included in a key cubist exhibition of 1911, but the next year he withdrew his 1912 *Nude Descending a Staircase, No. 2* from the Salon des Indépendants after cubists on the hanging committee objected to the painting's subject (indicated, unavoidably, by the title painted directly on the canvas). The work was nonetheless included in the 1913 Armory Show in New York, where popular press responses to this major exhibition of advanced European art singled out Duchamp's work for particular derision.

When Duchamp himself came to New York in 1915, his avant-garde credentials were firmly established by his Armory Show scandal. In 1913, however, Duchamp had turned away from cubist painting in favor of investigations of chance, optics, and theories of geometry exploring the concept of a fourth dimension, all of which reflected his engagement with an increasingly theoretical rather than a visual or "retinal" artistic experience. These ideas, as well as an overlay of sexual and machine imagery, were the basis for the two panels of a complex work on glass, *The Bride Stripped Bare by Her Bachelors, Even* (1915–1923), also known as *The Large Glass,* divided vertically between the bride's section on top and the domain of the bachelors below. Begun the year of Duchamp's arrival in New York and declared definitively unfinished by the artist in 1923, this work was in another sense completed with the publication of a series of related notes in 1934, *La mariée mise à nu par ses célibataires, même,* or *The Green Box,* which appeared as an edition of unbound facsimiles, and a later set of notes, *A l'infinitif,* issued in 1966. And the work received another final touch in 1936, when Duchamp reassembled the pieces that had shattered during shipping in 1927.

In 1913 Duchamp also mounted a bicycle wheel on a wooden stool, but even he required time to recognize the gesture's significance, adopting the term *readymade* only in 1915. By simply selecting everyday objects and designating them works of art, Duchamp redirected making from a physical to a conceptual act and also drew attention to the surrounding institutional conventions that allow the gesture to register. The series came to include such objects as a bottle rack, snow shovel, and an altered reproduction of Leonardo da Vinci's *Mona Lisa,* but the most famous was the urinal that Duchamp turned on its back, signed with the pseudonym R. Mutt, entitled *Fountain,* and submitted to the 1917 Society of Independent Artists exhibition in New York. After the work's rejection from an event that was supposed to be open to all who paid the entrance fee, Duchamp orchestrated a sequence of responses, including a photograph by Alfred Stieglitz (1864–1946) that provides the only visual record of an object that, like most of the other readymades, was lost soon after it was initially chosen.

At the time of his ostensible rejection of art in favor of chess in 1923, Duchamp's reputation was largely confined to avant-garde circles associated with Dada and surrealism. Yet over the course of the century his reputation burgeoned, gathering momentum particularly during the 1960s as a modernist aesthetic was supplanted by postmodernism in the context of Pop Art's engagement with everyday objects or images and as conceptual art began to emphasize the primacy of idea over physical entity.

Duchamp contributed to his reception through his *Box in a Valise,* a kind of miniature museum composed of small-scale reproductions of extant work as well as lost readymades that first appeared in 1941. Postwar attention was prompted by the Philadelphia Museum of Art's 1954 installation of a major collection of Duchamp's work acquired from Louise and Walter Arensberg and Robert Lebel's 1959 monograph, *Marcel Duchamp,* published in French and English editions. These were followed by a 1963 retrospective at the Pasadena Art Museum, limited edition versions of previously

***The Bride Stripped Bare by Her Bachelors, Even.*** By Marcel Duchamp, 1923. THE PHILADELPHIA MUSEUM OF ART/ART RESOURCE, NY

lost readymades issued in 1964, and, immediately following Duchamp's death, the public unveiling of his final, secret work, *Given: 1° The Waterfall; 2° The Illuminating Gas,* or *Étant donnés,* 1946–1966, which presents a startling tableau of a nude woman, head invisible and legs spread, that can only be seen through holes in a wooden door installed in an alcove near the *Large Glass* at the Philadelphia Museum of Art. Yet even if the complexity of Duchamp's work as a whole is one reason for his ever expanding reputation, the deceptively simple gesture of the readymade raised questions about the nature of artistic authorship, originality, and aesthetic judgment that continue to reverberate through art of the present day.

*See also* **Avant-Garde; Cubism; Degenerate Art Exhibit; Modernism; Pop Art; Postmodernism.**

BIBLIOGRAPHY

Ades, Dawn, Neil Cox, and David Hopkins. *Marcel Duchamp*. London, 1999.

Buskirk, Martha, and Mignon Nixon, eds. *The Duchamp Effect*. Cambridge, Mass., 1996.

Naumann, Francis M. *Marcel Duchamp: The Art of Making Art in the Age of Mechanical Reproduction*. New York, 1999.

Sanouillet, Michel, and Elmer Peterson, eds. *The Writings of Marcel Duchamp*. New York, 1989. Translation of *Marchand du sel: Écrits de Marcel Duchamp* (1958).

MARTHA BUSKIRK

---

# DUMONT, RENÉ (1904–2001), French agronomist; Third World activist and ecologist.

René Dumont was born into a staunchly republican family in the northern French city of Cambrai. His mother was a mathematician and school director and his father an agricultural engineer and publisher of the first French agricultural dictionary, *Larousse agricole* (1921). His close contact with the wounded soldiers who were treated in his mother's high school during World War I directed his political views toward an unshakable pacifism and a radical form of socialism. Although his admiration for the Soviet Union waned during the early 1920s, his overall left-wing orientation remained unchallenged during the rest of his life.

After graduating as an agronomical engineer from the Institut National Agronomique National and specializing at the Institut National D'Agronomique Coloniale at Nogent, Dumont became a colonial administrator in Indochina, where he inspected and studied the cultivation of rice in the Tonkin estuary (on which he wrote his first book, *La culture de riz dans le delta du Tonkin* [Rice culture in the Tonkin delta], 1935). Between 1933 and 1974, Dumont taught comparative agriculture at the Institut National Agronomique in Paris, where he became a full professor in 1953.

As an agronomist, Dumont combined a thorough empirical knowledge of agricultural techniques and practices (gathered during innumerable travels throughout Europe and the rest of the world) with a sociological approach to farmers' communities. His work was grounded in the belief that the organization of agriculture is inherently a political matter, and this fundamental assumption guided him in his analysis of French agriculture, which occupied him at the start of his academic career.

During World War II, Dumont contributed articles—primarily technical in nature—to *La Terre Française* (French earth), a Pétainist journal that pleaded for agricultural corporatism, that is, for a nonconflictual cooperation between growers and refiners for the sake of French national interests. Because of this and because his pacifism kept him out of the Resistance, some critics have, mistakenly, depicted Dumont as a fascist.

After World War II, Dumont became an agricultural expert in the team with which the leading public servant Jean Monnet embarked upon the economic modernization of France. A visit to the United States in 1946 (about which he wrote his *Les leçons de l'agriculture américaine* [The lessons of American agriculture, 1949]) imbued him with a productivist ideology, according to which agricultural growth had to be attained by drastically raising productivity. In line with these productivist tenets, he contributed greatly to the intensification and mechanization of agricultural methods throughout France.

When French decolonization began in the 1950s, Dumont focused his attention on the Third World, where he tried to apply his productivist approach in support of the newly independent states. He sympathized with and was solicited by those new regimes that recognized the importance of agricultural reforms as the starting point of economic and political emancipation. He particularly admired Mao Zedong's China until he was disenchanted by its ideological dogmatism and the priority it gave to industry, beginning with the Great Leap Forward (1958). Similar disillusionments awaited him with the new regimes in the Maghreb countries (in northwest Africa), in sub-Saharan Africa, and in Latin America (particularly Fidel Castro's Cuba). Whereas he relentlessly pointed to the colonial past and the neocolonial practices of the northern countries as the main impediments to the economic and social development of the southern ones, he nonetheless criticized the regimes of the decolonized countries for blindly imitating the model of the developed world. Most notably, he rejected the primacy given to industrial development and to urban elites at the expense of the peasantry. He expressed this provocatively in his book *L'Afrique noire est mal partie* (1962; *The False Start in Africa*). Opposing both the capitalist and the communist models, Dumont believed in the self-regulating capacities of small-scale communities reined in by internal democracy and adapting their agrarian and industrial production to local needs.

Also during the 1960s, Dumont began to abandon his belief in productivist agriculture. He had come to the conclusion that further enhancement of agricultural productivity would exhaust the world's fertile soils and render every form of social and economical progress impossible. As a consequence, his main objective became the reduction of consumption rather than the increase of production. With regard to the Third World, this ecological turn strengthened his support for population control, which he had embraced as early as the 1930s. Not only would overpopulation mortgage all chances of economic development, it would also lead to ecological catastrophes. With regard to the developed countries, his ecological awareness was translated into a sustained cry for austerity. If western overconsumption were to be transposed to the Third World, he argued, the world's natural resources would be exhausted within half a century. Hence his continuous struggle for reducing the use of private cars and the consumption of meat, since large parts of the Third World's agricultural production were aimed at feeding the livestock of the developed world. These convictions found their most powerful expression in his *L'utopie ou la mort* (1973; Utopia or death). Dumont drew heavily from the information in the report published by the Club of Rome in 1972, *The Limits to Growth*, but he criticized the report for its apolitical character. Dumont never left any room for doubt that ecological activism was, for him, a form of left-wing engagement, since the first victims of environmental damage were the poor peasants of the Third World.

When the formerly diffuse French ecological movement joined together to run a candidate in the presidential elections of 1974, Dumont became their candidate. Although he only won 1.33 percent of the vote, the campaign politicized the European ecological movement. With his direct, nonconformist style and his flair for mediation, Dumont demonstrated that ecology was not an aesthetic issue but a highly political one. After 1974 Dumont engaged sporadically in ecological politics, most notably when heading the Greens' Parisian list in the 1986 legislative elections and when promoting Dominique Voynet's presidential campaign in 1995. He also served as a symbol and spiritual guide to the French ecological movement, accounting for its overall leftist humanism. In a more marginal way, he played a similar role in the anti-globalization movement and was one of the founders of ATTAC-France.

*See also* **Agriculture; Colonialism; Decolonization; Globalization; Greens; Monnet, Jean.**

BIBLIOGRAPHY

Besset, Jean-Paul. *René Dumont: Une vie saisie par l'écologie.* Paris, 1992.

Dufumier, Marc, ed. *Un agronome dans son siècle: Actualité de René Dumont.* Paris, 2002.

Whiteside, Kerry H. "René Dumont and the Fate of Political Ecology in France." *Contemporary French Civilization* 21 (1997): 1–17.

MARNIX BEYEN

**DUNKIRK.** Dunkirk was the northern French port from which British and Allied troops were evacuated during the fighting that led to the fall of France in 1940. On 10 May, German forces invaded France and the Low Countries and within ten days had reached the Channel coast near Abbeville. The British Expeditionary Force (BEF), which had advanced into Belgium to meet the German attack, was in danger of being surrounded and cut off. General John Vereker, Viscount Gort, the commander in chief of the BEF, was authorized to withdraw his beleaguered force to the coast in order to be transported back to Britain. On 26 May, Operation Dynamo—the Dunkirk evacuation—began.

The Royal Navy hastily assembled a vast armada of some nine hundred ships to bring the troops home across the Channel. Dunkirk harbor became the main point of embarkation, but the nearby beaches were also used for this purpose, and a host of little ships, such as fishing boats and pleasure cruisers manned by civilian volunteers,

**British and French troops await evacuation on the beaches at Dunkirk, May 1940.** ©CORBIS

ferried the troops out to the bigger ships that could not get in close to the shore. The discipline of the rear echelon troops as they waited for evacuation was not always good. Officers organizing the long queues were on occasion forced to maintain order at the point of a gun. However, as the fighting troops arrived in the area, discipline improved and the rate of embarkation speeded up. In the meantime, the Wehrmacht attacked the perimeter around the town and the Luftwaffe pounded the harbor and the beaches. By 4 June more than three hundred thousand British and Allied troops had escaped from Dunkirk under the noses of the Germans. It was a staggering feat.

A number of factors combined to make possible this seemingly miraculous achievement. Dunkirk was a fortuitous bridgehead for such an evacuation. It had an extensive harbor and beaches, it was ringed by canals that acted as defense lines, and the sea dikes could be opened to flood the low-lying land and hamper the German tanks. The BEF played an important role in its own salvation. The skillful fighting retreat that it conducted back to

the coast, as well as the valiant defense of the Dunkirk perimeter, were essential in ensuring that so many troops got away. Nor should the part played by the French army be forgotten. Not only did it help to defend the port during the evacuation, but it also formed the final rearguard that allowed the last of the British troops to escape. Much credit should of course go to the Royal Navy for the success of the operation. Vice-Admiral Bertram Ramsey, flag officer for Dover, deftly coordinated the evacuation, and the navy gallantly brought out the troops despite heavy losses during the embarkation. The naval effort was greatly assisted by good weather and calm seas: this was perhaps the real miracle of Dunkirk. The troops criticized the Royal Air Force (RAF) for abandoning them to their fate on the beaches, but this view was too harsh. Although it was not possible to maintain continuous air patrols over Dunkirk, and essential that precious aircraft were not frittered away when they would be needed for the forthcoming defense of Britain, much damage was done to the Luftwaffe during the evacuation period.

The Germans themselves contributed to the escape of the BEF. On 24 May, Adolf Hitler issued the notorious halt order that prevented German tanks, which were close to Dunkirk, from advancing for three days. Various explanations have been put forward for this order, including a need to preserve the armored forces for the impending push south, a misplaced faith in the Luftwaffe to finish off the BEF, a desire on the part of the Fuhrer to reassert his authority over his commanders, and a reluctance to believe that a large-scale sea evacuation was possible. Whatever the reason, by the time the tanks began to roll again the BEF had strengthened its defense line, the troops were streaming into Dunkirk, and the chance to cut them off had disappeared. This proved to be a crucial mistake.

On 4 June, Churchill told the House of Commons that "wars are not won by evacuations," and there was no doubt that the withdrawal from Dunkirk was a serious military reversal. But the success of Operation Dynamo was vital to the British war effort. If the BEF had not got away, most of Britain's trained troops would have been lost, with serious consequences for the country's military position. The shock might have been so great that the British government would be forced to contemplate a negotiated peace. As it was, the returning troops greatly enhanced the country's home defense capability and formed the nucleus of a new citizen army that was built up after the debacle in France. Churchill was boosted in his conviction that the country must fight on alone in 1940, and he set about galvanizing the nation for the struggle ahead. For the British people the evacuation was an important psychological victory. The rescue of the troops against the odds electrified the public and gave them a new sense of purpose and national unity. Propagandists were quick to turn the event into a patriotic myth in which the little ships became a symbol of resistance to the might of the Nazis. The "Dunkirk spirit" entered the British lexicon: a mixture of improvisation and a stubborn refusal to give up when defeat seems inevitable.

*See also* **Britain, Battle of; World War II.**

BIBLIOGRAPHY

Divine, David. *The Nine Days of Dunkirk*. London, 1959.

Gardner, W. J. R., ed. *The Evacuation from Dunkirk: Operation Dynamo, 26 May–4 June 1940*. London, 2000.

Harman, Nicholas. *Dunkirk: The Necessary Myth*. London, 1980.

Lord, Walter. *The Miracle of Dunkirk*. London, 1982.

JEREMY A. CRANG

---

# DURAS, MARGUERITE (1914–1996), French author.

Marguerite Duras was known both for her style and for the diversity of her writings about passionate love and the madness of history. In novels, plays, and films she explored her childhood in Indochina, her political involvement during the Resistance in World War II, and the wartime deportation of her husband, Robert Antelme.

Born in 1914 in the Mekong Delta, Marguerite Donnadieu was strongly influenced by her Indochinese childhood. She grew up facing the hardships of poor white colons in a region under exploitative colonial rule. Her mother, for example, a young widow and elementary schoolteacher who in 1924 purchased land that turned out to be almost impossible to farm, struggled mightily to raise three children. In an early novel, *Un barrage contre le Pacifique* (1950; *The Sea Wall*), Duras described both the constant battles against the tropical environment and the personal torments of her female narrator. In 1932 she moved to Paris to continue her education and there found a low-level job at the colonial ministry. In 1943 she published her first novel, *Les impudents* (The insolent), under a pen name, Duras, because she believed that "a writer cannot write under the name of the father." She rapidly found the voice that would make her famous in the 1960s, treading the line between spoken language and poetry. In *Hiroshima mon amour* she wrote that "love allows one to die more comfortably to life." *Destruction* was a key word for Duras. She depicted herself in novels, plays, and films, making no distinction between these various forms of expression. Duras became closely identified with her work—forty novels and a dozen plays and films that she wrote or directed—in which, as in life, she did not like to acknowledge restrictive boundaries, whether the contradictory demands of the heart or physical frailties, such as those brought on by her alcoholism.

Duras married Robert Antelme in 1939 and three years later met Dyonis Mascolo, with whom she had a son. At about this time she became friendly with avant-garde writers and philosophers such as Jean Genet, Henri Michaux, Georges Bataille, Maurice Merleau-Ponty, René Leibowitz, and Edgar Morin. In World War II, Duras, her husband, and Mascolo joined the French Resistance, fighting alongside François Morland (that is, François Mitterrand, the future president of France), who remained a lifelong friend. Antelme was captured by the Gestapo and deported first to Buchenwald, then to Dachau. After the Liberation he wrote one of the most remarkable firsthand accounts of Nazi concentration camps, *L'espèce humaine* (1947; *The Human Race*). Duras transformed her own wartime experiences into literary and cinematic works. She wrote the screenplay for *Hiroshima mon amour*, the 1959 film directed by Alain Resnais, the theme of which was the devastation of the atomic bomb, and returned to the war in a collection of texts entitled *La douleur* (*The War: A Memoir*), published only in 1985, in which she recounts Antelme's return and his subsequent illness and death. Duras, who had joined the French Communist Party in 1943 but was expelled in 1950, remained an advocate of left-wing causes and came out against the Algerian War, signing the Declaration on the Right to Insubordination in 1960, under Charles de Gaulle's Fifth Republic. She also played a role in the events of May 1968. *Les yeux verts* (1980; *Green Eyes*) is a political text about the founding of an action committee of students and writers.

Duras shaped her fantasies into a variety of novels and films, from *Moderato Cantabile* (1958) to *India Song* (1975). Her characters seek to escape loneliness and to give meaning to their lives: through absolute love in *Le ravissement de Lol V. Stein* (1964; *The Ravishing of Lol Stein*), through madness in *L'amante anglaise* (1967; *The English Lover*). *Le ravissement* inaugurated a cycle of novels about the femme fatale Anne-Marie Stretter, a character that would continue to haunt Duras. In *Yann Andréa Steiner* (1992), she turned the man with whom she had been living since 1980 into a veritable Durassian hero.

Duras gradually became a major literary figure, a cult author much admired and sometimes hated. She was always interested in the world at large and in 1957 started writing for the news magazine *France observateur*. Her position on the Villemin affair, a famous case of alleged infanticide, expressed in her newspaper article "Sublime, forcément sublime" (Sublime, necessarily sublime; published in *Libération* in 1985), provoked hostility and controversy among feminists with whom she had until then been allied. In *L'amant* (1984; *The Lover*), Duras wrote frankly about her childhood in Indochina. The novel was awarded the Prix Goncourt and brought her extraordinary fame and popularity. It sold three million copies and was translated into forty languages, its worldwide success aided by the 1992 film adaptation directed by Jean-Jacques Annaud.

*See also* **France; Indochina; Mitterrand, François.**

BIBLIOGRAPHY

Blot-Labarrère, Christiane. *Marguerite Duras*. Paris, 1997.

"Duras, l'écriture mise à nu." *Le monde*, April 2003.

ANNETTE BECKER

---

# DUTCH COLONIAL EMPIRE.

The foundations of the Dutch Empire were laid in the seventeenth century by trading companies operating in Asia and the Atlantic. Business was, in all periods, the primary motive of Dutch colonialism, engendering a utilitarian colonial discourse. Despite commercial leanings, however, Dutch imperial drives were essentially ambiguous, and scholars argue about whether the Netherlands had an imperial drive similar to that of the larger European powers. Whereas in the last decades of the nineteenth century Britain and France embarked on imperial programs of annexation and conquest, the Dutch kingdom seemed to be more committed to concentration than expansion. As late as 1873, the Netherlands handed over its unprofitable African possessions on the Gold Coast to Great Britain. At the same time, the Dutch colonial state in the Dutch East Indies showed a marked urge toward securing colonial borders and extending its authority. In the last quarter of the nineteenth century, the

Dutch fought protracted wars in Aceh, the northern tip of Sumatra, and many other areas of the Indonesian archipelago in order to subdue indigenous states that were considered disobedient to Dutch hegemony. If by the mid-nineteenth century colonial rule was still limited to Java and to isolated pockets in other areas, by 1910 it extended over almost the entire archipelago. The Dutch imperialist drive remained limited to its Asian colonies, however. In contrast, the Netherlands' small possessions in the Americas—Surinam on the Guyana coast and the six small Caribbean islands of the Antilles—hardly attracted attention in the Netherlands. Demographically, they were negligible: the six small islands of the Antilles had about 55,000 inhabitants in 1910 and Surinam around 100,000, compared to about 45 million in the Dutch East Indies.

## COLONIAL ETHICS AND MODERNISM

By the turn of the twentieth century, Dutch colonialism developed its own brand of the "white man's burden," called the ethical policy. Its ethics consisted of a mixture of Christian philanthropy, an increasing awareness of state responsibilities toward the poor, and feelings of superiority packaged in a rhetoric of development and uplifting of indigenous peoples. As a consequence, in the popular press and even in official publications, terms such as *ereschuld* (debt of honor)—the moral duty of the Netherlands to return the profits of colonial exploitation to the Indies—appeared next to disparaging stories about the backwardness of the colonized.

The new imperialist atmosphere was tangible in the Netherlands, where the colonies became an instrument of national propaganda. Statues, friezes, monuments, and exhibitions extolled Dutch overseas exploits, military victories, and technological progress but also proudly showed the cultures of the colonized peoples. Despite this short-lived episode of imperial pomp, colonial rule remained in essence a technocratic affair. The colonies were scarcely the subject of political debate and figured only marginally in party programs and at political meetings. The Dutch East Indies were a place for investment and development. Even in socialist circles, only a few voices advocated the immediate end of colonial rule.

In the colonies, the beginning of the twentieth century was marked by the emergence of public opinion and political associations. The first Indonesian organization, Boedi Oetomo (Noble Endeavour), was established in 1908 and aimed primarily at protecting the interests of the Javanese administrative elite. An explicit call for autonomy was raised only a few years later by the Indische Partij (1912; Indies party), which was then banned by the government. In the following years, numerous other associations sprang up, stimulating the desire for a representative government. In 1918 a People's Council was established, although it was chosen by a very small constituency and invested with limited powers.

Due both to growing concerns in government circles about the nationalist movement's radicalization and to the conservative direction of the Netherlands after an abortive socialist revolution, political reform in the Indies stalled after 1918. Colonial government became increasingly repressive toward Indonesian movements, particularly after a violently repressed communist uprising in 1926. After that, radical opposition was silenced, and nationalist leaders were arrested and exiled.

Dutch colonialism in the 1930s was complacent and politically conservative. Independence was generally acknowledged as the ultimate aim, but the moment of its realization put off to an undefined future. But behind the facade of *rust en orde* (peace and order), the old structures were increasingly becoming unbalanced. The rise of western-educated indigenous elites eroded the boundaries between the separate elements of colonial society, which had once been separated by law and labeled native, foreign oriental, and European. The access of Indonesians and Indonesian-Chinese subjects to modern education and their entry into the colonial establishment stimulated their political ambitions and led to demands for constitutional reform. These changes were clearly visible to the Dutch regime, but reform was obstructed by Dutch economic interests in the colony and the conviction that the Dutch were indispensable for guiding the Indonesians to political maturity and prosperity. Despite the rapid changes in Indies' society, a redrawing of its political relationships proved to be impossible.

Eloquent radicals such as the engineer Sukarno and the lawyer Mohammad Hatta spent years in and out of prison or exile. Even pleas by such moderate Indonesian nationalists as Mas Soetardjo and Muhammad Thamrin for autonomy were turned down. Throughout the world, it was becoming clear that the colonial system was unsustainable. Other colonies, including India and Ceylon, went through a process of institutional and constitutional change, augmenting representative government and the participation of indigenous officials in the country's administration, and the Philippines were preparing for independence. But in the Netherlands, few advocated autonomy or even constitutional reform. Only on the brink of Pacific involvement in World War II, in September 1940, did a commission for political reform, the Visman Commission, present ambiguous proposals for reforms, which would in no way have granted autonomy and were in any case not implemented.

## PROFITS OF EMPIRE

During the first decades of the twentieth century, the economy of the East Indies was transformed. The economic center of gravity shifted from Java's plantations, which were primarily sugar estates, to the outer islands, in particular Sumatra and Borneo, where rubber and oil were the dominant exports. The economic boom in the outer islands was led by large, Dutch-based corporations with little intervention by the colonial government. In several regions, local smallholder enterprises, especially those producing rubber and copra, were successful in the 1920s, but they failed to generate growth outside the export sector. In contrast to the British colonies, the commercial ties between the Netherlands and the East Indies became weaker during the 1930s. The destination of exports gradually shifted from the Netherlands to other parts of the world, especially Japan and the United States. In the late 1940s, this eased the Dutch economy's adjustment to the loss of its colonies. According to economists of the period, the Dutch East Indies represented 13.7 percent of the Netherlands' gross national product in 1938.

Parallel statistics are not available for the Caribbean colonies, but they would make a bleak contrast. Only a handful of large Dutch companies operated in the west. Surinam and the Antilles attracted few investments from the Netherlands. Just before the abolition of slavery in 1863, Surinam had 245 plantations; by 1937 this number had dwindled to 42. Sugar cultivation, which had made Dutch entrepreneurs rich in the eighteenth century, had not disappeared but production had become concentrated on two plantations, one of which was run by the large Dutch company Nederlandsche Handel Maatschappij. During the 1910s and 1920s, Dutch governors initiated a program to stimulate small agriculture, which met with marked success: Surinam became an exporter of food products instead of an importer. But in colonial terms, the western colonies had little to offer to the Netherlands. The two exceptions were that Koninklijke Olie/Shell established refineries on Curaçao in 1915 and in Aruba in 1924 and that bauxite mining was started in Surinam in 1922 by the Surinaamse Bauxiet Maatschappij. These industrial complexes were a boost to the listless economies of Surinam and the Antilles, but they created lopsided economies, dependent on these single sources of income.

## DECOLONIZATION

World War II brought radical changes throughout the Dutch Empire. With the outbreak of the war in the Pacific on 7 December 1941, following Japan's attack on Pearl Harbor and the subsequent Japanese invasion of Southeast Asia, the Dutch colonial state fell like a house of cards. The colonial government sought refuge in Australia and had to bide its time until the Allied Powers would reconquer Indonesia. Most white and many Eurasian Dutch citizens were imprisoned by the Japanese army.

In the meantime, and largely out of sight of the Dutch government-in-exile, the Indonesian landscape changed fundamentally. Nationalist leaders were freed from exile and detention and assumed a leading role in government and mass organizations created to support the Japanese war efforts. Also important were the generation of young Indonesians, who now had the opportunity to assume public roles as journalists, artists, and administrators, and the military training the Japanese provided to Indonesian youth, whom they organized into an Indonesian military corps under Japanese command. These three developments were crucial in postwar period.

On 17 August 1945, two days after the Japanese capitulation, the Indonesian nationalist leaders Sukarno and Mohammad Hatta proclaimed the independent Indonesian Republic, which became a clarion call for revolution. Although the Dutch had discussed the possibilities of reform and autonomy, they were not prepared for confrontation. They made three mistakes: First, most Dutch politicians saw Sukarno as an agitator and a Japanese collaborator and were not aware that he embodied a wish for independence that was common to many educated and politically active Indonesians. Second, they misjudged nationalism's support among the Indonesian population. Third, they did not anticipate international opposition, in particular that of the United Nations and the United States, to armed conflict. It was this international pressure that eventually forced the Netherlands to a negotiated agreement in 1949.

During the Indonesian War of Independence, the Netherlands dispatched about 135,000 troops to Indonesia, in addition to 70,000 members of the Royal Netherlands East Indies Army. The war lasted four years, took the lives of about 4,500 Dutch troops, several thousand Dutch civilians, and an unknown number of Indonesians (the number 100,000 is often mentioned but remains a wild guess). Twice, in July 1947 and December 1948, the Dutch army launched large-scale offensives aimed at securing the main production areas of colonial businesses (the first attack was called Operation Product) and weakening the position of the Indonesian Republic. At the same time, outside Republican areas, the Dutch East Indies government started building the framework of a federal state. By 1949 sixteen states had been created, all of which were invested with democratic and administrative institutions of their own.

What the Dutch called the Indonesian question led to heated debates in the Netherlands. The conflict in Indonesia was not fought over the principle of independence—this had by and large been accepted by the main protagonists by mid-1946, but about the form it would take. Under pressure from the United States and the United Nations, talks were resumed between the Indonesian Republic, the newly created local governments, and the Netherlands. In the negotiations leading to the transfer of sovereignty on 27 December 1949, four issues were paramount: the protection of Dutch business interests in postcolonial Indonesia; the establishment of a United States of Indonesia, of which Sukarno's republic would be only one part; the construction of an Indonesian-Dutch Union; and the continuance of Dutch rule over New Guinea.

Within twelve years after the transfer of sovereignty, the Dutch lost on all four issues. The political arrangements were the first to fall. The federal structure was annulled by August 1950, when all states joined the unitary Indonesian Republic. A year later, Indonesia left the Indonesian-Dutch Union. In the following years, national leaders used labor unions to put pressure on Dutch companies, which had been a source of concern for the Indonesian government. In December 1957 Dutch business enterprises were occupied by Indonesian unions and the military and the last vestiges of Dutch colonialism were cleared away. By 1962 the Dutch were forced, again under U.S. pressure, to leave New Guinea and to hand it over first to the United Nations and in 1963 to Indonesia.

## DEVELOPMENT COLONIES

The years after 1950 saw the advent of the concept of development, which in many senses represented a stronger version of the old ethical policy. In order to legitimize the Dutch hold on New Guinea, which had been largely neglected before the war, the island became the testing ground for development. In a few years, many schools, roads, and settlements were built and local civil servants trained. Until well into the 1960s, most of the budget for development aid went to the Netherlands' own colonies. The same was true in Surinam and the Antilles, although they took an entirely different political path. Surinam and the Antilles had seen very little nationalist activity before World War II. In contrast to Europe and Southeast Asia, World War II brought not hardship to the Dutch Caribbean and South American colonies but an economic boom thanks to a heightened Allied demand for their oil and bauxite industries.

Promises of autonomy made by the Dutch government-in-exile during the war triggered political consciousness, in particular in Surinam. In the immediate postwar years, political parties sprang up and organized along community lines. In the first general elections in 1949, the National Party of Surinam, which was dominated by Creoles (the descendants of African slaves), won two-thirds of the seats in parliament, and it dictated internal politics for decades. Surinam and the Antilles gradually gained greater autonomy. Talks begun in 1948 resulted in a Charter of the Kingdom in 1954. According to the charter, Surinam, the Antilles, and the Netherlands were equal partners within the kingdom. The Netherlands would refrain from intervention in interior affairs, but in practice the colonies would become more financially dependent on the Dutch government than ever before.

A revolt of oil workers in Curaçao, in the Antilles, on 31 May 1969 over payment and racial inequality was quelled by the Dutch army, recalling the armed interventions in Indonesia twenty years earlier. The violent clashes caused the governments in the Netherlands, the Antilles, and Surinam to reassess their relationship. In 1973 a center-left government took office in The Hague under Prime Minister Joop den Uyl, a Social Democrat, and it accelerated the decolonization process. This concerned only Surinam; Antillean politicians unanimously considered the Antilles still unripe for independence. Although the self-determination of Surinam was the public justification for the move, the swelling stream of Surinamese immigrants to the Netherlands was the primary source of Dutch concern. Above all, after their experiences in Indonesia and New Guinea, the Dutch wanted a "clean" decolonization in Surinam. Surinam became independent on 25 November 1975, within two years of the opening of talks. Surinam received a promise for 3.5 billion guilders of financial help from the Dutch government. Aid was stopped in December 1982, however, after the murder of fifteen critics of the military regime.

By the 1980s empire had given way to postcolonial diaspora. In the aftermath of the decolonization of Indonesia and New Guinea, about 300,000 Europeans, most of them born in the Indies, came to the Netherlands, followed in the 1960s by several thousand Indonesian Chinese and political refugees from the terror that besieged Indonesian society since the violent advent of General Suharto in 1965. In the 1960s migration from the Caribbean increased. In 2005 the Surinamese community in the Netherlands includes roughly 330,000 people and is almost equal to the total population of Surinam. Similarly, 130,000 Antilleans migrated to the Netherlands since the 1960s.

Empire also left its traces in the awareness of both the Netherlands and its former colonies. Dutch business interests in Asia have for a long time been concentrated on former Dutch colonies, as has much of the Dutch tourist industry. Political relations between the Netherlands and its former colonies have often been strained, and Dutch criticism of Indonesia's human rights record angered the Indonesian government enough that it canceled development relations in 1992; they were resumed only after the fall of Suharto in 1998. Relations with Surinam are even more turbulent. Apart from recurrent bickering over the resumption of financial aid, former coup leader Desi Bouterse was convicted before a Dutch court to a sentence of eleven years' imprisonment on a charge of drug trafficking in 1999. As Surinam does not extradite its citizens, the case continued to hamper relations between the two states into the twenty-first century.

*See also* **Colonialism; Decolonization; Netherlands.**

BIBLIOGRAPHY

Jong, J. J. P. de. *De waaier van het fortuin: Van handelscompagnie tot koloniaal imperium: De Nederlanders in Azië en de Indonesische Archipel, 1595–1950.* The Hague, 1998.

Oostindie, Gert. *Paradise Overseas: The Dutch Caribbean: Colonialism and Its Transatlantic Legacies.* London, 2004.

Oostindie, Gert, and Inge Klinkers. *Decolonising the Caribbean: Dutch Policies in a Comparative Perspective.* Amsterdam, 2003.

Ricklefs, M. C. *A History of Modern Indonesia since c. 1200.* 3rd ed. London, 2001.

REMCO RABEN

**EASTERN BLOC.** In the closing months of World War II and the latter half of the 1940s, the Soviet Union oversaw the establishment of Communist regimes throughout central and Eastern Europe. Over the next four decades, those regimes constituted what was informally known as the Eastern bloc. Initially, China, which fell under Communist rule in 1949, was also part of the bloc. The first major breach in the Eastern bloc occurred in 1948, when Yugoslavia was expelled amid a deepening rift with the Soviet Union. A more serious breach occurred at the end of the 1950s, when a bitter dispute erupted between China and the Soviet Union and soon became irreconcilable. The Sino-Soviet rift also inspired Albania to leave the bloc. Aside from these three breaches, however, the Eastern bloc remained intact until 1989, when the collapse of communism in Eastern Europe put an end to the bloc once and for all.

### FORMATION OF THE BLOC AND THE STALINIST LEGACY

The establishment of communism in Eastern Europe proceeded at varying rates. In Yugoslavia and Albania, the indigenous Communist parties led by Josip Broz Tito (1892–1980) and Enver Hoxha (1908–1985) had obtained sufficient political leverage and military strength through their roles in the anti-Nazi resistance to eliminate their opposition and assume outright power as World War II drew to a close. In the Soviet zone of Germany, the Soviet occupation forces and control commission enabled the Socialist Unity Party of Germany (Sozialistische Einheitspartei Deutschlands, or SED) to gain preeminent power well before the East German state was formed in 1949. Similarly, in Bulgaria and Romania, Communist-dominated governments were imposed under Soviet pressure in early 1945.

Elsewhere in the region, events followed a more gradual pattern. Exiles returning from Moscow played a crucial role in the formation of what initially were broad coalition governments, which carried out extensive land redistribution and other long-overdue economic and political reforms. The reform process, however, was kept under tight Communist control, and the top jobs in the ministry of internal affairs were reserved exclusively for Communist Party members. From those posts, they could oversee the purging of the local police forces, the execution of "collaborators," the control and censorship of the media, and the ouster and intimidation of noncommunist ministers and legislators. Supported by the tanks and troops of the Soviet Army, the Communist parties gradually solidified their hold through the determined use of what the Hungarian Communist Party leader Mátyás Rákosi (1892–1971) called "salami tactics." Moscow's supervision over the communization of the region was further strengthened in September 1947 by the establishment of the Communist Information Bureau (Cominform), a body responsible for binding together the Eastern European Communist parties (as well as the French and Italian Communist parties) under the leadership of the CPSU (Communist Party of the Soviet Union). By the spring of 1948 "People's Democracies" were in place all over east-central Europe. Although the Soviet Union withdrew its support for the Communist insurgency in Greece and refrained from trying to establish a Communist government in Finland or even a Finno-Soviet military alliance, Soviet power throughout the central and southern heartlands of the region was now firmly entrenched.

Within a few weeks, however, at the June 1948 Cominform summit, the first—and in Eastern Europe the largest—crack in the Eastern bloc surfaced. Yugoslavia, which had been one of the staunchest postwar allies of the Soviet Union, was expelled from Cominform and publicly denounced. The rift with Yugoslavia had been developing behind the scenes for several months and finally reached the breaking point in the spring of 1948.

The split with Yugoslavia revealed the limits of Soviet military, political, and economic power. The Soviet leader, Joseph Stalin (1879–1953), used economic and political coercion against Yugoslavia, but these measures proved futile when Tito turned elsewhere for trade and economic assistance, and when he liquidated the pro-Moscow faction of the Yugoslav Communist Party before it could move against him. Stalin's aides devised a multitude of covert plots to assassinate Tito, but all such plans ultimately went nowhere. The failure of these alternatives left Stalin with the unattractive option of resorting to all-out military force, an option he declined to pursue.

If Yugoslavia had not been located on the periphery of Eastern Europe with no borders adjacent to those of the Soviet Union, it is unlikely that Stalin would have shown the restraint he did. Stalin's successor, Nikita Khrushchev (1894–1971), later said he was "absolutely sure that if the Soviet Union had had a common border with Yugoslavia, Stalin would have intervened militarily." Plans for a full-scale military operation were indeed prepared, but in the end the Soviet Union was forced to accept a breach of its Eastern European sphere and the strategic loss of Yugoslavia vis-à-vis the Balkans and the Adriatic Sea. Most important of all, the split with Yugoslavia raised concern about the effects elsewhere in the region if "Titoism" were allowed to spread. To preclude further such challenges to Soviet control, Stalin instructed the Eastern European states to carry out new purges and show trials to remove any officials who might have hoped to seek greater independence. The process took a particularly violent form in Czechoslovakia, Bulgaria, and Hungary.

Despite the loss of Yugoslavia, the Eastern bloc came under no further threat during Stalin's time. From 1947 through the early 1950s, the Eastern European states embarked on crash industrialization and collectivization programs, causing vast social upheaval yet also leading to rapid short-term economic growth. Stalin was able to rely on the presence of Soviet troops, a tightly woven network of security forces, the wholesale penetration of the Eastern European governments by Soviet agents, the use of mass purges and political terror, and the unifying threat of renewed German militarism to ensure that regimes loyal to Moscow remained in power. He forged a similar relationship with Communist China, which adopted Stalinist policies under Moscow's tutelage and subordinated its preferences to those of the Soviet Union. By the early 1950s, Stalin had established a degree of control over the Communist bloc to which his successors could only aspire.

## KHRUSHCHEV AND THE BLOC: CRISES, CONSOLIDATION, AND THE SINO-SOVIET RIFT

After Stalin died in March 1953, a shift began within the Eastern bloc, as the new leaders in Moscow encouraged the Eastern European governments to loosen economic controls, adopt "new courses" of economic and political reform, downgrade the role of the secret police, and put an end to mass violent terror. The severe economic pressures that had built up on workers and farmers during the relentless drive for collectivization were gradually eased, and many victims of the Stalinist purges were rehabilitated, often posthumously. The introduction of these changes spawned socioeconomic unrest that had been held in check during the Stalin era through pervasive violence and oppression. From 1953 until the late 1980s the Soviet Union had to come up with alternative means of defusing centrifugal pressures in Eastern Europe—a task that was often formidably difficult.

Within a few months of Stalin's death the Eastern bloc came under serious challenge. An uprising in Plzeň and a few other Czechoslovak cities in early June 1953 was harshly suppressed by the local authorities, but a much more intractable

Soviet premier Nikita Khrushchev (center) with Romanian state council president Gheorghe Gheorghiu-Dej (right) and premier Ion Gheorghe Maurer, during a visit to Bucharest, June 1962. ©BETTMANN/CORBIS

problem arose on 17 June in East Germany, where a full-scale rebellion erupted. Coming at a time of profound uncertainty and leadership instability in both Moscow and East Berlin, the rebellion threatened the very existence of the SED regime and, by extension, vital Soviet interests in Germany. The Soviet Army had to intervene on a massive scale to put down the rebellion. The intervention of Soviet troops was crucial both in forestalling an escalation of the violence and in averting a grave fissure within the Eastern bloc.

Despite the resolution of the June 1953 crisis, the use of Soviet military power in East Germany revealed the inherent fragility of the bloc. Over the next few years, most of the leaders in Moscow were preoccupied with the post-Stalin leadership struggle and other salient domestic issues, and they failed to appreciate the implications of changes elsewhere in the bloc. Even after a large-scale rebellion broke out in the Polish city of Poznań in June 1956, Soviet leaders did not grasp the potential for wider and

more explosive unrest in Eastern Europe. Not until the events of October–November 1956 did the Soviet Union finally draw a line for the bloc. Although a severe crisis with Poland in October was ultimately resolved peacefully, Soviet troops had to intervene en masse in Hungary in early November to suppress a violent revolution and get rid of the revolutionary government under Imre Nagy (1896–1958). The Soviet invasion, which resulted in heavy bloodshed, made clear to all the member states of the Warsaw Pact (the Soviet-East European military alliance formed in May 1955) the bounds of Soviet tolerance and the limits of what could be changed in Eastern Europe. The revolution in Hungary had posed a fundamental threat to the existence of the Eastern bloc, and the Soviet Union's reassertion of military control over Hungary stemmed any further erosion of the bloc.

Important as it was for the Soviet Union to consolidate its position in 1956, the bloc did not remain intact for long. A bitter split between the

Soviet Union and China, stemming from genuine policy and ideological differences as well as from a personal clash between Nikita Khrushchev and Mao Zedong (1893–1976), developed behind the scenes in the late 1950s. The dispute intensified in June 1959 when the Soviet Union abruptly terminated its secret nuclear weapons cooperation agreement with China. Khrushchev's highly publicized visit to the United States in September 1959 further antagonized the Chinese, and a last-ditch meeting between Khrushchev and Mao in Beijing a few days later failed to resolve the issues dividing the two sides. From then on, Sino-Soviet relations steadily deteriorated. Although the two countries tried several times to reconcile their differences; the split, if anything, grew even wider, leaving a permanent breach in the Eastern bloc.

Khrushchev feared that the schism in world communism would deepen if he did not seek to counter China's efforts to secure the backing of foreign Communist parties. In late 1960 and early 1961 the Albanian leader, Enver Hoxha, sparked a crisis with the Soviet Union by openly aligning his country with China, a precedent that caused alarm in Moscow. The "loss" of Albania, though trivial compared to the earlier split with Yugoslavia, marked the second time since 1945 that the Soviet sphere in Eastern Europe had been breached. When Soviet leaders learned that China was secretly trying to induce other Eastern European countries to follow Albania's lead, they made strenuous efforts to undercut Beijing's attempts. As a result, no further defections from the Eastern bloc occurred by the time Khrushchev was removed from power in October 1964.

## THE BREZHNEV AND EARLY POST-BREZHNEV ERA: RETRENCHMENT AND CONFORMITY

Khrushchev's successor, Leonid Brezhnev (1906–1982), had to overcome several challenges to the integrity of the bloc. The first of these was presented by Romania, which in the mid-1960s began to embrace foreign and domestic policies that were at times sharply at odds with the Soviet Union's own policies. Romania staked out a conspicuously neutral position in the Sino-Soviet dispute, refusing to endorse Moscow's polemics or to join in other steps aimed at isolating Beijing. In 1967 Romania became the first Eastern European

country to establish diplomatic ties with West Germany, a step that infuriated the East German authorities. That same year, the Romanians maintained full diplomatic relations with Israel after the other Warsaw Pact countries had broken off all ties with the Israelis in the wake of the June 1967 Arab-Israeli War. Romania also adopted an independent military doctrine of "Total People's War for the Defense of the Homeland" and a national military command structure separate from that of the Warsaw Pact. Although Romania had never been a crucial member of the Warsaw Pact, the country's growing recalcitrance on foreign policy and military affairs posed serious complications for the cohesion of the alliance.

The deepening rift with Romania provided the backdrop for a much more serious challenge that arose in 1968 with Czechoslovakia and what became widely known as the Prague Spring. The introduction of sweeping political reforms in Czechoslovakia after Alexander Dubček (1921–1992) came to power in early 1968 provoked alarm in Moscow about the integrity of the Eastern bloc. Both the internal and the external repercussions of the far-reaching liberalization in Czechoslovakia were regarded by Soviet leaders as fundamental threats to the cohesion of the Warsaw Pact, especially if the developments in Czechoslovakia "infected" other countries in Eastern Europe. Soviet efforts to compel Dubček to change course were of little efficacy, as all manner of troop movements, thinly veiled threats, and political and economic coercion failed to bring an end to the Prague Spring. Finally, on the evening of 20 August 1968, the Soviet Union and four other Warsaw Pact countries—East Germany, Poland, Bulgaria, and Hungary—sent a large invading force into Czechoslovakia to crush the reform movement and restore orthodox Communist rule. Although it took several months before the last remnants of the Prague Spring could be eradicated, the final ouster of Dubček in April 1969 symbolized the forceful restoration of conformity to the Eastern bloc.

For more than a decade thereafter, the bloc seemed relatively stable, despite crises in Poland in 1970 and 1976. But the facade of stability came to an abrupt end in mid-1980 when a severe and prolonged crisis began in Poland, a crisis that soon posed enormous complications for the integrity of the bloc. The formation of Solidarity, an independent and popularly based trade union that soon

**Workers at an auto parts factory strike in support of the growing revolution against the Communist government, Prague, Czechoslovakia, 1989.** ©DAVID TURNLEY

rivaled the Polish Communist Party for political power, threatened to undermine Poland's role in the bloc. Soviet leaders reacted with unremitting hostility toward Solidarity and repeatedly urged Polish leaders to impose martial law, a step that was finally taken in December 1981.

The Soviet Union's emphasis on an "internal solution" to the Polish crisis was by no means a departure from its responses to previous crises in the Eastern bloc. In both Hungary and Poland in 1956, and in Czechoslovakia in 1968, Soviet leaders had applied pressure short of direct military intervention and sought to work out an internal solution that would preclude the need for an invasion. In each case Soviet officials viewed military action as a last-ditch option to be used only if all other alternatives failed. An internal solution proved feasible in Poland in 1956, but attempts to reassert Soviet control from within proved futile in Hungary in 1956 and Czechoslovakia in 1968. During the

1980–1981 Polish crisis Soviet officials devised plans for a full-scale invasion, but these plans were to be implemented only if the Polish authorities failed to restore order on their own. Only in a worst-case scenario, in which the martial-law operation collapsed and civil war erupted in Poland, does it seem at all likely that the Soviet Union would have shifted toward an "external" option.

The successful imposition of martial law in Poland by General Wojciech Jaruzelski (b. 1923) in December 1981 upheld the integrity of the Eastern bloc at relatively low cost and ensured that Soviet leaders did not have to face the dilemma of invading Poland. The surprisingly smooth implementation of martial law in Poland also helped prevent any further disruption in the bloc during the final year of Brezhnev's rule and the next two-and-a-half years under Yuri Andropov (1914–1984) and Konstantin Chernenko (1911–1985). During an earlier period of uncertainty and leadership transition in the Soviet Union and Eastern Europe (1953–1956), numerous crises had arisen within the bloc; but no such upheavals occurred in 1982–1985. This unusual placidity cannot be attributed to any single factor, but the martial-law crackdown of December 1981 and the invasions of 1956 and 1968 probably constitute a large part of the explanation. After Stalin's death in 1953, the limits of what could be changed in Eastern Europe were still unknown, but by the early to mid-1980s the Soviet Union had evinced its willingness to use "extreme measures" to prevent "deviations from socialism." Thus, by the time Mikhail Gorbachev (b. 1931) assumed the top post in Moscow in March 1985, the Eastern bloc seemed destined to remain within the narrow bounds of orthodox communism as interpreted in Moscow.

## THE DEMISE OF THE EASTERN BLOC

Although Gorbachev initially carried out few changes in the Eastern bloc, he began shifting course within a few years of taking office, as he steadily loosened Soviet ties with Eastern Europe. The wide-ranging political reforms he was promoting in the Soviet Union generated pressure within Eastern Europe for the adoption of similar reforms. Faced with the prospect of acute social discontent, the Hungarian and Polish governments embarked on sweeping reform programs that were at least as ambitious as what Gorbachev was pursuing. By early 1989 it had become clear that the Soviet Union was willing to countenance radical changes in Eastern Europe that cumulatively amounted to a repudiation of orthodox communism.

In adopting this approach, Gorbachev did not intend to precipitate the breakup of the Eastern bloc. On the contrary, he was hoping to strengthen the bloc and reshape it in a way that would no longer require heavy-handed coercion. But in the end his policies, far from invigorating the bloc, resulted in its demise. In early June 1989 elections were held in Poland that led within three months to the emergence of a noncommunist government led by Solidarity. Political changes of similar magnitude were under way at this time in Hungary. Although the four other Warsaw Pact countries—East Germany, Bulgaria, Czechoslovakia, and Romania—tried to fend off the pressures for sweeping change, their resistance proved futile in the final few months of 1989, when they were engulfed by political turmoil. The orthodox Communist rulers in these four countries were forced from power, and noncommunist governments took over. In 1990 free elections were held in all the Eastern European countries, consolidating the newly democratic political systems that took shape after the Communist regimes collapsed.

By that point, events had moved so far and so fast in Eastern Europe, and the Soviet Union's influence had declined so precipitously, that the fate of the whole continent eluded Soviet control. The very notion of an "Eastern bloc" lost its meaning once Gorbachev permitted and even facilitated the end of Communist rule in Eastern Europe. This outcome may seem inevitable in retrospect, but it was definitely not so at the time. If Gorbachev had been determined to preserve the Eastern bloc in its traditional form, as his predecessors had been, he undoubtedly could have succeeded. The Soviet Union in the late 1980s still had more than enough military strength to prop up the Communist regimes in Eastern Europe and to cope with the bloodshed that would have resulted. Gorbachev's acceptance of the peaceful disintegration of the bloc stemmed from a conscious choice on his part, a choice bound up with his domestic priorities and his desire to do away with the legacies of the Stalinist era that had blighted the Soviet economy. Any Soviet leader who was truly intent on overcoming Stalinism at home had to be willing to implement drastic changes in relations with Eastern Europe. Far-reaching political liberalization and greater openness within the Soviet Union would have been incompatible with, and eventually undermined by, a policy in Eastern Europe that required military intervention on behalf of hard-line Communist regimes. The fundamental reorientation of Soviet domestic goals under Gorbachev therefore necessitated the adoption of a radically new policy vis-à-vis Eastern Europe that led, in short order, to the dissolution of the Eastern bloc.

*See also* **Berlin Wall; 1989; Prague Spring; Solidarity; Soviet Union; Warsaw Pact.**

BIBLIOGRAPHY

Brzezinski, Zbigniew K. *The Soviet Bloc: Unity and Conflict.* Cambridge, Mass., 1967.

Gati, Charles. *The Bloc That Failed: Soviet–East European Relations in Transition.* Bloomington, Ind., 1990.

Hutchings, Robert L. *Soviet–East European Relations: Consolidation and Conflict, 1968–1980.* Madison, Wis., 1983.

Kramer, Mark. "The Soviet Union and Eastern Europe: Spheres of Influence." In *Explaining International Relations since 1945,* edited by Ngaire Woods. Oxford, U.K., 1996.

Smith, Alan H. *The Planned Economies of Eastern Europe.* London, 1983.

MARK KRAMER

---

**EASTER RISING.** On 24 April 1916 (Easter Monday), a group of men and women seized a number of prominent public buildings in central Dublin and proclaimed an Irish Republic. The Rising ended in defeat on 30 April when Patrick Henry Pearse (1879–1916), president of the Irish Republic, ordered an unconditional cease-fire.

The Rising marked a major setback for the dominant constitutional strand of Irish nationalism, which had been coming under threat for three or four years. With the introduction of the 1911 Parliament Act removing the veto of the House of Lords, Ireland appeared to be on course to secure Home Rule—devolved government within the United Kingdom—in 1914. However, the majority Protestant population in the northeast was determined to prevent this, and in order to do so, they formed the Ulster Unionist Volunteers in 1913; the Ulster Volunteers landed guns at Larne in the spring of 1914. These actions prompted the tit-for-tat militarization of nationalist Ireland, with the formation of the Irish Volunteers (1913) and the Howth gun-running (June 1914). The Irish Volunteers were an essentially defensive body formed to defend Home Rule, however, they were infiltrated by the Irish Republican Brotherhood (IRB)—a militant republican group whose origins could be traced back to the 1850s. When war broke out in August 1914, the British authorities postponed the introduction of Home Rule until it ended, postponing the decision on Irish partition. While many Ulster and Irish Volunteers enlisted in the British army, a more militant minority of Irish Volunteers continued to meet and drill in Ireland. In May 1915 the IRB formed a military council, which eventually consisted of seven men, that went on to plan and to lead the 1916 Rising. The military council operated in such secrecy that the leadership of the Volunteers and the IRB were not informed about their plans for a rising. This obsession with secrecy reflected the belief that previous rebellions against Britain had failed because of informers. On this occasion, however, the secrecy resulted in such confusion that it made the Rising less effective.

In keeping with a long-standing tradition in Irish separatism, that "England's difficulty is Ireland's opportunity," efforts were made to enlist support from Germany, with Irish American leader John Devoy (1842–1928) as the major channel of communications. Germany dispatched a shipment of guns to Ireland, though not the hoped-for troops; a failure of communications, however, meant that there was nobody to meet the arms ship, the *Aud,* when it arrived off the southwest coast of Ireland on 20 April. When intercepted by the Royal Navy, the captain scuttled the boat rather than surrender.

The lack of communication was not confined to the rebels. British intelligence had advance knowledge of the planned uprising, having intercepted German transatlantic cables, but in order to protect the knowledge that Britain had broken German codes, they failed to pass on the information to the authorities in Dublin. The arrest of Roger Casement (1864–1916), who had landed from a German submarine in southwest Ireland on Good Friday, and the scuttling of the *Aud* gave Dublin Castle the first warning that a rising was imminent. The authorities in Dublin, however, assumed that the rising would not proceed after these setbacks, and they took no immediate steps to round up the probable ringleaders.

This decision had some justification because Irish Volunteers leader Eoin MacNeill (1867–1945), who was not privy to the plans for a rising, issued an order countermanding volunteer maneuvers for Easter Sunday (the cover for the planned rising), but the IRB army council determined to go ahead on the following day. Approximately 1,600 men and women took part in the rebellion: 200 of these were members of the Irish Citizen Army, which had been formed in the spring of 1914 by revolutionary socialists, in the final stages of a bitter dispute between radical trade unionists and Dublin employers. In January 1916 socialist leader James Connolly

(1868–1916) became the seventh member of the IRB Military Council.

The rebel headquarters were in the General Post Office (GPO) on Sackville Street (now O'Connell Street), the city's main thoroughfare. From the steps of the GPO, Pearse, poet and schoolteacher, read the proclamation of an Irish Republic "in the name of God and of the dead generations." The proclamation reflected the influence of Connolly with its affirmation of "the right of the people of Ireland to the ownership of Ireland" and commitment to "civil and religious liberty, equal rights and equal opportunities to all its citizens," but its greatest significance is that it revived the commitment to an Irish Republic, which was first enunciated by the United Irishmen of the 1790s.

The original plan was for simultaneous risings in Dublin and throughout Ireland, with a concentration on the west and the southwest, taking advantage of the expected landing of German troops and arms. There were no plans to fight in Ulster; Irish Volunteers from Ulster would have moved to northwest Connaught to hold the "line of the [river] Shannon." If the rebels had to retreat from Dublin, they planned to regroup in the west of Ireland. Because of MacNeill's countermanding order, however, the Rising was almost wholly confined to Dublin, with minor engagements in Wexford, north County Dublin, Galway, and Cork. In Dublin the rebels seized major public buildings dotted around the city, but they made no effort to break out from these positions in order to link up, and they failed to prevent British reinforcements from entering the city. The decision not to seize Dublin Castle—the headquarters of British administration in Ireland—and the failure to occupy the grounds of Trinity College or the city's telephone exchange were major strategic errors. The British authorities could call on 6,000 effective troops, plus a greater number who were on leave or convalescent. They also made extensive use of artillery to flatten buildings in central Dublin, including Liberty Hall, headquarters of Connolly's Irish Transport Workers' Union—contrary to Connolly's belief that capitalists would not destroy property.

It is unlikely that the rebellion would have succeeded, even if all had gone to plan, but many of the leaders saw it as an opportunity to move Irish nationalism from the compromise of Home Rule toward militant republicanism. Like many of the 1914–1918 generation, Pearse was convinced that a "blood sacrifice" could bring about a spiritual transformation; he claimed that "bloodshed is a cleansing and a sanctifying thing, and the nation which regards it as the final horror has lost its manhood."

The majority of the Irish population disapproved of the Rising, but the mood changed rapidly in subsequent weeks as 3,430 men and 79 women were arrested (more than double the number of participants), and 89 men and 1 woman, Constance Markievicz (1868–1927), were sentenced to death. Fifteen men were executed in Ireland, including all seven signatories of the proclamation, but the remaining death sentences were commuted in response to growing public outrage; the majority of the 1,836 men and 5 women who were interned in Britain were released by Christmas. Whether this upsurge of sympathy would have had a long-term effect on Irish opinion is debatable, but Britain's failed attempt to settle the Home Rule/Ulster Question in the summer of 1916, and the threat of conscription (which had not been introduced to Ireland in 1914), added fuel to the militant fire. When the final 1916 prisoners were released in the summer of 1917, they were greeted as national heroes.

In April 1916 the British authorities had described the Rising as the Sinn Féin rebellion, although this political party played no part in the event. In the autumn of 1917, however, Sinn Féin—a nonviolent party campaigning for greater autonomy than Home Rule—was taken over by 1916 veterans, and its mission was changed to securing an Irish Republic. A Sinn Féin landslide in the 1918 general election was interpreted as giving retrospective sanction for the 1916 Rising, and a mandate for the Anglo-Irish war of 1919–1921. The determining factor for those who rejected the 1921 Anglo-Irish Treaty, which granted a partitioned Ireland dominion status, was the belief that they were betraying the Republic proclaimed in 1916; this was the primary cause of civil war in 1922–1923.

Despite these violent beginnings, democracy triumphed in independent Ireland. The young men who fought in the 1916 Rising dominated Irish

**Soldiers and civilians shoot at each other in the street as an overturned cart burns in the foreground during the Easter Rising, April 1916.** ©GETTY IMAGES

politics until the 1960s: Eamon de Valera (1882–1975), the most senior surviving commander, retired as president in 1973. The fiftieth anniversary of the Rising in 1966 was marked by lavish official ceremonies of what was regarded as a historical event. By the early 1970s, however, the Provisional Irish Republican Army (IRA) was invoking Pearse's rhetoric of blood sacrifice and the fact that the 1916 Rising had been waged contrary to the wishes of the people as justification for their actions, prompting a lively debate over the legacy of 1916, and the respective importance of democratic and revolutionary traditions for contemporary Ireland. The seventy-fifth anniversary passed almost unnoticed, but the IRA cease-fire and the 1998 Belfast Agreement (also called the Good Friday Agreement) have made it more acceptable to acknowledge the Rising.

*See also* **British Empire; British Empire, End of; IRA; Ireland; Sinn Féin.**

BIBLIOGRAPHY

Caufield, Max. *The Easter Rebellion*. London, 1963.

Coates, Tim, ed. *The Irish Uprising, 1914–1921.* Papers from the British Parliamentary Archive. London, 2000.

Connolly, James. *Labour and Easter Week: A Selection from the Writings of James Connolly.* Edited by Desmond Ryan. Dublin, 1966.

Edwards, Ruth Dudley. *Patrick Pearse: The Triumph of Failure.* London, 1977.

Laffan, Michael. *The Resurrection of Ireland: The Sinn Féin Party, 1916–1923*. Cambridge, U.K., 1999.

Lyons, F. S. L. "The Revolution in Train, 1914–16"; "The New Nationalism 1916–18." In *A New History of Ireland*, Vol. 6: *Ireland Under the Union, 1870–1921*, edited by W. J. Vaughan, 189–222. Oxford, U.K., 1996.

Ní Dhonnchadha, Máirín, and Theo Dorgan, eds. *Revising the Rising*. Derry, 1991.

O'Brien, Conor Cruise. *States of Ireland*. London, 1972.

ó Broin, Léon. *Dublin Castle and the 1916 Rising*. Dublin, 1966.

Pearse, Pádraic. *Collected Works of Pádraic H. Pearse*. Dublin, 1917.

Shaw, Francis. "The Canon of Irish History: A Challenge." *Studies* 61 (summer 1972): 113–152.

Stephens, James. *The Insurrection in Dublin*. Dublin, 1916.

Thompson, William Irwin. *The Imagination of an Insurrection, Dublin, Easter 1916: A Study of an Ideological Movement*. Oxford, U.K., 1967.

Townshend, Charles. *Easter 1916: The Irish Rebellion*. London, 2005.

MARY E. DALY

---

# EBERT, FRIEDRICH (1871–1925), German Social Democratic politician.

Friedrich Ebert was born in Heidelberg. The son of an independent tailor, he studied to be a saddler and during travels as a journeyman joined the Social Democratic Party (SPD), becoming a trade union activist. Because of the repressive (anti) Socialist Laws, he moved from place to place continually until he settled in Bremen in 1891, becoming a leading local functionary in both the federation of trade unions and the SPD. He served on the city parliament from 1900 to 1905, when he entered national politics, becoming a secretary to the executive office of the SPD and moving to Berlin. Elected to the Reichstag in 1912, he became one of the two co-presidents of the SPD after the death of its founder, August Bebel.

During the crises of July 1914, following the assassination of Austrian archduke Francis Ferdinand, Ebert left Germany for some weeks to prepare for an executive office-in-exile in case the SPD was banned. Joining the majority of the party's parliamentary members in approving the war budget, he became the leading Social Democratic politician after the left-wing and pacifist opponents of the war left the party in 1916 and 1917. In January 1918 he attempted to settle a Berlin metalworkers strike smoothly and quickly, an effort that attracted polemics both from chauvinists and leftists, who denounced him as a traitor to the fatherland and the working class, respectively.

He stayed in contact with reform-oriented elements of the administration and supported the constitutional reforms of October 1918, which favored a constitutional monarchy, and joined the new government of Chancellor Prince Max von Baden as undersecretary of state. With the outbreak of revolution in November and the abdication of Emperor William II, Ebert became co-president of the Council of the People's Commissioners, the six-person committee leading the revolutionary movement, and he worked for a rapid transition to parliamentary rule. This policy was based on his personal alliance with the Supreme Army Command under General Wilhelm Groener, an alliance that enabled him to suppress left-wing attempts to establish alternative centers of revolutionary power—Räte, the equivalent of soviets—in Berlin, Bremen, and Bavaria.

On 11 February 1919 Ebert was elected president of the Reich by the National Assembly, which had adopted a republican constitution in Weimar, where the assembly met in order to escape an insecure situation in the capital (hence the name Weimar Republic). From the beginning of his term, Ebert came under ferocious attacks by right-wing opponents of the new political order, who accused him, and Social Democrats in general, of obstructing the German army during World War I. In a defamation trial, a local district court even deemed his participation in the Berlin strike high treason. On 28 February 1925, six month before his term as Reich president was to end, Ebert died of an untreated inflammation of the appendix.

To Social Democratic leaders of the German Empire, Ebert represented a generation of young pragmatists with a reformist worldview who were prepared to integrate the working class into the existing order if they were granted political equality and social rights in a modern welfare state. He remained true to this antirevolutionary approach during the postwar crisis of 1918 and 1919, when he decided that making a rapid transition to a constitutional government based on an agreement with the military leadership was more important than creating a broad alliance of the Left, which would have entailed cooperation with movements that wanted to complete the revolution's socialist agenda. This antirevolutionary partnership, however, led to the tragic end of his career as well as the fatal flaw in the Weimar Republic: that representatives of the ancient elites, who were spared a violent revolution thanks at least in part to Ebert's intervention, focused their opposition to the young republic on its top representative. In the last two years of his life, the republican center of the political landscape had already been deserted as a result of growing political polarization, making Ebert the head of a "republic without republicans." When the war hero General Paul von Hindenburg—an open opponent of the republic and a zealous proponent of the belief that Germany had been defeated from within during World War I—was elected to Ebert's former office of Reich president, the end of the first modern German democracy had begun.

Ebert's legacy is marked in his native city of Heidelberg, and as early as 1925 the German Social Democratic Party established a foundation named after him to support cultural, scholarly, and educational activities. It has become one of the largest foundations of its kind in the world.

*See also* **Germany; Hindenburg, Paul von; Social Democracy; World War I.**

BIBLIOGRAPHY

"Friedrich-Ebert-Stiftung." Available at http://forum.fes-international.de/sets/s_stif.htm

Mühlausen, Walter. *Friedrich Ebert, 1871–1925. Reichspräsident der Weimarer Republik.* Bonn, 2006.

THOMAS LINDENBERGER

---

# ECO, UMBERTO (b. 1932), Italian semiotician.

Umberto Eco's work on semiotics began in the 1960s, when his examination of mass culture in *Apocalittici e integrati* (1964; *Apocalypse Postponed*, 1994, a partial translation only) convinced him that a unified theory of signs was needed to study all cultural phenomena. In *La struttura assente* (1968; The absent structure), Eco provided an early formulation of such a theory. Elaborating on the insights of the two thinkers behind twentieth-century semiotics, the American pragmatic philosopher Charles Sanders Peirce (1839–1914) and the Swiss linguist Ferdinand de Saussure (1857–1913), Eco gives an overview of the fundamental concepts of semiotics: sign, code, message, sender, and addressee. Because *La struttura assente* is a work born of the debate with the ontological structuralism of Claude Lévi-Strauss and Jacques Lacan, however, Eco places a great deal of emphasis on the provisional and historical nature of systems of signs. He argues that semiotics studies the mechanisms governing closed, rigorously formalized systems but also analyzes the contextual variability and historical modifications to which these same systems are subjected. By doing so, Eco successfully integrates semiotics with a Marxist philosophical project whereby, "as in an ideal 'semiological' warfare" (Eco, 1968, p. 417), messages can be deciphered or encoded on the basis of oppositional, politically empowering codes.

Eco's semiotic reflection is pursued in *Le forme del contenuto* (1971; The forms of content) and especially in the monumental *A Theory of Semiotics* (1976), where he develops a twofold formulation of semiotics as a theory of codes and as a theory of sign production. The theory of codes, which remains indebted to Saussure, entails a semiotics of "signification" that deals with the codes underlying and governing the functioning of a great variety of natural and artificial languages, that is, of closed systems such as zoosemiotics (animal communication); olfactory signs; tactile communication; kinesics and proxemics (ritualized gesture); music; aesthetics; and visual codes, among others. Yet, in theorizing a semiotics of "communication," Eco replaces the Saussurean notion of the sign as a twofold entity composed of a signifier (material form) and a signified (concept) with that of the *sign-function*, a mutable and transitory correlation whereby one or more units of expression can be associated with one or more semantic units of content. Moreover, following Charles Morris and especially Peirce, Eco describes the production of meaning as an inferential process dependent upon three entities: the sign; its object, that for which the sign stands; and its interpretant, the mental effect created by the relation between sign and object. Therefore, the meaning of a sign, or its interpretant, comes to reside in another sign in a process of unlimited semiosis (sign production) that is only partially related to the real world. Eco's definition of the sign as inference also facilitates his departure from a structuralist semantics of dictionary definitions or a semantics based upon one-to-one equivalences, and allows him to develop the notion of the encyclopedia: an archive of meanings that, through a process of abduction (a metalinguistic operation that enriches a code), activates an infinite number of associations in the course of interpretation. The process of abduction, however, does not imply semiotic drift or the endless deferral of signs. Not only does it remain teleologically oriented toward the creation of a better, more developed sign but its potential for drift is contained by the notion of *ground* and *final interpretant,* or definitions agreed upon by the habit of interpretive communities.

Eco's mature semiotic theory has been interpreted as a partial retreat from the political implications of *La struttura assente.* While the code theory tends to eliminate the referent and bracket intention, the sign-production theory, in an attempt to regulate the potentially unlimited openness of interpretation, places limits on the inferential notion of the sign and reduces the social import of semiosis.

While pursuing a general theory of signs, Eco continued his empirical research, writing a number of essays and book chapters where semiotic methods are applied in the practical analyses of the many forms of communication in human collective life, including the media and popular novels. Eco's extensive theoretical and empirical work by necessity also infiltrated his activity as an author of fiction. Novels such as *The Name of the Rose* (1983), *Foucault's Pendulum* (1989), *The Island of the Day Before* (1995), *Baudolino* (2002), and *The Mysterious Flame of Queen Loana* (2005) can be read as endorsements of semiotic creativity and invention but also as tales warning readers about the dangers of the unbounded semiotic regress allowed by the encyclopedia. For example,

while *The Name of the Rose* exemplifies the process of semiotic abduction through the Franciscan William of Baskerville's investigation of the murders that have occurred in the northern Italian abbey, *Foucault's Pendulum* demonstrates the pitfalls of the unbridled, endless chain of semiotic production undertaken by the characters of Belbo, Diotallevi, and Casaubon. As such, Eco's fictional activity closely parallels the developments that have occurred in his theoretical and empirical work on signs.

*See also* **Lacan, Jacques; Lévi-Strauss, Claude; Saussure, Ferdinand de; Semiotics.**

BIBLIOGRAPHY

*Primary Sources*

Eco, Umberto. *Apocalittici e integrati: Communicazioni di masse et teorie della cultura di massa.* Milan, 1964.

———. *La struttura assente.* Milan, 1968.

———. *A Theory of Semiotics.* Bloomington, Ind., 1976.

———. *The Name of the Rose.* Translated by William Weaver. New York, 1983.

———. *Foucault's Pendulum.* Translated by William Weaver. London, 1989.

———. *Apocalypse Postponed.* Edited by Robert Lumley. Bloomington, Ind., 1994. Partial translation of *Apocalittici e integrati.*

———. *The Island of the Day Before.* Translated by William Weaver. New York, 1995.

———. *Baudolino.* Translated by William Weaver. New York, 2002.

———. *The Mysterious Flame of Queen Loana: An Illustrated Novel.* Translated by Geoffrey Brock. New York, 2005.

*Secondary Sources*

Bal, Mieke. "The Predicament of Semiotics." *Poetics Today* 13, no. 2 (fall 1992): 543–552.

Bouchard, Norma, and Veronica Pravadelli, eds. *Umberto Eco's Alternative: The Politics of Culture and the Ambiguities of Interpretation.* New York, 1998.

Caesar, Michael. *Umberto Eco: Philosophy, Semiotics, and the Work of Fiction.* Cambridge, U.K., 1999.

Capozzi, Rocco, ed. *Reading Eco: An Anthology.* Bloomington, Ind., 1997.

De Lauretis, Teresa. *Alice Doesn't: Feminism, Semiotics, Cinema.* Bloomington, Ind., 1984.

Robey, David. "Umberto Eco: Theory and Practice in the Analysis of the Media." In *Culture and Conflict in*

*Postwar Italy: Essays on Mass and Popular Culture,* edited by Zygmunt G. Barański and Robert Lumley, 160–177. New York, 1990.

NORMA BOUCHARD

---

# ECONOMIC MIRACLE.

The concept of an "economic miracle" in a strict sense has come to be associated with the development of the West German Federal Republic after 1945 and especially during the 1950s. These, as is reflected in the title of Hanna Schissler's anthology, were *The Miracle Years* of postwar reconstruction. However, the term has also been used with reference to the rapid growth of other European economies in this period.

## THE IMPACT OF WORLD WAR II

What happened in West Germany in the two decades after World War II did indeed have, to many contemporaries, the appearance of something miraculous. While an estimated 50 million people died in that war, and the suffering of other societies, especially of Eastern Europe, must not be forgotten or minimized, German human losses were also enormous. Some 7 million Germans had been killed or were presumed dead, around 3.2 million being civilians. To these figures must be added some 1.3 million Wehrmacht soldiers missing in action, the fate of many of whom the Red Cross was still trying to trace as late as 1962. There were at least 1 million disabled, and civilian health had deteriorated dramatically.

Material destruction was widespread. After several years of Allied carpet bombing, many cities had been reduced to rubble. Some 3.4 million apartments out of 17.1 million had been completely flattened. Another 30 percent were badly damaged. The housing shortage was exacerbated by the influx of some 11 million refugees and expellees from Eastern Europe. As late as August 1945 an estimated 25,000 to 30,000 of them were passing through Berlin day after day. In addition to mothers and their children who had been evacuated to the countryside to escape the bombings of the cities and demobilized soldiers on their way home, there were also some 1.5 million Russian DPs (displaced persons), 1.2 million Frenchmen, 600,000 Poles, 400,000 Dutch and Belgians, 350,000 Italians, 100,000 Yugoslavs, and scores of other nationals who had been recruited, most of them by force, as foreign laborers to work in German factories or on farms. In 1945 they, too, were wandering about or being accommodated in makeshift camps.

Industrial production was at a virtual standstill. Food was extremely scarce. By July 1945 the daily intake had fallen to 950–1,150 calories, well short of the 1,500 minimum that the British military government had laid down for its zone of occupation. The initial approach of the victorious Allies to the country that had surrendered unconditionally in May 1945 was severely punitive. Although not many decision makers supported the radical plans of a partial deindustrialization of Germany that the American treasury secretary Henry Morgenthau had proposed in 1944, most people expected the Germans to enjoy for many years to come no more than a minimum living standard after extensive dismantling of industrial machinery and installations and the denazification and punishment of the adult population for their involvement in the Hitler regime. Under the denazification laws that the Allies introduced, defendants could be imprisoned, have their property confiscated, have their pension and other entitlements cancelled, and be barred from future employment.

## RECONSTRUCTION AND RECOVERY

However, soon the "reconstructionists" won the day over the "Morgenthauians." Learning from the experience after 1918, they held that keeping the Germans down and not reintegrating them into the community of nations might merely produce a repetition of history—another rise of a radical revisionist movement, such as National Socialism, leading to yet another war. The reconstructionists were helped in their strategy by the onset of the Cold War between East and West, which divided Germany in the middle along the Iron Curtain into what was eventually to become the two semisovereign states of the West German Federal Republic and the East German Democratic Republic. This division reinforced the determination of the United States but also its Western European allies to make the West Germans partners in the emergent defense community against the Soviet bloc and in the concomitant program of building a Western European economic community. The promulgation of the European Recovery Program (ERP or Marshall Plan) for economic reconstruction and of the North Atlantic Treaty Organization (NATO) for military defense laid the foundations for the economic miracle in West Germany.

Other key factors were the currency reform of June 1948 and the completion of the decartelization and deconcentration programs that pushed West German industry, which had developed in a highly anticompetitive and monopolistic direction under Nazism, into an oligopolistic liberal-capitalist system based on the principle of market competition. There was also a keen desire on the part of the West German population to revive the economy and to reduce the massive unemployment. On closer inspection, industry's production capacity turned out to be much less heavily damaged than had been assumed at the end of the war at the sight of the bombed-out cities. A skilled workforce wanted to get the machines running again for civilian production to provide jobs and to hold out the prospect of renewed prosperity. This prosperity came in the 1950s during the "miracle years."

Here are a few statistics to demonstrate this recovery. The index of industrial production, which had been below 100 points in 1935 but had then seen a rapid rise as a result of Adolf Hitler's massive rearmament program before 1939 and after the start of the war had been given a further boost by Albert Speer's total war mobilization, stood, notwithstanding the bombings, at 146 points as late as 1944, a slight decline from its peak in 1943 by a mere 3 points. In 1945–1946 the index had dropped well below the 100 mark, which it reached again in 1950. By 1960 it had grown two-and-a-half-fold to 248, reaching 327 points in 1965 and 435 in 1970.

Coal and steel production—so vital for industrial reconstruction—had slumped to 18.7 and 14.6 points respectively in 1945–1946. It rose to 58.3 and 69.1 points respectively by 1950 and to 68.8 and 121.4 points respectively by 1955. The rekindling of heavy industrial production triggered a revival of manufacturing, quite dramatically reflected in the index of automobile production. Starting from a base level of 100 in 1913 and having seen a complete collapse in 1945, the index climbed back to 936 points in 1950, 2,656 in 1955 and 4,266 in 1959.

The chemical industry saw a less rapid but still impressive rise from 240 points in 1950 to 439.8 in 1955 and 630.9 in 1959. This expansion enabled West Germany, following the years of the Nazi quest for autarky and the inevitable wartime isolation, once again to join the multilateral world trading system that the United States had re-created after 1945 outside the Soviet bloc, buttressed by a number of new institutions and agreements, such as the International Monetary Fund, the World Bank, and the General Agreement on Tariffs and Trade (GATT).

Within this framework, the Federal Republic, by then well integrated into the Atlantic community both politically and commercially, once again became one of the major trading nations of the world that it had been before 1914. In 1950 exports had reached a value of 8.3 billion marks in current prices and imports 11.4 billion; by 1955 the respective figures were 25.7 billion and 24.5 billion and by 1960, 47 billion and 42.7 billion marks, showing by this time a healthy trade surplus. All this meant that the annual real growth of the West German economy reached no less than 10.4 percent as early as 1951, subsequently hovering around the 8 percent mark. It peaked at 12 percent in 1955 and, after two more meager years in 1957 and 1958, stood at 9 percent in 1960. Of course, by the standards of later years even the 5.7 percent for 1957 and the 3.7 percent for 1958 were impressive. Accordingly, the return on capital in joint-stock companies in industry and commerce was also high. The profit rate, which had reached 9 percent in 1950, fluctuated around 12 percent throughout the 1950s. Share prices calculated in relation to 100 points in 1965 rose steadily from 16 points in 1951 to 39 in 1955, 134 in 1960, and revolved around a 110-point average in the years thereafter.

### SOCIAL EFFECTS

Moving on to the impact of this growth on the population at large, it is clear that families who either owned companies or had invested in them did very well during the economic miracle, as did their managers. The upper and middle classes, whose assets had been destroyed or severely damaged during the war and whose savings were eaten up by inflation and the currency reform, did particularly well if they held (and had held on to) industrial or landed property or stocks on the western side of the Iron Curtain. These assets rapidly gained in value during the 1950s. Those millions who came as refugees or expellees from the East, however, had lost everything. In order to provide at least some compensation for the sake of creating social stability and integrating the newcomers, the first federal government under chancellor Konrad Adenauer insisted that a partial burden-sharing be instituted. This took the form of the Equalization of Burdens Law (LAG) of 1952. The underlying idea was to collect a contribution, amounting to half of the estimated asset values in 1950, from the "haves" who owned property above a current unit value of five thousand marks. This contribution was to be paid in installments over thirty years and to be allocated to refugees from the East but also to those who had been bombed out in the West.

Furthermore, the funds accumulated in this way were distributed in proportion to the size of the losses suffered. Small lump sums were paid for losses of household goods. Those who had lost more and could document their losses participated in the *Hauptentschädigung*. For example, persons who had lost documented assets of 2 million marks would get 8 percent of their former assets. A person with 50,000 marks would be given 19,000 marks in compensation; someone who had lost 5,000 marks would be given the full amount. The effect of the LAG was not only economic but also psychological. All West Germans had a sense that the material costs of the war were being shared, even if not equally. For those who had to make a contribution, it was reassuring that they were participating in a show of societal solidarity. Meanwhile, as the economic miracle unfolded and their assets grew rapidly well beyond the assessment date of 1950, their sacrifice appeared smaller and smaller and more and more bearable. Those who took part in the *Hauptentschädigung* obtained a windfall that enabled many of them to participate in the boom as founders of new companies or investors. Those who merely received a token at least had the feeling that they were restarting their lives on roughly the same level as those West Germans who, while not having lost anything, remained below the threshold at which a contribution to the LAG fund became due. This, of course,

was the overwhelming majority of the population that benefited from the economic miracle not by seeing their assets grow but by getting jobs and subsequently achieving raises of their pay and benefits.

In 1950 the Federal Republic had 1,869,000 unemployed. By 1955 this figure had declined to 1,074,000. In 1960 it was a mere 271,000. This reduction is all the more remarkable as it includes not only the refugees and expellees who had moved west in the late 1940s but also a steady stream of those who fled from East Germany before the building of the Berlin Wall sealed the East off completely. Between 1949 and 1960 over 2.5 million East Germans crossed into the Federal Republic. In the eight months of 1961 until the building of the wall another 160,000 came. They were all absorbed into the West German economy with relative ease and hence also participated in rising real incomes, the expansion of the social security system, and a reduction of work hours. In 1950 average annual wages in crafts and industry had grown to 3,046 marks. By 1955 they had increased to 4,475 and by 1960 to 6,148 marks for all workers and employees. The index of real wages, after deduction of inflation and calculated from a 1976 baseline of 100 points, had reached 31.4 points in 1950, 51.4 in 1960, and 69.0 in 1965. Meanwhile average work hours in industry fell from 48 per week in 1950 to 45.5 in 1959.

In short, all West Germans, except for some marginal groups who depended on welfare and small pensions, had more money in their pockets and more leisure time at their disposal, helping to create a gradual growth in the consumption of goods and "mass culture," with the United States, as the hegemonic power of the West, providing not only military security through NATO and the model of Fordist mass production but also the model of a modern consumer society. To be sure, spending power was still well below the American average and, above all, continued to be unevenly distributed. Between 1950 and 1963, almost 84 percent of all dependently employed households (workers, employees, civil servants, pensioners) owned 53 percent of the total national wealth. The other 47 percent was held by a mere 16 percent of the households of the self-employed and farmers.

These inequalities have led to a debate on how rapid the advent of a mass consumption society was that is usually associated with the economic miracle. It is probably safest to say that the expansion went through several phases, perhaps best reflected in the proliferation of motor vehicles. While expensive cars were quickly available for the well-to-do, the ordinary consumer was more likely to start off with a moped, scooter, or motorbike. A few years later, he would be able to afford a three-wheeled or four-wheeled "bubble car," at most a standard model Volkswagen. But by the 1960s, the full range of midsized mass-produced car models was coming within reach, as were many other consumer durables, such as refrigerators, radios, TV sets, and washing machines. Those goods became available not only because of rising wages but also because American ideas of mass production and mass marketing began to spread in the Federal Republic as well as in other West European countries. With Fordist production and management techniques, Henry Ford's idea of passing a larger portion of the gains of factory rationalization on to the consumer in the shape of lower prices also took root.

## GROWTH OUTSIDE OF WEST GERMANY

The notion of a mass production and mass consumption society, as first more fully developed in the United States, also reached West Germany's neighbors at about the same time. In Britain during the 1950s boom, Prime Minister Harold Macmillan alleged that the population had "never had it so good." Following the catastrophe of fascism and the war, Italy, too, experienced something like an economic miracle. Living standards rose and there was a new sense of participation in material wealth, democratic politics, and cultural enjoyment. However, in Italy, as in other parts of the Mediterranean, the gap between rich and poor remained more marked because poverty was more regional and systemic. While the urban-industrial centers of northern Italy prospered, the rural-agricultural parts of the south, with their small-scale farming, remained economically more backward. Only when agriculture in the Mezzogiorno witnessed an exodus of migrants to the industrial north similar to the population movements in Germany and Britain in the nineteenth century did the economic miracle begin to reach ever larger numbers of Italians.

It took even longer for it to spread to Eastern Europe. Here the communist regimes, like their Western neighbors beyond the Iron Curtain, were publicly committed to creating a mass consumer society. But while there was some improvement in living standards, especially after the end of Stalinism, the rulers and their bureaucracies kept a tight political control not only over their populations but also over industrial production. Centralized, lumbering, and under the pressure to divert scarce resources into the military and the nuclear competition in which the communist bloc was engaged with the capitalist West and its hegemon, the United States, these regimes proved incapable of unleashing to the full the potential of modern Fordist mass production for civilian purposes. It was only after the collapse of communism in 1989–1990 and the advent of a competitive liberal capitalism of the kind that had emerged in Western Europe since 1945 that the societies of Eastern Europe also experienced something like an economic miracle, though perhaps a more modest one.

*See also* **Germany; Marshall Plan.**

BIBLIOGRAPHY

Ardagh, John. *The New France.* 3rd ed. Harmondsworth, U.K., 1977.

Di Nolfo, Ennio. *Power in Europe? Great Britain, France, Germany, and Italy and the Origins of the EEC, 1952–1957.* Berlin, 1992.

Geppert, Dominik, ed. *The Postwar Challenge: Cultural, Social, and Political Change in Western Europe, 1945–1958.* Oxford, U.K., 2003.

Hallett, Graham. *The Social Economy of West Germany.* London, 1973.

Junker, Detlef, ed. *The United States and Germany in the Era of the Cold War.* Vol. 1: *1945–1968.* New York, 2004.

Kramer, Alan. *The West German Economy: 1945–1955.* New York, 1991.

Leaman, Jeremy. *The Political Economy of West Germany, 1945–1985.* London, 1988.

Maier, Charles S. *Dissolution.* Princeton, N.J., 1997.

Moeller Robert G., ed. *West Germany under Construction.* Ann Arbor, Mich., 1997.

Schissler, Hanna, ed. *The Miracle Years: A Cultural History of West Germany, 1949–1968.* Princeton, N.J., 2001.

VOLKER R. BERGHAHN

**EDEN, ANTHONY** (1897–1977), British politician, served as prime minister from 1955 to 1957.

Eden was born on 12 June 1897 into a gentry family in County Durham. He went directly from school to serve on the western front in World War I, where he was awarded the Military Cross. He was elected Conservative member of Parliament (MP) for Warwick and Leamington in 1923, and was one of the talented young MPs who supported Stanley Baldwin's (1867–1947) moderate outlook. From 1926 to 1929, Eden served as parliamentary private secretary to the foreign secretary, and from this point onward his career was dominated by foreign affairs.

Eden was the junior minister at the Foreign Office from 1931 to 1933, and then given responsibility for relations with the League of Nations as lord privy seal, though outside the cabinet. In 1935 he was promoted to the cabinet as minister for League of Nations affairs, and became foreign secretary in December 1935 following the downfall of Sir Samuel John Gurney Hoare (1880–1959). For most of his first period as foreign secretary, Eden followed a course of moderate appeasement. He hoped for negotiations with Adolf Hitler (1889–1945), and when German forces remilitarized the Rhineland in March 1936 his reluctance to act restrained the French from anything more than diplomatic protest. When Neville Chamberlain (1869–1940) became prime minister in May 1937, frictions between them over the control and direction of foreign policy led to Eden's resignation in February 1938. The immediate cause was Chamberlain's desire to make concessions to Italy, and Eden's resistance made him seem an opponent of appeasement in general. Although this was hardly true, it was to be the making of his career and reputation.

When war came in September 1939, Eden accepted the post of dominions secretary, but was not a member of the war cabinet. In May 1940, Churchill appointed him secretary for war, and he oversaw the evacuation from Dunkirk and the preparations against invasion. As the "anti-appeasers" rose to dominance, Churchill was able to restore Eden to the post of foreign secretary in December 1940. This established him as Churchill's heir apparent and the second figure within the Conservative Party, although he would also have to wait patiently for his inheritance. Eden worked closely with Churchill during the war, providing important support and advice on strategic and policy issues as well as handling the detailed work of relations with Britain's allies.

When the Conservatives were defeated in the 1945 general election, it seemed likely that Churchill would soon make way for his younger colleague. In fact, it was to be a decade before Eden secured the top post, and by then many of his colleagues felt that he had passed his prime. From 1945 to 1951, Eden acted as leader of the opposition during Churchill's lengthy absences, and he played a key role in fostering a moderate and modern identity for the Conservative Party, popularizing the aim of creating a "property-owning democracy."

He served again as foreign secretary in Churchill's second ministry of 1951–1955, although their relations were marred by Churchill's repeated postponement of his oft-promised retirement. Eden had several successes in this period, including the 1954 Geneva Conference on Indochina and the resolution of German rearmament and entry into the North Atlantic Treaty Organization (NATO). Ironically, he also secured an agreement with the Egyptian government on the withdrawal of British forces from bases near the Suez Canal in 1954.

He finally became prime minister in April 1955 and called a general election in which the Conservatives increased their majority. Within a few months, matters had deteriorated and criticism of his performance was mounting. The defining event was the Suez crisis of 1956: as well as the importance of the Suez Canal route for Britain's oil supply, Eden saw parallels with the failure to resist Hitler in the 1930s. He accepted a French plan for military seizure of the canal in collusion with Israel, concealing this from the House of Commons and most of the cabinet. The Israeli attack upon Egypt was followed by the landing of Anglo-French forces near the canal on 5 November 1956. However, Eden had failed to inform the U.S. administration of his intentions or to consider its response, and this led to the collapse of his strategy. Within a few days, American refusal of economic aid forced Eden to halt operations and promise to withdraw; it was a national humiliation that revealed Britain's eclipse as an independent world power. Eden had been under mounting stress, and his health—permanently damaged by a botched operation in 1953—gave way. On 9 January 1957 he resigned as prime minister; he was created Earl of Avon in 1961 and died on 14 January 1977.

*See also* **Chamberlain, Neville; Churchill, Winston; Suez Crisis; United Kingdom.**

BIBLIOGRAPHY

*Primary Sources*

Eden, Anthony, Earl of Avon. *Full Circle: The Memoirs of Anthony Eden.* London, 1960. Memoirs that are selective and misleading on key aspects of the Suez crisis. Also available in three separate volumes, listed below:

———. *Facing the Dictators: The Memoirs of Anthony Eden.* London, 1962.

———. *The Reckoning: The Memoirs of Anthony Eden, Earl of Avon.* London, 1965.

———. *The Eden Memoirs: Another World, 1897–1917.* London, 1976. Slim but elegant account of his early life.

*Secondary Sources*

Carlton, David. *Anthony Eden: A Biography.* London, 1981. Very critical biography.

Dutton, David. *Anthony Eden: A Life and Reputation.* London, 1997. A judicious and balanced assessment.

James, Robert Rhodes. *Anthony Eden.* London, 1986. The original official life.

Thorpe, D. R. *Eden: The Life and Times of Anthony Eden, First Earl of Avon, 1897–1977.* London, 2003. Early twenty-first-century life authorized by Eden's widow.

STUART BALL

# EDUCATION.

**EDUCATION.** European countries have a long tradition of education; schools and universities have existed in Europe for more than eight centuries. Early formal schooling was provided by religious orders, as part of training for the priesthood, or for the sons of the wealthy. State funding for education followed, although attendance was initially subject to the payment of fees. By 1914, compulsory, free elementary education was virtually universal throughout the twenty-five countries that comprised the European Union (EU) in the early twenty-first century: Austria, Belgium, Cyprus, the Czech Republic, Denmark, Estonia, Finland, France, Germany, Greece, Hungary, Ireland, Italy, Latvia, Lithuania, Luxembourg, Malta, the Netherlands, Poland, Portugal, Spain, the Slovak Republic, Slovenia, Sweden, and the United Kingdom.

The period since 1914 has seen very different political and economic developments, not least the occupation by—and subsequent liberation from—totalitarian regimes, which affected virtually all of Europe. Although all systems have been subject to increasingly frequent reforms, there are similarities in the patterns of control, structure, curriculum, and assessment, and evidence of convergence over time.

This article summarizes the key characteristics of the educational systems of the twenty-five EU countries in the early twenty-first century and explores the factors influencing convergence, namely, a shared heritage, common challenges, and, in particular, the increasingly powerful role played by the European Union.

## THE EDUCATION SYSTEMS

It should be noted that, for historic political reasons, in Belgium, Germany, and the United Kingdom, there are multiple education systems. The Flemish-, French-, and German-speaking communities in Belgium control separate (albeit similar) education systems for their respective areas. Each of the sixteen *Länder* (states) in Germany exercises autonomous power over the school system in its jurisdiction. As a result, there are differences, for example, in the duration of compulsory education and the ways in which schools are organized. Within the United Kingdom, Scotland has always exercised control over its education system. U.K. education legislation applied to England, Wales, and Northern Ireland until 1999, when the Welsh and Northern Ireland Assemblies gained devolved powers over education in their respective areas.

Despite the competition—and even wars—between nations, European education systems share many common characteristics.

***Aims and priorities*** The aims and priorities expressed in national documentation focus particularly on participation, learning experiences, and outcomes.

The first objective is to ensure that all young people participate actively in their education, during the compulsory phase and beyond. Yet, despite the high levels of investment, disaffection among secondary school students leads to disengagement and truancy, and up to 30 percent of students leave school without having satisfactorily completed compulsory education.

In terms of learning experiences and outcomes, education aims to enable young people to:

- master the basic skills of literacy and numeracy and demonstrate confident use of information and communication technologies and, in virtually all countries, at least one foreign language;
- lay the foundations for lifelong learning by developing the dispositions, motivation, and skills to learn, and to find, select, critically evaluate, and use information;
- develop the capacity to solve problems creatively and to work independently and with others, in preparation for (self-)employment;
- develop a shared knowledge of the histories, heritage, and values of the different groups in society, so that they can participate as active, informed and responsible citizens within a diverse (European) community.

**Policy and control** Initially under church control, education became a matter of state policy in Europe during the twentieth and twenty-first centuries.

**The role of the churches** The earliest "schools" were established by the (Christian) churches, initially to train clerics and subsequently to provide education for the sons of the wealthy. Nondenominational schools quickly followed—still for privileged boys—to promote literacy. The role of churches diminished over time. The role of the church and the state were separated in Finland (1869), France (1905), and Czechoslovakia (1948), and church schools were absorbed into the state-funded system (usually subject to their being allowed to continue to offer religious instruction) in England, Scotland, and Ireland.

In the Netherlands, the unequal treatment of public schools (founded by the municipality or the state) and private schools (founded by churches and other independent bodies) led to the so-called schools dispute, a political battle to achieve complete equality under the law for both types of school. Catholics and Protestants wanted their own schools with a pronounced Roman Catholic or Protestant stamp but with equal state funding. The Liberals, too, wanted the freedom of education guaranteed by the constitution to be reflected in equal financial treatment of public and private schools. The battle, which raged from the middle of the nineteenth century, was finally settled in the 1917 amendment to the constitution, in what is known as the Pacification of 1917. After 1917, the principle of financial equality was extended to secondary and higher education. There are now nearly twice as many privately run as state-run schools.

In Belgium, the inclusion of freedom of education in the 1831 Constitution has been the cause of much conflict and struggle. Educational establishments may not be subjected to any restrictive measure, and schools can be established without being in any way connected with the official authorities. Private schools, however, must satisfy certain criteria in order to receive state funding and to have the qualifications they award formally recognized.

In Northern Ireland, integrated schools have been established for children of both Roman Catholic and Protestant families, specifically to promote mutual understanding and reduce the tensions between these religious communities.

Religious values are reflected in curricula in different ways. For example, in France (except Alsace and Lorraine, which were under German control) religious instruction is banned in state schools. In the United Kingdom, religious education is a compulsory part of the curriculum, although parents can apply to have their children excused.

**The role of the state** In the early twenty-first century, education policy, structure, and financing are determined at national level, except in Germany, where responsibility for school education lies with the sixteen *Länder*, and Belgium, where responsibility lies with the three (Flemish-, French-, and German-speaking) communities.

Administration may be decentralized, whereby central policies are locally implemented without discretion (for example, in France) or devolved, whereby regional, district, or municipal authorities enjoy differing degrees of discretion. For example, the *Länder* in Germany have full devolved powers to determine funding, structure, curriculum, and inspection arrangements, while the Autonomous Communities in Spain can exercise some discretion within central policies and guidelines.

Since the early 1980s, European education has seen a tendency toward devolving financial, managerial, and curricular responsibility to schools (at the expense of local authorities' powers), within a framework of externally determined outcome targets, assessment, and inspection. School governing bodies or boards, especially in Belgium, England, Ireland, Italy, Malta, the Netherlands, and Wales, have considerable autonomy. Elsewhere (in Denmark, Portugal, the Slovak Republic, and Slovenia), they enjoy less autonomy or may have a purely advisory role. In both cases, they serve as a focal point for parental and community views.

***Duration and structure of compulsory education*** Virtually all the education systems in Europe had instituted compulsory education, at least for the primary years, by the beginning of World War I. Compulsory education, however, was not always free. For example, education was made compulsory in 1869 in Hungary, but was not free until 1908, and in Scotland the relevant dates were 1872 and 1890. The duration of compulsory education also varied, ranging from two years in Italy (1877, extended to eight years in 1948), through four years in Portugal (from 1956 for boys and 1960 for girls, extended to six years in 1974), to eight years in Czechoslovakia (1869), Slovakia (1927), and Spain (1931), and nine years in England (1870) and Luxembourg (1912).

During the twentieth century the period of compulsory education—whether at school or elsewhere—was extended so that it now starts between the ages of four and six and lasts between nine and twelve years. Preschool classes, although not compulsory (except in Hungary, Latvia, and Luxembourg) are attended by the vast majority of children.

Two main models of provision exist for compulsory education:

- The "single structure" model aims to avoid the transition between schools during the compulsory phase and is common in the Czech Republic, Denmark, Estonia, Finland, Hungary, Latvia, Portugal, the Slovak Republic, Slovenia, and Sweden. The school may have a lower and upper division, to reflect differences in the content and organization of the curriculum. Students leaving compulsory education progress to upper-secondary education, vocational training, or employment.

- The two-tier structure (prevailing in Austria, Belgium, Cyprus, France, Germany, Greece, Ireland, Italy, Lithuania, Luxembourg, Malta, the Netherlands, Poland, Spain, and the United Kingdom) involves a transfer from primary to secondary education, usually around age ten to twelve. Some schools cater to students over compulsory school age, but in other cases, students transfer again to upper-secondary or vocational education.

In most countries, compulsory education was provided in elementary schools; secondary education was restricted to an elite minority. This restriction was usually imposed by means of fees, although scholarships were available (for example, in England and Northern Ireland) for students who showed exceptional ability. Intelligence testing was used from early in the twentieth century onward to identify those suitable for academic education.

As (lower-) secondary education became compulsory for all (starting from the middle of the twentieth century), separate schools or tracks were established to provide general education (preuniversity academic and less advanced general courses), technical education, and vocational courses. This stratification was intended to meet the perceived needs of future leaders of society, workers, and housewives and mothers, respectively. The trend to early specialization was based on an assumption of inherent aptitude—or lack of it.

"Grammar" schools, which stressed the classics, the sciences, and theoretic knowledge, were to prepare the future leaders. Admission was often controlled by means of entrance examinations, and students were expected to continue their studies beyond the statutory school-leaving age to secure the qualifications necessary for admission to higher education. The Nordic countries tended to defer specialization to the postcompulsory (upper-secondary) phase.

**TABLE 1**

### Duration and structure of compulsory education

| | Start | Total Full-time | Total Part-time | Pre-school | Primary | Lower Secondary | Upper Secondary |
|---|---|---|---|---|---|---|---|
| Austria | 6 | 9 | | | Yr 1-4 | Yr 5-8 | Yr 9-12 |
| Belgium | 6 | 9[1] | 3 | | Yr 1-6 | Yr 7-10 | Yr 11-12 |
| Cyprus | 6 | 9 | | | Yr 1-6 | Yr 7-9 | Yr 10-12 |
| Czech Rep. | 6 | 9 | | | Yr 1-5 | Yr 6-9 | Yr 10-13 |
| Denmark | 7 | 9 | | | Yr 1-9 | | Yr 10-12 |
| Estonia | 7 | 9[2] | | | Yr 1-9 | | Yr 10-12 |
| Finland | 7 | 9 | | | Yr 1-9 | | Yr 10-12 |
| France | 6 | 10 | | | Yr 1-5 | Yr 6-9 | Yr 10-12 |
| Germany | 6 | 9/10 | 3 | | Yr 1-4 (or 1-6)[3] | Yr 5-9 (or 7-9) | Yr 10-12 |
| Greece | 6 | 9? | | | Yr 1-6 | Yr 7-9 | Yr 10-12 |
| Hungary | 5 | 1+10[4] | | 1 yr | Yr 1-8 | | Yr 9-12 |
| Ireland | 6 | 9 | | | Yr 1-6 | Yr 7-9 | Yr 10-12 |
| Italy | 6 | 9 | | | Yr 1-5 | Yr 6-8 | Yr 9-12 |
| Latvia | 5 | 2+9[5] | | 2 yrs | Yr 1-9 | | Yr 10-12 |
| Lithuania | 6/7 | 10 | | | Yr 1-4 | Yr 5-8 | Yr 9-12 |
| Luxemburg | 4 | 2+10 | | 2 yrs | Yr | Yr | Yr 10-13 |
| Malta | 5 | 10 | | | Yr 1-6 | Yr 7-11 | Yr 12-13 |
| Netherlands | 5 | 12 | 1-2 | | Yr 1-8 | Yr 9-11 | Yr 12-14 |
| Poland | 7 | 9[6] | | | Yr 1-6 | Yr 7-9 | Yr 10-12 |
| Portugal | 6 | 9[7] | | | Yr 1-9 | | Yr 10-12 |
| Slovak Rep. | 6 | 10 | | | Yr 1-9 | | Yr 10-12/13 |
| Slovenia | 6 | 8[8] | | | Yr 1-8 | | Yr 10-12 |
| Spain | 3 | 10 | | | Yr 1-6 | Yr 7-10 | Yr 11-12 |
| Sweden | 7 | 9 | | | Yr 1-9 | | Yr 10-12 |
| UK (England, Wales) | 5 | 11 | | | Yr 1-6 | Yr 7-11 | Yr 12-13 |
| UK (Scot) | 5 | 11 | | | Yr 1-7 | Yr 8-11 | Yr 12-13 |
| UK (N.Ireland) | 4 | 12 | | | Yr 1-7 | Yr 8-12 | Yr 13-14 |

[1] Students must complete Year 2 of secondary education. Those who achieve this after eight years may transfer to other types of education.

[2] Those who have not completed the ninth year must stay at school for a further year.

[3] Different transfer ages apply in different Länder.

[4] To be extended by two years for students starting school from 1998.

[5] Those who have not completed the ninth year must stay at school until they do, or until they are 18.

[6] Those who have not completed the ninth year must stay at school until they do, or until they are 18.

[7] There are proposals to extend this to twelve years.

[8] Nine years, phased in for students starting school from 1999/2000.

Technical schools emerged from the strong tradition of apprenticeships and guilds. These offered training for young people (especially boys) for technical and manual occupations. In Italy, for example, there were separate secondary schools offering courses (from age fourteen) in the classics, the humanities, and the sciences (leading to university education); technical schools; vocational schools; training for nursery and primary school teachers; and fine art schools offering early specialization. Indeed, until the 1960s or beyond, primary school teachers in many countries were trained in "secondary" schools.

A third category—general schools—emerged to provide for those deemed to be unsuited for either academic or technical education. These were sometimes designated as "extended primary" schools.

Two factors have led to the widespread adoption of all-ability (lower-) secondary education since the early 1960s. First, institutional differentiation in terms of status and funding led to calls for more egalitarian provision, and second, a higher level of basic education is required to meet the demands of a more highly mechanized and computerized society. During the second half of the twentieth century stratification was deferred until the upper-secondary phase in all countries except Austria, Belgium, the Czech Republic, Germany, Luxembourg, the Netherlands, and Northern Ireland. But results from the Organisation for Economic Co-operation and Development's Programme for International Student Assessment demonstrate that the gap between the best and weakest students tends to be wider in countries with differentiated systems. This finding may lead to a review of these structures.

***Curriculum*** Curricula that prescribe the aims and desired outcomes for each educational phase, the subjects to be studied, and the amount of time to be allocated to each, exist in virtually all countries to safeguard students' entitlement, to allow for mobility between schools, and, more recently, to facilitate a degree of local responsiveness or specialization.

Two countries provide examples of the ebb and flow of control. In the United Kingdom, religious education was the only compulsory subject until 1988. The national curriculum introduced that year in England, Wales, and Northern Ireland was very detailed, and proved to be unmanageable. (There is no compulsory curriculum in Scotland, although guidelines exist for all subject areas.) Successive reductions in prescription have culminated in "Curriculum 2000," a framework that sets a compulsory entitlement to learning for all students (aged five to sixteen years) in terms of content, attainment targets for learning, and requirements for the assessment and reporting of performance, but that gives schools discretion regarding the detailed content, timetable, teaching methods, and materials. In a contrasting example, the government in power in Italy in 2003 increased centralized control over the curriculum, thereby reversing its predecessor's trend toward devolving responsibility in these matters.

The status and political ideology of countries affect their approaches to the curriculum. The reestablishment of nation-states (for example, the unification of Italy in 1871; the unification of the Czech and Slovak lands and the Transcarpathian Ukraine into Czechoslovakia in 1918; the liberation from foreign occupation of Lithuania in 1918; and the liberation of the territories occupied by the USSR) was accompanied by education systems that sought to establish a sense of nationhood in the different territories brought together or to "replace the alien cultural foundations with its own." In these cases, the use of the national language and inculcation of the culture(s) were crucial.

Dictatorships and foreign occupations sought to impose particular ideologies and structures. Examples include the emphasis on Catholic and patriotic values during the regime of Francisco Franco in Spain, and the centralization and Russification of the territories incorporated into the USSR after World War II.

The education systems of these latter countries (Czechoslovakia, Estonia, the German Democratic Republic, Hungary, Latvia, Lithuania, and Poland) were subjected to a strict control of the Communist Party and central power, and therefore autonomy on the school level was minimal. Education was aimed at glorifying the Soviet Union and at educating pupils for the benefit of the collective Soviet nation; the development of individual abilities was encouraged only if it had potential value for the Soviet system. Regulations issued by the party and the government were the supreme guidelines in designing the education system, dictating the operation of education institutions and the organization of instructional work in schools. Schools worked on the basis of a statute approved by the USSR Council of Ministers, and the Ministry of Education of the individual Soviet republics established the foundations for educational and instructional work in general schools; approved syllabuses, curricula, and statutes of instructional work organization in schools; and gave specifications and orders to direct the schools' activities and performance of tasks.

Despite the ideological pressure and restrictions set, some differences were maintained, especially in Estonia, Latvia, and Lithuania. In Estonia, for example, Estonian was retained as a language of instruction, alongside Russian; textbooks were written in Estonian by Estonian authors; the syllabus of upper-secondary schools was longer by one year—providing eleven years; and the volume of studies in some subjects differed. In Latvia, some schools still provided some "nationally oriented" education with Latvian language of instruction. In Lithuania, despite the intensive process of russification, the national cultural resistance continued. A network of secret Lithuanian schools operated for forty years. Training at these schools was very poor, but they offered an opportunity to study, and they encouraged interest in reading the illegal Lithuanian press. In terms of education, these small schools played a unique role in promoting the patriotism of the people and expanding their experience.

In early-twenty-first-century Europe, the areas of "essential" learning are remarkably consistent, namely: national and regional language(s) and literature, mathematics, science, information technology, technology, the humanities (history, geography, social studies), physical education and health, the arts (fine arts, music, dance, drama), citizenship, and moral or religious education. The place of foreign languages is particularly interesting. Although member states may have resisted the intervention of the European Community in their school curriculum, "foreign" occupation, proximity to a border, and the size of a country has led to the teaching of more than one language. Foreign languages are compulsory in virtually all countries (often from primary school), and most schools teach a second foreign language. English is the most popular choice, probably because it is the principal language of the entertainment industry and the Internet.

For a number of reasons, however, foreign languages are less widely studied in some parts of the United Kingdom and Ireland. First, students in Ireland and Wales are required to learn Irish and Welsh, respectively (in addition to English), and these are not classed as foreign languages. Second, the prevalence of English speakers reduces the motivation of students, and there is no obvious "first" foreign language for them to learn. Finally, a serious shortage of foreign-language teachers in England and Wales made it impossible to implement the requirement for compulsory foreign-language teaching to all students aged eleven to sixteen. Despite several government initiatives to encourage the teaching and learning of foreign languages, many students in the United Kingdom lag behind their continental peers in this area.

The school timetable is generally organized by subject or subject areas. Concern about students' failure to transfer knowledge and skills across subject boundaries and the need for higher-order skills for employment in a "knowledge society" are leading to a greater emphasis on the understanding, evaluation, and application of knowledge in different contexts. Learning outcomes are therefore increasingly expressed in terms of key skills such as communication, problem solving, creativity, cooperative working, and the appropriate use of new technologies.

*Assessment* Diagnostic assessment takes place regularly as part of the teaching and learning process in all countries, and periodic tests provide a summative record of student progress. Grades are based on classroom participation, homework, extended projects, tests, and end of term/year examinations. Many countries have official grading schemes and performance criteria, and all the teachers of a school-year group collectively determine whether a student has mastered the knowledge and skills required for promotion to the next class. Internal school grades are used to award school-leaving certificates (in fifteen countries) and upper-secondary qualifications (in ten countries). The remaining countries require students to take an externally set examination.

The use of high-stakes, external assessment of student performance as an indicator of the quality of schools and the education system is not widespread in the EU. Samples of the school population are assessed in Hungary (throughout compulsory education) and Spain (at ages 12 and 16), and standardized assessment is compulsory for all students in England (at ages 7, 11, and 14), France (ages 8 and 11), and Wales (ages 11 and 14). The results of standardized assessments are published in England (by school) and in France and Spain (anonymously). Standardized assessment is optional in Ireland, the Netherlands, and Sweden.

## INFLUENCES ON CONVERGENCE

Factors that have most influenced the convergence of European education systems are heritage, political and ideological values, economic and technological change, social change, and international "competition."

*Heritage* Geographical, political, and linguistic boundaries have shifted as a result of colonization, invasion, and wars. This may result in shared or "inherited" aspects of control and provision. The thirty countries described herein have experienced numerous geographical and political changes. The following serve as examples:

- Finland was ruled by Sweden for four hundred years, then Russia for one hundred years, before gaining independence in 1917. Finland joined the EU in 1995.

- Poland was successively invaded by the Swedes and Turks; suffered partition by the Russians, Prussians, and Austrians; was annexed by the German Third Reich; and then fell under the USSR's sphere of influence (until 1989). Lithuania united with Poland (as self-governing partners) in the eighteenth century and subsequently followed the fate of Poland. Both countries joined the EU in 2004.

- Slovakia has been, successively, part of Hungary, Czechoslovakia, and the USSR (until 1989). It joined the EU in 2004.

- Slovenia sought—unsuccessfully—to unite the Slovenes, Croats, and Serbs occupying Habsburg lands as a new nation in 1918. To resist further territorial raids by Italy, Slovenia became part of Yugoslavia in 1929. World War II saw Yugoslavia divided between Germany, Italy, and Hungary. Following the Yugoslav resistance and the break with Soviet Union (1948), a milder version of socialism, based on common ownership and self-management, was established. Slovenia achieved independence in 1991 and joined the EU in 2004.

While the Swedish and Russian occupations do not appear to have had a negative influence on the education system of Finland, the same cannot be said for the political changes that affected the other three examples cited above.

Invading powers and totalitarian regimes have used education to influence and control behavior and thought (or at least the expression of thought) by means of the form and content of education and, in many cases, the medium of instruction. Hence, several countries have more than one official language (for example, Belgium, Ireland, Luxembourg, Malta, and Wales), and the languages of former regimes may continue to be taught because of the prevalence of their use (for example, Russian in Estonia). Regions that were absorbed into nation-states or kingdoms have vigorously defended their right to retain their language (for example, Flemish in Belgium, Friesian in the Netherlands, Catalan and Basque in Spain, and Welsh in Wales).

***Challenges*** When governments identify economic and social problems, they often attribute the cause to education systems, which therefore undergo frequent reforms. The speed and nature of changes has increased during the past century as a result of a number of factors.

***Political and ideological values*** Following the introduction of universal suffrage, governments have had to take account of a wider range of expectations. The approach of elections therefore stimulates a rethinking of education policies so that values, their interpretation, and their enactment match the perceived preferences of the electorate. Thus, systems that offer differentiated provisions intended to meet the needs of different groups (as in the selective secondary education systems common during the middle of the twentieth century) are replaced by those that stress a common, equal entitlement for all.

In the past, education was respected as an unquestioned public good, whose aims, nature, and resources were centrally determined. As indicated above, some schools exercise devolved responsibility for school governance and management and have developed particular curricular or philosophical approaches, to raise student achievement. Indeed, in a few countries, an education "market" is developing, as parents are encouraged to express a preference, and schools compete to attract students and the funding that accompanies their enrollment. Such competition is intended to "drive up standards." Within a market model, however, it may be difficult to manage demands and expectations on the one hand, and the individual actions of providers (schools) on the other, and there are cases in which parents or students seek legal redress and compensation for perceived inadequacies of the system.

***Economic and technological change*** Advances in information and communications technology enable people to do more, faster, more cheaply, and from a distance. Many routine jobs are computerized, and higher-order skills are required from those seeking employment. As a result, career paths become fragmented, and those unable or unwilling to update their skills may become unemployable. In this context, education must

- be overtly "relevant" both in the eyes of students (to reduce the dropout rate and disengagement from the learning process) and of employers (who complain that young people are ill-equipped for employment);

- incorporate new approaches in the teaching and learning process, with the emphasis moving from learning facts to the selection, evaluation, and application of knowledge and skills; and

- change the focus from one-off, standardized initial education and training to flexible and lifelong learning.

*Social change* At the turn of the twentieth century, European societies were largely rural, predominantly Christian, and relatively homogenous. Subsequently, mobility within Europe—stimulated by political unrest, persecution, or pursuit of higher living standards—and immigration from beyond its borders have created heterogeneous societies that must recognize, tolerate, and accommodate differences in culture, religion, language, and traditions. Compulsory education, therefore, has to find a balance between transmitting the traditional or predominant culture, and raising awareness and understanding of the diversity within the community and beyond. Education systems are also expected to secure economic and social advancement for the individual and for society as a whole.

*International "competition"* Education policy is increasingly seen in a global context, with outcomes expressed in terms of "world-class" benchmarks, as policy makers assess the performance of their students relative to those in other countries. For example, between thirty and forty countries worldwide participate in international surveys and education databases and studies that compare education systems and outcomes. Pressure to overcome perceived deficiencies weighs particularly heavily on governments, which seek to demonstrate achievements within three- to five-year electoral cycles. This may lead to ad hoc policy changes, which may be neither feasible, nor even desirable, given the social, cultural, and educational context and the long-term educational aims in the country concerned.

The elements assessed in international surveys reflect the collective—but not necessarily the individual—priorities of the participating countries. Thus, as each new survey is reported, changes are introduced to compensate for perceived national deficiencies, and priorities are realigned. For example, the findings of the 1995 Third International Mathematics and Science Study caused England to change the focus of mathematics teaching from higher-order skills to basic computation (in which students from, in particular, Singapore and Hungary outperformed those from England). Subsequently, the Programme for International Student Assessment for 2000 focused on "young people's capacity to use their knowledge and skills in order to meet real-life challenges, rather than merely looking at how well they had mastered a specific school curriculum," which redirected attention to higher-order skills. This focus has given rise to growing curricular emphasis on core or transferable skills and independent learning. Yet, it may be difficult for teachers who were trained and spent much of their professional life under totalitarian regimes to model and encourage open-ended, autonomous learning.

A further example of the influence of international surveys is the possible introduction of national standards in core subjects for school leavers in Germany, in apparent contravention of educational autonomy accorded to the *Länder* by the constitution.

*The emerging European response* During the second half of the twentieth century there emerged an understandable desire to avoid a repeat of the devastation caused within this small continent by the two world wars. The early steps focused on economic cooperation and a common market allowing free movement of individuals, goods, and services. The contribution of vocational training to enhancing mobility was recognized as crucial and therefore a "legitimate" concern of the emerging European Economic Community (EEC). Hence, the Treaty of Rome (1957), which established the EEC, proposed a common policy on vocational training (Article 128), in pursuit of improved living and working conditions (Article 117), cooperation with respect to the initial training and ongoing development of professionals (Article 118), and the guarantee of free movement, nondiscrimination, and the mutual recognition of qualifications (Article 57). Higher education was included under the umbrella of "vocational education" but—possibly understandably, given the Continent's history—all external intervention in education was rigorously resisted, on the grounds that it was, and should remain, a matter of national sovereignty.

There are tensions between retaining national sovereignty over the transmission of values, heritage, and culture, and a willingness to accept common education and training objectives, and to support collective programs and initiatives, with a view to enhancing economic strength and social and political harmony. Nevertheless, in 1992, thirty-five years after the signing of the Treaty of Rome, member states agreed to include education as a legitimate area for community policy. This was achieved through a four-pronged action plan:

1. the establishment of a legal basis and administrative structures
2. the dissemination of information on education systems and policies
3. the creation of programs to support cooperation between institutions, teachers, and students
4. the development of education policies that contribute to the achievement of European economic, social, and political objectives.

***Legal basis and supporting structures*** In 1974 the (nine) ministers of education adopted a Resolution—a voluntary commitment, with no legislative power—that set the ground rules for cooperation and established the Education Committee. The Resolution recognized the different educational policies and structures and acknowledged that their harmonization could not be an explicit objective. Starting in 1978, the Education Committee, comprising civil servants from all member states, met regularly to discuss matters of common interest and prepare for the biennial meetings of the ministers of education in council. The European Commission provided the secretariat.

An administrative support structure was gradually built by bringing together the (separate) education and training divisions within the Directorate-General V (Employment, Social Affairs and Education) in 1981. In 1989 a Task Force on Human Resources, Education, Training and Youth was established; it achieved the status of a Directorate-General (XII) in 1995, and was redesignated the Directorate-General Education and Culture (incorporating culture and audiovisual media) in 1999.

Careful progress, by means of exchange of information and a series of Community Programmes to promote voluntary cooperation, prepared member states to open up aspects of their education policy to cross-national and EC involvement. A watershed was reached in 1992 with the signing of the Treaty on European Union. Article 126 of the treaty formally recognized the importance of education in the creation of a single Europe and assigned to the European Commission the role of supporting and complementing this work. However, the principle of added value and subsidiarity restricted the commission's involvement to those actions collectively approved by member states and that added value to national initiatives. Crucially, the Act respected member states' responsibility for the content and organization of education and for cultural and linguistic diversity; all harmonization of education systems was excluded.

***Exchange of information and study visits*** In 1976 the ministers of education identified the collection of documentation and statistics as a priority action. Eurydice, the European education information network, became operational in 1980 and provided a question-and-answer service, primarily for educational policy makers. In this way it was hoped that national education policy would take account of good practice elsewhere. By 1990, the network had produced detailed descriptions of the education systems, and its primary role became the preparation of comparative studies (1992) and indicators (1994) to support the work of the Education Committee. The Eurydice network was enlarged to include thirty countries in 1996, and participation in the network served as an introduction to cooperation within the EU framework for countries that were candidates for admission into the EU.

A program of study visits (later named Arion) was instituted to bring together senior school staff, regional policy makers, inspectors and other professionals from several member states. Each visit focused on a specific aspect of education (for example, teacher training in Finland, or special educational needs provision in Italy), but participants invariably broadened their discussions to include general priorities and issues in their respective countries. The number of participants grew from eighty-five in 1978 to twenty-one hundred in 2005.

The National Academic Recognition Information Centres (NARIC) were set up in 1984 to advise higher education institutions and students on the recognition of courses of study and qualifications.

***Actions and programs*** The first Resolution adopted by the ministers of education (1976) identified six priority actions. But the lack of a legal basis paralyzed action for three years (1978–1980), and proposals relating to the introduction of a European dimension in secondary education, the teaching of foreign languages, the admission of students to higher education institutions in other EEC member states, and equal opportunities for girls in education and vocational training, were blocked. Nevertheless, the Resolution gave rise to some transnational pilot projects and laid the groundwork for Eurydice and Arion.

During the 1980s, the member states agreed to finance a series of Programmes to support and facilitate cooperation in priority areas. The main education Programmes were Erasmus (student mobility and cooperation between universities) and Lingua (the development of foreign language teaching). After the signing of the Maastricht Treaty (1992), the education Programmes were reorganized as elements of the Socrates program and expanded for a second phase of funding (1995–1999). New actions were added to support secondary school cooperation and exchange (Comenius), open and distance learning, and adult education. These programs were progressively opened to participants from the nations that joined the EU in 2004: Cyprus, the Czech Republic, Estonia, Hungary, Latvia, Lithuania, Malta, Poland, the Slovak Republic, and Slovenia.

The programs were extended for a third phase (2000–2006), and a fourth phase (2007–2013), as of 2006 still being planned, aimed to bring together Socrates and the former vocational training program (Leonardo da Vinci) into a single "lifelong learning" program. Funding increased tenfold from 0.1 percent of the community budget (in 1986) to more than 1 percent for the fourth phase.

***Development of policy*** Article 126 of the Maastricht Treaty provided the legislative basis for the European Commission to make policy proposals in the field of education for consideration by member states. Accordingly, the EC published a series of papers stressing the important role of education and training systems in the development of a single Europe; the need for systems to adapt to meet the challenges of globalization; the information society, and the scientific and technical developments; and the importance of lifelong learning and the creation of a knowledge society.

The four-pronged action plan has led—surprisingly quickly—to the development of shared aims and indicators, and agreed-upon monitoring processes to create a European educational space in both the university and school sectors, known as the Bologna Process and the Lisbon Strategy, respectively.

***The Bologna Process*** In 1998 the education ministers called for the harmonization of higher education structures, to make the sector more comparable and competitive and to create a "European higher education space." The resulting Bologna Process involves thirty countries in the convergence of higher education systems. It builds on, and is supported by, a number of established initiatives: Erasmus, NARIC, transferable credit units of study (ECTS), and the Internet Portal on Learning Opportunities throughout the European Space (Ploteus). The Erasmus Mundus program aims to make higher education in Europe (and not only in the United Kingdom, France, and Germany) more attractive to students from within and beyond the European Union by offering a cross-national master's degree involving study at two or more of three participating institutions, drawn from three countries.

***The Lisbon Strategy*** The Lisbon Strategy, proposed by the education ministers in 1999, aims to make Europe the most competitive knowledge economy, by modernizing and harmonizing education and training systems to achieve "world-class" standing by 2010. The strategy comprises the adoption of the (first) EC framework of common benchmarks, together with an implementation program and agreed-upon monitoring and reporting procedures. Because it aims to promote the exchange of good practice, the development of indicators to measure progress, and peer review, the so-called open method of coordination goes far beyond the "rolling agenda" that ministers had originally envisaged. This was not achieved without reservations on the part of some member states, who did not wish their policies to be so closely aligned with that of other countries. The method nevertheless has enormous potential for a higher shared quality and efficiency of education and training systems in Europe, while respecting the principle of subsidiarity.

The process depends heavily, however, on the ability and willingness of individual member states to adopt the common objectives at a national level. Interim progress reviews conducted in 2003 and 2004 reveal that, despite widespread reforms in all countries, progress toward the creation of a knowledge society is lagging behind that of major international competitors, and national investment in human resources is deemed inadequate to meet the challenge. The Education Council and the EC therefore called on member states to make greater and more efficient efforts and investments to implement global and coherent lifelong education and training strategies and to develop a knowledge society and a European education and training space. The qualifications framework and the European dimension in education are seen as especially important.

**CONCLUSION**

The diverse political, economic, and social contexts of the participating countries mean that the objectives set for the Bologna Process and the Lisbon Strategy are ambitious. Member states resist what they perceive as unreasonable pressure from the center, as the rejection of the proposed European Constitution by France and the Netherlands in 2005 shows. Nevertheless, educational cooperation in Europe has come a very long way since the 1950s, and, provided that the spirit, as well as the letter, of subsidiarity is respected, the omens for increasing cooperation are very positive.

*See also* **Child Care; Childhood and Adolescence; Citizenship; Welfare State**

BIBLIOGRAPHY

European Commission. Eurydice. "Eurybase." Available at http://www.eurydice.org.

Organisation for Economic Co-operation and Development (OECD). "Programme for International Student Assessment." Available at http://www.pisa.oecd.org.

———. *Problem Solving for Tomorrow's World: First Measures of Cross-Curricular Competencies from PISA 2003.* Paris, 2004. Also available at http://www.pisa.oecd.org.

———. *Education at a Glance, 2005.* Paris, 2005.

Pépin, Luce. *Histoire de la coopération européenne dans le domaine de l'éducation et de la formation.* Luxembourg, 2006.

JOANNA LE MÉTAIS

**EDWARD VIII** (1894–1972), king of Great Britain, Ireland, and the British dominions, and emperor of India.

Edward was born in Richmond, Surrey on 23 June 1894, the first child of the duke and duchess of York (later King George V [r. 1910–1936] and Queen Mary [1867–1953]). He was also known as Prince Edward, Duke of Windsor, and in full, Edward Albert Christian George Andrew Patrick David.

With the death of Edward VII (r. 1901–1910) and the accession of his father on 6 May 1910, Prince Edward (as he was officially known) became heir to the throne. On his sixteenth birthday he was created Prince of Wales. After a stint as midshipman with the Royal Navy, he matriculated in October 1912 at the University of Oxford. He left university at the start of the war in 1914 and was commissioned in the Grenadier Guards on the Continent but did not see direct action. In civilian life, Prince Edward was noted for his charm, good looks, romantic liaisons, and unconventional wearing of hats. He became a leader of fashionable London society and something of a modern celebrity.

In January 1931 the prince met Wallis Simpson (1896–1986), an American citizen then living in London with her second husband. By 1934 the prince had cast aside his other lovers and saw in Mrs. Simpson his natural life partner.

George V died on 20 January 1936, and the Prince of Wales was proclaimed King Edward VIII on 21 January. Once on the throne, Edward VIII showed a marked indifference toward public affairs and the intricacies of state business.

Prime Minister Stanley Baldwin (1867–1947) belatedly learned of the king's hopes to marry Mrs. Simpson, who had begun divorce proceedings against her second husband. By early November,

Baldwin's cabinet was discussing the constitutional problem of a king's potential marriage to a divorcée. For many ministers, the Simpson affair illuminated wider uncertainties about Edward's competency to be king. Public opinion was strongly hostile to the marriage, and he faced opposition from both the Church of England and Parliament.

On 10 December, the king signed the instrument of abdication and left for Europe the next day. Edward VIII is the only British monarch ever to have resigned the crown. His reign lasted from 20 January to 10 December 1936—327 days—the shortest of any recognized monarch since Edward V (r. 1483). George VI (r. 1936–1952) then titled him "his royal highness the duke of Windsor."

The Windsors married in France on 3 June 1937. No member of the duke's family attended. Though a duchess, his wife was denied the prefix Her Royal Highness, to the duke's great disappointment.

In October 1937 they visited Germany. The Windsors were honored by Nazi officials and met Adolf Hitler (1889–1945); the duke reportedly made a modified Nazi salute and on two other occasions a full Nazi salute. As a Nazi sympathizer, the Duke of Windsor may have entertained thoughts of becoming an alternative monarch should Britain be defeated by Hitler. Evidence suggests the Germans expected that the duke would inaugurate an "English form of Fascism and alliance with Germany." He was doubtful about Britain's ability to withstand a German attack in 1940 and favored a negotiated peace with Hitler.

When war began, the Windsors were returned to Britain from France. George VI did not appreciate the duke's presence in the United Kingdom. The duke shortly afterward became a member of the British military mission in France and served as a major-general for the duration of the war.

Upon the fall of France in June 1940, the Windsors escaped to Madrid, where Edward was part of a fanciful plan of the Nazis to remake him king and to use him against the established government in England. He moved to Lisbon at the start of July. From his friend Winston Churchill (1874–1965), now prime minister, the duke was offered the governorship of the Bahamas.

He and his wife arrived in Nassau on 17 August 1940. The duke worked on policies for agricultural

Former king Edward VIII of England with his wife, Wallis Warfield Simpson, on their wedding day, 3 June 1937. ©BETTMANN/CORBIS

improvement, to diminish black unemployment, and helped quell riots in June 1942. Unsatisfied with his lot, he resigned as governor of the Bahamas on 16 March 1945. The couple henceforth divided their time between the United States and France until the duke's death.

In February 1952 the duke attended the funeral of George VI, though the two had scarcely met since the latter's accession. He was not invited to Queen Elizabeth II's coronation. In 1966, however, the duke and duchess were invited by Elizabeth II (r. 1953– ) to attend the unveiling of a plaque to Queen Mary, the duchess being presented to the queen for the first time.

The duke's health faded fast in the late 1960s. In 1972 he suffered cancer of the throat. In these final days, he was visited by Elizabeth II during her state visit to France. On 28 May 1972 the duke of Windsor died at his home in Paris. His body lay in state in St. George's Chapel, Windsor, and was buried in a plot beside the Royal Mausoleum at Frogmore, where the duchess was also interred in 1986.

See also **Aristocracy; United Kingdom.**

BIBLIOGRAPHY

Bloch, Michael. *The Duke of Windsor's War: From Europe to the Bahamas, 1939–1945.* New York, 1982.

Donaldson, Frances Lonsdale. *Edward VIII.* London, 1974.

McLeod, Kirsty. *Battle Royal: Edward VIII & George VI, Brother against Brother.* London, 1999.

Ziegler, Philip. *King Edward VIII: The Official Biography.* London, 1990.

STEPHEN VELLA

---

**EGYPT.** Egypt, the most populous nation in the Arab world, and strategically straddling the Suez Canal and the Nile River, has had a major role in Europe's relations with the Middle East since 1914. Great Britain, the de facto ruler of Egypt from 1882, retained significant control and an extensive military presence there until 1956, despite ever-growing resistance from Egyptian nationalists. The 1952 Revolution, led by Gamal Abdel Nasser (1918–1970) and the Suez Crisis of 1956 brought British influence in Egypt to an abrupt end. In the 1950s the charismatic Nasser was a strong exponent of pan-Arab unity and emerged as a leader of the Non-Aligned Movement in the conflict between the superpowers. By the 1960s, however, he increasingly relied on military and economic aid from the Soviet Union to implement his plans for modernization and economic growth. The defeat of Egypt and its Arab allies in the June 1967 war against Israel dealt a severe blow to Nasser's policies, and his successor, Anwar el-Sadat (1918–1981), initiated peace talks with Israel. The Camp David Accords of 1978 brought peace with Israel and aid from the United States, and although Sadat was assassinated in 1981 his successor, Hosni Mubarak (b. 1928), has preserved much of his legacy. Over these decades, Egypt's society and economy have been strained by explosive population growth and rapid urbanization, and its authoritarian government has often suppressed domestic dissent, most notably that led by Islamic radicals.

**EGYPT AND EUROPE BEFORE 1914**
Egypt's modern history began abruptly in 1798 with the French invasion and occupation led by Napoleon I (1769–1821). The French forces left within a few years, but European influence in Egypt—especially Anglo-French influence—grew steadily thereafter. Throughout the nineteenth century Egypt remained under the suzerainty of the Ottoman sultan, but its rulers, Mehmet Ali (also known as Muhammad Ali, 1769–1849) (r. 1805–1849) and his successors, were de facto independent. Their efforts to modernize Egypt's military and economy along Western lines saw little success, and Egypt's growing debt to European lenders culminated in the British invasion and occupation of Egypt in 1882. The occupation allowed the British to consolidate their control of the Suez Canal, completed in 1869, which they saw as the lifeline of the empire, a crucial communication link to its possessions in Asia. Though Egypt's monarch retained his crown, after 1882 its de facto ruler was the British consul general in Cairo. Under Lord Cromer (Evelyn Baring, 1841–1917) (r. 1883–1907) and his successors, Egypt attained a measure of stability: a legislative assembly was established and modern political parties and press developed. At the same time, the period saw the beginnings of a nationalist sentiment to resist British rule.

**WARTIME PROTECTORATE AND THE 1919 REVOLUTION**
When the Ottoman Empire declared war on the Allied powers in November 1914, London immediately declared Egypt a British protectorate. Egypt served as a staging ground for the British offensive against the Ottoman possessions in the Levant. Martial law was declared, and wartime requisitions and conscription made life difficult for the population at large and aroused widespread anti-British sentiments. When the armistice was announced, Egyptian nationalists demanded that Egypt be granted independence in line with the principle of self-determination. The British government refused, and widespread protests broke out across Egypt, launching the "1919 Revolution," which augured a new era of Egyptian nationalism.

If prior to 1919 the nationalist movement had been largely limited to urban intellectual elites, it now mobilized far broader sections of the middle classes and the peasantry. The Wafd, the new nationalist party that led the movement, would dominate Egyptian politics until 1952.

## BRITISH POWER AND EGYPTIAN NATIONALISM UNDER THE MONARCHY (1922–1952)

Continued Anglo-Egyptian negotiations could not make progress, and in 1922 London issued a unilateral declaration granting Egypt formal independence, but retaining control of the Canal, external defense, protection of foreigners and minorities, and the Sudan. In 1923 Egypt officially became a constitutional monarchy under King Fuad I (1868–1936, r. 1917–1936). The next two decades were marked by internal political conflict between the Wafd, which advocated the expansion of parliamentary democracy and had a broad support base among Egypt's growing middle classes, and the royal court, which aimed to curtail the power of parliament and was supported by the large landowners and industrialists. Early on the British saw the king as a pliable instrument for their influence, but by the 1930s they began to recognize the Wafd as the representative of the Egyptian people, with whom they must reach an accommodation. The Italian invasion of Ethiopia in 1935, which highlighted British weakness as well as Egypt's own vulnerability to attack, helped break the impasse. In the ensuing Anglo-Egyptian Treaty of 1936 the military occupation of Egypt was declared terminated, and Egypt was admitted to the League of Nations in 1937. The treaty recognized Egyptian sovereignty over the Suez Canal but allowed British troops to remain in the Canal Zone to secure it for the empire.

In Egypt, as elsewhere in the world, the 1930s were a time of economic crisis and the concomitant rise of new ideas about politics and society. If the 1920s in Egypt had been a "liberal era," a period of experimentation with constitutionalism and parliamentary democracy, in the 1930s fascism seemed to be the wave of the future, and its attractions in Egypt added another facet to anti-British sentiments. The interwar period also saw a significant evolution in the ideological nature of Egyptian nationalism. If in the 1920s it had been largely liberal-secular and territorial, the 1930s saw a growing interest in Egypt's identity as an Islamic and Arab nation. The Muslim Brotherhood, founded in 1928 to advocate moral and social reform, became increasingly politicized in the ensuing years. The 1930s also saw Egypt's emergence as a leader on pan-Arab issues, culminating in the formation of the Arab League in Cairo in 1945.

When World War II broke out Egypt remained neutral even after Axis troops invaded its territory from Libya, and large sections of the public openly hoped for Axis victory. At the same time, Britain's military presence in Egypt during the war far exceeded the limits set in the 1936 treaty, as did its involvement in politics, and tensions remained high. The United Nations decision to partition Palestine between Arabs and Jews, creating the State of Israel, precipitated military intervention by the surrounding Arab states in May 1948, but military weakness and conflicting interests led to an Arab defeat. The trauma of 1948 underscored, for many Egyptians, the corruption and ineptitude of the old elites—the royal court, large landlords, big industrialists—who bowed before foreign imperialists and enjoyed decadent privilege while most Egyptians remained mired in poverty. The escalating tensions culminated in July 1952 with a bloodless coup by a group of young military men, the Free Officers, led by the thirty-four-year-old Gamal Abdel Nasser. Nasser was a charismatic leader who wanted Egypt to lead the Arab nations out of their political, social, and economic malaise to become strong and prosperous. His powerful persona and ideology of pan-Arab nationalism and socialism would dominate the politics of Egypt, and much of the Arab world, in the 1950s and 1960s.

## THE NASSER ERA: ARAB NATIONALISM AND SOCIALISM (1952–1970)

The new regime moved quickly to transform Egyptian society. Land reform came first, with large estates broken up and divided among the peasantry, and old aristocratic titles eliminated. The 1956 constitution laid out the new regime's vision: Egypt was an Arab and Islamic nation; the state would provide social welfare; imperialism, feudalism, and monopoly capital would be dismantled. Although it was formally constituted as a democracy, Egypt in fact became a presidential dictatorship; political parties were banned, and potential competitors for power, such as the Muslim Brotherhood, were suppressed.

Nasser's early years in power saw a string of victories in the international arena. First came the Anglo-Egyptian agreement of 1954, which provided for the withdrawal of the remaining British forces from the Canal Zone within twenty months, and in 1955 Nasser emerged as a major world leader at the Bandung Conference of Non-Aligned Nations. In 1956 Egypt's nationalization of the Suez Canal led to a combined Anglo-French-Israeli invasion of Egypt. Nasser remained defiant, however, and firm pressure from the United States government forced the invaders to retreat. Nasser emerged from the "Triple Aggression," as it is known in Egypt, the clear victor. After seventy-four years of military occupation, British power in Egypt abruptly ended, and the efforts of the United States to replace Britain as Egypt's patron met with failure. Nasser's prestige in the Arab world reached new heights. He was the first Arab leader to harness the power of radio to influence public opinion across the region, and his fiery speeches against the imperialists and their collaborators among the "reactionary" Arab regimes helped topple the pro-Western monarchy in Iraq in 1958; King Hussein (r. 1952–1999) of Jordan only narrowly avoided the same fate. Nasser's vision of pan-Arab unity seemed to materialize in 1958 when Egypt and Syria formed the United Arab Republic (UAR) under Nasser's leadership.

Nasser's regional ambitions, however, soon came up against the divergent interests of other Arab governments, as well as U.S. power. With the "Eisenhower Doctrine" of 1957, which promised to defend any Middle Eastern nation threatened by "international Communism," the United States managed to preserve the pro-Western regimes in Lebanon, Jordan, and Saudi Arabia. Iraq's new leaders resisted Egyptian meddling in their internal affairs, and Egypt's union with Syria collapsed in 1961. As Nasser's domestic agenda grew more socialist, with widespread nationalization of industry, Egypt became increasingly dependent on the Soviet Union for military and economic aid. In 1962 Egyptian troops became entangled in the civil war in Yemen, and Nasser's support for Palestinian incursions into Israel further escalated regional tensions. By May 1967 the battle over Arab opinion pushed Nasser to take a stand against Israel: he demanded the removal of

United Nations observers in the Sinai Peninsula and closed the Red Sea straits to Israeli shipping. Nasser may not have intended to bring about a full-scale war, but for Israel Nasser's actions were casus belli, and Israel launched a preemptive attack. After six days of fighting, the armies of Egypt, Jordan, and Syria were decisively defeated, and Israel occupied territory on all three fronts: the Sinai Peninsula, the West Bank, and the Golan Heights, respectively. The defeat of 1967 dealt a mortal blow to Nasser's stature, both regional and domestic, and his ideal of pan-Arab unity; and Egypt's efforts to regain some of its lost territory in the War of Attrition (1969–1970) against Israel also ended in failure. When he died in September 1970, at the age of only fifty-two, he was, personally and politically, a broken man.

## SADAT: WAR, PEACE, AND THE TURN WEST (1970–1981)

Nasser's vice-president, Anwar el-Sadat, succeeded him upon his death. Like Nasser, Sadat came from humble origins, rose through the ranks of the military, and took part in the Free Officers coup of 1952. Like Nasser, he wanted to make Egypt strong and prosperous; but the road he chose to these goals was, in many respects, the polar opposite of Nasser's. If Nasser relied on the Soviet Union for economic and military aid, Sadat led Egypt into the American camp; and while Nasser restructured the Egyptian economy along the lines of state socialism, Sadat would turn to capitalism and seek foreign investment. Like his predecessor, however, Sadat suppressed political dissent and kept a large role for the state in the economy.

Sadat's first mission when he came to power was to erase the shame of the 1967 defeat. In this he achieved spectacular success, engineering a coordinated surprise attack on Israel by Egyptian and Syrian forces in October 1973 (The Yom Kippur War or the October War). Although the Arabs did not achieve a decisive military victory, they scored a major psychological and strategic coup. The 1973 war proved that Arab armies could match Israel on the battlefield, restored Arab confidence, and shook the Israeli leadership out of its post-1967 hubris. But 1973 was only the first part of Sadat's plan. In 1977 he shocked the world with an unprecedented trip to Jerusalem, launching negotiations that led to a peace treaty between

Egypt and Israel. The Camp David Accords, signed in 1978 under American auspices, restored all of the Sinai to Egypt. But early hopes that the accords would serve as a basis for a comprehensive Arab-Israeli peace did not materialize; after 1977 Egypt was ostracized in the Arab world for more than a decade. The peace with Israel, and Sadat's continued suppression of domestic dissent, also alienated many in Egypt itself, and in October 1981 Sadat was assassinated by a member of the outlawed Muslim Brotherhood. He was succeeded by his vice president, Hosni Mubarak.

## EGYPT UNDER MUBARAK (1981–)

The Mubarak regime has largely kept Sadat's legacy in place. It remained committed to peace with Israel but gradually managed to improve relations with the Arab states—in 1989 Egypt was readmitted into the Arab League. Egypt also remained an ally of the United States and a major recipient of U.S. military and economic aid, providing important support to the U.S.–led coalition during the Gulf War of 1991. Domestically, Mubarak experimented with a tentative opening of the political system. But in the mid-1990s, a wave of terror attacks by Muslim radicals against foreign tourists—one of Egypt's most important sources of income—led to a renewed crackdown on opposition groups, with dozens of Muslim militants arrested and executed. By 2004, after almost a quarter-century in power, the seventy-six-year-old Mubarak had yet to designate an heir, and it remained unclear in which direction Egypt would go after he was no longer on the scene.

## POPULATION AND ECONOMY

As in much of the developing world, Egypt's population grew rapidly over the course of the twentieth century due to improvements in hygiene, healthcare, and diet. From 1900 to 1950 the population doubled from about 10.5 million to 21 million, and since then it has more than tripled, reaching an estimated 77 million by 2005. At the same time, large-scale migrations from the countryside have swelled the urban population. In 1914 more than 85 percent of the populace farmed the arable strip of land along the Nile—less than 5 percent of Egypt's total land area—where the density of rural population is among the highest in the world. By 2004 only about a third of the Egyptian workforce was employed in farming, although population growth has meant that arable land is still intensively farmed. Cairo, Egypt's capital and largest city, had some 2 million inhabitants by midcentury and 7.6 million in the city proper by 2004. Ninety-four percent of Egyptians are Sunni Muslim, and most of the rest belong to the Egyptian Coptic Orthodox Church. Although Egypt's major cities had thriving multicultural communities—Greeks, Jews, Armenians, Syrian Christians, and Italians—until the 1950s, those dwindled in the years after the 1952 Revolution and have since largely disappeared.

The years since 1914 saw marked improvements in education and health services in Egypt: literacy rates grew from less than 10 percent to an estimated 58 percent in 2005, and life expectancy more than doubled from thirty-three to sixty-nine years. Efforts at industrialization have helped to diversify the economy away from its early twentieth century dependency on cotton exports, but Egypt remains a relatively poor country, with gross domestic product per capita of $4,400 at purchasing power parity (which adjusts for differences in price levels). Cotton and textiles remain major exports, though in 2005 they are increasingly threatened by competition from Asia. Petroleum products and natural gas are also important exports, and tourism is major source of foreign currency. Since development efforts, especially after 1961, were based on socialist models and included large-scale nationalization of industry, the state has owned much of the economy and played a decisive role in planning; it continues to do so despite some market-oriented reforms in the 1980s and 1990s.

*See also* **Cold War; Islam; Israel; Palestine; Suez Crisis; Terror.**

BIBLIOGRAPHY

Daly, M. W., and Carl F. Petry, eds. *The Cambridge History of Egypt.* 2 vols. Cambridge, U.K., and New York, 1999. A useful collection of essays. Vol. 2 covers Egypt since 1517.

Gershoni, Israel, and James P. Jankowski. *Egypt, Islam, and the Arabs: The Search for Egyptian Nationhood, 1900–1930.* New York, 1987. An analysis of the evolution of modern Egyptian national identity.

Hahn, Peter L. *The United States, Great Britain and Egypt, 1945–1956: Strategy and Diplomacy in the Early Cold War.* Chapel Hill, N.C., 1991. A study of Anglo-American tensions over Egypt in the early postwar years.

Ibrahim, Saad Eddin. *Egypt, Islam and Democracy: Critical Essays with a New Postscript.* Cairo and New York, 2002. Essays by a prominent Egyptian sociologist, imprisoned between 2000 and 2003 for pro-democracy activism.

Mahfouz, Naguib. *The Cairo Trilogy.* New York, 2001. Nobel Prize–winning author's epic depiction of life in Cairo from World War I to the 1950s.

Qutb, Sayyid. *Milestones.* Indianapolis, Ind., 1990. A manifesto of modern Islamic radicalism, written while the author (1903–1966) was awaiting execution in an Egyptian jail.

el-Sadat, Anwar. *In Search of Identity: An Autobiography.* New York, 1978. Self-serving, as expected from an autobiography of a sitting ruler, but interesting nevertheless for its insight into Sadat's self-image.

Vatikiotis, P. J. *The History of Modern Egypt: From Muhammad Ali to Mubarak.* 4th ed. Baltimore, 1991. A standard text, covering the nineteenth and twentieth centuries.

EREZ MANELA

---

# EICHMANN, ADOLF (1906–1962),
German Nazi and one of the chief architects of Jewish extermination during World War II.

Adolf Otto Eichmann was born Karl Adolf Eichmann in Solingen, an industrial town in the German Rhineland. His father was a bookkeeper who worked for an electric and electronics company. In 1913 his employer moved him to Linz, Austria, where his family joined him in 1916. Affiliated with the Evangelical Church and holding deep German national convictions, Eichmann *père* enrolled Adolf in an ultranational youth movement.

Adolf Eichmann was a mediocre student; he studied mechanical engineering but finished school without an occupation and without completing vocational training. Initially he made a living by working for a company that his father had established. In 1927, using his father's business connections, he went to work for a U.S. oil company as an itinerant agent who sold fuel products and negotiated for his employer in the establishment of filling stations. He was dismissed in 1933. The events that elevated the Nazi Party to power in Germany fired his imagination and he began to take a growing interest in politics. In 1932 he joined the Nazi Party in Austria.

After joining the party Eichmann made the acquaintance of an SS member named Ernst Kaltenbrunner, who recruited him for service in his organization. Kaltenbrunner arranged Eichmann's transfer to Germany for training purposes. The relationship between the two men became especially meaningful in subsequent years, as in 1942 Kaltenbrunner was appointed to the vastly powerful post of commander of the SS Security Police (RSHA) after the assassination of Reinhard Heydrich. After his transfer to Germany, Eichmann visited Dachau, the first Nazi concentration camp (established in 1933), where he spent his training period. Afterward he joined the SD (Sicherheitsdienst; the Security Service of the Nazi Party), and was posted to the SD office in Berlin.

## AN EXPERT ON THE JEWISH QUESTION
Eichmann quickly adopted the "Jewish question" as his main area of concern in his service for the SD. He began to take an interest in Jewish history, the doings of the Zionist movement, the development of the Jewish community in Palestine, and the activities of Jewish organizations around the world. Noticing the SD's mounting concern about the Jewish problem and the growing interest of the Reich leadership in solving the problem of German Jewry by means of emigration, Eichmann visited Palestine in 1937. Returning to Germany, he concluded that the idea of Jewish statehood was useless and that the Jews could never sustain a state that would solve the problem of their presence in Germany. Events in early 1938 gave Eichmann an opportunity for rapid professional advancement. After the Germans annexed Austria in March of that year, the SD sent him to Vienna as its representative and tasked him with organizing the emigration of Austrian Jewry.

Finding ways to facilitate the emigration of Jews from the Reich became Eichmann's main vocation during this time. As soon as he had set up his office in Vienna, he engineered a harsh campaign of terror against the Jews, including violence and humiliation in the streets and public places by thugs of the Austrian Nazi Party and members of the SA. Concurrently Eichmann established the Central Emigration Office, in which several organizations and administrative authorities joined forces to arrange the Jews' emigration expeditiously and efficiently. The office developed a modus operandi that facilitated the rapid actualization of the Jews' departure. Within days, Jews were forced to dispose of property and belongings and received their emigration papers from the state. This program, combining emigration and deportation action accompanied by terrorism and violence, was wildly successful. Several months after it began some 150,000 Jews, almost 75 percent of the pre-annexation population, had left Austria.

Eichmann's success in inducing the emigration of Austrian Jewry, in contrast to the difficulties that beset this cause in Germany, inspired the leaders of the SD in 1939 to establish a general emigration office along similar lines in Berlin and to station Eichmann at its head. In October 1939 Eichmann was placed in charge of Department IV B4 of the Gestapo, the secret political police of the SD. This department was tasked with dealing with the Jewish problem. After World War II began, its purview included millions of Jews who had come under German rule as inhabitants of occupied Poland and the annexed areas of Czechoslovakia.

In 1939–1940 Eichmann's office strove intensively to devise a territorial solution to the Jewish question. Eichmann himself visited Poland to follow the attempts of the SS to deport hundreds of thousands of Poles and Jews from the annexed areas in western Poland to the General Government, the area in central Poland that had been placed under a severe German occupation regime. Eichmann then proposed that the Jews of the Reich be deported to a "Jewish reservation" in the Lublin area of occupied eastern Poland. Several thousand Jews from Austria and from the Protectorate of Bohemia and Moravia were deported to that area. In 1940, however, in view of difficulties that had surfaced in deporting Jews from the Reich to occupied Poland, Eichmann began to work intensively on another scheme, the Madagascar Plan. His intention now was to transform this eastern African island, a French colony, into a vast territorial ghetto to which the millions of Jews in Europe would be deported. Although Eichmann invested immense efforts in the Madagascar Plan during 1940, it had become clear by the end of that year that the realities of the war and other limitations made this baneful idea totally unworkable.

In March 1941, shortly before the German invasion of the Soviet Union, Eichmann's department of the Gestapo was reorganized. Its staff was expanded to 107, mostly in administrative and white-collar posts. The Final Solution of the Jewish question was imminent, and Eichmann took part in the discussions that were held in the summer and autumn of 1941 about how to expedite and streamline the murders of Jews that had begun in the summer. Branches of his department were then established in various cities in the Reich and in the annexed Polish areas. In autumn 1941 Eichmann participated in discussions and decisions about the establishment of mass-murder facilities and the use of gas for this purpose in the Lublin area and the Auschwitz concentration camp. He also made preliminary visits to locations in eastern Europe where mass murders of Jews were being carried out.

In January 1942 Eichmann participated in preparing the working meeting at Wannsee, where the modus operandi and responsibilities of various players in the German ruling system for the evacuation of the Jews were worked out. Eichmann wrote the invitations to the meeting and, in coordination with Heydrich, took the minutes. From early 1942 Eichmann's office was in charge of organizing and managing the transports that had begun to head for the newly established extermination centers in eastern Europe. His staff members organized the deportation of Jews from Germany, Austria, France, Belgium, the Netherlands, Slovakia, Greece, and Italy to the death camps.

In March 1944, after the Wehrmacht invaded Hungary, Eichmann and members of his office staff moved to that country to direct the deportation of Hungarian Jewry. Within a few months, from May to July 1944, some 440,000 Jews were deported from Hungary to Auschwitz for extermination. Concurrently Eichmann pursued contacts with Jewish activists in Budapest who sought to halt the mass murder by negotiating what became known as the "Trucks for Blood" program. These contacts were part of a scheme by Heinrich Himmler, head of the SS, to build a bridge to the Western Allies in order to conclude a separate accord with them to end the war. Eichmann left Hungary but returned in October 1944 to organize the death marches of some 76,000 Jews to the

**Adolf Eichmann at his trial in Jerusalem, May 1961.** ©BETTMANN/CORBIS

Austrian border, where they were to build defensive fortifications against the advancing Red Army.

### THE EICHMANN TRIAL AND ITS SIGNIFICANCE

Although captured by U.S. soldiers and interned in a detention camp for SS men, Eichmann obfuscated his identity and escaped from the camp in early 1946. Under a false identity, he lived in a small town south of Hamburg, Germany, and worked as a lumberjack for four years. In early 1950 he made contact with an organization of SS veterans that smuggled Nazi war criminals to South America. He moved to Italy and thence, in July 1950, to Argentina, where he began a new life under the name Ricardo Klement. His wife and children in Germany joined him in summer 1952.

On 11 May 1960 Israeli agents captured Eichmann and had him secretly flown to Israel. In April 1961, after months of interrogation, his trial in Jerusalem District Court began. Eichmann was indicted for crimes against the Jewish people, crimes against humanity, and membership in a hostile organization (the SS and the Gestapo). Refusing to confess, he claimed that he did not consider himself guilty of responsibility for murder in the sense of the indictment. Eichmann was willing to confess only to having aided the commission of a crime, arguing that he had never committed the crimes attributed to him. His attorney raised additional questions, such as the extent to which Jewish and Israeli judges could conduct the trial without prejudice and whether it was just to bring the defendant to trial in Israel, because Eichmann had been abducted from a country in which he held citizenship and taken for trial to a country where the offenses attributed to him had not been committed. The defense also argued that the basis in Israeli jurisprudence for the prosecution of Eichmann—the 1950 law that allowed Nazis and their accomplices to be tried in Israel—was being applied retroactively, that is, to crimes committed before it had been enacted.

The court rejected these arguments on the grounds of U.S. and British legal precedents and specific examination of the crimes attributed to the defendant that had been perpetrated under the criminal Nazi German regime. More than one hundred witnesses, most of whom were Holocaust survivors, gave testimony, and more than sixteen hundred documents were entered into evidence. The trial marked the first systematic, step-by-step presentation of how Nazi Germany had dealt with the "Jewish question" and, especially, the progression of the Final Solution and Eichmann's centrality in it. On 15 December 1961 the court sentenced him to death. Eichmann appealed the verdict to the Supreme Court, which on 29 May 1962 upheld the outcome of the trial. After the president of the State of Israel rejected his application for clemency, Eichmann was executed on the night of 31 May–1 June 1962. It was Israel's first and the only court-ordered execution.

In subsequent years the Eichmann trial became a central event in the academic and public debate over the Holocaust and the Nazis' crimes. The philosopher and intellectual Hannah Arendt covered the trial for the *New Yorker* and her articles were gathered together in the book *Eichmann in Jerusalem,* published in May 1963. Arendt's book touched off a far-reaching debate, mainly due to her view of Eichmann as a bureaucrat devoid of ideological, moral, and value considerations—the archetype of a murderer who acts within a totalitarian society that promotes terror, murder, and genocide as ordinary phenomena. She also defined Eichmann as representative of a human phenomenon that she termed the "banality of evil." Arendt's arguments attracted fierce resistance, especially among Holocaust survivors, but they led to extensive research that has continued into the early twenty-first century on issues related to the Nazi murderers' motivation and the relationship between ideology and bureaucracy in the process that led to the Final Solution.

The Eichmann trial was also an important landmark in the attitude of Israeli society toward the Holocaust. It was the first time that the story of the extermination of the Jews had been presented systematically, almost day-by-day, to the Israeli public. At the time the trial was held, nearly one-fourth of the population of the young State of Israel was composed of Holocaust survivors. They retold their experiences to Israeli society not as personal recountings for family or friends but rather in a public and state setting, on the witness stand at a trial that was broadcast on Israel Radio every day. The trial and, especially, the survivors' testimonies launched a process of coping with the Holocaust that has continued ever since in Israel, in the United States, and in Western Europe. The implications of this process continue to affect Israeli society and the patterns of commemoration and memorialization of a historical event that has shaped the historical consciousness of the Jewish people.

*See also* **Heydrich, Reinhard; Holocaust; SS (Schutzstaffel); Wannsee Conference; World War II.**

BIBLIOGRAPHY

Arendt, Hannah. *Eichmann in Jerusalem: A Report on the Banality of Evil.* New York, 1963.

Lozowick, Yaacov. *Hitler's Bureaucrats: The Nazi Security Police and the Banality of Evil.* Translated by Haim Watzman. London and New York, 2002.

Safrian, Hans. *Die Eichmann-Männer.* Vienna, 1993.

Wojak, Irmtrud. *Eichmanns Memoiren: Ein kritischer Essay.* Frankfurt, Germany, 2002.

DANIEL BLATMAN

# EINSATZGRUPPEN.

The Einsatzgruppen (Special Action Groups), were mobile units trained by the Third Reich's organizations of oppression—the Gestapo (Geheime Staatspolizei), its criminal police department known as Kripo (Kriminalpolizei), and SS (Schutzstaffel) security forces, called SD (Sicherheitsdienst des Reichsfuehrer). Their aim was to secure order through each phase of the Nazi empire's expansion. The best known of these groups were those formed in preparation for the invasion of Poland and the Soviet Union. Although their internal organization remained essentially unchanged and their missions apparently fixed during the entire course of their operations, their activity would undergo a series of modifications that transformed them, especially in the Soviet Union, into agencies of genocide.

## ORGANIZATION

In 1938 the Gestapo, the SD, and the Kripo were instructed to organize commandos for security missions in occupied countries. These units operated in Austria, Sudetenland, Czechoslovakia, Poland,

and the USSR, and later in Tunisia, Croatia, and Slovakia. Their composition varied greatly—the units set up for Operation Barbarossa, with three thousand commandos, had by far the largest contingent—but all were trained in the same way.

The units were composed of the Sonderkommandos (Special groups) that operated in the Soviet Union near the front lines, and the Einsatzkommandos, whose missions, conducted inside the war zone, were the more conspicuous. In the Soviet Union they were assigned zones of operation as follows:

In the Baltic, Einsatzgruppe (EG) A, with one thousand men, had Leningrad as its objective.

In Byelorussia, Einsatzgruppe B, with eight hundred men, had Moscow as its objective.

In Ukraine, Einsatzgruppe C, with seven hundred men, had Kiev as its objective.

In Crimea and the Caucasus, Einsatzgruppe D, with five hundred men.

Initially conceived as motorized mobile units, they would be settled after several weeks of activity and converted into Gestapo and SD local officers under regional commanders. It was exceptional for recruits to serve in different units; for example, commandos in Poland did not serve in Russia.

Recruitment methods did change, however, consonant with the general evolution of EG activities. Composed initially almost exclusively of Gestapo functionaries and SS officers of the SD, the units became more heavily armed; the presence of armed guards of the Waffen SS marked the transition between the "peaceful" campaigns prior to 1939 and the principal theaters of operation in Poland and the Soviet Union during the war.

## MISSIONS: FROM SECURITY TO GENOCIDE

Throughout these operations, the structure of command under which the units acted remained remarkably fixed. A directive from Reinhard Tristan Eugen Heydrich (1904–1942), chief of the Gestapo and the SD, summarized the units' duties at the end of the invasion of Czechoslovakia:

1. Protection (*Sicherung*) of the new order against any attack or turmoil

2. Arrest of all persons known to be hostile to the Reich

3. Seizure of all archives and files regarding the activities of individuals or organizations hostile to the Reich

4. Elimination of organizations that are hostile or that pursue goals hostile to the Reich

5. Occupation of all offices of the Czech criminal and political police as well as those of all the organizations pursuing political or criminal police activities (Krausnick and Wilhelm, p. 17)

However rigid the judicial and police structure, the units underwent a critical change in Poland and the Soviet Union. Like the Gestapo, they had always used brutal but traditional police techniques, but policy changed in Poland. The security mind-set operating there had already lowered the threshold of violence, and Operation Barbarossa, which may be viewed as an exercise in racial annihilation, brought with it for the first time orders to systematically kill specific categories of victims. During the invasion of Poland, Einsatzgruppen units liquidated partisans (the franc-tireurs) as well as members of the bourgeoisie and members of the Polish nationalist parties. In the Soviet Union, repression was anti-Semitic, with four categories by which Jewish adult males, supposedly guilty of all the "offenses against public order," became the first and primary targets. Executions constantly increased in number through the first six weeks of the campaign. However, around the end of July 1941, the units started to kill women under the pretext that they belonged to the Communist Party or to other partisan groups. A key modification, in place by mid-August 1941, was that the groups started executing children. Finally, between the end of August and mid-October, all units were murdering whole communities. Over the course of several months the Einsatzgruppen had evolved into mobile killing units.

Unit members were for the most part low-ranking police functionaries supervised by SS officers of the Gestapo and of the SD. None who were sent to Russia had any experience in putting to death large numbers of human beings. Neither were they selected for murderous predisposition or anti-Semitic militancy. The various steps that led them to willingly commit genocide were preceded by an intense work of legitimation on the part of their superior officers. Speeches, "evenings of comradeship," and murderous acts by the officers themselves all aimed at persuading the men to execute what Heinrich Himmler (1900–1945) in a speech in Posen in 1943 called "the most horrible of all tasks."

Despite deeply internalized anti-Semitism and clear evidence of racial hatred revealed in recovered correspondence, and even in spite of mechanisms for habituating soldiers to murder—such as those Christopher R. Browning describes in *Ordinary Men* (1992)—extermination remained a transgressive act in the eyes of those who became mass murderers, a traumatic activity that created alcoholics and generated nervous breakdowns. Aware of these problems after invading the Soviet Union, unit leaders created strategies to reduce what the chief of Einsatzgruppe A called the "psychological tensions" induced in the executioners by the massacres. One such strategy, for example, was to mobilize local militias to murder children; they also pressured Gestapo headquarters in Berlin to provide mobile gassing units. Whether their thoughts and actions led to the procedures for mass extermination by gas is difficult to determine. In any event, genocide committed by men with machine guns, such as that carried out by the Einsatzgruppen in the Soviet Union, was a system of extermination that wrought havoc with the executioners and was poorly adapted to many situations.

At the end of 1941 the units became sedentary, forming the security police (BdS) of the Nazi-occupied Soviet Union. Their genocidal activities did not stop, however, but continued until the summer of 1943, by which time virtually all communities of Russian Jews had been eradicated. Their activities henceforth consisted in fighting the thriving partisan movements, particularly in Byelorussia. There again, the executioners left a bloody imprint throughout the Soviet Union.

Together, the four units of the Einsatzgruppen in the Soviet Union exterminated some 550,000 individuals, mainly Jews, between June and September 1941. Each member of each unit committed an average of one murder per day for six months. Overall, the Einsatzgruppen murdered between 850,000 and 1,000,000 victims, the vast majority Jewish. Their role in the deaths of the millions of Russian civilians who were victims of deliberate famine or of operations to eliminate partisan fighters is somewhat more difficult to evaluate.

## WAR CRIMES TRIALS

Activities of the Einsatzgruppen units are well known thanks to daily reports submitted to Berlin, which the RSHA compiled and dispatched to a restricted list of recipients. Seized by the American forces at the end of the war, these compilations constituted the grounds of the indictment filed during the ninth Nuremberg trial, against the high-ranking leaders of the units arrested by the American army. General Otto Ohlendorf (1907–1951), chief of Einsatzgruppe D, which had operated in Crimea, was sentenced to death together with a dozen other defendants, although the American-run judiciary gave out reduced sentences for most others, except chiefs of the units and Paul Blobel (1894–1951), who was prominent in the Babi Yar massacre. Most of the others accused, although sentenced to long prison terms, were released after 1955.

Beginning in the late 1950s, Germany systematically pursued prosecution for crimes perpetrated by the Einsatzgruppen, laying the groundwork for famous trials at Ulm and Darmstadt, in which severe sentences were meted out to high-ranking and other officers of the Einsatzgruppen. What appears to be the last known investigation ended with the condemnation in 1975 of Kurt Christmann, one of General Ohlendorf's adjuncts in the Crimean operation.

*See also* **Babi Yar; Germany; Gestapo; Holocaust; Jews; Nazism; Occupation, Military; Operation Barbarossa; SS (Schutzstaffel); World War II.**

BIBLIOGRAPHY

Angrick, Andrej. *Besatzungspolitik und Massenmord: Die Einsatzgruppe D in der südlichen Sowjetunion, 1941–1943.* Hamburg, Germany, 2003.

Browning, Christopher R. *Ordinary Men: Reserve Police Battalion 101 and the Final Solution in Poland.* New York, 1992.

Headland, Ronald. *Messages of Murder: A Study of the Reports of the Einsatzgruppen of the Security Police and the Security Service, 1941–1943.* Rutherford, N.J., 1992.

Hilberg, Raul. *The Destruction of the European Jews.* Revised and definitive edition. 3 vols. New York, 1985.

Klein, Peter, and Andrej Angrick, eds. *Die Einsatzgruppen in der besetzten Sowjetunion 1941/42: Die Tätigkeits- und Lageberichte des Chefs der Sicherheitspolizei und des SD.* Berlin, 1997.

Krausnick, Helmut, and Hans-Heinrich Wilhelm. *Die Truppe des Weltanschauungskrieges: Die Einsatzgruppen der Sicherheitspolizei und des SD, 1938–1942.* Stuttgart, Germany, 1981.

Ogorreck, Ralf. *Die Einsatzgruppen und die Genesis der "Endlösung."* Berlin, 1996.

Wilhelm, Hans-Heinrich. *Die Einsatzgruppe A der Sicherheitspolizei und des SD, 1941/42.* Frankfurt, 1996.

CHRISTIAN INGRAO

---

# EINSTEIN, ALBERT (1879–1955),
German-born American physicist.

Albert Einstein, the most important theoretical physicist of the twentieth century, was born in Ulm, Germany, on 14 March 1879. He was the first child of Hermann Einstein, a featherbed merchant, and Pauline (Koch) Einstein, who would pass her love of music on to her only son. When Albert was one year old, the family moved to Munich, where Hermann became a partner with his youngest brother, Jakob, in a small electrical engineering firm. On 18 November 1881 Albert's sister Maria (Maja) was born, and they had a close relationship throughout her life. Albert's speech development was worrisomely slow, but he later attributed this to his ambition to speak in complete sentences. He also remembered that, early in his childhood, he began to wonder about space, time, and the mysteries of magnetism.

In 1885, when Albert was at the statutory school age of six, he began attending Petersschule, a nearby Catholic elementary school, where he, the only Jew, was often at the top of his class and where he already manifested what would become his lifelong love of isolation. On 1 October 1888 Albert enrolled in the Luitpold Gymnasium, where he was a very good student, even in such subjects as Latin and Greek, which he disliked. In school his favorite subject was Euclidean geometry, and outside of school his favorite readings were books of popular science, which contributed to his increasing skepticism about biblical stories (he was never bar mitzvahed). In 1894, when Einstein & Cie went into liquidation, Hermann moved his wife and daughter to northern Italy, where he and Jakob set up another factory. Albert was left with relatives to complete his secondary-school education, but after a few months, he left the gymnasium without graduating and joined his parents in Milan.

During the autumn of 1895 Albert took the entrance exam for the Swiss Polytechnic in Zurich, and, though he did well in mathematics and physics, he failed other subjects, necessitating remedial work at a cantonal school in Aarau, from which he graduated on 3 October 1896. He immediately began attending the Zurich Polytechnic where he was enrolled in the "School for Specialized Teachers in the Mathematical and Scientific Subjects." He rarely attended classes, relying instead on his friend Marcel Grossmann's excellent class notes to complete the formalities of his education. He preferred learning on his own, and he immersed himself in the writings of such physicists as the Scot James Clerk Maxwell (1831–1879) and the Austrian Ernst Mach (1838–1916). During his freshman year he met Mileva Marić, the only female student in the school, and although she was an Orthodox Christian Serb, they shared a love of physics, and their friendship deepened into love.

After graduating from the Polytechnic in the spring of 1900, Einstein was unable to obtain a permanent job, even though he wrote to physicists all over Europe. He was forced to take temporary positions as a tutor or teacher. His frustration was exacerbated by Mileva's pregnancy, which led to her dropping out of school and returning to her parents' home in Hungary where, early in 1902, Lieserl, the illegitimate daughter of Mileva and Albert, was born. Despite assiduous efforts of scholars, what later happened to Lieserl remains cloaked in mystery. Through the efforts of Marcel Grossmann's father, Albert Einstein was finally able to get a well-paying job. On 16 June 1902 he was engaged as an "Expert III Class" at the patent office in Bern, Switzerland. Because of his need to become established and because of the death of his father, Albert was not able to marry Mileva until 6 January 1903.

## EARLY CAREER AND ACHIEVEMENTS
In 1904, following a probationary period, Einstein obtained a permanent post at the patent office with a raise in salary, and on 14 May 1904 his first son Hans Albert was born. The next year, 1905, has been called Einstein's annus mirabilis (wonderful year) because of a revolutionary series of papers he published on fundamental issues in physics.

Another puzzling phenomenon that engaged Einstein's attention was Brownian motion. Early in the nineteenth century the Scottish botanist Robert Brown (1773–1858) had discovered that pollen grains in water exhibited random movements. Though discovered by a botanist, Brownian motion actually had far-reaching consequences for physicists, chemists, and mathematicians. When Einstein became interested in Brownian motion in the spring of 1905, it was in the context of his desire to find facts that would confirm the existence of atoms. By mathematically proving that the movement of these pollen particles was due to a difference in the number of water molecules colliding on opposite sides of each of the particles, he was able to account for not only the motion but also the exact numbers of molecules in a particular volume of the fluid. Since the numbers, sizes, and masses of atoms could now be precisely determined, skeptical physicists were forced to accept the atom's existence.

The final two papers Einstein wrote in 1905 were on the special theory of relativity, and they were even more revolutionary than the first two. He called this theory of space, time, matter, and motion "special" because it was restricted to uniformly moving systems, though he was aware that a more appropriate name for it than "relativity" would have been "invariance," since its two basic postulates assumed the invariance of light's speed and the invariance of physical laws in uniformly moving systems. Reasoning from these postulates and using various "thought experiments," Einstein proved that an event interpreted as simultaneous by one observer will be interpreted as nonsimultaneous by another (the relativity of simultaneity). This meant that there were no absolute "nows" throughout the universe. Further nonintuitive consequences of the special theory were the slowing of time and the contraction of length for systems moving at extremely high speeds. In September Einstein also published a supplement to his relativity paper, and it contained the formula $E = mc^2$, explaining how inertial mass ($m$) and energy ($E$) were equivalent, with a gigantic proportionality constant (the square of the speed of light, $c$).

Although Einstein continued to work at the patent office, his interactions with academia increased. For example, in 1906 he received his doctorate from the University of Zurich, and in 1908, after an earlier

**Albert Einstein gives a lecture to the American Association for the Advancement of Science, December 1934.** ©BETTMANN/CORBIS

His first paper provided an exciting explanation to a puzzling phenomenon that had been discovered at the end of the nineteenth century. When electromagnetic radiation, especially visible light, hit a metal, electrons were ejected (the photoelectric effect). By studying this phenomenon, physicists discovered that the greater the intensity or brightness of the light, the greater the number of ejected electrons. They further found that the energy (or speed) of the ejected electrons depended on the color (or frequency) of the incident light. What puzzled physicists about the photoelectric effect was that it could not be explained by the wave theory of light. However, Einstein made sense of these perplexing observations by interpreting the incident light as a stream of particles instead of waves. To explain quantitatively how these "light quanta" (later called photons) interacted with the metal, Einstein used an equation developed by the German physicist Max Planck (1858–1947) in his quantum theory of the emission and absorption of radiation. So successful was Einstein's quantum theory of the photoelectric effect that he was later given his only Nobel Prize for this discovery.

rejection, he became a *privatdozent* (an unsalaried lecturer) at Bern University. In 1909 he left the patent office to become an extraordinary professor of theoretical physics at Zurich University. After the birth of his second son, Eduard, in 1910, Einstein took his family to Prague where, in 1911, he assumed his position as full professor of theoretical physics at the German University.

During these early years in academia he was already working on his general theory of relativity, in particular the equivalence principle whose basic idea was the impossibility of distinguishing between a gravitational and an accelerating force. This theory, which applied to nonuniformly moving systems, challenged Einstein with daunting mathematical difficulties, which he attempted to resolve while at Prague and, after 1912, in Zurich, where he became a full professor at the Polytechnic. By this time his marriage was in turmoil because of his adulteries and his emotional separation from Mileva and his two sons. He had already begun a relationship with his cousin Elsa (Einstein) Löwenthal, a divorcée with two daughters. He was able to escape from his marital troubles by attending scientific meetings and conferences and by visiting Elsa in Berlin. His first marriage was essentially over when, in 1914, he, as a new member of the Prussian Academy of Sciences, accepted a position at the University of Berlin (he would later become director of its Kaiser Wilhelm Institute for Physics). Although Mileva and the boys spent a few months in Berlin, they quickly returned to Zurich, and the family was never whole again.

Early in 1916 Einstein published his first systematic treatment of the general theory of relativity. By using a non-Euclidean geometry to handle the four dimensions of space and time, he was able to fundamentally change Newton's conception of the universe and solve problems that had baffled Newtonian physicists. Whereas Isaac Newton (1642–1727) had conceived of space as absolute and homogeneous, Einstein understood that space must be related to the gravitational objects in it. He actually conceived of space as curving around these objects. He was able to use these ideas—that "matter tells space how to curve" and "curved space tells matter how to behave"—in explaining what had been inexplicable to Newtonian astronomers, for example, the shift of the point in the planet Mercury's orbit when it is closest to the sun (the so-called precession of the perihelion point of Mercury). More famously, Einstein predicted that, because of the curvature of space around the sun, starlight would be deflected when it neared the sun. So confident was Einstein of the truth of his theory that he predicted precisely how much starlight would be bent during an eclipse of the sun. This prediction was unable to be tested until after World War I, but when it was, in 1919, Einstein's prediction was confirmed, an event that made front-page news in many countries, transforming Einstein into a worldwide paragon of the scientific genius.

## LATER CAREER AND ACHIEVEMENTS

Because of Einstein's fame, his strong opposition to German militarism in World War I did not have a negative effect on his academic positions; neither did his divorce from Mileva and his marriage to Elsa on 2 June 1919. During the 1920s he received many honors and invitations to speak in countries around the world. For example, in 1922 he retroactively received the 1921 Nobel Prize in Physics for his explanation of the photoelectric effect. His sensitivity to a resurgent anti-Semitism led him to accompany Chaim Azriel Weizmann (1874–1952), a Zionist leader who later became Israel's first president, on a two-month lecture tour of the United States. Einstein later traveled to Japan, Palestine, and South America. After his travels, he devoted himself, when in Berlin, to a project that would dominate his scientific efforts for the rest of his life: the search for a unified field theory that he hoped would result in a common explanation for both electromagnetism and gravity. Einstein also took an interest in a new theory of physics, quantum mechanics, that was being formulated by Werner Heisenberg, Erwin Schrödinger, Max Born, and Niels Bohr. By analyzing radiations emitted from atoms these physicists were able to describe in considerable detail how electrons behaved in these atoms, which had significant implications for physics and chemistry. However, Einstein had serious misgivings about quantum mechanics, particularly with those physicists who interpreted the behavior of subatomic particles statistically or, in the case of Heisenberg, indeterministically (in his famous "uncertainty principle"). In his intensive debates with Niels Bohr about these issues, Einstein insisted that "God does not play dice." Einstein was an ardent supporter of causality and determinism in the physical world (and an incisive critic of chance and indeterminism).

During the early 1930s Einstein dedicated much of his time to his growing interests in internationalism, pacifism, and Zionism. From 1930 to 1932 he made three trips to the United States, where he spent time doing research at the California Institute of Technology (CIT) in Pasadena. Here he learned from CIT astronomers that the universe was expanding, contrary to the static universe Einstein had depicted in his general theory of relativity (he called this the "biggest mistake of his life"). In August 1932 he accepted an appointment to the new Institute for Advanced Study in Princeton, New Jersey, intending to spend half a year in Princeton and the other half in Berlin, but when the Nazis seized power in Germany in 1933, he announced publicly that he was resigning from the Prussian Academy of Sciences and his other positions, and he promised that he would never return to Germany (a promise he kept). During the spring and summer of 1933 he spent time in Belgium and England, but on 17 October 1933 he arrived in the United States with his wife, his secretary Helen Dukas, and an assistant to take up residence in Princeton.

While at the Institute for Advanced Study, Einstein continued to work on his unified field theory, but in 1935, in collaboration with Boris Podolsky and Nathan Rosen, he published an influential paper attempting to show that the quantum mechanical description of physical reality is incomplete. A central argument in this paper, which came to be known as the "EPR Paradox," concerns what occurs when a part of a system is measured while another part, previously connected to it, is at a great distance. For example, if an electron pair is created, and the spin of one of these electrons is measured, then the electron spin of the other is instantly determined. Although Einstein hoped that this paradox would convince physicists that quantum mechanics is not the final word, subsequent research has made it very much a part of the quantum-mechanical vision of reality.

After his wife, Elsa, died in 1936, Einstein was reunited, in 1939, with his sister Maja, who remained with him until her death in 1951. On 2 August 1939 Einstein signed a letter to President Franklin Delano Roosevelt (1882–1945), warning him of the possibility that the Germans might develop an atomic bomb. This letter led to the Manhattan Project, the American program that successfully produced the world's first atomic bombs. During World War II Einstein abandoned his pacifism, supported the cause of the Allied Powers, and became an American citizen on 1 October 1940. When the atomic bombs were used against Japan, Einstein was horrified because he had hoped that they would have been used against the Nazis.

During the postwar years he rededicated himself to pacifism and campaigned against nuclear weapons and the arms race. He was also an active participant in the movement for a world government, and his socialist sympathies led to his surveillance by the Federal Bureau of Investigation (FBI). In 1952, after the death of Weizmann, he was offered but refused the presidency of Israel. In response to a request from the British philosopher Bertrand Russell (1872–1970), he signed what became known as the Russell-Einstein manifesto, a plea for all government to renounce nuclear weapons. On 13 April 1955, after the rupture of an aortic aneurysm, Einstein was brought to a Princeton hospital, where, on 18 April, he died. His last words, in German, were not understood by the attending nurse. Against his wishes, his brain was preserved (and its many travels have become the subject of a book). The rest of his body was cremated, and his ashes were scattered at a location that has never been disclosed to the public.

*See also* **Bohr, Niels; Quantum Mechanics; Science.**

BIBLIOGRAPHY

*Primary Sources*

Einstein, Albert. *Relativity, the Special and General Theory: A Popular Exposition.* Translated by Robert W. Lawson. London, 1920.

———. *Ideas and Opinions.* Translated by Sonja Bargmann. Edited by Carl Seelig. New York, 1954. Translation of *Mein Weltbild* (1934).

———. *Autobiographical Notes.* Translated and edited by Paul Arthur Schilpp. LaSalle, Ill., 1979.

———. *The Collected Papers of Albert Einstein.* Translated by Anna Beck. Consultation by Peter Havas. 9 vols. Princeton, N.J., 1987–2004. This massive project is expected to reach twenty-five volumes when completed. Introductions and scholarly apparatus are in English, and every document appears in its original language, but each volume is also supplemented by English translations of the non-English materials.

*Secondary Sources*

Fölsing, Albrecht. *Albert Einstein: A Biography.* Translated by Ewald Osers. New York, 1997. This English translation of the 1993 German edition has been called the best general account of Einstein's life now available.

Frank, Philipp. *Einstein: His Life and Times.* Translated by George Rosen. Edited and revised by Shuichi Kusaka. New York, 1947. According to contemporary friends and colleagues, this was the best biography of Einstein published in his lifetime. Scholars prefer the 1979 German edition, since it contains an introduction by Einstein and much material left out of the English edition.

Galison, Peter. *Einstein's Clocks, Poincaré's Maps: Empires of Time.* New York, 2003. This widely praised book uses history, biography, and science to make some of Einstein's most important work accessible and engrossing to general readers.

Pais, Abraham. *"Subtle Is the Lord . . .": The Science and Life of Albert Einstein.* Oxford, U.K., 1982. Pais, a physicist who knew Einstein, has used previously unpublished papers and personal recollections to present a detailed analysis of Einstein's most significant scientific contributions for those readers with backgrounds in physics and mathematics.

ROBERT J. PARADOWSKI

---

# EISENSTEIN, SERGEI (1898–1948), Russian film director and theorist.

The son of a prominent architect and civil engineer, Sergei Mikhailovich Eisenstein began to study engineering in his native Riga but was called up for service in World War I. In the 1917 Bolshevik Revolution and civil war, Eisenstein fought with the Reds. In 1920 he settled in Moscow, where he began to study under and work with the outstanding modernist theater director Vsevolod Meyerhold. Eisenstein also worked independently in the theater and had a stint with the Proletkult (short for "proletarian culture") Workers Theater where, as part of the 1923 avant-garde staging of a nineteenth-century Russian play, he created a short film piece called *Glumov's Diary* (*Dnevnik Glumova*). He then began to concentrate on film, and in 1925 he made *Strike* (*Stachka*), his first full-length work. Depicting a workers' uprising and its violent suppression, *Strike* reflects Eisenstein's tendency in his first films to make sharp propaganda statements that reflect Bolshevik ideology. The brilliant cinematography,

which features scenes that are unforgettable in their vividness and brutality, is by Eduard Tisse, who worked on all of Eisenstein's films.

Eisenstein's next work, *The Battleship Potemkin* (*Bronenosets Potyomkin*, 1926), is widely regarded as one of the greatest films ever made. Made to commemorate the 1905 uprising in Russia, it too deals with a rebellion and the harsh suppression of the masses, though it ends on a far more optimistic note. While the film is loosely based on actual events, the famous Odessa steps scene, in which advancing soldiers gun down civilians during a sequence that lasts significantly longer than real time, was Eisenstein's invention. Notable qualities include striking crosscuts, contrasts in mood between violence and almost idyllic quiet, and the use of shapes and lighting to create symbolic effect. *October* (*Oktyabr*, 1927; U.S. title *Ten Days That Shook the World*, 1928), served to mark the tenth anniversary of the Bolshevik Revolution. In depicting the storming of the Winter Palace, Eisenstein provided a convincing mass spectacle that gave his exaggerated version of the events an aura of authenticity; as with the fictional Odessa steps sequence, his film account became the historical reality for many viewers. By now Eisenstein's theory of montage—essentially the bold use of cutting to emphasize mood or meaning through the juxtaposition of shots—had evolved; rather than just crosscutting between scenes to create visual and emotional contrasts, he wrote about and in his films employed what he termed "intellectual montage," where editing creates metaphors. Thus in *October* shots of the proud prime minister, Alexander Kerensky, are intercut with those of a mechanical peacock.

Eisenstein had political difficulties with his next film, originally called *The General Line* (*Generalnaya liniya*). That title refers to the Bolshevik policy for the countryside, which at first was to have peasants gather voluntarily into collectives. The policy shifted toward a harsher line while the film was being made, and thus it was recut and released as *The Old and the New* (*Staroye i novoye*, 1929). That was to be the last of his silent films and his last released project for nine years. He left for Europe and the United States in 1929, but his efforts to find support for projects in Hollywood came to naught. Financed by Upton Sinclair, he shot

**Sergei Eisenstein editing the film *October*, 1928.** THE BRIDGEMAN ART LIBRARY

the footage for *Qué viva México!* on location. A souring relationship with Sinclair resulted in Eisenstein's never receiving the footage to edit the film, which has been released by others over the years in several versions and under various titles. After returning to Russia in 1932 he had growing difficulties with the authorities, who were now trying to exert greater ideological control over film as well as the other arts. The original script for *Bezhin Meadow* (*Bezhin lug*), which treated collectivization, came in for sharp criticism; even the rewrite resulted in a film that was never released. The only remaining copy perished in World War II.

Eisenstein's career revived with *Alexander Nevsky* (1938), on the thirteenth-century victory by the eponymous hero against Teutonic invaders, a topical subject in the late 1930s. Besides the famous Battle on the Ice sequence, the film featured a fruitful collaboration between Eisenstein and Sergei Prokofiev, who composed the score. Eisenstein's last works were again historical: the two parts of *Ivan the Terrible* (*Ivan Grozny*). If Part 1 premiered in 1945 to great acclaim, Part 2 was too obvious in drawing historical parallels between Stalin and an increasingly megalomaniacal and isolated Ivan, and was not released until 1958. A planned third part was not completed. The *Ivan the Terrible* films, with their probing psychological depictions and their remarkable visual texture (including the final segment of Part 2, the only scene Eisenstein ever shot in color) are widely regarded as his crowning achievement. Eisenstein's pioneering filmmaking and insightful theoretical writings have assured enduring fame for the person who brought Soviet cinema to world attention.

*See also* **Cinema.**

BIBLIOGRAPHY

Bordwell, David. *The Cinema of Eisenstein.* Cambridge, Mass., 1993.

Goodwin, James. *Eisenstein, Cinema, and History.* Urbana, Ill., 1993.

LaValley, Al, and Barry P. Scherr. *Eisenstein at 100: A Reconsideration.* New Brunswick, N.J., 2001.

Nesbet, Anne. *Savage Junctures: Sergei Eisenstein and the Shape of Thinking.* London and New York, 2003.

BARRY P. SCHERR

## EISNER, KURT (1867–1919), German revolutionary leader.

Kurt Eisner served as one of the leaders of the Bavarian revolution of 1918–1919 that toppled the Wittelsbach dynasty and introduced republican government to that southern German state. As provisional prime minister of the new government, Eisner proved incapable of gaining control over the chaotic political situation in postwar Bavaria and fell victim to assassination in February 1919. His brief moment in the political spotlight exemplified both the soaring aspirations and the fumbling incompetence of the Bavarian revolutionaries.

Kurt Eisner was undoubtedly one of the most unlikely figures ever to hold political power in Bavaria. Unlike most of the power brokers in that land, he was neither a Bavarian native nor a Catholic, but a Jew from Berlin. Physically, he was the antithesis of the earthy Bavarian; he had a spindly frame, sallow skin, and a long gray beard. It was impossible to imagine him in lederhosen. He had moved to Munich in 1910 to take up a post as drama critic for the socialist newspaper *Die Münchner Post.* Soon he became a regular at the Café Stefanie, a coffeehouse in Schwabing, the bohemian district that gave birth to the Bavarian revolution.

Eisner might have remained an obscure coffee-house intellectual had it not been for World War I, which, as it brought increasing misery to the German home front, generated an impassioned antiwar movement. In 1917 Eisner emerged as a spokesman for the newly formed Independent Social Democratic Party (USPD), which, unlike the more moderate Social Democratic Party (SPD), argued that only a socialist revolution could bring an end to the war. A follower of the philosopher Immanuel Kant, Eisner delivered speeches filled with glowing abstractions and idealistic slogans. Nebulous though Eisner's rhetoric was, however, his fiery idealism had a genuine appeal at a time when misery and deprivation set people dreaming of a new epoch for mankind.

Eisner's call for strikes to cripple the German war effort resulted in his imprisonment in January 1918, but the Bavarian government released him in October of that year in an effort to placate the militant left. Eisner was not to be placated. He immediately resumed his revolutionary activities, which gained even more resonance when it became clear that Germany was losing the war. On 7 November 1918, he and his followers instigated mutinies among the royal regiments stationed in Munich and quickly asserted control over the city. The Bavarian monarch, King Ludwig III, fled into exile. Eisner proclaimed the birth of the Bavarian Republic and called on people to help him build a new democratic order.

As the new regime's provisional prime minister, Eisner sought to steer a middle course between embittered monarchists and advocates of a communist order modeled on the Bolshevik experiment in Russia. He brought moderate SPD figures into his coalition government. Eisner had never held office before, however, and lacked the leadership skills and tough-mindedness to shift from the world of coffeehouse philosophizing and revolutionary speechmaking to the harsh realities of political administration in a time of extreme volatility. He angered the right by publishing some secret reports that showed how the German imperial government had pushed for war in 1914. He alienated the far left by refusing to place large agricultural, industrial, and financial institutions under state ownership.

Perhaps if he had been granted several years in office, Eisner might have found a way to translate his Kantian vision into political reality, but at a time when thousands were going hungry and armed bands roamed the streets of Munich, few Bavarians were willing to concede their new leader that luxury. Realizing this, Eisner decided to resign after a mere one hundred days in office. However, on 21 February 1919, as he was on his way to the parliament building to resign, Eisner was shot dead by

Count Anton Arco auf Valley, a former army officer who despised "the Jew from Berlin."

Because in retrospect Eisner's brief rule seems benign in comparison to what followed his assassination—a short-lived "Bavarian Soviet" run by Schwabing intellectuals; a bloody suppression of the soviet conducted by rightist Free Corps soldiers; and finally years of archconservative rule that made Bavaria a haven for right-wingers from all over Germany—Eisner has been treated by historians rather better than he was by his contemporaries. While recognizing his inadequacies as a political leader, most scholars give him credit for a deeply humane sensibility and a genuine desire to put Bavaria and Germany on a democratic footing. A plaque now marks the spot in Munich where Eisner was assassinated.

*See also* **Communism; Germany; Social Democracy.**

BIBLIOGRAPHY

Geyer, Martin H. *Verkehrte Welt: Revolution, Inflation und Moderne: Munchen 1914–1924.* Göttingen, Germany, 1998.

Large, David Clay. *Where Ghosts Walked: Munich's Road to the Third Reich.* New York, 1997.

Mitchell, Allan. *The Revolution in Bavaria, 1918–1919: The Eisner Regime and the Soviet Republic.* Princeton, N.J., 1965.

DAVID CLAY LARGE

# EL ALAMEIN, BATTLE OF.

El Alamein transformed British military fortunes in World War II and its victorious general took the name as part of his aristocratic title after the war. The settlement itself was an unremarkable railway halt short of the Libyan-Egyptian border and fifty miles west of Alexandria, with the extremely inhospitable, if not impassable, Qattara Depression lying forty miles to the south.

Prior to the October 1942 battle of El Alamein, the British Eighth Army had been consistently outperformed and out-maneuvered in North Africa by a German-Italian force known by the name of its German contingent, the Afrika Korps. In June 1942 the British-led Commonwealth army had been defeated at Al-Gazala by Field Marshal Erwin Rommel, an outstanding armored commander whose skill, daring, and tempo on the battlefield outclassed his rivals. During the subsequent withdrawal eastward, the British lost the deepwater port of Tobruk, which had held out against all Axis attacks since April 1941 and had become a worldwide symbol of defiance to Germany. (A chance insult by Nazi propagandist Joseph Goebbels, who called its defenders "the rats of Tobruk," led the Eighth Army to call itself the Desert Rats, an accolade its successor formations adopt to this day.)

General Sir Claude Auchinleck, commander-in-chief for the Middle East, retreated from Libya eastward to the Egyptian border, pausing at Matruh to buy time while defenses at the next choke point, El Alamein, could be prepared. The survival of British interests in the Middle East would depend on the successful defense of El Alamein, the final position before Alexandria that could not be outflanked, with the Qattara Depression an obstacle to the south and an ocean to the north. As Rommel harried the Eighth Army throughout its withdrawal, his lines of supply and communication grew ever more extended and vulnerable to air attack. His fuel supplies could only be sent by sea, where they were also vulnerable to both air and submarine attack. Most German supplies came through Tripoli, some 1,400 miles away. As a result, German formations arrived in the area too weak for a major engagement, whereas the British supply line was a mere fifty miles long: a two-hour drive to Alexandria.

Rommel, ever the cavalier with his logisticians, attempted to break through at El Alamein before he was ready, which Auchinleck first blocked and then countered with a series of assaults. At the battle of Tell el Eisa (10 July 1942), the British XXX Corps attempted to outflank the Germans from the northern end of the El Alamein Line. Although two divisions (the First South African and Ninth Australian) secured their immediate objectives, Rommel stalled them. Next, in the first battle of Ruweisat Ridge (14–16 July 1942), Gott's XIII Corps pounced on two Italian divisions, Brescia and Pavia, but German counterattacks successfully retook the positions. A second battle at Ruweisat (21–23 July 1942) was a night attack that, although initially successful, again was blocked by a German counterattack. In these battles, coordination and cooperation between Allied infantry and armor divisions was poorly rehearsed and both arms tended to blame each other for the failure.

In August 1942, with Rommel threatening to dine out in Alexandria, Churchill flew to Africa to see why his Eighth Army could make no progress. He reorganized the command structure, sacking generals and appointing Gott to replace Auchinleck as commander of the Eighth Army, fast becoming a demoralized and defeated force. However fate intervened and Gott's aircraft was shot down by Messerschmitts on 7 August, leading Churchill to appoint Bernard L. Montgomery to command the Eighth Army. Montgomery's arrival in the desert proved to be the beginning of a turnaround in the Allied fortunes. The changes—doctrinal, psychological, and physical—that he wrought in the Eighth Army in August and September 1942 are a model of how to transform a demoralized force of losers into a confident, capable, and winning team, and are studied by businesspeople as well as soldiers to this day. In two months, Montgomery, fresh from England with no desert experience, personally altered the outlook of his army. The results were quickly apparent. At the battle of Alam Halfa (30 August–7 September 1942), Rommel's next attack was blunted, but Montgomery was cautious and refused to counterattack and pursue, feeling that conditions were not yet overwhelmingly in his favor: German morale had not been dented and he needed more tanks, men, and time to build up combat supplies. Instead, firmly in command of a confident force that had tasted victory, Montgomery waited for his moment.

Against the strategic background of Operation Torch (the Anglo-American landings in North Africa planned for November 1942), Montgomery's moment arrived on the evening of 23 October 1942, when he attacked Rommel's 100,000 men and 500 tanks (half of which were Italian) with the Eighth Army's 230,000 men and 1,030 tanks, including 250 M4 Sherman tanks, deployed in combat for the first time. On the eve of combat Montgomery held a press conference and accurately predicted the course and duration of the battle. His assault, code-named Lightfoot, was choreographed in three phases. During the break-in, XIII Corps (under Horrocks, who followed Montgomery to Normandy) made a diversionary attack in the south while the XXX Corps (under Leese, who would eventually succeed Montgomery as army commander) attacked Rommel's center, which was heavily fortified and defended by minefields, but were unable to break through as hoped. The next phase, which Montgomery termed the dogfight, lasted from 26 to 31 October, when Rommel's defenses were systematically crumbled by attrition, characterized by overwhelming artillery firepower. German and Italian counterattacks were repulsed by close air support, coordinated by Air Vice Marshal Sir Arthur Coningham (who also followed Montgomery to Normandy with the same formula), whose command post was positioned with Montgomery's.

The last phase, the breakout, commenced on 1 November. Using the reinforced New Zealand Division, Montgomery punched a hole through the weakened Axis lines and fed X Corps through the gap to roll up the Axis rear. Shattered by the tactical effect of ten days' attritional combat and with his own front disintegrating, Rommel withdrew, counterattacking constantly; the Afrika Korps was nevertheless unable to stem the tide: while the mechanized divisions managed to get away, the less mobile infantry and their supporting formations were left to their fate. By 4 November 1942 Rommel's Afrika Korps had been routed, but the Eighth Army's pursuit was far less certain, leading to criticisms (which were to resurface in Normandy) of Montgomery's excessive caution and inability to exploit operational opportunities with due speed. Days later, the Torch landings took place to the west in Morocco and Algeria, sandwiching Rommel in Tunisia, while on 23 January 1943 Montgomery reached the Axis main port of Tripoli.

Many historians feel that the battle of El Alamein was won by the code-breakers, deception, and the quartermasters. Although Montgomery did not know the exact details of the Axis defensive battle plan, Ultra decryptions from Bletchley Park (the British top-secret code breaking center) gave him Rommel's precise troop and tank strengths on the eve of battle. Ultra also enabled the British to track and sink vital German ammunition and fuel supplies in the Mediterranean. Meanwhile Rommel's own eyes and ears, the

621st Intelligence Company, had been overrun by an Australian battalion in the early fighting at Alamein on 10 July; they were irreplaceable, so the main battle started with a startling German ignorance of their enemy.

On the eve of battle, Allied tanks disguised as trucks assembled in the north; while inflatable armored vehicles, supported by dummy stores dumps and a fake water pipeline constructed from tins, fooled the Germans into thinking the attack would occur later and be launched from the south. Even the Eighth Army's mass batteries of artillery were disguised as trucks or expertly camouflaged, encouraging Rommel to fly to Europe for urgently needed rest and ensuring his absence for the first forty-eight hours of battle. In the final analysis, El Alamein showcased Allied materiel superiority for the first time while Rommel had stretched his logistics elastic to the maximum.

*See also* **Afrika Korps; World War II.**

BIBLIOGRAPHY

Barnett, Corelli. *The Desert Generals.* London, 1983.

Barr, Niall. *Pendulum of War: The Three Battles of El Alamein.* London, 2004.

Bungay, Stephen. *Alamein.* London, 2002.

Latimer, Jon. *Alamein.* Cambridge, Mass., 2002.

McKee, Alexander. *El Alamein: Ultra and the Three Battles.* London, 1991.

PETER CADDICK-ADAMS

---

**ELECTORAL SYSTEMS.** Revolutionary changes in electoral laws occurred repeatedly in Europe in the twentieth century. There were four shifts from majority systems to proportional representation. The first occurred after 1918; the second, after the collapse of the totalitarian regimes of Germany and Italy in 1945; the third in 1989–1991, after the implosion of the Warsaw Pact countries and the Soviet Union; the fourth emerged in 1989–1991. In the fourth shift, proportional representation was introduced after the fall of dictatorships in Southern Europe: Greece (1974), Portugal (1975), and Spain (1976).

ELECTORAL SYSTEMS
The history of the two postwar eras with the consolidation of democracies first in Western Europe, then, after the fall of the Berlin Wall in 1989, in Central and Eastern Europe, has taught at least two lessons: no electoral laws, even from the same "typology"—a majoritarian system or a proportional one—is found to be identical in different historical contexts and within different nations. Major changes were often possible because electoral laws are not part of the constitution.

Nevertheless, electoral reforms did not always operate according to the will of their promoters, who tested the impact of the reform in their political "laboratories." Real poll results may differ from any theoretical prevision made before the vote. A change to electoral law also needs a stabilization period before it will be understood by the electorate and fruitfully used by the political actors.

The case of the 1953 so-called Italian tricky law is one of the most obvious misuses of electoral engineering and a defeat of those who were thinking to use electoral laws on behalf of a precise political strategy. During the Cold War, at the end of the Korean War (1951–1953), Italy had to confront the most important Communist Party (PCI) outside the Soviet bloc: proportional representation, reintroduced after the war, was not able to give a stable majority to Alcide De Gasperi's (1881–1954) Catholic Party and his allies. A new electoral law was planned to ensure stability; this law granted a "premium" to the coalition of parties who would have won more than 50 percent of the votes. This coalition would have then gathered two-thirds of the seats in the national Chamber of Representatives. No premium was activated because the Christian Democratic Party secured only 49.8 percent of the valid votes and no absolute majority.

**ENFRANCHISING LIBERAL DEMOCRACIES AFTER WORLD WAR I**
Before 1914 much progress had been made in establishing a franchise in most European countries and in extending it to the male population. But only after World War I was it possible to abolish formal barriers to the vote for all men over age twenty-one. It was through the participation of men in the war that the voting rights

TABLE 1

### Introduction of male and female universal suffrage in Europe

| Countries | Universal male suffrage | Universal female suffrage |
|---|---|---|
| Greece | 1844 | 1956 |
| France | 1848 | 1944 |
| Switzerland | 1848 | 1971 |
| Germany | 1848 | 1919 |
| Spain | 1869 | 1932 |
| Bulgaria | 1877 | 1945 |
| Belgium | 1894 | 1948 |
| Austria | 1897 | 1919 |
| Norway | 1900 | 1915 |
| Finland | 1906 | 1906 |
| Portugal | 1911 | 1975 |
| Sweden | 1911 | 1921 |
| Denmark | 1915 | 1915 |
| Iceland | 1916 | 1916 |
| Latvia | 1917 | 1917 |
| Lithuania | 1917 | 1917 |
| Estonia | 1917 | 1917 |
| Russia | 1917 | 1917 |
| Poland | 1918 | 1918 |
| Hungary | 1918 | 1918 |
| Czechoslovakia | 1918 | 1920 |
| Netherlands | 1918 | 1922 |
| Ireland | 1918 | 1923 |
| United Kingdom | 1918 | 1928 |
| Italy | 1918 | 1946 |
| Luxembourg | 1919 | 1919 |
| Romania | 1922 | 1945 |
| Malta | 1947 | 1947 |
| Liechtenstein | 1984 | 1984 |

were enlarged to every male citizen after 1918. In some cases the franchise was extended to women. Belgian mothers and widows of soldiers who had died in the Great War were included in the suffrage in 1919; Belgium did not introduce universal female suffrage until 1948. Everywhere in Europe the war and the collapse of the Central Empires and Russia played a decisive role in the wave of enfranchisement. In Weimar Germany the Social Democrat Chancellor Friedrich Ebert (1871–1925) introduced universal franchise for men and women aged twenty or older in 1919. Nevertheless, in many countries at that time, there were marked differences in the "weight" of votes to elect a representative across constituencies. In sum, between 1918 and 1920, male—and sometimes female—universal suffrage became accepted practice in most European democracies.

## PROPORTIONAL REPRESENTATION AGAINST MAJORITY

During the second half of the nineteenth century the idea of proportional representation was spread all over Europe. Scientific societies and, later, political pressure groups promoted the proportional representation of all political opinions into parliamentary debates against the majority systems within single or multimember constituencies.

Proportional representation is a system of electing representatives to a legislative assembly in which it is possible to have a number of members representing any opinion in the electorate. The number of successful candidates representing each political opinion or party is directly proportional to the percentage of votes won.

The 1864 meeting of the Association Internationale pour le Progrès des Sciences Sociales (International association for the progress of the social sciences) encouraged the study and the diffusion of proportional representation against plurality systems. These systems were underrepresenting political, ethnic, and linguistic minorities and together with them, many electors' opinions in "bourgeois" parliaments. Proportional representation was used with different formulas to transform the vote into parliamentary seats. Thomas Hare (1806–1891) and John Stuart Mill (1806–1873) in England, Eduard Hagenbach-Bischoff (1833–1910) with the Association réformiste of Geneva in Switzerland, and Victor D'Hondt (1841–1901) with the Association réformiste pour l'adoption de la représentation proportionnelle in Belgium diffused the proportional idea and offered new electoral formulas for a proportional representation of opinions. During the international meeting of the Association réformiste pour l'adoption de la représentation proportionnelle of 1885 in Antwerp, Belgium, a resolution stated that: "1. the system of elections by absolute majorities violates the liberty of elector, provokes fraud and corruption and can give a majority of seats to a minority of the electorate; 2. the proportional representation is the only means of assuring power to the real majority of the country, an effective voice to minorities and exact representation to all significant groups of the electorate; 3. while the particular needs of each country are recognised, the D'Hondt system of competing lists with divisors, adopted by the Belgian Association, is a considerable advance on the systems previously proposed, and constitutes a practical and efficient means of achieving proportional representation," (Carstairs, p. 3).

**TABLE 2**

### First introduction of proportional representation (different forms) for legislative elections in Europe

| Countries | Introduction | Withdrawal |
|---|---|---|
| Belgium | 1899 | |
| Finland | 1907 | |
| Bulgaria | 1910 | |
| Sweden | 1911 | |
| Denmark | 1918 | |
| Netherlands | 1918 | |
| Romania | 1918 | |
| Austria | 1919 | |
| Germany | 1919 | |
| Italy | 1919 | |
| Luxembourg | 1919 | |
| Switzerland | 1919 | |
| Czechoslovakia | 1920 | |
| Estonia | 1920 | |
| Lithuania | 1920 | |
| Poland | 1921 | |
| Norway | 1921 | |
| Malta | 1921 (STV) | |
| Latvia | 1922 | |
| Ireland | 1922 (STV) | |
| Greece | 1926 | |
| France | 1945 | 1958 (PR again in 1986 and FPTP again in 1988) |
| Iceland | 1959 | 1988 |
| Portugal | 1975 | |
| Spain | 1976 | |
| Hungary | 1989 (mixed with FPTP) | |
| Slovakia | 1993 | |
| Czech Republic | 1993 | |
| Russia | 1993 (mixed with FPTP) | |
| United Kingdom | Never introduced | |

STV=single transferable vote
FPTP=first past the post
PR= proportional representation

Proportional representation was an attempt to integrate better the new elites and the masses and their political parties in the political system and to try to build parliaments, which were the "mirror" of public opinion. At that time it was becoming impossible for liberal democracies and constitutional monarchies with restricted access to suffrage not to take care of the new radical, republican, socialist, and Catholic parties representing the economic and political interests of new social classes derived from processes of industrialization and urban concentration. Proportional representation was not only a liberal and democratic solution to integrate in parliamentary regimes these new political aspirations but also a way to prevent old nineteenth-century conservative and/or liberal bourgeois parties (as in Belgium and Germany) from being removed from the parliaments.

Belgium first introduced proportional representation in 1899 and most European countries followed after 1918–1919, choosing at the same moment to introduce the universal male suffrage. Many countries, except the oldest and more stable democracies, such as Great Britain, abolished their majority systems.

## PLURALITIES AND THE REPRESENTATION OF MINORITIES

After World War I the aim of electoral reform was for a fair representation of opinions and universal suffrage. After World War II the legislators in most countries discussed instead the best electoral system to introduce stability in modern democracies through a fair representation of many strands of thought and opinion in the population. Proportional representation was the answer in most cases.

Proportional representation and the different formulas adopted to put it into practice have always had strong opponents and not only in Great Britain, where proportionality was never introduced. The collapse of liberal regimes between the two world wars raised the question of the impact of proportional representation on "governmental instability." The political economist Ferdinand Aloys Hermens (1906–1998), in the United States during his exile from Germany during the Nazi era, wrote "Democracy or Anarchy" and made a radical criticism of proportional representation that found many positive echoes after the war. Hermens's most famous criticism was that proportional representation had driven Italy to Benito Mussolini's (1883–1945) fascism in 1922 and Germany to Adolf Hitler's (1889–1945) Nazi regime in 1933. Weimar Germany and postwar liberal Italy were chosen by Hermens as the outstanding examples of how proportional representation was unable to secure a strong democratic government.

There were different solutions to this problem after 1945. The quest for stability in France was solved in 1958 with the introduction of a two-stage vote, with a majority system in single-member constituencies. This was at the heart of Charles de Gaulle's (1890–1970) rule in the Fifth Republic. Another solution was the introduction of an election threshold together with proportional representation in order to oblige a party to win a minimum number of votes to be eligible to win any seats. The purpose of an election threshold is generally to keep very small parties from fragmenting the parliament. A reinforced mixed system of single-member constituencies with proportional representation was introduced in the Federal Republic of Germany in 1949 together with a threshold of 5 percent; parties would have to obtain at least 5 percent of the votes in an election to ensure any representation.

Most of the continental European countries have operated some variant of strict PR. Only after the fall of the Berlin Wall (1989), German reunification (1990), the dissolution of the Warsaw Pact (1991), and the birth of the new Community of Independent States (CIS) out of the former Soviet Union (1991) were mixed systems of majority and proportional representation electoral systems, with threshold clauses, adopted in ex-communist countries as well as in Italy (1993).

*See also* **Minority Rights; Suffrage; Suffrage Movements.**

BIBLIOGRAPHY

Bartolini, Stefano. *The Political Mobilization of the European Left, 1860–1980: The Class Cleavage.* Cambridge, U.K., and New York, 2000.

Bartolini, Stefano, and Peter Mair. *Identity, Competition, and Electoral Availability: The Stabilisation of European Electorates 1885–1985.* New York, 1990.

Carstairs, Andrew McLaren. *A Short History of Electoral Systems in Western Europe.* London and Boston, 1980.

Caramani, Daniele. *Elections in Western Europe since 1815: Electoral Results by Constituencies.* London, 2000.

Colomer, Josep M., ed. *Handbook of Electoral System Choice.* Houndmills, Basingstoke, U.K., and New York, 2004.

Duverger, Maurice. *Political Parties: Their Organization and Activity in the Modern State.* London and New York, 1962.

Farrell, David M. *Electoral Systems: A Comparative Introduction.* New York, 2001.

Hart, Jenifer. *Proportional Representation: Critics of the British Electoral System, 1820–1945.* Oxford, U.K., and New York, 1992.

Hermens, Ferdinand Aloys. *Democracy or Anarchy? A Study of Proportional Representation.* 1941. New York, 1972.

Hobsbawm, Eric J. *The Age of Extremes: A History of the World, 1914–1991.* New York, 1994.

Laurent, Annie, Pascale Delfosse, and André Paul Frognier, eds. *Les systémes électoraux: permanences et innovations.* Paris, 2004.

Lijphart, Arend. *Electoral Systems and Party Systems: A Study of Twenty-Seven Democracies, 1945–1990.* Oxford, U.K., and New York, 1994.

Lijphart, Arend, and Bernard Grofman, eds. *Choosing an Electoral System: Issues and Alternatives.* New York, 1984

Mackie, Thomas T., and Richard Rose. *International Almanac of Electoral History.* 3rd ed. London, 1991.

Maier, Charles S. *Recasting Bourgeois Europe: Stabilization in France, Germany, and Italy in the Decade after World War I.* Princeton, N.J., 1975.

Martin, Pierre. *Les systèmes électoraux et les modes de scrutin.* Paris, 1997.

Mayer, Arno J. *The Persistence of the Old Regime: Europe to the Great War.* New York, 1981.

Michels, Robert. *Political Parties: A Sociological Study of the Oligarchical Tendencies of Modern Democracy.* New York, 1962.

Nohlen, Dieter. *Elections and Electoral Systems.* New Delhi, 1996.

Noiret, Serge. *La nascita del sistema dei partiti nell'Italia contemporanea: la proporzionale del 1919.* Manduria, Italy, 1994.

———. "Ferdinand Aloys Hermens y la Crítica de la Representación Proporcional Introducida en Italia en 1919." In *Elecciones y Cultura Política en España e Italia (1890–1923)*, edited by Rafael A. Zurita, Rosanna Gutiérrez, and Renato Camurri, 89–102. Valéncia, 2003.

Noiret, Serge, ed. *Political Strategies and Electoral Reforms: Origins of Voting Systems in Europe in the 19th and 20th centuries.* Baden-Baden, Germany, 1990.

O'Gorman, Frank. *Voters, Patrons, and Parties: The Unreformed Electoral System of Hanoverian England 1734–1832.* Oxford, U.K., and New York, 1989.

Perrineau, Pascal, and Dominique Reyni, eds. *Dictionnaire du vote.* Paris 2001.

Rae, Douglas W. *The Political Consequences of Electoral Laws.* 2nd ed. New Haven, Conn., 1971.

Rokkan, Stein. *Citizens, Elections, Parties: Approaches to the Comparative Study of the Processes of Development.* Oslo, Norway, 1970.

Romanelli, Raffaele, ed. *How Did They Become Voters? The History of Franchise in Modern European Representation.* The Hague and Boston, 1998.

SERGE NOIRET

## ELIAS, NORBERT (1897–1990), German sociologist.

Two experiences appear to have been fundamental to the intellectual development of the German sociologist Norbert Elias (1897–1990); each influenced his work in a different way. The first, World War I, was virtually the antithesis of Elias's model of the "process of civilization." The second, his own complex experience of marginalization, Elias explicitly distilled in a book entitled *The Established and the Outsiders* (1965).

Little is known about Elias's life during World War I; he wrote and said little about this period. But his experience as a telegraph operator on the eastern and western fronts seems to have had a profound effect on him. Suffering from shell shock, he was nearly amnesiac at the end of the war.

Returning to Breslau, Elias, who was from a Jewish bourgeois family, undertook studies in medicine and philosophy. Although Germany's hyperinflation in 1922–1924 forced him to leave school and work in a factory for a time, in 1924 he nevertheless managed to successfully defend his doctoral thesis in philosophy, *Idee und Individuum* (Idea and individual). Once finances stabilized he went to Heidelberg to study sociology, beginning a *Habilitation* under the sociologist and economist Alfred Weber (1868–1958). He also became close friends with another early and influential sociologist, Karl Mannheim (1893–1947), serving as his assistant; during this period he also frequented the famous Institute for Social Research directed by Max Horkheimer (1895–1973) in Frankfurt.

When Adolf Hitler's rise to power in 1933 effectively forced Elias into exile, he attempted to find work in Switzerland and in France. He did not succeed, despite two published articles, one on "The Kitsch Style and the Age of Kitsch" (1935) and the other on the "The Expulsion of the Huguenots from France" (1935); and in a sense he found himself more marginalized than ever in terms of a teaching career. He moved to England in 1935 and three years later he saw his parents for the last time. His father died in 1940 and his mother was deported and was probably killed in Auschwitz.

Elias found it difficult to publish his books. His major work *Über den Prozess der Zivilisation* (The civilizing process), which he started in 1935 with a small grant from a Jewish refugee organization, was published in 1939 by a small Swiss publishing house but it went largely unnoticed, only to be republished to acclaim thirty years later. The work of *Habilitation* from 1933, *Die höfische Gesellschaft,* was published only in 1969.

With the beginning of World War II Elias was interned in Britain as an "enemy alien" on the Isle of Man. After the war he worked in London at an adult learning center. Finally, at the age of fifty-seven, he obtained his first real academic post at the University of Leicester. He remained in England until 1975, except for two years, 1962–1964, during which he taught in Ghana. He was a visiting professor at several universities, particularly in Germany and the Netherlands, where he settled definitively in 1984. Enthusiasm for Elias's work came only late in his career.

Elias eventually took up the question of mores and civilization once again when he examined, with Eric Dunning, the nature of sport as "controlled violence" and in his *Studien über die Deutschen* (1989; The Germans). He there developed the hypothesis of a *Habitus* or "second nature," a key concept in Eliasian sociology that refers to the psychological structures shaped by social environment, and applied it to the peculiarities of German society. He further developed the concept of "de-civilization" as the mirror-image to reflect the recession of civilization and allow the development of "modern barbarism" as happened during the Nazi era.

Isolated and marginalized most of his life, in the early twenty-first century Elias is one of the most read, studied, debated and controversial of all sociologists. His work is at once processual, collective, and individual; one of his books is entitled *The Society of Individuals* (1987). His lenses are psychoanalytical, anthropological, and historical, and he focuses on a range of original subjects such as the emotions, the body, sport, death, and socialization. He has recourse to a repertoire of concepts adequate to such a task, including sociogenesis, psychogenesis, self-control, informalization, *Habitus,* "controlled decontrolling emotions" and others. Elias aspired, as

Robert van Krieken has written, to "cut through many of the central dilemmas in sociology, especially the apparent opposition between action and structure, individual and society."

*See also* **Frankfurt School; Germany; Holocaust.**

BIBLIOGRAPHY

*Primary Sources*

Elias, Norbert. *Reflections on a Life.* Translated by Edmund Jephcott. Cambridge, U.K., and Cambridge, Mass., 1994.

———. *The Germans: Power Struggles and the Development of Habitus in the Nineteenth and Twentieth Centuries.* Translated by Eric Dunning and Stephen Mennell. New York, 1996.

*Secondary Sources*

Mennell, Stephen. *Norbert Elias: An Introduction.* Oxford, U.K., 1989.

van Kriecken, Robert. *Norbert Elias.* London and New York, 1998.

NICOLAS BEAUPRÉ

---

# ELIOT, T. S. (1888–1965), American/British poet, critic, and dramatist.

Born in St. Louis, Missouri, Thomas Stearns Eliot moved to New England in 1906, the home for 300 years of Puritan relatives, to study literature at Harvard, and then to England in 1914, the home of even earlier forbears, to study philosophy at Oxford. He married, undertook jobs as teacher, banker, and editor, and became a British subject in 1927. He can be said to have died a European in 1965, having received the Hanseatic Goethe Award in Germany (1955), the Dante Gold Medal in Italy (1959), the Order of Merit in Britain (1948), and the Nobel Prize for literature in Sweden (1948) as acknowledgements of career-long dedication to development of what he called "the mind of Europe" (Eliot, 1975, p. 39).

Pursuing Harvard doctoral work at Oxford, but prevented by World War I from returning to America to defend his thesis (*Knowledge and Experience,* 1964), Eliot engaged the work of leading philosophers: Francis Herbert Bradley, Henri Bergson, William James, Charles Sanders Peirce, Edmund Husserl, Bertrand Russell. He also learned

Sanskrit to study Indian philosophy. During the decade of his serious philosophical work, Eliot moved from a traditional conception of signs as *re*-presentation of the real to our contemporary conception of signs as *presentation* of the real.

In London in 1914, Eliot met Ezra Pound (1885–1972) who arranged for publication of "The Love Song of J. Alfred Prufrock" (1915), declaring astonishment that Eliot had modernized himself. Eliot admired the work of imagists like Pound and T. E. Hulme and published early poems in Wyndham Lewis's vorticist journal *BLAST,* but developed his distinctive early poetic idiom (widely imitated, thereby becoming a distinctively modern idiom) from study of metaphysical poetry, Jacobean drama, French symbolism, and Dante. Eliot's focus upon squalid urban imagery and demoralized human behavior, his practice of speaking ironically through personae, and his preference for opaque narratives comprising clipped grammar and unusual, unpoetic words offended critics expecting poets speaking in their own voice, developing a steady current of ideas, and animated by the spirit of beauty.

Eliot launched his literary criticism with *Ezra Pound: His Metric and Poetry* (1917), defending modern poetry's difficult meter, unfamiliar use of language, and displays of erudition. In several essays published between 1919 and 1923, Eliot defined a hermeneutic relationship between past and present literature, implicitly rejecting the anti-past futurism of Filippo Tommaso Marinetti (1876–1944), and encouraged a formalism foundational to Anglo-American New Criticism, disallowing genetic and affective accounts of literature as compromising the integrity of the work of art as art. Against Romantic celebration of poetry as an exceptional person's experience, he argued that "honest criticism and sensitive appreciation is directed not upon the poet but upon the poetry" (Eliot, 1975, p. 40). Against Walter Pater's impressionism, he argued that a critic's sensitive and cultivated "impressions are as much created as transmitted by the criticism" (Eliot, 1975, p. 51). After baptism and confirmation into Anglican Christianity in 1927, however, Eliot came to regard literary criticism as necessarily completed by cultural criticism grounded in religious belief.

With publication of *The Waste Land* (1922), Eliot confirmed his position as preeminent English modernist poet, soon to rival William Butler Yeats (1865–1939) as most famous living poet. The poem presents fragments of 1920s London experience (zombie-like commuters, pub conversations, bored couples, banking business, abortion), weaving them together with parallels from the past (prophets thunder, Cleopatra sails the Nile, Tereus rapes Philomela, Augustine and the Buddha enjoin asceticism, Christ dies), all presented alongside hallucinated images of exhausted, drought-stricken lands made waste, according to Eliot's references to J. G. Frazer's *Golden Bough*, because the gods no longer bless humankind with fertility. Sometimes measuring the present against the past to show contemporary degeneration, at other times deploying immortal seers Tiresias and the Sybil to suggest that all time is the same, the poem projects personal spiritual dispossession and sexual enervation (which biographical criticism identifies as Eliot's own) as a timeless narrative of a culture's strikingly contemporary and disturbingly continuous dysfunctions. Baffling many, it struck a poetic avant-garde as faithfully rendering an intensely literary consciousness's kaleidoscopic impressions of European cultural collapse following World War I. Regarded in its own time as both the ultimate expression of high modernist aesthetics and important social criticism, its dramatic and sometimes violent juxtapositions of language, imagery, mood, times, events, and ideas continue to engage new readers.

Eliot's lifelong interest in theater expressed itself first in notable criticism of Renaissance dramatists and then in plays of his own. An uncompleted experimental verse play about inhabitants of a bed-sit wasteland in the modernist spirit of his early poetry was followed by *Murder in the Cathedral* (1935), verse drama focused on the martyrdom of Thomas à Becket (c. 1118–1170): Eliot uses a chorus, makes an act of a sermon, and has medieval murderers directly address the modern audience to justify their crime. Determined to reestablish verse drama on the modern stage, between 1938 and 1958 Eliot wrote several popular drawing-room comedies that present implicitly religious studies of sin, guilt, vocation, forgiveness, and love beneath their realistic surface.

From lines left over from *Murder in the Cathedral*, Eliot began a sequence of poems published during World War II as *Four Quartets* (1943). Affirming the value of the social, religious, and intellectual life that British history had fostered, the poems were a comfort and encouragement to many during the war. Continuing the meditative, penitential, and mystical mood of poems like *Ash Wednesday* (1930), still difficultly learned in their allusions but much more discursive and occasionally conversational in style, the poems explore questions of faith and fate, time and eternity, experience and expression—all from points of view ranging from the personal to the communal, and from the contemporary to the historical. Eliot regarded these poems as his best work.

Between the wars, Eliot expressed his commitment to continuity and coherence in contemporary European culture through his editorship of *The Criterion* (1922–1939). Soliciting contributions from intellectuals across Europe representing widely ranging aesthetic and political beliefs, Eliot declared himself "classicist in literature, royalist in politics, and anglo-catholic in religion" (Eliot, 1975, pp. 18–19). In *The Idea of a Christian Society* (1939), Eliot rejected fascist and communist solutions to Europe's modern social problems but bemoaned Europe's liberalism, regarding its laudable determination to free people from illegitimate constraints as ultimately a negative ideology that could oppose no positive vision to communism and fascism. In radio broadcasts and publications after World War II, Eliot discussed rebuilding European culture in the context of a new global order. Contemplating in *Notes Towards the Definition of Culture* (1948) the difficulties of the secular experiment of building the good society by means of reason, Eliot suggested that since thinking the way to a radically different future cannot anticipate the way such a future would feel to its inhabitants, society should pursue a pragmatic conservatism.

Eliot's work continues to find itself at the center of contemporary cultural debates. Rapturous reception of his work as modern antidote to the poison of nineteenth-century convention was replaced by complaints in the postmodern last half of the twentieth century that his work was elitist, misogynistic, homophobic, fascistic, and anti-Semitic. A new generation of readers has returned to Eliot, finding that his deep and sophisticated engagement on so many fronts with the stresses and strains of modern life allows his work still to disclose new and challenging perspectives on the contemporary concerns (about relationships between high and low culture, gender, sexuality, ideology, racism, and so on) that we bring to it. "The mind of Europe," Eliot noted, "is a mind which changes, and ... this change is a development which abandons nothing *en route*, which does not superannuate either Shakespeare, or Homer, or the rock drawing of the Magdalenian draftsmen"—or the work of Eliot himself (Eliot, 1975, p. 39).

*See also* **Avant-Garde; Pound, Ezra; Theater; Yeats, William Butler.**

BIBLIOGRAPHY

*Primary Sources*

Eliot, T. S. *The Complete Poems and Plays of T. S. Eliot.* London, 1969.

———. *Selected Prose of T. S. Eliot.* Edited by Frank Kermode. London, 1975.

*Secondary Sources*

Gordon, Lyndall. *T. S. Eliot: An Imperfect Life.* New York, 1999.

Laity, Cassandra, and Nancy K. Gish, eds. *Gender, Desire, and Sexuality in T. S. Eliot.* Cambridge, U.K., 2004.

Moody, A. David, ed. *The Cambridge Companion to T. S. Eliot.* Cambridge, U.K., 1994.

Smith, Grover. *T. S. Eliot's Poetry and Plays: A Study in Sources and Meanings.* 2nd ed. Chicago, 1974.

DONALD J. CHILDS

---

# ELTSIN, BORIS. *See* Yeltsin, Boris.

---

# ÉLUARD, PAUL (1895–1952), French poet.

Paul Éluard was born Eugène Émile Paul Grindel on 14 October 1895 in the Paris suburb of Saint-Denis. His mother was a seamstress who rose to become a manager of a dressmaking shop; his father, Clément Grindel, was an accountant who in about 1900 started a real estate business that became successful and prosperous.

Éluard received a scholarship to the elite Primaire Supérieure Colbert in Paris, but in 1912 he fell ill with tuberculosis. With his mother he traveled to England for a cure and then to a Swiss sanitarium. There he fell in love with a young Russian woman, Helene Deluvina Diakonova—to whom he gave the nickname "Gala." A voracious reader, he began writing poetry and in 1913 published *Premiers poèmes* (First poems). At the beginning of the First World War, the young Éluard was recruited by the army and later assigned to an evacuation hospital as a nurse. He self-published, in an edition of seventeen copies, ten poems with the meaningful title *Le devoir* (Duty) and signed "Paul Éluard," employing the maiden name of his maternal grandmother. He spent most of the war in the hospital, whether as patient or nurse. In 1917 he married Gala and the same year published *Le devoir et l'inquiétude* (Duty and disquietude), followed a year later by *Poèmes pour la paix* (Poems for peace). These texts won the attention of the French editor and publisher Jean Paulhan (1884–1968), who introduced Éluard to the men who were soon to found the surrealist movement.

**SURREALISM**

Éluard participated in the first public demonstrations of the Paris dadaists and became involved with the magazine ironically called *Littérature,* founded by André Breton (1896–1966), Philippe Soupault (1897–1990), and Louis Aragon (1897–1982). At about the same time, he published *Les animaux et leurs hommes, les hommes et leurs animaux* (Animals and their men, men and their animals) and in 1921 started a short-lived Dada publication, *Proverbe.* As Dada gave way to surrealism, Éluard took part in the surrealists' earliest demonstrations. Taking as their slogan the imperative to "change life," which was coined by the French poet Arthur Rimbaud (1854–1891), the surrealists engaged in a rebellion against the values that had led to the enormous massacres of the First World War. Meanwhile, Éluard continued to work with his father on construction projects in the Parisian suburbs—and to him is owed a street named Rue Jacques Vaché, after one of the early surrealist heroes.

The arrival in Paris of the German painter and sculptor Max Ernst (1891–1976), his friend but also Gala's lover, complicated Éluard's life with conflicting feelings of amity and jealousy. In 1924 the poet went off on a "fugue" that fed rumors about his mysterious disappearance while he traveled around the world. About the time he returned, Breton published the first of his two major surrealist manifestos. Éluard was immediately and in all ways committed to the group. He took part in *Une vague de rêves* (A wave of dreams), the first surrealist collective text, collaborated with Benjamin Péret (1899–1959) on *152 proverbes mis au goût du jour* (1925; 152 tasteful proverbs for today), and with André Breton and René Char (1907–1988) on *Ralentir travaux* (Slow down—construction ahead), and again with Breton on *L'immaculée conception* (1930; The immaculate conception).

## COMMUNISM

In 1926, with his surrealist friends, Éluard joined the French Communist Party (PCF). The next several years saw publication of his major works, including *Au défaut du silence* (1925; For want of silence), *Capitale de la douleur* (1926; Capital of pain), *L'amour de la poésie* (1929; The love of poetry). In 1929 he met Maria Benz, also called Nusch, who would become his companion and muse for the next seventeen years; they married in 1934. Éluard published more poetry—*Facile* (1935; Easy), a hymn to love and newfound happiness, and *Les yeux fertiles* (1936; Fertile eyes).

Relations between surrealists and communists became stormy, especially around divergent views concerning a nascent organization of avant-garde writers. The party preferred conventional cultural values and opposed the artistic nihilism associated with surrealism, and the Soviet predilection for "proletarian art" did not help matters. On 15 August 1930 the surrealist group repudiated two of its members, Louis Aragon and Georges Sadoul, because they had attended the Second International Congress of Revolutionary Writers, and the surrealists were at odds with the theses coming out of that congress. While Aragon distanced himself from Breton, Éluard remained his ally and took his side during the "Aragon affair" even while attending the antiwar Amsterdam-Pleyel Congress and participating in the anticolonialist exhibition organized by the Communist Party, entitled "The

Truth about the Colonies." Expelled from the party in 1933, Éluard appeared on the behalf of the surrealists at the antifascist International Congress of Writers for the Defense of Culture held in Paris in June 1935.

While in Spain in 1936 for a series of conferences on Pablo Picasso (1881–1973), Éluard saw that country erupt into civil war. Now he committed his poetry to the service of politics, published "Novembre 1936" in the French Communist newspaper *L'humanité*, and renewed ties with the PCF, which fully supported the Spanish republicans. Éluard also wrote "Victoire de Guernica" (Victory of Guernica), which together with Picasso's famous painting was on display in 1939 at the Spanish Pavilion at the New York World's Fair. In spite of this work with the Communists, Éluard helped Breton organize the International Exhibition of Surrealism in Paris, which opened in January 1938, and he also collaborated on the *Dictionnaire abrégé du surréalisme* (1938; Brief dictionary of surrealism). He also published *L'évidence poétique* (1937; Poetic evidence), *Les mains libres* (1937; Free hands), *Cours naturel* (1938; Natural course), and *Médieuses* (1939).

In 1942 Éluard rejoined the French Communist Party and during the German occupation became an important player in framing party policy concerning artists. He belonged to the Comité Nationale des Écrivains and, among other works, published *Poésie et vérité* (1942; Poetry and truth). This collection includes the famous poem, "Liberté," which circulated throughout the occupied region of France.

> On my school notebook
> On my school desk and on the trees
> On sand on snow
> I write your name (translated from the French)

During the war Éluard published a number of collections of poetry that carried similar messages of hope: *L'honneur des poètes* (1943; The honor of poets), *Le livre ouvert* (1940; Open book I), *Sur les pentes inférieures* (1941; On the lower slopes), *Le livre ouvert II* (1942; Open book II), *Les sept poèmes d'amour en guerre* (1943; Seven poems of love in wartime), *Le lit la table* (1944; The bed the table), and *Les armes de la douleur* (1944; Weapons of pain).

After Liberation and with the end of the war, Éluard was renowned and widely respected. In September 1946, however, Nusch died suddenly. The poet's suffering exploded in *Le temps déborde* (1947; Time overflows). However, he kept to his commitments and became a prominent spokesperson for the World Congress of Intellectuals for Peace in Wrocław, Poland, in 1948 and in Mexico in 1949, where he met Dominique (née Odette Lemort), who became his last wife in 1951.

Éluard's death on 18 November 1952 occasioned a grand funeral, and he was laid to rest in the famous Parisian cemetery, Père Lachaise, beside other celebrated French Communists.

*See also* **Aragon, Louis; Breton, André; Communism; Dada; Ernst, Max; Spanish Civil War; Surrealism.**

BIBLIOGRAPHY

*Primary Sources*

Éluard, Paul. *Uninterrupted Poetry: Selected Writings.* Translated by Lloyd Alexander. New York, 1975.

———. *Oeuvres complètes.* 2 vols. Preface and chronology by Lucien Scheler; text edited and annotated by Marcelle Dumas and Lucien Scheler. Paris, 1990–1991.

*Secondary Sources*

Nugent, Robert. *Paul Éluard.* New York, 1974.

Vanoyeke, Violaine. *Paul Éluard: Le poète de la liberté: Biographie.* Paris, 1995.

PAUL ARON

---

# ÉMIGRÉ LITERATURE.

The experience of exile is not exclusive to twentieth-century literature. It was a central theme in the work of Homer and Plato, as well as in Euripides (*The Heracleidae*). Seneca, who had himself been forced into exile in Corsica, related this experience in his *Ad Helviam matrem, De consolatione* (Consolation to his mother Helvia). Nor was it uncommon prior to the twentieth century for writers to take refuge outside their native countries. Voltaire, for instance, settled in Ferney on the Swiss border in order to be able to cross over in case of any trouble, and Victor Hugo fled his hated oppressor Napoleon III to live in Guernsey. However, in the twentieth century the phenomenon took on a completely new scale. The emigration and exile (voluntary or enforced) of hundreds of writers, artists, and intellectuals, generally as a result of oppressive and censorious political regimes, was a defining characteristic of the century.

The largest wave of intellectual migration was unquestionably that which followed Hitler's accession to power in Germany in 1933: intellectuals fled Nazi Germany in large numbers because of their Jewish origins, their stated political views, or simply to preserve their freedom of speech. As in the Nazi case, the totalitarian and authoritarian nature of the political regime in question was often one of the major causes of exile for intellectuals who, under these regimes, were confronted with censorship and sometimes a threat to their lives. However, the nature of the regime was not always the reason for exile. Sometimes wars produced a flood of exiles. At other times certain cultural centers acted as magnets, attracting writers and intellectuals from all over the world.

## WARTIME AND INTERWAR EMIGRATION

World War I marked the first milestone in the history of exiled writers in the twentieth century. Neutral countries were receiver states. Switzerland was a refuge for pacifist artists, poets, and writers. The Frenchman Romain Rolland is probably the most famous example here. However, Switzerland also welcomed many younger German writers who were at the forefront of the Dada movement, which emerged in Zurich during the war. After 1918 most of the émigrés returned to their countries of origin and the Paris Dada and Berlin Dada movements were nurtured by this preliminary experience.

During the interwar period London, Vienna, Berlin, and Paris exerted an attraction for intellectuals born elsewhere. In part this was a revival of prewar cultural trends. Paris is probably the prime example: the City of Light attracted an entire generation—F. Scott Fitzgerald, Ernest Hemingway, and others, termed "lost generation" by Gertrude Stein—who settled there by choice and fled their countries of origin for a period, either temporarily or, like Stein, permanently. The peak in the history of intellectual emigration was not, however, represented by voluntary emigration but by the enforced flight from Nazism from 1933 onward. Moreover, as the Reich's dominion spread, emigration grew apace.

From 1933 both Jewish and non-Jewish Germans fled Hitler's Reich in order to escape censorship and, above all, political and racial persecution. One of the most prominent cases is that of the Mann family—the novelist Thomas Mann, his wife, Katia, their six children, and Thomas's brother Heinrich—who settled in the United States and were in exile at the height of the anti-Nazi struggle. They used radio broadcasts, articles, novels, essays, and every other possible medium to expose the workings of Nazism to those in the West still unaware of the threat Hitler's regime posed to the world.

As German imperialism spread, countries that had been exile havens became traps that closed on the exiles or generated new waves of departures. This is what happened in Austria after its annexation in 1938: some German writers who had taken refuge in Vienna had to flee once again, and some Austrian citizens had to leave in their turn. At an advanced age Sigmund Freud had to flee; he died in London. What had happened in Vienna was repeated in early 1939 in Prague.

When World War II broke out in September 1939 some refugees suddenly became "enemy aliens" and were therefore suspects in the countries that were at war with the Reich. France thus interned in camps large numbers of refugees, some of whom were then handed over to the Nazis by the Vichy regime that was set up after the defeat of France in 1940. Others fled—accompanied this time by anti-Nazi or anti-Vichy French writers—toward Switzerland or the United States. One group, including the artists Marc Chagall and Jean Arp, escaped through the work of an American socialite turned smuggler, Varian Fry, in Marseille. Some did not make it and committed suicide, as did the German literary critic, writer, and philosopher Walter Benjamin when turned back at the neutral border of Spain. Others took their lives in despair at the attitude of their host country—such as the German poet Walter Hasenclever after he had fled to France—or gave in to despair about the apparent triumph of Nazism and the destruction of the Europe they knew. The Viennese writer Stefan Zweig said farewell to the world at war by taking his own life in Brazil in 1942.

The USSR, which had served as a refuge for communist writers and intellectuals persecuted in their own countries, also proved to be a death trap for many. The Moscow trials of 1936–1937 descended first on many intellectuals who had taken refuge in the USSR. The German-Soviet pact of 1939 then had its own tragic consequences. Imprisoned in the gulag following Stalin's purges, the writer Margarete Buber-Neumann was then handed over to the Nazis and transferred to the camp at Ravensbrück.

## POSTWAR EMIGRATION AND EXILE

The experience of exile had a devastating impact on many individuals. In his novel *Ignorance* (2000), Milan Kundera describes the reception given to Czech émigrés in France after World War II: "In the fifties and sixties, émigrés from the Communist countries were not much liked there; the French considered the sole true evil to be fascism: Hitler, Mussolini, Franco, the dictators in Latin America. Only gradually, late in the sixties and into the seventies, did they come to see Communism, too, as an evil" (p. 11), one that had produced wave after wave of out-migration. The periods in which these regimes took a particularly hard line following popular revolts, such as in Berlin in 1953, Budapest in 1956, or the Prague Spring of 1968, then led to departures on a wider scale. In 1968 many Polish intellectuals of Jewish origin were forced or strongly encouraged into exile following the anti-Semitic campaign orchestrated by the ruling Communist Party. To deal with certain particularly undesirable cases, states would sometimes simply force them into exile instead of imprisoning or assassinating them. In 1976, during a West German tour of his music, the East German poet and songwriter Wolf Biermann found that he was blocked from ever returning to the GDR. Two years earlier, the Nobel Prize–winner for Literature (1970), Alexander Solzhenitsyn, had been forcibly exiled from the USSR to the United States.

## EXILE: FROM EXPERIENCE TO LITERARY EXPLORATION

Even those who chose to stay, or who were prevented from leaving, sometimes described themselves as "inner exiles," blocked from access to the media. These people withdrew into the private domain, which is what the authorities wanted in the first place. Inner exile was a slightly veiled alternative to expulsion. One famous example is the German expressionist poet Gottfried Benn, who accommodated himself to Nazism in preference to starting life again elsewhere.

Exile itself constituted a source of literary exploration. Many novels and short stories therefore relate this experience, such as *Transit Visa* by Anna Seghers (1944), *Escape to Life* (1939) by Klaus and Erika Mann, and *Party in the Blitz* (2003), the recently discovered and published texts that Elias Canetti wrote in England.

In some cases exile even led writers to make a permanent change in their working language, as with Milan Kundera, who gradually moved from Czech to French, and Vladimir Nabokov, moving from Russian to English. For others, the conscious or passive choice to continue writing in the language of their country of origin could, however, represent resistance to the contamination of the language by totalitarian jargon. The Romanian-born writer Paul Celan changed his surname (he was born Antschel) but continued to write in German, the language of his youth in Czernowitz and the language of those who killed his family and—again through suicide—who brought him to his death in 1970 in Paris.

Exile also stimulated the creation of new international networks and literary circles within the country of refuge. New York thus became a center of French literature from 1940 to 1945, just as Paris had become a center of American literature twenty years earlier and a haven for German writers in the 1930s. Paris was a magnet for exiled Polish intellectuals, who were haunted by the memory of the exile of their compatriots Frédéric Chopin and Adam Mickiewicz in the nineteenth century. Most of these men and women were determined to continue working in the literary field despite the difficulties. They formed networks around émigré publishing companies (such as Querido in Amsterdam) and literary magazines, which have been a recurrent feature in the history of literary exile in the twentieth century.

After years in exile some of these groups and their publications became permanent fixtures of their adopted countries' cultural life. One such survivor is the Polish dissident magazine *Kultura*, founded in Italy in 1947 and then published in Maisons-Laffitte near Paris by Jerzy Giedroyc until his death in 2000. This magazine helped to publicize some of the finest authors in contemporary Polish literature both in Poland and in the West, while also being smuggled home to nurture the dissident movement.

The ends of wars or the collapse of regimes that had generated the exile presented émigrés with the dilemma of whether to return to their homelands. In the case of Germans after 1945, there also arose the question of choosing their country of return, the FRG (West Germany) or the GDR (East Germany). Thomas Mann chose neither, opting instead for a home near Zurich, Switzerland, while Bertolt Brecht ultimately settled in East Berlin.

The circles of exile and the exiles themselves, despite the fact that they were sometimes accused of leading an isolated existence, often played the role of intermediary between the host country and the country they had left, creating a form of diasporic writing of great importance in the later twentieth century and beyond.

*See also* **Immigration and Internal Migration; Purges; Refugees.**

BIBLIOGRAPHY

*Primary Sources*

Canetti, Elias. *Party in the Blitz: The English Years.* Translated by Michael Hofmann. London, 2005.

Kundera, Milan. *Ignorance.* Translated by Linda Asher. London, 2002.

Seghers, Anna. *Transit Visa.* Translated by James A. Galston. London, 1945.

*Secondary Sources*

Betz, Albrecht. *Exil et engagement: Les intellectuels allemands et la France, 1930–1940.* Paris, 1991.

Jasper, Willi. *Hotel Lutetia: Ein deutsches Exil in Paris.* Vienna, 1994.

Mehlmann, Jeffrey. *Émigré New York: French Intellectuals in Wartime Manhattan.* Baltimore, Md., 2000.

Meller, Stefan, and Thierry de Montbrial, eds. *Mémoires d'un combat: Kultura 1947–2000.* Cahiers de l'Ifri 32. Paris, 2000.

Palmier, Jean-Michel. *Weimar en exil: Le destin de l'émigration intellectuelle allemande antinazie en Europe et aux Etats-Unis.* 2 vols. Paris, 1990.

NICOLAS BEAUPRÉ

# ENIGMA MACHINE.

The "Enigma machine" was a family of electromechanical rotor cipher-machines whose components and operating procedures evolved over time. It was the principal

German military and civil cipher device from the late 1920s through World War II. Messages enciphered on Enigma were decrypted ("broken") from December 1932—just as Adolf Hitler was about to take power in Germany—by the Polish General Staff's Cipher Bureau and during World War II also by Great Britain's Bletchley Park ("Ultra") operation.

The foundations for Enigma decryption were laid by the mathematician Marian Rejewski soon after he joined the Cipher Bureau as a civilian cryptologist in September 1932. He used a mathematical theorem that has been called "the theorem that won World War II." Permutation theory and documents supplied by French military intelligence officer Gustave Bertrand, which had been bought from Hans-Thilo Schmidt ("Asché")—an employee of the German Armed Forces' Cipher Office—enabled Rejewski to reconstruct the wirings of the military Enigma's rotors and reflector. He guessed correctly (to the later chagrin of British cryptologist Alfred Dillwyn Knox) that the letters of the alphabet were wired into the machine's entry ring simply in alphabetical order.

With the Enigma reconstructed, Rejewski and fellow mathematician-cryptologists Henryk Zygalski and Jerzy Różycki devised techniques to regularly break messages. They used the "grill" and "clock," the "cyclometer" and its derivative "card catalog," and from late 1938 the "cryptological bomb" and "perforated sheets." They also exploited the machine's design quirks and German cipher clerks' security lapses. In January 1938 the Poles were reading a remarkable 75 percent of Enigma intercepts.

On 25 July 1939, in the Kabaty Woods south of Warsaw, with World War II a month off, the Poles revealed their achievements to British and French intelligence representatives. The British mathematician Gordon Welchman has written: "Ultra would never have gotten off the ground if we had not learned from the Poles, in the nick of time, the details both of the German military ... Enigma machine, and of the operating procedures that were in use." Welchman subsequently contributed an important innovation to a British-produced "bomb": a "diagonal board" that increased the device's efficiency.

In September 1939 key Cipher Bureau personnel were evacuated from Poland via Romania to France. At "PC [Command Post] Bruno" outside Paris, during the "Phony War," they resumed breaking Enigma ciphers. They collaborated with Bletchley Park, eventually by teletype (for maximal security, they corresponded in Enigma, closing dispatches with a "Heil Hitler!"). The mathematicians were visited by Alan Turing, conceptual founder of the first programmable electronic computer, Colossus; the latter would come into use in late 1943 to break still more complex German ciphers that the British christened "Fish."

Enigma decryption created sustained opportunities (sometimes inadequately exploited) to look over enemy leaders' shoulders. It took time for Britain to master large-scale interception, decryption, translation, assessment, and secure distribution of Enigma traffic. Eventually Ultra provided the Allies near-unprecedented tactical and strategic advantages in the North African, Mediterranean, European, and Atlantic theaters, and—through official as well as clandestine sharing of Ultra intelligence with the Soviets—on the eastern front. Ultra enabled the Allies not only to counter German moves but also to deceive Germany about Allied intentions, most notably on the eve of the Normandy landings (June 1944).

Ultra's influence on the war has been assessed variously. A common opinion holds that Ultra shortened it by two years. Such estimates of duration, however, beg the question of outcome.

British prime minister Winston Churchill's greatest fear was that German submarine wolf packs might strangle his sea-locked country. The major factor that staved off Britain's defeat in the Battle of the Atlantic was its regained mastery of Naval-Enigma decryption, thanks to captures of Enigma machines and key tables from German submarines and weather trawlers. Had Britain capitulated, a United States deprived of the British Isles as a forward base could not have entered the European or North African theaters. The war in Europe would have been played out essentially between Germany and the Soviets. Germany, given two years' grace time, might have developed a crushing advantage in jet aircraft, missiles, perhaps atom bombs.

At war's end, Supreme Allied Commander Dwight D. Eisenhower described Ultra as having been "decisive" to Allied victory. Churchill told King George VI: "It was thanks to Ultra that we won the war."

Ultra remained secret, at Churchill's behest, until F. W. Winterbotham published *The Ultra Secret* in 1974.

*See also* **Espionage/Spies; Intelligence.**

BIBLIOGRAPHY

Bertrand, Gustave. *Enigma ou la plus grande énigme de la guerre 1939–1945.* Paris, 1973.

Hinsley, F. H., and Alan Stripp, eds. *Codebreakers: The Inside Story of Bletchley Park.* Oxford, U.K., and New York, 1993.

Kahn, David. *Seizing the Enigma: The Race to Break the German U-Boat Codes, 1939–1943.* Boston, 1991.

Kozaczuk, Władysław. *Enigma: How the German Machine Cipher Was Broken, and How It Was Read by the Allies in World War Two.* Edited and translated by Christopher Kasparek. Frederick, Md., 1984.

Rejewski, Marian. "Remarks on Appendix 1 to [volume 1, 1979, of] *British Intelligence in the Second World War* [edited] by F. H. Hinsley." Translated from the Polish by Christopher Kasparek. *Cryptologia* 6, no. 1 (January 1982): 75–83.

Welchman, Gordon. *The Hut Six Story: Breaking the Enigma Codes.* New York, 1982.

Winterbotham, F. W. *The Ultra Secret.* New York, 1974.

CHRISTOPHER KASPAREK

---

# ENSOR, JAMES (1860–1949), Belgian painter.

A painter, printmaker, and musician, James Sydney Ensor was also a writer who expressed his deepest aspirations in various texts, lectures, and an extensive correspondence. Critics have often sought to compare him to Joseph Mallord William Turner (1775–1851) for his use of light; to Hieronymus Bosch (1450–1516) for his cynicism; and to Rembrandt (1606–1669), Antoine Watteau (1684–1721), and Francisco José de Goya y Lucientes (1746–1828) for his remarkable etched engravings. In fact, Ensor was a unique and unclassifiable artist who opened a path that helped painters acquire the freedom to express their most intimate thoughts by the use of rare and original chromatic choices.

James Ensor was born on 13 April 1860 in the city of Ostend, Belgium, on the North Sea coast. His father, who was English, and his mother owned a souvenir shop and sold seashells, masks, and chinoiseries to the tourist trade. Ensor's entire universe was already present in his parents' small shop, often visited by his maternal grandmother, who was fond of costume disguises and carnival folklore. Later, Ensor would say that this exceptional background enabled him to develop his artistic faculties, and he credited his grandmother as his great inspiration.

On 1 October 1877 Ensor enrolled at the Fine Arts Academy in Brussels, where he proved to be a mediocre student. Three years later he returned to Ostend and settled back to live with his parents. He put up a small studio in the attic with a beautiful view of Ostend and its environs. Here he created his first major paintings, including *Chinoiseries aux éventails* (Chinoiseries with fans), *Le lampiste* (The lamplighter), *Une coloriste* (A colorist), *Le salon bourgeois* (The bourgeois salon), and *Musique russe* (Russian music). In addition to his immediate surroundings, Ensor let himself be guided by ambient light, his major source of inspiration, which transfigures the real and blurs the classical line. But he was not associated with the impressionists, who sought to reproduce the vibrancy of light itself; Ensor aspired to give it a solid, particulate form. His search for a vision led him to destroy many of his early canvases, although personal rancor over their uneven reception may have also played a role.

As a young artist, however, Ensor also won acceptance in several artistic circles, including the Chrysalide, L'Essor, and Les XX, which was directed by a lawyer, Octave Maus. Although he contributed to every exhibition of the latter group, his participation was much discussed, and some of his works were rejected, including *L'entrée du Christ à Bruxelles* (Christ's entry into Brussels) in 1889. The same year, he finally hit upon the use of pure color. After having painted seascapes, landscapes, interiors, flowers, and still-lifes, he now started a series of masks and carnival crowds, caricatures of the bourgeoisie, scenes of death and evil, and self-portraits both burlesque and Christ-like.

Despite his fecundity during this period, Ensor progressively became a recluse in Ostend. Surrounded by females, including his mother, aunt, and sister "Mitche"—as well as his faithful friend Mariette Rousseau, to whom he often wrote—he became increasingly misogynist. Feeling himself criticized by family and misunderstood by the avant-garde, Ensor, fearful of being forgotten,

**Christ's Entry into Brussels.** Painting by James Ensor, 1889. BRIDGEMAN ART LIBRARY

became obsessed with creating an enduring reputation. To this end, he developed skills as an engraver, which through printmaking provided him with an ideal way to disseminate works otherwise deprived of audience or outlet.

In 1894 Ensor mounted his first one-man show in Brussels, thanks to support from his friend Eugène Demolder, the author of an 1892 book about Ensor subtitled *Mort mystique d'un théologien* (Mystical death of a theologian). In 1916 came the first complete monograph devoted to his work, by Emile Verhaeren, another friend. After 1900, although he continued to paint prolifically, it seemed to be with diminished inspiration; his major works were behind him. At the same time, the new century brought recognition both within Belgium and internationally, beginning with the acquisition of one hundred etchings from the Albertine of Vienna. In 1903 King Leopold II (r. 1865–1909) knighted Ensor, and in 1923 Ensor was admitted to the Royal Academy of Belgium. During the same period, his musical talent was encouraged by his friends Albin and Emma Lambotte, who gave him a harmonium in 1906. He wrote the score for a ballet-pantomime *La gamme d'amour* (The scale of love), which he finished in 1911, having not only composed the music but also designed the sets, costumes, and texts. Ensor wrote a great deal and so became not only a painter but also ENSOR; he put himself on stage, so to speak, becoming the incarnation of his favorite pun, "Hareng-saur" (literally, "salted herring"; phonetically, "Ensor's Art"). His writings shared the sense of provocation found in his paintings. But it was the painter who was admired, recognized, and ennobled—his title of baron came in 1929. Ensor died on 19 November 1949 in Ostend, his cradle of inspiration.

*See also* **Painting, Avant-Garde; Surrealism.**

BIBLIOGRAPHY

France, Hubert de. *James Ensor: Proeve van gecommentariëerde bibliografie = essai de bibliographie commentée.* Brussels, 1960.

Taevernier, August. *James Ensor: Catalogue illustré de ses gravures, leur description critique et l'inventaire des plaques.* Ledeberg, Belgium, 1973.

Tricot, Xavier. *James Ensor: Catalogue Raisonné of the Paintings.* 2 vols. London, 1992.

VIRGINIE DEVILLEZ

# ENVIRONMENTALISM.

Environment-alism is a social movement animated by the goal of bringing about deep changes in how humans perceive and behave toward the natural world. It aims at a fundamental shift in society's vision of humankind's home planet: from a world perceived as offering a virtually limitless cornucopia of resources for human use to a world perceived as fragile, finite, and requiring careful stewardship on the part of its increasingly powerful human inhabitants. Although the movement's roots lie in the nineteenth century, environmentalism really only took off during the cultural ferment of the 1960s, spreading rapidly throughout Western Europe and the other industrial democracies during the 1970s and 1980s. By the early 2000s, environmentalist ideas have come to constitute a prominent feature in the political, economic, and cultural landscape of virtually all the major industrial democracies. Environmentalism still has a very long way to go before its ambitious goals of economic and ecological restructuring come close to full realization—but it has made a most impressive (and incisive) start.

## THREE HISTORICAL PHASES

In Europe, three major phases in the rise of environmentalist awareness can be discerned from the eighteenth to the twenty-first century. The first, situated in the eighteenth and nineteenth centuries, might be described as the era of utilitarian conservationism, marked by concern over soil erosion or the accelerating depletion of certain key resources such as timber, and by the development of new strategies for managing natural areas with an eye to husbanding those resources for the future. Thus the earliest signs of a modern environmental sensibility can be traced to the Enlightenment period, as naturalists first began putting together the systematic picture of Earth's plants and animals that would gradually mature into the full-fledged science of modern biology. Yet this emergent conservationist attitude remained quite far removed from the worldview of twenty-first-century environmentalists because it only assigned value to nature's plants and animals insofar as those creatures—or their products—might prove useful to humans. A tree was a good thing, according to this vision, because it offered wood for fuel or for building such objects as houses, boats, or furniture; its value lay solely in its utility to humankind. This homocentric vision of nature would predominate in Europe throughout the nineteenth century (and still continues to play a key role in the advancement of environmentalist agendas in some quarters even in the early twenty-first century).

Toward the late nineteenth century, however, a new vision began to emerge—an attitude that might be described as aesthetic conservationism. Partly through the far-reaching influence of the artistic currents of Romanticism, and partly as a reaction against the rapid spread of urban society and industrialism, more and more citizens of Europe and North America began to place a value on nature simply because they deemed it beautiful to behold. The first major sign of this new attitude can be seen in the creation of Yellowstone Park by the United States government in 1872. Yellowstone was of no "use" to anyone because it consisted of a large tract of territory fenced off from further development or human intervention: its value lay simply in its very wildness, in the beauty people found through the contemplation of nature in a relatively primal and untouched state. During the succeeding decades, many nations followed the example set by the United States, creating national parks throughout the world: in Australia (1879), Canada and New Zealand (1880s), South Africa (1890s), Sweden (1909), and France and Switzerland (1914). This current of aesthetic protectionism gave a powerful boost to the efforts of the more utilitarian conservationists, and the two groups often formed alliances around the turn of the twentieth century in getting laws passed for the defense of natural sites.

Yet one should not read too much into these early efforts. Throughout the first half of the twentieth century, the vast majority of Europeans, like the citizens of the world's other industrial democracies, continued to believe unabashedly in endless material progress through unrestrained economic growth, in the seemingly limitless bounty that human ingenuity could extract from nature. Only a small minority even became aware of conservationist issues, and even fewer actively campaigned for nature protection.

All this changed quite dramatically in the 1960s—the decade that marked the birth and rapid

Greenpeace members hang from a bridge across the Rhine to block river traffic in a protest inspired by contamination incidents in late 1986, Leverkusen, Germany. ©REUTERS/CORBIS

rise of modern environmentalism. Several factors came together to bring about this sudden shift: a keen awareness among scientists of the increasingly grievous (and in some cases irreversible) damage being done to the earth's ecosystems by the accelerating growth of industrial society; a new radicalism among scientists and nature lovers, no doubt emboldened by the activism and protests of the 1960s counterculture; and a new sophistication in the science of ecology itself, offering truly alarming forecasts of a full-scale environmental collapse if human beings continued to exploit nature with the reckless abandon that had thus far prevailed. For the first time, many ordinary citizens began using the metaphor of a spaceship to describe Planet Earth: a finite environment, from which only limited resources could be drawn, and into

which only a limited quantity of pollutants and effluents could be cast. Once humankind crossed a critical threshold, the spaceship would simply become uninhabitable, a spherical tomb floating in the blackness of space. It was this attitude of profound alarm, coupled with an urgent and hopeful effort to mobilize the requisite social and economic changes for long-term survival, that distinguished modern environmentalism from its conservationist predecessors.

## THE GROWTH OF ENVIRONMENTALISM

The movement spread with extraordinary swiftness, flowing across borders and winning converts by the thousands throughout the industrialized democracies. A pullulating variety of organizations formed to spread the message: from small neighborhood groups promoting recycling to international networks such as Friends of the Earth and Greenpeace; from the Environmental Protection Agency in the United States (1970) to the Ministry of the Environment in France (1971) to the creation of the United Nations Environmental Program (1972). Between 1965 and 1975, vast numbers of books, newspaper articles, and TV programs devoted to environmentalist topics spread across the cultural scene; and public opinion polls consistently showed that citizens placed environmental issues near the top of their list of priorities for public policy. While the number of hard-core environmental activists remained relatively small (probably in the thousands throughout Europe), the number of Europeans who considered themselves ardently "pro-environment" clearly numbered in the tens of millions by the mid-1970s.

Not surprisingly, the politicians responded with alacrity. As fledgling environmentalist (or "green") political parties began to form in the 1970s, somewhat hesitantly submitting their first candidates in regional and national elections, the mainstream parties of both Left and Right quickly took notice: they soon co-opted various portions of the environmentalist message within their own party platforms, and declared themselves to be ardently "greener than thou." Green parties formed and began contesting elections in the late 1970s in England, Germany, and France; other West European nations, such as Spain, Italy, Sweden, and the Netherlands, followed suit in the 1980s. These new green parties tended to receive between 2 percent and 10 percent of the vote in national elections, and rarely succeeded in pushing beyond those levels; but their influence far exceeded these modest statistics because their very existence—and their vocal advocacy on behalf of environmental issues—forced the larger mainstream parties in government to begin institutionalizing significant measures for environmental protection.

## ENVIRONMENTALISM'S IMPACT

During the 1980s, and even more markedly during the 1990s, a dense blanket of environmental legislation and regulation gradually spread over the societies of Western Europe (with the newly liberated societies of Eastern Europe following suit after the collapse of the Soviet empire). In France by the early 1990s, for example, more than one thousand specialized laws on the environment were in place, as well as eighty-three ordinances and regulations at the level of the European Union and some three hundred international treaties. A commensurately complex thicket of French governmental agencies, institutes, and regulatory bodies had come into being to implement and enforce these new laws.

Here indeed lay one of the great ironies of the environmental movement's history: despite the fact that most green activists deeply distrusted the centralized bureaucracies of the nation-state and advocated a devolution of power to more decentralized and local forms of democratic power, the fact remained that several decades of successful environmental activism had resulted in more, not less, government. The sheer complexity of most environmental issues, and their close imbrication in virtually every aspect of a modern industrial economy, all but forced the management of environmental problems into the hands of governmental authorities—from the municipal level all the way up to the supranational institutions of the European Union. The "greening" of Europe had only proved possible through a significant growth in state power.

A second great irony also faced Europe's green activists. During the movement's early years, in the 1960s, most environmentalists earnestly believed that the main "enemy" lay in Big Industry—the huge factories with their belching smokestacks, the captains of industry who had strong economic interests in blocking environmental regulation and who possessed powerful political connections to help them do so. But the activists turned out to be wrong. By the year 2000, it was the industrial sector that exhibited far and away the most impressive "greening" of any facet of European society. Partly the changes were voluntary—undertaken by industrial firms because of tax incentives or because of concerns about maintaining a positive image before an environmentally aware public opinion; and partly the changes were coerced by ever rising standards of environmental legislation and regulation. Yet, whatever the reason, the factories of the 1990s emitted only a small fraction of the pollutants they had spewed a mere three decades earlier; they were far more energy efficient; and a great many of the products they created were being

**Okohaus (Eco-house), an environmentally friendly housing development in Berlin, was built in 1987.** ©Angelo Hornak/Corbis

designed with tough environmental standards in mind, so that they might minimize the harm done to the natural world throughout their product life cycle, from manufacturing to disposal. The combined pressures of public opinion and stringent legislation had made a major impact.

Far less successful in the "greening" effort were the important economic sectors of transportation, the consumer economy, and agriculture. Europeans drove more cars, faster cars, bigger cars in the 2000s than they had four decades earlier; and although these modern vehicles emitted far fewer particle pollutants than the models of the 1960s, they still belched forth greenhouse gases on an ever growing scale—and most consumers

apparently did not care enough about this fact to switch to eco-friendly modes of transport, such as buses, bicycles, or trains. The consumer economy, meanwhile, was pouring out a cornucopia of products that would have astonished even the most brazenly optimistic economists of the 1960s: despite substantial efforts at recycling, the volume of trash produced in most European countries in the 2000s had grown by 300 percent since the 1960s. Energy consumption had just about quadrupled in the four decades between 1960 and 2000, and the portion derived from renewable sources such as hydroelectric, wind, or solar power constituted a paltry 8 percent of the overall energy equation: the other 92 percent of energy came from sources that would sooner or later run out.

As for European agriculture, in 2004 it still remained premised on the same model that had dominated the 1950s: pour on the fertilizers, squeeze the most possible out of the land, ignore erosion and soil depletion, and place faith in the invention of new chemicals to fix the problems that will inevitably arise down the road. Overfishing of the seas around Europe, meanwhile, has resulted in the near extinction of many species that once provided a plentiful bounty of seafood; efforts by national governments and by the European Union to rein in the destructive practices of industrial-scale fishing enterprises had, by the 2000s, spectacularly failed to yield positive results.

**LOOKING TOWARD THE FUTURE**

The "bottom line," therefore, remains mixed. On one level, it is astonishing to observe just how many areas of European society have been deeply affected by environmentalist changes—and all this in the relatively short span of a mere four decades. Attitudes, habits, practices, laws, and institutions have all undergone a significant green transformation. And yet the transformation remains incomplete—appallingly so, when one considers the high stakes in play. European society, it is fair to say, has taken the first important steps down the road to a truly sustainable economic and cultural order; but the road yet to be traveled remains dauntingly long.

A pessimist might argue that environmentalism has failed, because modern industrial society has proved incapable of making a sufficiently swift transition into a fully sustainable economy, and (more importantly) because the hardest changes— those involving real sacrifices—still lie in the future. An optimist, on the other hand, could argue that the most difficult phase has already occurred: the phase in which large numbers of citizens first become aware of the environmentalist challenge and begin to adjust their horizons commensurately. According to this vision, a generation newly educated in environmental values, and energized by the grim prospect of looming environmental collapse, will prove ready to make the sacrifices, and to meet the challenges, that undeniably still lie ahead.

*See also* **Consumption; Greenpeace; Greens.**

BIBLIOGRAPHY

Bess, Michael. *The Light-Green Society: Ecology and Technological Modernity in France, 1960–2000.* Chicago, 2003.

Cronon, William, ed. *Uncommon Ground: Toward Reinventing Nature.* New York, 1995.

Dalton, Russell J. *The Green Rainbow: Environmental Groups in Western Europe.* New Haven, Conn., 1994.

Dominick, Raymond H. *The Environmental Movement in Germany: Prophets and Pioneers, 1871–1971.* Bloomington, Ind., 1992.

Latour, Bruno. *Politics of Nature: How to Bring the Sciences into Democracy.* Translated by Catherine Porter. Cambridge, Mass., 2004.

Lipietz, Alain. *Green Hopes: The Future of Political Ecology.* Translated by Malcolm Slater. Cambridge, Mass., 1995.

McNeill, J. R. *Something New under the Sun: An Environmental History of the Twentieth-Century World.* New York, 2000.

Nash, Roderick. *The Rights of Nature: A History of Environmental Ethics.* Madison, Wis., 1989.

Oelschlaeger, Max. *The Idea of Wilderness: From Prehistory to the Age of Ecology.* New Haven, Conn., 1991.

Worster, Donald. *Nature's Economy: A History of Ecological Ideas.* Cambridge, U.K., 1994.

MICHAEL BESS

**ERASMUS PROGRAM.** In 1987 the European Commission started funding a mobility program for European students. This program, named Erasmus after the cosmopolitan scholar (1465–1536), was the culmination of the European partners' political will to cooperate and also the starting point for the harmonization of the European Space for Higher Education. In the construction of Europe, the Europe of knowledge and learning has often lagged behind. Yet in 1955 it was decided that an intergovernmental institute for research and training should be created. It would take more than twenty years to see this hope fulfilled by the inauguration in 1976 of the European University Institute of Florence. Success lay ahead but university cooperation was limited to graduate students, doctoral students, and a few dozen professors. Europe wished to develop a wider process and to target a more varied audience. In 1986 Europe launched the Comett program of cooperation between universities and companies.

Finally, in 1987, the Europe of education became reality, although it was still fragile and patchy. When the Erasmus program was launched in 1987, 3,244 students from all over the European Community went to study in a university of one of its twelve member states. They were pioneers, and enthusiasm for the program soon became widespread. In 1992 eighty thousand students had benefited from the program and ten years into it, four hundred thousand had taken advantage of the grants allocated by the commission.

But these figures are still well below the target set in 1987 of mobility for 10 percent of students moving among universities in Europe. All parties agree on the beneficial effects of the program: the students come back transformed, wiser. They acquire not only exposure to different teaching methods and different research themes but also language skills and a new life—and love—experience. In 2002 the French director Cédric Klapisch (b. 1961) developed this almost mythical dimension of the experience in a movie. L'auberge espagnole (The Spanish apartment), a widely acclaimed Franco-Spanish production, focuses on Xavier, a French student on an Erasmus exchange in Barcelona, where he shares a flat with students from all over Europe. This saga highlights the changes and cultural shock that are also part of the Erasmus experience.

The European Union's voluntarist policy, which permits a sharp development of the mobility of European students, has also been the butt of criticism. In practice, students have faced many obstacles: red tape, a striking lack of accommodation in the host universities, lack of information, welcomes that left much to be desired, differences between school schedules, difficulties in validating credits obtained, and insufficient grants. During the 1990s, a few studies pointed out these weaknesses, along with the gaps and risks entailed by the Erasmus program. The program seemed in danger of becoming an exchange program for wealthy students. Aware that their public images were also at stake, the universities started making considerable efforts to improve their implementation of Erasmus. A specific logistics for Erasmus students was implemented in each university. Student mobility also became a local or regional political issue. Further subsidies were allocated by territorial and regional authorities, national grants, and supplementary grants offered by local powers (for

instance the Regions in France) complemented the European Community grants. Aware that the international reputation of local universities could become an asset, towns or regions implemented specific and very public policies to improve the image of their educational institutions. They pampered the incoming students, offering them local tours, language classes, and even gourmet tasting sessions—a far cry from the anonymity of the major universities that welcome thousands of Erasmus students each year. All countries actively joined the Erasmus project. Germany and France head the list, and Spain and Italy, which also attract many students, follow. The United Kingdom's participation in the program, however, is deeply unbalanced; it welcomes many students but "exports" far fewer. The English-speaking or English-teaching universities are sought after by European students, which has increasingly led these institutions to restrict access.

In 2006, 2,199 higher education institutions in thirty-one countries—twenty-five European Union member states, three countries belonging to the European Economic Area (Iceland, Liechtenstein and Norway), and three candidates (Bulgaria, Romania, and Turkey)—are part of the Erasmus program. Since its creation, 1.2 million students have benefited from studying abroad. In 2004 the Erasmus budget added up to 187.5 million euros. On 1 January 2004 Erasmus opened up to the world with the launch of Erasmus Mundus. This cooperation and mobility program aims to improve the quality of European higher education through collaboration with new countries. Erasmus Mundus is designed to create new centers of excellence for European teaching and research by supporting high-quality graduate degrees and welcoming students, researchers, and teaching staff from other countries.

But the "Europe of Knowledge" is based on more than a student-mobility project. Erasmus has given rise to many different projects and fits into a much wider European education policy. Subsequent to the launch of Erasmus, seven other operations were set up to promote cooperation between European partners. They include programs that promote the professional training of youth (Petra), promoting foreign languages (Lingua), encouraging continuing education (Force), and spurring technological innovation (Eurotechnet). All these operations, Erasmus included, have now been brought together as Socrates, which is intended to build a Europe of knowledge and contribute to a common European identity. Socrates includes different operations such as Comenius (school education), Erasmus, Grundtvig (adult education), and Lingua and Minerva (information and communication technologies in education). These different operations have highlighted the weaknesses of a Europe of knowledge, notably the diverging national traditions of each country and the uncountable difficulties in following a truly European program. Although it is possible to take classes for a few months or a year in another European country, it is still difficult to validate the degrees obtained outside the national borders. Yet the economic world demands multilingual employees, trained in different cultures and prepared for work in an international environment. Thus the homogenization of higher education has become a European priority.

At the Sorbonne in May 1998 , Germany, Italy, the United Kingdom, and France made a formal appeal (known as the Sorbonne Declaration) for a European University: "The Europe we are building is not only that of the Euro currency, of banks and economy, it must also be a Europe of knowledge." The European Commission encouraged the use of the European Credit Transfer System (ECTS), already used in Erasmus exchanges, a system adopted to ensure that credits and diplomas obtained are acknowledged and validated. In June 1999 all the European education ministers pursued the process by signing the Bologna Declaration, which harmonizes the European Space for Higher Education. The changes in the European University Space go deep: acknowledged and clear degrees; a program divided into three cycles (bachelor's, master's, and doctorate levels); a system of credit transfer and accumulation; student, teacher, and researcher mobility; and the development of a culture of quality evaluation. This famous Bologna Declaration has had a tremendous impact. All European universities have been asked to revise their syllabi, degrees, and the way in which these are valued. Implementation of the Bologna policies has not always been easy, particularly for the many institutions that had to shift suddenly from a two- to a three-year syllabus for the first part of their degree courses. Ultimately, this small revolution will permanently transform the shape of higher education in Europe.

*See also* **Education; European Union.**

BIBLIOGRAPHY

Berning, Ewald, in cooperation with Margit Weihrich and Wolfgang Fischer. *Accommodation of ERASMUS-students in the Member States of the Europe-Community: Study Carried Out for the Commissioners of the European Communities.* Munich, 1992.

European Union education information. Available at http://www.Europa.eu.int/comm/education.

VALÉRIE PIETTE

## ERNST, MAX

**ERNST, MAX** (1891–1976), a major artist of the German Dada and French surrealist movements.

Born in Brühl, Germany, Max Ernst studied philosophy at the University of Bonn, where he first encountered Sigmund Freud's psychoanalytic theories. Traumatic events and dreams of his childhood often formed the creative foundation of his imagery. In Bonn, he joined the Young Rhineland movement, encouraged by August Macke. His early paintings were influenced by cubism and German expressionism, such as *Crucifixion* (1913), a work also inspired by the German Renaissance master Matthias Grünewald. After reluctantly serving in the German artillery during World War I, Ernst established the Cologne Dada movement with his wife, Luise Straus-Ernst, and Johannes Theodor Baargeld (Alfred F. Gruenwald). Sexual and machine imagery in *Katharina Ondulata* (1920) find parallels in Marcel Duchamp's *Large Glass* and the futile Dada machines of Francis Picabia.

At a printer's shop, Ernst discovered a teaching-aids manual. Its assorted botanical, zoological, geological, microscopic, and anatomical illustrations sparked an outpouring of new work: collages, overpaintings onto full-page plates, and oil paintings that duplicated found imagery, as in *Elephant of the Celebes* (1921) and *Oedipus Rex* (1922). Giorgio de Chirico influenced his spatial environments. Jean Arp and Tristan Tzara encouraged his contact with other Dada groups, including the Parisians. Ernst exhibited his collages at the Galerie au Sans Pareil in May 1921, a seminal exhibition for establishing the direction of later surrealist imagery. Ernst and Paul Éluard published *Répétitions* (1922) and *Les malheurs des immortels* (1922; The misfortunes of the immortals), collaborative books that juxtaposed Ernst's collages with Éluard's

***Elephant of the Celebes.*** Painting by Max Ernst, 1921. TATE GALLERY, LONDON/ART RESOURCE, NY

poetry. In the fall of 1922, Ernst moved to Paris and soon painted the first surrealist group portrait, *The Rendezvous of Friends* (1922). His most emblematic alchemical painting, *Of This Men Shall Know Nothing* (1923), includes a sun, a moon, and a sexually conjoined couple, inspired by Herbert Silberer's psychoanalytic interpretation of alchemy.

In 1924 André Breton's *Manifeste du surréalisme* called for automatic methods to tap the creative powers of the unconscious mind. Ernst responded with the "invention" of several automatic techniques. He produced *frottages* by rubbing graphite and charcoal on paper placed over rough surfaces to produce textures that inspired images of forests and other natural forms, as in his *Histoire naturelle* series (1926). He created *grattage* paintings by layering paints onto canvas, then placing the canvas over rough surfaces and scraping to produce patterns to provoke his imagination. The resulting *grattage* paintings of forests, shell-flowers, and bird families continue into the late 1920s. Loplop, a birdman and Ernst's alter ego, presents paintings within paintings from 1928 onward.

Ernst also produced three collage novels—*La femme 100 têtes* (1929; The hundred headed woman), *Rêve d'une petite fille qui voulut entrer au carmel* (1930; A little girl dreams of taking the veil), and *Une semaine de bonté* (1934; A week of kindness)—assembling multiple collages into novels with only short captions or title pages. To create these collages, Ernst collected illustrations from nineteenth-century serial novels. Unlike the tattered edges and abstracted imagery of the cubist collages of Pablo Picasso and Georges Braque, Ernst's collage pieces were carefully clipped and joined to create unified images that heightened the shock of his strange hybrid figures and environments. These chaotic novels reflect many of the surrealist themes and interests of the 1930s—politics, sexuality, religion, psychoanalysis, violence, natural history, Oceanic art, and alchemy. He also created sculptures, incising river rocks with bird imagery during a summer in 1934 spent with Alberto Giacometti. Paintings of overgrown jungles date to the late 1930s. He developed Oscar Dominguez's technique of decalcomania, compressing paint between canvas and glass to produce spongy and mottled textures. References to his relationship with Leonora Carrington, the English surrealist, can also be found. Works of the late 1930s and early 1940s, such as *Europe after the Rain* (1941), reflect mounting political tensions in Europe, and Adolf Hitler included several works, including Ernst's earlier *La belle jardinière* (1923; The beautiful gardener), in the Degenerate Art Exhibition in 1937.

From 1941 to the early 1950s Ernst lived in the United States, first in New York with the collector Peggy Guggenheim, among exiled surrealists. Living in Sedona, Arizona, with his fourth wife, the American surrealist Dorothea Tanning, Ernst painted western landscapes and created his most famous sculpture, *Capricorn* (1948), a "family portrait." Tanning and Ernst returned to France, where they lived until his death. He was awarded the Venice Biennale Prize in 1954. He continued abstract technical experiments, while his late paintings often included cosmological imagery inspired by space exploration. Throughout his life, he illustrated books of his own poetry, other surrealist writers, and his favorite authors, including Lewis Carroll.

*See also* **Cubism; Dada; Surrealism.**

BIBLIOGRAPHY

Camfield, William A. *Max Ernst: Dada and the Dawn of Surrealism.* Munich, 1993.

Legge, Elizabeth. *Max Ernst: The Psychoanalytic Sources.* Ann Arbor, Mich., 1989.

Russell, John. *Max Ernst: Life and Work.* New York, 1967.

Spies, Werner. *Max Ernst, Loplop: The Artist in the Third Person.* Translated by John William Gabriel. New York, 1983.

———. *Max Ernst: Collages.* Translated by John William Gabriel. New York, 1991.

Spies, Werner, ed. *Max Ernst: A Retrospective.* Translated by John William Gabriel. Munich, 1991.

Warlick, M. E. *Max Ernst and Alchemy.* Austin, 2001.

M. E. WARLICK

**ESPERANTO.** Esperanto was intended as an international language, a language of wider communication to exist beside local and national languages, and was first introduced in 1887. The work of a young Polish Jewish ophthalmologist and intellectual, Lazar Ludwik Zamenhof (1859–1917), the language is based primarily on European languages, particularly Latin, with words drawn also from Germanic and Slavic sources. The grammar, however, has many features linking it with agglutinative and isolating languages in other parts of the world. It is both a spoken and a written language, using the Roman alphabet, and is based on fairly simple rules, making it relatively easy to learn.

Esperanto was one of several languages proposed in the late nineteenth century, among them Volapük (1881), the work of Johann Martin Schleyer (1831–1912), which proved difficult to learn, so that many of its adepts moved to Esperanto. Zamenhof limited his own contribution to Esperanto to a basic vocabulary and a set of grammar rules: he left its development to its users, thereby combining a planned core with free-flowing expansion of the language through active use. The language flourished initially in the Russian Empire, where Leo Tolstoy was among its earliest converts (1894), and then in the 1890s in Germany, France, and beyond. Esperanto clubs were formed in numerous communities, books and magazines appeared, and vigorous international correspondence began. Zamenhof translated major literary

## ARTICLE 7 OF THE UNIVERSAL DECLARATION OF HUMAN RIGHTS, IN ESPERANTO AND ENGLISH

Ĉiuj homoj estas jure egalaj, kaj rajtas sen diskriminacio al egala jura protekto. Ĉiuj rajtas ricevi egalan protekton kontraŭ kia ajn diskriminacio, kiu kontraŭas tiun ĉi Deklaracion, kaj kontraŭ kia ajn instigo al tia diskriminacio.

[All are equal before the law and are entitled without any discrimination to equal protection of the law. All are entitled to equal protection against any discrimination in violation of this Declaration and against any incitement to such discrimination.]

(In Esperanto, the accent in all words falls on the second-to-last syllable; j is pronounced like y, ŭ like w, and ĉ like ch.)

works, including *Hamlet* and the entire Old Testament, into Esperanto, beginning a tradition that continued into the early twenty-first century. The first international congress of Esperanto speakers took place in Boulogne-sur-Mer, France, in 1905, and the Universal Esperanto Association (UEA), linking Esperantists in Europe and beyond, was founded in 1908. In France the language was supported particularly by business people and scientists. During World War I, UEA was active in relaying communications among families divided by the war.

After the war, UEA, based in Geneva, promoted Esperanto at the League of Nations. Despite a favorable report, a proposal to promote the teaching of Esperanto in schools (among other measures) was defeated, primarily through the diplomatic efforts of the French. However, Esperanto found ready acceptance among working people in many countries, and soon a strong socialist and proletarian movement grew up beside the politically neutral UEA, gaining particular force in the newly established Soviet Union, where some revolutionaries saw Esperanto as the future language of worldwide socialism. But a schism opened between the primarily Western European members and the

Esperanto Union of the Soviet Republics (SEU) from 1928 to 1930. SEU soon came under attack from Joseph Stalin, under whose regime SEU leaders were rounded up and executed as cosmopolitans and enemies of the people. A similar fate awaited the large Esperanto movement in Central Europe. The German Esperanto Association was closed down by Heinrich Himmler in 1936, despite its efforts to accommodate itself to the Nazi regime, and a large percentage of Esperanto enthusiasts (including the extensive Zamenhof family) fell victim to the Holocaust in Germany, Poland, Hungary, and other countries.

Following World War II, Esperanto re-emerged in Western Europe. Organizations were established or re-established in most Western European countries, and in Latin America, North America, and parts of Asia. The annual World Esperanto Congresses, the thirty-first of which occurred in Bern in 1939, were revived in 1947. Efforts to interest the United Nations in Esperanto began early, with an Esperanto delegation sent to the UN's first headquarters at Lake Success. The question was referred to the UN Educational, Scientific, and Cultural Organization (UNESCO), resulting in a resolution (1956) noting the achievements of Esperanto in the promotion of international intellectual exchanges. This action was reinforced in 1985 by a similar resolution encouraging member states to introduce Esperanto and the study of language problems in schools and universities.

Stalin and his legacy slowed the re-establishment of official Esperanto organizations in Eastern Europe, although Yugoslavia under Josip Broz Tito, himself an Esperantist, actively promoted the language. Poland Esperantists were among the first to reorganize, hosting the World Esperanto Congress in 1959, and associations revived in Bulgaria and Hungary, with Czechoslovakia emerging after 1968, and the German Democratic Republic in the 1960s. But Esperanto activity in Eastern Europe was extensive, since the language offered a way of making international contacts outside official channels. In 1987 the World Congress in Warsaw drew almost six thousand people.

The electronic revolution of the 1990s saw a significant shift in Esperanto activity as more and more people learned the language over the Internet and began to use it for informal communication.

Although membership in the UEA and the organized Esperanto movement in general have declined in the early twenty-first century, the number of Esperanto users appears to have increased, particularly outside Europe, in such places as China and parts of Africa. Web sites for self-instruction, large electronic libraries of Esperanto materials, and online magazines and radio are easily available.

Esperanto's future in Europe depends in part on the future of European institutions. The European Esperanto-Union has proposed Esperanto, in combination with the languages of European Union (EU) members, as a solution to the increasingly polarized language situation in EU institutions. The language is taught on a voluntary basis in a number of EU universities and schools. Above all, it is used by ordinary Europeans as a neutral alternative to English and a way of accessing international culture through its wealth of original and translated literary works, its numerous meetings and festivals, and its highly developed communication networks.

*See also* **European Union; League of Nations; Pacifism; United Nations and Europe.**

BIBLIOGRAPHY

Eco, Umberto. *The Search for the Perfect Language.* Oxford, U.K., 1995.

Janton, Pierre. *Esperanto: Language, Literature, and Community.* Albany, N.Y., 1993.

Nuessel, Frank. *The Esperanto Language.* New York, 2000.

Richardson, David. *Esperanto: Learning and Using the International Language.* Eastsound, Wash., 1988.

*Lernu.* Available at http://www.lernu.net. For learning Esperanto.

HUMPHREY TONKIN

---

**ESPIONAGE/SPIES.** Ancient religious and historical texts such as the biblical Old Testament or Sun Tzu's *Art of War* (chapter 13, "On the Use of Spies") underpin the continued importance in military strategy and operations of the twin processes of gaining and analyzing information about one's enemy. Lumped together, these have become known as "military intelligence" and in the late twentieth century a specific genre of intelligence

history emerged. Although popular myth associates most of this military information gathering with the James Bond school of intelligence warfare, from World War II onward military intelligence has relied on four types of sources: human intelligence (HUMINT) gained from the interrogation of prisoners, censorship of mail, and analysis of captured documents; traditional espionage; photographic intelligence (PHOTINT) of aerial reconnaissance images; and signals intelligence (SIGINT).

Traditionally, much of this intelligence work was ad hoc, or a function of the diplomatic communities that shape national and coalition policies, rather than a specifically military activity. This is illustrated by the observation that the organizations to control and coordinate intelligence gathering and analysis in the United Kingdom were formalized only late in the nineteenth century: the British army and Royal Navy established permanent intelligence departments in 1873 and 1883 respectively. Those of the U.S. Navy and War Department were established in 1882 and 1885. It may be observed that much of their early activities involved collating open-source material and preparing maps. Other, more covert organizations such as the British Secret Intelligence Service were formalized even later, in 1909. Indeed, until World War II it can be observed that the military frequently ignored the intelligence community, dismissing its observations and scorning its personnel. It is remarkable how many nations went to war in the years 1939–1941 in total ignorance of their opponents. Throughout the Allied armies in World War II, unit intelligence officers were usually the least experienced, newest arrivals, and the British only established a regular army intelligence corps in 1957, followed by the U.S. Army Intelligence Corps in 1961.

### HUMAN INTELLIGENCE (HUMINT)

The post–World War II reliance that western governments have put on technological solutions to intelligence gathering, particularly SIGINT, overshadows the contribution that traditional HUMINT has made in the twentieth century. Spies can provide character insights that SIGINT cannot, as well as the view of a target denied by weather to photo reconnaissance. Some spies have been casual sources with information of a specific nature, but many have traditionally been attached to diplomatic missions or run by personnel from embassies and legations. During World War II, both the British Special Operations Executive (SOE) and its U.S. counterpart, the Office of Strategic Services (OSS) trained and relied on spies, as much for sabotage purposes as for intelligence gathering. Part of the dividend was comprehensive knowledge of the German Atlantic Wall (*Atlantikwall*) defenses in Normandy prior to D-Day. Most of the data was obtained by French spies in the traditional manner and conveyed back to England. The German *Abwehr* (counterintelligence) spies deployed into the United States, Canada, and the United Kingdom were all rounded up and either executed or "turned" (by the Double Cross XX-Committee) to provide false information to the Third Reich.

The effectiveness of spies increased exponentially with the development of longer range and more portable wireless sets. This was both their strength and Achilles' heel, for most spy networks penetrated by the *Abwehr* in Europe or MI5 in the United Kingdom seem to have been compromised initially by radio direction finders. Counterintelligence efforts during World War II were directed by the dictators more against their own than against foreign subversives. Both the Nazi Gestapo and Security Service of the SS (Sicherheitsdienst der SS) and the Soviet OGPU (and its successor, the People's Commissariat of Internal Affairs, or NKVD) spent more resources on monitoring the politically suspect or unreliable than on uncovering real spies. The Soviets' greatest wartime spying achievements were not against the Germans but against their allies. It is significant that while the spy ring of U.K. agents (Anthony Blunt, Guy Burgess, and Donald Maclean, along with John Cairncross, and Kim Philby) and perhaps a dozen U.S. agents passed vital information to Moscow throughout World War II, there was no equivalent Anglo-American success against the USSR (who were, after all, wartime allies). In the Pacific, Japanese spy rings provided much useful data before the attack on Pearl Harbor, the Malay Peninsula, and Singapore.

Of course, spies can be brilliant but disbelieved by their military overlords. The German-born Soviet spy Richard Sorge (1895–1944) warned the Soviets of the impending German invasion (Operation Barbarossa) in June 1941 but was ignored by Joseph Stalin (1879–1953), and U.S. authorities were cavalier in listening to warnings of a Japanese raid on Hawaii (Pearl Harbor, December 1941) or a German counterattack in the Ardennes (December 1944). British military intelligence ignored the warnings of Dutch Resistance spies that SS armored units were concentrated around Arnhem prior to the September 1944 parachute drop. Other intelligence revelations can be hampered by interdepartmental rivalry. SD-Gestapo-*Abwehr* conflict was often to blame for German intelligence blunders, as have been FBI-CIA (and other agency) tensions in the United States as well as Europe, post–World War II. British authorities have tended to coordinate all intelligence activity through a Joint Intelligence Committee, to resolve such problems in advance.

## WIRELESS COMMUNICATION

In each world war, the military intelligence communities appear to have had to relearn the skills required to establish networks of agents and collect their products, sift and interrogate prisoners of war, interpret SIGINT (signals intelligence), analyze PHOTINT (photographic intelligence), draw up reliable intelligence estimates, and collate all these activities for national and coalition benefit. Although these functions were reduced or disbanded after 1918, the Cold War threat ensured their continuation after 1945 to the present day. The key enabler for the deployment of spies and growth in twentieth-century intelligence has been the development of wireless communication. The transcripts and other records of these broadcasts to and from field operatives at every level provides modern historians with unprecedented access to the process of military espionage, impossible in earlier centuries.

The best example of how this process has impacted on the traditional understanding of military history was the publication in 1974 of *The Ultra Secret* by Frederick William Winterbotham. The author was a liaison officer at Bletchley Park in the United Kingdom, where signals traffic encoded by German Enigma machines was intercepted, collected, and systematically deciphered in conditions of great secrecy. The material thus gathered provided the western Allies (but not the Soviet Union) with strategic intelligence and is variously credited with saving tens of thousands of lives and/or of shortening the European theater by at least a year. Such was the importance of the ULTRA material (reference to which was prohibited in the United Kingdom prior to 1974) that many World War II military histories (whether general, or on air, maritime, or land operations) written before the ULTRA revelation have needed substantial revision. It can be argued that *The Ultra Secret* directly triggered the trickle into the public domain of Bletchley Park decrypts and other material at the United Kingdom's Public Record Office. The release of U.K. World War I–era intelligence files followed in 1976, though the release of intelligence material generated in peacetime has remained very restricted. Yet even today, the intelligence communities remain secretive about their long-past activities—this is partly out of habit, and partly for fear of compromising their operational methods and procedures. This may prompt the reflection that more is known about intelligence failures than successes—the controversy about how much was known prior to the attacks of 11 September 2001 or the 2003 invasion of Iraq are useful cases in point.

*See also* **Enigma Machine; Intelligence; Radio.**

BIBLIOGRAPHY

Andrew, Christopher. *Secret Service: The Making of the British Intelligence Community.* London, 1985.

Godson, Roy, ed. *Comparing Foreign Intelligence: The US, the USSR, the UK, and the Third World.* London, 1988.

Hughes-Wilson, John. *Military Intelligence Blunders and Cover-Ups.* London, 2004.

Winterbotham, Frederick William. *The Ultra Secret.* London, 1974.

PETER CADDICK-ADAMS

---

**ESTONIA.** The cauldron that was the twentieth century made Estonia a nation-state with a strong sense of its own identity, one that Estonians themselves see rooted fundamentally in history. The twentieth century witnessed two births of Estonia as an independent state and also the creation of a modern Estonian-language culture. The survival of both was put into question by the horrors of war, occupation, and the long, enervating decades of Soviet rule.

During World War I, the areas of Estonian settlement in the tsarist empire—the province of Estland and northern Livland province—escaped most of the violence and population dislocation that affected Latvian areas to the south. As many as one hundred thousand Estonian men were mobilized into the Russian army, but it is unknown how many of these were wounded or killed.

Estonian independence came almost as a surprise. Only when the troops of the Russian provisional government, successor to the tsarist regime, failed to prevent the German army from capturing Riga in August 1917 did it occur to Estonians that independence was a reachable goal. The provisional government agreed to Estonians' demands for the unification of Estland and northern Livland into one administrative unit, and Baltic German provincial assemblies were abolished. The political Left grew strong in 1917, though mainly in Tallinn, which was also home to about two hundred thousand tsarist troops, among whom leftist views were popular. When Bolsheviks seized power in Petrograd (present-day St. Petersburg) in late October 1917, Bolsheviks in Tallinn took power from the commissar of the provisional government for Estonia, the former Tallinn city mayor. Their popularity was clearly falling when they were forced to flee eastward in February 1918 before a renewed German advance. On 24 February 1918, the day before the Germans' arrival in Tallinn, representatives of the Estonian provincial assembly, elected in May 1917, declared Estonia an independent, democratic republic.

The German occupation of Estonia, which lasted until Germany's capitulation in November 1918, restored former Baltic German elites to power; Estonian societies were closed, and strict press censorship was maintained. Estonian forces, aided by British war matériel and Finnish loans and volunteers, drove back a Bolshevik offensive by the end of February 1919, a conflict known in Estonian historiography as the War of Independence.

## THE INTERWAR REPUBLIC

Estonia was a liberal, parliamentary democracy for most of the interwar period. A number of leading politicians had been central figures in the Estonian national movement in the late tsarist period. Land reform was the new state's first major step; in 1919 a constituent assembly enacted the expropriation of large estates (held mainly by Baltic German nobles). The number of smallholdings increased, with land either purchased or leased from the state. Independent Estonia's economy was primarily agricultural; main trading partners were Germany and Great Britain.

In the five elections held from 1920 to 1932, seats in the Riigikogu, or parliament, were evenly divided between parties of the Right, Center, and Left, though the Right and Center dominated in Estonian cabinets. Estonian Communists attempted a coup in Tallinn on 1 December 1924; their failure furthered the Communist Party's electoral weakness, which the agrarian reform had initiated.

Economic problems in Estonia and elsewhere in the world in the early 1930s helped pave the way to a political crisis. Particularly destabilizing was the far rightist League of Veterans, styled after fascist organizations elsewhere in Europe, which sought to undermine parliament and force elections for a strong, directly elected president. The reforms advocated by the League received overwhelming support in an October 1933 referendum, and the League was poised to enter its own candidate to elections to be held in April. The acting head of state Konstantin Päts (1874–1956) responded on 12 March 1934, declaring martial law and canceling the elections; he then outlawed the League's organizations and arrested its leaders. In March 1935 Päts went further, banning all political parties and introducing press censorship. During his authoritarian rule, which lasted until occupation by the Soviet Union in 1940, Päts ruled by decree, though in 1938 he engineered the election of a reorganized, docile parliament.

## SOVIET OCCUPATION AND WORLD WAR II

With the signing of a nonaggression pact between the USSR and Nazi Germany on 23 August 1939, the Soviets forced on Estonia the following month a mutual assistance agreement permitting Soviet military bases in the country. The failure of the interwar Baltic states to establish a military alliance made it unthinkable to resist these Soviet demands as Finland did. Full occupation followed in June 1940. Rigged elections were held in July to a new parliament that requested inclusion into the USSR, but the real power in Estonia was the Communist Party. In the year of Soviet rule before the arrival of German forces in July 1941, an estimated eight thousand Estonian citizens, including virtually all of the country's political elite, were arrested. Some two thousand people were executed in Estonia; the rest were sent to prison camps in Soviet Russia, an experience only about two to six hundred survived. In June 1941, at least ninety-two hundred persons were deported to the interior of the USSR, including women, children, and elderly; about half of these either were executed or perished in adverse conditions. No fewer than 33,000 men of military service age were seized, of whom at least 10,400 perished within a year in forced labor camps. Nationalization of the economy moved forward, especially in urban areas, and vast changes were forced on the educational system.

Killings, population dislocations, and further suffering continued under Nazi German occupation (1941 to 1944), though time did not allow the occupying authorities to implement plans for the Germanization of Estonia and the rest of the Baltic region. A prominent leader in the League of Veterans was made head of an Estonian self-administration. Some eight thousand persons were executed or died in prison camps, including nearly one thousand Estonian Jews. Soviet air raids killed about eight hundred. An estimated fifty to sixty thousand Estonian men were mobilized into the German army; over half of these joined in 1944, hoping to prevent a Soviet return after the anticipated German defeat. An estimated seventy thousand people fled to the West as refugees in the summer of 1944 before the Soviets' recaptured the Baltic region in the late summer and early fall. In all, between 1940 and 1945 the number of people in Estonia fell by as many as two hundred thousand, a loss of nearly a fifth of the country's population.

## THE SOVIET DECADE

Re-sovietization began with a third consecutive violent campaign to remake Estonia's population in line with the ideology of its ruling power. In

**The Baltic Way.** Residents of Tallinn, Estonia, participate in the 23 August 1989 Baltic Way protest, demanding independence from the Soviet Union. The protest was staged by citizens of the three Baltic nations—Estonia, Latvia, and Lithuania—who joined hands to form a human chain that stretched over hundreds of miles. GETTY IMAGES

1945 and 1946, those who had served in the German military or affiliated Estonian support units were sent to Soviet prison camps. In a single massive action in late March 1949, 20,700 people were deported from the countryside to collective farms in Siberia, primarily family members of men already executed or deported. This had the expected effect of breaking resistance to collectivization of Estonian agriculture, which was completed by 1952. An anti-Soviet Estonian partisan movement in the countryside was effectively stemmed by the early 1950s. In 1950 and 1951, several hundred cultural figures, educators, and native Estonian communists were arrested or removed from their positions, accused of being "bourgeois nationalists."

Between 1945 and 1953, over two hundred thousand Russians were relocated to the Estonian SSR (Soviet Socialist Republic) to help carry out the rapid industrialization ordered by Moscow. Some of these new immigrants were russified

Estonians who had grown up in Russia and were now sent to occupy key positions in society, such as in the Estonian Communist Party. The result of these demographic shifts was a severe drop in the portion of the population who were Estonians: from 88.2 percent in 1934 to an estimated 72 percent in 1953. With the return of surviving deportees after 1956, the portion of Estonians rose slightly, to nearly 74.6 percent in 1959. Immigration of Russians and others from elsewhere in the Soviet Union continued, however, and the percentage of Estonians within the Estonian SSR hit a low in 1989, at 61.5 percent, with 30.3 percent being Russians and 8.2 percent of other nationalities. Estonians made up only 47.4 percent of the population of Tallinn in 1989.

The cultural thaw permitted by Soviet leader Nikita Khrushchev (1894–1971) in the 1950s allowed for the first period of Estonian cultural development since the interwar era. Particularly noteworthy were the massive national song festivals, held in 1947 and then every five years beginning in 1950, a tradition that had begun in the nineteenth century and continued in the interwar period. Living standards rose in the 1960s and early 1970s, and there was an increase in the proportion of Estonians in the Estonian Communist Party, with an attendant strengthening of local control and greater sensitivity to Estonian national issues. The optimism resulting from these developments flagged, however, by the mid- to late-1970s as economic stagnation set in and the russification of Estonian society escalated. Increased immigration of non-Estonians and greater emphasis on the use of Russian in education and public life increased social tensions by the early 1980s.

## NATIONAL REAWAKENING AND NEWLY INDEPENDENT ESTONIA

The reform initiatives of the new Communist Party chief Mikhail Gorbachev (b. 1931), named general secretary in March 1985, perestroika (restructuring) and glasnost (openness) were intended to reinvigorate the USSR, not hasten its end. Estonians, Latvians, and Lithuanians used the new political atmosphere to launch popular reform movements in 1987. While autonomy within the USSR was the initial goal, these became by the fall of 1989 fullfledged independence movements supported by the overwhelming majority of members of each titular nationality and by large numbers of local minorities.

In Estonia, public opposition to environmental threats in 1987 rapidly mushroomed into wideranging demands for change as expressions of Estonian national feeling became more explicit. In April 1988 a "popular front" democratic movement was formed at the initiative of economist Edgar Savisaar (b. 1950). The heightening of popular national sentiments was evident at a number of mass meetings that combined political speeches with the traditions of the Estonian song festival. Gatherings of this "singing revolution" regularly drew crowds of a hundred thousand and more, and once even three hundred thousand—20 percent of the entire population of Estonia. Intra-Baltic cooperation, both between elected representatives and on the popular level, was substantial in the last several years before independence.

Elections to the Supreme Council of Estonia (formerly, the Supreme Soviet of the Estonian SSR) in March 1990 represented a key break with the Soviet past. This democratically elected body was essentially a national parliament, with Savisaar as prime minister. The only significant division among Estonians concerned the status of existing political structures. A minority rejected the legitimacy of the Supreme Council because of its Soviet-era roots, establishing "citizens' committees" of those born in the interwar republic and their descendants, and then organizing elections to an "Estonian Congress" in February 1990. In a March 1991 referendum, 77.8 percent of voters said they were in favor of the restoration of Estonia's independence. While nearly all ethnic Estonians supported independence, non-Estonians (overwhelmingly Russians and Russophones of other nationalities) were divided, with an estimated 30 percent voting for independence, 40 percent voting against, and 30 percent failing to cast a ballot.

The Supreme Council reacted to the launching of the attempted coup against Gorbachev on 19 August 1991 with a declaration of Estonia's independence the following day. By April 1992, a constitutional assembly had completed work on a new constitution, based on that of the interwar republic. A new parliament, called the Riigikogu as in the interwar republic, was elected in September.

Governments of post-Soviet Estonia have changed frequently, with eleven governments in office from 1991 to 2005, all of them coalitions. Parties on the right and center have dominated. Throughout much of the 1990s, parties tended to coalesce around individual politicians, resulting in weak party institutionalization. By the mid-2000s this trend was beginning to abate with changes in leadership in several popular parties. As in neighboring Latvia, relations between ethnic Estonians and non-Estonians have been the most important social issue in the post-Soviet period. Those who are not descendants of citizens of interwar Estonia (or themselves born in interwar Estonia)—which includes the vast majority of Russians and other non-Estonians—must become citizens through naturalization. Except for children born in Estonia beginning in 1992, this requires knowledge of Estonian. Some non-Estonians have criticized the naturalization process and other policies favoring the use of Estonian in the workplace and in education as discriminatory. As of 2000, 39.7 percent of those who were not ethnic Estonians (overwhelmingly Russians) were citizens of Estonia, 19.7 percent had taken Russian citizenship, and 38.2 percent were stateless.

Bold economic reform in the early 1990s ended Soviet-era state subsidies and produced a stable, market economy, though this entailed several years of painful belt-tightening. Income disparities are significant, with workers in new, modernized economic sectors (such as services) in Estonia's urban areas—particularly in Tallinn—earning much more than agricultural workers and workers in the eastern parts of the country.

On 14 September 2003, 66.8 percent of voters approved Estonia's accession to the European Union, which took place on 1 May 2004. Dissenting voters feared a loss of sovereignty within the European Union. Estonia became a member of NATO on 29 March 2004.

*See also* **Latvia; Lithuania; Soviet Union.**

BIBLIOGRAPHY

Misiunas, Romuald J., and Rein Taagepera. *The Baltic States: Years of Dependence, 1940–1990.* Expanded and updated edition. Berkeley, Calif., 1993.

Rauch, Georg von. *The Baltic States: The Years of Independence: Estonia, Latvia, Lithuania, 1917–1940.* Translated from the German by Gerald Onn. Berkeley, Calif., 1974.

Raun, Toivo U. *Estonia and the Estonians.* Updated 2nd ed. Stanford, Calif., 2002.

Salo, Vello, et al., eds. *The White Book: Losses Inflicted on the Estonian Nation by Occupation Regimes, 1940–1991.* Translated by Mari Ets et al. Tallinn, Estonia, 2005.

Smith, David J. *Estonia: Independence and European Integration.* London, 2001.

Taagepera, Rein. *Estonia: Return to Independence.* Boulder, Colo., 1993.

BRADLEY D. WOODWORTH

---

**ETA.** Euskadi Ta Askatasuna (ETA; Basque Homeland and Freedom) is a clandestine organization dedicated to establishing the Basque provinces of Spain and France as an independent state through armed struggle and terror. ETA was founded in 1959 by student activists frustrated by what they saw as the excessive passivity of the historic party of Basque nationalism, the Partido Nacionalista Vasco (PNV).

The turn to armed struggle was a response to the repression of the Basque language by the regime of Francisco Franco as well as to the influence of Marxism and movements of national liberation in the colonial world. ETA's initial acts were to set off bombs in major cities in the region and, in 1961, to attempt to derail a train. In 1968 ETA carried out its first planned killing, and by 1975 ETA had killed forty-five people: members of the army or police and political figures. Its most spectacular act was the assassination of Franco's handpicked successor, the prime minister Admiral Luis Carrero Blanco, in 1973. Even though ETA was concerned only with freeing the Basque country, acts such as this, and the 1970 Burgos trial of ETA activists and sympathizers, earned the organization considerable solidarity among anti-Franco groups.

The death of Franco in November 1975 and the subsequent transition to democracy only increased ETA's activity. For *etarras* (ETA members), a democratic Spanish state was no better than a dictatorial one. Indeed, a democratic state that granted the Basque region considerable self-government, as the new "state of the autonomies" did, was an even more dangerous enemy. Consequently, the number of assassinations increased sharply in the late 1970s. Military figures were favored targets, as ETA believed that the military was the real power in Spain. This upsurge in ETA violence was an important part of the backdrop to the failed military coup of 23 February 1981.

Over the years, ETA has undergone a number of schisms and changes of tactics, as some groups renounced armed struggle in favor of strictly political action. In September 1998 it announced a cease-fire, but then announced a return to violence in November 1999.

Since the restoration of democracy, ETA has had close links to a broader social movement known as the "patriotic Left." From 1978 until 1998, a party called Herri Batasuna (HB) acted as ETA's political wing. During the 1980s, in

**Masked policemen stand guard outside the home of a man arrested as a suspected ETA member, Zaldibia, Spain, August 2001.** Basque regional police, known as Ertzainas, often wear masks to prevent their identification by ETA members. ©REUTERS/CORBIS

particular, HB enjoyed significant electoral support in the region, winning as much as 18 percent of the vote in regional elections. This support dropped during the 1990s, and in 1998 HB changed its name to Euskal Herritarrok (EH).

Another aspect of political violence connected to ETA was the emergence in the 1990s of what was called *kale borroka*, struggle in the streets. This was carried out primarily by gangs of young people who would set fire to municipal buses and cause other damage of this sort. The *kale borroka* peaked in 2000, when there were 581 reported incidents; in 2003 there were only 150, largely as a response to changes in the laws making it possible to prosecute minors.

At the same time, ETA has suffered a continuous and serious loss of public support in the Basque country. A grassroots civic organization called Basta Ya! (Enough Is Enough) began to organize street demonstrations against ETA, and surveys done by the Universidad del País Vasco show that the percentage of Basques who supported or justified ETA's actions fell from 12 percent in 1981 to only 2 percent in 2003, while the percentage who totally rejected ETA rose from 23 percent to 64 percent in the same period.

Over time, ETA's violence became more indiscriminate. Victims included businessmen, academics, and journalists, as well as people who happened to be in the wrong place at the wrong time.

TABLE 1

**ETA victims, 1968–2003**

| Year | Victims |
|------|---------|
| 1968 | 2 |
| 1969 | 1 |
| 1970 | 0 |
| 1971 | 0 |
| 1972 | 1 |
| 1973 | 6 |
| 1974 | 19 |
| 1975 | 16 |
| 1976 | 17 |
| 1977 | 10 |
| 1978 | 66 |
| 1979 | 76 |
| 1980 | 92 |
| 1981 | 30 |
| 1982 | 37 |
| 1983 | 32 |
| 1984 | 32 |
| 1985 | 37 |
| 1986 | 43 |
| 1987 | 52 |
| 1988 | 21 |
| 1989 | 19 |
| 1990 | 25 |
| 1991 | 46 |
| 1992 | 26 |
| 1993 | 14 |
| 1994 | 12 |
| 1995 | 15 |
| 1996 | 5 |
| 1997 | 13 |
| 1998 | 6 |
| 1999 | 0 |
| 2000 | 23 |
| 2001 | 15 |
| 2002 | 5 |
| 2003 | 3 |
| **Total** | **817** |

SOURCE: Minister of the Interior, Spain

According to government statistics, 339 of ETA's 817 victims have been civilians. In effect, the Basque country has been living through a low-level civil war, as violence and insecurity have become widespread. Many academics, journalists, and politicians in the region have permanent bodyguards.

The government of Spain has taken a hard line with ETA. In the early 1980s, the Socialist government engaged in a "dirty war" in which suspected ETA militants were killed by hit squads. When this became public, it contributed significantly to the discrediting of the Socialist Party and led to one former minister being sent to jail.

ETA itself is a small organization. It is believed to have some twenty core members and a few hundred supporters. Its money comes from kidnappings, robberies, and extortion, what it calls "revolutionary taxes." ETA has ties with the IRA (Irish Republican Army).

From early in its existence, ETA took advantage of the proximity of the border with France, often using southern France as a base for its operations. Until the early 1980s, the French government tolerated this, so long as ETA did not commit any crimes in France itself. French policy changed after the Socialists came to power in Spain: with Socialist governments in both countries, the French agreed to withdraw their previous tolerance and to collaborate in efforts to combat terrorism. ETA thus found it harder to use southern France as a sanctuary. Such collaboration increased still further following the events of 11 September 2001; in October 2004, French police arrested the suspected leader of ETA and discovered large hidden caches of arms.

*See also* **Basques; IRA; Terrorism.**

BIBLIOGRAPHY

Clark, Robert P. *The Basque Insurgents: ETA, 1952–1980.* Madison, Wis., 1984.

———. *Negotiating with ETA: Obstacles to Peace in the Basque Country, 1975–1988.* Reno, Nev., 1990.

Núñez Seixas, Xosé M. "The Reawakening of Peripheral Nationalisms and the State of the Autonomous Communities." In *Spanish History since 1808,* edited by José Alvarez Junco and Adrian Shubert, 315–330. London, 2000.

Sullivan, John. *ETA and Basque Nationalism: The Fight for Euskadi, 1890–1986.* London, 1988.

ADRIAN SHUBERT

**ETHIOPIA.** The year 1914 was a watershed in Ethiopia's age-old history. Emperor Menelik II (1844–1913), victor of the battle of Adwa over the Italians in 1896 and founder of the modern Ethiopian state, had died in December 1913 after a four-year illness that had left him incapacitated. His eighteen-year-old grandson and heir, Lij Iyasu (1896–1935), sought to steer a course between the dominant Christian Orthodox Church and the Muslims of the surrounding lowlands. He also maneuvered between Menelik's old courtiers, who came mainly from Shawa in the Christian center of the country, and the hitherto subordinate chiefs of other areas, many of them Muslim. Knowing that his father, Ras Mikael of Wallo, had been forcibly converted from Islam, and that Menelik had sought to circumscribe the church's power, Iyasu attempted to win Muslim support.

Things came to a head with the outbreak of World War I in 1914 when Iyasu favored the Central Powers. He did so partly because three of the Allies—Britain, France, and Italy—had colonized the neighboring coastline, thereby blocking his access to the sea, and partly because an Ottoman alliance reflected his rapprochement with Islam. His policies alienated the church, the Shawan nobility, and the Allied Legations. He was accordingly deposed in 1916.

The Shawan nobles thereupon chose Menelik's daughter Zawditu (1876–1930) as empress, and a cousin, Lij Tafari Makonnen (1892–1975), as heir to the throne and regent. This led to an uneasy sharing of power between the two leaders, each with their own palace, courtiers, and policies: a traditionalist empress, with all the trappings of royalty, and a younger, partly French mission–educated regent, given the title of Ras, who sought to bring the country into the modern world.

Ras Tafari, who adopted a pro-Western stance, improved the ministerial system, built roads, and curtailed the slave trade. In 1923 he obtained Ethiopia's entry into the League of Nations. In the following year, together with his courtiers, he visited the principal countries of western Europe. In ensuing years he founded a printing press, a reformist newspaper, a new school, and a hospital; dispatched several dozen students for study abroad, many to France; protested to the League of Nations in 1926 against a joint Anglo-Italian attempt to pressure him into granting economic concessions; and, overcoming traditional conservatism, imported the first airplane to Ethiopia in 1929.

On Zawditu's death in 1930 Tafari assumed the throne as Emperor Haile Selassie and staged an impressive coronation. He introduced a new written constitution and a parliament in 1931 and accelerated the speed of reform, nationalizing the old private Bank of Abyssinia, introducing a new currency, setting up a radio station, legislating against slavery, employing foreign advisors, and sending more students abroad for study. Faced by

**The Cake of the King, of Kings.** A cartoon from the French journal *Le Pelerin,* 1936, depicts Haile Selassie handing his country to Mussolini. BRIDGEMAN ART LIBRARY

the threat of invasion by Fascist Italy (which had colonies in Eritrea to the north and Somalia to the south) he also attempted to modernize his armed forces and imperial bodyguard.

Benito Mussolini's seizure of power in Italy in 1922 and the emergence of the chauvinistic and expansionist Fascist regime had far-reaching consequences for Ethiopia. Relations between the two countries were initially cordial—a mutual Friendship Treaty was signed in 1928. However in 1933 the Duce decided to invade Ethiopia "not later than 1936." A confrontation between Ethiopian troops and infiltrators from Italian Somalia at Wal Wal (one hundred kilometers within Ethiopian territory) led to an "incident" in December 1934 that Mussolini used as a pretext for war. He proclaimed his intention to "avenge Adwa" (Emperor Menelik's victory of 1896) and win Italy "a place in the [African] sun."

Fascist Italy's invasion of Ethiopia, which shocked international opinion, particularly in Britain, began without any declaration of war on 3 October 1935. Eight days later the League of Nations found Italy guilty of aggression but imposed only ineffective economic sanctions. The invaders enjoyed overwhelming military superiority and complete control of the air. They made extensive use of mustard gas, outlawed by the Geneva Convention of 1926; bombed foreign Red Cross hospitals and ambulances; and shot Ethiopian prisoners in cold blood. On the northern front Emperor Haile Selassie was defeated at May Chaw at the end of March 1936 and left his capital, Addis Ababa, on 2 May to go into exile. Italian troops under General Pietro Badoglio (1871–1956) occupied the town three days later. The emperor proceeded to Jerusalem and later to England. He addressed the League in Geneva on 30 June, but member-states ignored his appeal, abandoned sanctions, and recognized Italy's "conquest." The United States, USSR, New Zealand, Haiti, and Mexico, however, refused to do so. Although Mussolini had declared the war's victorious conclusion in 1936 Ethiopian patriots continued to resist in much of the country: Italian control was largely confined to the towns, where the Fascists built roads and introduced strict racial segregation. The attempted assassination of the Italian viceroy Rodolfo Graziani (1882–1955) in February 1937 was followed in Addis Ababa by the massacre of thousands of defenseless Ethiopian men, women, and children.

Mussolini, assuming that Adolf Hitler (1889–1945) would win the war, and wanting a seat at the ensuing peace conference, declared war on Britain and France on 10 June 1940. This threatened Britain's position on the route to India and obliged the British to embark in January 1941 on the Ethiopian Liberation Campaign. British, Commonwealth, and Allied forces, under General William Platt (1885–1975), attacked from Sudan into Eritrea, and others, under Alan Cunningham (1887–1983), from Kenya into Somalia, while the emperor, with Colonel Orde Charles Wingate (1903–1944) as his field commander, advanced with patriot support from Sudan into Gojjam province. Addis Ababa fell to South African troops on 6 April, and the emperor entered it on 5 May—exactly five years after its occupation by the Italians in 1936.

The emperor faced major post–liberation period problems. The Italians had killed many modern-educated potential administrators. The British, who had come as liberators, emerged as occupiers who proposed the country's partition and the establishment of a virtual protectorate. Ethiopia was, however, a founding member of the United Nations, and Anglo-Ethiopian agreements recognizing the African country's increasing freedom of action were signed in 1942 and 1944. Ethiopia then turned increasingly to the United States but took increasing interest in anticolonialist struggles in Africa. In 1952 the United Nations federated the former Italian colony of Eritrea with Ethiopia under the Ethiopian crown and in 1955 a new Ethiopian constitution was promulgated. Institutions founded at this time included a State Bank of Ethiopia (which issued a new currency), Ethiopian Airlines, and a University College that developed into Haile Selassie I (later Addis Ababa) University. The Ethiopian capital became the headquarters of the UN Economic Commission for Africa and the Organization of African Unity, OAU (later the African Union).

Discontent at the country's slow pace of development led in 1960 to an abortive coup d'état by the Imperial Bodyguard, followed by antigovernment student demonstrations. A serious famine was followed by a "creeping coup," by the armed forces, which led to the 1974 revolution. Power was thereafter exercised by a Derg (literally [military] "committee"). It dissolved parliament; crushed opposition; deposed and imprisoned the emperor, who died under mysterious circumstances; nationalized land and large businesses; and embarked on resettlement, villagization, and mass literacy campaigns. With the rise of Colonel Mengistu Haile Mariam as president (and dictator) the Derg turned increasingly toward the USSR and established a Soviet-style Workers Party of Ethiopia (WPE).

Opposition to the Derg, which was initially contained, came from monarchists, traditionalists, regional separatists (in Eritrea, Tegray, Oromo, and Afar), and Marxists (particularly the Ethiopian Peoples Revolutionary Party [EPRP]). An invasion by Somalia in July 1977 was repulsed with Soviet, Cuban, and South Yemeni help, but insurgency in Eritrea by the Eritrean People's Liberation Front (EPLF) proved intractable. The largely Tegre-based

Ethiopian People's Revolutionary Democratic Front (EPRDF), supported by the EPLF, defeated the Soviet-supported Derg army in 1991, occupied Addis Ababa in May, and established the Federal Democratic Republic of Ethiopia. Eritrea, although it had long been economically linked to Ethiopia, became a separate independent state in 1993. War between the two states nevertheless followed in 1997–1999, and hostility was not yet defused as of 2005. The postrevolutionary turmoil was accompanied by the emigration of over a million Ethiopians, the majority to the United States, but fifty thousand Beta Esra'el (or Ethiopians of supposed Jewish origin) went to Israel, and as many Muslims went to Saudi Arabia and the Gulf states.

*See also* **Badoglio, Pietro; British Empire; Italy; Mussolini, Benito.**

BIBLIOGRAPHY

*Primary Sources*

Haile Sellassie I. *The Autobiography of Emperor Haile Sellassie I.* Translated by Edward Ullendorff. Oxford, U.K., 1976.

Spencer, John H. *Ethiopia at Bay: A Personal Account of the Haile Sellassie Years.* Algonac, Mich., 1984.

*Secondary Sources*

Henze, Paul B. *Layers of Time: A History of Ethiopia.* New York, 2000.

Marcus, Harold G. *Ethiopia, Great Britain, and the United States 1941–1974: The Politics of Empire.* Berkeley, Calif., 1983.

Mockler, Anthony. *Haile Selassie's War.* London and New York, 1984.

Pankhurst, Richard. *The Ethiopians: A History.* Oxford, U.K., and Malden, Mass., 2001.

Tiruneh, Andargachew. *The Ethiopian Revolution 1975–1987: A Transformation from an Aristocratic to a Totalitarian Autocracy.* Cambridge, U.K., and New York, 1993.

Zewde, Bahru. *A History of Modern Ethiopia 1855–1974.* Athens, Ohio, and Addis Ababa, 1991.

RICHARD PANKHURST

---

**ETHNIC CLEANSING.** *Ethnic cleansing* is similar to the main term used to describe Joseph Stalin's terror, *chystki* (purges), as well as Adolf Hitler's word for racial "hygiene," *Säuberung.*

The term *cleansing* appeared in various languages (Polish, Czech, and Ukrainian) in the 1940s in the context of national violence. In the 1990s a mass viewing public was introduced to practices known as ethnic cleansing as they took place. During the Yugoslav wars of the 1990s, the term *ethnic cleansing* found its way from Serbs to the world mass media. The term opened new paths of interpretation of the history of Europe in the twentieth century. In general, these emphasized the continuity of national violence, the connections between the First and the Second World Wars, the similarity of practices between Nazi Germany and the Soviet Union, and the importance of war in the social history of modern Europe.

There is no accepted definition of ethnic cleansing as a term of scholarly investigation, although it is perhaps most often used in the sense of "coercive actions justified in national terms designed to clear territories of putatively undesirable populations without aspiring to their total physical extermination." Ethnic cleansing occupies a middle position between voluntary migration and total genocide. People can be ethnically cleansed without being killed, although the credible threat of murder is a basic tool of ethnic cleansers. Ethnic cleansing refers to the cleansing of a territory rather than the cleansing of a population. It and similar expressions are employed in a military or partisan context, when forces are used to eliminate civilians and thus putatively secure territory. As a term of analysis, *ethnic cleansing* captures the willingness to use force, which need not include the aim or desire to murder the entire population. The perpetrators of ethnic cleansing are usually acting on behalf of a state, although in some important cases they have been revolutionaries or partisans.

**ETHNIC CLEANSING AND NATIONALISM**
If ethnic cleansing is analytically distinct from earlier forms of politically motivated mass violence against civilians, this is because it contains a certain modern assumption about the national identity of populations. Modern nationalists believe that legitimate political power over a given territory flows from the national identity of its inhabitants. Many modern nationalists also believe that the national identity of populations is determined by factors that transcend human choice, such as

mother tongue or family origin. These two views, taken together, are usually referred to as ethnic nationalism. Ethnic cleansing is a practical reconciliation of these two ideas of the nation and power. If political legitimacy rests with the nation, and the nation is defined in ethnic terms, minority groups have a poor claim to political rights. Yet political actors who express such views can rarely put them into practice, absent other favorable circumstances. These ideas may be more or less widely held, but they will generally seem more cogent at moments of threat, especially in times of war. Ethnic minorities connected to foreign powers during warfare are at special risk.

Over the course of the twentieth century, ethnic cleansing has taken place in much of Europe, from the Baltic Sea to the Black Sea, from the Rhine to the Volga. Although the circumstances and actors present a tremendous variety, most cases, when examined closely, exhibit most or all of the following conditions: (1) the prior collapse of state authority; (2) the cover of a larger war or the plausible threat thereof; (3) the practical anticipation that the political map of the region in question can be redrawn, borders changed, and new states created; (4) the presence of a dedicated and committed group of ethnic cleansers, usually at work far from home; (5) historical propaganda that only seems plausible because of ongoing cleansing, and that seems to justify that cleansing projects be completed; (6) a conscious escalation by dedicated propagandists, who seek to transform the individual experience of loss into a social commitment to national war; (7) a property motive that attracts and implicates large numbers of people who have no apparent political or ideological motivation.

The popular explanation of ethnic cleansing, which also became current in the 1990s, can be summarized as "ancient hatred." Yet the very idea that the groups who cleanse and are cleansed are ancient is itself an artifact of modern nationalism. That such an explanation found credulous listeners testifies to the persuasiveness of nationalism itself. Even if national groups were antique and ever hostile, such a presentation of the issue can never provide an explanation of a given episode of ethnic cleansing. If the existence of ethnic groups and their hostility are taken as constants, they cannot explain the variable: a sudden eruption of forced population movements. In most recorded cases of ethnic cleansing in Europe, international or domestic political actors created, intentionally or unintentionally, a propitious moment for the expression of ethnic nationalism and the fulfillment of its program. At the level of high politics, those who resort to or profit from ethnic cleansing need not themselves be convinced ethnic nationalists. In some cases, especially in the communist world, leaders seek rather to divert national energy away from themselves.

At the level of society, ethnic cleansing, once it has been started, tends to self-perpetuate. Perpetrators initiated into murder and rape acquire the habit. Victims who respond with armed force, and even victims who flee, can be presented as evidence that the initial action of cleansing was justified. Since some kind of self-defense or revenge can be expected, ethnic cleansers consciously or unconsciously are targeting their own group when they attack another. Once attacks on civilians of different groups are underway, the question of blame becomes a matter of propaganda. In general, populations that are attacked will believe that they are the victims, even when organizations acting in their name initiated the violence. A situation can quickly emerge in which rival organizations kill civilians in the name of the self-defense of their own civilians. In some cases of ethnic cleansing, this moment of general violence seems to destroy older social norms of cohabitation and create fertile ground for the spread and reception of nationalist propaganda. In a situation that seems senseless, nationalism seems to provide an explanation for what is happening and a program for collective survival. In the proper conditions, an armed attack on a small number of civilians can become a war of nation against nation.

This dynamic of escalation well describes the Yugoslav wars of the 1990s, the Ukrainian-Polish ethnic cleansing of the 1940s, and the Greco-Turkish violence of the 1920s. It need not obtain in all cases. In Nazi Germany and the Soviet Union, the state carried out massive policies of ethnic cleansing at a moment when it enjoyed a monopoly or a near monopoly on the use of force. Soviet and Nazi policies of ethnic cleansing generally met little or no effective resistance. Yet even in such cases, many of the same conditions hold. Both

Moscow and Berlin justified ethnic cleansing by the threat of war. Both, and especially Nazi Germany, radicalized their approach to enemy groups when war was actually underway. Both redrew the map of Europe, using national propaganda to justify their actions. Both deployed bureaucratic cleansers, trained security policemen or soldiers of paramilitary forces. In both cases, but far more in the German case than the Soviet one, venal motives drew in collaborators. People who are cleansed leave behind more property than the cleansers can themselves exploit. When Germany invaded the Soviet Union in 1941, this motive of property was especially important. After the Red Army defeated the Germans, many Soviet citizens retained the apartments they had seized from murdered Jews.

One of the most controversial questions is the distinction between ethnic cleansing and genocide. In a legal sense the question is badly put, because the legal definition of genocide is rather broad. It includes the motivated murder of part of a national group, for example. In this sense, almost all examples of ethnic cleansing are genocidal. Legally speaking, there can also be instances of genocide that do not involve ethnic cleansing. "Causing serious bodily or mental harm to members of the group" is legally genocide if motivated by the intention to destroy that group. Such a policy need not involve ethnic cleansing. Even directly murderous policies of genocide need not involve ethnic cleansing. If part of a population (its educated classes, for example) is murdered in situ without the intention to expel the rest, this is legally genocide, but is not ethnic cleansing. In popular usage, however, *genocide* is sometimes taken to mean the attempt to exterminate an entire national or racial group. In this sense, not all episodes of ethnic cleansing are genocidal. The example of the Holocaust of the Jews, however, shows that episodes of genocide in this strong, popular sense of the term may be preceded by attempts at ethnic cleansing.

### TWENTIETH-CENTURY EXAMPLES

After Germany occupied western Poland in 1939, it encountered large Polish and Jewish populations. Between 1939 and 1941 Germans expelled a few hundred thousand Jews from the expanded Reich, and compelled their settlement into ghettos. At this time, the Germans ethnically cleansed more Poles than Jews and placed far more Poles than Jews in concentration camps such as Auschwitz. In the Jewish case, ethnic cleansing preceded a policy of total extermination; in the Polish case, it coincided with a policy of eliminating the educated classes. During this period, the German leadership considered what to do with the large Jewish population under German rule. Two of the plans discussed, expulsion east to the Soviet Union and forced transport to Madagascar, would have been further and more radical ethnic cleansing. Had they been carried out, they likely would have led to mass murder by neglect or starvation. The decision to murder all the Jews of Europe, taken after the German invasion of the Soviet Union, was no longer ethnic cleansing. From autumn 1941 the German goal was no longer the removal of Jews from territory, but their total physical elimination as a people.

During the 1930s, Stalin ordered Soviet security forces to deport all or part of every national group that inhabited both the Soviet Union and one of its neighbors. The entire Korean minority, for example, was deported to central Asia. Poles were probably the first national group in the Soviet Union to be targeted as such for deportations. In 1936 some sixty thousand Poles were ethnically cleansed from the western border of the Soviet Union. Some one hundred thousand Soviet citizens were also executed in 1937 and 1938 for supposed contact with Polish intelligence. This episode, the bloodiest part of the Great Terror, cannot be defined as ethnic cleansing. Although Poles predominated in that number, members of other nations were killed as well. Something similar holds for the famine of 1933, in which millions of Ukrainians and others perished. By directing resources in one way rather than another, the Soviet leadership chose which Soviet citizens would starve to death. This was not a policy of ethnic cleansing as such, since there was probably no intention of cleansing territory. Ethnic cleansing provides a useful lens through which to see important policies, but does not exhaust the possibilities for state violence against national groups.

At the end of the Second World War, after direct contact with German policy, the Soviet Union modified its policies in one respect. Throughout the 1930s, no group was actually deported from the Soviet Union. The official hope remained that individuals and communities could redeem themselves in exile or in the gulag, and one day become loyal Soviet citizens. In 1944, for the first time, the Soviet Union dispatched some of its own citizens beyond its borders. Stalin deported Poles and Jews from the Soviet far west, from territories that had been Polish before 1939. As before the war, the concern after the war was the consolidation of communist power. The Soviet Union was anything but a national state. Its leaders, however, were perfectly aware of the importance of nationalism. Initial optimism that national loyalties could be channeled to communist faith by way of administrative concessions was exhausted by about 1930. The less optimistic view that national questions could be resolved by deportation and execution no longer held by the 1940s. By 1944 the Soviet Union had in effect conceded a defeat to nationalism, treating Poles and Jews in its western territories as inassimilable, their ethnic identity as determinative of their future loyalty.

The negative moral coloration of ethnic cleansing obscures an important fact of the twentieth century: that many states, not only Nazi Germany and the Soviet Union, believed that the forced resettlement of peoples was justified for political reasons. In several cases, ethnic cleansing was actually regulated by treaty. The first such instance was apparently a treaty between Turkey and Bulgaria of 1913, which provided for the mutual transfer of civilian populations at the end of the Balkan Wars. Its implementation was interrupted by the First World War. The Treaty of Lausanne of 1923 regulated the mutual expulsions of Greeks and Turks after the Greco-Turkish War that followed the First World War. Mutual ethnic cleansing was already underway, and the treaty was seen as a way to regulate and civilize a process that should be brought to its conclusion rather than reversed. At Potsdam in 1945, not only the Soviet Union but the United States and Great Britain took for granted that the expulsion of Germans from Eastern Europe was inevitable and desirable for the cause of future peace. While Potsdam led to an informal agreement between great powers rather than a formal peace settlement, it nevertheless stands

as an important example of the attempt to regulate a process of ethnic cleansing seen as desirable. The Soviet Union did sign formal agreements with its satellite regime in Poland regarding the transfer of Poles westward and Ukrainians eastward.

In the Europe of the twentieth century, only Soviet state power and ideology seem to provide an exception to the general observation that ethnic cleansing is enabled by war. If the ideologies most associated with ethnic cleansing are Nazism and communism, the points of temporal concentration are the First and Second World Wars. Major examples of the ethnic cleansing in twentieth-century Europe are: (1) the Bulgarian-Greco-Turkish "exchanges" of 1913–1922; (2) the mass murder of Armenians in Turkey in 1915–1919; (3) the deportation of "enemy nations" by the Soviet Union in 1935–1938; (4) the expulsion of Poles and Jews from the expanded Reich by Nazi Germany in 1939–1941; (5) the deportation of "collaborating nations" by the Soviet Union during the Second World War; (6) the mass murder of Poles by Ukrainian insurgents in Volhynia in 1943–1944 and the Polish response; (7) the "repatriations" of Poles and Ukrainians between the Soviet Union and communist Poland in 1944–1946; (8) the forced resettlement of Ukrainians in communist Poland in "Operation Vistula" in 1947; (9) the expulsion of Germans (and some Hungarians) from Czechoslovakia in 1945–1946; (10) the expulsion of Germans from Poland in 1945–1947; and (11) the murder of Bosnian Muslims, Kosovars, and others in the Yugoslav wars of 1992–1999.

The United States, Britain, and their NATO allies fought a war against Yugoslavia (Serbia) in 1999 with the aim of halting ethnic cleansing. By the end of the century, *ethnic cleansing* was a term not only of perpetrators and victims but of scholars, reporters, diplomats, and human-rights activists.

*See also* **Concentration Camps; Deportation; Genocide; Gulag; Holocaust; War Crimes; Warfare.**

BIBLIOGRAPHY

Browning, Christopher R. *Nazi Policy, Jewish Workers, German Killers.* Cambridge, U.K., 2000.

Ladas, Stephen P. *The Exchange of Minorities: Bulgaria, Greece, and Turkey.* New York, 1932.

Martin, Terry. *The Affirmative Action Empire: Nations and Nationalism in the Soviet Union, 1923–1939*. Ithaca, N.Y., 2001.

Naimark, Norman M. *Fires of Hatred: Ethnic Cleansing in Twentieth-Century Europe*. Cambridge, Mass., 2002.

Snyder, Timothy. *The Reconstruction of Nations: Poland, Ukraine, Lithuania, Belarus, 1569–1999*. New Haven, Conn., 2002.

Ther, Philipp, and Ana Siljak, eds. *Redrawing Nations: Ethnic Cleansing in East-Central Europe, 1944–1948*. Lanham, Md., 2003.

TIMOTHY SNYDER

---

# EUGENICS.

*Eugenics* refers to the study and cultivation of conditions that may improve the physical and moral qualities of future generations. Derived from the Greek word *eugenes,* meaning "good in stock" or "hereditarily endowed with noble qualities," eugenics is understood historically to be a reaction to perceptions of industrial society being in states of decline and decay.

## ORIGINS

Sir Francis Galton, cousin of the British naturalist Charles Darwin, coined the term *eugenics* in 1883 after reflecting upon Darwin's seminal work *On the Origin of Species by Means of Natural Selection, or the Preservation of Favoured Races in the Struggle for Life* (1859). Here, Darwin advanced his theory of evolution by describing natural selection, the process in nature by which only the organisms best adapted to their environment tend to survive and transmit their genetic characteristics in increasing numbers to succeeding generations, while those less adapted tend to be eliminated. *On the Origin of Species* prompted Galton to consider the idea of human civilization potentially thwarting, instead of being changed by, mechanisms of natural selection. In his book *Inquiries into Human Faculty and Its Development* (1883), Galton reasoned that because many societies sought to protect the underprivileged and weak through charitable and other social interventions, those societies stood at odds with the natural selection responsible for eliminating individuals deemed to be "less fit." As a natural application of knowledge about breeding to the human life, Galton concluded, the science of eugenics was a means to changing these social policies and preventing what Galton described as "reversion towards mediocrity." Galton highlighted dysgenic tendencies in British society (behavior that caused degeneration instead of improvement in offspring produced), such as the late marriages of eminent people and the paucity of their children, and advocated the encouragement of eugenic marriages by supplying incentives for the "most fit" to have children.

Eugenics differed from social Darwinism in that while both concepts claimed that intelligence was hereditary, eugenics actively promoted policies to move the status quo toward a more "eugenic" state. Social Darwinists argued that nature would naturally "check" the problem of the status quo if no welfare policies were enacted. Poor and unhealthy individuals, they reasoned, might reproduce more to yield a potentially greater population of poor and unhealthy individuals, but nature would intervene to "select" this group to encounter higher mortality rates.

Contributing to Galton's influence on European eugenics movements after the turn of the century—and no less to the work of others who were seeking a solid theory of inheritance to apply to eugenics—was the rediscovery in 1900 of Gregor Mendel's midcentury research on the mechanisms of heredity. Mendel's laws demonstrated that specific inherited characteristics are determined not by the environment but rather by the combination of a pair of hereditary units, what are now understood to be genes, from each of the parental reproductive cells, or gametes.

## EUGENICS POLICIES, INITIATIVES, AND OUTCOMES

Eugenic policies have historically been divided into two categories, positive and negative. Examples of "positive eugenics" policies are those advocated by Galton and others who sought to increase reproduction of individuals seen to have advantageous hereditary traits. "Negative eugenics" refers to the discouragement of reproduction by those with hereditary traits that are perceived as poor. During the course of the twentieth century, European eugenics movements advocated a variety of positive and negative eugenics policies that found their way into national life with varying degrees of success.

Formed in the United Kingdom in 1907, the Eugenics Education Society, later the British

Eugenics Society, promoted policies to improve levels of industrial and personal efficiency among members of the working class. Legislative efforts of the society fell short, but its promotion of sterilization for mental defectives and individuals with physical disabilities became part of a larger dialogue among British social Darwinist organizations about national "social hygiene." These organizations included the National Council for Mental Hygiene, the Central Association for Mental Welfare, the People's League of Health, and the National Institute for Industrial Psychology.

Established in 1912, the French Eugenics Society was a response to the perception that French society was in a state of decline, due in part to fears of a shrinking population. To varying degrees, scientists and policy makers affiliated with the society adopted policies of birth control, premarital examinations, sterilization, and immigration control as ways to affect not only the quality of the population but also its quantity.

Following its establishment in 1922, Sweden's National Institute for Race Biology sponsored research in social engineering that ultimately led to the forced sterilization of an estimated sixty thousand "unfit" men and women between 1936 and 1976. The governments of Norway, Finland, Denmark, Estonia, Switzerland, and Iceland instituted comparable programs as part of large-scale social welfare efforts. In each of these countries, policy leaders held that economic prosperity and social progress depended in part upon preventing the reproduction of individuals who were poor, uneducated, or deemed to be mentally or physically weak or disabled. Although each these programs reached far fewer individuals than did the Swedish case, many remained in effect toward the third quarter of the twentieth century. The Swiss programs to control the country's Gypsy population ended in 1972. Finland outlawed forced sterilization two years earlier; its own program of sterilization reached nearly fifteen hundred individuals between 1930 and 1955.

## THE CASE OF NAZI GERMANY

The most infamous case of eugenics in twentieth-century Europe was Nazi Germany under Adolf Hitler. Radicalizing what had been a relatively moderate national eugenics movement, Hitler's Third Reich transformed eugenics into a pseudoscientific means to achieve a "pure" German race. "Racial hygiene" programs included awards to "Aryan" women who had large numbers of children and impregnation of "racially pure" single women by members of the Schutzstaffel Protection Squad (SS), which formed the basis of the Nazi police state and was the major instrument of racial terror in the concentration camps and occupied Europe. Nazi eugenics programs also involved forced sterilization of hundreds of thousands of people who were viewed as mentally and physically "unfit," compulsory "euthanasia" programs that killed tens of thousands of institutionalized individuals with disabilities, and the systematic killing during the Holocaust of millions of "undesirable" Europeans, including Jews, Gypsies, and homosexuals. Such programs existed alongside extensive experimentation on live human beings to test Nazi genetic theories, ranging from simple measurement of physical characteristics to horrific experiments carried out in concentration camps.

## DISCREDITING AND RECONFIGURATION AFTER 1945

Following the Holocaust and the Nuremberg Trials against former Nazi leaders, which helped to reveal fully the genocidal policies of the Nazi regime, politicians and members of the scientific community almost universally rejected eugenics programs. The cases of Sweden and others, including the forced sterilization of Romani women in Slovakia during the final years of the twentieth century, may be considered exceptions to this view. However, they should not overshadow the broader postwar reaction to the abuses of the Nazi regime, which involved the development of the Universal Declaration of Human Rights adopted by the United Nations in 1948, the subsequent statements on race and racial prejudice by the United Nations Educational, Scientific and Cultural Organization (UNESCO), and medical ethics policies that promoted the involvement of informed and concerned medical and scientific professionals in their respective disciplines.

## SCHOLARLY INTERPRETATIONS AND DEBATES

Since the late twentieth century, interpretations of eugenics have revealed several new ideas and debates.

While historians continue to credit Galton for coining the term *eugenics* and for helping to spread its influence across Europe, they have paid increasing attention to the fact that eugenics ideas and movements outside Britain, particularly in France, developed through their own indigenous circumstances and leadership, both simultaneously with and independently from Galton's ideas and the British eugenics movement. However, such nationally focused studies of eugenics history have not slowed efforts to reveal the interplay of eugenics ideas and programs across borders, particularly between the United States, which had its own robust eugenics movement, and Germany. Scholars have shown that when Nazi administrators appeared at Nuremberg, they justified the mass sterilizations by citing the United States as their inspiration. Historical interpretations have also revealed the significant degrees to which medical professionals in Germany and elsewhere not only promoted and facilitated negative eugenics programs but also profited professionally and financially from them.

Advances in science have also helped to shape new debates related to eugenics. During the late nineteenth and early twentieth centuries, eugenics was widely accepted in European scientific circles as a logical way to improve the physical and moral qualities of future generations. At the beginning of the twenty-first century, and in the wake of the abuses of the past, European governments, including the European Commission, and members of the European scientific community, including the European Society of Human Genetics and the European Society of Human Reproduction and Embryology, approached discussions of new genetic technologies with reference to the past, the acknowledgement of ethical issues such as patient confidentiality and reproductive autonomy versus professional duty, and the recognition of the economic impact of new technologies, such as the commercialization and profitability of gene therapy, genetic testing and screening, and genetic counseling.

*See also* **Nazism; Public Health; Racism; Science.**

BIBLIOGRAPHY

*Primary Sources*

Darwin, Charles. *On the Origin of Species by Means of Natural Selection, or the Preservation of Favoured Races in the Struggle for Life.* London, 1859.

Galton, Francis. *Inquiries into Human Faculty and Its Development.* London, 1883.

Mendel, Gregor. *Experiments in Plant Hybridisation.* Translated by the Royal Horticultural Society of London. Cambridge, Mass., 1965.

*Secondary Sources*

Broberg, Gunnar, and Nils Roll-Hansen, eds. *Eugenics and the Welfare State: Sterilization Policy in Norway, Sweden, Denmark, and Finland.* East Lansing, Mich., 1996.

Jones, Greta. *Social Hygiene in Twentieth-Century Britain.* London, 1986.

Kühl, Stefan. *The Nazi Connection: Eugenics, American Racism, and German National Socialism.* New York, 1994.

Proctor, Robert. *Racial Hygiene: Medicine under the Nazis.* Cambridge, Mass., 1988.

Schneider, William H. *Quality and Quantity: The Quest for Biological Regeneration in Twentieth-Century France.* Cambridge, U.K., 2002.

Weindling, Paul. *Health, Race, and German Politics between National Unification and Nazism, 1870–1945.* Cambridge, U.K., 1989.

JEFFREY S. REZNICK

**EURASIANISM.** Eurasianism (*evraziistvo*) was a complex and controversial intellectual and political movement developed by Russian émigrés in Europe in response to the collapse of the Russian Empire in World War I, the Russian Revolution (1917), and the Russian civil war (1918–1920). Eurasianism reflected developments in prerevolutionary Russian culture and in interwar Europe and attempted to reconcile an illiberal vision of modernity with the legacy of the multinational Russian Empire. Its central concern was with describing Russian imperial diversity as a cultural, political, and geographic unity, thus offering a "supranational" identity for the imperial space.

Eurasianism operated from 1920 to the late 1930s and was founded by Prince Nikolai Trubetskoy (1890–1938), a famous linguist and originator of structuralist phonology; Peter Suvchinsky (1892–1985), an essayist, philosopher, publisher, and influential connoisseur of music; Georgy Florovsky (1893–1979), an Orthodox thinker and church historian; and Peter Savitsky (1895–1968), a geographer and economist.

Eurasianism pulled into its orbit a number of prominent intellectuals: the historians Peter Bitsilli, George Vernadsky, and Sergei Germanovich Pushkarev; the literary scholar Dmitri Svyatopolk-Mirsky; the diplomat and scholar of Iran, V. P. Nikitin; the philosopher Lev Karsavin; and the legal scholar N. N. Alexeyev; as well as less prominent figures such as Sergei Efron, Konstantin Chkheidze, and Konstantin Rodzevich. A Kalmyk officer, Dr. Erzhen Khara-Davan, remained the only representative of the "Turanian peoples of Eurasia" (peoples who speak languages of the Ural-Altaic group) among the Eurasianists.

Several prominent intellectuals cooperated with the Eurasianists without becoming members of the movement formally: the church historian Anton Kartashev, the philosophers Semen Frank and Ivan Ilin, and the composer Artur Vincent Lourié (1892–1966). Roman Jakobson (1896–1982), one of the greatest linguists of the twentieth century, worked together with the Eurasianists in the 1920s and early 1930s. Although he never shared the Eurasianist political program, Jakobson took part in the intellectual exchanges of the Eurasianists.

### INTELLECTUAL PREDECESSORS

Eurasianism was rooted in the debate on Russia's identity vis-à-vis Europe and Asia, in which "Europe" often stood for undesired elements of modernity: in the nineteenth century many Russian intellectuals expressed ambiguity about Russia's "Europeanness." Peter Chaadayev (c. 1794–1856) and the Slavophiles had stressed Russia's difference from western Europe and its ties with Byzantium. The historian Nikolai Karamzin (1766–1826) granted the Tatar khans the honor of securing the unity of the Moscow state and the rise of Russian autocracy. Nikolai Danilevsky (1822–1865) and the pan-Slavists envisioned a specific Slavic civilization, as opposed to the world of the "Romano-Germans." Vladimir Soloviev (1820–1879) saw Russia's messianic destiny in saving the Christian civilization from the "yellow peril" of the Orient, and Fyodor Dostoyevsky (1821–1881) suggested a civilizing path for the Russians in Asia. By the end of the nineteenth century the symbolist poet Alexander Blok (1880–1921) and others associated the repressed masses of Russians with "Asia" and expected the social explosion to assume anti-

European cultural form. Velimir Khlebnikov (1885–1922), a leading futurist poet, projected the new liberating role for revolutionary Russia in Asia, while the Bolsheviks saw the world of the colonized peoples as a major source of social transformation. On the eve of the revolution Russian arts, music, and literature saw an unprecedented fascination with the Orient; Eurasianism inherited this interest from Russian modernism.

### A MODERNIST MOVEMENT

The Eurasianists were described as "Slavophiles of the era of futurism": the author of the Eurasianist aesthetics, Peter Suvchinsky, saw the Russian Revolution as a climactic event of a religious nature, which inaugurated a "new Romantic order" (despite the superficial adherence to ideas of progress and materialism by the Bolsheviks). As many Russian intellectuals, in particular the poet Blok, had suggested, the Russian Revolution (through the "Asian" masses of the Russian people) destroyed the old world of philistine bourgeois culture of Europe and unleashed the search for new forms of social, cultural, and political organization. For Suvchinsky, this search was reflected in developments in art and music, where traditional descriptive art gave way to a merging of form and content. He saw the future of art in a combination of this new creativity with Romantic and religious foundations. Suvchinsky's modernist aura attracted artists, musicians, and writers to Eurasianism. In 1926 Suvchinsky coorganized a literary journal *Versty*, which featured the philosopher Lev Shestov; the poetess Marina Tsvetayeva (1892–1941); the composers Igor Stravinsky (1882–1971) and Lourié; and the writers Alexei Remizov (1877–1957), Isaac Babel (1894–1941), and Boris Pasternak (1890–1960). In 1928 the newspaper *Evrazia* was founded and published among others Alexandre Kojève (1902–1968), who was the future interpreter of the philosopher Georg Wilhelm Friedrich Hegel (1770–1831), and the literary critic Emilia Litauer.

### EURASIA AS A GEOGRAPHICAL AND CULTURAL WHOLE

Utilizing the Romantic ideas of the German geographer Friedrich Ratzel (1844–1904), Savitsky envisioned Eurasia as a homogeneous territorial complex. Following nineteenth-century Russian geographers such as Vladimir Lamansky, Savitsky rejected a division of Russia into "Europe" and "Asia." He believed that no important geomorphologic obstacles existed in the territory of Eurasia, which was governed by the regularity of climatic change. This regularity was defined by the coincidence of two principles, that of the alteration of humidity, and that of the amendment in temperatures. In Eurasia, the vectors of these two principles coincided along the line south-north. Hence, Eurasian territory was constructed not on the basis of "vertical" division into "Europe" and "Asia" but on the grounds of three "horizontal" zones (steppe, forest, and tundra) stretching from the Baltic Sea to the Pacific.

Hence the dynamics of Eurasian history were defined by the interaction of the three natural zones, in particular of the steppe and the forest. Any state that took control of the "Eurasian highway," the steppe zone, was predestined to control the entire Eurasian continent, and modern Russia was thus an heir to the nomadic empires of Asia. The geographical and historical processes helped define Eurasia as a union of languages (*Sprachbund*): Jakobson and Trubetskoy stressed common characteristics acquired by genetically different languages in the course of their historical cohabitation within the Eurasian space. Reflecting on themes that had already been discussed by Russian historians such as Vasily Klyuchevsky (1841–1911) and Afanasy Shchapov, the Eurasianists suggested that Eurasia was a whole as an ethnographic mixture of peoples: the Russian national character had much in common with the Turkic peoples of Eurasia, and the nomadic "Turanians" played an essential role in Russian state and culture. The Russian state was a natural protector of the non-European culture of Eurasia. Tsar Peter I (Peter the Great; r. 1682–1725), violated the organic correspondence between that state and the underlying culture, and created a cleavage between Russia's Europeanized elite and its Eurasian masses of population. The alien bureaucratic regime of the tsars collapsed during the Russian Revolution, which was not just a revolt of one class against the other, but an uprising of colonized Eurasians against the alien Europeanized regime. In their rejection of European civilization, the Eurasianists became forebears of the poststructuralist critique of "orientalism": Trubetskoy wrote that all European disciplines were a tool of European colonial domination and need to be purged of judgments about superior and inferior cultures. The Eurasianists proclaimed Russia-Eurasia to be part (indeed, the potential leader) of the world of colonized peoples.

## EURASIANISM AND STRUCTURALISM

Eurasianism exercised significant influence on development in the humanities. The Eurasianist rhetoric implied terms such as "structure" and placed the "uncovering" of Eurasia in the context of the epistemological revolution. Trubetskoy, Savitsky, and Jakobson proposed to move away from describing "atomistic" facts and to employ notions of scientific regularity in order to discover hidden structures below the surface of visible phenomena. This rhetoric was translated into linguistics through the medium of the Prague Linguistic Circle, where Eurasianist scholars took part in the proceedings. Although scholars disagree on the extent to which Eurasianist "structuralism" differed from views of the Swiss linguist Ferdinand de Saussure (1857–1913), there is little doubt that Eurasianist "practical" structuralism had far-reaching impact on further developments in the humanities. After World War II Jakobson helped spread many of the ideas that emerged in the Eurasianist milieu of the 1920s and 1930s and thus contributed to the emergence of the structuralist paradigm in the humanities and social sciences.

## THE POLITICS OF EURASIANISM

Politically, Eurasia was envisioned as a federation of peoples re-created by the "state instinct" of the Bolsheviks, whom the Eurasianists welcomed as saviors of the Russian state tradition, but despised as representatives of European atheist and materialist culture. The Eurasianists' conception of history argued that a revolution was the replacement of the "ruling layer [of the population]" with a new class formed by a powerful idea. The Bolsheviks, by emancipating Russia from its old elite, cleared the way for this new ruling class. This class was predestined to create a true "ideocratic" state. The conception of the "ideocratic state," ruled by a single ideology, was elaborated by Trubetskoy, who was directly influenced by the *Ständestaat* theory of the Austrian philosopher, sociologist, and economist Othmar Spann (1878–1950): Trubetskoy met Spann in Vienna and discussed Eurasianist ideas with him. Such a state would preserve the Soviet demotic nature and its "natural selection" of the ruling class, yet it would get rid of Marxist theory and replace it with Eurasianism.

The Eurasianists translated ideas into political practice. In 1922 a group of émigré monarchist officers, led by Peter Arapov (later the agent of the Soviet intelligence) and Baron Alexander Meller-Zakomelsky (future leader of the Russian Nazis), joined the movement, which quickly developed from an intellectual venture into a clandestine political organization, whose aim was to convert as many people as possible, both émigrés and those living in the USSR, to Eurasianism. The converted members of the Soviet leadership in particular would help transform the USSR into a true "ideocratic state" based on the principles of Eurasianism. Contacts with clandestine émigré organizations led to penetration of the movement by Soviet agents. The Eurasianist leaders conducted negotiations with Soviet representatives (for instance, with G. L. Pyatakov, the Soviet trade representative in Paris, in 1927) and cherished hopes of turning their movement into a "laboratory of thought" at the service of the Soviet opposition.

Eurasianism was funded by the British philanthropist and theologian Henry Norman Spalding, who mistakenly believed that it could distract elites of colonial countries from communism. Spalding's money made possible an extensive publishing program of the movement in the 1920s. Yet, Eurasianism split in 1928–1929 on the issue of the evaluation of the Soviet power: the "orthodox" Eurasianists, Trubetskoy and Savitsky, refused to become instruments of Soviet propaganda, which was the conscious choice of the "left" group of the movement, led by Suvchinsky and Svyatopolk-Mirsky and supported by the Soviet agent Arapov. The left Eurasianists monopolized the newspaper *Evrazia*, and in response Trubetskoy left the movement. Savitsky managed to exclude the "left" group and to cut their funding. After 1929 Trubetskoy occasionally contributed to Eurasianist editions and Eurasianism gradually declined. In 1938 Trubetskoy died after arrest and interrogation by the Gestapo in Vienna. Suvchinsky became an important figure in the Parisian artistic scene and influenced the work of such composers as Pierre Boulez (b. 1925) and Gérard Masson (b. 1936).

Savitsky was arrested by Soviet counterintelligence in Prague and spent ten years in the gulag. After his return to Prague in 1956, he was arrested by the Czechoslovak political police, freed again, and died in 1968. After World War II, only George Vernadsky in the United States and Lev Gumilev (a geographer and a Eurasianist follower and son of the poet Anna Akhmatova) in the USSR continued to write in the Eurasianist vein.

## EURASIANIST REVIVAL

Post-Soviet Russia saw a revival of interest in Eurasianism, which provides hope for the restoration of the Russian imperial space, suggests a world-historical mission for the Russians, and gives form to widespread anti-Western sentiment. Books by the Eurasianist follower Gumilev became bestsellers after the fall of communism, while the neo-Eurasianist movement of Alexander Dugin has become an important phenomenon in post-Soviet Russia. The leaders of the Russian Communist Party, lacking ideological novelties, often utilize Eurasianist rhetoric. Intellectuals and politicians of some minorities, especially Turkic peoples, have a different motivation to use Eurasianism: in Tatarstan, Bashkortostan, and Sakha (Yakutia) it is often employed to counter ethnic Russian nationalism (while sharing in the post-Soviet anti-Western sentiment) and to carve out a space for Turkic peoples in Russian culture and history. In some former Soviet republics Eurasianism serves as a means to reconcile numerous Russian minorities with the titular nationality: the Kazakhstan president, Nursultan Nazarbaev, established a "Eurasian University" in Astana and named it after Gumilev. Eurasianism even became the name for a theory in international relations, which argues for an anti-Western Russian diplomacy and opposes "Atlantism." The new economic and political union of post-Soviet countries was named the "Eurasian Economic Community" (EvrAzES). Scholars in the West often use the term *Eurasia* to describe peoples who have had historical experiences of the Russian Empire and the Soviet Union but remain wary of the imperialist implications of Eurasianism.

*See also* **Russia; Soviet Union.**

BIBLIOGRAPHY

Böss, Otto. *Die Lehre der Eurasier: Eine Beitrage zur Russische Ideengeschichte des 20 Jahrhunderts.* Munich, 1961.

Glebov, Sergey. "The Challenge of the Modern: Eurasianist Ideology and Movement and the Legacy of the Russian Empire." Ph.D. diss., Rutgers University, 2004.

Laruelle, Marlène. *L'idéologie eurasiste russe; ou, Comment penser l'empire.* Paris, 1999.

Riasanovsky, Nicholas. "Prince N. S. Trubetskoi's 'Europe and Mankind.'" *Jahrbücher für Geschichte Osteuropas* 13 (1964): 207–220.

———. "Asia through Russian Eyes." In *Russia and Asia: Essays on the Influence of Russia on the Asian Peoples,* edited by Wayne S. Vucinich. Stanford, Calif., 1972.

———. "The Emergence of Eurasianism." *California Slavic Studies* 4 (1967): 39–72.

Sériot, Patrick. *Structure et totalité: Les origines intellectuelles du structuralisme en Europe centrale et orientale.* Paris, 1999.

Smith, G. S. *D. S. Mirsky: A Russian-English Life, 1890–1939.* Oxford, U.K., 2000.

Toman, Jindrich. *The Magic of a Common Language: Jakobson, Mathesius, Trubetzkoy, and the Prague Linguistic Circle.* Cambridge, Mass., 1995.

SERGEY GLEBOV

---

**EURO.** The euro became the single currency of the European Union (EU)—for exchange and financial markets—on 1 January 1999, the starting date for the third and final stage of the Economic and Monetary Union (EMU), one of the key components of the ongoing integration of Europe. The euro replaced the European Currency Unit (ECU), created in 1979, against which it was exchanged at the rate of 1 to 1. All obligations and contracts in ECUs were pursued in euros in a seamless transition. The euro is used in all operations (revenue and expenditure) linked to the EU's 110 billion euro budget and to EU financial activities (such as loans and bonds). A further evolution of the currency came on 1 January 2002 when the euro became the national currency for twelve of the fifteen EU member states: Austria, Belgium, Finland, France, Germany, Greece, Ireland, Italy, Luxembourg, the Netherlands, Portugal, and Spain.

In order to qualify to have the euro as the national currency, an EU member must fulfill three economic criteria linked to areas of sound management of public finance (public deficit and public debt, stability of exchange rates, and low inflation and interest rates). Failure to meet these criteria is the reason why the ten nations that entered the EU on 1 May 2004 could not, as of 2005, use the euro as their national currency, although they are aiming to meet the criteria by 2014. Thus, although by EU treaty all member states have the obligation to participate in the EMU, they may not be permitted to participate in all of its provisions. Moreover, three states, Denmark, Great Britain, and Sweden, although fully part of the EMU, negotiated to postpone their adoption of the euro until a later stage, when the nation's government and citizenry decide that the time is ripe.

## FUNCTIONING RULES

As the EU is not yet a federal state, management of the Economic and Monetary Union is based on functioning rules, on strong interstate cooperation and policy coordination, and on a division of tasks between member states' economic policy ministers and the European Central Bank (ECB). Monetary and economic management rules are defined by treaty and specified by EU regulations. The main economic policy element is the Growth and Stability Pact, which obliges member states to pursue sound budgetary policy aimed at economic growth. The European Commission continuously monitors member states' economic situations and reports to the Council of Economic and Finance Ministers (ECOFIN). Breaches to the pact may lead to sanctions, if the ECOFIN decides so on the basis of the commission's recommendations. Although less strict for the countries that have not adopted the euro, treaty obligations and potential sanctions do apply to all EU members. The European Court of Justice is charged with dealing with disputes that arise concerning these matters. Monetary policy is the domain of the fully independent ECB. It defines objectives (such as inflation rates and growth of the money supply) and fixes reference interest rates accordingly as well as the amount of coins and notes in euro to be issued. Its treaty obligation is to ensure the stability of the euro both internally (inside the EU) and externally (outside the EU). The role of the European Parliament (EP) is very limited. The institutions in charge have an obligation to inform the EP of their actions, and it may issue nonbinding recommendations.

## THE ECONOMIC RATIONALE

During Europe's nearly 2,500-year history as a politically organized but divided continent, Europeans had many occasions to use common monetary instruments and monies. The euro, however, is the first currency in world history willingly accepted by citizens from nation-states who used to fight one another, in a move toward building a commonwealth and political unity.

The story certainly starts with the development of economics as a science during the eighteenth century. Economists such as David Hume (1711–1776) and Anne-Robert-Jacques Turgot (1727–1781) demonstrated the interdependence of national economies and policies and developed the theories now called the "monetary approach of the balance of payment" and the "optimal currency area." From these derive liberal and monetarist economic policies, and the economic rationale for creating the euro. Briefly, the theory stipulates that when two (or several) rather small countries widely open their borders to mutual trade, they have no more control over their individual monetary policies and by consequence over their economic cycles. Therefore it is beneficial for the countries to create a monetary union, with a single currency. And this is the case with the EU members. Obviously, in an increasingly globalized world, there are many other economic reasons to create a single currency, including the reduction of transaction costs, economies of scale, productivity gains, and the creation of a large economic space that permits greater consolidation. Nevertheless, these economic rationales, if necessary, are not sufficient to explain why EU members made such an extraordinary decision—through a treaty signed in Maastricht, Netherlands, on 7 February 1992—to abandon one of the main hallmarks of national sovereignty. Politics and geopolitics certainly also played a major role.

**A one-euro coin.** ©MATTHIAS KULKA/CORBIS

## A BRIEF HISTORY OF THE ROAD TO THE EURO

The process has been long and difficult, even bloody. It necessitated the failure of the gold standard and of the limited monetary unions of the nineteenth century, the latter failures resulting mainly from the incapacity of European nations to cooperate and from their rivalry for dominance of the world—based on excessive nationalism and dictatorial ideologies—culminating in two world wars that killed millions and destroyed economies. Lessons were drawn during the last years of World War II. Some European federalists, such as Luigi Einaudi (1874–1961), argued in favor of a European political and monetary union, whereas others, such as John Maynard Keynes (1883–1946), wanted, along with some Americans, to establish an international monetary order. The latter succeeded with the creation, via the Bretton Woods Conference (1944), of the international monetary system monitored by the International Monetary Fund (IMF). The United States led the negotiations. It was by then the largest and strongest economy in the world and possessed 90 percent of the world's gold reserves. Therefore, the U.S. dollar was chosen as the reference currency against which all others had to define their value.

To work smoothly, such a system needed the U.S. government to adopt a multilateral and cooperative approach to its economic policy that could lead the world economic cycle. Starting in the late 1950s, this was not the case. By the late 1960s, the United States' "benign neglect" approach, its growing indebtedness and money supply to finance its economic growth, and its wars made the dollar—which, up to then, had been considered "as good as gold"—an inconvertible currency (the crises of 1968 and 1971–1973) and led to the collapse of the Bretton Woods system in 1976.

In the meantime, the Europeans, thanks to the U.S. Marshall Plan (1948–1951) and the European Payments Union (1950–1958), reconstructed their economies. To suppress one cause of war, they decided to pool their coal and steel industry (European Coal and Steel Community, formed 1952), then to create, through the Rome Treaty of 1957, a broader economic and political community known initially as the European Economic Community (later simply the European Community). To succeed, an economic union needed internal and external monetary stability. The mismanagement of the dollar was putting the entire enterprise at risk. As early as 1960, a gold pool had to be created to maintain the value of the dollar against gold. The growing crisis of the dollar led to a formalized strengthening of the monetary cooperation of the European Community central banks in 1964, and the dissolution of the gold pool prompted the first project with a goal of creating a European common currency (Plan Barre, 1968). The Council of the European Union asked one of its members, Pierre Werner (1913–2002), the prime minister of Luxembourg, to prepare a road map. Adopted in 1971, the plan's policy tools and monetary practices were aimed at achieving a common currency by 1980.

## THE LAST STEPS: FROM THE ECU TO THE EURO

The international monetary crisis precipitated by the crises of the dollar (1971, 1973, and 1976), reinforced by the first oil crisis (1973–1975), disrupted the European Community economies, placing their cooperation at stake, and leading to the partial failure of the agreement to maintain the fluctuations of the European currencies within a small band (a system known as the "European monetary snake"). But the negative consequences on growth and unemployment were such that the monetary unification process was reinitiated in 1978. In March 1979 the European Monetary System (EMS), based on the ECU, a weighted basket of the EC national currencies, was adopted, with the ECU becoming the monetary unit of account of the EC budget. The ECU was managed by the European Monetary Cooperation Fund, which later evolved into the European Central Bank, and the Committee of the Governors of the EC central banks. The second oil crisis (1979–1981), as well as the initial unbalanced practices of the monetary cooperation in favor of Germany, made its debut difficult. Two reforms (in 1985 and 1987) solved these problems, ensuring real cooperation in the definition of monetary policies and bringing about a better share of EMS management costs. In the meantime, the ECU developed as an international currency. By 1991 it was the third most used international currency on the financial markets.

The success of the EMS in stabilizing the national currencies internally and externally, the growing convergence of economic indicators, the interdependence and integration of the EC economies, the large swings in the value of the U.S. dollar, the collapse of the communist systems of central and eastern Europe and the end of the Cold War, and the vital necessity of Europe to contribute to world monetary stability were the main developments that enabled the adoption of a three-step plan toward the creation of the EC monetary union. The Maastricht Treaty that formalized it also contained elements to build a political union. The reluctance of Great Britain, Sweden, and Denmark to abandon their monetary sovereignty in order to slow down the process of political union did not compromise the monetary union of which they are part without using the single European currency. The transition to the full use of the euro (1999–2002) in the twelve other countries was an incredible challenge: all coins and notes had to be exchanged, the new euro had to be designed and produced, all systems—financial, banking, accounting—had to be modified, vending machines had to be changed, and so on. A changeover plan was adopted in December 1995. As planned, the euro was introduced as the international currency and the accounting currency of banks on 1 January 1999. At that point, the twelve national currencies of the union disappeared from exchange and financial markets. Only coins and notes continued to circulate internally. Their exchange for euro coins and notes started on 1 January 2002 and was achieved in two months, far quicker than expected.

Although there are some political tensions surrounding the application of the Growth and Stability Pact that could lead to some limited modifications, the whole system is functioning smoothly. Very quickly, the ECB was able to gain strong international credibility. In a few short years, the euro has become the second most used international currency in world trade—on all types of financial markets—standing just behind the U.S. dollar (at a ratio of 3 to 4). In some countries, complaints were raised from citizens contending that the changeover to the euro permitted professionals to increase their prices, but all are using the euro coins and notes without major problems and benefit from the low or nil electronic transaction costs for payments. The euro is generally considered to be a major European success.

*See also* **European Union.**

BIBLIOGRAPHY

Collignon, Stefan. *Monetary Stability in Europe.* London, 2002.

Dyson, Kenneth, ed. *European States and the Euro: Europeanization, Variation, and Convergence.* Oxford, U.K., 2002.

Dyson, Kenneth, and Kevin Featherstone. *The Road to Maastricht: Negotiating Economic and Monetary Union.* Oxford, U.K., 1999.

Mundell, Robert, and Armand Clesse, eds. *The Euro as a Stabilizer in the International Economic System.* Boston, 2000.

Padoa-Schioppa, Tommaso. *The Road to Monetary Union in Europe: The Emperor, the Kings, and the Genies.* 2nd ed. Oxford, U.K., 1996.

Pelkmans, Jacques. *European Integration: Methods and Economic Analysis.* 3rd ed. Harlow, U.K., 2003.

Triffin, Robert. *Gold and the Dollar Crisis.* New Haven, Conn., 1960.

Vissol, Thierry. *The Euro: Consequences for the Consumer and the Citizen.* Dordrecht, Netherlands, 1999.

THIERRY VISSOL

# EUROCOMMUNISM.

Eurocommunism was a political movement that came to prominence in the second half of the 1970s in several European Communist parties, influenced by the ideas of Santiago Carrillo (b. 1915), the secretary of the Spanish Communist Party (PCE) from 1960 to 1982.

## THE ROOTS OF EUROCOMMUNISM

In 1956 destalinization and Soviet repression in Hungary provoked unease and a certain confusion among the Communist parties of Europe, though these feelings were for the time being overcome. Faith in the USSR was restored by Soviet successes in space, by the Cuban Revolution, and by Nikita Khrushchev's assurance of the inevitable triumph of socialism. Support for Soviet policy was expressed even by opponents of the Communist parties upon the launch of the process of European economic integration, which was portrayed as another step in a capitalist-imperialist reorganization designed to benefit the United States.

All the same, the breakdown of relations between the USSR and China, which revealed the "indestructible friendship" between the two communist powers as a fiction, followed by Khrushchev's deposition in the shadow of conspiracy, the Chinese Cultural Revolution, and finally the 1968 invasion of Czechoslovakia, increasingly undermined faith in the Soviet myth.

In 1968 the French and Italian Communist parties, taking an unprecedented stance, publicly condemned the invasion of Czechoslovakia, albeit as an error and certainly not for what it was, a manifestation of Soviet "power politics." In any case, the condemnation of the event indicated that the Soviet myth was by then shaken and that the two parties had assumed a degree of political autonomy that betokened a turnaround in policy. This turnaround found its institutional expression in the birth of the movement that came to be called Eurocommunism.

## ORIGIN OF THE TERM

It appears that the word *Eurocommunism* was coined not by a Communist leader but by a Yugoslav journalist, Frane Barbieri, who used it in his article "Le scadenze di Brezhnev" (Brezhnev's ticking clock), published in *Il giornale nuovo* of 26 June 1975, and whose political and ideological views were opposed to those of the Italian Communist Party (PCI). The new term came to represent Carrillo's policy of seeking to conform less and less with the strategic vision of Moscow while showing new openness to the European Community. According to Barbieri, *Eurocommunism* had been chosen over *neocommunism* because it represented a perspective that was geographical and not ideological, whereas the second term seemed to stand for a concept too ideologically loaded.

About a year after Barbieri's article, on the occasion of the rally of the PCI and the French Communist Party (PCF) on 3 June 1976 at La Villette, near Paris, Enrico Berlinguer (1922–1984; secretary of the PCI from March 1972 to 1984) first used the neologism, which he placed in quotation marks. Referring to the great interest in many circles of the "bourgeois" international press regarding "Eurocommunism," he defined the term generically as a label for certain common positions shared by various Communist parties.

On the occasion of the pan-European conference of Communist parties, held in East Berlin on 29–30 June 1976, Berlinguer emphasized the way in which certain Communist and workers' parties in Western Europe had arrived, by way of independent efforts, at similar perspectives on the route best followed to establish socialism. According to Berlinguer, it was to these novel perspectives and inquiries that the name *Eurocommunism* had been given.

On a preceding occasion, at the Twenty-fifth Congress of the Communist Party of the Soviet Union, held in Moscow in February 1976, Berlinguer had already, without using the word, elaborated what the PCI considered to be its fundamental characteristics: the principle according to which relations between Communist parties were to be imbued with a spirit of friendship and solidarity, with an open concourse of diverse experiences and positions; recognition of and respect for the full independence of every Communist Party; and the idea that the construction of a socialist society ought to constitute the culminating moment in the forward progress of all democratic reforms and guarantee respect for all individual and collective liberties.

Carrillo first used the word *Eurocommunism*, which he likewise placed in quotation marks, on the occasion of the Berlin conference, proclaiming that the principle of internationalism was going to be profoundly modified. For Carrillo too, Eurocommunism implied a new conception of democracy, conditioned by the fact that the Communist parties of developed capitalist nations had to confront a particular set of circumstances tied to the exigencies of promoting class struggle in such environments. This reality led toward trajectories and types of socialism that would not be the same as those in other countries. The rule of the forces of labor and culture would not be imposed through dictatorial mechanisms but rather with respect for political and ideological pluralism and without a single-party system.

Finally, after demonstrating more circumspection in the adoption of the new term, the PCF at last entered into the new movement, abandoning in sudden and spectacular fashion the principle of the dictatorship of the proletariat, and thus ushering in a new conception of democracy, at its Twenty-second Congress in February 1976. At the Berlin conference, Georges Marchais (1920–1997; secretary of the PCF from 1972 to 1994) affirmed the principles of Eurocommunism without ever uttering the word, proclaiming that the PCF would follow an independent path in the struggle for socialism.

## THE FUNDAMENTAL ELEMENTS OF EUROCOMMUNISM

The innovations introduced by Eurocommunism in the field of international communism were ranged on three different planes: international, national, and party-level. On an international level, it advanced a new concept of internationalism, definitively purged of the legacy of Joseph Stalin and the Communist International gatherings. No longer was a single international center of communism recognized, nor was any one party or state henceforth considered a model to be followed. The Eurocommunist parties sought to establish a more marked autonomy from Moscow and from communism of a Soviet stamp, and they indeed criticized the USSR more and more frequently for the grave limits it placed on democracy, for its treatment of dissidents, for its disturbing shortcomings in the field of human rights, and for its ossified bureaucratic apparatus, which paralyzed every process of social transformation the world over.

While Leonid Brezhnev (1906–1982; leader of the USSR from 1964 to 1982) continued to affirm that the Soviet brand of socialism was the best possible, the French, Italian, and Spanish Communist parties evinced the conviction that in the West, it would be necessary to follow a "third road" separate from that followed by the Communist bloc, where "socialist democracy" had failed to develop, and from that of Western social democracy, which remained subordinate to capitalism.

On a national level, the three parties maintained similar positions regarding the crises that had struck the advanced capitalistic societies of Western Europe, beginning with the oil crisis. The situation was defined as global—because it did not pertain only to the economy but to all aspects of society, including politics and ethics—and therefore systemic. The only solution was to set out on the road to socialism. The architects of this new type of society rejected the Soviet model above all, preferring instead to emphasize the universal values of liberty and democracy, which were "inseparable from socialism."

At a party level, while they remained structured according to the principle of centralized democracy in the Leninist tradition, the three Eurocommunist parties, inspired both by their own membership and by the climate abroad, opened themselves to more democratizing reforms, albeit in very different ways.

## THE BILATERAL MEETINGS AND THE MADRID SUMMIT

After the meeting of 12 July 1975, the policy of Eurocommunism was enunciated at Livorno by Berlinguer and Carrillo in a joint communiqué, in which they affirmed the solemn declaration of Italian and Spanish Communists that, in their conception of a democratic advance toward socialism in peace and liberty, they intended not tactical maneuvering but a strategic conviction, born of reflection on the collective experiences of the workers' movement and on the specific historic circumstances of their respective countries.

At the second summit between the PCI and the PCF in November 1975, a second communal declaration proclaimed that the two parties were acting under different material circumstances and that each of them would therefore pursue a policy designed to meet the needs and suit the characteristics of their own nation. At the same time, given their struggle in developed capitalist countries, they stated that the problems they confronted presented common characteristics and required similar solutions.

The Madrid summit of 2–3 March 1977 constituted an important and indeed spectacular moment in the Eurocommunism movement, and the definitive testimonial to the links between the three parties. The summit, attended by Berlinguer, Marchais, and Carrillo, was considered the first and only joint conference of Eurocommunism. Rather than the apogee of Eurocommunism, however, it in fact represented the beginning of its decline. The secretaries of the three parties (particularly Marchais and Berlinguer) appeared more preoccupied with affirming that the real purpose of the summit was to show solidarity with the Spanish Communist Party, which still lacked formal legal authorization, than with giving their backing to a novel conception of the communist world.

After the meeting, in fact, due to the fragility of the accord that was reached, the absence of a common regional strategy, the resistance the new initiatives met from proponents of the old order, and the support that these proponents received from the Soviets, a period of discord began that would rapidly lead to the decline of Eurocommunism.

## LEADERS, PARTICIPANTS, AND ASSOCIATED MOVEMENTS

Eurocommunism, with its intent to bring about a transition to socialism while respecting democratic politics and pluralism, found its most authoritative leader in Berlinguer, who was inclined even to recognize the positive function of NATO (in an interview of 15 June 1976 in *Il corriere della sera*). The other protagonist was Carrillo, who harshly criticized the Soviet model in the study *"Eurocomunismo" y estado* (1977;

"Eurocommunism" and the state), which focused chiefly on a Spanish and European context and was characterized by strong declarations in favor of pluralism and "Europeanism," in open polemic with Soviet ideology.

In addition to the Italian, Spanish, and French Communist parties, the Communist parties of England, Belgium, Switzerland, and Greece (in the last case, an internal faction born in 1968 from a schism in the Greek Communist Party) participated in the movement. Support also came from the Dutch Communist Party, whose total autonomy from the USSR had long been established. The same ideas were espoused outside of Europe, though with different motives, by the Communist parties of Japan, Australia, and Mexico, as well as by political factions that had broken off from Communist parties, such as the MAS (Movement toward Socialism) in Venezuela.

In Western Europe, the ranks of the Eurocommunist parties were in this period opposed by the Communist parties of Portugal, Greece (in exile), Austria, Luxembourg, and Norway.

### THE REACTION OF MOSCOW

The 1976 Berlin conference of twenty-nine European Communist parties made still clearer the difficulties facing the proposal, advanced repeatedly on Soviet initiative, to organize a new worldwide conference on the model of the one held in Moscow in 1969 (where on 11 June Berlinguer had reiterated the condemnation of the Soviet intervention in Czechoslovakia) for the purpose of eliminating, or at least reducing, the contrasts that continued to manifest themselves within the international Communist movement.

In order to redress a political climate conditioned by such diverse influences, the USSR promoted a series of regional conferences. The most important, aside from those in East Berlin and later Paris (April 1980), the latter boycotted by the Eurocommunists, took place between 1981 and 1985. These were "theoretical" conferences to which the presence of Soviet officials imparted a clear political hue. They were organized on the initiative of the journal *Problems of Peace and Socialism*, born in Paris in 1958 as a forum for interaction and debate in the wake of

the dissolution of Cominform (the Communist Information Bureau).

### THE CRISIS OF EUROCOMMUNISM

The crisis became explicit at the moment of the Soviet invasion of Afghanistan in December 1979, and thereafter with the Polish "affairs" of 1980 (the Baltic strike and the birth of the Solidarity union), followed in 1981 by the Polish government's proclamation of a state of siege. Such events shattered the Eurocommunist ranks. The Italian, Spanish, Belgian, English, Swedish, Swiss, Dutch, Mexican, and Japanese Communist parties criticized Brezhnev's policies, though other parties took a different stance, most notably the PCF. Furthermore, some of the parties that had continued to adhere to Eurocommunism were quick to experience serious internal divisions. As a result of the pressures exerted on party leadership by factions still faithful to old pro-Soviet policies, as well as through the direct intervention of the USSR, discord and fractures broke out that afflicted above all the Spanish, Finnish, and English Communist parties, precipitating rapid and dramatic losses at the polls.

Still more decisive, however, was the split that had come about between the leading parties. Though the PCF would never openly renounce its positions of the preceding period (from the Champigny Manifesto of 1968 to the documents of the Twenty-second Congress on "socialism in French colors" and on the abandonment of the formula of the "dictatorship of the proletariat"), it effectively sanctioned the Soviet invasion of Afghanistan and proceeded, together with the Polish Communist Party, to promote a meeting of nineteen parties that occurred in East Berlin in March 1979. At the Twenty-fourth Congress, the leadership of the PCF abandoned its reservations about past Soviet policy and moreover defined as "globally positive" the cumulative effects of the "real socialism" of the Brezhnev years. The adoption of these new positions not only failed to impede but indeed contributed to the electoral collapse suffered by the PCF in the subsequent administrative and political elections.

So too in the PCE, internal fragmentation resulted in a series of grave electoral defeats. The crisis led to Carrillo's resignation from the secretariat of the party in 1982, from which he was expelled entirely in 1985 (Carrillo then formed the group Unidad Comunista, from 1987 an official party).

The choices made by the PCI were different and in fact opposed, though they too were accompanied by a decline in the polls, after the positive results of the first phase. By way of carrying forward the critiques advanced in 1956 and 1968 on the problems of change in advanced capitalist societies and on the rapport between socialism and democracy, as well as on what came to be called the "new internationalism," in March 1979 the Italian Communists proposed the idea of a "third road" or a "third phase" as an alternative to the Soviet example and to that of the social democrats, both of which were considered ineffective.

In the process, the PCI came to its "rupture," with the declaration of Berlinguer in December 1981 regarding the defunctness of the "forward push" of the October Revolution and the Soviet exemplar, and the consequent necessity of following other paths to arrive at a "diverse" socialism and a greater integration of the PCI with the circle of the Western European Left.

Among the Eurocommunist parties in Europe, besides minorities in Finland, England, and France, only that of Greece (the internal faction) maintained positions similar to those of the PCI, against which there was an extremely harsh backlash from the Russian and Polish Communist parties, as well as from numerous other parties.

Thanks to its deep social and political roots in Italy, the PCI managed during the first half of the 1980s to achieve a significant electoral consensus and put an end to the opposition to European integration. Mikhail Gorbachev's rise to power in the Soviet Union gave hope that the time had come for an internal reform of Soviet communism and for the recovery of communism on an international level. The failure of Gorbachev's program inevitably drew the PCI and the other Communist parties of Western Europe into an irreversible crisis, which was accelerated after 1989. Indeed, by the end of the 1980s, with the dissolution of the USSR, the fall of the Communist regimes of Eastern Europe, the increase of repression in China, and the crisis of many pro-communist regimes in the Third World, the framework of world communism was thrown into total chaos.

In 1991 the PCI dissolved itself at its Twentieth Congress, giving life on the one hand to a Democratic Party of the Left, which placed itself under the aegis of European socialism with its adherence to the Socialist International, and on the other to a Party of Communist Refoundation, spawned from the secession of a minority. The Communists in France and Spain, for their part, saw a net decline in their collective influence. At the same time, such events and circumstances marked the culmination of the process of crisis and turned the debate on the future of communism toward an analysis of the prospects of existing communist nations and a recap of a historical phenomenon.

*See also* **Berlinguer, Enrico; Brezhnev, Leonid; Communism; Gorbachev, Mikhail; Italy; 1968; 1989; Soviet Union.**

BIBLIOGRAPHY

Agosti, Aldo. *Bandiere rosse: Un profilo storico dei comunismi europei.* Rome, 1999.

Argentieri, Federigo, ed. *La fine del blocco sovietico.* Florence, 1991.

Aspaturian, Vernon V., Jiri Valent, and David P. Burke, eds. *Eurocommunism between East and West.* Bloomington, Ind., 1980.

Cafagna, Luciano. *C'era una volta—: Riflessioni sul comunismo italiano.* Venice, 1991.

Del Noce, Augusto. *L'Eurocomunismo e l'Italia.* Rome, 1976.

Italian Communist Party, ed. *Socialismo reale e terza via: Il dibattito sui fatti di Polonia nella riunione del Comitato centrale e della Commissione centrale di controllo del Pci (Rome, 11-13 gennaio 1982) I documenti sulla polemica con il Pcus.* Rome, 1982.

Kiegel, Annie. *Eurocommunism: A New Kind of Communism?* Translated by Peter S. Stern. Stanford, Calif., 1978. Translation of *Autre communisme?*.

Leonhard, Wolfgang. *Eurocommunism: Challenge for East and West.* Translated by Mark Vecchio. New York, 1978. Translation of *Eurokommunismum*.

Marcou, Lilly. *Le mouvement communiste international depuis 1945.* Paris, 1980.

Middlemas, Keith. *Power and the Party: Changing Faces of Communism in Western Europe.* London, 1980.

Rizzo, Aldo. *La frontiera dell'eurocomunismo.* Rome, 1977.

Salvatori, Massimo L. *Storia dell'età contemporanea: Dalla restaurazione all'eurocomunismo.* Turin, 1976.

Tőkés, Rudolf. *Eurocommunism and Détente.* New York, 1978.

Valli, Bernardo. *Gli eurocomunisti.* Milan, 1976.

MARIA TERESA GIUSTI

---

# EUROPEAN COAL AND STEEL COMMUNITY (ECSC).

The European Coal and Steel Community (ECSC) was an international organization that was established on 25 July 1952 by the Treaty of Paris. In the treaty the Federal Republic of Germany, Italy, Belgium, the Netherlands, and Luxembourg agreed with France to renounce part of their sovereignty by placing their coal and steel production in a common market, under a supranational authority. Later, as the European integration process progressed, the incoming members of the European Union also became part of the ECSC (that is, Denmark, Ireland, and United Kingdom in 1973; Greece in 1981; Portugal and Spain in 1986; and Austria, Finland, and Sweden in 1995). In 1990, when East and West Germany reunified, the country joined the organization in its turn. First established in the city of Luxembourg, the ECSC headquarters finally moved to Brussels in 1967. As agreed in the treaty, after fifty years of functioning, the ECSC came to an end on 25 July 2002, its competences being transferred to the European Community.

## THE SCHUMAN PLAN AND ITS OBJECTIVES

On 9 May 1950 Robert Schuman, French minister for foreign affairs, invited all European countries to join France and Germany in pooling production of coal and steel. The idea of international cooperation among European heavy industries was not completely new, as similar projects had been developed in the aftermath of World War II in France, in Germany, and inside the American administration. The so-called Schuman Plan, secretly conceived by Jean Monnet but politically endorsed by Schuman, was innovative in two respects; first, from a functionalist perspective, it was expected to bring about further European integration: the two pioneering branches would attract other sectors in the process and, by a so-called spill-over effect, lead gradually to a European federation; second, it implied a revolutionary method of governance characterized by the delegation of national powers to a supranational institution.

Beyond economic and social objectives—the development and modernization of European production, the expansion of import-export exchanges inside and outside the pool, and a converging improvement of living standards for the workers—the Schuman Plan was also defined along essential political objectives. By bringing France and Germany to a factual solidarity, it was expected that any future war between them would be both unthinkable and impossible. French-German relations had reached a deadlock on unresolved questions (the status of the Saar, the German rearmament, and free access to the Ruhr's coal), paralyzing, if not jeopardizing, the European integration process. In Monnet's view, similar to the United States' position, such a situation could not last given the Cold War's context: a fast and ambitious initiative was needed, on the one hand, to anchor Western Germany to the West and make it participate in Western Europe's defense and, on the other hand, to keep German industrial cartels and rearmament capacities under close control. In exchange for this economic concession, an opportunity was given to Germany to reenter international politics with equal rights for the first time since the end of the war. By accepting and endorsing the idea, despite strong opposition in his country (mainly social democrat and communist parties), Konrad Adenauer, the German chancellor, played a decisive role in the success of the plan. After Germany, the Benelux countries (Belgium, Netherlands, and Luxembourg) and Italy agreed to enter the discussions by accepting the idea of a supranational authority. The categorical rejection by the United Kingdom brought much disappointment and doubt, but could not stop the process. The extent to which the United States influenced the Schuman Plan is not clear and has long been debated, with some scholars suggesting that it may have considered the project as an ideal extension of the previous Marshall Plan. At least, the United States showed itself eager to defend the supranational character of the treaty and to make Europe move away from past cartels.

## THE CONFERENCE OF PARIS

Ten months was not a long time to reach an agreement on the matters at stake considering their

**French foreign minister Robert Schuman presents the plan for the European Coal and Steel Community to a meeting of European representatives, Paris, June 1950.** ©BETTMANN/CORBIS

complexity and novelty, particularly if one thinks of the harsh discussions that arose in institutional, political, and economic terms. Thus, at the very beginning of the conference, the small Benelux countries called for some essential guarantees: a clear delimitation and definition of supranational prerogatives and a fair balance of powers between small and big member-states inside the different organs. Belgium and Italy, for their part, insisted that a transitional period should be agreed to ease the integration of their industries in the future common market. The negotiations led to the Treaty of Paris, signed on 18 April 1951. Opposition arose in all six countries: the communist parties considered that the plan was against the USSR's interests; the German social democrats refused any kind of national concessions; the French Gaullist party opposed any loss of national sovereignty; but also industrialists, such as

the Belgian coal producers and the French, Luxembourg, and Belgian steelmakers, particularly feared the future High Authority's interventionism.

### THE ECSC TREATY
In contrast with the subsequent European treaties, which provided a general framework of action but few directly applicable rules, this treaty was composed of detailed rules fixing once and for all the supranational competences (treaty-law). Comprising one hundred articles, it resulted from numerous compromises between different political and economic visions, mainly between dirigisme (i.e., strong economic state interventionism) and laissez-faire, (or "let do," i.e., free-market economics).

***General principles*** Liberal in essence, the treaty established a common market for coal and steel by banning state-aid, subsidies, discrimination, and restrictive practices. It aimed to promote economic expansion by modernizing and rationalizing coal and steel production; avoiding an unconsidered exhaustion of their resources; developing employment and improving living and working standards in the member-states; and favoring international trade. As part of this, it sought to reduce prices on the internal market by imposing tariff transparency. However, the treaty was also characterized by different interventionist mechanisms, enabling the High Authority to regulate the market.

*Institutions* The High Authority was the supranational executive body. Its composition (eight members, nominated by national governments, plus one co-opted, that is, chosen by the nominated members) was intended to ensure a balanced representation of large and small states. Financially autonomous, this collegial organ was also politically independent, as its nine members were required to act without any external instruction. Supported by a secretariat, it was assisted by an Advisory Committee constituted of coal and steel producers, consumers, and trade unions. Empowered to impose levies and direct sanctions on firms, the High Authority had a far more significant power than the future European Commission. To counterbalance and control it, an intergovernmental body, the Special Council of Ministers, was established, composed of member-states' representatives: this second executive body was meant to harmonize the supranational and national policies. In certain areas involving direct controls, the decisions of the High Authority had to be approved by the Council of Ministers. Furthermore, the Court of Justice (seven judges nominated by consensus by national governments) exerted a judicial control upon the High Authority and the member-states. The Common Assembly (seventy-eight delegates from national parliaments) was created to provide more legitimacy to the new institutions. Despite having relatively limited powers (such as the power to review the High Authority's annual report, and to sack the members of the supranational body), this paved the way for a future European Parliament. The same fourfold structure would be given to the European Economic Community and the Euratom treaties in 1957.

In essence, this "dual executive" structure created tensions between national and community forces and between large and small member-states. The latter insisted that every country be represented in every institution, and particularly in the High Authority and the Common Assembly. Within the Council of Ministers, votes were weighted in function of respective coal and steel production and, depending upon the issue, a unanimous vote, a simple majority, or a qualified majority was requested. The system enabled the small states to counterbalance the large ones, if the former decided to act together.

*Policies* All types of discrimination (quotas, prices, taxes, subsidies, or transport costs) were forbidden and, for the first time in Europe, precise antitrust legislation was applied: cartels, concentrations, and mergers were allowed by the High Authority only if they helped the market to function better. Social dumping was prohibited and the free circulation of qualified workers inside the community was promoted. Besides this, the supranational body was also empowered to intervene actively in the market: in cases of nonrespect of competition and nondiscrimination rules, it could pronounce direct sanctions; it was also empowered to help (by loans) limit and influence the financing of investment programs. Furthermore, in certain conditions, after having consulted the Advisory Committee and the Council of Ministers, the High Authority could fix minimum and maximum prices. In periods of crisis, with the Council of Ministers' approval, it could, as a last resort, fix quotas on production (in the case of overproduction) or allocate scarce supplies (in the case of shortage). Like governments, the High Authority could borrow money and was allowed to impose levies on the firms: these were shared across functioning costs, loan interests and guarantees, investments, and research expenditures. A portion of the levies was put in an international readaptation fund, meant to help workers and firms affected by the new open market.

A complementary part to the treaty, more flexible, defined a series of actions and duties to be undertaken during a five-year transition period: aside from establishing the ECSC's organs, time was needed to unify the markets, negotiate with third countries, and readapt the industries. Some specific dispositions concerning French, Belgian, and Italian coal production and Italian and Luxembourg steel production, were also agreed in order to cushion the immediate effects of the common market.

## FIFTY YEARS OF FUNCTIONING

The existence of the ECSC can be divided in two distinct periods, as the High Authority stopped functioning as such in 1967. All its competences were then transferred to the Commission of the European Communities (by the Merger Treaty).

The High Authority began operating in August 1952 with Monnet as its first president (followed by René Mayer (France), Paul Finet (Belgium), Piero Malvestiti (Italy), and, finally, Dino Del Bo (Italy). In July 1952 the ECSC countries produced 19.4 percent of the coal and 16 percent of the steel in the world. At that time, coal met about 70 percent of European energy requirements. Germany was by far the biggest producer in the Community responsible for more than a half of the coal, almost three-fifths of the coke, and a third of pig iron and steel. With two-thirds, France was the biggest ECSC producer of iron ore. During the spring of 1953, the High Authority gradually opened the common markets (i.e., coal, iron ore, scrap, pig iron, and steel) with some exceptions to the rule (e.g., Italian steel). During this period, and for the next five years, the transitional measures were in operation (e.g., aid regime for Belgian coal). After a short recession period between 1949 and 1951, the High Authority profited from the favorable economic situation to implement an active policy of modernization and research and, in social terms, a policy of building housing for ECSC workers. By 1958 trade in steel inside the community had increased by 151 percent; 21 percent for coal and 25 percent for iron ore. In terms of European integration, the results were rather disappointing and left the ECSC's functionalist and federalist conceivers a little disillusioned. Handicapped by too specialized a scope and too precise a mandate, hampered by growing bureaucracy, the High Authority could not expand its competences. By contrast, the intergovernmental body had successfully imposed its presence and role in European Community politics. Because of national divergences and interferences (even inside the High Authority itself), it became difficult to ensure the strict application of the treaty or any coordinated action that went against national interests, as illustrated by the antitrust policy and the coal

crisis of the late 1950s. Despite its will, the High Authority did not succeed in remaining a key player in the integration process, and the initial functionalist path toward a European federation was left aside as the next European treaties were being negotiated. After 1967 the ECSC treaty was applied with more efficiency and visibility, under the responsibility of the European Commission in Brussels. In front of the steel crisis (mid-1970s to mid-1980s), three successive plans (named after their responsible commissioners Spinelli, Simonet, and Davignon) attempted to deal with the situation: these consisted of a process of restructuring, accompanied by a program of public aids. Despite its enormous complexity (considerable costs and competing national interests), and thanks to a better application of the treaty, the commission was successful when facing the steel crisis, where the High Authority had been powerless in front of the coal crisis. During the 1990s the ECSC was confronted simultaneously with the privatization, amalgamations, globalization, and transnational specialization in the European steel industry (about 20 percent of the world production by 2000). On 23 July 2002, after fifty years, as agreed in the treaty, the ECSC officially came to an end, its responsibilities and assets having been transferred gradually to the European Community since 1992. In any event, coal and steel, by which the Schuman Plan had been justified, had completely (or almost completely) lost their strategic character by that stage; the number of workers employed in the ECSC sectors had been reduced from 1,365,697 workers in 1953 to 364,500 in 2001.

*See also* **European Commission; Industrial Capitalism.**

BIBLIOGRAPHY

*Primary Sources*

European Community for Coal and Steel–High Authority. *E.C.S.C., 1952–1962. Results. Limits. Perspectives.* Luxembourg, 1963.

European Commission. *CECA EKSF EGKS EKAX ECSC EHTY EKSG. 1952–2002. Fifty Years of the European Community for Coal and Steel. 34 Different Perspectives.* Luxembourg, 2002.

*Secondary Sources*

Diebold, William, Jr. *The Schuman Plan. A Study in Economic Cooperation, 1950–1959.* New York, 1959.

Gillingham, John R. *Coal, Steel and the Rebirth of Europe, 1945–1955: The Germans and French from Ruhr*

*Conflict to Economic Community.* Cambridge, U.K., and New York, 1991. Reprint, 2004.

Mény, Yves, and Vincent Wright, eds. *The Politics of Steel: Western Europe and the Steel Industry in the Crisis Years (1974–1984).* Berlin and New York, 1986.

Milward, Alan S. *The Reconstruction of Western Europe, 1945–51.* London and Berkeley, Calif., 1984.

Schwabe, Klaus, ed. *Die Anfänge des Schuman-Plans 1950/51.* Baden-Baden, Germany, 1988.

Spierenburg, Dirk, and Raymond Poidevin. *The History of the High Authority of the European Coal and Steel Community: Supranationality in Operation.* London, 1994.

Wilkens, Andreas, ed. *Le Plan Schuman dans l'histoire: intérêts nationaux et projet européen.* Brussels, 2004.

ROCH HANNECART

---

# EUROPEAN COMMISSION.

While drafting the treaty that established the European Coal and Steel Community (ECSC)—adopted in Paris in 1951—the negotiators decided on a novel institutional model. Motivated by a concern for efficiency and a desire to overcome partisan and nationalist divisions but with a federal structure impossible, they conceived a system whose central element would be an executive and supranational body called the High Authority. Independent and drawing upon the technical skills of its individual staff members, the High Authority would ensure the efficacy of ECSC common policies while serving its interests. The High Authority would wield considerable power with a good deal of autonomy yet operate within a narrow judicial framework determined by its representatives.

## THE EUROPEAN COMMISSION AS A MAJOR INSTITUTIONAL INNOVATION

Some years later, in negotiating the treaty that created the European Economic Community (EEC)—adopted in Rome in 1957—this institutional model was used again, although the more sober Commission replaced the High Authority. In contrast to the ECSC treaty, the framework of the EEC gave its institutions greater autonomy to serve more general objectives. As a consequence, the executive function no longer consisted in the mere application of treaties but in developing legislative initiatives, creating policy, and determining the significance of commitments undertaken by the various nations. To balance intergovernmental and supranational interests, the negotiators reinforced the decision-making role of the Council of the EEC but entrusted to the Commission both control of the European policy agenda and executive powers for the enforcement of norms.

In spite of considerable structural evolution in the European Union (EU) since its founding in 1957, the original institutional scheme has never been redesigned. However, two important developments in the 1980s must be mentioned. The European Parliament, whose members have been directly elected since 1979, gradually and ineluctably imposed itself upon the Commission as its partner and obligatory interlocutor. In addition, the Council began making decisions that no longer required unanimity but only a qualified majority.

These developments subtly altered the Commission's equilibrium. It now had to persuade not one but two organizations of its proposals. However, the qualified majority voting system in the Council, together with the European Parliament's participation in most legislative decisions, gave the Commission greater room to maneuver when it could win the support of ministers within the Council or political groups within the European Parliament. Equilibrium in the actual decision-making process—symbolized by the co-decision-making procedure—has forced the Commission, Council, and Parliament to negotiate compromises satisfactory to all.

The institutional system of the European Union is not specifically bound by the principle—common to all democratic regimes, whether presidential or parliamentary—of the distribution of power. It rests instead on another principle of equilibrium: representational plurality. Whereas the European Parliament's task is to protect the interests of peoples and to express their viewpoints and the Council's is to ensure arbitration of national interests, the neutral or supranational European Commission represents the community as a whole. (In practice, this power-sharing arrangement is not so neatly divided. The Commission does not in fact exclude national or partisan interests.) The role of the European Court of Justice is to ensure that the various institutions and member states respect the treaties and laws adopted on their behalf.

## DESIGNATION OF THE COMMISSION

The meaning of the term *commission* is ambiguous. It refers to the group of twenty-five commissioners chosen by member states and the Parliament, but it also refers to the institution itself, with its numerous civil servants. Commissioners are appointed every five years and are chosen in the six months after parliamentary elections. Prior to 1999, the terms of the Commission and Parliament did not coincide and the European Parliament had no formal authority over the Commission's appointment process. In response to chronic complaints about deficiencies in the European Union's democratic processes, however, representatives coordinated the election of Parliament with the Commission's investiture and set their terms to run concurrently. This allows for the possibility of European elections affecting the Commission's composition and policy-making activity and enables Parliament to exercise more rigorous control over the Commission.

The Commission's nominating process has often been reformed and is complex. First, the European Council, composed of chiefs of state or government leaders, chooses by qualified majority vote a candidate for president. Then Parliament must approve the choice. After that, each government submits the name of the person it intends to appoint to the Commission. The European Union's president-elect must then approve these choices and assign to the candidates the various portfolios and vice presidencies that will form the Commission College (the twenty-five commissioners). This slate is submitted to the European Parliament for approval. To judge the qualifications of the commissioners-elect, deputies interview them before the parliamentary commissions qualified to judge individual portfolios. The European Parliament then pronounces on the whole college. Only after this vote does the newly appointed Commission begin to function.

Commissioners are chosen on the basis of experience and qualifications. Although it is not a requirement, all have occupied a political post—the proportion of commissioners with an important political experience has risen continuously since 1957—and many have been ministers. Once appointed, however, they are required to act in the best interests of the European Union as a whole and they may not, in principle, receive

### TABLE 1

| Presidents of the European Commission | | |
| --- | --- | --- |
| **Name** | **Country** | **Period of tenure** |
| Walter Hallstein | Germany | 1958–1967 |
| Jean Rey | Belgium | 1967–1970 |
| Franco Maria Malfatti | Italy | 1970–1972 |
| Sicco Mansholt | Netherlands | 1972–1973 |
| François-Xavier Ortoli | France | 1973–1977 |
| Roy Jenkins | United Kingdom | 1977–1981 |
| Gaston Thorn | Luxembourg | 1981–1985 |
| Jacques Delors | France | 1985–1995 |
| Jacques Santer | Luxembourg | 1995–1999 |
| Romano Prodi | Italy | 1999–2004 |
| José Manuel Barroso | Portugal | 2004– |

instructions from their home governments. The president of the Commission distributes portfolios, can change appointments, and—if a majority of the commissioners agree—may request a resignation.

In terms of policy, the Commission reports and must answer to the Parliament, which can dismiss it with a no-confidence vote. Although such motions have been submitted often enough, mainly by very small minorities, none has ever won the requisite majority: the Commission has never been censured since 1957. This is true in part because the European Commission and Parliament are objective supranational allies and because, given the subsidiary character of partisan interests in the relationship between Parliament and the Commission, censure does not provoke political change but punishes poor administration and bad practices. In March 1999, with a vote of censure in the offing, the commission led by Jaques Santer had to resign because independent experts criticized its financial management.

## HOW THE COMMISSION FUNCTIONS AND WHAT IT DOES

The Commission College meets once per week, generally on Wednesdays, in Brussels. Commissioners make presentations concerning items on the agenda in their areas of expertise; the commission then takes collective decisions. In theory, decisions are made by a majority but they are most often consensual. The Commission is served by a large staff, including about 25,000 administrators, experts, translators, interpreters, secretaries, and service employees. These posts are distributed among the directorates-general, which draft legislative proposals that the commissioners subsequently sponsor and each of which has a director and specific responsibilities.

The European Commission has four major missions: First, it wields exclusive control of the legislative initiative, drafting all the proposals for European norms that will be voted on by Parliament and Council in accord with the best interests of the European Union and its citizens while disregarding the interests of individual states. However, in order to make appropriate legislative proposals, the Commission keeps in close touch with a wide range of interest groups, with the national administrations, and with experts of all kinds. According to what is known as the subsidiary principle, each proposal must be justified. The Union does not take action (except in the areas that fall within its exclusive competence) unless it is more effective than action taken at the national, regional, or local level.

Second, the Commission is charged with carrying out EU policy. With well-developed policies—for example, those concerning competition, agriculture, and structural funds—the Commission possesses extensive executive powers. The Commission dispenses funds with oversight by the European Court of Auditors and the European Parliament, on a budget determined by the council and the European Parliament on a Commissions' proposal.

Third, the Treaty of Rome grants the Commission powers as "the guardian of the treaties." In collaboration with the Court of Justice, it oversees appropriate application of European law in all member states. In the case of transgression, it takes the necessary measures to bring the offending state back into line.

Fourth, the Commission speaks for the European Union on all international matters within its sphere of activity—for example, in organizations such as the International Trade Organization—and it negotiates international treaties in the name of the European Union.

## CONTRIBUTION OF THE COMMISSION TO EUROPEAN INTEGRATION

The Commission has always played a key role in the process of European integration because of its treaty-making assignment; in addition, the individuals who serve on it are in favor of a unified Europe, from which arises a natural tension between its own interests and those of the Council. The Commission's capacity to promote European integration, however, has changed considerably since 1957. At the beginning, it functioned as a political spur, taking most of the initiatives that favored the development of common policies and actively promoting integration. A strong collective spirit characterized the first colleges, as did stable composition and highly influential presidents who were close to the national leaders of the period. This enabled the Commission to put into place the Common Agricultural Policy (CAP) and to accelerate the introduction of the single customs union.

However, the Commission's activism, its project for financing CAP through the EEC's resources, and the impending installation of the qualified majority voting process in the council, led Charles de Gaulle, in 1965, to oppose what he called the "federalist" deviation of the European integration. A crisis ensued, called the empty chair crisis, that brought the leadership of the Commission into question. During the 1970s, a dull economic outlook, the enduring dominance of intergovernmental logic (derived from the veto power of national representatives within the council) and the growing autonomy of the Commission's directorates-general further weakened the Commission's capacity to develop legislative initiatives. The establishment of the European Council in 1974 confirmed this fall from grace; states or government leaders now took charge of policy creation and the settlement of intergovernmental conflicts, which until then had been the province of the Commission.

The appointment of Jacques Delors as president of the Commission in 1985 renewed its influence and marked the revival of European integration, first through the creation of the single market (31 December 1992) and subsequently through the establishment of the European Union. The Commission played a major role in charting the framework of the single market. It was also central to the policy of "enlargement and deepening" that was decided upon in the 1990s as a way of reinvigorating the process of European unification. But the situation soon took a turn for the worse because of its lack of democratic policy; the commissions led by Jacques Santer and Romano Prodi from 1995 to 2004 could not claim major achievements, with the exception of the European Union's enlargement.

With a union that since 2004 has twenty-five members, it is doubtful that the Commission will recover its leadership role or its ability to propel future European integration. It faces three major hurdles. The first is the political context of the enlarged union, in which the visions and expectations held for some institutions have become more divergent than ever, making legislation an ever more delicate operation. The second is the continuing crisis of legitimacy facing the European Union and its policies. Euroskepticism is an entrenched element of the national political landscapes, and the Commission is a main target of criticism. The third, which partly explains these problems of legitimacy, is the intrinsic originality of the Commission. Europeans are unsure whether it is a sort of political entrepreneur, an agency, an institution for mediation, an executive secretariat, or the European Union's future government. Thus the Commission is confronted with two dangers: confinement to executive tasks, which would diminish both its capacity as an initiator and its political role, and excessive politicization, made possible by the European Union Constitution, which would prevent the Commission from creating consensus and a cooperating spirit among member states.

*See also* **Common Agricultural Policy; European Coal and Steel Community (ECSC); European Court of Justice; European Parliament; European Union; Rome, Treaty of.**

BIBLIOGRAPHY

Cini, Michelle. *The European Commission: Leadership, Organisation and Culture in the EU Administration.* Manchester, U.K., 1996.

Coombes, David. *Politics and Bureaucracy in the European Community: A Portrait of the Commission of the EEC.* London, 1970.

Cram, Laura. "The European Commission as a Multi-Organization: Social Policy and IT Policy in the EU." *Journal of European Public Policy* 1, no. 2 (1994): 195–217.

Dimitrakopoulos, Dionyssis G., ed. *The Changing European Commission.* Manchester, U.K., 2004.

Nugent, Neill. *The European Commission.* Basingstoke, U.K., 2001.

Ross, George. *Jacques Delors and European Integration.* New York, 1995.

Smith, Andy, ed. *Politics and the European Commission: Actors, Interdependence, Legitimacy.* London, 2004.

OLIVIER COSTA

---

**EUROPEAN CONSTITUTION 2004–2005.** On 29 October 2004 the twenty-five member states of the European Union (EU) signed the Treaty establishing a Constitution for Europe (hereinafter Constitution). If it enters into force, the Constitution will replace all existing treaties that first established the European Communities and then reformed them over the years. While much of the Constitution is taken directly from the earlier treaties, there are a number of novelties, such as the creation of a permanent post of President of the European Council and the establishment of the office of EU Foreign Minister, supported by a new External Action Service. The Constitution includes 448 articles and 36 protocols. Its substantive provisions are grouped together in four parts:

- Part I deals with the EU's general objectives, competences, and institutional framework;

- Part II incorporates the EU's Charter of Fundamental Rights;

- Part III contains more specifics on the EU's internal and external policies and functioning; and

- Part IV deals with the EU's general and final provisions, such as the procedure for revision.

The route toward the Constitution was launched at the Laeken European Council of 14 and 15 December 2001. The EU's heads of state or government considered institutional reform essential in view of the EU's upcoming expansion from fifteen to twenty-five member states in 2004. Earlier attempts to adjust the EU's institutional functioning had produced only meager results. The Treaty of Nice, signed on 26 February 2001, forms the most notorious example of a complex agreement including only minimal achievements. The Treaty of Nice and its predecessors had been negotiated at Intergovernmental Conferences (IGCs). These are meetings of government representatives behind closed doors. In an attempt to open up the preparatory process of treaty reform, the heads of state or government decided at Laeken to establish a Convention. The Convention brought together representatives of all member states, national parliaments, the European Parliament, and the European Commission. It debated in public between February 2002 and July 2003. Under the strong leadership of former French President Valéry Giscard d'Estaing (b. 1926), the Convention succeeded in adopting—by consensus—a draft treaty establishing a Constitution for Europe. The draft was submitted to the President of the European Council on 18 July 2003. While the Convention prepared the Constitution, it had no legal powers to formally amend the existing treaties. This required another traditional IGC. After a year of tough IGC bargaining among the member states, the Constitution was signed in Rome.

The Constitution can enter into force only after having been ratified by all twenty-five member states. The ratification process takes place in accordance with the constitutional requirements that are proper to each member state. This sometimes involves a referendum. By January 2006, thirteen member states had successfully ratified. In the referenda in France and the Netherlands, a majority of the voters expressed themselves against the Constitution. In France, the referendum was held on 29 May 2005. With a turnout rate of 69 percent, the "no" obtained 55 percent of votes. The actual text of the Constitution motivated only a fifth of "no" voters. The unemployment situation in France was given as the main reason for the "no" vote. The Dutch referendum was held on 1 June 2005. With a turnout rate of 63 percent, the "no" obtained 62 percent of votes. Among the "no" voters, 28 percent indicated that their key motivation was the economic and social situation in the Netherlands, 23 percent voted "no" because of their negative overall opinion on the EU, and a further 21 percent held that they specifically opposed the text of the Constitution.

In reaction to the results in France and the Netherlands, the European Council of 16 and 17 June 2005 called for a period of reflection to enable a broad debate in each of the member states. While the heads of state or government declared that the negative referenda in France and the Netherlands would not call into question the validity of continuing with the ratification processes, the British government had already decided on 6 June 2005 to suspend the ratification procedure indefinitely. The negative referenda in France and the Netherlands did not bring the EU to a halt. The European institutions continued functioning on the basis of the existing treaty framework.

*See also* **Constitutions; European Union.**

BIBLIOGRAPHY

Devuyst, Youri. *The European Union Transformed: Community Method and Institutional Evolution from the Schuman Plan to the Constitution for Europe.* Brussels, 2005.

European Commission. *Flash Eurobarometer 171: The European Constitution: Post-Referendum Survey in France.* Luxembourg, 2005.

———. *Flash Eurobarometer 172: The European Constitution: Post-Referendum Survey in the Netherlands.* Luxembourg, 2005.

Milton, Guy, Jacques Keller-Noellet, and Agnieszka Barto-Saurel. *The European Constitution: Its Origins, Negotiation and Meaning.* London, 2005.

YOURI DEVUYST

---

# EUROPEAN COURT OF JUSTICE.

From the outset, the authors of the Paris (1951) and Rome (1957) treaties accorded a decisive role to law in the process of European construction. Confronted with the impossibility of political integration and a federal model, they chose a system that was based on law in order to facilitate the decision-making process and to make the integration both effective and surreptitious. In order to ensure that member states complied with their obligations and with the European Community standards adopted by supranational European institutions, in order to anticipate potential conflicts between member states or between states and community institutions, and in order to guard against excessive prescriptiveness on the part of the European executive, the negotiators assigned great importance to establishing a European court. This was a remarkable choice, given that the principle of constitutional justice was not widespread at that time in Europe; the prevailing view was that judicial power should not interfere with the work of political bodies. The court was, therefore, intended to be both an international and an administrative court. The history of the European project reveals, however, that the Court of Justice has exercised a third function, the importance of which was not perceived at the outset: the interpretation of community law.

## STRUCTURE AND FUNCTIONS

The Court of Justice is based in Luxembourg. It consists of one judge from each member state (twenty-five as of the 2004 elections) and eight advocates-general, each appointed by common accord of the governments for a renewable six-year term. Since 1989, the court has been assisted by a Court of First Instance; since the implementation of the Nice Treaty (February 2003), this has functioned as the court of ordinary law for all direct actions. In these matters, the Court of Justice is the appeal body.

The primary task of both the Court of Justice and the Court of First Instance is to ensure compliance with the law, whether this relates to the treaties directly or to legal measures adopted in accordance with them. Several types of direct action exist. The first, the "action for failure to fulfill obligations," enables the judges—at the request of the Commission of the European Union or, less frequently, of a state—to monitor member states' compliance with community law. In the event of a breach, the commission first makes contact with the representatives of the state concerned to give them an opportunity to remedy the problem. If this course of action fails, the commission can refer the matter to the court. In case a state violates a court judgment, the court can order it to pay a fine. The second, the action for annulment, authorizes a state, a European Union institution, or a private party directly concerned to petition the court for an annulment of an institution's act. The third, the action for failure to act, enables the Court of Justice to penalize any inactivity on the part of community institutions.

The treaties also give the court the jurisdiction to interpret community law within the procedure called "reference for a preliminary ruling." This procedure is unique to the European Union and arises because the Court of Justice is not the only court that applies community law. Given that the national implementation of community law falls under the jurisdiction of the member states, national courts are required to monitor compliance with it. The community treaties and standards adopted by the institutions of the European Union (primarily the Commission, the Council, and the European Parliament) create rights to benefit natural and legal persons (collective organizations, such as associations, companies, and public bodies, considered as having a legal personality distinct from the natural individuals who comprise them), which the national judges are required to protect. In order to prevent community law from being interpreted and applied in excessively divergent ways in the various member states, the treaties authorize member states—and, in certain cases, require them—to petition the Court of Justice to interpret community law when a doubt arises concerning the conformity of national legislation with the community law or, conversely, the validity of an act of community law. The Court of Justice then gives a judgment or an explanatory ruling that binds the national courts to an interpretation of community law. However, the court does not intervene in the substance of the matter. The court is not looking at the original case; it is only giving the answer to a question regarding interaction between national and community law. The court's interpretation forms case law at the community level.

This procedure, called reference for a preliminary ruling, although ostensibly neutral, has had a decisive impact on the construction of the European Community by enabling the Court of Justice to develop a specific and innovative case law, which is uniformly imposed in the community domain. It has also enabled the court to establish some of the major principles of community law and helped to bring citizens and economic agents closer to the process of community construction by allowing them to obtain clarification of the rights that it grants them. Citizens involved in proceedings before a national court may request the national court to submit an appeal to the Court of Justice, and the procedure has often been used by private parties. The reference for a preliminary ruling is also a means of opening community law to debate, because the Court of Justice does not act unilaterally and can summon the parties concerned, the member states, and the commission to state their views on the matter.

The Court's interpretive function, which was intended to be peripheral, has become predominant. To the extent that monitoring the compliance of states with their obligations falls broadly under the Commission's jurisdiction, the judges have been able to concentrate on their role of interpreting community law. Moreover, the Court of Justice has done nothing to facilitate the access of private parties to its courtrooms by means of direct appeals; in practice, it has always given a restrictive interpretation of community treaties. Natural and legal persons have thus been encouraged to pursue the route of a reference for a preliminary ruling, which enables the court to undertake a consideration at the community judicial level rather than conduct complex investigations into what are often highly technical special cases.

## THE COURT'S ROLE IN EUROPEAN INTEGRATION

Since 1952, more than ten thousand cases have been brought before the court, which has given rise to nearly six thousand judgments, covering all the community's fields of jurisdiction. Retrospective analysis of the drafting of the Paris and Rome treaties has shown that the negotiators did not set out to grant the Court of Justice a leading role in European integration. However, the court has evolved into a form of federal European constitutional court. Although some of the negotiators may have anticipated this development, it was not inscribed in the treaties and it stems from a deliberate and skilful strategy on the part of the judges.

At the outset and until the early 1960s, the judges took a cautious approach. The scale of their activities was limited and most of the appeals issued from member states or economic agents who were dissatisfied with decisions made by the High Authority of the European Coal and Steel Community or the Commission of the European Economic Community, and the court operated in accordance with the function that the treaties had assigned to it.

After the early 1960s, however, the court played an increasingly active role and acquired some latitude in the interpretation of community law. The judges specified the scope of the legal

obligations signed by the member states by giving interpretations that systematically favored a reinforcement of the effects of European integration. To this end, the judges in Luxembourg sought to establish relationships of trust with national courts. As the latter were not required to petition the court for interpretations of community law, the Court of Justice took care not to encroach on their jurisdictions or adopt an imperialist approach. National judges were quick to understand the advantage that they could derive from the reference for a preliminary ruling, which reinforced their own authority at the national level. The interpretations given by the Court of Justice authorized them to reject national standards on the grounds that they were contrary to the treaties or to the laws derived from them, which led national courts to carry out a form of constitutionality monitoring. Most of the national courts have no powers of judicial review. National constitutional courts have, however, persistently shown some reserve toward the Court of Justice. They have been demonstrably protective of their jurisdiction in monitoring the constitutionality of laws and have looked unfavorably on claims made by European judges to do likewise. In the early twenty-first century these courts have nevertheless all accepted the principal aspects of Court of Justice case law.

## INNOVATIVE CASE LAW AND FEDERAL INTEGRATION

In the 1960s, the court laid the foundations of the European legal system through some particularly innovative judgments, which had a broad impact. First of all, the court asserted, during a reference for a preliminary ruling, the principle of the direct effect of community law (*Van Gend en Loos* judgment, 1963). The judges considered that community law creates rights that citizens can cite directly, whether or not member states have explicitly made provision for this. This creates a clear distinction between the European Community and any previous international organization and establishes the existence of a legal system that is federal in nature.

The court went further than this. In its *Costa v. ENEL* judgment (1964), it also asserted the primacy of community law over national law. The court inferred from this that national judges should refuse to apply national standards, even constitutional ones, if they were contrary to community law

(*Simmental*, 1978). The court thereby asserted a federal type of hierarchical principle, which places primary community law (treaties) and community law derived from this (rulings and directives) above national law. The assertion of the principles of direct effect and primacy, as well as the broad understanding applied to the reference for a preliminary ruling procedure, have led the court to establish the treaty as a form of constitutional charter, something the authors of the treaties had not anticipated.

The court continued this course of action in the 1970s and 1980s by giving equally innovative interpretations to the fundamental rules of the community legal system, such as the freedom of movement or equality of treatment for European citizens irrespective of nationality. It thereby contributed to the commission's project of negative integration, which consisted in the repeal of national regulations restricting the free movement of goods, services, and workers.

In the 1990s the court, ever sensitive to the prevailing climate of opinion, embarked on a process of positive integration. It supported efforts at regulation made by citizens and by economic and social agents, whether in the domain of environmental protection, consumer protection, or public health. When the European single market was established (31 December 1992), the court promoted the adoption of common standards to ensure market regulation.

Given that a substantial proportion of the technical documentation relating to European integration emphasizes the fundamentally inter governmental nature of the process, how has it come about that governments should have accepted this increase in the court's power and submitted to its case law? The explanation contains three parts. First and foremost, the governments needed the court and often appealed to it themselves, particularly to resolve their disagreements with the Commission. Second, juridical culture is important in European Union countries; few European political officials dare to enter into open conflict with a court, whether national or European. Third, the court enjoys strong guarantees of independence, and governments have only weak methods of exerting pressure on it. The principal means would be to reform the treaties and restrict the court's powers, but this would require unanimity among the governments, which is an unlikely eventuality.

The governments have thus been content to follow the work of the Court of Justice more closely and to submit observations to it in a growing number of cases. When treaties have been reformed, national governments have sought to define the scope of certain rights and principles in order to prevent the court from interpreting them too widely; the drafting of treaties has thus become increasingly precise, if not prolix. The governments have also removed some new policies, such as the common foreign and security policy, from the court's jurisdiction.

### THE ERA OF SELF-RESTRAINT

The legitimization crisis that has affected the European project since the beginning of the 1990s has marked the dawn of a new era for the Court of Justice. The European project, which had hitherto taken place away from the glare of public opinion and partisan controversies, suddenly became a matter for impassioned debate during the ratification proceedings of the Maastricht Treaty (1992–1993). At this time, many citizens, civil organizations, and political officials discovered the full scale of the transfers of sovereignty granted by the member states to European Union institutions and the role played in this process by the Court of Justice. The court's judgments began to attract wide media coverage and commentary. Having previously explained its case law only to judges and national leaders, the court was obliged to defend it among a broader public and to develop a wide-ranging media strategy. Moreover, as the jurisdiction of the European Union increased, the court came to deal with increasingly sensitive matters such as human rights, bioethics, and social affairs. Finally, the deep political and national divergences that have surrounded the European project and the lack of consensus concerning the objectives and modes of European integration made the work of the judges into a highly delicate matter. All these pressures have led them to demonstrate a cautious and moderate approach and to adopt an attitude of self-restraint that is more in keeping with the existing realities of integration.

*See also* **Council of Europe; Maastricht, Treaty of; Nice Treaty; Rome, Treaty of.**

BIBLIOGRAPHY

Arnull, Anthony. *The European Union and Its Court of Justice.* Oxford, U.K., 1999.

Mattli, Walter, and Anne-Marie Slaughter. "Revisiting the European Court of Justice." *International Organization* 52, no. 1 (1998): 177–209.

Shapiro, Martin. "The European Court of Justice." In *The Evolution of EU Law,* edited by Paul Craig and Gràinne De Bùrca. Oxford, U.K., 1999.

Slaughter, Anne-Marie, Alec Stone-Sweet, and Joseph H. Weiler, eds. *The European Court and National Courts: Doctrine and Jurisprudence: Legal Change in Its Social Context.* Oxford, U.K., 1998.

Weiler, Joseph H. "The Transformation of Europe." *Yale Law Journal* 100 (1991): 2403–2493.

OLIVIER COSTA

# EUROPEAN FREE TRADE ASSOCIATION.

After World War II the introduction of free trade was discussed on and off in Western Europe. It could take the form of either a customs union—with common external tariffs—or a free trade area with the abolition of internal tariffs and national trade policies. Free trade was strongly advocated by the United States and also favored by trade-dependent low-tariff countries such as Belgium and Sweden. In 1947, Western European countries for the first time studied the possibility of creating a customs union or free trade area in the context of the Marshall Plan. During the 1950s, the Scandinavian countries Sweden, Norway, and Denmark discussed the formation of a customs union, but failed to bridge major differences, especially over the inclusion of agriculture. The main incentive for the formation of the European Free Trade Association (EFTA) came from the creation of a continental European customs union with strong supranational political dimensions in the form of the European Economic Community (EEC), the present-day European Union (EU), in 1957–1958. As the EEC was to abolish internal tariffs and impose common external tariffs, it would give its member-states—France, Italy, West Germany, the Netherlands, Belgium, and Luxembourg—privileged access to the newly created internal market. This in turn threatened to undermine the competitive position of industrial producers from other European countries. When

the British plan to create an all–Western European free trade area as a roof over the EEC failed at the end of 1958, when the French President Charles de Gaulle vetoed the ongoing negotiations in the OEEC, Britain, Sweden, Norway, Denmark, Switzerland, Austria, and Portugal opted for the creation of the small EFTA in 1959–1960. Finland became associated with EFTA in 1961 through the FIN-EFTA treaty.

Unlike the EEC, EFTA was characterized by strictly intergovernmental market integration in the form of an industrial free trade area with weak institutions. It had limited provisions for majority voting to enforce treaty provisions, a general consultation and complaints procedure, escape clauses intended mainly for balance-of-payments problems, and a set of rules of origin. The EFTA treaty defined industrial commodities in a set of process lists and lists of basic materials. Commodities could claim EFTA treatment when containing more than 50 percent value added in EFTA. In agriculture the EFTA treaty merely included a general commitment to the removal of agricultural export subsidies and to consultations about the expansion of agricultural trade among member states. The signing of the treaty was combined with the conclusion of bilateral treaties, especially of Britain, Sweden, and Switzerland with Denmark, to accommodate the economic interests of the agricultural export countries.

With the creation of EFTA the so-called Outer Seven European states demonstrated that an industrial free trade area was technically feasible and could operate with a loose institutional framework. The EFTA states actually succeeded in abolishing internal tariffs one and a half years before the EEC, by 1 January 1967. This helped to increase trade among them at a faster rate than trade with the EEC in a period of rapid trade expansion in the 1960s. From 1959 to 1969 EFTA's trade with the EEC grew by 130 percent, but intra-EFTA trade grew by 186 percent. Trade among the Scandinavian countries even rose by 284 percent during the same period. Yet none of the member-states regarded EFTA as an aim in itself. Rather, they hoped that it would act as a bridge to the EEC to reopen negotiations about the creation of a larger Western European free trade area. This strategy failed, however, as the EEC was preoccupied with developing its institutions and policies and strengthening its internal cohesion, and because de Gaulle was strongly opposed to a greater political role for Britain in the integration of Europe.

Compared to the EEC, EFTA suffered from a number of weaknesses. Its economic cohesion was relatively low as it was geographically disparate and lacked reciprocal export advantages in agriculture, which the Common Agricultural Policy (CAP) provided within the EEC. British leadership was weak, too. Britain actually broke the EFTA treaty in the autumn of 1964 when it imposed a tariff surcharge to deal with balance-of-payments problems, provoking the organization's most severe crisis, comparable to the "empty chair" crisis in the EEC in the following year. Moreover, the United States was hostile to EFTA and to a wider settlement between the EEC and EFTA. As U.S. balance-of-payments problems intensified during the 1958–1961 period, it led to fears that a larger Western European free trade area would effectively exclude U.S. goods from the European market without the compensatory political benefit of strengthening the cohesion of the West in the Cold War.

The conflict between EFTA and the EEC was finally resolved in 1972–1973 when Britain and Denmark as well as Ireland became members of the EEC in its first round of enlargement. Norway stayed outside of the EEC after a marginally negative referendum result. It, as well as the other EFTA states, concluded free trade treaties with the EEC to safeguard their core trade interests. EFTA continued to exist, but it increasingly developed into a waiting room for future full EEC/EC/EU membership. Portugal joined the EC in 1986 and Austria, Finland, and Sweden in 1995. In the early twenty-first century, only Switzerland, Liechtenstein, Norway, and Iceland, which joined EFTA in 1970, remain. Of the four, only Liechtenstein and Norway (after a second negative EU referendum in 1994) are associated with the EU through the European Economic Area. The present-day EFTA sees its main role in advancing global trade liberalization, although its member-states actually have highly protectionist agricultural and fisheries policies, but it no longer plays a significant role in European politics.

*See also* **European Union.**

BIBLIOGRAPHY

Kaiser, Wolfram. "Challenge to the Community: The Creation, Crisis and Consolidation of the European Free Trade Association, 1958–72." *Journal of European Integration History* 3, no. 1 (1997): 7–33.

———. "A Better Europe? EFTA, the EFTA Secretariat, and the European Identities of the 'Outer Seven,' 1958–72." In *Institutions européennes et identités européennes,* edited by Marie-Thérèse Bitsch et al., 165–184. Brussels, 1998.

———. "The Successes and Limits of Industrial Market Integration: The European Free Trade Association 1963–1969." In *Crises and Compromises: The European Project 1963–1969,* edited by Wilfried Loth, 371–390. Baden-Baden, Germany, 2001.

Kaiser, Wolfram, and Jürgen Elvert, eds. *European Union Enlargement: A Comparative History.* London and New York, 2004. Includes chapters on the postwar European policies of the EFTA member-states Britain, Denmark, Austria, Sweden, Finland, and Portugal.

Malmborg, Mikael, and Johnny Laursen. "The Creation of EFTA." In *Interdependence versus Integration: Denmark, Scandinavia and Western Europe, 1945-1960,* edited by Thorsten B. Olesen, 197–212. Odense, Denmark, 1995.

Wolfram Kaiser

**EUROPEAN PARLIAMENT.** At the founding of the European Communities (1951 and 1957), the European Parliament was essentially a consultative institution. It was established to serve four functions: as a symbol of reconciliation between the member states; to establish a balance between the institutions (as the house of the peoples, it was designed as a counterweight to the Council, the body that represented the governments); to mirror the other international organizations created in that period (including the United Nations, the Western European Union [WEU], the Council of Europe, and the North Atlantic Treaty Organization [NATO]), all of which had parliamentary assemblies; and to legitimize the European Community by exercising some control over the activities of its executive.

Since the 1950s, many changes have been made to the treaties. The European Parliament has emerged as a powerful institution in the context of international pressure to parliamentarize the European Community's institutional system. The assembly has gradually taken on all the typical characteristics of a national parliament: financial independence, an internal physical and administrative organization, an election process, and immunities and privileges for its members. The European Parliament has thus become a powerful force in the EU's political system, exercising multiple functions.

First and foremost, the European Parliament can adopt declaratory resolutions on all the matters that fall under the EU's jurisdiction, which makes it the principal forum for political debate at the supranational level. Second, it controls the activities of the European Commission and, to a lesser degree, of the Council. Third, it plays a central role in the appointments procedure for the Commission and other Community institutions. Fourth, it exercises major budgetary powers, both in allocating funds and in controlling the implementation of the budget. Fifth and most conspicuously, it exercises legislative powers; although at the outset the Parliament had only a consultative role, which deprived it of any influence, in the early twenty-first century it participates with the Council in adopting most legislative texts, and its status is equal to the Council's.

Initially, the European Parliament was composed of delegates from the national parliaments. The Treaty of Rome (1957) nevertheless provided for the possibility of its members being elected by universal direct vote. This was done for the first time in 1979 and has been done ever since at five-year intervals. These elections, which take place within the member states, have not generated the excitement among citizens anticipated by federalists. This can be explained by the lack of scrutability of the European Parliament's functions, weak media coverage of its activities, and the tendency of national parties to downplay the event. In 2004, when the European Union membership rose to twenty-five states, the assembly was made up of 732 deputies divided among the states roughly according to population. At one extreme, Malta had five deputies; at the other, Germany had nine-nine.

The European Parliament has always sat in political groupings, although this is not required under the Treaty of Rome. After 2004 elections, it contained seven groups, which corresponded to

**Members of the European Parliament vote to open membership talks with Turkey, Strasbourg, 15 December 2004.** ©Vincent Kessler/Reuters/Corbis

the main party groupings within the member states. Until the end of the 1990s, the Parliament was dominated by a split between supporters and opponents of the quest for European integration, which led the two main groups—the Christian Democrats and the Socialists—to make common cause regularly. Because of the criticisms generated by this convergence, as well as because of European policies that have led to ideological conflicts, a traditional split between left and right has become increasingly apparent. However, the assembly's functioning remains highly complex. The determining factor in the dominant split varies according to the decision-making procedures and the subject of the texts. When the Parliament is taking decision at simple majority, mainly to adopt declarative resolutions, a split between left and right is very common. But when it is voting on legislative texts, it must reach the majority of its members, and not only voters; this is a strong incentive for the two main groups to find a compromise. National conflicts remain fairly muted, however, and the statistical cohesion of the political groupings remains strong. By contrast, relations between the European Parliament and the Commission are not governed by party affiliation, because the Commission does not resemble a government and the two institutions continue to operate independently.

In addition to the increase in its powers, the assembly's history is also characterized by a progressive rationalization of its functioning. As a supranational assembly, the European Parliament is confronted with manifold and growing pressures: a broad cultural and political heterogeneity; the use of many languages (twenty in 2004); a dispersal across three working sites (Strasbourg, Brussels, and Luxembourg); a large number of members; an overcrowded agenda; the frequent obligation to vote placed on the majority of its members rather than voters; delays in legislative and budgetary matters; a strict application of the "personal and individual" nature of the deputies' voting rights (i.e., only members who are in the room at the voting time can vote; they cannot delegate their voting right); and the constant need to protect the interests of the institution against those of the Council and the Commission. In confronting all these pressures, the deputies enjoy certain powers: the total independence of their institution, which cannot be dissolved; complete freedom as to how they organize their deliberations and define their agenda; substantial autonomy with regard to national parties; and a progressive institutional framework that is conducive to the extension of the assembly's powers.

In order to overcome the pressures on their deliberation, the deputies have regularly adapted the assembly's regulations in order to rationalize its functioning. Since the early 1990s, the assembly has been characterized by a meticulous organization of all the plenary assembly's activities and institutions and the precise timing of plenary sessions. This process has reinforced the assembly's hierarchical institutions through increasing delegation of legislative work and control to parliamentary committees. It has also conferred a leading role on the political groupings and their officials, to the detriment of individual initiative on the part of the deputies. The European Parliament's internal organization is therefore the object of frequent and contentious debate, both between those who subscribe to differing views of the parliamentary work (mainly a "Latin" tradition of political debate vs. a "Nordic" tradition of policy making) and between members of the small as opposed to the two large political groupings.

The European deputies have always played an important, albeit indirect, role in deepening European integration. Pro-European members, who want to promote a more federalized Europe, have always held a large majority. This objective has associated the objective of European integration with that of reducing the "democratic deficit" (a concept invoked in the argument that the European Union and its various bodies suffer from a lack of democracy and seem inaccessible to the ordinary citizen because their method of operating is too complex), which is generally understood to necessitate an increase in the European Parliament's powers.

*See also* **Council of Europe; European Union; Rome, Treaty of.**

BIBLIOGRAPHY

Corbett, Richard, Francis Jacobs, and Michael Shackleton. *The European Parliament.* 5th ed. London, 2003.

Costa, Olivier. *Le Parlement européen, assemblée délibérante.* Brussels, 2001.

Kreppel, Amie. *The European Parliament and the Supranational Party System: A Study in Institutional Development.* Cambridge, U.K., 2002.

Magnette, Paul. "Appointing and Censuring the Commission: The Adaptation of Parliamentary Institutions to the Community Context." *European Law Journal* 7, no. 3 (2001): 289–307.

OLIVIER COSTA

# EUROPEAN UNION.

The European Union (EU) came into being on 1 November 1993 when the Treaty on European Union, negotiated and ratified by the twelve member states of the European Communities (EC)—Belgium, Denmark, France, the Federal Republic of Germany, Greece, Ireland, Italy, Luxembourg, the Netherlands, Portugal, Spain, and the United Kingdom—took effect. The treaty was negotiated in an Intergovernmental Conference of the member states that began in December 1990 and concluded in December 1991 in the Dutch city of Maastricht (hence the frequent reference to it as the "Treaty of Maastricht"). The treaty was formally signed on 7 February 1992.

Article A of the treaty states that it "marks a new stage in the process of creating an ever closer union among the peoples of Europe" and that the Union "shall be founded on the European Communities, supplemented by the policies and forms of cooperation established by this Treaty." The Communities, commonly referred to as the European Community, consisted of the European Coal and Steel Community (ECSC), which came into being on 23 July 1952 as a result of the Treaty of Paris signed by France, the Federal Republic of Germany, Italy, Belgium, the Netherlands, and Luxembourg on 18 April 1951; and the European Economic Community (EEC) and European Atomic Energy Community (Euratom), both of which came into being on 1 January 1958 as a result of the Treaties of Rome signed by the six member states of the ECSC on 25 March 1957.

After withdrawing from discussions in the early and mid-1950s about possible membership in the ECSC and the EEC the British government, as well as those of Ireland, Denmark, and Norway, applied for membership in the EC in August 1961. President Charles de Gaulle (1890–1970) of France vetoed British membership in January 1963, saying that Britain lacked a "European vocation," and one week later signed a Treaty of Friendship with the Federal Republic of Germany. A subsequent British government applied again for membership in May 1967, but again de Gaulle vetoed British membership.

De Gaulle resigned after a referendum defeat in April 1969. His successor, Georges Pompidou (1911–1974), signaled that the EC would welcome an application from Britain and in July 1969 Britain, Ireland, Denmark, and Norway applied for the third time. After the completion of accession negotiations Norwegian voters rejected membership in a referendum in September 1972. Britain, Ireland, and Denmark joined the EC on 1 January 1973.

On 21 April 1967 a military coup led by Colonel George Papadopoulos (1919–1999) and other colonels took power in Greece. After seven years of a repressive dictatorship the regime collapsed in August 1974 in the wake of the invasion and occupation of northern Cyprus by Turkey. Democracy was restored, the Greek government applied for membership in the EC in June 1975, and Greece joined the EC on 1 January 1981.

In April 1974 a military coup in Portugal launched by a group of army captains and other lower-level officers opposed to the government's colonial policies in southern Africa brought an end to a lengthy period of authoritarian rule and inaugurated a short-lived period of social revolution. A democratic regime was established in 1975 and the government applied for EC membership in March 1977.

In Spain, Francisco Franco (1892–1975) died in November 1975. Franco had come to power when his Nationalist forces, aided by Nazi Germany and Benito Mussolini's (1883–1945) Italy, defeated the supporters of the Second Republic in the Civil War of 1936–1939. After some uncertainty as to the nature of the post-Franco regime, a government headed by Adolfo Suarez (b. 1932) engineered, with the vital assistance of King Juan Carlos I (r. 1975– ), who had become head of state upon the death of Franco, engineered a transition to a democracy that culminated in the first free election of the Congress of Deputies in June 1977. One month later Spain applied for membership in the EC. After a prolonged accession negotiation, complicated by the fears of French, Italian, and Greek agricultural producers, Spain and Portugal entered the EC on 1 January 1986.

The Treaty on European Union, which took effect on 1 November 1993, transformed the existing European Communities (EC) into the European Union (EU). All of the existing treaties, laws, regulations, directives, court rulings, and institutions of the Communities continued in the EU. The treaty changed the Communities into a single Community and added new functions, responsibilities, and institutions to those that had existed in the EC. Most notably, it committed the member states to the establishment of an Economic and Monetary Union (EMU); implementation of a Common Foreign and Security Policy (CFSP), including the eventual framing of a common defense policy that might in time lead to a common defense; close cooperation in the area of justice and home affairs (JHA); creation of citizenship in the Union; and an increase in the legislative power of the European Parliament. The treaty provided, however, that both the Common Foreign and Security Policy and cooperation in the area of justice and home affairs would be pursued solely through intergovernmental cooperation. The treaty thus defined three "pillars" of activity, the first of which involved the institutions and domains of policy of the existing European Community, the second of which involved the CFSP, and the third of which involved cooperation in the area of JHA.

## THE ANTECEDENTS OF EMU

The idea of economic and/or monetary union had been on the agenda of the European Communities in some form for several decades prior to the negotiation of the Treaty on European Union. Indeed, Belgium and Luxembourg had created the Belgium-Luxembourg Economic Union (BLEU) on 25 July 1921. BLEU removed the economic frontier between the two countries and created a monetary union in which the exchange rate for the two currencies, the Belgian franc and Luxembourg franc, was fixed at 1:1 with no fluctuation range. The Belgian central bank assumed the role of the central bank for the two countries and the Luxembourg central bank became, instead, the Luxembourg Monetary Institute.

On 5 September 1944 the governments-in-exile of Belgium, the Netherlands, and Luxembourg, meeting in London, agreed to institute after World War II a common tariff regime with a common external tariff and, eventually, a customs union that would, in time, evolve into an economic union in which there would be a single internal market in which goods could move freely and without barriers across the national borders. The Benelux Customs Union came into being in 1948 and in 1960 it was replaced by the Benelux Economic Union.

The Benelux countries played a major role in the creation of the European Economic Community in 1958. As early as 1950 one or more of the Benelux governments proposed that a customs union be created that would include additional countries beyond the Benelux three. In June 1950, after the French politician Robert Schuman (1886–1963) had proposed the creation of what would become the ECSC, the Dutch government proposed a sector-by-sector plan of trade liberalization that would eventually result in a free-trade area. Known as the Stikker plan after its proponent, the Dutch foreign minister Dirk Stikker (1897–1979), it was followed in 1953 by another Dutch proposal put forward by the foreign minister, Willem Beyen (1897–1976), which aimed to create a customs union.

In August 1954 the French National Assembly rejected a treaty negotiated by the six founding member states of the ECSC to create a European Defense Community. With that defeat and the resignation of Jean Monnet (1888–1979), who had devised the Schuman Plan and had served as the first president of the High Authority of the ECSC, the ambition to integrate the economies of the six member states appeared to be thwarted. In an effort to relaunch the effort to integrate Europe, the foreign ministers of the Benelux countries—Paul-Henri Spaak (1899–1972) of Belgium, Joseph Bech (1887–1975) of Luxembourg, and Beyen—put forward a series of proposals in early 1955 to relaunch European integration. In April 1955 they resurrected Beyen's 1953 proposal for a customs union, combined it with proposals to extend supranational regulation to other sectors, such as atomic energy and transportation, and submitted it for consideration by the ECSC foreign ministers at their meeting in Messina, Italy, in June 1955. At the conclusion of the meeting the ministers agreed to create a committee of experts to study the proposal that, by then, featured the creation in stages of a customs union, the institution of a common external tariff, fiscal and monetary harmonization, and the development of common policies in agriculture, energy, and transportation.

The committee of experts, chaired by Spaak, began meeting in the fall of 1955 and submitted a report to the foreign ministers in April 1956 that proposed the creation of a customs union as well as an atomic energy community and a common agricultural policy. The ministers, meeting in Venice in May 1956, agreed to start negotiations aimed at implementing the proposal and did so in October 1956. The Treaties of Rome, creating the EEC and Euratom, were signed on 25 March 1957. The treaty establishing the EEC promised to eliminate in stages all tariffs and quotas limiting trade between the member states; establish a common external commercial frontier; coordinate the economic policies of the member states; and provide for the free

**French farmers drive tractors to Paris to protest the Maastricht Treaty, September 1992.** ©REUTERS/CORBIS

movement of goods, services, capital, and people. In its preamble, the signatories stated they were "determined to lay the foundations of an ever closer union among the peoples of Europe."

Why were the Benelux countries the leading proponents, from the advent of BLEU in 1921 to Messina, Venice, and Rome in 1955–1957, of trade liberalization and the creation of a customs union and eventually an economic and monetary union in Europe? The answer lies in the fact that their economies are unusually open in the sense of being highly dependent on trade. Throughout the twentieth century many of the goods these countries produced were purchased by consumers in other countries and many of the goods they consumed were produced in other countries. In 1958, for example, Italian and French exports were equivalent to roughly 12 percent of GDP and German exports to roughly 22 percent of GDP. Belgian exports, by contrast, represented one-third of GDP, those of the Netherlands nearly one-half of GDP, and those of Luxembourg more than

three-quarters of the country's GDP. And those countries were also much more dependent on trade with their large neighbors than those large neighbors were on trade with them. Thus, in 1958, roughly 25 percent of all of the exports of France, Italy, and Germany went to the other five member states of the EC. In contrast, more than 40 percent of the exports of Belgium, Luxembourg, and the Netherlands went to the other member states. As countries that were highly dependent on trade, including trade with larger neighbors that maintained protective barriers to their national markets, the Benelux countries had a strong national interest in liberalizing trade both among themselves and with their larger neighbors.

The Treaty of Rome anticipated the creation of a common market in which all internal tariffs, quotas, and other barriers to trade would be removed by 1970. But the move to a common market occurred more rapidly than anticipated and elimination of the last remaining internal tariffs was advanced to July 1968. In anticipation of that development, as well as the scheduled introduction at that time of a common pricing scheme in the Common Agricultural Policy, Pierre Werner (1913–2002), the prime minister and minister of finance of Luxembourg, proposed in January 1968 that the six member states irrevocably lock the exchange rates among their currencies and create a fund that could intervene in foreign exchange markets in order to maintain the fixed rates. It was hardly surprising, of course, that the first call for a monetary union of the Six would come from Luxembourg; by that time it had participated for nearly a half-century in the BLEU, a central feature of which was the irrevocably locked 1:1 exchange rate without a fluctuation range between the Belgian and Luxembourg francs.

Werner's proposals prompted several memoranda to the Counsel from Raymond Barre (b. 1924), the vice president of the commission in charge of monetary affairs. Barre did not fully endorse Werner's proposals but did call for a reduction in the margins of fluctuation between the EC currencies, provision for multilateral negotiation of currency realignments, a fund and mechanism for joint intervention in currency markets, and a common exchange rate vis-à-vis other EC currencies.

In July 1969 the council approved Barre's recommendation for the creation of some form of joint consulting and decision-making mechanism in the domains of monetary and exchange-rate policy. At their summit in The Hague in December 1969 the leaders of the six member states endorsed the idea of creating an Economic and Monetary Union and recommended that the council accept Barre's proposal that an EMU be created in three stages, with the third and final stage coming into existence in December 1980. The council approved the plan in March 1970 and created a working group, chaired by Werner, to develop the plan. In October 1970 the Werner group proposed that in the first stage the fiscal and monetary policies of the member states be coordinated and harmonized, regulatory restrictions in financial markets be eliminated, and the range of fluctuation among exchange rates be narrowed. New supranational monetary institutions would come into being in the later stages.

The council accepted the Werner Committee's report at its meeting in February 1971 and stage one of what was anticipated would be a ten-year transition to an economic and monetary union

began shortly thereafter. But only months later the first of several crises in the International Monetary Fund's exchange-rate regime, in which the value of the American dollar was fixed vis-à-vis gold and all other currencies were pegged to the dollar, took place. Pressure from holders of dollars who sought to exchange them for gold as the United States experienced trade and budget deficits and an acceleration of the rate of change in prices led President Richard Nixon (1913–1994) to close the gold window in August 1971. Shortly thereafter the dollar was devalued vis-à-vis gold and the margin of fluctuation between the dollar and other currencies was increased from plus or minus 0.75 percent to 2.25 percent.

The threefold increase in the range of fluctuation between the dollar and other currencies meant, of course, that rather than narrowing, the fluctuation range among the EC currencies had increased dramatically. The widening range of fluctuation among the currencies would of course create havoc for the trade among countries with highly interdependent economies and common prices in the agricultural sector. In order to reduce that fluctuation, the member states agreed in April 1972 to limit the fluctuation in the exchange rates among their currencies to a range equal to one-half that allowed by the IMF, and they reaffirmed the objective of achieving EMU by 1981 in summit conferences in October 1972 and again in December 1974. By 1976, however, it became obvious that the widened fluctuation range, coupled with the absence of any mechanism to keep the currencies in a more narrow range, spelled the end—at least for the time being—of the ambition to create an economic and monetary union.

The EC continued to face the problem of maintaining an internal market among highly interdependent economies in the face of continuing fluctuation of each EC currency vis-à-vis the other EC currencies, since the fluctuations translated into immediate changes in the prices of goods produced in one member state relative to the prices of goods produced in the other member states. That meant that producers might obtain competitive advantages or, on the other hand, be harmed in both their home markets and other markets through fluctuations in the value of the currencies. It also greatly complicated the task of setting common prices for agricultural commodities in the CAP.

The necessity of dampening the fluctuations among the currencies of highly interdependent economies belonging to a common market led the EC, after the large fluctuations in inflation rates and exchange rates in the wake of the first "oil price shock" and subsequent economic downturn in 1973–1975, to search for a new way to limit the fluctuations among their currencies and create a zone of monetary stability. Following a proposal in October 1977 by Roy Jenkins (1920–2003), the president of the commission, chancellor Helmut Schmidt (b. 1918) of Germany and president Valery Giscard d'Estaing (b. 1926) of France—both former finance ministers who were knowledgeable about exchange-rate and monetary policy—agreed to create a new European Monetary System (EMS). The EMS, which came into being in March 1979, created a bilateral parity grid among all the currencies, limited the fluctuation range among them to plus or minus 2.25 percent, provided a means of monitoring the fluctuations among the currencies, and provided for a means of negotiating realignments in the values of the currencies.

Not all of the member states participated in the EMS. Britain, for example, refused to join until 1990. But those that did participate gradually came to understand EMS constraints on monetary and fiscal policy. A critical period in the development of the EMS occurred during the first two years of the administration of President François Mitterrand of France. Mitterrand, a Socialist, was elected in 1981 with the support of the Communist Party. Coming to power for the first time since the advent of the Fifth Republic in 1958 and in the midst of a recession marked by an increasing rate of unemployment, the Left-dominated government sought to pursue a reflationary policy that tolerated large increases in wages, a substantial increase in public spending, a budget deficit, and an acceleration in the rate of inflation to 12–13 percent. The predictable result was a deteriorating balance of trade and downward pressure in the currency markets on the franc relative to the German mark. As it approached its floor against the mark, France was forced to negotiate a devaluation of the franc within the EMS on three occasions in the first two years of the Mitterrand-led government—in October 1981, June 1982, and March 1983.

Since any devaluation of the franc involved, by definition, a revaluation of other currencies that would hurt the competitive position in the EC of goods produced in the revaluing countries, the devaluations were always modest. Moreover, agreement on a devaluation—even a modest one—came only with a French agreement to scale back public spending, first in a *pause,* then in a policy of *rigueur,* then in a policy of austerity.

The French experience conveyed a lesson to the rest of the EC. Participation in the EMS required countries to emulate the macroeconomic policy of the strong-currency countries, such as Germany, which sought to stabilize prices through a tight monetary policy and a balanced fiscal policy. As that lesson was internalized by the participating member states in the 1980s, the frequency of realignments decreased. But countries such as France and Italy continued to object to what they regarded as the asymmetry of influence and benefit in the EMS. The German Bundesbank in effect set monetary policy for the countries participating in the EMS, since its interest rates established the de facto floor for interest rates in the other countries. And Germany, along with the Netherlands, which shadowed German monetary and fiscal policy, enjoyed substantial gains from trade since participation in the EMS in effect caused their currencies to be undervalued, especially as realignments—which invariably involved revaluation of the mark and the guilder—became less frequent.

The decreasing frequency of realignments in the exchange rates of the EMS currencies created the impression that the EC might someday approach the stability of a fixed-exchange-rate regime such as would exist in an EMU with irrevocably locked rates. And perhaps for that reason, EMU reappeared, albeit surreptitiously, on the agenda of the EC in the mid-1980s. The preamble of the Single European Act (SEA) of 1986, which was designed to remove the non-tariff barriers that still interfered with the free movement of goods and services in the internal market of the EC, claimed as one of the objectives of the Act "the progressive realization of economic and monetary union." And the SEA amended the Treaty of Rome by adding an ambiguously titled chapter, "Cooperation in Economic and Monetary Policy (Economic and Monetary Union)."

The preamble and reference to EMU in the SEA were apparently the work of Commission President Jacques Delors (b. 1925). Soon after the SEA was agreed to in February 1986 Delors convened a group of economists to analyze the effects of the SEA. In their report, published in 1987, they concluded that completion of the internal market by 1992—the overarching objective of the SEA—would require greater coordination of monetary policy and a strengthening of the EMS. They noted the incompatibility of nationally determined monetary policies with EC–wide free movement of goods, services, and capital, on the one hand, and an exchange-rate regime that, because of the decreasing frequency of realignments, was becoming increasingly analogous to a fixed-exchange-rate regime.

It was, however, a dispute between France and Germany over exchange-rate policy that ultimately led to the resurrection of the Werner plan to create in stages an Economic and Monetary Union. Very soon after taking power after the election of March 1986, the French cohabitation center-right government headed by Prime Minister Jacques Chirac (b. 1932)—Mitterrand was still president—negotiated another devaluation of the franc, which by then had become significantly overvalued in the EMS. Yet despite that devaluation, the franc remained overvalued and under pressure in the foreign exchange markets. As the franc moved toward its floor against the mark in January 1987, the French finance minister Édouard Balladur (b. 1929), taking the view that the problem was caused in part by the systematic undervaluation of the mark, let the franc go through its floor in order to force the Bundesbank to intervene in support of the franc.

Eventually the German government revalued the mark by a modest amount. But the French government remained dissatisfied with the operation of the EMS. In July 1987 and again in August 1987 Balladur called upon the EC to strengthen the EMS and alleviate the asymmetry that existed between Germany and its partners. The result was the Basel-Nyborg Agreements of September 1987, in which the governors of the EC central banks and the ministers of finance agreed on a credit facility to support intra-margin interventions in the currency markets. In December 1987, with the franc again under attack in the markets and the government

again forced to raise interest rates to support the currency, Balladur called again for reform of the EMS. He proposed a greater degree of symmetry in the operation of the EMS—especially in the defense of currencies at their floors—and strengthening of the European Monetary Cooperation Fund. And in order to present a common front vis-à-vis the American dollar and Japanese yen, he called for the EC to create a common currency and assign the responsibility for monetary policy to a single central bank—in short, for EMU.

The French proposal, soon supported by the Italian government, was placed on the agenda of the June 1988 meeting of the heads of state and government in Hanover, Germany. The leaders created a committee, chaired by Delors and composed largely of the central-bank governors, to study the issue. In April 1989 the committee recommended, very much along the lines of the earlier Werner committee, creation in three stages of an Economic and Monetary Union. Meeting in Madrid in June 1989, the leaders accepted the report as defining a process leading to EMU, agreed that the first stage would begin on 1 July 1990, and agreed that an Intergovernmental Conference would be convened sometime after the start of the first stage to negotiate the treaty amendments necessary for the later stages. At a meeting in Strasbourg in December 1989 the leaders agreed the IGC would begin one year hence.

## THE TRANSITION TO EMU

Title VI of the Treaty on European Union committed the member states to coordinating their economic policies through the formulation of broad guidelines for their economic policies and multilateral surveillance and assessment of those policies by the Commission, Council, and Parliament of the EU. The treaty stipulated that the member states would avoid "excessive deficits," defined as a ratio of the combined deficit of all levels of government to Gross Domestic Product in excess of 3 percent unless the ratio had declined substantially and continuously to a level close to 3 percent or the excess was exceptional and a ratio of government debt to GDP in excess of 60 percent unless the ratio was diminishing and approaching 60 percent. The treaty established sanctions, including fines, to be levied on countries that did not repair their excessive deficits.

The treaty committed the member states to the creation of an EMU in stages by 1999. The first stage of EMU had begun, by agreement of the heads of state and government, on 1 July 1990. The treaty provided for a transitional second stage beginning in 1 January 1994 and a third and final stage to begin on 1 January 1999 at the latest. In the second stage the member states were to undertake programs to ensure their lasting economic convergence, the achievement of price stability, and avoidance of excessive deficits. They were also required, if it was necessary, to begin the process leading to the independence of their central banks. At the start of the second stage a European Monetary Institute (EMI) was to be created. The EMI was to be headed by a council consisting of a president appointed by the heads of state and government and the governors of the national central banks. The EMI was mandated to strengthen the cooperation between the national central banks and the coordination among their monetary policies, oversee the functioning of the European Monetary System, and prepare for the third and final stage of EMU.

The treaty stipulated that in the third and final stage of EMU the EMI would be transformed into a new European Central Bank that would assume responsibility from the national central banks for the formulation and implementation of monetary policy in the participating member states. The Governing Council of the ECB, which would be located in Frankfurt, Germany, would consist of the six members of the ECB's Executive Board—a president, a vice-president, and four other members, appointed by the heads of state and government—and the governors of the national central banks of the participating member states. The exchange rates among the national currencies of the participating member states would be irrevocably locked and the national currencies would, in time, be replaced by a new single currency, the euro.

The treaty stipulated that during the second stage the EMI and the commission would report periodically to the council on the fulfillment by the member states of the criteria, set forth in the treaty, by which the achievement of the high degree of sustainable convergence necessary for participation in the third and final stage of EMU would be judged. Those criteria, often referred to as the "convergence criteria," included: (1) the achievement of price stability as reflected in a rate of inflation close to that of the three best-performing member states; (2) the achievement of a sustainable budgetary position as reflected in the absence of an "excessive deficit;" (3) the observance of the normal fluctuation margins in the Exchange Rate Mechanism of the European Monetary System for at least two years without a devaluation; and (4) the durability of convergence as reflected in long-term interest rates that were close to those of the three best-performing member states.

The treaty provided that the Council, meeting as the heads of state or government, would vote no later than 31 December 1996 whether a majority of the member states satisfied the "convergence criteria" and thereby fulfilled the necessary conditions for participation in the third and final stage of EMU and, if so, when that stage would begin. It stipulated, also, that if by the end of 1997 a date for the start of the third stage had not been set, it would start on 1 January 1999 and the leaders would decide, prior to 1 July 1998, which member states fulfilled the conditions for participation.

By the time the decisions pertaining to movement to the third stage of EMU were to be taken, three more states—Austria, Finland, and Sweden—had joined the EU, all having acceded on 1 January 1995.

Meeting in Cannes in June 1995, after the finance ministers of the fifteen member states had agreed that the earliest possible date for entry to the third stage of EMU—1 January 1997—was "not realistic," the heads of state and government stated their "firm resolve" to move to the third stage by 1 January 1999. Meeting at Madrid six months later, the leaders confirmed "unequivocally" that the third stage would begin on that date. They also adopted the EMI's scenario for the move to the third stage, according to which the exchange rates among the participating currencies would be irrevocably locked with each other and with the euro as of 1 January 1999 and the national currencies and the euro would circulate as "different expressions of the same money" until the first half of 2002, at which time the national currencies of the participating member states would be withdrawn from circulation and the euro would become the sole legal tender, and single currency, of the participating states.

Meeting in Brussels in May 1998, the leaders of the fifteen member states decided that eleven of the fifteen member states—all but the United Kingdom, Denmark, Sweden, and Greece—fulfilled the necessary conditions for adoption of a single currency and would, therefore, enter the third and final stage of EMU on 1 January 1999. The United Kingdom had negotiated an "opt-out" at the concluding meeting at Maastricht of the Intergovernmental Conference by which it is not obliged or committed to move to the third stage without a separate decision to do so by its government and parliament. In October 1997 the British government set forth five criteria by which it would assess whether it was appropriate to enter. It did not carry out an assessment prior to the May 1998 meeting. In fact, it did not carry out an assessment until 2003, at which time it found some of the criteria had not been satisfied. Moreover, Britain had not participated in the Exchange Rate Mechanism of the EMS since September 1992, when it had been forced by unabated downward pressure on the exchange rate of the pound vis-à-vis the German mark to withdraw the pound.

After the Treaty on European Union was signed in early 1992 the Danish Storting had overwhelmingly approved it. But ratification of the treaty required, also, approval by the Danish electorate in a referendum. Despite the fact that the Danish government had obtained at Maastricht an "opt-out" from the third and final stage of EMU, in the referendum, held on 2 June 1992, 50.7 percent of the voters rejected the treaty. The government subsequently obtained additional "opt-outs" at a meeting of the heads of state and government at Edinburgh in December 1992 that allowed it to call another referendum, on 18 May 1993, at which 56.7 percent approved the treaty. But at Edinburgh, Denmark gave notice that it would not participate in the third stage. (Later, in 2000, the Danish government had second thoughts about participating in the third stage of EMU and called another referendum on the issue but 53.1 percent voted against participation on 28 September 2000.)

In June 1997 the Swedish government announced that it would not enter the third stage in 1999 and that it would hold an election or referendum on the issue if it decided to recommend entry. Moreover, Sweden, like the United Kingdom, refused to participate in the Exchange Rate Mechanism of the EMS, thereby failing to satisfy one of the necessary "convergence criteria" for participation. Like the Danish government, the Swedish government did subsequently have second thoughts about participating in the single currency and called a referendum on the matter. In the referendum, which took place on 14 September 2003, only three days after the murder of Anna Lindh (1957–2003), the Swedish foreign minister who had become the chief spokesperson supporting participation, 53.1 percent of the Swedish electorate voted against participation.

On the basis of its economic performance in 1997 Greece did not satisfy all of the "convergence criteria" and was barred from entering the third stage with the eleven other participating member states. However, it did subsequently qualify and joined as of 1 January 2001.

At their May 1998 meeting the leaders of the fifteen member states chose the president, vice president, and four other members of the Executive Board of the European Central Bank. The meeting was marked by a heated dispute between Helmut Kohl (b. 1930), the German chancellor, who supported Wim Duisenberg (1935–2005), the Dutch central-bank governor, for president and Chirac, the French president, who favored Jean-Claude Trichet (b. 1942), the governor of the Banque de France. Chirac reasoned that since the ECB was to be located in Frankfurt and since it embodied the German Bundesbank's priorities, which favored price stability above all else, it would only be fair for France to hold the presidency. Ultimately, it was agreed that the initial eight-year term would be split, with Duisenberg holding the presidency until some time after the national currencies had been withdrawn from circulation in early 2002. He assumed the presidency on 1 June 1998 and held it until 31 October 2003, at which time Trichet became president.

In late 1998 the exchange rates among the currencies of the eleven participating countries were irrevocably locked and the third and final stage of EMU came into being on 1 January 1999. The ECB assumed responsibility for monetary policy in the eleven states as of that date. In early 2002 the national currencies were withdrawn from circulation and replaced with bills and coins denominated in euros.

## THE COMMON FOREIGN AND SECURITY POLICY

In addition to creating the European Union and committing the member states to the creation of an Economic and Monetary Union, the Treaty on European Union committed them to defining and implementing a Common Foreign and Security Policy (CFSP). The CFSP would be designed to safeguard the common values and interests of the EU, strengthen the security of the EU and its member states, preserve peace and strengthen international security and cooperation, and develop and consolidate democracy and the rule of law and respect for human rights and fundamental freedoms. It was designed to deal with all questions related to the security of the EU, including "the eventual framing of a common defense policy, which might in time lead to a common defense."

The CFSP was designed to achieve these objectives by establishing systematic cooperation between the member states and gradually implementing joint action in the areas in which they had important interests in common. The member states were mandated to consult with each other on any matter of foreign and security policy and they could, when necessary, define a common position in the Council. In such cases they were to ensure that their national policies conformed to the common position and they were mandated, further, to coordinate their action in international organizations in order to uphold the common positions. The Council could also decide, on the basis of general guidelines established by the heads of state and government, that a particular matter should be a subject of joint action and, if so, by what means that action would be undertaken. The presidency of the Council was designated as the representative of the EU in matters falling within the CFSP and the office responsible for the implementation of common measures.

Having been negotiated at a time in which Europe was undergoing a historic geopolitical transformation with the collapse of communist regimes throughout central and eastern Europe and in the Soviet Union, it was inevitable that the Treaty on European Union would attempt to empower the EU as an international actor. But the commitment to the pursuit and implementation of a CFSP was nearly derailed even before the formal signing ceremony of the treaty in February 1992 by developments in the former Yugoslavia.

After the former Yugoslav republics of Slovenia and Croatia declared their independence in June 1991 and the Yugoslav army undertook military action in both, the EC became deeply involved in efforts to resolve both conflicts. An effort by the EC to end the Yugoslav intervention in Slovenia was facilitated by the unexpected ability of the Slovenian National Guard to defeat the Yugoslav army's contingent in a "ten-day war" in July 1991. But in Croatia, where the Yugoslav army came to the defense of the Serb population concentrated in the Krajina and shelled Vukovar in eastern Slavonia and Dubrovnik, the EC found itself unable to prevent a full-fledged war. By December five hundred thousand Croats and two hundred thousand Serbs had been displaced, Vukovar had been destroyed, and the Yugoslav army occupied one-third of Croatia.

In the fall of 1991, as the negotiations on the Treaty on European Union were drawing to a close, the EC faced the issue of whether it should recognize Slovenia, Croatia, and perhaps other Yugoslav republics as independent. In November 1991 it created a five-person commission headed by Robert Badinter (b. 1928) to develop criteria for international recognition.

Meeting only a week after the heads of state and government had agreed to the treaty and its provisions for a CFSP the German foreign minister, Hans-Dietrich Genscher (b. 1927), made it clear that if the EC refused to recognize Croatia and Slovenia, Germany would do so unilaterally. The ministers agreed that any Yugoslav republic seeking EC recognition should apply immediately, the applications would be considered by the commission, and the commission would report in January 1992. Several member states opposed immediate recognition. But Germany had already told Slovenia and Croatia they would be recognized by Christmas. Four republics applied—Slovenia, Croatia, Macedonia, and Bosnia and Herzegovina. The Badinter commission recommended that Slovenia and Macedonia be recognized,

**Irish president of the European Parliament Pat Cox (left) and former Polish president Lech Wałęsa photographed at a ceremony marking the admission of ten nations, including Poland, to the European Union, 3 May 2004.** ©JEAN-MARC LOOS/REUTERS/CORBIS

that Croatia not be recognized until it guaranteed the rights of the Serb minority, and Bosnia not be recognized until it had held a national referendum on the issue. Greece vetoed the recognition of Macedonia, Croatia was recognized despite the commission's recommendation, and Bosnia and Herzegovina was advised to hold a referendum on independence. The Bosnia referendum had the entirely predictable effect of precipitating a three-year war. The sizable Serb population in Bosnia abstained from the referendum since it was obvious their desire to remain in Serb-dominated Yugoslavia would lose. As a result the vote overwhelmingly endorsed independence; Bosnia immediately received international recognition; hostilities broke out immediately between the Bosnian Serbs, Muslims, and Croats; and the Yugoslav army entered the fray.

The inability of the EC to deal collectively with the recognition issue was amplified by its inability to terminate the conflict. Lacking the military capacity and will to take on the Yugoslav army in a ground war, the EC could only stand by and watch as two hundred thousand were killed and two million displaced in a war that ended only in 1995. Eventually, the war came to an end, but only after the United States had engineered a coalition of Bosnian Croats and Muslims in 1994 and provided assistance to the Croatian military, which, beginning in May 1995, swept through the Serb-controlled areas of the country and took control of a significant portion of Serb-occupied Bosnia. In the wake of the Bosnian Serb army's massacre of eight thousand Bosnian Muslims at Srebrenica in July 2005 the air power of the North Atlantic Treaty Organization was brought into the battle and the war ended with the signing of the Dayton Accords (negotiated at an American air base in Ohio).

In 1998, as NATO prepared to once again use military force to bring to an end Serbia's effort to defeat the Kosovo Liberation Army and remove large numbers of ethnic Albanians from the territory, it became apparent once again that the EU lacked the military capacity to carry out a Common Foreign and Security Policy even in the unlikely event that it could adopt a "common position." That realization, shared by Prime Minister Tony Blair (b. 1953) of the United Kingdom and President Chirac of France, the two countries that had made the largest contributions to a United Nations peacekeeping force in Croatia and Bosnia in 1992–1995, resulted in an agreement at St. Malo in December 1998 that set the stage for the development of an EU Rapid Reaction Force and a European Security and Defense Policy. Both the Force and the ESDP came into being in 1999.

The EC and EU's failure to prevent and then terminate the genocidal wars of the 1990s in the Balkans made it apparent that the pursuit and implementation of a Common Foreign and Security Policy requires more than a substantially increased capability to conduct military operations, important as such capability may be. The failure made it apparent that pursuit and implementation of CFSP requires, also, the articulation of a "common position" and the binding commitment of the member states to that position. The articulation of and adherence to a binding "common position," depending as it does upon a convergence of the national interests of the member states in the domains of foreign, security, and defense policy, may be difficult—if not impossible—to achieve. That difficulty was perhaps best illustrated in the acrimonious dispute within the EU in the run-up to the American-led war in Iraq in 2003. In that dispute, some member states—most notably, the United Kingdom but also Spain, Italy, and several others—enthusiastically supported and joined the American "coalition of the willing" while other member states—most notably, France, Belgium, and Germany—strongly objected to the American effort to use military force, rather than the efforts of the International Atomic Energy Agency and United Nations, in dealing with Iraq.

## THE ENLARGEMENT OF THE EUROPEAN UNION

The negotiation of the Treaty on European Union took place in the immediate aftermath of the historic events of 1989–1991 in central and eastern Europe and the Soviet Union. As the communist regimes collapsed many of the new governments looked toward the EC and EU and sought arrangements that would enable them, in time, to become members. As early as 1990, for example, governments in Poland and Hungary negotiated "Europe Agreements" with the EC that anticipated eventual membership.

The EC sought initially to create a new entity, the European Economic Area, in which the postcommunist states would participate, enjoying many of the economic benefits of the single market without, however, participating in the institutions of the EC. But it soon became obvious that, armed with the slogan "Return to Europe," most if not all of postcommunist Europe wanted nothing less than full membership.

In June 1993 the leaders of the twelve member states of the European Communities, in Copenhagen for their recurring summit meeting, approved criteria by which the applications of states for membership would be evaluated. The criteria, known as the Copenhagen Criteria, require that in order to be considered for membership a country must be democratic and abide by the rule of law; must respect the rights of minorities and human rights; must have a functioning market economy; and must be able to administer and implement the *acquis communautaire*, the body of all treaty obligations, laws, regulations, directives, and policies of the EU.

By 1996 the Czech Republic, Estonia, Hungary, Latvia, Lithuania, Poland, the Slovak Republic, Slovenia, Bulgaria, and Romania had applied for membership in the EU. (Prior to the demise of the postcommunist regimes in central and eastern Europe, two small island countries in the Mediterranean—Cyprus and Malta—had applied for membership in the EC, and Turkey had applied as early as 1987.) Applying the "Copenhagen Criteria," the EU opened accession negotiations with the Czech Republic, Poland, Hungary, Slovenia, Estonia, and Cyprus in early 1998. In 1999 it agreed to open the negotiations as well with the Slovak

Republic, Latvia, Lithuania, Malta, Bulgaria, and Romania and did so in early 2000.

By late 2002 those negotiations had reached agreement on all but a few of the most difficult aspects of the *acquis communautaire*. Negotiations on two of the most contentious chapters of the *acquis*—agriculture and financial and budgetary provisions—were completed with ten of the twelve candidates—all but Bulgaria and Romania—at the Copenhagen meeting of the heads of state and government in December 2002. The accession treaty was signed in Athens on 16 April 2003 and the ten candidates, as well as the fifteen member states, set about the process of ratifying the treaty. All did so and the ten entered the EU on 1 May 2004. As of that date, therefore, the EU increased from fifteen to twenty-five member states.

Bulgaria and the EU concluded their accession negotiations in December 2004, at which time the EU expressed the view that it anticipated that Bulgaria would enter in January 2007. However, the accession treaty signed in April 2005 allows the EU to postpone Bulgaria's entry one year to January 2008 if there is clear evidence that it is unprepared for membership. Any such delay would, however, have to be approved by all of the member states.

Like Bulgaria, Romania completed its accession negotiations with the EU in December 2004, signed the accession treaty in April 2005, and anticipates accession on 1 January 2007. However, as with Bulgaria, its entry can be postponed one year upon a unanimous vote of the twenty-five member states that clear evidence exists that it is unprepared for membership.

In November 2000 a summit meeting between the EU and the governments of the Western Balkans—Croatia, Bosnia and Herzegovina, Serbia and Montenegro, the Former Yugoslav Republic of Macedonia, and Albania—agreed upon a Stabilization and Association Process (SAP) that supports the development of the Western Balkan countries and prepares them for eventual membership in the EU. The SAP is designed to support the countries through a Stabilization and Association Agreement, trade, and financial assistance. An SAA is regarded as a precursor of an application for membership.

Croatia applied for membership in the EU in February 2003. After Croatia addressed a number of issues pertaining to minority rights, the return of refugees, and judicial reform, the EU set March 2005 as the date for the start of accession negotiations, provided the government cooperated fully with the International Criminal Tribunal for the former Yugoslavia (ICTY) in The Hague. Unable or unwilling to turn over a popular former general, Ante Gotovina (b. 1955), who had led the Croatian military in its 1995 victory over the Serb and Bosnian Serb armies, the start of Croatia's negotiations was delayed until October 2005. After being assured by the Chief Prosecutor of the ICTY, Carla del Ponte (b. 1947), that Croatia was cooperating fully, the negotiations began on 3 October 2005. Gotovina was arrested in December 2005 in the Canary Islands.

Macedonia reached agreement with the EU on an SAA in April 2001 and it applied for membership in March 2004. In December 2005 the EU concluded that Macedonia was officially a candidate for membership, but it did not set a date for the start of accession negotiations pending continued progress in a variety of economic and political domains of policy.

Albania opened negotiations with the EU for an SAA in January 2003. Both sides hoped to complete the negotiations in the first half of 2006.

Serbia and Montenegro opened SAA negotiations in October 2005 and Bosnia and Herzegovina opened the same negotiations a month later. The EU made it clear that in both cases progress in the negotiations would depend upon the countries' full cooperation with the ICTY.

In addition to the ongoing negotiations between the EU and the five countries that are part of the Stabilization and Association Process for the Western Balkans, the EU opened accession negotiations in October 2005 with Turkey, which had applied for membership in April 1987.

In the event all of the countries that, as of 2006, were acceding countries (Bulgaria, Romania), candidates for membership (Croatia, Macedonia, Turkey), or potential candidates for membership (Albania, Bosnia and Herzegovina, Serbia, and Montenegro) join the EU, it will have thirty-three states encompassing nearly six hundred million citizens. In addition, it should be noted that some of the non-Baltic states of the former Soviet Union—most notably, Georgia after its "Rose Revolution" of 2004 and Ukraine after its "Orange Revolution" of 2005—have expressed a strong desire to join the EU. In 2006 the EU declared that Ukraine had a functioning market economy, thereby satisfying one of the criteria for membership set forth at Copenhagen in June 1993.

*See also* **Benelux Economic Union; Euro; European Coal and Steel Community (ECSC); European Commission; European Constitution 2004–2005; Maastricht, Treaty of; Monnet, Jean; Rome, Treaty of; Schuman, Robert.**

BIBLIOGRAPHY

Cameron, David R. "Transnational Relations and the Development of European Economic and Monetary Union." In *Bringing Transnational Relations Back In: Non-State Actors, Domestic Structures, and International Institutions,* edited by Thomas Risse-Kappen, 37–78. Cambridge, U.K., 1995.

———. "Creating Supranational Authority in Monetary and Exchange-Rate Policy: The Sources and Effects of EMU." In *European Integration and Supranational Governance,* edited by Wayne Sandholtz and Alec Stone Sweet, 188–216. Oxford, U.K., 1998.

Dinan, Desmond. *Ever Closer Union: An Introduction to European Integration.* 3rd ed. Boulder, Colo., 2005.

Duff, Andrew, John Pinder, and Roy Pryce, eds. *Maastricht and Beyond: Building the European Union.* London and New York, 1994.

Gillingham, John. *European Integration, 1950–2003: Superstate or New Market Economy?* Cambridge, U.K., and New York, 2003.

Hitchcock, William I. *The Struggle for Europe: The Turbulent History of a Divided Continent, 1945–2002.* New York, 2003.

Hix, Simon. *The Political System of the European Union.* 2nd ed. New York, 2005.

Judt, Tony. *Postwar: A History of Europe Since 1945.* New York, 2005.

Kenen, Peter B. *Economic and Monetary Union in Europe: Moving Beyond Maastricht.* Cambridge, U.K., and New York, 1995.

Milward, Alan S. *The Reconstruction of Western Europe, 1945–51.* Berkeley, Calif., 1984.

Milward, Alan S., with the assistance of George Brennan and Federico Romero. *The European Rescue of the Nation-State.* Berkeley, Calif., 1992.

Moravcsik, Andrew. *The Choice for Europe: Social Purpose and State Power from Messina to Maastricht.* Ithaca, N.Y., 1998.

Silber, Laura, and Allan Little. *Yugoslavia: Death of a Nation.* Rev. and updated ed. New York, 1997.

Wallace, Helen, William Wallace, and Mark A. Pollack, eds., *Policy-Making in the European Union.* 5th ed. Oxford, U.K., and New York, 2005.

DAVID R. CAMERON

---

**EUTHANASIA.** Until the eighteenth century, a doctor could do little to save the life of a dying person and it was rare for doctors to be called to a person's deathbed. The word *euthanasia* generally referred to a "good death," a death without pain.

## HISTORICAL BACKGROUND

With advances in medicine, doctors began to play a larger role at the deathbed. The term *euthanasia* came to be associated with old age, with life prolonged beyond the point at which it was meaningful for the patient, and with the doctor's duty to make the transition from life to death as comfortable as possible. Toward the end of the nineteenth century, the modern discussion about euthanasia emerged, a discussion in which it is taken for granted that (1) a doctor is at the deathbed, (2) the doctor disposes over the means of hastening death, (3) shortening the dying process is a possible aim or effect of the medical treatment, and (4) the patient asks for euthanasia. In short, the behavior of doctors is the subject of debate and the central question is to what extent the state should forbid or regulate euthanasia.

In the late nineteenth and early twentieth century, the discussion of euthanasia took place chiefly in England and Germany. In England, the discussion resulted, among other things, in the establishment of the Voluntary Euthanasia Society, which tried unsuccessfully to achieve legalization in 1935, 1959, 1969, and 2003–2005. In Germany, the question of whether human life always has to be preserved was answered in the negative by authors who argued that it is sometimes permissible for a doctor to terminate the life of a patient, both in cases of incurably ill competent patients who ask for euthanasia and also in cases of severely mentally defective persons and patients in irreversible coma. In the English discussion, too, the border between the voluntary and nonvoluntary ending of life was not always clear-cut, and the early euthanasia movement had connections with the eugenics movement. After World War II, the idea of euthanasia became severely discredited by the Nazi euthanasia program, which had aimed to purify the German "race" of physically and mentally handicapped persons.

## THE MOVEMENT TO LEGALIZE EUTHANASIA

In the years after World War II, euthanasia was hardly discussed. This began to change toward the end of the 1960s. Several reasons have been suggested for the renewed interest: death ceased to be a taboo subject; medicine had gained the ability to keep terminally ill patients alive far longer than they or those close to them wanted; and the demand for personal autonomy over matters of life and death increased. Beginning in the 1970s, proponents of voluntary euthanasia established organizations to promote their views in most Western European countries. The most important principles invoked were autonomy, beneficence, and freedom from state control. Opponents argued that the law should respect the absolute value ("sanctity") of life and that legal euthanasia would undermine patient confidence in doctors; they invoked the danger of the "slippery slope": the idea that legitimizing voluntary euthanasia would lead inevitably to a situation in which involuntary termination of life is practiced.

The public discussion of these questions often found its stimulus in a dramatic court case. Examples include cases concerning the continued medical treatment of a person in irreversible coma (the Bland case in England in 1993 and the Versluis case in the Netherlands in 1969); prosecutions resulting from a person having acceded to the insistent requests of a family member to put an end to his or her misery (the Postma case in the Netherlands in 1973 and the Humbert case in France in 2003); and civil cases brought by people demanding the right to be helped with suicide without exposing others to the risk of prosecution

(the Sanpedro case in Spain in 2000 and the Pretty case in England in 2002).

Although it is generally assumed that euthanasia takes place with some regularity in most countries, the Netherlands was the only country in which doctors were regularly prosecuted for performing euthanasia. These prosecutions led in the 1980s to judicial recognition of a justification for euthanasia if it is performed according to a number of "rules of careful practice" first formulated within the medical profession itself. Since 2002 legislation in the Netherlands and Belgium has exempted from criminal prohibition euthanasia performed by a doctor under strictly defined circumstances.

## DEFINITION AND LEGAL STATUS

Although the term *euthanasia* has been used historically to refer to a wide variety of conceptions of or ways of achieving a good death, in the postwar public debate over whether and under what conditions euthanasia should be legal it has come to have a much narrower definition: medical behavior that causes the death of another person at that person's request (usually in the context of unbearable suffering accompanying the terminal stage of a fatal disease, such as cancer). Until the end of the twentieth century, euthanasia in this narrow sense was illegal in all European countries.

Closely related to euthanasia in the narrow sense (and included under that term in the rest of this entry) is assistance with suicide. In general, assistance with suicide is not illegal unless specifically prohibited; in some countries where it is not itself illegal, it can nevertheless entail criminal liability for failure to rescue or some other offense. Where assistance with suicide is not a criminal offense, in some countries it is still considered a violation of the Code of Medical Ethics for a doctor to give such assistance. In Switzerland there is an institutionalized practice of assistance with suicide by non-doctors, and since the 1990s partisans of a greater role for patient autonomy at the end of life have been exploring the possibilities for humane (assisted) suicide in other countries without the involvement of a doctor.

Two sorts of medical behavior that are often closely related to euthanasia in both intention and effect were in the past sometimes considered varieties of euthanasia. The first, abstention (withholding or withdrawing life-prolonging treatment), was called *passive euthanasia*. A special case of abstention is when the doctor honors the request of a patient to abstain (including requests made in advance in a written advance directive); abstention in such a case is based on the absolute right of the patient—recognized at least in principle in most European countries—to refuse medical treatment. In other cases, abstention is legal in most countries if treatment has become "futile." The second, pain relief in doses expected to cause earlier death, was called *indirect euthanasia* and is usually deemed legitimate so long as the doctor's intent is to relieve pain and the earlier death of the patient is only a byproduct (often referred to the doctrine of double effect). In most European countries, both abstention from futile treatment and pain relief that may hasten death are considered normal medical practice and attract no specific legal control.

A final category is the termination of life without an explicit request. In practice, this is often difficult to distinguish from abstention and pain relief, and also from euthanasia at a patient's request. It includes what amounts to ordinary murder as well as cases in which the patient's request for euthanasia does not meet legal standards, some cases of abstention and pain relief, and what is sometimes called "assistance in dying." While generally illegal, in the Netherlands termination of life without an explicit request has been held to be legally justifiable in a narrowly defined category of cases (e.g., in the case of babies born with extreme birth defects, where treatment has been withdrawn on grounds of futility but the baby does not die quickly and in a humane way).

## EMPIRICAL DATA

Opinion polls in most countries show strong and generally increasing support for the legalization of euthanasia since the late twentieth century. Although outside the Netherlands all medical associations are strongly opposed, opinion polls among doctors suggest a more positive attitude toward legalization.

The frequency with which euthanasia is actually practiced is difficult to establish because of serious criminal prohibitions and the taboo that surrounds

**TABLE 1**

**Frequencies of MBSL in the Netherlands (percentages of all deaths)**

|  | 1990 | 1995 | 2001 |
|---|---|---|---|
| euthanasia | 1.9 | 2.6 | 2.8 |
|    death on request | (1.7) | (2.4) | (2.6) |
|    assistance with suicide | (0.2) | (0.2) | (0.2) |
| termination of life without a request | 0.8 | 0.7 | 0.7 |
| death due to pain relief | 18.8 | 19.1 | 20.1 |
| death due to abstinence | 17.9 | 20.2 | 20.2 |
| total MBSL | 39.4 | 42.6 | 43.8 |
| total deaths | 128,824 | 135,675 | 145,377 |

Source: G. van der Wal et al., *Medische besluitvorming aan het einde van het leven*, Utrecht, 2003, p. 67 (report of the national research conducted in 2001).

the subject. Only in the Netherlands have reliable data over a long period been produced. Table 1 shows that medical decisions that shorten life (MBSL) account for about two-fifths of all deaths in the Netherlands (something generally true of countries with modern health care systems). Abstention and pain relief each account for almost half of these cases. Euthanasia, physician-assisted suicide, and termination of life without a request together account for well under 5 percent.

The first national research in the Netherlands was conducted in 1990 and led to a vigorous international debate on the interpretation of the data. Critics have argued that a significant number of cases allocated to the pain relief and to abstention categories really amount to euthanasia, making the euthanasia rate higher than the data suggest and thereby, it is suggested, much higher than in countries where euthanasia is illegal. And some critics argue that the existence of cases categorized as termination of life without request shows that the legalization of euthanasia will indeed be the beginning of a slippery slope toward medical killing on a wider scope. The weakness of both arguments is that no comparable data exist for other countries or for the Netherlands prior to the legalization of euthanasia, so the suggestion that legalization is responsible for the Dutch data lacks any empirical support.

## THE PROBLEM OF EFFECTIVE CONTROL

The difficulty in effectively controlling euthanasia—whether that means legal euthanasia, as in the Netherlands and Belgium, or illegal, as elsewhere—arises from two sources: in practice, euthanasia is often hard to distinguish from abstention or pain relief, and control depends on self-reporting by doctors. The debate over control has focused on the question of how much of the euthanasia that in fact takes place can be scrutinized by the authorities, which in turn hinges on how many doctors accurately report the cause of death. As is still the case elsewhere, the Dutch reporting rate was essentially zero until the beginning of the 1990s, when a formal reporting procedure was established and the rate gradually increased until by 2002 it was more than 50 percent of all cases in which euthanasia is in fact performed. The remaining cases are reported as natural deaths (due to abstention or pain relief) and therefore escape legal control. In countries where euthanasia is illegal, the reporting rate is of course essentially zero and whatever cases there are go entirely unexamined.

Some research has been done into why doctors do not report euthanasia. Apart from a dislike of state involvement in medical practice and a distaste for red tape, the most important reasons seem to be uncertainty about the consequences of reporting, or the inclination to characterize their behavior so that it falls within the legal category of pain relief, for example, rather than euthanasia. Both the Netherlands and Belgium have—partly in order to deal with the problem of doctors' reluctance to report—recently established systems of non-criminal assessment of reported cases.

**BIBLIOGRAPHICAL NOTE**

The references included in the bibliography are restricted as much as possible to publications in English. Extensive references to the non-English (in particular, the Dutch) literature can be found in Griffiths, Bood, and Weyers, 1998; a second edition, containing more recent literature, is due to appear in 2006.

*See also* **Death Penalty; Eugenics; Old Age.**

BIBLIOGRAPHY

Benzenhöfer, Udo. *Der Gute Tod?: Euthanasie und Sterbehilfe in Geschichte und Gegenwart.* Munich, 1999.

Brody, Baruch A. *Suicide and Euthanasia: Historical and Contemporary Themes.* Dordrecht, Boston, and London, 1989.

Deliens, Luc, Freddy. Mortierm et al. "End-of-Life Decisions in Medical Practice in Flanders, Belgium: A Nationwide Survey." *Lancet* 356 (2000): 1806–1811.

Friedlander, Henry. *The Origins of Nazi Genocide: From Euthanasia to the Final Solution.* Chapel Hill, N.C., and London, 1995.

Griffiths, John, Alex Bood, and Heleen Weyers. *Euthanasia and Law in the Netherlands.* Amsterdam, 1998.

Kemp, Nick D. A. *Merciful Release: The History of the British Euthanasia Movement.* Manchester, U.K., and New York, 2002.

Keown, John. *Euthanasia, Ethics, and Public Policy. An Argument against Legalisation.* Cambridge, U.K., and New York, 2002.

Klijn, Albert, Margaret Otlowski, and Margo Trappenburg. *Regulating Physician-Negotiated Death.* The Hague, 2001.

Lavi, Shai. "Euthanasia and the Changing Ethics of the Deathbed." *Theoretical Inquiries in Law* (2003): 729–762.

Maas, Paul Johann van der. "Euthanasia, Physician-Assisted Suicide, and Other Medical Practices Involving the End of Life in the Netherlands, 1990–1995." *New England Journal of Medicine* 335 (1996): 1699–1705.

Maas, Paul Johan van der, Johannes Joseph Marten van Delden, and Ludovica Pijnenborg. *Euthanasia and Other Medical Decisions Concerning the End of Life.* Amsterdam, 1992.

Otlowski, Margaret. *Voluntary Euthanasia and the Common Law.* Oxford, U.K., and New York, 1997.

JOHN GRIFFITHS, HELEEN WEYERS

**EVTUSHENKO, EVGENII.** *See* Yevtushenko, Yevgeny.

**EXISTENTIALISM.** Existentialism began as an obscure philosophical movement and ended up as a way of life. The term *existentialism* now embraces thinkers who did not necessarily see themselves as members of a common enterprise. That makes identifying a core set of beliefs difficult. But there is no doubt at all about the identity of its best-known champion or about the moment of its

No text better captures both the apparently demobilizing implications of existentialism, which seemed to undermine the basis for any commitment, and the simultaneous desire to find some grounds for action, than the memorable concluding passage of Sartre's *Being and Nothingness:* "All human activities are equivalent . . . and all are destined in principle to fail. So it amounts to the same thing whether one gets drunk alone or leads nations. If one of these activities is superior to the other, it is not because of its objective in the world, but because of the degree of consciousness involved in its adoption; in this sense, it is possible that the quietism of the solitary drunk will take precedence over the vain agitation of the leader of nations. . . . The ontology [of this work] cannot allow the formulation of moral prescriptions by itself. It nevertheless allows one to imagine what an ethics will be that rethinks responsibility in light of *human reality in situation.* . . . But we will return to these problems in a future work" (*L'être et le néant: Essai d'ontologie phénoménologique* [Paris, 1943], pp. 690–692; author's translation). In spite of writing many pages of "notebooks" for a prospective work on ethics, no sequel to *Being and Nothingness* ever appeared in Sartre's lifetime.

greatest recognition. Although forever linked with the Frenchman Jean-Paul Sartre (1905–1980) and his famous intellectual coterie just after World War II, when the themes of existentialism, and the term itself, entered global consciousness, the philosophy had begun its history long before.

## EXISTENCE AND ESSENCE

The name *existentialism* referred to the movement's radical new position on the long-standing opposition between essence and existence. Ancient philosophers and their medieval heirs defended the priority of essences. A thing, they argued, is what it is independent of any transformations it undergoes. Like ordinary things, human beings have an essence. That premise allowed the ancients a robust (and highly restrictive) theory of human virtues and vices supposed to follow from man's

unchanging nature. Monotheistic religion found a compromise with this view by holding that it is God, the creator, who bestows an essence on each thing (including human beings). Existentialists argued, quite simply, that the ancient and monotheistic thesis was false. Humans have no essence, whether naturally appointed or God-given, and therefore no foreordained purpose, no matter how profoundly they may desire one: in Sartre's famous formula from his central text, *Being and Nothingness* (1943), "man is a useless passion" (p. 784). Human beings, at least, are wholly defined by their choices, acts, and transformations, and therefore by their ongoing existence. For this reason, existentialism, like no other philosophical movement before or since, stressed the temporality of human consciousness and action. Few failed to notice that the existentialist destruction of the ancient and monotheistic position on human nature also endangered traditional ethical—and political—teachings.

## HEIDEGGER AND THE QUESTION OF BEING

Existentialists often claimed that the lineage of their movement stretched far back in the annals of philosophy. Its history, they said, ran through the decisive nineteenth-century figures of Søren Kierkegaard (1813–1855) and Friedrich Nietzsche (1844–1900), thinkers who were, however, ciphers in their own time and owe their present renown to existentialism itself. But by common consent, the founder of existentialism is the German philosopher Martin Heidegger (1889–1976). In his masterpiece, *Being and Time* (1927), Heidegger embarked on a clarification of the "question of being," a philosophical subject he thought had been recognized by the ancients but since forgotten. But this investigation, Heidegger said, admitted of a strategy that placed humanity at the center, since the problem of being in general could be addressed through an "existential" analysis of human being in particular. The most famous parts of the book gave memorable analyses of various "existential" states and created, almost overnight, a new style of philosophical inquiry. What emerges from *Being and Time* is the groundlessness and relativity of human beings' inherited systems of value and purpose, leading to an abyss of meaning, a frightening situation to be remedied, if at all, only by a decisive or "resolute" affiliation with reactivated elements of the past. Scandalously, when Heidegger chose to affiliate himself with the Nazi Party six years later, in

1933, he claimed that the Germans were doing exactly what his text dictated.

## SARTRE, CAMUS, AND THE QUESTION OF FREEDOM

Sartre, who drank deep at Heidegger's well and anticipated his existential philosophy in brilliant pieces of fiction such as his famous *Nausea* (1938), separated Heidegger's focus on human being from its larger justifying framework. Sartre's analyses were intended to illustrate the truth that there are no safe or certain values and that the anguished fate of humans is to make choices without any self-evident criteria for doing so. Unlike Heidegger, Sartre was a gifted prose stylist. In his conclusion to *Being and Nothingness,* he bitterly suggested that "it amounts to the same thing whether one gets drunk alone or leads nations." The emotionally numb hero of *The Stranger* (1942)—by Albert Camus (1913–1960), the other star French existentialist, and, like Sartre, a Nobel Prize winner for literature—draws the implication that if there is no authority governing action in the world, then none exists to enforce traditional prohibitions either, and therefore he shoots an Arab for no reason at all. Of particular interest in existentialism, not surprisingly, was its internal debate about the status of other people, the relation of the wayward human being to his fellows. For Heidegger, community seemed both the disease—the source of false reassurance about the existence of stable values—but also potentially the cure. For Sartre, other people appeared only as threats, lures. The act of submitting to them or of loving them might provide comfort, but it would be an inauthentic escape from freedom. As he put it in his drama *No Exit* (1944), "hell is other people" (p. 45).

The freedom depicted in existentialism, then, is not triumphant but anguished. No doubt it was Sartre's friend Camus who most vividly illustrated the "absurd" predicament of freedom. The two alternatives for human beings, he declared, were clarity and escape. Camus advocated staring unflinchingly at the painful truth—embracing "a total absence of hope (which has nothing to do with despair), a continual rejection (which must not be confused with renunciation), and a conscious dissatisfaction (which must not be compared to immature unrest)" (p. 31). Escape, Camus argued in his *Myth of Sisyphus* (1942), amounted to metaphorical suicide. Existentialists had to be strong enough to surf on a "dizzying crest" (p. 31) from which others might take the leap of faith to a suicidal end; they must embrace meaninglessness because of "the unyielding evidence of a life without consolation" (p. 60). The title of Camus's essay refers to the figure from Greek mythology, condemned in hell to the eternal task of rolling a boulder up a hill, only to watch it roll back down to the bottom again and again. Sisyphus thus serves as the very symbol for the correct approach to an agonizingly meaningless existence. "I want to know whether I can live with what I know and with that alone," Camus wrote (p. 40).

## RELIGIOUS, PSYCHOANALYTIC, AND FEMINIST EXISTENTIALISM

Existentialism appeared in a riot of conflicting forms. In a development that might at first seem surprising, an important school of religious existentialism arose, with Gabriel Marcel (1889–1973) as perhaps its most important representative. Its members were right to point out that existentialism had historically emerged out of the thought of a religious figure, Kierkegaard, and concluded that the obsolescence of tradition and the new emphasis on the individual did not mean God had died, as Nietzsche famously claimed. Rather, existentialism provided a new confirmation of the old religious theme of human neediness. Other existentialists, such as Karl Jaspers (1883–1969) and Ludwig Binswanger (1881–1966), tried to ally Heidegger's philosophy with Sigmund Freud's thought, arguing that existentialism in effect provided a new foundation for psychoanalysis by showing that symptoms were not biologically caused but freely chosen by an escapist self. Simone de Beauvoir (1908–1986), Sartre's companion and lover, influentially applied the insights of existentialism to gender relations, suggesting in *The Second Sex* (1949) that the discovery of the obsolescence of tradition and the relativity of values spelled the end of the validity of sexual hierarchies as well.

## EXISTENTIALISM AND ETHICS

Having spawned existentialism, which was already multiplying into many variants, Heidegger vehemently disavowed it at the moment of its triumph. He claimed that in *Being and Time* he had only introduced the focus on human existence as a means of addressing the far more important question of being in general; and in his "Letter on Humanism" (1947), addressed to his French enthusiasts, he indicted his legacy and his own earlier text as "anthropocentric." By then, however, existentialism had grown too fashionable for its repudiation by its founder to matter.

Since the fall of communism, the ethical ambiguity of existentialism—its challenge to all inherited systems of moral certitude—along with the political choices of its most famous exponents led scholars to lose interest in its intellectual content in order to focus on its putatively disastrous real-world consequences. Heidegger became a National Socialist and Sartre, shortly after World War II, broke with the apparent relativism and quietism of *Being and Nothingness* and, in an atmosphere of intellectual leftism, began a long campaign to combine his existentialism with Marxist theory and practice. How exactly to make existentialism compatible with Marxism, a deterministic science of history that would seem to be wholly at variance with existentialism's emphasis on human freedom, remained problematic and obscure in Sartre's work, even in his second major book of theoretical philosophy, *The Critique of Dialectical Reason* (1960). In any event, Sartre's turn to radicalism led, scandalously for many post–Cold War observers, to his apology for the communist Soviet Union, including the excesses of Joseph Stalin's violent reign. Sartre's one-time school friend and lifelong rival, the liberal thinker Raymond Aron (1905–1983), found it curious that a philosophy of freedom could lend its support to repression, and pilloried Marxism as a dangerous myth in *The Opium of the Intellectuals* (1955) and other writings. But other existentialists, such as Maurice Merleau-Ponty—probably the most philosophically enduring of the French band of thinkers, important notably for his attempt to ground the existentialist analysis of consciousness in the corporeal nature of human being—joined Sartre's campaign. In his *Humanism and Terror* (1947), Merleau-Ponty, who for a time coedited the main existentialist organ *Les temps modernes* with Sartre, defended violence as a morally plausible response to the deficiencies of liberal societies, since, he said, bourgeois rule also involved terror and, unlike the Soviet Union, did not promise a world beyond it. Merleau-Ponty later broke with both Sartre and Marxist politics. For his part, Camus, who could

never bring himself to join Sartre's Marxist reinvention of existentialism, dissented from the Parisian intellectuals' sympathy for communism in *The Rebel*, whose publication in 1951 led to a bitter public quarrel between the two leading lights of the movement. For Camus, a dreamy utopian future did not justify immorality now; Sartre replied that *not* to resort to violence in effect ratified existing immorality, and he supported the insurrectionary struggle of Algerians against French rule. Camus, who came from a French family in the Algerian colony, revealingly admitted preferring "[his] mother to justice."

In fact, there was little connection between philosophical existentialism and political extremism, and its founders were wrong to posit a necessary one. After all, their discovery of the relativity of values precluded all attempts at the commitment they desired, and in retrospect the popularity of existentialism may well have served liberal capitalism better than it did its rivals. Undermining all traditions and emancipating the individual from inherited obligations, even religion and community, existentialism forced the human beings it influenced to embark on pained quests for meaning, aware in advance that little lasting satisfaction might follow but condemned to the search nevertheless. As modern life has continued to provide human beings with a way to cultivate ever-new and always-transitory tastes, to engage in experiments in living for every season, and to purchase products with planned obsolescence, it has allowed increasing numbers of people to embrace absurdity without regret, as Camus would have wanted. Narcissism and consumerism, rather than illiberal extremism, were perhaps in the end the main historical legacy of the existentialist movement.

*See also* **Aron, Raymond; Camus, Albert; Cold War; Communism; Jaspers, Karl; Merleau-Ponty, Maurice; Sartre, Jean-Paul.**

BIBLIOGRAPHY

*Primary Sources*

Camus, Albert. *The Myth of Sisyphus and Other Essays.* Translated by Justin O'Brien. New York, 1955.

Sartre, Jean-Paul. *Being and Nothingness: An Essay on Phenomenological Ontology.* Translated by Hazel E. Barnes. New York, 1966.

———. *No Exit and Other Plays.* New York, 1989.

*Secondary Sources*

Aronson, Ronald. *Sartre's Second Critique*. Chicago, 1987.

Carman, Taylor, and Mark B. N. Hansen. *The Cambridge Companion to Merleau-Ponty*. Cambridge, U.K., 2005.

Cotkin, George. *Existential America*. Baltimore, Md., 2003.

Dreyfus, Hubert L. *Being-in-the-World: A Commentary on Heidegger's "Being and Time," Division I*. Cambridge, Mass., 1991.

Izenberg, Gerald N. *The Existentialist Critique of Freud: The Crisis of Autonomy*. Princeton, N.J., 1976.

Judt, Tony. *Past Imperfect: French Intellectuals, 1944–1956*. Berkeley, Calif., 1992.

———. *The Burden of Responsibility: Blum, Camus, Aron, and the French Twentieth Century*. Chicago, 1998.

Sprintzen, David A., and Adrian van den Hoven, eds. and trans. *Sartre and Camus: A Historic Confrontation*. Amherst, N.Y., 2001.

Todd, Olivier. *Albert Camus: A Life*. Translated by Benjamin Ivry. New York, 1997.

Wahl, Jean. *A Short History of Existentialism*. Translated by Forrest Williams and Stanley Maron. New York, 1949.

Wolin, Richard, ed. *The Heidegger Controversy: A Critical Reader*. New ed. Cambridge, Mass., 1993.

SAMUEL MOYN

---

**EXPOSITIONS.** The exhibitions of the twentieth century reflect the technological advances of their period. A marked difference can be seen between, on the one hand, universal exhibitions, such as those that emphasize science and technology or movements in painting, sculpture, or photography, all of which reflect aesthetic, political, or historical issues, and, on the other hand, commercial exhibitions, even when they are international in nature. Generally, an exhibition presents the international public with a national phenomenon (art, sciences, products) through signs, objects, and a range of communications. The term *exhibition* implies the showing of objects in a particular temporal and spatial context.

Exhibiting is motivated by several aims and objectives and therefore has a number of functions. The first is the symbolic function, in which the objective is largely political. The second is the commercial function: objects are for sale. The third is a scientific function: exhibitions have an informative purpose, explaining and interpreting the items on display. This function is usually in play at museums of science, technology, and ecology. Some expositions have explanatory notices or plaques for attendees to read, or films for them to view. The surrounding sound, the lighting, and the way visitors move within the exhibition space also vary according to the function of the exhibition and depend on the exhibition's intended public and the social space in which it takes place. However, every exhibition conforms to a single goal, which is to facilitate the relationship between production and reception.

## CATEGORIES OF EXHIBITIONS

With the exception of art exhibitions, which have specific traditions of their own that do not stem from the same concerns, conceiving of an exhibition involves embracing several perspectives that all relate to the concept of heritage: paying tribute to the past, leaving traces for posterity, and transmitting and interpreting movements and innovations in the exposition's particular field.

Toward the end of the twentieth century, a major upsurge of art exhibitions took place. These can be divided into several categories:

- The biennial: for example, the first São Paulo Biennial in 1951; the first biennial of contemporary African art in Dakar—Dak'Art—in 1992; and the first Montreal Biennial in 1998.
- The month of the photograph: for example, in 1980, the month of photography was launched in Paris.
- The manifesta: the first manifesta was created in Rotterdam in 1996. The encounter: for example, the 1973 opening of the International Photography Encounter at the Arles Festival.
- The fair: for example, the International Fair of Contemporary Art in Paris, which began in 1973.

What all these exhibitions had in common was that they traced and displayed a multitude of experiences—the most contemporary creation—occurring at the time they took place.

## UNIVERSAL EXHIBITIONS

In universal exhibitions, the different focuses and functions of other exhibitions are combined. In the

**A Malayan mosque under construction for the 1924 British Empire Exposition.** ©Hulton-Deutsch Collection/Corbis

nineteenth and twentieth centuries, universal exhibitions brought major technological and artistic trends together with minor phenomena in a single space. However, universal exhibitions have tended to highlight the politics of their periods, becoming concrete examples of competition between the organizing states. The first universal exhibition, The Great Exhibition of the Works of Industry of All Nations, took place in London in 1851 and featured two major themes: technological innovation and "exotic items" originating from the exhibitors' colonies. Universal exhibitions continued to have a colonial character and became stage sets for the display of products from the colonies of the European industrial powers. This culminated in 1883 with the first international colonial exhibition in Amsterdam.

Universal exhibitions were also the setting for many conferences and led to the adoption of the

meter as an international unit of measurement in 1875. The 1930s were a difficult period for universal exhibitions because they were flanked by the two world wars and the Great Depression, which began in 1929. Nevertheless, world's fairs took place in Chicago in 1933, Brussels in 1935, and Paris in 1937, and they were important political events; by contrast, Rome was forced to cancel its world's fair in 1942. World War II and the reconstruction that followed led to a suspension of universal exhibitions. It was not until 1958 that the next universal exhibition took place, in Brussels, and it reflected a profound change in attitudes toward Europe's colonies, which had begun pressing for emancipation.

Most international exhibitions have left their mark on the architecture of the cities in which they took place. For architects, these exhibitions are the privileged site of daring innovations and a source of new styles, such as art deco, which arose from the Paris exhibition of 1925. The first universal exhibition in London took place in a single building: the Crystal Palace, designed by Joseph Paxton and constructed entirely of glass and iron. The Paris exhibition in 1867 marked a radical departure in that the participants assembled in several buildings. All the universal exhibitions that have taken place in Paris left a permanent mark on the urban landscape: the 1889 exhibition brought the construction of the Eiffel Tower and the inauguration of the Paris metro; the 1900 exhibition was the occasion for several architectural achievements, including the Pont Alexandre III and the Grand and Petit Palais, as well as a Chinese pagoda that later became the site of a famous Parisian cinema; the 1937 universal exhibition brought the construction of the Palais de Tokyo and Palais de Chaillot. Just before the outbreak of World War II, the 1937 Paris exhibition was the setting for a German-Soviet architectural duel, with the Germanic eagle that crowned Albert Speer's building standing in opposition to the Soviets' vast block of marble. This exhibition was also the setting for a universal testimony against barbarism. In the Spanish pavilion, Pablo Picasso presented *Guernica*, a painting depicting the German bombing of a Basque town.

Paris was not the only city where exhibitions left an architectural legacy; other examples include Saint Louis with its Pike (1904), San Francisco with its Gay Way (1939), Brussels with its Atomium (1958), San Antonio with its the Tower of America (1968), and Osaka with its Expoland (1970). The Osaka exhibition also marked the advent of an unprecedented collaboration between artists and engineers, culminating in the creation of the Pepsi-Cola pavilion. The exhibition was also marked by an innovative use of modern architecture. These few examples illustrate a change in the universal exhibition. Initially, they were held in European countries but gradually became more genuinely international.

Universal exhibitions celebrate economic changes and demonstrate the increased power of certain states. A hundred years after it first took part in exhibitions, Japan celebrated its accession to the ranks of the great industrial powers in Osaka in 1970. The 1992 universal exhibition in Seville

The entrance to the Côte d'Or building at the Brussels exposition of 1935, a classic example of art deco architecture. ©HULTON-DEUTSCH COLLECTION/CORBIS

marked the emergence of modern Spain and reaffirmed its European membership. The same was true of Lisbon in 1998. In 2000 Hanover inaugurated the first universal exhibition of the second millennium, but it was with the 2005 Aichi exhibition, near Nagoya in Japan, dedicated to sustainable development, that the visitor entered a world of robots and technological innovations that can no longer be termed futuristic.

**ART EXHIBITIONS**

Art exhibitions generally focus on a single artist, although some present an artistic movement or a particular period: an example of this is Reconsidering the Object of Art 1965–1975 at the Museum of Contemporary Art in Los Angeles in 1995 and 1996. Others focus on a specific object or set of themes. Relations between two cities—generally major artistic centers—can also form the subject of exhibitions: for example, the Paris-Berlin exhibition in 1978, followed by

Paris-Moscow the following year at the Georges Pompidou Center in Paris.

Art exhibitions can arise from profound deliberation on the part of the curator, who then presents his or her viewpoint on how to approach the art works. This is what Harald Szeemann did in 1969 with When Attitudes Become Form at the Kunsthalle in Berne or what Norman Rosenthal and Christos M. Joachimides did in 1982 with Zeitgeist at the Martin-Gropius-Bau in Berlin.

Some exhibitions treat a work of art as a document within a historical, political, and ideological context. The exhibition's purpose is then to illustrate this entire context, as was done in the Berlin Myths of the Nations: Arena of Memories exhibition at the Deutsches Historisches Museum in 2004 and 2005. The historical dimension of some art exhibitions enables the viewer to visit a part of the past that is otherwise obscured by ideology or propaganda and make comparisons. The Berlin-Moscow 1900–1950 exhibition at the Berlinische Galerie in 2004 is a good example of this. As the philosopher and art critic Yves Michaud observed, "There are as many kinds of exhibition as there are methods of classifying objects and since everything resembles something else in some respect, there is a confusing multitude of ways of assembling objects or art works" (Michaud, p. 129).

## ART INSTITUTIONS AND EXHIBITIONS

Since the nineteenth century, artists have dealt with institutions. In 1855, after his canvases had been rejected thirteen times for the universal exhibition, Gustave Courbet presented forty canvases in his own pavilion on Avenue Montaigne, financed by his patron, Alfred Bruyas. This was the first solo exhibition held by an artist in his own lifetime.

The exhibition can be the site of a battle between artistic movements, as happened with Paul Cézanne's triumph and the creation of the fauvist movement at the Salon d'Automne in 1904 or, in the realm of abstract painting, the Degenerate Art exhibition in Munich in 1937. The Armory Show, which was held in the New York armory and then in Chicago in 1913, remains one of the major art exhibitions and is credited with disseminating throughout the world the works of European avant-garde artists such as Alexander Archipenko, Georges Braque, Constantin Brancusi, Claude Monet, and Vincent van Gogh.

In the twentieth century, institutions emerged that were historically important for their architectural modernity and their acquisition policies; they were also notable for exhibitions that are remembered both for their innovations and for the scandals they generated. Examples include the creation of the Museum of Modern Art in New York in 1929, the Paris opening of the Musée National d'Art Moderne in 1947, and the inauguration of the UNESCO building in Paris in 1958. In 1977 the Georges Pompidou Center opened its doors with two major exhibitions: Paris-New York and a Marcel Duchamp retrospective. In the last quarter of the twentieth century, two events are worthy of note: the inauguration of the Ludwigsmuseum in Cologne and the Reina Sofía Art Center in Madrid in 1986.

As showcases for contemporary art, galleries have played a major role in the development of art movements. The Denise René Gallery played a significant part in the dissemination of abstract art and brought renown to the kinetic artists in France after 1944. In a relatively rare phenomenon in the art world, in 2001 the Georges Pompidou Center paid tribute to the substantial role played by this gallery.

Museums and other art institution are not the only sites for art exhibitions, however. Joseph Beuys organized an exhibition in the stables at the Van der Grinten house in Kranenburg in 1963, and in 1973 the Contemporanea exhibition was held in the underground parking lot at the Villa Borghese in Rome. Such nontraditional spaces form a symbolic extension of the museum.

The history of exhibitions can be traced through the scandals that they have generated. At the exhibition 1960–1972: Douze ans d'art contemporain en France (1960–1972: Twelve years of contemporary art in France), the Swiss artist Ben Vautier displayed a flask of his urine, incurring the wrath of politicians and sparking police intervention. In 2000 the machine produced by the Belgian artist Wim Delvoye, *Cloaca*, which artificially reproduces the human digestive system, was placed on public view and has been the object of polemic ever since. The same has happened to the wax sculpture by Maurizio Cattelan, *La nona ora* (The ninth hour), which represents the pope being crushed by a meteorite.

## CONCLUSION

In the twentieth century, exhibitions, whether international or commercial, have served to create, display, and influence art and technology. In doing so, they served as an important catalyst for the idea, for its dissemination and eventual commodification.

*See also* **Architecture; Art Deco; Colonialism; Duchamp, Marcel; Guernica; Picasso, Pablo.**

### BIBLIOGRAPHY

Allwood. John. *The Great Exhibitions.* London, 1977.

Bennett, Tony. *The Birth of the Museum: History, Theory, Politics.* New York, 1995.

Kavanagh, Gaynor, ed. *Museum Languages: Objects and Texts.* New York, 1991.

Michaud, Yves. *L'artiste et les commissaires: Quatre essais non pas sur l'art contemporain mais sur ceux qui s'en occupent.* Collection Rayon Art, Jacqueline Chambon. Nimes, France, 1989.

Miles, Roger, and Lauro Zavala, eds. *Towards the Museum of the Future: New European Perspectives.* London, 1994.

Ory, Pascal. *L'expo universelle.* Brussels, 1989.

CYRIL THOMAS

---

**EXPRESSIONISM.** Expressionism at the beginning of the twentieth century was a central and eastern European movement that brought together painters, sculptors, writers (of literature and for the theater), art critics, architects, filmmakers, engravers, and musicians. More specifically, in 1912 the magazine *Der Sturm* used the term *expressionism* to characterize the art scene of the day in contrast to impressionism. Paul Fechter, in his book *Der Expressionismus,* published in Munich in 1914, was the first critic to use the word *expressionism* to refer to a trend in German art. For Fechter, expressionism had come to embody the spirit of the times—a spirit that, in the realm of the arts in Germany, took the form of a fight against

governmental authority; a rupture defined by the formation of "secessions" or "new secessions" of groups of artists independent of the official culture of William II (r. 1888–1918). In 1897 the Vienna Secession had freed artists from academic painting, proclaiming a more individual art and thus paving the way for the Berlin Secession the following year. Until 1913 the Berlin New Secession helped open up access to European, and especially French, art (the exhibition of impressionist paintings in Berlin museums was forbidden by the government). These new approaches were immediately disseminated through the reviews. The founding in 1910 of the Berlin magazine *Der Sturm* by Herwarth Walden (pseudonym of Georg Lewin, 1878–1941) and the subsequent founding of *Die Aktion* provided a way to convey the new ideas, reflecting the desire for liberty and freedom from institutional constraints—the basic elements of the avant-garde in Europe.

## DIE BRÜCKE

The rejection of academic art and teaching allowed four students at the Technische Hochschule (Technical School) in Dresden—Ernst Ludwig Kirchner (1880–1938), Fritz Bleyl (1880–1966), Erich Heckel (1883–1970), and Karl Schmidt-Rottluff (1884–1976)—to form an association in 1905. Schmidt-Rottluff proposed to call it "Die Brücke" (The bridge); the choice of this name was made explicit by a woodcut made the same year representing Dresden's Augustus Bridge, which links the old town to the new town. Other group members were Max Pechstein (1881–1955) and (briefly) Emil Nolde (1867–1956). Subject matter linked to their environments—such as lake scenes from the Bavarian landscape, in which nude figures are merged with nature (Otto Muller), or nostalgia for the landscapes of northern Germany (Nolde)—contrasted with the context of urban development and rapid industrialization that inspired the futurists. With the exception of Pechstein, the artists of Die Brücke were not academically trained and were thus unencumbered by doctrine. They painted twisted, angular shapes with violent contrasts and pure colors outlined in black: yellow faces, red trees, or blue streets, inspired by *The Scream* (1893, considered the first "expressionist drama") by Edvard Munch (1863–1944) or the violent colors of Vincent Van Gogh (1853–1890).

***Almanach Der Blaue Reiter.*** Cover illustration by Wassily Kandinsky, 1912. ERICH LESSING/ART RESOURCE, NY

Taking their inspiration from non-European sculpture, the artists produced series of sculpted and painted nudes (from 1910 to 1914) with exaggerated thighs and breasts, their curves accentuated with black paint, that show a return to a primitivism recalling that of Paul Gauguin (1848–1903). Until 1913 the artists of Die Brücke also reinvigorated the graphic arts through their recurrent use of the technique of woodcut engravings.

## DER BLAUE REITER

Wassily Kandinsky (1866–1944) and Alexej von Jawlensky (1864–1941), Russian painters who had emigrated to Germany, settled in Murnau (south of Munich), near Lake Staffel, in 1908. Kandinsky's concrete references in his work were becoming increasingly enigmatic: his gestures were expressive, his palette essentially freed from the real appearance of objects.

In January 1909 Kandinsky and Jawlensky founded the Neue Künstler-Vereinigung München (New association of Munich artists, NKVM). This heterogeneous group, whose members had varying objectives, organized its first exhibition in December 1909 at Heinrich Thannhäuser's Moderne Galerie (the second exhibition was in September 1910). The painter Franz Marc (1880–1916), who met Kandinsky for the first time in 1911, explained that "This bold enterprise, which consists in sublimating the 'matter' that impressionism clings to, is a necessary reaction that began at Pont-Aven with Gauguin. . . . What seems to us so promising in these new experiments by the Association of Artists is that fact that these works . . . provide valuable examples of the manipulation of space, rhythm, and chromatic theory" (quoted in *Figures du moderne*, p. 199; translated from the French).

In 1911 Kandinsky resigned as president of the association because one of his *Compositions* was rejected during preparation for the next exhibition. Immediately, Marc and Kandinsky founded the group Der Blaue Reiter (The blue rider) and organized an alternative exhibit to coincide with the third NKVM show. Fifteen artists with varying artistic visions, including musicians such as Arnold Schoenberg (1874–1951), presented their works. Kandinsky and Marc used terminology that they hoped to use in their publishing projects; those projects culminated in the publication in May 1912 of the *Almanach Der Blaue Reiter*. This rich and eclectic publication combined avant-garde works with examples of Egyptian and Far Eastern art, folk art, children's drawings, and paintings by amateurs. That same year Paul Klee (1879–1940) joined the second Blaue Reiter exhibit, while Kandinsky's work began to combine figurative elements (such as knights and trees) and nonfigurative elements and to dissociate color from line through the use of watercolor. He published *Concerning the Spiritual in Art*, developed the concept of "internal necessity," and laid the first foundations for abstraction. Kandinsky left Germany in 1914.

## EMERGENCE OF AN AVANT-GARDE
In this context of their hatred of social conventions and the struggle against traditional values and authority, some German artists saw in the war of 1914 the potential to destroy the old order and build a better society. Kirchner, August Macke (1887–1914), and Marc voluntarily enlisted. Marc (whose *Letters from the Front* provides valuable testimony), Macke, and Wilhelm Morgner (1891–1917) died in combat. After the signing of the Treaty of Versailles, in the context of the payment of war reparations owed to France and severe unemployment, the young Weimar Republic, its government dominated by the Social Democrats, awarded positions of responsibility in teaching as well as honorific titles: Nolde, Schmidt-Rottluff, and Kirchner were elected to the Prussian Academy of Arts. Most of the Blaue Reiter artists fled Germany. After the rise of Nazism, the works of German expressionist artists were deemed "degenerate"; they were "displayed" in 1938 at the *Entartete Kunst* (Degenerate art) exhibit.

Die Brücke and Der Blaue Reiter were two complementary groups that contributed to the establishment of the avant-garde in Europe at the beginning of the twentieth century.

*See also* **Avant-Garde; Kandinsky, Wassily; Klee, Paul; Modernism.**

BIBLIOGRAPHY

*Primary Sources*

Fechter, Paul. *Expressionismus.* Munich, 1914. Rev. ed., Munich, 1920.

Kandinsky, Wassily. *Uber das Geitige in der Kunst.* Munich, 1912. Translated as *Concerning the Spiritual in Art.* New York, 1947.

*Secondary Sources*

*Figures du moderne: L'expressionism en Allemagne, Dresden, Munich, Berlin, 1940–1914.* Paris, 1992. Exhibition catalog.

Gordon, Donald. "German Expressionism." In *"Primitivism" in 20th Century Art*, edited by William Rubin. New York, 1984.

Lloyd, Jill. *German Expressionism: Primitivism and Modernity.* New Haven, Conn., 1991.

Myers, Bernard. *Expressionistes allemands: Une génération en révolte*, translated by Jean Rousselot. Paris, 1967.

CAROLINE TRON-CARROZ

---

**EZHOV, NIKOLAI.** See **Yezhov, Nikolai.**

**FALANGE.** The Spanish political party commonly called the Falange was founded on 29 October 1933 as the Falange Española by José Antonio Primo de Rivera (1903–1936), a young lawyer and son of the former military dictator, Miguel Primo de Rivera. In February 1934 the party merged with a small Castilian Fascist party, the Juntas de Ofensiva Nacional Sindicalista (JONS). Primo de Rivera became supreme leader of the new organization, the Falange Española de las JONS, in October 1934. That same month the new party adopted most of its official paraphernalia, including the blue shirt, the red and black flag (a variation of the anarchist flag), and, significantly, the yoke and arrows adopted by the Spanish sovereigns Isabella and Ferdinand in the late fifteenth century. This set of symbols pretended to combine the semiproletarian nature of the new party with its roots in the supposedly best aspects of Spanish tradition. Although Primo de Rivera rejected being called a fascist and always insisted in the exclusive Spanish character of his party, he received financial backing from the Italian Fascist leader Benito Mussolini. By the same token, despite his proclaimed independence from both rightist and leftist groups, Primo de Rivera repeatedly obtained financial and political support from rich patrons and was elected to parliament in 1933 as part of an electoral ticket that included prominent conservative politicians and businessmen.

The ideological discourse of the Falange shared many fundamental traits with fascist groups elsewhere: the rejection of both liberal politics and class struggle, the cult of the state, vaguely worded ideas of social reform, exaggerated nationalism, the exaltation of youth, sublimation of violence, and the necrophilia surrounding the cult of the "fallen ones." The exaltation of Catholicism—despite some anticlericalism—and of the glorious imperial past of the nation gave the party its differentiating aspects. The group attracted a relatively youthful militancy, with a disproportionate presence of students. Most of the leaders came from middle- and upper-class backgrounds, but some workers also joined. The frequent violent confrontations with left-wing groups led the Popular Front government to ban the Falange shortly before the start of the civil war in July 1936. The Falange was deeply involved in the military uprising that precipitated the civil war, and although its role was subordinate to the military, its militias offered the initially weak rebel forces valuable support in many parts of the country. Primo de Rivera, who had been arrested in March 1936, remained trapped in the Republican zone and on 20 November 1936 was executed.

The Falange lost its highly charismatic leader at a critical moment. On the eve of the war, the party had scarcely ten thousand militants. The dynamic of political radicalization and social militarization that the war brought made the Falange militias very attractive to both militants of traditional conservative parties and political neophytes. Hundreds of thousands of them flocked to its ranks, which reached around one million by the end of the conflict in March 1939. In the meantime, roughly half of the "old shirts," or prewar militants, had perished. But the party changed from the top as well as from below. The surviving leaders of the Falange moved to rebuild the organization, but they were deeply divided. The elected successor of Primo de Rivera, the plebeian, and not too skillful, Manuel Hedilla, was constantly undermined by the circle around the aristocratic relatives of the party founder. Tensions grew high and in April 1937 led to a brief armed confrontation in Salamanca, where Francisco Franco's headquarters were located. Franco, who did not have a party of his own, seized the opportunity: he detained Hedilla, forced the merger of the Falange with the other party/militia in the rebel zone, the ultraconservative Comunión Tradicionalista (also called the Carlists), and made himself head of the newly born single party, the Falange Española Tradicionalista y de las JONS. With this maneuver, the military and the conservative forces of Spain, so many times bitterly criticized by Primo de Rivera, had put the Falange at their service.

From then until the end of the dictatorship in 1975, the role of the Falange was to serve Franco's political needs. It gave him an organization to discipline politics in his "new Spain," to organize mass rallies showing support for his regime, and to dispense sinecures to his followers. Because the nascent Francoist regime was a coalition of different social and political forces and institutions (including the army, the church, monarchists, urban and rural bourgeoisie, and landowning peasants), the Falange was constantly used by the dictator as a counterweight to pressure from those forces. Officially the Falange was given responsibility for the regime's social policies, and particularly control over the official unions. In reality, the party owed whatever influence it had to the dictator's wishes, and its weight in the government's decision-making process was minimal. Its popular support was always very limited, while the image of its leaders and militants as rough opportunists was widespread, even among the regime's supporters.

See also Fascism; Franco, Francisco; Spanish Civil War.

BIBLIOGRAPHY

Ellwood, Sheelagh M. *Spanish Fascism in the Franco Era: Falange Española de las JONS, 1936–1976.* Basingstoke, U.K., 1987.

Payne, Stanley G. *Falange: A History of Spanish Fascism.* Stanford, Calif., 1961.

Preston, Paul. *Franco: A Biography.* London, 1993.

ANTONIO CAZORLA-SANCHEZ

---

**FALKLANDS WAR.** The Falklands War broke out in 1982 because the United Kingdom and Argentina claimed sovereignty over the islands. Neither country had an unambiguously legitimate claim to the territory, and the dispute was further complicated by the settlement of the islands by British people in the nineteenth century, whose descendants claimed the right to self-determination—a claim that was heard with increasing sympathy in British politics. United Nations Resolution 2065 of 1965 called for "self-determination of all peoples," but also for the end of colonization in all its forms, including the Falklands (for Argentina, the "Malvinas"). Attempts to resolve the dispute made little progress, even though the British were reluctant possessors of the Falklands, and in 1975 Argentina warned that its patience was not inexhaustible. British hopes that a compromise could be found by an arrangement whereby Britain would cede Argentina's sovereignty claim but lease back the islands for seventy years were frustrated in 1982 by the islanders.

In 1981 Britain conducted a defense review, concentrating its military and naval assets on the NATO area and withdrawing the HMS *Endurance* from its patrol of the Falklands. Argentina tested British resolve following the landing of some scrap dealers on 19 March 1982 on the British dependency of South Georgia. This incident was a catalyst. When the British ordered Argentina to remove the dealers, the Argentina Junta on 30 March decided to implement an invasion plan drawn up at the end of 1981. On 2 April Argentina seized the Falklands. The British Government led by Margaret Thatcher responded by preparing a Task Force, despite some doubts on the part of the Defense Secretary John Nott. They also asked U.S. President Ronald Reagan to mediate. The Task Force was ordered to sail on 5 April.

This was a risky enterprise. The Falklands were 8,000 miles away; the South Atlantic winter was near. The British were fortunate that the United

States allowed the use of the airstrip on Ascension Island as a staging post. Other military assistance was given covertly. The European Union imposed economic sanctions on Argentina. Argentina had the advantage of occupying the islands, proximity to the mainland, and the possibility of spinning out negotiations. The British Task Force commander, Admiral John Forster "Sandy" Woodward, was aware that time was not on his side and that if he lost even one of his two aircraft carriers he might well lose the war. Air power would therefore play an essential role in the conflict, and the Argentine Air Force possessed Exocet missiles and skilled pilots. On 28 April the British imposed a total exclusion zone around the islands. On 2 May Woodward asked for a change to rules of engagement to enable the submarine HMS *Conqueror* to sink the Argentine warship ARA *General Belgrano*. This ended the Argentine navy's part in the war, though it cost the British some good opinions, and was followed by the sinking of HMS *Sheffield*. The war was now in earnest.

U.S. mediation failed, and it is difficult to see how these and subsequent mediations could have succeeded, since for both Argentina and Britain the bottom line was that their claim to sovereignty could not be compromised, though other items, such as the administration of the Falklands while a final settlement could be worked out, were negotiable. The diplomatic situation influenced the military and was influenced by it. When the British landed unopposed at San Carlos Bay on 21 May, and the second battalion Parachute Regiment won the hard-fought Battle of Goose Green on 28 May, it was tempting for the British government to envisage military victory and disentangle itself from negotiations. The superior professionalism of the British forces suggests that (in retrospect) a British victory was assured. But the British lost mobility when the *Atlantic Conveyor,* containing the bulk of the helicopter force, was sunk in San Carlos Bay. The British army had to march across rough terrain in harsh weather, and with an increasingly large logistical "tail." Not all Argentine forces fought with resolution, but many of them did, and had the advantage of standing on the defensive in prepared positions. A British military reverse might damage public support for the campaign, which was complicated by the continuing efforts by the United Nations to resolve the conflict by

negotiation. As the British forces moved close to Stanley, where the Argentine army waited (increasingly cold and uncomfortable), such negotiations were of greater value to Argentina.

On 11 June British forces attacked the Argentine defensive positions around Stanley. A series of hard-fought battles on the hills and ridges, with the British attacking at night and engaging the Argentine forces in bitter close-quarter fighting, resulted in an Argentine surrender on 14 June. Argentina suffered 655 casualties; British losses were 255 (including two Falkland Islanders).

For Thatcher, the war marked the end of a "nation in retreat" and the beginning of a recovery of national confidence. For Argentina, it ended the rule of the military junta, ushered in democracy, and struck a blow at Argentine assumptions about its preeminence in South America—but not the end to Argentine claims to the Malvinas. The Falklands War was a small one, but remained the object of fascination. This is because it was a "regular" war, one fought by armies in uniform using a range of weapons, from the latest technology to trench warfare, and deploying land, sea, and air forces. In an age when the only conflict anticipated was one with the Warsaw Pact, the Falklands offered some kind of guide to modern war as a conflict that must hold lessons for the future. British and Argentine methods of directing the campaign, including the political control of the war, were likewise examined closely. The war turned out for the British to be a last one, in the sense that their forces would probably never again fight as a separate military machine, but would work with other European or American forces, in Bosnia, Kosovo, and Iraq, and in the "War on Terror."

*See also* **British Empire; United Kingdom.**

BIBLIOGRAPHY

Boyce, George. *The Falklands War.* New York, 2005.

Brown, David. *The Royal Navy and the Falklands War.* London, 1987.

Ethell, Jeffrey, and Alfred Price. *Air War South Atlantic.* London, 1983.

Freedman, Lawrence, and Virginia Gamba-Stonehouse. *Signals of War: The Falklands Conflict of 1982.* London, 1990.

Freedman, Lawrence. *The Falklands War: The Official History.* 2 vols. London, 2005.

Hastings, Max, and Simon Jenkins. *The Battle for the Falklands.* London, 1983.

Middlebrook, Martin. *The Fight for the "Malvinas": The Argentine Forces in the Falklands War.* London, 1989.

Moro, Rubén O. *The History of the South Atlantic Conflict: The War for the Malvinas.* New York, 1989.

D. GEORGE BOYCE

---

# FAMINE, UKRAINIAN. *See* Ukraine.

---

# FANON, FRANTZ (1925–1961), writer, psychiatrist, and revolutionary.

Frantz Fanon was born a French citizen on the West Indies island of Martinique. He fought for the Free French Forces during World War II, took his medical training in Paris, and practiced psychiatry. His training and his life offered Fanon the evidence and the terms for grappling with some of the most important problems of his time. What made him a radical was his certainty that political analysis, by leading to the diagnosis of social problems, could help popular revolt to produce fundamental change. Fanon's work remains of scholarly and political interest primarily because of his efforts to identify the foundations of what he termed "Manichean thinking": how terms such as *native* and *colonizer* or *white* and *black* came to confine people in polarized relationships. His aim was to open possibilities for more complex, and more fully human, understanding.

Fanon was born on 25 July 1925 to a family whose racial background, economic position, comfort with the French language, and embrace of French culture led local society to identify as white. The arrival in Martinique of French troops in 1940, sent by the collaborationist Vichy state, disrupted this local economy of race. Yet even the troops' crude assertion that skin color rather than culture was the primary marker of race did not fully prepare Fanon for how color defined him, first in the Free French Forces and then as a medical student in the French metropolis. His encounters with the

certainty among the common people and among the elite that blacks could not be French because they were different from whites inspired the work he presented as his doctoral thesis, which appeared in 1952 as *Black Skin, White Masks.*

In his analysis of racism, Fanon insists that it arises historically, in specific times and places, and that it now had systematic effects. He argued that in the current context it had become the most visible aspect of an interlocking network of economic, military, and political organizing structures because of the centrality of colonialism, which directly depended on racism. Fanon's novel focus was on how colonialism as a system controlled people's psychological options. He claimed that the colonial situation enabled disdain to determine white conceptions of blacks to such a degree that blacks struggled simply to be recognized as an "Other," as comparable to the white "Self." Because no dialectical relationship was possible, colonial racism wreaked psychological havoc on both blacks and whites. Steeped in Freudian assumptions though not himself a psychoanalyst, Fanon focused on sexual desire and the complications of sexual and gender identities in order to understand how colonial racism structured individuals. In his reading, the type of racist dynamic that colonialism had produced made it necessary for blacks to engage in struggle against both their own desire to be recognized as white and against the colonizers.

During the year he spent as the head of a psychiatric hospital in Algeria, Fanon came to see that Algeria's independence struggle offered revolutionary possibilities. In 1956 he moved to Tunis, where the men leading that fight had set up their headquarters. He continued to practice psychiatry, but also taught, wrote for the official newspaper, and advised the leaders of the Algerian Front de Libération Nationale (FLN; National liberation front), which he later represented as ambassador to Ghana. Drawing on his understanding of what revolutionary action could mean, Fanon published his final book in 1961. His goal in *The Wretched of the Earth* was to provide an ideological roadmap that would allow colonized peoples to benefit from the cascading series of decolonizations. His prescriptions sought to avoid the dangers inherent in any struggle that took place at a national level and, in addition, to allow the revolt against colonial racism's "thingification" of the colonized to succeed. In his preface to Fanon's book, Jean-Paul Sartre proclaimed that "the Third World finds *itself* and speaks to *itself* through his voice." Because it offered a convincing alternative to Marxism's privileging of the proletariat and of class relations, the book immediately became a touchstone for New Left radicals in Western Europe and the United States.

Like his other wartime writings, *The Wretched of the Earth* emphasizes that violence lies at the foundation of the colonial relationship. Western colonialism, rather than take responsibility for its use of violence, created racial groups as a schematic overlay to explain relations of domination, which recast the violent maintenance of the colonizers' control as a natural relationship of superior to inferior. In his final works, Fanon argued that only violence by the colonized could both destroy the colonial system and set the stage to move beyond the destructive effects of the colonizer/colonized dyad. Despite his cogent recognition of the dangers of embracing violence, Fanon is often vilified for his supposed celebration of revolutionary violence. He died of leukemia in 1961 at the age of thirty-six.

*See also* **Algerian War; Colonialism; Sartre, Jean-Paul.**

BIBLIOGRAPHY

*Primary Sources*

Fanon, Frantz. *Studies in a Dying Colonialism.* Translated by Haakon Chevalier. New York, 1965. Translation of *L'an V de la révolution algérienne.*

———. *Black Skin, White Masks.* Translated by Charles Lam Markmann. New York, 1967. Translation of *Peau noire, masques blancs.*

———. *Toward the African Revolution, Political Essays.* Translated by Haakon Chevalier. New York, 1967. Translation of *Pour la révolution africaine. Écrits politiques.*

———. *The Wretched of the Earth.* Translated by Constance Farrington. New York, 1968. Translation of *Les damnés de la terre.*

*Secondary Sources*

Cherki, Alice. *Frantz Fanon: Portrait.* Paris, 2000.

Gates, Henry Louis, Jr. "Critical Fanonism." *Critical Inquiry* 17, no. 3 (Spring 1991): 457–471.

Gendzier, Irene L. *Frantz Fanon: A Critical Study.* New York, 1973.

Macey, David. *Frantz Fanon: A Biography.* New York, 2001.

Sekyi-Otu, Ato. *Fanon's Dialectic of Experience.* Cambridge, Mass., 1996.

Sharpley-Whiting, Denean T. *Frantz Fanon: Conflicts and Feminism.* Lanham, Md., 1997.

TODD SHEPARD

---

**FASCISM.** Even in the early twenty-first century, the term *fascism* remains one of fundamental ambiguity and controversy. Unlike many other "-isms," it still invites competing perceptions of what it is and what it stood (or even stands) for. Originally a word borrowed from the ancient Roman imagery (*fasces* = bundle of rods surrounding an ax) coined in the Italian post–World War I context to express radical collective action in defense of the nation (*Fasci della Difesa Nazionale*), it was appropriated by Benito Mussolini (1883–1945) to label his nascent ultranationalist movement that eventually became the National Fascist Party (*Partito Nazionale Fascista*, PNF). Already in the early 1920s socialist observers ascribed a generic import to the term, as a historically specific reactionary vehicle for recasting monopoly capitalism and crushing socialist mobilization. At the same time, fellow travelers, disciples, and imitators across the Continent in the 1920s and 1930s invoked the term or alluded to a sort of ideological-political affinity with the Italian model. The alliance between Mussolini's regime and Adolf Hitler's (1889–1945) National Socialist Germany was similarly founded on the premise of such a deep kinship in search of a universal post-liberal and postsocialist order. The impressive diffusion of *fascism* as ideology and type of regime in the interwar period led the controversial German historian Ernst Nolte to declare that the 1918–1945 period was the indisputable "era of fascism" and thus cast the phenomenon as the product of a particular continent-wide set of historical circumstances that manifested itself in a plethora of national permutations.

Yet, *fascism* remains superlatively hard to define in a way that generates academic consensus. One prominent analyst has described the fray of fascist studies as a "deserted battlefield." Its allegedly generic nature has been fiercely contested by those who still perceive it as either a purely Italian phenomenon or a descriptive term that relates to style rather than substance. Some would deny it any degree of ideological import, thereby reducing it to a set of ad hoc practices that have been inflated into something more by subsequent academic wishful thinking. While historians tend to agree with Nolte that 1945 represented the cataclysmic end of the "fascist era," others discerned an allegedly wider conceptual relevance that goes far beyond historical periods or geographic settings. And the catalog of controversy goes on: irrational and antimodern or an alternative radical modern formula? Antiliberal, antisocialist, or both? Revolutionary or counterrevolutionary/reactionary? Right-wing or syncretic or even a "scavenger"? What about its relation to other concepts, such as authoritarianism, totalitarianism, and dictatorship, with which it shared some crucial but partial similarities? Finally, if "fascism" had any intellectual substance, where did it come from and how did it shape its ideological content?

### INTELLECTUAL ORIGINS: THE SEARCH FOR ALTERNATIVES TO LIBERALISM

Even the task of searching for an intellectual origin of fascism before World War I is fraught with controversy. For, unlike other contemporary "-isms," the term was not used specifically by thinkers to designate a specific body of thought in opposition to existing doctrines. A plethora of potential derivations have indeed been suggested: the break with and revision of Marxian socialism by the French theorist Georges Sorel (1847–1922) and subsequently by the National Syndicalism movement; the concept of an all-encompassing ethical state developed by the German philosopher Wilhelm Friedrich Georg Hegel (1770–1831); the mystic conception of the "nation" professed by the Italian liberal nationalist Giuseppe Mazzini (1805–1872); and the fascination with heroic politics conveyed through the philosophy of Friedrich Nietzsche (1844–1900). In fact, the search for fascism's origins has implicated even the critique of the French Revolution and the Enlightenment by the French theorist Joseph De Maistre (1753–1821), articulated as far back as the last years of the eighteenth century.

For some this search for fascism's intellectual derivation appears as a dubious attempt to read history backward. This, however, should not prevent seeking to locate fascism in the context of generic historical conditions in the late nineteenth and early twentieth century that subsequently found fertile ground in particularly national contexts. Essentially, the origins of what later came to be identified as fascism lay in a milieu of disillusionment with the condition of civilization and society at a time of a seeming liberal ascendancy and at the dawn of a radical socialist alternative. This meant that fascism was a "latecomer" as a political ideology, attempting to occupy a precarious position in the overcrowded spectrum of visions for the future of civilization. Already in the second half of the nineteenth century certain thinkers across Europe had launched a wholesale attack against the liberal focus on individualism, rights, and pluralism. The function of the liberal state as an agnostic (neutral) agent of promoting freedom had been identified as the primary source of moral decline, social malaise, and cultural degeneration. Parliamentarism and representative government became the soft target of a multiple radical critique that focused on corruption, the cynicism of political elites, the empty rhetoric of social justice accompanied by very limited reforms, the yawning gap between government and people, and the moral relativism of "modern" society. Whereas some of the critics opted for a retreat into antimodern, nostalgic prescriptions in an attempt to reset the clock of history, many had already assumed the advent of modernity and sought to recast it in a decidedly *postliberal* fashion. In other words, the revision of the course of history sought by disparate observers in the second half of the nineteenth century had a common target (liberalism and modern society) but explored fundamentally divergent paths for a different order.

In the four decades before World War I socialism provided the main modern alternative to liberalism, organizing and channeling radical energies across the Continent into a supranational movement in search of a postliberal society. However, by the turn of the century the ambitious prediction of collective revolutionary action predicated on socialist ideology appeared further than ever before. Thinkers initially steeped in revolutionary socialism vented their frustration through seeking a new type of modern alternative that, while still seeking a postliberal order, also antagonized Marxism's stress on materialism and class struggle. Fusing revolution, modernity, and irrational myth, they sought to identify a different vehicle for historical change. At a time of growing populist mobilization and participation in the political arena the "nation" appeared a far more potent conduit for collective action than did social "class"—the focus of socialism. This new alternative grew not only in opposition to liberalism but also as an absolute antithesis of the socialist formula in search for a "third way." It was not about simple reform or retreat into a premodern golden age; instead, it capitalized on the drive of both liberal empowerment of the masses and socialist revolutionary dynamics but sought to redirect the course of modernity in a predominantly ultranationalist direction.

The devastating experiences of World War I and the Bolshevik Revolution in Russia provided crucial ammunition for an urgent synthesis of previously disparate strands of radical thought. They also further alienated large sectors of the European societies from the liberal experiment while turning the socialist alternative into a tangible—and therefore threatening—reality that could spread from Russia across the Continent on the basis of the professed "world revolution." As a chauvinistic version of nationalism was continuously being nurtured in the decades leading to the Great War and received a further boost in its aftermath (the Versailles Treaty of 1919 and the complications of redrawing the boundaries of post-1918 Europe), the appeal of radical nationalism intensified. The impression that liberal Europe had entered a phase of terminal decline at a time that the socialist experiment in Russia threatened to engulf the Continent with its internationalist revolutionary creed had two crucial effects: first, it robbed parliamentary democracy of its last vestiges of legitimacy; and, second, it afforded a sense of historic urgency to nationalist populist politics as the only effective antisocialist radical alternative.

Thus fascism emerged from the ashes of World War I as a revolutionary, radical nationalist ideology, based on the glorification of an idealized "nation" and on collective activism. It was populist in terms of its political conduct, obsessed with reversing the process of alleged national decline,

and offering instead a vision of wholesale regeneration ("rebirth") for the members of the "national community"—and only them. Fascism was a particularly historical articulation of nationalism—of an extreme, radical, exclusive, and holistic nationalism that rejected violently any form of dissidence and nonconformity to its vision. Although France had been the intellectual incubator of protofascist ideologies, Italy became the testing ground for its first political articulation. Within the course of five years (1914–1919) Mussolini completed an astounding ideological transformation from renegade revolutionary socialist leader into the Duce of an ultranationalist populist movement that preached wholesale national collective action as the only meaningful path to regeneration. The synthesis that Mussolini spearheaded in Italy between 1917 and 1921 was rooted in exactly this sense of liberalism's political impasse and socialism's allegedly impending onslaught. But, rather than harking back to premodern ideals, it sought to involve the nation in a history-making collective struggle for a revolutionary break with a recent historical course dominated by liberalism and socialism. Such a synthesis was essentially negative: disparate forces ranging from conservative radical nationalists to the (ultramodern and antitraditionalist) futurists came together in an open-ended struggle for a postliberal order that ought to be spared from the socialist experiment—a struggle in which the nation as an organic, culturally homogenous, and indivisible unity would be the uncontested protagonist.

### THE "FASCIST EPOCH": 1922–1945

The period between the political formation of the fascist movement and the appointment of Mussolini as head of a coalition government in October 1922 was too brief to allow the resolution of ideological ambiguities or even tensions. By 1925, when the Duce ushered Italy into the era of the Fascist dictatorship, fascism had already been arbitrarily associated with disparate trends: a generic reactionary offspring of monopoly capitalism for the Communist International; a new, highly promising system of rule for antiparliamentary elites across the Continent; and a source of inspiration for a novel style of politics that could be appropriated by radical movements beyond Italy in search of the same goal of a postliberal transformation. It took Mussolini himself a bit longer to

**Fascists burn socialist literature, Rome, November 1922.** ©BETTMANN/CORBIS

declare a wider relevance for his Italian experiment: in 1929 he spoke of fascism as an "export product" and a few years later (1932) went so far as to claim that the twentieth century would be a truly fascist epoch, just like the eighteenth and the nineteenth centuries belonged to liberalism and socialism respectively.

But what did it mean to be a fascist? Unlike socialism in the Bolshevik Soviet Union, there was no Marxian gospel or Leninist scripture from which to draw dogmatic inspiration. Even Mussolini's attempt to codify the fascist doctrine in 1932 in cooperation with the prominent philosopher Giovanni Gentile (1875–1944) came too late to have a real impact on the formation of the fascist experiment in Italy. What the doctrine emphasized, however, was fascism's emphasis on open-ended, heroic collective action for the spiritual regeneration of the nation. This goal was the necessary

condition for the realization of Fascist Italy's historic mission: as a "third Rome" (heir to the universalist legacies of the Roman Empire and of Catholicism) the rekindled national spirit would be the harbinger of a global political, socioeconomic, and cultural revolution. The absence of a sacrosanct doctrine was regarded as a blessing, for a fixed ideology could curtail the spontaneity of collective action. Instead, fascism promised an open-ended, "holistic" radical utopia-in-the-making of which the whole nation would be the primary agent and the beneficiary.

The growing idea that Mussolini alone incarnated the fascist doctrine bred an overreliance on the "cult of the duce" and a consequent monopolization of the movement by him. Mussolini made a series of fundamental choices in the second half of the 1920s that established the broad parameters of the fascist political experiment and provided a more tangible definition of what fascism stood for. The institutional-judicial reforms of Alfredo Rocco (1875–1935)—a prominent nationalist with far more conservative leanings than many early fascists (*fascisti della prima ora*) would have desired—set the foundations for an all-encompassing state that would function as the primary vehicle for national mobilization. As a result, the party was formally placed under the institutional tutelage of the state and of the Duce. Furthermore, calls from more radical members for a "continuous revolution" and a wholesale break with the past were crushed under the institutional rigidity of Rocco's reforms and the doctrine of "*all within the state, nothing outside the state, nothing against the state.*" The signing of the Lateran Pacts with the Vatican in 1929 also sent mixed signals: on the one hand, the agreement settled the only remaining obstacle to the full legitimation of the Italian state by resolving the "Roman Question" (the schism between church and state that had beset the Italian state ever since the completion of its national unification in 1870); on the other, it appeared as a crucial step further away from revolution and in the direction of "normalization," that is accommodation with the establishment forces that fascism was meant to fight.

The emerging blending of order and change that fascism came to encapsulate involved a careful balancing act, as exemplified in the case of the experiment with "corporatism" in the late 1920s and early 1930s. Corporatism professed a fundamental socioeconomic transformation of societal relations, promising new, radical modes of collective action as well as a total framework for negotiating differences in a truly organic manner. Yet, its eventual failure and abandonment in the 1930s signified the impasse of fascism's formula of a controlled revolution "from above." By the early 1930s Italian fascism appeared to manage what the Italian historian Renzo De Felice (1929–1996) termed a *totalitarian state* but appeared to have lost a large part of its earlier radical edge.

By that time a pan-European trend away from liberal-parliamentary democracy had already been in motion. The majority of this generation of dictators did not hide their admiration for—or even imitation of—Mussolini's experiment in Italy. Even conservative observers across the Continent recognized the developmental utility of fascism, even

if some of them acknowledged that this sort of political system was not perhaps suited for all countries. Winston Churchill (1874–1963), who visited Rome in 1927 as Chancellor of the Exchequer, remarked "If I were an Italian, I am sure that I would have been with you entirely from the beginning of your victorious struggle against the bestial appetites and the passions of Leninism." Even in the United States the fascist experiment found admirers, with the New York Congressman Sol Bloom (1870–1949) going so far as to state that fascism "will be a great thing not only for Italy but for all of us if he [Mussolini] succeeds." An array of antiliberal and anticommunist regimes that started to replace unstable parliamentary systems embarked on partial borrowing, appropriating fascist ideas such as the single mass-party, the emphasis on parades and ritual celebrations, the cult of the leader, and the myth of national renewal. Within less than a decade from Mussolini's appointment in 1922, Italian fascism had been established in the eyes of contemporary observers as a genuine political alternative to both liberalism and socialism; for many in the right, it was indeed *the most* effective and modern political solution. Mussolini cherished his role as the public face of a new political creed that had been pioneered in Italy: Mohandas Gandhi (1869–1948) visited; so did the renegade British member of Parliament Oswald Mosley (1896–1980), who immediately afterward experienced a deep ideological conversion that turned him into the purveyor of fascism in Britain.

### NATIONAL SOCIALISM: FASCIST, TOTALITARIAN, OR UNIQUE?

The second crucial watershed in the history of interwar fascism came in 1933. On 30 January, Hitler, the leader of the National Socialist German Workers Party (Nationalsozialistisches Deutsches Arbeiterpartei, NSDAP), was appointed chancellor of the German Republic, in a form of power-sharing with Paul von Hindenburg (1847–1934), the veteran nationalist and World War I hero who had held the office of president since 1925. The political arrangement was strikingly reminiscent of the coalition government over which Mussolini had presided between October 1922 and January 1925. Hitler's subsequent measures against the more radical segments of his party (for instance, the leadership of the SA [Sturm Abteilung], purged during the "Night of the Long Knives" in June 1934) echoed Mussolini's less violent but comparably determined suppression of the fascist squads and militia (*squadri, MVSN*) in the 1920s. For many contemporary observers (particularly on the left) the assumption of power by Hitler constituted further evidence of the wider pan-European shift away from liberalism, in fundamental opposition to socialism and in search of a new type of populist politics.

Hitler's movement shared many crucial ideological themes and priorities with Mussolini's regime: the emphasis on national regeneration; the vision of an organic, indivisible nation; the belief in the need for a different, postliberal and antisocialist, modernity; the fetishization of spectacle; the cult of leadership; and the stress on spontaneous collective action as the vehicle for history-making. Unlike fascism in Italy, however, it featured an obsession with racial engineering and anti-Semitism—both notoriously absent or even derided in the Italian case. Furthermore, the geopolitical interests of the two countries, although broadly concordant with regard to revising the Versailles settlement, collided over the issue of Austria. Nazi Germany wished to absorb Austria into a new pan-German Reich while Italy, fearing secessionist demands from its own German-speaking minority in the newly acquired province of South Tyrol, preferred it to remain independent as a bulwark against further German expansion southward. Thus, in spite of Hitler's intense admiration for Mussolini and the latter's funding of German radical nationalist parties (including the NSDAP) in the pre-1933 era, the two regimes found themselves at loggerheads until 1935–1936. In fact, an abortive coup in July 1934 in Vienna against the Austrian fascist-like government of Chancellor Engelbert Dollfuss (1892–1934) brought the two countries to the verge of a military confrontation that was avoided only after Hitler backed down.

Although relations between the two regimes improved in the aftermath of Italy's military campaign against Ethiopia (1935–1936) and generated a dynamism that led to their eventual military alliance in 1939 (the "Pact of Steel"), their fundamental ideological divergence could not be easily glossed over. The majority of the fascist leaders in Italy viewed the rapprochement with Nazi Germany as not only unjustified but also harmful to the spirit of fascism. The Nazi obsession with race and anti-Semitism found very few disciples in the ranks of the PNF and the seeming fascination of the NSDAP with the rigid *volkisch* tradition appalled many fascists who had been steeped in modernism and a more eclectic attitude to culture. Equally, many of Hitler's colleagues did not share their leader's loyalty to Mussolini, seeing in the Fascist regime a half-baked experiment compromised by an overreliance on the state, power-sharing with the monarchy, and concessions to the church. Even after the introduction of anti-Semitic legislation in Italy (1938, Manifesto for the Defense of the Race), such misgivings did not abate. Apparently, the Italian racial laws had nothing to do with any form of German pressure; in fact, they could have been partly derived from the racial legislation that Italy had introduced in occupied Ethiopia in 1936. However, the perceived emulation of Nazi Germany left unconvinced Fascists even more disgruntled, whereas the milder, watered-down version of Italian racial politics and its less fanatical pursuit by the fascist authorities failed to allay the doubts of Nazi observers about the overall radical dynamics of Italian fascism.

The issue of "race"—and the subsequent anti-Semitic terror that was unleashed in the context of the Nazi "new order"—raises reasonable doubts about the aptness of the term *fascism* for the case of National Socialist Germany. Even if fascism is recognized as a generic phenomenon with relevance to the whole of European—or even global—history, race remained fundamental to the Nazis in a way that found no parallel in any other movement or regime. In fact, National Socialism can be viewed as the political vehicle for a genuine *racial* revolution with an open-ended scope that went far beyond the boundaries of even the most extreme version of a pan-German (*Gesamtdeutsch*) Reich. As a result, National Socialism appeared to diverge from the Italian model in both degree and kind.

Differences, however, do not mean that comparison is futile. Broadly speaking, fascism acquired its particular ideological and political shape in the circumstances of a particular generic "crisis" situation that affected different European societies in ways that could not possibly be identical. The rise of interwar fascism was rooted in the ambiguous combination of generic (supranational) and specific (national) historical factors. Its emphasis was on *action,* radical experiment, and self-generating dynamism. This did not mean that fascism did not possess a vision in itself; but it meant that its particular manifestations in each case were far more contingent on national specificities than in the cases of either liberalism or socialism. Racism, anti-Semitism, religious mysticism, Catholic-inspired corporatism, and imperialism were not related to fascism per se; they became part of the fascist prescription only to the extent that the latter found such trends in national traditions and then radicalized them in the search for a new framework for collective action for the whole (regenerated) nation.

It is therefore essential to distinguish between three potential understandings of fascism. The first, located in the pre–World War I crisis of liberal modernity, revolved around the search for a radical alternative model for national collective action but was far too open-ended and diverse to constitute a defined ideology. The second—what may be called "generic fascism"—captured this trend at a particular historical moment in the immediate post–World War I period, establishing a more concrete ideological framework (negations, expectations, prescriptions) for a radical modern alternative to the existing triptych of conservatism-liberalism-socialism. The third understanding involved the plurality of national manifestations of fascism in the 1920s and 1930s, their devices of collective action, experiments, limitations, successes, and failures; in other words, fascism's aggregate political record of the interwar period. While the first two perceptions of fascism had to do with ideas and intentions, the latter notion involved the result of political agency so diverse and particular that it requires an acute awareness of each context in order to separate the specific from the generic.

## VARIETIES OF FASCISM

The impressive spread of fascist ideas and influences across the Continent in interwar Europe generated an array of country-specific manifestations, as fascist movements began to appear in almost all countries. In Romania the League of Archangel Michael (founded in 1927 and later known as the Iron Guard) combined the goal of national rebirth with a strong emphasis on religious Christian mysticism

and an extreme cult of self-sacrifice. Fascist variants in many Catholic countries displayed a similar conceptualization of "rebirth" along (dissident) religious lines: in Belgium the main fascist movement glorified Christus Rex as the vehicle for national regeneration (hence the common collective name *Rexists* for its membership). Equally, corporatism (in itself an idea rooted in Catholic doctrines of self-organization) proved particularly popular in countries with a similar religious background (Italy, Portugal, Belgium) but left fascists in Germany and elsewhere decidedly unenthusiastic. The institution of the state, so instrumental in the process of "fascistizing" society under Italian fascism, was also used by António de Oliveira Salazar (1889–1970) in Portugal (with his model corporatist constitution for the "New State"), General Francisco Franco (1892–1975) in Spain, and Ioannis Metaxas (1871–1941) in Greece, but was rejected by National Socialists in Germany and the Legionaries of the Iron Guard in Romania as an impediment to the spontaneous collective action of the movement.

Biological racism was nowhere as strong as in the case of National Socialism in Germany, but anti-Semitism remained a common focus of many movements; in fact, its cultural roots stretched too far beyond the constituency of fascists for it to be considered a strictly fascist contribution. Again, prescriptions varied greatly: Italian fascism welcomed "Jewish Italians" to the ranks of its movement until the late 1930s; in Hungary the Arrow Cross movement espoused the doctrine of "a-Semitism," which entailed in theory the nonviolent excision of the Jews from the national body; in Greece, Jews fared much better under the fascist regime of General Metaxas in the second half of the 1930s than under its liberal predecessor that had advocated a far more ethno-exclusive notion of nationalism; in Britain, quite like in Italy, anti-Semitism for Mosley's British Union of Fascists started as a nonissue but became a bizarre knee-jerk obsession in the years before the outbreak of World War II that convinced few and galvanized even fewer. Although Italy joined Germany in the Axis alliance in 1939, other fascist movements and regimes refused to join an alleged fascist alliance: in France fear of German expansionism kept many fascists away from declaring an ideological and political loyalty to National Socialism, and those who did so committed political suicide; the Francoist regime that was established in 1939 after a bitter civil war that became a proxy confrontation between the emerging Axis alliance and Soviet Union remained stubbornly neutral during World War II; General Metaxas in Greece saw his policy of "equidistance" (even-handed diplomatic attitude to both western and fascist coalitions) collapse after the Italian attack in 1940 that eventually delivered the country to the western Allies.

Fascist movements and regimes appropriated or adapted the emerging fascist style of politics. Most of them shared the fascist emphasis on leadership: Mosley in Britain, Corneliu Zelea Codreanu (1899–1938) in Romania, Léon Degrelle (1906–1994) in Belgium, José Antonio Primo de Rivera (1903–1936, leader of the Falange fascist movement) in Spain, and even such uncharismatic leaders as Franco, Metaxas, Dollfuss in Austria, or the head of the collaborationist regime in Norway, Vidkun Quisling (1887–1945), were charismatized and glorified by propaganda, supported by carefully choreographed rituals of popular adulation. They displayed a striking fascination with militarism, order and discipline, parades and uniforms, spectacle, symbols, and collective rituals. They endeavored to combine ultranationalist ideology with populist mobilization and activism, cultivating the impression of a society in constant flux and unity. They recast particular national traditions as devices for communal action and consensus. The variety of these national traditions and historical circumstances bred variation and specificity. The inherent paradox of fascism as a generic trend rooted in—and articulated by—national agency may explain the failure of Mussolini to establish a sort of Fascist International in 1934 (an initiative that was boycotted by Nazi Germany from the very start). It may also help us understand why Italy and Germany remained locked in mutual suspicion and competition, not only before the rapprochement of 1935–1936 but also as allies in the build-up to, and the conduct of, the war.

## FROM MOVEMENT TO REGIME: THE FASCIST RULE

In spite of fascism's ideological diffusion across Europe in the 1920s and 1930s, the number of fascist regimes was relatively small. Apart from Fascist Italy and National Socialist Germany, other examples of fascist rule may be found in countries of southern, central, and eastern Europe (Spain,

Portugal, Greece, Romania, Hungary, Poland), with western Europe proving to be rather resistant to the fascist political challenge. A further wave of regimes that were sympathetic to the Nazi "new order" and appropriated many fascist ideological and political elements were installed in the Axis-occupied countries after 1939, but the circumstances in which the latter climbed to power were determined by military developments and external (German) pressure rather than by the dynamics of the domestic political field.

One of the paradoxes of fascism's transition to political power was that, in spite of its professed "revolutionary" orientation, it never seized power in opposition to established political and economic elites. In fact, even in the cases of Italy and Germany, the fascist movements cast aside many of their original revolutionary demands (e.g., anti-capitalist rhetoric) in order to become more acceptable to potential elite sponsors and thus acquire power through seemingly legal means. Both Mussolini and Hitler were finally appointed through constitutional channels (the latter having won a decisive victory in parliamentary elections) as heads of coalition governments and under the supervision of established institutions (monarchy in Italy; presidency in Germany). It was only in January 1925 that Mussolini took the crucial steps toward the establishment of a fascist dictatorship and embarked on the construction of a "totalitarian state" through suppression of freedoms, the establishment of secret police, censorship, and one-party rule. Hitler had to wait until President Paul von Hindenburg's death in August 1934 before abolishing the institution altogether and assuming full control of the German government. From that point he oversaw the gradual transformation of the existing state structures into a "totalitarian" system geared to the needs of racial revolution.

In both cases, the same established elites that had been so instrumental in propelling the fascists to power in a seemingly legal/constitutional arrangement did so in the belief that they would be able to control fascism or "normalize" it under the weight of government responsibility. When, however, they realized in the process that their controlling powers were limited (and rapidly shrinking), they did not oppose the fascist regimes; in fact, on many occasions powerful elite interests continued to work relatively smoothly with the fascist regimes until the very end. In Italy, King Victor Emmanuel III (r. 1900–1946) oversaw the dismantling of the liberal system and the pursuit of aggressive foreign-policy goals by the Fascist regime until July 1943, when—in the shadow of the Allied invasion of Sicily and disquiet among leading Fascists—he took the initiative to remove Mussolini from power.

Others proved equally accommodating, with powerful industrial interests working in tandem with the Fascist regime to offset the impact of the 1929 world economic crisis or supplying the Italian armed forces with military equipment in support of the regime's expansionist policies. In Germany, too, powerful industrial giants, such as Krupp and IG Farben, benefited from the National Socialist regime's autarkic policies from 1936 onward, as well as from the drive toward rearmament that Hitler authorized in contravention to the provisions of the Versailles Treaty. The composition of bureaucracy, industry, diplomacy, and the military displayed relative continuity between the prefascist and the fascist period; a process of "fascistization" did take place but it was gradual, often aided by the compliance of the institutions themselves, and never truly "revolutionary." What is instead striking about all fascist regimes was the degree of elite complicity in bringing fascists to power and tolerating their excesses until the very end.

Barely a year after Mussolini's appointment, in September 1923, a military coup d'état in Spain headed by General Miguel Primo de Rivera (1870–1930) ushered in a seven-year dictatorial rule, during which many of the features and ongoing experiments of Italian fascism were adopted. Indeed, coup d'état, whether military or political, proved another popular avenue to fascist rule. In Portugal in May 1926 a similar *pronunziamento* brought the military to power, with General António Óscar Carmona (1869–1951) becoming president of the republic. Six years later he appointed his former finance minister, António de Oliveira Salazar as head of the executive. Salazar, an economics professor, had been instrumental in creating a single national movement/party (União Nacional, National Union) along the lines of the Italian Fascist mass party. As prime minister, he appropriated the fascist rhetoric of "corporatism" and launched a new constitution heavily influenced by the Italian experience, which was approved in 1933.

Salazar described his political reforms as an attempt to create a "new state" (*Estado Novo*), promising to regenerate modern Portugal and resolve all socioeconomic tensions on the basis of national unity. His combination of fascist and conservative (for example, religious) elements emerged as an alternative route to the more blatant radicalism of the Italian and German variants of fascism—and an example for many subsequent dictatorships in southern Europe and in Latin America. Interestingly, his "fascism from above" did not have any space for "revolutionary" fascist alternatives: instead of co-opting it, Salazar violently suppressed the more radical Blue Shirt (National Syndicalist) movement, headed by Rolão Preto (1893–1977), and embarked upon building his "new state" in virtual continuity with preexisting sociopolitical structures.

Generally, the 1930s witnessed an overwhelming shift to dictatorial rule across the Continent; and this was a shift, coupled with a fundamental rejection of liberalism and an uncompromising, violent opposition to communism, that had an increasingly fascist flavor. Coups d'état put an end to democratic rule in Poland (1926), where Marshall Józef Piłsudski (1867–1935) used his popularity and the support of the armed forces to overthrow the elected government and in 1930 eliminated any form of political opposition; in Austria (1933), after the elected chancellor Engelbert Dollfuss suspended the constitution, outlawed political parties, and introduced a corporatist system under the tutelage of Mussolini; and in Greece (1935–1936), where an unstable liberal system faced the concerted opposition of the military, the royalists, and the nationalist Right, eventually succumbing after two coups to the hands of retired General Ioannis Metaxas.

But it was in 1930s Spain that the most symbolic shift from democracy to dictatorship and fascism occurred. Five months after the electoral victory of the Left and the formation of a Popular Front government in February 1936, the military staged a coup in Spanish Morocco that soon spread into the Spanish mainland under the leadership of General Francisco Franco. The ensuing three years of civil war became a genuine proxy confrontation between fascism and socialism. As Italy and

**Nationalist troops pass a block of ruined buildings in the Basque city of Guernica, 1 October 1937.** Earlier in 1937, in one of the most notorious episodes of the Spanish civil war, the city had been bombed and strafed by the German Luftwaffe to aid the Nationalist insurgency. ©BETTMANN/CORBIS

Germany became increasingly involved on the side of the Nationalists, and the Soviet Union did the same for the Republican camp, the conflict became internationalized and highly symbolic of the continent-wide shift toward dictatorship, antiliberal/antisocialist rule, and fascism. By April 1939, with Barcelona and Madrid eventually capitulating to the siege of the Francoist forces, the Nationalists could declare victory and set about constructing a fascist-like state in close cooperation with the indigenous Falange Español movement. Ideologically and socially conservative, affording a new lease of power to traditional elites (particularly the powerful families, including the landowning aristocracy and the Catholic Church), but ruthless toward its political opponents to the point of suppressing freedom, the Francoist regime remained in effect until its figurehead's death in 1975.

The "fascist epoch" reached its peak between 1938 and 1941. By the time the war broke out only the British Isles, France, the Low Countries, and Scandinavia had not succumbed. Austria eventually gave in to Nazi pressure under the threat of military invasion in March 1938, thus paving the way for its incorporation (Anschluss) into the "Greater German" Reich (this time, unlike in 1934, Mussolini did not stand up for Austrian independence). Even Czechoslovakia—for many a model of democratic transition for the "successor states" of the Austro-Hungarian Empire—was first dismembered in September 1938 and finally erased from the map in March 1939. In this case, the assault on the state emerged from a combination of Nazi expansionism intent on incorporating the Czechoslovak lands inhabited by a sizable German-speaking minority (Sudetenland) and internal Slovak designs for independence, spearheaded by the fascist-like Hlinka party headed by Josef Tiso (1887–1947).

In the course of the subsequent two years, most European countries were subjugated to the Axis "new order" in Europe, supervised by installed collaborationist regimes. Vidkun Quisling, erstwhile head of the small Nasjonal Samling (National Union) fascist party, declared himself head of the Norwegian state in the immediate aftermath of the Nazi invasion of the country, thereby setting an example of how domestic collaborators could be deployed by the Axis occupiers as puppet administrators of the occupied states. Marshall Philippe Pétain (1856–1951)—a World War I hero—was installed by the Nazis as head of the dismembered Vichy state of France. After Germany had invaded and occupied the Balkans in spring 1941, collaborationist regimes were installed in all countries under Axis control and borders were shifted in order to reward those who had contributed to the success of the operation. Notorious among them was the "Independent State of Croatia," headed by Ante Pavelić (1899–1959), the leader of the indigenous fascist movement, Ustaše, which immediately embarked upon a genocidal policy of ethnic cleansing against Serbs, Jews, and Sinti/Roma (Gypsies). Even in cases of milder occupation policies that tolerated a degree of civilian self-government (Denmark, the Netherlands), the trend after 1941 was for tighter control by Nazi Germany, more oppressive measures against the populations, and loss of even the last remaining vestiges of independence.

With the launch of Operation Barbarossa against the Soviet Union in June 1941 the moment of triumph came very close but eluded the fascist alliance: in December 1941, within a few miles from Moscow, the military coalition headed by the German Wehrmacht failed in the end to capture the capital of the Soviet Union—and, through it, to bring about the collapse of international socialism confidently predicted by Hitler. Military defeat proved impossible for interwar fascism to survive: first on the freezing Russian steppe, then on the beaches of Normandy and Sicily, finally inside the territories of the German Reich and of Italy, the fascist epoch came to a shattering end. One by one previous allies and fellow travelers abandoned the sinking boat and sought separate agreements with the advancing western Allies and the Soviet Union. Underground resistance movements became emboldened and fought even more resolutely against the domestic fascist order. The almost simultaneous demise of Mussolini and Hitler, in the last two days of April 1945, proved a fitting epilogue to the disaster that fascism brought upon Europe and eventually upon itself: the former was arrested on his way out of Italy by partisans and executed on the spot along with his mistress, their bodies ending up in a public display of hatred in a Milanese piazza; Hitler at least chose the manner and moment of his death, committing suicide inside the labyrinth of his Berlin bunker.

## THE FASCINATION WITH FASCISM

Thus the fascist epoch came to an end, symbolically defeated by a peculiar wartime coalition between its two ideological archenemies, western liberalism and Soviet communism. The postwar endeavors to understand why such a radical ideological phenomenon moved from the intellectual fringes of the late nineteenth century to a position of hegemony during the interwar period have produced a plethora of insights but also of ambiguities. The horrifying evidence from the killing camps of occupied Poland, where millions of Jews, Sinti and Roma, Poles, and other minority groups considered as "nonconformist" by the Nazi authorities perished, the chilling awareness of the so-called euthanasia program against disabled people and the overall brutality of the Nazi occupying forces across the Continent have proved painfully difficult to explain. Although branding fascism as a parenthesis in the otherwise assumed progress of Enlightenment-derived reason has afforded some measure of reassurance for post-1945 humanity, the unnerving hypermodernity of the Nazi genocide and its realization under the auspices of an utterly technological and bureaucratic system are hard to dispel.

Far from "nihilistic" or confined to conditions of "deviant personality" or located in particular national traditions, interwar fascism was popular, even fascinating to many. The disenchantment with the particular management of the transition to the modern world that liberalism had epitomized had led even certain liberals to the path of alternatives from within the modern project. For example, the prominent Italian philosopher Benedetto Croce (1866–1952) experienced a short-term conversion to fascism's promise of a new type of democratic alternative to the one that representative democracy had betrayed. Whereas many read fascism as an unacceptable assault on individualism and plurality, others welcomed its emphasis on voluntary mobilization and collective action on the basis of clearly defined and emotive grand schemes.

The agnosticism of the liberal state, unable or unwilling to adjudicate social tensions or anchor individual action in comfortable ideological havens, beset by a fixation with *negative* freedom even if this entailed paralyzing conflict and division, was a soft target for many—and not just those inhabiting the extreme right-wing fringe of the ideological spectrum. Prominent modernists, such as the French architect Le Corbusier (Charles-Édouard Jeanneret, 1887–1965), saw in fascism (in his case, of Mussolini's experiments with corporatism) the design for a more harmonious, creative, and sustainable social arrangement. Others, such as the futurist movement in Italy, embraced fascism as a radical break with the ghost of tradition, offering new, legacy-free alternatives for an ultramodern civilization. Its leader, Filippo Tommasso Marinetti (1876–1944), rejected nationalism, imperialism, and heritage in favor of a wholesale embrace of timeless modernity, succumbing to the exhilarating possibility for new, previously unthinkable modes of action and expression in its pure context.

But fascism's early ideological versatility attracted further admirers from other unlikely backgrounds. It was primarily Italian fascism and the Mussolini of the 1920s that appealed to intellectuals including Sigmund Freud (1856–1939) and the American poet Ezra Pound (1885–1972). The latter moved to Italy and remained an unapologetic admirer of the Italian fascist experiment until the end of his days. Pound admired fascism's radical potential and ability to generate a sense of dynamism that was in sharp contrast to the alleged stagnation of liberal democracy. In cooperation with Wyndham Lewis (1884–1957)—with whom he founded vorticism as an avant-garde movement preaching a revolutionary break with obsolete tradition in search of a novel, radical aesthetic and dynamic synthesis—Pound rejected the internationalism of the capitalist system and castigated the absence of humanism in the particular kind of modernity epitomized in western civilization. However, he was vehemently anticommunist and thus a fierce critic of the Soviet experiment, while Lewis saw the desired transgression in a combination of fascist and Soviet methods of power centralization. Similarly, the British playwright George Bernard Shaw (1856–1950) identified fascism and communism in tandem as a joint genuine solution to the perceived disintegration of the modern world, praising the two doctrines' emphasis on activism and collective mobilization.

Fascism also recruited admirers from the ranks of the political theorists who sought an alternative to the representative model of liberal democracy and a radical prescription against the alleged decline of western civilization. From the ranks of the "conservative revolution" movement that gathered momentum in the first half of the twentieth century a series of thinkers courted fascism; some, like the prominent sociologist Robert Michels (1876–1936) and the philosophers Martin Heidegger (1889–1976) and Julius Evola (1898–1974), ended up heavily involved in the development of fascist political experiments, lending crucial intellectual support to them. Others, such as the theoretician of "total mobilization" in Germany Ernst Jünger (1895–1998) and the politician and writer Edgar Jung (1894–1934) (who was assassinated during the "Night of the Long Knives" after having assumed an openly critical stance toward the Nazi regime), followed the rather familiar path of initial attraction followed by disillusionment and alienation. What is interesting in all these cases was the promise that fascism appeared to hold in the far-reaching quest for a postliberal order, steeped in fundamental anxiety about the moral collapse of modern civilization and in a deep pessimism about the ability of the masses to effectively control their own fate. Fascism appeared to them for a variety of reasons to offer a viable, ethically and historically superior, pathway to the rebirth of European culture and society.

The variety of backgrounds from which fascism recruited or received ideological support, as well as the diversity of motives that underpinned such support in each case, highlight a central problem in defining the concept and reconstructing its intellectual history. Fascism appeared so flexible and open-ended in the 1920s that it was co-opted by highly disparate parallel projects, from the Left and Right alike. Becoming closely identified with the particular evolution of Fascist Italy and National Socialist Germany produced a far narrower and restricted understanding that has obscured its ambiguous intellectual matrix. As a historically specific articulation of anxiety and search for alternatives, the concept of fascism remains tied to the political experiments of the 1920s and 1930s, with 1945 as a definitive watershed. As a particular instance, however, of a wider search for radical alternatives, constantly updated in the light of shifting supranational and national circumstances, fascism remains highly relevant—not necessarily as an ongoing project in itself but as a diachronic reminder of how widespread disaffection with established norms and directions may breed radical alternatives and of how these alternatives may appear dangerously fascinating to many.

*See also* **Anticommunism; Antifascism; Anti-Semitism; Communism; Corporatism; Franco, Francisco; Hitler, Adolf; Metaxas, Ioannis; Mussolini, Benito; Nazism; Racial Theories; World War II.**

BIBLIOGRAPHY

Ben-Ami, Shlomo. *Fascism from Above: The Dictatorship of Primo de Rivera in Spain, 1923–1930.* Oxford, U.K., and New York, 1983.

Bessel, Richard, ed. *Fascist Italy and Nazi Germany: Comparisons and Contrasts.* Cambridge, U.K., and New York, 1996.

Blinkhorn, Martin, ed. *Fascists and Conservatives: The Radical Right and the Establishment in Twentieth-Century Europe.* London and Boston, 1990.

Burleigh, Michael, and Wolfgang Wippermann. *The Racial State: Germany 1933–1945.* Cambridge, U.K., and New York, 1991.

Costa Pinto, Antonio. *Salazar's Dictatorship and European Fascism: Problems of Interpretation.* Boulder, Colo., 1994.

De Grand, Alexander J. *Fascist Italy and Nazi Germany: The "Fascist" Style of Rule.* New York, 1995.

Goldhagen, Daniel Jonah. *Hitler's Willing Executioners: Ordinary Germans and the Holocaust.* New York, 1996.

Eatwell, Roger. *Fascism: A History.* London and New York, 1995.

Griffin, Roger. *The Nature of Fascism.* London and New York, 1993.

Griffin, Roger, ed. *Fascism.* London and New York, 1995.

Griffin, Roger, ed., with Matthew Feldman. *Fascism: Critical Concepts in Political Science.* London, 2004.

Higham, Robin, and Thanos Veremis, eds. *The Metaxas Dictatorship: Aspects of Greece, 1936–40.* Athens, Greece, 1993.

Ioanid, Radu. *The Sword of the Archangel: Fascist Ideology in Romania.* Boulder, Colo., and New York, 1990.

Kallis, Aristotle A., ed. *The Fascism Reader.* London and New York, 2003.

Kershaw, Ian. *Hitler.* Harlow, U.K., and New York, 2000.

Kershaw, Ian, and Moshe Lewin, eds. *Stalinism and Nazism: Dictatorships in Comparison.* Cambridge, U.K., and New York, 1997.

Knox, MacGregor. *Common Destiny: Dictatorship, Foreign Policy, and War in Fascist Italy and Nazi Germany.* Cambridge, U.K., and New York, 2000.

Larsen, Stein Ugelvik, Bernt Hagtvet, and Jan Petter Myklebust, eds. *Who Were the Fascists? Social Roots of European Fascism.* Bergen, Norway, and Irvington-on-Hudson, N.Y., 1980.

Laqueur, Walter, ed. *Fascism: A Reader's Guide: Analyses, Interpretations, Bibliography.* London, 1976.

Mann, Michael. *Fascists.* Cambridge, U.K., and New York, 2004.

Milza, Pierre. *Fascisme français, passé et présent.* Paris, 2000.

Nolte, Ernst. *Three Faces of Fascism: Action Française, Italian Fascism, National Socialism.* New York, 1966.

Payne, Stanley G. *A History of Fascism, 1914–1945.* Madison, Wis., 1995.

Peukert, Detlev J. K. *Inside Nazi Germany: Conformity, Opposition, and Racism in Everyday Life.* Translated by Richard Dereson. New Haven, Conn., 1989.

Preston, Paul. *The Politics of Revenge: Fascism and the Military in Twentieth-Century Spain.* London and New York, 1995.

Soucy, Robert. *French Fascism: The Second Wave 1933–1939.* New Haven, Conn., 1995.

Sugar, Peter F. *Native Fascism in the Successor States, 1918–1945.* Santa Barbara, Calif., 1971.

ARISTOTLE A. KALLIS

**FASHION.** During the twentieth century, European fashion evolved from its aristocratic and bourgeois roots in Paris and London into a democratic, global phenomenon. The couture system had been established in France since the 1860s, and in Britain the arts of tailoring had produced the man's suit, a cornerstone of modern clothing design. In the sphere of mass production, the sewing and cutting technologies necessary for the manufacture of cheap ready-made clothing had been in operation since the 1840s. This was supported by a well-established retail network crowned by the department store and a sophisticated advertising and publishing industry set up to foment desire for fashionable goods. By 1914 all the elements were in place for the expansion of a sector that, by the turn of the twenty-first century, would come to symbolize the consumerist nature of modern life itself.

### THE PARISIAN FASHION DESIGNER

Although the concept of fashion encompasses the design, manufacture, distribution, marketing, and retailing of clothing, together with its role in the formation of identity and the practice of everyday life, in the twentieth century it was the figure of the designer who came most powerfully to symbolize fashion's particular character. The designer's ability to communicate novel ideas around design and dressing smoothed the relationship, necessary in a capitalist system of provision, between the production and consumption of goods, and ensured that new products carried the requisite cachet to stand out in a busy marketplace. In essence, the modern fashion designer had to master the creative skills associated with dressmaking, theater, and art, and also of business, mass marketing, and self-promotion. Paradoxically, most of the key designers in the twentieth century were primarily associated with the traditions of couture, which had only a small and elite clientele. Yet the expert management of their reputations was vital to the democratization of fashion and the expansion of markets. This was largely achieved through the association of their names and ideas with diffusion (wholesale) lines, the distribution of syndicated patterns, the sale of branded perfumes and accessories, and tie-ins with the mass media through magazines and films.

The Englishman Charles Frederick Worth (1825–1895) had pioneered this system in Paris, setting a precedent for later generations. The first to follow his lead was Paul Poiret (1879–1944), who opened his couture house in Paris in 1903 and became famous for producing "exotic" garments that drew on current crazes for orientalist fantasy and for rejecting the nineteenth-century corseted feminine form in favor of a more fluid ideal. By 1914 he had also made an unprecedented contribution to the modernization of the French fashion industry through his innovative promotion of design. This was especially marked in his collaboration with avant-garde illustrators such as Paul Iribe and George Lepape, who produced lavish volumes celebrating Poiret's vision. In a similar vein he promoted interior design at the Atelier Martine and the manufacture of perfume and makeup at the House of Rosine, of paper goods at the Colin workshop, of fabric painting at the Petite Usine, and of fine art at his own commercial gallery. This catholic understanding of fashion as a complete "lifestyle" extended ideas of the *Gesamtkunstwerk*, the total work of art, first developed in Vienna at the turn of the twentieth century, and laid the foundations for future understandings of high fashion as a Parisian practice.

After World War I a trio of female designers continued Poiret's legacy. The Frenchwoman Coco Chanel (1883–1971) was adept at turning her personal taste into a powerful commodity. By 1930 she had built up an impressive network of patrons and had honed her design and marketing expertise to such an extent that her name had become synonymous with a symbolic modernization of women's clothing styles that was equated with Henry Ford's impact on the American automobile industry, though her "little black dress," the so-called Model T of the modern woman's wardrobe, was launched to a rather more select market. Nevertheless, in 1935, her most productive year before the outbreak of World War II, Chanel employed four thousand workers and sold twenty-eight thousand designs across the globe. Chanel's contemporary Madeleine Vionnet (1876–1975) was more of a technical pioneer; her work bears closest comparison to that of modernist architects such as Adolf Loos or Le Corbusier. She approached couture as a problem of structure and engineering, constructing dynamic forms that combined classic grace with purist abstraction. The reality of dealing in the fashion marketplace, however, also necessitated an attention to commercial issues, and the novelty of her designs obliged Vionnet to protect her copyright by photographing

**Dinner dress by Vionnet c. 1925.** ©CONDÉ NAST ARCHIVE/CORBIS

and numbering each product. Individual creativity was thus subordinated to a concern with standards and control, which was in tune with the fetishization of the machine so dominant in Western culture in the interwar period. This extended to Vionnet's interest in the welfare of her employees, who worked under the most advanced conditions. In many ways her persona was closer to that of the philanthropic industrialist than the autocratic old-style couturier. The Italian Elsa Schiaparelli (1896–1973), in her work, looked more toward the antirational impulses of surrealism. Based in Paris from 1922 on, she built up a reputation for her knitwear, which clung provocatively to the body and used extraordinary trompe l'oeil motifs. Her later collaborations with the artists Salvador Dalí and Jean Cocteau traded on the shock of unlikely connections and a fetishistic attention to de-contextualized details such as zippers, hair, and mirrors; and lip, newsprint, and hand patterns. Her significance as a designer lay in her idiosyncratic and eclectic avant-garde vision and her understanding of the fragility of the fashion psyche (i.e., the creative practice and the psyche of the fashion consumer). These characteristics would resurface in the spectacular couture shows produced by a later generation of designers in Paris at the end of the twentieth century.

After World War II, when the German occupation of Paris brought a temporary halt to that city's global dominance, the 1950s witnessed a flowering of designer-led couture. The leading personality in this period was Christian Dior (1905–1957), who in 1947 launched the "New Look." His attitude toward fashion differed somewhat from that of his predecessors in that he rejected the forward-looking vision of Chanel for a more nostalgic and conservative interpretation of traditional ideals of femininity. This coincided with a return to more constrained domestic and decorative roles for women in the postwar years. Dior's New Look models promoted a romantic style that required the use of nineteenth-century-style boning and support structures and many yards of fabric (it is no coincidence that Dior was funded by Marcel Boussac, a French textiles magnate, for whom the generous use of fabric was a boon). Austerity tempered the initial reception of the collection in Europe, and several governments and journalists condemned it as wasteful and reactionary. For many consumers, however, it offered a welcome escapism and beauty and it translated well to the American market, where its voluptuous surfaces were especially well suited to a new era of conspicuous consumption. Dior's most famous competitor was the Spanish-born Cristóbal Balenciaga (1895–1972), whose signature collections also stressed luxury but were more self-consciously artistic, making reference to seventeenth-century paintings and contemporary art in their innovative draping and sculptural form. Balenciaga's imperious yet reserved personality refined the idea of the designer once again, presenting a model of tortured genius that would be taken up by several of his followers.

The social and political revolutions of the 1960s issued a challenge to the dominant traditions of Parisian couture, and the bourgeois sensibility of the salon no longer seemed relevant. Yves Saint Laurent (b. 1936) continued the artistic traditions of Dior and Balenciaga, but adapted them to the new demands of pop culture. His influences were diverse, spanning the formal simplicity of his Mondrian collection in 1965, the cartoonlike "Pop Art" of 1966, and safari suits and African art in 1968. But perhaps Saint Laurent's most lasting contribution to the history of fashion was his pioneering of tailored evening suits for women, first presented in 1967. Beyond the design of clothing, the designer's body, name, and opinions were used to an unprecedented degree to promote the YSL brand. Diversifying from couture, he launched the boutique chain Rive Gauche in 1966 and posed naked for an advertising campaign for his men's fragrance in 1971. This adoption of outrageous tactics was shared by Saint Laurent's contemporaries, such as Pierre Cardin and André Courreges, whose futuristic "space age" designs in new synthetic fabrics were quite at odds with the soigné elegance of old-style couture. The 1960s generation of Parisian designers opened up a world of freedom and opportunity, which was enjoyed by French designers, including Jean Paul Gaultier and Christian Lacroix in the 1980s and Rei Kawakubo, Hedi Slimane, and others in the 1990s and 2000s. But by the opening of the twenty-first century the idea of Paris as the capital of fashion had become diluted. Its supremacy was challenged by other European and world centers. The market for couture had disappeared, and the global nature of a fashion industry now controlled by a limited number of luxury brand companies meant that the epoch of the independent autocratic designer and of specialized craft skills, on which Paris's preeminence had been based, had come to an end.

## LONDON AND MILAN

If Paris was widely perceived as the capital of couture during the twentieth century, then London was equally lauded as a center for street style and innovative dressing. As a world trade city and the political hub of an empire during the nineteenth century, it was more closely associated with the production of elite tailoring for powerful men, and Savile Row, the source of the gentleman's wardrobe, continued to attract statesmen, film stars, and celebrities from across the world for most of the following century. As for women's clothing, most wealthy socialites looked to Paris, but from 1914 to the early 1960s London did sustain a small

**Christian Dior's New Look, 1951.** ©BETTMAN/CORBIS

couture industry whose wares drew on strong tailoring traditions and were suitable for the social pursuits of the British Social Season. Couturiers including Norman Hartnell, Hardy Amies, Victor Steibel, and Digby Morton joined forces during World War II to form the Incorporated Society of London Fashion Designers. But although they had some success in designing a series of ingenious fabric-saving garments as part of the Utility scheme—a British government-sponsored wartime initiative that supported the production of fashionable garments designed to save on materials and labor while boosting consumer morale—their work did not really deserve international recognition on a par with Paris fashions. The challenge to French

models and the introduction of a more democratic and avant-garde form of London fashion did not occur until the rise of Mary Quant in the late 1950s and the whole "swinging" phenomenon of the 1960s.

Mary Quant opened her boutique Bazaar on the Kings Road in London's bohemian Chelsea in 1955. A graduate of Goldsmith's College of Art, she had no formal training in fashion design, but with her partner, Alexander Plunkett-Green, she worked up collections of garments that were more attractive to her peers than the formal dress associated with their mothers' generation. Her happy childlike designs with their simple cut, abstract pattern, and clear colors were a real departure from tradition, and the informality of the shop with its quirky window displays offered a new relaxed way of buying clothes. The success of Bazaar brought invitations for Quant to design for the American market via J. C. Penney in 1962. In 1963 she set up the diffusion label "Ginger Group" and diversified into makeup and hosiery. Most important, her example opened up the terrain for a generation of young designers and entrepreneurs such as Foale and Tuffin, John Stephen, Ossie Clark, Barbara Hulaniki, and Zandra Rhodes, whose work pushed at the boundaries between high and popular culture, art and fashion, and craft and commerce in a distinctively "London" manner.

The reinvention of British fashion on the Kings Road was echoed in the West End's Carnaby Street with its colorful men's boutiques, and soon London had caught the attention of the international media, which equated the London fashion revolution with the global success of pop bands such as the Beatles. In 1966 *Time* magazine produced its famous "Swinging London" edition, which sealed the reputation of the city as the new center of "cool." But it is important not to lay all the credit at the feet of the designers and boutique owners. They were simply responding to the demands of a new market of teenagers who had more disposable income than ever before and an iconoclastic attitude toward outdated ideas of respectability or conformity. For the first time, new fashion trends were not being dictated by remote designers in Paris but by working-class subcultures such as the Mods, whose taste for sharp styling and a distinctive image set in motion a new form of conspicuous consumption that "bubbled up" from the British street. Much of the variety of the "scene" was captured in and driven by London's style publishing industry. Pioneering magazines such as *Nova* in the 1960s and 1970s and *I.D., Face,* and *Dazed and Confused* in the 1980s and 1990s, superseded *Vogue* as the most influential fashion publication. London's art schools were also a source of inspiration, as was the city's multi-ethnic culture, and by the 1970s, 1980s, and 1990s, with the rise first of punk and then of the club scene as their backdrop, London-based designers such as Vivienne Westwood, John Galliano, and Alexander McQueen were able to sell

**Mary Quant poses with models wearing fashions from her spring 1967 collection.** GETTY IMAGES

a distinctive postmodern look back to Paris and the world.

As London was reinventing itself as a center for quirky iconoclastic fashions in the 1960s, Milan was also undergoing a transformation as a slick industrial and retail challenger to Paris. American financial support, administered through the Marshall Plan of the late 1940s, guaranteed that the struggling textile factories of northern Italy had access to capital, new technologies, and raw materials. As this process of reconstruction continued through the 1950s and 1960s, Italian manufacturers and consumers also embraced an American idea of modernity, filtered through Hollywood film and television, which promoted the positive aspects of a consumer society. An ensuing domestic boom coincided with a very favorable reception for new mass-produced Italian goods in the rest of Europe and America. Alongside clothing and textiles, Italian food and drink, furniture, and automobiles were universally celebrated for their modern styling, high quality, beautiful materials, and urbane characteristics. Working within such a context, fashion designers, including the Fontana sisters at couture level, Emilio Pucci at made-to-measure, and the company MaxMara at the ready-to-wear end of the industry pioneered a distinctive Italian look during this period.

By the early 1970s Milan had overtaken Rome and Florence as the new capital of the Italian fashion industry, mirroring a shift from the promotion of couture to a celebration of ready-to-wear. A younger generation of designers, including Spazio Krizia, Ottavio Missoni, Gianni Versace, and Giorgio Armani, who had enjoyed a more wide-ranging experience of design, manufacturing, marketing, and retailing of clothing than their predecessors, found the commercial and manufacturing infrastructure of Milan to be a more congenial base than the stuffier cultures of the older centers. Many of these new names benefited from the financial backing of large corporate sponsors whose interest lay in anticipating the desires of a mass market through the adoption of new research practices borrowed from architecture, philosophy, and advertising. This conceptual radicalism went hand in hand with an entirely practical approach, borrowed from long-established merchant trading houses such as Fendi and Gucci, who sold branded luggage and accessories and maintained a belief in the importance of "craft." The success of the "second economic miracle" of the 1980s also owed much to the dolce vita attitudes of the Italian consumer and the materialist culture of Milan itself, evident in the cosmopolitan shopping streets, exhibition halls, and design studios of the city and the glamorous products of a design community that by the 1990s included Domenico Dolce, Stefano Gabbana, and Miuccia Prada.

The experience of Paris, London, and Milan in the twentieth century suggests that modern sartorial goods operate in the "realm of values." The stereotypical products and images of each city are never entirely fixed by their geographical location, even though their meanings are informed by a concrete social and industrial history and aesthetic heritage. Instead, their coherence has been constantly challenged by the global nature of their production and reception and the subjective ordering of their merits in the media. Beginning in the 1970s, for example, much of the manufacturing of garments associated with European centers took place in the Far East, and Paris, London, and Milan also competed with New York and Tokyo as world-class fashion cities. Indeed, it is precisely the fluid nature of such values that endows the modern fashion system with the extraordinary capacity to create and overturn social realities and identities on an unprecedented scale; but it also means that the continuing cultural and economic dominance of European fashion capitals can never be guaranteed.

*See also* **Avant-Garde; Chanel, Coco; Consumption; Surrealism.**

BIBLIOGRAPHY

Breward, Christopher. *Fashion.* Oxford, U.K., 2003.

Evans, Caroline. *Fashion at the Edge: Spectacle, Modernity and Deathliness.* New Haven, Conn., 2003.

Lipovetsky, Gilles. *The Empire of Fashion: Dressing Modern Democracy.* Translated by Catherine Porter. Princeton, N.J., 1994.

White, N. *Reconstructing Italian Fashion: America and the Development of the Italian Fashion Industry.* Oxford, U.K., 2000.

CHRISTOPHER BREWARD

# FASSBINDER, RAINER WERNER
(1945–1982), German filmmaker.

During his lifetime, much of what was written about Rainer Werner Fassbinder gave the year of his birth as 1946. It seems that Fassbinder may have encouraged the publication of that erroneous date, perhaps as a means of making his extraordinary productivity—he directed more than forty films between 1969 and 1982—appear all the more prodigious. It is worth entertaining the possibility, though, that the substitution of 1946 for 1945 might have other kinds of significance with regard to Fassbinder's films and his controversial politics. Perhaps the most famous filmmaker of the so-called New German Cinema of the 1970s and 1980s, Fassbinder saw film as "a political instrument, in the sense that it can describe and expose the underlying problems of society" (Whitney, sec. C). He made the recent history of Germany, and of West Germany in particular, the focus of much of his work as a director.

**Hanna Schygulla as Maria Braun in a scene from Rainer Werner Fassbinder's *Marriage of Maria Braun,* 1978.** TRIO/
ALBATROS/WDR/THE KOBAL COLLECTION

Central to Fassbinder's understanding of the history of West Germany was his conviction that "in 1945, at the end of the war, the chances which did exist for Germany to renew itself were not realized. Instead, the old structures and values . . . have basically remained the same" (Elsaesser, 1996, p. 25). In light of that remark, Fassbinder's endorsement of the publication of 1946, rather than 1945, as the year of his own birth might be seen as a way of dissociating himself from the history of the nation that several of his most important films recount in melodramatic allegories.

Beginning in the mid-1970s, Fassbinder was continually caught up in political controversies concerning his approach to representing German history, in particular the place of anti-Semitism in that history. Fassbinder repeatedly declared that in his films he "wanted to show that National Socialism wasn't an accident but a logical extension of the bourgeoisie's attitudes, which haven't altered to this

day" (Thomsen, p. 95). In line with that belief, Fassbinder's 1975 play *Der Müll, die Stadt und der Tod* (Garbage, the city, and death) draws connections between Jewish property speculators, prostitution rings, and corrupt politicians in contemporary Frankfurt, which provoked inflammatory accusations of left-wing anti-Semitism in the press and ultimately led to the cancellation of the production of the play scheduled for that year at Frankfurt's Theater am Turm. Fassbinder's so-called BRD Trilogy (BRD stands for Bundesrepublik Deutschland or Federal Republic of Germany), a suite of films comprising *The Marriage of Maria Braun* (1979), *Lola* (1981), and *Veronika Voss* (1982), frames the history of West Germany allegorically in its melodramatic depiction of the lives of the title characters of the three films. The films incorporate references to—and sometimes, by means of the montage of both film and sound recordings, direct citations of—the transmission of recent German history in the media of photography, film, and radio.

In the BRD Trilogy and elsewhere, Fassbinder's work brings together his emulation of the formal techniques of both the early-twentieth-century avant-garde and classic Hollywood cinema, the former represented, for example, by the German novelist Alfred Döblin, whose monumental novel *Berlin Alexanderplatz* (1929) Fassbinder adapted in 1980 as a fourteen-part serial for West German television, and the latter epitomized for Fassbinder by the melodramas or so-called women's films directed by the German-born Hollywood filmmaker Douglas Sirk in the 1950s. Fassbinder's films also include adaptations of Theodor Fontane's novel *Effi Briest* (1894) (*Fontane Effi Briest*, 1972/74) and of Marieluise Fleisser's 1929 play *Pioniere in Ingolstadt* (Recruits in Ingolstadt), which Fassbinder set in the present when he directed his film version in 1970.

In addition to his work as a film director, Fassbinder had a significant career as a writer, director, and actor in the theater, and he appeared as an actor in films directed by others, as well as in many of his own. In 1978 Fassbinder took part in the production of the film *Deutschland im Herbst* (Germany in autumn), which was made as a collective work by thirteen German filmmakers and writers, including Heinrich Böll, Alexander Kluge, and Volker Schlöndorff, in response to the interrelated events of the so-called Deutscher Herbst (German autumn) of 1977: on 5 September, the kidnapping of the German business executive, right-wing public figure, and former National Socialist Hanns-Martin Schleyer by members of the Red Army Fraction (RAF; sometimes rendered into English as Red Army Faction); on 13 October, the hijacking of a Lufthansa jet, which resulted in the death of the plane's pilot, by members of the RAF in collaboration with members of the Popular Front for the Liberation of Palestine as an attempt to exert pressure on the German government to agree to release prisoners in exchange for the release of Schleyer; on 18 October, the suspicious deaths, in Stammheim Prison near Stuttgart, of three members of the RAF (Andreas Baader, Gudrun Ensslin, and Jan-Carl Raspe); and the subsequent murder of Schleyer on 19 October. In his part of the film, Fassbinder insists on the problematic and sometimes paradoxical connection between authoritarianism, violence, and domination in politics and public life, especially in recent German history, and in intimate, especially familial, interpersonal relationships. Fassbinder's portrayal of himself as he berates his mother and his male lover for their expressions of sympathy with the positions taken by the German chancellor Helmut Schmidt's government in response to the RAF's acts of terrorism is at once unflinching and self-indulgent, with Fassbinder, drunk and high on drugs, embodying a political problematic that preoccupied him throughout his brief but exceptionally productive career.

*See also* **Döblin, Alfred; Cinema; Germany; Wenders, Wim.**

BIBLIOGRAPHY

Elsaesser, Thomas. *New German Cinema: A History.* New Brunswick, N. J., 1989.

———. *Fassbinder's Germany: History, Identity, Subject.* Amsterdam, 1996.

Fassbinder, Rainer Werner. *The Anarchy of the Imagination: Interviews, Essays, Notes.* Edited by Michael Töteberg and Leo A. Lensing. Translated by Krishna Winston. Baltimore and London, 1992.

Kaes, Anton. *From Hitler to Heimat: The Return of History as Film.* Rev. ed. Cambridge, Mass., and London, 1989.

Kardish, Laurence, and Juliane Lorenz, eds. *Rainer Werner Fassbinder.* New York, 1997.

Santner, Eric L. *Stranded Objects: Mourning, Memory, and Film in Postwar Germany.* Ithaca, N.Y., 1990.

Thomsen, Christian Braad. *Fassbinder: The Life and Work of a Provocative Genius.* Translated by Martin Chalmers. Minneapolis, 2004.

Whitney, Craig R. "Fassbinder: A New Director Movie Buffs Dote On." *New York Times,* 16 February 1977, sec. C.

BRIGID DOHERTY

---

# FEBVRE, LUCIEN (1878–1956), French historian.

The historian Lucien Febvre left his intellectual imprint on both historiography and the French intellectual world of his time. Born into a Burgundian family in Nancy, he always remained strongly attached to his regional origins, even though he spent most of his life in Paris. He was a student at the École Normale Supérieure from 1898 to 1902 and was a member of the student generations strongly marked by the Dreyfus affair. He also sympathized with the labor movement, and from 1907 to 1909 he wrote for a socialist paper in Besançon. Later he was close to the Socialist Party of Léon Blum (1872–1950), but he also maintained contacts with the Radical Party and among the Communists. His closest friend, for example, the psychologist Henri Wallon (1879–1962), was a member of the French Communist Party. Their relationship broke off only during the Cold War.

Febvre was mobilized into the army on 3 August 1914 and served at the front until February 1919, with the exception of several months of hospitalization and convalescence after being seriously wounded. By the end of the war he was a captain in command of a machine gun regiment in the Rhineland. However, unlike his colleague and friend Marc Bloch (1886–1944), he felt no nostalgia for those years of "butchery," as he took to calling them: he thus always advocated policies whose aim was to avoid any return to war. He abandoned this pacifist stance only during the Spanish civil war, when he argued for aiding the Republicans, and later at the time of the Munich pact, when he criticized the opportunistic politics of the government of Édouard Daladier (1884–1970).

In 1911 Febvre defended his thesis on the politics of the Spanish king Philip II (r. 1556–1598) in Franche-Comté. He was first appointed professor of Burgundian history at Dijon; in 1919 he was one of the first professors to be named to the new University of Strasbourg. There he met the medievalist Marc Bloch, eight years his junior, with whom he shared the project of renewing historiography based on a critical conception strongly influenced by the sociology of Émile Durkheim (1858–1917) and the geography of Paul Vidal de la Blache (1845–1918). Together they founded a new interdisciplinary journal that revolutionized the human sciences, *Annales d'histoire économique et sociale,* whose approach combined socioeconomic history with a new type of cultural history that would come to be known as the "history of mentalities." But Febvre, who divided his time and energies between the *Annales* and the *Revue de synthèse historique,* which Henri Berr (1863–1954) had headed since 1900, had a tendency to spread himself thin. Thus, in 1932 he took on the

editorship of another major endeavor, the *Encyclopédie française,* of which some ten volumes appeared by 1939. The aim of this project, in which Febvre demonstrated a singular talent for "making connections," comparable to that of Denis Diderot (1713–1784), was to present the most advanced state of human knowledge in all the scientific disciplines.

Alongside these tasks, in which he had help from efficient collaborators such as the writer Pierre Abraham (born Pierre Bloch, 1892–1974) and the Austrian-born historian Lucie Varga (1904–1941), Febvre taught at the Collège de France, to which he had been elected in 1933, and wrote a great many articles and book reviews that enabled him to participate directly in the debates of his times. His own works, by contrast, took time to come to fruition: after *Un destin: Martin Luther* (1928) and *Le Rhin* (1931; The Rhine), his subsequent books (on François Rabelais, Marguerite de Navarre, and Bonaventure Des Periers) took much longer than anticipated and were completed only during the occupation, when the author enjoyed long periods of solitary work. It was during this same period that relations between Febvre and Marc Bloch soured over the issue of whether publication of the *Annales* should continue under the regime imposed by the Germans. Whereas Bloch, after some hesitations, argued for suspending publication until the end of the war, Febvre was prepared to adapt it, as a matter of form, at least, to the new conditions to preserve this forum for French historical science; he consequently asked Bloch to remove his ("Jewish") name from their common enterprise. Bloch finally agreed to this strategy, but only after bitter debate; from May 1942, he signed his contributions, which remained numerous, with a pseudonym, "M. Fougères."

After the liberation, Febvre was the sole editor of the *Annales* and headed many other projects: a revitalized *Encyclopédie française,* the sixth section (social and economic sciences) of the École Pratique des Hautes Études, created in 1948, and several other journals and series. He was also a member of the Langevin-Walon Commission for educational reform from 1945 to 1948 and was one of the French delegates at the founding of UNESCO. In short, until his death he was a central figure in the French academic world and the founding father of the "new" historiography that, thanks to Fernand Braudel (1902–1985) in particular, soon became a sweeping international success.

*See also* **Annales School; Bloch, Marc; Braudel, Fernand.**

BIBLIOGRAPHY

Burke, Peter, ed. *A New Kind of History and Other Essays.* London, 1973.

Candar, Gilles, and Jacqueline Pluet-Despatin, eds. *Lucien Febvre et l' "Encyclopédie Française."* Special issue of *Cahiers Jean Jaurès,* no. 163/164 (2002).

Massicotte, Guy. *L'histoire problème: La méthode de Lucien Febvre.* Paris and Québec, 1981.

Müller, Bertrand. *Lucien Febvre, lecteur et critique.* Paris, 2003.

Schöttler, Peter. *Lucie Varga: Les autorités invisibles: Une historienne autrichienne aux "Annales" dans les années trente.* Paris, 1991.

PETER SCHÖTTLER

---

# FELLINI, FEDERICO (1920–1993), Italian film director, screenwriter, and cartoonist.

After showing precocious talent as a cartoonist and sketch artist in provincial Rimini, the young Federico Fellini moved to Rome in 1939 and began work on the humor magazine *Marc'Aurelio,* a periodical with an enormous circulation that included many journalists working in the cinema. Fellini became quite well known by contributing comic gags, cartoons, serial narratives, and humorous vignettes and was introduced to the social circles of Italian cinema.

In 1943 he married the actress Giulietta Masina (1920–1994), began scriptwriting in earnest, and befriended Roberto Rossellini, who hired Fellini as one of his scriptwriters for *Open City* (1945), the international hit that announced the birth of Italian neorealism in the cinema and won for Fellini his first of many Oscar nominations (this one for best script). Fellini made major contributions to neorealist scripts for such directors as Rossellini, Pietro Germi, Alberto Lattuada, and Luigi Comencini before making his debut as a director, collaborating with Lattuada on *Variety Lights* (1951). This first film, followed by *The White Sheik* (1951) and his first critical and box office success, *I vitelloni* (1953; The loafers), begins a trilogy of character that moves Italian cinema away from neorealist emphasis on socially defined characters and toward a more fanciful consideration of how a character's personality may conflict with society's demands. The subsequent trilogy of grace or redemption, three films dealing with the nature of innocence in a cruel and unsentimental world— *La strada* (1954), *Il bidone* (1955; The swindle), and *The Nights of Cabiria* (1957)—employs the only superficially Catholic notions of salvation and conversion to examine secular crises in the lives of his willfully fanciful characters. The first and third of the films in this trilogy garnered Oscars for best foreign film and made his wife an international star. The stupendous commercial success of *La dolce vita* (1960), beginning Fellini's long collaboration with Marcello Mastroianni (1924–1996), left neorealist cinema behind in its baroque imagery, its picaresque plot structure, and its exuberant treatment of high society corruption. The film's very title became synonymous everywhere and in numerous languages with the society life depicted by Rome's gossip column photographers, or *paparazzi,* a word that Fellini contributed to the English language.

The film that critics regard as Fellini's masterpiece, *8½* (1963), cast Mastroianni as a film director and Fellini's alter ego, earning the director his third Oscar. The high modernist aesthetics of *8½* have become emblematic of the very notion of free, uninhibited artistic creativity and have been imitated by many other directors since its appearance. Fellini would subsequently be forever linked to the vogue of the postwar European art film, even though he was one of the few non-American directors who could be counted upon by his producers to score at the box office. Fellini's post-*8½* works deal with the myth of Rome, the cinema, and his own subjective fantasy world, and some were quite successful both critically and commercially. *Fellini Satyricon* (1969) demonstrated his mastery of a dreamlike cinematic language in an original adaptation of Petronius's Latin classic. *Fellini's Roma* (1972) provided a personal portrait of the Eternal City. *Amarcord* (awarded Fellini's fourth Oscar in 1974), offered a nostalgic portrait of Fellini's provincial adolescence during the Fascist period. Other, later films encountered both critical objections and commercial difficulties. The

**Marcello Mastroianni as the anguished film director in Fellini's autobiographical 8 ½.** CINERIZ/THE KOBAL COLLECTION

breathtaking sets of *Fellini's Casanova* (1976), the satire of a feminist convention in *The City of Women* (1980), his humorous portrait of opera singers on an ocean voyage in *And the Ship Sails On* (1983), and his biting satire of television in *Ginger and Fred* (1985) and in his last film, *The Voice of the Moon* (1990), demonstrated the maestro's genius but somehow failed to find a large commercial audience. In his penultimate work, *Interview* (1987), Fellini provided a moving homage to the art of the cinema that won at least critical acclaim. During the last years of his life, Fellini received career awards from Venice's Biennale and Lincoln Center (1985), as well as a lifetime achievement Oscar (1993).

Fellini's death was rightly seen by Italians as the end of a great era of artistic creativity in their national cinema. His works have influenced such very different directors as Martin Scorsese, Francis Ford Coppola, Peter Greenaway, Ettore Scola, Lina Wertmüller,

Giuseppe Tornatore, François Truffaut, Bob Fosse, Woody Allen, Nanni Moretti, and Spike Jonze.

*See also* **Cinema; Italy.**

BIBLIOGRAPHY

Bondanella, Peter. *The Cinema of Federico Fellini.* Princeton, N.J., 1992.

————. *The Films of Federico Fellini.* New York, 2002.

Costantini, Costanzo, ed. *Conversations with Fellini.* Translated by Sohrab Sorooshian. San Diego, Calif., 1996.

Fellini, Federico. *Fellini on Fellini.* Translated by Isabel Quigley. New York, 1996.

Kezich, Tullio. *Federico Fellini, la vita e i film.* Milan, 2002.

PETER BONDANELLA

**FEMINISM.** The terms *feminism* and *feminist*, as they are used throughout the world, connote, respectively, movements that have advocated the idea of women's emancipation and the individuals who have supported these movements. Nineteenth-century French political discourse commonly used the term *féminisme* as a synonym for women's emancipation. Its exact origin remains uncertain, but dictionaries do not record its use in this sense before the 1870s. In the following decade, it was used by the first self-proclaimed feminist, Hubertine Auclert (1848–1914), in her periodical *La citoyenne* (The woman citizen) and gained currency after a number of "feminist" congresses in the 1890s. Before the turn of the twentieth century, the term appeared first in British, then in Belgian, French, Spanish, Italian, German, Greek, and Russian publications.

**SENSE OF THE TERM**

In European societies, *feminism* often acquired various cultural meanings. It connotes a political ideology as well as a social movement. The historian Karen Offen has aptly defined it as "the name given to a comprehensive critical response to the deliberate and systematic subordination of women as a group within a given cultural setting" (p. 20). As a historical phenomenon, feminism can accordingly be defined as an "encompassing program of sociopolitical critique and remediation, with gender issues at its very core" (p. 24). European feminist movements addressed imbalances of power between the sexes, raised issues concerning personal autonomy or individual freedoms, and supported ideas and movements for sociopolitical change, often intersecting with other concerns such as class, race, age, or religion.

## FORMS OF FEMINIST POLITICS

Since the eighteenth century, European feminists have debated the distribution of political, social, and economic power between the sexes and have challenged women's subordination to men in the family and in society. The fortunes of European feminism have varied greatly from one society to another, often depending on the possibilities for voicing dissent. Most feminist movements in Europe were transnational in scope and addressed common themes. In the first half of the twentieth century, national politics and population issues figured prominently; in the second half, European feminists continued to fight for women's economic opportunities and equal legal status with men but also turned to new issues, as the "personal" became "political."

In the history of European feminist thought, historians have identified two basic approaches, not necessarily distinct and often intertwined. The so-called relational argument proposes a gender-based but egalitarian organization of society, emphasizes the rights of women in relation to those of men, and insists on women's distinctive contributions to society. The "individualistic" argument sees the individual, irrespective of its sex, as society's basic unit and stresses more abstract concepts of individual human rights as well as the quest for personal independence. Although it is tempting to categorize each European women's movement as either "relational" or "individualistic," the great historical and political heterogeneity of these movements argues against simple categorizations. Not all women's organizations were feminist, some can indeed be seen as antifeminist, yet their activities outside the domestic realm generally contributed to the development of a feminist consciousness.

## NATIONAL MOVEMENTS

By the beginning of the twentieth century, national feminist movements had emerged in many western,

central, and northern European countries. These movements were largely liberal, Protestant, and middle-class. Their members organized against the subordinate legal status of women and their exclusion from higher education and the professions, for women's suffrage and a variety of social and moral reforms. In Great Britain, Germany, France, Scandinavia, and Italy, feminists became increasingly concerned about the fate of the bourgeois marriage and shared the general anxiety about the falling birthrate in their countries. Working-class women also organized and joined socialist organizations in Britain, France, Germany, Italy, and Russia. Although some of their leaders proclaimed a "clean separation" from bourgeois feminism, European feminists increasingly crossed class barriers, especially after transnational cooperation came to a temporary halt during World War I and national movements united to support the war effort. The aftermath of the war saw not only the reorganization of Europe's political landscape but also the development of new feminist movements.

Feminists in the successor states to the Austro-Hungarian Empire got off to a shaky start. Newly enfranchised women activists in the new Austria were certainly pleased when the son of Marianne Hainisch, the founder and president of the Bund Österreichischer Frauenvereine (BÖFV; League of Austrian women's associations, founded in 1902) was elected president of the republic. Yet widely divergent views on feminist issues in the two major parties, the Social Democratic and the Conservative, kept them from enacting significant feminist policies. While Social Democratic women, often exhibiting an anti-Catholic bias, addressed the double burden of women workers and protested restrictive laws on abortion and on contraceptive information, the middle-class feminists of the BÖFV emphasized peace and harmony in postwar Austrian society. They pressed for better educational opportunities and changes in Austrian women's legal and economic situation, and they promoted international peace.

Feminists fared differently in smaller Catholic countries, especially when nationalist issues were also at stake. When the monarchy in Portugal, a rural and Catholic nation, was replaced by a republic in 1910, a small but enthusiastic feminist movement, the Liga Republicana das Mulheres

Portuguesas (Republican league of Portuguese women), emerged in Lisbon. Its leaders worked for the economic autonomy of married women, a divorce law, and a number of other legal reforms, but their efforts were hampered by World War I and came to a standstill in 1926, when the authoritarian regime of António Salazar took control. The Portuguese feminists had no choice but to succumb to its Catholic, nationalist, and corporatist principles. After World War II, "unofficial" women's organizations were dissolved and coeducation in the schools was abolished. The constitution of 1966 reestablished the husband's marital authority. Feminist activism reemerged only after the end of the authoritarian regime in 1974.

In the neighboring country of Spain, the program of the Asociación Nacional de Mujeres Españolas (National association of Spanish women), founded by educated urban women in 1918, also called for major changes in civil legislation, women's access to education and the professions, equal opportunity, and equal pay. High illiteracy rates—especially among women—poverty, infant mortality, prostitution, and discriminatory laws provided a broad agenda for both middle-class and socialist feminists. In 1930 the constitution of the Second Republic gave women full political rights and secularized civic life. The republican government soon came under attack from the Right, especially after the disastrous election of 1933, for which the Left blamed women voters. When civil war ensued in 1936, a number of women's organizations emerged on both sides, but feminist issues were rarely at the top of their agenda. Under the regime of the victorious General Francisco Franco (1892–1972), abortion was redefined as a "crime against the state," coeducation ceased, male authority in marriage was restored, and marriage loans (incentive programs offering government grants to newlyweds for the purchase of household goods) were paid along with birth premiums. Yet feminism reemerged in the 1970s and gained momentum after Franco's death.

Irish feminists had to contend with Catholicism and nationalism as well, but the outcome was different from that in Spain, Austria, and Portugal. The proclamation of the Irish Republic in 1916 stipulated equal political rights for both sexes, and militant Irishwomen became activists

for independence during the years of undeclared war with England that followed. When Irishwomen were partially enfranchised in 1918, Cumann na mBan, the women's organization associated with the nationalist party Sinn Féin, called upon women voters to support the cause of Irish independence. After Ireland achieved legislative independence in 1921, the constitution of the Irish Free State gave equal rights to both sexes. In the 1920s and 1930s, Irish feminists waged a battle on matters concerning divorce, access to contraceptive information, the age of consent for girls, the legal situation of unmarried mothers, and prostitution. When Ireland finally gained independence in 1937, the new constitution discriminated against women. Irish feminists did not challenge this until the 1970s, and the constitutional clauses on women's status were still in effect in the 1990s.

The development of Scandinavian feminist movements took yet another path. Postwar Swedish society, for example, was still relatively poor and predominantly agricultural; however, high literacy rates, Protestant traditions, and a Social Democratic Party that was more nationalist, more populist, and less Marxist than some of its counterparts in other countries contributed to the formation of a particular brand of "feminism." Nineteenth-century Swedish feminists rejected the term and named their movement *kvinnosaken*, or "woman's cause," a name that by the 1920s was widely connected with a radical liberal faction that supposedly promoted mostly the interests of single, childless women. Its representatives founded a school for women's civic education at the Fogelstad estate, which contributed a new dimension to European feminism by emphasizing environmental issues, the skills of rural women, and women's special qualities and contributions to society. This Swedish brand of what could be called antimilitarist ecofeminism enjoyed a revival around the turn of the twenty-first century. "Classic" feminist demands such as the abolition of legal, state-regulated prostitution, full legal rights for married women, educational equality, access to the civil service, and motherhood insurance were largely met in the 1920s. With increasing industrialization and modernization of the country, many Swedish feminists became associated with the Social Democratic Party and committed themselves to solving the dilemma of combining employment and motherhood. A number of reforms after the 1936 elections, including the legalization of contraceptives, promoted women's economic independence and created facilities for child care and household support services but also addressed the division of domestic labor and the perpetuation of gender roles. Framed in terms of Sweden's national interest, this program was central for Swedish society beginning in the 1960s and ensured the success of the Social Democrats for many decades.

### PHASES OF PROTEST AND POLITICAL NEGOTIATION

Woman suffrage was undoubtedly one of the most prominent causes of feminist movements in Europe. At the beginning of the twentieth century, they could already look back on decades of struggle. The road to full political participation for women varied but was characterized by similar developments: European suffragists often based their demands for inclusion on women's special contribution to society while at the same time raising questions of equal rights and representation. By 1922 twenty-one European countries had passed woman suffrage laws. The vote was won in Finland in 1906 and Norway in 1913; seventeen countries followed between 1915 and 1922; Spain and Portugal joined the ranks in 1931. Yet four European countries denied the vote to half their population until the end of World War II (France until 1944 and Italy until 1945) or even longer (Greece granted woman suffrage in 1952, Switzerland in 1971).

The postwar successes of the European suffrage movements, or so the conventional argument goes, were largely "a reward" for women's participation in the war effort, though woman suffrage was passed in some neutral countries and women in warring countries such as France still stood empty-handed. As in the United States, woman suffrage in Europe was actually the result of a transnational development that originated in the suffragist movements of the nineteenth century and depended on other factors as well, for example, different democratic traditions, the intensity of the class struggle, the extension of male suffrage, or changing coalitions between liberal and conservative or socialist parties.

No European country allowed women to vote before the suffrage had been extended to all males, and even then restrictions applied: in Great Britain, for example, only married women, female heads of households, or women over thirty with university degrees could vote between 1918 and 1928; Belgium introduced *suffrage des morts* in 1920 for mothers and widows of war casualties; Austria initially excluded prostitutes from voting; and Portugal, which demanded a literacy test for male voters, in 1931 extended the suffrage only to women with "higher education."

Italy passed local woman suffrage for "educated" women as well as for mothers and widows of slain soldiers in 1925, shortly before Benito Mussolini abolished all elections. The discourse and tactics of the feminist movements in France and Switzerland did not differ much from those in the rest of Europe, and the French feminist movement achieved some prominence. Women in these countries counted on being granted the vote after World War I. The necessary referenda in several Swiss *Kantone* (states), however, produced overwhelmingly negative results until 1971. In France, the cause of the feminists was primarily defeated by anticlerical republican forces, which feared that women would vote against the republic. This argument turned up in other Catholic countries as well, but was of special significance for the *Gauche démocratique* (democratic Left) in France. Only in 1944 did woman suffrage finally become part of the program of Charles de Gaulle's provisional government.

After World War I, many newly enfranchised European feminists would have sided with Marie Juchacz, who, in the first speech given by a woman elected as a representative to the German parliament, claimed that "political equality has given my sex the possibility to fully develop its powers" (quoted in Offen, p. 252). Thus, equal suffrage rights not only epitomized civil and political equality but was also considered the gateway to women's social rights. European feminists did not merely aspire to participation in the male political sphere but sought to redefine that sphere. Whereas the social rights demanded by men centered on questions of wages, hours, and insurance for disability and old age, the respective feminist discourses concentrated on gender-neutral social insurance,

**Emmeline Pankhurst (center) leading a protest march, July 1915.** Pankhurst and other feminists voice their demand that women be used to replace male workers called to the front during World War I. ©UNDERWOOD & UNDERWOOD/CORBIS

protective laws for women workers, and maternity benefits for all mothers, employed or not (*protection des mères* in France, *Mutterschutz* in Germany). The developing European welfare states traveled different roads to insuring the risks of sickness, old age, and unemployment, notably in Great Britain, where insurance systems were largely tax funded and thus comparatively gender neutral, and in Germany, where they were often tied to the male "breadwinner" and thus disadvantaged women. Nevertheless, the "feminization of poverty" remained a problem throughout Europe and the need to remedy it was uncontested within feminist movements.

The question of protective laws for women workers was a different matter. Before 1914, most countries had passed laws prohibiting night work as well as dangerous employment for women workers

and limiting their hours. This transnational development was facilitated by the founding of the International Labor Organization (ILO) in 1919. Protective labor legislation for women was highly contested. The debate centered on gender roles, gender relations, and the "welfare" of the family and the nation. Feminists could be found on both sides of the issue. The fight about protective labor legislation was mostly symbolic, however, and had relatively few practical consequences. In most European countries and for the greater part of the twentieth century, women represented only a minority of industrial workers; night work was never prohibited for nurses and the eight-hour day and minimum wage legislation never applied to sweatshops. Laws could be easily abolished, for example, during both world wars and the Soviet civil war, when the number of women workers increased sharply, or could be circumvented by both employers and women workers.

European feminist movements were far more unified when it came to maternity legislation, demanding not only restrictions on employment but also financial support for pregnant women and mothers. Feminists throughout Europe declared motherhood a "social function" of the state and demanded public maternity funds, maternity insurance, paid leave, and cash allowances for mothers and children. They thus continued a debate that had originated in the nineteenth century, when some rudimentary legislation was also enacted. In 1913 Great Britain passed more comprehensive maternity laws; Norway followed suit in 1915, Germany in 1924, France in 1928, and Sweden in 1931. Even though these laws were passed somewhat hesitantly and with minimal benefits, they provided a base for making employment compatible with family responsibilities. Benefits for mothers and children were extended as the European welfare states developed, with France introducing family allowances in 1931, Italy and Germany in 1936, Sweden in 1937, Spain in 1938, Portugal in 1942, and Great Britain and Norway in 1945. Originally a demand of feminists that envisioned a "mother's salary," family allowances now functioned as a kind of financial compensation for families. Generally, the checks were sent to the fathers.

As woman suffrage gradually expanded throughout Europe after World War I, women became more visible in national and, to a more limited extent, international politics. Women activists tried to influence the terms of peace in 1919 and, while their achievements seem limited, the Treaty of Versailles did include certain provisions for equal rights and specified the inclusion of women in the work of the ILO and the League of Nations. Building on the work of the International Council of Women (founded in 1888) and the International Women Suffrage Alliance (founded in 1904), the Women's International League for Peace and Freedom emerged in 1919 to support a broad feminist network, whose members worked for the newly founded international organizations. They promoted laws that would secure the citizenship of women married to foreigners, end state-regulated prostitution and the "trade" in women

and children, and defend women's employment at all levels.

Paradoxically, those national feminist movements that had fought so vehemently for woman suffrage did not necessarily profit from it after the war, and vice versa. Suffragists had been somewhat underrepresented in the German women's movement, yet the Reichstag had the highest percentage of women representatives in 1919 (10 percent, followed by Finland with 9 percent and the Netherlands with 7 percent). In contrast, the British Parliament had only one female member in 1919 and fifteen (less than 3 percent) in 1931. Without a common cause, many feminist movements disintegrated into special interest groups. Although adult women outnumbered men in many countries after the massive casualties of the war, coalitions of women voters on behalf of women's supposed common interests did not materialize anywhere in Europe. Plans to found women's parties were either quickly abandoned or resulted in short-lived and unsuccessful experiments, as in Sweden and Austria, for example.

During the decade of the *garçonne* (boyish girl) and of the flapper, who sported knee-length dresses and the *Bubikopf* (short-cropped hair), many feminists lamented not only the "loose morals" of a new generation of women but also the lack of interest in feminist issues. Although European women had entered public life at an unprecedented scale, the younger generation did not necessarily seek emancipation as understood by more traditional feminists, nor did they appreciate the role feminist movements had played in opening the opportunities of modern life to them.

Overall, the interwar decades were not characterized by a triumph of democracy but rather by a sense of crisis, as a growing number of countries succumbed to authoritarian or totalitarian regimes, which often meant a strengthening of traditional gender roles. Socialist women in Russia thought their dream had come true when the Bolsheviks came to power in 1917, but some of them soon faced exile and even imprisonment for criticizing party leaders. Although the new Soviet government completely refashioned marriage and family law, legalized abortion on demand, and addressed the problem of prostitution—issues firmly rooted in nineteenth-century progressive thought—most of the much-hailed benefits for working women, including transformation of work, child care, the household, and gender roles, were on paper only. The prewar generation of liberal feminists, largely opposed to the Bolsheviks, was effectively silenced and lost the enfranchisement gained under the provisional government. But the fate of feminist movements was sealed as well in the right-wing authoritarian regimes that came to power in Italy in 1922, in Germany and Portugal in 1933, in Greece in 1936, and in Spain in 1938. In Germany, where for a decade the women's movement had been under attack from the Right for being too liberal, too dominated by Jewish women, too international, and too pacifist, the National Socialists declared "women's emancipation from women's emancipation."

Feminist organizations in these countries were outlawed outright or forced to cooperate with the government under a strict set of guidelines. Fascist and military dictatorships were both anticommunist and antifeminist and fiercely supported the reconsolidation of male authority over women. Specifically, they objected to higher education, many forms of paid employment for women, and their political participation, which was confined to the party's mass organizations. While the percentage of female party members was small (4 percent in Portugal, 6 in Germany in 1936, and 8 in Soviet Russia in 1924), with virtually no representation in the higher ranks, every totalitarian party founded special organizations to "meet women's needs" or to "educate" them: the Zhenotdel in the Soviet Union, the Fasci Femminili in Italy, the Nationalsozialistische Frauenschaft in Germany, and the women's Falange in Spain all proclaimed a private role for women but at the same time functioned as important instruments of public mass mobilization.

In the 1920s European feminists had warned against the dangers of totalitarian regimes, which would reduce women to "servants of men" and "childbearing machines." Wherever these regimes came to power, all politically active women were ostracized. In Germany, the lives of Jewish, socialist, and pacifist women were in extreme danger—women could be arrested and sent to concentration camps just like men. Some feminist leaders managed to escape, but life in exile proved depressing

and difficult, even if they could rely on international women's networks. Others suffered long years of imprisonment or were murdered in concentration camps. As the Nazis extended their grip over Europe, feminists in democratic countries joined the war effort, not the least because they did not want to share the fate of their German peers. In the words of the British feminist Margery Corbett Ashby, in 1940 "the problem was no longer how to force democracies logically to include women, but how to protect democracy itself" (quoted in Offen, pp. 367–368). Women became involved in the war effort as both perpetrators and victims of its violence. As feminists faced the ruins of half of Europe, campaigns for "peace and bread" often seemed more important than those for equal rights.

## EMERGENCE OF NEW MOVEMENTS AFTER 1945

In contrast to the development of feminist movements after 1918, organized feminism barely survived World War II; its aging leadership was dispersed, imprisoned, or had been executed, and large parts of its records were lost or destroyed. The first half of the twentieth century had seen dramatic progress for women, first and foremost equal political rights, increased literacy, better access to schooling at all levels and to the professions, changes in marriage and property laws, increasing equity in the developing welfare states, and even early proposals to restructure the domestic division of labor. The legal status of married women, the question of their employment, and the dilemma of combining employment and family responsibilities still figured prominently on the list of problems, however.

International feminist organizations hailed the United Nations Charter, which declared equal rights in 1945, the Universal Declaration of Human Rights, including equal rights for married women and equal pay, in 1948, and the establishment of a UN Commission on the Status of Women. In postwar Europe, many political parties, and the resurgent communist parties in particular, wooed women voters, but female elected officials remained few and far between in most European countries. On both sides of the Iron Curtain, women's "organizations" increasingly replaced feminist movements. After the catastrophe of World

War II, women and men throughout Europe, overwhelmed by problems of survival and rebuilding, longed most for a return to "normalcy," often defined in terms of traditional gender roles.

## NEW FEMINIST MOVEMENT AFTER 1965

Whereas European feminist movements had developed rather gradually in the nineteenth and early twentieth century, the "new" women's movement made a rather sudden appearance on the political stage in the late 1960s. "Second wave feminism" was characterized by highly provocative campaigns and a close-knit international communications network. Taking their name from a New York organization, the Danish Redstockings paid only 80 percent of the price of a bus ticket, arguing that they earned only 80 percent of a man's salary; in France, feminists placed a wreath commemorating the "unknown wife of the unknown soldier" at the Arc de Triomphe and stormed the offices of the fashion magazine *Elle;* British feminists supported striking women workers and protested against beauty contests; in Germany, women turned against the traditional gender roles practiced in leftist student protest movements and founded self-help institutions such as cooperative child care centers and women's shelters. Feminists in Rome and Milano "took back the night" in protest marches, a movement that spread throughout Europe. Many campaigns were inspired by the "new" feminist movement in the United States, in particular the founding of encounter and self-help groups and the emergence of a lesbian feminist movement. Inspired by what Betty Friedan had termed the "problem without a name," women in Italy and Great Britain started to demand payment for housework, a campaign that extended into Germany, Canada, and the United States. In 1976 the protests of prostitutes against state regulation and police harassment in France, Germany, Italy, and Great Britain and the protests of black feminists in Germany against racism culminated in the International Tribunal on Crimes against Women in Brussels.

The major issue for almost all Western European feminist movements, however, was the controversy about abortion. In the wake of massive campaigns in which French and German feminists admitted they had had abortions, laws were

**Women's rights demonstrators gather in Trafalgar Square, London, 1971.** ©HULTON-DEUTSCH COLLECTION/CORBIS

gradually liberalized. Great Britain had already reformed its laws in 1967, and feminists defended the reforms in 1975, the same year French abortion laws were liberalized. In 1974 Italian feminists were thrust into action by a mass trial in Trent, and in 1977 their campaign resulted in a highly controversial law that allowed termination of pregnancies under certain circumstances. A similar law in West Germany legalized first-trimester abortions on ethical, eugenic, medical, and social grounds in 1974. This law became a major issue during the unification process fifteen years later, since abortion had been legalized without any restrictions in East Germany. The feminist discourse about abortion, however, did not limit itself to legal issues but addressed issues of unwanted pregnancy and, ultimately, sexual power relations. While safe abortions on demand had become the epitome of women's liberation for some feminists, others saw them as a last resort and tried to spread information about contraceptive methods instead.

There were some significant exceptions to the "autonomous" European women's movements that defined abortion rights as their central issue: questions of sexuality and male domination were discussed less openly in Ireland; Scandinavian women generally worked closely with the Social Democratic parties in their countries and took the legislative road to articulate and respond to feminist grievances; women activists in Spain and Portugal were first closely tied to authoritarian regimes and later contributed to building democratic nations.

Many "second wave" feminists not only were at odds with the "New Left" but also distanced themselves from the older feminist movements, which they criticized for demanding "only" legislative reforms and "mere" equality with men instead of fundamental social changes. Initially, even the term *feminism* was discredited (and replaced by *women's liberation*). It ultimately prevailed, and feminist debates focused increasingly on the relationship of "difference and equality," a debate that continued into the twenty-first century. The debates of the "new" feminists, debates about hierarchies and women's liberation, employment and housework, families and reproductive rights ultimately revealed that neither businesswomen nor factory workers, neither housewives nor mothers were homogenous groups that could be represented as such, but rather individuals claiming the right to make their own decisions.

## MULTIPLE FRONTS AT THE END OF THE TWENTIETH CENTURY

The second half of the twentieth century witnessed the developments many early-twentieth-century feminists had envisioned: women's political representation in Europe rose to unprecedented levels, with Scandinavian countries once more leading the way. In 1999 women made up 43 percent of the parliament in Sweden, 37 percent in Denmark, 34 percent in Finland, 31 percent in the Netherlands, and 30 percent in Germany, but only 9 percent in France and 6 percent in Greece. In Russia, the figure was 6 percent in 1992.

Throughout Europe, the gender gap in higher education narrowed. By the mid-1980s, women made up more than 40 percent of all university students in most countries and more than half in Poland, Hungary, Norway, Portugal, and France. Still, they often clustered in certain fields such as education, language, and literature studies and were underrepresented in some of the fields leading to prestigious (and well-paid) jobs, such as engineering and science. The same was true for women's participation in the labor market: labor conditions improved and wages rose, yet the discrepancy in men's and women's wages remained.

In the early years of the twenty-first century, solving the dilemma of combining wage work with family responsibilities was still widely considered a mother's job. Although some European countries created family policies to help deal with this problem, for example, by contributing to old age insurance for parents who stay at home or by introducing generous paid family leave policies, the percentage of fathers availing themselves of these opportunities remained in the low single digits, even in countries such as Sweden, where these policies had been in effect since 1974. Often, this was a rational choice to secure the family income. While Eastern European countries propagated full-time employment for women, mainly for economic reasons, and developed an extensive system of public day care, Western European women generally saw part-time work as the solution. Yet most European women still worked a double shift, taking over the lion's share of childrearing and unpaid housework. Also, family patterns changed significantly. Birthrates dropped throughout Europe, as did rates of marriage, while divorce rates and the number of children born outside marriage climbed. In spite of a multitude of social programs, the average poverty rate of children in the European Union stood at 20 percent in 1993.

Apart from changes in political representation, employment, and family patterns, the second half of the twentieth century saw a host of legal reforms concerning marriage, divorce, and women's economic opportunities. These reforms occurred on three levels, the national, European, and international, where the ILO and the United Nations continued to work for women's rights. After the decade of the woman was declared in 1975, feminist networks became visible at a number of international conferences, from Mexico City to Beijing. Undoubtedly, the need for feminists to speak about and act on women's rights and women's issues inside and outside Europe did not vanish with the twentieth century.

*See also* **Gender; Suffrage.**

BIBLIOGRAPHY

Akkerman, Tjitske, and Siep Stuurman, eds. *Perspectives on Feminist Political Thought in European History, from the Middle Ages to the Present.* London, 1998.

Anderson, Bonnie. *Joyous Greetings! The First International Women's Movement, 1830–1860.* New York, 2000.

Banks, Olive. *The Politics of British Feminism, 1918–1970.* Aldershot, U.K., 1993.

Bock, Gisela, and Pat Thane, eds. *Maternity and Gender Policies: Women and the Rise of the European Welfare States, 1880s–1950s.* London, 1991.

Bridenthal, Renate, Susan Mosher Stuard, and Merry E. Weisner, eds. *Becoming Visible: Women in European History.* 3rd ed. Boston, 1998.

Caine, Barbara. *English Feminism, 1780–1980.* Oxford, U.K., 1997.

Coulter, Carol. *The Hidden Tradition: Feminism, Women, and Nationalism in Ireland.* Cork, U.K., 1993.

Daley, Caroline, and Melanie Nolan, eds. *Suffrage and Beyond: International Feminist Perspectives.* New York, 1994.

Evans, Richard J. *The Feminist Movement in Germany 1894–1933.* London, 1976.

———. *The Feminists: Women's Emancipation Movements in Europe, America, and Australasia, 1840–1920.* London, 1977.

———. *Comrades and Sisters: Feminism, Socialism, and Pacifism in Europe, 1870–1945.* New York, 1987.

Fraisse, Geneviève, and Michelle Perrot, eds. *Emerging Feminism from Revolution to World War.* Vol. 4 of *A History of Women in the West,* edited by Georges Duby and Michelle Perrot. Cambridge, Mass., 1993.

Frevert, Ute. *Women in German History: From Bourgeois Emancipation to Sexual Liberation.* Translated by Stuart McKinnon-Evans in association with Terry Bond and Barbara Norden. Oxford, U.K., 1989.

Good, David, Margarete Grandner, and Mary Jo Maynes, eds. *Austrian Women in the Nineteenth and Twentieth Centuries: Cross-disciplinary Perspectives.* Providence, R.I., 1996.

Haan, Francisca de. *Gender and the Politics of Office Work: The Netherlands 1860–1940.* Amsterdam, 1998.

Hause, Steven C., with Anne R. Kenney. *Women's Suffrage and Social Politics in the French Third Republic.* Princeton, N.J., 1984.

Jackson, Margaret. *The Real Facts of Life: Feminism and the Politics of Sexuality, c. 1850–1940.* London, 1994.

Kaplan, Gisela T. *Contemporary Western European Feminism.* New York, 1992.

Koven, Seth, and Sonya Michel. *Mothers of a New World: Maternalist Politics and the Origins of Welfare States.* New York, 1993.

Offen, Karen. *European Feminisms, 1700–1950: A Political History.* Stanford, Calif., 2000.

Offen, Karen, Ruth Roach Pierson, and Jane Rendall, eds. *Writing Women's History: International Perspectives.* Houndmills, U.K., 1991.

Owens, Rosemary Cullen. *Smashing Times: A History of the Irish Women's Suffrage Movement, 1889–1922.* Dublin, 1984.

Pugh, Martin. *Women and the Women's Movement in Britain, 1914–1959.* Houndmills, U.K., 1992.

Rupp, Leila J. *Worlds of Women: The Making of an International Women's Movement.* Princeton, N.J., 1997.

Scott, Joan Wallach. *Only Paradoxes to Offer: French Feminists and the Rights of Man.* Cambridge, Mass., 1996.

Sklar, Kathryn Kish, Susan Strasser, and Anja Schüler, eds. *Social Justice Feminists in the United States and Germany: A Dialogue in Documents, 1885–1933.* Ithaca, N.Y., 1998.

Slaughter, Jane, and Robert Kern, eds. *European Women on the Left: Socialism, Feminism, and the Problems Faced by Political Women, 1880 to the Present.* Westport, Conn., 1981.

Smith, Harold L., ed. *British Feminism in the Twentieth Century.* Amherst, Mass., 1990.

Smith, Paul. *Feminism and the Third Republic: Women's Political and Civil Rights in France, 1918–1945.* Oxford, U.K., 1996.

Stites, Richard. *The Women's Liberation Movement in Russia: Nihilism, Feminism, and Bolshevism, 1860–1930.* Princeton, N.J., 1978.

Thébaud, Françoise, ed. *Toward a Cultural Identity in the Twentieth Century.* Vol. 5 of *A History of Women in the West,* edited by Georges Duby and Michelle Perrot. Cambridge, Mass., 1994.

ANJA SCHÜLER

# FILM (DOCUMENTARY).

Early European documentary film relied on preexisting forms of popular culture as sources of inspiration. During this period, documentary films carried news stories, exhibited celebrity tours and sporting occasions, and showed exotic locales. However, the ability of documentary to render everyday realities was also a factor, as is evident in the fascination that the brothers Auguste-Marie-Louis-Nicolas and Louis-Jean Lumière provoked with *La sortie des usines Lumiére* (1895; Workers leaving the Lumière factory) and *Arrivée d'un train à la Ciotat* (1895; Arrival of a train at Ciotat). Early documentaries also played a public relations role for corporate enterprise, as in *Life on the Oxo Cattle Ranch* (1911). However, after the advent of World War I, films of greater substance such as *The Battle of the Somme* (United Kingdom, 1916) and *On the Firing Line with the Germans* (Germany, 1915) appeared, and during this period documentary also became increasingly employed as a form of state propaganda.

## EARLY DOCUMENTARIES

The first important movement of documentary film was the British documentary film movement. John Grierson (1898–1972), the movement's founder, hoped that the documentary film might provide an effective channel of communication between government and people and thus play a role in defending European democracy against the inroads of fascism, communism, and unregulated capitalism. However, although the films of the documentary film movement had a social purpose they were also characterized by a modernist aesthetic inclination, apparent in Grierson's *Drifters* (1929), a film that combines modernist technique with the more expository imperatives of the information film. Other important films produced by this movement include *Industrial Britain* (dir. Robert Joseph Flaherty and others, 1933), *The Song of Ceylon* (dir. Basil Wright, Alberto Cavalcanti, 1934) and *Night Mail* (dir. Harry Watt, Wright, 1936). Grierson himself was a producer rather than a director, as was (at this time) the other major figure within the documentary film movement, Cavalcanti. However, one important director who did emerge from the movement was Humphrey Jennings, who directed exceptional films such as *Spare Time* (1939), *Listen to Britain* (1942), and *Fires Were Started* (1943).

Around 1925 a modernist tradition of documentary filmmaking emerged in France, influenced by the nineteenth-century naturalist tradition and the pictorialist, naturalist, and cinematic impressionist schools of cinema of the 1910–1929 period. Films such as *Voyage au Congo: Retour des souverains* (1928; Voyage to the Congo, dir. Marc Allégret), *Rien que les heures* (1926; Nothing but the hours, dir. Cavalcanti), *Études sur Paris* (1928; Studies of Paris, dir. André Sauvage), *La Zone* (1928; *The Slum Belt*, dir. Georges Lacombe), *Nogent, Eldorado du dimanche* (1929; Nogent, Sunday's Eldorado, dir. Marcel Carné), and *À propos de Nice* (1930; On the subject of Nice, dir. Jean Vigo) emphasized film's capacity for rendering subjective vision through evocative suggestion, and employed impressionistic delineations of the urban environment to create poetic, expressive effects.

This school of French, poetic, modernist documentary can also be associated with the "city symphony" cycle of documentary films, which emerged in the late 1920s and includes German director Walter Ruttmann's *Berlin: Die Sinfonie der Großstadt* (1927; Berlin: Symphony of a Great City), Soviet director Dziga Vertov's *Chelovek s kino-apparatom* (1929; Man with a movie camera), the Belgian Henri Storck's *Images d'Ostende* (1929; Images of Ostend), and, from the Netherlands, Joris Ivens's *Regen* (1929; Rain). The narrative structure in these films is composed of sequences that display activities taking place within the city during the course of a single day, and the films employ modernist techniques to convey an impression of the interconnected character of the modern city.

The works of Grierson, Storck, Vertov, Ruttmann, Ivens, Cavalcanti, Allégret, Sauvage, Lacombe, Carné, and Vigo, together with films such as the Soviet documentaries *Turksib* (1929; dir. Victor Turin) and *Mekhanikha golovnogo mozga* (1929; Mechanics of the brain, dir. Vsevolod Pudovkin), make up a body of modernist documentary filmmaking that appeared across Europe during the silent period. As with other forms of experimental filmmaking, this modernist paradigm went into decline after 1930, as the sound film became increasingly prominent, and as countries such as the Soviet Union, Germany, Spain, and Italy placed censorial diktat over what was perceived to be a reactionary form of modernist cinema.

**A scene from John Grierson's *Drifters*, 1929.** Grierson's documentary about herring fishermen in the North Sea is considered a landmark in the development of the genre. COI/THE KOBAL COLLECTION

## POLITICAL INFLUENCES

The early documentaries considered here were also influenced by a dual imperative to constitute the documentary as an art form and to distinguish documentary from the superficiality of the commercial cinema. In many cases both these imperatives were influenced by political motives, as documentary filmmakers sought a more active political role for the medium. During the 1930s European documentary film became increasingly involved in the political sphere. In Germany, Leni Riefenstahl's *Olympia 1. Teil—Fest der Völker* and *Olympia 2. Teil—Fest der Schönheit* (1938; Olympia, Part one: festival of the nations, and Part two: festival of beauty) and *Triumph des Willens* (1935; *Triumph of the Will*) were appropriated as propaganda vehicles by the Nazi regime, although these ground-breaking films were more than mere propaganda

pieces. In Britain, filmmakers such as Ivor Montagu and Ralph Bond made films such as *Spanish ABC* (1936) in support of the Republican cause during the Spanish civil war while the directors Norman MacLaren and Helen Biggar made the antiappeasement film *Hell Unlimited* (1936). Elsewhere in Europe, filmmakers such as Joris Ivens and Henri Storck made films with a political dimension, as in Storck's *Histoire du soldat inconnu* (1932; *The History of an Unknown Soldier*), and Ivens's *Borinage* (1933; *Misery in Borinage*) while political organizations such as the Workers' Film Association in Britain made films such as *Advance Democracy* (1938) as a means of promoting socialism.

During the war, a number of films produced by government agencies also achieved levels of accomplishment, including Germany's *Feuertaufe*

(1940; Baptism of fire, dir. Hans Bertram), *Feldzug in Polen* (1940; Campaign in Poland, dir. Fritz Hippler), *Sieg im Westen* (1941; Victory in the West, dir. Svend Noldan), Vichy France's *La Tragedie de Mers-el-Kébir* (1940; The Tragedy of Mers-el-Kébir), the United Kingdom's *Fires Were Started* (1943, dir. Jennings), *Desert Victory* (1943, dir. Roy Boulting and James Lansdale Hodson), the Soviet Union's *Stalingrad* (1943; dir. Leonid Varlamov), and *Pobeda na Pravoberezhnoi Ukraine i izgnaniye nemetsikh zakhvatchikov za predeli Ukrainskikh sovietskikh zemel* (1945; Victory in Ukraine and the expulsion of the Germans from the boundaries of the Ukrainian Soviet earth, dir. Alexander Dovshenko and Yuliya Solntseva). Mention should also be made of Germany's highly anti-Semitic *Der ewige Jude* (1940; The eternal Jew, dir. Fritz Hippler), although many other anti-Semitic documentaries were made in France and Germany during the war years.

After the war, films such as the *World of Plenty* (1943; dir. Paul Rotha [U.K.]), *Berlin im Aufbau* (1946; Building up Berlin, dir. Kurt Maetzig [GDR]), *Le retour* (1946; The return, dir. Henri-Cartier Bresson [France]), and *Diary for Timothy* (1945; dir. Jennings [U.K.]) portrayed the problems of postwar reconstruction.

## MIDCENTURY

During the 1950s and 1960s the European art cinema became increasingly influential, and its corollary can also be found within the documentary films of the period. Feature filmmakers such as Michelangelo Antonioni and Alain Resnais turned to the documentary, while auteurist documentary filmmakers such as Georges Franju, Bert Haanstra, Chris Marker, Arne Sücksdorff, Lindsay Anderson, Karel Reisz, Michel Brault, Frederic Rossif, and others came to prominence. Resnais's *Nuit et brouillard* (1955; Night and fog; 1955), with its striking portrayal of the Nazi death camps, and his *Toute la mémoire du monde* (1956; All the world's memory), were two of the finest documentaries of the period. Other important contributions included Rossif's *Mourir à Madrid* (1963; To die in Madrid), Chris Marker's *Le joli mai* (1963; The happy May), Jacques-Yves Cousteau's series of underwater films such as *Le Monde du silence* (1956; *The Silent World*, with Louis Malle), Arne

Sücksdorff's *Det stora äventyret* (1953; The great adventure), and Franju's *Hôtel des Invalides* (1952; Hotel of the invalids), with its contemplation of the tragic consequences of war. Pier Paolo Pasolini's *Comizi d'amore* (1965; Love meetings) and Jean Rouch and Edgar Morin's *Chronique d'un été* (1961; Chronicle of a summer) also broke new ground in exploring tensions between the subjective and "objective" dimensions of documentary filmmaking. In Eastern Europe, documentary film was often used as a form of state propaganda and suffered as a consequence; perhaps the most significant film of note to emerge during this period is the East German *Die Windrose* (1956; The windrose), directed by Ivens and Cavalcanti as well as Yannick Bellon, Sergei Gerasimov, and Alex Viany.

One of the most important films to appear during the 1970s, Marcel Ophüls's *Le chagrin et la pitié* (1969; The sorrow and the pity), provided moving testimony to French complicity in the appeasement of Adolf Hitler. Werner Herzog also made documentary films during this period, including *Fata Morgana* (1971), and *Land des Schweigens und der Dunkelheit* (1971; Land of silence and darkness), the latter a powerful study of deaf and blind people. Also in West Germany, filmmakers such as Alexander Kluge and Hans-Jürgen Syberberg developed a modernist documentary style, while in Poland, Krzysztof Kieslowski made, among others, *Bylem zolnierzem* (1970; I was a soldier) and *Pierwsza milosc* (1974; First love), the latter a portrayal of the contradiction between romantic love and the harsh realities of life in communist Poland. From the 1940s to the late 1970s, distinctions between the documentary and the feature film also became blurred, as schools of documentary-based feature filmmaking, the most important of which was Italian neorealism, emerged in France, Germany, Italy, the United Kingdom, Spain, and elsewhere.

## THE LATE TWENTIETH CENTURY

During the 1980s and 1990s European documentary filmmaking become absorbed into new, more commercial subgenres such as reality TV. At the same time, the weakening of public service television broadcasting and the impact of globalization led to a decline in critical documentary filmmaking. However, although these factors dulled the

***Night and Fog.*** A photograph from Alain Resnais's 1955 documentary film shows huge piles of shoes discovered in a Nazi concentration camp. Resnais juxtaposed newsreel footage and black-and-white photographs of the era with later scenes of the deserted camps to create an overwhelming vision of the human tragedy of the Holocaust. ARGOS/COMO/THE KOBAL COLLECTION

potential of the genre, the more critical traditions of the European documentary were carried on by filmmakers such as Nick Broomfield, Molly Dineen, Nicholas Barker, and others. Bertrand Tavernier's *La guerre sans nom* (1992; *The Undeclared War*), which explores the Franco-Algerian War, deserves mention here, as do René Allio's *L'heure exquise* (1981; The delightful hour), Agnès Varda's *Les glaneurs et la glaneuse* (2000; The gleaners and I) and Claude Lanzmann's highly influential *Shoah* (1985).

In the USSR, following the implementation of Mikhail Gorbachev's policy of glasnost, critical documentaries such as *Vlast Solovetskaya. Svidetelstva i dokumenty* (1988; Solovki regime, dir. Marina Goldovskaya) and *Vai viegli but jaunam?* (1987; Is it easy to be young?, dir. Juris Podnieks) also appeared. The documentary drama has also built on the foundations provided by such works as

*Cathy Come Home* (1966; dir. Ken Loach), *The War Game* (1965; dir. Peter Watkins), and *Death of a Princess* (1980; dir. Antony Thomas) to produce influential films such as *The Investigation: Inside a Terrorist Bombing* (1990; dir. Mike Beckham for Granada Television). Important television documentary series have also appeared, such as *The World at War* (1974–1975; Thames Television), *The Nazis: A Warning from History* (1997; dir. Laurence Rees and Tilman Remme for the BBC) and *The Death of Yugoslavia* (1995; BBC).

*See also* **Cinema; Workers' Theatre Movement.**

BIBLIOGRAPHY

Aitken, Ian, ed. *The Documentary Film Movement: An Anthology.* Edinburgh, 1998.

———. *The Encyclopedia of the Documentary Film.* New York, 2005.

Barnouw, Eric. *Documentary: A History of the Non-Fiction Film.* Oxford, U.K., 1983.

Barsam, Richard M. *Nonfiction Film: A Critical History.* Bloomington and Indianapolis, Ind., 1992.

Grant, Barry Keith, and Jeannette Sloniowski, eds. *Documenting the Documentary: Close Readings of Documentary Film and Video.* Detroit, Mich., 1998.

Jacobs, Lewis, ed. *The Documentary Tradition.* New York, 1979.

IAN AITKEN

---

**FINLAND.** In retrospect, the history of Finland in the twentieth century may seem, in almost every sense, like an incredible success story. Within three generations the country located on Europe's northeastern periphery developed from a poor and in many ways backward province affiliated with the Russian Empire into one of the most modern industrial welfare states. This evolution did not proceed in a straight line and was expected by hardly anyone at the beginning of the century; it resulted from a combination of favorable external circumstances, policies displaying farsightedness at the right junctures, and a number of historical coincidences.

The country had been part of the Swedish Empire for more than six centuries before becoming joined to Russia as an autonomous grand duchy in 1809 (Peace of Hamina). With the special linguistic position of Finnish as a starting point and under the autonomy guaranteed by the tsar, a Finnish national identity evolved in the course of the nineteenth century that was directed as much against Swedish cultural dominance as against any political tutelage by Russia. However, in 1899 a policy of russification was instituted with the aim of removing Finland's autonomous status, and this was met with widespread—though largely passive—resistance. To be sure, the Finns' traditionally strong loyalty to the person of the Russian tsar, who was also grand duke of Finland, remained unbroken for the time being. But russification spurred political participation in wide sections of the Finnish population, leading to the constitutional reform passed in 1905–1906 that, among other things, introduced for the first time anywhere in the world women's unqualified active and passive voting rights. Finland thus turned away from the corporatist diet toward a modern unicameral system, which would remain the foundation of Finnish parliamentarism throughout the entire twentieth century. In doing so, the country suddenly catapulted itself into the ranks of the Continent's politically most advanced polities, despite continuing economic backwardness.

**WORLD WAR I AND INDEPENDENCE**
Nevertheless, at the outbreak of World War I, Finland's eventual emergence from the conflict as an independent republic along democratic-parliamentary lines was by no means foreseeable. Only the revolutionary changes in Russia in 1917 provided the conditions necessary for that outcome. The fall of the tsar during the February Revolution of 1917 shook the constitutional foundations in Finland too, in that it was unclear who should take over supreme state authority at the time. Thus Russia's destabilization created a power vacuum in Finland as well; as it turned out, the dissolution of the Finnish parliament (Eduskunta), ordered by the provisional government in St. Petersburg in July 1917, was the last significant show of power in Finland by the Russian central authority. At this point the political forces quickly began to reorganize and polarize. The backdrop to these developments was the war-related escalation of economic and social problems in Finland, which temporarily led to hunger crises even in Finnish cities. Between 1913 and 1917 the cost of living rose approximately fourfold, while at the same time the Finnish mark dramatically decreased in value. Industry also sustained heavy losses. A wave of labor disputes, growing unemployment, and mass impoverishment provided the setting for political conflicts that were gradually shifting to the extra-parliamentary realm. The presence of a growing number of politicized Russian soldiers—close to one hundred thousand by the fall of 1917—exacerbated the situation.

On 15 November the newly elected Eduskunta, now dominated by bourgeois forces, declared itself the supreme authority in Finland. Three weeks later, on 6 December (today's national holiday), the parliament approved a declaration of independence introduced by the new senate under the leadership of Pehr Evind

Svinhufvud. Against the backdrop of the October Revolution, which had meanwhile erupted in Russia, the bourgeois parties were attempting to create a fait accompli as quickly as possible. The Socialists also favored the country's independence, striving in the process for a reorganization along socialist lines but without Lenin's proletarian dictatorship. They denied the legitimacy of the bourgeois government as much as the legality of the armed Defense Corps raised by the government to disarm the Russian troops still remaining within Finnish territory. Instead the Socialists banked on contractual agreements with the new Russian government, which indeed formally recognized the independence of Finland on 31 December 1917. A revolutionary government formed in late January 1918 in Helsinki, led by Kullervo Akilles Manner and supported by armed forces of its own (Red Guards), quickly gained control over large parts of southern Finland, especially the urban centers of Helsinki and Tampere. Nonetheless, within weeks the White Guards concentrated in the area of Vaasa (Ostrobothnia) managed to turn the tide, and at the beginning of May resistance by Red forces broke down completely. The outcome of the war reflected the military-professional superiority of the White troops, who had a well-trained and experienced commander in chief in the person of Carl Gustav Mannerheim, a former tsarist general. In addition, starting in 1915 numerous volunteers had already obtained secret military training in Germany and gained combat experience as members of the Königlich-Preußisches Jägerbatallion (Royal Prussian Riflemen Battalion) 27. This *Jäger* movement, comprising close to two thousand men overall, would become a cornerstone of the Finnish army in subsequent decades.

In other respects too Germany contributed to the victory of the Whites in the civil war. On 3 April 1918 the German Baltic Sea Division commanded by General Rüdiger von der Goltz landed in Finland and managed to enter Helsinki ten days later. With this event German influence in Finland appeared to have reached its climax—much against Mannerheim's will. According to the wishes of the Finnish parliament, the country's army was to be built up by German officers, and a Hessian prince, the brother-in-law of the German kaiser, was to be crowned king of Finland. However, by fall 1918 the collapse of Imperial Germany had already eliminated the basis for any pro-German policy in Finland. Instead, following new parliamentary elections in March 1919, passage of the constitution (21 July 1919), and the election of a committed republican (Kaarlo Juho Ståhlberg) as first president, the new polity began consolidating into a durable democratic republic.

The events of 1917–1918 represent one of the great turning points of Finnish history and have been subject to widely differing interpretations. It is certain that the conflicts of that period represented the convergence of efforts toward national sovereignty, the struggle for a reorganization of society, and interventionist interests from abroad. As a result the young republic incurred a difficult legacy: the war had cost about 29,000 deaths overall, for the most part victims of terror and inhuman internment conditions, and for at least two decades Finnish society remained internally divided. It is all the more remarkable that among the countless new states arisen from the "disposable assets" left by World War I, Finland was one of the few that managed to retain its democratic form of government throughout. One essential reason for this was that during the constitutional struggles of the previous decades, the beginnings of a party system had already formed, which now underwent rapid consolidation. In addition to the already existing Agrarian Party (Maalaisliitto) and the party of the Swedish-speaking minority (Swedish People's Party), the National Progressive Party (Edistys), which had grown out of the liberal movement of Young Finns, was now emerging as the main party in support of the republic; by contrast, the political Right saw the hitherto mainly pro-monarchical "old Finns" join forces in the National Coalition Party (Kokoomus). On the left, the outcome of the war resulted in a split of the workers' movement. Whereas the Social Democratic Party (SDP) under Väinö Tanner oriented itself programmatically toward its West European sister parties and reassumed the responsibility of government as early as 1926, the Communist Party of Finland, founded in Moscow in 1918, was forced to work underground; thousands of Finnish Communists who emigrated to the Soviet Union subsequently fell victim to the Stalinist purges.

## INTERWAR PERIOD

Despite political normalization and societal modernization, Finland remained a "White" republic during the interwar years. Ideological anticommunism among large parts of the bourgeoisie, the rekindled language controversy between the Finnish majority and the Swedish minority, and the effects of the world economic crisis felt in Finland by the late 1920s encouraged the development of extraparliamentary and extreme right-wing protest movements. Temporary influence was exerted above all by the Lapua movement, the Academic Karelia Society (AKS), and the Patriotic People's Movement (IKL), which also participated in the parliamentary elections during the 1930s, albeit with moderate success. That in the end none of these organizations succeeded in making a breakthrough as a mass movement was primarily due to three reasons: first, the deep-rootedness of democratic traditions among the Finnish people; second, determined government intervention against public attempts to instigate turmoil (the Mäntsälä revolt in 1932); and finally, the fact that, despite numerous linkages, the antidemocratic Right among the country's conservatives and among the associated paramilitary Defense Corps (Suojeluskunta) received only halfhearted support.

Finland also faced major foreign policy problems. On the western frontier, relations with Sweden initially suffered from the quarrel over possession of the Åland Islands; in 1921 the League of Nations decided that the islands would remain with Finland but that the purely Swedish-speaking population be granted far-reaching autonomy. The situation in the east was more threatening. Though on 14 October 1920 Finland had managed to conclude the Peace Treaty of Tartu (Dorpat) with the Soviet Union, the situation along the East Karelian frontier remained uneasy. Under these circumstances Helsinki initially worked toward a defense alliance with other neighboring states of the Soviet Union (Poland, Estonia, and Latvia). After the failure of this so-called border states policy Finland decided on a nonalignment policy combined with close affiliation with the League of Nations. In the 1930s the foreign political situation at first appeared to ease off. Following the nonaggression pact with the Soviet Union signed in January 1932 there was intensified cooperation with the Scandinavian countries along the lines of a "Nordic neutrality." By sheer lack of realistic alternatives, Helsinki adhered to this policy even though its fragility became increasingly apparent as international tensions mounted in 1938.

## WORLD WAR II

Whereas Finland was involved only indirectly in the Great Power conflicts of World War I, it became embroiled in World War II very early on and repeatedly in the most ominous way. Under circumstances varying in each case, the country experienced three wars in those years: in 1939–1940 the so-called Winter War, waged with the Soviet Union without any foreign assistance; in 1941–1944 the Continuation War, once again waged with the Soviet Union but now side by side with Germany; and finally, the Lapland War against Germany, beginning after the armistice with the Soviet Union in the fall of 1944. Each of the three wars had its own significance for Finland's internal and external development. In the Winter War, Finland fell victim to the German-Soviet Nonaggression Pact concluded in August 1939, whose secret accompanying protocol had ceded the country to the Soviet sphere of influence. During the negotiations about redrawing borders and about military bases, which the Soviet Union demanded shortly afterward, Helsinki had proved intransigent—in contrast to the Baltic republics—and as a result faced military attack by the Soviets on 30 November. The unexpected defensive successes of the greatly outnumbered Finnish army excited worldwide admiration; they failed, however, to spare Helsinki from having to accept a peace treaty on 12 March 1940. The agreement not only granted the Soviet Union a naval base in southern Finland (Hanko) but also afforded Moscow territorial gains in East Karelia and, on the Karelian Isthmus, Viipuri (Vyborg). Despite heavy losses (approximately 25,000 war dead), in domestic politics the Winter War contributed substantially to Finnish national unity and to overcoming the trauma of the civil war. In terms of foreign policy it strengthened the general belief that lasting security vis-à-vis the Soviet Union could only be achieved at the side of a strong military ally.

This conviction led the Finnish government in 1941 to cooperate with Germany. Within the framework of a "loose comradeship in arms" without further contractual commitments, the leaders in Helsinki hoped to recapture the territories lost by the Treaty of Moscow and move the country to a strategically stronger position in relation to the eastern neighbor. Great initial military successes during the Continuation War beginning in late June 1941 stirred up hopes among nationalist circles of a substantially expanded "Greater Finland." However, following the British declaration of war (5 December 1941) and the first German setbacks in the winter of 1941, the Finnish government adopted a policy of wait-and-see, and the military campaign became defensive. By February 1943—after the German defeat in Stalingrad and the reverses in front of Leningrad—politicians in Helsinki began looking for ways to get out of the war. These efforts were made difficult by two circumstances: on the one hand by the heavy economic and military dependence on Germany, which had stationed an army of its own (20. *Gebirgsarmee*) in northern Finland; and on the other by the fact that neither the United States nor Great Britain was in a position to guarantee Finnish independence in the face of Soviet demands. Considering this situation, in retrospect it appears as a particular success of Finnish politics to have been able to withdraw from the war on 2 September 1944 by means of an armistice with the Soviet Union, without having to undergo the experience of a German or Soviet occupation. The Lapland War between German and Finnish troops, resulting from the terms of the armistice, represented a short though bloody end to the "comradeship in arms" of previous years and led to the large-scale devastation of northern Finland by withdrawing German troops.

## POSTWAR YEARS AND COLD WAR FOREIGN POLICY

The Lapland War marked the final chapter of a policy seeking to secure Finnish independence through political dependence on Germany. It cleared the way for a fundamental reorientation of Finnish foreign and security policy, which now for the first time relied consistently on reconciliation of interests with Moscow to serve as reinsurance for the country's own sovereignty. This policy, subsequently named the "Paasikivi-Kekkonen line" (for Juho Kusti Paasikivi and Urho Kekkonen, the successive presidents who shaped it) was set down contractually in the Paris Peace Treaty of 1947 and

above all in the Moscow Treaty of Friendship, Cooperation and Mutual Assistance concluded in 1948. Finnish foreign policy, based on this agreement from then on until the collapse of the Soviet Union, was by no means undisputed in the West. In fact, the pact of cooperation, in conjunction with the limitations on Finnish armaments stipulated in the peace treaty and a naval base in Porkkala (near Helsinki) granted to the USSR (returned to Finland in 1955), represented a considerable strain on Finland's claim to a policy of neutrality. There is also no doubt that Finnish postwar policies—both with respect to foreign policy and security issues and in terms of domestic and economic questions—was geared toward making far-reaching concessions to Soviet demands in order to defuse potential conflicts with Moscow before they arose. Not without good reason, commentators sometimes spoke of a "Second Republic" to differentiate this political culture from that of the prewar era. Nevertheless, the characterization by some analysts of the Finnish-Soviet relationship as, in John P. Vloyantes's words, "silk-glove hegemony," misses the crux of the matter insofar as Finland was the only European neighbor of the Soviet Union that managed to retain its sovereignty as a parliamentary democracy. Moreover, despite a number of serious crises (the "Night-Frost" crisis in 1958; the "Note" crisis in 1961), Finnish foreign policy managed to play an increasingly independent role in international affairs, as demonstrated by diverse activities under the auspices of the United Nations, participation in the Nordic Cooperation organization (Nordic Council), and in relation to the policy of détente (the Conference on Security and Co-operation in Europe in 1975, which produced the broad-based international agreement that came to be known as the Helsinki Accords).

With respect to domestic policy, the end of World War II brought new challenges, particularly in the initial postwar years. Monitored by a Soviet-dominated Allied Control Commission, Finland's army (which had incurred losses of some ninety thousand during the war years) had to be demobilized completely in very short order, and the leading politicians of the war years (except Mannerheim) were tried in court. About 420,000 refugees from the areas ceded to the Soviet Union—about 12 percent of the total Finnish territory, mainly

Karelia and the Petsamo region—had to be resettled and integrated into Finland. Reconstruction was also hampered by reparations payable to the USSR and the fact that, out of consideration for Moscow, Finland abstained from participating in the Marshall Plan. The resulting economic and social problems, election successes of the Left, and the temporarily dominant role of the Moscow-oriented Communist Party (allowed again since 1944) caused many observers to perceive the early postwar period as "years of danger," during which the transformation of the country into a Soviet-style "people's democracy" did not seem completely out of the question. Nonetheless, several factors contributed to the country's economic recovery. As opposed to other Soviet adversaries, Finland had withdrawn from the war early on and remained unoccupied; there had been few civilian casualties; and, with the exception of Lapland, the material war damages had been relatively small. Thus economic output recovered to prewar levels as early as 1948.

## ECONOMY AND SOCIETY SINCE 1970

In subsequent decades the Finnish economy and society underwent the type of modernization process experienced much earlier on by most central and Western European countries. Between 1910 and 1970 the population of Finland grew from 3 million to 4.6 million (4 million in 1950); at the same time, the share of the workforce employed in agriculture and forestry declined from 80 percent to 20 percent (47 percent in 1950). The breakthrough into a modern industrial and service economy was accompanied by a rural exodus, urbanization, and growing economic involvement abroad. The standard of living rose significantly (per capita gross national product in 1975 was $5,100), even though it continued to lag considerably behind the country's major Nordic neighbors. Free-trade agreements with the European Community, its key economic partner, and with the European Free Trade Association, which Finland joined later on, secured Finland's international competitiveness; at times, the Soviet Union's share in Finnish foreign trade reached close to 20 percent.

The 1980s and 1990s brought Finland fundamental change both in domestic and foreign politics. The end of the "Kekkonen era" (Urho Kekkonen held the office of president from 1956 to 1981) brought a loosening of the country's party political designations and cautious modifications of the domestic balance of power, which culminated in the constitutional reform of 1999. For Finland, the limitation of presidential jurisdiction prescribed in this reform in favor of expanded parliamentary and governmental prerogatives marked the transition from a semi-presidential to a full-fledged parliamentary system of government. The breakup of the Soviet Union had an even more important effect, substantially extending the scope of Finnish politics. To be sure, the collapse of trade to the east in the early 1990s initially led to an escalation of the country's economic recession, but successful countermeasures laid the groundwork for an economic boom unprecedented in Finnish history.

Despite Finland's continuing claim to neutrality in the realm of security policy, the country's accession to the European Union in 1995 and to the European Economic and Monetary Union in 1999 fundamentally changed the framework of Finnish politics. With good reason, one may refer to the beginning of a "Third Republic." Thanks to a society largely pacified politically and socially, major investments in education and infrastructure, and specific promotion of high-tech industries (especially Nokia), Finland appears to be succeeding better than most other European countries in combining the prerequisites of international competitiveness with the continuously high social standards of a Scandinavian-style welfare society. In spite of some ongoing structural problems, mainly due to its geographic location, Finland appears to be as well prepared as any European country for the new challenges of the twenty-first century.

*See also* **Germany; Helsinki Accords; Sweden; World War I; World War II.**

BIBLIOGRAPHY

Jussila, Osmo, Seppo Hentilä, and Jukka Nevakivi. *From Grand Duchy to a Modern State: A Political History of Finland since 1809.* London, 1999.

Kirby, D. G. *Finland in the Twentieth Century.* London, 1979.

Paasivirta, Juhani. *Finland and Europe: The Early Years of Independence, 1917–1939.* Edited and translated by Peter Herring. Helsinki, 1988.

Ruddy, T. Michael, ed. *Charting an Independent Course: Finland's Place in the Cold War and in U.S. Foreign Policy.* Claremont, Calif., 1998.

Screen, J. E. O. *Mannerheim: The Finnish Years.* London, 2000.

Upton, Anthony F. *The Finnish Revolution, 1917–1918.* Minneapolis, Minn., 1980.

Vehviläinen, Olli. *Finland in the Second World War: Between Germany and Russia.* Translated by Gerard McAlester. Houndmills, U.K., 2002.

BERND WEGNER

---

# FISCHER, JOSCHKA (b. 1948), foreign minister of the Federal Republic of Germany and the leading figure in the environmentalist Green Party.

Joschka Fischer was born in the small German town of Gerabronn. His family were so-called Danube Schwabs (ethnic Germans expelled from Hungary following the end of the Second World War) and were grounded in the solidly middle-class German "burgher" tradition. The odd combination of bourgeois respectability and the trauma of expulsion shaped Fischer's political worldview, which over his lifetime has encompassed the personae of extreme left-wing firebrand and the paragon of the internationally respected statesman that he later became. Depending on their political views, observers have interpreted Fischer's ability to embrace both roles without disowning either as evidence of supreme political acumen or a lack of real political moorings.

Fischer's first foray into active politics took place in the late 1960s and early 1970s as part of the turbulent student's movement and "Extra-Parliamentary Opposition." Although not a student himself, Fischer immersed himself in the student-led hard-left milieu in the city of Frankfurt and was highly active in the anarcho-Marxist "Revolutionary Struggle" group—better known as the "Spontis." While they rejected the urban guerrilla strategies of groups such as the Red Army Faction (RAF), many Spontis did indulge in street violence. Fischer was a leading member of the Spontis' fighting force the "Proletarian Union for Terror and Destruction" (PUTZ), which was a fixture of political demonstrations in Frankfurt during this period. Ultimately some PUTZ members did drift toward the terrorist strategy espoused by the RAF and others.

Fischer's street-fighting past almost dealt a fatal blow to his career in 2001, when two separate issues became the center of public debate. The first was the trial of the former PUTZ member Hans-Joachim Klein for his part in an armed attack on an OPEC conference in Vienna in 1975. Klein had been on the run in France before being captured in 2000, and although a quarter of a century had passed in the meantime, his trial reopened the national debate about the violence of the 1970s. For Fischer this debate was made very personal because he was ordered to give evidence at the trial. At the same time, a second scandal erupted over photos of Fischer and his PUTZ colleagues beating up a police officer during a demonstration in Frankfurt in 1973. Characteristically Fischer survived what for many lesser politicians would have been a mortal blow to their careers. Nevertheless, the scandals demonstrated how much political terrain Fischer had traveled in the years since 1973.

By 2001 Fischer had become foreign minister of Germany and the second most powerful member of the ruling "Red-Green" coalition between the Social Democratic Party (SPD) and the Green Party. The coalition had assumed power nationally in 1998, following years of political cooperation between the two parties at the state level in Germany from the early 1980s onward. It was during this period of state-level cooperation that Fischer had made his political mark. He served two terms as environment minister in the state of Hessen, from 1985 to 1987 and again from 1991 to 1994, and gained a reputation as a highly effective minister who was capable of securing the stringent application of existing environmental laws. At the same time, he was able to gain an ascendancy within the Green Party.

The Greens had emerged from the antinuclear and "citizens' initiative" groups of the late 1970s and entered the German Bundestag for the first time in 1983. In the early 1980s the Greens were very much the "anti-party party" described by the late Petra Kelly, but by the mid-1990s Fischer and his moderate colleagues within the party had transformed it into a center-left environmentalist party that was fit for national government. During this process previously nonnegotiable ideological shibboleths such as pacifism, anti-Americanism, and withdrawal from NATO were either removed or deemphasized within the party's ideological profile. Thus, by the end of the 1990s, the Greens had changed to such an extent that they were able to accept the need for armed intervention in Bosnia and, after coming to power, even actively consent in the 1999 NATO campaign in Kosovo and the 2001 U.S.-led campaign in Afghanistan. Nevertheless, the party (along with the SPD and a majority of the German population) was deeply hostile to U.S.-led plans to invade Iraq and opposed the 2003 Iraq campaign.

During the second term of the SPD-Green government (2002–2005) Fischer had begun to show some impatience with the Greens and even his role in the government. At the same time, critics within his party also displayed an increased readiness to question Fischer's political motivations and to demonstrate irritation with the manner in which he appeared to dominate the party. There was some speculation that he might move on to a more "dignified" role within the European Union or the United Nations—as befitting his established role as international statesman. Following the defeat of the SPD-Green government in the 2005 federal elections, Fisher left his post as foreign minister and adopted a much lower profile within the Green Party.

*See also* **Environmentalism; Germany; Greens.**

BIBLIOGRAPHY

Frankland, E. Gene, and Donald Schoomaker. *Between Protest and Power: The Green Party in Germany.* Boulder, Colo., 1992.

Hülsberg, Werner. *The German Greens: A Social and Political Profile.* Translated by Gus Fagan. London, 1988.

Kaase, Max. "A New Government—A New Democracy? The Red-Green Coalition in Germany." *Japanese Journal of Political Science* 1 (2000): 129–149.

Kolinsky, Eva, ed. *The Greens in West Germany.* Oxford, U.K., 1989.

Lees, Charles. "The Red-Green Coalition." *German Politics* 8, no. 2 (1999): 174–194.

———. *The Red-Green Coalition in Germany: Politics, Personalities, and Power.* Manchester, U.K., 2000.

Poguntke, Thomas. *Alternative Politics: The German Green Party.* Edinburgh, 1993.

Scharf, Thomas. *The German Greens: Challenging the Consensus.* Oxford, U.K., 1994.

Sylvia, Stephen J. "The Fall and Rise of Unemployment in Germany: Is the Red-Green Government Responsible?" *German Politics* 11, no. 1 (2002): 1–22.

CHARLES LEES

---

**FIUME.** At the end of World War I, the city of Fiume (Croatian Rijeka) became a major source of international tension, and events there in 1919 and 1920 marked an important moment in the emergence of Italian fascism. Fiume, a major seaport and industrial center in western Croatia, had a population of 50,000 in 1919, of whom Italians formed a plurality, followed by Croatians and Hungarians. In 1915 Italy had entered the war in exchange for concessions specified in the secret Treaty of London (1915). As a victorious power, Italy expected as a matter of right to expand at the expense of the now-dismembered Habsburg Empire. Italians assumed that military victory would result in the annexation of Fiume and northern Dalmatia, allowing Italy to dominate the Adriatic. At the peace conference, however, the Great Powers regarded Italian contributions to victory as undeserving of significant recognition. Furthermore, U.S. president Woodrow Wilson viewed the secret treaty as invalid and at odds with the democratic principles of his new diplomacy.

On the Italian political right, the failure to gain Fiume was symbolic of the illegitimacy of the Liberal regime. Despite the years of slaughter in the trenches and of hardship behind the lines, Italy emerged with "empty hands" and a "mutilated victory." The bitter disappointment of nationalists and patriotic veterans focused on Fiume. Here was a predominantly Italian city just beyond the border that had been paid for in copious Italian blood. Furthermore, its assignment to newly created Yugoslavia rather than Italy seemed hypocritical in view of Wilson's principle of self-determination. The majority of Fiume's inhabitants were Italian, and the local government had declared its desire for the city to be annexed to Italy.

In this inflamed context, the poet and ardent expansionist Gabriele D'Annunzio (1863–1938) took the decisive initiative. Placing himself at the head of a volunteer army of patriots and war veterans, D'Annunzio marched on Fiume, entering the city on the morning of 12 September 1919. Unable to dictate events through military force, D'Annunzio and his band of 2,500 "Legionnaires" succeeded because no attempt was made to stop them. Disloyal troops sympathetic to the poet were hopeful both of staking Italian claims to Dalmatia and of overthrowing Liberal prime minister Francesco Saverio Nitti. They did not, therefore, obey orders to arrest the Legionnaires. Instead the army allowed D'Annunzio to seize the town unopposed. In the heady early days of the adventure it was thought that Fiume might be the prelude to a second march on Rome itself to overthrow the state.

In the occupied city, D'Annunzio established a charismatic personal dictatorship that established much of the rhetoric, tactics, and choreography that Benito Mussolini adopted on a much larger stage when he marched on Rome in 1922 and inaugurated Fascist rule. At Fiume, D'Annunzio pioneered a demagogic mass populism. Speaking to crowds of Italians, D'Annunzio promised to redeem Italian national greatness. He also called for new wars, initiated a cult of youth, and adopted fire as the symbol of the newly proclaimed City of the Holocaust that would set a decadent nation alight in a blaze of purification. At the same time he exploited the ethnic tensions of the largely middle-class Italian majority against the working-class minorities of Croatians and Hungarians. Gathering full power into his hands, the "Commander" imposed his new order from on high and sacralized his rule as that of a secular messiah.

At the same time that Fiume marked a local triumph for the subversive political Right against the Liberal state, D'Annunzio borrowed "revolutionary" symbols from the political arsenal of the Left, briefly giving his movement unprecedented élan. From the French Revolution he appropriated the idea of a new calendar, with his march into Fiume as the beginning of the Year I. He appointed the former revolutionary syndicalist Alceste De Ambris to the task of producing a dazzling new constitution for the city. Drafted but never implemented, the constitution, the Carta del Carnaro, promised direct democracy, a republic with equal rights for women, universal suffrage, and corporate institutions to regulate production.

D'Annunzio's rule increasingly invoked the rhetoric of the Left as he struggled to maintain the ardor of his followers while difficulties mounted. Unwilling to test the loyalty of the army in a direct assault on D'Annunzio's outpost, the Liberal leadership decided to blockade the rebel city. As enthusiasm for D'Annunzio waned, the poet devised no practical strategy for survival. As the months passed, supplies of food and fuel ran low; the economy collapsed; citizens deserted the cause and departed; divisions deepened among the leaders; and strikes and demonstrations erupted. By late 1920 Giovanni Giolitti, who succeeded Nitti as prime minister, felt that the balance of power had shifted. In December he ordered the fleet to bombard Fiume and evict the Legionnaires.

*See also* **D'Annunzio, Gabriele; Italy.**

BIBLIOGRAPHY

De Felice, Renzo. *D'Annunzio politico, 1918–1938.* Rome, 1978.

Gentile, Emilio. *The Sacralization of Politics in Fascist Italy.* Translated by Keith Botsford. Cambridge, Mass., 1996.

Ledeen, Michael A. *Annunzio: The First Duce.* New Brunswick, N.J., 2002.

FRANK M. SNOWDEN

---

**FIVE-YEAR PLAN.** Administrative plans were one of the instruments by which the leaders of the Soviet Union sought to impose their preferences on the economy. The Five-Year Plans for national economic development were the best known of these, but this reflects their important ceremonial functions; other plans and decisions were often more significant from a practical point of view.

In all, there were thirteen Soviet Five-Year Plans. The first ran from the autumn of 1928 to 1933; at that time the accounting year began in October with the end of the harvest. The third plan (1938–1942) was interrupted in mid-1941 by World War II. Five-year planning began again with the fourth (1946–1950). The sixth (1956–1960) was abandoned and replaced by a Seven-Year Plan (1959–1965). After that, everything went in step until the unlucky thirteenth plan (1991–1995), barely adopted when the Soviet Union collapsed at the end of 1991.

Five-year planning was not limited to the Soviet economy. The socialist economies of Eastern Europe copied it after World War II. Joseph Stalin's Five-Year Plans also provided symbolic inspiration for Adolf Hitler's two "four-year plans" (1933–1940) for Germany's self-sufficiency and war preparations, but there was little or no similarity in underlying respects.

## THE FIRST FIVE-YEAR PLAN

The first "five-year plan of development of the national economy of the USSR" was adopted in April 1929, although it nominally covered the period from October 1928 to September 1933. It called for the country's real national income to double in five years and investment to treble, while consumption per head was to rise by two-thirds. There were ambitious targets to increase the production of industrial and agricultural commodities. The purpose of the plan was not just to expand the economy but to "build socialism"; associated with it was a vast program of new large-scale capital projects that would embody the new society in steel and cement. Indeed a five-year period was chosen partly in the belief that it would allow time to complete these major projects; another motivation was to permit the smoothing of harvest fluctuations.

The character of the First Five-Year Plan reflects complex underlying political and institutional changes of the time. In the 1920s leading Soviet political and economic officials disputed the nature of economic planning. Some believed that the task of administrative plans was essentially to replicate a market equilibrium without the mistakes to which they believed the market mechanism was prone; hence, a planned economy could balance public and private wants more efficiently, eliminate unemployment, and smooth out cyclical fluctuations. More radical figures regarded planning as an instrument for mobilizing resources into government priorities, breaking with the limitations of a market economy, and transforming the economic and political system as rapidly as possible. The radicals' victory was completed at the end of the 1920s by Stalin's left turn in favor of forced

industrialization and the collectivization of peasant agriculture.

It took several years for Gosplan, the USSR's state planning commission, to prepare the First Five-Year Plan; the growing power of the radicals was expressed in increasingly ambitious targets that were set out in successive drafts. The optimism continued to grow even after the plan had been adopted, and this resulted in further upward revisions to particular targets in the course of 1930. The single most ambitious change was the decision to "fulfill the First Five-Year Plan in four years." Halfway through its implementation, the Soviet authorities decided to symbolize the country's transition to an industrial basis by replacing the old, harvest-oriented "economic year" with calendar-year accounts. To accommodate this transition a "special quarter" of extra effort was announced for the last three months of 1930. After that, the targets for 1931/32 and 1932/33 were brought forward to 1931 and 1932, respectively.

Judged by its targets, the First Five-Year Plan must be counted a ridiculous failure. The value of national income in 1932 was nearly twice that of 1928, but unacknowledged price increases and other statistical biases accounted for most of the increase. Many of the big projects that had been started remained unfinished. Instead of rising by two-thirds, consumption collapsed; by the end of 1932 the country was in the grip of a catastrophic famine. One reason for the famine was that the efforts to industrialize as rapidly as possible had stripped the countryside of food.

On other criteria, however, the same plan was a great success. Real investment had doubled and, under the Second Five-Year Plan (1933–1937), the unfinished projects would be completed and pay off. Although many specific targets were not met, industry's results for 1932 still showed remarkable progress over the starting point. Rapid industrialization was under way; it was the temporary collapse of agriculture that was to blame for the disappointing growth of national income and the severe decline in living standards.

Resources were now directed by administrative decrees, not markets and prices. Just as importantly, the critics of planning as all-out economic mobilization had been silenced. As much as

**A Soviet poster promoting the Five-Year Plan, 1928, shows a wealthy businessman in tears because of the plan's success.** BRIDGEMAN ART LIBRARY

anything Stalin used the First Five-Year Plan as a political instrument to flush out moderate opinion, expose critics, taint them with guilt by association with the political opposition to Stalin, and subject them to censorship, dismissal, and arrest. The underfulfillment of detailed targets was important only to the extent that it gave him a weapon with which to beat the oppositionists and fainthearts alike.

### FIVE-YEAR PLANS IN CONTEXT
In the mid-1930s the Soviet economy overcame the crisis and settled down to a more "normal" style of economic planning. The Second and Third Five-Year Plans were enacted, and by the end of the decade leading officials were thinking in terms of plans with an even longer fifteen- or twenty-year horizon. But these "perspective" plans did not have much practical significance for

management of the economy; Eugène Zaleski later described them as no more than "visions of growth" (1971, p. 291). The plans through which the authorities exerted "operational" control over resources were for shorter periods: yearly, quarterly, and monthly.

How did the operational plans work? In theory there was a process of breaking the perspective plans down into shorter time periods and distributing them across production ministries so that the annual and quarterly branch plans were nested arithmetically within the perspective plans for the economy as a whole. In practice, however, operational plans tended to creep away from perspective targets as the economy evolved. Investigations in the Soviet archives of the 1930s have also shown that, even at the "operational" level, the planners' control over day-to-day transactions was much less than might be expected. Gosplan projected supply and demand for a few broad commodity groups in the aggregate, but left it to the ministries in charge of each industry to plan the detailed assortment and distribution of commodities and to link up particular producer and user factories. When there were tens, then hundreds of thousands, and eventually millions of commodities, and tens of thousands of producers, these tasks could not be centralized. Planning was also much less "physical" than the stereotype; planners set targets for the value of industry output using plan prices that were supposedly fixed, but in fact the factories themselves exerted considerable influence over the prices, and could push them up under certain conditions to make the plan easier to fulfill. Finally, the plans themselves were relatively fluid; they were subject to continual revision, and secondary targets were often agreed upon during or after the event, when results were predictable or already known. Most detailed plans existed only in draft form and were never finalized.

It is not surprising, therefore, to find that the Soviet record of fulfillment of five-year and other plans tended to improve over time. There were three reasons for this. First, planners adjusted their expectations to results, and became less likely to set targets that were beyond the capacity or desire of the producers to fulfill them. Second, plans remained negotiable, and producers could often bargain inconveniently demanding targets downward during the plan period. Third, producers could also fulfill plans for output by manipulating prices upward, and "hidden" inflation became a persistent phenomenon.

Administrative plans never covered the whole Soviet economy. The labor market was planned, if at all, only on the demand side. For much of the Stalin period the supply of labor was fairly harshly regimented, but these controls had nothing to do with economic planning, even in the loose sense described here. Food supplies were partly planned and partly left to a legal unregulated market in which collective farmers sold their sideline private produce directly to households. Many goods and services were diverted out of the planned economy and retraded in illegal markets.

The planning system on its own does not fully explain the success of the Soviet state in allocating resources to investment and defense. This is reflected in the fact that, as is now known, Stalin and his immediate colleagues paid relatively little attention to five-year or annual plan figures other than for grain. They gave much closer consideration to the billions of rubles allocated to investment and defense through the state budget. Plan targets for output helped to ensure that output would be produced and resources would be available for use in the aggregate, but did not determine how these products would be used or by whom. Given this, the cash made available to military procurement departments and construction organizations through the budget was critically important in fixing the pattern of final uses. In short, money was more important in the Soviet economy than has sometimes been recognized, and in this sense the role of plans was more to influence the context than to decide outcomes.

### THE FAILURE OF SOVIET-TYPE PLANNING

A fundamental problem of planning was the volume of detailed information that it required the planners to acquire and use. To plan the economy efficiently in theory required planners to have accurate knowledge of the specific needs and resources of every firm and household. In decentralized market economies this information does not have to be transmitted or shared directly because it is carried by price signals. In the command system, in contrast, the authorities aimed to direct resources in a comprehensive way despite very limited information and an even more limited capacity to process it.

As a result the planners evolved rules of thumb to take the place of the information they lacked. One such was to plan "from the achieved level." This rule solved the following problem: planners had to set targets for output, not knowing what industry was really capable of producing. In fact, producers took care to conceal their true resources from the planners in the hope that they would be given an "easy" plan. In turn, the planners knew that every factory was probably capable of more than it would admit, but they did not know by how much more. The standard solution was to set the next target on the basis of the most recent results, that is, the "achieved level," plus an increment. The benefit of this rule was that it resulted in plans that were likely to be feasible while also "stretching" the producers a little. But there were also drawbacks. One was that the rule tended to make plans conservative; planning "from the achieved level" inhibited structural change, especially the downsizing of industries that should have been allowed to decline. Another was that the same rule gave the producers an instrument to manage planners' expectations; by keeping down the "achieved level" today, they could ensure a still easier plan tomorrow.

In the 1960s and 1970s the Soviet Union, like other socialist economies, experimented with planning reforms. These reforms typically aimed to motivate producers to tell the truth about their capabilities and to cut costs by working harder without being watched all the time. In practice the experience of reform was almost entirely fruitless. To get incentives right the planners needed to set prices for outputs and inputs that reflected their social value, but this depended on information that producers controlled. But the producers did not trust planners with this information because it could also be used to make them work harder. Therefore, producers continued to work at concealing the truth from the planners rather than at being more efficient. In turn the planners had to continue to watch and control them with plans.

In the end the failure of this type of planning is symbolized by the declining growth rates of the Soviet-type economies. The lag of productivity and living standards behind Western Europe and the United States, which closed somewhat in the 1950s and 1960s, widened steadily thereafter. While the immediate causes of the collapse of socialism in Europe at the end of the 1980s are debatable, it seems beyond doubt that Soviet planning failed to adapt to changing tastes and technologies at the end of the twentieth century.

*See also* **Collectivization; Industrial Capitalism; New Economic Policy (NEP); Soviet Union; Stakhanovites; Stalin, Joseph.**

BIBLIOGRAPHY

Birman, Igor. "From the Achieved Level." *Soviet Studies* 30, no. 2 (1978): 153–172.

Davies, R. W., Melanie Ilic, and Oleg Khlevnyuk. "The Politburo and Economic Policy-Making." In *The Nature of Stalin's Dictatorship: The Politburo, 1924–1953,* edited by E. A. Rees, 108–133. Houndmills, Basingstoke, U.K., 2004.

Ellman, Michael. *Socialist Planning.* 2nd ed. Cambridge, U.K., 1989.

Gregory, Paul R. *The Political Economy of Stalinism: Evidence From the Soviet Secret Archives.* Cambridge, U.K., 2004.

Gregory, Paul R., and Robert C. Stuart. *Soviet Economic Structure and Performance.* New York, 1974. Rev. ed. as *Soviet and Post-Soviet Economic Structure and Performance.* New York, 1994.

Hanson, Philip. *The Rise and Fall of the Soviet Economy: An Economic History of the USSR from 1945.* London, 2003.

Harrison, Mark. *Soviet Planning in Peace and War, 1938–1945.* Cambridge, U.K., 1985.

Kontorovich, Vladimir. "Lessons of the 1965 Soviet Economic Reform." *Soviet Studies* 40, no. 2 (1988): 308–316.

Zaleski, Eugène. *Planning for Economic Growth in the Soviet Union, 1918–1932.* Translated by Marie-Christine MacAndrew and G. Warren Nutter. Chapel Hill, N.C., 1971.

———. *Stalinist Planning for Economic Growth, 1933–1952.* Translated and edited by Marie-Christine MacAndrew and John H. Moore. Chapel Hill, N.C., 1980.

MARK HARRISON

**FLEMISH BLOC.** The Vlaams Blok, or Flemish Bloc, a Flemish political party of the extreme Right, was founded in 1979, as the result of a fusion between two dissident factions that had broken away from the then dominant Flemish nationalist party, the Volksunie (People's Union). It represented the hard-liners within that party, who cultivated the heritage of the radical nationalism of the interwar and World War II period and who often belonged to a subculture in which the collaboration with the Nazis was justified as an act of Flemish idealism. They were frustrated by the "progressive" course followed by the Volksunie leaders and by their willingness to participate in negotiations with the other parties about the federalization of Belgian institutions. The final aim of these radical nationalists was not federalization but the independence of Flanders (with Brussels as capital).

During the first years of its existence, when the party was unequivocally led by its founder Karel Dillen, this secessionist claim formed the core of its program. From the interwar Flemish nationalism, however, the Vlaams Blok had inherited not only secessionist ideals but also authoritarian party structures (without an explicit rejection of parliamentary democracy) and an ethnocentric nationalism with xenophobic overtones (but without any overt anti-Semitism). During the second half of the 1980s, this latter element started to overshadow the original Flemish nationalism, making of the Vlaams Blok a primarily anti-immigrant party. The driving force behind this evolution was the young and popular Antwerp politician Filip Dewinter. The shift toward this anti-immigrant program allowed not only for the recruitment of new party officials but also for a considerable extension of the electorate. The real breakthrough for the Vlaams Blok occurred with the parliamentary elections of 24 November 1991, when the party trebled its 1987 share of the vote, thus covering more than 10 percent of the Flemish electorate. Ever since, the party's electoral results have shown further progress. During the 2004 elections for the Flemish parliament, it obtained more than 24 percent of the vote, thus becoming Flanders's largest single party. In its main stronghold, Antwerp, it reached a monster score of more than 34 percent, outdoing its own result in the 2000 local elections in that town by 1 percent.

This overwhelming success was mainly due to the party's ability to adapt a long-lasting tradition of right-wing Flemish nationalism to current concerns about politics and society. Only a minority of the Vlaams Blok's electorate seems to be inspired by Flemish nationalist concerns. It consists largely of young people from socially disadvantaged backgrounds, with a relatively low degree of education and only weak ties to civil society. The Flemish nationalist background of the party, however, does provide an organizational and ideological framework within which this group's feelings of political alienation and welfare chauvinism can gain political momentum. The often mentioned tension within the party between the neoconservative Flamingantism represented by Gerolf Annemans and the anti-immigrant populism represented by Dewinter appears therefore as a matter of style and strategy rather than ideology. Karel Dillen judiciously averted the threatening potential of this tension in 1996 by appointing as his successor to the party's presidency the intermediate figure Frank Van Hecke.

If all these factors have made the Vlaams Blok the strongest extreme-right party of Western Europe, it has so far been deprived of political power, in spite of its (since 1994) often expressed willingness to accept governmental responsibilities. This exclusion from power is due to the so-called *cordon sanitaire,* an agreement (1989, renewed in 1994) between all the other Flemish political parties represented in parliament not to engage in any coalition or political initiative with the Vlaams Blok. Because of this agreement, the party has not yet been compelled to make the potentially disrupting choice between maintaining ideological purity or transforming into a broad right-wing party participating in the games of party politics.

A judicial sentence in April 2004 (confirmed by the Court of Cassation in November of that year) that condemned some of the party's affiliated organizations for their transgressions of the law on racism ended the official existence of the party. As early as 14 November 2004, however, a new party was founded under the name Vlaams Belang (Flemish Interest). Although this "new" party shuns an overtly racist discourse, the structures and the party summit are inherited from the Vlaams Blok. Because of this evident continuity, the other political parties have decided not to abandon the cordon sanitaire.

*See also* **Belgium; Flemish National League.**

BIBLIOGRAPHY

Billiet, Jaak, and Hans de Witte. "Attitudinal Disposition to Vote for an Extreme Right-wing Party: The Case of the 'Vlaams Blok.'" *European Journal of Political Research* 27 (1995): 181–202.

Buelens, Jo, and Kris Deschouwer. *De verboden vleespotten: De partijorganisatie van het Vlaams Blok tussen oppositie en machtsdeelname.* Brussels, 2003.

Delwit, Pascal, Jean-Michel De Waele, and Andrea Rea, eds. *L'extrême droite en France et en Belgique.* Brussels, 1998.

Mudde, Cas. *The Ideology of the Extreme Right.* Manchester, U.K., and New York, 2000.

———. "De (non-)transformatie van Vlaams Blok naar Vlaams Belang." *Samenleving en politiek* 11, no. 10 (2004): 16–22.

Spruyt, Marc. *Wat het Vlaams Blok verzwijgt.* Louvain, Belgium, 2000.

Swyngedouw, Marc. "The Extreme Right in Belgium: Of a Non-existent Front National and an Omnipresent Vlaams Blok." In *The New Politics of the Right: Neopopulist Parties and Movements in Established Democracies,* edited by Hans-Georg Betz and Stefen Immerfall, 59–75. New York, 1998.

MARNIX BEYEN

**FLEMISH NATIONAL LEAGUE.** The Vlaams Nationaal Verbond was a Flemish nationalist political party of the extreme Right from 1933 to 1945. Flemish nationalism arose during World War I as a reaction against the absence of a language rights settlement for Dutch-speaking Flemings in the Belgian state, which was dominated by Francophones. Despite the fact that some postwar language laws met several of the Flemish demands, Flemish nationalism developed a strong anti-Belgian streak. The rejection of the Belgian state went hand in hand with a growing aversion to democracy. The Flemish National League was the most important emanation of this development.

The party was founded in 1933 when Staf De Clercq, a prominent Flemish nationalist politician, united a number of anti-Belgian, Flemish nationalist organizations into one party. The new party's program was inspired by the German Nazi party and other European nationalist movements of the extreme Right. The FNL had a pan-national goal: it wanted to annex Flanders to the Netherlands because all speakers of Dutch were considered to form one "Diets" people. This remained a merely theoretical point because interest was lacking in the Netherlands, even in Anton Mussert's National Socialist Movement (Nationaal Socialistische Beweging; NSB), which was theoretically in favor of "Dietsland." The FNL saw itself as the revolutionary vanguard of the "Diets" Flemish and as not bound by the laws of the Belgian state, which was depicted as an unnatural and unnational construction to be destroyed. In reality the FNL stayed within the bounds of Belgian lawfulness, and it tried to gain power by participating in elections. The party was succesful. In the last prewar elections in 1939 it rallied 15 percent of the Flemish votes (8 percent of the Belgian electorate). On the local level, the party had formed coalitions with branches of the Catholic Party, on the basis of a pro-Flemish and right-wing program.

The socialists, liberals, and the Christian labor movement fought the FNL as a fascist and pro-German party. For good reason. Staf De Clercq and other FNL leaders had secret contacts with the Abwehr, the German military secret service. They offered their services to the German army in case of war. Concrete arrangements were never made, but a few days after the German invasion De Clercq contacted the Abwehr. On 4 June he offered the German occupation administration his party's cooperation. De Clercq wanted to realize the FNL program with the occupier's help, obtaining total power, founding Dietsland, and destroying the Belgian state. This last wish was never granted as Berlin did not want a new state on its western border. Yet the FNL became the privileged partner of the occupation administration because Hitler wanted to favor the "Germanic" Flemings as opposed to the "Latin" Walloon. With German help the country's administration was massively infiltrated by FNL members, though the occupation administration kept the Belgian state structure formally intact because Hitler did not want to make a definitive decision about Belgium's political

future. The FNL remained outside important centers of power such as the Belgian judiciary, the economic centers of decision, and the Catholic Church. In return for its rather limited acquisition of power, the FNL had to engage itself completely in the German war effort, many of its members joining the Waffen-SS on the eastern front.

From very early on, the FNL rank and file questioned the political guarantees that were offered for their efforts. Talking about Dietsland was prohibited, and the Belgian state remained intact. They also saw how the Walloon-Belgian collaborationist Léon Degrelle and his Rexist movement gained influence. At the same time, the SS leaders in Berlin and Flanders started building a Greater German movement against the FNL. The German-Flemish Labor Community became an important pawn in the imperialist agenda of the Nazi leadership. When Hitler decided to annex Flanders as Reichsgau to Germany on 12 July 1944, the FNL was ousted from power. At that moment thousands of FNL members were enlisted in German military or paramilitary organizations or were engaged in the administration of the country. The FNL leaders could not offer them any way out. This partly explains why the party kept collaborating until the very end.

After the war the FNL was outlawed by the Belgian authorities as a collaborationist organization. FNL members in high administrative positions and in German military service were severely punished. Many ordinary members lost their civil rights. After some years a generous mercy policy set most punished FNL members free and gave them back their political rights. Some became politically active in postwar Flemish nationalist political parties that followed a democratic path to gain political autonomy for Flanders. However, ideologies of the extreme Right survived latently and resurfaced in 1979, when the Flemish Bloc (Vlaams Blok) was founded as a Flemish nationalist party with an explicitly xenophobic program.

*See also* **Belgium; Flemish Bloc.**

BIBLIOGRAPHY

De Wever, Bruno. *Greep naar de macht: Vlaams-nationalisme en Nieuwe Orde: Het VNV 1933–1945.* Tielt-Ghent, Belgium, 1994.

BRUNO DE WEVER

## FOOTBALL (SOCCER).

**FOOTBALL (SOCCER).** Football (soccer) emerged as the great popular sport in Europe during the second half of the nineteenth century. With its roots in the industrial towns of England and Scotland, football was originally the game of the industrial working classes. In the late twentieth century it was transformed by television and sponsorship revenue and is now the largest sport in the world. The world governing body of football, the Fédération Internationale de Football Association (FIFA), estimates that between 2003 and 2006 it will generate 1.64 billion dollars in revenue, of which 144 million dollars will be profit.

By the time of World War I many of the European nations had national football associations that were responsible for organizing league and cup tournaments and selecting the national squad for international matches. The English Football Association was the first to be formed, in 1863, followed by similar national governing bodies in Switzerland and Belgium (1895), Italy (1898), Germany (1900), Hungary (1901), and Finland (1907). The first international match was played between English and Scottish teams in 1872, and such contests became popular rapidly. Some leagues, such as the Boldspil league in Denmark (the second-oldest in the world), predated the formation of a formal national association. The French Federation of Football was not formed until 1919, although teams had been in existence since 1872 (Le Havre), and France played its first international match (against Belgium) in 1904. Despite the strong amateur ethic that dominated many British and empire sports, such as cricket and rugby, football moved swiftly toward professionalization, and by the time of World War I the majority of elite players were paid for their services.

The international spread and organization of football was underpinned in 1904 by the establishment of FIFA in Paris. The founding members were Belgium, Denmark, France, the Netherlands, Spain, Sweden, and Switzerland. Despite being the most powerful force in football at the time, the English decided not to participate and did not sign up until 1906. FIFA's original statutes effectively made those countries the owners of world football. They would decide who could join, set the rules of the game, and organize international matches. The European domination of FIFA would take decades to be broken down.

### INTERNATIONAL COMPETITION

In 1919, in the wake of World War I, FIFA had to work hard to revive the game. European divisions meant that the British associations, for example, were reluctant to assist in reviving FIFA alongside the national representatives of their former enemies. FIFA's first major postwar step was the organization of the football tournament at the 1924 Olympics. Entry was restricted to amateur players, and the final was played out between Switzerland and Uruguay, who won. The victory of the South Americans demonstrated not only how the game had spread beyond its European origins but also how the balance of power in the world game was also being transformed.

In 1928, in a decision that would formalize international football competitions in a global setting, FIFA decided to work toward the establishment of a world championship. The first World Cup finals were held in Uruguay in 1930, but because of the Depression only four European countries took part. The idea of the World Cup as an attractive event to host, and to win, really took hold in the European context in 1934 and 1938, when the finals were held in Italy and France, respectively. The Italian tournament, which was used, in part, to promote the achievements of Benito Mussolini's Fascist regime, demonstrated the political possibilities and positive publicity that could be accrued by staging a major sporting event. Signaling the advances in technology and the power of football to appeal to an audience beyond the stadium, the 1934 finals were the first to be broadcast live on radio.

FIFA, and thus world football, has been predominantly controlled by a European leadership. Its first key president was the Frenchman Jules Rimet, who was succeeded by a Belgian, Rodolphe William Seeldrayers, and then two Englishmen, Arthur Drewry and Stanley Rous. From 1974 to 1998 the presidency moved for the first time to a non-European, João Havelange from Brazil. He was succeeded by another European, Joseph Blatter from Switzerland.

Although Rimet, Seeldrayers, Drewry, and Rous were prone to championing the cause of

European nations above others, they were instrumental in restoring the game to its preeminent position as the world's number one sport. Rous in particular played a key role in allowing television cameras into international matches and ensuring that the World Cup became a television spectacular. Also, because of the relative weakness of the United States and South Africa in football terms, FIFA did not get embroiled in the politics of the Cold War and the apartheid issue in the same way that the Olympic Games did. As qualification for the World Cup finals was based on a series of continental groupings, European teams always competed in relative harmony, and the finals themselves were not overly plagued by political and ideological concerns. Politically charged incidents did occur, however. In May 1938 the English team played Germany in Berlin and its members were roundly criticized for giving the Nazi salute so as not to offend their hosts. In 1966 the qualification of the Democratic People's Republic of Korea caused the British hosts difficulties as they did not recognize that state. Playing under the name of North Korea, the team performed well as underdogs and the political dimension was forgotten.

Under the Brazilian Havelange, FIFA was transformed into a truly global entity, and the European dominance of the organization was reduced. Under Havelange the organization also secured major sponsorship and television deals that transformed its finances. He oversaw the increase in the number of teams at the World Cup finals, increased the organization's involvement in youth and women's football, and cleared the way for the entry of Israel into the world of football. Blatter has continued to work with a global focus, and while Europe remains centrally important to FIFA, the rise of South Asian and African teams and their ability to effectively host major championships have reduced its power at the heart of the organization of world football. Whereas the European nations hosted five of the eight World Cup finals from 1930 to 1966, and won four of them, the Continent has only been the location for four of the nine finals since then, and its teams have won only four.

### EUROPEAN COMPETITION

Given the global focus of FIFA, a specifically European football organization emerged in 1954.

**World Cup finals in Paris, 1938.** Giuseppe Meazza of Italy (left) and Gyorgi Sarosi of Hungary shake hands before the match. The Italian team won with a score of 4–2. ©HULTON-DEUTSCH COLLECTION/CORBIS

The Union of European Football Associations (UEFA) was formed in Switzerland after discussions between the French, Italian, and Belgian associations. Initially twenty-five associations joined UEFA. By 2004, with the collapse of the Soviet Union and the plethora of new nations that came into existence, the membership of UEFA had grown to fifty-two associations.

UEFA functions as the administrative body that controls European football. It organizes competitions for both club-level and international teams. In the 1955–1956 season it began the European Champion Clubs Cup, which quickly established itself as the leading club competition in the world. European football benefited from having a large number of high quality and competitive national leagues, including those in England, Italy, Spain, France, and Germany. These clubs were able to attract the best players from around the world, and the transfer of stars accelerated rapidly during the 1960s. These major football nations dominated European competition, and clubs such as Real Madrid, Liverpool, Ajax, Bayern Munich, and Milan became synonymous with winning the trophy.

In the 1992–1993 season the competition was reorganized to take advantage of the growing commercial opportunities that were available to UEFA. Rather than being a knockout tournament, the competition was expanded so that it became an almost weekly league competition that allowed for additional television coverage and sponsorship opportunities. In the 2001–2002 season the marketing income of the league was estimated at 667 million dollars. Of the total revenue, 75 percent went to those clubs that had taken part and the remainder to UEFA. The popularity of the competition is obvious. In the 2002–2003 season the cumulative viewing figures worldwide totalled four billion people (some 17,200 hours of live football across the globe), and television companies paid an estimated 500 million dollars for the rights to cover the games.

Given the strength and appeal of European football, UEFA also began an international tournament for its member associations. Played every four years, the European Football Championship is structured around a two-year qualification process, culminating in a finals tournament. The first finals were played in 1960, when the Soviet Union beat Yugoslavia. The tournament has been staged without a break ever since and has been won most often by the Germans (three times) and the French (twice). As well as working with single host nations, UEFA has also embraced the idea of smaller nations cohosting the tournament. In 2000 Belgium and the Netherlands were cohosts, and in 2008 it will be the turn of Austria and Switzerland.

At the beginning of the twenty-first century, Europe stands as the most successful home of football in the world. Its leagues and associated UEFA competitions are the most competitive on the globe and attract huge viewing numbers and sponsorship income. The best players and coaches are attracted to Europe by large salaries. It is estimated that David Beckham earns two hundred thousand dollars per week at Real Madrid, with a total income from salary and endorsements of over twenty million dollars per year. This makes him the eighth-highest paid sports star in the world. This wealth, despite the long-standing popularity of football on the Continent, is a recent phenomenon.

## PROBLEMS IN SOCCER

Up to the 1960s football teams were, with the odd exception, little known outside their national league. Many players were drawn from the local area, as was the spectator base. While football was popular, the game and the facilities of the 1960s were little changed from three decades earlier. During the 1960s, however, English and Scottish football regularly witnessed incidents of violence at football matches. The spate of hooliganism was seen initially as a specifically British problem, and one that had its roots in the social dislocation of young white males as economic security in Britain declined.

The problem was so extreme that it had a negative effect on attendance and television-viewing figures, and many commentators in the 1980s talked about the death of English football as the main national pastime. Things came to a head in three disastrous incidents: the Bradford stadium fire that killed fifty-six in 1985; the disaster at a European Cup final in 1985 in Heysel, Belgium, where thirty-eight Italian supporters and one Belgian were killed when a wall collapsed on them after clashes with Liverpool fans; and the Hillsborough tragedy, where ninety-six Liverpool supporters were crushed to death in 1989. These events, accompanied by violent incidents at English international matches, galvanized the British government into action. Stadiums were modernized, with seats replacing the areas where fans had previously stood, and increased police surveillance made football matches much safer. With the advent of satellite television in the late 1980s, the Football League was able to gain significant income by selling its products, and the game rapidly moved to a new level of prosperity.

These trends were followed across Europe. From the 1980s Italy developed a significant hooligan problem, which was echoed in Germany and the Netherlands. Since the 1990s, the former

Soviet states have also suffered from high levels of football-related violence. At the same time, due to changes in the selling of television rights and the success of the Champions League, most European leagues have seen a significant increase in revenue.

In addition to legislation by individual countries to control stadium design and facilities and to prevent the hooligan problem, European law has also impacted the game. In 1990 a Belgian second-division player, Jean-Marc Bosman, was out of contract with his club, RFC Liege, and wanted to move to Dunkerque in France. The transfer fee offered by Dunkerque was not high enough, and Liege refused to allow him to move. Bosman took his case to the European Court of Justice, arguing that he was being prevented from plying his trade. He won a landmark judgment that guaranteed all players freedom of movement, at the end of their contract, within the European Union (EU). The ruling also prevented clubs or leagues from imposing restrictions on the number of foreign (non-EU) players on each team. The case had significant ramifications for players, empowering them in negotiations with clubs and inflating salaries for top players. The ruling also demonstrated how football, as a business, was not immune from the reach of European legislation.

*See also* **Leisure; Popular Culture; Television.**

BIBLIOGRAPHY

Armstrong, Gary. *Football Hooligans: Knowing the Score.* Oxford, U.K., 1998.

Conn, David. *The Beautiful Game? Searching for the Soul of English Football.* London, 2004.

Kuper, Simon. *Football against the Enemy.* London, 2003.

Lanfranchi, Pierre, and Matthew Taylor. *Moving with the Ball: The Migration of Professional Football Players.* Oxford, U.K., 2001.

Lanfranchi, Pierre, Christiane Eisenberg, Tony Mason, and Alfred Wahl. *100 Years of Football: The FIFA Centenary Book.* London, 2005.

Martin, Simon. *Football and Fascism: The National Game under Mussolini.* Oxford, U.K., 2004.

Szymanski, Stefan, and Andrew Zimbalist. *National Pastime: How the Americans Play Baseball and the Rest of the World Plays Soccer.* London, 2005.

MIKE CRONIN

**FORCED LABOR.** As defined by the International Labour Organization (ILO) in 1930, *forced labor* is "all work or service which is exacted from any person under the menace of any penalty, and for which the said person has not offered himself voluntarily." In historiography a clear delineation of forced labor is rather difficult. It has to be distinguished from specific forms of unfree labor that have been commonly accepted, especially work obligations during war and catastrophes, and work by prisoners of war; by persons in penitentiary institutions or workhouses; and by persons in debt bondage on the one side and in slavery on the other, discussions of which include questions of individual property rights related to the laborers.

Unfree labor is not a new phenomenon of the twentieth century. It has existed since ancient times in different forms, especially the work obligations of peasants in feudal societies and slavery in Africa, America, and Asia. Twentieth-century forced labor was a mass phenomenon organized by modern states, predominantly in dictatorships. Its characteristics were imprisonment, often deportation to other places, inhumane living and working conditions, and little or no payment.

According to the fourth Hague Convention (1907) on the rules of law in ground warfare, services forced on a population by an occupier had to be restricted to the actual necessities of the occupying army and in relation to the resources available. The International Labour Organization, after a convention on slavery in 1926, brought forward a convention on forced labor in 1930.

At the beginning of the twentieth century, most European states allowed forced labor in their colonies. Russia since the eighteenth century had located its penal exile and forced labor system (*katorga*) in Siberia. Among the first cases of mass recruitment for forced labor in Europe were German deportations from occupied Belgium and Poland during World War I. The German government in 1915 ordered that civilians in these occupied areas be forcibly recruited and transported to the Reich for work in the armament industry. These deportations were stopped in 1917. After the war they constituted a major war crimes allegation against German officials.

## THE SOVIET GULAG

The first modern dictatorship to organize forced labor on a mass scale was Bolshevik Soviet Russia. Already in mid-1918 the government of Vladimir Lenin (1870–1924) introduced compulsory labor service in the constitution of the Russian Soviet Federated Socialist Republic (SFSR) and installed camps for alleged political or class enemies. In 1921, more than one hundred thousand citizens were imprisoned in the different camp systems. The precursor of the gulag, the Northern Camps of Special Tasks at the Solovetsky Islands was installed in 1922–1923 by the political police (then OGPU).

The expansion of imprisonment was connected to the collectivization drive under the Soviet dictator Joseph Stalin (1879–1953) from 1929 to 1930. New camp systems, now explicitly called labor correction camps (*ispravitelno-trudovye lageri*) and networks of so-called labor colonies were installed, most of them in Siberia. In October 1934, after the reorganization of the camp system into the Main Administration for Camps (Glavnoe Upravlenie Lagerei, or GULag) of the NKVD (People's Commissariat of Internal Affairs), more than a million persons lived in these camps, most of them farmers and their families. Forced labor now became integrated in the economic planning of the state, which prevailed from the first Five-Year-Plan of 1928. The camps were subordinated to specific economic People's Commissariats, or ministries, especially for construction or forestry works.

Connected to the terror waves especially in 1937–1938, hundreds of thousands of alleged "enemies of the people" were arrested and detained in camps or colonies. Already before the war 1.6 million persons had been imprisoned; after the annexation of Polish and Baltic territories in the west, this figure rose to 1.9 million persons. During the war, the death rate reached its high point at 25 percent of prisoners a year, which means that from 1941 to 1945 almost one million gulag prisoners died in camps and labor colonies. More than three hundred thousand ethnic Germans were forcibly recruited into the labor army (*trudarmiya*) beginning in late 1941. The majority of the three million Axis prisoners of war (POWs) in the Soviet Union were put under a hard labor regime from 1944 on, especially in order to reconstruct the devastated western areas. The gulag system reached its culmination during the years 1948–1952, with approximately 2.5 million prisoners. In 1943 an extreme category of special camps was introduced (katorga camps), with the hardest working conditions and low food rates. According to Soviet statistics, which present rather minimal figures, at least two million persons died in the gulag, more than one million in the labor colonies, and another million in the POW and internment camps. During the course of early destalinization, from 1954 on, a large number of the surviving prisoners were released, but the gulag remained in action until 1960. Other forms of forced labor, as in prison, continued to exist until the collapse of the Soviet Union in the late 1980s.

Under the control of the Soviet Union, the regimes of Eastern European states operated forced labor camps immediately after the war, from 1945 for German minorities or alleged collaborators, and from 1947–1948 on for persons considered as enemies of the new communist regimes. Some of these prisoners were exploited for forced labor, sometimes under very hard conditions. Most of the camps remained in operation until the mid-1950s.

## NAZI GERMANY

Another type of forced labor system was installed by Nazi Germany and, to a certain extent, by its Axis allies. Beginning in 1933, the regime of Adolf Hitler (1889–1945) installed concentration camps, intended to detain first alleged political enemies, later groups considered as "racial" enemies. The concentration camp system was in decline until 1937, when new types of big camps were introduced, and the number of inmates rose considerably from 1938 on. From 1938 on, four types of forced labor can be distinguished under Nazi rule: (a) forced labor inside the expanding concentration camp system, (b) forced labor in the occupied territories, (c) the recruitment of foreign laborers for the Reich, and (d) forced labor of Jews.

The number of concentration camp inmates rose with each military expansion. But their workforce until 1941–1942 was predominantly used for SS-owned firms. The SS (Schutzstaffel) failed in their efforts to introduce work for German enterprises inside the big concentration camps. Instead

**Women in Ukraine are forced to spin wool for German uniforms under Nazi occupation, 1942.** ©BETTMANN/CORBIS

in 1942 the installation of concentration camp branches in or near the enterprises started and expanded massively in 1943–1944. In the beginning of 1945, more than seven hundred thousand persons were imprisoned in the camps, the majority of whom worked in subcamps either for the armament industry or for SS purposes. Death rates among concentration camp inmates were very high. Out of the estimated 1.5–2 million concentration camp prisoners, approximately eight hundred thousand did not survive the war.

Forced labor recruitment inside the occupied territories especially affected Jews and other criminalized groups and was used for defense works. People suspected of working for the Resistance were interned and forced to work for German purposes, as were farmers who did not fulfill the German grain quota. The latter were put into specific labor camps. In the occupied Soviet territories, work columns were introduced in several regions. During the German retreats, from 1943–1944 on, tens of thousands of eastern Europeans were recruited to build fortifications.

The major part of the foreign workforce during World War II was civilians deported to the Reich.

Until early 1942 direct force was not much used in recruitment, this changed with the establishment of the General Plenipotentiary for Labor (Generalbevollmächtigter für den Arbeitseinsatz), which organized manhunts especially in Poland and the Soviet Union. Working and living conditions were generally hard, but varied according to workplace, less dangerous in agriculture, more in coal mining. Approximately eight million civilians were thus forcibly employed in the Reich, the majority from Poland ("P-Arbeiter") and the Soviet Union ("Ostarbeiter"). The latter groups suffered the most, approximately 150,000 to 300,000 persons died. In general, forced labor of POWs has to be distinguished as a separate issue, but during the war there were overlapping cases: Polish and (from 1943) Italian POWs were stripped of their legal POW status and used as civilian forced laborers. Soviet POWs who survived the mass starvation of 1941–1942 were put under an extreme labor regime, with high rates of mortality especially in mining.

German and Austrian Jews were recruited for forced labor beginning in 1938, Polish Jews from 1939. Beginning in 1941, the murder of Jews in the Soviet Union paralleled the exploitation of Jews as forced laborers. The majority of eastern European Jews had been killed by the end of 1942, but approximately 10 percent of them had been kept alive in order to use them as a workforce in ghettos, in specific labor camps for Jews, and finally in concentration camps. For Jews, forced labor often turned out to be important for individual survival. Nevertheless the majority of Jewish forced laborers were killed like all other Jews by the end of the war.

The other Axis states also kept forced labor facilities, especially for Jews. Adult Jewish men were recruited for work battalions in Hungary, Slovakia, Romania, and Bulgaria. In the Hungarian case, Jews were required to support the Hungarian army inside the occupied Soviet territories. The camps installed by the Croatian Ustaše (a fascist group) for Serbs, Jews, and Roma served predominantly for internment and extermination, less for forced labor. Even fascist Italy established labor camps for Jewish foreigners in the country, and for "suspects" in the occupied regions of southeastern Europe. Other authoritarian dictatorships introduced forced labor for political prisoners. Francisco Franco's Spain during World War II forced Republican prisoners in camps to set up the "Valley of the Fallen" (Valle de los Caídos), with high mortality rates among the laborers.

## AFTER WORLD WAR II

In Western Europe, unlike in dictatorships in Asia, South America, and Africa, conventional forced labor lost its significance after the war. The ILO issued another convention against forced labor in 1957. Specific forms of unfree labor still exist in Europe, especially in southeast European countries. The ILO twice, in 1973 and 1999, organized conventions against child labor. In 2001 the ILO created the Special Action Programme to Combat Forced Labour. It is a question of definition whether prostitution under coercion can be counted as forced labor. In general, since the 1970s, forced and slave labor have been a phenomenon of the non-European world.

Usually, forced labor is defined according to legal patterns, but is considered first a moral problem. On the other hand, there is a constant discussion among forced-labor administrations (and among researchers) concerning the economic

efficency of forced labor. In most cases, labor regimes try to reduce their costs by fully exploiting their victims, but productivity is low since the laborers are put under extreme physical conditions and receive few incentives. The endemic violence in detention centers further reduces productivity. It is still under debate whether totalitarian regimes like Nazi Germany or the Soviet Union intentionally applied programs of "annihilation through labor," that is, totally exhausting the laborers within weeks and killing them right afterward. This effect was visible especially regarding some Nazi concentration camps and labor camps for Jews, and to a certain extent even in the katorga camps of the gulag. But evidence for such a specific intention exists only in a limited number of cases of Nazi policy, especially regarding Jews doing construction work in the east, and so-called asocials in 1942–1943. But there is no doubt that labor administrations anticipated the death of hundreds of thousands by forced labor under specific circumstances. For most survivors, forced labor led to severe physical damage for the rest of their lives, especially if they had worked under extreme environmental circumstances or in construction works, mining, or heavy industry.

Already during the 1950s the issue of indemnification for forced labor came up, first during the German "Wiedergutmachung" for victims of National Socialism, then from the 1960s in negotiations with individual German firms that had used forced labor during the war and now wanted to enter the U.S. market. But a systematic approach only came into being with the new discussion on compensation during the 1990s. In 2000 the German Stiftung "Erinnerung, Verantwortung und Zukunft" (Foundation Remembrance, Responsibility, and Future) was established in order to support the forced laborers who are still alive. Almost simultaneously the issue of compensation for forced labor under communist regimes was being addressed, but by the mid 2000s the issue had not yet been resolved.

*See also* **Concentration Camps; Germany; Gulag; Jews; Political Prisoners; Soviet Union; World War II.**

BIBLIOGRAPHY

Applebaum, Anne. *Gulag: A History.* New York, 2003.

Brass, Tom, and Marcel van der Linden, eds. *Free and Unfree Labour: The Debate Continues.* Bern, 1997.

Carlton, Richard K., ed. *Forced Labor in the "People's Democracies."* New York, 1955.

*Forced and Slave Labor in Nazi-Dominated Europe: Symposium Presentations.* Washington, D.C., 2004.

Gregory, Paul R., and Valery Lazarev, eds. *The Economics of Forced Labor: The Soviet Gulag.* Stanford, Calif., 2003.

Herbert, Ulrich. *A History of Foreign Labor in Germany, 1880–1980: Seasonal Workers, Forced Laborers, Guest Workers.* Translated by William Templer. Ann Arbor, Mich., 1990.

———. *Hitler's Foreign Workers: Enforced Foreign Labor in Germany under the Third Reich.* Translated by William Templer. Cambridge, U.K., and New York, 1997.

Kotek, Joël, and Pierre Rigoulot. *Le siècle des camps: Emprisonnement, détention, concentration, extermination: Cent ans de mal radical.* Paris, 2000.

Smirnov, M. B., ed. *Sistema ispravitelno-trudovykh lagerei v SSSR, 1923–1960: Spravochnik.* Moscow, 1998.

Spoerer, Mark. *Zwangsarbeit unter dem Hakenkreuz: Ausländische Zivilarbeiter, Kriegsgefangene und Häftlinge im Deutschen Reich und im besetzten Europa, 1939–1945.* Stuttgart, 2001.

Weinmann, Martin, ed. *Das nationalsozialistische Lagersystem (CCP).* Frankfurt am Main, 1990.

DIETER POHL

---

**FORDISM.** The term *Fordism* emerged between the world wars. At that time, it designated the economic and social system pioneered by Henry Ford. In the last two decades of the nineteenth century engineer Frederick Taylor had developed the techniques of "scientific management," showing how productivity could be increased by closely studying workers' movements and eliminating time-wasting gestures. Ford extended Taylor's methods from the individual laborer to the "collective worker" on the moving assembly line at his Highland Park, Michigan, factory. In January 1914, Henry Ford introduced the unprecedented wage of five dollars for eight hours of work—more than twice the going rate in the automobile industry at the time.

The retail sale price of Ford's Model T fell from $950 to $490 between 1909 and 1914, and in the same period Ford went from being just one among hundreds of automobile companies to controlling 48 percent of the automobile market. Admirers of Ford used the term *Fordism* to refer to a system they found baffling, due to its combination of a "constant reduction of prices" with "powerfully superelevated wages" (Gottl-Ottlilienfeld, p. 3). The tradeoff for these high wages, however, was a relentless increase in the pace of production. Manufacturing workers had been paid a survival wage in the nineteenth century; the Ford workers were paid enough that they could to purchase their own product. Ford also meddled in his workers' private lives, although he was by no means the only capitalist to do so at the time. Workers received the full five-dollar wage only if inspectors from the company's "Sociological Department" determined that their personal life met certain standards of sobriety, cleanliness, and adherence to an "American" lifestyle. These traits were seen as the basis for efficiency in the workplace. Ford's Sociological Department vetted prospective employees, inspected workers' homes, and taught workers to become Americans. For example, in 1916 Ford rented the largest public meeting hall in the city. On the stage stood a replica immigrant ship and in front of it a giant kettle, a "melting pot." The ceremony literally stripped the worker of his past identity and gave him a new one: "Down the gangplank came the members of the class dressed in their national garbs … [then they descended] into the Ford melting pot and disappeared." Teachers used long paddles to "stir" the pot. Before long, "the pot began to boil over and out came the men dressed in their best American clothes and waving American flags" (Zieger and Gall, p. 17).

In 1919 Ford began moving his workforce to the new Rouge Plant in Dearborn, Michigan, which embodied another element that came to be seen as central to Fordism: the horizontal integration of the production process. The Rouge was composed of "sawmills, blast furnaces, foundries, body and glass departments, a power house," and more (Bucci, p. 48). Ford soon opened factories in Canada, Latin America, Europe, and the Soviet Union, and two rubber plantations in Brazil.

Some of Ford's social interventions during the Great Depression constituted a sort of corporate alternative to the New Deal in the Detroit area. Ford created commissaries in towns with large concentrations of his workers, selling food at low prices, and provided loans to keep his unemployed workers off public welfare. Ford bailed out the bankrupt Detroit suburb of Inkster, where many of the company's African American workers lived, and offered loans and construction help to workers who wanted to improve their homes. Although Ford hated the New Deal, a Detroit politician claimed that Ford's relief programs "became the model for Harry Hopkin's WPA [Works Projects Administration] in President Roosevelt's New Deal recovery program" (Gomon, box 10, p. 34). This points toward the centrality of the welfare state in postwar Fordism. Ford's involvement in the improvement of his employees' homes related to another dimension of Fordism: its effects on urbanism. Like many other industrial metropolitan areas that emerged in this period, Detroit was not so much a city as "a series of buildings held together by transportation and communications" (Bucci, p. 11). Detroit became the quintessential low-rise city, with high rates of working-class home ownership.

During the prewar and interwar period the term *Fordism* typically referred to the combination of mass production on the assembly line, rationalization of the labor process, comparatively high wages, and efforts to shape working-class culture to fit the requirements of industry. Because Ford resisted labor unions and was the last Detroit automaker to recognize the United Auto Workers after a 1941 sit-down strike at the Rouge plant, socialists and unionists used *Fordism* as a label for the company's fierce repression of unions and relentless increases in productivity. The lasting theoretical contribution to this interwar discussion is an essay called "Americanism and Fordism" by Antonio Gramsci, written during his imprisonment in fascist Italy. Gramsci suggested that recent developments in the United States could be characterized as constituting a novel form of social "hegemony"—a word Gramsci used to mean not simply leadership or the use of force, but a web of informal and formal persuasive devices located not just in the state but also in the interstices of civil society, and within families, bodies, and psyches. These loosely coordinated devices, he argued, combine to stabilize and reproduce capitalism. He argued that Ford's "so-called high wages" were necessary to "maintain and restore the strength that has been worn down by the new form of toil" and that these wages made possible "a larger internal market" and "a more rapid rhythm of capital accumulation" (pp. 310, 291). This made it necessary to forge a more disciplined type of worker who was able to tolerate the strenuous monotony of the assembly line. Frederick Taylor's experiments had already determined that only a small proportion of workers could keep pace with the rationalized process. Gramsci interpreted Prohibition and campaigns for monogamy in this light.

Some of Ford's other activities fit the definition of hegemony as a process of generating consent through persuasion rather than force. Some U.S. employers in this period sowed racial hatred in order to weaken labor unity. Although Ford was the first Detroit automaker to pay equal wages to whites and blacks, the latter typically worked in the foundry or in janitorial jobs. In the 1930s, Ford built separate schools in black and white districts in towns west of Dearborn. Ford's Greenfield Village, a collection of historic structures established in 1933 in Dearborn, celebrated a rural America that his cars and factories were helping to destroy. Ford also established a Motion Picture Department in 1914, "the first of its kind at a major commercial company," and began producing short documentaries and longer historical and educational films. By 1920 these Ford films "were shown in a minimum of 4,000 theatres and were seen by approximately one-seventh of the weekly motion picture audience in the United States" (Grieveson). The mass culture that played a central role in analyses of postwar Fordism was represented here in microcosm.

Gramsci's essay was rediscovered in the 1970s, when the socioeconomic crisis led European theorists to speculate on the sources of the prosperity during the preceding decades. Fordism had developed in the meantime and differed in part from the Fordism of the first half of the century. What remained was the virtuous cycle between mass production and mass consumption, grounded in a disciplined working class. The postwar model encompassed a much more elaborate system for stabilizing labor relations through agreements like the Treaty of Detroit in the U.S. auto industry or the neocorporatist practices that emerged across Western Europe. Unions offered to control their members' militancy in exchange for increased benefits and participation in managerial decisions and wages that were pegged to profits. This new social contract was buttressed by a welfare state and Keynesian fiscal policies that buffered workers' incomes during cyclical downturns in the economy, illness, accident, and retirement. Workers' ability to develop longer time horizons led to increased levels of home ownership and raised aggregate demand for manufactured goods. In geographic terms Fordism concentrated economic circuits within the boundaries of the nation-state while partly evening out regional inequalities. Another signal feature of postwar Fordism was the pervasiveness of middle-brow culture, broadcast through the mass media. Although French social theorist Michel Aglietta followed Gramsci in situating (postwar) Fordism in the United States, others argued that northwestern European countries such as Sweden and West Germany represented the model's apotheosis, whereas Fordism in the United States (and the United Kingdom) was less complete due to the relative underdevelopment of social insurance there.

Those who reintroduced the concept of Fordism were associated with regulation theory, an approach that presents Fordism as a model of organizing and governing society that allows continuing increases in profitability despite the intrinsically contradictory dynamics as capitalist economies, that is, the adversarial interests of business and labor. Fordism was understood as a "mode of regulation," that is, as a cluster of economic, political, and social institutions that undergirded economic growth and permitted social relations to perpetuate themselves, at least for a limited period of time. In contrast to traditional Marxist theories, regulation theory does not assume that capitalist systems will automatically find a solution to every socioeconomic crisis; prolonged economic stagnation and social chaos are distinct possibilities. The institutions and practices that made up Fordism were not necessarily invented with that mode of regulation in mind, but arose instead from a variety of disparate historical contexts and were subsequently woven together into a temporary social structure. For example Keynesian economic theory was developed with the aim of promoting economic growth, while the nuclear, male-breadwinner family was the product of very different interests, but both institutions played a central role in postwar Fordism. Like postmodern social theory, regulation theory emphasizes accident and causal contingencies in the creation of new social forms. Regulation theory also traces the emergence of postmodern culture itself to the decline of Fordism and to the rise of new, post-Fordist social conditions. The new social movements of the 1960s and the scientific culture of the 1950s have also been explained in terms of specific features of Fordism.

Since the late twentieth century social theorists have realized that the category of Fordism is best suited for analyzing the period before 1980. The 1980s marked the beginning of a rollback of the welfare state and a decline in unionization; a spiraling increase in economic and regional inequalities; a focus within industry on just-in-time production and flexible specialization; production for niche rather than mass markets; and the ascendance of neoliberalism as a dominant economic ideology. Centers of Fordist manufacturing, such as Detroit and the German Ruhr Valley, suffered massive disinvestment, leaving the vast hulking ruins of factories in their wake. Some theorists analyzed the emergent social formation as "post-Fordism" and tried to specify its contours, whereas others suggested that regulation theory could not be extended to eras other than the Fordist one. In Europe many right-wing extremists based in the disempowered working class attributed their plight to immigrants and looked back nostalgically at an idealized Fordist era of prosperity, equality, and national homogeneity. Left-wing critics targeted post-Fordism and globalization as the culprit.

*See also* **Keynes, J. M.; Labor Movements; Postmodernism.**

BIBLIOGRAPHY

Aglietta, Michel. *A Theory of Capitalist Regulation: The U.S. Experience.* Translated by David Fernbach. London, 1987.

Amin, Ash, ed. *Post-Fordism: A Reader.* Oxford, U.K., 1994.

Bucci, Federico. *Albert Kahn: Architect of Ford.* New York, 2002.

Fox, R. M. "Fordism: A Critical Evaluation." *The Nineteenth Century and After* 101 (February 1927): 234–241.

Gomon, Josephine. "The Poor Mr. Ford." Unpublished manuscript. Bentley Historical Library, Gomon Papers. Gomon was executive secretary to Detroit Mayor Frank

Murphy (1930–1933) and later director of the Detroit Housing Commission.

Gottl-Ottlilienfeld, Friedrich von. *Fordismus? Paraphrasen über das Verhälnis von Wirtschaft und Technischer Vernunft bei Henry Ford und Frederick W. Taylor.* Jena, Germany, 1924.

Gramsci, Antonio. "Americanism and Fordism." In *Selections from the Prison Notebooks,* edited and translated by Quintin Hoare and Geoffrey Nowell Smith. New York, 1971.

Grieveson, Lee. 2005. "Watching Henry Skate: The Films of the Ford Motor Company." Available at http://humanities.uwe.ac.uk/bristoldocs/Detroit/Background.htm.

Harvey, David. *The Condition of Postmodernity: An Enquiry into the Origins of Cultural Change.* Cambridge, Mass., 1989.

Jessop, Bob. "Conservative Regimes and the Transition to Post-Fordism: The Cases of Great Britain and West Germany." In *Capitalist Development and Crisis Theory: Accumulation, Regulation, and Spatial Restructuring,* edited by Mark Gottdiener and Nicos Komninos. Houndmills, U.K., 1989.

McIntyre, Stephen L. "The Failure of Fordism: Reform of the Automobile Repair Industry, 1913–1940." *Technology and Culture* 41, no. 2 (2000): 269–299.

Meyer, Stephen. *The Five Dollar Day: Labor, Management, and Social Control in the Ford Motor Company, 1908–1921.* Albany, N.Y., 1981.

Steinmetz, George. "Regulation Theory, Post-Marxism, and the New Social Movements." *Comparative Studies in Society and History* 36, no. 1 (1994):176–212.

——. "Scientific Authority and the Transition to Post-Fordism: The Plausibility of Positivism in American Sociology since 1945." In *The Politics of Method in the Human Sciences: Positivism and Its Epistemological Others.* Edited by George Steinmetz. Durham, N.C., 2005.

Zieger, Robert H., and Gilbert J. Gall. *American Workers, American Unions: The Twentieth Century.* 3rd ed. Baltimore, Md., 2002.

GEORGE STEINMETZ

---

# FORTUYN, PIM (1948–2002), Dutch author and politician.

Born in Velsen, Wilhelmus Simon Petrus Fortuyn studied sociology at the Free University of Amsterdam and then taught Marxist sociology at the University of Groningen, but he left academic life to work in the private sector as a management consultant. In an odyssey characteristic of his generation, he abandoned Marxism to become a social democrat and ultimately a neoliberal. He was a prolific author, and during his last ten years published a dozen books. As a weekly columnist for *Elseviers Weekblad* he consistently castigated the consensus policies adopted by the so-called purple liberal-socialist cabinet of Wim Kok (1994–2002). In his view this consensus democracy had degenerated into a cartel democracy, with deals being struck by the ruling parties. Kok's personalized authority had been assumed to be popular in the years of economic growth, but this apparent popularity masked the increasing discontent with the lack of immigrant integration and with the public sector, especially education and public health care, where its growing bureaucracy and expensive managers had not delivered a better service. In reaction to Nazi policies during World War II, political elites not only avoided any discrimination between cultures and races but also denied that there were any real problems. Their espousal of "multiculturalism" led to growing social tensions, primarily in inner-city areas. Fortuyn warned against immigration because he considered Islam to be a threat to a tolerant, liberal Dutch society, and he did not want the emancipation of homosexuals and women to be put under threat. He blamed his generation, the spoiled baby boomers, for decadence in the Netherlands, as their irresponsible egoism took no account of the interests of future generations.

On 20 August 2001 Fortuyn announced that he would participate in the parliamentary elections of May 2002. He became the leader of a new party, Leefbaar Nederland (Livable Netherlands), that was born out of popular frustration with the policy of Wim Kok's "purple cabinet." The terrorist attacks on the United States on 11 September 2001 brought the hidden tensions within Dutch society to the surface, in particular the slumbering antagonisms between the Dutch and the Muslim immigrants and the fears of certain marginalized sections of the Dutch middle classes, who felt threatened by globalization. They no longer felt themselves represented by elites who pretended to be cosmopolitan. Fortuyn came at the right moment to mobilize these estranged voters by calling for a halt to immigration. He considered television an ideal instrument for a direct form of personalized democracy, as opposed to the "old" democracy of political parties, and he was the first Dutch politician who used an image culture. With his aggressive rhetoric and mastery of television as a medium, he was able to outmaneuver his political opponents.

On 9 February 2002 Fortuyn contended that Holland was full, that Islam was a backward culture, and that Article 1 of the constitution, which penalized discrimination, should be rescinded. This perceived shift to the right proved unacceptable to Leefbaar Nederland, and Fortuyn was dismissed as party leader. On 14 February Fortuyn founded his own national party, the Lijst Pim Fortuyn (List Pim Fortuyn, LPF). The local splinter party, Leefbaar Rotterdam (Livable Rotterdam), which still retained Fortuyn as its leader, became the largest party in Rotterdam in the municipal elections of 6 March. With his remarkable political style, the flamboyantly dressed dandy Fortuyn had his finest hours during the many television debates that preceded the parliamentary elections. His ever growing popularity allowed him to frame the political debate, especially on the integration of foreigners and the treatment of criminals.

Fortuyn was murdered on 6 May 2002 in Hilversum by an ecological extremist only nine days before the elections. The Left was blamed for his death, having "demonized" Fortuyn, and other politicians who were threatened went into hiding or employed bodyguards. His funeral gave birth to hitherto unknown expressions of mass grief in the Netherlands. On 15 May, the Labor and Liberal Parties of the "purple" coalition were severely defeated. The LPF won twenty-six parliamentary seats and thus became the largest party after the Christian Democrats. The ascendancy of populism can be observed elsewhere in Europe, but unlike right-wing populists such as Jean-Marie Le Pen in France and Filip Dewinter in Belgium, the overtly homosexual Fortuyn, the "pink populist," could not be classified as a traditional fascist or racist. After his assassination the *Frankfurter Allgemeine* called him "the first genuine postmodern populist of Europe" (8 May 2002).

This unique landslide in Dutch politics can be seen as the consequence of a longer process, in which traditional political parties based on ideology had been overtaken by more consumerist behavior and an increasing volatility among the Dutch electorate. After Fortuyn's death, the movement failed to maintain momentum, losing eighteen seats in a subsequent election, primarily because of its lack of experience and organization. However, the agenda set by Fortuyn had to be addressed by the traditional mainstream political parties.

*See also* **Immigration and Internal Migration; Le Pen, Jean-Marie; Minority Rights; Netherlands.**

BIBLIOGRAPHY

Fortuyn, Pim. *De verweesde samenleving in het informatietijdperk.* Amsterdam, 2001.

Holsteyn, Joop J. M. van, and Galen A. Irwin. "Never a Dull Moment: Pim Fortuyn and the Dutch Parliamentary Election of 2002." *West European Politics* 26, no. 2 (April 2003): 41–66.

Holsteyn, Joop J. M. van, Galen A. Irwin, and Josje M. den Ridder. "In the Eye of the Beholder: The Perception of the List Pim Fortuyn and the Parliamentary Elections of May 2002." *Acta Politica* 38 (spring 2003): 69–87.

Pels, Dick. *De geest van Pim: Het gedachtegoed van een politieke dandy.* Amsterdam, 2003.

Wansink, Hans. *De erfenis van Fortuyn: De Nederlandse democratie na de opstand van de kiezers.* Amsterdam, 2004.

DICK VAN GALEN LAST

**FOUCAULT, MICHEL** (1926–1984), French poststructuralist and philosopher.

Michel Foucault studied at the École Normale Supérieure and took his degrees in philosophy and psychology. His most influential teachers were in the emerging field of science studies, Georges Canguilhem and Jean Cavaillès. He later taught in Sweden, Poland, Germany, and Tunisia, and in 1970 assumed a chair in the history of systems of thought in France's most prestigious institution of higher learning, the Collège de France. Foucault was consistently aligned with the political Left, espousing causes such as prisoners' rights and gay rights. At times sympathetic to Marxist thought, he did not join any communist or socialist parties. Although he began his writing career exploring the limits of the Enlightenment, he always maintained the stance of a social and cultural critic. His critique of the "humanism" of the Enlightenment, for example, did not lessen his commitment to what he called, in his essay "What Is Enlightenment?" (1984), "the spirit of critique."

Foucault's first major work, *Madness and Civilization* (1961), aligned him with the antipsychiatry movement. Its leading figures, R. D. Laing (1927–1989) in England and Félix Guattari (1930–1992) in France, sought to redefine mental illness through a critique of the notion of reason. Foucault's book contributed to this project by tracing a history of "madness" as a product of the modern Cartesian concept of reason. *Madness and Civilization* was quickly followed by *The Birth of the Clinic* (1963), which continued his critique of the modern notion of health by outlining a cultural and social history of the formation of the modern medical profession.

But Foucault's most influential work of the 1960s was no doubt *The Order of Things* (1966), with its companion methodological volume, *The Archaeology of Knowledge* (1969). In these books Foucault turned to structuralist linguists to pursue the critique of reason he had begun in the early 1960s. Although he denied that he was ever a structuralist, Foucault undertook a study of the forms of reason embodied in various emerging disciplines in the eighteenth century (the life sciences, economics, and linguistics) by deploying a structuralist analysis of the epistemological assumptions that formed these bodies of thought. Very much influenced by the early-twentieth-century work of Ferdinand de Saussure (1857–1913), which was enjoying popularity at the time, Foucault sought to get beneath the consciousness of thinkers by analyzing the general patterns that both enabled and restricted their ideas. This tendency would continue in Foucault's writings of the 1970s and 1980s in his most general intellectual project: the history of the formation of the subject or self in Western culture.

## POSTSTRUCTURALIST SOCIAL AND CULTURAL THEORY

After the student and worker protests of May 1968, Foucault emerged as one of the leaders of an important group of French intellectuals known in the United States as poststructuralists and sometimes as postmodernists. This group includes Gilles Deleuze, Jacques Derrida, Jacques Lacan, and Jean Baudrillard and did much to transform intellectual life in Western society beginning in the 1970s and continuing into the twenty-first century. The lesson Foucault drew from the unrest of the late 1960s was that cultural history must include not only discourse but also practice. His major works of the 1970s, *Discipline and Punish* (1973) and *The History of Sexuality, Volume 1* (1976) were enormously influential studies of the systems of discourse and practice that contributed to the formation of the modern individual. In sympathy with other poststructuralists, Foucault carried out these projects by rejecting totalizing intellectual gestures, reductionist theory, and positions that rely on strong explanatory concepts, such as cause and certain truth.

In his effort to develop a method of studying the formation of the modern, rational self, Foucault perforce spurned all discursive gestures that relied upon the figure of the rational agent. One could not understand the cultural construction of the modern individual by resorting to explanatory strategies that presumed such a figure of the self. This basic theme of his work, very much characteristic of poststructuralism, led Foucault into controversies with intellectuals and academics who relied upon humanist thought in its liberal and Marxist forms. Foucault was accused of undermining the basis of political action, of all rational discourse, and of Western culture more generally. Yet he was also seen, perhaps by a smaller number, as laying the foundation for a new kind of cultural history that would for the first time not simply celebrate Western values against all others but configure those values as historical in nature. In other words, Foucault established the very possibility of a history of Western culture.

## DISCIPLINARY POWER

Pursuant to this end, *Discipline and Punish* examined the history of punishment systems in such a way that the modern penitentiary system appeared not as the culmination of the humane treatment of criminals, divergent from the "torture" methods of most earlier practices, but as the beginning of a new "technology of power," a new way of exerting force upon the larger population, which Foucault termed "discipline." This novel form of "power" was not centralized in the state and embodied in its leader, the monarch, but was dispersed throughout the social fabric, implicating everyone in its tentacles. Modern individuals, Foucault argued, would be "constructed" into "subject positions" through their participation in the mechanisms of disciplinary power. Power in this sense was not embodied in individuals and at their disposal, as in the earlier form of power Foucault called "sovereignty." Rather, it was characterized by the discourse/practice of individuals understood as nodes in a network, receiving and transmitting in turn the "power" that coursed through social relations.

Foucault used the occasion of writing a history of punishment practices to develop a critique of modern, disciplinary power, but he also inscribed into *Discipline and Punish* a highly novel method of writing cultural history, one he termed "genealogy," in an allusion to the work of Friedrich Nietzsche. *Discipline and Punish* was no ordinary chronological narrative of agents who created new social formations. Foucault began with punishment practices of the Old Regime that he called "torture," shocking the reader with minute details of the justice meted out to Robert-François Damiens (1715–1757), who attempted to assassinate King Louis XV of France. But he viewed such horrors not through the lens of the Enlightenment, which saw them as barbaric, but as a "system" of procedures that worked and that, however repugnant to modern eyes, operated as an established set of methods most contemporaries regarded as normal and legitimate. Treating the "torture" method of punishment in this way enabled Foucault to find a cultural specificity and to accept the way it differed from modern conventions.

The text of *Discipline and Punish* was not organized as a linear narrative tracing the formation of modern incarceration and implicitly or explicitly legitimizing it. Rather, Foucault arranged the bits and pieces of historical materials—the practices related to the scheduling of military training, the organization of monasteries and schools from the early modern period, the ideas of the jurist Cesare Beccaria (1738–1794) on humane punishment, the architectural model of the prison outlined by Jeremy Bentham (1748–1832), and so forth—into a patchwork design. In this way he constructed a

"polyhedron of intelligibility," a multiple, heterogeneous array of practices that might be understood as preceding and informing the birth of the modern prison. He thereby outlined the cultural formation of the modern self without relying upon rational agents as its ultimate "cause."

## SEX AND GENDER

*The History of Sexuality, Volume 1* opened the way for a historical investigation of sex outside the then-dominant framework built on the idea of sexual repression. Against Freudo-Marxists, Foucault argued that forms of sexuality thought of as modern in the early twenty-first century did not undergo a kind of disappearance in the Victorian era, but actually flourished and expanded through the multiplication of discourses on the topic. The discourse/practice around sex that Foucault termed "sexuality" contributed a new form of power to the modern world, "biopower." Here individuals were constructed as cultural figures of "sexuality" through the discursive effects of the medical profession, psychoanalysis, governmental efforts at population control and health management, ideas of perversity, and educational institutions.

Volumes 2 (*The Care of the Self*) and 3 (*The Uses of Pleasure*) of *The History of Sexuality* traced the story from the ancient Greek and Hellenistic eras. Here again Foucault depicted a form of sex among the Greeks very different from that of modern "sexuality." Ruling-class Greek men were both heterosexuals, in that they governed a household of wives, children, and servants, and what is currently called "homosexual," because they had erotic relations with younger men. This homosexual practice, however, was framed as part of the education of the younger men into the ruling class and as a method of self-fashioning, especially for the older males. Again Foucault, in *The History of Sexuality*, had opened a field to historical investigation in a promising if controversial manner.

This time it was feminists and historians of gender who took up Foucault's claims. A spate of books appeared, starting in the late 1980s, that examined and often criticized Foucault's initiative. One of the earliest of these was Judith R. Walkowitz's *City of Dreadful Delight* (1992), which examined the condition of women in nineteenth-century London, combining a Foucaultian sensitivity to discourse and a feminist and socialist attention to new forms of women's agency. Irene Q. Diamond and Lee Quinby's edited volume, *Feminism and Foucault* (1988), contained many pieces questioning how Foucault could outline a project for a history of sexuality without even mentioning gender.

## THE HISTORY OF RACE

Foucault's lectures at the Collège de France in 1975–1976, collected as *Society Must Be Defended* (2003), showed how opposition to monarchical power in early modern France led to a discourse of race. Foucault argued that the formation of modern society was commensurate with the emergence of racial thought. In *Race and the Education of Desire* (1997), Ann Laura Stoler pioneered an investigation of Foucault's method for writing the history of racial thought while expanding it to explore the repercussions of European colonization, the racism developed in that context, and its impact on Europe.

## ETHICS OF THE SELF

One final area of influence of Foucault's writing was a renewed interest in the self as agent. Nikolas Rose's *Inventing Our Selves* (1998) explores this question, raising a concern that the project of constituting the self might itself be mired in a new form of power: postmodernity constructs the self as something that must be constituted. In this line, the collection of essays edited by Jack Z. Bratich, Jeremy Packer, and Cameron McCarthy (2003) asks whether neoliberalism is not promoted by the injunction to fashion oneself. Thus Foucault's work has continued to inspire new directions in the humanities and social sciences.

*See also* **Baudrillard, Jean; Crime and Justice; Derrida, Jacques; Lacan, Jacques; May 1968; Postmodernism; Saussure, Ferdinand de; Sexuality.**

BIBLIOGRAPHY

Bratich, Jack Z., Jeremy Packer, and Cameron McCarthy, eds. *Foucault, Cultural Studies, and Governmentality.* Albany, N.Y., 2003.

Diamond, Irene Q., and Lee Quinby. *Feminism and Foucault: Reflections on Resistance.* Boston, 1988.

Foucault, Michel. *Society Must Be Defended: Lectures at the Collège de France, 1975–1976.* Edited by Mauro Bertani and Alessandro Fontana. Translated by David Macey. New York, 2003.

Rose, Nikolas. *Inventing Our Selves: Psychology, Power, and Personhood.* New York, 1998.

Stoler, Ann Laura. *Race and the Education of Desire: Foucault's History of Sexuality and the Colonial Order of Things.* Durham, N.C., 1995.

Walkowitz, Judith R. *City of Dreadful Delight: Narratives of Sexual Danger in Late-Victorian London.* Chicago, 1992.

MARK POSTER

---

**FRANCE.** The history of France in the twentieth century was shaped by global developments. This European power was drawn into the economic, social, political, and cultural realignments of Europe and the world after World War I, and then shared in the mixed history of economic growth in the interwar years. After ten years of prosperity, it was drawn into the crisis of the 1930s that culminated in World War II, then went through three decades of prosperity, called the "trente glorieuses" (the glorious thirty years) by French historians, before making the shift toward neoliberalism that began in 1973. Its history is thus particular and characteristic of all European countries passing through "the short twentieth century."

France is a country whose political history and social structures were permanently marked by the effects of the Revolution of 1789, and therefore presents distinctive features, including a bumpy political history with major ruptures. The following pages attempt to combine the conventional economic divisions ("the crisis of the 1930s," "modernization," "the neoliberal shift") with a specific political chronology ("the structural effects of the Republican compact," "the Vichy regime," "Liberation," "the Fourth Republic," "the Fifth Republic," "1968"). They attempt to reveal both the factors of convergence that place France within the scope of global developments and the strong political singularities that have long been preserved and that today are being eroded.

## STRUCTURAL EFFECTS OF THE REPUBLICAN COMPACT

On the eve of World War I, France was a parliamentary democracy with young institutions comparable to those of greater antiquity in Britain. Its constitutional system, more or less contemporary to those of Italy and Germany when it was defined by the constitutional laws of 1875, changed course when the republicans prevailed over their opponents and established enduring hegemony (1880). They taught and "trained for" universal (male) suffrage, a prerogative restored in 1875, by deploying a political pedagogy in which a mandatory draft, political dramaturgy (Bastille Day, "La Marseillaise," Marianne), and compulsory, free, and secular primary education were the most effective instruments. These measures consolidated their social base (the middle classes) because these policies appeared to be the best means of protecting independent producers and property owners. As the politician Léon Gambetta (1838–1882) put it, "with each property that is created, a citizen is born." To these ends, a broad political reformism designed to solidly integrate the individual-citizen into the state was combined with selective protectionism (the Méline Tariff of 1892). Thus defined, the Republican system ended the constitutional instability that had characterized France since the Revolution.

In 1914 France was unquestionably a great imperial and financial power with powerful technology-based industries (electricity, automobile manufacturing, and cinema). However, small-scale businesses remained the norm in all sectors; the rate of rural flight was therefore lower than in other industrialized countries and industrial concentration was less marked. This enabled Germany to catch up to and overtake France as an economic power before the war. The persistence of small-scale units of production was reflected in France's social structures: 58 percent of the labor force was salaried on the eve of the war (as compared with 66 percent in Germany), and there were 4.7 million French industrial workers, compared to 9.5 million in the United Kingdom and 11 million in Germany. In France, only 28 percent were employed by businesses with more than fifty employees; in contrast, in the United Kingdom and Germany, there were 36 percent and 47 percent in large enterprises.

These factors help to explain the relative weakness of state social reform in France as compared with some neighboring countries, including Germany. Finally, owing to an earlier pattern of low fertility, France was the only European country with significant immigration at the time (1.2 million foreigners in 1913), at rates that still put its population behind that of Germany.

World War I permanently established American economic dominance and, without radically changing the hierarchy of economic powers in Europe, challenged the traditional bases of France's prosperity. The country's financial power was savaged by debt, inflation, and the loss of loans to Russia. Its currency was stabilized late and greatly devalued by comparison with the prewar period; the franc was worth 20 percent of the gold franc of 1914. Russia, where more than 25 percent of French exported capital had been invested before the war, escaped from France's sphere of influence. These new circumstances and the widely held (but entirely illusory) hope for a return to the prewar world corresponded to a fierce determination to "make Germany pay" for the war. It also reflected France's increased stake in its colonial empire. In 1928 that empire became the mother country's lead trading partner. Colonies mobilized forced labor to create those infrastructures needed to produce a profit from the French capital invested there. It is hardly surprising, therefore, that many prominent and propertied people were proud of the French Empire. This self-interested story was well represented in the Parisian Colonial Exhibition of 1931.

A very small minority called for a more radical modernization of the French economy in the belief that it was the only way to respond to the broad economic changes induced by the war. However, putting these changes into effect would involve profound shifts in the structure of French society and thus an attack on the government's social base. Modernization was therefore subordinated to state reforms intended to strengthen the executive branch and free it from pressures. Fundamental economic and social reform was politically impossible, but modernization plans were formulated time and again (by Georges Clemenceau in 1919, by Alexandre Millerand in 1924, and by André Tardieu in 1930). Thus a stalemate ensued: everyone wanted modernization, but no one could achieve it without alienating the social base on which the Third Republic stood. Thus the institutions of prewar political culture survived the conflagration, and the Radical Party, the expression of the middle classes, although weakened, remained a pivotal party that made and unmade parliamentary majorities throughout the interwar period. Governments of both the Right (1919–1924, 1926–1932) and the Left (1924–1926) were consequently forced to continue along the path of a politics designed to protect the middle classes, thus perpetuating the political order established before World War I. However, economic depression exposed the weaknesses in this arrangement, weaknesses that would have political consequences in the late 1930s and 1940s.

It would certainly be inaccurate to speak of total stasis in France's economy and society. After the short-lived postwar crisis and the easing of monetary difficulties, the country enjoyed a prosperous decade (the Roaring Twenties) like elsewhere. The country returned to prewar levels of prosperity in 1923 and experienced growth in its Gross Domestic Product (GDP) of nearly 5 percent per year until 1929. The key branches of the second wave of industrialization had shifted to Taylorist "scientific management" to meet the needs of the wartime economy, and these changes were accentuated when peace returned. Fueled by inflation, growth lightened the debt burden and encouraged investment. Transformations in the organization of labor and work, their technical and financial structures, and the organization of markets allowed for marked increases in productivity.

In contrast, older trends put brakes on development. The losses incurred in the war (1.4 million dead, 3 million wounded) and flat birthrates reinforced slow rates of demographic growth. The French population got older, and immigration was the main source of growth (2,715,000 foreigners in 1931, or 7.1 percent of the French population). Women (at least some of them) had access to more skilled jobs, but their employment rate fell beginning in 1921 in comparison to their employment rate in 1911. Women still were denied the vote. The loss of assets invested in Russia, inflation, and the tax system hurt recipients of interest income and changed the distribution of wealth. Farmers took advantage of inflation to pay off their debts, and the number of small, family-owned businesses, protected by duty tariffs and weak competition, remained high. Agriculture (36 percent of the working population) retained its lead over industry (34 percent) and the service sector (30

**Demonstration at the Place de Concorde, Paris, 6 February 1934.** The economic crises of the early 1930s culminated in protests by right-wing groups in Paris, which quickly became violent. ©Bettmann/Corbis

percent), and the rural population outnumbered the urban population until 1931. The traditional industries and agriculture enjoyed far less growth than the technological sector. The Taylorist revolution did not bring with it rising wages capable of sustaining a growth in consumption, and the agricultural sector was not sufficiently integrated into the national market to support an expansion of output.

Consequently, domestic consumption declined after the franc was stabilized in 1928, at a time when industrial production no longer benefited from the export effects of devaluation. The economic crisis of the 1930s arose from a blending together of these two vectors, matched by international economic disorder.

**THE CRISIS OF THE 1930S**
The first symptoms of the crisis preceded the Wall Street crash: a drop in exports beginning in 1927, an early decrease in wholesale prices, especially in

agriculture, and a falling stock market beginning in February 1929. But this economic downturn was not perceived by contemporaries. The crisis became apparent to them only starting in 1931, when the devaluation of the British pound resulted in a collapse of industrial production and a manifold increase in bankruptcies, creating the lasting, although erroneous, sense of a belated crisis that had originated abroad. The crisis further rigidified the structures of an agricultural sector that withdrew into self-subsistence. Its effects on the various branches of industry were uneven, but everywhere it caused a decrease in investment that put a halt to modernization and resulted in aging machinery. From 1928 to 1938, the annual growth rate of GDP stagnated at around 0.3 percent. Farm revenues, in particular, were hard hit; many artisans and merchants were affected by the decline in industrial and commercial profits; and many workers had to leave France owing to rising short-term and long-term unemployment and the influx of tens of thousands of foreign workers.

This situation obliterated the policies of modernization and updating of equipment initiated by Tardieu in 1929. It contributed to the defeat of the Right in favor of the Radical Party (supported by the Socialists) in the elections of 1932. It also fed into the propaganda of the extreme Right groups that had emerged in the 1920s. These groups seized on a political and financial scandal (the Stavisky affair) to push their offensive. On 6 February 1934, they organized a protest in Paris that turned into a deadly riot, and forced the Radical prime minister to resign despite his party's majority, thereby enabling the Right to return to power.

This political crisis was radically different from the German crisis of 1933. It did not affect the existing structures of the system and was resolved within their framework. It did not produce reforms in the working of the state, although an attempt in that direction was made by the Right when it returned to power. It did, however, profoundly weaken the political culture that had ensured government stability. Radicalism had presented itself as the embodiment of the values and ethic of the Republic. Its capitulation in the face of the rioting of February 1934 destabilized the groups that had identified with it, allowing them to make other choices and thus making new political coalitions

possible. This crisis plunged the country into a phase of institutional instability that rivaled those of the early nineteenth century in France: three constitutions from 1940 to 1958 that were, moreover, preceded or marked by serious ruptures that led to profound changes in political coalitions, culture, and choices. In the short term, however, the political crisis seemed to come down to the rapid succession of governments of the Left (1932–1934) and the Right (1928–1932, 1934–1936), all of which responded to the economic crisis in the same way.

All of these governments emphasized defense of the franc and the maintenance of sound finance to revitalize the economy. They refused devaluation, although it was needed to restore the competitiveness of French goods; they attempted to reduce state spending to reduce the budget deficit; they responded to the drop in agricultural prices by encouraging farmers to reduce production; and then, in 1935, they embarked on a policy of deflation that hit both white-collar and blue-collar government workers and veterans especially hard. There were the beginnings of a recovery, but discontent over these policies contributed to the victory of the Popular Front in May 1936.

This victory resulted from an unprecedented political reconfiguration. Communists, Socialists, and Radicals united to combat the crisis by depriving the "fascist" groups of the key political support of the destabilized middle classes. The Popular Front was thereby able to defend its commitment both to peace and to democracy, threatened both internally and beyond France's borders, especially in Spain entering its civil war. The economic orientations of the program the Popular Front ratified were consequently shaped by the need to consolidate the economic alliance between the middle classes and the working classes against the "two hundred families," the metaphor for financial and propertied elites that supposedly ran the country.

Léon Blum, prime minister during the early days of the Popular Front, oriented his economic policy around these political realities. He drew inspiration from the policies of the New Deal of the U.S. president Franklin Delano Roosevelt (1882–1945), and thus reflected what is now termed a Keynesian interpretation of the crisis, in total contrast to the interpretation of his predecessors. In the short term, Blum wanted to respond to the contraction of international trade by enlarging the domestic market and to "prime the pump" by boosting public consumption and initiating major public works projects, for instance the electrification of rural areas and the construction of roads, bridges, schools, and stadiums. In the longer term, he hoped to modernize the French economy. Massive strikes forced him to act quickly and under pressure. The measures adopted were in line with his initial program. Wage increases were meant to increase purchasing power, as did the new laws reducing working hours and establishing paid vacations, in that these measures were intended to create more jobs. The few structural reforms envisioned in the program were implemented on the heels of these changes. There was reform of the status of the Bank of France, with stronger state control; there was the creation of a National Wheat Office that guaranteed grain prices and thereby farm prices; and there was nationalization of war-related industries to remove them from the control of arms dealers, all within a stated objective of "moralizing" economic life.

This increase in the role of the state in the economy was not specific to France. However, it had the particularity of favoring economic and financial concentration rather than helping unemployed workers. This targeting of economic measures in the 1930s helped buffer French institutions and preserve the specificities of its economic structures. There were half the number of bankruptcies in 1937 as in 1935, and there was no great migration out of the countryside. France remained the most rural of the industrialized countries.

In the short term, French political and economic life was preserved in its older forms. Yet the experience of the Popular Front did have a lasting impact on French political culture. The Communist Party was integrated into the political mainstream; the Socialist Party (Section Française de l'Internationale Ouvrière, or SFIO) became a governing party; and the Left, henceforth defined in relation to both Republican culture and working-class culture, sought out accommodations, as did portions of the political Right. Others on the right moved in more extreme directions, proclaiming that they would "sooner have Hitler than the Popular Front."

Similarly some employers accepted the new atmosphere in which industrial conflict was conducted; others grew increasingly worried about the shifts in power relations that successful strikes and the exponential growth in union membership brought about. Small employers rejected the modernizing of social relations in companies initiated by the framework of collective bargaining, and the creation of a framework for worker representation in the governing of industry, known as the Matignon agreements. These hardliners engaged in what they termed a "Battle of the Marne" in the face of what they felt to be a major attack on their prerogatives. Their freeze on investment and hiring and the massive flight of capital made any sustained recovery in production impossible, despite a devaluation of the franc, intended as an economic stimulus, to which Blum resigned himself.

The combination of increased demand and constraints on supply arising from the stance of employers caused a sharp rise in prices and doomed the economic policies of the Popular Front to failure. On the eve of the war France had not emerged from the crisis: its industrial production was 10 to 20 percent lower than in 1929, national revenues were similarly down, and the colonial markets accounted for 30 percent of exports (12 percent in 1913). Moreover, as the country fell back on its traditional structures it appeared to be turning into an old country—becoming "Malthusian" in the language of the day. The mortality rate surpassed the birthrate; only 30 percent of the population was younger than age twenty in 1936, and the population was scarcely larger than it had been in 1914, despite the reintegration of Alsace-Lorraine into the Republic.

## THE VICHY REGIME

"Not enough arms, not enough children, not enough allies," was the accusation soon made by Marshall Philippe Pétain (1856–1951), who blamed the defeat of 1940 on the "spirit of exuberance" that the Popular Front had supposedly encouraged, thereby undermining France's institutions. Pétain ignored the considerable armament effort initiated in April 1938 and the passing of a pronatalist policy, known as the "Family Code" in 1939, a set of measures that could not have had any effect when the war came. Pétain also ignored the

**French Communist election poster, 1937.** Members of the most prominent banking families in France are declared to be "against the nation." BRIDGEMAN ART LIBRARY

serious mistakes made by France's high command. More generally he underestimated the way Frenchmen and women approached the problem of war and peace, which in 1940 was by reflecting on the massacres of 1914–1918. Veterans were pacifists in France, opposing assertive nationalism as a recipe for another bloody war. These men, four million of them in veterans' associations, knew what war was. They believed it must never happen again. They were agents of cultural demobilization, not at all like German or Italian veterans of the period. French veterans were trapped between their revulsion at the idea of another war and the growing threat of a European war, following the Italian invasion of Ethiopia, the Spanish civil war, and successful conquest of Austria and Czechoslovakia by Adolf Hitler (1889–1945).

Once war broke out in 1939, and the German army succeeded in its daring breakthrough of 1940, the French Third Republic was effectively dead. Few mourned its passing. Defeat enabled the new authorities under Marshall Pétain to succeed where "modernizers" of every stripe had previously failed. After the signing of the armistice, parliament voted to give full powers to the "hero of Verdun." Marshall Pétain took advantage of this unique moment to lay the foundations of what he termed a "national revolution." More than half of France was occupied; the Communist Party was outlawed; most elite groups rallied around him; most people breathed a sigh of relief that another bloodbath like that of 1914–1918 was not imminent. Thus Pétain and his circle could break not only with the 1930s but also with the political model and principles inherited from 1789. An authoritarian French state replaced the Republic. This hybrid regime, sometimes described as a "pluralist dictatorship," drew its support from traditional conservatives, but also from promoters of a "new order" that came out of the "nonconformists of the 1930s": young technocrats who advocated a strong, centralized state; modernizers disillusioned by the compromises of the Third Republic; and some adherents to Christian socialism or fascism. The national community promoted by the regime presupposed the elimination of "anti-France" elements through policies of exclusion and repression targeting communists, Freemasons, and Jews. Thus the politics of Léon Blum, symbolizing the 1930s, were what had to be stamped out, well in advance of any German requirements to do so. In its place a new political order valorized "work, family, homeland." However, this conservative and paternalistic discourse came hand in hand with interventionist and modernizing programs. Restrictions on raw materials and the need for reconstruction after defeat in 1940 made at least some planning of production and infrastructures indispensable, and private business management collaborated closely with state engineers within the organizational committees established by the regime. Its economic strategy, however, was impeded or complicated by the combined circumstances of the war and the presence and demands of the Germans. From the end of 1942, France was increasingly a police state, increasingly dominated by extremists more and more tied up in a civil war with the Resistance, a dirty war that has left scars on France to this day.

## LIBERATION AND MODERNIZATION

The political landscape at the end of World War II was different in all respects from that after World War I. Liberalism, which was held responsible for the crisis of the 1930s, for fascism, and for the war, was unanimously condemned, and the desire for a return to the status quo ante bellum that had prevailed in 1919 was replaced by the exact opposite, a general hope for radical change and a nearly unanimous rallying to the principle of state regulation of the economy and society.

In France this orientation was formulated while the war was going on, clandestinely in March 1944, when various elements in the Resistance against the occupying forces and the Vichy government, united around General Charles de Gaulle, ratified the National Council of the Resistance (Charter of the Conseil National de la Resistance, or CNR). From 1940 to 1944, the defeat, shortages, German greed, and the needs of the French state greatly increased employers' willingness to accept a certain amount of state

interventionism. At the same time, state intervention was supported by the trade union federation, the Confédération Générale du Travail (CGT), which had emerged from the Resistance strengthened and unified, and by the French Communist Party (Parti Communiste Français, or PCF), now the foremost party in France (26.1 percent of the vote in May 1946). The charter of the National Council of the Resistance called for a "true economic and social democracy" that would redefine the Republican social contract. In particular, it provided for the nationalization of key industrial sectors, thus removing them from the influence of "financial feudal systems;" it established mechanisms for democratic economic planning, and for a system of social security.

It is evident that the two shocks of 1940 and 1944—defeat and liberation—converted skeptics into supporters of state intervention. This consensual embrace of the welfare state and expansionist and voluntaristic policies to encourage returns on investment then, and only then, allowed for structural responses to the economic and social crises that had begun in the early 1930s. Owing to the new power relations, it was possible even to adopt and adapt some structural reforms made by the Vichy regime, to the extent that they did not particularly reflect its ideological and political orientations. France's economy underwent a lasting shift into a type of mixed economy in which private enterprise coexisted with a nationalized sector and incentive-based economic planning. It was supported by a new generation of modernizing technocrats and the newly created state instruments of national economic planning and public finance. The central role of the state in the money markets and in the structures of production and distribution thus became a characteristic trait of French capitalism that persisted into the 1960s, despite the return to power of the "liberals" in 1952.

The signatories of the CNR charter almost unanimously rejected the idea of a return to the political institutions of the Third Republic, but they were acutely divided on what should replace them. The recent experience of the Vichy government undermined any idea of strengthening the powers of the executive, even under de Gaulle. The latter, who believed a strong executive was indispensable, preferred to leave the provisional

**German Field Marshall Erwin Rommel and his staff inspect Atlantic sea wall fortifications in France, March 1944.** The fortifications failed to repel the Allied D-Day assault that began ten weeks later. ©Bettmann-Corbis

government in January 1946 rather than yield to opposing views.

The new constitution, adopted in October represented a compromise within a tripartite coalition (the SFIO, the PCF, and the Mouvement Républicain Populaire, or MRP, a new political formation coming out of the Christian Resistance that soon attracted large portions of the prewar Right). This constitution opened with a preamble reaffirming the rights and freedoms of man and the citizen consecrated in 1789, and established as constitutional principles the reforms put into effect by the provisional government, including the extension of universal suffrage to women, relatively late in comparison with most countries in Western Europe. It laid the foundations for a union of French-speaking peoples, but nonetheless spectacularly ignored the hopes for independence of France's colonies, although those hopes had been magnified

everywhere by the war. Apart from these innovations, the new regime was not much different from that of the previous Republic and it remained a regime founded on inherently unstable coalitions.

**THE FOURTH REPUBLIC**

The structural reforms put in place with the Liberation, the rebuilding of French industry, aid under the Marshall Plan, the relative stabilization of Western finances and economies from 1947 to 1949, and the first two plans that coordinated public investment and allocated American aid to the priority sectors enabled the French economy by 1950 to return to and then to surpass its 1929 industrial and agricultural levels. France entered an unprecedented phase of economic expansion. Growth, mainly channeled into the industrial and service sectors, was nonetheless general. From 1950 to 1958, there was a 40–50 percent increase in national income, in purchasing power, consumption, industrial production, exports, and returns on investment. These trends reflected better integration into the international marketplace, and a marked growth in domestic consumption owing to the baby boom, producing a population of 47 million in 1962 as opposed to 40.3 million in 1946. There was a wider distribution of income, in part reflecting the fact that there were twice as many salaried workers in 1967 as in 1949. Owing to a marked increase in the average period young people spent in education and a generalization of the system of retirement benefits, the total working population barely increased during these years.

Industry and, to a lesser extent, agriculture responded to increased demand with increases in productivity made possible by growth in investments and an increase in the length of the workday that made it longer than in neighboring countries. These changes caused the country to enter a "silent revolution" that accelerated from 1954. Self-employment decreased in favor of salaried employment (65.7 percent of the workforce in 1954), and agriculture entered a phase of a growing concentration of farms and an acceleration of rural flight.

The traditional support base of radicalism remained more numerous (and more powerful) than elsewhere. In 1954, 26 percent of the workforce was still in agriculture, accounting for 14 percent of the GDP. Their discontent, unable to make itself heard via traditional channels, was expressed in unprecedented forms: roadblocks by farmers, and the creation of the Union for the Defense of Tradesmen and Artisans, led by Pierre Poujade.

Some believed that the "ball and chain" of colonialism was putting a brake on the processes of modernization. However, they had difficulty making themselves heard by a France clinging all the more tightly to its colonial empire inasmuch as it served as a "compensatory myth" after the trials undergone from 1940 to 1944. The mother country was intent on retaining its sovereignty within the framework of a unilaterally defined French Union that it declared to be inviolable. It granted reforms but refused to negotiate them, describing any other attitude as "capitulation." It repressed insurgencies in Sétif and Madagascar; it entered the war in Indochina in 1946, and seemed to begin decolonization after the French defeat at Dien Bien Phu in 1954. Prime Minister Pierre Mendès-France worked to end colonial domination in Tunisia and Morocco, but no one seemed willing or able to avoid a bloody war over Algerian independence, which lasted until 1962.

Reluctant decolonization was one facet of French history at this time; political paralysis was another. The weakness of the constitutional structure was evident. There were twenty-five governments formed between 1947 and 1958, all unable to hold together unstable coalitions when hard choices had to be made over finance, education, and the European Defense Community. Then the country entered into the Algerian "war without a name"—nameless in part because it was a domestic revolt: Algeria was not a colony but an integral part of France. This brutal struggle, marked by widespread torture practiced by French soldiers within living memory of the torture of Resistance fighters by the Nazis and their allies, hastened the process of disintegration of the Fourth Republic. There was an attempted coup d'état in Algeria on 13 May 1958, uniting the defenders of "French Algeria" and those fiercely opposed to "party government." In some ways similar to the violent protests of 1934, the coup of 1958 was crushed through the mobilization of the Republican mainstream. But this time, instead of leading to a Popular Front, the failed right-wing plot brought General de Gaulle to power. The Gaullist republic he inaugurated was one in which he had full powers to restore calm to Algeria and prepare a new constitution, that of the Fifth Republic.

## THE FIFTH REPUBLIC

The constitution, submitted to the country in a referendum in September 1958, was approved by 80 percent of French voters. It maintained a parliamentary framework but ensured the dominance of the executive, endowing it with increased powers. For the first time since the 1930s, a government structure emerged that offered both legitimacy and stability. In 1962 a constitutional amendment was passed instituting the principle of direct election of the president of the Republic by universal suffrage. De Gaulle's party, the Union for the New Republic (Union pour la Nouvelle République, or UNR), won 256 out of 475 seats in the legislative elections of 1962. The UNR's growth came at the expense of the traditional parties of the Right. In opposition, the Socialist Party remained divided over the question of Algeria and entered a major crisis from which it did not recover; consequently, the Communist Party became the main opposition party but fell below the 20 percent share of the electorate for the first time since the Liberation of 1944. "There is nothing left between us and the Communists," summed up the novelist André Malraux (1901–1976), one of de Gaulle's most able allies.

The crisis of 1958 and de Gaulle's undeniable charisma enabled him to succeed where Pierre Mendès-France (and so many others before him) had failed. He managed to reform the government; he resigned himself to decolonization after four more years of war in Algeria that led France to the brink of civil war; and he hastened the course of the "silent revolution" that French society had entered from the mid-1950s.

General de Gaulle was always imbued with a "certain idea of France" and believed that it "could not be France without grandeur," that the country was "only truly herself in the first rank." He held modernization of its political institutions to be the necessary condition for fulfilling his plans. With the aim of freeing the country from American domination, and becoming "the greatest of the small," he separated French armed forces from NATO; he made overtures to the Eastern bloc countries, and oversaw France's emergence as a nuclear power.

France's acceptance of the Treaty of Rome (1957) and full membership in the European Union, coincided paradoxically with the return to power of the one French leader who had elevated the defense of national sovereignty into an absolute imperative. General de Gaulle opposed an integrated Europe of "Esperanto and Volapuk," and conceived of the building of Europe only as an instrument for the generalization and extension of French ideas and French power. To this end, he established closer ties with Germany, "still divided and weakened," and opposed European Economic Community (EEC) membership for Great Britain, which he viewed as America's Trojan Horse in Europe.

The problem remained, though, that France could not maintain its standing in the first "rank"

of world powers without a strong and competitive economy. The postwar break with more than half a century of protectionism underscored this need. The state implemented policies to update the country's industrial plant and infrastructure. At the same time, steps were taken both to increase agricultural productivity and to reduce the number of agricultural workers (15.6 percent of the workforce in 1968). Demographic growth and the development of consumer demand also supported economic growth. The birthrate decreased beginning in the mid-1960s, as it did everywhere else in Europe and North America, but the French population continued to grow because of immigration. First there was the return of more than a million French citizens from North Africa to the mainland in the 1960s. Secondly, immigrant workers were welcomed to fill in gaps in an expanding workforce, especially at low skill levels. The foreign population thus doubled between 1954 (1.7 million) and 1975 (3.4 million). Under the influence of these combined factors, the 1960s were the most productive of the three postwar decades of growth. The structural changes that had been under way since the mid-1950s accelerated. Independent employment decreased, with a corresponding increase in salaried workers (about 85 percent of the workforce in the mid 1970s). The number of agricultural workers remained higher than in other countries (12 percent of the workforce), but these men and women modernized their equipment and strategies, enabling the average size of farms to increase.

There were other massive changes in the structure of the workforce in these years. The relative decline in the number of skilled workers, the emergence of a new working class, and the growing ranks of managers, engineers, and technicians (almost 10 percent of the workforce) profoundly affected the secondary sector of industrial workers (40.2 percent of the workforce in 1968). The tertiary or service sector (44.2 percent) was revolutionized too.

These changes produced tension and conflict. Miners affected by the country's conversion from coal to oil energy went on a long strike in 1963. In 1966, trade unions struggled against Gaullist labor policies. At the same time, the baby boom generation was coming of age. Many groups of young people broke with the bureaucratic, authoritarian, and hierarchical structures that they encountered everywhere, in school, in universities, in business, and in the state. Here is the background to 1968.

## 1968

This crisis was part of a global phenomenon that mainly (but not exclusively) affected industrialized countries. Two decades of economic growth did not still doubts about what kind of society France had become. Demographic growth, an increase in the period of life in education for a substantial part of the population, changing sexual mores—the contraceptive pill became widely available in the mid-1960s—and growing consumer demand brought into high relief a new social group: youth. The crisis that was born in the Latin Quarter before igniting all of France cannot be understood without reference to these structural and generational factors at work everywhere. However, France's tradition of trade unionism, the nature of the Gaullist regime, and the extent of the upheavals within French society combined to render the crisis more complex and more polyvalent than it was elsewhere. France was the only industrialized country that had to face this transnational crisis with a Republican structure and government that was barely ten years old. Influenced by anxieties raised by the economic and social changes of the postwar period, the country experienced what could be described either as a "crisis of belated modernity" or as an accumulation of crises (generational and cultural, social, and political) that in other countries remained apart. In France, a wide array of developments lay behind the upheaval of 1968, at which time the country passed from an industrial crisis and a general strike markedly broader in scope than that of 1936, and then into a political crisis.

The increased importance of the presidency within the government and de Gaulle as the personal embodiment of power almost immediately made him the major target of all those who took to the streets in 1968. But his power also gave him the institutional and political means to prevail, when a crisis of this kind would have swept from power any of the governments of the Fourth Republic. In the short term the crisis of 1968 ended in a victory of the Gaullists that strengthened their parliamentary majority. An embittered de Gaulle attributed this paradoxical victory to "the party of fear." For him personally, the victory was

ephemeral. The crisis had revealed the extent of the imbalances between the demands and values of a rejuvenated and modernized France and those of power structures that in many respects remained patriarchal. This lack of fit between politics and society was tacitly recognized within the Gaullist camp. In 1969 General de Gaulle chose to retire after his defeat in a referendum that had the air of a last will and testament. After Georges Pompidou's brief presidency, the election of Valéry Giscard d'Estaing put an end to the "Gaullist state."

The regime survived the crisis of 1968, and then showed its resiliency in adjusting to the shift of power to the Socialist Party in 1981, under François Mitterrand, and then to various moments in 1986 and 1995 when the president was a man of the Left or Right and the prime minister was of the opposite party. Crises in governments became less important as European integration proceeded apace.

As in 1934, so in 1968: French Republican political culture survived a systemic crisis. But also as in 1934, albeit in a radically different mode, the political system and the founding culture of the Gaullist Republic underwent marked changes. So did French society. After 1968 we can see a clear path toward cultural liberalization, marked by the lowering of the voting age to eighteen, liberalization of radio and television, and the passage of liberal abortion and divorce laws. Older family forms began to atrophy, as was the case throughout Western Europe.

## THE NEOLIBERAL SHIFT

In the 1970s and 1980s a major downturn in the international economy produced major shifts in political life. First came a move to the Left to cope with the problems of the time; then a move to the Right, which is now termed the "neoliberal shift." In 1981, the victory of the Left united behind François Mitterrand seemed to underscore a return to a Popular Front. There were four Communists in the government. Prime Minister Pierre Mauroy responded to the situation triggered by the 1973 oil crisis by returning to a Keynesian approach. The first measures adopted were rooted in the traditions of the Left: taxation of the wealthiest, a new wave of nationalization that affected some large banking and industrial sectors, lowering the retirement age to sixty, and the thirty-nine-hour work week. Subsequent measures turned toward cultural liberalization: the abolition of capital punishment, the creation of a high authority to guarantee the independence of radio and television. These measures set the country on the path to decentralization.

But the Left's return to power coincided with the deepening of an economic crisis whose causes and effects proved to be more complex and more permanent than they had first appeared during the crisis of 1973: the slowing of growth, technological revolution in all sectors that meant the end of full employment and the emergence of structural unemployment (around 10 percent), saturation of the market in durable consumer goods, and so forth. These new circumstances and external constraints (integration into the European monetary system that made currencies interdependent) led France to abandon its path of singularity in relation to Europe. The French political system, now fairly similar to those of neighboring countries, accepted alternating governments or cohabitation between a liberalized Right and a Social-Democratized Left. The emergence of the Green Party and the National Front attest, in different modes, to the broadscale changes at work within it.

Beginning in 1983 the government shifted to a neoliberal approach, one that for a long time remained less radical than in Great Britain. In some twenty years it dismantled the structure of nationalized industries, and redefined its social security and pension systems. In 2000, 16 percent of the population was older than sixty-five, 25 percent younger than nineteen. Paying for the elderly was a problem looming in the future. This was true everywhere, and throughout these years, the notion of French particularism, its otherness, began to fade. Scientific and technical advances, a greater emphasis on European integration, globalization, and outsourcing underscored the disappearance of the structural differences that had characterized France for two centuries. Now France was just as "postindustrial" as everyone else. In 2001 the primary sector of employment had fallen to 3.5 percent of the workforce and the secondary sector to 25.4 percent (of which 2.6 million still consisted of skilled workers), as compared with 71.1 percent for the service sector (75.2 percent of the GDP). At the same time economic insecurity and regionally concentrated unemployment, especially among immigrant youth became endemic.

These upheavals hurt the welfare state and the foundations of the Republican social contract as redefined at the Liberation. They undermined social cohesion and "French-style" Republican integration. After World War II, France generally succeeded in integrating a very substantial number of immigrants. The number of foreigners doubled from 1945 to 1965, and their enlarged recruitment pool became more markedly Mediterranean. In 1999, one French citizen out of four had foreign ancestry within fewer than three generations. Among them, 38.4 percent were from Europe and 22.3 percent from North Africa. Beginning in the 1980s, protectionist measures restricted immigration. In 1993, the government considered reforming citizenship rules; until then based on place of birth; if you were born in France, you were French. School dropout rates, unemployment, and the crisis of the inner cities above all affected first- and second-generation immigrants (the "beurs"). France's colonial past and the Algerian war, that "past that will not pass," brought with them negative perceptions of the North African immigrant population. These tensions were expressed in the upsurge of the National Front, which outpolled the Socialist Party in the presidential elections of 2002. On the other side, Muslims increasingly rejected the notion that all French were the same. Many retreated into identity politics, defending the wearing of the veil by Muslim girls in schools, thereby undermining the French model of secularism and integration.

It was in this environment that France experienced a national identity crisis magnified by the emergence of new regional, European, and international forms of political decision making. A crisis in the political realm was characterized, as it was everywhere else in Europe, by a decrease in trade union and political affiliation, by voter abstention, and by the increasingly salient role played by groups on the margins of the political system.

*See also* **Algerian War; European Union; French Empire; Gaulle, Charles de; Indochina; 1968; Riots in France.**

BIBLIOGRAPHY

Agulhon, Maurice. *La république*. Paris, 1990.

Hazareesingh, Sudhir. *Political Traditions in Modern France*. Oxford, U.K., 1994.

Kritzman, Lawrence D., ed., *The Columbia History of Twentieth-Century French Thought.* New York, 2006.

Kuisel, Richard F. *Capitalism in Modern France: Renovation and Economic Management in the Twentieth Century.* Cambridge, U.K., 1981.

Margairaz, Michel. *L'état, les finances, et l'économie: Histoire d'une conversion, 1932–1952.* 2 vols. Paris, 1991.

Mendras, Henri. *La fin des paysans: Suivi d'une réflexion sur la fin des paysans, Vingt ans après.* Arles, France, 1992.

———. *La séconde révolution française, 1965–1984.* Paris, 1994.

Popkin, Jeremy P. *A History of Modern France.* 2nd ed. Upper Saddle River, N.J., 2000.

Rémond, René. *La république souveraine: La vie politique en France, 1879–1939.* Paris, 2002.

Sowerine, Charles. *France since 1870: Culture, Politics and Society.* New York, 2001.

DANIELLE TARTAKOWSKY

---

# FRANCO, FRANCISCO (1892–1975), Spanish general and dictator.

On the cover of its 6 September 1937 issue, *Time* magazine presented a diminutive, balding, and increasingly pot-bellied forty-four-year-old Spanish general, Francisco Franco Bahamonde, to America as the de facto head of Spain. This incongruity between Franco's appearance and his power represents just one of many contradictions of the Spanish dictator who ruled until 1975. While Franco was most often associated with fascism (*Time*'s accompanying article in fact placed him in the dubious pantheon of Europe's fascist leaders), his own political makeup was essentially conservative and traditional. His personal beliefs were dominated by a devout sense of loyalty and propriety, and yet he rose to power in a revolt against a democratically elected government to which he had sworn allegiance. He projected calm and efficient command, yet he bewildered friend and foe with an apparent utter lack of political guile or intellectual heft. His significance in twentieth-century European history is seemingly contradictory: an intellectually incurious pillar of Spanish conservatism in the twentieth century, Franco was also the one leader tied to the Axis who survived World War II and remained in power well into the future.

## EARLY LIFE AND EDUCATION

Born in the northwestern province of Galicia in the coastal town of El Ferrol on 4 December 1892, Franco saw his early life prefigured by his nation's military failures. As the main port of Spain's Atlantic fleet, El Ferrol experienced the military defeat in the Spanish-American War in 1898 and the loss of the last remnants of Spain's overseas empire as a direct affront not just to Spanish pride but also to the town's institutions. In particular, the closing of the Naval Administration School that the young Franco would have attended denied the future *generalísimo* the naval career that occupied his brothers, his father, and his grandfather. His decision in 1907 to attend the army's Infantry Academy in Toledo played a far more direct role in creating the values, politics, and also the ambiguous personality that guided Franco's career.

For one, the departure to Spain's ancient capital allowed Franco to escape an overbearing father known best for the philandering and gambling that created, in some historians' view, the social rigidity that defined Franco's lifelong demeanor. The education at Spain's military academies also helped forge the conservative and nationalist outlook that served as the only consistent element of Franco's personal politics. Franco learned that Spain's glorious past was shaped by the intermingling of imperial conquest, strong monarchy, Catholicism, and rigid social hierarchy, all of which were defended, protected, and occasionally revived by Spain's warrior class, the military. While he absorbed these values well, Franco's military education was not a stunning success; in 1910 he graduated 251st in a class of 312 cadets.

## MOROCCO, WAR, AND A GROWING RUTHLESSNESS

The creation of a Spanish protectorate in Morocco in 1912 to defend small but long-held colonies offered Franco the chance to develop his military prowess. Dispatched to Morocco in 1912, Franco quickly gained a reputation as a ruthless and courageous leader who seemed to possess an unusual amount of luck. After he survived a number of serious injuries, Moroccan troops fighting for the Spanish began to ascribe to Franco a kind of divine or mystical protection they called *baraka*. Franco never lost this sense that his life possessed a divine purpose. He also began to demonstrate in battle an unusual ruthlessness toward his enemies. Throughout his first published work, *Diario de una bandera* (1922; Diary of a battalion), Franco detailed in an unsettlingly casual tone the presentation of enemy heads to his own troops as awards for valor or as souvenirs to visiting journalists and dignitaries. His later treatment of opponents both during and after the Spanish civil war was no less violent.

His book also demonstrated that Franco's political attitudes were aligned with those of the close-knit group of military leaders in Morocco known as the *africanistas*. These figures generally blamed Madrid politicians for failing Spanish troops, both overseas in 1898 and then in Morocco. Yet the *africanistas* were only one part of a broader attack on Spain's political system from across the political spectrum. Regional independence movements, anticlerical movements, and the growing socialist and anarchist parties and trade unions all attacked a system that had generally worked to favor wealthy landowners, industrialists, the church, the military, and other conservative institutions. Despite this ferment, Franco offered little of a political philosophy throughout the 1920s. Even with the arrival of a military dictatorship in 1923 under General Miguel Primo de Rivera, Franco served the new leader but never made clear whether he truly supported Primo or preferred other solutions to the political crisis. The price Franco paid for his ambiguity was negligible, as he was nevertheless promoted to brigadier general in 1926. At the age of thirty-three, Franco had become the youngest general in Europe since Napoleon.

## THE SPANISH SECOND REPUBLIC AND THE CIVIL WAR

Franco's hesitation to declare his politics proved prescient when Primo's dictatorship ended and pro-Republican parties trounced monarchical and other conservative parties in subsequent municipal elections in April 1931. Shortly thereafter, on 14 April 1931, the Spanish Second Republic was declared. Still, Franco continued to hide his true political opinions. While he offered some speeches and articles that seemed obliquely critical of the Republic, he also resisted the numerous military coup plots that immediately began to emerge. It remains unclear whether Franco was biding his time or actually reluctant to decry the Republic in

its early days. Yet, experiencing the same political instability that dominated much of Europe in the 1930s, the Second Republic struggled for legitimacy. Beset by revolutionary groups on the left and the right, including one of Europe's most powerful anarchist movements, and by intractable social and economic problems formed over centuries, Republican leaders faced mounting problems in the Republic's first years.

Their reforms against the pillars of Spanish conservatism, among them the separation of church and state, military reforms, and the recognition of regional autonomy, proved the most deleterious. Increases in street violence, revolutionary insurrections, and the number of military plots signaled the growing recourse toward nonlegal means among the Republic's conservative opponents. After the election of a Popular Front government in February 1936 and ever growing political violence, Franco openly began to advocate a coup to other military leaders, many of whom were former *africanistas*. On 18 July 1936 Franco helped lead the insurrection. The plotters captured much of northwestern and parts of southern Spain but failed to take many of Spain's major cities, and a three-year civil war began. Franco gradually emerged as the leader of the insurgents, as they came to be called, after all of Spain's other leaders and Franco's potential rivals died in the early days of the war. In the fall of 1936 Franco officially became *generalísimo*, or supreme military leader of Spain, and head of state. In April 1939 the war ended.

## WAS FRANCO A FASCIST?

The political context in Europe in the late 1930s partially explains why Franco remains associated with European fascism. Yet whether Franco was ever truly a fascist in the mold of Hitler and Mussolini remains debatable. Certainly, the energetic military aid that Hitler and Mussolini provided Franco during the civil war suggested their view that Franco was a kindred spirit. However, the question better posed is not whether Franco was a fascist but rather when was he a fascist. Franco clearly admired both Hitler and Mussolini and aped their personal styles of leadership early in his regime. During some of World War II, the Franco regime also mimicked its fascist counterparts.

**Francisco Franco salutes German troops on parade, May 1939.** ©BETTMANN/CORBIS

Franco gave speeches to mass rallies, incorporated the Roman salute, established the rudiments of a corporative state, inveighed against the dual enemies of liberal democracy and communism, and created youth and women's sections of the ruling party. Yet Franco never truly cultivated the almost mystical image of the fascist "new man." Even the title Franco adopted, *Caudillo*, reached back to older military traditions in Spain and Latin America, unlike the titles *Führer* or *Duce*.

The regime's political party, the Falange Española Tradicionalista (Spanish Traditional Phalanx), knit together forces that were unified only by their opposition to the Second Republic. In fact, the "Traditional" of the party name was added to appease many of the more conservative political forces that joined Franco. Among them were monarchists, who throughout the course of the regime bristled at Franco's imperious hold on power and were chastened only in 1947 with the

passage of the Law of Succession, which declared Franco "regent for life," with the tacit promise of a later return to monarchy. Carlists, an ultraconservative, ultra-Catholic political formation from northern Spain that favored the return of a different monarchical line, were constantly working to have Franco follow their tradition. The original Spanish fascist party, itself a collection of disparate political groupings, harbored deep resentments because of Franco's hesitation to join the Axis powers in World War II and then the banishment of many of its leaders from positions of power in the Francoist state. Franco's political gift lay in keeping these coalition members divided and thus always working to curry the *caudillo*'s favor against the interests of other coalition partners.

While Franco's image as a fascist was more a product of his wartime alliances, his own behavior toward the Axis powers reflected a political agenda geared more toward staying in power than promoting fascism. Despite Franco's personal desire for an Axis victory and his feeling of kinship with Hitler and Nazism (he even entitled his 1941 screenplay *Raza* [Race] to echo the language of his German counterparts), he continuously frustrated the efforts of Hitler and Mussolini to have Spain join the Axis. Franco's mixture of promises and delays led Hitler to call Franco the "Latin charlatan." Despite ongoing sales of raw materials to Germany and logistical support for U-boats, Franco gradually began to distance his regime from the Axis in 1942.

Franco demonstrated far less delicacy with his enemies. The ruthlessness he demonstrated in Morocco returned with the postwar repressions of former Republican soldiers, communists, anarchists, regional separatists, and other political opponents. The repressions were both vicious and well publicized. Though the civil war was particularly brutal, killing perhaps up to five hundred thousand Spaniards, Franco kept the bloodshed continuing after the war, executing an estimated twenty-eight thousand after 1939. He often personally called for execution by garrote, a metal clamp tightened around the neck of the victim. He imprisoned tens of thousands more during his regime.

**THE FRANCO REGIME**

At the end of World War II, Western Europe remained wary of Franco and succeeded in keeping Spain out of the United Nations and NATO, at least until 1955 and 1982 respectively. In the effort to refashion Spain's image, Franco benefited most from changing international circumstances. The United States, for example, increasingly focused on Franco's ardent anticommunism and saw Spain as a bulwark against the Soviet Union on Europe's important southwestern edge. Promising more than 1.5 billion dollars of aid, the United States signed the Pact of Madrid with Spain in 1953 and secured military bases in the Iberian Peninsula. While Franco enjoyed the international benefits of his anticommunism, his economic policies only served to isolate Spain further. Immediately after the civil war the regime pursued autarkic economic policies of self-sufficiency that ushered in what Spaniards still remember as the years of hunger. Only as a result of technocratic changes in his regime in the late 1950s and an increasing opening

of Spain to international tourism did economic conditions and Spain's image begin to improve.

These changes did not signal a loosening of Franco's personal politics or unitary view of the Spanish nation. His repression of political enemies, real and imagined, remained an essential facet of his dictatorship. The ferocity of his response to regionalist movements, in particular the Basque separatist group ETA (Euskadi Ta Azkatasuna—Basque Homeland and Freedom), after 1968 led to greater ostracism of the regime in Europe and demonstrated that Franco's basic conservative values remained virtually unaltered. His appointment of thirty-one-year-old Juan Carlos de Borbón (b. 1938), the grandson of Spain's last monarch, as his successor in 1969 represented his undying belief in monarchy as an essential element of Spanish national identity. Ironically, following Franco's death on 20 November 1975, Juan Carlos became the linchpin in Spain's transition to democracy and reintegration with the rest of the modern world.

*See also* **Basques; ETA; Juan Carlos I; Primo de Rivera, Miguel; Spain.**

BIBLIOGRAPHY

*Primary Sources*

Andrade, Jaime de [Francisco Franco Bahamonde]. *Raza anecdotario para el guión de una película.* Barcelona, 1997.

Franco, Francisco. *Diario de una Bandera.* Madrid, 1922.

*Secondary Sources*

Ellwood, Sheelagh. *Franco: Profiles in Power.* London, 1993.

Hodges, Gabrielle Ashford. *Franco: A Concise Biography.* London, 2000.

Jensen, Geoffrey. *Franco: Soldier, Commander, Dictator.* Washington, D.C., 2005.

Payne, Stanley G. *The Franco Regime, 1936–1975.* Madison, Wis., 1987.

Preston, Paul. *Franco: A Biography.* New York, 1994.

JOSHUA GOODE

**FRANK, ANNE** (1929–1945), German-born diarist, writer, and Holocaust victim.

Anne Frank was born in Frankfurt am Rhein, Germany, on 12 June 1929. Her ancestors had lived in that city for centuries, achieving a modest position of wealth and prestige in the world of commerce and banking. Her father, Otto Frank, belonged to a family of cultivated, liberal, assimilated German Jews. After the Nazis came to power, he arranged for his family to emigrate to Amsterdam, where he had established a Dutch branch of a chemical firm. Anne joined her parents and elder sister, Margot, in March 1934, and both girls soon adapted to life in the Netherlands. The German invasion on 10 May 1940 had few immediate effects, but anti-Semitic measures were gradually introduced and Anne was forced to transfer to a Jewish school in September 1941. When the Nazis began to deport the Jews in July 1942, the Frank family went into hiding almost immediately, using the attic (*Achterhuis*) above Otto Frank's office at 263 Prinsengracht in the old center of Amsterdam. Anne meticulously recorded in her diary the events of the following two years in this secret annex. She quickly developed her skills as a writer and on 11 May 1944 wrote that she wished to become a journalist and writer. To that end she started to rewrite her original diary.

On 4 August 1944, two months after the Allied landing in Normandy, Otto Frank and his family were arrested, having been betrayed to the Germans. On 8 August they were deported to the Westerbork transit camp in the northeastern part of the Netherlands. On 3 September, as the Allied armies were approaching the Dutch frontier, the Frank family was deported on the very last train to leave Westerbork for Auschwitz. Anne and her sister were transported to Bergen-Belsen at the end of October, leaving their mother, Edith, in Auschwitz, where she died of exhaustion. Like many other inhabitants of the overpopulated Bergen-Belsen camp, the Frank sisters died of typhus before the British Army liberated it on 15 April 1945.

After returning from Auschwitz, Otto Frank learned that his family had not survived the camps but that most of Anne's diary had been preserved. In 1947 he decided to publish an abridged version

**Anne Frank at her desk c. 1940.** AP/Wide World Photos

under the title *Het Achterhuis* (The secret annex). For the sake of propriety, the good name of third parties, and in order to maintain interest, Otto Frank and the Dutch publisher felt they had to omit certain passages. International acclaim followed in the mid-1950s, and reprints, translations, and new editions followed in quick succession. The diary became the most widely read nonfiction book in the world after the Bible. A critical edition of Anne Frank's diary appeared in Dutch in 1986 to rebut neo-Nazi allegations that it was a hoax.

In 1957 the Anne Frank Foundation was created with the aim of propagating the ideals expressed in the diary. The foundation acquired the house on the Prinsengracht and created a museum there in 1960. It became one of Western Europe's most popular shrines. The foundation and its museum addressed many of the broader ideological preoccupations of society until the 1990s, when there was a return to assessing Anne Frank as an individual; several biographies were published and more emphasis was put on the literary qualities of her writings.

For many people, Anne Frank provides a human face to the six million Jews who died, and her diary is of enduring importance in memorializing the victims of the Holocaust. Although she was initially seen as an icon of Dutch innocence and resistance, this view of the population as a whole was later undermined by historians, who demonstrated that the vast majority were indifferent to the fate of their fellow citizens and many were even actively involved in their deportation. More than 102,000 of the Netherlands' 140,000 Jews were murdered, a proportion equaled only in the countries of occupied Eastern Europe. More recently, Anne Frank became a ready-made icon for those who, in the words of Ian Buruma, have turned the Holocaust into a kind of secular religion.

There has also been intense criticism of those who have used her experiences as an emblem of the Nazi persecution of the Jews. Because her diary ends at the moment of her deportation, it can give no attention to the suffering of the millions of Jews in the camps and the ghettos of Eastern Europe, as Anne herself recognized in her entry of 13 January 1943. In the age of "identity politics," many were also shocked by the "de-Judaizing" of Anne Frank, for example in the play and film by Frances Goodrich and Albert Hackett in the 1950s, where Anne expresses her belief in the goodness of men, thus becoming a symbol of innocence and hope, and where her suffering was taken as the symbol of the suffering of all humanity. These changing perspectives go a long way toward illuminating the different phases of contemporary and cultural history since the diary was written. Her writings also show the many faces of Anne Frank herself, as a recalcitrant adolescent, a young girl in love, and, in her letters to her fictitious friend Kitty, a penetrating and witty observer.

See also **Childhood and Adolescence; Holocaust; Netherlands.**

BIBLIOGRAPHY

*Primary Sources*

Frank, Anne. *The Diary of a Young Girl.* Translated by B. M. Mooyaart-Doubleday. London, 1952.

———. *The Diary of Anne Frank.* Edited by David Barnouw and Gerrold van der Stroom. Translated by Arnold J. Pomerans, B. M. Mooyaart-Doubleday, and Susan Massotty. Rev. critical ed. New York, 2003.

*Secondary Sources*

Enzer, Hyman Aaron, and Sandra Solotaroff-Enzer, eds. *Anne Frank: Reflections on Her Life and Legacy.* Urbana, Ill., 2000.

Galen Last, Dick van, and Rolf Wolfswinkel. *Anne Frank and After: Dutch Holocaust Literature in Historical Perspective.* Amsterdam, 1996.

Müller, Melissa. *Anne Frank: The Biography.* Translated by Rita Kimber and Robert Kimber. New York, 1998.

Rittner, Carol, ed. *Anne Frank in the World: Essays and Reflections.* Armonk, N.Y., 1998.

DICK VAN GALEN LAST

# FRANKFURT SCHOOL.

The phrase *Frankfurt School* refers to an illustrious group of German-Jewish thinkers who came of age during the tumultuous years of the Weimar Republic. Their number included Theodor Adorno, Walter Benjamin, Erich Fromm, Max Horkheimer, Otto Kirchheimer, Leo Lowenthal, Herbert Marcuse, Franz Neumann, and Friedrich Pollock. Later, they achieved a remarkable degree of intellectual renown in the United States, where they fled following Adolf Hitler's seizure of power.

## FRANKFURT

The Frankfurt School's organizational base was the Institute for Social Research, which was established by Felix Weil in the liberal milieu of Frankfurt in 1923. The institute was originally conceived as an intellectual ally of the German working-class movement, whose 1918 through 1919 revolution had been brutally subdued by the reigning social democrats and their right-wing allies. The institute's charge was to undertake research on working-class politics in order to facilitate the eventual triumph of the "progressive social forces" that had been defeated in Weimar's early years. However, the Frankfurt School as it is known today was given its definitive shape under the directorship of Max Horkheimer, who succeeded Carl Grünberg in 1930.

Horkheimer articulated a new program in his inaugural address as director, "The Present State of Social Philosophy and the Tasks of an Institute for Social Research." The new approach centered on the research methodology of "interdisciplinary materialism." By this term, Horkheimer sought to map an intellectual course that would navigate between two prevalent scholarly extremes: on one hand, philosophical speculation entirely ungrounded in fact and on the other hand narrow-minded social scientific fact-gathering uninformed by theoretical directives.

The institute's approach to social philosophy followed a course that had been charted by the Western Marxist revival of the 1920s. In 1923 Karl Korsch's *Marxism and Philosophy* and Georg Lukács's *History and Class Consciousness* appeared. Both works vigorously rejected the determinist conception of Marxism purveyed by Soviet theoreticians. Lukács argued that Soviet Marxism's "objectivism" was incompatible with the notion of human freedom. Marxism, Lukács contended, was in essence a superior theory of human self-determination. However, it differed from earlier, bourgeois theories in stressing the "material" side of freedom: the component of social justice, without which freedom shrinks to a formal attribute relevant to the privileged classes alone. (In this vein, Horkheimer was fond of quoting the maxim, "Capitalism is inherently democratic; it forbids the right to sleep under bridges to millionaires and vagrants alike.") In many respects, Western Marxists like Lukács, Korsch, and the Frankfurt School foresaw the degeneration of Soviet Marxism into an oppressive and dogmatic "science of legitimation."

The collaborative research project that was meant to implement the Frankfurt School's interdisciplinary research program was Studies on Authority and the Family, in which Fromm's social psychology played a pivotal role. The study's thematic focus was the structural transformation of the bourgeois nuclear family, one of the institute's dominant concerns in the 1930s. But another aspect of the project highlighted the increasingly precarious status of Weimar democracy: the cultural transmission, via the family, of authoritarian patterns of socialization that undermined autonomy and bred obedience, thereby paving the way for dictatorship—a model that would soon cast its net across the Continent. During the 1950s, many of the concepts and research methods employed in the 1936 study were utilized in *The Authoritarian Personality* (1950), co-edited by Adorno and sponsored by the American Jewish Committee as part of its Studies in Prejudice series.

Hitler's seizure of power put an end to the Frankfurt School research program in its original incarnation: in March 1933, institute offices and property were confiscated by the Gestapo. Empirical research of the sort Horkheimer envisioned had become ideologically impossible in Germany. In 1934 the institute relocated to New York, where it established ties with Columbia University. Until 1940 its members continued to publish in German in order to preserve intellectual and cultural traditions that the Nazis sought to efface. Institute studies appeared in the *Zeitschrift für Sozialforschung,* a repository of strikingly innovative work in philosophy, cultural criticism, and social theory.

## EXILE

The institute focused on the economic, political, cultural, and psychological preconditions behind the rise of fascism. In his own programmatic contributions, such as the 1937 essay "Traditional and Critical Theory," Horkheimer strove to articulate the theoretical foundations of critical theory, a term that had become a deliberate euphemism for reflexive, nondogmatic Marxism. Unlike orthodox Marxism, critical theory had shed all vestiges of economic determinism, remaining sensitive to the multifarious causalities of the total social process—political, legal, and cultural developments that possessed their own immanent logic. Unlike "traditional theory"—the conventional bourgeois disciplines that Horkheimer sought to integrate—critical theory rejected the positivist ethos that accepted bourgeois society at face value, in its sheer immediacy or givenness. By casting its lot with the downtrodden and oppressed, critical theory sought to inform processes of social emancipation—or, as Horkheimer phrased it, the "rational organization of society."

As prospects for emancipation receded with the triumph of fascism in Europe and "state capitalism" (the New Deal) in the United States, critical theory's approach became increasingly abstract and philosophical. In his essays from the late 1930s, Horkheimer began to rely on the ideals of "Philosophical Reason" as a transhistorical touchstone of humanity's emancipatory hopes. In Horkheimer's view, reason, by stressing the tension between the "real" and the "rational," brought to light the deficiencies of contemporary social life. By emphasizing the ways in which reality failed to measure up to the sublimity of reason's demands, philosophy preserved the idea of a radically different, utopian social order. Many of these themes were also central to Marcuse's important 1940 study of Hegel, *Reason and Revolution.*

Horkheimer presided over the institute's effective dissolution, apparently due to financial constraints, in 1941, at which point the *Zeitschrift* ceased to appear. He and Adorno relocated to Pacific Palisades, California, where they coauthored *Dialectic of Enlightenment* (1944–1947), an influential presentation of the Frankfurt School's philosophy of history. Here Adorno's influence clearly predominated, because the new outlook on reason was a highly critical one. The authors argued that the very process of human ratiocination—intellection itself—underwrote the modern totalitarian impulse. The most basic expression of domination, they argued, was the attempt to make the dissimilar similar by subjecting it to the abstract imperatives of logical thought.

Despite fascinating chapters on the Enlightenment, Homer's *Odyssey,* the Marquis de Sade, and anti-Semitism, their perspective seemed oblivious to some important and potentially devastating objections and counterarguments; the authors had abandoned the original methodological promise of interdisciplinary materialism in favor of a schematic philosophy of history. Horkheimer and Adorno concluded that the rise of totalitarianism had revealed the inner logic of the Western cultural development in toto. They never explored the converse possibility that fascism represented a last-ditch effort to overturn the ideas of the French Revolution, the rule of law and democratic republicanism.

One of the book's major innovations was its systematic treatment of the phenomenon of mass culture ("The Culture Industry: Enlightenment as Mass Deception"). Similar misgivings about mass culture as a species of socially administered, ideological conformity would be voiced by American critics such as Dwight MacDonald, Clement Greenberg, and Irving Howe. Yet in this instance, too, one suspects that, despite the chapter's undeniable analytical brilliance, the authors indelicately grafted the experience of European totalitarianism onto the American situation. As a result, their analysis of the culture industry became monolithic: they readily assumed that mass culture, as a new form of ideological control, resulted in the "total integration" of American society. The distinctiveness of American political traditions—rule of law, republicanism, civil liberties—as a counterweight to culture industry conformity played no role in their account.

### POSTWAR DISCOURSE

In 1950, Horkheimer and Adorno returned to Frankfurt to accept teaching positions. Other former institute members—Kirchheimer, Lowenthal, Marcuse, and Neumann (who died in 1953)—remained in the United States, where they enjoyed distinguished university careers. Although Horkheimer and Adorno's major philosophical works were only translated during the 1970s, the Frankfurt School's interpretive framework was introduced to an American public via a number of influential works by Herbert Marcuse. During the 1960s, reading books such as *Eros and Civilization* (1955) and *One-Dimensional Man* (1964) served as an obligatory rite of passage for many members of the New Left. Marcuse's critique of the repressive nature of advanced industrial society, whose survival was predicated on rechanneling desire in accordance with the strictures of mass consumption (a process he famously characterized as "repressive desublimation") proved prophetic, for it anticipated the "libidinal politics" that a subsequent generation of student radicals would soon adopt.

Thus, whereas the Frankfurt School's critique of domination was first elaborated in the 1930s and 1940s, its doctrines were received under very different conditions. As a result of this unexpected confluence of German social thought and indigenous American radicalism, a generation of young American scholars (inspired in part by Martin Jay's pioneering history *The Dialectical Imagination* [1973]) sought to renew and adapt critical theory to the changed political and social realities of the post-1960s America, making the Frankfurt School framework an integral component of postwar American intellectual discourse.

During the 1950s and 1960s, Horkheimer and Adorno, for their parts, were extremely active in refashioning German politics. In his capacity as university rector, Horkheimer rubbed elbows with

German political elites and had an important influence on postwar educational policy. The resurrected institute's new annual, *Frankfurter Beiträge zu Soziologie*, published influential studies of German occupational life that revealed a marked continuation of authoritarian character structure.

Adorno was an especially active participant in the reeducation process. He delivered a series of public lectures and radio addresses urging his fellow citizens to actively confront the German past rather than simply bury it. In the aftermath of Auschwitz, contrition and restitution became the twin preconditions for Germany's return to the fold of civilized nations. The Frankfurt School, with Adorno in the lead, stressed the imperatives of *Vergangenheitsbewältigung*, or "Coming to terms with the past." For these reasons, in their study of the School's postwar influence Clemens Albrecht et al. credited it with establishing the intellectual and moral foundations of postwar Germany.

In "Education towards Maturity," Adorno praised the Kantian virtue of *Mündigkeit*, or autonomy. Thereby, he acknowledged that one of the key factors in Nazism's precipitous rise was a widespread dearth of *Zivilcourage* on the part of the German civil population. The traditional authoritarian state had excelled at producing quiescent and obedient subjects (*Untertanen*) rather than citizens. Only a far-reaching transformation in socialization patterns would remedy this debility and set Germany on the path to stable democratic government. Consequently, the Frankfurt School consciously downplayed its earlier hopes for radical social change—to the point where for many years Horkheimer categorically refused requests to republish books and articles from the 1930s and 1940s.

However, this change in political tone was apparently lost on postwar German youth. To the chagrin of Horkheimer et al., they found the Frankfurt School's more radical doctrines of the 1930s timely and congenial. Their impatience was, in many respects, understandable. After all, during the 1950s the Americans had sacrificed denazification to the ends of anticommunism. But this policy meant that there was a discomfiting continuity in personnel from the Third Reich to the Federal Republic.

The German SDS (Sozialistischer deutscher Studentenbund) saw itself as antifascist, and its goal was to oppose the authoritarian continuities in German politics. But this put it on an explosive collision course with the reincarnated Institute for Social Research, since one of the political lessons that Horkheimer and his colleagues had learned during the 1930s was that the Left's failure to rally around the values of liberal democracy had greatly facilitated Hitler's seizure of power—a scenario they were anxious to forestall in the postwar era. The inevitable political clash between the two groups came to pass in 1968, when Adorno felt compelled to summon the police to expel student radicals who had illegally occupied institute premises.

Jürgen Habermas, Adorno's assistant in Frankfurt during the 1950s, has continued to build on his mentor's legacy. Yet he has taken exception to the philosophy of history propounded in *Dialectic of Enlightenment*, which he perceives as an exaggerated "inverted" teleology, in which linear decline supplants the positive teleology of progress. Unlike Horkheimer and Adorno, Habermas has been eager to stress the redeeming or positive features of political modernity: the values of civil society, the public sphere, the rule of law, human rights, and participatory democracy, all of which he perceives as an important bulwark against political authoritarianism.

At the same time, Habermas shares the Frankfurt School's critical verdict on "instrumental reason": like Adorno, he fears that the technocratic imperatives of economic management and state administration have taken precedence over human capacities for undistorted intersubjectivity—the ability to reach agreement through the beneficent capacities of mutual understanding. In *The Theory of Communicative Action* (1981), Habermas coined the phrase *administrative colonization of the lifeworld* to describe the process whereby the formal imperatives of economic and administrative rationality increasingly subsume informal modes of human interaction: friendship, intimacy, and principled political will-formation. Unlike his intellectual forebears, he has sought to reconcile critical theory's emancipatory thrust with contemporary developments in philosophy and the social sciences.

Thus, his view of traditional theory is markedly less confrontational than was Horkheimer's. His theory of "universal pragmatics"—the "ideal speech situation" that constitutes the philosophical basis for the theory of communicative action—was developed via an encounter with the linguistic philosophies of J. L. Austin and John Searle.

Habermas's own work, which has had a profound and extensive impact on a variety of intellectual fields, is significant testimony to the continuing relevance of the Frankfurt School vision.

*See also* **Adorno, Theodor; Benjamin, Walter; Fromm, Erich; Habermas, Jürgen; Marcuse, Herbert.**

BIBLIOGRAPHY

Albrecht, Clemens, et al. *Die Intellektuelle Gründung der Bundesrepublik: Eine Wirkungsgeschichte der Frankfurter Schule.* Frankfurt, 1999.

Arato, Andrew, and Eike Gebhardt, eds. *The Essential Frankfurt School Reader.* New York, 1978.

Bernstein, Richard J., ed. *Habermas and Modernity.* Cambridge, Mass., 1985.

Bronner, Stephen Eric, and Douglas MacKay Kellner, eds. *Critical Theory and Society: A Reader.* New York, 1989.

Horkheimer, Max. *Critical Theory,* translated by J. Cummings. New York, 1972.

McCarthy, Thomas. *The Critical Theory of Jürgen Habermas.* Cambridge, Mass., 1978.

Seidman, Steven, ed. *Jürgen Habermas on Society and Politics: A Reader.* Boston, 1989.

Wiggershaus, Rolf. *The Frankfurt School: Its History, Theories, and Political Significance.* Cambridge, Mass., 1994.

Wolin, Richard. *The Terms of Cultural Criticism: The Frankfurt School, Existentialism, Poststructuralism.* New York, 1992.

RICHARD WOLIN

---

**FRENCH EMPIRE.** In 1914 the French Empire was the second largest colonial empire in population and extent/territory. A century earlier, France had already lost most of a substantial previous empire in India and North America, retaining only a few slave islands in the Caribbean and the Indian Ocean, tiny colonial fragments in India, and some coastal footholds and trading stations in Africa and Asia. By a curious irony, therefore, modern French imperialism coincided and was indelibly associated with the rise of French republicanism and the modern state. This irony became more acute with time, haunting the troubled French experience of decolonization.

In 1848, the short-lived Second Republic began to forge a republican conception of empire by setting two formidable precedents. First, it abolished slavery (which had been abortively abolished once before, in 1791) and created citizens of former slaves, who thus could vote in French parliamentary elections. Second, the Republic incorporated the newly conquered territories of Algeria—which had been invaded in 1830 and brutally "pacified" thereafter—within the administrative structure of metropolitan France: Algeria was divided into *départements* under the control of a prefect. When François Mitterrand, interior minister at the outbreak of the Algerian War in 1954, infamously claimed that "Algeria is France," he was thus doing no more than stating the official truth. Algeria constituted the keystone of the French Empire until it gained its independence in 1962. The colonies emancipated in 1848 (now the overseas *départements* of Martinique, Guadeloupe, French Guiana, and Réunion), were still outposts of the French Republic—and of the European Union—in 2004, along with a few other quasi-colonial "overseas territories."

France's empire expanded most rapidly, alongside that of other colonial powers, in the 1880s and 1890s, with the internationally sanctioned occupation and, where necessary, armed conquest, of vast territories in West and Central Africa, Madagascar, and Southeast Asia, along with divers islands and archipelagos in the Atlantic, Indian, and Pacific Oceans. Prized protectorates over Tunisia and Morocco were also secured in this period, and Algeria acquired its Saharan extension through the cartographic skills of the French army. This "scramble for Africa" (and Asia) coincided with the dynamic consolidation of the values and institutions of the modern French state by the Third Republic after 1870. The territorial contiguity of French-ruled territory in Africa inspired the enduring rhetorical trope of a *"Françafrique"* stretching "from Flanders to the Congo" (one of

Mitterrand's more fanciful slogans from the 1950s); plans for a Trans-Saharan Railway, which might have lent substance to the rhetoric, were much discussed but never realized. Even so, by 1914 the French imperial map revealed impressive stretches of French rule, commanded by powerful proconsuls in Algiers, Rabat, and Tunis, Dakar (French West Africa), Brazzaville (French Equatorial Africa), Tananarive (Madagascar), and Hanoi (Indochina, a French creation comprising the modern-day states of Vietnam, Cambodia, and Laos). The map was completed only after 1919, when France was granted mandates by the newly formed League of Nations to administer former German colonies in Africa (Cameroon, Togo) and former Ottoman territories in the Middle East, where French soldiers and proconsuls created the states of Syria and Lebanon with their modern boundaries. The dominant doctrine underpinning French colonial rule was assimilation, allied to the looser conception of a *"mission civilisatrice"* (civilizing mission). As late as 1944, at the time of the Brazzaville Conference organized by the Free French movement, a prominent Gaullist declared that France's aim was to "transform French Africans into African Frenchmen." This French mission took various practical forms, the most important being the inculcation, through education, of French norms, culture, and language. Chiefly remembered for the apocryphal stories of African schoolchildren reciting how "our ancestors the Gauls had blond hair and blue eyes," in reality the French colonial school system never reached more than the few—very few beyond primary level—though it was bolstered by the efforts of Catholic missionaries (since the core republican doctrine of *laïcité,* the separation of church and state, was largely ignored overseas). In addition, "civilization" was to be imposed through the supposedly virtuous instruments of taxation and labor; indeed, as in pre-1789 France, the two were often combined in the form of labor impressments for public works. French administrators and their intermediaries also acted as recruiting agents for labor on major projects, such as the notorious Congo-Ocean Railway, which claimed the lives of thousands of Africans, or for seasonal work on European-owned plantations. Although banned by the International Labor Organization in 1930, forced labor continued in various guises until it was finally abolished after World War II.

Assimilation also implied the application of French legal norms, but this principle too was readily manipulated to French ends. Most notably, French law in Algeria, France's principal settler colony, was used to justify the expropriation of the best agricultural lands by European farmers, thus forcing upon indigenous Algerians the choice between laboring in the European farms and vineyards, migrating to poorer, mountainous regions, electing a precarious existence in the coastal cities, or, from the 1920s on, immigrating to metropolitan France to serve as cheap, transient, industrial labor. More generally, French administration relied on an often cruel and arbitrary *indigénat,* or "native" code of justice, which was abolished only after 1945. In theory, the colonized could attain equal status through citizenship. In fact, for most of the colonial period, citizenship had to be earned by meeting stringent criteria, though these were sometimes arbitrarily applied: literacy, property ownership, office holding, military service, or, for Muslims, the humiliating renunciation of rights and duties possessed under Islamic law and custom. Even when universal suffrage was eventually broached in the 1940s, it was clear that it could never be practiced on the basis of "one person, one vote" because demography dictated that France would then become "the colony of her former colonies." Voters were thus corralled into demeaning electoral colleges, which discounted their suffrage, so that African or Algerian *députés* (members of parliament) represented constituencies that were up to ten times more populous than those of French metropolitan *députés.* Even this double standard was not enough for the Algerian settlers, or *pieds noirs* (approximately one-eighth of the Algerian population), and in the 1948 elections to the new Algerian Assembly, massive electoral fraud excluded all but the most pro-French voices. By contrast, politics in post-1945 French sub-Saharan Africa showed how the rhetoric of assimilation could be turned to the advantage of the colonized, as a new generation of politicians and trade unionists campaigned with some success for equal rights for African workers, with the creation of an African Labor Code in 1952. In this case at least, French colonial rule was starting to become too costly to maintain.

Although assimilation remained the dominant ideal—or rather, fiction—of French republican imperialism, colonial officials came to learn the advantages of a less intrusive policy of association, which accompanied or supplanted assimilationist grand designs. Association had its philosophical basis in an ambiguous relativism, which purported to respect cultural difference in conquered societies, but for the most part simply considered some "ancient" civilizations as yet unfit for the benefits of Western rule. More pragmatically, association recognized the costs of prolonged resistance to French rule or to its harsher policies, such as military recruitment during World War I. It also took into account the necessary paucity of French administrative resources, since by law French colonies had to remain fiscally autonomous. French colonial officials thus restored, or sometimes invented, institutions of local rule, which compensated for an overstretched colonial administration. Assimilationist and associationist doctrines came together in the increasingly professionalized training of colonial administrators at the École Nationale de la France d'Outre-Mer (ENFOM, National academy for overseas France), then counted among France's more prestigious *grandes écoles,* which in 2004 still trained French administrative, political, intellectual, and business elites. Cadets at ENFOM studied law and administration, but also ethnography, languages, and basic applied sciences, so that they could operate effectively as technocratic modernizers, lonely but resourceful "kings of the bush." Unlike their typical British counterparts, they were often men of the Left, drawn from France's provincial periphery, from lower-middle-class or peasant backgrounds.

What was the importance of empire for French public opinion? Parisian high culture between the wars drew heavily on contact with the colonized cultures of Africa and Southeast Asia. The Parisian intelligentsia reveled in exotic ethnographic discoveries; enthused over African and Asian artifacts pillaged for French museum collections; admired the poetry and manifestos of the negritude movement, whose leading lights included future politicians, Léopold Sédar Senghor of Senegal and the Martiniquan Aimé Césaire; and danced to the music of African American jazz musicians. This fascination with the exotic Other was periodically tempered by unease at the colonial abuses revealed by the left-wing intellectuals André Gide, Andrée Viollis, and

Cover of the novel *Datine le Berba* by French novelist Joseph Huchet. Huichet was a French missionary in Dahomey who wrote popular novels depicting the life of indigenous people in the region. BRIDGEMAN ART LIBRARY

Michel Leiris, but by few others before the 1950s. French popular culture was saturated with imperial clichés in film, popular song, commercial advertising, and official propaganda. Yet the staging in 1931 of a Grand Colonial Exposition in a park outside Paris, under the prestigious direction of Marshal Louis Lyautey, "pacifier" of Morocco, indicates that the government felt some anxiety that the French public was not sufficiently "empire-minded." Millions of visitors took up the invitation to voyage "round the world in one day," marveling at replicas of temples, mosques, palaces, and mud huts, and ogling the spectacle of costumed "natives" acting out the tamer fantasies of their colonial masters. It is doubtful that this experience stiffened popular imperialist resolve.

Colonial affairs were never high on the political agenda, even at moments of crisis, and the French colonial enterprise was supported, albeit unenthusiastically, by a broad consensus of French political opinion. In the days of conquest, the empire had depended on the vigorous lobbying of a small but influential *parti colonial,* a loose coalition of imperial interests including businessmen, geographers, soldiers, and missionaries. Within the political parties, colonial questions were the province of a few "experts" rather than a matter for mainstream party debate. On the Left, the Socialist Party (Section Française de l'Internationale Ouvrière, or SFIO) campaigned against the scandals associated with colonialism, rather than against colonialism itself. Even the French Communist Party's anticolonialism, a Leninist article of faith, turned out to be conditional: after the Party rejoined the republican mainstream with the formation of the Popular Front in 1934, its stance came to reflect that of the secretary-general Maurice Thorez, in December 1937, recalling Vladimir Lenin's maxim that "the right to divorce does not mean the obligation to divorce." After World War II, the party line equated separatist nationalism with fascism (for example, in Algeria in 1945) and decolonization with U.S. imperialism. The Cold War made it easier for the party to oppose French actions in Indochina and Madagascar, but its solidarity with Communist brethren such as Ho Chi Minh was signally more wholehearted than its subsequent support for the Algerian National Liberation Front (FLN). Conversely, the same Cold War logic constrained the other parties, even the SFIO, to back *Algérie Française.* Before the cautious or compromised party leaderships, it was individual party militants and independent intellectuals—mostly on the Left, but also among liberal Catholics—who supported the Algerian cause: denouncing torture, encouraging desertion by French servicemen, or acting as *porteurs de valises* (couriers, or literally, suitcase-carriers) for the FLN.

The empire mattered to businesses and investors and was a crucial source of foodstuffs and raw materials, from West African cocoa and peanut oil to Indochinese rubber and coal. But French imperialism increasingly acted as a brake on economic modernization, as it was old-fashioned, unprofitable industries, such as food oils and textiles that benefited from the colonies. Colonial development was first mooted in the 1920s, under the utilitarian guise of the proposed *mise en valeur* (valorization) of the colonies, but virtually nothing happened until 1946, when an Investment Fund for Economic and Social Development (FIDES)

was created to channel metropolitan funds into major development projects. Ironically, the scheme's very success made a powerful case for decolonization, when it was argued, most prominently by the editor of the popular magazine *Paris-Match,* that the money would be better spent at home. By a further irony, the Algerian economy—hitherto largely perceived as competition for French farmers and winegrowers—promised to benefit France only when it was almost too late, with the discovery of the Saharan oil fields in the late 1950s. By this time, governments and multinational enterprises were coming to realize that the resources of the developing world could be exploited more profitably without the hindrance of colonial rule: so it proved in Algeria, where independence barely interrupted the pace of French investment in Algerian oil and gas, or of Algerian labor migration to France.

The French Empire remained a prop for French claims to the status of a great power, even after 1945. Although imperial rivalries with Britain were resolved almost amicably when the Entente Cordiale was concluded in 1904, the more practical purpose of "Greater France" (*la plus grande France*) was as a demographic counterweight to a Germany whose sixty million citizens otherwise outnumbered France's forty million. France alone deployed non-European colonial troops on the western front during World War II, including a *Force Noire* (black force) of some 170,000 African *tirailleurs* (infantry troops). In 1940 colonial troops fought in the Battle of France, which left many Africans among the 1.25 million French prisoners of war in Germany. General Charles de Gaulle's Free French army was largely a colonial army, which fought in the Western Desert and in Italy, before spearheading the secondary Allied landings in southern France in August 1944. France continued to rely on colonial levies and the much-romanticized mercenaries of the Foreign Legion in its various wars of decolonization, in Indochina, Madagascar, and North Africa. In Algeria, locally recruited troops and auxiliaries (*harkis*) were in the thick of the fighting; at independence, they were faced with a tragic nonchoice between exile and massacre. Although the Algerian War (1954–1962) was the first and only colonial campaign in which French conscripts were deployed, allowing the army to field a force of up to 450,000 men, it also represented the last stand for the imperial ethos of the professional French officer corps. For de Gaulle (who, for reasons of background and temperament, did not share that ethos), ending the war in Algeria was an opportunity for France to "marry her century"; this included modernizing the French army and revolutionizing French strategy by switching to a policy of nuclear deterrence based on a nascent French *force de frappe* (strike force). Even de Gaulle regretted losing the Algerian Sahara, which offered facilities for nuclear testing far preferable to the Pacific atolls used after 1962.

Any account of the end of the French Empire must begin by examining its inescapable contradictions. It must also consider the continuity of resistance to French rule, which found expression between the wars in the emergence of nationalist movements, and in various revolts, insurrections, and conspiracies—all brutally and effectively repressed. The French Empire might still have limped along, sustained by a circular argument that legitimized colonialism within an international system dominated by colonial powers—claims that seemed almost acceptable alongside the ambitions of the Axis. World War II, however, changed everything, perhaps for France especially: when it was defeated in 1940, its colonial territories were divided between Free France and the old order represented by Vichy. France's authority was undermined by the presence, from 1942 on, of Allied troops on French colonial soil, and its very status as a power was threatened by the two new, and anticolonialist, superpowers. Most immediately, Japanese occupation in Southeast Asia effectively spelled the end of European colonialism in that region, although the British, French, and Dutch all resorted to arms to avoid the writing on the wall—which was finally translated into French only at the battle of Dien Bien Phu in 1954, after eight years of futile combat against the forces of Ho Chi Minh's Communist Revolution. France's vestigial Indian city-colonies were peacefully incorporated into the surrounding states of independent India in 1950 and 1954.

Crucially, however, the end of the war initially led to an attempt by the European powers to reinvigorate colonial rule as an integral part of postwar reconstruction, though as it turned out, what was at stake was not the maintenance of colonial rule but the manner, timing, and outcomes of eventual decolonization. France made a last attempt to reconcile the Republic with its empire through a raft of political and economic reforms contained within the constitutional framework of a new French Union (a name chosen in homage to the USSR). This unwieldy monster was too readily compromised by concessions to the Right in the constitutional debates of 1946, or, in Algeria, was subverted by the obdurate *pieds noirs* and a complaisant administration. A more stable, less divided, better-led regime, less troubled by the legacy of defeat in 1940 than the postwar Fourth Republic (1946–1958), might still have fought in Indochina or shown the same ruthlessness in crushing the Malagasy insurrection of 1947–1948, or the same reluctance to concede Tunisian and Moroccan independence; but it might not have managed any better in setting up the institutional framework that paved the way for rapid decolonization in sub-Saharan Africa. Even with new, dynamic leadership and a radically reshaped French constitution, more of the Algerian War took place after de Gaulle's return to power in May 1958 than before. Conversely, a different postwar regime might just have forced through timely reforms in Algeria, however limited, thus providing openings for moderate nationalists, who might then have eschewed the all-out violence of the FLN, the French army, and settler vigilantes, or the last-ditch scorched-earth campaign of the Secret Army Organization (OAS), a terrorist movement of settler extremists and dissident army officers. In sum, decolonization would have been difficult and traumatic in any event, but surely anything would have been preferable to the infernal Franco-Algerian escalation of massacres, terrorism, and torture—especially the increasingly systematic use of torture that has stained the French conscience ever since. The population transfers and "ethnic cleansing," the political and personal traumas, were still unhealed in the early years of the twenty-first century, more than fifty years after the FLN's declaration of war.

The sense of relief that accompanied decolonization may help explain the readiness with which French people "turned the page" in 1962, given that it took almost forty years before there was any widespread public debate about the appalling memories and troublesome legacy of the Algerian War (officially so designated only with a National

Assembly vote in June 1999). Surely most French people concurred (if for divergent reasons) with de Gaulle's assertion in 1961 that "decolonization is in the French interest, and is therefore French policy." Indeed, notwithstanding the French Fifth Republic's dubious history of neocolonial adventures in Africa and nuclear posturing, there was little sense that France had "lost an empire but not yet found a role," as U.S. Secretary of State Dean Acheson caustically characterized Britain's situation. France's role was at the heart of another nascent union of sovereign and democratic European nations.

*See also* **Algeria; Algerian War; British Empire; British Empire, End of; Fanon, Frantz; Indochina; Morocco; Negritude; Senghor, Léopold Sédar; Suez Crisis; Vietnam War.**

BIBLIOGRAPHY

Branche, Raphaëlle. *La torture et l'armée pendant la Guerre d'Algérie, 1954–1962.* Paris, 2001.

Brocheux, Pierre, and Daniel Hémery. *Indochine: La colonisation ambiguë, 1858–1954.* Paris, 1995.

Conklin, Alice L. *A Mission to Civilize: The Republican Idea of Empire in France and West Africa, 1895–1930.* Stanford, Calif., 1997.

Cooper, Frederick. *Decolonization and African Society: The Labor Question in French and British Africa.* Cambridge, U.K., 1996.

Horne, Alistair. *A Savage War of Peace: Algeria, 1954–1962.* Rev. and updated ed. London, 2002.

Le Sueur, James D. *Uncivil War: Intellectuals and Identity Politics during the Decolonization of Algeria.* Philadelphia, 2001.

Marr, David G. *Vietnam 1945: The Quest for Power.* Berkeley, Calif., 1995.

Marseille, Jacques. *Empire colonial et capitalisme français. Histoire d'un divorce.* Paris, 1984.

Ross, Kristin. *Fast Cars, Clean Bodies: Decolonization and the Reordering of French Culture.* Cambridge, Mass., 1995.

Ruedy, John. *Modern Algeria, the Origins and Development of a Nation.* Bloomington, Ind., 1992.

Shipway, Martin. *The Road to War: France and Vietnam, 1944–1947.* Oxford, U.K., 1996.

Thomas, Martin. *The French Empire at War 1940–45.* Manchester, U.K., 1998.

MARTIN SHIPWAY

# FRENCH NEW WAVE.

French new wave cinema was an explosion of hundreds of motion pictures made by young new directors between 1958 and 1964. This was surely one of the richest, most important movements in film history. The new wave was the result of very specific social and technological developments of post–World War II France. Moreover, during the decade after the war, the rise in film criticism created conditions that welcomed drastic changes in French cinema. The legendary film critic André Bazin and scores of other critics engaged in a frenzy of filmgoing and critical writing. This was the era of *ciné-clubs* and daring new film journals, especially Bazin's *Cahiers du cinéma* (formed in 1951). Bazin featured articles and reviews by a group of very young cinephiles, including Eric Rohmer, Claude Chabrol, François Truffaut, and Jean-Luc Godard, all of whom would go on to direct films. *Cahiers du cinéma* celebrated a wide range of distinctive directors, or auteurs, but the restless critics also attacked many of France's most successful commercial filmmakers. And their rebelliousness was not isolated.

During the 1950s, there were fundamental changes under way within nearly every aspect of French society. As the decade progressed, there was a growing perception of a distinct youth culture, or "new wave" (*nouvelle vague*) generation, defined in part by a rejection of many of France's traditions. *Express* magazine even launched a survey to investigate new wave morals, politics, and general behavior. The new wave dismissed old institutions and authority figures, while its core constituents, urban, well-educated young people, flocked to jazz clubs, read New Novels, and mocked mainstream movies as outdated. By 1958 and 1959, when an unprecedented rise in movies by and for young people appeared, the label *new wave* became permanently attached to a new sort of film, shot cheaply with daring new techniques. "Papa's cinema" was now under attack from new wave cinema, led by some of the same critics who had written for *Cahiers* and who were now directors. International audiences took notice. Parisian culture seemed once again the envy of Europe.

## BIRTH OF NEW WAVE CINEMA

France has a long tradition of individual directors with distinctive narrative styles. Never before, however, had conditions allowed so many first-time directors to experiment with telling new stories in new ways. A handful of creative individuals working during the late 1940s and early 1950s pointed the way toward change. The critic Alexandre Astruc (b. 1923) called for new strategies in a famous 1948 article on *"la caméra stylo,"* challenging directors to make their camera equivalent to a novelist's pen. Jean-Pierre Melville (1917–1973) provided a practical example for the eventual new wave. His first feature, *Silence of the Sea* (1947), was shot on a tiny budget, completely outside the system of production, by his own small production company. Melville went on to write and direct a number of films independently, including *Bob le Flambeur* (1955), which synthesized traits from French art cinema and American genre films alike, inspiring other young directors.

Another key role model was Agnès Varda (b. 1928). As a twenty-six-year-old woman with no film experience, Varda shot *La pointe courte* (*Short Point*) in a Mediterranean fishing village in 1954. For this very personal film, Varda formed her own company, Ciné-Tamaris, which she still operated fifty years later. The movie, shot on location with local residents and several fresh young actors, combined aspects of documentary cinema and Italian neorealism with a very modern narrative structure. Bazin hailed it as a miraculous film, and it too was made outside the rules and regulations of commercial cinema. She went on to make scores of documentaries and fiction films, including her new wave–era masterpiece, *Cleo from 5 to 7* (1961).

One of the first people to follow Astruc, Melville, and Varda's path was the young Louis Malle (1932–1995). At the age of twenty-five, Malle directed an elegant crime melodrama, *Elevator to the Gallows* (1958), featuring a sound track by the jazz legend Miles Davis and a stunning visual style. Malle immediately went to work on the controversial *The Lovers* (1958), a tale about a bourgeois wife who leaves both her husband and her lover for a man she had met the same day. Both films launched the rising new wave star Jeanne Moreau. By the late 1950s, such frank presentations of romance had shaken up French cinema, and the natural acting styles, casual visual look, and jazzy sound tracks broke away from more classically stagy

conventions. Malle's movies were hailed for announcing a new, long-awaited era.

By 1959 most film critics were convinced a true new wave cinema had arrived. The *Cahiers du cinéma* critic Claude Chabrol (b. 1930) premiered his first two movies, *Le beau Serge* and *The Cousins,* in February and March 1959; *The Cousins* became the fifth biggest hit of the year. In May, Truffaut (1932–1984) won the best director award at the Cannes Film Festival for his *The 400 Blows* (1959), and Alain Resnais's *Hiroshima mon amour* (1959) was shown outside competition to a sensational response. Truffaut and Resnais earned huge international distribution contracts, motivating other young producers and directors to get into the cinema. The new wave accelerated in 1960 with the arrival of *Breathless* by Jean-Luc Godard (b. 1930), Truffaut's *Shoot the Piano Player,* and Chabrol's *The Good Girls,* as well as Eric Rohmer's *The Sign of Leo* (1959) and Jacques Rivette's *Paris Belongs to Us.* Gradually, observers narrowed their definition of the new wave to former critics from *Cahiers du cinéma,* and Truffaut and Godard certainly became its central spokesmen, but other exemplary members included Jacques Demy (*Lola,* 1961; *Umbrellas of Cherbourg,* 1964) and Jacques Rozier (*Adieu Philippine,* 1962).

## DEFINING NEW WAVE AESTHETICS

Unlike previous film movements, such as German expressionism, Soviet montage, or Italian neorealism, the new wave did not have any fixed style or tactics. Instead, a wild variety of stories were told and styles were employed, in part because these young directors considered themselves auteurs. They strove to establish their own personal styles rather than copy one another. It is nonetheless possible to define shared general traits of new wave films. Most were shot on location with a low budget and quick shooting schedules, thanks in part to new, lightweight film equipment designed for small documentary and television crews. The actors were typically fresh faces, rethinking their craft in opposition to the theatrical acting, makeup, and costuming of mainstream cinema. A new generation of stars, including Moreau, Jean-Paul Belmondo, and Jean-Pierre Léaud, resulted.

A casual filming style required stories set in the present day and loosely organized around characters

**Jean Seberg and Jean-Paul Belmondo in a scene from Jean-Luc Godard's *Breathless*.** WALTER DARAN/TIME LIFE IMAGES/ GETTY IMAGES

spontaneously meandering from one encounter to another. Visually, these movies defied professional standards of three-point lighting, continuity editing, and smooth camera movements. Instead, they fore-grounded their cheap aesthetics, with hand-held cameras, amateurish lighting, disjointed editing, and bold, peppy sound tracks. Cinema for this generation was a cultural practice, not just an industry. Some mainstream critics dismissed such movies as poorly made, even ugly, but international audiences lined up behind the Parisians, making *The 400 Blows, Breathless,* and Truffaut's *Jules and Jim* (1961) three of the most important movies in the world.

New wave films truly reworked cinema from the ground up. The whole notion of who could make a movie was challenged. These directors shot in their apartments and favorite cafés and employed a new generation of cinematographers willing to

experiment. For instance, Godard filmed long con-versations for *Breathless* by pushing his camera ope-rator in a mail cart along the sidewalk. Truffaut's cinematographer sat in the trunk of a tiny car, dangling his legs out as he filmed. Malle filmed Jeanne Moreau strolling through Paris at night, with only the shop windows for illumination. The sound tracks also contributed to the sense of urgency and honesty, with lively dialogue peppered with modern slang and spoken with natural pauses and accents. Cheap, creative techniques became chic; it was acceptable to use wheelchairs for track-ing shots, jump cuts for a hectic pace, and freeze frames for suspended endings. Film language changed forever.

## LEGACY

The new wave inspired young filmmakers across Europe and the world to follow their mode of production. Its wide range of styles—from Malle and Truffaut's sensitive, sexy tales of betrayal to Godard and Varda's formal experimentation to Demy's singing melodramas and Resnais's labyrinthine narratives—allowed nearly everyone to find something engaging. In France, however, the new wave proper can be said to have ended by 1965. The number of first-time directors declined dramatically. Moreover, some new wave directors could not be considered so "new" anymore. In 1965 Chabrol completed his eleventh feature film, and Godard his tenth. The key new wave filmmakers had moved into the heart of French cinema, and ever since, their movement has been hailed as one of the most joyous and mythic moments in world cinema.

*See also* **Cinema; Godard, Jean-Luc; Truffaut, François.**

BIBLIOGRAPHY

Douchet, Jean. *French New Wave.* Translated by Robert Bonnono. New York, 1999. Translation of *Nouvelle vague* (1998).

Marie, Michel. *The French New Wave: An Artistic School.* Translated by Richard Neupert. Oxford, U.K., 2003. Translation of *La nouvelle vague: Une école artistique* (1997).

Monaco, James. *The New Wave: Truffaut, Godard, Chabrol, Rohmer, Rivette.* New York, 1976.

Neupert, Richard. *A History of the French New Wave Cinema.* Madison, Wis., 2002.

RICHARD NEUPERT

# FREUD, SIGMUND (1856–1939), Austrian psychiatrist, founder of psychoanalysis.

Sigmund Freud was fifty-eight years old in 1914 when the long nineteenth century came to an abrupt end and Europe plunged into four years of intense, internecine war. The adventure in thought that was his career was roughly half over, and the core ideas of classic Freudian psychological theory, known as psychoanalysis, were already in place. Formulated between the years 1893 and 1911 in a series of essays, case histories, and scientific monographs, psychoanalysis centered on the concepts of unconscious mental activity, childhood psychosexuality, the Oedipal scheme of psychological development, the repressive origins of neurotic symptoms, and the symbolic role of dreams in mental life. Although familiar in the early twenty-first century, these ideas were strikingly original when Freud first published them. A tiny group of intellectuals, mostly in the Germanic world, was familiar with and excited by Freud's work before 1914. A larger minority found his teachings improbable, subversive, or disgusting. Most Europeans remained unfamiliar with Freud up to this time.

## FREUD'S CAREER AFTER 1914

This situation changed dramatically in the years following 1914. During and after the First World War, Freud continued his tireless productivity. His intellectual career during the interwar period is marked by a continuing rethinking and refashioning of his ideas in the light of new clinical and historical experience. His major psychological publications during the war and postwar years concerned the psychological drives and psychical structure and function as well as ancillary subjects such as psychological sublimation and the nature of femininity. He also devoted himself to exploring the implications and applications of psychoanalysis to nonclinical domains, including anthropology, sociology, religion, literature, art, and biography. Another characteristic of the latter half of Freud's career is the drive to achieve a comprehensive model of human psychology capable of accounting for everyday normal mental life as well as psychopathology. Freud also during the 1920s and 1930s addressed the training of psychoanalysts and aspects of psychoanalytic psychotherapy. And he produced highly readable codifications of his ideas that succeeded in publicizing psychoanalysis to a wider audience. During these same years, Freudian psychology developed from a small, sectarian community in a few central European cities into both a highly dynamic professional movement and a radical cultural force across the European American world.

Two texts—*Beyond the Pleasure Principle* (1920) and *The Ego and the Id* (1923)—lie at the center of Freud's postwar output. In the latter, Freud announced his famous tripartite or "structural" theory of the human psyche. Entirely unconscious, the Freudian id, he proposed, was laid down at birth and consists of the deepest, inherited human desires and instincts. In contrast, the super-ego is an internalized composite of the many authority figures—parents, babysitters, educators, public heroes—encountered in a person's upbringing that collectively form his or her conscience. The ego attempts rationally to mediate between the imperious and persistent id, the strictures of the superego, and the outside environment with its incessant demands for sociable, civilized behavior. Freud's three psychic agencies or processes correspond, in short, with what one wants to do, what one feels one ought to do, and what one will do. An additional line of thought that flowed from *The Ego and the Id* was the concept of "mechanisms of psychological defense." Freud, and later his psychoanalyst daughter Anna Freud (1895–1982), hypothesized that in daily life people routinely deploy a series of psychological strategies to avoid ideas, situations, and realizations would cause anxiety or "unpleasure." These mechanisms, in Freud's terminology, include denial, rationalization, projection, externalization, and displacement.

*Beyond the Pleasure Principle* offered Freud's new theory of the human drives. Freud previously had conjectured that Eros, consisting of the intertwined instincts for love, sex, propagation, and self-preservation, was the central psychological drive in human life. In a controversial modification in 1920, however, he broadened his drive theory to include a second, primary impulse derived from the human capacities for aggression, destruction, and self-destruction. This change reflects in part Freud's growing pessimism as he observed the carnage of World War I. Freud labeled this second drive "Thanatos" or "the death instinct," which in his rather biologized view reflected a desire for organic life to return to its original, unorganized, and inorganic state. The concept of a human death instinct tends to be rejected by most psychoanalysts in the twenty-first century, although Freud's wider emphasis on aggression's role in human nature is accepted.

Freud's vision of the psychoanalytic project during the generation following 1914 was stunning in breadth. In several memorably titled monographs, he applied his new system of ideas to social and cultural phenomena outside medical psychology. *Totem and Taboo* (1913) explores the speculative origins of patriarchal authority in society and the family. In *Group Psychology and the Analysis of the Ego* (1921), Freud ventured into social psychology. Individuals in crowds, organizations, and movements, he maintained, tend to submerge their personal identities into that of a charismatic leader in return for a sense of security and group identity. "The Moses of Michelangelo" (1914) and "Dostoevsky and Parricide" (1928) are among Freud's explorations in psychoanalytic art and literary criticism. Finally, in *The Future of an Illusion* (1927), he took on organized religion. Candid and courageous in his atheism, Freud argued in this provocative work that the idea of God was an illusion, created by humanity in order to comfort it in the face of its mortality and helplessness when individuals outgrew the protection of their parents. Despite its moral and psychological consolation, he continued, the belief in an absolute, supernatural authority should be jettisoned as the human species matures intellectually. Theologians, cultural conservatives, and believers of all sorts, needless to say, furiously contested Freud's critique of religion.

Freud's most widely read interwar publication was *Civilization and Its Discontents* (1930). Appearing in the aftermath of the stock market crash in New York City, Freud's famous rumination interprets human civilization as a continuing and precarious balance between the deep-seated human tendency toward destructive behaviors and the unique capacity to channel or "sublimate" primitive aggression into constructive, nonviolent cultural activities, such as economics, sports, art, science, and the life of the mind. The necessary psychological cost, or "price of civilization," was the frustration and suffering that follows the continual renunciation of instinctual gratifications required by stable, communal living. This in the Freudian view is the essential human predicament. If *The Future of an Illusion* features Freud as a latter-day Enlightenment thinker championing rational, critical thinking over age-old dogmatic superstition, *Civilization and Its Discontents* showcases Freud's increasingly despairing view of human nature as dark forces began to gather across Europe. Freud brought this latter line of thinking to bear on current events in "Why War?" (1932; published 1933), a magnificent exchange of letters with the physicist Albert Einstein, written at the invitation

**Sigmund Freud at his desk in his office in Vienna, Austria, 1930.** ©BETTMANN/CORBIS

of the League of Nations, that addresses the reasons for human warfare and its possible prevention.

Despite the troubling historical circumstances of these years, Freud continued to push his ideas in ever more directions. This drive toward theoretical and clinical comprehensiveness is yet another distinctive feature of his overall intellectual career. The *Introductory Lectures on Psychoanalysis* of 1916 clarifies and systematizes his ideas for a general reading public. *From the History of an Infantile Neurosis* (1918), known colloquially as the Wolf Man case, is Freud's longest published case history. And in *Inhibitions, Symptoms, and Anxiety* (1926), he revised his earlier theory of psychological anxiety. As more people sought to study psychoanalysis formally, Freud needed to set out the guidelines for proper training. In *The Question of Lay Analysis* (1926), he rejected the notion that psychoanalysts

must be medical doctors. Other publications addressed questions about the psychodynamics of the doctor/patient relationship—or, in psychoanalytic parlance, the analyst/analysand relationship. In a well-known essay written near the end of his life titled "Analysis Terminable and Interminable" (1937), Freud forthrightly acknowledged the limitations and even dangers of psychoanalytic therapy with certain types of patients. In all of his later writings, his focus remained on the neurotic, rather than psychotic, forms of psychopathology. Within the field of the neuroses, he concentrated in the second half of his career on anxiety, obsessions, narcissism, and melancholia rather than the hysterical neuroses, which had absorbed his attention in the 1890s.

Biographically, the last fifteen years of Freud's life were intensely difficult, plagued by two mounting menaces. First, in 1923, at the age of sixty-seven, Freud underwent an operation on his jaw and palate for what turned out to be cancer. Soon thereafter he began wearing a painful and unwieldy prosthesis. Many other surgeries followed; he was in continual, growing pain throughout these years. Second, after a decade of electoral vicissitudes, Adolf Hitler was appointed chancellor of Germany late in January 1933. Freud had struggled against Austrian anti-Semitism since the 1880s, but the ascent to power of the Nazis ushered in a new level of racism across German-speaking Europe. In the spring of 1933, Freud's books were included in the book burnings carried out in Berlin; later that year the Nazis began to close down psychoanalytic societies across Germany. Across the 1930s, vandalism against Jews rose steadily. With the annexation of Austria in March 1938, the Nazis entered the native city of psychoanalysis. They dissolved the Vienna Psychoanalytic Society and briefly seized Freud's daughter Anna. Two months later, Freud departed Vienna for London, via Paris, in order "to die in freedom," as he put it. On 23 September 1939, at the age of eighty-three, he died peacefully in his new home in the north London suburb of Hampstead. Three weeks earlier, Hitler had invaded Poland, confirming, it seemed, Freud's somber assessment of humanity's self-destructiveness. Because Hitler clamped down early in his murderous regime on psychoanalysis, the overwhelming majority of analysts were able to leave Germany and Austria safely. Most emigrated, in body, mind, and spirit, to Britain or the United States. The so-called psychoanalytic diaspora enriched immeasurably the psychological communities in these countries.

### THE SPREAD OF PSYCHOANALYSIS

Knowledge of and fascination with psychoanalysis spread extensively between the two world wars. During the first decade of the twentieth century, small groups of admirers and enthusiasts had gathered at Freud's own home in Vienna and in a few other central European cities to ponder his ideas. With the diffusion of psychoanalysis, however, Freud found it more and more difficult to control or contain his creation. The post-1914 years are marked by schisms within the psychoanalytic community, with participants emerging as loyalists or dissidents. Freud had already, in 1913, broken with

the Swiss psychologist Carl Jung, once judged his most important adherent. *The History of the Psycho-Analytic Movement*, published in 1914, is Freud's reckoning with a number of newly independent followers, including Jung and Alfred Adler. In 1924 Otto Rank, another early enthusiast, published his own twist on psychoanalytic theory in *The Trauma of Birth*. Freud was troubled by and intolerant of these departures, which he saw as misguided defections rather than independent, psychoanalytically oriented explorations. From this time onward, factionalism plagued the movement.

At the same time, psychoanalysis as a formal doctrine and practice—with its own conferences, organizations, publications, and membership—spread widely. In 1908 the Vienna Psychoanalytic Society had been founded and the first international congress of psychoanalysts had met in Salzburg. In 1919 the International Psychoanalytic Press was established. A year later, Freud's devoted British disciple Ernest Jones launched the *International Journal of Psycho-Analysis*. As Freudian psychology gained a foothold in one Western country after another, a striking pattern emerged: distinctive national schools or trends took shape that reflected the cultural and intellectual heritages, as well as medical and scientific traditions, of different countries.

Snubbed by the prudish public and conservative medical establishment in Freud's native Austria, psychoanalysis nonetheless achieved brilliant prominence in the German capital during the interwar period. In 1920 a psychoanalytic polyclinic or outpatient clinic, the first of its kind in the world, opened in Berlin. The Berlin clinic assembled a gifted coterie of theorists and therapists, and it accepted paying and nonpaying clients alike from all social classes. Psychoanalytic societies were also founded during the 1920s in Heidelberg, Dresden, and Hamburg. Typically, the staffs of these early societies were heavily Jewish, with political sympathies overwhelmingly on the left. Imperial Wilhelminian Germany had been conservative and repressive in its official moral atmosphere. In contrast, Freud's frank, exploratory attitude toward sexuality corresponded well with the freer, experimental environment of the German Weimar Republic.

Characteristically, Freud's ideas in France followed their own path. Although French intellectuals were slow initially to embrace Freud—they argued that Jean-Martin Charcot, Henri Bergson, and Pierre Janet had been there first—the first translations of Freud's texts into French appeared in the mid-1920s, and the Société psychanalytique de Paris was registered in 1926. Still, at the time of Freud's death and the fall of France in 1939–1940, there was no mass movement around psychoanalysis in the country. "French Freud," as it came to be called, emerged only after the 1968 uprisings in Paris. Since then, a rich, if somewhat overheated, psychoanalytic culture formed in France, dedicated to the working out of Freud's ideas in literature, philosophy, linguistics, and feminist theory.

For a decade after the Bolshevik Revolution of 1917, Freud's thinking found quite receptive ground in Soviet Russia. In the 1920s his most important books and articles were translated into Russian. A Russian psychoanalytic journal appeared, and institutes with sizable memberships were founded in St. Petersburg and Moscow. Peaking in 1921–1923, Soviet Freudianism was drastically curtailed by the late 1920s as Joseph Stalin consolidated his dictatorship.

The British reaction to Freud's ideas was divided: residual Victorianism caused much of the British public to recoil at Freud's forthright discussion of childhood sexuality. Nevertheless, in 1913 Ernest Jones established the London Psycho-Analytic Society. The Bloomsbury circle of avant-garde intellectuals also took up Freud's work with alacrity. In 1924 the Hogarth Press, which had recently been founded by Leonard and Virginia Woolf, began to publish an ambitious and authoritative edition of Freud's complete psychological writings in English. This definitive edition, which eventually ran to twenty-four volumes, was immensely influential in the spread of Freudian thought throughout the anglophone world. Furthermore, for different reasons both Melanie Klein and Anna Freud eventually moved to London and set up psychiatric shop. A productive institutional and intellectual rivalry developed between the two woman psychoanalysts. Child psychoanalysis became a national specialty, and the prestigious Tavistock Clinic in London was heavily psychoanalytic in orientation.

Beyond doubt, psychoanalysis found its most enthusiastic and wide-ranging reception in the United States. Freud personally disdained America. In 1909, however, he had delivered a powerful set of lectures at Clark University in Massachusetts, which launched a movement in the country. The New York Psychoanalytic Society opened its doors in 1911. In 1914 Boston followed suit, and an American Psychoanalytic Association was created. New translations into English of key texts, as well as the larger libertine social and sexual atmosphere associated with the decade, allowed intellectual and popular interest in psychoanalysis to burgeon in the 1920s. A long period of American enchantment with Freud ensued that waned only in the last quarter of the twentieth century. The American psychoanalytic community's requirement that practitioners obtain a medical license deeply influenced the character of Freudian practice in the country.

The decades from the 1920s to the 1950s also witnessed a remarkable cultural diffusion of Freud's ideas. In many forms—some of them inaccurate, simplified, or bastardized—Freudian motifs flooded films, novels, plays, paintings, advertising, and popular culture during the second quarter of the twentieth century. The distinctive Freudian vocabulary of id, ego, superego, wish fulfillment, sibling rivalry, penis envy, Oedipus complex, and the like cropped up ubiquitously. Not only physicians and mental health workers but the general educated public read Freud's writings, which were clear and concise, full of memorable coinages, and cast in compelling metaphorical language. Inevitably, cultural and popular responses to Freud—in his time and in the early twenty-first century—ranged extravagantly from fascination and adulation to skepticism and hostility.

The "golden age of psychoanalysis" extended into the 1970s. After that time, a new wave of biologically oriented psychiatry supplanted psychoanalysis institutionally and intellectually in many parts of the world. Likewise, shorter-term therapies aimed at symptomatic relief gained currency. After Freud's death, a tendency also developed among some of his well-meaning but reverential followers for his many profound and original insights to harden into doctrine and then dogma.

At the outset of the twenty-first century, Sigmund Freud's standing and legacy are warmly contested. But this much is certain: among European thinkers, only Karl Marx has had as great an influence on the thought and culture of the twentieth century as Freud. For fifty years, he was incontestably the central psychological thinker of the age. During these years, the cultural appeal and prominence of his ideas were tremendous. The volume of his output and the breadth of his thinking remain astonishing. Much of his lifework has become integrated into commonsense psychology and entrenched in modern thought generally. This heritage includes the ideas that a person's early biography is crucial to his or her subsequent psychological development, that psychosexuality is a fundamental part of human personality, that repressed painful or traumatic experiences can over time be harmful, and that speaking systematically with a trained and sympathetic listener about psychological difficulties can be beneficial. This last practice in particular represents the beginnings of the so-called verbal psychotherapies—what the early psychoanalytic patient "Anna O." dubbed "the talking cure"—and may well be his most basic and enduring contribution.

*See also* **Jung, Carl; Psychiatry; Psychoanalysis; Sexuality.**

BIBLIOGRAPHY

Capps, Donald, ed. *Freud and Freudians on Religion: A Reader.* New Haven, Conn., and London, 2001.

Cocks, Geoffrey. *Psychotherapy in the Third Reich: The Göring Institute.* 2nd ed. New Brunswick, N.J., 1997.

Fine, Reuben. *A History of Psychoanalysis.* New expanded ed. New York, 1990.

Freud, Sigmund. *The Standard Edition of the Complete Psychological Works of Sigmund Freud.* Translated from the German under the general editorship of James Strachey in collaboration with Anna Freud. 24 vols. London, 1953–1974.

Gay, Peter. *Freud: A Life for Our Time.* New York, 1988.

Gellner, Ernst. *The Psychoanalytic Movement: The Cunning of Unreason.* 3rd ed. Malden, Mass., 2003.

Hale, Nathan G., Jr. *The Rise and Crisis of Psychoanalysis in America: Freud and the Americans, 1917–1985.* New York, 1995.

Kahn, Michael. *Basic Freud: Psychoanalytic Thought for the Twenty-First Century.* New York, 2002.

Kurzweil, Edith. *The Freudians: A Comparative Perspective.* New Haven, Conn., and London, 1989.

Laplanche, Jean, and J.-B. Pontalis. *The Language of Psychoanalysis.* Translated by Donald Nicholson-Smith. London, 1973.

Miller, Martin A. *Freud and the Bolsheviks: Psychoanalysis in Imperial Russia and the Soviet Union.* New Haven, Conn., and London, 1998.

Neu, Jerome, ed. *The Cambridge Companion to Freud.* Cambridge, U.K., 1991.

Roazen, Paul. *Freud and His Followers.* New York, 1975.

Roudinesco, Elisabeth. *Jacques Lacan and Co.: A History of Psychoanalysis in France, 1925–1985.* Translated by Jeffrey Mehlman. Chicago, 1990.

Sayers, Janet. *Mothers of Psychoanalysis: Helene Deutsche, Karen Horney, Anna Freud, Melanie Klein.* New York, 1991.

Zaretsky, Eli. *Secrets of the Soul: A Social and Cultural History of Psychoanalysis.* New York, 2004.

MARK S. MICALE

---

# FROMM, ERICH (1900–1980), German-born intellectual and social critic.

Few European intellectuals in the twentieth century played the role of the global public intellectual and interdisciplinary scholar as successfully as the controversial social critic Erich Fromm. He was the author of such influential books as *Escape from Freedom* (1941), *The Sane Society* (1956), and *To Have or to Be* (1976). Fromm was born in Germany in 1900 and was a member of the "critical theorists" of the Frankfurt School in the 1930s. Exiled from Nazi Germany with the rise of Adolf Hitler, Fromm moved to the United States and wrote bestselling and critically acclaimed books on Nazism, communitarian socialism, disarmament, Freudian theory, and humanistic Marxism. Moving to Mexico City in the early 1950s, and then back to Europe in the last decade of his life, Fromm's influence was truly global.

Fromm was one of the most articulate and courageous psychoanalytic revisionists, building on Freud's intellectual legacy while moving beyond some of the outmoded aspects of orthodoxy. Like earlier psychoanalytic rebels Carl Jung, Otto Rank, and Alfred Adler as well as his contemporaries Karen Horney and Harry Stack Sullivan, Fromm was skeptical of traditional libido theory and the organized dogma of the psychoanalytic movement.

Unlike some of Freud's less imaginative followers, Fromm was an internal critic of orthodoxy committed to Freud's insights into character, the irrational and the unconscious. Fromm's account of both the greatness and the limitations of Freud's thought was outlined in a number of highly influential and bestselling books such as *Psychoanalysis and Religion* (1950), *Sigmund Freud's Mission* (1959), and *The Crisis of Psychoanalysis* (1970). Fromm practiced psychoanalysis from the late 1920s well into the 1960s, gaining a reputation as an insightful, caring, and committed although not uncontroversial clinician. A European intellectual to the core, few writers, paradoxically, were as successful at popularizing Freud in America. Some of his Freudian detractors, however, felt that Fromm had gained his fame in the United States by diluting Freud's stoic European pessimism and challenging theoretical insights for the allegedly more shallow and optimistic Americans, particularly in his hugely popular *The Art of Loving* (1956). Ultimately, Fromm is best seen as one of Freud's loyal but most creative and innovative followers.

Fromm was also an influential public intellectual and social scientist who had been trained in sociology at Heidelberg by Alfred Weber. Fromm was an early critic of the consumerism of modern globalizing culture, an opponent of traditionalism and neo-liberalism in the global south, and a leading voice against both the American military and corporate empire and communist dictators. Fromm's *Escape from Freedom* (1941), in particular, will be remembered as one of the classic works of social psychology of the twentieth century. His thesis about how the breakdown of community can lead to a fascist "escape from freedom," moreover, is all too relevant today as we reflect on the breakdown of communism in Eastern Europe, the rise of Islamism, and the re-emergence of right-wing authoritarianism throughout Western Europe and the United States in the early years of the twenty-first century. Fromm's association with the Frankfurt School has often been forgotten, but he worked on an early empirical study of working-class support for Nazism that led directly to the famous *The Authoritarian Personality* (1950) project. Furthermore, the Harvard University sociologist David Riesman's bestselling classic *The Lonely Crowd* (1950) came partly out of a dialogue with

Fromm, an example of the creativity that flowed from "critical theory meeting America." Unfairly characterized as a simplistic popularizer, Fromm's work from the 1970s, particularly *Social Character in a Mexican Village* (1970) (written with Michael Maccoby) and *The Anatomy of Human Destructiveness* (1973) combined sophisticated theory, detailed engagement with empirical evidence, and true interdisciplinary range.

Fromm was not without his critics. The Berkeley liberal political theorist John Schaar viewed Fromm as an unrealistic utopian proponent of an "Escape from Authority." Fromm was widely attacked by neo-conservatives for his opposition to the Vietnam War, American-led "modernization," and the nuclear arms race and for his radical democratic ideas on education. Allan Bloom's bestselling book *The Closing of the American Mind* (1987) famously made Fromm a key villain in the importation of European ideas that had led to alleged "Nietzscheanization of the American Left" (Bloom, 1987). Ironically, given these critiques of Fromm's alleged ultra leftism, Fromm was also accused of being a liberal conformist by Herbert Marcuse, Theodor Adorno, and various interpreters of "critical theory." Contrary to these polarized views that were reinforced during the late twentieth-century attacks on humanism during the debates on postmodernism, Fromm's contribution to twenty-first-century political philosophy and social criticism will likely be remembered as a European moderate democratic socialist communitarian humanism. When Fromm returned to his European roots in the last decade of his life, his popular "radical humanist" radio broadcasts in the early 1970s and his bestselling book *To Have or to Be* had a significant influence on the emergence of the Green movement. Given Fromm's own religious Jewish roots, and his conflicted relationship with both Marxism and psychoanalysis, Fromm's career might best be summed up as a constant and creative "escape from orthodoxy" along the road to his emergence as a truly engaged global public intellectual.

*See also* **Freud, Sigmund; Psychiatry; Psychoanalysis; Social Democracy; Socialism.**

BIBLIOGRAPHY

Bloom, Alan. *The Closing of the American Mind.* New York, 1987.

Brunner, Jose. "Looking into the Hearts of the Workers, or: How Erich Fromm Turned Critical Theory into Empirical Research." *Political Psychology* 15, no. 4 (1994): 631–654.

Burston, Daniel. *The Legacy of Erich Fromm.* Cambridge, Mass., 1991.

Maccoby, Michael. "The Two Voices of Erich Fromm: The Prophetic and the Analytic." *Society* 32 (July-August 1995): 72–82.

McLaughlin, Neil. "Nazism, Nationalism, and the Sociology of Emotions: *Escape from Freedom* Revisited." *Sociological Theory* 14, no. 3 (1996): 241–261.

———. "How to Become a Forgotten Intellectual: Intellectual Movements and the Rise and Fall of Erich Fromm." *Sociological Forum* 13 (1998): 215–246.

———. "Origin Myths in the Social Sciences: Fromm, the Frankfurt School and the Emergence of Critical Theory." *Canadian Journal of Sociology* 24, no. 1 (1999): 109–139.

———. "Optimal Marginality: Innovation and Orthodoxy in Fromm's Revision of Psychoanalysis." *Sociological Quarterly* 42, no. 2 (2001): 271–288.

Richert, John. "The Fromm-Marcuse Debate Revisited." *Theory and Society* 15, no. 3 (1986): 181–214.

Roazen, Paul. *Political Theory and the Psychology of the Unconscious: Freud, J. S. Mill, Nietzche, Dostoevsky, Fromm, Bettelheim and Erikson.* London, 2000.

———. *On the Freud Watch: Public Memoirs.* London, 2003.

Schaar, John. *Escape from Authority: The Perspectives of Erich Fromm.* New York, 1961.

NEIL MCLAUGHLIN

---

**FUTURISM.** Proclaimed in a manifesto by Filippo Tommaso Marinetti that appeared in *Le Figaro* on 20 February 1909, futurism was the first twentieth-century avant-garde movement to aim at a total reconstruction of modern culture and society. In the prewar years, Marinetti relentlessly promoted the movement throughout Europe, developed a futurist version of nearly every art form (including poetry, literature, music, painting, sculpture, architecture, theater, photography, and dance), and sparked an international debate about his vision of modernity.

## DEFINING A MOVEMENT

Futurism was at once a cultural vision devoted to the ideals of speed, machinery, anti-passéism, the love of danger, the glorification of war, the destruction of museums, and scorn for the traditional ideal of woman *and* a new sort of intellectual association: a close-knit group of stalwarts who publicly displayed themselves in performances called *serate futuriste* (futurist evenings) and used Marinetti's manifestos as the basis for a total rethinking of art and life.

Until February 1912, when the first exhibition of futurist painting opened in Paris, Marinetti promoted his movement by recruiting artists such as Giacomo Balla, Umberto Boccioni, Carlo Carrà, Aldo Palazzeschi, Luigi Russolo, and Gino Severini; holding *serate;* and publishing more and more manifestos. In general, the manifestos preceded the reform of artistic practice. Thus, although the "Manifesto of the Futurist Painters" appeared in February 1910, only in late 1911 did the painters settle on a way to depict motion dynamically in painting, as their manifesto required. Similarly, the "Technical Manifesto of Futurist Literature" (1912) appeared well before efforts (such as Marinetti's "Zang Tumb Tuuum" in 1914) to deploy its declared preference for "words-in-freedom." In music, Marinetti recruited the composer Francesco Balilla Pratella in 1910 and Pratella promptly wrote a manifesto, but his participation in futurism was erratic, and the task of creating a "futurist art of noises" ultimately fell to the painter Russolo. The exception was the manifesto on cinema, which Marinetti published a month after the first futurist film, *Vita futurista,* (1916; Futurist life), by Arnaldo Ginna. Oddly, futurism did little to further develop futurist film, despite film's obvious compatibility with futurism's celebration of the machine.

Marinetti wrote two early political manifestos, the second and more detailed one when Italy went to war in Libya in October 1911. A still fuller discussion appeared as the "political program" of futurism in the 15 October 1913 edition of the Florentine review *Lacerba.* These texts linked libertarian, nationalist, irredentist, antisocialist, and anticlerical themes to the futurist cultural vision.

The futurists engaged in many other forms of public spectacle, such as hurling futurist leaflets from the top of the campanile overlooking Venice's Piazza

San Marco. Marinetti also reported from war scenes such as Tripoli and the Bulgarian trenches of Adrianopolis. No expense was too great if publicity resulted from it, for Marinetti was a man of substantial inherited wealth who probably understood as well as anyone of the day the power of visual spectacle, sloganeering, and vivid typography in a world that moved too fast for long books and long-winded speeches.

While Marinetti was in Tripoli, Boccioni, Carrà, and Russolo were in Paris assessing the cubist scene under Severini's guidance. French poet Guillaume Apollinaire would soon charge that they had stolen cubist ideas, and many issues of the early *Lacerba* were devoted to the question of who owed what to whom. One result of their Paris sojourn was an important new recruit, Valentine de Saint-Point, a dancer who wrote manifestos on the futurist woman and, even more scandalously, on lust. Although women were noticeably absent from the early futurist movement, many women writers joined in during World War I, especially in connection with the second journal of Florentine futurism, *L'Italia futurista* (1916–1918).

In 1913 Marinetti wrote a manifesto on variety theater, which addressed the urban working classes and sought to destroy "art with a capital A." By 1914 some striking images of the futurist city had emerged in the manifesto on architecture by Antonio Sant'Elia, which appeared in *Lacerba* on the day World War I broke out. Sant'Elia, like Boccioni, would die in the coming conflagration.

### THE WAR AND EARLY POSTWAR YEARS

In 1915 Balla and Fortunato Depero published a design manifesto on the "futurist reconstruction of the universe." It anticipated the futurism of the interwar years, which became associated with a certain style of design for fascist and capitalist culture to appropriate rather than with an avant-garde movement aiming to put the futurists themselves in charge of reconstructing modern cultural life.

The war took the futurists to the front and largely ended the frenetic theorizing and theatrical self-display of their first years. When Marinetti stepped back into the public realm in 1918, he aimed to found a futurist political party that would take power and direct the effort at postwar

***Mercury Passes the Sun.*** Painting by Giacomo Balla, 1914. ERICH LESSING/ART RESOURCE, NY

reconstruction. This grand illusion lasted until May 1920, when at the Second Fascist Congress Benito Mussolini split with the futurists, moved to the right, and began an ascent to power that culminated two and half years later in his March on Rome. Once fascism had consolidated its power, futurism was reduced to competing to become fascism's official art rather than being a comprehensive movement in its own right. This later aesthetic futurism is often called second futurism, but there are really three futurisms, corresponding to the prewar, immediate postwar, and fascist periods.

The political futurism of 1918 through 1920 was anticipated by Marinetti's jocular pamphlet, *Come si seducono le donne* (1917; How to seduce women), which, noting the transformations that had occurred in women's lives during the war years, argued that society was moving in the direction of universal free love and, toward that end, that divorce should be made easy and women given the right to vote. Then, in *Al di là del comunismo* (Beyond communism), written in the wake of the November 1919 elections in which the futurist-fascist ticket had suffered a crushing defeat, Marinetti fantasized about a coming counter-bourgeois political order in which futurists would rule, parliamentarism would be abolished along with prisons and police, and a new, free artistic sphere would flourish.

Post–World War I political futurism was a curious blend of leftist and rightist attitudes, and an independent left-futurism persisted well into the 1920s. Its main manifestation was in Turin, where the communist Antonio Gramsci led a section of Proletkult, a Comintern-sponsored cultural organization that included a number of futurists, including Arturo Cappa (the brother of Benedetta Cappa, who married Marinetti in 1923), and Luigi Colombo, known as Fillia, who would become close to Marinetti later in the decade.

Turin Proletkult was part of a general fragmentation of 1920s futurism. Some of the greatest futurist talents had died in the war. Others who survived it, like Carlo Carrà, had grown conservative and joined earlier defectors from futurism, such as Ardengo Soffici in calling for a "return to order." Still others, such as Mario Carli, Emilio Settimelli, and Giovanni Bottai, split with Marinetti over political questions, the first two launching an independent futurism of an apparently monarchist (but covertly fascist) stripe, and Bottai abandoning futurism altogether for a straightforward embrace of fascism. Finally, some futurists, such as Enrico Prampolini, launched independent futurist journals of a purely aesthetic sort. His early *Noi* (1917–1920; We) showed dadaist sympathies, and his second series (1923–1925) pursued machine aesthetics in relation to theater and design, with some influence from Russian constructivism. The only prewar futurist who remained loyal to Marinetti in this period was Balla.

## WITHIN THE FASCIST REGIME

Beginning in 1923, Marinetti openly embraced Mussolini, seeking in vain to make futurism into the regime's state art. He moved to Rome in 1925, was among the inaugural members of the Reale Accademia in 1929, and then used his hitherto anticlerical avant-garde theory to advocate "sacred art." A manifesto on this topic, coauthored with Fillia, appeared in 1931 and undergirded futurist efforts in "aeropainting," "aeromusic," and "aeropoetry"—art forms inspired by transatlantic aviation—that had begun with a 1929 manifesto. These forms of "sacred art" lent themselves especially well to regime propaganda, for example in the celebration of Italo Balbo's 1933 spectacular flight from Orbetello to Chicago and back. In 1935 a futurist "war aeropainting" helped to promote the war in Abyssinia.

Despite Marinetti's obsequious efforts, the futurists were marginalized by the regime. They were not invited to participate in the 1924 Venice Biennale, which featured a number of works by Russian futurists. They were also denied any role in the Italian pavilion at the 1925 Paris Exposition, although they were allowed to display their work in a separate pavilion—a fitting symbol of their relationship with the fascist regime. They were consigned to two rooms on the upper level of regime's Mostra della Rivoluzione Fascista (1932), the most lavish and popular artistic spectacle it ever staged. Meanwhile, a group of right-intransigent fascists led by Roberto Farinacci conducted a feverish campaign in the early 1930s against all forms of avant-garde modernism, including futurism. Parroting Adolf Hitler's argument that modernism was "degenerate art," they succeeded by 1937 in having futurism officially declared decadent in Italy. In 1939 the suppression of Mino Somenzi's futurist journal *Artecrazia* (Artistocracy) meant that an independent futurism had been stamped out in Italy. During the 1940s, futurism survived only as fascist war propaganda.

*See also* **Fascism; Marinetti, F. T.**

BIBLIOGRAPHY

Apollonio, Umbro, ed. *Futurist Manifestos.* Translated by Robert Brain et al. Boston, 2001.

Blum, Cinzia Sartini. *The Other Modernism: F. T. Marinetti's Futurist Fiction of Power.* Berkeley, Calif., 1996.

Caruso, Luciano, ed. *Manifesti, proclami, interventi, e documenti teorici del futurismo, 1909–1944.* 4 vols. Florence, 1990.

Crispolti, Enrico, and Franco Sborgi, ed. *Futurismo: I Grandi temi 1909–1944.* Milan, 1997.

De Felice, Renzo. *Futurismo, cultura e politica*. Turin, 1988.

Gambillo, Maria Drudi, and Teresa Fiori. *Archivi del futurismo*. 2 vols. Rome, 1958.

Perloff, Marjorie. *The Futurist Moment: Avant-garde, Avant-guerre, and the Language of Rupture*. Chicago, 1986.

Salaris, Claudia. *Storia del futurismo: Libri, giornali, manifesti*. Rome, 1985.

Tisdall, Caroline, and Angelo Bozzolla. *Futurism*. London, 1977.

WALTER L. ADAMSON